PLANET OF THE GREEKS

THE GREAT TIME WARP OF HISTORY

MERES J. WECHE

AMUN-RA PUBLISHING

PLANET OF THE GREEKS

Copyright © Meres J. Weche 2000-2003
All rights reserved.

Amun-Ra Publishing

www.worldagesarchive.com

All rights reserved. Except for the quotation of short passages for the purpose of criticism and review, no part of this publication may be reproduced, stored in a retrieval system, or transmitted in any form or by any means, electronic, mechanical, photocopying, recording or otherwise, without the prior permission of the author.

ISBN 0-9684282-1-5 (paper)
ISBN 0-9684282-0-7 (cloth)

A CIP catalogue record for this book is available from the National Library of Canada.

Charts, maps and photographs © Meres J. Weche. (except Figs. 1b, 1g, 2d, 2i).
All ancient monument and artifact drawings taken from publications now out of copyright.

Typeset and designed by author.
Printed and bound in Canada in 2003.

...ANET OF THE GREEKS

...osmogony of Thinis-Abydos and the Memphite Theology ...ited (140) — Mesopotamia and Early Dynastic Egypt (142) ...e Asiatic Threat (145) — More Sethian Chaos: The Universal ...er is Disturbed (146) — The Reaffirmation of the Memphite ...ology's Central Importance in Egypt's Historical Cycle (147) ...The Black Land Reasserts its Power Over the Red Land (148) — ...aven on Earth: The Gizah Pyramids and the Great Sphinx (150) — The Divine Bull and the Leviathan (158).

Chapter 3: The Archaeotheology of Creation 161

The Seven Heavens (163) — The Fifty-Two-Year Cycle (164) — The Fall (169) — The Gilgamesh Epic (172) — The African Roots of the Biblical Noah (174).

Part II — 2,730 BCE to 1,953 BCE

Chapter 4: The Supremacy of Horus, Son of Re 179

King Sneferu as Successor of Khnum-Khufu: The Unification of the Horus Kingships (180) — The Dominance of the Dynastic Race (186) — The Inventory Stela: On the Anteriority of the Gizah Plateau Pyramids (188) — The Rebirth of Osiris-Orion and the Khemetic Renaissance (189) The Antiquity of the Osiris and Isis Cults (192) — The Day the Earth Shook (194).

Chapter 5: Coping with the Asiatic Threat 197

The Arrival of the C-Group Asiatic Nubians (197) — The Sixth Dynasty (200) — The Old Akkadian Empire (201) — The Sentence of the Heavens (202) — The Gutian Invasion of Akkad (205).

Chapter 6: And the Waters of Heaven Came Down 207

The Kings of Herakleopolis (208) — The Great Flood (208) — The Hermopolitan Cosmogony: An Egyptian Account of the Flood (214) — Other Flood Narratives from around the World (218) — Abraham Descends Into the Land of Pharaoh (220) — Behold

Table of Contents

Preface and Acknowledgements ....
Introduction ....
Partial Map of the Ancient World ....
Standard Chronology of Ancient Egypt ....
New Chronology Table 6*
Historical Periods, Catastrophes and World Ages Table 73

Part I — 4,413 BCE to 2,730 BCE

Chapter 1: The Formative Period 81

Upper Egypt: The Black Land (84) — The first Calendar (88) — The Heliopolitan Theology (91) — The Primordial Cosmology (93) — A Red Crown in Upper Egypt (99) — The Gerzean Period (3,600 - 3,200 BCE) (100) — Pharaoh Narmer and the Expansion of Khemetic Culture (101) — King Narmer as Osiris (104) — Seth-Mercury as Instigator of Primeval Chaos (107) — King Djoser-Netjerykhet and the Memphite Theology (109) — The Qustul Pharaohs: The First Disciples of Seth (113) — The end of Typhon Season#1 and the Primordial Flood (119).

Chapter 2: A New Beginning 121

The New Dynastic Horus: Horus the Child (122) — The Classic Ptolemaic Age (123) — Hathor, Mistress of Punt and the Dynastic Race Theory (131) — The Primordial Victory of Horus the Child Over Seth (136) — The Great Battle of the Sixth Generation of Ta-Seti (The Emergence of the Egyptian Dynastic State) (139)

the Vile Asiatic!: The C-Group Nubians to the South and their Threat to Egyptian Hegemony (221) — Birth of the Zodiacal Seasons (223) — The End of the Theban Supremacy (228) — The Third Dynasty of Ur (229).

Part III — 1,953 BCE to 1,330 BCE

Chapter 7: A King-Less Egypt Under Foreign Occupation 235

Taking advantage of Egypt's Nakedness (235) —Seeking Refuge in Ethiopia: The Egyptian Exodus (236) — Reunifying the Two Lands (238) — Mesopotamia after the Elamites (245) — Joseph the Patriarch (246) — The Venus Shift of 1,787 BCE and the Seven Years of Want (247).

Chapter 8: The Pharaohs Who Knew Not Joseph 251

Recovering from Civil Strife (252) — The Move of the State Capital from Thebes to Lisht-Memphis: The Death of Noah 256) — The Influence of 12th Dynasty Kings in Palestine and the Aegean (259) — The Nubian Policy (267) — Year 7 of Sesostris III and the Threat of Doomsday (268) — The Thera Eruption and the Papyrus Ipuwer (270) — Death Upon the Firtsborn of Egypt: Of Exodus and Conquest (275).

Chapter 9: The Hyksos Invasion 283

Dismantling the Manethonian Framework (284) — A Change in the Balance of Power: The Hyksos in Avaris (288) — Tell el-Dab'a After Pharaoh Neferhotep (291) — MBIIc in Palestine: The Hebrews After the Conquest (296) — The Hyksos Colonization of Crete and Greece (299) — The MBIIc Indo-Aryan Invasions: Why a Hurrian is Not a Hyksos (303) — Typhon Season #4: Mercury and Venus Embark on Yet Another Collision Course with Earth (304) — To Divide and Conquer (306) — Egypto-Nubian Relations Under Sobekhotep IV and the Conquests of Moses (307) — The End of an Era: Venus, Ammisaduga and the Demise of the Xia Dynasty in China (310).

Chapter 10: The Missing Link 317

Was Ahmose Responsible for the Destruction of the Middle Bronze Age Canaanite Cities? (318) — The Road Towards Peaceful Coexistence (321) — The Osirid Statues of Late Bronze Age Egypt and the Cult of Mentuhotep-Nebhepetre as Divine Ancestor (326) — The Kingdom of Meroë: The Lion-God Apedemak and the Mandate of Leo (331) — The Day of the Lord (338) — The Late Bronze Age Aegean: The Lost Pre-Homeric Civilization (342) — King David and the Continuing Hyksos-Amalekite Challenge (346) — Solomon the Builder King (348) — A Peace Coming Undone: The Second Hyksos Invasion and Tuthmosis II's Reunification of the Two Lands (350) — Solomon and the Queen of Sheba (353) — Tuthmosis III Drives the Hyksos Out of Avaris (360) — A Hyksos Palace in Jerusalem (365) — The Men with Horses: The Hurrian Invasion of Canaan and the Transmission of Horse-drawn Chariots in Egypt (368) — The Tell el-Amarna and Boghazköy Records (371) — Amenhotep IV and the Turbulent End of the Theban Renaissance (375).

Part IV — 1,330 BCE to 747 BCE

Chapter 11: The New Kingdom Begins 385

Seti I's Victorious Campaigns in Asia (386) The Battle of Kadesh (387) — Pharaoh Ramses II's "Hyksos" Division (389) — After Year 8: Foreigners in Pharaoh's Land (390) — The Rage of Typhon-Poseidon Strikes Again (394) — An Invasion from the North: The Sea Peoples Storm Through Egypt and Libya (396) — A Philistine Solider in Meroë: A Look at an Inconceivable Idea (399) — Arsa the Atlan and the Invasion of the Atlanteo-Napatans (409).

Chapter 12: Learning the Art of Chariot Warfare 421

The Hyksos Once Again (422) The Horse-Drawn Chariot: An African War Apparatus Changes the Course of Egyptian History (424) — King Ramses III, the Great Papyrus Harris, and the Battle of the Peoples of the Sea (427) — The Trojan War and

Stonehenge Revisited (432) — A Fight for Avaris (435) — Ahmose the Saviour (440) — The Great Exodus (446) — The Egypto-Phoenician Colonization of the Aegean at the End of the Late Bronze Age (448) — The Birth of Mycenaean-B Culture: Homers' Heroic Age Begins (453) — A Change of Seasons in China (455) — Moses the Lawgiver and the Hyksos Giants (458).

Chapter 13: The Imperialistic Age: In Search of the Glory of Saul, David and Solomon 465

Can the Real Israels Please Stand in Line? (467) — Hail the King: Tuthmosis I as the Founder of the New United Monarchy (473) — The Mycenaean-B Domination of Crete (476) — The Neo-Hittites: An Intermediary Iron Age Power (478) — The Many Layers of the Temple of Karnak (482).

Chapter 14: The Western Hemisphere 485

The Fifth Sun at the End of the Second World (486) — Olmec Civilization (490) — The Feathered Serpent from the East: The Hyksos, the Danaans and Phoenicians Beyond the Pillars of Herakles (492) — The Venus Calendar (495) — The Aztecs: Carriers of a Lost Knowledge (498) — The Legacy of the Catastrophic World View in Native American Traditions (500) — The Seventh Sun (502).

Chapter 15: The Libyans and Ethiopians Take Control of the Two Lands 505

The Libyan Renaissance Era (506) — The Biblical Shishak (508) — The Ethiopian Invasion (513) — Akhenaten: The Heretic King (517) — The Amarna Letters: A Continuing Story (520) — The Dark Age of Greece (525) — The End of the Amarnian Heresy (532) — Bubastis, Soleb and the Heb-Sed Festival (535) — The Temple of Osiris-Apis (536) — King Moeris & the Labyrinth (538) — King Minos, Ruler of the Iron IIb Aegean, and the Sethian Minotaur (542) — Chariots of Fire: Venus and the Olympiads (549) The Freudian Moses, the Fourth Exodus, and the Pharaoh of the Exodus (551) — The Ethiopia-bound Israelites and the Ark of the Covenant

(560) — A Changing of the Guard (564) — Setting the Record Straight (566) — Mars: The Velikovskian Scenario (567).

Part V — 747 BCE to 404 BCE

Chapter 16: Descendants of Ancient Kings 573

A Dark Age in Nubia? (575) — A Chronological Enigma at Gebel Barkal (580) — Governing Petty Kings (582) — Mars, Venus, and the Trojan War (587) — The Typhonian Cycle and the End of Napatan Dominance (592).

Chapter 17: Changing the Course of History:
The Tale of the Victor 595

The Abydos King-lists and the Dark Age of Egyptian History (596) — The Move to Tanis and the Four-Hundred-Year Stela (601) — The Community of Workmen at Deir el-Medina: A Post-Napatan Ramesside Town (604) — The Myth of the Transfer to Meroë (607) — The Battle of Kadesh: An Iron Age Poetic Account (608) — The Two Chief Queens of Ramses II: Myth or Reality? (612) — The Ashkelon Wall and the Ramesside Succession Line (615) — Venus, the Solar Eclipse and the Northern Coalition (617) The End of the Sixth Sun (624) — A Funny Thing Happened on the Way to Ethiopia (627) — The Identity of the "Ruler of Khemet" (632) — The Second Persian Invasion and the Completion of the Red Sea Canal (638) — Child of Jacob, Where's Thy Brother? (643).

Part VI — 404 BCE to 31 BCE

Chapter 18: The Last Centuries 651

The Great Religious Renewal (652) — The Second Persian Occupation, Alexander the Great, and the advent of the Greek Ptolemaic Dynasty (655) — The Cult of the Fish (659) — The Revolt in the South (662) — Ramses III: Ruler of the Greek Ptolemaic Age (663) — The Rise of the Priest-Kings (672) — The Khonsu Cosmogony (676) — The Anomalies from Tanis (677) — The Tomb Robberies and the Renaissance Era (681) — The Mummies of the Royal

Cache and the Missing Bulls (687) — The Ourmai Papyrus: Record of the End of a Civilization (695).

Part VII — Returning to Ceasar What Belongs to Ceasar

Chapter 19: After Cleopatra: The Rise of Rome and the Uniformitarian World View 699

Manetho's History of Egypt (700) — Ethiopia During the Graeco-Roman Era (702) — Mankind in Amnesia? (Stolen Legacies, Fallen Skies and the Triumph of the Axial Age) (708).

Chapter 20: Catastrophist Christology and the New Testament 715

The New Moses: The Jesus Narratives and their Old Testament Sources (716) — Jesus-Christ as Catastrophist (718) — On the Osirian Aspects of Christ (723).

Bibliography 731

Preface and Acknowledgements

> *" Almost always the men who achieve these fundamental inventions of a new paradigm have either been very young or very new to the field whose paradigm they change."*
>
> - Thomas Kuhn
> The Structure of
> of Scientific Revolutions

> *" Every great advance in science has issued from a new audacity of the imagination."*
>
> - John Dewey
> The Quest For Certainty

> *" There are only two powers in the world, the sword and the pen; and in the end the former is always conquered by the latter."*
>
> - Napoleon I

If there is such a thing as ownership of knowledge, then this book is a blatant act of theft. For nearly four years, I have had the temerity of trespassing into diverse established strongholds of Western scholarship—uncovering glaring inconsistencies and endeavouring to overturn, redefine and synthesize an armada of scholarly and scientific paradigms which, supported by traditional institutional pillars, have stood the test of time. Stripping science to its bare essentials, the present work issues the following challenge: Could the edifice of Western scholarship withstand a rigorous multi-disciplinarian critique of its most fundamental paradigms? How much of what universally, and uncritically, passes for objective science today is supported by mere convention? These are some of the central issues tackled here. In the eyes of most "reasonable" observers, I had no right to write this book. But perhaps it's precisely this "outlaw and lone ranger" status which gives me the freedom to journey through forbidden territories which desperately need to be explored. Whether or not my theories are ultimately accepted by the scholarly pundits, the provocative questions raised cannot be ignored. Many readers will probably be tempted to dismiss this work altogether from the first few pages. I will, however, make a cogent appeal for flexibility and consideration. Moreover, a cursory reading of this book would certainly not serve any purpose whatsoever. Many of the statements therein may, quite understandably, seem improbable until the volume has been read in its entirety. I do not claim to be an accredited expert in any of the fields covered therein. However, I believe that, as a member of a younger generation, I am in a position to offer a fresh and non-hegemonic perspective to the many fields tackled therein. My methodological approach is simply based on common sense. Indeed, to quote author Louis Jacot: " *True cognition of the world is only possible if knowledge and common sense are closely interlinked.*"[1] Through an exhaustive analysis of the extant archaeological and textual evidence used by historians throughout the ages to write history, I shall undertake to explain why I believe that much of this same body of evidence has been gravely misinterpreted. This *"organized confusion"* which is the conventional chronology of the ancient world is responsible for many embarrassing gaps and so-called "Dark Ages" throughout ancient history. The real problem is not that critical archaeological evidence is missing. It is rather that historians have simply missed the forest for the trees. The goal of the present volume is to critically reinterpret the entire history of the ancient world through the window of ancient pharaonic culture. This objective can only be achieved by radically altering the traditionally accepted chronology of ancient Egypt. With the new chronology, it will finally be possible to bridge the gap between biblical and pharaonic history, as well as to synchronize well-known accounts of ancient Greek historians with the world's "lost history."

At any rate, my fascination with ancient Egypt began in 1993, as an undergraduate student of economics and political science, during a summer internship with the National Bank of Egypt in Cairo. Upon my return home to Canada, at the end of the summer, I endeavoured to learn as much as I could about what I had seen in the Land of the Pharaohs. My studies in those totally unrelated domains would, however, limit my research for the time being. During the last year of my university studies, much indeed concerned with creative pursuits, I developed a portfolio of thirty photographs of Egyptian antiquities which I had taken at Cairo's Egyptian Museum in 1993. I converted them digitally into poster format and, after completing my Bachelor of Social Sciences (political science) degree, I ventured to New York city in June of 1995 to try my luck with art publishers. Unfortunately, I was repeatedly told that my work was not commercial enough, and that it was too specialized for a mainstream market. After six months of unsuccessful attempts at getting published, I returned to Canada to revamp and expand the subject-range of my portfolio and, undaunted, I was determined to give New York another try once I believed that the imperfections had, to the best of my abilities, been ironed out. I thought that a good way to make the prints

---

[1] Louis Jacot (1986) *A Heretical Cosmology (The Catastrophic Dislocation of Galaxies, Stars and Planets)*, Exposition-Banner: Pompano Beach, Fl., p. xi.

more palatable to a mainstream public would be to include short descriptive paragraphs along with each photograph. Thus grew my interest in ancient Egypt from a mainly artistic and cultural perspective to its considerably more rigorous archaeological aspects. My return voyage to New York city's art scene was however never to take place because of a fateful trip to a local Ottawa municipal library, in February of 1996, that would change my life forever. While searching for books on ancient Egypt to complete my art project, I accidentally came across Dr Immanuel Velikovsky's infamous best-selling book *Worlds in Collision*. For reasons which would subsequently be made much clearer to me, I had never heard of this man before; and was entirely unaware of the controversy that this book had caused within scholarly circles just a generation or two ago. The efforts of established academia to suppress his views had made sure that most young people of my generation would be free of his memory and legacy. Undeterred, I went on to read several of his other books with keen interest. As a result, I was simply stunned at the amount of apparent inconsistencies present within the conventional chronology of ancient Egypt — which, up until then, I had actively resisted to seriously question. Even more astounding to me, were his radical theories about cosmic catastrophes in the ancient past which allegedly wrought havoc upon the earth. I attempted to discuss Velikovsky's ideas with some of my former university classmates — whom I thought would be genuinely interested in the implications of his work. Much to my amazement, despite being all open-minded and critical readers, none of them had ever heard of him either. I convened two or three small meetings with five of my history and political science classmates (Ajani Ajamu, Copperfield Jean-Louis, Patrick Fry, Fuad Farage-Holm, and Derrick Haye), and began to tell them about what I had discovered. Shortly after our initial meeting, one of them approached a philosophy of science professor at the University of Ottawa and asked him what he thought of Immanuel Velikovsky. His emphatic response was: *"He was a raving lunatic"* and that intelligent young people such as ourselves ought to occupy our minds to more constructive matters. Hearing that only put fuel to my fire. I was more than ever determined to find out why this man was so feared and scorned by so many people. I sought to discover why, despite the fact that *Worlds in Collision* had been published in 1950, this book was still the subject of incessant debate among scholars and laymen alike — all over the world. I felt that Velikovsky had raised many important questions which seemingly still remained largely unanswered to this day. Some of the blatant inconsistencies of conventional wisdom, I thought, simply could not be over looked. Although I went on to complete my research project entirely on my own, this initial group of classmates, although understandably skeptical, offered me valuable encouragement, and were always eager to hear about the latest developments in my theories. I must especially thank my good friend (and African-centered librarian) Ajani Ajamu, who successfully went on to pursue post-graduate and legal studies, and served as my window into some of the harsh realities of being a critical and independent thinker even at the graduate level. He also passed on to me his very cleaver definition of the title of Ph.D. as: *"Please Honour my Degree."* I am also very grateful to my long-time friend, and big brother I never had, David MacLeod, from Scotland, for having unflagging been there for me through the thick and thin over the years. I thank him especially for always taking the time to listen to my unconventional ideas. Last but not least, I wish to thank my good friend and lost-and-found-again relative Copperfield Jean-Louis for believing in me and offering sound and valuable advice. Even though my stubborn reluctance to settle into a traditional path of work or study was sometimes interpreted by them as aloofness, and even sheer insanity on my part, they still understood that a maverick's road is often a lonely, unpredictable and treacherous one.

As I got more and more immersed into Velikovskian research, I soon realized that several other independent "new chronologists" were continuously hard at work, long after Velikovsky's death, to devise a revised chronological scheme for the ancient world. New chronologists hold among their ranks several *bona fide* historians and Egyptologists whom, whilst recognizing the validity of Dr Immanuel Velikovsky's call for a radical reshaping of the conventional chronology of the ancient world, often reject most of the latter's solutions. Some of them have been labelled by strict Velikovskians as " *the Peters of the revisionist movement"* — for on the one hand, working from Velikovsky's foundations, and on the other hand, failing to fully acknowledge their scholarly debt to him. Their principal motivation, it is often alleged, being to immune themselves from the Velikovskian stigma and ultimately shield themselves from the unavoidable backlash. New chronologists generally reply by saying that it isn't fair to lump all chronological revisionists along-side the Velikovskian legacy. Currently, two of the most well-known of those new chronologists are British scholars Peter James and David M. Rohl. James and Rohl were originally part of the same group of ancient historians who began to work on revising the chronology of ancient Egypt during the late 1970s.

It is evident that their initial efforts had been sparked by Velikovsky's *Ages in Chaos* series. But from the late 1970s on, there has been a general tendency for neo-catastrophists and new chronologists to go their own separate ways, after Immanuel Velikovsky's attempt to make both revolutionary fields combine. The unfortunate result has been that Immanuel Velikovsky is being ignored, and even denounced, by those who owe a lot more to him than they are willing to admit. Given the circumstances, I wholeheartedly agree with Professor Bruce G. Trigger of McGill University who, in a personal correspondence, related to me that any such attempt to enact a chronological revolution in ancient history, without acknowledging the central importance of Velikovsky, is tantamount to trying to "reinvent the wheel."

PREFACE AND ACKNOWLEDGEMENTS | xxiii

It must, however, be said that both Peter James and David Rohl have helped maintain a forum for Velikovskian debate through their active involvement within various inter-disciplinarian associations and initiatives open to Velikovskian research.[2] Yet, had they been more forthcoming about such Velikovskian ties while advancing their chronological revisionist research, many insiders would have rendered them a verdict of "guilty by association" without even taking the time to consider their independent ideas — of which there are indeed plenty.

One particular scholar who's been eager to make use of the "guilt by association" card is Prof. Kenneth A. Kitchen of Liverpool University (now retired). Following the publication of Peter James's Centuries of Darkness in 1990, Kitchen referred to the new chronologists as *"sons of Velikovsky."* Other reviewers were some what more sympathetic, and cautioned that the chronological revisionists' work was *"too impressive for them [James and his team] simply to be smeared as reincarnations of Velikovsky."*[3] Ironically, Dr K. Kitchen's 1973 book *The Third Intermediate Period in Egypt* had served as an important benchmark for James *et al.* and Rohl's scholarly quests. By using the detailed evidence provided by Kitchen concerning the Third Intermediate Period in Egyptian history, Peter James and his team concluded that the TIP had been artificially extended. They identified this error as the primary cause for the apparent "Dark Age" which engulfed much of the ancient world after 1,150 BCE. Being a staunch supporter of the orthodox chronology, Prof. Kitchen dismissed their theories by claiming that any revision of the standard chronology inevitably brings up unsolvable anomalies.[4] Consequently, as of now, the debate still rages between the defenders of the orthodox chronology and those who would propose a new chronological framework. As I now prepare to enter the battlefield, it would not be surprising if Professor Kitchen were to refer to me as *"the Prodigal Son of Velikovsky!"*

---

[2] See David M. Rohl & Peter James (1983) 'An Alternative to the Velikovskian Chronology of Ancient Egypt: A Preview of Some Recent Work in the Field of Ancient History', *Society for Interdisciplinary Studies Workshop* Vol. 5 - Num. 2, pp. 12-21. Peter James was also one of only two scholars (the other being biblical Conquest scholar John Bimson) at a Glasgow symposium in 1978 to suggest that Velikovsky's chronological revision might resolve long-standing archaeological conundrums — see Jerome Burn (1978) 'Velikovsky Spawns More Controversy', *New Scientist* Vol. 78 - Num. 1099, p. 134. Additionally, James and Rohl have been actively involved with both the Society for Interdisciplinary Studies (SIS) and the Institute for the Study of Interdisciplinary Sciences (ISIS) — both organizations act as prime forums for neo-Velikovskian research.

[3] Graeme Auld (1992) 'BOOK REVIEW: Centuries of Darkness: A Challenge to the Conventional Chronology of Old World Archaeology. P. James *et al.* 1991', *Journal of Theological Studies* Vol. 43 - Num. 1, p. 142.

[4] Kenneth A. Kitchen (1991) 'Egyptian Chronology: Problem or Solution?', *Cambridge Archaeological Journal* 1, pp. 235-239. See also Kitchen's review of P. James *et al.* in *London Times Literary Supplement* (17 May 1991), p. 21.

Being an independent scholar, I stand with nothing to lose by identifying myself as a critical but proud disciple of Immanuel Velikovsky. As an internationally renowned Egyptologist and ancient historian, as well as an expert on chronology, I certainly do not underestimate the validity of the objections raised by Dr Kitchen. It is evident that any new or novel chronological paradigm must, in order to be viable, take account of and be tested against the abundant extant archival material (i.e. king-lists, annals, inscriptions, political patterns, etc). In spite of my innumerable disagreements with Professor Kitchen, I still, and will continue, to hold him in high regard for his very comprehensive and remarkably multi-disciplinarian approach to the study of the ancient past. His increasingly rare ability to combine breadth and depth of scholarship is a trait which I have sought to emulate. In an era plagued with the modern disease of exaggerated specialization, his case is certainly more of an exception than the rule. In any event, I hope that this book will serve as a much needed antidote, and ultimately encourage scholars, in all disciplines concerned, to begin engaging in much more extensive inter-disciplinarian research, based upon open and honest discourse.

By the time *Centuries of Darkness* was published, David Rohl had already split from the original group, since the late 1980s, and later went on to pursue a Ph.D. in Egyptology at University College, London. In 1995, he released the first volume of his series *A Test of Time* subtitled *The Bible – From Myth to History*. It is through David Rohl's work that I was initially exposed to the ideas of chronologists. I first began taking Rohl's work seriously shortly after having read Velikovsky's *Worlds in Collision* and *Ages in Chaos*. My original contact with David Rohl's theories had occurred only a month earlier, in January of 1996. Again, this was a chance discovery, as while flicking through television channels, I stumbled across his international three-part television special entitled *Pharaohs and Kings: A Biblical Quest*. At that time, I was merely trying to familiarise myself with ancient Egyptian history and chronology; and I thought that this heretic's ideas would cloud my still young and impressionable mind with "false teachings." So I made a conscious effort to remain skeptical. Never before had I even entertained the idea of questioning the validity of the accepted chronology of the ancient world. As it was my practice with every television programs on ancient Egypt which I encountered, I recorded the series for my personal archives. It was again only during the following month of February, after having read Velikovsky, that I blew off the dust from the videotape containing David Rohl's documentary, and decided to take another look at his work. I was mostly struck by the fact that Rohl presented very compelling evidence to suggest, as Velikovsky had earlier, that the period of the Hebrew sojourn in the land of Egypt should be situated at the end of the epoch of Egyptian history known as the "Middle Kingdom." With this striking concordance, I was convinced that this theory was accurate. Shortly thereafter, I began devising my own new chronology for the ancient world with Velikovsky and Rohl's dating for the Hebrew sojourn as a major building block.

After having spent the months of February to May 1996 absorbed in Velikovsky's books, I decided to set out to London, England for six months, in June of 1996, in order to fully devote myself to my research. I spent much of my time at the British Museum, getting acquainted with the available archaeological evidence. My evenings were spent back in my bedsit (bachelor room) in Islington (north London) — where I entered the information I gathered everyday from the British Museum and the School of Oriental and African Studies library into my computer. Slowly but surely, I ventured to reconstruct the ancient past. It had actually escaped my memory, by the time I had arrived in London, that David M. Rohl's television documentary had been based on a book of his. It was only sometime during the late summer of 1996 that, while strolling along Charing Cross Road in London, that I suddenly noticed an entire pile of Rohl's book *A Test of Time* exposed in a bookshop window — as part of a promotional sale. Enchanted with this unexpected find, I promptly purchased a copy. I found Rohl's analysis to be thoroughly detailed and well researched. Although I would ultimately develop very different theories of my own, his style of investigation between the realms of presumed biblical myth and archaeology served as an invaluable source of inspiration and evidence for much of the present work. A trained Egyptologist, Rohl nonetheless purposely wrote *A Test of Time* with a popular audience in mind. Some critics hurriedly suggested that, despite the fact that he claimed to speak to a general audience, the highly technical nature of his arguments betrayed his true hidden agenda of convincing his skeptical Egyptological colleagues. Many trained insiders believed that such a detailed analysis would ultimately "*lose*" half of the intended readership. Such comments only serve to highlight academia's notoriously high-handed attitude toward the masses of lay people. This unfortunately widespread tendency among professional scholars to underestimate the intelligence and capacity to reason of non-academics has, for centuries, been part and parcel of the "rarefaction" culture which characterizes much of modern scholarship.

My views about ancient Egypt had however started taking shape long before having encountered the works of Velikovsky and Rohl. After having had the life-changing experience of reading Alex Haley's *The Autobiography of Malcolm X* in February of 1992, I first began thinking about the possible African origins of ancient Egyptian civilization. Like most people however, my very first experience with the study of the ancient world occurred in secondary school — in an eighth grade class on ancient civilizations given by an Alexandrian Egyptian. I remember finding this subject a total bore. During a particular lecture on ancient Egypt, noticing that I was not paying attention, the teacher immediately decided to surprise me with the following question: "Meres! Where is Egypt?" Having been suddenly startled out of an engaging conversation about the previous night's Montreal Canadiens' hockey game with my friend sitting next to me, I quickly glanced down at the map from my class textbook, and replied: "in Africa?" This response was immediately followed by a thunderous burst of laughter from the entire class. Somewhat taken aback, the teacher simply glanced at me with a puzzled look, neither correcting or approving of my answer, and asked the same question again to another student. I believe the answer he sought was "the Near East." Looking back at this episode, I would say that it was the beginning of a journey of self-discovery which has culminated with this volume. I went on believing that my answer was indeed wrong until I read Malcolm X a few years later, in 1992, at the age of nineteen. It was in Malcolm X's footsteps that I ventured to Egypt for the first time during the summer of the following year. For this opportunity, I must express my deepest gratitude to Mr Mohammed Abushadi — former Chairman of the National Bank of Egypt, for having personally given me, as a mere undergraduate student and complete stranger, the chance to live and work in Egypt during that summer. My idea to approach Mr Abushadi was very much like throwing a bottle in the sea. I had inadvertently come across his name in *The International Who's Who*, and decided to send him a resume at his Paris office in the hope of obtaining a summer internship in Cairo. Much to my surprise, this rather unorthodox method actually paid off. My main motivation for making the trip, at the time, was not really to learn about ancient Egyptian history, but rather to understand the political, economic and social climate of Africa and the Middle East. I did not even take the time to visit the Cairo Museum until several weeks after my arrival in Egypt. I spent many hours discussing issues of politics, race and religion with my Egyptian colleagues at the bank. Although I have unfortunately not been very good at keeping in touch with my friends in Cairo, I would wish to especially thank my friend Abdal Moneim Aufy, and everyone else at the NBE: Mrs Laila Kamel, Mrs Mona Hossny, Mrs Fadia Metwally, and all of my comrades from the Economic Research Department for their warm welcome and friendship. I hope you can all forgive me for my prolonged silence.

Those very engaging and stimulating discussions, as well as my various readings, would eventually lead me to the study of African liberation theology and Afrocentricity (also commonly known as Afrocentrism). I was first introduced to Afrocentric scholarship upon my return from Egypt through some political science classmates at the University of Ottawa. Our interactions eventually evolved into lengthy weekly informal discussions every Sundays — in which we analysed the works of scholars such as W.E.B. Du Bois, Cheikh Anta Diop, Theophile Obenga, Maulana Karanga, Harold Cruse, Jean Price-Mars, Jacob Carruthers, Molefi Kete Asante, George G. M. James, Carter G. Woodson, Yosef Ben-Jochannan, Ivan Van Sertima, Wayne B. Chandler, Chancellor Williams, Marimba Ani, Frantz Fanon, John G. Jackson, St. Clair Drake and many others. This collective formative period would later prove to be a crucial asset in my efforts to critically analyse the scholarly establishment, and in equipping me a greater awareness of the cultural biases which often go hand in hand with archaeological interpretation. The writings of Dr Cheikh Anta Diop, in particular, would have a truly lasting impact on me. The same way I would be struck by Immanuel Velikovsky's ideas three years later, Dr Diop would from then on become a life-long mentor of mine.

Cheikh Anta Diop was born on December 23rd 1923 in Diourbel, Senegal. He studied sociology, anthropology, ancient history, classical antiquity, Egyptology, linguistics and mathematics at the Sorbonne in Paris between 1946 and 1960. He additionally studied physics under Frederick Joliot-Curie, Madame Curie's son-in-law, and later translated Einstein's theory of relativity into his native Wolof. From him, I've learned of the crucial importance of a multi-disciplinarian and rigorous scientific approach to the study of African history and culture. Moreover, his steadfast belief in excellence first — rhetoric later, has been and continues to serve as a prime model for me. Dr Diop's first book, *Nations nègres et culture*, published in 1954, is considered a classic of Afrocentric scholarship. In the prophetic words of Diop: *"The history of Africa will remain suspended in air and cannot be written correctly until African historians connect it with the history of Egypt."* As a young man of Afro-Haitian descent, it is in the spirit of my pioneering ancestors Baron P.V. Vasty and Prince Sanders[5] that I have taken up Dr C. A. Diop's challenge. I found in Diop's work many of the answers I was seeking about Egypt's African heritage and it's many contributions to world civilization. I was nonetheless strangely convinced that Dr Diop's pioneering journey had not been completed and that fundamental questions had remained unexplored. For three years, the missing piece of the puzzle would elude me. It is only once I became confident that the accepted chronology of ancient Egypt was inaccurate that everything instantly fell into place. The principal reason why African history, to paraphrase C. A. Diop, remained suspended in air is because African scholars had failed to realize that African history is the prisoner of an erroneous chronology and history of ancient Egypt. It became evident to me that the only way to connect ancient African history with the history of Egypt was to devise an African-centered chronology of the ancient world. This had become my mission and pioneering objective.

Another scholar to whom I am immensely indebted for this work, is British scholar Prof. Martin Bernal of Cornell University. His (1987-1991) book series *Black*

---

[5] see Introduction, p. 13.

Athena: The Afroasiatic Roots of Classical Civilization (Volumes I & II), created a storm of controversy throughout much of the academic world. His major crime was that he, a scholar of European descent to boot, had dared to commit the unspeakable sacrilege of proposing that the ancient Greeks owed much of their culture to ancient Egyptian and Phoenician colonists.[6] He, moreover, vehemently denounced what he perceives as having been the overt racism and anti-Semitism of nineteenth century European scholars. I only first heard of Martin Bernal in 1994, through the Sunday discussion group which I attended while at the University of Ottawa. Since I was not very much interested in the classics at the time, I was merely contented to gain a general understanding of his theories through others in the group who had actually read *Black Athena*. It wasn't until the Fall of 1996, while conducting my research in Britain, that I finally acquired a copy of *Black Athena* (Vol. I) and, for the first time, read Bernal's work for myself. It was truly an eye-opening experience. Immediately, I began establishing links between my then fast-evolving Egypto-biblical synchronism and extant literature and archaeological evidence from ancient Greece. I must indeed credit Professor Martin Bernal with providing the all-important initial spark which ultimately led me to delve a lot deeper into the classical epic tales on Afroasiatic colonizations of early Greece, the classics in general, and even ancient Chinese history. While Martin Bernal cannot be categorized as an Afrocentric scholar,[7] his work has been well received within the Afrocentric community. Bernal describes himself as "lumper," and denounces many of his academic colleagues' narrow style of academic inquiry as that of "splitters." Like many of the scholars already mentioned, Bernal recognizes the need for an inter-disciplinary approach to ancient world scholarship. In the present climate where mainstream institutional scholarship and forwardly focused Afrocentric discourse are on a collision course, such attempts at universal consolidation, based on respect for truth and open-mindedness, are certainly needed.

Other authors (deceased or living) to whom I am likewise thankful for their inspiring scholarship are: Cyrus H. Gordon, Michael C. Astour, John Philip Cohane, Barry Fell, Vine Deloria, Jr., Graham Hancock, Robert Bauval & Adrian Gilbert, Giorgio de Santillana & Hertha Dechend, Jane B. Sellers, Cain Hope Felder, Thomas S. Kuhn and Noam Chomsky. With absolute certainty, this book would never have been written – and especially not in such record time – had it not been for all of the

---

[6] See Martin Bernal (1992) 'The Case for Massive Egyptian Influence in the Aegean', *Archaeology* Vol. 45 - Num. 5, pp. 53-55, 82-86. For a critique of Bernal's thesis see: John E. Coleman (1992) 'Did Egypt Shape the Glory that Was Greece?', Ibid, pp. 48-52, 77-81 and James M. Weinstein (1992) 'BOOK REVIEW: Black Athena: The Afroasiatic Roots of Classical Civilization. Vol. II: The Archaeological and Documentary Evidence. M. Bernal. 1987', *American Journal of Archaeology* 96, pp. 381-383.

[7] Martin Bernal & Mary R. Lefkowitz (1992) 'Correspondence: Martin Bernal Responds to Afrocentric "Myths." An Exchange', *New Republic* (March 9), p. 5.

PREFACE AND ACKNOWLEDGEMENTS | xxix

thirty-some aforementioned scholars' significant influence upon my own perception of ancient history and/or the sociology of knowledge. However, the readers will now be required to brace themselves for not only the explosive amalgamation of those radical approaches, but also for the revolutionary and progressive historical, theological and scientific theories necessary to both correct them and glue them together.

It must at this point be made very clear that I have conducted my research independently; and that though I have been influenced by the theories of the cited scholars, I am in no position to assume, or suggest, that they would automatically, wholly or partly, support my own findings. My scholarly and political views are entirely my own. Since the scholars who have inspired me do not even agree amongst one another, it is difficult to imagine how a combination of all of these approaches might easily be accepted by the disparate individuals. If, for instance, Immanuel Velikovsky, Cheikh Anta Diop, David Rohl & Martin Bernal were metaphorically made to sit together on a discussion round table, one would most certainly bear witness to a much heated debate. For example, Dr Diop, as a physicist, would have, and probably has, laughed at Immanuel Velikovsky's scenario of planetary collisions. Prof. Martin Bernal has likewise not hesitated to relegate those ideas to the realms of cranks and charlatans.[8] Moreover, both Diop and Bernal would also likely be very critical of Velikovsky and Rohl's attempts to devise a radical new chronology for the ancient world. On the other hand, David M. Rohl actually believes that Immanuel Velikosky's *"whole thesis degenerated into farce."*[9] Finally, with regards to the issue of Afrocentrism, Rohl and Velikovsky might have joined forces to question the evidence and methodologies of both Diop and Bernal. Having said that, it is also noteworthy that Professor Bernal has sought to distance himself from Diop's ideas on the racial make-up of ancient Egyptian society.[10] The reader may therefore wonder how, in the world, could anyone attempt to condense and vindicate the works of these four scholars in a single volume! Of course, while I support the overall themes of each author's scholarship, I must disagree with many details of their respective historical reconstructions. Despite the fact that this All-Star Dream Team of heretics have, in my opinion, made some important methodological mistakes, we must remember, as in the words of Nietzsche, that *"the errors of great men often prove more fruitful than the truths of little men."*

---

[8] Martin Bernal (1987a) *Black Athena (The Afroasiatic Roots of Classical Civilization) — Vol. I: The Fabrication of Ancient Greece 1785-1985*, Vintage: London, p. 6.
[9] David M. Rohl (1991) *A Test of Time — Vol. I: The Bible – From Myth to History*, Century: London, p. 402.
[10] See Clyde Ahmad Winters (1994) 'Afrocentrism: A Valid Frame of Reference', *Journal of Black Studies* Vol. 25 - Num. 2, pp. 175-176.

To be sure, catastrophism, chronological revisionism and Afrocentricity have historically been like three feared sharks swimming in different oceans, but hunting for the same prey. This radical new approach, which I hereby propose, of combining all three rebel disciplines, can without a doubt, be seen as the worst nightmare of every conventional scholar come true. The very last thing that traditional academics now want to deal with or even hear about is of an "Afrocentric Velikovskian chronologist!" But, as mentioned earlier, there is neither any guarantee that this merger will be welcomed by the proponents of each individual discourse themselves. It is however quite clear to me that all three revolutionary schools, while having had some effect independently in addressing important inconsistencies of conventional science and history, their ultimate combination represents their one and only salvation.

The year 1997 was arguably the most important year of my life. Back in Canada, I faced a major dilemma. After laborious research and writing efforts in England, the sheer enormity of this project had finally dawned on me. Though I had by then managed to devise what I, at the time, thought was a viable new chronology, it remained incomplete and many vital questions still begged to be answered. I knew that if I had any chance of closing over this endeavour once and for all, in order to move on with my life, I would need to continue devoting most of my time to it. To quote my mentor Immanuel Velikovsky, I had become the "prisoner of an idea." I would not and could not rest until I finally saw the light at the end of the tunnel. Much to the dismay of my understandably concerned relatives and entourage, I sacrificed everything for this pursuit. Like a hermit, I spent countless hours in several academic libraries in my hometowns of Montreal and Ottawa, and accumulated many sleepless nights.

It was on the landmark date of December 28th 1997, that the firm chronological framework for my revised history of the ancient world was at last established. As much as this meant for me, as a personal achievement, an equally challenging set of tasks still lay ahead — a process that would keep me busy through much of the following year and a half. These final steps of refining the historical details of each Egyptian dynasties, and linking the various ancient theological constructs with cyclical celestial events in order to ultimately perform a gigantic balancing act across the ages, were to form the backbone of this novel historiography. Several more people are to thank for their invaluable support throughout this often difficult but rewarding quest. I am first of all grateful to Ms Carmen Nesbeth for her precious advice gained through her numerous years in the book trade. Others friends and family I especially wish to thank are: Alain-Ralph David, Yves J. David, Andrée

Brunache, the Antoine cousins, Ralph Adrien, Surpris Latouche, Jean St-Vil, Elizabeth Vorlicky, Keeli Smith, Yvon Villarceaux, and Beth Cumming. Finally, to Professors Cain Hope Felder and Vine Deloria, Jr., whose demonstrated enthusiasm for the finished project provided me with much encouragement, I extend my most heartfelt gratitude.

Meres J. Weche
Ottawa, 2000

Introduction

> *" The basis for any analysis of an ancient literary text is the establishment of the text itself through critical comparison of all extant witnesses to the textual tradition. Variants and aberrations must be weighed so as to arrive at the most reliable ancient witness to the original text."*
>
> - Robert H. O'Connell
> (Egyptologist)

Professional historians, it is oft-alleged, write history on the basis of objective and dispassionate analysis of extant primary materials such as archaeological and textual evidence. It must however be borne in mind that history is not merely a mechanical accumulation of primary evidence. Scholars necessarily interpret archaeological evidence in a manner which is consistent with their own preconceived notions about the past. Therefore, the preeminent role of interpretation in historiography should never be underestimated. Interpretation of historical evidence can be shaped by such things as culture, politics, current sociological mores, religious beliefs and nationalism. Historians are, generally speaking, only too little aware of the real extent to which these often unconscious biases affect their own formulation and treatment of history. Indeed, to quote author Marc Ferro: *"It is always possible to doubt the scientific innocence of the historian who, also as a product of his century, is as much guided by passion as by reason."*[1] Since all historiography is suspect, it becomes necessary to evaluate all extant ancient documents with a critical eye. Such caution, again, must not only be directed against the given ancient chroniclers but also against the prevalent interpretation of contemporary scholarship. Which kind of evidence, emerging from which cultural context, should be employed as a measuring tool to assess the validity of the multitude of textual and archaeological remains?

Following the Napoleonic expedition into North Africa and Palestine, early nineteenth century European scholars undertook the monumental task of deciphering ancient scripts which had not been read in many centuries. Archaeologists, philologists, artists and mapmakers flocked from Britain, France, Germany, Austria and Italy to unravel the mysteries of the ancient Near East and Africa. Most of these excavators and explorers having been raised according to the prevailing strict doctrines of the Judeo-Christian faith, it comes as no surprise that many of them went

---

[1] Marc Ferro (1985) *L'histoire sous surveillance,* Calmann-Lévy: Paris, p. 148 (my translation).

2 | PLANET OF THE GREEKS

there looking for evidence to prove the accuracy of the biblical narratives. When, in 1822, the Frenchman Jean-François Champollion finally deciphered the Egyptian hieroglyphs, their task was both eased and complicated. Pharaoh Ramses II, for instance, was immediately identified as the Pharaoh of the Oppression. Also, Pharaoh Shoshenk I was at once recognized as the biblical Pharaoh Shishak who plundered the temple of King Solomon. To this very day, these two identifications remain central synchronizing pillars of ancient Egypto-biblical chronology. However, as archaeological remains continued to be unearthed, and an apparently workable ancient Egyptian chronology was established, the embarrassing incompatibility of the extant Egyptian king-lists, archaeological remains from prominent ancient Near Eastern sites, and the biblical narratives became increasingly evident. Meanwhile, classical scholars were likewise attempting to correlate the accounts of the early Greek historians (i.e. Herodotus and Diodorus of Sicily) with the fast-developing scholarly knowledge about ancient Egypt. There again, classicists quickly discovered that the ancient Greek texts did not always appear to be vindicated by the Egyptian archaeological remains. As the inconsistencies incrementally accumulated, Western scholars, over time, developed what has come to be known as the "historical-critical" method. According to this principle, traditional texts like the Hebrew Bible or the *History* of Herodotus could no longer be looked upon as "historical" documents if their contents could not be verified by independent archaeological or scientific inquiry. With the rapidly declining power of the Church, such overt criticism of the Bible became more and more common place within scholarly circles.

In the following chapters, I shall endeavour to argue that Western scholars have somewhat disproportionately applied the rigorous standards of the historical-critical method upon textual evidence written on paper and not enough on textual records inscribed in stone. Why should excavators and philologists be more suspicious about the Bible's narratives and less cynical when confronted, for example, with the Egyptian official king-lists carved upon the temple-walls of Abydos? What makes a textual source more credible when it is written in stone as opposed to paper? Furthermore, there is the thorny question of culture. Were the ancient Egyptian scribes more credible than the Israelite biblical redactors? Moreover, why should the accounts of ancient Greek historians be perceived as being more "rational" or "objective" than the contemporary historical annals of any other ancient culture? Who should decide who's right? Is anyone right? Most excavators would reply that the "physical evidence" is right. But again, what guarantee do we really have that the supposedly objective primary evidence has not been tainted by faulty modern interpretation?

The truth is, historians of antiquity were just as susceptible to historiographical propaganda as modern historians are. The straightforward reason why the extant textual records or narratives from ancient Egypt, Israel and Greece fail to accord with one another is because they each represent a set of politically biased records of the people who composed them. There is no reason why the Egyptian Turin Canon for instance, as detailed as it may be as an official king-list, should be considered as being any more historical than the biblical genealogy from the Book of Kings, or vice versa. For generations, scholars have attempted to establish a continuous link between the biblical texts and the ancient Egyptian cultural records. Such endeavours have, however, mostly proved unfruitful as, too often, scholars either tried forcing the biblical texts to fit with the archaeological evidence or, in equally futile efforts, struggled to mould the archaeological records around the traditional Bible stories. Quite understandably, many scholars have despaired. It is a generally accepted fact today that much of the biblical narratives are not supported by the archaeological remains from the ancient Near East and Africa. The same dire verdict has been cast upon many of the classical accounts concerning ancient Egypt. The scientific age had, so it seemed, silenced the ancient chroniclers.

However, I am thoroughly convinced that it *is* actually possible to reconstruct history from the Egyptian archaeological remains and king-lists, the biblical narratives and the classical textual evidence. Indeed, I hereby claim to have at long last solved the eternal riddle presented by the elusive Egypto-biblical textual synthesis and its link with the classical authors' narratives. This trilateral correlation unifying Egyptology, biblical exegesis and the classics can only come together once it is acknowledged that the ancient Egyptian, Israelite and Greek chroniclers' ultimate goal never was to write objective accounts of their people's history. What we modern observers must do is attempt to read between the lines. To unravel not what the ancients actually wanted us to know but what they *didn't* want us to know.[2] The historical-critical method must go far beyond mere assessment of competitive plausibility and into determining probable motives for clearly misleading historical accounts on the part of ancient chroniclers. It is precisely through the latter process that a genuine history of the ancient world can be gleaned. The truth does not lie at the surface, but in the hidden recesses of inter-disciplinarian exegesis. Ancient historians, from Mesoamerica to China, spoke in a metaphorical language unknown to the modern rationalistic mind. History was hidden in myth as often as myth was hidden in history. Deciphering this ancient historiography is as important as deciphering the scripts in which the ancient histories were written. The positivist mentality of contemporary scholars have unfortunately prevented such vital methodologies from developing within institutional circles. Anyone who as much as attempts to tread the thin line between science and, dare we say it, esoteric speculation

---

[2] *See* William G. Dever (1995a) 'Cultural Continuity, Ethnicity, and the Question of Israelite Origins', *Eretz-Israel* 24, pp. 22-33.

is at once labelled a crank or heretic. If my search for truth makes me a heretic then this book is indeed a heresy. My objective is to write "Total History."³ The ancient world cannot be properly understood unless historians study it through the eyes of the ancients themselves. This means being open to such diverse realms as mythology, folkloric legends, comparative religion and archaeoastronomy. Gaining insight on how the ancients related to these traditions will, in itself, set the path towards establishing more accurate relative chronologies between the major cultures of the ancient world. And once the chronologies are readjusted, many of the motivations behind the ancients' desire to circumvent, or even altogether falsify, historical records will be made apparent.

The Bible as History

> *" The historical-critical method of Bible interpretation is indispensable , [...] Proper understanding [of the Bible] not only admits the use of this method but actually requires it. [Holy Scripture is the] Word of God in human language. [it] has been composed by human authors in all its various parts."*
>
> - Pontifical Biblical Commission of the Roman Catholic Church. (Vatican, 1993)

Without a doubt, no other book has had more influence on Western culture and the rest of the world than the Hebrew Bible. Yet, many of its mysteries continue to elude scholars. Modern archaeology has unfortunately raised more questions than it has answered. Confronted with the embarrassing incompatibility of the biblical narratives and archaeology, many excavators no longer dare to speak of "biblical archaeology" but instead prefer the term "Syro-Palestinian archaeology." Having pronounced the death of biblical archaeology,[4] certain professional excavators, and even some theologians, today dismiss most of the biblical narratives, such as those concerning the Exodus and Conquest, as idealized fictitious accounts. While I likewise contend that the traditional biblical narratives, specifically covering the period before the Divided Monarchy, have indeed little to do with historical reali-

---

[3] The concept of "Total History" is largely associated with the Annales school. The Annales school of historical research originated in France with the publication, in 1929, of the journal *Annales d'Histoire Sociale et Economique [Annales: ESC since 1955]*. This approach promotes the total reconstruction of history through the use of a broad and diverse set of perspectives, disciplines, or database. See John Bintliff (editor) (1991) *The Annales School and Archaeology*, Leicester University Press: Leicester and London.

[4] See William G. Dever 'Biblical Archaeology: Death and Rebirth.' In A. Biran & J. Aviram (editors) (1993a) *Biblical Archaeology Today, 1990 (Proceedings of the Second International Congress on Biblical Archaeology — Jerusalem, June-July 1990)*, pp. 706-722.

ty, I am nonetheless persuaded that they hide reliable information necessary to reconstruct the ancient Israelites' past. Altogether dismissing the first five books of the Bible (the Torah) represents a grave mistake. The Torah (or Pentateuch) is an indispensable tool toward the accurate reconstruction of not only Israelite history, but also of the entire history of the ancient Near East. The key to unlocking the Torah's secrets is not found in its literal interpretation but in one's ability to divine its hidden story lines. As the ancient Jewish historian Flavius Josephus observed, the Torah is a document laden with fanciful allegory and symbolism.

The countless mysteries and allegories found in the Bible can only be genuinely understood once the biblical narratives have been reintegrated within their true historical context. Indeed, as it could not have been conveyed better, Bible scholar George E. Mendenhall remarks: *"The misunderstanding of the Bible that derives from an inability to understand it in a historical context is a luxury that the religious tradition can no longer afford."*[5] In addition, where matters complicate themselves is when we come to the realization that certain major biblical stories, in order to fit with extant archaeological evidence, must be shifted to entirely different ages than the ones in which they are portrayed in the Bible. One such example is the Conquest narrative from the Book of Joshua. It will be argued in this book that the Conquest of Joshua did not take place at the end of the archaeological period known as the Late Bronze Age, as the Bible implies, but during the Middle Bronze Age. Needless to say, such a radical chronological shift carries important ramifications for biblical archaeology. Placing the Conquest in an entirely new context opens up a myriad of new possibilities. For instance, quite surprisingly, the Syro-Palestinian archaeological remains from the Middle Bronze Age strata fit perfectly well with the Conquest narratives. Whereas when the Conquest narratives are staged in the context of the closing Late Bronze Age, scholars can only conclude that the Book of Joshua's contents belong to the realms of myth. In essence, archaeologists have looked for evidence of the Conquest in the right places, but in entirely the wrong time. Precisely the same difficulties present themselves when attempting to date the biblical Exodus. I shall refrain from going into further details for now about my revised dates for the Exodus and Conquest — as the topic will be dealt with at length shortly. What must be borne in mind, however, is that the archaeological context in which the biblical stories are placed plays an infinitely important role in determining their probable veracity. The following work in chronological revisionism endeavours to relocate ancient historical narratives into their proper archaeological context. Received chronologies and histories taking second place, the ancient records are reexamined with the naked eye of archaeology.

---

[5] George E. Mendenhall (1973) *The Tenth Generation (The Origins of the Biblical Tradition)*, Johns Hopkins University Press: Baltimore and London, p. 3.

The Velikovsky Affair: A Twentieth Century Inquisition

> " Daring ideas are like chessmen moved forward. They may be beaten, but they may start a winning game."
>
> - Goethe (1749-1832)

> " If Dr. Velikovsky is right, the rest of us are crazy."
>
> - Dr Harlow Shapley
> Director of the Harvard
> Observatory (1946)

One of the most original, and certainly most controversial, quests to reconstruct ancient history independently of the received chronologies was undertaken by Dr Immanuel Velikovsky. Since Velikovsky's work is so prominently featured in this volume, it would be relevant for the reader to first gain an adequate understanding of his life and works. To begin with, Immanuel Velikovsky was born in Vitebsk, Russia on June 10th 1895. As a youngster, he was schooled at Moscowat Medvednikov Gymnasium. After graduating with honours in 1913, he studied briefly in Montpellier, France, travelled to his ancestral home of Palestine and, in 1914, began pre-medical studies in Edinburgh, Scotland. With the outbreak of World War I, Velikovsky was forced to abandon his studies abroad and enrolled at the Free University in Moscow — where he studied law and ancient history for a few years. Meanwhile, in 1915, he began taking classes at the University of Moscow to complete his medical degree in Psychiatry — which he obtained in 1921. Trained under Sigmund Freud's pupil, Wilhelm Stekel, Velikovsky, between 1921 and 1924, lived in Berlin — where, in collaboration with Heinrich Loewe, he founded and published the academic journal Scripta Universitatis. He also worked very closely with Albert Einstein, editor with the new journal, who was responsible for the mathematical-physical section. Scripta Universitatis would later become the cornerstone for the advent of the University of Jerusalem. While in Berlin, Dr Velikovsky met violinist Elishiva Kramer, whom he married in 1924. That same year, the newly-weds settled in Palestine, where Velikovsky opened a medical practice. What would ultimately prove to be a major turning point in his life occurred fifteen years later. On March of 1939, while meandering down a Tel Aviv street, Velikovsky by chance noticed two intriguing books displayed in a store window. One of them was Adolf Hitler's *Mein Kampf,* and the other Sigmund Freud's then latest book *Moses and Monotheism*. After briefly hesitating about which book to buy, his choice finally rested upon Freud's volume.

Sigmund Freud's controversial belief in the Egyptian origins of Jewish monotheism had a profound effect on Velikovsky. Disagreeing in principle with Dr Freud's thesis, Velikovsky saw in the former "a still-unresolved conflict with respect to his Jewish origins and in his own father."[6] Enthralled with a new-found fascination with Sigmund Freud's psyche, Immanuel Velikovsky at once got to work on a book on Freud's dreams. Entitled "Freud and His Heroes," the manuscript focused on Freud's heroes: Oedipus, Akhenaten, and Moses. It was precisely to complete his research for this intended book that Dr Velikovsky journeyed, along with his family (wife and two young daughters), to the United States. They arrived by boat at Ellis Island, in New York, on July 26th 1939. Velikovsky's initial plan was to stay in America for eight months, but he had enough means to stay for up to two years. Dr Velikovsky immediately plunged himself into his library research. With his work finally nearly completed by the spring of 1940, he began making plans to return home to Israel. But on the day before he was supposed to sail across the Atlantic, a publisher unexpectedly expressed interest in publishing his manuscript on Freud. Immanuel Velikovsky hence decided to stay; only to eventually see that publisher gradually lose interest in the manuscript. This last setback no longer mattered though — since, to again use his own words, he had become the "prisoner of an idea."

In the fall of 1940, while pondering on the biblical narratives describing the Hebrew Exodus and Conquest, Velikovsky began wondering if the cataclysmic upheavals which purportedly accompanied those pivotal episodes in the Old Testament could not have been caused by a genuine natural catastrophe of global scale in ancient times. He hypothesised that if the Israelites' journey out of Egypt took place in the midst of a natural conflagration, then evidence for this paroxysm of nature must also be available among the ancient Egyptian records. Velikovsky discovered this corroborating evidence in an ancient Egyptian document know as the Papyrus Ipuwer (from the name of its author, Ipuwer). The text in question was a lament composed during Egypt's Middle Kingdom. It related, in amazingly similar details as found in the Bible's Exodus narratives, how the land of Egypt was abruptly hit by a terrible plague which turned the waters of the Nile into blood. When Immanuel Velikovsky sent the parallel texts to the British Egyptologist, and excavator at Jericho, Prof. John Garstang, the latter informed Velikovsky that the two documents, despite their obvious similarities, could hardly describe one and the same event since the Papyrus Ipuwer, according to received wisdom, is supposed to have been written long before the time of the Israelite Exodus. Dr Velikovsky, still convinced that both texts described the same cataclysm, therefore surmised that one of the histories, either that of pharaonic Egypt or of the Israelite nation, was out of step by several centuries. Simi-

---

[6] Immanuel Velikovsky (1983) *Stargazers and Gravediggers (Memoirs to Worlds in Collision)*, William Morrow: New York, p. 28.

larly to what I have argued above, Velikovsky moved the Exodus and Conquest upwards by several centuries, to coincide with the archaeological context of the Papyrus Ipuwer. He believed that the close of the Middle Kingdom in Egypt witnessed a major cosmic upheaval which manifested itself throughout the ancient world. Dr Velikovsky spent the following six years avidly searching for corresponding evidence in Mesoamerica, China and other ancient cultures documenting this same, and other, catastrophes. His radical thesis was that, sometime during the Early Bronze Age, a powerful convulsion inside the planet Jupiter caused a huge molten mass to be expelled from the planet's body as a comet. This comet, according to Velikovsky, subsequently became the planet Venus. But before becoming a fully-formed planet he argued that the fiery comet hurtled across space — threatening the stability of the entire solar system. Then, in around 1,500 BCE, according to Velikovsky's scenario, the earth passed through the tail of the comet. He ascribes the disaster recounted in the Book of Exodus and the Papyrus Ipuwer to that encounter between the earth and the comet's tail. Velikovsky believed that a record of Venus' ejection for Jupiter had survived in the ancient Greek myth concerning the goddess Athena (whom Velikovsky identified with Venus) who sprang from the head of Zeus (commonly identified with Jupiter). Then, from the Mesoamerican annals, Velikovsky concluded that fifty-two years after the Venusian comet's tail caused the earth's polar axis to tilt, another cosmic catastrophe resulted from the, by then fully-formed, planet Venus' settling into an erratic orbital path around the sun. The second conflagration, Velikovsky contended, was responsible for the sun and the moon standing still, as the Bible relates, in the days of the Conquest led by Joshua. The new planet remained in this highly precarious orbital path until the seventh century BCE — at which time Venus finally appeased itself into its current stable orbit.

Assessing the impacts of this radical reconstruction of the history of the solar system, Velikovsky predicted that the planet Venus (1) was still hot as a result of its recent birth and violent history, (2) is covered in hydrocarbon clouds (3) travels in an abnormal rotational pattern because of its turbulent past. As the earth went into the comet's tail in c.1,500 BCE, Velikovsky believed that the hydrocarbon gases rained down to Earth — exploding in great bursts of fire as it turned into petroleum. The exchange of electromagnetic charges with the fiery comet caused the earth's polar axis to tilt, resulting in the swift destruction of several major city-states of the ancient Near East. By 1946, Velikovsky's labours has produced two manuscripts, namely: Ages in Chaos (a detailed chronicle of his revised chronology of the ancient world spanning from c.1,500-300 BCE) and *Worlds in Collision* (devoted mainly to providing global evidence for cosmic catastrophes in ancient times and establishing their sequence). *Worlds in Collision* would be the first one to be published.

Between June and October 1946, Velikovsky submitted his manuscript to several publishers — but to no avail. Then, in May of 1947, he finally managed to sign a publishing contract with the Macmillan Company. James Putnam, the trade-books editor at Macmillan, saw great potential in the book. Three years would pass before the release of *Worlds in Collision*. In the mean time, Velikovsky's manuscript underwent several thorough readings by professional reviewers from various fields — whom Macmillan sought for publication recommendation. By March 1949, word had gotten out about the controversial book that Macmillan was preparing to publish. What followed became notoriously known as the "Velikovsky Affair." Commenting on these developments, Alfred de Grazia observes:

> What must be called the scientific establishment rose in arms, not only against the new Velikovsky theories but against the man himself. Efforts were made to block dissemination of Dr. Velikovsky's ideas, and even to punish supporters of his investigations. Universities, scientific societies, publishing houses, the popular press, were approached and threatened; social pressures and professional sanctions were invoked to control public opinion. There can be little doubt that in a totalitarian society, not only would Dr. Velikovsky's reputation have been at stake, but also his right to pursue his inquiry, and perhaps his personal safety.
>
> As it was, the "establishment" succeeded in building a wall of unfavorable sentiment around him: to thousands of scholars the name of Velikovsky bears the taint of fantasy, science-fiction and publicity.[7]

Even before *Worlds in Collision* was published, a concerted campaign of defamation was already in the works to discredit Dr Velikovsky. The seeds of this scientific inquisition were first planted when, in April of 1946, Velikovsky approached Dr Harlow Shapley, then director of the Harvard College Observatory, to introduce himself and the rudimentary outlines of his novel paradigm. The idea of recent changes in the order of the solar system was not welcome by Prof. Shapley — who viewed that as a fundamental violation of gravitational theory. Nonetheless, Harlow Shapley initially agreed to perform spectroscopic tests to investigate Velikovsky's claims about the elusive properties of the planet Venus. Immanuel Velikovsky wanted to prove that Venus was littered with petroleum gases and hydrocarbon dust. But, having bluntly refused to even read Velikovsky's manuscript, Shapley later declined to perform the tests, quipping the now famous phrase: *"... if Dr. Velikovsky is right, the rest of us are crazy."* Like Dr Shapley, many other scientists

---

[7] Alfred de Grazia (editor) (1966) *The Velikovsky Affair (The Warfare of Science and Scientism)*, University Books: New York, p. 1.

10 | PLANET OF THE GREEKS

began to attack Velikovsky's unpublished manuscript without having even read it. What's more, several scientific journals who were publishing factually erroneous summaries of *Worlds in Collision* refused to either retract their misguided statements or even allow Velikovsky to reply to his critics.

At the time of Worlds in Collision's publication, on April 3rd 1950, the "first three printings were sold out before publication ... and within a week of publication there were 55,000 copies in print..."[8] By May, "[it] was being outsold by only one book — the Bible."[9] *Worlds in Collision* occupied the top-spot on the best-seller lists of the New York Times and the New York Herald Tribune for a period of twenty consecutive weeks in 1950. At the height of his book's success, Immanuel Velikovsky was summoned, on May 25th 1950, to a meeting with the president of Macmillan, George Brett. Immediately, Brett got straight to the point. The Macmillan publishing company had been threatened by a conglomerate of universities, libraries and scientific institutions who were menacing to boycott Macmillan's vital textbook division unless they dropped Velikovsky's *Worlds in Collision* from their publishing roster. Several influential scientists, whose books had likewise been published by Macmillan, demanded that their work cease to be published. So on June 8th 1950, with Immanuel Velikovsky's approval, the rights to *Worlds in Collision* were entirely transferred from Macmillan to Doubleday & Company. With no precarious textbook division to protect, Doubleday was able to guarantee Velikovsky that they would be immune from such pressures. Ten days later, on June 18th 1950, the *New York Times* reported:

> The greatest bombshell dropped on Publishers' Row in many a year exploded the other day... Dr. Velikovsky himself would not comment on the changeover. But a publishing official admitted, privately, that a flood of protests from educators and others had hit the company hard in its vulnerable underbelly — the textbook division. Following some stormy sessions by the board of directors, Macmillan reluctantly succumbed, surrendered its rights to the biggest money-maker on its list. ... Was it censorship? Or public opinion?[10]

Many fingers pointed to Harlow Shapley as the orchestrator of this scientific inquisition. But when confronted about these allegations, Dr Shapley replied:

---

[8] (1950) *Publishers' Weekly* 157 (June 17), p. 2645.
[9] David Dempsey (1950) 'In and Out of Books: $4.50 Question', *New York Times Book Review* (May 21), p. 8.
[10] David Dempsey (1950) 'In and Out of Books: New Horse, Old Rider', *New York Times Book Review* (June 18), p. 8.

"I didn't make any threats and I don't know anyone who did." James Putnam, the editor who had acquired Velikovsky's best-selling manuscript for Doubleday, was summarily fired. Several established scientists who had dared to be sympathetic to the Velikovskian heresy likewise saw their careers suddenly come to an end. To this day, the mere mention of Immanuel Velikovsky by any reputable scientist or scholar is tantamount to professional suicide.

Over the course of the following years, Immanuel Velikovsky would publish several more books. In 1952, *Ages in Chaos* finally appeared. The controversy which, two years earlier, had rocked the scientific establishment now ruffled feathers in the spheres of ancient history, archaeology and religion. The *Ages in Chaos* series, concentrating on old world chronology amendments, continued throughout the following decades with the publication of *Peoples of the Sea* in 1977 and *Ramses II and His time* in 1978. Much of Dr Velikovsky's time was however, and perhaps unfortunately, spent responding to his scientific critics. With the advent of the space age, new discoveries seemed to confirm several of Velikovsky's predictions. In 1961, radio astronomers detected radiation emanating from Venus, which revealed that the planet's surface temperature was as high as 600°F. Two years later, in February of 1963, new findings from the Mariner II mission raised the estimate of Venus' temperature to 800°F. Mariner II also demonstrated that the 15-mile-thick envelope which blankets the planet Venus was not composed of carbon dioxide or water as it had been heretofore thought, but that was instead made up of heavy molecules of hydrocarbons. Moreover, in 1962, the Washington-based U.S. Naval Research Laboratory announced its groundbreaking observation that the planet Venus, unlike any other planet of the solar system, travelled in a slow retrograde motion. To Immanuel Velikovsky, these finds went a long way toward proving his theory that Venus was a youthful planet with a violent history.

While I do not agree with Immanuel Velikovsky's hypothesis that Venus is a youthful planet ejected out of Jupiter, the present volume nonetheless seeks to pursue Velikovsky's idea that the planet Venus has a recent violent past. A dreaded god in Antiquity, Venus (also known as Ishtar, Inanna, Anat, Astarte, etc) brought several destructions of major centres of civilization. Immanuel Velikovksy's major legacy has certainly been his unique contribution to comparative mythology. His truly revolutionary thesis that many ancient myths contain the genuine memory of major cosmic cataclysms involving diverse planets like Venus, Mars and Mercury has set the foundation for my own reconstruction of the histories of the ancient world and the solar system. Several other neo-Velikovskian scholars have helped in keeping this legacy alive since Dr Velikovsky's passing on November 17th 1979.

To enumerate a few: Charles Ginenthal,[11] Benny J. Peiser,[12] Gunnar Heinsohn, Ev Cochrane, Clark Whelton, and several others. Nearly half a century after the eventful publication of Worlds in Collision, this latest foray into planetary catastrophism, comparative mythology and chronological revisionism is, in my own view, just as explosive and potentially defining as in the days of Velikovsky. The ages are still in chaos, and the time is ripe for a new heresy. A grand heresy to end all heresies.

The Afrocentric Debate: Past and Present

> *" The inability to 'see' from several angles is perhaps the one common fallacy in provincial scholarship."*
>
> - Molefi Kete Asante
> *The Afrocentric Idea*

> *" In the end, ideology is everywhere. It is rather the pretence of its absence that is suspicious."*
>
> - François-Xavier Fauvelle
> *L'Afrique de Cheikh Anta Diop*

The past half century has not only seen Immanuel Velikovsky's renewed catastrophist challenge to Western scientific uniformitarianism, but has likewise witnessed an intense reinvigoration of fundamental challenges to Western *cultural* uniformitarianism. Charles Darwin's evolutionary paradigm, favouring both an infinitely slow pace of change in the natural world and a gradual evolutionary process from barbaric caveman to supercivilized modern man has undoubtedly been at the very heart of Western scientism from the nineteenth century onwards. The Darwinian ethos has in addition, quite naturally, made its way into Western scholarship's assessment of the role played by various cultures in the evolution of world civilization. Favouring an exceedingly Eurocentric approach to the study of the ancient world, the majority of modern Western historians and archaeologists, as Immanuel Velikovsky has demonstrated, have largely dismissed the pre-Socratic

---

[11] See Charles Ginenthal (1995) *Carl Sagan & Immanuel Velikovsky*, New Falcon Publications: Tempe, AZ; (editor) (1996) *Stephen Jay Gould and Immanuel Velikovsky (Essays in the Continuing Velikovsky Affair)*, IVY Press Books: Forest Hills, NY. Charles Ginenthal is also editor of *The Velikovskian* — a journal dedicated to Velikovskian research.

[12] See Benny J. Peiser, Trevor Palmer & Mark E. Bailey (editors) (1998) *Natural Catastrophes During Bronze Age Civilizations: Archaeological, Geological, Astronomical and Cultural Perspectives*, Archaeopress: Oxford, U.K.

catastrophic world-view held by ancient peoples the world over. Viewed as "pre-logical" or superstitious cultures, the annals of the ancient Mesoamerican, Chinese and Afroasiatic peoples are routinely set against and defined according to the standards of post-Axial Age Europe. Scholars use the term "Axial Age" to mark the turning point in history, starting in the days of Socrates, when it is believed that the ancients' cyclical view of the world, dominated by their irrational fear of the gods' wrath and recurring turmoil of the inconsistent heavens, was overturned to finally make way for a much more "realistic" understanding of phenomena — as if Aristotelianism shook the ancient world out of its traumatic infantile fantasy world. The rise of European positivism, particularly in the nineteenth century, incorporated this pre-Socratic skepticism with the new historical-critical methodology of ancient text exegesis. Particularly suspect in the minds of nineteenth century European scholars were the early Greek historians' accounts about the colonization of Greece by the ancient Egyptians and Phoenicians. The concept that Greece, the fountainhead of Western civilization, could owe the basis of its arts and sciences to Afroasiatic peoples ran smack against nineteenth century scholars' racial preconceptions.

At the vanguard of recent scholarly criticism of the overly hegemonic and Eurocentric interpretation, and outright dismissal, of ancient Pre-Socratic textual sources, such as the writings of the early Greek historians Herodotus and Diodorus of Sicily, have been Afrocentric scholars. Challenging the monopoly and ideology of Western historiography, Afrocentricity endeavours to formulate a more culturally holistic view of ancient history. The term "Afrocentricity" was coined by the Pan-African scholar Prof. Molefi Kete Asante of Temple University in an effort to develop a paradigm which would be independent from Eurocentric philosophies and methodology.[13] While the term *"Afrocentrism"* is most frequently used, many contemporary Afrocentric scholars generally prefer employing the term "Afrocentricity." It has rarely been understood by the majority of the critics of the Afrocentric movement that genuine Afrocentricity isn't geared toward the blanket "Africanization" of world history. Rather, Afrocentricity, when properly understood, is primarily, once again, a form of intellectual inquiry which seeks to distance itself from the dominance of a one-sided Eurocentric view of phenomena — be that philosophy, history, sociology, psychology or literature. Not a monolithic or hegemonic philosophy, various African theorists, hailing from Africa and its Diaspora, have offered differing perspectives to this movement which holds a long history.

For example, as early as the first two decades of the nineteenth century, Haitian pioneers Baron P.V. Vasty and Prince Sanders[14] had already been advancing the

---

[13] See Molefi Kete Asante (1987) *The Afrocentric Idea*, Temple University Press: Philadelphia.
[14] Prince Sanders (editor) (1969) *Haytian Papers*, Negro University Press: Westport, Conn.

revolutionary claims that pharaonic Egypt was a fundamentally African civilization. Vasty fought under Toussaint L'Ouverture as well as in Dessalines' army. He was also chief advisor to King Christophe. For his part, Sanders was an Afro-American immigrant who advocated Afro-American migration to Haiti. In the 1840s, the African-American scholar John H. Johnson, of Philadelphia, published a ground breaking monograph entitled *Arguments and Observations of the Ethiopians or African Race*, in which he argued that the ancient Egyptians had been Black Africans. Up until his time, the majority of Black scholars in the United-States advocating the same position did so mainly on scriptural grounds.[15] Therefore, Johnson's monograph can be seen as the first scientifically-based attempt to prove ancient Egypt's African roots in the U.S. In it, he sought chiefly to dispel Dr Samuel Morton's thesis that the ancient inhabitants of the Nile Valley were "Asiatics in origin and Caucasian in race."[16] Another great African-American champion of the early Afrocentric school was William Leo Hansberry — who had been drawn to the study of African history after having read W.E.B. Du Bois' classic book *The Negro*. Relating the story of Hansberry, who studied at Harvard under the eminent Egyptologist George A. Reisner (1867-1942) at the turn of the century, James G. Spady writes:

> ... Hansberry meanwhile offered Reisner serious challenges in the classroom. On the basis of his research as an undergraduate at Harvard, he challenged the prevailing interpretation of African cultures and civilizations along the Nile. It has been reported that Reisner was so infuriated on one occasion that he told Hansberry in the presence of his class: *"I do not believe Negroes found those great civilizations. You are a brilliant student, Hansberry, but you are a product of our civilization."*[17]

In 1922, Hansberry went on to join the faculty at Howard University. He also lectured extensively at the grassroots level in churches, schools and community centres all over the U.S. — teaching about African contributions to Nile Valley civilizations (living up to his Harvard nickname of "Little Nile"). At the universities he visited, Hansberry constantly induced serious students to enter formal disciplines that could equip them with the necessary tools to formulate a new history of ancient Egypt. In 1929, he returned to Harvard and, after two years, he completed his Master's thesis in African archaeology entitled: "The Political and

---

[15] James G. Spady (1989) 'Dr. Cheikh Anta Diop and the Background of Scholarship on Black Interest in Egyptology and Nile Valley Civilizations', *Présence Africaine* 149-150, p. 295.
[16] Ibid, p. 296.
[17] Ibid, p. 299.

Cultural History of Nilotic Ethiopia Prior to the Christian Era with Special Emphasis on the Ethiopian Conquest and Rehabilitation of Egypt by the Napatan Kingdom of Ethiopia in the eighth and seventh centuries B.C."

Other African-American contemporaries of William Leo Hansberry likewise articulated their strong belief in the Ethiopian origins of Egyptian civilization, and the latter's influence of early Western civilization. In an address delivered before the Omaha Philosophical Society on April 1st 1917, G. W. Parker, describing an academic climate amazingly similar to today's, said:

> To claim an African origin for the Grecian civilization is hardly in keeping with the historical traditions inherited from our school days. It savors of a sort of heresy and passes far beyond the limits of popular opinion. There is a peculiar unanimity among all historians to state without reservation that the greatest civilization the world has ever known was preeminently Aryan, but historians are not always to be relied upon. They write for their own race and times [and] are careful to give as little credit as possible to races and events which fall within the pale of their prejudice.[18]

Speaking of what he saw as archaeologists' denial of evidence pointing to the African origins of Western civilization, Parker later utters:

> We wonder, then, why the historians continue to ignore those remains and persist in continuing falsehood. There can be but one answer and that is racial vanity prefers falsehood to truth and prejudice demands suppression rather than expression.[19]

The theory that historians write for their own cultural universe and times is a topic which was extensively explored about forty years later in Africa by the Senegalese Pan-African scholar Cheikh Anta Diop. Indeed, a central and consistent theme common to most Afrocentric scholarship is that European historiography's traditional claim to objectivity is illusional. Cheikh Anta Diop saw in Western historiography an extension of European colonialism and cultural imperialism. Diop wrote what many consider his magnum opus, *Nations nègres et culture*, between 1948 and 1953 — at the apex of the anti-colonial struggle in Africa. One of Diop's major vehicles for the dissemination of his ideas, over many years, was the African journal *Présence Africaine* [African Presence]. Inaugurated by Alioune Diop, as both

---

[18] G. W. Parker (1917) 'The African Origins of Grecian Civilization', *Journal of Negro History* 2, p. 334.
[19] Ibid, p. 338.

a journal and publishing house, the idea for *Présence Africaine* was first conceived between 1942 and 1943. In 1947, Alioune Diop's work finally came to fruition with the establishment of the journal in Paris. Alioune Diop's objective, far from merely being driven by ambition of personal renown, was "to rehabilitate the collective memory of the peoples of Africa."[20] Cognizant of the necessity for African culture to take its place within the consciousness of humankind in general as well, Alioune Diop sought, in his own words, to make the rehabilitation of the Black world the concern "of all men of good will (white, yellow, or black) capable of helping us to define the African originality and to hasten its insertion into the modern world."[21] Proving his commitment to working with a cross-section of dedicated minds, Alioune Diop formed a Committee of Patrons which incorporated such names as: Jean-Paul Sartre,[22] Léopold Sédar Senghor, Albert Camus, Aimé Césaire, and several others. *Présence Africaine* initiated over the years many landmark scholarly events in African intellectual history: including, among others, the First International Congress of Black Writers and Artists (Paris, 1956),[23] the Second International Congress of the African Society of Culture (Rome, 1959), the World Festival of Black Arts (Dakar, Senegal, 1966; and Lagos, Nigeria 1977). Even after the death of Alioune Diop, *Présence Africaine* continues to act as an important forum and contributor to the African experience in our time.

Sharing *Présence Africaine*'s stated commitment to internationalism, Cheikh Anta Diop made it clear that "culture" and not "race" was his primary interest.[24] Indeed, Cheikh A. Diop respected, and widely cited, the works of non-African scholars but always remained resolutely dedicated to an African-centered perspective to the study of ancient African history and culture. The very first known publication of C. A. Diop, 'Origins of the Wolof Language and Race,' appeared in *Présence Africaine* in 1948. In 1959, Dr Diop published the two sections of his doctoral dissertation: *L'unité culturelle de l'Afrique noire* [The Cultural Unity of Black Africa].[25] In these work, the Senegalese scholar clearly articulated his belief, resorting to physical anthropology and linguistics, that the basis of ancient Egyptian civilization was Black African. He used the concept of African cultural

---

[20] Christiane Yandé Diop. Foreword to V. Y. Mudimbe (editor) (1992) *The Surreptitious Speech: Présence Africaine and the Politics of Otherness 1947-1987*, p. xiii.
[21] Alioune Diop (1947) 'Niam n'goura ou les raisons d'être de Présence Africaine', *Présence Africaine* 1, p. 7.
[22] Jean-Paul Sartre (1947) 'Présence noire', *Présence Africaine* 1, pp. 28-29.
[23] That event was the catalyst for the formation of the African Society of Culture.
[24] J. D. Walker (1995) 'The Misrepresentation of Diop's Views', *Journal of Black Studies* Vol. 26 - Num. 1, p. 78.
[25] For a review of this work see Molefi K. Asante (1992) 'BOOK REVIEW: Cultural Unity of Black Africa (The Language Question)', *Research in African Literatures* Vol. 23 - Num. 1, pp. 191-195.

unity, or continuity, to argue that modern Africans are racially and culturally related to the ancient Egyptians. Dr Diop found evidence of Africa's pharaonic heritage in Africa's use of totems, practice of circumcision, structure of monarchy, linguistic kinship and, among others, parallel cosmological concepts.[26] Starting in the late 1950s, C. A. Diop amassed a considerable following among young African and Caribbean intellectuals, who looked to him as a mentor figure. One such young disciple, who became a close associate, was the Congolese Egyptologist Théophile Obenga. Born in Brazaville in 1930, Obenga was educated both in France (Sorbonne and Collège de France) and in the United-States (University of Pittsburgh). C. A. Diop and T. Obenga jointly attended, in 1974, the UNESCO-sponsored Cairo Symposium which was attended by twenty eminent Egyptologists and observers. From 1971, Diop and Obenga had already been busy gathering information to bolster their arguments supporting the linguistic and cultural affinity hypothesis between pharaonic Egypt and the rest of Africa. At the 1974 Cairo conference, Profs. Diop and Obenga dominated the lively discussions. To quote Cheikh A. Diop himself, "African historiography indeed wrote a memorable page at the Cairo Symposium."[27] With Egyptologists of such prestigious renown as Jean Vercoutter, Serge Sauneron and Jean Leclant present at the Cairo conference, Diop and Obenga demonstrated that it was possible for Afrocentric scholars, quoting again C. A. Diop, to place themselves "on the field of scientific rigour and not on that of ideology."[28] Turning the tables on the Western myth of objectivity, Cheikh Anta Diop maintained that the true ideologues were found within the established academe itself. In his mind, Western scholars, far from simply being wrong and much more than mere victims of innocent errors, are in fact guilty of systemic efforts to obfuscate, deceive, and obscure the truth. Their methodologies being irremediably tainted with desires of cultural hegemony and racial prejudice.[29] To be sure, Cheikh Anta Diop sought to engage in a debate where Africa would no longer merely be the *object* but the *subject* of knowledge.[30] He believed that this could only be achieved if African intellectuals actually "decolonized" their cultural universe by taking into their own hands the scientific tools necessary to write their own history. This, he contended, was necessary not merely for ideological purposes, but for the benefit of science. For as the Cameroon scholar Jean-Marc Ela wrote:

---

[26] Chris Gray (1989) *Concepts of History in the Works of Cheikh Anta Diop and Theophile Obenga*, Karnak House: London, p. 8.
[27] Cheikh A. Diop (1975) 'L'Antiquité africaine par l'image', *Notes Africaines* 145-146, pp. 6-7. Trans. by and cited in Gray (1989).
[28] Ibid.
[29] Cheikh Anta Diop (1979 [1955]) *Nations nègres et culture (De l'Antiquité nègre égyptienne aux problèmes culturels de l'Afrique Noire d'aujourd'hui) — Tome I*. Troisième édition. Présence Africaine: Paris, pp. 16-17, 57.
[30] Jean-Marc Ela (1989) *Cheikh Anta Diop ou l'honneur de penser*, L'Harmattan: Paris, p. 23.

> To exclude Black Africa from the community of universal history isn't to rely on the exact sciences but on science-fiction and on accumulated clichés which leave in the dark the objective facts of human phenomenon.[31]

During the early 1970s, Dr C. A. Diop's scholarship had finally found its way in the United-States — thanks largely to his interactions with John Henrik Clarke. Although not all of his works were translated into English, efforts were made by American publishers to both condense the contents of his major works and to provide extensive translations. The rapid proliferation of Black Studies departments in American university campuses, as a result of the U.S. Civil Rights movement, provided an unprecedented impetus for the study of African history. It is however evident, to paraphrase historian Chris Gray, that Diopan scholarship finds its most direct line of succession among the proponents of Afrocentricity.[32]

As the afrocentric method emerges as a critical discourse, one of the most vociferous voices currently denouncing Afrocentricity comes from American classicist Mary R. Lefkowitz of Wellesley College. Lefkowitz first encountered Afrocentricity in 1991, and was appalled to discover that such "fallacies" were being taught and discussed from grade schools up to even her own university campus. In Prof. Martin Bernal's words: "... *she [Lefkowitz] has felt obliged to stand up and be counted against what she sees as the Afrocentrist assault on the basic principles of education, respect for the facts, logical argument and open debate.*" While I must agree with Lefkowitz's premise that some of the theories advanced by Afrocentric scholars are indeed historically incorrect, the same could be said about the claims supported by conventional historians. The only difference being that because Eurocentric historical fallacies have been part and parcel of humanity's collective consciousness for so long, they have now been accepted as fact. It is commonly known that if a lie is repeated often enough, and for long enough, it eventually becomes regarded as truth. In 1996, Lefkowitz authored a work entitled *Not out of Africa*. This book was an expanded follow-up to an article published in *The New Republic* in 1991 in which she sought to expose some of the so-called myths of Afrocentrism. She attacked the Afrocentrists' claims that nineteenth century European scholars had been biased in their treatment of history. Prof. Lefkowitz also defended the widespread view within modern classical scholarship that the ancient Greeks themselves were misguided about their own early history. In the same year Dr Lefkowitz co-edited, with Guy MacLean Rogers, another book entitled *Black Athena Revisited*. This publication is a collection of essays by twenty renowned academics from a variety

---

[31] Ibid, p. 52.
[32] Chris Gray (1989) p. 73.

of fields, intended to discredit Martin Bernal's *Black Athena* volumes. In addition to M. Lefkowitz and G. Rogers, leading academics such as Egyptologists John Baines of Oxford University and Frank J. Yurco of the University of Chicago, as well as classicist Frank M. Snowden, Jr.[33] formerly of Howard University — offered passionate rebuttals of Bernal's theories. But as Eric H. Cline of Xavier University pointed out: "... *rather than Black Athena Revisited, the present volume might have been more aptly entitled Black Athena Revilified.*"[34] Indeed, no effort was made throughout the entire volume to offer a truly balanced review of Bernal's work. Professor Bernal was even denied the basic opportunity to include an essay in his own defence. For scholars who speak of academic freedom, this conspicuous "more bang for the buck" attempt to sway a misinformed lay public, dangerously resembles the tactics used by the academic establishment during the Velikovsky Affair.

The myth of objectivity is a constantly recurring theme in *Black Athena Revisited*. Interpretation of evidence becomes regarded as the evidence itself. As soon as scholars begin to use defined paradigms as primary evidence, they no longer practice science, but engage in ideology.[35] While they freely accuse revisionists of ignoring scientific evidence, their own preconceived notions have blinded them. They are utterly unable, or unwilling, to see the blatant contradictions ingrained within their own institutional paradigms. Outright denial of pathological behaviour serves as the best tool for its propagation. They are also very quick to denounce underlying political agendas; but while I admittedly share Lefkowitz & company's valid concerns about ideological sectarianism within certain elements of Afrocentric discourse, theirs is really a case of "the pot calling the kettle black." The featured scholars of *Black Athena Revisited* are indeed conspicuously silent about the culture of "elitist tribalism" which characterizes much of modern mainstream scholarship. Moreover, the manner in which they seem to have so easily dismissed so many accounts of the ancient Greeks, and the mountain of evidence, pointing to the Afroasiatic roots of Western civilization forces me to question their scholarly, or perhaps ideological, motives. In my opinion, they are either guilty of premeditated deception, or of inexcusable narrow-mindedness for scholars of their position.

I would be the first to point out that many specific points in Professor Bernal's historical reconstruction need to be drastically revised. My own view is that his strategy of adopting a historically revisionist stance, whilst nevertheless relying on the accepted chronology of Egypt and the ancient world, has dealt him a considerable disservice by leaving him open to justified methodological criticism. Can there

---

[33] See Burkard Bilger (1997) 'The Last Black Classicist', *The Sciences* Vol. 37 - Num. 2, pp. 16-19.
[34] Eric H. Cline (1996) 'BOOK REVIEW: Black Athena Revisited. M. R. Lefkowitz & G. M. Rogers. 1996', *American Journal of Archaeology* Vol. 100 - Num. 4, p. 782.
[35] François-Xavier Fauvelle (1996) *L'Afrique de Cheikh Anta Diop (Histoire et idéologie)*, Karthala / Centre de recherches africaines: Paris, pp. 20-26.

be a new history without a new chronology? I think not.[36] Notwithstanding, the overall direction of Bernal's inquiry is valid, honourable, and long overdue.

Ironically, the following is also an open challenge, as well as being a rallying cry, to Afrocentric scholars themselves. This is brought about by my belief that, since Cheikh Anta Diop's death, the Afrocentric movement, as a whole, has failed to carry on his ground breaking research to the next level[37] — that of devising an independent Afrocentric paradigm for the study of ancient pharaonic culture — especially from an archaeological perspective. Superb work certainly has, and is, being done on Afrocentric epistemology and social theory by distinguished Pan-African theorists whom the present writer can only defer to. However, significant shortcomings continue to plague Afrocentric scholarship with respect to Afrocentric Egyptology. It's in fact my opinion that a certain sense of "false triumphalism" has been allowed to settle itself into Afrocentric Egyptology by well-meaning scholars, and adepts alike, who feel that Diop had unequivocally proven his case during his life-time. And that we, his proud students, need not bother ourselves much with the archaeological minutia of Egyptological research. In other words, the epistemological ends ultimately justify the ideological means. Yet, this is exactly the kind of intellectual laxity which Cheikh Anta Diop fought against his whole life. Prof. C. A. Diop fully realized that his arguments remained to be proven; and that what he had really provided through his defining scholarship is a series of paths towards further scientific research. To reiterate Cheikh A. Diop's challenge:

> For us, the return to Egypt in all domains is the necessary condition for reconciling African civilizations with history, in order to be able to construct a body of modern human sciences, in order to renovate African culture. Far from being a revelling in the past, a look toward the Egypt of antiquity is the best way to conceive and build our cultural future. In reconceived and renewed African culture, Egypt will play the same role that Greco-Latin antiquity plays in Western culture.[38]

---

[36] While it is true that Bernal's "revised chronology" — arguing for a lengthening of the Egyptian First Intermediate Period by about 300 years [see Bruce Trigger (1992) 'Brown Athena: A Postprocessual Goddess?', *Current Anthropology* Vol. 33 - Num. 1, p. 122.] — breaks with the rigid standard chronological scheme, I believe that a much deeper paradigmatic shift or revolution is required.

[37] For a critical analysis of the reasons why Diopan research has stagnated since Diop's death, see Mamadou Diouf & Mohamad Mbodj 'The Shadow of Cheikh Anta Diop.' In V. Y. Mudimbe (editor) (1992) *The Surreptitious Speech: Présence Africaine and the Politics of Otherness 1947-1987*, pp. 118-135.

[38] Cheikh Anta Diop (1991 [1981]) *Civilization or Barbarism (An Authentic Anthropology)*. Trans. by Yaa-Lengi Meema Ngemi. Lawrence Hill Books: Brooklyn, NY, p. 3.

This meaningful and significant endeavour is what's behind my own efforts to create a new field of study which I have called "Khemetology." A full definition of Khemetology will be given later in this *Introduction*, but suffice it to say for now that this revolutionary new science will, I should hope, serve not necessarily to replace but to complement Afrocentricity. This "new Black African school,"[39] of which Cheikh Anta Diop's disciple Theophile Obenga spoke, is to be heralded by a new breed of Pan-African scholars who belong to:

> ... that category of Africans who, driven by a real intellectual courage, have sought to take up a position in the field of research in order to aid the psychological liberation, the de-alienation and the edification of the historical consciousness of their people.[40]

There is indeed, now more than ever before, a pressing need for a renewed commitment by African scholars in terms of developing a serious and committed archaeological methodology — in order to build a strong scientific base for Afrocentric epistemology. The complete absence of any Afrocentric voices in the current heated debates over ancient world chronology and archaeology is an urgent and alarming signal to the effect that Afrocentric scholarship has, for far too long, shied away from any serious involvement in such spheres.

The Faulty Compass of Egyptian Chronology:
The Case of the Blind Leading the Blind

> " ... it is important that scholars in other disciplines understand that absolute dates for Egypt are not as clear and well-established as they are often thought to be ... A thorough reassessment of the accepted chronological structure of Egypt during the second millennium B.C.E. is currently underway and scholarship on the subject is in some disarray."
>
> -William A. Ward (1992)
> Brown University

---

[39] Theophile Obenga (1973) *L'Afrique dans l'Antiquité (Egypte pharaonique — Afrique Noire)*, Présence Africaine: Paris, p. 90.
[40] Thiero Mouctar Bah (1974) 'Compte rendu: Obenga, L'Afrique dans l'Antiquité', *Afrika Zamani* 3, p. 163 (Trans. by Chris Gray).

22 | PLANET OF THE GREEKS

The chronology of ancient Egypt is the most important yardstick for the parallel dating of practically every other culture in the ancient Near East[41] and the Aegean. The dates ascribed to a particular culture, as in the case of Mycenae, can be determined simply by the discovery of Egyptian artifacts at those archaeological sites. For example, if the cartouche (i.e. name rink) of a particular Egyptian pharaoh is found at a specific site, the culture associated with that site is automatically dated to the reign of that given pharaoh of Egypt. It therefore becomes evident that if the Egyptian chronology is *wrong*, then it automatically follows that the dates for all the other cultures, which depend on the accuracy of Egypt's chronology, also have to be revised. That confusion about the proper dating of the Egyptian pharaohs, in relation to other cultures, is, I believe, largely responsible for what ancient historians refer to as "Dark Ages." Hence, the chronological misalignment of diverse archaeological remains can lead to serious misinterpretations of ancient history. Chronology represents the backbone and blueprint of history. Any undertaking to revise history without amending the chronological framework upon which it is built is therefore doomed to failure.

That is why there is absolutely no doubt in my mind that the traditional hegemony of Eurocentric historiography derives from Western scholars' mastery of ancient chronology. Thus, there can be no adequate understanding of ancient pharaonic history unless there is first and foremost an attempt to formulate an Afrocentric chronology of ancient Egypt. Certainly, no other ancient historiography has been more victimized by the faulty Egyptian chronology than that of the African continent. It will therefore always remain a mystery to me as to why Afrocentric scholars have never (at least to my knowledge) questioned the validity of the standard chronology of ancient Egypt. As a direct result, and unbeknownst to them, Afrocentric scholars are struggling within a framework which is systematically set up against African culture. Unfortunately, this situation has created a "siege mentality" in which European scholars are seen as holding the monopoly over archaeological interpretation. As an inevitable consequence, African-centered scholars' agenda for reclaiming ancient Egypt's African past is often methodologically misguided. Those who are seeking to reinterpret the history of African classical civilization, within its indigenous cultural context, must be weary not to fall into the trap of intellectual isolationism. Admittedly, any effective course of action requires that. This, as Professor Henry Louis Gates, Jr. of Harvard University aptly put it, "means using the most sophisticated critical theories and methods available to re-appropriate and to define our own 'colonial' discourse."[42]

---

[41] See Amihai Mazar (1990) *Archaeology of the Land of the Bible — 10,000 - 586 B.C.E.*, Doubleday: New York, pp. 28-29.
[42] Henry Louis Gates, Jr. 'Writing, "Race," and the Difference it Makes.' In H. L. Gates, Jr. (editor) (1986) *"Race," Writing, and Difference*, University of Chicago Press: Chicago, p. 14.

Since most historiography is political and ideological, the prevailing social climate in which scholarly conventions are adopted, and passed on, are of immense importance. For instance, Western scholarship's rigid adherence to social Darwinism, and its concept of "evolutionism" has condemned European scholars to perpetually view African, and non-European, historiography as part of a "stage" or "step" which European historiography has long passed.[43] This attitude leads Western scholars, generally speaking, to inaccurately believe that classical Greek civilization had nothing, or little, to learn from ancient African and other non-European cultures. Quite naturally, these fundamental assumptions are reflected in Western academia's conceptions of ancient chronology. So, once again, dismantling the methodological basis of Eurocentric chronology, particularly as it has been applied to pharaonic chronology, is a vital prerequisite to any liberating historiography.

In a sense, Afrocentric scholarship is certainly not alone in having fallen victim to the faulty compass of Egyptian chronology. Even catastrophists and chronologists, who have traditionally had no qualms in questioning the accepted version of Egyptian chronology and history, still continue holding on to many sacred cows of conventional wisdom. The basic fact is that most historians, be they conventional, Afrocentric, catastrophist or revisionist scholars, have, without exception, been trained to accept long-established tenets of ancient chronology. They can also be described as time detectives. Indeed, as the eminent biblical scholar Richard E. Friedman observes: *"The research of scholars does resemble detective work in a variety of ways — clues, deduction, false starts, breakthroughs, patience, unexpected twists — presumably because so much of life is, after all, a mystery."*[44] As in the tradition of all great detective stories, they make use of available evidence to reconstruct the ancient past and, in this process, either confirm or challenge accepted views. But what if that very basic evidence (annals, king-lists, and archival remains), used as objective primary sources today, had themselves been tainted by political circumstances in Antiquity? What if those deceptive processes were set in motion long before the very archival evidence used to interpret history had even come into existence? What if even the most radical of anti-establishment scholars used that evidence as an unquestioned departure point for further investigation? What if those ancient culprits were not only beyond suspicion, but were in fact disguised as great heroes? We would then be witnessing the perfect crime. All those attempting to solve the riddle would already find themselves in a checkmate

---

[43] See Bruce G. Trigger (1989) *A History of Archaeological Thought*, Cambridge University Press: Cambridge, U.K., p. 113; Vine Deloria, Jr. (1994 [1972]) *God is Red (A Native View of Religion)*. Updated edition. Fulcrum: Golden, Col., p. 63; Théophile Obenga (1980) *Pour une nouvelle histoire*, Présence Africaine: Paris, p. 80.

[44] Richard Elliott Friedman (1997) *The Hidden Face of God*, Harper: San Fransisco, pp. 3-4.

position even before stepping on to the proverbial chess board. Errors of interpretation made in one field are automatically transferred into other disciplines, until the original source of the confusion is lost forever. Such misunderstandings in relative chronology have had a devastating domino-effect upon the entire history of the ancient world. In spite of his strict adherence to the isolationist "model of autochthonous origins,"[45] Professor Colin Renfrew of Cambridge University, acknowledges that:

> The first step, however, is to recognize the depths of our ignorance. To realize how the existing 'chronologies' in different parts of the Mediterranean are bolstered up by circular arguments, where specialists in one area believe that those in other areas must know what they are talking about, and blindly use dating systems which are no better than their own. ... a chronological revolution is on its way.[46]

While Prof. Renfrew and others might argue that modern Western archaeology's isolationist perspective may have in fact little to do with its reluctance to acknowledge the circular nature of their established chronologies, I believe that a strong case can indeed be made to the contrary. Organized confusion is the state in which, in my view, ancient world scholarship currently finds itself. The lay public's widespread view that archaeologists and ancient historians have answered most of the questions concerning ancient chronology has little to do with reality. If anything, modern excavations have raised new questions and exposed the shortcomings of received models. In any event, the "chronological revolution" which Prof. Renfrew has prophetically heralded is now close at hand.

A Panoply of Myths

> " All history is saga and myth, and as such the product
> of the state of our intellectual powers at a particular time:
> of our capacity for comprehension, the vigour of
> our imagination, our feeling for reality."
>
> - Janheinz Jahn, *Muntu*

---

[45] The 'Model of Autochthonous Origin'— an anti-diffusionist paradigm — contends that ancient Greece, and other ancient cultures, developed indigenously. Meaning that Greek culture did not result from some outside Indo-European impetus, but that the Indo-European element was already there from early Neolithic times. See Colin Renfrew (1972) *The Emergence of Civilisation (The Cyclades and the Aegean in the Third Millennium B.C.)*, Methuen: London, p. xxv.

[46] Colin Renfrew – Foreword to Peter James et al. (1991) *Centuries of Darkness (A Challenge to the Conventional Chronology of Old World Archaeology)*, p. xv. Evidently, Renfrew does not anticipate that this "chronological revolution" ultimately demands the acknowledgement of the central importance of cultural diffusionism.

INTRODUCTION | 25

What this chronological revolution will primarily bring about is the repudiation of many myths which have been accepted as historical fact over the centuries. Doubtlessly, historical myths that were both the cause and effect of the fallacious chronology of the ancient world. While such examples abound, the following is a list of just seven of the greatest myths of and about Antiquity which continue to plague ancient world scholarship.

Myth no.1: **The uniformitarian universe**

" ... at certain periods the universe has its
present circular motion, and at other periods it
revolves in the reverse direction. ... there is at that time
great destruction of animals in general, and
only a small part of the human
race survives."

- Plato
Politicus, 270

" A brief look at the succession
of cultures in ancient Palestine might
almost convert us to a cyclical view of history.
It seems that civilizations rose briefly,
only to fall, then repeat the process
over and over."

- William G. Dever (1987)

It was during the late eighteenth century CE that illustrious Scottish physician James Hutton's Theory of the Earth established the foundations of modern geology with his theory of "uniformitarianism." The basic principle of uniformitarianism postulates that present physical, chemical, and biological laws operating today are constant phenomena which can be used to evaluate the geological past. In other words, what is now has always been and always will be. The same forces which currently shape our world have been at work for time immemorial. With the publication, in 1830, of English geologist Charles Lyell's (1797-1875) magnum opus *Principles of Geology*, the uniformitarian view of the earth's physical history was further entrenched in the scientific world. According to Lyell, geological changes on the earth's surface do, and always have, occurred through the same gradual process — at the same rate and magnitude. The scientific concepts of Charles Lyell were later taken up by Charles Darwin (1809-1882) in his theory of evolution. With the subsequent widespread acceptance of Darwin's theory of evolution, uniformitarianism automatically became the binding law and Gospel in science. But at this time, there was a fiercely fought battle between the two nascent views of celestial mechanics: catastrophism and uniformitarianism. To quote author Herbert Butterfield:

> The clean and comparatively empty Newtonian skies ultimately carried the day against a Cartesian universe packed with matter and agitated with whirlpools, for the existence of which scientific observations provided no evidence.[47]

But if we rely upon the pre-Aristotelian literature from around the world, we get the very clear impression that the present stable solar system was indeed, as the Cartesian model postulates, a turbulent place. The big question is: did the ancients' view of the planetary system radically change as a result of the Greeks' "rational mode of thinking" or was it because, at the pivotal time of the Axial Age, the solar system had suddenly stabilized itself? The prevailing uniformitarian paradigm is wholly against any sudden change in the solar system's dynamic nature. This is indeed very true of the solar system as we've known it for around the last two millennia. But, in this book, I will attempt to demonstrate, using historical records, inscriptions, sacred annals and mythologies from around the ancient world, that the agitated Cartesian universe was a concrete reality for the pre-Hellenistic world. Dismantling the myth of uniformitarianism is hence a necessary first step to understanding the pre-Socratic world. Without appreciating the catastrophic world-view, it is virtually impossible to fully elucidate the Bible, pharaonic and Mesoamerican religion, ancient Chinese legends, Homeric poetry and the history of the ancient world in general.

It was Dr Velikovsky's implied aim to "reinstate Descartes as a rightful contestant of Newton in the understanding of the texture of the universe."[48] Furthermore, Velikovsky remained adamant that, while gravitation and inertia were important forces governing celestial motions, electromagnetic forces also played a significant role in celestial mechanics. That point remained a hotly debated issue during his personal interactions with Albert Einstein — who remained steadfastly convinced that the sun and the planets were electronically neutral and that space must be free of magnetic fields and plasma. Disputing Dr Harlow Shapley's contention that denying gravitation the sole role in astronomy meant denying gravitation *any* role in astronomy, Velikovsky argued that his theories did not violate any of the laws of

---

[47] Herbert Butterfield (1958) *The Origins of Modern Science: 1300-1800*, G. Bell & Sons: London, p. 158.
[48] Livio C. Stecchini (1963) 'The Inconsistant Heavens: Velikovsky in Relation to Some Past Cosmic Perplexities', *American Behavioral Scientist* Vol. 67 - Num. 1, p. 19.

gravitation. Far from denying the role of gravitation, Dr Velikovsky was simply of the opinion that gravitation was only "one" of the important factors governing celestial mechanics. Therefore, the thrust of his criticism wasn't that Newtonian mechanics was *wrong*, but that is was *incomplete*. In the years following the controversial publication of *Worlds in Collision*, astronomers have indeed increasingly been aware of the major role that electromagnetism plays in cosmic processes.

All the same, I am fully prepared to acknowledge that my very limited knowledge of the natural sciences represents my Achilles' heel in this project. Nonetheless, it must not be forgotten that this book is primarily a work of history. One that is much more likely to be of immediate concern and interest to biblical scholars, ancient historians, archaeologists, classicists, Egyptologists and Nubiologists. I nevertheless must recognize that by pulling the sleeping lion's tale, it is beyond my control how the beast will react. Resurrecting the spectre of Velikovskian scholarship, I leave myself open to constructive and developmental criticism from a myriad of concerned parties. Because much of the following evidence in support of cosmic catastrophes in historical times lies outside of the realms of the natural sciences, I indeed recognize that much remains to be done before my case is irrefutably proven in the realm of the physical sciences. However, I hope that, by providing a chronological sequence in which I posit these planetary cataclysms occurred, those who *do* possess the required scientific skills would have both the open-mindedness and the courage to undertake the necessary research. As Velikovsky said about his own revolutionary undertaking: *"My work is first a reconstruction, not a theory; it is built upon the human testimony as preserved in the heritage of all ancient civilizations ..."*[49] In addition, I am reminded of an uncharacteristically frosty encounter in Princeton, NJ in August of 1952, between Drs Einstein and Velikovsky. When approached by Velikovsky, Einstein defiantly asked him: "But what do you know of astronomy?" — to which Velikovsky replied: "I know to put questions."

As an introduction to how such planetary cataclysms could have affected the earth in ancient times, I will, once again, quote Velikovsky himself:

> Let us assume, as a working hypothesis, that under the impact of a force or the influence of an agent — and the earth does not travel in an empty universe — the axis of the earth shifted or tilted. At that moment and earthquake would make the globe shudder. Air and water would continue to move through inertia; hurricanes would sweep the earth and the seas

---

[49] Immanuel Velikovsky 'My Challenge to Conventional Views in Science.' In Lewis M. Greenberg & Warner B. Sizemore (1977) *Velikovsky and Establishment Science*, p. 5.

would rush over continents, carrying gravel and sand and marine animals, and casting them on the land. Heat would be developed, rocks would melt, volcanoes would erupt, lava would flow from fissures in the ruptured ground and cover vast areas. Mountains would spring up from the plains and would travel and climb on the shoulders of other mountains, causing faults and rifts. Lakes would be tilted and emptied, rivers would change their beds; large land areas with their inhabitants would slip under the sea.[50]

Scientists do not deny the fact that such cataclysmic events *could* occur, or that Velikovsky's scenario of planetary catastrophes goes against the laws of physics. Indeed, the late renowned American scientist Carl Sagan admitted that "there is nothing absurd in the possibility of cosmic collisions."[51] He recognizes that in *"the 4.6 billion-year history of the solar system, many collisions must have occurred."*[52] So what's the entire tumult all about then? The controversial issue is Immanuel Velikovsky's contention that such cosmic cataclysms took place in *"historical times."* University of Texas astronomer J. Derral Mulholland clarifies the position of establishment science as follows:

> *If* a planet-sized object were to pass close by the Earth, then giant tides would be raised; there would be global earthquakes; the north pole would change direction; the day, the month, the seasons, the year would all change. Faith is not involved here; these are unavoidable consequences of the laws of motion as we presently know them. We must accept that the dynamical aspects of Velikovsky's vision of hell on Earth are largely acceptable. This is not to admit that the events he described ever happened ...[53]

By comparison, my own reconstruction of the history of the solar system differs considerably from that of Immanuel Velikovsky. For starters, I do not believe that the planet Venus was ever a comet ejected out the planet Jupiter before eventually becoming a fully-formed planet. In addition, I do not challenge the Big Bang theory which contends that *all* the planets of the solar system were simultaneously formed in a single cataclysmic event billions of years ago. Velikovsky's theory that Venus is a young planet, on account of its extreme heat, can, in my own view, be otherwise explained. I think that the basic contention of recent violent activity suffices to account for it's infernal temperature of $c.800°F$.

---

[50] Immanuel Velikovsky (1955) *Earth in Upheaval*, Doubleday: Garden City, NY, p. 136.
[51] Carl Sagan 'An Analysis of Worlds in Collision.' In Donald Goldsmith (editor) (1977) *Scientists Confront Velikovsky*, pp. 46-47.
[52] C. Sagan (1979) *Broca's Brain (Reflections on the Romance of Science)*, Random House: New York, p. 86.
[53] J. Derral Mulholland 'Movements of Celestial Bodies—Velikovsky's Fatal Flaw.' In Donald Goldsmith (editor) (1977) *Scientists Confront Velikovsky*, p. 106.

In fact, the role which the planet Venus plays in my own tumultuous solar system of Antiquity is actually even more active than in the Velikovskian model. In the following pages, I will outline no less than 9 occasions in which Venus veered from its peaceful orbital path, provoking a cataclysmic tilting of the earth's polar axis, between the years 3,114 BCE and 612 BCE. Along with other similar sudden orbital shifts involving Mercury, Mars and the moon, I believe that the total number of cosmic catastrophes in historical times elevates itself to 22. Indeed, twenty-two times, the ancients feared the destruction of the world. Twenty-two times, they watched helpless as the ancient skies grew dark with smoke and fire, the waters of the ocean seabeds invaded the inhabited lands, and the entire earth grumbled. Although some catastrophes were less severe than others, the most destructive ones were caused by the planet Venus. In most instances, the planet Venus wrought its havoc in tandem with its fellow inner planet Mercury. These two particular planets, Mercury and Venus, are known as "inner" planets because they are both positioned between the sun and the earth. Mercury, the closest one to the sun, is hardly visible to the naked eye due to the fact that it bathes in the sun's rays. Yet, to the ancients, Mercury was a mighty deity — identified with heroes like Hermes or Nebo. Temples were built to this feared planet to appease it's periodic wrath. Why? Similarly, Venus was notoriously know by ancient peoples throughout the globe as a vengeful deity sporadically punishing the earth-dwellers for their inequities. Where did these widespread beliefs come from?

Mercury and Venus earned their vengeful reputation because, together, they terminated great World Ages by fiery destruction. Known as Sun Ages in Mesoamerica and Mandates of Heaven in ancient China, these ancient World Ages' cataclysmic culmination portended the coming of a new era, or covenant, through which humankind was given another chance to walk in a righteous path. The planetary deities, Mercury and Venus, dutifully exacted the judgment of the gods by decimating the degenerating previous World Age. It was afterwards entirely up to the earth-dwellers themselves to ensure the continuity of the new world order. The ancients ascribed each of these World Ages to a particular constellation of the zodiac. Mythological tales and theological constructs correlating these twelve constellations and the succeeding World Ages abounded. According to ancient chroniclers Hesiod and Porphyrius, the twelve labours of Herakles symbolized the twelve signs of the zodiac.[54] In Charles François Dupuis' *Origine de tous les cultes (Origin of all Religious Worship)*, first published in 1795, the latter contended that all ancient religions had been essentially inspired by the movement of the twelve constellations. Referring specifically to the Twelve Labours of Herakles, Dupuis writes:

---

[54] Charles François Dupuis (1984 [1872]) *The Origin of All Religious Worship*, Garland: New York and London, p. 89.

> It is under the name of Hercules Astrochyton, or of the God clad in the mantle of Stars, that the poet Nonnus designates this Sun-God, worshipped by the Tyrians. The titles of the **King of Fire, Lord of the World and of the Planets**—of nourisher of mankind, of the God, whose glowing orb, revolves eternally around the Earth ... daughter of Time and mother of the twelve Months, draws along in regular succession the seasons, which renew themselves ...'[55]

While Charles F. Dupuis, following these ancient traditions, sees the twelve labours of Herakles merely as a "solar fable, which can have reference only to the twelve months and to the twelve signs ..."[56], I shall propose that an even deeper allegory is hidden in this legend. Hercules (the Roman pronunciation of Herakles) was known as the "King of Fire, Lord of the World and of the Planets" for a very specific reason. Each of the World Ages which came to an end in a great destruction were associated with one of Herakles' twelve constellations. So the annihilating fire, spattered by the angered planetary deities at the termination of the World Ages, came about under the jurisdiction of Herakles — hence his title. Criticising Martin Bernal's attempt to find meaning in Dupuis' theory, Professor Robert Palter of Trinity College remarked that:

> ... Dupuis's text discloses the suspicious fact that in only three of the twelve cases (Leo the lion, Aries the ram, and Taurus the bull) does the object represented by the zodiacal sign actually occur in the narrative of the corresponding Herculian labor.[57]

Why do only these three particular zodiacal constellations play a central role in the Herculean myth? It is because the last three World Ages prior to the one in which we currently live, the Age of Pisces, were, in sequence, that of Aries, Leo and Taurus. These are the only works which Herakles had fully completed since the ancients started to correlate the World Ages with the twelve zodiacal constellations. The first thing that now comes to the informed reader's mind however is that this is not the order in which the constellations are supposed to have succeeded themselves. Moreover, the phenomenon of precession, which allows for the rotational passage of the various zodiacal constellations along the earth's polar axis, insures that every zodiacal signs remains at the vernal equinox for a period of 2,160 years each. So this should signify that, in order

---

[55] Ibid, pp. 87-88.
[56] Ibid.
[57] Robert Palter 'Eighteenth-Century Historiography in Black Athena.' In Mary R. Lefkowitz & Guy M. Rogers (1996) *Black Athena Revisited*, p. 357.

just to complete the three aforementioned works (Aries, Leo and Taurus), Herakles would have needed 6,480 years! What's more, if one were to stick to the traditional ordering of the precessional movements, getting through these three constellations would take considerably longer — assuming that Herakles would take a rest during the intervening constellations. How could the ancient Greeks have kept records dating to such exceeding Antiquity? This is unthinkable; so another explanation has to be found.

The phenomenon of precession is the result of the earth's "wobble" motion in space. What causes the earth to constantly wobble is the gravitational pull exerted by both the sun and the moon upon the earth's equatorial bulge. So at the time of the Spring Equinox (March 21) the firmament is never in quite the same position as in previous year. This is because, due to the wobbling effect, there is a very slight annual lag of around 50 seconds which over a period of 72 years amounts to one full degree (50 seconds x 72 years = 3,600 seconds = 60 minutes = 1 degree).[58] In the course of 2,160 years, the shift amounts to 30 degrees — which is the equivalent of one of the signs in the zodiac. The ancients divided the celestial zodiac into twelve equal parts of 30° — each representing a sign corresponding to a particular zodiacal constellation. The designated constellation, or Pole Star, changes over the millennia as the north celestial pole migrates along the precessional cycle. This total circuit of 360° is completed in a period of about 26,000 years (the time it takes for the earth's vernal equinox to travel through all 12 constellations by remaining 2,160 years under each zodiacal sign). Quoting Harvard University astronomer Charles A. Whitney: "Three thousand years ago and perhaps longer — astronomers chose the sun signs according to the corresponding zodiacal constellations ..."[59] Therefore, the idea of dividing the sky into the twelve constellations of the zodiac is in itself very ancient. Most modern scholars do not however believe that the actual precessional cycle was discovered until the fourth century BCE. In fact, I suggest that the division of the sky, into its 12 parts of 30° each, took place in c.2,130 BCE — thus becoming the standard throughout the ancient world, from Egypt to China. But contrary to modern scientific opinion, I believe that the ancient astronomers in fact *did* have a sophisticated understanding of the precessional movement of the constellations. Although they never were able to compute the cyclical period of 2,160 years attributable to individual constellations — which the ancient Greeks discovered. The pre-Aristotelian stargazers' inability to divine the actual length of the precessional cycle, as we know it today, was not due to any lack of intellectual capacity on their part, but simply because they lived within an inconsistent solar system.

---

[58] Joseph Campbell (1962) *The Masks of God: Oriental Mythology*, Viking: New York.
[59] Charles A. Whitney (1985) *Whitney's Star Finder*. Cited in Jane B. Sellers (1992) *The Death of Gods in Ancient Egypt*, p. 171.

The ancients emphatically believed that the precessional transition from one zodiacal constellation to the next was a bad omen because it heralded the destruction of the current world order, or World Age. The extremely slow, gradual succession of the zodiacal constellations along the vernal equinox did not yet exist in pre-Aristotelian times. At the time when the Herculean myth was composed, the Pole Star shifted unexpectedly and at highly irregular intervals. These instant precessional vacillations were precipitated by the swift movements of the earth's polar axis caused by the planet Venus' cycle-ending cataclysmic orbital shifts. Because the polar displacements along the precessional cycle occurred so violently, and without regard for the prescribed order of the zodiacal signs, the earthlings experienced major natural disasters. The ancient Chinese interpreted a change in the vernal equinox's constellation as a message from the gods that a new divine covenant, or Mandate of Heaven, was in order. The ancient Israelites held very similar beliefs; and denoted such an event as a Day of the Lord. The following represents the order, and time span, in which I believe that the zodiacal ages succeeded themselves, from the beginning of the Middle Bronze Age to the advent of the present Age of Pisces:

Aries Mandate: 2,130 BCE to 1,559 BCE
Leo Mandate: 1,559 BCE to 1,135 BCE
Taurus Mandate: I) 1,135 BCE to 776 BCE
II) 776 BCE to 612 BCE

None of these zodiacal Mandates of Heaven persisted for their full potential length of 2,160 years. In a matter of centuries, the earth's axis would abruptly shift and travel erratically along the precessional cycle. At such occasions, a World Age would come to an end and be replaced by another in the midst of a great catastrophe. This is why the ancients were so utterly terrified of transitions between precessional constellations. In modern times, the solar system is stable. So we need not fear the coming transition between the ages of Pisces and Aquarius. The earth's polar axis is peacefully following its preordained path along the precessional cycle. This is why modern scholars have so much difficulty understanding why the ancients dreaded the precessional transition between zodiacal signs. Because the dominant uniformitarian paradigm dictates that current observable phenomena have always been and always will be, the very notion that the tranquil precessional cycle could have been repeatedly interrupted by cosmic catastrophes in Antiquity has never been fathomed. Yet, such was the reality of Antiquity and the basis for many ancient myths.

To quote archaeoastronomer Jane B. Sellers, I believe that "myths were the carriers of information of celestial movements and events."[60] While Sellers would probably

---

[60] Jane B. Sellers (1992) p. 5.

be horrified at being associated with Velikovskian catastrophism, the basic thrust of this particular argument is at the heart of my catastrophic reconstruction of the history of ancient man and his myths. The practice of animal-worship in Egypt, for instance, was in part inspired by the shifting World Ages and their associated zodiacal signs. What may appear to modern observers as a primitive worship of animals, devoid of any meaning was, in fact, part of an intricate priestly mystery system concealing a profound knowledge of precession.[61] The ancients often portrayed their deities according to the constellation which occupied the northern celestial pole at any given time. The Mandate of Heaven, represented by a given zodiacal constellation, would finally expire when a two-pronged cosmic attack by the planets Mercury and Venus came along to herald a new World Age.

The planet Mercury's cataclysmic orbital shift was not, in itself, responsible for the cycle-ending axial shift, but it always hailed the coming of a devastating Venusian catastrophe. From the Mesoamerican annals, we can deduce that the length of time elapsed between the Mercury and Venus shifts was of fifty-two years. In the civilizations of ancient Mexico, that fifty-two-year period, inaugurated by a Mercury-induced cosmic cataclysm, was seen as a precursor to a new World Age, or Sun Age. Fifty-two years was the length of the Aztec century. This period known under the name of *xiuhmolpilli*, "a bundle of years," was tabulated by setting aside a peeled wand every year for fifty-two years and, once the 52 years had passed, they were bundled together and buried in a special ritual. The following period of fifty-two years was then seen as a time of great renewal.[62] The fifty-two-year cycle is attested from very early on in Mesoamerican rituals. The Aztecs strongly believed that if the transition rituals performed in between the fifty-two-year periods were somehow disturbed or neglected in the slightest was, then at the termination of the following fifty-two-year cycle: "catastrophe ensued and the celestial demons descended to kill and eat the last of mankind."[63] During the late nineteenth century, Ignatius Donnelly wrote:

> The ancient Mexicans believed that the sun-god would destroy the world in the last night of the fifty-second year, and that he would never come back.[64]

While the Aztecs had never themselves experienced the cataclysmic destructions carried out by the planetary gods, they had acquired this ancient knowledge con-

---

[61] See Diodorus of Sicily, Book I: 86.
[62] Burr Cartwright Brundage (1979) *The Fifth Sun (Aztec Gods, Aztec World)*, University of Texas Press: Austin and London, p. 21.
[63] Ibid, p. 22.
[64] Ignatius Donnelly (1882) *Atlantis: The Antediluvian World*, Harper & Bros.: New York, p. 146.

cerning the fifty-two-year cycle from their Mesoamerican ancestors like the Olmecs and Maya. The Olmec Calendar Stela found at Tres Zapotes, during the excavations of American archaeologist Matthew Stirling in 1939-1940, starts in the year 3,114 BCE. This year marks the beginning of the First Sun or First World in the Mayan and Aztec world-view, as I shall extensively argue. Since Venus was the one planet responsible for inaugurating new World Ages, we can conclude that the very first catastrophic orbital shift of the planet Venus, in historical times, took place in 3,114 BCE. Moreover, since the axial-shifting Venusian catastrophes were always preceded, by fifty-two years, by a Mercury shift, we may likewise date the first Mercury shift to 3,166 BCE. There were in total seven 52-year destructive cycles in Antiquity. Each one of them separating two great World Ages. All over the ancient world, we can find records and mythological traditions describing in detail these great 52-year-long Typhon Seasons. The term "Typhon Season" is used, throughout this book, in reference to these recurring lapses into universal chaos. The Greek deity Typhon, the equivalent of the Egyptian Seth, was known as the god of chaos. A major function of the pharaoh in ancient Egyptian culture was to maintain the order of nature so that it would not be reabsorbed into chaos. Periods of chaos were seen as times when the universal balance tilted in favour of Seth (or Typhon) — the archdemon.[65] Referring to the Platonic dialogues, classical scholar Phyllis Young Forsyth writes: *"The idea of world cycles, separated by natural catastrophes, is the core around which Plato constructs his myth."*[66] Forsyth also cites the following from J. A. Stewart: *"The doctrine of periodical terrestrial 'catastrophes', universal or local, leaving on each occasion a few scattered survivors ... was part of the 'science' of Plato's day..."*[67] The following is a list of the seven Typhon Seasons as they occurred in Antiquity:

Typhon Season #1:	3,166 BCE to 3,114 BCE
Typhon Season #2:	c.2,780 BCE to c.2,730 BCE
Typhon Season #3:	c.2,180 BCE to c.2,130 BCE
Typhon Season #4:	1,579 BCE to 1,559 BCE
Typhon Season #5:	1,187 BCE to 1,135 BCE
Typhon Season #6:	828 BCE to 776 BCE
Typhon Season #7:	664 BCE to 612 BCE

The only exceptionally short Typhon Season out of the seven was TS#4, which lasted a mere twenty years. These seven Typhon Seasons will be used as vital anchor points for the new chronology. They will be used to effectively synchronize the

---

[65] See H. Te Velde (1967) *Seth, God of Confusion (A Study of his Role in Egyptian Mythology and Religion)*. Trans. by G. E. van Baare-Pape. E. J. Brill: Leiden.
[66] Phyllis Young Forsyth (1980) *Atlantis (The Making of Myth)*, McGill-Queen's University Press: Montreal; Croom Helm: London, p. 71.
[67] J. A. Stewart (1960) *The Myths of Plato*, Centaur Press: Sussex, p. 192.

mythological traditions from ancient civilizations the world over. In many major cultural centres of Antiquity, the concept of the seven World Ages, and their intervening Typhon Season, were well known. In the Buddhist sacred book *Visuddhi-Magga*, it is professed in a particular chapter entitled "World Cycles" that there are seven ages.[68] Each cycle is said to have ended in a cataclysmic upheaval. Likewise, seven solar ages are recorded in Mayan manuscripts — each "sun" meaning a new "age." The reference to the sun as a synonym for world ages stems from the fact that the sun rose at a different point in the sky at the culmination of each Typhon Season. As there were seven Typhon Seasons, there necessarily were Seven Suns.

First Sun:	3,114 BCE to c.2,780 BCE	
Second Sun:	c.2,730 BCE to c.2,180 BCE	
Third Sun:	c.2,130 BCE to 1,5 79 BCE	Age of Aries
Fourth Sun:	1,559 BCE to 1,187 BCE	Age of Leo
Fifth Sun:	1,135 BCE to 828 BCE	Age of Taurus
Sixth Sun:	776 BCE to 664 BCE	Age of Taurus (cont.)
Seventh Sun:	612 BCE to present	Age of Pisces

It is only from the time of the Third Sun onwards that the ancients began taking account of precession. At the same time, in China, the tradition of the Mandate of Heavens took shape. The end of a Great Sun was believed to denote the rage of Heaven against the rebellious earth-dwellers who had strayed away from the righteous path. The Taoist text of Wen-Tze reveals that the following sequence of events occurs during the transition between the ages:

> When the sky, hostile to living beings, wishes to destroy them, it burns them; the sun and the moon lose their form and are eclipsed; the five planets leave their paths; the four seasons encroach one upon another; daylight is obscured; glowing mountains collapse; rivers are dried up; it thunders then in winter, hoarfrost falls in summer; the atmosphere is thick and human beings are chocked; the state perishes; the aspects and the order of the sky are altered; the customs of the age are disturbed [thrown into disorder] ... all living beings harass one another.[69]

As a matter of fact, my historical reconstruction will demonstrate that during the transition periods between the World Ages, major social, economic and political upheavals engulfed the notable states of Antiquity. Powerful kingdoms were at

---

[68] H. C. Warren (1896) *Buddhism in Translations*, pp. 320 ff.
[69] Wen-Tze in *Textes taoistes*. Trans. C. de Harlez (1891).

once overthrown, bloody civil wars erupted, foreign invaders infiltrated their neighbours' domains, etc. Civilizations would completely collapse to subsequently rise up again under entirely new foundations with the new World Age. The sky, planets and constellations also experienced substantial alternations. Entirely new cosmologies and cosmogonies were formulated to account for the changing pattern of the universe.

Myth no.2: **Ethiopia as student of Egypt**
" They say also that the Egyptians are colonists, sent out by the Ethiopians, Osiris having been the leader of the colony."

- Diodorus of Sicily
(Book III: 3)

How African was the ancient Nile Valley's celebrated pharaonic civilization? Had proto-dynastic Egypt, as the illustrious ancient Greek historian Diodorus of Sicily proclaims above, been colonized by Ethiopians? These questions continue to fuel many contemporary debates. European Egyptologists have generally tended to treat Diodorus of Sicily's remark with much skepticism. Since the infancy of modern Egyptology in the nineteenth century, scholars have interpreted the foundation of the Egyptian pharaonic state as an essentially "Asiatic" phenomenon. Epitomised in the acclaimed American Egyptologist James Henry Breasted's "Great Northwest Quadrant" hypothesis, Western scholars have situated Egypt within a civilization nucleus comprising of Europe, southwestern Asia and northern Africa. Ancient Egypt had, for all intents and purposes, been artificially divorced from the rest of Africa. As a result, Egyptologists' view of dynastic Egypt's relations with the rest of Africa, as Robert G. Morkot testifies, amounts to one of master versus subordinate — or civilization versus barbarism:

> It is a common place in Egyptological discussions to regard Egypt's attitude to Nubia as totally different from its attitude to the Western Asiatic dominions. This received view derives from the pre-conceptions about African societies prevalent in the nineteenth and early twentieth centuries. Inherent is the attitude that the Egyptians thought like 'us' in relation to the south.[70]

To quote just one particularly blatant example of such modern tendencies, British

---

[70] Robert G. Morkot 'Nubia in the New Kingdom: The Limits of Egyptian Control.' In W. Vivian Davies (editor) (1991) *Egypt and Africa (Nubia from Prehistory to Islam),* p. 294.

Egyptologist Peter Clayton asserts that: *"In ancient Egypt, Nubia and its indigenous population were the butt of many jokes, as with much ethnic humour today."*[71] Since most historians' view of the past is inevitably influenced by the times in which they live, it is always necessary to guard against such preconceived notions — particularly when setting out to analyse so ancient a culture. Nineteenth century European racism and colonialism are, in my estimation, largely responsible for distorting modern scholars' perception of the relationship between dynastic Egypt and Nubia. So remote is the concept that ancient Egypt's pharaonic culture might have been fundamentally African that early Egyptologists developed the "dynastic race" theory — which essentially argued for an invasion from without by a superior non-African Asiatic race, possibly from Mesopotamia, that was responsible for introducing civilization into the Nile Valley in the late fourth to early third millennium BCE. The dynastic race instituted, under the leadership of Pharaoh Menes, the very first of the thirty-one dynasties of ancient Egypt. As the masters of the Nile, these dynastic Egyptians, according to Egyptologists, had always seen themselves as being separate, both culturally and racially, from the Ethiopians living below their southern border. The dynastic race is believe to have, throughout pharaonic history, exploited the land and inhabitants of Nubia for such valuable resources as gold, incense and mercenaries. With the establishment of Egyptian garrisons, and eventually of a formal viceregal administration in Nubia, the Ethiopians allegedly "adopted" pharaonic culture. After Egypt's New Kingdom, they had supposedly become so thoroughly Egyptianized that a Kushite (Nubian) dynasty, the conventional 25th Dynasty, even came to rule Thebes itself. A period which British Egyptologist Arthur Weigall (1880-1934) spiteful qualified as "a period of nigger domination." The obsequious pupil had actually managed, perhaps through subterfuge, to transcend the master.

Over recent years, however, a radically new interpretation of Ethiopia's role in the formation of ancient pharaonic culture has emerged. To quote Prof. Ivan Van Sertima of Rutgers University:

> What is equally significant is the more recent discovery that there was some pharaonic-type civilization developing parallel to Egypt through the centuries. Bruce Williams, in a letter to me in 1984, maintained that a Kushite continuity sustained the pharaonic impulse through the ages, from A-group (3,300 B.C.) right through to X-group (550 A.D.) This, to put it in his own words, represents a new departure in the examination of Egypt's place in the African context.[72]

---

[71] Peter Clayton (1993) 'Nubia: A Drowned Land and its Re-emerging Civilization', *Minerva* Vol. 4 - Num. 1, p. 26.
[72] Ivan Van Sertima (editor) (1989a) *Egypt Revisited*, Journal of African Civilizations / Transaction Books: New Brunswick, NJ, p. 86.

American Nubiologist Bruce Williams has indeed pointed to the existence in Nubia of a pharaonic culture predating, by sixth generation, the advent of the 1st Dynasty in Egypt.[73] Ultimately, this is clear evidence that pharaonic culture's birthplace was in Africa. The model proposed in this book is that an African colony of civilizers known as the "Anu," as Diodorus of Sicily proposes, moved northwards along the Nile from below the Fifth Cataract in the Sudan, during the fifth millennium BCE, and set the very foundations of pharaonic culture. They inaugurated the calendar, instituted the religious rituals, organized the state theology, and developed the hieroglyphic system of writing. All this was accomplished before Pharaoh Menes founded the 1st Dynasty.

Egyptologists and ancient historians have long been baffled at the staggering speed with which the proto-dynastic Egyptians marshalled the necessary ingredients to constitute such a complex and enduring civilization. It was principally this "Egyptian miracle," as it may be called, which prompted scholars to search for the origins of pharaonic culture outside of the Nile Valley. Perhaps surprisingly to some, I personally do not discount at all the theory of the dynastic race. It is true that the dynastic Egyptians hailed from southwestern Asia. Pharaoh Menes was not, racially speaking, an African king. Nonetheless, the pharaonic culture which he, and his dynasty, inherited, was fundamentally African. My hypothesis is that a thriving Black pharaonic civilization existed in the Nile Valley centuries before the advent of dynastic Egypt; and that, through colonization, the African pharaonic culture was exported to southwestern Asia in the historical period commonly referred to as the predynastic era (3,200 BCE to 2,950 BCE). With this knowledge, partially adapted to their Asiatic heritage, the dynastic race, headed by Menes, descended upon Memphis and founded dynastic Egypt.

Meanwhile, in Upper Egypt or Khemet (i.e. the Black Land), the Ethiopian descendants of the Anu continued to reign from Egypt's southern border near the First Cataract region — at Edfu and Philae. Therefore, up until the end of the 3rd Dynasty, two separate kingships, one (the senior) in southern Egypt and the other (the junior) in northern Egypt peacefully shared the royal title of Horus the Falcon — ruler of Egypt. The unification of the Horus kingship only came with Pharaoh Sneferu of the 4th Dynasty. King Sneferu ensured the supremacy of the dynastic race for the entire duration of the Old Kingdom (2,730 BCE to 2,180 BCE). As a result, Horus the Elder and Horus the Child were for the first time united into a single divine king. The Khemites from the Black Land (southern Egypt) had retreated to their ancestral homeland below the Fifth Cataract in the Sudan. Behind them, the Khemites had left the founding iconography and theology which

---

[73] See Bruce Williams (1980) 'The Lost Pharaohs of Nubia', *Archaeology* 33, pp. 12-21.

would, millennia later, serve as an inspiration for the Ptolemaic architecture of the Hellenistic era. Thus, what I boldly portend is that what is today known as Ptolemaic architecture, dating to the Hellenistic era (fourth to first centuries BCE), has its roots in proto-dynastic times. Therefore, the rise of the celebrated Ptolemaic period in the fourth century BCE was, in reality, a renaissance era commemorating the classic Ptolemaic Age of the Early Bronze Age (fourth to third millennia BCE). Only within Ptolemaic theology, can the lost record of the primeval division between Horus the Elder and Horus the Child be found. The Ptolemaic texts hold within them the key to understanding the true context in which the early pharaonic state was formed. Hence, they must be interpreted as genuine historical accounts hidden in elaborate myth.

Myth no.3: **Ancient Egyptian history's 'Intermediate Periods'**

The close of the Old Kingdom in ancient Egyptian history conventionally coincides with an era of civil disorder and confusion known as the First Intermediate Period. Egyptologists have identified a total of three such Intermediate Periods in ancient Egyptian history. The First Intermediate Period (2180-2,040 BCE), the Second Intermediate Period (1,674-1,559 BCE), and last the Third Intermediate Period (1,080-715 BCE). The common distinguishing feature between these three periods is that two or more Egyptian dynasties reigned simultaneously, but from different capitals. The reason why I believe that the designation of those eras as Intermediate Periods is a myth is because there was in fact nothing unusual with such dynastic arrangements. In the new chronology I propose, the eras when a single Egyptian pharaoh reigned from a single capital are overwhelmingly out-numbered by periods in which more than one dynasty shared power simultaneously. The ancient Egyptian dynasties did not, generally speaking, succeed each other in an orderly and sequential fashion — as Eusebius of Caesarea (*c*.264-340 CE) relates:

> It seems ... that different kings held sway in different regions, and that each dynasty was confined to its own nome [province]; thus it was not a succession of kings occupying the throne one after the other, but several kings reigning at the same time in different regions.
> (Manetho, *Aegyptiaca*, FR.1)

Obviously, this statement contradicts what Egyptologist Helen J. Kantor of the University of Chicago's Oriental Institute proclaims — when she informs us that: *"... in contrast to western Asia, the difficult chronological problems of co-ordinating the dynastic sequences of contemporary states [in ancient Egypt] do not exist, except for the*

40 | PLANET OF THE GREEKS

periods of decline."[74] Viewing epochs when dynasties ruled contemporaneously as periods of decline is a major flaw of modern Egyptology. As I shall endeavour to prove with the new chronology, three dynasties reigned contemporaneously at the height of dynastic Egypt's imperial age — during the reign of Pharaoh Ramses II.

An immediately foreseeable consequence of such a revolutionary rearrangement of the accepted order of the pharaonic dynasties is the creation of important gaps in the overall chronology of ancient Egypt. Making two or more conventionally consecutive dynasties suddenly synchronous implies that previous rulers would have to move down chronologically — hence creating a myriad of other chronological problems. Ancient world scholars would then be faced with the monumental task of reconstructing the entire history of the ancient world. Undoubtedly, this is the main argument of conventional scholars against chronological revisionism.[75] As a result, orthodox Egyptologists and ancient historians, much to the detriment of scientific truth, have been extremely reluctant to question the accepted ordering of the dynasties. The repercussions of such a drastic shift in time would be nothing less than momentous.

Myth no.4: **Manetho's 'History of Egypt', the Abydos King-lists and the Turin Canon**

Historians believe that, in 280 BCE, a Graeco-Egyptian chronicler by the name of Manetho of Sebennytos compiled a formal history of pharaonic Egypt. This elusive document is now long lost but proclaimed versions of the Manethonian history of Egypt have come down to us in the writings of first century CE Jewish historian Flavius Josephus and from the third to eighth centuries CE chronographers Sextus Julius Africanus (c.221 CE), Eusebius of Caesarea (c.264-340 CE), and George Syncellus.[76] Intriguingly though, there is no firm evidence to prove that Manetho ever existed. Despite this eerie silence, scholars accept that Manetho is a genuine historical figure and that his history of Egypt is a reliable source. According to the renowned Egyptologist and ancient historian Donald B. Redford of the University of Pennsylvania:

---

[74] Helen J. Kantor 'The Relative Chronology of Egypt and Its Foreign Correlations before the Late Bronze Age.' In Robert W. Ehrich (editor) (1965) *Chronologies in Old World Archaeology*, pp. 2-3.
[75] For an excellent analysis of the problems associated with radical chronological revisions, see William H. Stiebing, Jr. (1985) 'Should the Exodus and the Israelite Settlement be Re-dated?', *Biblical Archaeology Review* Vol. 11 - Num. 4, pp. 58-67.
[76] Kenneth Kitchen (1991) 'The Chronology of Ancient Egypt', *World Archaeology* Vol. 23 - Num. 2, pp. 201-208.

INTRODUCTION | 41

Although no contemporary references of him exist and nothing of his writings survives, no reputable scholar today would deny the historicity of Manetho of Sebennytos.[77]

It is therefore safe to say that these "reputable scholars" base their assumptions more on faith and convention than on verifiable historical fact. As Prof. D. B. Redford's statement plainly outlines, Manetho of Sebennytos, the "King Arthur of Egyptology," has served as a cornerstone to ancient world scholarship for generations despite the complete absence of any hard evidence pointing to his historicity. Contrary to the prevailing "article of faith," I shall contend that the simple reason why no contemporary records attesting to his existence have, or ever will, surface is because Manetho of Sebennytos *never* existed! My theory is that the Manethonian history of dynastic Egypt was concocted during, and not before, the first century of the common era by the Romans.

The Manethonian tradition divides the history of Egypt into thirty-one dynasties of kings succeeding each other in a linear fashion. Egyptologists further subdivide Manetho's thirty-one dynasties into such classifications as the New Kingdom and the three Intermediate Periods. In addition to the Manethonian chronology, Egyptologists rely on an even more ancient king-list drafted by the native dynastic Egyptians themselves. This king-list, dated by scholars to the standard 19th Dynasty, is known as the Royal Turin Canon (or Turin Papyrus). It is now conserved at the Museo Egizio in Turin, Italy (no. 1874) — hence its name. Referring to the Turin Canon, Egyptologist Jaromir Malek writes:

> Whatever the character of its no doubt more detailed primary source may have been, the list was intended to be an official administrative reference aid and thus, presumably, an objective (non-selective) and unbiased document. It provides us, therefore, with a rare insight, limited though it may be, into the Egyptians' own view and awareness of their past. The list has attracted scholars since J.-F. Champollion studied it in 1824 and is, consciously or unconsciously, the corner-stone of all chronological schemes for Egyptian history before the Ramessides, even thought outwardly Egyptologists range in their attitude towards the information provided by the 'Royal Canon of Turin' from 'fundamentalists' to 'rejectionists.'[78]

There is no question however that the "fundamentalists" still run the show. Although, behind closed doors, professional Egyptologists might still quietly

---

[77] Donald B. Redford 'The Name Manetho.' In Leonard H. Lesko (editor) (1986) *Egyptological Studies in Honor of Richard A. Parker*, Brown University Press: Hanover and London, p. 118.
[78] Jaromir Malek (1982) 'The Original Version of the Royal Canon of Turin', *Journal of Egyptian Archaeology* 68, p. 93.

bicker over the true accuracy of that list, they maintain a "united front" when confronted with the lay public. As with the Manethonian texts, I am very disinclined to view the Turin Canon as an accurate and unbiased record of dynastic Egypt's history. I don't of course deny the undisputable fact that the dynastic Egyptians themselves drafted the Royal Turin Canon. But, as will be delineated, I contend that it was devised many centuries later than conventionally believed. In my view, the Turin Canon is actually a very selective and subjective list of the ancient Egyptian monarchs. There is nothing to completely assure us that the ancients Egyptians did not compile a politically or ideologically motivated king-list to reflect their own idealized version on Egyptian history. For instance, we know that another ancient king-list drafted by the Egyptians at around the same time, the Abydos King-list, altogether ignores the Hyksos pharaohs — who belonged to a race of foreign Asiatic invaders who took over the reigns of power in Egypt temporarily. Likewise omitted were Egyptian pharaohs whom the Abydos priesthood had disliked. Therefore, as Austrian excavator Manfred Bietak observes below, such ancient written sources must be taken with a dose of skepticism:

> In contradistinction to archaeology, the philological disciplines dealing with ancient civilizations depend on sources which already at the outset are burdened with the biases and tendentious opinions of their ancient writers. The written source material is, therefore, by no means objective to begin with.[79]

In my own view, it is just as dangerous for professional Egyptologists to rely on either the Manethonian history of Egypt or the extant Egyptian king-lists for historical accuracy as it is for biblical scholars to depend on the Hebrew Bible as an authoritative source for the study of Syro-Palestinian archaeology. The same way that the biblical redactors could, and certainly were, more than occasionally guided by nationalistic or ideological fervour, the compilers of the extant Egyptian king-lists must be treated with equivalent caution. That's because, as I will undertake to prove throughout the present work, the remaining archaeological evidence from Egypt *does not* support the official native Egyptian king-lists themselves! To borrow a term from biblical studies, the Egyptological "maximalists" who blindly follow the Turin Canon and the Manethonian genealogies do so in spite of glaring inconsistencies prevalent within these traditions. A thorough reevaluation of the reliability of the native king-lists, in full light of recent archaeological discoveries, is truly long overdue. By placing archaeology first, and being willing to ultimately confront the fallibility of the king-lists, a more plausible and scientific historical account of ancient Egypt can be arrived at.

---

[79] Manfred Bietak (1979a) 'The Present State of Egyptian Archaeology', *Journal of Egyptian Archaeology* 65, p. 157.

INTRODUCTION | 43

Myth no.5: **The Aryan Model and the Dark Age of Greece**
" *Does the Eagle know what is in the pit?*
Or wilt thou ask the Mole? "

- William Blake

Starting as early as the 1820s, European scholar Karl Otfried Müller began using the historical-critical method to refute all classical traditions supporting the notion of an Egyptian colonization of ancient Greece. Moreover, in late nineteenth century Germany, following K. O. Müller, European scholars, under the leadership of Julius Beloch,[80] set out on a relentless crusade to once and for all debunk all the ancient so-called myths of Afroasiatic colonization of Greece. The accounts of the classical authors had, at all cost, to be shown to bear no historical value whatsoever. Even in contemporary academic circles, this view has not changed very much — as is demonstrated in the following commentary by Nubiologist David O'Connor: *"Such theories were invented in antiquity to explain the origins of Greek and Egyptian civilizations, which otherwise seemed mysterious."*[81] To quote Semitist Michael C. Astour, this polemic "was conducted with such passion that its motivation seemed to be derived from external considerations."[82] Furthermore, Cornell University historian Martin Bernal has dedicated his *Black Athena* book series to figuring out what these "external considerations" were. In Prof. Bernal's mind, Western scholars' outright denial of the Afroasiatic colonization of Greece in Antiquity stems chiefly from European racism. What Bernal refers to as the "Ancient Model," supporting the hypothesis of Afroasiatic colonization was, in his opinion, replaced with the so-called "Aryan Model" during the early nineteenth century by European scholars who found it unbearable to think that "Egyptians and other non-European 'barbarians' had possessed superior cultures, from which the Greeks had borrowed massively."[83] Citing Martin Bernal:

> The Aryan Model has dominated scholarship for the last 150 years. It holds that Greece was originally inhabited by a non-Indo-European speaking but

---

[80] Julius Beloch (1894) 'Die Phoeniker am aegäischen Meer', *Rheinisches Museum* 49, pp. 111-132.
[81] David O'Connor (1993) *Ancient Nubia: Egypt's Rival in Africa*, University Museum of Archaeology and Anthropology – University of Pennsylvania: Philadelphia, p. 2.
[82] Michael C. Astour (1967) *Hellenosemitica (An Ethnic and Cultural Study in West Semitic Impact on Mycenaean Greece)*, E. J. Brill: Leiden, p. xvii.
[83] Martin Bernal (1987a) *Black Athena (The Afroasiatic Roots of Classical Civilization) — Vol. I: The Fabrication of Ancient Greece 1785-1985*, Vintage: London, p. 310.

44 | PLANET OF THE GREEKS

'racially' 'Caucasian' population. Some time in the third or second millennium B.C. these people or peoples were conquered by Indo-European-speaking invaders from the north. Greek culture is viewed as the result of this fusion, some elements being Indo-European and the rest derived from the conquered aborigines.[84]

In the revised model which I suggest, I retain the idea of an Indo-European invasion during the second millennium BCE. However, the Aryan Model's proposition that Homeric Greek culture resulted from the merging of the Early Helladic population and the invading Indo-Europeans is a fallacy. To illustrate, the Greeks of Homer's Heroic Age descended from a Nordic band of invaders from the Baltic region who spoke a language intimately related to the Indo-European family. Known as the Danaans, these blond-haired and blue-eyed invaders arrived in the Mediterranean region, and the ancient Near East, as part of a northern coalition of maritime peoples. Collectively referred to as the "Peoples of the Sea," they arrived in the Aegean during the thirteenth to twelfth centuries BCE. During that time in mainland Greece, powerful Asiatic rulers dominated the Mediterranean. The latter, whom I shall identify as the Hyksos, had retained control of mainland Greece throughout the Late Bronze Age (1,559 BCE to 1,135 BCE). Only the Minoans (the Eteocretans), inventors of the Linear-A script and masters of Middle and Late Bronze Age Crete, remained wholly independent of the Asiatic Mycenaeans of the Late Bronze Age. Nonetheless, a very close trilateral alliance existed Minoan Crete, mainland Greece and the Egyptian Delta. Contrary to what conventional wisdom would purport, I believe that the Hyksos held sway over both the Egyptian Delta and Mycenae during much of the Late Bronze Age. Hence, the Danaans, the proto-Hellenic Greeks, had inevitably come under the partial authority and influence of the Mycenaean Hyksos during the twelfth century BCE.

It is indeed precisely during this pivotal time that the legendary colonizing waves, from the Egypto-Phoenicians principally, shaped what was to become Homeric Greece during the Iron Age. As Diodorus of Sicily wrote:

> ... the belief prevailed that the Egyptians were the first men to effect the discovery of the stars. Likewise the Athenians, although they were the founders of the city in Egypt men call Sais, suffered from the same ignorance because of the flood. And it was because of reasons such as these that many generations later men supposed that Kadmos, the son of Agenor, had been the first to bring letters from Phoenicia to Greece ...
> (Diodorus of Sicily, Book V: 57)

---

84 Martin Bernal (1986) 'Black Athena Denied: The Tyranny of Germany over Greece and the Rejection of the Afroasiatic Roots of Europe 1780-1980', *Comparative Criticism* 8, pp. 3-4.

This radical redating for the composition of the Greek alphabet, through the transmission of the Kadmean letters, to the twelfth century BCE is extremely consequential. To begin with, it offers a solution to the enduring enigma of the "Dark Age of Greece" — since classicists have long be confounded by the apparent absence of any evidence whatsoever of writing in Greece from the twelfth century BCE to the eighth century BCE. Somehow, with the sudden demise of the Late Bronze period's Heroic Age, the ancient Greeks inexplicably forgot how to read and write their own script. Supposedly, the tales of Agamemnon, Kadmos, Aegyptus and Danaos were preserved in orals traditions and were only finally committed to writing in the eighth century BCE during the days of Homer. How is it possible to explain this strange hiatus? Again, the answer lies in the radical revision of the accepted chronology of the ancient world. In the new chronology, Kadmos is identified with an Egyptian monarch of Phoenician heritage who, in 1,135 BCE, leads an Egypto-Phoenician colonising expedition into mainland Greece. Therefore, the five hundred year period traditionally attributed to Homer's Heroic Age moves downward, by about five hundred years, from the Late Bronze Age to the Iron Age. The five hundred-year-long Dark Age is then automatically eliminated. Since Agamemnon, Kadmos, Aegyptus and Danaos, as well as the transmission of the alphabet resulting from the Afroasiatic colonization, all belong to the twelfth century BCE, then we may presume that Homer, in the eighth century BCE, inherited a continuous tradition. There is, in fact, no allusion whatsoever in the classical records to a Dark Age of Greece. This concept is nothing more than an invention of modern scholarship born out of an erroneous Egyptian chronology.

Myth no.6: **The Biblical Exodus**
Perhaps no other quest has been more frustrating for Bible historians and archaeologists than locating the exact date of the Hebrew Exodus. How much of the Book of Exodus is mere fiction? How much of it is historical? Where should one draw the line? Most scholars who still believe in the historicity of the Hebrew Exodus, date the event to the reign of King Ramses II — whom they identify with the biblical "Pharaoh of the Oppression." The accepted dating for the biblical Exodus among these conservative excavators ranges from 1,280-1,220 BCE. But numerous archaeological digs in Syria-Palestine, during the past fifty years especially, have revealed embarrassingly little proof pointing to the historicity of the Book of Exodus. So dire is the situation that many excavators no longer use the term biblical archaeology but instead use the term "Syro-Palestinian archaeology."

The preeminent problem is that the archaeological record from Syria-Palestine during the closing Late Bronze Age does not corroborate the biblical model of a conquest from without. In an attempt to find a solution to the impasse, alternative theories explaining the emergence of an Israelite nation have developed in recent years. The first one, known as the Alt-Noth school or the Peaceful Infiltration Model, argues that the twelve Israelite tribes entered Canaan peacefully over a long period of time in successive migratory waves. Another slightly more successful theory, the Mendenhall-Gottwald school or Peasant Revolt Model, suggests instead that the Israelites had been indigenous Canaanites who rose up against the degenerate Canaanite ruling class and rallied around Yahwism in order to identify with a unifying divine symbol (the god Yahweh).

Ultimately, it is entirely self-evident, given the dearth of archaeological proof, that the Conquest Model found in the Book of Joshua is not suitable to the time period conventionally consecrated to the Hebrew Exodus. The question is then: should one dismiss completely the historicity of the biblical Exodus? If taken word for word, the Books of Exodus and Joshua are indeed myths. Joshua never conquered Canaan at the end of the Late Bronze Age. While Ramses II was indeed the Pharaoh of the Oppression, Joseph the Patriarch lived five hundred years before that king, in the Middle Bronze Age. In the revised chronological model I will put forward, earnest efforts will be applied to resolving many of such perplexing contradictions. For example, by carefully dissecting the biblical version of the Exodus, it will be made apparent that the biblical redactors have very skillfully woven together no less than "four" different historical Exoduses together spanning a period of over eight hundred and fifty years! Hence, the totality of the biblical Exodus must not be interpreted as a veritable historical account. Furthermore, virtually every major details of the story, if taken away from the sum total of the its parts, reflect genuine historical circumstances. To use an analogy, if a journalist were to use short clippings from various newspapers and then carefully paste them together to form a new story, the individual clippings would still tell parts of a real story but the totality of the manufactured story would be very misleading. Therefore, taking the manufactured Exodus story apart, I have identified and dated the following four Exoduses: the First Exodus took place in 1,628 BCE, Second Exodus in 1,380 BCE, Third Exodus in 1,135 BCE and finally the Fourth Exodus in 776 BCE. All four of these separate historical Exoduses contain within themselves kernels of truth — which can be gleaned from the biblical Exodus account. For instance, while the Pharaoh of the Oppression ruled about a century prior to the Third Exodus, the Pharaoh of the Exodus (who chased the fleeing Israelites) reigned during the Fourth Exodus. Likewise, while Joshua's Conquest of Canaan took place following the First Exodus, the Israelites' forty years of wandering in the Sinai desert occurred during the Third Exodus.

Myth no.7: <u>**The Five Books of Moses**</u>
*" Moses received the Torah on Sinai, and
delivered it to Joshua, and Joshua to the elders,
and the elders to the prophets, and the prophets delivered
it to the men of the Great Synagogue. These said three
things: Be deliberate in judging, and raise up many
disciples, and make a hedge for the Torah."*

- Jewish Mishnah
Abot 1.1

Having thus identified four different historical Exoduses, the next question inevitably has to be: how many Moses characters were there? Equally relevant questions are: when was the biblical Exodus story concocted from the four historical Exoduses? Who wrote the composite Exodus account? Why had the biblical redactors gone through such lengths? Did they have something to hide or an ideological agenda to fulfil? All these questions can be explored by thoroughly analysing the first five books of the Bible — i.e. the Five Books of Moses or the Pentateuch. The Five Books of Moses have been at the centre of one of the oldest puzzles in the world. The first five books of the Bible: Genesis, Exodus, Leviticus, Numbers, and Deuteronomy have been wrestled with by scholars, clerics and faithful laymen alike ever since the Bible was completed. The Five Books of Moses are also commonly known as the *Pentateuch* (from Greek, meaning five scrolls) or as the *Torah* (from Hebrew, meaning instruction). Ancient Jewish and Christian traditions commonly held that Moses himself authored the Pentateuch. Though Moses is the central figure through most of these five books, nowhere does it actually say that Moses *himself* wrote them. The theory that a single person, the biblical Moses, wrote the Pentateuch presents many important contradictions. For example, Moses describes his own death[85] and actually relates events which should have occurred *after* his death. To get around such blatant inconsistencies, some suggested that the later accounts were written by Joshua — Moses' successor. This explanation was however challenged by Carlstadt, a contemporary of Luther, during the sixteenth century. He pointed to the fact that the account of Moses' death is written in the same style as the texts that precede it.[86] During the seventeenth century, the renowned British philosopher Thomas Hobbes became the first to out rightly express his belief that the majority of the Pentateuch was not written by Moses. He cleverly observed that the author used the expression: *"to this day."* That very statement, "to this day," would logically only be applicable to the author's

---
[85] *Talmud*, Baba Bathra 15a.
[86] Richard Elliott Friedman (1987) *Who Wrote the Bible?*, Summit Books: New York, p. 19.

description of events not contemporaneous to his own time. Four years later, French Calvinist Isaac de la Peyrère would make another insightful observation by referring to the statement: *"These are the words that Moses spoke to the children of Israel across the Jordan ..."* Again, this passage presents a serious problem. The author's use of the phrase "across the Jordan," would necessarily suggest the perspective of someone situated in Israel — west of the Jordan. The problem is, Moses was never supposed to have reached the Promised Land! After his book was promptly banned and burned, De la Peyrère was arrested, forced to become a Catholic, and was required to offer an official apology accompanied by a retraction to the Pope in exchange for his freedom.[87] However, the controversy was not silenced — as the philosopher Spinoza aptly observed in the following phrase: *"There never arose another prophet in Israel like Moses..."* Undoubtedly, this sounds like the words of an author who lived long after the time of Moses. This would be the only plausible explanation as to how the author could have compared Moses to the prophets who came *after* him. What's more, the Book of Genesis (36:31) speaks of *"... the kings that reigned in the land of Edom, before there reigned any king over the children of Israel."* Once again, how could Moses have known that Israel would eventually be ruled by kings?[88] In the words of Spinoza: *"It is ... clearer than the sun at noon that the Pentateuch was not written by Moses, but by someone who lived long after Moses."*[89] So, who then was the author of the Five Books of Moses?

Since the end of the nineteenth century, it's safe to say that most Bible scholars have agreed that the biblical Moses had not written the first five Books of the Bible. The scholarly consensus ultimately formed around the idea that the Pentateuch was the result of the intricate weaving together of four separate documents, commonly referred to as J, E, D, and P. As a result, biblical scholars believe that these ancient Jewish documents were written down in numerous stages — from the time of the United Monarchy to the Babylonian Exile. These letters stand for: J = Yahwist (Jahwist in German), E = Elohist, P = priestly codes, D = Deuteronomist, and also R = redactor or editor. In full agreement with the current body of scholarship which advocates a late composition, I believe that "all" of these texts were both written and consolidated during the Babylonian Exile in the sixth century BCE.

With respect to the authorship, I contend that the Torah was indeed written, or at the very least edited by Moses. Naturally, the concept of Moses living in the sixth century BCE, during the Babylonian Exile, should strike any reasonable person as

---

[87] Ibid, p. 20.
[88] William H. Stiebing, Jr. (1989) *Out of the Desert? (Archaeology and the Exodus/Conquest Narratives)*, Prometheus Books: Buffalo, NY, p. 21.
[89] Richard Elliott Friedman (1987) p. 21.

INTRODUCTION | 49

completely preposterous. But, as with the case of the composite biblical Exodus, I believe that there were no less than "six" historical Moses upon which biblical tradition was based. The author of the Pentateuch or Five Books of Moses was the last among them — the Sixth Moses. That Sixth Moses was none other than the prophet Ezra. With the last three of the four historical Exoduses had developed the enduring tradition of an anointed saviour or Messiah whose mission it was to rescue God's people from bondage or oppression. That recurring saviour's name, or title, was Moses — the Messiah. I shall argue that it is precisely on this ancient Mosaic tradition that the Jews' anticipation of a redeeming Messiah, as crystallised in the Book of Isaiah, emanates from. If there were indeed six different Moses characters in Jewish history, and that their cyclical succession formed the basis for the Messianic tradition, then why would the Bible be so blatantly silent about something so important? To answer that question, we must consider the following two passages from the Old and New Testaments. The first one, from the Book of Exodus, recounts:

> 32 And afterward all the children of Israel came nigh: and he gave them in commandment all that the Lord had spoken with him in mount Sinai.
> 33 And till Moses had done speaking with them, he put a veil on his face.
> (Exodus 34: 32-33)

Why does Moses put on a veil? This has, for time immemorial, been a mystery. In most ancient rabbinical texts, Moses is cloaked in mystery. The date of his birth and death are obscure and there had always been a powerful taboo associated with inquiring too much about the mysteries surrounding Moses. Quite interestingly, we find an eerily similar caution and reference to the veiled face of Moses in the New Testament writings of Paul of Tarsus:

> 12 Seeing then that we have such hope, we use great plainness of speech:
> 13 And not as Moses, which put a veil over his face, that the children of Israel could not steadfastly look to the end of that which is abolished:
> 14 But their minds were blinded: for until this day remaineth the same veil untaken away in the reading of the old testament; which veil is done away in Christ.
> (2 Corinthians 3:12-14)

In the New Testament, we detect a certain hostility against Moses' decision to wear a veil. Evidently, Paul implies that the veil is a metaphor indicating a form of deceit on the part of Moses. The redactor of the Torah has Moses wear a veil because he, Ezra — the Sixth Moses, is well aware that there had been several Moseses before the Pentateuch was written. Wishing to place sole emphasis on the composite Moses, Ezra put a veil on the former's face to hide his multiple identities. As long as that veil remains on the face of the composite Moses, Paul of Tarsus is entirely right to claim that a veil shall likewise pervade over Old Testament exegesis.

The Birth of a New Science

" People don't beg other people to restore their history; they do it themselves. ... If other people's hands secure it for us, other people's hands can take it away from us."

- John Henrik Clarke
Africans at the Crossroads

With this book, I wish to introduce a new science by the name of *Khemetology*. By definition, Khemetology seeks to study ancient pharaonic civilization from an African-centered cultural perspective. This particular approach is based on the premise that the civilizations of ancient Khemet (usually used as a synonym for Egypt) and Egypt represented two distinct cultural entities, and that the latter emerged out of the former. Khemetology likewise recognizes ancient pharaonic cosmogony and cosmology as crucial tools toward the proper chronological and theological reconstruction of ancient Khemeto-Egyptian history. It is, indeed, my belief that the science of Egyptology is seriously flawed; mainly due to its heavy reliance on the Turin Canon, as well as other official dynastic Egyptian king-lists (specifically the Abydos King-lists), and the Graeco-Egyptian Manethonian chronology of dynastic Egypt. This fundamental paradigmatic set of mistakes has led to a grave modern misunderstanding of not only ancient Egyptian civilization, but also of the entire ancient world.

As has just been delineated in the seven principal myths of ancient history, the ancient king-lists, and other annals of Antiquity, must be extremely critically analysed — taking into account ideological motivations and dissimulated cultural biases. Having taken an exceedingly maximalist stance with respect to ancient Egypt's extant king-lists, modern Egyptology's virtually uncritical acceptance of the Manethonian classification of pharaonic rulers into single succeeding dynasties has isolated dynastic Egyptian history from its early Ethiopian or Khemetic roots. As a result, Egyptology fails to properly understand the theological and historical developments of ancient pharaonic civilization. While Western Egyptology concerns itself preeminently with dynastic Egypt, Khemetology deals with the entire spectrum of ancient pharaonic culture — recognizing that pharaonic culture does not begin with dynastic Egypt but holds more ancient African roots.

Finally, since the chronology of ancient pharaonic civilization is crucial for the parallel dating of virtually every other culture in Antiquity, Khemetology also acts as a reliable common denominator for the accurate chronological classification of the entire history of the ancient world. The radical reordering of the pharaonic dynasties' sequence, which will be proposed, carry truly devastating effects for the accepted historiographies of ancient Greece, Syria-Palestine and Anatolia — among others. The multi-disciplinarian exegesis of historical and religious texts from these many ancient cultures, tackled throughout these pages, will likewise be pivotal for the reconstruction of the historiography of Antiquity. Toward this venture, it will be necessary to resort to a field of study which I have called archaeotheology. As the name implies, archaeotheology draws parallels between ancient religious traditions, or national myths/theologies, and genuine historical developments in Antiquity. For instance, an archaeotheological analysis of the ancient Greek colonization myth of Kadmos and Aegyptus reveals that the presumably mythical tale recounts a real colonization of ancient Greece by Phoenicians and Egyptians during the Late Bronze Age.

The daunting challenge which I have taken on of completely destroying the conventional chronology of the ancient world, and rebuilding it from top to bottom, requires me to rely on very meticulous evidence and tightly woven forms of argumentation. To illustrate, as a prosecution lawyer who must prove his case beyond the shadow of a doubt, my main objective is to convince a jury comprised of both my peers as well as an army of highly qualified scholars, that something is fundamentally wrong with the conventionally accepted version of world history. Although I have attempted to make the material as accessible as possible, to as wide an audience as possible, the nature of this undertaking dictates that my analysis be quite detailed and comprehensive. Moreover, since I don't believe that such truths should solely be made available to the "high priesthood of academia," I estimate that the controversial debates enclosed within the pages of professional academic journals ought to be displayed for all to see. Not only is the general public virtually always excluded from these debates, but scholars from other disciplines, engrossed in their own isolated dialogues, are only too often unaware of inconsistencies prevalent within other scholarly fields which regularly affect their own domains. Organized confusion continues to reign largely because overspecialization in contemporary ancient world scholarship has fostered an unhealthy climate where the synthesis of knowledge is perceived as being the realm of dilettantes and charlatans.

4,500 - 3,200 BCE PREDYNASTIC PERIOD

Badarian **(4,500 to 4,000 BCE)**
Naqada I (Amratian) **(4,000 to 3,600 BCE)**
Naqada II - III (Gerzean A - B) **(3,600 to 3,200)**

3,200 - 2,180 BCE THINITE PERIOD

1ˢᵗ Dynasty (3,200 to 2,980 BCE)
Menes (The Horus Narmer)
Ity I (The Horus Aha)
Ity II (The Horus Djer)
Ity III (The Horus Wadjit / Djet)
Khasety (The Horus Den)
Merpibia (The Horus Adjyeb)
Irynuter (The Horus Semerchet)
Ka-aseny (The Horus Ka'a)
2ⁿᵈ Dynasty (2,980 to 2,780 BCE)
Hotep (The Horus Hetepsekhemwy)
Nubnefer (The Horus Reneb)
Nynetjer
Weneg
Sened
Pery-yebusen (Seth)
Khasekhem / Khasekhemwy

2,780 - 2,180 BCE OLD KINGDOM

3ʳᵈ Dynasty (2,780 to 2,680 BCE)
Djoser I (The Horus Netjerykhet)
Djoser II (The Horus Sinakhte)
Sekhemkhet
Tety (The Horus Khaba)
Nebku
Huny
4ᵗʰ Dynasty (2,680 to 2,560 BCE)
Snefru
Khufu (Cheops)
Djedefre
Khafre (Chephren)
Menkaure (Mycerinus)
Shepseskaf

5th Dynasty (2,560 to 2,400 BCE)
Userkaf
Sahure
Neferirkare (Kakai)
Shepseskare
Neferefre
Niuserre (Ini)
Menkauhor (Kaiu)
Djedkare (Isesi)
Unas
6th Dynasty (2,400 to 2,180 BCE)
Teti
Userkare
Pepi I
Merenre I
Pepi II
Merenre II
Nictoris

2,180 - 2,040 BCE FIRST INTERMEDIATE PERIOD

7th and 8th Dynasties (2,180 to 2,160 BCE)
Many short-lived kings including:
Wadjkare and Qakare Iby
9th and 10th Dynasties (Herakleopolis) (2,160 to 2,040 BCE)
Meryibre Khety I
Neferkare
Nebkaure Khety II
Neferkare Meryibre
Merikare
11th Dynasty (Thebes) (2,160 to 2,040 BCE)
Inyotef I
Inyotef II
Inyotef II
Mentuhotep I
S'ankhibtawy-Mentuhotep II

2,040 - 1,674 BCE MIDDLE KINGDOM

11th Dynasty (All Egypt) (2,040 to 1,991 BCE)
Nebhepetre Mentuhotep II
Mentuhotep III
Mentuhotep IV
12th Dynasty (1,991 to 1,785 BCE)
Amenemhat I
Senusret I
Amenemhat II
Senusret II
Senusret III
Amenemhat III
Amenemhat IV
Queen Sobeknefru
13th Dynasty (1,785 to 1,674 BCE)
Wegaf
Sobekhotep I
Auyibre (Hor)
Sobekhotep II
Khendjer
Sobekhotep III
Neferhotep I
Sobekhotep IV
Neferhotep II
Sobekhotep V
Sobekhotep VI
Sobekhotep VII
Sobekhotep VIII

1,674 - 1,559 BCE SECOND INTERMEDIATE PERIOD

14th Dynasty	15th Dynasty	16th Dynasty	17th Dynasty
Dudimose I	Sheshi	Anather	
Menthu-Emsaf			
Dudimose II	Yakhuber	Semken	Rahotep
Nehesy			Sobek-Emsaf II
	Khyan	Khaworsere	Nebiryerawet I
	Apophis I	Yakobaam	Shedwast
	Apophis II	Ahetepre	Inyotef VII
	Khamudy	Sekenre	Tao I
		Amu	Tao II (Sekenenre)
		Apophis III	Kamose

1,559 - 1,069 BCE NEW KINGDOM

18th Dynasty (1,559 to 1,295 BCE)
Ahmose
Amenophis I
Tuthmosis I
Tuthmosis II
Tuthmosis III
Hatchepsut
Amenophis II
Tuthmosis IV
Amenophis III
Amenophis IV
Akhenaten
Smenkhkare
Tutankhaten / Tutankhamun
Ay
Horemheb

19th Dynasty (1,295 to 1,185 BCE)
Ramses I
Seti I
Ramses II
Merneptah
Amenmesses
Seti II
Siptah
Twosret

20th Dynasty (1,185 to 1,069 BCE)
Sethnakhte
Ramses III
Ramses IV
Ramses V
Ramses VI
Ramses VII
Ramses VIII
Ramses IX
Ramses X
Ramses XI

STANDARD CHRONOLOGY OF ANCIENT EGYPT

1,080 - 715 BCE THIRD INTERMEDIATE PERIOD

21st Dynasty (1,080 to 945 BCE)

Thebes	Tanis
Herihor (Siamun)	
Pi-Ankhy	Smendes I
Pinudjem I	
Masaherta	
Menkheperre	
	Amenemnisu
	Psusennes I
	Amenemope
Smendes II	
Pinudjem II	
	Osorkon The Elder
	Siamun
Psusennes (III)	Psusennes II

22nd Dynasty (945 to 715 BCE)

Bubastis	Thebes (Chief Priests)
Shoshenk (Sosenk) I	Iuput
Osorkon I	Shoshenk
Shoshenk II	Smendes
Takelot I	Iuwelot
	Harsiese
Harsiese	
Osorkon II	Nimlot
Takelot II	Prince Osorkon

23rd Dynasty (825 to 715 BCE)

Shoshenk III	Pedubast I	
	Osorkon III	
Pimay		
	Takelot III	
Shoshenk V		
25th Dynasty	Rudamon	**24th Dynasty (Sais)**
Kashta	Iuput II (754-715 BCE)	Tefnakht (727-720 BCE)
Pi-Ankhy (747-716 BCE)		Bocchoris (720-715 BCE)

745 - 525 BCE LATE PERIOD

25ᵗʰ Dynasty (747 to 656 BCE)
Pi-Ankhy
Shabaka
Shebitku
Taharqa
Tanutamun

26ᵗʰ Dynasty (664 to 525 BCE) (Sais)
Nekau I (672-664 BCE)
Psamtik (Psammetichus) I
Nekau II
Psamtik II
Apries
Amasis
Psamtik III

525 - 404 BCE FIRST PERSIAN PERIOD

27ᵗʰ Dynasty (525 to 404 BCE)
Cambyses II
Darius I
Xerxes I
Artaxerxes I
Darius II
Artaxerxes II

404 - 343 BCE INDEPENDENT DYNASTIES

28ᵗʰ Dynasty (404 to 399 BCE)
Amyrtaeus
29ᵗʰ Dynasty (399 to 380 BCE)
Nepherites I
Psammuthis
Achoris
Nepherites II
30ᵗʰ Dynasty (380 to 343 BCE)
Nectanebo I
Tachos
Nectanebo II

343 - 332 BCE SECOND PERSIAN PERIOD

31st Dynasty (343 to 332 BCE)
Artaxerxes III
Arses
Darius III

332 - 305 BCE MACEDONIAN KINGS

Alexander (The Great) III
Philip Arrhidaeus
Alexander IV

305 - 30 BCE PTOLEMAIC DYNASTY

Ptolemy I (Soter I)
Ptolemy II (Philadelphus)
Ptolemy III (Euergetes)
Ptolemy IV (Philopator)
Ptolemy V (Epiphanes)
Ptolemy VI (Philometor)
Ptolemy VII (Neos Philopator)
Ptolemy VIII (Euergetes II)
Ptolemy IX (Soter II)
Ptolemy X (Alexander I)
Ptolemy XI (Alexander II)
Ptolemy XII (Neos Dionysos)
Queen Berenice IV
Queen Cleopatra VII
Ptolemy XV (Caesarion)

PART I

KHEMET	**EGYPT: Hierakonpolis** (ADAM)	**Naqada II (Ombos)**		(EVE)	**(3600 BCE)**
- "*Cults of Re and Khnum*"	- Narmer (Osiris)			**BYBLOS/ CANAAN**	**(3200 BCE)**
(Horus of Behdet)	"*First unification of Egypt*"	**Naqada III**	**Ombos (Ta-Seti)**	- "*Land of Punt — God's Land*"	**(3166 BCE)**
- Djoser (The Horus Netjerykhet)			- "*Cult of Seth*"		
KHEMET (First Cataract)		**UPPER / LOWER EGYPT**		**Troy I**	**(3114 BCE)**
- "*Cult of Horus the Elder*"	**Philae / Dendera**	- "*Cult of Horus the Child*"			
Edfu	- "*Cult of Isis / Hathor*"	**Abydos / This / Memphis (Noph)**			
(Horus the Behdetite / of Mesen)	- Cleopatra I	**Horus Name** **King Name**			
- Ptolemy I		**1st Dynasty** "*Egyptian invasion of Ta-Seti*"			**(2953 BCE)**
- Ptolemy II	**Ombos (Ta-Seti)**	- Aha / Menes (CAIN) - Ity I			
- Ptolemy III	- Sixth gen. (ABEL)	- Djer - Ity II			
- Ptolemy IV		- Wadji - Ity III		**SYRIA / CANAAN**	
- Ptolemy V		- Den - Khasety		(Asiatics / Bowmen)	
- Ptolemy VI	**Kom Ombo**	- Adjyeb - Merpibia		**MESOPOTAMIA**	
- Ptolemy VII	- "*Cult of Sobek*"	- Semerchet - Irynuter		- "*Early Dynastic I*"	
- Ptolemy VIII	- Cleopatra II	- Ka-a - Ka-aseny			
- Ptolemy IX		**2nd Dynasty**			
- Ptolemy X	- Cleopatra III	- Hotepsekhemwy - Hotep			
- Ptolemy XI		- Reneb - Nubnefer			
- Ptolemy XII	- Cleopatra IV	- Nynuter - Nynuter			
- Ptolemy XIII		- Weng			
- Ptolemy XIV	- Cleopatra V	- Sened			
- Ptolemy XV	- Cleopatra VI				
	- Cleopatra VII				
KHEMET	**UPPER EGYPT (Ombos)**	**LOWER EGYPT**		**MESOPOTAMIA**	**(2780 BCE)**
Elephantine	**2nd Dynasty (Continued)**	**3rd Dynasty**		- "*Ancient Sumer*"	
- "*Cults of Re and Khnum*"	- Pery-yebusen (Seth)	- Tety (The Horus Khaba)		- Gilgamesh	
- Khufu	- Khasekhemwy (Seth / Horus)	- Nebku		**PHOENICIA**	
"*Gizah Pyramids built*"	- Djoser (The Horus Sinakhte)	- Sekhemkare, - Neferkare		- "*Founding of Tyre*"	
		- Huny			**(2730 BCE)**

PART II

	(Birth of Noah)	
UP. / LOW. EGYPT	**MESOPOTAMIA**	**(2730 BCE)**
4th Dynasty	- "*Early Dynastic II*"	
- Sneferu	**Thebes**	
- Khufu (Cheops)	**(Deir el-Bahri)**	
- Djedefre	- "*Cult of Hathor*"	
- Khafre (Chephren)		
- Menkaure (Mycerinus)		
- Shepseskaf		
5th Dynasty	**MESOPOTAMIA**	
- Userkaf, - Sahure, - Neferirkare, - Shepseskare,	- "*Early Dynastic III*"	
- Neferefre, - Niuserre (Ini), - Menkauhor (Kaiu),	- King Lagash	
- Djedkare (Isesi), - Unas (*Pyramid Texts*)	**ELAM** **Troy II**	**(2560 BCE)**
	- "*Dynasty of Awan*"	

UPPER NUBIA
(Early Kerma)
(Kushites)

	Akkad	**Syria**	**(2400 BCE)**
6th Dynasty	- Sargon	(Asiatics / Amorites)	
- Teti, - Userkare	- Rimush	- "*Settlement of Terqa*	
- Pepi I (Meryre)	- Manistusu	*city walls built*"	

LOWER NUBIA
(Wawat)
(Medjay)

- Merenre I	- Naram-Sin		
- Pepi II, - Merenre II, - Nictoris	- Sharkalishari		
7th & 8th Dynasties	- Dudu	**ELAM**	**(2180 BCE)**
- Wadjkare	- Shu-durul	- "*Dynasty of*	**Troy III**
- Qakare Iby		*Shimashki*"	- Huang Ti
			- Ti Ku

	SHEM	**JAPHTEH**	
UPPER / LOWER EGYPT	**Elam**	(Indo-Europeans)	
Herakleopolis	**Ashur**		**CHINA** **(2150 BCE)**
9th & 10th Dynasties	**Lud / Arphaxad / Aram**	**Mari (Terqa)**	- Ti Chih
- Meryibre (Akhtoy I)	- Terah	- "*Sakakkanakku Period*"	- Yao
....	- Abraham		
- Khety (Akhtoy III)	- Isaac	**Troy IV**	**THE GREAT** **(2130 BCE)**
- Merikare	- Jacob & Esau		**FLOOD)**
			"*Luni-solar calendar*"

HAM			
Canaan	**Arabia**	**Akkad**	**ASSYRIA**
(Canaanites)	- Ishmael	"*Ur III*"	- Sulili, - Kikkiya
Put		- "*Tower of Babel*"	- Akiya
(Libyans)			

Thebes
11th Dynasty

- Inyotef I	
- Inyotef II	**Cush**
- Inyotef III	(Kushites / Amorites)
- Mentuhotep I	**Mizraim**
- Mentuhotep-S'ankhibtawy	(*Medjay*)

(1953 BCE)
- Shun

PART III

KHEMET	EGYPT				ELAM	AEGEAN: "Middle Minoan"	Troy V-VI (1953 BCE)

KHEMET — *"Egyptian retreat to Meroë during Asiatic occupation of Egypt"*

11th Dynasty (cont.) — **MESOPOTAMIA: BABYLONIA** — **ELAM** *"Period of Sukkalmahs (1953 - 1559 BCE)"*

KHEMET / 11th Dyn. (cont.)	BABYLONIA			
- Mentuhotep-Nebhepetre	- Sumuabum			
- Mentuhotep III	- Sumulael			
- Mentuhotep IV *"Joseph the vizier"*	- Sabium			

EGYPT (12th Dynasty)	MARI (Terqa)	ASSYRIA		Hattusa (Hittites)	CHINA (Xia Dynasty)	(1820 BCE)
		- Shamshi-Adad I		- Pithana		
		- Ishme-Dagan I	*"Khana I"*	- Anitta		

Upper Egypt	Delta / Avaris	CANAAN (Hazor)		BABYLONIA (Amorites)		Troy VI (1780 BCE)
- Sesostris I	- Wegaf	- Kashtiliashu	- Yapah-sum			
- Sesostris II	- Auyibre (Hor)	- Yabin-Hadad	- Apilsin	- Sinmuballit		
- Sesostris III	- Khendjer	**PHOENICIA**	- Ammi-Madar			
- Sobeknefru	- Neferhotep	- Yantin-Ammu	- Zimri-Lim	- Hammurabi		

Upper Egypt (13th Dynasty)	Lower Egypt (13th Dynasty)	Avaris	ISRAEL			Hattusa (Hittites)	(1628 BCE)
- Dudimose I (Tutimaius)	- Sobekhotep I	- Sheshi I (Salatis)	- Joshua	*"Kassite / Hittite invasion"*	- Hanaya	- Labarna	
- Menthu-Emsaf	- Amenemhat VI (Sobekhotep II)		- Othniel		- Iddin-Kakka	- Hattusilis I	
- Dudimose II	- Sekemres (Sobekhotep III)	- Bnon			- Isar-Lim	- Mursilis I	
- Nehesy	- Khaneferre (Sobekhotep IV)		- Deborah	- Samsuiluna	- Iggid-Lim	- Hantilis	**CHINA**
	- Sobekhotep V	- Apachnas	- Abimelech	- Abiesha	- Isih-Dagan	- Zidanta I	- Kwei
				- Ammiditana	- Hammurapih		
				- Ammisaduga			

KHEMET	14th Dynasty	13th Dyn. (cont.)	Avaris	ISRAEL		Troy VI (cont.)	CRETE (Minoans)	(1559 BCE)
- Amanitekha	- Ahmose	- Sobekhotep VI	- Apophis	- King Saul			*"Late Minoan"*	*"Shang replaces Xia."*
- Arnekhamani	- Amenhotep I	- Sobekhotep VII		- King David				
- Queen ...pnayka	- Tuthmosis I	- Sobekhotep VIII	- Jannas				**ASSYRIA**	
- Amanitekha	- Tuthmosis II	- Sobek-Emsaf I	- Seshi II	- King Solomon		**MITANNI**	- Ashir-rabi	
- Arqamani	- Hatchepsut (Queen of Sheba)	*"Second Exodus / Salem built"*				- Parattarna		(1418 BCE)
- Tabirqa	- Tuthmosis III / IV		**Avaris**	**BABYLONIA**		- Sausatar		
- Shanakdakhete	- Amenhotep II			- Karaindash		- Artatama		
- Naqrinsan	- Amenhotep III (Nap-huria)	(*Egyptian lepers*)		- Kurigalzu I		- Sutarna	- Ashur-uballit	(1380 BCE)
- Tanyidamani	- Amenhotep IV (Nibhururiya)	- Osarsiph				- Tushratta		
						- Mattiwaza		

Hittites (right column, Troy VI cont. section):
- Ammuna
- Huzziya I
- Telipinu
- Hantili II
- Tudhaliya II
- Arnuwanda I
- Tudhaliya III
- Hattusilis II
- Suppiluliumas I

(1330 BCE)

PART IV

KHEMET (Meroë/Napata)	EGYPT 15th Dyn.	Thebes (Phoenicians) 17th Dyn.	Avaris (Amalekites) 16th Dyn.	BABYLONIA	HATTUSA	ASSYRIA	(1330 BCE) Troy VIIa
- Amanikhabale	- Ramses I			- Kurigalzu II	- Mursilis II	- Enlil-Nerari	
- Teriteqas	- Seti I	- Rahotep	- Anather	- Nazimaruttash	- Muwatalis II	- Adad-Nerari I	Troy VIIb
- Amanirenas	- Ramses II	- Sobek-Emsaf II	- Semken	- Kadashman-Turgu	- Mursilis III	- Shalmanaser I	
- Akinadad	....	- Nebiryerawet I	- Khaworsere	- Kadashman-Enlil II	- Hattusilis III	- Tukulti-Ninurta I	
- Amanishakhete	- Merneptah	- Shedwast	- Yakhuber	- Kashtiliash IV	- Tudhaliya IV	....	(1200 BCE)
- Natakamani	- Setnakhte			**Boeotia / Avaris / Canaan**	- Suppiluliumas II	- Enlil-kudurri-usur	
- Atlanarsa				- Apap I **(Agag I)**	- Tudhaliya V		
- Senkamanisken	- Ramses III	- Inyotef VII	- Ahetepre	**"Sea People / Ionian invasion"**	**Troy VIIb2**		(1180 BCE)
- Anlamani	- Ramses IV	- Tao I		- Apap II **(Agag II)**			
- Aspelta	**18th Dyn.**	- (Tao II/Sekenenre- Sekhenre)		**"Third Exodus" / "Ogyges flood of Attica"**		**ASSYRIA**	
- Amtalqa	- Ahmose	- Kamose/**Kadmos**- Amu				- Wen Wang	(1135 BCE)
- Malenaqen	- Amenhotep I		- Apap III **(Agag III)**			- Tiglath-Pileser I **" Zhou replaces Shang"**	
KHEMET	**UP./LOW. EGYPT**			**CANAAN**	**AEGEAN**	**PHOENICIA**	**BABYLONIA** (1117 BCE) **ASSYRIA**
....	**18th Dyn. (cont.)**			*(Israelites)*	*(Mycenean-B)*		- Nebuchadnezzar I
- Siaspiqa	- Tuthmosis I (King Saul)				- *"Late Helladic II"*		- Tiglath-Pileser II
- Nasakhma	- Tuthmosis II (King David)						- Marduk-ahhe-eriba
- Malewiebamani	- Hatchepsut/ Tuthmosis III (King Solomon)					- Ahiram	- Nabu-shum-libur
KHEMET	**EGYPT**	**Tanis** *(Libyans)*			- *"Late Helladic III"*	- Itobaal	**ASSYRIA (Nimrod)** (945 BCE)
- Talakhamani	Thebes	**19th Dyn.**		**JUDAH**	**ISRAEL**	- Yehimilk	- Ashur-dan II
- Aman-yerike	- (Amenhotep II ---	- Shoshenk I)		- Rehoboam	- Jeroboam	- Abibaal	- Adad-nirari II
- Baskakeren	- (Tuthmosis IV ---	- Osorkon I)		- Abijam	- Baasha	- Elibaal	- Tukulti-Ninurta II
- (Harsiotef	- **Harsiese)**	- Shoshenk II		- Asa	- Omri	- Shipitbaal	- Ashurnasirpal II
- (Akhraten	- **Akhenaten)**	- Takelot I		- Jehosaphat	- Ahab **(Ayab)**		- Shalmanaser III
Thebes	- Amenhotep III	- Osorkon II		- Joash	- Jehu		- Shamshi-Adad V
- Tutankhamun	Shoshenk III /**Moeris**	- Takelot II			- Jehoahaz	**CRETE**	- Adad-nirari III
- Ay **"Fourth Exodus"**	- Osorkon III /	- Osorkon III /		- Amaziah	- Jeroboam II	**CHINA**	- King Minos
	- Horemheb	- Takelot III		- Uzziah	- Menahem	- Yen-Yang	- Shalmaneser IV
							- Ashur-nirari V
							GREECE
							-**"Olympiads"**
							(747 BCE)

PART V

KHEMET / EGYPT   **(747 BCE)**

Napata/Thebes	Thebes	Tanis / Sais	JUDAH	ISRAEL	ASSYRIA	BABYLONIA	PHRYGIA
20th Dynasty	**21st Dynasty**		(-Uzziah)	- Pekahiah	- Tiglath-Pileser III	- Nabonassar	- Midas
- Kashta	- Rudamon	- Pedubast	- Jotham	- Pekah			
- Piye (Pi-Ankhy)	- Iuput, - Pimay	- Nimlot					**SYRIA**
- Shabaka	- Osorkon IV	- Tefnakht			- Shalmaneser V	- Nabu-Mukin-zeri	- Rezin
- Shebitku	- Shoshenk IV	- Bocchoris	- Ahaz	- Hoshea	- Sargon II		**Troy VIII**
- Taharka	- Osorkon V	- Shoshenk V	- Hezekiah		- Senacherib		*-"Iliad"*
- Tanutamun			- Manasseh		- Esarhaddon		**(664 BCE)**

Thebes (*Macedonians*)   - *"Assyrian sack of Thebes"*   - Ashurbanipal

22nd Dynasty	**MEMPHIS**	JUDAH	ASSYRIA			
- Nekau I — Ramses I	- *"Cult of Apis"*	- Amon	(- Ashurbanipal)			
- Psamtik I — Seti I (Sethos)		- Josiah			**BABYLONIA**	**GREECE**
- Nekau II — Ramses II (Ozymandias)		- Jehoahaz	- Ashur-etil-ilani		(*Chaldeans*)	- *"Byzantium founded by Greeks"*
- *"Building of Red Sea canal"*		- Jehoiakim	- Sin-shumu-lishir		- Nabopolassar	
		- Zedekiah	- *"Nineveh destroyed by Chaldeans and Medes"*		- Nebuchadnezzar II	- *"Draconian Laws"*

- Psamtik II — Khamweset
- Apries — Merneptah   - Ashur-uballit II   **(612 BCE)**

"Israel Stela"   - *"Exile of Judah to Babylon"*   - Amel-Marduk   **GREECE**

	PERSIA	**PHOENICIA**			- Neriglissar	- *"Solon visitis Amasis in Egypt"*
- Amasis	- Cyrus I	- Ahiram III			- Labashi-Marduk	**CHINA**
- Psamtik III	- Cambyses I				- Nabonidus	**(561 BCE)**

23rd Dynasty (*Ethiopians*)   **ISRAEL**
- Actisanes-Amenemhat   - Cyrus II   - *"Return of Jews from Babylonian Exile"*   - Confucius (b. 551 BCE)
- Sesostris   **(525 BCE)**

24th Dynasty (*Persians*)   - *"Battle of Marathon"*
- Cambyses II   - *"Athens founds Delian League"*
- Darius I   - Socrates (b.469 BCE)
- Xerxes   - Plato (b.429 BCE)
- Artaxerxes I
- Darius II   - *"Ezra introduces the Five Books of Moses"*   **(404 BCE)**

PART VI

UPPER / LOWER EGYPT

25th Dynasty
- Amyrtaeus

26th Dynasty
- Nefaarad I (Nepherites I)
- Hakor (Achoris)

27th Dynasty
- Nakhtnebef (Nectabo I)
- Djedhor (Theos)
- Nakhthoreb (Nectanebo II)

28th Dynasty
- Artaxerxes III
- Arses
- Darius III

GREECE   (404 BCE)

- *"Long Walls rebuilt in Athens"*
- *"Socrates condemned to death (399 BCE)"*
- *"Plato founds Academy"*
- Aristophanes (Athenian dramatist)
- Aristotle (b.384)   (380 BCE)
- Demosthenes (b.384 — Orator)

ROME
- *"Gauls sack Rome"*
- *"City walls of Rome built"*
- *"Temple of Concordia"*
- *"Latin Wars"*
- *"First Roman coins"*

- *"Battle of Chaeronea: Macedonians conquer Athens"*
- *"Pan-Hellenism of Isocrates"*

CHINA
- *"Tsi's army defeats Wei's forces"*

GREEK PTOLEMAIC KINGS

29th Dynasty (Alexandria)
- Alexander III (the Great)
- Soter I (Ptolemy I)
- Philadelphus (Ptolemy II)
- Euergetes I (Ptolemy III)
- Philopator (Ptolemy IV)
- Ptolemy V-VI **"Rapid decline of empire"**
- Neos Philopator (Ptolemy VII)
- Euergetes II (Ptolemy VIII)
- Soter II (Ptolemy IX)
- Alexander I-II (Ptolemy X- XI)
- Neos Dionysos (Ptolemy XII)
- Cleopatra VII
- Caesarion (Ptolemy XV)

GREECE   (332 BCE)

- *"Revolt of Greeks against Macedon"*

CHINA
- *"Burning of the Books"*   (145 BCE)

"Battle of Actium"   (31 BCE)

THEBES
31st Dynasty
(Khons-in-Thebes)
- Pi-Ankhy
- Pinedjem I
- Masaherta
- Menkheperre
- Smendes
- Pinedjem II
- Psusennes III
- Osorkon VI

TANIS
(Horus-of-the-Camp)
- Amenemnisu
- Psusennes I
- Osorkon The Elder
- Amenenope
- Siamun (Herihor)
- Psusennes II
- Shoshenk VI

UP./LOW. EGYPT
30th Dynasty
- Ramses III
- Ramses IV
- Ramses V-VI
- Ramses VII-VIII
- Ramses IX
- Ramses X-XI
- Ramses XII

DATES AND PERIODS			EVENTS OF IMPORTANCE
5,000 BCE	HELIOPOLITAN ERA/ HIERAKONPOLITAN & MEMPHITE PERIODS		▶ The African early pharaonic culture of Anu settles in Heliopolis. ▶ First observation of the heliacal rising of Sirius.
4,413			▶ First calendar introduced by Khemites.
3,600			▶ Beginning of Gerzean period.
3,200		Early Bronze I	▶ Beginning of Naqada III period. ▶ First unification of Egypt under Narmer (Osiris).
3,166			▶ **Mercury shift** ▶ Seth of Naqada kills Osiris.
3,114 BCE	NEW HORUS PERIOD		▶ **Venus shift** (End of TS#1) ▶ Classic Ptolemaic temples built in Edfu, Philae and Dendera. ▶ The sixth generation of Ta-Seti reigns in Qustul and Ombos.
2,953		Early Bronze II	1st Dynasty — ▶ Heliacal rising of Sirius. 2nd Dynasty — ▶ Min-Horus (Menes) reunifies Egypt and defeats Ta-Seti. ▶ Egyptian conflict with Asiatic bowmen.
2,780	OLD KINGDOM	Early Bronze III	3rd Dynasty — ▶ **Mercury shift** ▶ Egypt divided between Seth and Horus. ▶ Khufu of Khemet builds Gizah pyramids.
2,730 BCE			▶ **Venus shift** (End of TS#2) ▶ Sneferu reunifies Egypt under Horus.
			5th Dynasty — ▶ Cult of Horus, son of Re is established. ▶ Fifth Dynasty observes Orion rising. ▶ Dynastic Egyptians adopt cult of Osiris.
2,400		Early Bronze IV	6th Dynasty — ▶ **Mercury shift** ▶ Infiltration of Asiatics into Nubia (C-Group). ▶ Old Akkadian empire in Mesopotamia.
2,180 BCE			▶ **Mercury shift**

DATES AND PERIODS

EVENTS OF IMPORTANCE

Dates	Period	Dynasty	Sub	Bronze Age	
2,180 BCE	MIDDLE KINGDOM — DILUVIAN PERIOD	7-8th 9-11th Dyns.	Aries Mandate	Middle Bronze I	EB IV
2,130					
	KINGLESS PERIOD			Middle Bronze IIa	
1,953 BCE					
1,820 BCE		11th Dyn. (Con.)			
1,780 BCE		12th Dyn.		M. Bronze IIb	
1,628		13th Dyn.		M. Bronze IIc	
1,579					
1,559 BCE					

- Emperor Yao begins ruling in China.
- Herakleopolitan kings rule Egypt.
- **Venus shift** (End of TS#3)
- The Great Flood.
- Theban nomarchs appear after in in the south after the Flood.
- Abraham and his family seek refuge in the land of Egypt.
- Sakakkanakku period in Mari.
- Luni-solar calender in China.
- The Third Dynasty of Ur in Akkad.
- **Venus shift**
- Elamites invade the Near East.
- Indo-Aryan invasion of the Aegean.
- Dynastic line in Egypt is interrupted.
- Theban monarchy finds refuge in Ethiopia.
- Mentuhotep-Nebhepetre reunifies the Two Lands.
- The states of Babylonia, Mari and Assyria emerge after Elamite decline.
- Joseph the Patriarch becomes vizier of Egypt.
- **Venus shift** (1,787 BCE)
- Twelfth Dynasty introduces the cult of Amun-Re.
- The capital of Egypt is moved from Thebes to Memphis.
- Heliacal rising of Sirius is recorded.
- **Moon shift**
- Thera eruption.
- First Exodus and Conquest of Joshua.
- Hyksos invasion of Egypt.
- **Mercury shift**
- First Moses fights Nubians under Pharaoh Khaneferre.

DATES AND PERIODS					EVENTS OF IMPORTANCE
1,559 BCE	THEBAN RENAISSANCE	14th Dyn.	Leo Mandate	Late Bronze I	➤ **Venus shift** (End of TS#4) ➤ Shang Dynasty replaces Xia in China. ➤ Ahmose (Moses) founds new 14th Dyn. ➤ Cult of Amun gains supremacy. ➤ Heliacal rising of Sirius. ➤ Rise of Meroïtic kingdom in Ethiopia. ➤ Original unified monarchy in Israel.
1,418				Late Bronze II	➤ The Hyksos attack Egypt once more. ➤ Two Lands unified under Tuthmosis II. ➤ Queen of Sheba visits Solomon.
1,380					➤ Tuthmosis III expels Hyksos in Avaris. ➤ Second Exodus/ founding of Jerusalem. ➤ First correspondences between the Hittites and Amenhotep IV. ➤ Lepers and Amalekites take over Egypt.
1,346					
1,330 BCE	NEW KINGDOM	15th Dyn.		Late Bronze III	➤ Amenhotep IV and Ramses I regain ➤ Cult of Amun-Re becomes state religion in Egypt once again.
		16th/ 17th Dyns.			➤ Seti I and Ramses II establish Egyptian imperial age by campaigning in Syria-Palestine and turning several city-states into vassal regions. ➤ Battle of Kadesh between Egypt and Hatti ends in peace treaty. ➤ Hyksos dynasty in Egypt gains power.
1,187					➤ **Mercury shift** ➤ Arsa of Atlantis rules Khemet and Egypt. Is later defeated by Setnakhte.
1,135 BCE		18th Dyn.	Taurus Man.	Iron I	➤ **Venus shift** (End of TS#5) ➤ Third Exodus and settling of Greece. ➤ Rise of he Neo-Hittites. ➤ Tuthmosis III attacks Carchemish.
1,117					
945		19th Dyn.		Iron IIa	➤ Shoshenk I (Shishak) and his Libyan line rule in Egypt. ➤ Ethiopian conquest of Egypt. ➤ Akhenaten rules at Amarna.
828					➤ **Mercury shift** ➤ Kings Moeris and Minos.
776 747 BCE				Iron IIb	➤ **Venus shift** (End of TS#6) ➤ Fourth Exodus (of Manasseh).

DATES AND PERIODS

EVENTS OF IMPORTANCE

Dates	Period	Dynasty	Mandate	Iron Age	
747 BCE	NAPATAN PERIOD	20th/21st Dyns.	Taurus Mandate	Iron Age IIIa	Iron IIc
687					
664 BCE	MACEDONIAN PERIOD	22nd Dyn.		Iron Age IIIa	
612			Pisces Mandate	Iron IIIb	
561 BCE	ETHIOPIAN AND PERSIAN CONQUESTS	23rd Dyn.			
525		24th Dyn.			
404 BCE					

> **Mars shift**
> - Ethiopians rule the Two Lands.
> - Midas rules in Phrygia.
> - Shalmanaser V renders Israel tributary to Assyria.
> - Hoshea asks King So (Shoshenk IV) to join with him in a coalition against the Assyrians.

> **Mars shift**
> - Homer composes the *Iliad*.
> - Kings Taharka, Hezekiah of Judah and Sennacherib are contemporaries.

> **Mercury shift**
> - Macedonian pharaohs rule Egypt.
> - The Turin Canon and Abydos king-lists are composed in Egypt.
> - Kingdom of Judah reigns alone in Palestine.
> - Nekau-Ramses II builds the Red Sea canal.
> - Nebuchadnezzar wars against Nekau II.
> - Chaldeans and Medes destroy Nineveh.

> **Venus shift (End of TS#7)**
> - Israelites forced to exile in Babylon by the Persians.
> - Ethiopian king Actisanes-Amenemhat takes over reigns of power in Egypt.
> - Confucius is born in China.
> - King Cyrus II returns Jews from exile.
> - Persians become masters of Egypt through conquest.
> - Battle of Marathon in Greece.
> - Socrates and Plato rise to prominence.
> - The prophet Ezra compiles the Five Books of Moses (Torah) in Israel.
> - The Persian king Artaxerxes permits the rebuilding of Jerusalem's walls.

DATES AND PERIODS | EVENTS OF IMPORTANCE

Dates	Period	Dynasty	Mandate
404 BCE	INDEPENDENT DYNASTIES	25th Dyn.	Pisces Mandate
4,413		26th Dyn.	
		27th Dyn.	
343 BCE	SECOND PERSIAN OCCUPATION	28th Dyn.	
332 BCE	LATE PERIOD	29th Dyn.	
		30th/31st Dyns.	
31 BCE			

- Native Egyptian rulers reclaim the pharaonic throne.

- Socrates is condemned to death.

- Plato founds Academy.

- Gauls sack Rome.

- Aristotle is born.

- Ptolemaic renaissance in Egypt. The temples of Edfu and Philae near the First Cataract are reconstructed.

- Persians regain control of Egypt.

- Latin Wars in Rome.

- Macedonians conquer Athens.

- Coins are first used in Rome.

- The Persian king Darius III faces a Macedonian invasion headed by Alexander the Great and is defeated by the latter in several major battles.

- The Macedonian army of Alexander the Great conquers Egypt.
- Macedonians set up a neo-Ptolemaic dynasty in Alexandria.
- Hellenization of Nubia.
- Native Upper Egyptians reassert their authority over Thebes and Tanis.
- The neo-Ptolemaic Macedonians' sphere of influence is limited to Alexandria.
- Diodorus of Sicily visits Egypt.
- High priests supplant power in Egypt.
- Battle of Actium.

Isis, Hathor & Osiris, by author

Part I

Heliopolitan Era
4,413 BCE to 3,166 BCE

Memphite Period
3,166 BCE to 3,114 BCE

New Horus Period
3,114 BCE to 2,730 BCE

1

The Formative Period (4,413 BCE to 3,114 BCE)

Did ancient pharaonic culture have fundamentally African origins? By starting the book with this question, I engage myself in a debate which is literally thousands of years old. According to some of the most well-known ancient Greek historians, like Diodorus of Sicily, the first ancient Egyptian pharaohs had been colonists from Ethiopia. In more recent times, one of the most ardent supporters of this theory has been the distinguished Senegalese historian and scientist Cheikh Anta Diop (1923-1986). Building on the ground breaking research of the eminent French Egyptologist Abbé Émile Amélineau (1850-1916), Diop argued that the very first pharaohs to occupy the Nile Valley belonged to a Black race known as the "Anu" — an African culture tracing its roots in remote antiquity.[1] According to Amélineau, this Black race of civilizers moved down the Nile from Ethiopia towards Egypt, founding the cities of Esneh, Erment, Qouch, and Heliopolis.[2] Diop, as I quite strongly concur, saw the obvious relationship between the name of the Anu and the original name of the sacred town of Heliopolis — home of the primordial pharaonic cosmogony of the sun-god Re. Evidently, ancient Heliopolis (suburb of modern Cairo) owes its very name to these ancient African civilizers. Indeed, the original name of Heliopolis was "Annu." The actual name of "Annu" was always written with three columns. Many scholars, following the argument of Samuel B. Mercer of the University of Toronto, believe that "Annu" meant "pillar-city" — since ancient Heliopolis was known for its scared primordial pillar.[3] But that is purely a matter of conjecture. If we can indeed identify the ancient Anu as the founders of Heliopolis, then we have a very credible name-source for the ancient city itself. Heliopolis was the primeval sacred city of pharaonic Egypt. According to ancient Khemetic cosmogony, it was the home and birthplace of the sun-god Re (Atum-Re). Heliopolis, the chosen religious capital of the Anu civilization, was, therefore, the place of beginnings.

---

[1] Cheikh Anta Diop (1962) 'Histoire primitive de l'Humanité: Évolution du monde noir', *Bulletin de l'IFAN* Vol. 24 (Série B) - Num. 3-4, p. 466.
[2] Émile Amélineau (1916) *Prolégomènes à l'étude de la religion égyptienne*, Éditions Leroux: Paris; Cheikh Anta Diop (1974) *The African Origin of Civilization: Myth or Reality?*, Lawrence Hill: Westport, Conn., p. 76.
[3] Samuel B. Mercer (1946) *The Religion of Ancient Egypt*, London, p. 127.

Egyptologists unanimously accept that the Heliopolitan cosmogony was the earliest state theology ever devised in ancient Egypt. It is likewise generally agreed that it served as a primary model for all subsequent cosmologies.[4] The Heliopolitan cult was moreover privileged in the sense that it was recognized everywhere in Egypt. The Anu, who devised the Heliopolitan Theology, were hence responsible for the birth of pharaonic religion in the Nile Valley. While the Anu's religious capital was based at Heliopolis, the administrative centre was located at Edfu, near the First Cataract. The earliest Khemites, the Anu, also paid homage to Khnum, Lord of the First Cataract (see Fig. 1b). There are a series of six cataracts from Aswan down to Khartoum. Cataracts are a grouping of rocks, across the River Nile, which obstruct the stream and make navigation difficult. Again, the First Cataract, which separates Egypt and Nubia, is located near Aswan; and was the primordial home of Horus the Behdetite or Horus the Elder.

Upper Egypt: The Black Land

The colonization of Upper Egypt in the middle of the fifth millennium BCE by the Anu of Ethiopia stands as a defining moment in human history. From their base in Upper Egypt, the Black Land, the Ethiopians exported the rudiments of their arts and sciences to the Nile Delta and early Syria-Palestine. Afrocentric scholarship is based on this fundamental development. A number of African scholars have defended this thesis using various methods ranging from physical anthropology to linguistics. According to Cheikh A. Diop, Khemet, "the Black Land," must be read as: "the Land of the Blacks."[5] Following the lead of Diop, most Afrocentric scholars maintain that *Km.t* "does not in any way refer to the colour of the Nilotic ground,"[6] but solely to the colour of the ancient inhabitants of the Black Land. Egypt, in Antiquity, was commonly referred to as the "Two Lands" — as in Upper and Lower Egypt. Because the ancient pharaohs' world-view pointed south, toward Africa, Upper Egypt was meant to symbolize southern Egypt, while Lower Egypt represented northern Egypt (see Fig. 1a). Upper Egypt was known as the "Black land" while Lower Egypt denoted the "Red Land." Scholars have traditionally maintained that the Black Land appellation designated the black colour of the fertile alluvial soil found in the Upper Nile Valley. While, in contrast, the Red Land was an indication of the desert-like nature of Lower Egypt's soil. Needless to say, the inevitable clash between Afrocentric scholars and traditional Egyptologists persists.

---

[4] Nicholas Grimal (1992) *A History of Ancient Egypt*. Trans. by Ian Shaw. Blackwell: Oxford, U.K., p. 41.

[5] Cheikh Anta Diop (1979 [1955]) *Nations nègres et culture (De l'Antiquité nègre égyptienne aux problèmes culturels de l'Afrique Noire d'aujourd'hui)*. Tome II. Troisième édition. Présence Africaine: Paris, p. 368.

[6] Oscar Pfouma (1993) *Histoire culturelle de l'Afrique Noire*, Éditions Publisud: Paris, p. 10.

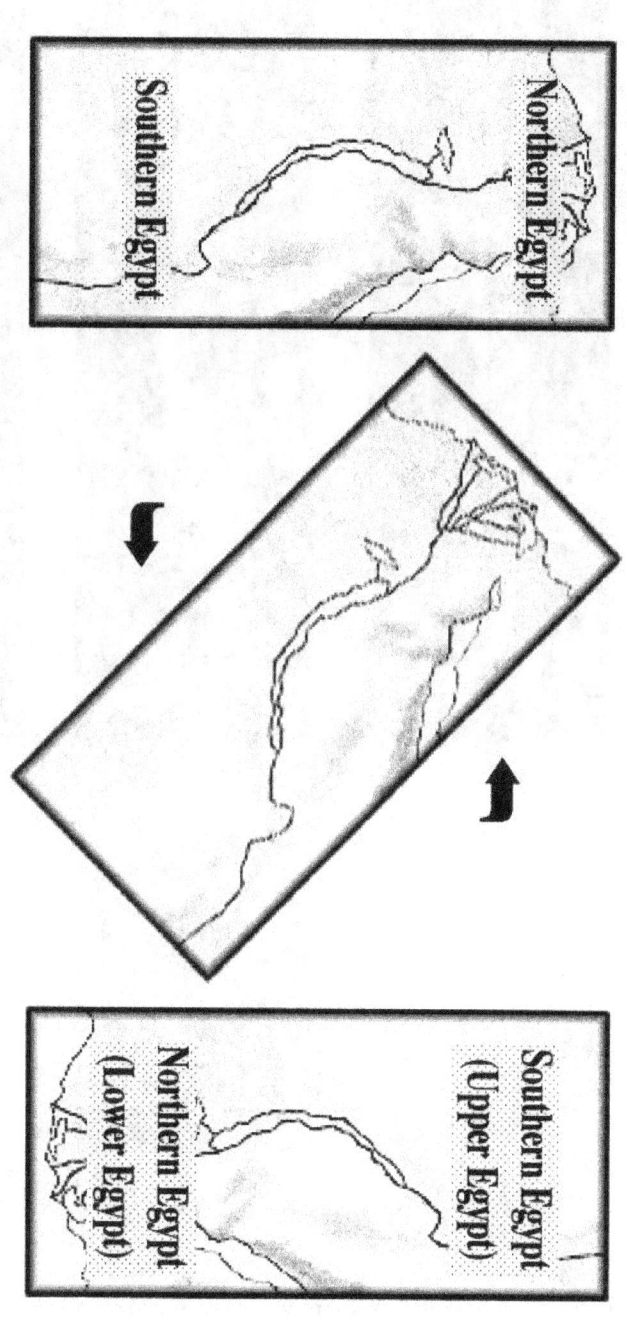

Fig. 1a

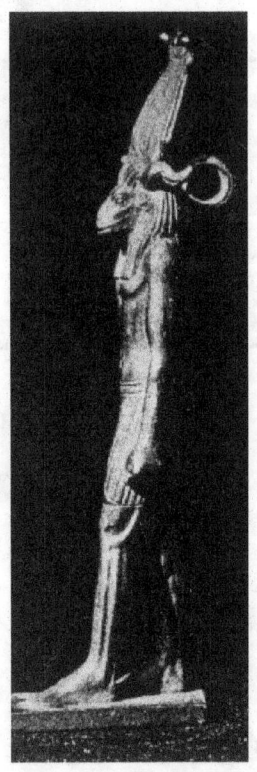

Fig. 1b: The Khemetic god Khnum of the First Cataract.

But an answer to the impasse may be found in the following legend of the Nilotic Shilluk people:

> ... we find the legend of the creation of mankind out of clay among the Shilluks of the White Nile, who ingeniously explain the different complexions of the various races by the different coloured clay out of which they were fashioned. They say that the creator Juok moulded all men of earth, and that while he was engaged in the work of creation he wandered about the world. In the land of the whites he found a pure white earth or sand, and out of it he shaped white men. Then he came to the land of Egypt and out of the mud of the Nile he made red or brown men. Lastly, he came to the land of the Shilluks, and finding there black earth he created black men out of it.[7]

Therefore, if we look at the traditions of the Shilluks, who have dwelt along the Nile for millennia, the association of the "Black Land" with the skin colour of the inhabitants of Upper Egypt is, in basic principle, based on fact. However, we must likewise deduce that the colour of the land played the primary role in establishing the names of Black Land and Red Land. Since the Shilluks convey that the Creator used various colours of clay, taken form the land, to create the different races, we can see that the black colour of the land in Upper Egypt had always been highlighted. The case is furthermore bolstered by the following statement by Herodotus:

> ... it (Khemet) is a land of black and crumbling earth, as if it were alluvial deposit carried down the river from Aethiopia; but we know that the soil of Libya is redder and somewhat sandy, and Arabia and Syria are lands rather of clay and stone.
> (Herodotus, Book II: 12)

As the Shilluks postulate, it so happens that the inhabitants of the Black Land (Ethiopia and Upper Egypt) had also been Black, racially speaking, since the colour of their skin matched with the colour of the land. This legend could not have been devised if this association was not based on factual observation. As the passage from Herodotus' *History* implies, the land of Lower Egypt, which includes the Libyan desert, is reddish and sandy. These attributes are likewise reflected in the racial characteristics of the peoples who live in this particular area.

---

[7] J. G. Frazer (1919) *Folklore in the Old Testament*, London, pp. 22-23. Translating and abridging W. Hofmayr (1906) 'Die Religion der Schilluk,' *Anthropos* VI, pp. 128 ff.

Once they took effective control of fertile alluvial lands of Upper Egypt, the Ethiopians turned to the task of civilizing the lands north of them. Turning to Dr Cheikh Anta Diop:

> According to Amélineau, this Black race, the Anu, probably created in prehistoric times all the elements of Egyptian civilization which persist without significant change throughout its long existence. These Blacks were probably the first to practice agriculture, to irrigate the valley of the Nile, build dams, invent sciences, arts, writing, the calendar. They created the cosmogony contained in *The Book of the Dead* ...[8]

Long before the advent of the Egyptian 1st Dynasty, the Ethiopians had set up the foundations of pharaonic culture and science. As the ancient histories affirm, the proto-dynastic Egyptians had learnt their sciences and religious observances form the Ethiopians, and not vice versa. Therefore, we will now begin to uncover that the evolutionary, or linear process perspective, adopted by a number of Egyptologists — dictating that predynastic Egypt was a cultural backwater until the arrival of the 1st Dynasty, is nothing more than a myth.

The First Calendar

It is a generally well accepted fact that the ancient Egyptians first began recording the successive heliacal risings of the star Sirius in the fifth millennium BCE.[9] Naturally, the first calendar was also introduced in the fifth millennium BCE.[10] The ancient Greeks called Sirius "The Dog Star" or "The Dog of Orion" because this bright star lies at the heel of the constellation of Orion — his master (the great hunter).[11] The Khemites, for their part, saw Sirius as a companion to Orion.[12] As "a hunstman striding across the sky,"[13] Orion was seen by the

---

[8] Cheikh Anta Diop (1974) p. 77.
[9] M. F. Ingham (1969) 'The Length of the Sothic Cycle', *Journal of Egyptian Archaeology* 55, pp. 36, 39.
[10] James H. Breasted (1962[1906]) *Ancient Records of Egypt: Historical Documents from the Earliest Time.* Vol. I. Russell & Russell: New York, p. 40; Cheikh Anta Diop (1991) *Civilization or Barbarism (An Authentic Anthropology).* Trans. by Yaa-Lengi M. Ngemi. Lawrence Hill Books: Brooklyn, NY, p. 279.
[11] Joseph Fontenrose (1981) *Orion: The Myth of the Hunter and Huntress,* University of California Press: Berkeley, Cal.
[12] G. A. Wainwright (1936) 'Orion and the Great Star', *Journal of Egyptian Archaeology* 22, p. 45.
[13] Ibid.

ancients as taking the appearance of a standing man because of the particular pattern of this constellation. The right shoulder of the standing man, or hunter, was the bright red star Betelgeuse — located at the upper left corner of Orion. His waist was made up of the three stars of the Belt of Orion (Zeta, Epsilon, and Delta Orionis). The star Rigel, at the lower right of the hourglass symbolises his knee. Finally, a crucial component, his sword was represented by the three stars hanging from his waist (the Belt of Orion). To the ancient Khemites, that constellation with the appearance of a standing man was the god Osiris. Hence his common name of Osiris-Orion.

The first calendar was a lunar one. Based on a "Civil Year," it was kept in place by the star Sirius. Thus, originated the common calendar of 365 days — made up of three seasons of four 30-day months, plus 5 days added at the end. The important religious significance of these five additional days will be explored shortly. Once the 30-day month was divided into three 10-day weeks, the fixed 24-hour day was arrived at through the observation of stars known as decans rising at nightfall. Since the calender had only 365 days to the year, it was naturally short one day every four years. The heliacal rising (*prt Spdt*) of Sirius, or "the Coming-Forth of Sopdet," or any other star, would occur one day later every four years. While Sirius would reappear heliacally each July, the "Great Year" began with the year when the heliacal rising of Sirius appeared on the first of Thoth. After four years, it would rise on the second of Thoth. Going along the cycle, after 1,461 years of 365 days, or 1,460 years of 3651/4 days, Sirius ultimately again rose on the first of Thoth. That complete cycle was known as the Sothic period. In essence, the first of Thoth, or the New Year, engenders an incremental movement through the four seasons of the Sothic period. Despite heliacally rising each July, Sirius rises on the first of Thoth only once (for four consecutive years) in 1,460 years.

These consecutive periods of 1,460 years have served as the backbone of ancient Egyptian chronology. Knowing on which pharaohs' reigns two different heliacal rising of Sirius occurred, Egyptologists can determine the actual time span that separated these two rulers. For instance, on the basis of an ancient document known as the Papyrus Ebers, Egyptologists have determined that a heliacal rising of Sirius took place during the lower half of the sixteenth century BCE — in the ninth year of Pharaoh Amenhotep I's reign. From this anchor point, scholars can then approximate the dates for both the previous and succeeding heliacal risings.

As I will delineate subsequently, I start from the premise that the star which was observed by the Magi on the year of Christ's birth, according to the New Testament, was the star Sirius, or Star of David, during its cyclical heliacal rising. For reasons that will be made clear in Chapter 20, I have concluded that Jesus-Christ was born in 33 BCE. Since the cycle of the "Great Year" is of 1,460 days, the previous heliacal rising of Sirius must have taken place early in the fifteenth century BCE. Therefore, I am convinced that Year 9 of Amenhotep I, the year of the heliacal rising of Sirius, fell in 1,493 BCE. That date is somewhat lower than the one accepted by historians, but it fits perfectly well with the new chronology. As a result, starting with the new Sothic year of 33 BCE, we may move backwards all the way through to the fifth millennium BCE as follows: (33 + 1460 = 1493), (1493 + 1460 = 2953) and (2953 + 1460 = 4413). Consequently, we end up with four important dates: 33 BCE, 1,493 BCE, 2,953 BCE and 4,413 BCE. These four dates mark the years in which a heliacal rising of Sirius was observed in the ancient skies. Although unequivocal precision is impossible to achieve, since a certain margin of error must be accounted for, I am confident that these are highly plausible dates.

The heliacal rising of 2,953 BCE is a particularly important one — as I would argue that it heralded the reunification of Egypt under the pharaohs of the 1st Dynasty. I here stress the word *"re*unification" because I believe that Upper and Lower Egypt had already been unified long before the coming of the dynastic period. The 1st Dynasty references to a heliacal rising of the star Sirius on the first of Thoth ought therefore not to be seen as the very first observance of a heliacal rising of Sirius. If the Sothic cycle was known to the 1st Dynasty Egyptians, then it would logically signify that the proto-dynastic Egyptians must have had access to carefully recorded knowledge about the exact length of the Great Year. As Cheikh Anta Diop rightly observes, this kind of knowledge could only have been acquired through time:

> One gets lost in conjectures in order to figure out *how* the Egyptians were able to arrive at such a result from protohistory, because it is known with certainty that the sidereal calendar was in use from 4236 B.C. onward. Supposing that a celestial phenomenon as fleeting as the heliacal rising of Sirius had accidentally caught the attention of the Egyptians from the fourth millennium onward, how could they have guessed at and verified, within a few minutes, its rigorous periodicity, in a time span of 1,460 years, and thus invented a calendar on this basis? Did they arrive at this result through empirical or theoretical means? Assuredly, the disparagers of Egyptian civilization have their work cut out for them![14]

Incidentally, Cheikh Anta Diop's figure of 4,236 BCE amounts to my own date of 4,413 BCE as the earliest occurrence of an observation of the heliacal rising of Sirius. A genuinely thorough attempt at establishing the length of the Great Year from that remote time on must have been undertaken. It's really the only way to explain how the proto-dynastic Egyptians could have known about it.

---

[14] Cheikh Anta Diop (1991) *Civilization or Barbarism*, pp. 279-280.

The Heliopolitan Theology

The proto-dynastic Egyptians ultimately owned their wealth of knowledge to the ancient Anu. When these ancient African civilizers came from inland Africa in the fifth millennium BCE, they brought along with them the building blocks of pharaonic culture. From their name was formed the ancient district of Annu (Heliopolis). According to the pioneering Egyptologist Wallis Budge, the Book of Coming Forth by Day (more commonly known by its misnomer the Book of the Dead) was originally drafted by the priests of Heliopolis — although the original is now long lost. It is therefore very appropriate to consider Heliopolis as the oldest sacred district in Egypt. I believe that ancient Heliopolis (Annu) became the religious centre of pharaonic culture under the Anu from the mid-fifth millennium BCE. In that ancient religious capital was, naturally, developed the "Heliopolitan Theology." The sun-god Re was the preeminent deity of this original Khemetic cosmogony. Re himself had emerged from Nun, the primeval water (often equated with chaos). Nun had no creator but had within itself the ability to create life. A giver of life, Nun paradoxically also had an uncontrolled element of chaos which perpetually threatened to disturb the cosmic order. Hence, while Nun gave life to the universe, it nonetheless remained outside the boundaries of the structured universe — standing ready to attack should the universal order (or Ma'at) be transgressed.

It was from this primordial watery chaos that Re (also spelled Ra), the sun-god, emerged as ruler of the regulated universe. Re first emanated out of Nun in the form of a protruding primeval mound or standing stone, the *benben*, which became the focus of the Heliopolitan cult. The sun-god Re likewise manifested himself in the form of Atum (the ultimate perfect being) or alternately as Khepri (taking the form of a scarab and meaning "transformation"). The Heliopolitan Theology went as follows:

> Ra the Sun, The Almighty God, appeared and said:
> "I am Who I Am! I am Khepri the lifegiver!
> When I — Ra the Sun — appeared, life appeared, every living creature appeared after I appeared.
> There was no Heaven and no Earth, there was no dry land and no reptiles in Egypt.
> Then, I spoke and living creatures appeared.
> I put all of them to sleep in Nun, the primeval sea, until I could find a place to stand.
> When I began thinking about Egypt, began planning everything, began designing every creature by myself, I had not exhaled Shu the Wind,

> I had not spat Tefnut the Rain, not a single living creature had appeared.
> Then I decided:
> Let there be a multitude of living creatures, let there be children and grandchildren.
> And so I copulated with my own fist, I masturbated with my own hand.
> I ejaculated into my own mouth.
> I exhaled Shu the Wind, I spat out Tefnut the Rain.
> Old Man Nun, the primeval sea, reared them,
> Eye the Overseer looked after them during the ages when I was away.
> At first, I — Ra the Sun — was alone, then, there were three more.
> I — Ra the Sun — appeared in Egypt, but Shu the Wind and Tefnut the Rain — played in Nun the primeval sea, and Eye the Overseer looked after them there.
> After I had copulated with my own fist, I wept for joy.
> Human beings appeared, from the tears I shed.
> Eye the Overseer was angry with me, for replacing it with another.
> I had replaced Eye the Overseer, I had made Eye the Glorious.
> I gave Eye the Overseer a place of honour, I made Eye the Overseer of all Egypt.
> Tears of anger became tears of joy, what was lost had been recovered.
> I took the tears of Eye the Overseer, and created all the Reptiles, and all their companions.
> Shu the Wind and Tefnut the Rain gave birth to Geb the Earth and Nut the Sky.
> Geb the Earth and Nut the Sky gave birth to the brothers: Osiris and Seth, and their wives: Isis and Nephthys, and Horus, son of Osiris and Isis.
> One born right after another from the body of Geb the Earth, and they gave birth to all the people of Egypt.[15]

The Heliopolitan Theology is the world's very first Creation account. It later served as an inspirations for several other Creation cosmogonies — including the biblical version in the Book of Genesis. As Table 1-2 illustrates, Re-Atum engendered Shu, the god of air and space (or wind), and Tefnut, the goddess of moisture (or rain). He created the universe alone by causing himself to ejaculate of his being all the elements of nature. Therefore, Shu and Tefnut were born without a mother. When Shu and Tefnut became husband and wife, they in turn engendered Geb (the Earth) and Nut (the sky-goddess). To complete the Heliopolitan Ennead (pantheon

---

[15] Papyrus Bremner-Rhind, XXVI - XXVII.

of nine deities), Geb and Nut finally had four children: Osiris, Isis, Seth, and Nephthys. Osiris and Isis would later unite to give birth to Horus, while Seth and Nephthys' union would remain infertile. The fact that the Heliopolitan cosmogony ends just before the respective unions of the children of Isis and Osiris, hence not including Horus in the Ennead, has vital archaeotheological significance. It tells us that the Heliopolitan cosmogony was composed before the prodigious duel between Horus and his uncle Seth. As the term "archaeotheology" implies, I assert that it is possible to use major ancient theological constructs to gain some much-valued insight about the archaeological context in which they were communicated. So-called mythical genealogies from antiquity very often obscure genuine historical records that have gone unrecognized by contemporary scholars. The ancient Khemetic story about the death of Osiris and the ensuing confrontation between Horus and Seth is just such a case as will be made clear shortly.

The Primordial Cosmology

Plutarch (*De Iside et Osiride,* Chap. 12) informs us that the five epagomenal days added at the end of the Egyptian 360-day calendar represented the days when five principal Egyptian gods were born. The first day marks the birth of Osiris, the second day Horus the Elder, the third day Seth (or Typhon), the fourth Isis, and the fifth and final day, Nephthys. These "five days out of time" were placed between the 30th of the last month and the first day of the new year in order to bring the total to 365 days. Since the New Year, indicated by the rising of Sirius (First of Thoth) fell on August 29th, the five epagomenal days were from August 24th to 28th.[16] Among the five, epagomenal days, the third, the day of Seth's birth, had been omitted from the Edfu Horus Temple calendar.[17] To the people of ancient Khemet the planet Mercury, as the dreaded precursor of Typhon Seasons, exemplified the element of chaos and cosmic disorder — hence this particular planet's identification with Seth, the arch-demon of chaos. Ma'at, the divine order of nature, would be periodically disturbed toward the end of a World Age when Mercury, shifting from it's set orbital path, came along to disrupt the order of nature. The temples' main function being to pay tribute to the gods in order for the world *not* to be summarily reabsorbed into chaos, the inclusion of the day of Typhon-Seth's birth would have be counterproductive. Naturally, in the historical time we are currently dealing with, the second half of the fifth millennium BCE, the planets had not yet gone off their course within recent human memory. Seth-Mercury only first disturbed the natural order in 3,166 BCE. But the earliest

---

[16] The date of August 29th was set in 22 BCE, when the Julian calendar was introduced into Egypt.
[17] Anthony Spalinger (1995) 'Some Remarks on the Epagomenal Days in Ancient Egypt', *Journal of Near Eastern Studies* Vol. 54 - Num. 1, p. 39.

calendar's five epagomenal days nonetheless set the stage for the later crucial correlation between five principal Egyptian deities and the five visible planets of the solar system. In the Ramesseum astronomical ceiling, the five planets are given the following roles:

The Five Planets and their Roles:

Jupiter: "Horus-who-bounds-the-Two-Lands" or
        "Horus-who-illuminates-the-Two Lands"
Saturn: "Horus-bull-of-the-sky" or "Horus-the-bull"
Mars: "Horus-of-the-horizon" or "Horus-the-red"
Mercury: "Seth"
Venus: "the crosser" or "the-star-which-crosses"

Table 1-1 (*from* R. A. Parker, 1974)

As the above table illustrates, the planets are listed in the order of the most distant down to the closest one to the sun. Therefore, it is particularly significant that the planets Jupiter, Saturn and Mars are all depicted as manifestations of Horus. Then, for reasons which elude ancient historians, the planets Mercury and Venus are labelled differently. Mercury is, again, identified with Seth — Lord of chaos. On many monuments, the first three planets were deliberately separated from the last two. Why would such a distinction have been necessary? As I have already argued in the introduction, the planets Mercury and Venus worked in tandem to bring the ancient World Ages to their catastrophic end. The attack of Mercury, the incarnation of Seth, totally destabilized the order of nature by bringing plagues which incited foreigners to invade Egypt, and precipitated domestic civil strife. Then, fifty-two years later, Venus would violently drift from its stable orbital path — passing dangerously close to the earth. This recurring catastrophic incident would result in the swift oscillation of the earth's polar axis. This is why the planet Venus is named "the-star-which-crosses" in the Ramesside astronomical ceilings. The first three planets, Jupiter, Saturn and Mars, which were all incarnations of Horus, also had important meaning. As the "Unifier of the Two Lands," Osiris could naturally be identified with the planet Jupiter[18] — the planet associated with the "Horus-who-bonds-the-Two-Lands." Here, we can see a clear relationship with the first of the five epagomenal days. As Jupiter is listed first in the order of the five planets, Osiris is also born on the first of the five epagomenal days. We can therefore observe that there was definitely a clarity of thinking and unity of purpose in these ancient cosmologies.

---

[18] The Greek god Zeus, traditionally identified with the planet Jupiter, is the equivalent of the Egyptian Osiris.

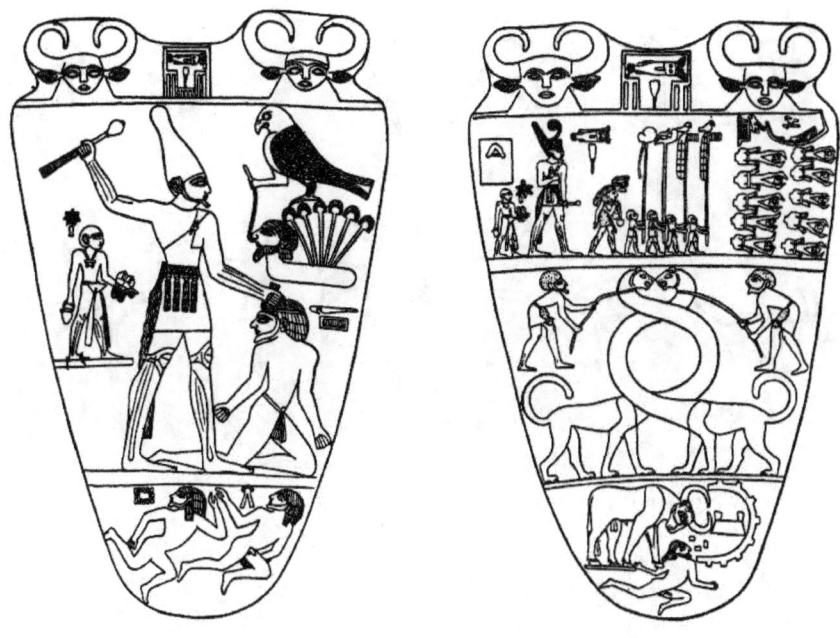

Fig. 1c: The famous Narmer Palette.

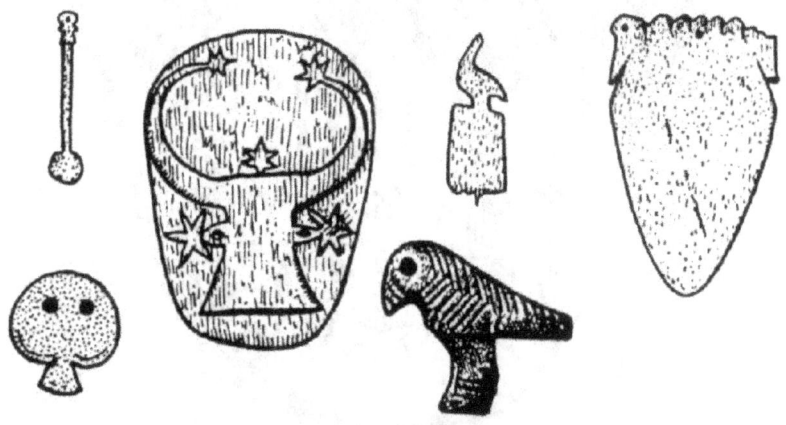

Fig. 1d: Predynastic combs and amulets representing the bovine deity Hathor and the Horus falcon.

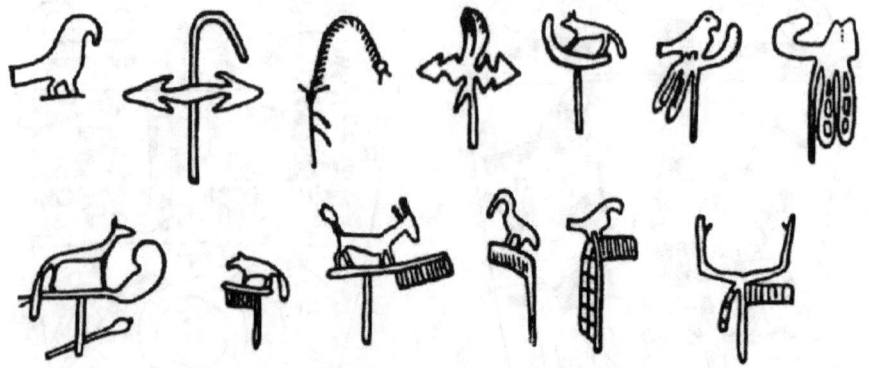

Fig. 1e: Predynastic totems representing various clans.

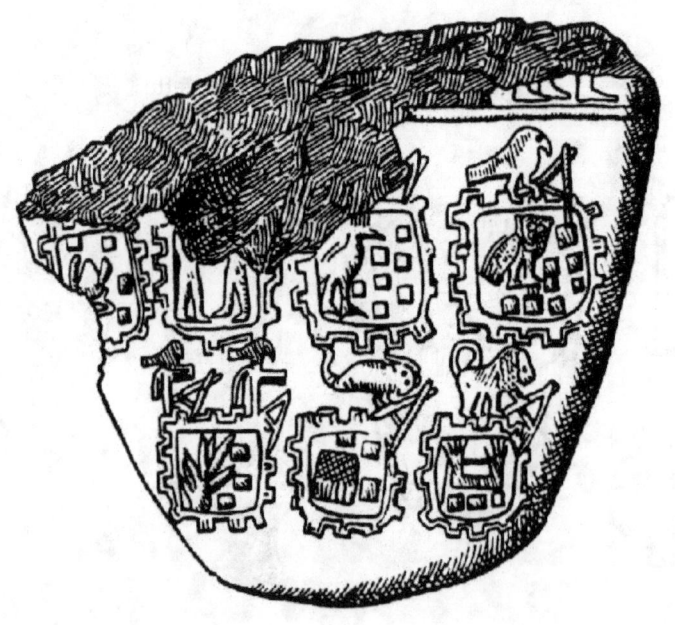

Fig. 1f: Outline of the different clans with their corresponding deities.

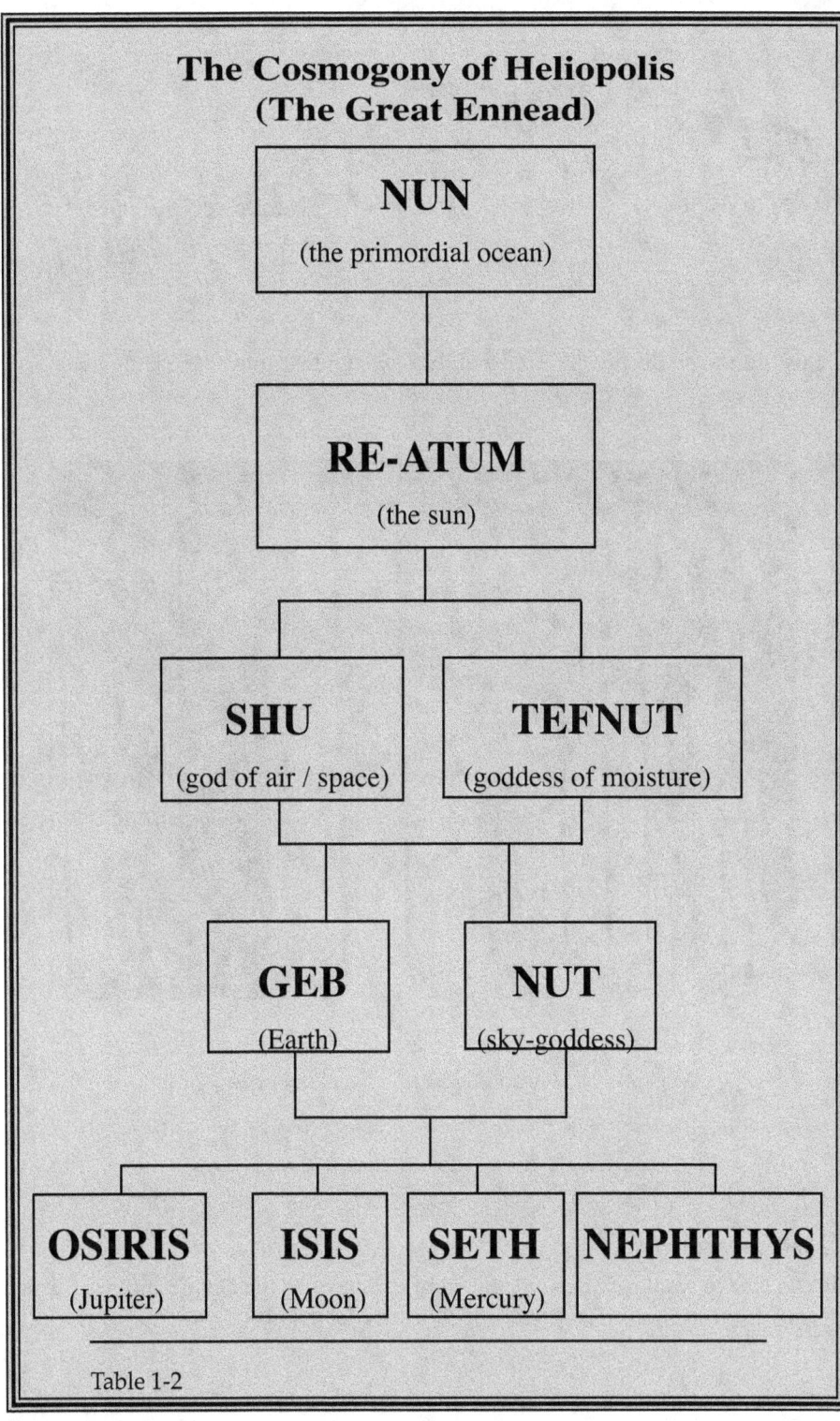
Table 1-2

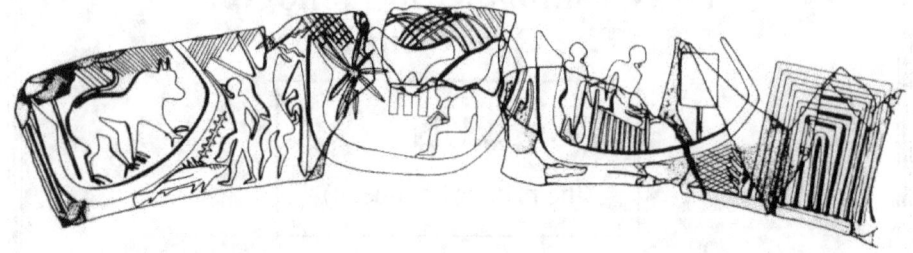

Qustul Incense Burner (Courtesy of the Oriental Institute of the University of Chicago).

Mastaba of Pharaoh Djoser-Netjerykhet at Saqqara.

Fig. 1g: Notice similarity between far right structure on the Qustul Incense Burner and the mastaba of Djoser-Netjerykhet.

A Red Crown in Upper Egypt

During Badarian (4,500 - 4,000 BCE) and Naqada I (4,000 - 3,600 BCE) times, Egypt (the Red Land) was populated by small settlements scattered about from Asyut in the north, down to Edfu to the south. The most prominent of those towns was Naqada, situated just north of Thebes. Egyptologists believe that it is at this site that the very first occurrence of the Egyptian red crown, representing Lower Egypt, is to be found.[19] Dating from around the end of Naqada I to early Naqada II, the relief in question was found by the eminent British excavator W. M. Flinders Petrie (1853-1942) carved on a sherd of black-topped ware. This piece of artifact, now kept in the Ashmolean Museum in England, is supposedly one of the earliest pharaonic emblems to be found in Egypt. There is no question that the crown-drawing on the potsherd dates to Naqada I times, and was not later applied, since it was clear to archaeologists that the crown had "been moulded in the clay of the vessel when it was wet and before it was burnished, for the burnishing marks run round it and into the various corners."[20] Adding to the existence of a calendar in the Naqada I period, the presence of this red crown provides irrefutable evidence of a pharaonic presence centuries before the emergence of dynastic Egypt. How is one to explain the presence of a red crown in such remote times? Moreover, what was it doing in Upper Egypt if the red crown was later known as a symbol of Lower Egypt? Pondering on those very questions, Egyptologist G. A. Wainwright, in the early 1920s, wrote:

> The first thought, of course, is one of surprise at the existence of this emblem of dynastic Egypt at so early a date—so very far removed from the beginning of the dynasties. Another is what was this northern symbol doing near Thebes some four hundred miles south of Cairo, when it is proper to the Delta, and more accurately to Sais, some eighty-five miles or so north-west of Cairo.[21]

To be sure, all this tells us that the early inhabitants of the Red Land, who carved this early representation of the red crown, did not necessarily know about its true significance. Moreover, I'm convinced that they were merely *imitating* a royal insignia which they'd observed the rulers of the Black Land employ. Indeed, I would maintain that by the end of Naqada I, the Anu began to colonize the native inhabitants of Upper Egypt in particular. The interactions

---

[19] Elise J. Baumgartel (1975) 'Some Remarks on the Origins of the Titles of the Archaic Egyptian Kings', *Journal of Egyptian Archaeology* 61, p. 28.
[20] G. A. Wainwright (1923) 'The Red Crown in Early Prehistoric Times', *Journal of Egyptian Archaeology* 9, p. 26.
[21] G. A. Wainwright (1923) p. 26.

between the Anu from the Sudan and the ancient Upper Egyptians were not hostile in nature but instead became an opportunity for the Upper Egyptians to, for the first time, familiarize themselves with pharaonic culture. Quite understandably, the Upper Egyptians' first attempts at reproducing the pharaonic regalia were very crude. This explains the very rudimentary delineation of the red crown found on the Ashmolean Museum potsherd. The tradition held among ancient Greek historians that the archaic Egyptians had learnt their arts and sciences from the Ethiopians traces its roots back to those early relations between the Anu and the Upper Egyptians. As Nubiologist and anthropologist Bruce G. Trigger adequately points out: *"... evidence that both the Red and the White Crowns were originally southern Egyptian symbols suggests that most of the iconography originated in Upper Egypt."*[22] However, where I believe Prof. Trigger is mistaken is in his belief that the red and white crowns "originated" in Naqada and Hierakonpolis (respectively). The main reason why the archaic kings of Egypt, bearing both the red and white pharaonic crowns, came from Upper Egypt is because they lived in relatively close proximity to the ancient Khemetic kings of the First Cataract. They were therefore a lot more likely to be directly influenced and inspired by Khemetic culture rather than by the predynastic Egyptians living up in the Delta.

The Gerzean Period (3,600-3,200 BCE)

The early native Egyptian pharaonic twin districts of Hierakonpolis and Naqada really evolved into small states ruled by kings during the Naqada II (or Gerzean) period.[23] Religious activity became increasingly organized, and burgeoning trade relations with southwestern Asia flourished. Consequently, the Gerzean period signalled a stage of maturation when the pupil Horus kingship of the native Upper Egyptians became sophisticated enough to be nominally independent from the Khemetic Horus kingship (that of Horus the Elder). Hence, the seat of the Egyptian Horus was at Hierakonpolis. As a manifestation of Horus the Behdetite from Edfu, the Hierakonpolite Horus became known as "Horus of Nekhen." The belief of most Egyptologists that Horus the Behdetite (or of Behdet), whom they argue originated from the western Delta (where the district of Behdet is located), was a northern god who "civilized" the archaic Upper Egyptians is, from the perspective of this revised history, entirely inaccurate. The home of Horus the Behdetite was in Upper Egypt, specifically in Edfu. Ironically, Egyptologists do recognize the Upper Egyptian attributes of Horus the Behdetite but, again, maintained that he hailed from the Delta marshes. The fact remains however that

---

[22] Bruce Trigger (1987) 'Egypt: A Fledging Nation', *Journal of the Society for the Study of Egyptian Antiquities* Vol. 17 - Num. 1-2, p. 63.
[23] Bruce Trigger (1976) *Nubia Under the Pharaohs*, Westview Press: Boulder, Col., p. 32.

CHAP. I: THE FORMATIVE PERIOD | 101

the Upper Egyptian town of Edfu was called "Behdet" by the ancient Egyptians. So one could just as easily assume that Horus the Elder came from the south and later travelled north. Indeed, as the son and heir of Re, Horus of Behdet could well have chosen, as Re in Heliopolis, a northern Egyptian town where his divine rulership could be manifested. The marshy northern land of the Delta was indeed often depicted in pharaonic mythology as a common dwelling place of the gods.

Thus, the Khemetic attributes of Horus of Nekhen at Hierakonpolis are particularly evident by the fact that the Horus-falcon of Nekhen is portrayed wearing a double-plume crown. This double-plume crown (see Fig. 2b) was the characteristic headdress of Horus the Elder. The later dynastic Egyptian pharaohs would very rarely be portrayed with this particular crown. In the Red Land, only the gods, such as Re, Amun-Re, and Sobek, would regularly be represented wearing a double crown in dynastic iconography. And as I will demonstrate further, all of the dynastic Egyptian pharaohs who later adopted that particular crown were culturally related to the Ethiopian Khemetic legacy. Since Horus of Behdet was the son and heir of Re, and Horus of Nekhen at Hierakonpolis a manifestation of Horus of Behdet, all of them had in common the purely Khemetic double-plume crown.

To sum up, throughout the Gerzean period (i.e. Naqada II), the followers of Horus of Nekhen at Hierakonpolis and the disciples of Seth in Naqada cohabited in Upper Egypt relatively peacefully. The centre of culture however appears to have remained at Naqada. The twin districts equally benefited from the tutelage of the Khemites at Edfu.

Pharaoh Narmer and the Expansion of Khemetic Culture

By the end of Naqada II, the town of Hierakonpolis had replaced Naqada as the most vital town of the Red Land.[24] The Hierakonpolitan deity Horus of Nekhen became the dominant figure. The rapid ascent in prominence of Hierakonpolis at that particular time was largely due to the advent of the illustrious King Narmer — a Khemetic ruler from the Sudan. Pharaoh Narmer adopted the title of Horus of Nekhen and single-handedly engineered Hierakonpolis' rise to prominence over the Sethian district of Naqada. This was the very first unification conquest geared towards joining both the domains of Horus and Seth ever undertaken in Egypt. The excavations of archaeologist S. Yeivin at Gath during the 1950s,[25] have demonstrated, on the basis of an Egyptian jar bearing the name of King Narmer, that this pharaoh reigned during the Early Bronze I period (3,200-2,950 BCE). This evidence pointing to an EBI archaeological context for the reign of

---

[24] Elise J. Baumgartel (1975) p. 29.
[25] S. Yeivin (1960) *A Decade of Archaeology in Israel, 1948-1958*, Publications de l'institut historique et archéologique néerlandais de Stamboul, VII.

King Narmer has led some scholars to date the beginning of dynastic Egypt to somewhere around 3,100-3,200 BCE — as Narmer, on his famous Narmer Palette (see Fig. 1c) discovered at Hierakonpolis, obviously narrates his victorious unification of the Two Lands. But since many EBII remains have been uncovered in early dynastic tombs, the trend has been to adopt the lowest possible date, i.e. c.3,100 BCE, for the beginning of EBI. In the words of the late influential American archaeologist William F. Albright (1891-1971):

> It had long been known that Palestinian (or coastal Syrian) pottery of early E.B. II type is often found in the royal tombs of the middle and late First Dynasty, and consequently it may be inferred that the critical shift from E.B. I to E.B. II took place during the first third of the dynasty.[26]

Accepting a date of c.3,100 BCE for the beginning of the EB I phase, Albright would have Narmer reign sometime between 3,000 and 2,800 BCE.[27] With dynastic Egypt officially beginning sometime around 2,950 BCE, a date commonly attributable to the EBII era, an EBI context for artifacts bearing the seal of King Narmer poses a rather thorny problem. On the one hand, one has to contend with undeniable proof of EBII pottery remains within 1st Dynasty royal tombs and, on the other hand, an equally compelling body of evidence anchors the reign of Narmer to the EBI period. Albright's attempt to conciliate such obvious contradictions by positioning the pivotal transition point between EBI and EBII somewhere during the first third of the 1st Dynasty requires too much of a drastic lowering of the EBI phase according to the presently argued chronological framework. In actuality, there is no real need to artificially extend the EBI phase into the thirty-first century BCE since, as I now contend, Pharaoh Narmer reigned between c.3,200 BCE and 3,166 BCE. No less than two hundred and fifty years separated the start of Egypt's 1st Dynasty from the beginning of Pharaoh Narmer's reign in Hierakonpolis. Furthermore, Narmer, contrary to popular opinion, was not a dynastic Egyptian king. He was an EBI Khemetic ruler hailing from the ancient First Cataract town of Edfu, who greatly helped civilize predynastic Egypt.

In fact, in the considered opinion of some Egyptologists,[28] Egypt was already politically united from as early as 150 years before the 1st Dynasty. Egyptologist Bruce

---

[26] William F. Albright 'Some Remarks on the Archaeological Chronology of Palestine before about 1500 B.C.' In Robert W. Ehrich (editor) (1965) *Chronologies in Old World Archaeology*, p. 50.
[27] W. F. Albright (1920) 'Menes and Narâm-Sin', *Journal of Egyptian Archaeology* 6, pp. 89-98.
[28] See Werner Kaiser (1964) 'Einige Bemerkungen zur ägyptischen Frühzeit', *ZÄS 91*, pp. 86-125.

CHAP. I: THE FORMATIVE PERIOD | 103

Williams has even gone so far as saying that certain objects found in Naqada I and Naqada II contexts are "completely pharaonic."[29] There is in fact no question that a vibrant pharaonic culture existed, in Upper Egypt particularly, from the earliest days in Naqada I — long before the emergence of Egypt's dynastic state. The single crucial mistake that Egyptologists and ancient historians have made is to equate Narmer with Menes — the founder of the 1st Dynasty of pharaonic Egypt. Since nineteenth-century scholars could not conceive of a unified pharaonic state prior to the establishment of dynastic Egypt during EBII, they searched far and wide for justifications to support this erroneous equation. In reality, there is not a shred of solid evidence to back up this important pillar of modern Egyptology. Nowhere in the Hierakonpolite documents associated with the reign of King Narmer is there a mention of a "Pharaoh Menes." The correlation is purely a matter of convention.

Thus, since Narmer came to Hierakonpolis as an outsider from the Sudan, it is improbable that he had been an heir descendant from the local Hierakonpolite monarchy. The notion of an outside input seems evident namely from the drastic upsurge in sophistication within the overall cultural landscape at Hierakonpolis following the end of the Gerzean period. It is only from the time of Pharaoh Narmer that we can truly speak of a united Upper and Lower Egypt. As we've seen, the twin districts of Horus and Seth during the Gerzean period were both located in Upper Egypt. But Narmer, after unifying Upper Egypt under the Hierakonpolite Falcon-god Horus, officially divided Egypt between its southern and northern kingdoms (the Two Lands). Pharaoh Narmer established the northern capital at Pe (or Buto as it was later called), in the western Delta — the dwelling place of the cobra-goddess Udot. The southern capital remained at Hierakonpolis and now became the domain of the vulture-goddess Nekhebet. Narmer also divided the Two Lands into the following districts:

District of the:	Corresponds to the city of:
1. Falcon	Hierakonpolis
2. Two Falcons	Koptos
3. Wolf	Lykopolis
4. Ibis	Hermopolis
5. Dog	Kynopolis

Naturally, the capital of Hierakonpolis, as the seat of power of the falcon-god Horus of Nekhen, became known as the district of the falcon. From Hierakonpolis, King Narmer ruled over both the southern and northern territories. The chief

---

[29] Bruce Williams 'The Qustul Incense Burner and the Case for a Nubian Origin of Ancient Egyptian Kingship.' In Theodore Celenko (editor) (1996) *Egypt in Africa*, pp. 95-97.

symbol of his dual dominion from the Hierakonpolite palette is the portrayal of Pharaoh Narmer wearing both the royal crowns of Upper and Lower Egypt (see Fig. 2h), defeating his northern enemies. This indubitably implies that Narmer held unquestioned suzerainty over both territories, and that he had gained power over the north by means of conquest.

King Narmer as Osiris

In the view of the vast majority of ancient scholars and Egyptologists, the extent of Pharaoh Narmer's unification conquest limited itself geographically to the Nile Valley. The northern battle scenes illustrated on the Narmer Palette are mainly thought to have involved various Asiatic groups who peopled the Egyptian Delta at the dawn of the Early Bronze Age. On the verso of the Narmer Palette is, for instance, written: "Narmer demolishes the fortress(es) and loots the storehouses (granaries) of the 'long-haired.'"[30] An important knife handle from the Metropolitan Museum of Art in New York seems to confirm the comprehensive victory of King Narmer over the people of Lower Egypt. According to the University of Chicago's Bruce Williams, *"the parallel to the Narmer palette is decisive."*[31] Like in the Narmer Palette, the picture of the defeated foes is accompanied by the small "Ta-mehu" sign, denoting Libyans dwelling in Lower Egypt. But did King Narmer's northern foray really end there? Is there more to Narmer Palette than a record of a victorious military drive into Lower Egypt? According to the celebrated Israeli excavator Yigael Yadin (1917-1984), Egyptologists have indeed failed to fully grasp the extent of King Narmer's campaign. Yadin writes:

> This interpretation suggests that *not all* of the scenes depicted on the palette are dedicated to the unification of the Nile Valley; in other words, it seems that this votive slate-palette records the victories and achievement of Narmer *including* the unification of Egypt ...[32]

What does Yadin mean when he enigmatically says that the Narmer Palette merely "includes" the unification of Egypt? Could he actually dare to suggest that Narmer could have conquered lands *beyond* the borders of Egypt? Indeed, that is exactly what Yigael Yadin proposes. In this relatively little known revolutionary aspect of his works, Yadin has theorized that:

---

[30] W. A. Fairservis, Jr. (1991) 'A Revised View of the Na'rmr Palette', *Journal of the American Research Center in Egypt* 28, p. 18.

[31] Bruce Williams & Thomas J. Logan (1987) 'The Metropolitan Museum Knife Handle and Aspects of Pharaonic Imagery Before Narmer', *Journal of Near Eastern Studies* Vol. 46 - Num. 4, p. 247.

[32] Yigael Yadin (1955) 'The Earliest Record of Egypt's Military Penetration into Asia? (Some Aspects of the Narmer Palette, the 'Desert Kites' and Mesopotamian Seal Cylinders)', *Israel Exploration Journal* Vol. 5 - Num. 1, pp. 10-11.

CHAP. I: THE FORMATIVE PERIOD | 105

The lower field of the reverse of Narmer's slate-palette records Egypt's military penetration into Trans-Jordan and possible Palestine.'[33]

Recent excavation work in Syria-Palestine have confirmed that the conquests of Pharaoh Narmer extended well beyond the confines of the Egyptian Delta. In actual fact, numerous Early Bronze I pottery vessels inscribed with Narmer's *serekh*, his royal seal, have been found as far north as the town of Silo in Canaan.

> The 1994 excavations (at Halif Terrace, Silo) have revealed large quantities of Egyptian prestige goods including Egyptian Late Ware ceramic vessels, a small faience jar, Egyptian storage jars, and administrative artifacts such as a clay bullae, or stamp impression, depicting a flag hieroglyph (NTR) which generally represents the concept of God in ancient Egyptian. ... In addition to these special finds, the analysis of *ca.* 990 kilograms of pottery recovered during the 1994 Silo Site excavations indicate a sharp increase in Egyptian pottery in the late EBI (Stratum IIB) ca. 3200-3000 BCE.[34]

The Silo site discussed above, excavated under the auspices of the new Nahal Tillah Regional Archaeology Project, is located in Israel's northern Negev desert. Confirming Yadin's hypothesis, these finds give considerable credence to the theory that King Narmer had colonized the archaic Near East. The Khemetic administrative centre appears to have been located on the Halif Terrace.[35] In order to prove this radical hypothesis one must be ready, needless to say, to confront the momentous repercussions upon the accepted understanding of world history that such a revolutionary theory entails. If the Narmer Palette, as Yadin suggests, records Pharaoh Narmer's "lost" conquest of *both* the Egyptian Delta and Syria-Palestine, then the importance of the reign of this pioneering ruler has been gravely underestimated.

To the eyes of the ancient Egyptians, the exploits of Narmer went far beyond the realms of a mere mortal. Thus, if I am right to propose that Pharaoh Narmer was not Menes, then how is it possible to explain the fact that the dynastic Egyptians do not appear to have held King Narmer at a higher pedestal than they did for King

---

[33] Ibid, p. 10.
[34] Thomas E. Levy *et al* (1995) 'New Light on King Narmer and the Protodynastic Egyptian Presence in Canaan', *Biblical Archeologist* 58:1, p. 28.
[35] Ibid; see also B. Brandle 'Evidence for Egyptian Colonization in the Southern Coastal Plain and Lowlands of Canaan During EB I Period.' In E.C.M. van den Brink (editor) (1992) *The Nile Delta in Transition: 4th-3rd Millennium B.C.*, Israel Exploration Society: Jerusalem, pp. 441-477.

Menes? In fact, King Narmer doesn't even appear in a central capacity *anywhere* other than on the famous palette from Hierakonpolis. As the founding father of the pharaonic Egyptian state, shouldn't we expect Narmer to have lived on for millennia in dynastic Egyptian legend? Why then the eerie silence? Or could it be that, in reality, there is no such silence — only just a case of unrecognized identity?

Pharaoh Narmer, because of his pioneering role as a great civilizer, became identified with the god Osiris. And like Osiris, Narmer travelled wide distances — spreading the knowledge of the pharaonic arts, crafts and civil administration. Thus, the predynastic objects found in the Red Land, displayed in Fig. 1d, were undoubtedly contemporaneous with the Narmer Palette itself. Yet, the difference in the quality of craftsmanship is obvious. Unquestionably, those who manufactured the objects shown in Fig. 1d were far less technically advanced than the Khemites who carved the Narmer Palette (Fig. 1c). These embryonic predynastic attempts at reproducing the arts of the Black Land attest to King Narmer's success at exporting pharaonic culture into the archaic Egyptian Delta and beyond.

As the 1994 Silo excavations have revealed, the primordial god-king Narmer-Osiris carried on his civilizing quest to southern Palestine. There, in the Halif Terrace, he instituted a pharaonic colony. From as far as ancient Byblos in Phoenicia, Asiatic craftsmen and artisans benefited from their exposure to a new cultural influx from Africa. Archaeologists maintain that the multitudinous Egyptian-style pottery found in EBI Syria-Palestine were of "local" make — meaning that they were not imported from the Nile Valley. Certainly, the EBI Asiatic inhabitants would not have, all of a sudden, started to reproduce these foreign objects without significant exposure to African culture. The historical traces of Osiris' sojourn in Syria-Palestine has survived in the belief of some scholars that Osiris entered Egypt from western Asia.[36] But as the work of Egyptologist Bruce Williams has made amply clear, evidence for an Osirian kingship in the Sudan largely antedates the Egyptian finds in Palestine. So the origins of the Osirian kingship, as we've already seen in this chapter, are irrefutably African.

So having secured his suzerainty over both Lower Egypt and Syria-Palestine, Narmer-Osiris, as the legend of Osiris and Isis relates, reigned in peace. However, that peace would be short-lived. In our archaeotheological analysis, we now come to the culmination of the historical era covered by the Heliopolitan Theology. Thus, we are now ready for Osiris' son Horus and the latter's uncle Seth to enter into the picture. At the height of the god-king's glory, Osiris suddenly saw his dominion threatened by a ferocious rebellion orchestrated by his brother Seth.

---

[36] Michael Rice (1991) *Egypt's Making (The Origins of Ancient Egypt 5000-2000 BC)*, Routledge: London and New York p. 54.

Seth-Mercury: Instigator of Primeval Chaos

> " Seeing that the birth of Seth disturbs
> the regular process of creation [in the Heliopolitan
> Theology], we can understand that the birth
> itself is represented as irregular."
>
> - H. Te Velde
> Seth, God of Confusion

As documented earlier in the Introduction, the ancient Mayan astronomers believed that "the current Great Cycle began in darkness on 4 Ahau 8 Cumku, a date corresponding to 13 August 3,114 BC in our own calendar."[37] This was known as "the Birth of Venus." Why did the ancient Maya single out the planet Venus? Moreover, what kind of Great Cycle were they talking about? The year 3,114 BCE introduced the very first Venus-induced pole shift which altered the map of the sky. That Great Cycle which "began in darkness" in 3,114 BCE consummated the first of the seven 52-year-long Typhon Seasons which occurred in ancient times. During these occasions the planet Venus would radically swerve from its prescribed orbital path and produce a major natural cataclysm upon the earth's surface. While these Typhon Seasons unfailingly ended in Venus-induced paroxysms, they always begun, fifty-two years prior to the Venus shift by a similar, albeit somewhat less devastating Mercury orbital shift. The two inner planets, which orbit between the sun and the earth, worked in tandem to usher in and terminate Great Cycles which the ancients also referred to as World Ages. Therefore the Venus shift which, according to the ancient Maya, inaugurated the first World Age in 3,114 BCE, was preceded fifty-two years earlier, in 3,166 BCE (3,114 + 52 = 3,166) by a Mercury-induced cataclysm. Since these conflagrations were naturally global in nature, their effects were certainly felt in Egypt and the ancient Near East.

As we've already described, the ancient Khemites identified the planet Mercury with the god Seth of the Great Heliopolitan Ennead. Hence, a universal cosmic disturbance involving the planet Mercury would evidently be blamed upon that god. The birth of Seth in the Heliopolitan theology takes place in a state of utter chaos — hence Seth's traditional role as a god of confusion. Seth's very existence poses a threat to the divine order of nature. Like his biblical counterpart Satan, Seth represents venomous reptiles who torment earth dwellers. It is therefore beyond doubt that, as a destabilizing force in the universe, Seth

---

[37] Graham Hancock (1996 [1995]) *Fingerprints of the Gods (A Quest for the Beginning and the End)*, Seal Books: Toronto, p. 174; Michael D. Coe (1992) *Breaking the Maya Code*, Thames & Hudson: London, p. 275.

represented a threat to his brother Osiris — who was ultimately responsible for the good order of nature. Hence, a sudden breakdown in the order of nature, induced by the actions of the planet Mercury, was duly interpreted as a defeat of the god Osiris by the Mercury-god Seth. Pharaonic legend has retained this episode in the form of the tale of Seth's murder of his brother Osiris. It's probably unlikely to think that Narmer-Osiris was actually murdered by followers of Seth but, one thing I believed is for sure, his reign ended in 3,166 BCE — the year of the primeval Mercury shift.

The story of Isis and Osiris reveals to us that Isis, in search of her murdered husband, followed the path of her deceased husband's casket until she arrived at Byblos, on the coast of Syria and Phoenicia. Once she finally found the remains of Osiris in Phoenicia, Isis took the tree trunk which had shielded the casket of her husband Osiris on the shores of Syria. She then ceremoniously erected it, wrapped it in pure white linen bands, in the temple of Byblos.[38] This ancient association of Osiris with Byblos has led to much speculation among Egyptologists. For instance, Weill[39] had expressed his belief that the myth was meant to symbolise a close trade relationship between Egypt and Byblos in earliest times. Weill even went so far as theorizing that the cult of Osiris originated in Byblos. Other ancient world scholars (e.g. Helck) who went along a similar path, believed that the name of Osiris was "non-Egyptian;" and attempted to equate it with the name of a god from a particular Syro-Palestinian or eastern Mediterranean pantheon.[40] Once again, while the Osirian cult's ancient presence in Syria-Palestine is undeniable, the god Osiris himself had African origins. Nonetheless, partially concurring with Weill and Helck, I strongly believe that the traditional link between Osiris and Byblos has genuine historical foundations, and that the archaic Syro-Palestinian pantheon was widely influenced by the Osirian cult. To begin with, it has already been demonstrated that Narmer-Osiris had made extensive forays into Syria-Palestine. This is, in my view, reflected in the legend of Isis and Osiris. The fact that Isis had to travel to Byblos to recover the body of her deceased husband can point to the possibility that the anti-Osirian rebellion erupted in that particular region of Narmer-Osiris' Asiatic empire. It is moreover evident that Byblos, as will be outlined in the following chapter, had been a very important neo-pharaonic centre during EBI. I will also argue that it is precisely from there that the kings of dynastic Egypt hailed from. I base this assertion on the fact that while in Byblos, Isis had befriended the queen of Byblos and her child. Isis is said to have "burned the mortal parts of the child's body and

---

[38] Norma Lorre Goodrich (1960) *Ancient Myths*, The New American Library: New York, pp. 30-32.
[39] R. Weill (1940) *Phoenicia and Western Asia*, E. F. Row: London.
[40] See John Gwyn Griffiths (1980) *The Origins of Osiris and His Cult*, E. J. Brill: London, p. 29.

CHAP. I: THE FORMATIVE PERIOD | 109

flew around the pillar [containing the chest bearing the body of Osiris] in the form of a swallow."⁴¹ After having, in this manner, rendered the princely child of Byblos immortal, Isis nursed him by allowing the babe to suckle her divine finger. That child, known as Horus the Child, would later grow up to avenge the murder of his divine adoptive father Osiris. The Khemites' adoption of an Asiatic heir to the Phoenician throne as the founding father of dynastic Egypt, proves the status of Byblos as an important neo-pharaonic centre during the reign of King Narmer-Osiris. Finally, with respect to the strong Osirian influence upon the Syro-Palestinian pantheon during EBI, we may turn to the following quote by Egyptologist Michael Rice:

> If the theory of his (Osiris') western Asiatic origins is at all feasible then Osiris might be identified with that god who was eventually best known as Dummuzi (or, in the Semitic form, Tammuz), the Sumerian divinity who brought the arts of husbandry and agriculture to the black-headed folk and then was killed and descended to the underworld.⁴²

Obviously, a strong case could indeed be made for establishing the Osirian origins of the Syro-Palestinian/Sumerian cult of Dummuzi. Like Osiris, Dummuzi was a great civilizer who benevolently passed on his premier body of knowledge to his subjects. Subsequently, like Osiris, Dummuzi was killed by his enemies. The kinship between Syro-Palestinian theology and the Osirian cult at the dawn of the Early Bronze Age is self-evident. No other explanation could be offered to rationalize these striking similarities but through the fact that Pharaoh Narmer-Osiris' reverberant sphere of influence reached well beyond the Nile Valley and into Syria-Palestine.

The murder of Osiris under the hands of Sethian forces, hereby dated to 3,166 BCE, would in turn necessitate the formulation of a new, or amended, pharaonic theology to fit with the new historical realities of the post-Osirian era. Although it would indeed continue to be piously used throughout pharaonic history, the Heliopolitan theology had run its course. The entire Sethian conflict had reshuffled the cards.

King Djoser-Netjerykhet and the Memphite Theology

That revised theological paradigm ultimately presented itself in the form of the "Memphite Theology." Following the murder of his father Osiris, Horus sought revenge by confronting his uncle Seth. Thus, in an effort to find a peaceful resolu-

---

⁴¹ Ibid, p. 32.
⁴² Michael Rice (1991) p. 54.

tion to the discord between Horus and Seth, Geb, who presided over the territorial dispute, decreed that the Two Lands should be divided equally between Horus and Seth. Horus was bequeathed the governorship of Lower Egypt while Seth was appointed ruler of Upper Egypt. The first unusual circumstance that we notice here is that Horus is all of a sudden depicted as a king of Lower Egypt. The principal domain of Horus was initially in Upper Egypt. How had he lost control of the Black Land? For most Egyptologists, no particular explanation needs to be found for this. The apparent anomaly is widely dismissed as yet another fanciful twist in the already much convoluted pharaonic theological plot. I, however, think that there is much more to this than mere creative license on the part of the ancient scribes. In fact, I am thoroughly convinced that we are dealing with an historical event of truly gargantuan importance. As a result of the Sethian rebellion, which erupted in 3,166 BCE, the Black Land (Ethiopia and Upper Egypt) fell under the rule of the followers of Seth. The Horus kingship was forced to relocate its administrative base north to Memphis in Lower Egypt. The Memphite Theology was thence devised by the high priests of the new northern capital (the High Priests of Ptah or HPP) with the disposition of reconciling the divine order with these new developments. The new cosmogony would have at its centre the god Ptah. Inspired by the previous Heliopolitan Ennead, the Memphite cosmogony postulated that Ptah, the creator-god, gave life to all things by means of his divine speech (logos) — much as in the manner of Yahweh in the Hebrew scriptures. The dominant importance of the tongue, teeth and lips of Ptah in the Memphite Theology, as primary agents of Creation, represents the principal differentiating feature between the Memphite and Heliopolitan Theologies. Delineating this pivotal difference, ancient historian James B. Pritchard wrote:

> His Ennead is before him in (the form of) teeth and lips. That is (the equivalent of) the semen and hands of Atum. Whereas the Ennead of Atum came into being by his semen and his fingers, the Ennead (of Ptah), however, is the teeth and lips in this mouth, which pronounced the name of everything, from which Shu and Tefnut came forth, and which was the fashioner of the Ennead.[43]

Ptah transmits life by thinking and commanding everything that he wishes. Re-Atum did so making love to his fist and ejaculating forth Creation from his erect divine phallus. What also characterized the Memphite Theology is that it was conceived during, and likewise sought to find a remedy to, dire times of chaos or universal disorder. In order to fulfil that function, Ptah, the creator-god of

---

[43] James B. Pritchard (editor) (1958) *ANET*, pp. 1-2.

Memphis, incarnated himself into the sacred "Apis bull." Classical authors held that the Apis was conceived "by a light or fire from heaven."[44] As the Mercury shift of 3,166 BCE was responsible for bringing forth this primeval universal chaos, the ancient belief that the birth of the Apis bull was accompanied "by a light or fire from heaven" is naturally a reference to the cosmic conflagration induced by the planet Mercury. Although he was identified as a deity responsible for the primeval rupture of the cosmic order (Ma'at), as "Master of the Sky," the function of Ptah–the-demiurge (the Apis bull) was to "uphold the sky" and prevent it from falling upon the earth (hence maintaining the cosmic equilibrium).[45] Ptah-Apis was therefore in a sense both Seth's counterpart, as instigator of primeval chaos, and Seth's rival, as the preserver of Ma'at in the time of the Sethian rebellion. For these reasons, the Memphite Theology would, throughout pharaonic history, resurface as the central state cosmogony during times of Sethian chaos, or Typhon Seasons.

The next step is to identify under which Khemetic pharaoh, ruling during the primordial Typhon Season (3,166-3,114 BCE), the Memphite Theology was formulated. Necessarily, he would have had to have reigned from Memphis and have immediately succeeded King Narmer-Osiris. I propose that this ruler was Pharaoh Djoser-Netjerykhet — the builder of the stepped pyramid at Saqqara. Of course, this is a very radical theory. King Djoser-Netjerykhet is traditionally dated to the 3rd Dynasty. Yet, in the new chronology, we find him ruling during the late pre-dynastic era! How can this be possible? Well, to begin with, it's important to differentiate between two pharaohs named Djoser. Near the cenotaph of King Djoser-Netjerykhet, archaeologists have found the cenotaph of another King Djoser who bore the Horus name of "Sinakhte." Because of the close proximity of the two cenotaphs, Egyptologists came to the conclusion that Djoser-Sinakhte, whom they called Djoser II, was the son of Djoser-Netjerykhet, or Djoser I. I would argue however that a gap of four hundred years separated the construction of the cenotaph of Djoser-Netjerykhet from the building of Djoser-Sinakhte's own cenotaph. King Djoser-Sinakhte is the dynastic Egyptian pharaoh whom the Manethonian chronology refers to. This Djoser did not build the step-pyramid at Saqqara. The well-know funerary complex of Djoser was constructed in predynastic times, during the reign of the Khemetic pharaoh Djoser-Netjerykhet.

Evidence that the Saqqara's step-pyramid was erected in predynastic times *does* in fact exist; but archaeologists were, as they often do, forced to rationalize the irrational. Within the subterranean chambers of Djoser-Netjerykhet's step-pyramid were uncovered scores of 1st and 2nd Dynasty artifacts. Describing these finds,

---

[44] John Gwyn Griffiths (1970b) 'BRIEF COMMUNICATIONS: "The Pregnancy of Isis": a comment', *Journal of Egyptian Archaeology* 55, p. 195.

[45] Jocelyne Berlandini (1995) 'Ptah-Demiurge et l'exaltation du ciel', *Revue d'Égyptologie* 46, pp. 11-14.

American Egyptologist William C. Hayes wrote:

> From its subterranean passages and chambers, many adorned with fine reliefs and brilliant blue faience "matting" tiles, were recovered more than thirty thousand vessels of alabaster and other ornate stones, many bearing the names of kings of the First and Second Dynasties.[46]

The obvious problem here is, if Djoser's step-pyramid *was* built during the 3rd Dynasty, then what would objects from the 1st and 2nd Dynasties possibly be doing in the subterranean area of the structure? Egyptologists hypothesise that Pharaoh Djoser himself had these proto-dynastic artifacts placed inside his pyramid. But upon closer examination, does this explanation make any sense at all? Why would Djoser-Netjerykhet take the time to gather up over thirty thousand vessels from his predecessors' reigns if he wanted the step-pyramid to be an everlasting testament to his own reign? What would be a lot more logical to assume is that these artifacts were placed there by the early dynastic kings themselves. But common sense is unfortunately not always common. Preconceived notions often take precedence over empirical evidence. This all goes to show just how deeply the Manethonian tradition is ingrained in the minds of professional Egyptologists.

There is no doubt that the step-pyramid at Saqqara was erected by the Khemetic king Djoser-Netjerykhet and not the dynastic king Djoser-Sinakhte. The monuments excavated at Saqqara, directly associated with the step-pyramid, all belong to King Djoser-Netjerykhet.[47] Referring to a particular monument of the sort, Egyptologist Zahi Hawass observes:

> The representation of the *serekh* and Horus on the front face of the monument is similar to that on the reliefs inside the king's southern tomb and on the passages below the Step Pyramid. Also, on the base of the statue of Djoser in the Cairo Museum, there is an exact parallel for the *serekh* as found on this piece, i.e. Horus with the double crown. **This base belongs to the Djoser statue that includes the name of Imhotep.**
>
> The occurrence of the jackal is not unusual for a royal monument. It undoubtedly represents the god Anubis, an important deity from the First Dynasty on. The jackal was assimilated with the gods of both Abydos (Khenti-Amentiu) and Saqqara (Sokar).[48]

---

[46] William C. Hayes (1990 [1959]) *The Scepter of Egypt*, Vol. I: p. 60.
[47] See Zahi Hawass (1994) 'A fragmentary Monument of Djoser from Saqqara', *Journal of Egyptian Archaeology 80*, pp. 45-56.
[48] Ibid, p. 49.

CHAP. I: THE FORMATIVE PERIOD | 113

The monuments from Saqqara therefore confirm that the famed vizier and architect Imhotep was indeed an official of Pharaoh Djoser-Netjerykhet. It is also of interest to note the relative importance of the jackal-god Anubis during the reign of Djoser-Netjerykhet. In the new chronology, the order of influence would be reversed. The early dynastic pharaohs at Abydos were the ones who adopted the cult of Anubis from Saqqara, not vice versa. In fact, the proto-dynastic Egyptians modelled their own cosmogony upon the Memphite model instituted under their Khemetic predecessor Pharaoh Djoser-Netjerykhet. Under the early dynastic rulers of Thinis-Abydos, as will be outlined in the next chapter, the Memphite Theology would continue to develop, adapting to new historical realities, during proto-dynastic times.

As mentioned a bit earlier, the Memphite Theology did not mark a complete break from the more ancient Heliopolitan Theology. King Djoser-Netjerykhet was the first pharaoh to adopt the title of "The Golden Horus."[49] He is also known to have held the title of high priest of Heliopolis.[50] In spite of these obvious attachments to the Black Land, Djoser-Netjerykhet's was compelled to flee northwards to the Red Land because, as the Memphite Theology postulates, the Black Land had become the domain of the followers of Seth.

The Qustul Pharaohs: The First Disciples of Seth

But who were these enigmatic followers of Seth who forced Pharaoh Djoser-Netjerykhet to establish his capital north to Memphis/Saqqara? Evidently, they must have hailed from the Black Land. Also, for them to have been disciples of Seth, and been recognized by Geb as legitimate heirs, they must have likewise been a pharaonic culture. To be sure, I believe that we must look for the source of this Sethian culture in the ancient Sudan. Specifically, to the predynastic A-Group Nubian culture of "Ta-Seti" — whose burial remains have been excavated at Qustul in Lower Nubia. The Sethian attributes of the Ta-Seti civilization can be gleaned from their name alone. Recently, debates have raged over the real significance or influence of this early Lower Nubian culture upon the development of proto-dynastic Egyptian culture. Among the questions raised was: did pharaonic culture emerge out of Africa? While I would certainly answer that question in the affirmative, I would add one more stage of development by saying that these A-Group Nubians were themselves taught by the Anu, the more ancient Khemetic culture. Therefore, it would be very misleading to look for the early roots of pharaonic culture among the Ta-Seti of Lower Nubia — despite the fact that they were also Africans. Aesthetically and culturally speaking, the Ta-Seti were less advanced and sophisticated than the Horus kingship at Hierakonpolis which they had mana-

---

[49] Michael Rice (1991) p. 191. More will be said about the Golden Horus in Chapter 4.
[50] Nicholas Grimal (1992) p. 65.

ged to displace in 3,166 BCE. Nonetheless, their impact upon pharaonic culture would be long-felt.

As soon as it became known, in 1959, that plans were in the works for the construction of the High Dam at Aswan, there was an immediate surge of interest in Nubian archaeology. Since the projected 111 feet-high dam would flood the Nile Valley over 200 kilometres south of the modern Sudanese border, efforts were undertaken to salvage any possible archaeological remains of value from the fast-rising Nile. The most famous and expensive of those campaigns was the removal of the gigantic rock-cut temple of Ramses II at Abu-Simbel from its original site, onto the plateau above the flooded cliffs. Among several UNESCO-sponsored projects was an excavation carried out at Qustul — near the modern-day border between Egypt and the Sudan. While surveying sites of potential importance, archaeologist Keith C. Seele of the University of Chicago's Oriental Institute, took it upon himself, in 1962, to excavate the remains at Qustul. And so, between 1963 and 1964, the Oriental Institute, with Keith Seele at the helm, pursued the Qustul campaign under the auspices of UNESCO. As his work progressed, Seele was astonished by what he had uncovered. In an area which became known as "Cemetery L," Seele found an impressive complex of thirty-three A-Group tombs. Most of them had been robbed in antiquity but, despite their dilapidated state, Seele immediately suggested that these tombs had belonged to "princes" or "kings."[51] If there had indeed been actual pharaohs in Nubia in such remote times, as some would later argue, wouldn't that bring into question the primacy of the early dynastic Egyptian line in the formation of the pharaonic state?

Scholars have dated the beginning of A-Group settlements in Lower Nubia to around 3,100 BCE.[52] In the present historical reconstruction, that estimation narrows itself down to the year 3,166 BCE. The year that the disciples of Seth, Ta-Seti, took control of the Sudan and Upper Egypt. The A-Group Nubians of Ta-Seti were not the lone disciples of Seth in predynastic times however. They had powerful allies among the Libyans — whom the Greek historian Herodotus qualified as the earliest followers of Seth:

> ... save only Poseidon, of whom they learnt the knowledge from the Libyans. Alone of all nations the Libyans have had among them the name of Poseidon from the first, and they have ever honoured this god.
> (Herodotus, II: 50)

---

[51] Bruce Williams (1980) 'The Lost Pharaohs of Nubia', *Archaeology* 33, p. 14.
[52] A. J. Arkell (1974) *A History of the Sudan (From the Earliest Times to 1821)*, Greenwood Press: Westport, Conn., p. 37.

CHAP. I: THE FORMATIVE PERIOD | 115

The very name of Nubia may even find its roots in this ancient association between the A-Group Nubians and the Libyan. Indeed, according to the renowned British Egyptologist Arthur Weigall (1879-1964):

> These Set-tribes seem to have been scattered throughout Egypt, living in communities distinct from those of the other Egyptian races, and it may be that they were the remnants of the original inhabitants of the country. ... Their main capital was the city of **Nubi,** "The Golden," **the Ombos of the Greeks** ... Possibly there was some racial connection between the Set-tribes and the Libyans, for Nubi was situated near the head of important caravan routes to the Oases, where the Libyans dwelt, and the emblem of the goddess Neit, who was perhaps Libyan in origin, is painted on pre-Pharaonic pottery found at Nubi (Petrie, *Nagada*, LXVI, 10, etc.) ... In early times these Set-tribes were a very powerful factor in Egyptian affairs, the god Set being the equal of the Hawk-god, Horus ... [53]

That strong kinship between the A-Group Nubians and their Sethian counterparts the Libyans would, as will be made amply evident in Chapters 11 and 15, foment a bond that these two peoples would rekindle more than once later on in history. That is why properly understanding their early union is crucial for grasping the nature of later events. The Sethian rebellion of Typhon Season #1, which brought the Ta-Seti and the Libyan cultures together spelled disaster for the followers of Horus. Modern archaeologists have however not been able to discern the magnitude of the threat that the Early Bronze Age I Nubian inhabitants of Qustul posed to Lower Egypt. In fact, no such conflict has been recorded in history books. Again, until relatively recently, scholarly interest in this predynastic Lower Nubian culture was virtually nonexistent.

It was only in 1977, after Prof. Seele's unfortunate death that the University of Chicago's Oriental Institute began an extensive study of the material found at Qustul. It was an associate researcher by the name of Bruce Williams who, in 1978, brought international scholarly attention to some intriguing drawings carved on a cylindrical incense burner from the site. According to Williams, the artifact in question pointed to the existence of a hitherto unknown sophisticated predynastic pharaonic culture in Lower Nubia. This discovery, and its implications, raised many eyebrows because, as far as professional Egyptologists were concerned, no indigenous pharaonic state was supposed to have existed in Nubia until the eighth century BCE! Bruce Williams' evidence rested on what clearly appears to

---

[53] Arthur Weigall (1925) *A History of the Pharaohs — Vol. I: The First Eleven Dynasties,* Thornton Butterworth: London, pp. 90-91.

depict, upon the Qustul Incense Burner (see Fig. 1g), a pharaoh wearing the white crown of Upper Egypt, seated on a sacred bark. Within the large body of evidence which, according to Williams, unequivocally confirms that the Qustul tombs indeed belonged to Nubian "pharaohs," is an important collection of similar inscribed incense burners. Those cylindrical objects were incised with unmistakably royal symbols such as serekhs.[54]

Most Egyptologists[55] and Nubiologists[56] however disagree with Williams' interpretation of the evidence. Nubiologist William Y. Adams argues, with little evidence in my view, that the A-Group culture at Qustul was probably contemporaneous with, or even later than, the early dynastic Egyptian rulers of Thinis-Abydos. However, refuting this argument, Williams writes:

> Adams appears to believe that pharaonic iconography and the appearance of monarchy were contemporary. In fact, specifically pharaonic motifs occur well before the monumental developments of the early Thinite Period, including, for example, features of the Hierakonpolis Painted Tomb and a red crown shown in relief on a black-topped vessel of earlier Naqada II times. However, such evidence as can be deduced from the geographical dispersal of outstanding tombs of the Hierakonpolis Tomb 100 type indicates that a number of rulers shared Upper Egypt simultaneously as late as the end of Naqada II times.[57]

While Williams certainly does not go as far as I do, with regards to the extent of pharaonic cultural sophistication and chronology in predynastic times. He nonetheless effectively discredits W. Y. Adams' position by pointing out that the latter "discards the chronological relationship between A-Group and Naqada period Egypt entirely."[58] In accordance with the chronological scheme being used here, Bruce Williams dates the Qustul Incense Burner to the Late Gerzean, or Naqada IIIa, period.[59] Moreover, if the archaeological remains from the Qustul cemetery are

---

[54] Bruce Williams (1980) p. 16.
[55] See Joseph W. Wegner 'Interaction between the Nubian A-Group and Predynastic Egypt: The Significance of the Qustul Incense Burner.' In Theodore Celenko (editor) (1996) *Egypt in Africa*, pp. 98-100.
[56] William Y. Adams (1985) 'Doubts about the Lost Pharaohs', *Journal of Near Eastern Studies* Vol. 44 - Num. 3, pp. 185-192.
[57] Bruce Williams (1987) 'Forebears of Menes in Nubia: Myth or Reality?', *Journal of Near Eastern Studies* Vol. 46 - Num. 1, pp. 15-16.
[58] Ibid, p. 16. To confirm the presence A-Group pottery in Naqada II context in Egypt, B. Williams cites: E. Baumgartel (1947) *The Cultures of Predynastic Egypt I*, London, pp. 100-101; F. Ll Griffith (1921) 'Oxford Excavations in Nubia', *LAAA* 8, p. 9; H. de Morgan (1909) 'L'Égypte primitive (suite)', *Revue de l'École d'Anthropologie de Paris* 19, p. 271, fig. 130.
[59] Bruce Williams & Thomas J. Logan (1987) 'The Metropolitan Museum Knife Handle and Aspects of Pharaonic Imagery Before Narmer', p. 252.

CHAP. I: THE FORMATIVE PERIOD | 117

contemporaneously datable with Late Gerzean or Naqada period artifacts, then they cannot possibly postdate the proto-dynastic pharaohs as Williams postulates.

A crucial test for this revised chronology would be to find some evidence that the A-Group Ta-Seti Nubians were contemporaries of Pharaoh Djoser-Netjerykhet. I am indeed entirely convinced that such a confirmation can be gleaned from the Qustul Incense Burner itself. In his final volume *Civilization or Barbarism*, Dr C. A. Diop makes the following observation about the Qustul Incense Burner:

> Even though the object was damaged, the parts that remained clearly showed a king sitting in a "royal" boat, wearing the long (white) crown of Upper Egypt; in front of him, the royal banner and the falcon-god Horus. One could also observe the wall of a palace, the style of which was reminiscent of the wall of the funeral domain of Pharaoh Zoser at Saqqara. The architecture, in cut stones of the IIIrd Dynasty, could not have been created *ex nihilo*.[60]

Diop, who had never actually challenged the accepted chronology of Egypt itself, did not mean to suggest that the structure depicted on the incense burner, which was reminiscent of Djoser's mastaba, was a portrayal of Djoser's actual funeral domain. This would have of course appeared to defy all logic since, as I have just argued, quoting Bruce Williams, the Qustul Incense Burner belongs to the Late Gerzean period. If the incense burner must necessarily antedate the 1st Dynasty, then surely it cannot be dated contemporaneously with Djoser's 3rd Dynasty! But according to the revised chronology, King Djoser-Netjerykhet — who built his funerary complex at Saqqara, reigned in predynastic times. The 3rd Dynasty Pharaoh Djoser of the extant king-lists was another king who bore the Horus name of Sinakhte. The Qustul Incense burner plainly delineates ceremonial activities from the court of Pharaoh Djoser-Netjerykhet. Citing Bruce Williams again:

> ... certain features of the iconography are fairly certain, including representations of incense burners in use; D-shaped altars or pylons associated with the Heb-Sed festival, the jubilee celebrated by a pharaoh first in his thirtieth year and periodically there after; and a man seated in a chair saluting the bow symbol.[61]

The Memphite temple-complex of King Djoser-Netjerykhet indeed hosted the very first elaborate Heb-Sed festivals in pharaonic history. Since the initial Heb-Sed fes-

---

[60] Cheikh Anta Diop (1991 [1981]) p. 103-105.
[61] Bruce Williams (1980) p. 19.

tival later became particularly significant for pharaohs who achieved a long reigned in the midst of a Typhon rebellion. The Apis, as the earthly representative of Ptah, naturally occupied a prominent position the Heb-Sed festivals.

The Typhonian characteristics of Djoser-Netjerykhet's reign are apparent in a particular text, dated to his eighteenth regnal year, attributed to the vizier Imhotep — Djoser's illustrious chief royal architect.

> To let thee know. I was in distress on the Great Throne, and those who are in the palace were in heart's affliction from a very great evil, since the Nile had not come in my time for a space of seven years. Grain was scant, fruits were dried up, and everything which they eat was short. Every man *robbed* his companion.[62]

As the upheavals of nature multiplied during Typhon Season #1, the population became increasingly agitated and restless. Like the legend of the Typhonian rebellion relates, extensive civil disorder ensued. The astronomer-priests dreadfully anticipated the end of the Typhon Season. The above citation, as I will further discuss in Part III, is highly reminiscent of the Old Testament story of Joseph the Patriarch. As it were, in both cases, the seven year famine came in conjunction with a violent Venus orbital shift. During the reign of Djoser-Netjerykhet, the Venus shift came at the end of the seven-year famine. His vizier Imhotep had been particularly concerned with appeasing the wrath of the Typhonian gods. Through Imhotep's plea to the gods, we can likewise gain a valuable perspective on the African origins of pharaonic religion. Returning to the roots of all worshipping traditions and the birthplace of the Nile, Imhotep reveals:

> ... *He said* to me: There is a city in the midst of the waters [*from which*] the Nile *rises*, named Elephantine. **It is the Beginning of the Beginning, the Beginning Nome, *(facing)* toward Wawat.** ... The Two Caverns is the name of the water; they are the two breasts which pour forth all good things. It is the couch of the Nile, in which he becomes young (again) ... **Khnum is there a god.**[63]

The reference to the First Cataract town of Elephantine, facing towards Nubia (Wawat), as the place of beginning of beginnings substantiates Amélineau and Diop's thesis that the Anu, in their northwards journey from Ethiopia, established the

---

[62] James B. Pritchard (editor) (1958) *ANET*, pp. 25-26.
[63] Ibid.

first centre of pharaonic worship in Egypt at Elephantine. The association of the god Khnum with this specific Nome has also been clearly articulated earlier. Imhotep's preoccupation with the First Cataract deity Khnum in this era of Typhonian disorder was no haphazard connection. The surviving Ptolemaic texts identify Khnum and the goddess Neith, a divine pair at Esna, as two forms of the same world-creating divinity. Neith, in her aspect of the divine creative cow, embodies the nurturing aspect of the creative force which regenerates the natural order as the World Age dies.

The End of Typhon Season #1 and

the Primordial Flood

A mythological work known as the "Memphite Drama" — which scholars believe was composed at the beginning of the Old Kingdom, i.e. during the conventional 3rd Dynasty[64] — speaks of the "Destruction of Mankind" by the sun-god Re. This tale of the "primeval wrath" of Re, recorded in what is referred to as the "Apophis Book," was the work of high priests of Ptah. The ancient legend relates that the sun-god Re ordered the lion-goddess Sekhmet to carry out Mankind's destruction on his behalf. Incidentally, the lion-goddess Sekhmet is also recognized as the wife or consort of Ptah in Memphis.[65] Along with Ptah and Nefertem, Sekhmet formed what was part of the Memphite divine triad. In this legend of the Destruction of Mankind, the lion-goddess Sekhmet is equated with the goddess Hathor. The two female deities' names are used interchangeably in the narrative. This Destruction of Mankind came at the end of Typhon Season #1 with the Venus shift of 3,114 BCE.

The year 3,114 BCE also incidentally corresponds with the Olmec and Mayan year zero in the Gregorian calendar. On that year, according to the Mesoamericans, the Great Cycle "began in darkness." It brought to a fiery culmination the first of seven 52-year periods where civilization was destroyed and regenerated. According to the Finnish catastrophist Timo Niroma:

> The first so-called "Dark Age", meaning a period from which little is known despite much information before and after that period, occurred about 3100 BC to 3000 BC. For example in Mesopotamia this period is called Jemdet Nasr. About 3100 BC there was suddenly a change to more primitive ages compared to the preceding Uruk period. For example the numerical token system dwindled. 3000 BC however there was a sudden

---

[64] William C. Hayes (1990 [1959]) *The Scepter of Egypt*, Vol. I: p. 75.
[65] Siegfried Morenz (1973) *Egyptian Religion*. Trans. by Ann E. Keep. Cornell University Press: Ithaca, NY, p. 17.

recovery. This is called the Early Dynasty, which can be described as the first known culture that began to have a some kind of centralized system. ... What happened 3100 BC, maybe right in 3114 BC? There is not any great crater on the continental areas, but 2/3 of the Earth's area is covered by water, and flood they speak of.[66]

Mesopotamian civilization thrived from c.4,500 BCE to c.2,000 BCE with only two major interruptions: one in around 3,100 BCE and the other in about 2,100 BCE. These two cataclysmic events, which manifested themselves more precisely in 3,114 BCE and 2,130 BCE, were two Great Floods. I contend that while the biblical Great Flood legend was based on the second conflagration, that of 2,130 BCE, the actual Hebrew chronicle of Noah is a later adaptation of an older Sumerian flood narrative based on the first Great Flood of 3,114 BCE. Both catastrophes were caused by the planet Venus — the flood carrier. Later Roman mythology related that Jupiter, angered by humanity's wickedness, resolved to destroy it by fire. But he then realized that he risked setting heaven itself on fire, so he sent a great flood.[67] Ancient mythologies from around the world embodied the cosmic forces of chaos in the form of a dragon or feathered serpent. Commenting on the eschatological role of the reptilian demon of chaos, author Joseph Fontenrose writes:

> The chaos demon (or demons) represented not only primeval disorder, but all dreadful forces that remain in the world and periodically threaten the god-won order: hurricane, flood, fire, volcanic eruption, earthquake, eclipse, disease, famine, war, crime, winter, darkness, death. They [the ancients] imagined either that the demon himself came back to life and renewed the combat, or that his progeny continued the war against the cosmos, ever striving for disorder and a return to primeval inactivity. His death amounted to no more than the banishment from the ordered world: he was cast into the outer darkness beneath the earth or beyond it, that is, he was thrown back into primeval chaos from which he came, where he and his minions lived on, ever ready to invade the god-established order and undo the whole work of Creation. For the cosmos has been won from the chaos that still surrounds it, as a cultivated plot from the encompassing wilderness.[68]

---

[66] Timo Niroma. Internet resource: http://personal.eunet.fi/pp/tilmari/tilmari3.htm
[67] Ovid, Book I.
[68] Joseph Fontrose (1959) *Python (A Study of Delphic Myth and its Origins)*, University of California Press: Berkeley, Cal., p. 219.

2

A New Beginning
(3,114 BCE to 2,730 BCE)

The Venus shift of 3,114 BCE, as was the case during all Typhon Seasons, had principally affected Egypt's eastern Delta and the Mediterranean world. Due to its fortunate geographical location, Upper Egypt (the Black Land) had continually been spared from the harshest ravages caused by the rising waterbed of the raging Mediterranean sea — as it overwhelmed the lands along its destructive path. Thus, the dawning of the Early Bronze Age II period saw the Red Land submerged, as the legend of Re's Destruction of Mankind suggests, in the bloody waters of the planetary gods' manifested indignation. It is also within this context of post-diluvian devastation that dynastic Egypt emerges. Moreover, in the Manethonian history of Egypt, Africanus and Eusebius relate that King Menes, the first king of Dynastic Egypt, came to rule in Egypt "after the Flood."[1] Herodotus also made the assertion that:

> The first human king of Egypt, they said, was Min. In his time all Egypt save the Thebaic (southern Upper Egypt) province was a marsh: all the country that we now see was then covered by water, north of the lake Moeris ...
> (Herodotus, Book II: 4)

The ancients, whether in China or the ancient Near East, traditionally considered their ancestral monarchs who lived and reigned before a great primeval flood as Gods. Herodotus' statement also makes clear that the only part of Egypt's territory which was inundated in proto-dynastic times was the Delta (beyond the Fayum). Therefore, while pharaonic history originates in the middle of the fifth millennium BCE, *dynastic* Egyptian history begins *after* the Great Flood which terminated Typhon Season #1. The various extant king-lists and annals from dynastic Egypt are, consequently, not to be interpreted as complete records of the Nile Valley's pharaonic history. The traditional Manethonian framework is, as a manner of speaking, an Egyptocentric historiography. This means that it does not concern itself with the formative historical period in which the Anu emerged from Ethiopia

---

[1] Manetho, *Aegyptiaca*, FR. 6-7.

to colonize the Nile Valley. That ante-diluvian period symbolized for the dynastic Egyptian the era of the gods. The fact that Pharaoh Narmer became know as Osiris to the dynastic Egyptians is one major example of that.

At this point, pharaonic history breaks into two branches: the original cult of Horus the Elder and the new dynastic cult of Horus the Child. The big problem with Egyptological historiography heretofore is its continuing inability to discern, or even as much as to acknowledge, the dual nature of early pharaonic kingship. While the majority of Egyptologists indeed recognize that, at some point during proto-dynastic times, the cults of Horus the Elder and Horus the Child merged into one, never has it been suggested that the two cults represented two distinct Horus kingships. Yet, this is precisely the thesis which will be advanced in this chapter.

The New Dynastic Horus: Horus the Child

Horus the Elder is traditionally known as the primordial patron god of Upper Egypt, Horus the Behdetite. As his name duly denotes, Horus the Elder is considered to have preceded another Horus figure — namely, Horus the Child, who was the son of Isis and Osiris. Horus the Elder, a son and heir to Re, was identified as the husband of Isis — who bore him four children. Egyptologists contend that Horus the Elder became one with the younger Horus early in Egyptian history to become the one Horus. Is there a hidden historical foundation at the root of this supposed mythological kinship between Horus the Elder and Horus the Child? I personally believe that there is. As a result, I have chosen to designate this era in ancient pharaonic history, beginning in 3,114 BCE and finishing in 2,730 BCE, the "New Horus Period." Because it is precisely between those years that Horus the Child, the New Horus, would come into prominence and coexist with Horus the Elder. This fusion between Horus the Elder and Horus the Child which Egyptologist erroneously believe took place prior to dynastic Egypt, only in actuality came to be at the "end" of the New Horus Period — during the Old Kingdom. Hence, prior to 2,730 BCE, we must contend with "two" Horus kingships — a Khemetic one (that of Horus the Elder) and a dynastic Egyptian one (of Horus the Child). As the titles' hierarchy indicates, the Khemetic Horus kingship is naturally the oldest of the two. Horus the Elder is the counterpart of Horus the Behdetite. As the founding Horus, he is akin to the African Anu who came to establish themselves at Edfu in Upper Egypt, and Heliopolis in Lower Egypt, during the fifth millennium BCE. As the primeval civilizer, Horus the Elder brought the fruits of pharaonic culture into the Red land (Egypt) from Khemet, the Black land (Ethiopia and Upper Egypt).

In predynastic times, the colonizing thrust of the Khemetic Horus kingship resulted, in two specific occasions, in the Horus cult's adaptation to new environments where pharaonic culture had implanted itself. Thus, the first manifestation of the cult of Horus was in Hierakonpolis — during Naqada II. At Hierakonpolis, Horus the Behdetite was transformed into his exclusively Upper Egyptian form of Horus of Nekhen. The Hierakonpolite Horus kingship had by then become sufficiently independent of the Ethiopic Edfu cult to establish a sort of "second generation" Khemeto-Egyptian domestic kingship. Subsequently, as the Horus of Nekhen himself, specifically incarnated by Narmer-Osiris, began to colonize lands further north — into Early Bronze Age I Syria-Palestine — the foundations of yet another Horus kingship fomented itself — that of Horus the Child. Therefore, unlike the earlier Horus kingships of Behdet and Nekhen (which were fundamentally African), the cult of Horus the Child was at its base Levantine, but wholly nurtured under African tutelage. When Horus the Child descended into Lower Egypt from his Canaanite homeland, he founded what is known as dynastic Egypt.

The Classic Ptolemaic Age

Shortly following the beginning of the third millennium BCE, the newly-formed dynastic line of Horus the Child at Thinis-Abydos (with Pharaoh Menes as its founder) would not actually dislodge the more ancient kingship of Horus the Elder at Edfu in Upper Egypt. Both kingships would coexist harmoniously throughout most of the New Horus Period.

The cataclysmic Venus shift of 3,114 BCE came in the middle of the archaeological period known as Early Bronze Age I. That year also brought the end of King Djoser-Netjerykhet's reign in Memphis and the beginning of the classic Ptolemaic age. Evidently, speaking of a "Ptolemaic" age during the Early Bronze II period is hardly in keeping with conventional scholarship. Such a radical thesis is certainly without precedent, and is sure to be scornfully received by virtually all academics. Yet, this is precisely the theory I now intend to bring forward. I certainly do not quarrel with the well-established fact that, following the conquest of Egypt by Alexander the Great in 332 BCE, Greek Ptolemaic kings and queens ruled in Alexandria, on Egypt's Mediterranean coast, in the third century BCE. The evidence for that is overwhelming and undisputable. Nonetheless, it is also a unanimously accepted fact among scholars that the Late Period Ptolemaic temples at Edfu, near the First Cataract, were constructed on top of much "earlier" temples. It is therefore entirely legitimate to deduce that a cult of Horus the Behdetite existed in Edfu long before the fourth century BCE. As I shall seek to demonstrate, the extant wall-temple scenes of the Late Period Ptolemaic temples recount the events of a much earlier period than the time of those who carved them in the fourth century BCE.

In Chapter 18, I will argue that, beginning about fifty years before the conquest of Alexander the Great, there was a massive religious renaissance in Egypt which vigorously revived these later dynastic Egyptians' interest in the classic Ptolemaic age — which I believe flourished between 3,114 BCE and 2,780 BCE. Immediately following the end of Pharaoh Djoser-Netjerykhet's reign, there arose in Edfu a new line of kings who bore the name of Ptolemy. Simultaneously, in the nearby Upper Egyptian town of Philae, a matriarchal succession of queens bearing the name of Cleopatra ruled in equal power. The central position occupied by Pharaoh Djoser and his vizier Imhotep in the Ptolemaic temple-wall reliefs is, in my estimation, a powerful hint pointing to the actual proximity of King Djoser-Netjerykhet's reign to the advent of the Ptolemaic rulers. Egyptologists hold on to the view that the fourth century BCE rulers had only *then* deified King Djoser and his vizier Imhotep. I instead contend that both Djoser and Imhotep were deified very shortly after their deaths. The revived Late Period interest in them stemmed directly from the fourth century BCE pharaohs' renewed fascination with the classic Ptolemaic age. Beginning with the standard 30th Dynasty, the native Egyptians' earnest desire to return to the roots of their pharaonic culture, following long periods of foreign domination, lured them to look to the classic Ptolemaic age for inspiration. An era of insatiable interest in anything neo-Ptolemaic was thus ignited. As a result, when Alexander came to Egypt, there *already* was much interest for the *classical* Ptolemaic dynasty — which had come to an end about 2,400 years earlier. Ptolemy, Alexander's famous general, had adopted this name as his own because of the many wondrous accounts he had heard about the classic Ptolemaic age while in Egypt. The Greeks' interest in the long-gone Ptolemaic dynasty of Upper Egypt only added to an already widespread fascination with the classic Ptolemaic age during Egypt's Late Period. The historical scenes depicted on the walls of the First Cataract Ptolemaic temples therefore do not actually attempt to articulate events which occurred during the rule of the Greek Ptolemaic kings in Alexandria, but illustrate historical events from the Early Bronze II period.

There can perhaps be no better way to review the important events of the previous chapter, as well as to situate ourselves within the ensuing historical context, than by turning to a crucial hieroglyphic text from the temple of Edfu. The inscription in question describes a pivotal rebellion, said to be historical, undertaken by Seth against Horus. In the story, Horus returns to Egypt from abroad, only to find that the country had fallen under the control of his evil uncle Seth. Unquestionably, Seth's new powers over the Two Lands had been in direct result of the rebellion in question. The relief on the Edfu temple-wall shows the famed vizier and architect, Imhotep, recounting the story of the rebellion to his king, Djoser-Netjerykhet. That conflict between Horus and Seth was sparked by the Mercury shift of 3,166 BCE. As the planet Mercury is identified in the Ptolemaic temples with Seth, the ravages that

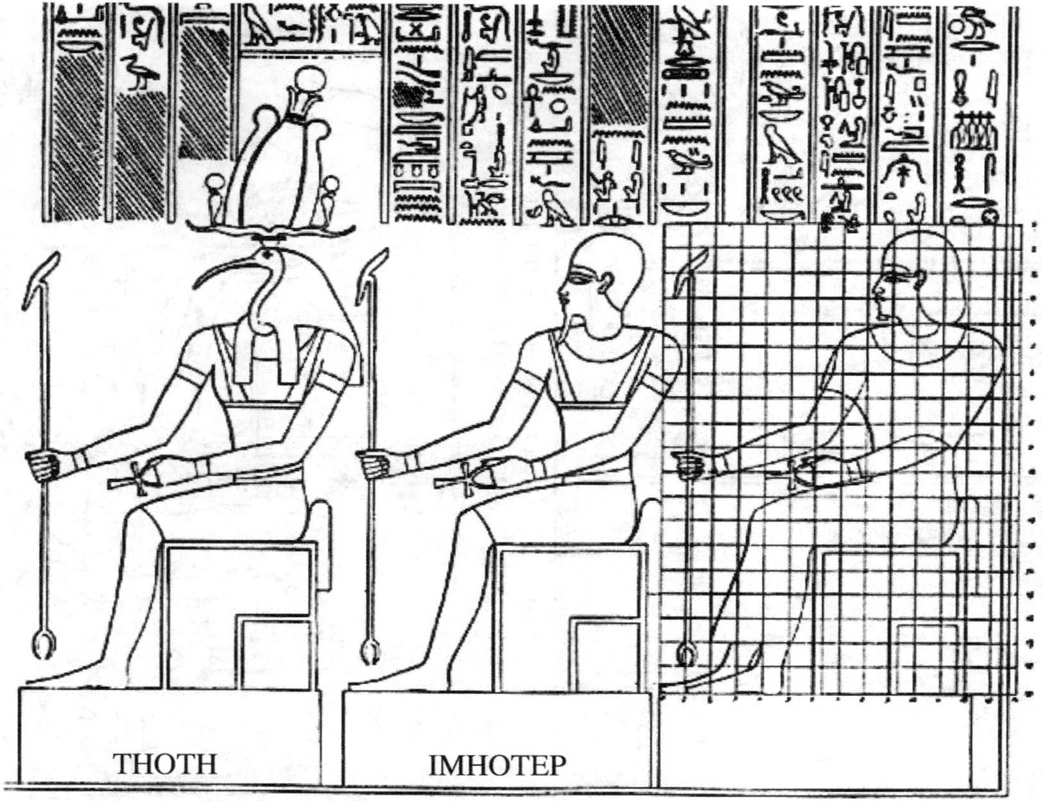

Fig. 2a: Thoth and Imhotep.

Fig. 2b: Ptolemy V (wearing double-plume crown) making offerings to deified Imhotep and other deities.

Fig. 2c: Ptolemy XI (wearing *atef*-crown) making offerings to Ptah, Hathor and Imhotep.

Fig. 2d: The goddess Isis.

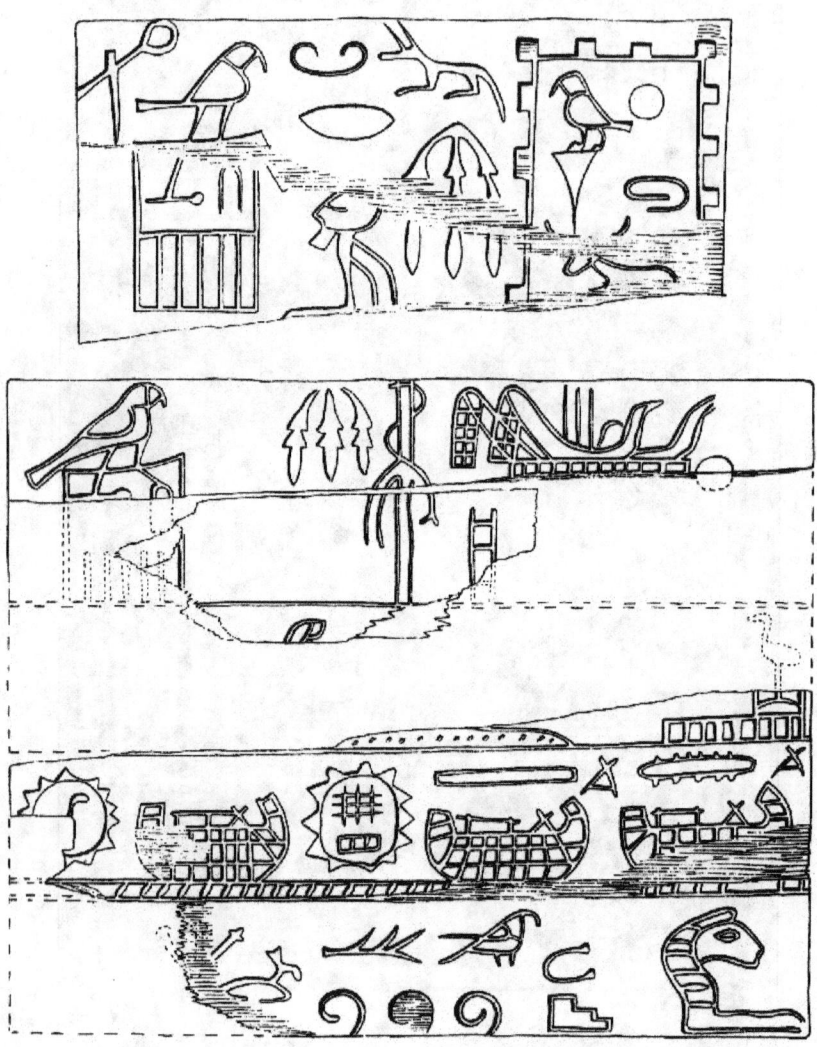

Fig. 2e: Scenes from the court of Pharaoh Aha-Menes.

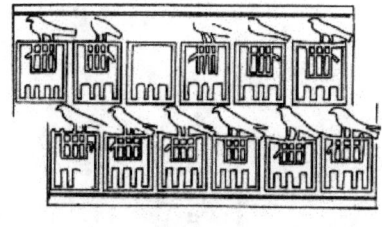

Fig. 2f: Sealings of King Djer at Abydos.

Fig. 2g: Ivory tablet of King Ka-a at Abydos.

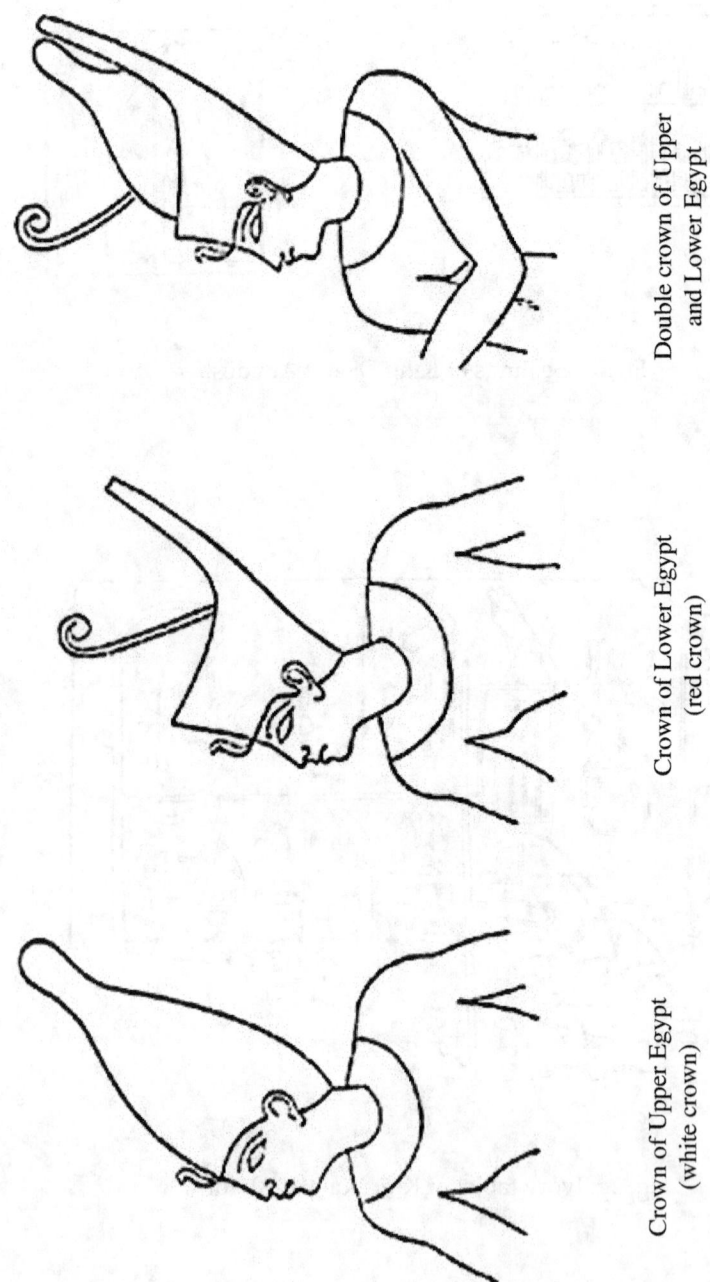

Fig. 2h: The royal crowns of ancient Egypt.

the planet Mercury inflicted upon Egypt, the domain of Horus, was likened to a wanton act of aggression by Seth against Horus. With the advent of Typhon Season #1, the inhabitants of the district of Ombos (Naqada), the African A-Group Nubians of Ta-Seti, spearheaded the rebellion by declaring themselves followers of Seth. For the first time, Seth had the ambition of becoming the equal, if not a superior, of Horus. The Sethian A-Group Nubians of Typhon Season #1 unilaterally acquired for themselves full pharaonic titles — without the approval of the Horus kingship. This rebellion would set an important precedent which would resolutely be followed by the disciples of Seth throughout much of dynastic Egyptian history whenever a Typhon Season came about. As we will ultimately see, at the time of other Typhon Seasons (particularly Typhon Seasons #2, 4 and 5) the governorship of Egypt tended to be separated between the disciples of Horus in the south and the followers of Seth in the north. In the previous chapter, it has been demonstrated that the Memphite Theology was particularly patterned with this division of power in mind. And, not surprisingly, elements of the Memphite Theology, as expressed through the worship of Ptah or the Apis bull, would periodically take centre-stage at the time of those Typhon Seasons. Be that as it may, the Horus kingship always held the genuine balance of power.

Thus, the scene depicting the rebellion of Seth during Typhon Season #1, which we find carved on the fourth century BCE Ptolemaic temple-wall, was undoubtedly reproduced from an earlier version belonging to the original Ptolemaic temple from the EBII period. There is no evidence whatsoever during the Late Period for a rebellion of that scale involving disciples of Seth. But since historians fail to realize that this so-called myth is actually historical, no attempt has been made to reconcile the details of that story with real events in Egyptian history. Undoubtedly, the genesis of the Sethian rebellion saga goes back to Early Bronze Age times. As a result, the classic Ptolemaic rulers of Edfu, who immediately succeeded Pharaoh Djoser-Netjerykhet, were recounting historical events very close to their own time.

Hathor, Mistress of Punt and the Dynastic Race Theory

*"... it is clear that she (Hathor) was believed to
be the personification of the entire Ennead and,
in that sense, the mother of Horus."*

- Leonard H. Lesko

In the Khemetic epic concerning the "Destruction of Mankind," we are told that after humankind had rebelled against the sun-god Re, their creator, Re sent his eye to earth, in the form of the goddess Hathor, to deliver his message of destruction.

In a single day of terror, Hathor devastated the earthly realm — causing much of humanity to perish at once, and went to sleep afterwards. Satisfied with Hathor's mission, Re poured down beer over the earth during the night — causing the liquid to mix with the Nile waters and giving it the appearance of blood. When Hathor woke up in the morning, she drank the excess water and became drunk. With this benevolent action on the part of the sun-god Re, humankind was saved from irrevocable devastation. Once again, this legend retelling Re's destruction of mankind has, in my view, a strong historical basis. It recounts the destruction which came at the end of Typhon Season #1 in the form of the orbital shift of the planet Venus, in 3,114 BCE. The theme of humankind's destruction at the culmination of a Typhon Season resonated throughout many ancient world cultures. As will be argued in Chapter 3, the biblical theme of the Fall of Adam and Eve was also inspired by this ancient Khemetic concept.

Incidentally, Re's choice of Hathor, in the form of the former's eye, as his prime agent of destruction also has a very consequential historical meaning. Accepting that Re's destruction of mankind is to be equated with the Venus-induced global catastrophe of 3,114 BCE, we should then expect to find Hathor occupying a position of some prominence during the transition period between EBI and EBII. In fact, this is what we see. The name Hathor actually means "House of Horus." In that capacity, she was often seen, in her hybrid identity of Hathor-Isis, as the mother of Horus. Hathor-Isis ruled as a "double-goddess" at Dendera.[2] The dynastic cult of Horus the Child owes its very existence to Hathor-Isis — the mother of Horus the Child. Since the dynastic Egyptian kinship of Horus the Child hails from the Levant, the Levantine aspects of Isis-Hathor should now be worthy of discussion.

It is a rather peculiar thing that Hathor is thought to have hailed from two different places: one of these locations is the Land of Punt (principally thought to have been located on the Red Sea coast of Somalia) and the other is Byblos in Phoenicia (hence Hathor's familiar title of "Lady of Byblos"). However, the problem is that these two places are miles away on opposites sides of Egypt, with Somalia in the south and Byblos (Phoenicia) in the north. Any impartial observer would find it difficult to understand how the goddess Hathor could have hailed from two different, and not to mention very distant, places at the same time. To me, this problem does not exist because, accepting Immanuel Velikovsky's theory, I believe that the Land of Punt and Byblos (Phoenicia) were in fact meant to refer to one and the same place. According to Velikovsky:

---

[2] Sylvie Cauville (1990) 'Les inscriptions dédicatoires du temple d'Hathor à Dendera', *Bulletin de l'Institut Français d'Archéologie Orientale* 90, p. 89.

The name Punt or Pont can be traced to "Pontus, father of Poseidon and Sidon," as narrated by Sanchoniaton, the early Phoenician writer.[3] Sidon was a Phoenician metropolis.[4]

Indeed, the Land of Punt, also referred to as "God's Land," was in fact located in the Levant, not the Sudan. The dynastic Egyptians identified the Levant as the land of the gods because the founder of Egypt's 1st Dynasty, Pharaoh Aha-Menes, came from Syria-Palestine. It had furthermore been in the Levant that Narmer-Osiris had come from Africa to instruct the ancestors of the dynastic Egyptians on the rudiments of pharaonic culture. In an Egyptological essay on the origin and meaning of the term "God's Land," Abdel-Aziz Saleh wrote:

> It has rightly been noted that the *"God's Land"* formula was not considered a strictly definite name of any specific land with clearly drawn boundaries. It seems to have two, more or less, traditional and coextensive significances: mythological and practical. The prevalent idea, held at present, is that in its mythological sense, the term pointed quite often to the Orient. A. Erman has ingeniously equated it with the indefinite forerunner of the *"Levant"* general term of modern times signifying countries vaguely situated to the east of the Mediterranean. However, with this broad identification, there are two different views with regard to the underlying trend of the meaning. According to the more common opinion, the mythical Orient, meant by "God's Land", came rather to represent the risen Sun-god. The other and less tenable opinion is inspired by the much-debated hypothesis that a certain people, known as the *"Followers of Horus,"* had entered Egypt from the East during the late Predynastic times under the guidance of the old Falcon-god Horus. In consequence, it has been inferred that *"God's Land"* namely the Orient, must represent the cradle of the Falcon-god of those early eastern invaders. Their god Horus is he who became afterwards the dynastic and royal deity of Egypt.[5]

As Saleh aptly observes, early Egyptologists rightly believed that the young Horus had foreign origins — specifically Levantine roots. In addition, it was thought that he might have reached the Nile Valley from as far away as Arabia or Asia Minor.

---

[3] Philo of Byblos as quoted by Eusebius in *Preparation for the Gospel*, I, 10, 27.
[4] Immanuel Velikovsky (1952) *Ages in Chaos*, Doubleday & Co.: Garden City, NY, p. 110.
[5] Abdel-Aziz Saleh (1981) 'Notes on the Ancient Egyptian T3-N*T*R " God's Land"', *Bulletin de l'Institut Français d'Archéologie Orientale* 81, pp. 107-108.

Eminent Egyptologists Sir Flinders Petrie[6] and Walter B. Emery[7] both believed that the land of Egypt was civilized by an invading dynastic race from southwestern Asia. The great Swiss Egyptologist Édouard Naville likewise related that:

> ... a vague and ancient tradition that they [the dynastic Egyptians] originally came from the land of Punt, and that it had been their home before they invaded and conquered the lower valley of the Nile.[8]

Accordingly, he was given the name of "the distant one."[9] In any event, the mysterious identity of this "dynastic race" has served as a source of much controversy over the last century or so. The unquestionable evidence of a mass infiltration by unknown aliens from the east just before dynastic Egypt's unification by Pharaoh Aha-Menes of the 1st Dynasty has led many historians to speculate that pharaonic Egypt sprung out as a result of a substantial cultural impetus from without — possibly Sumeria. In recent decades however, the dynastic race theory has somewhat been swept under the carpet. The apparently racist implications of a veiled "master race" theory supporting the concept of a northern race civilizing the "savages" of Africa has made the dynastic race theory unpopular in the post-modern era. The very mention of it, even in the most conservative of circles, brings out the embarrassing ghosts of imperialism and colonialism.[10] Therefore, it may seem very strange to many readers that I, an Afrocentrists of all people, would support the Aryanist and seemingly racist dynastic race theory. It is my personal opinion that the abandonment by modern scholars of the dynastic race theory has, in truth, been more beneficial to the Eurocentrists than to Afrocentrists. Afrocentric scholars have been the most outspoken critics of the dynastic race theory because, in their view, it denies the fundamental African origins of pharaonic culture and civilization. This exceedingly Egyptocentric view of pharaonic culture is, in my opinion, something that Afrocentrists can much do without. The truth is that pharaonic culture *did not* begin with dynastic Egypt. Again, the ancient African "Anu" settlers first imported pharaonic culture into Upper Egypt (Khemet or the Black Land) and Pharaoh Narmer-Osiris of Hierakonpolis later went on to colonize the Levantine territories — bringing to the Asiatics the fruits of pharaonic culture. Having been nurtured in their Levantine homeland during EBI, the proto-dynastic Egyptians then moved south into the Egyptian Delta,

---

[6] Sir Flinders Petrie (1899) *A History of Egypt*, Charles Scribner's Sons: New York, p. 10.
[7] Walter B. Emery (1967) *Archaic Egypt*, Penguin: Baltimore, p. 39.
[8] Édouard Naville, *Deir el-Bahari*, pt. iii, p. II.
[9] Michael Rice (1991) *Egypt's Making (The Origins of Ancient Egypt 5000-2000 BC)*, Routledge: London and New York, p. 51.
[10] See David M. Rohl (1998) *A Test of Time — Vol. II: Legend (The Genesis of Civilization)*, Century: London, pp. 315-316.

early in EBII, and founded the 1st Dynasty under Aha-Menes. Therefore, it is evident that the dynastic race (Horus the Child) somewhat adapted the more ancient African pharaonic culture to their own cultural reality by adapting certain aspects of Phoenician and Mesopotamian traditions.

In addition to the obvious influence of Narmer-Osiris, the matriarchal roots of dynastic Egypt are likewise evident. As it has already been mentioned, the goddess Isis-Hathor, as the mother of Horus the Child, also took an important part in grooming the young Horus. In the previous chapter, we saw that when Isis arrived in Phoenicia in search of the body of Osiris, she stayed as a guest of the goddess Ishtar, Queen of Syria, in the palace of Byblos. There, the coffin of her husband was hidden inside a wooden pillar (the sacred tamarisk tree which she later erected in Byblos). Since she did not reveal that she was a goddess herself, Ishtar ordered Isis to remain in the palace to nurse her eldest son.

> Isis kept her anonymity for some time, remaining in the palace of Byblos to nurse the son of its rulers. Whenever the child was hungry, she let it suck on her divine fingers instead of her breast. Every evening when the palace courtiers had gone to bed, Isis held the little boy over a flame because in this way she knew how to singe away those parts of him which were mortal only and confer upon this future king the precious gift of eternal life.[11]

This "future king" was none other than Horus the Child — founder of dynastic Egypt. It is also particularly interesting to note that the young Horus is often portrayed sucking his thumb. This may well be a symbol of the manner in which he had been nursed by Isis as in infant in God's Land. The matriarchal role of Isis-Hathor may also be observed during the transitional period in Egypt between the end of Pharaoh Djoser-Netjerykhet's reign and the advent of Aha-Menes. Shown on the Palermo Stone wearing the red crown of Upper-Egypt,[12] this ephemeral line of predynastic kings counted among them one named King Scorpion. Since, according to this revised historical scheme, a cult to the goddess Isis existed at the time of King Scorpion, a link between the goddess Isis and those predynastic Egyptian pharaohs of the Delta ought to be detectable. Incidentally, just such an association may be contemplated with the cult of Isis-Scorpion, Mother of Horus. The common symbol of the scorpion, however elusive the meaning of it may be,

---

[11] Norma Lorre Goodrich (1960) *Ancient Myths*, The New American Library: New York, p. 31.
[12] Elise J. Baumgartel (1975) 'Some Remarks on the Origins of the Titles of the Archaic Egyptian Kings', *Journal of Egyptian Archaeology* 61, p. 28.

establishes a relationship between King Scorpion and the cult of Isis at Philae at the beginning of the Early Bronze II period. The same way the Ptolemaic kings of Edfu were identified with the god Horus the Behdetite, it would seem that the Cleopatra queens of Philae held divine power under the guise of Isis-Hededet. Additionally, textual evidence from the Ptolemaic temple-walls confirms that this title of "Isis-Hededet" was synonymous with the designation "Isis-Scorpion." The evidence in question is an inscription from the temple of Edfu which mentions a goddess by the name of "Hededet" Isis-Scorpion. In addition, she was believed to hold powers over venomous reptiles.[13] Isis-Hededet's reputation as a subduer of venomous reptiles would appear to come from the fact that the Isis cult was established immediately after the first Typhon Season. The serpentine Sethian demon of chaos had evidently been tamed by the goddess Isis. It therefore follows that, in all probability, the scorpion symbolized the defeat of the Sethian forces of chaos.

The Primordial Victory of Horus the Child Over Seth

The kinship of Isis-Hathor with the proto-dynastic Egyptians is further demonstrated in Isis-Hathor's antipathy towards Seth — the sworn enemy of Horus the Child. In addition to her traditional role as the mistress of the Sethian serpent of chaos, we find the goddess Isis-Hathor actively participating in the altercations waged by both Horus the Elder, her husband, and Horus the Child, her son, against the archdemon Seth. She is sometimes seen as an active participant in the battle, and at other times, she acts as an encouraging bystander. As such, Isis-Hathor becomes a central figure in the reunification effort of Egypt undertaken by both Horus kingships following Typhon Season #1. Understanding this entire dynamic is pivotal since, as I shall now argue, records of these latest unification bouts have survived, gone wholly unrecognized by scholars, onto the walls of the Ptolemaic temples.

In the foreground, our quest begins with the examination of one of six hymns dedicated to Isis, from the sanctuary of her temple at Philae, associated with the reign of Pharaoh Ptolemy II. Hymn (I) from Room X is accompanied by a relief of King Ptolemy II paying homage to Isis-Hathor with the following words: " *Son of the Sun, Ptolemy, has come before you, O Isis, the Great, God's Mother, kissing the ground before your beautiful face; give him your love forever."* [14] Moreover, inscribed above the hymn, we can also read Isis's words to Ptolemy: " *I have given you the life-span of Re in heaven (itself) with what is in it; I have given you victory over the south."* Elsewhere, Isis is

---

[13] Jean-Claude Goyon (1978) 'Hededyt: Isis-Scorpion', *Bulletin de l'Institut Français d'Archéologie Orientale* 78, p. 442-446.
[14] L. V. Zabkar (1983) 'Six Hymns to Isis in the Sanctuary of Her Temple at Philae and their Theological Significance — Part I', *Journal of Egyptian Archaeology* 69, p. 116.

very precise about the identity of those people from the south whom King Ptolemy II had taken under his tutelage: *"O my beloved son, son of the Sun, Ptolemy, I have given you the south as far as Kenset, Ta-Seti, bent down for ever, belongs to you."* The fact that Isis mentions "Ta-Seti" is somewhat of an oddity, within the context of conventional scholarship, since we know that "Ta-Seti" was the appellation used to qualify the A-Group Nubians of the Early Bronze Age. If the Ptolemaic texts really originated in the Late Period, why would Isis-Hathor choose to refer to the Nubians by the name of their distant ancestors? These enemies of Horus the Behdedite, King Ptolemy II, whom the goddess Isis-Hathor speaks of are none other than the disciples of Seth, the A-Group Nubians of Ta-Seti, whose rebellion the kingship of Horus the Elder had successfully managed to quell with the help of Isis-Hathor.

I am not the first to suggest that the conflict between Horus and Seth recounted on the walls of the Late Period Ptolemaic temples mirror actual historical events dating to early dynastic times. During the 1920s, Percy Edward Newberry had suggested that the Horus myth of the Edfu Temple essentially narrated a Sethian rebellion under King Pery-yebusen of the 2nd Dynasty.[15] Also, John Gwyn Griffiths' seminal 1960 book *The conflict of Horus and Seth*, convincingly shows that the Horus and Seth saga was based on genuine historical events involving feuding followers of the two gods in predynastic Egypt.[16] The research of both Newberry and Griffiths therefore conclude, as I myself contend, that the epic feud between Horus and Seth dissimulates the record of an actual conflict between the ancient followers of these two gods. As Newberry astutely concludes, that conflict arose as a result of a rebellion of the disciples of Seth. Significantly, Newberry places that rebellion during Typhon Season #2. I indeed agree that a *second* Sethian rebellion erupted during the reign of Per-yebusen — one much modelled on the original rebellion. The Edfu Temple texts however are a record of the first Sethian rebellion during predynastic times.

Returning to the six hymns dedicated to Isis-Hathor from her temple at Philae, we find that the revengeful victory of Horus the Child over the perpetrators of the Sethian rebellion is likewise clearly delineated. In one particular hymn, we read:

> Praise to you Isis-Hathor,
> God's Mother, Lady of Heaven,
> Mistress of Abaton, queen of the gods.
> You are the divine mother of Horus,

---

[15] P. E. Newberry 'The Seth Rebellion of the IInd Dynasty.' In *Ancient Egypt* (1922), pp. 40-46.
[16] J. Gwyn Griffiths (1960) *The Conflict of Horus and Seth (From Egyptian and Classical Sources)*, Liverpool University Press: Liverpool, U.K.

> The Mighty Bull, avenger of his father,
> **Who causes the rebels to fall.** ...
> You are the divine mother of Horus,
> **Min-Horus,** the hero who smites his enemy,
> And makes a massacre thereby.[17]

Herodotus named Menes, the first dynastic Egyptian king, "Min." The God Min was already known during the predynastic era, but the title "Min-Horus" originates with Menes — whose name is obviously a variation of "Min" as Herodotus himself seems to have been aware of. In this hymn to Isis-Hathor, Min does not appear in his common guise of a fertility god, but more as an avenger god. Like Zabkar remarks:

> Horus identified with Min does not appear here in the capacity of a god of fertility and procreation, but in the role of Min as a redoubtable god, conqueror of hostile forces, as he is described in some Middle Kingdom hymns, which refer to him as 'Min-Horus, the powerful ... who overthrows his enemies, who avenges his father, and strikes the disaffected of heart' ... Having been incorporated into the Osirian cycle, Min became son of Isis and Osiris, another Horus, Min-Horus, and as such he could appropriately be addressed as protector and avenger of his father.[18]

Since Pharaoh Menes, as the primordial incarnation of Horus the Child, came along to avenge the death of his father Osiris by decimating the disciples of Seth, it becomes easy to identify Menes with Min-Horus. Thus, in the New Chronology Table, we find that the classical Khemetic pharaoh Ptolemy II, in whose reign the hymn to Isis-Hathor mentioning Min-Horus, presumably for the first time, was composed, was a contemporary of the dynastic Egyptian king Menes. This personification of Min-Horus becomes a vital anchor point in this revised history. The hymn cited earlier specifically identifies Isis-Hathor as the divine mother of Min-Horus — Horus the Child. We also learn that Min-Horus overcame the "rebels" who had been responsible for Osiris' death and the ensuing disorder in the balance of nature or Ma'at. All these attributes and events fit perfectly well with Aha-Menes and the circumstances which brought him to power.

An oft-repeated refrain in the texts of the Edfu Temple, which reads: "Hold fast, Horus, Hold fast!", urges Horus on in his fight against "Him" — Seth in hippopotamus form.[19] Horus is repeatedly encouraged "to seize, take possession of"[20] the

---

[17] L. V. Zabkar (1983) p. 118.
[18] Ibid, p. 120.
[19] John Gwyn Griffiths (1976b) 'BRIEF COMMUNICATIONS: A refrain in the texts of the Edfu Temple', *Journal of Egyptian Archaeology* 62, pp. 186-187.
[20] Ibid, p. 187.

dominion of Seth. We recall that after Horus the Behdetite, who had transformed himself into a winged sun-disk, had mercilessly annihilated the Sethian disciples under the orders of Re at the end of Typhon Season #1, the perpetrators of the Sethian rebellion changed themselves into crocodiles and hippopotami. Chronologically speaking, we behold that it was Horus the Elder's fight against Seth that preceded the confrontation between Horus the Child and Seth's disciples. Therefore, the Ptolemaic hunting scene — where Horus sets out to capture and kill the Sethian hippopotamus — represents the historic confrontation between the proto-dynastic Egyptians and the A-Group Ta-Seti Nubians. Another place where we find a contemporary record of this very same battle is in the territory of the Ta-Seti themselves — in the royal cemetery of Qustul; where we will now turn our attention.

The Great Battle of the Sixth Generation of Ta-Seti

(The Emergence of the Egyptian Dynastic State)

An increasingly large number of Egyptologists have, over the past fifty years, begun to question the long-accepted understanding that the first Egyptian dynasty arose in the thirty-second century BCE.[21] Many of them, like Albright,[22] Stock,[23] Scharff & Moortgat,[24] and slightly earlier, Heinrich Schäfer (1868-1957)[25] of the 'Berlin School,' have advanced the view that dynastic Egypt saw its beginning later — somewhere around 2,900 BCE. Favouring this lower-dating trend, I have opted for a date of *c.*2,950 BCE for the advent of Pharaoh Aha-Menes at Thinis-Abydos. Therefore, the great Nubian campaign in which Pharaoh Aha-Menes records the smiting of Ta-Seti early in his reign must necessarily date to *c.*2,950 BCE. At the A-Group royal cemetery at Qustul, scholars have unearthed evidence for just such a devastating proto-dynastic Egyptian attack at the end of the sixth generation of the Ta-Seti pharaohs. According to Nubiologist Bruce Williams, the royal

---

[21] Michael Rice (1991) pp. xvi, xviii.
[22] William F. Albright 'Some Remarks on the Archaeological Chronology of Palestine before about 1500 B.C.' In Robert W. Ehrich (editor) (1965) *Chronologies in Old World Archaeology*, p. 50.
[23] Hanns Stock (1949) *Studia Aegyptiaca II: Die erste Zwischenzeit Ägyptens*, Analecta Orientalia, 31.
[24] Alexander Schraff & Anton Moortgat (1950) *Ägypten und Vorderasien im Altertum*, Bruckmann: Munich.
[25] Heinrich Schäfer (1974) *Principles of Egyptian Art*. Trans. and ed. by John Baines. Clarendon Press: Oxford, p. 9.

tombs at Qustul diminished considerably in size and, subsequently, A-Group culture altogether vanished from Lower Nubia. Quoting Prof. Bruce Williams:

> Apparently, the demise of Qustul coincides with the campaign of Aha in Nubia, the first king of the Egyptian First Dynasty, who recorded the smiting of Ta-Seti. Afterward, the A-Group culture ceased to exist in Lower Nubia.[26]

Likewise, McGill University anthropologist Bruce Trigger writes:

> For all practical purposes, the A-Group appears to have vanished from Lower Nubia before the end of the First Dynasty.[27]

If archaeologists accept a thirty-second century BCE date for the beginning of the A-Group cemetery at Qustul, and that its ultimate destruction from the hands of Aha-Menes took place at the end of the sixth generation of Ta-Seti, how is it then possible for these very same scholars to accept a thirty-second century BCE date for the advent of the 1st Dynasty at Thinis-Abydos? Logically speaking, this is impossible. Egyptologists accept that a generation lasted from thirty to forty years. In the present chronology, we observe that the six generations of active Ta-Seti culture in Lower Nubia lasted from between 3,166 BCE and c.2,950. As we have demonstrated earlier in Chapter 1, we can actually fine tune the date for the establishment of the 1st Dynasty by correlating it with the heliacal rising of 2,953 BCE. Therefore, the lapse of time between the beginning of Ta-Seti culture to the rise of dynastic Egypt amounts to about thirty-six years per generation. At the end of those six generations, in 2,953 BCE, the proto-dynastic Egyptians decimated these Sethian disciples. For that reason, Horus the Child had at last exacted his revenge for the murder of his father Osiris in the hands of Seth. Having rid Egypt of the rebellious disciples of Seth, both Horus kingships, i.e. Horus the Elder in the Black Land and Horus the Child in the Red Land, reigned supreme over the Khemeto-Egyptian horizon. Meanwhile, at Philae and Dendera, Isis-Hathor, the wife of Horus the Elder and mother of Horus the Child, completed this harmonious royal triad.

The Cosmogony of Thinis-Abydos and the Memphite Theology Revisited

There is a strong possibility that the unification of dynastic Egypt under Pharaoh Aha-Menes was triggered by the heliacal rising of Sirius in 2,953 BCE. As the con-

---

[26] Bruce Williams (1980) 'The Lost Pharaohs of Nubia', *Archaeology* 33, p. 21.
[27] Bruce Trigger (1976) *Nubia Under the Pharaohs*, Westview Press: Boulder, Col., p. 44.

stellation of Orion which accompanied the dog star Sirius represented the god Osiris, Horus the Child, then still dwelling in God's Land, seized upon this symbolic opportunity to avenge the murder of his heavenly father. Therefore, the timing of the final extermination of the disciples of Seth was connected to a meaningful celestial event. Incidentally, Osiris-Orion had returned as a celestial deity — seeking justice for the crime perpetrated against him by Seth. Likewise, the proto-dynastic pharaohs' decision to, not only continue to adhere to the Memphite Theology, but also to rewrite it in order to acknowledge the final victory of Horus the Falcon was very determinant. Thus, the Memphite Theology continued to be a "work in progress" long after the death of Djoser-Netjerykhet. The only extant version of the Memphite Theology which modern Egyptologists rely upon was written down during the Ethiopian dynasty of the eighth century BCE — in the form of a document known as the Shabaka Stone. Therefore, we can only be entirely certain that the Memphite Theology was composed, as it is know today, from this time on. Furthermore, since the Memphite Theology of Pharaoh Shabaka's time included within it obvious aspects of both the Heliopolitan and Hermopolitan theologies, Egyptologists assume that the Memphite Theology was the last of these three ancient cosmogonies to be devised — with the Heliopolitan Theology as the most ancient one of course. But as I shall argue throughout Chapter 6, the Hermopolitan Theology was only composed during the twenty-second century BCE. Therefore, the Memphite Theology must have in reality been the second cosmogony, followed by the Middle Egyptian Hermopolitan Theology several centuries later.

Where we last left the Memphite Theology, during the reign of King Djoser-Netjerykhet, the followers of Seth and Horus each occupied a part of the Two Lands. Such was the arrangement, as decreed by the earth-god Geb, following the murder of Osiris. As we have observed, there was a very real historical background to this mythical tale. But the story does not end there. Later on, we are told that Geb realized that he had made a mistake, and decided that it was not right to have divided Egypt equally between Horus and Seth. So, revising his initial decision, he awarded the whole of Osiris' inheritance to Horus. Archaeotheologically speaking, King Aha-Menes of the 1st Dynasty, personified the Horus figure who ultimately won the eschatological battle against Seth, the god of chaos. From that point onwards, the clear setting of the conflict is that Horus "was the leading god of Lower Egypt in a predynastic conquest of Upper Egypt."[28] As a result, the notion of a Horus-led conquest of Upper Egypt was never raised at the time of the Memphite Theology's original inception during Typhon Season #1. It had been understood that Seth occupied Upper Egypt and that Horus was meant to rule Lower Egypt. It is only after the end of King Djoser-Netjerykhet's reign that Horus sought to regain control of Upper Egypt. Thus, taking advantage of the turmoil which resulted from the Venus shift of

---

[28] J. Gwyn Griffith (1960) p. 140.

3,114 BCE, the kingship of Horus the Elder retook Upper Egypt, their former capital at Edfu, from the hands of the disciples of Seth. Nonetheless, the seed of Ta-Seti's power would not be entirely eradicated until Horus the Child, through Pharaoh Aha-Menes' punitive expedition, drove them out of Lower Nubia altogether. With these crucial new developments, the Memphite Theology had to be amended.

Mesopotamia and Early Dynastic Egypt

The new Horus kingship which established itself at Thinis-Abydos in 2,950 BCE imported into Egypt many elements of it's Levantine culture. It has often been observed by scholars that the languages spoken by the dynastic Egyptians and the desert Asiatics had a common origin. Indeed, Semitic elements are distinctively present in the language of the dynastic Egyptians.[29] This leaves no doubt that the origins of the dynastic Egyptians were indeed Asiatic. As I've already pointed out, those Early Bronze I Asiatics, who later became the proto-dynastic Egyptians, were taught the pharaonic arts and language during the colonization of Syria-Palestine by Narmer-Osiris. As we know, this is not how modern Egyptologists interpret the rise of dynastic Egypt. Ancient historians have long puzzled over how the predynastic Egyptians managed to formulate such a complex writing system as the pharaonic hieroglyphics in such a short period of time. Quite inexplicably, the necessary foundation for a civilization which would last for over three thousand years, came to fruition in a comparatively fleeting moment. Egyptologists, like the late William C. Hayes, have indeed long been acutely perplexed by this enigma:

> Owing to the scantiness of the material from the Late Predynastic period, the written language seems to appear suddenly, already at an advanced stage of development, at the beginning of the First Dynasty.[30]

Many scholars have argued that this unequivocally proves that the system of writing was introduced into Egypt from abroad — specifically Sumeria.[31] But Hayes argued that this is not likely to be the case,[32] as we can clearly discern its epigraphic roots in earlier prehistoric Egyptian Dynasties. Yet, the Mesopotamian influence on early dynastic Egypt remains undeniable. In my revised historical scheme, these apparent contradictions do not exist. As Hayes rightly points out, the epigra-

---

[29] Michael Rice (1991) p. 65.
[30] William C. Hayes (1990 [1959]) *The Scepter of Egypt*, Vol. I: p. 37.
[31] See John A. Wilson (1968) *The Culture of Ancient Egypt*, University of Chicago Press: Chicago, Ill., pp. 38-39.
[32] William C. Hayes (1990 [1959]) Vol. I: p. 37.

CHAP. II: A NEW BEGINNING | 143

phic roots of the pharaonic script indeed belong in the Nile Valley. Once the hieroglyphic script was carried into Syria-Palestine by Narmer, it was partially modified by the Asiatic locals who introduced some Asiatic loan-words into this newly acquired language. It was that Afro-Asiatic language which later, during EBII, came to characterize dynastic Egyptian civilization. Therefore, the intrinsically illusory meteoric speed with which the dynastic race whipped up pharaonic culture can be explained by the fact that they had borrowed from the much older Khemetic culture. The following chronological table sums up the development of pharaonic culture prior and up to dynastic times in Egypt, in relation to pre/proto-dynastic Mesopotamia:

Comparative Table of Early Mesopotamian and Early Egyptian Chronologies:

MESOPOTAMIA		EGYPT	
Ubaid I	5,000 to 4,500 BCE	Fayum	5,000 to 4,500 BCE
Ubaid II	4,500 to 4,000 BCE	Badarian	4,500 to 4,000 BCE
Early Uruk	4,000 to 3,500 BCE	Naqada I	4,000 to 3,600 BCE
Uruk IV	3,500 to 3,200 BCE	Naqada II	3,600 to 3,200 BCE
Uruk III	3,200 to 2,900 BCE	Hierakonpolite	3,200 to 3,166 BCE
		Memphite	3,166 to 3,114 BCE
		Transitional	3,114 to 2,950 BCE
Early Dynastic	2,900 BCE - ...	Early Dynastic	2,950 BCE - ...

Table 2-1

The new chronology removes a great deal of the sheer abruptness with which dynastic pharaonic culture appears in the mid-thirtieth century BCE. Hence, we find that searching for the origins of pharaonic culture in Mesopotamia is wholly unnecessary. What is true nonetheless is that archaic Syria-Palestine lay in the joint sphere of influence of the two cultural superpowers of the time: Khemet and Mesopotamia. The dynastic Egyptian kinship of Horus the Child, emanating from Phoenicia (or God's Land), is partially the result of the meeting of these two mother civilizations. Although the most direct influence came from Khemet.

As we have found plausible traces of the Osiris legend in the Syro-Palestinian pantheon in the previous chapter, it is likewise intriguing to find striking similarities between the myth associated with the "Eridu figures" from Sumeria, and the Egyptian story as it develops after the slaying of Osiris by Seth.[33] As we know, once Osiris had been torn to pieces by his jealous brother, Isis conceived a god-child from the semen of her deceased husband, and protected her divine offspring (the future

---

[33] Michael Rice (1991) p. 54.

avenger of his father) from the serpentine deity, Seth. In the Sumerian tale, the pottery figures from Eridu likewise feature a snake-figure epitomizing evil, who is opposed to a female goddess whose role it is to protect a divine infant from the menacing clutches of a reptilian creature. While it is difficult to ascertain whether or not this was *entirely* a Khemetic influence, we can at least presume that these two eerily similar legends were born out of the same celestial observation of the catastrophic movements of the heavenly bodies. Certainly, both the dynastic Egyptian and Mesopotamian early dynasties of the thirtieth century BCE were at a some level influenced, either through direct contact or trade relations, by the ancient Khemetic interpretation of these cataclysmic heavenly battles. Indeed, as Sir E. A. Wallis Budge observes:

> It would be wrong to say that the Egyptians borrowed from the Sumerians or the Sumerians from the Egyptians, but it may be submitted that the literati of both peoples borrowed their theological systems from some common but exceedingly ancient source.[34]

That "exceedingly ancient source" was none other than the Khemetic culture of the Anu. With the expansion of Narmer-Osiris' Asiatic empire during Naqada III times, and Mesopotamia's own distant forays,[35] varying version of the basic Osirian story spread throughout the ancient Near East. The Khemetic story of the goddess Hathor's Destruction of Mankind likewise finds its counterparts in various ancient legends about other goddesses representing the planet Venus. The Sumerian goddess Inanna, like her Akkadian counterpart Ishtar (both Venus-goddesses), symbolized "thunderstorms, war, and the morning and evening stars."[36] The correlation of the planet Venus with these elements of chaos and universal disorder was a universal characteristic of the religious paradigms or cosmogonies of the ancient civilizations from the nascent Bronze Age. Evidently, all these peoples had experienced the very same ruinous ravages wrought on by the Venus shift of 3,114 BCE. Their shared ordeal and collective apprehension were rendered into epic legends of planetary gods fighting amongst each other and against the earth dwellers.

---

[34] Sir E. A. Wallis Budge (1934) *From Fetish to God in Ancient Egypt*, Oxford University Press: London, p. 155.

[35] Archaeological evidence have been found to substantiate the theory of the existence of ancient trading networks (3,300-2,000 BCE) linking the Nile Valley with Iran and Mesopotamia with Afghanistan. See Martin Bernal (1991) p. 69.

[36] Walter R. Bodine 'Sumerians.' In Alfred J. Hoerth, Gerald L. Mattingly & Edwin M. Yamauchi (editors) (1994) *Peoples of the Old Testament World*, pp. 24-25.

The Asiatic Threat

No sooner had the dynastic race established itself in the Egyptian Delta, that the proto-dynastic pharaohs already found themselves in conflict with their Asiatic cousins in the Levant. It is indeed abundantly evident that from the 1st and 2nd Dynasties, the Egyptians were conducting warfare against "the Asiatics" of the Levant. Available evidence form early EBII sites in Syria-Palestine demonstrates this fact conclusively. The early dynastic Egyptians considered the Asiatics as unkempt and uncivilized barbarians. They would often described those EBII Palestinians as "beyond the pale," "kilt wearers" and "people of the bow."[37] The Asiatics owed the latter appellation to their characteristic use of the bow and arrow for means of subsistence hunting and war. These "wild men of Asia," as the Egyptians also called them, frequently hijacked and harassed Egyptian caravans and troops. The fact that they were likewise specifically referred to as "those-who-are-across-the-sand," is an obvious indication that they also dwelled beyond the Sinai Peninsula. It appears as though these Asiatic hordes from the Sinai moved into the Syro-Palestinian territories left behind by the proto-dynastic pharaohs. This theory is supported by the sudden appearance of Asiatic fortifications at Arad in the Negev of Israel from the start of the EBII period.[38] From the extant archaeological evidence, we can surmise that clear trade relations existed between the Egyptians and the Asiatics. But scholars have yet to explain exactly how the 1st and 2nd Dynasty kings could have managed to extend their sphere of influence beyond the Sinai. Much less clear is the exact nature of the relationship between the two peoples.

It is entirely probable that the early dynastic Egyptians had already developed a form of trade alliance with those Asiatics from beyond the Sinai back during the time when they dwelled in the Syro-Palestinian territories. Those regions were now occupied by these new Asiatic settlers. This means that their *continuing* relationship with them, once they relocated in the Egyptian Delta, would serve to explain how those trading links were formed. Therefore, in retrospect, the proto-dynastic Egyptians' sphere of influence did not expand from Egypt to the Levant, but from the Levant to Egypt's Delta. The early trading links with the Asiatics were actually already fomented *before* King Aha-Menes unified dynastic Egypt. The fact that the dynastic Egyptians no longer had their base in Palestine during the EBII period might have caused hostilities to flare between the two peoples. The Asiatics saw this as an opportunity to extend their territorial power beyond the Arabian peninsula and into Syria-Palestine. To the dynastic Egyptians, their advance denoted an ever-pending threat to both their regional hegemony and internal security.

---

[37] Donald B. Redford (1992) *Egypt, Canaan, and Israel in Ancient Times*, Princeton University Press: Princeton, NJ, pp. 31-32.
[38] Ibid, p. 35.

As later events would ultimately reveal, those Egyptian fears for their domestic security were well founded. These wild men of Asia would eventually come to exemplify the very chaotic elements of nature. Positioned beyond the borders of the divinely regulated world of Ma'at, the Asiatic multitudes came to be seen as the new disciples or agents of Seth. But for the time being, yet another cosmic paroxysm would once again, and quite unexpectedly, force the dynastic Egyptians to contend with Sethian disciples within their own borders.

More Sethian Chaos: The Universal Order is Disturbed

According to both Africanus and Eusebius (Manetho, FR. 8), a chasm or earthquake opened at Bubastis during the 2nd Dynasty — causing many to perish. They also maintain that in the reign of King Kaiechôs (Khasekhemwy) three different cults were practised in Egypt. Namely, that of the Apis bull in Memphis, Mnevis at Heliopolis, and the Mendesian goat. The natural catastrophe that caused many to perish during the 2nd Dynasty was a Mercury shift dated to c.2,780 BCE. Heralding the second 52-year-long Typhon Season, the planet Mercury's violent erring from its set orbital path once again set loose the disruptive elements of Sethian chaos. Amidst the ensuing civil turmoil, a second Sethian rebellion erupted in Egypt. As was the case during Typhon Season #1, the Two Lands became divided between the followers of Horus and the disciples of Seth. This time around, the rebellious Sethian disciples were not foreigners, but actually the kings of the second half of the 2nd Dynasty themselves. As was the case during the primeval Sethian rebellion, the followers of Seth governed the southern part of Egypt. Meanwhile in the Egyptian Delta, were found the followers of Horus — as the Memphite Theology dictated should be the case during a Typhon Season. As the 2nd Dynasty fulfilled the role of Seth in Upper Egypt, a brand new dynasty – the 3rd Dynasty – was inaugurated in Lower Egypt. So this means that the 3rd Dynasty was contemporaneous with the 2nd Dynasty. Since Egyptologists, like W. C. Hayes,[39] accept that the 3rd Dynasty began in 2,780 BCE, the date fits perfectly with the beginning of Typhon Season #2. Since there are no exact dates to pin-point when the 52-year-period began and ended in this case, the closest possible round estimation falls between c.2,780 BCE and c.2,730 BCE.

The elusive reason why certain kings of the 2nd Dynasty oddly chose to dedicate their reign to Seth has long been debated among scholars. The notion of a rebellion by a group of Seth's followers has been a popular explanation. As mentioned earlier, Egyptologist John Gwyn Griffiths had rightly conjectured that King Pery-yebusen had headed a Sethian rebellion. Quite abruptly, he adopted a Sethian prenomen

---

[39] William C. Hayes (1990 [1959]) *The Scepter of Egypt*, Vol. I: p. 58.

and became openly hostile to the followers of Horus in Lower Egypt — who had no choice but to form a Horus dynasty of their own under King Tety (The Horus Khaba). The Sethian capital was set up at Ombos in Upper Egypt. In open defiance, Pharaoh Pery-yebusen proclaimed himself king of the Two Lands by declaring that: *"The Ombite (Seth – Lord of Ombos) has given the Two Lands to his son Peribsen."* His immediate Sethian successor at Ombos, King Khasekhemwy, recorded on a vase inscription:

> The year of **fighting the Northern enemy** within the city of Nekheb the goddess Nekheb grasps the rebels, and unites Egypt before the Horus Khasekhem (Kasekhemwy)[40]

Pharaoh Khasekhemwy, as the above inscription indicates, was eager to continue the hostilities against the 3rd Dynasty monarchs in the north. But he appears to have nonetheless been sympathetic to the Horus cult. His ambivalence was reflected by his rather enigmatic dual allegiance to both Seth and Horus. Perhaps his attempt was to unify the Sethian and Horus kingships under the Upper Egyptian vulture-goddess Nekhebet, as the above text clearly implies. Khasekhemwy's efforts seem to have partially successful; but the final unification, under a Horus pharaoh, did not come about until the end of Typhon Season #2.

The Reaffirmation of the Memphite Theology's

Central Importance in Egypt's Historical Cycle

The emplacement of Bubastis as the site where the mid-2nd Dynasty Mercury-induced chasm manifested itself, according to Africanus and Eusebius, is of primary significance. Bastet, the daughter of Re, consort of Ptah, and mistress of Bubastis, was closely assimilated with the furious lion-goddess Sekhmet. All of these associations are intimately Typhonian in nature. It therefore comes as no surprise that the Memphite Theology reasserts its dominance during this time of political disunity between the followers of Seth and Horus. Adequately reflecting the very divisive religious and political situation prevalent during Typhon Season #2, the Shabaka Stone records:

> [Geb, lord of gods, commanded] that the Ennead gather to him. He judged between Horus and Seth; he ended this quarrel. He made Seth king of Upper Egypt in the land of Upper Egypt, up to the place where he was born, which is Su. And Geb made Horus king of Lower Egypt in the land of Lower Egypt,

---

[40] M. E. Moncton Jones (1924) *Ancient Egypt from the Records*, Methuen: London, p. 14.

up to the place where his father (Osiris) was drowned, which is 'Division of the Two Lands'. Thus Horus stood over one region, and Seth over one region. They made peace over the Two Lands at Ayan. That was the division of the Two Lands.[41]

Naturally, the archaeotheological context is precisely the same as we find in Typhon Season #1. The similarity is not, by all means, coincidental. The Mercury shift of 2,780 BCE triggered a series of events which were, premeditatedly, patterned after the theological crisis which was engendered by the precedent setting Mercury shift of 3,166 BCE. The followers of Seth who suddenly erupted unto the scene during the middle of the 2nd Dynasty did not choose their moment haphazardly. They took their cue from the Mercury-induced conflagration. Recognizing the significance of this parallel, the priesthood of the Two Lands reasserted the primacy of the Memphite Theology.

The Black Land Reasserts its Power Over the Red Land

The period between the establishment of dynastic Egypt under King Aha-Menes and the Mercury shift of 2,780 BCE was quite peculiar in the sense that two Horus kingships, Horus the Elder in Upper Egypt (Black Land) and Horus the Child in Lower Egypt (Red Land), reigned in relative independence from each other. The arrangement between the older African Horus kingship and the new Asiatic one seems to have carried on smoothly. What's more, as it's worth noting, from the beginning of the 2nd Dynasty there was a clear rapprochement between the Seth district of Kom Ombo, aligned to the classic Ptolemaic kingship, and the Memphite pharaohs. This can especially be gleaned from the throne name which the first pharaoh of the 2nd Dynasty chose to adopt: Hotepsekhemwy — which stands for "the two powers are at peace." An increased openness to Khemetic culture was also evident on the part of the proto-dynastic kings with Pharaoh Reneb, Hotepsekhemwy's immediate successor, choosing to include the name of the Heliopolitan sun-god Re in his own name. These trends were all leading to the eventual unification of power under one theological construct. But before this were to take place, a tremendous power struggle ensued between these two disparate ruling centres.

Along with the outbreak of the second Sethian rebellion in 2,780 BCE, a *coup d'état* was taking place in the Black Land. A new Khemetic ruler, apparently not affiliated with the classic Ptolemaic succession line, emerged and deposed the Edfu and Philae monarchs. Objecting to the conciliatory stance adopted by the classic Ptolemaic rulers toward the nascent Horus kingship in the north, he sought to revive the

---

[41] Barry J. Kemp (1989) *Ancient Egypt: Anatomy of a Civilization*, Routledge: London and New York, p. 30.

CHAP. II: A NEW BEGINNING | 149

old Khemetic imperialist traditions of Pharaohs Narmer and Djoser-Netjerykhet's days. A staunch follower of Horus, he instituted his capital at the Anu's primeval capital at Elephantine and adhered to the cults of Re and Khnum. The name of this Khemetic pharaoh was Khufu. Indeed, in the words of Herodotus, Pharaoh Khufu at once had all the temples of Egypt closed down.[42] I am convinced that Herodotus, probably unbeknownst to himself, was not transmitting an account from the reign of the 4th Dynasty Egyptian pharaoh Khufu, but of an earlier Khemetic namesake. I propose that the name of the Pharaoh Khufu who reigned from Elephantine, contemporaneously with the 2nd and 3rd Dynasties, was *Khnum-khuefui* (or Khnum-Khufu) — meaning: "Khnum is protecting me." Probing this controversy, African-centered scholar Wayne B. Chandler writes:

> The name Khufu and Khnum-Khuf has been found in various locations throughout Egypt. Though they appear together it is not really known if Khnum-Khuf is another name for Khufu or if it is truly another individual. Both of these names appear in the Great Pyramid but the cartouches of Khnum-Khuf are far more numerous. As stated earlier, we know virtually nothing of this king, with the exception that he is purported to have built the greatest structure on earth.[43]

My hypothesis is that Khnum-Khufu was indeed "truly another individual." Seizing power coercively in *c.*2,780 BCE, he went on ruling for the entire fifty-two-year duration of Typhon Season #2. According to Herodotus (II: 127), Khufu reigned for fifty years. Most Egyptologists however estimate the length of the 4th Dynasty pharaoh Khufu's reign in the vicinity of twenty-five years. Hence, the majority of contemporary scholars would argue that Herodotus' figure for the length of Khufu's reign is much inflated. That's only of course if one accepts the hypothesis that Herodotus is referring ultimately to the 4th Dynasty ruler. Throughout much of ancient Egypt's history, Pharaoh Khufu was remembered particularly for his alleged cruelty. Even today, many Egyptologists speak of his "despotic" rule. In the words of Herodotus:

> ... but Cheops, who was the next king, brought the people to utter misery. For first he shut up all the temples, so that none could sacrifice there; and next, he compelled all the Egyptians to work for him, appointing to some to drag stones from the quarries in the Arabian mountains to the Nile ... For ten years the people were afflicted in making the road whereon the stones were

---

[42] Herodotus, Book II: 128.
[43] Wayne B. Chandler 'Of Gods and Men: Egypt's Old Kingdom.' In Ivan Van Sertima (editor) (1989a) *Egypt Revisited*, p. 161.

> dragged ... The pyramid [of Khufu] itself was twenty years in the making.
> (Herodotus, Book II: 124)

Herodotus observes also that the people of Egypt "hated the memory" of Khufu. Citing an ancient Egyptian papyrus, contemporary Egyptologist Barry J. Kemp imparts:

> Papyrus Westcar tells the story as a prelude to introducing the ultra-pious kings of the succeeding 5th Dynasty, the point evidently being that by arrogant and offensive behaviour, Khufu brought doom to his house.[44]

Since, as Wayne B. Chandler illuminates, the majority of the royal cartouches affiliated with the Great Pyramid at Gizah belong to the Khemetic pharaoh Khnum-Khufu, and that, as Herodotus claims, his reputation as a cruel monarch was partially earned from his pyramid building activities, then we must deduce that Pharaoh Khnum-Khufu was indeed the builder of the Great Pyramid. King Khnum-Khufu enlisted labourers from dynastic Egypt to bring his gigantic project to fruition. While his work force was not composed of slaves, it is indeed very likely that the physical and economic expenses incurred for the construction of the Great Pyramid were very taxing on the people of dynastic Egypt. Pharaoh Khnum-Khufu may have actually viewed the construction of the Gizah complex as a golden opportunity to subdue the Asiatic proto-dynastic kings — whom he thought had grown much too independent and powerful.

Heaven on Earth: The Gizah Pyramids and the Great Sphinx

The notion that the Great Pyramid at Gizah could have been built decades before the advent of the 4th Dynasty raises several fundamental questions. First, it's always been thought that the three pyramids on the Gizah plateau were erected by three different pharaohs of the 4th Dynasty, namely: Khufu, Khafre and Menkaure. Only the name of Khnum-Khufu appears inside the Great Pyramid. The other two pyramids bear no royal inscriptions whatsoever. How can we then be sure that these three pharaohs built the three pyramids in the order traditionally prescribed? Two authors who've pondered these questions in recent years are Robert Bauval and Adrian Gilbert:

> Why did Sneferu, Khufu (Cheops) and the others not inscribe their pyramids? Never mind posterity, why leave the gods guessing who was responsible for these monuments? Did the Fourth Dynasty kings not re-

---
[44] Barry J. Kemp (1989) p. 24.

Fig. 2i: Pharaoh Khnum-Khufu.

Fig. 2j: The Gizah pyramids (Khufu & Khafre).

Fig. 2k: The Great Sphinx.

Fig. 21: Exterior and interior of Khnum-Khufu's Great Pyramid.

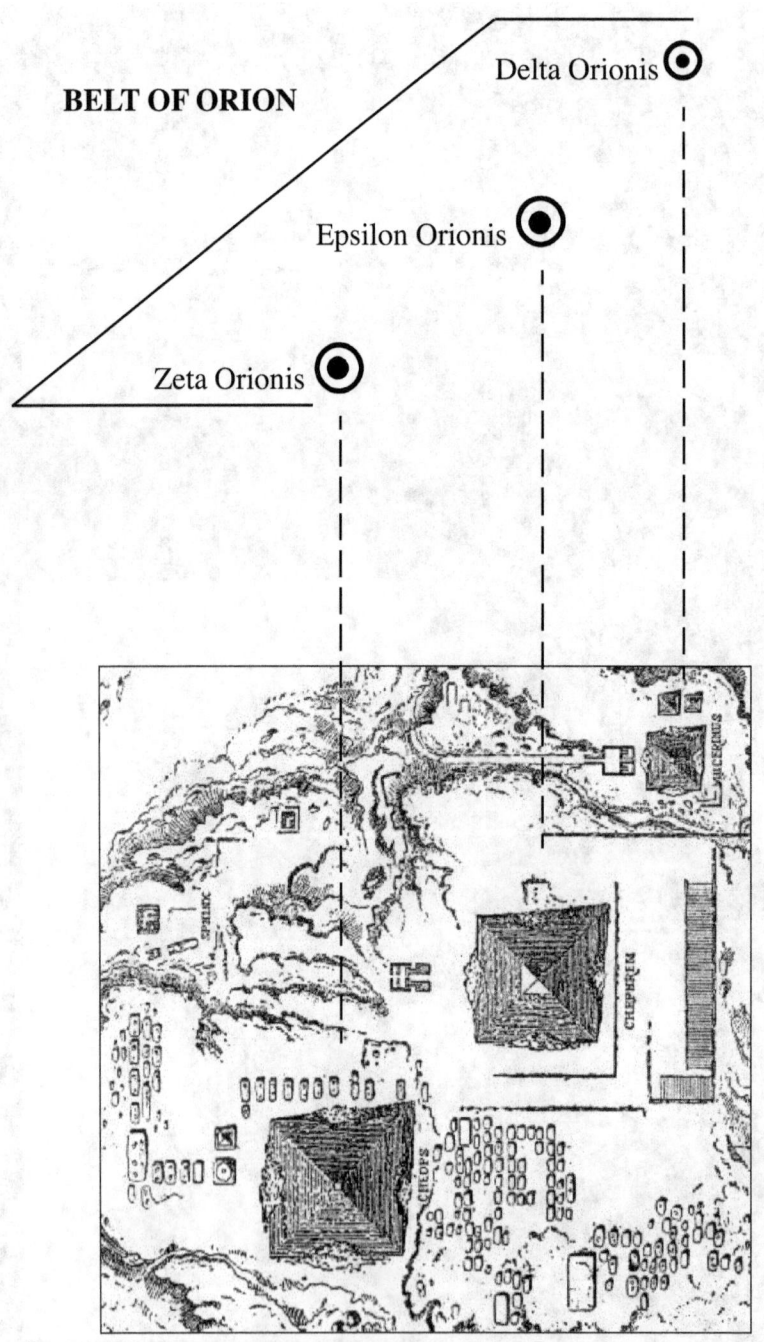

Fig. 2m: Star correlation pattern.

gard themselves as individual owners of the pyramids? Is it possible that all the Fourth Dynasty pyramids were part of a single scheme, which required the building of seven different pyramids at specific locations?[45]

I believe that Bauval and Gilbert are on the right track when they postulate that the three Gizah pyramids were part of a single overall plan. Moreover, I am convinced that Pharaoh Khnum-Khufu was himself responsible for the construction of all three pyramids, including the Great Sphinx. What exactly could have motivated Khnum-Khufu to undertake such an enormous project? Why three pyramids? What was the significance of the Great Sphinx? To begin answering these perplexing questions, I turn once again to the ground breaking work of Bauval and Gilbert. For example, in their best selling book entitled *The Orion Mystery*, Robert Bauval tells of a fateful camping expedition he undertook in Saudi Arabia's desert, on a clear night, in early November of 1983. He, along with family members and friends, sat on the dunes admiring the starry sky. Later that night, Bauval and a friend awoke to gaze at the constellation of Orion. Out of the blue, Bauval's companion observed that the three stars of Orion's Belt are not perfectly aligned and that the smallest of them is slightly offset to the right. Then, in a striking moment of inspiration, Robert Bauval came to the sudden realization that up there was the enigmatic pattern of the Gizah plateau's three pyramids. The pyramids on the ground were a reproduction of the Belt of Orion (see Fig. 2m). Subsequently extending his search for an even grander pattern, Robert Bauval also discovered a possible continuation of this Orion constellation outline by carefully observing the emplacement of two other pyramids: that of Zawyat-al-Aryan, located just six kilometres to the northwest of the Gizah plateau, and the pyramid of Abu Ruwash, situated in the south-east. Since we've seen in the previous chapter that the ancient Khemites associated the constellation of Orion with the god Osiris, these two distant pyramids appear to delineate, respectively, the right shoulder and knee of Osiris-Orion. The fact that an inscription from the pyramid of Zawyat-al-Aryan suggests that the edifice was constructed by either King Nebku or King Neferkare would in turn indicate that the pyramid was erected during the 3rd Dynasty.[46] Confirming this notion, French Egyptologist Nicholas Grimal has recently hypothesised that this pyramid erected at Zawyat-al-Aryan *"dates stylistically to the Third Dynasty."*[47] Therefore, on the basis

---

[45] Robert Bauval and Adrian Gilbert (1994) *The Orion Mystery (Unlocking the Secrets of the Pyramids)*, Doubleday Canada: Toronto, p. 33.
[46] Nicholas Grimal (1992) *A History of Ancient Egypt*. Trans. by Ian Shaw. Blackwell: Oxford, U.K., p. 66.
[47] Nicholas Grimal (1992) p. 67.

of the star-correlation theory, the three pyramids of the Gizah plateau must likewise date to the 3rd Dynasty — when Khnum-Khufu reigned from Elephantine.

Pharaoh Khnum-Khufu's preoccupation with the constellation of Orion, and hence the cult of Osiris, is not at all difficult to comprehend. His wholehearted longing to reinvigorate the primeval Khemetic religious traditions, which his revered ancestors – the Anu – had instituted, can arguably have Pharaoh Khnum-Khufu credited with saving Heliopolitan Theology from the brinks of extinction. Not particularly concerned with the sophomoric squabbles between the dynastic followers of Horus and Seth, a domain of the Memphite Theology, he placed pre-eminent emphasis on the solar cult of Re. The pyramid complex at Gizah, including the Great Sphinx, was therefore meant to be an everlasting testament to the Khemetic Heliopolitan Theology.

The connection which I hereby make between the Sphinx of Gizah and Pharaoh Khnum-Khufu is, as pretty much everything else in this book, quite controversial. It still is largely the Gospel around Egyptological circles that the Great Sphinx of Gizah was carved by the 4th Dynasty pharaoh Khafre, in his own image. Challenging this accepted view, I maintain that the Great Sphinx was not carved to represent any given living pharaoh at all, but instead symbolized the Khemetic deity Atum Kheprer (or Khepri). The following passage (utterance 600) from the Pyramid Texts, dating to the Old Kingdom's 5th Dynasty, articulates the duties and characteristics of Atum-Khepri:

> Atum Kheprer, you have come to be high on the hill, you have arisen on the Benben stone in the mansion of the Benben in Heliopolis, you spat out Shu, you expectorated Tefnut, and you put two arms around them as the arms of a ka symbol, so that your ka (personality) might be in them. O Atum, place your arms around the king, around this edifice, around this pyramid as the arms of a ka, so that the King's ka may be in it, firm forever and ever. O Atum, place your protection over this king, over this pyramid of his ...
> O great Ennead which is in Heliopolis - Atum, Shu, Tefnut, Geb, Nut, Osiris Isis, Seth, Nephthys - children of Atum, extend his heart (good-will) to his child (the king) in your name of nine Bows.[48]

In the Heliopolitan Theology, the *benben* is the incarnation of the sun as creator. The *benben* stone was also meant to symbolize the petrified rays of the sun which would lead the king on his journey up to the heavens.[49] Carved from a symbolic *benben* stone, the Great Sphinx was there to assist the pharaoh in his final journey

---

[48] Leonard H. Lesko 'Ancient Egyptian Cosmogonies and Cosmology.' In Shafer, Byron E. (editor) (1991) *Religion in Ancient Egypt (Gods, Myths, and Personal Practice)*, p. 92.
[49] Nicholas Grimal (1992) p. 127.

as he became one with Osiris. Again, the Heliopolitan theological aspects are at the forefront. Highlighting this pivotal correlation between the Great Sphinx and Atum-Khepri, James Henry Breasted writes:

> Now, the very great statue (the Great Sphinx) of Khepri, rests in its place; the great in prowess, the splendid in strength; upon which the shadow of Re tarries. ...
> A vision of sleep seized him (Tuthmosis IV) at the hour (when) the sun was in the zenith, and he found the majesty of this revered god speaking with his own mouth, as a father speaks to his son, saying: "Behold thou me! See thou me! my son Thutmose. I am thy father, Harmakhis Khepri-Re-Atum, who will give to thee my kingdom on earth at the head of the living."[50]

The Sphinx must be seen as the embodiment of the three major solar deities of Khemet: Khepri (the morning sun), Re (the sun during the day), and Atum (the setting sun). As a manifestation of Khepri, the rising sun, the Sphinx was also there, as alluded to previously, to symbolize the return to life or "resurrection" of Osiris-Orion.

The principal piece of evidence to which Egyptologists cling for identifying the Great Sphinx with the Old Kingdom king Khafre is the following excerpt from the New Kingdom pharaoh Tuthmosis IV's Sphinx Stela:

> ... and we shall give praise [to] Wenofer, ... Khaf [re], the statue made for Atum-Harmakhis [...][51]

Egyptologists can only read the first syllable of Khafre's name, "Khaf" (the "re" was hypothetically added by scholars), so it cannot be proven with absolute certainty that the text actually refers to that king. Even James H. Breasted admitted that this theory was "a conclusion which does not follow"[52] — since no actual cartouche of this pharaoh was present. In my historical reconstruction, I again propose that the Great Sphinx was really built by the Khemetic king Khufu himself, along with all three pyramids at Gizah, to symbolize Atum-Khepri. Later on, in the Old Kingdom, the 4th Dynasty king Khufu claimed the Great pyramid for himself, while his son (Pharaoh Khafre) and grandson (Pharaoh Menkaure) respectively took credit for the construction of the second and third Gizah plateau pyramids — evidently on a first come first serve basis. Because the Great Sphinx (Atum-Khepri)

---

[50] J. H. Breasted, *Ancient Records of Egypt*, Vol. II - § 814-815.
[51] Ibid, § 815.
[52] See footnote (e) to ibid.

was intimately linked with this second pyramid, Khufu's son took on the throne name of "Khafre" in the likeness of the Great Sphinx akin to the pyramid he had usurped. Khafre's father, for his part, had adopted the name of the Typhon Season #2 Khemetic pharaoh Khufu. As we'll shortly further examine, the dynastic Egyptian king Khufu, in an effort to solidify the new-found domination of Horus the Child during the Old Kingdom, had felt it necessary to minimize any lingering influence of the older Horus kingship. He did not accomplish that by neglecting the Heliopolitan Theology, but by instead usurping and Egyptianizing the Khemetic legacy.

The Divine Bull and the Leviathan

Returning again to Africanus and Eusebius' reports from the Manethonian tradition, we ascertain that, during the 2nd Dynasty, three different divine bulls were worshipped in Egypt: Apis at Memphis, Mnevis at Heliopolis, as well as the Mendesian goat. This diversity in worship reflects the historical cohabitation, during Typhon Season #2, of the three major denominational districts: the followers of Horus in Memphis (Apis), the First Cataract Khemites who adhered to the sun-god Re (Mnevis), and the disciples of Seth from Ombos. In Memphis the Apis bull was a manifestation of Ptah while in Heliopolis Mnevis naturally personified the sun-god Re. The faithful adherents to both Apis and Mnevis put the blame for the prevailing universal chaos on the shoulders of Seth's disciples and vigorously hunted them down, as Diodorus of Sicily relates:

> The sacred bulls — I refer to the Apis and the Mnevis — are honoured like the gods, as Osiris commanded ... Red oxen, however may be sacrificed, because it is thought that this was the colour of Typhon, who plotted against Osiris and was then punished by Isis for the death of her husband. Men, also, if they were of the same colour as Typhon, were sacrificed, they say, in ancient times by the kings at the tomb of Osiris; however, only a few Egyptians are now found red in colour, but the majority of such are non-Egyptians, and this is why the story spread among the Greeks of the slaying of foreigners by Busiris ...
> (Diodorus of Sicily, Book I: 88)

Echoing Diodorus of Sicily, Plutarch (Manetho, *Aegyptiaca*, FR. 86) writes:

> ... as Manetho has related, they used to burn men alive, calling them "Typhôn's followers"; and their ashes they would winnow and scatter broadcast until they were seen no more.

CHAP. II: A NEW BEGINNING | 159

Bull sacrifices accompanied by the murderous pursuit of disciples of the demon of chaos in times of Typhonian instability were not unique to the ancient Nile Valley. In ancient Mesoamerica, cultic 52-year periods (Typhon Seasons) were designated by astronomer-priests in which foreign enemies faithful to an antagonist deity were hunted and sacrificed to appease the recurring fury of Heaven. In ancient Mesopotamia, the classic myth of "Gilgamesh and the Bull of Heaven"[53] recounts an epic battle between the forces of good versus the Bull of Heaven — who personifies universal chaos. According to Prof. Cyrus H. Gordon:

> The Sumerian Bull of Heaven is an evil monster, partly bovine and partly human in form, slain by the heroes of the epic.[54]

Evidently, the Sumerian Bull of Heaven was closely associated with Typhon Season rituals — as were the Apis and Mnevis bovine deities in Egypt. Indeed, as the next chapter will illuminate, the Sumerian hero Gilgamesh lived during the second Typhon Season. In Sumerian epic literature, Gilgamesh and Enkidu join forces to defeat the evil serpentine dragon Humbaba (the Sumerian counterpart of Seth). Such legends of an epic duel opposing divine heroes and evil primordial dragons abounded in early Antiquity. The Greeks believed that, in just such a conflict, the Apis bull was slain "at the hands of Typhon."[55] Most legends however portray the Apis as being ultimately victorious. His primary functions, as the Greek dramatist Aischylos relates, were to protect and heal humanity from the destructiveness of the serpentine demon of chaos.

> For Apis, seer and leech, the son of Apollo, came from Naupaktos on the farther shore and purged well this land of monsters deadly to man, which Earth, defiled by the bloody deeds of yore, caused to spring up — plagues charged with wrath, a baleful colony of swarming serpents. Of these plagues Apis worked a cure by surgery and spells ...
> (Aischylos, *The Suppliant Maidens*, 260-265)

From Aischylos' statement, we may surmise that a preeminent reason why Typhonian chaos was associated with serpents is because the tremors which the earth would experience, as it violently convulsed from the gravitational pull exercised on its axis from the erratic movements of Mercury and Venus, caused serpents and other normally submerged pernicious creatures to surface in great

---

[53] See Walter R. Bodine 'Sumerians.' In Alfred J. Hoerth, Gerald L. Mattingly & Edwin M. Yamauchi (editors) (1994) *Peoples of the Old Testament World*, p. 29.
[54] Cyrus H. Gordon (1962) *Before the Bible (The Common Background of Greek and Hebrew Civilizations)*, Collins: London, p. 52.
[55] Diodorus of Sicily, Book I: 85.

numbers. The Typhonian serpent tradition therefore had both a literal and allegorical (cosmic) meaning. The eschatological duel opposing the evil serpent and the divine is of course amply illustrated in the Bible as well. The Book of Isaiah for instance says:

> In that day the Lord with his sore and great and strong sword shall punish leviathan the piercing serpent, even leviathan that crooked serpent; and he shall slay the dragon that is in the sea.
> (Isaiah 27:1)

The symbol of the cyclical cosmic serpent, or Leviathan, is therefore common to Egypt, Sumer, Israel and Mesoamerica. All viewed this serpent as the catalyst of global cosmic catastrophes. Were these just legends? Clearly, the fiery conflagrations had been universal in nature. The ancients, with striking concordance, articulated that floods and fire ravaged the entire world and left it in ruins.

3

The Archaeotheology of Creation

> " In the beginning God created the
> heaven and the earth. And the earth
> was without form, and void; and darkness
> was upon the face of the deep. And the
> spirit of God moved upon the
> face of the waters."
>
> - Genesis 1:1-2

With the above words, the Old Testament's book of Genesis begins. It isn't difficult to notice a similarity between this passage, from the Hebrew Bible, and the Khemetic Heliopolitan Theology. Nun, the primeval watery mass of the unformed universe, gave birth to the sun-god Re who appeared in the shape of a primordial mound. How much had the Jewish biblical redactors been influenced by these ancient so-called pagan myths? Significantly more than the Judeo-Christian tradition has been willing to admit. The similarities are indeed quite striking since virtually all ancient religions were, at their very source, theological explanations of past cosmic catastrophes. For instance, in the Hebrew book of Genesis, the waters of the face of the deep which the spirit of God hovers over symbolises the primordial Venus-induced Great Flood of 3,114 BCE. Naturally, the world did not actually begin during the fourth millennium BCE. It would be very illusory to take the Bible literally in this, or many other, cases. The traditional story of Creation in the Book of Genesis must, for all intents and purposes, be deciphered in order to unveil its allegorical meanings.

According to the "Maimonides," whom C. F. Dupuis describes as the wisest of rabbis:

> We must not understand or take in a literal sense what is written in the book of creation, nor form of it the same ideas, which are participated by the generality of mankind, otherwise our ancient sages would not have so much recommended to us, to hide the real meaning of it, and not to lift the allegorical veil, which covers the truth contained therein. When taken in its literal sense, that work gives the most absurd and most extravagant ideas of the Deity. Whosoever should divine its true meaning, ought to take great care in not divulging it. This is a maxim, repeated to us by all our sages,

> principally concerning the understanding of the work of the six days. It is possible, that somebody, either through himself, or by means of the light obtained from others, may succeed to divine its meaning; then let him be silent, or if he speaks of it, let it be done only in as veiled in a manner as I do, leaving the remainder to be guessed, by those who can hear me.[1]

Once again, the theme of the veil, already explored in the book's Introduction — as in Paul's (2 Corinthians 3:12-14) reference to the mystifying veil of Moses being intertwined with the secrets of the Torah, returns in connection with the Book of Genesis. The enigma of the "work of the six days" which the Maimonide sages considered sacred knowledge is the key to the decipherment of the Book of Genesis' allegories. As mentioned above, the biblical authors had purposely written the Creation account in coded jargon so that only the initiated could understand the hidden content.

One man whom the Scriptures say did possess the knowledge of the "work of the six days" is Enoch. That man is said to have "walked with God" and had not known death for he had been taken to heaven directly by the Almighty (Gen. 5:24). Enoch had been initiated to the wisdom of the seven heavens and the mysteries of Creation. In the Seventh Heaven, Enoch saw how the earth had gone through seven creations and that God had attempted to destroy the world six times following the initial Creation.

> He saw fifteen myriads of angels who go out with the sun and attend him during the day, and the thousand angels who attend by night.
> Each angel had six wings, and they go before the chariot of the sun, while one hundred angels keep the sun warm, and light it up ...
> They showed him also the six gates in the east by which the sun goes forth, and the six gates where he sets, and also the gates by which the moon goes out, and those by which she enters. ...
> In the seventh heaven he saw the seven bands of archangels who arrange and study the revolutions of the stars and the changes of the moon and the revolution of the sun, and superintended the good and evil conditions of the world.[2]

The symbolism of the six gates through which the heavenly bodies travel represent the six times in which the earth had nearly been destroyed following the initial Creation. The angels bear six wings because they, as the agents representing the planets, carried out the destructions under the directions of God. As a result,

---

[1] In Charles François Dupuis (1984 [1872]) *The Origin of All Religious Worship*, Garland: New York and London, pp. 226-227.
[2] The Jewish Aggada.

establishing an archaeotheological link between the biblical story of Creation and the Sun Ages is therefore the first step toward unravelling the enigmas of the Book of Genesis.

The Seven Heavens

> " *God created the seven heavens in harmony.*"
>
> - Qur'an 7.15

The six destructions of the world which Enoch witnessed following the primeval Creation represent the seven Typhon Seasons. Each World Age amounted to one Creation. When God was no longer pleased with humanity, he resolved to destroy his work and start anew. From the primeval Flood, God created the First Creation and subsequently destroyed the world six times — until he became satisfied with the current Seventh Creation. In their holy book Sidra Rabba, the gnostic sect of the Mandaeans wrote that the history of civilization is separated into seven ages. Each one of those ages is said to have come about, as well as ended, in catastrophe.[3] Ancient Jewish legend also relates that seven heavens had been created. Each of those times, the earth rose on new foundations.[4] The earliest of these seven ages, according to rabbinical tradition, is the one in which Adam lived: the Seventh Erez. Referring to those ancient Jewish traditions, Immanuel Velikovsky writes:

> Six times this earth was rebuilt — without entire extirpation of life upon it, but with major catastrophes new conditions were created after each of these catastrophes; new chances were given to men to improve their inclinations, evil from the beginning. This is the seventh creation, the time in which we live.[5]

The belief that Adam lived at the time of the First Creation, or Seventh Erez, is recorded, as follows, in the Jewish Aggada:

> Several heavens were created, seven in fact.
> Seven earths were created: the most removed
> the seventh Erez,
> the sixth Adamah,

---

[3] M. Norberg (editor) (1815) *Ginza: Codex Nasareus, Liber Adami Apellatus*, London, Vol. III: pp. 69-73.
[4] L. Ginzberg (1925) *The Legends of the Jews*, Vol. I: 10f.
[5] Immanuel Velikovsky 'A Hebrew Cosmogony': unpublished material.

the fifth Arka,
the fourth Harabah,
the third Yabbashah,
the second Tebel,
and our own land called Heled, and like the
others, it is separated [from the foregoing]
by abyss, chaos, and waters.

As Table 3-1 illustrates, these seven Creations correspond to the seven World Ages. The ancient rabbis' firm conviction that the seven Creations of God were separated by "abyss, chaos, and waters" reveals their intimate knowledge of the cycle-ending Typhon Seasons. According to the first century CE Jewish historian Flavius Josephus, Adam had promptly forewarned his descendants that "the world was to be destroyed at one time by the force of fire, and at another time by the violence and quantity of water."[6] These two recurring catastrophes were caused, respectively, by the planets Mercury and Venus. The diluvian aspect of the planet Venus is indeed particularly relevant to the Adam narrative since the latter emerged into the First Creation, aware of the secrets of the cyclical seasons, after the Venus-induced primeval Great Flood. In learning of the mystery of recurring destructions of the world, brought about by God's displeasure with humanity, Adam and Eve lost their innocence. In essence, the Fall marked an act of "presumption which brought the Golden Age to an end."[7] With the advent of Typhon Season #1, the imperturbable and orderly pattern of the universe came undone.

The Fifty-Two-Year Cycle
In the Book of Enoch, it is recounted how, in a vision, the righteous Enoch came to be revealed the details of how the earth became engulfed in fiery destruction at the divinely appointed time of Heaven's collapse.

> I had laid me down in the house of my grandfather when I saw a vision how the heaven collapsed and was borne off and fell to the earth. ... And when I fell to the earth, I saw how the earth was swallowed up in a great abyss, and mountains were suspended on mountains, and hills sank down on hills, and high tress were rent from their stem, and hurled down and sunk in the abyss.
> (Book of Enoch 83:3-5)

---

[6] Flavius Josephus, *Antiquities of the Jews*, Book I: 2, 3.
[7] Norman Powell Williams (1929) *The Ideas of the Fall and Original Sin (A Historical and Critical Study)*, Longmans, Green & Co.: London, p. 51.

The Seven Creations of the Aggada

FIRST CREATION	Seventh Erez	3,114 BCE — 2,730 BCE
SECOND CREATION	Sixth Adamah	2,730 BCE — 2,130 BCE
THIRD CREATION	Fith Arka	2,130 BCE — 1,559 BCE
FOURTH CREATION	Fourth Harabah	1,559 BCE — 1,135 BCE
FIFTH CREATION	Third Yabbashah	1,135 BCE — 776 BCE
SIXTH CREATION	Second Tebel	776 BCE — 612 BCE
SEVENTH CREATION	First Heled	612 BCE — Present

Table 3-1

The Seven Typhon Seasons

TYPHON SEASON #1	➤ 3,166 BCE to 3,114 BCE - Temptation of Adam and Eve in the Garden of Eden. - Satan is symbolised by Seth, the demon of chaos.	**TYPHON SEASON #6**	➤ 828 BCE to 776 BCE
TYPHON SEASON #2	➤ 2,780 BCE to 2,730 BCE - Seth, the son of Adam and Eve who replaced Abel is born. Again, name is based on Sethian god of chaos. - Noah is born, 2,780 BCE.	**TYPHON SEASON #7**	➤ 664 BCE to 612 BCE
TYPHON SEASON #3	➤ 2,180 BCE to 2,130 BCE - The Great Flood of Noah in 2,130 BCE.		
TYPHON SEASON #4	➤ 1,579 BCE to 1,559 BCE		
TYPHON SEASON #5	➤ 1,187 BCE to 1,135 BCE		

Table 3-2

CHAP. III: THE ARCHAEOTHEOLOGY OF CREATION | 167

These fiery destructions which Enoch speaks about were caused by the Typhon Seasons which terminated each Creation or World Age (see Table 3-2)[8]. According to the ancient rabbinical literature: *"The celestial light ceased, to the consternation of Adam, who feared that the serpent would attack him in the dark."* We of course recognize here the pernicious Typhonian serpents which we discussed in the previous chapter. The Typhonian serpents came out, as the celestial light ceased, on account of the Mercury shift inaugurating the tumultuous Typhon Season. Adam had become wise in matters of the cyclical Typhonian seasons because, following the collapse of the Golden Age, he asked god: *"Grant me knowledge and understanding, that I may know what shall befall me, and my posterity, and all the generations that come after me, and what shall befall me on every day and in every month."* Complementing Flavius Josephus, the Aggada states:

> ... they were the inventors of that peculiar sort of wisdom which is concerned with the heavenly bodies and their order.
> And that their inventions might not be lost before they were sufficiently known, they made two pillars upon Adam's prediction that the world was to be destroyed at one time by the force of fire and at another time by the violence and quantity of water.

"They" whom the Aggada speaks of were the children of Seth — Adam's progeny. As followers of Seth, they were amply aware, by the time of second Typhon Season, of the fifty-two-year cycle flanked by two great catastrophes of fire and flood. In Greek mythology, these Sethian pillars are the equivalent of the Pillars of Hercules. Both the Jews and the Greeks maintained that these sacred pillars salvaged mankind's extensive reservoir of knowledge from the imminent threat of a great natural conflagration. As Table 3-2 delineates, the children of Seth, Adam's progeny, lived during the time of Typhon Season #2 or second Sethian rebellion. The biblical character of Seth, Adam's second son, is therefore, archaeotheologically speaking, the namesake of the Sethian followers of the 2nd Dynasty in Upper Egypt. The name of "Seth" as Adam's son, and replacement of Abel, was not haphazardly selected. The link between Abel and Seth was their common allegiance to the cult of Seth. Like the New Chronology Table demonstrates, Abel symbolized the first disciples of Seth: the Ta-Seti of Lower Nubia and Upper Egypt. The conquest of Qustul by Aha-Menes, whom I identify with Cain, therefore symbolized the murder of Abel

---

[8] Table 3-2 tabulates all seven Typhon Seasons with all the dates corresponding to the beginning and end of each fifty-two year cycle — although the dates for Typhon Seasons #2 and #3 have been arrived to at the closest round estimation. Typhon Season #4, which lasted for an exceptionally short period of twenty years, was the only one of the seven Typhon Seasons not to have lasted fifty-two years.

by his jealous brother Cain. That is precisely why, when the second Sethian rebellion erupts, the biblical redactors recognise the leaders of the second Sethian rebellion (Seth) as the third son of Adam who comes along to replace the murdered Abel. Since the Jews were Asiatics, it is perfectly understandable how the moralistic roles of Horus and Seth have been totally reversed. From the Asiatic perspective, the aggressor was Horus (Cain). However, the knowledge which Abel and Seth had acquired from Adam, concerning the movement of the heavenly bodies and the need for the building of the great pillars, was definitely Khemetic in origin. The Greek pillars of Hercules, which represent the Sethian pillars, are intricately linked with the ancient Khemetic cult of Apis. Indeed, Hercules, in Greek mythology, is equated with the Graeco-Egyptian god Serapis — the equivalent of Apis. Since the sacred Apis bull was particularly worshipped during the cycle-ending Typhon Seasons, the association is very consequential. In fact, the mysterious ancient legends alleging that the Gizah pyramids contained a vast deposit of sacred knowledge, kept safe from the ravages of an impending great cataclysm, probably have their roots in this tale of the Sethian pillars. This is because, as I have postulated earlier, the Gizah pyramids were erected, precisely, during the second Typhon Season. Whether Pharaoh Khnum-Khufu actually did dissimulate records of a sacred science inside the Great Pyramid cannot be known for sure but at the very least the thesis of the contemporaneity of the Gizah pyramids and the 2nd Sethian Dynasty is considerably bolstered by this legend — which has survived millennia after the decline of pharaonic civilization. In the seventeenth century, a British astronomer from Oxford by the name of John Greaves collected, while in Egypt, a series of ancient traditional accounts which preserved the memory of an ancient king, presumably Khufu, who had built the Pyramids at Gizah at the eve of a great natural conflagration. He writes:

> The occasion of this was because he saw in his sleep that the whole earth was turned over, with the inhabitants of it lying upon their faces and the stars falling down and striking one another with a terrible noise ... And he awaked with great feare (sic), and assembled the chief priests of all the provinces of Egypt ... He related the whole matter to them and they took the altitude of the stars, and made their prognostication, and they foretold a deluge. The king said, will it come to our country? They answered yes, and it will destroy it. And there remained a certain number of years to come, and he commanded in the mean space to build the Pyramids ... And he engraved in these Pyramids all things that were told by wise men, as also all profound sciences — the science of Astrology, and of Arithmeticke, and of Geometry, and of Physicke. All this may be interpreted by him that knowes (sic) their characters and language ...[9]

---

[9] John Greaves, *Pyramidographia*. Quoted in Graham Hancock (1996 [1995]) *Fingerprints of the Gods*, p. 518.

While virtually no inscriptions have been discovered inside the Gizah pyramids, speculations continue to grow among "pyramidologists" that somewhere inside the hidden passages and inaccessible chambers of the Great Pyramid or even deep below the ground surface below the paws of the Great Sphinx, such a repository of lost knowledge exists. However, with no conclusive evidence to date, these speculations remain at the level of conjecture. Nonetheless, even if these assumptions prove to be spurious, these ancient correlation between the pyramids of Gizah and the Sethian pillars, again, go a very long way toward proving that the pyramids had indeed been erected during the second Typhon Season. The later traditions postulating that Khufu had brought doom onto his people's land no doubt stems from the memory of the Venus shift of 2,730 BCE, at the end of Typhon Season #2, which terminated King Khnum-Khufu's reign. Whether Khnum-Khufu's reputation as a tyrant was warranted or not, as Immanuel Velikovsky relates below, the ancients often blamed the sitting monarch, who ruled at the time of a cycle-ending Typhon Season, for the breach in the good order of nature.

> In his great fright and looking back on what did happen to a former generation, the thinking man imagined that the catastrophe must have been provoked by the iniquity of the ancestors, their vices and evils. Such thought could provide a hope for a non-repetition of catastrophes: should humankind abstain from wretched acts, it would be spared. By this, man assumed that the planetary gods could be kept at bay by his own decency — and if he already formulated for himself what is good and what is evil, or ate already from the tree of knowledge of good and evil, he needed a covenant with the outraged deity and commandments for behavior.[10]

Such was the legacy of Khnum-Khufu. His decision to close the temples of Edfu and Philae was a heresy which the Horus purists had likely not forgiven.

The Fall

> *"The sun had grown dark the instant Adam became guilty of disobedience."*
>
> - Aggada

Having identified Abel with the Sethian disciples and Cain with the proto-dynastic Egyptians, the obvious question is: who were Adam and Eve? Were they likewise akin to ancient lands and peoples? Indubitably, they were. Naturally, the birth of

---

[10] Immanuel Velikovsky 'World Catastrophes as Punishment': unpublished material.

Adam and Eve must precede the Venus shift of 3,114 BCE — which corresponds with the demise of the Golden Age of innocence. It is my hypothesis that Adam and Eve are the ancient Hebrew equivalent of the Khemetic divine couple Osiris and Isis. As the great primeval civilizer of the Hebrews' homeland, the Hierakonpolite Osiris (Adam) left his mark in the earliest of Hebrew theologies. Evidently, Osiris' wife, Isis-Hathor, was symbolized by Eve. The expanse of Osiris' Asiatic conquests had given him and his wife a truly international standing. The homeland of Eve (Isis-Hathor, the august Mistress of Punt or God's Land) in the Hebrew tradition had been in Syria-Palestine. With respect to Adam, his name literally meaning: "red ground" (as in Red Land), indicates that his original dwelling place was indeed in Egypt.

The fatal temptation of Adam and Eve, induced by the arrival of the serpent on the scene, coincided with the first Sethian rebellion of 3,166 BCE in which the Typhonian serpent manifested himself for the first time. By succumbing to the Typhonian serpent's seditious advance, Adam and Eve tacitly joined into the rebellion against God. The result of their disobedience was their instantaneous expulsion from the Garden of Eden (Gen. 3:23-24). The Book of Genesis relates that a "flaming sword" was placed by God himself at the entrance of the Garden of Eden in order to prevent humanity from ever returning. As ancient Hebrew legends transmit:

> When Adam was cast out of Paradise, he first reached the lowest of the seven earths, the Erez, which is dark, without a ray of light, and utterly void. Adam was terrified, particularly by the flames of the ever-turning sword.

This ever-revolving flaming sword, which darkened the skies of the nascent Seventh Erez (or the First Creation), represents the fiery conflagrations which brought about Typhon Season #1. In the excellent book *Hamlet's Mill*, Giorgio de Santillana wrote:

> The theory about "how the world began" seems to involve the breaking asunder of a harmony, a kind of cosmic "original sin" whereby the circle of the ecliptic (with the zodiac) was tilted up at an angle with respect to the equator, and the cycles of change came into being.[11]

---

[11] Giorgio de Santillana & Hertha von Dechend (1969) *Hamlet's Mill (An Essay on Myth and the Frame of Time)*, Gambit: Boston, p. 5.

CHAP. III: THE ARCHAEOTHEOLOGY OF CREATION | 171

Indubitably, the notion of the "original sin" corresponds with a violent shift of the earth's axis caused by a close encounter with the planet Venus. There most likely never was an actual Garden of Eden. The real Garden of Eden was the Golden Age prior to the cataclysmic unravelling of the cosmic order. From the time of the Fall, the Typhonian serpent, albeit disabled by God for his transgression, intermittently tempted humanity to rebellion. Thus, each time the serpent would succeed, God destroyed his Creation and built it anew. Interestingly, in the Khemetic Book of Coming Forth by Day, the disrupting role of the Typhonian serpent is acknowledged and described in a very similar way as in the Old Testament:

> Thoth and the goddess Maat mark out thy course for thee day by day and every day. Thine enemy the Serpent hath been given over to the fire. **The Serpent-fiend Sebau hath fallen headlong, his forelegs are bound in chains, and his hind legs hath Ra carried away from him. The Sons of Revolt shall never more rise up.**
> (Book of Coming Forth by Day)

The above passage's mention of the "sons of revolt" is a direct reference to the great Sethian rebellion which erupted with the intervention of the Typhonian serpent in 3,166 BCE. Strikingly mirroring the Old Testament text, the Khemetic Book of Coming Forth by Day reveals:

> The Sebau-fiend hath fallen to the ground, his fore-legs and his hind-legs have been hacked off him ...
> (Book of Coming Forth by Day)

Similarly, the Book of Genesis relates:

> 14 And the Lord God said unto the serpent, because thou hast done this, thou art cursed above all cattle, and above all cattle, and above every beast of the field; upon thy belly shalt thou go, and dust shall thou eat all the days of thy life:
> 15 And I will put enmity between thee and the woman, and between thy seed and her seed; it shall bruise thy head, and thou shalt bruise his heel.
> (Genesis 3:14-15)

In effect, we may recall that the goddess Isis-Hededet (Isis-Hathor), mother of Horus the Child and wife of Horus the Elder, held special repelling powers over the venomous Typhonian reptiles. Moreover, Hathor was recognized in Phoenicia as a serpent-goddess. Again, this is plainly reflected in the Book of Genesis — where

Eve, the Hebrew Isis-Hathor, is given powers to crush the head of the serpent with her heel. Quoting from ancient sources, renowned British Egyptologist Barry J. Kemp of Cambridge University writes:

> ... the goddess Isis (a clever woman. Her heart was craftier than a million men) schemes to discover the secret name of the sun-god Ra, depicted as an old man who succumbs to the pain of a snake bite and reveals his hidden name to Isis.[12]

In the Khemetic and Hebrew mythologies, Isis and Eve plot to uncover the secrets of the Almighty. Both of them succeeded in divining the eternal enigmas in conjunction with the evil Typhonian reptile — with whom they both subsequently developed a strong enmity. Can all this be mere coincidence? Evidently, the Hebrew story of Creation had heavily borrowed from ancient Khemetic mythology.

The Gilgamesh Epic

Another ancient source which the ancient Jewish biblical redactors largely relied upon was the Sumerian Epic of Gilgamesh. The story of Gilgamesh, a Mesopotamian king who reigned at Uruk at the time of Typhon Season #2, recounts as well the cosmic catastrophes of the first two Typhon Seasons. The chronicle is told by an unnamed narrator who states: "I will proclaim to the world the deeds of Gilgamesh." According to the unnamed narrator, upon his return from his travels and resting from his labours, Gilgamesh engraved the entire story on a clay tablet. Therefore, the extent Epic of Gilgamesh, by the unnamed narrator, is a transcription of an oral telling of the original text carved by Gilgamesh himself. Gilgamesh was two-thirds god and one-third man but the story maintains that he was a historical king. When the epic begins, Gilgamesh is portrayed as a tyrannical ruler of Uruk who kills and rapes its citizens. Helpless, the citizens pleaded with the gods of Sumer to save them from the abuses of Gilgamesh. Hearing the laments, the gods created Enkidu, who was himself half man and half god, as a counterpart of equal strength for Gilgamesh. When Enkidu and Gilgamesh engaged in battle, neither could overcome the other — for both were of equal strength. In the heat of battle, their eyes met and, immediately, both erupted into laughter. Their anger vanished and, from that day on, they became inseparable. One night, as Gilgamesh and Enkidu were asleep, the former suddenly awoke frightened. The legend relates:

---

[12] Kemp, Barry J. (1989) *Ancient Egypt: Anatomy of a Civilization*, Routledge: London and New York, p. 25.

CHAP. III: THE ARCHAEOTHEOLOGY OF CREATION | 173

> Toward morning Enkidu awoke to find Gilgamesh leaning over him. "It is I who have dreamed," he said. "Or did you awaken me from my slumber? I must have dreamed, for lo! the earth shook, and the heavens rained fire! All around me death fell from the clouds!" Enkidu listened to the dream and reassured Gilgamesh, saying that his dream surely presaged the destruction of Huwawa. Then, as they prepared for battle, Huwawa breathed.[13]

Like his contemporary Pharaoh Khnum-Khufu in Egypt, Gilgamesh's nightly vision convinced both himself and Enkidu that the World Age was coming to an end. The Huwawa monster whose imminent demise had been heralded by Gilgamesh's dream was, unequivocally, the Sumerian equivalent of the Typhonian serpent or Seth — the demon of chaos. Since King Gilgamesh reigned during a Typhon Season – perhaps explaining, as in his Khemetic contemporary Pharaoh Khnum-Khufu's case, his reputation as a ruthless ruler – his dream could only have foretold of the impending Venus shift. It is indeed evident that the Typhonian monster was already present when Gilgamesh had the dream. The approaching end of the Typhon Season, as Enkidu postulated, meant that his power was waning. So Gilgamesh and Enkidu set out to do battle with Huwawa.

> Back and forth the battle raged between Gilgamesh and the monster. his dagger was soon red with blood from the gushing wounds he had inflicted. Harder and harder Gilgamesh pressed the monster. His courage and strength welled up in him as he fought. Harder and faster he swung his war club, unmindful of his own danger. Finally, the monster fell over backward; and before he could get his footing and rise again, Enkidu rushed over him and hacked off his head.[14]

As in Egyptian mythology where the Horus-king harpoons the Sethian beast, the Sumerian epic depicts a hero-king who ensures the safety of his people by killing the very embodiment of chaos. But all was not well for long.

> After the battle the heroes cleansed themselves of blood, put on fresh garments, and made offerings to the gods. Gilgamesh was so handsome in his gold helmet and white tunic that the goddess of love, Ishtar, appeared suddenly before him. While she was congratulating him on his victory, she began to caress his face provocatively and to stroke his shoulders, asking

---

[13] Norma Lore Goodrich (1960) *Ancient Myths*, New American Library: New York, p. 17.
[14] Ibid.

him if he did not begin to love her. Gilgamesh answered her sharply, "What do you do to your loves, Ishtar? When the stallion worships you, do you not put him into the harness and condemn him to pull the heavy war cart? When the shepherds of the hills are charmed by you, do you not transform them into leopards that eat the little lambs?"[15]

Deeply offended by Gilgamesh's comments, the goddess Ishtar, who represents the planet Venus, plotted her revenge.

By the time Gilgamesh and Enkidu had felled the cedars and returned to Uruk, the sultry Ishtar had planned a terrible revenge. She had persuaded her father An to send the Bull of Heaven into the city to trample the people, destroy the temples, and slaughter the warriors by the thousands.[16]

The destruction of Uruk by Ishtar and the Bull of Heaven incontrovertibly denotes the cataclysmic Venus shift of 2,730 BCE. The dreams of Gilgamesh and Khnum-Khufu, heralding the termination of Typhon Season #2, had come true. The goddess Ishtar, symbolizing the planet Venus in the Gilgamesh Epic, annihilated everything in her way. Therefore, it is amply evident that the plot for this great Sumerian story is a beautifully crafted metaphor explaining the various cosmological events taking place during Typhon Season #2 — in which time Gilgamesh reigned. As in ancient Israelite, Egyptian and Greek theology, the wisdom to divine the carefully concealed meanings behind those myths was reserved for an initiated elite. But the common citizen of any of these great ancient civilizations could easily relate to the tales of their national heroes.

The African Roots of the Biblical Noah

In her wrath, Ishtar had likewise imposed a curse on Enkidu, the dear companion of Gilgamesh. Enkidu was sick for twelve days and died on the thirteenth day. Heartbroken, Gilgamesh embarked on a journey to learn the secret of immortality from Ut-napishtim, in the hope of resurrecting Enkidu. To reach Ut-napishtim, the king of Shuruppak, Gilgamesh had to travel far from Uruk. It was Ut-napishtim himself who recounted to Gilgamesh the story of the Great Flood, in times past, when the god of wisdom commissioned the construction of a great ship. The tale was not foreign to Gilgamesh, for he had heard it many times on his mother's lap. The

---

[15] Ibid, p. 19.
[16] Ibid.

gods had decreed that for six days and six nights, rain would be poured upon the earth, destroying all living things — save those who had been spared by entering the ark. When, on the seventh day, the boat finally landed on the mountain of Nizir, King Ut-napishtim, the Mesopotamian Noah, sent out a dove, a swallow, and raven that never returned. It was at that precise moment, King Ut-napishtim told his guest Gilgamesh, that he won eternal life. This Great Flood which King Ut-napishtim spoke to Gilgamesh about was the primeval Venus-induced Flood of 3,114 BCE. Ut-napishtim had managed to survive the ravages of this Typhon Season. Therefore, Gilgamesh hoped that King Ut-napishtim would transmit to him the secret for surviving the latest Typhon Season.

The story has a very familiar ring to it since it anticipates the story of Noah in the Book of Genesis. Biblical scholars generally agree that the Gilgamesh Epic served as a model for the biblical redactors. But there is also a much less, if at all, acknowledged Egyptian influence in the biblical story of Noah. This influence is to be found in the name of Noah itself. I believe that the name of Noah came from the ancient Egyptian sacred city of Thebes — the "No" or "No Amon" of the Old Testament (Jer. 46:25). More will be revealed about this ancient association in the following chapters but suffice it to say for now that the biblical redactors, having borrowed from the Gilgamesh Epic to establish the plot of the Flood story, turned to the Egyptian city of Thebes to fashion the tale's leading character. Ascribing the birth of Noah to the year 2,730 BCE, in the new chronology, we shall find that the story of Noah's life, as described in the Hebrew Bible, mirrors the history of the ancient Egyptian capital of Thebes during the 950 years which make up Noah's life. But why would the biblical redactors choose the city of Thebes to symbolize the patriarch Noah? To answer this pivotal question, one must first remember that the tale of Gilgamesh served as the foundation for the Israelite story and that, in the Sumerian epic, King Ut-napishtim imparts that he was saved from the devastation of the Great Flood by building a large ark in which he and his hosts found refuge. The significant connection with Thebes is precisely through this "ark." According to Martin G. Bernal:

> ... before the advent of the Extreme Aryan Model it was generally accepted that the Greek city of Theba came from the Canaanite *tebåh* (ark, chest). This itself came from the Egyptian *tbi*, or *dbt* (box) ... Hesychios, the lexicographer of the 5th or 6th century AD, wrote that Theba 'was a city of Boiotia' and 'a chest' (*kibotos*). **Kibotos is used to translate the *tebåh* (ark) in the Noah story in the Septuagint.**[17]

---

[17] Martin G. Bernal (1991) *Black Athena* II, p. 475; *Black Athena* I (1987) p. 51. See also David M. Rohl (1998) *A Test of Time — Vol. II: Legend (The Genesis of Civilization)*, Century: London, p. 144.

Therefore, Noah's "ark" (*tebâh* in Hebrew or *arca* in Latin — meaning "chest"), is the ancient root of the common appellation for the Egyptian sacred capital of Thebes. Since the Hebrew name for Thebes was "No," the protagonist of the Flood story, Noah, was named accordingly.

Triad of Menkaure, by author

Part II

Old Kingdom

2,730 BCE to 2,180 BCE

Diluvian Period

2,180 BCE to 1,953 BCE

4

The Supremacy of Horus, Son of Re (2,730 BCE to 2,400 BCE)

The Old Kingdom, often dubbed as the "Pyramid Age," is traditionally dated with the 3rd Dynasty as its starting point. According to received wisdom, the step-pyramid of Pharaoh Djoser, built at Saqqara in the beginning of the Old Kingdom, introduced an era of monumental pyramid building which culminated with the construction of the Gizah pyramids. From their relatively miraculous ascent about two centuries earlier, the dynastic Egyptians, once again in an unexplained meteoric advance in cultural and technological sophistication, are supposed to have erected these stupendous edifices which still boggle the mind today. Objecting to this traditional view, I assert that the Pyramid Age was in actual fact drawing to an end during the Old Kingdom. The pyramids of the 5th Dynasty are indeed notable for their lack of sophistication compared to the pyramids built under Pharaohs Djoser-Netjerykhet and Khnum-Khufu. In all evidence, the golden age had passed. Scholars are greatly puzzled by the sheer speed with which the architectural standard collapsed after the 5th Dynasty. It would in fact appear as though, from one dynasty to the next, the dynastic Egyptians completely forgot how to build fantastic pyramids. Various theories have been proposed in search of a solution to this conundrum. To some, this was the result of a sudden lack of economic resources following the extravagance of the 4th Dynasty rulers.[1] The traditional stories describing Pharaoh Khufu as a tyrant pushing down on his people to feed his insatiable self-glorifying ambitions has provided much ammunition to this school of thought. The Old Kingdom pyramids of the 5th and 6th Dynasties, to quote Egyptologist Rosalie David, "suffered a lessening of standards." Instead of the expert masonry which characterizes the pyramid of King Khufu, we find that the 5th and 6th Dynasty pyramids were constructed with inferior materials. Brick and rubble had entirely replaced the stone used to erect the earlier pyramids. The cause for this sharp decline in architectural standards has, in my own view, more to do with the fact that the later pyramids were built by a less experienced work force. As Robert Bauval

---

[1] See Rosalie David (1996) *The Pyramid Builders of Ancient Egypt (A Modern Investigation of Pharaoh's Workforce)*, Routledge: London and New York, pp. 24-25.

appropriately remarks: *"... it was not a collapse that occurred but something more like the handing over of the state's authority to a less experienced government after a large-scale event."*[2] As I have proposed in Part I, the step-pyramid at Saqqara and the Gizah pyramids were not constructed by dynastic Egyptians but by Khemetic kings. The dynastic Egyptians were just coming out of their infancy, as an organized pharaonic state, when the Old Kingdom began. Their first effort at erecting a pyramid is exemplified by the bent pyramid of King Sneferu of the 4th Dynasty at Dashur — a few kilometres south of the step-pyramid. This structure, a noble but rather naive attempt at reproducing Khemetic architecture, retained at least some of the sophistication found at Saqqara and Gizah but the pioneering verve had altogether faded. Pharaoh Sneferu's bent pyramid at Dashur, I maintain, was the only major pyramidal edifice erected during the 4th Dynasty. The Gizah pyramids were *all* built by King Khnum-Khufu during Typhon Season #2's divided kingship era. Some of the reasons why these famous pyramids, from early antiquity, came to be regarded as Old Kingdom edifices will be tackled in this chapter. Other topics to be investigated include how the dynastic Egyptians of the Old Kingdom came of age, as the all-powerful sole rulers of Egypt, on the heels of the cycle-ending Venus shift of 2,730 BCE. Indeed, it is under the reign of the dynastic pharaoh Sneferu that the two kingships of Horus the Elder and Horus the Child first merged into a single kingship.

King Sneferu as Successor of Khnum-Khufu:

The Unification of the Horus Kingships

Several important factors came into play during the latter half of the 2nd Dynasty, which would ultimately induce the kingship of Horus the Child to seek its full independence — which it acquired during the Old Kingdom. Although the proto-dynastic Egyptians had enjoyed a peaceful, and even parental, relationship with the Khemetic kingship of Horus the Elder, the advent of King Khnum-Khufu during Typhon Season #2 forever altered the amicable rapport between Horus the Elder and Horus the Child. By closing down the Ptolemaic temples, Khnum-Khufu made a strong statement that "he" was now in charge and that the traditional Khemetic crown of Horus the Elder would reclaim its full suzerainty over the Red Land. Therefore, the legends claiming that Khufu had been an ironhanded monarch must have had at least some grain of truth in them. Secondly, Typhon Season #2 also rekindled the threat of a Sethian rebellion. The perpetual role of Horus as sole ruler of the Two Lands was in jeopardy. The stage was set for a grand and definitive

---

[2] Robert Bauval and Adrian Gilbert (1994) *The Orion Mystery (Unlocking the Secrets of the Pyramids)*, Doubleday Canada: Toronto, p. 50.

Fig. 4a: Tablet of Sneferu smiting an Asiatic enemy in Wadi-Magharah.

Fig. 4b: King Khafre (Cairo Museum).

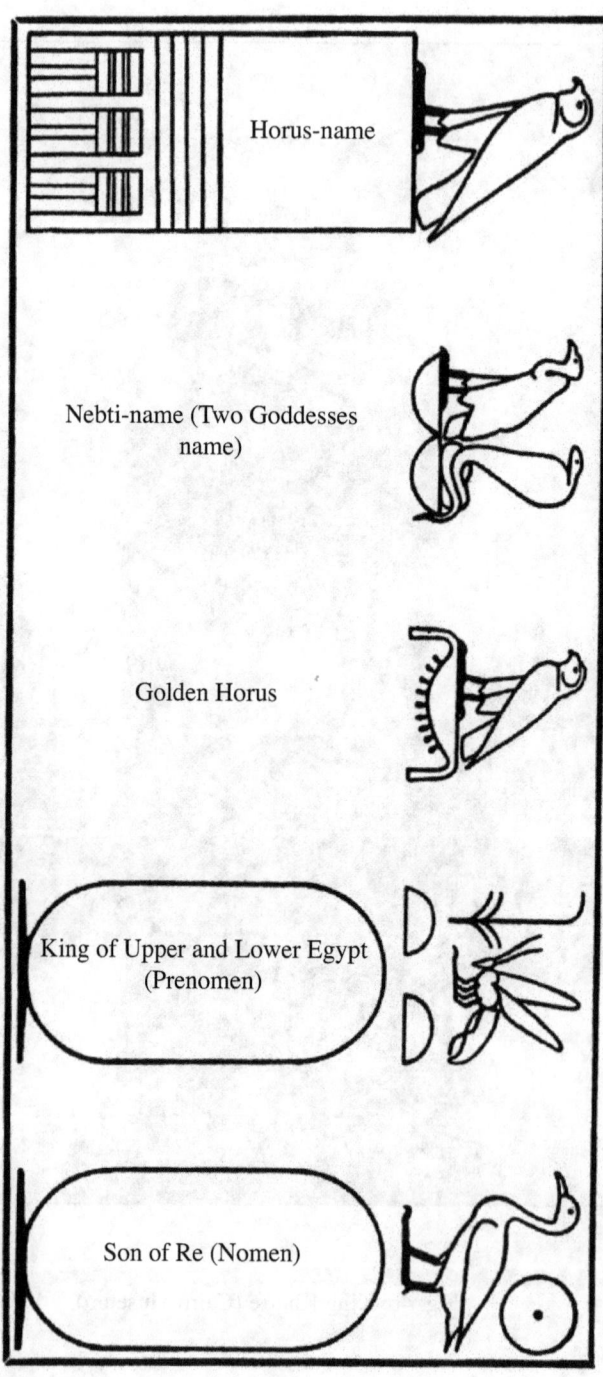

Fig. 4c: The five names of the dynastic Egyptian pharaoh.

Prominent Gods of the Old Kingdom and their Places of Worship

God:	Nome:	Special roles:
1. Neith (war goddess)	Sais	- Divinity of war.
2. Osiris (god of vegetation)	Busiris	
3. Horus (falcon god)	Behdet	- Associated with the sun.
4. Ram god	Mendes	
5. Udot (cobra goddess)	Buto	
6. Bastet (cat goddess)	Bubastis	- Goddess of joy and love.
7. Seth	Ombos	- God of the South / storms.
8. Up-wawet (wolf god)	Si ut	- Divinity of war.
9. Anubis (dog god)	Kynopolis	- Presides over burials.
10. Min (anthropomorphic gods)	Koptos	- Gods of generation.
Amun	Thebes	and fertility.
11. Vulture goddess	Nekhab (el Kab)	
12. Khnum (other ram god)	Elephantine	- God of the First Cataract.

Table 4-1 (*after* W. C. Hayes, 1990)

Fig. 4d: The vizier Rahotep and his wife Nofret.

unification of Upper and Lower Egypt under a single ruler who could bend all other dissenting powers to his will. With the Venusian global conflagration of the end of Typhon Season #2 being blamed on the iniquitous behaviour of Horus the Elder, in the guise of Pharaoh Khnum-Khufu, Horus the Child was in a perfect position to act. The Sethian rebellion had moreover been due to be quelled with the advent of the Venus shift of 2,730 BCE. This latest "Destruction of Mankind" by the sun-god Re, as it was the case at the end of Typhon Season #1, called for the falcon-god Horus to reclaim the domain of Osiris from the usurping hands of the followers of Seth. Hence the Venus-induced paroxysm gave Pharaoh Sneferu, the first ruler of the 4th Dynasty, divine sanction to oversee the good order of nature on behalf of Re. True to the Memphite Theology, we thence find that the kingship of Horus regains, once and for all, his uncontested dominion over the Two Lands. As the Shabaka Stone relates:

> ... Then it seemed wrong to Geb that the portion of Horus was like the portion of Seth. So Geb gave to Horus his inheritance, for he is the son of his firstborn son. Geb's words to the Ennead: 'I have appointed Horus, the firstborn' ... He is Horus who arose as King of Upper and Lower Egypt, who united the Two Lands in the Nome of the Wall (Memphis), the place in which the Two Lands were united.[3]

As the son of the firstborn of Geb, Horus the Falcon prevails over the disciples of Seth — god of chaos. This time, the supremacy of the Horus kingship would go unchallenged virtually throughout the remainder of Egyptian history. No other dynastic Egyptian pharaoh would ever again take a Sethian prenomen in open defiance of the supremacy of Horus. Although, as we shall see, other kings did adopt Sethian throne names (e.g. Sesostris and Seti), they nonetheless maintained a Horus prenomen and reigned as Horus kings. The only kings of Egypt who did rule as exclusively Sethian monarchs in post Old Kingdom times were foreigners (Hyksos) who usurped the Egyptian throne.

This latest unification was carried out by Pharaoh Sneferu — the son of King Huni and Meresankh I, a wife of the latter. As soon as Sneferu ascended the throne, he began persecuting the traditional enemies of Horus who dwelt outside of the ordered territory of Ma'at. The new pharaoh sent out several bellicose expeditions against the Libyans and the Nubians — in which he claims to have captured over 7,000 prisoners. In all evidence, Pharaoh Sneferu was following on the footsteps of Aha-Menes — the first dynastic ruler to unify the Two Lands. But one could easily argue that Sneferu's unification campaign was just as, if not even more, consequential than Menes' own unification. In my personal view, scholars have consid-

---

[3] Barry J. Kemp (1989) *Ancient Egypt: Anatomy of a Civilization*, Routledge: London and New York, pp. 30-31.

erably underestimated the significance of Pharaoh Sneferu's reign. Pharaoh Sneferu was remembered throughout Egyptian history as one of the greatest dynastic kings because, like King Aha-Menes, he single-handedly ensured the continued supremacy of the Horus kingship at a time when Sethian forces were threatening to usurp the inheritance of Osiris. Moreover, this time around, Horus the Child was the first to reply to the sun-god's Re's appeal to crush the Sethian rebellion following the cycle-destroying Venusian catastrophe. When the sun-god Re once again sent his vengeful eye to earth in the form of the Venusian goddess Hathor, King Sneferu was there to reinstate the universal order.

Since Horus the Child owed his supremacy over the Two Lands to the divine will of the sun-god Re, it was only fitting that the 4th Dynasty pharaohs be known as the sons of Re. Hence, starting with the reign of Sneferu, the dynastic Egyptian kings began using two additional titles — namely: "Son of Re" and "The Golden Horus."[4] In total, that raised the number of titles used by the dynastic Egyptian kings to five (see Fig. 4c). Also, for the first time, the dynastic Kings began writing their throne names in a royal cartouche (or name ring) — a privilege which had hitherto been exclusively reserved to the kingship of Horus the Elder. The classic Ptolemaic kings and queens indeed appear to have been the first ones to make use of the royal cartouche. The graffiti of King Khnum-Khufu's name found inside the Great Pyramid at Gizah was likewise written inside a cartouche. So as the two kingships of Horus the Elder and Horus the Child merged during the reign of Pharaoh Sneferu, such distinctions at once disappeared and the dynastic pharaohs freely began writing their names in royal cartouches. A changing of the guard had taken place. The dynastic Egyptians were coming into their own, and so, undertook concerted efforts to take over the duties and trappings traditionally reserved to Horus the Elder.

The Dominance of the Dynastic Race

As the new "Golden Horus," a title originally carried by Pharaoh Djoser-Netjery-khet, King Sneferu divided the Land of Egypt into several administrative Nomes — each with a particular deity associated with it (see Table 4-1). The deities were allocated their Nomes in keeping with their traditional places of worship and characteristics (see Table 4-1). The famous seated diorite statue of Pharaoh Khafre (see Fig. 4b) illustrates very well the theological turn taken during the 4th Dynasty. In this statue, a Horus falcon is incorporated in Khafre's headgear. Yet, contemporary religious developments in the primeval Nome of Heliopolis, which continued

---

[4] Vassil Dobrev (1993) 'Les titulaires des rois de la IVe Dynastie', *Bulletin de l'Institut Français d'Archéologie Orientale* 93, pp. 180-204.

to maintain the supremacy of Re, gained increased impetus throughout Egypt. The fact that Khafre, and several other 4th and 5th Dynasty pharaohs, included Re in their throne names highlights this phenomenon. Horus the Child priests were however able to rationalize this fusion by making the living pharaoh the child of the sun-god Re. The pharaohs of the Old Kingdom's 4th Dynasty, perhaps in a concerted effort to prove themselves as worthy inheritors of ancient Khemetic traditions, devised an intricate cultic and civil bureaucracy around the living Horus — more so than had been done in the past. The rows of royal tombs built around the Gizah pyramids, for instance, undoubtedly date to the time of the 4th Dynasty. They stand as testament to the highly sophisticated administrative complex erected around the pharaoh as god-king during the Old Kingdom.[5] The prevailing notion that the Gizah pyramids where built as tombs for the pharaohs of the 4th Dynasty originates from this period. But, as I have argued, the Gizah pyramids antedates the advent of the 4th Dynasty.

Hence, the dynastic race of Horus the Child has unduly been given the credit for building the Gizah pyramids. It is however evident that they attempted, and obviously succeeded, in making it seem as though they were the original architects. At around the middle of the past century, excavator D. E. Derry became convinced that the dynastic Egyptians dating from the 4th to 6th Dynasties were of a different racial stock than the predynastic Egyptians — whom Derry believed had much more pronounced African characteristics.[6] Of course, this is because the 4th Dynasty kings belonged (as Derry contends himself) to the "dynastic race" that came to Egypt from the Levant at the start of the New Horus Period. More recently, Derry's work was retaken by critics of African-centered scholarship like Kathryn A. Bard of Boston University, who wrote:

> D. E. Derry, who studied the physical remains of Old Kingdom elites buried at Gizah (excavated in the first decade of this century by Georges Reisner of Harvard University), took skull measurements and concluded, like Petrie and Emery, that the pyramid builders were a dynastic race of invaders, probably from the East, "who were far removed from any negroid element."[7]

While Dr Bard goes on to say that craniometry is no longer considered as a reliable means for determining race, she nevertheless maintains the view that ancient

---

[5] See Ann Macy Roth (1988) 'The Organization of Royal Cemeteries at Saqqara in the Old Kingdom', *Journal of the American Research Center in Egypt* 25, pp. 201-214.
[6] D. E. Derry (1956) 'The Dynastic Race in Egypt', *Journal of Egyptian Archaeology* 42, pp. 81, 84.
[7] Kathryn A. Bard 'Ancient Egyptians and the Issue of Race.' In Mary R. Lefkowitz & Guy M. Rogers (editors) (1996) *Black Athena Revisited*, p. 105.

Egyptians were a "Mediterranean people" — not indigenous Africans. Such conclusions have however been reached on the basis of incomplete evidence. True, the 4th Dynasty pharaohs were of Asiatic racial stock. But if it can be proven that the Gizah pyramids were *not* constructed during the 4th Dynasty, then the issue of the origins of pharaonic culture is by no means settled.

The Inventory Stela: On the Anteriority of the Gizah Plateau Pyramids

A crucial ancient document, dating to the 4th Dynasty itself, which confirms the anteriority of the Gizah pyramids is the Inventory Stela. According to this stela, the Gizah pyramids and the Great Sphinx were already erected at the time of Pharaoh Khufu's accession in the 4th Dynasty. The Inventory Stela records:

> Live the Horus: Mezer, king of Upper and Lower Egypt: Khufu, who is given life. He found the house of Isis, Mistress of the Pyramid, **beside the house of the Sphinx** of [Harmakhis] on the north-west of the house of Osiris, Lord of Rosta. **He built his pyramid beside the temple of this goddess**, and he built a pyramid for the king's-daughter Henutsen beside this temple.[8]

Oddly enough, Egyptologists do not think that the reference to the Sphinx in the Inventory Stela represents any problem whatsoever for the accepted chronology of Egypt because, as they see it, the document in question was not contemporaneous with Khufu. The main reason they give is that the cult of Isis only became prominent very late in Egyptian history.[9] It is also thought that the title of "Isis, Mistress of the Pyramid" could not have been used as early as the Old Kingdom. Few would even concede that the Inventory Stela is a copy of an older document. The text however unequivocally says that the temple of Isis and the Great Sphinx were already standing in Gizah even before the Egyptian king Khufu ascended the throne. Bewildered by such a scenario, James Henry Breasted wrote:

> According to this statement (from the Inventory Stela), the little Isis-temple east of the Great Pyramid was standing on the Gizeh plateau before any of the pyramids were built![10]

---

[8] J. H. Breasted, *Ancient Records of Egypt*, Vol. I - § 180.
[9] Ibid, § 177.
[10] Ibid, § 180 (footnote "j.").

CHAP. IV: THE SUPREMACY OF HORUS, SON OF RE | 189

It is therefore little wonder that scholars have dismissed the Inventory Stela as a pure fabrication. Moreover, admitting to the accuracy of this ancient stela's account is tantamount to overthrowing the entire basis of the science of Egyptology. If King Khufu built a pyramid next to a temple of the goddess Isis (Mistress of the [Great] Pyramid), itself erected in the vicinity of the house of the Great Sphinx, then we must acknowledge at least three fundamental things: (1) the extreme antiquity of the cults of Osiris and Isis, (2) that the Great Sphinx was not carved in the image of Pharaoh Khafre and (3) that Kings Khufu, Khafre and Menkaure were not the original builders of the three pyramids of the Gizah plateau. The first of these three realities is of special importance for comprehending the genuine historical place of the dynastic race. As will be shortly examined, the dynastic Egyptians, until the close of the 4th Dynasty, had never acknowledged the traditional Khemetic worship of Osiris and Isis. That was seen as the exclusive dominion of the Upper Egyptian descendants of the Anu. But all that changed with the accession of the 5th Dynasty pharaohs.

The Rebirth of Osiris-Orion and the

Khemetic Renaissance

" Behold him who is come as Orion! Behold
Osiris who is come as Orion!"

- *Pyramid Texts* 819c

According to the Manethonian tradition, the 5th Dynasty rulers hailed from the primeval Nome of Elephantine. They had no obvious familial links with the preceding 4th Dynasty. Under the 5th Dynasty, the Heliopolitan priesthood wielded unprecedented influence. The new dynasty's first king, Userkaf, had a sun temple built at Abusir which appears to have been an exact replica of the Heliopolis temple.[11] A great Khemetic renaissance was ushered in. As these two districts, Elephantine and Heliopolis, were the original centres of the Anu civilization, the archaeotheological relationship is not difficult to establish. This was a very conscious effort to reinvigorate the legacy of Horus the Elder. The name of the sun-god Re permeated the royal titulary as well as everyday life. Six of the nine kings of the 5th Dynasty are known to have erected sun-temples bearing such names as "Pleasure of Re," "Horizon of Re," and "Field of Re." With this resurgence of Khemetic theology naturally came a renewed interest, a first for dynastic Egypt, in the cults of Osiris and Isis. In essence, this Khemetic renewal was very similar to the theological revolution enacted under Pharaoh Khnum-Khufu.

---

[11] Nicholas Grimal (1992) p. 75.

I would even go so far as claiming that the 5th Dynasty was a natural progression of Khnum-Khufu's vision which was partially interrupted by Horus the Child's unification of the Horus kingship during the 4th Dynasty. Albeit not necessarily abandoning the dynastic cult of the unified Horus, the 5th Dynasty, as Khnum-Khufu had done before, resurrected the traditional association between the Khemetic civilizer-god Osiris and the constellation of Orion. Why was *that* particular time chosen for this Khemetic renaissance?

The advent of the 5th Dynasty, in 2,560 BCE,[12] was accompanied by a very important astronomical event. It was on that very year that the constellation of Orion lined up perfectly with one of the shafts of Khufu's Great Pyramid at Gizah. The Egyptologist and architect Alexander Badawy had pioneered the idea in recent times that the tomb shafts of Khufu's pyramids were "channels to the stars." Convinced that the "star-shaft" of the king's chamber pointed directly and deliberately to the Belt of Orion, Badawy sought the help, in 1964 of an American astronomer by the name of Virginia Trimble to investigate the matter fully. With the aid of advanced precessional calculations, Dr Trimble indeed came to the most sensational conclusion that the southern shaft, pointing towards the meridian at a slope of 44 degrees and 30 minutes, was pointed like a gun barrel to the constellation of Orion. Had Pharaoh Khnum-Khufu constructed the Great Pyramid with the grand design of this eventual correlation in mind? Or was the Great Pyramid's star-shaft pointing directly toward the constellation of Orion during the reign of Khnum-Khufu and again at the beginning of the 5th Dynasty? Was that the elusive foundation for the Khemetic renaissance? Either of these explanations, in my view, are probable.

Recent debates over the true significance of the Great Pyramid star-shafts have been spearheaded by authors Robert Bauval, Adrian Gilbert and Graham Hancock. In his book *Fingerprints of the Gods*, Graham Hancock informs us that:

> The roots of Bauval's discovery at Giza go back to the 1960s when the Egyptologist and architect Dr Alexander Badawy and the American astronomer Virginia Trimble demonstrated that the southern shaft of the King's Chamber in the Great Pyramid was targeted like a gun-barrel on the Belt of Orion during the Pyramid Age — around 2600 to 2400 BC.[13]

Amazingly, those dates fit *exactly* with the time frame of the 5th dynasty's rule over Egypt! It is evident that a primary catalyst behind the Khemetic revival, coinciding with the rise of the 5th Dynasty, was this alignment of the Great Pyramid star-shaft and the Belt of Orion. The great Osiris-Orion had returned or was resurrected.

---

[12] William C. Hayes (1990 [1959]) *The Scepter of Egypt*, Vol. I: p. 58.
[13] Graham Hancock (1996 [1995]) *Fingerprints of the Gods (A Quest for the Beginning and the End)*, Seal Books: Toronto, p. 468.

CHAP. IV: THE SUPREMACY OF HORUS, SON OF RE | 191

In support of their theory that the Great Pyramid's shafts were astronomical markers pointing to the sky, Bauval, Gilbert and Hancock refer to the Neoplatonist Proclus who, in the fourth century CE, claimed on the basis of his study of Plato's writings that the Great Pyramid functioned as an astronomical observatory. They also refer to the work of Victorian author Richard A. Proctor who, in his 1883 book *The Great Pyramid: Observatory, Tomb and Temple,* reiterated that very same idea.[14] Proctor theorized that the Great Pyramid's various corridors had been used to observe the stars in the sky while the structure was being constructed. Most conventional Egyptologists however maintain that the Great Pyramid shafts had been used merely for ventilation purposes. But, joining Bauval and Gilbert, I remain convinced that the shafts were in fact channels to the stars.

A truly fascinating corpus of ancient religious texts, dating to the 5th Dynasty, offering valuable insight on this star-shaft theory, have been found inscribed on the walls of the pyramid of Pharaoh Unas. While the earlier pyramids had been virtually devoid of text, several 5th and 6th Dynasty pyramids were full of these esoteric texts. Known collectively as the *Pyramid Texts,* these hymns praised the coming of Osiris in the form of Orion:

> Behold he has come as Orion, behold Osiris has come as Orion ... O King, the sky conceives you with Orion, the dawn-light bears you with Orion ... you will regularly ascend with Orion from the eastern region of the sky, you will regularly descend with Orion in the western region of the sky ... your third is Sothis [Sirius]...
> (*Pyramid Texts,* 820-822)

This passage identifies Osiris with the constellation of Orion (Osiris-Orion) and his queen Isis with Orion's companion star Sirius (conferring her the title of Isis-Sirius). Sirius was closely related to the constellation of Orion because the former rose immediately after the latter. Hence, as the companion-star of Osiris-Orion, the ancient Egyptians identified Sirius with the goddess Isis — the celestial couple. The same manner in which the star-shaft from the King's Chamber in the Great Pyramid points towards the Belt of Orion, it was found, thanks to the diligence of independent Egyptologist Robert Bauval, that the southern shaft from the Queen's Chamber aimed directly at the star Sirius. In Bauval's mind, this was no mere coincidence. The examination of the Queen's Chamber by German engineer Rudolf Gatenbrink, in March of 1993, had shown that, unlike what Egyptologists had long thought, the southern shaft from the Queen's Chamber had not been abandoned in the midst of construction. In fact, it had been an integral ritualistic component of the Great Pyramid.

---

[14] See Robert Bauval and Adrian Gilbert (1994) *The Orion Mystery (Unlocking the Secrets of the Pyramids),* p. 43.

The Antiquity of the Osiris and Isis Cults

Regardless of the existing disagreements between scholars, with respect to the interpretation of the Pyramid Texts, one thing everyone agrees on is that they record the rebirth hymns reenacting the story of Osiris and Isis and their divine procreation of Horus.[15] As summarised earlier, this marks a significant return to the ancient Heliopolitan theology. Moreover, a New Kingdom document known as the Westcar Papyrus, now in the Berlin Museum, relates that the 5th Dynasty had been formed under the divine directions of Re, the Heliopolitan sun-god. Although the Westcar Papyrus is a conventional New Kingdom document, it is widely accepted to have been a copy of a 5th Dynasty original. Since the Heliopolitan Theology predates dynastic Egypt in my revised history, the return to prominence of Osiris presents no particular contradiction. However, to conventional Egyptologists, the issue is not so simple. While recognizing the antiquity of the cult of Osiris itself, Egyptologists, as it has been most thoroughly argued by John Gwyn Griffiths, believe that the Osirian element was "added" to the story of the conflict between Horus and Seth during the 5th Dynasty.[16] In other words, modern Egyptologists believe that the Heliopolitan Theology, which establishes the familial relationship between Osiris, Horus and Seth, cannot predate the 5th Dynasty. Therefore, my theory that the 5th Dynasty pharaohs inaugurated a Heliopolitan theological "renaissance" is entirely incompatible with orthodox views. But how can the cults of Horus and Seth actually be precursors to the cult Osiris? This fundamental question is posed by author Jane B. Sellers:

> It is disconcerting that some Egyptologists accept an early date for the conflict between Horus and Seth more readily than for the origin of the stories of Osiris. This acceptance is based on what are believed to be representations of Horus and Seth dated to a millennium before historical times.[17]

How could there have been a conflict between Horus and Seth in predynastic times if the god Osiris had not existed prior to the 5th Dynasty? Furthermore, the battle between Horus and Seth was fought over which one of them would gain the "inheritance" of Osiris! How could the cult of Osiris have not existed prior to the 5th Dynasty?

---

[15] Ibid, p. 92.
[16] J. Gwyn Griffiths (1980) *The Origins of Osiris and His Cult*, E. J. Brill: Leiden, pp. 7-8.
[17] Jane B. Sellers (1992) *The Death of Gods in Ancient Egypt (An Essay on Egyptian Religion and the Frame of Time)*, Penguin Books: New York, p. 23.

CHAP. IV: THE SUPREMACY OF HORUS, SON OF RE | 193

Based on the research that I've so far outlined, there is absolutely no doubt in my mind, to again quote Sellers, that "Osiris' story was cloaked in the veil of distant antiquity even at this early date."[18] Likewise, long before Jane B. Sellers, Cheikh Anta Diop had emphatically asserted that the myth of Isis and Osiris was "at the origin of the Egyptian nation."[19] Hence, unlike what Egyptologists would like to believe, despite being the first "dynastic Egyptian" text to mention the god Osiris, the pyramid texts of the 5th Dynasty were certainly not the first "pharaonic" records to mention Osiris. Ultimately, Osiris was a Khemetic god and, as such, absence of evidence from the dynastic Egyptian's records before the 5th Dynasty is, by no means, evidence of absence. As the Inventory Stela proves, the cults of Osiris and Isis antedates, by centuries, the ascent of the 5th Dynasty. In an attempt to rationalize Egyptology's paradoxical position, Griffiths explains:

> The most distinctive claim concerning the story of Osiris is that he is represented as the god who died. He is said to have died through the action of an enemy, Seth, but this enemy emerges, in an older myth, as the enemy of Horus. The reason for Seth's enmity to Osiris is plainly the fact that Horus was identified with the living king and Osiris with the dead father, so that the enmity is transferred, in death, to another god.[20]

While this is certainly an ingenious proposition, it does not, in the light of the body of evidence presented thus far, stand up to close scrutiny. As a result, far too much would have to be summarily explained away. But profoundly entrenched assumptions die hard. Following James H. Breasted's "increased Osirinization"[21] hypothesis, contemporary Egyptologists have unfalteringly upheld the view that, from a powerful Horus kingship, the supremacy of Re and Osiris later ensued. Perhaps there can be no finer example to delineate the fundamental difference between traditional Egyptology and Khemetology. Egyptologists, basing their assumptions on the supremacy of dynastic Egypt (or the dynastic race), as the primordial cradle of pharaonic culture, naturally cannot endorse the notion of the predynastic antiquity of Osiris. So the sudden emergence of the god Osiris, the father of Horus, so late in dynastic Egyptian history represents a primary contradiction which can only be explained in two ways: (1) either, as J. Gwyn

---

[18] Ibid, p. 21.
[19] Cheikh A. Diop (1982) *L'unité culturelle de l'Afrique Noire*, Présence Africaine: Paris, p. 56.
[20] J. Gwyn Griffiths (1980) p. 22.
[21] Leonard H. Lesko 'Ancient Egyptian Cosmogonies and Cosmology.' In Byron E. Shafer (editor) (1991) *Religion in Ancient Egypt (Gods, Myths, and Personal Practice)*, Cornell University Press: Ithaca & London, p. 100.

Griffiths postulates, the cult of Osiris was an oddly applied later addition or, (2) as logic itself would seem to dictate, the origins of the cult of Osiris and his familial links with Horus were already well established before the advent of the 1st Dynasty. Khemetology adopts the second deduction. To be sure, the proto-dynastic Egyptians were not ignorant of the cult of Osiris prior to the 5th Dynasty; but, in fact, respectfully recognized it as a cardinal constituent of the cult of Horus the Elder. Once the traditional Khemetic and dynastic Egyptian kingships of Horus the Elder and Horus the Child finally coalesced into a single dynastic crown during the Old Kingdom, this basic distinction was forever abandoned and Osiris became a fully-fledged dynastic Egyptian god.

The Day the Earth Shook

Similarly, it has caught the attention of Egyptologists that the scribes who compiled the Turin Canon presented the end of the 5th Dynasty as the closing stage of a great era — beginning with King Menes. This perception that the termination of the 5th Dynasty marked the culmination of an era was probably partly inspired by the catastrophic traditions associated with the World Ages. If such is indeed the case, then one should expect to find some evidence of a major cosmic conflagration at the end of Pharaoh Unas' reign. This evidence in fact does exist. But the conflagration dated to the end of the 5th Dynasty was not a typical cycle-ending Venus shift. Instead, it was a relatively modest Mercury shift which announced the forthcoming third Typhon Season. Pharaoh Unas was undoubtedly aware of the coming period of chaos as, from an isolated block from Unas' Causeway, he had carved images of helpless people suffering from famine and of complete social disorder. Since the editors of the Turin Canon were obviously not following the order of the ending World Ages, the great era which they were referring to, from the 1st to the end of the 5th Dynasty, most likely alludes to the period which covered the progression from the birth of Horus the Child to the final and total unification of the Horus the Elder and Horus the Child kingships (including the Osirinization of dynastic Egypt). Nevertheless, the culmination of this historical process was likewise accompanied by a degeneration in the social and natural order.

The sense of impending disaster, also experienced earlier by Khnum-Khufu, another past pyramid builder, is amply demonstrated in the Pyramid Texts. Pyramid Text 509 reveals:

> The sky thunders, the earth quakes, Geb quivers,
>   the two districts of God roar, the earth is hacked up.
> ... The encircling of Horus was in Abydos, and Osiris was
>   embalmed so that he might go forth to the sky among
>   the imperishable stars.

CHAP. IV: THE SUPREMACY OF HORUS, SON OF RE | 195

> His companion is Sothis, his guide is the morning star,
> > and they grasp his hand at the Field of Hetep.
> He sits on this iron throne,
> > the faces of which are those of lions ,
> > the feet of which are the horns of the Great Wild Bull.[22]

Commenting on these Pyramid Texts, John Gwyn Griffiths writes:

> The *Pyramid Texts* contain several instances of spells beginning in this way with the suggestion that cosmic disturbances precede an important event. Thus the 'Cannibal Hymn' begins, 'The heavens pour water, the stars are darkened' (393a); Spell 477, which portrays a trial scene in Heliopolis, begins, 'The heaven is agitated, the earth trembles' (956a); Spell 503, a solar composition, starts with 'The door of heaven is opened, the door of earth is opened' (1078a) ...[23]

Pharaoh Unas' unambiguous report that the entire earth trembled and that the skies were darkened undoubtedly refers to yet another planetary catastrophe. The planet which shifted from its set orbital path at the end of Pharaoh Unas' reign was Mercury. There is a telling episode described in the Pyramid Texts concerning the trial of Seth — the god of confusion and chaos. The 5th Dynasty texts relate that Seth was summoned to face the Great Ennead at Heliopolis in order to answer for his actions in disturbing the cosmic order. Geb, the presider at the trial, found Seth guilty of committing violent acts against Osiris. As punishment, Seth was condemned to carry Osiris as the latter traversed the firmament; so that Seth may tremble under Osiris as the earth quivers.

> The Lord of the storm, it is forbidden him to spit when he carries thee.
> It is he who will carry Atum.
> (*Pyramid Texts* 1261a-b)

The 5th Dynasty context of this mythical trial is very translucent. The Ennead of Heliopolis, reflecting the Khemetic renaissance, occupies a central leadership position. What is more, the traditional enmity between Seth and Osiris supersedes the conflict between Seth and Horus. Once again, Seth-Mercury is responsible for disturbing the cosmic order. As a result, I contend that this tale represents a genuine historical event. The Mercury-induced conflagration, the intemperate attack

---

[22] Leonard H. Lesko (1991) pp. 99-100.
[23] John Gwyn Griffiths (1970b) 'BRIEF COMMUNICATIONS: 'The Pregnancy of Isis': a comment', *Journal of Egyptian Archaeology* 55, p. 195.

against Osiris, took place in *c*.2,400 BCE. The astronomer-priests of Pharaoh Unas' court knew that the great tremors experienced by the earth and the darkened skies were caused by Seth-Mercury.

5

Coping with the Asiatic Threat (2,400 BCE to 2,150 BCE)

The Mercury shift of *c*.2,400 BCE at the end of the 5th Dynasty did not precipitate a Typhon Season but nonetheless foreshadowed a relatively long period of intense economic, social and natural upheavals. It was the beginning of the end of a great era for the dynastic race. The resilience of the dynastic Egyptian state was to be tested in the process by foreign invasions from Syria-Palestine. Elsewhere in the ancient Near East, the period covered in the present chapter also witnessed foreign invasions into ancient Mesopotamian city-states. Overflowing movements of Asiatic peoples, often synonymous with Sethian rebellions, were readily associated with Mercury shifts. Typhon Season #3 was incidentally ushered in by a Mercury shift in *c*.2,180 BCE. Hence, within a period of 220 years two Mercury shifts prompted Asiatic invasions by disciples of Seth. Weakened by Mercury's ravages, Egypt and Mesopotamia helplessly saw their borders invaded by Asiatic intruders.

The Arrival of the C-Group Asiatic Nubians
At the beginning of the Old Kingdom, the Lower Nubian town of Buhen was founded by the Egyptians — mainly for the purpose of copper production. The town was an important centre throughout the New Kingdom. King Khufu used the city and its vicinities as sites for diorite quarries. Then, quite unexpectedly, the fortress of Buhen was abandoned near the end of the 5th Dynasty. All the nearby quarries were immediately closed. The reason for that divestiture, according to most Egyptologists, is that the chaotic state of affairs in Egypt at the end of the Old Kingdom allowed for a band of northern invaders — the C-Group Nubians — to settle in Nubia, and ultimately overtake Upper and Lower Nubia. From then on, faced with hostile new neighbours to the south, the dynastic Egyptians could no longer roam all over Nubia unopposed.

I date this invasion to *c*.2,400 BCE when, at the close of the 5th Dynasty, the planet Mercury shifted from its prescribed orbit — causing a global cataclysm. The C-Group Nubians were not natives of Nubia but were Asiatic invaders from Syria-Palestine — the Land of Punt. As the goddess Hathor, Mistress of Punt/ Phoenicia who arrived in Egypt from Syria-Palestine in the beginning of the New Horus

Period, the Asiatics settlers who invaded Upper Nubia at the end of the 5th Dynasty, and who later became known as the C-Group Nubians, hailed from the land of Pontus — father of Seth-Poseidon. As I've argued at length in Chapter 2, the original Land of Punt was located in the Syria-Palestine — homeland of the Asiatic followers of Seth-Poseidon. It is therefore only fitting that a Mercury-induced invasion should emanate from the primordial Land of Punt. Nubia only came to be known as the Land of Punt when the Asiatics came to settle the region *en masse* at the end of the 5th Dynasty. Hence, the widely accepted notion that the Land of Punt, or God's Land, was exclusively located in the Somali coast is erroneous. Referring to this accepted view about the land of Punt's location, Egyptologist Michael Rice likewise points to the possibility that "Punt" might not have always been synonymous with Nubia:

> ... this does not mean that it (the land of Punt) was always located there (east Africa or south Arabia). There are many examples of place names changing their actual location, a process which is initiated by a number of different circumstances.[1]

This special circumstance was dictated by the fact that Nubia became a prime haven for the followers of Seth dwelling outside of the divinely regulated (*ma'at*) borders of the Egyptian state. Having established the equation, or equivalence, of the terms "Land of Punt" and "Land of the Asiatics," there is no inherent contradiction with viewing both east Africa and Syria-Palestine as authentic locations of God's Land or Land of Punt.

The hybrid culture which the C-Group Asiatic Nubians initiated in 2,400 BCE was largely based on the local Nubian culture (Pre-Kerma) which they found upon arriving in Upper Nubia. Nevertheless, the C-Group Asiatic Nubians and the earlier A-Group Nubians, quite obviously, belonged to different racial categories. Outlining these transitions, Nubiologist William Y. Adams writes:

> Elliot Smith and Derry had no difficulty in recognizing significant racial differences among the skeletons from the various Nubian grave types. The people of the 'A-Group' they believed to be identical with the pre-dynastic Egyptians, while in the 'B-Group' they perceived a much stronger Negro strain. This element was still believed to be present, although much diluted, in the 'C-Group' — a circumstance which led both Elliot Smith and Reisner to postulate a second migration of northerners into the Sudan at this time.[2]

---

[1] Michael Rice (1991) *Egypt's Making (The Origins of Ancient Egypt 5000-2000 BC)*, Routledge: London and New York, p. 64.
[2] William Y. Adams (1977) *Nubia: Corridor to Africa*, Princeton University Press: Princeton, NJ, p. 91.

CHAP. V: COPING WITH THE ASIATIC THREAT | 199

As W. Y. Adams illuminates, the C-Group Nubian settlement (Early Kerma) at the ancient Third Cataract town of Kerma marked a sudden departure, racially speaking, from the earlier African settlements. The only plausible explanation has to be that an Asiatic invasion, in c.2,400 BCE, brought in a substantial influx of non-African blood to the region. The Early Kerma Asiatic Nubians, in a very short time, transcended the Pre-Kerma African B-Group Nubians (whom Nubiologists perceive as having had "stronger Negro strain") and significantly altered the military and political realities south of Egypt's border.

	Standard Chronology	**New Chronology**
Pre-Kerma	3,000 - 2,400 BCE	2,950 - 2,400 BCE
Early Kerma	2,400 - 2,050 BCE	2,400 - 1,953 BCE
Middle Kerma	2,050 - 1,750 BCE	1,953 - 1,780 BCE
Classic Kerma	1,750 - 1,580 BCE	1,780 - 1,628 BCE
Final Kerma	1,580 - 1,500 BCE	1,628 - 1,559 BCE

Table 5-1

These Syro-Palestinian newcomers established themselves in both Upper and Lower Nubia. The name "Wawat" was used to describe all of Lower Nubia — which represents the land between the First and the Second Cataract. "Yam," the precursor of "the land of Kush,"[3] was itself used to designate Upper Nubia — between the Second and the Fourth Cataract. The Egyptians of the 6th Dynasty referred to the inhabitants of the territory of Wawat (Lower Nubia) as the Medjay, while those from the Land of Kush (Upper Nubia) were naturally known as the Kushites. Other names used to denote the Nubians of Wawat and Kush were *Ta-Seti* (evidently a throwback to the A-Group Nubians) and *Ta-Nehesy* (*nehesy* means "Nubian" and *Panehesy* signifies "the Nubian"). Yet another common Egyptian designation for the C-Group Nubians was "People of the Bow." This name is, of course, not without reminding us of the similar term employed in proto-dynastic times to denote the Syro-Palestinian "wild men of Asia" who were known as "people of the bow"[4] — in reference to their characteristic use of the bow in warfare. The bow, which was imported from Asia, is another crucial example of the commanding influence of Syria-Palestine over Nubia at the close of the Old Kingdom.

---

[3] Marianne Cornevin (1998) *Secrets du continent Noir révélés par l'archéologie*, Maisonneuve et Larose: Paris, p. 109.
[4] Donald B. Redford (1992) *Egypt, Canaan, and Israel in Ancient Times*, Princeton University Press: Princeton, NJ, pp. 31-32.

The Sixth Dynasty

Despite the natural upheavals which accompanied the transition from the 5th to 6th Dynasties, there does not appear to have been any antagonism, or strife, between the rulers of these two dynasties. King Teti had married a daughter of King Unas: Iput — who later gave birth to King Pepy I. The difficult period which preceded the rise of the 6th Dynasty is nonetheless apparently acknowledged in the prenomen of King Teti who adopted the Horus name of *Seheteptawy*, meaning: "He who pacifies the Two Lands." According to both Eusebius and Africanus, King Teti was assassinated by guards from his own court.[5] Some Egyptologists believe that Pharaoh Userkare, his immediate successor, might have had a hand in his murder.[6] Other Egyptologists, like W. C. Hayes and Nicholas Grimal, however believe that Pharaoh Userkare was instrumental in ensuring the smooth transition between Pharaohs Teti and Pepi I's reigns by providing legitimacy to the line.

The 6th Dynasty rulers, following the 5th Dynasty Khemetic renaissance, continued to grant preeminence to the Heliopolitan cult. But again, the prevailing state theology was adjusted to fit current political circumstances. This, for instance, is made amply evident in Pharaoh Merenre's Northern Inscription (cut on a block of granite south of the first cataract on the eastern bank of the Nile, facing the southern extremity of the island of El-Hesseh):

> The king stands leaning upon his staff, with the lion's tail as his only symbol of royalty. Behind him is the god Khnum, and before him the chiefs of Nubia. Over his head are the usual names and titles: *"King of Upper and Lower Egypt, Mernere;"* behind him the words: *"Beloved of Khnum, Lord of the Cataract;"* below him the date: *"Year 5, second month of the third season (tenth month), day 28."* [7]

King Merenre's title as "Beloved of Khnum," as King Khnum-Khufu had likewise called himself, accentuates Merenre's adherence to the ancient Khemetic traditions. Now confronted with the inimical presence of the C-Group Asiatic Nubians, Merenre emphasises his dominance over his Sethian enemies — collectively referred to as the "Nine Bows." Two copper statues representing King Pepy I and Merenre, now in the Cairo Museum, were found in Hierakonpolis — showing the kings trampling the Nine Bows under their feet.

---

[5] Manetho, Aegyptiaca, FRS. 19(a-b)-20.
[6] Michel Baud & Vassil Dobrev (1995) 'De nouvelles annales de l'Ancien Empire égyptien (Une «Pierre de Palerme» pour la VIe dynastie)', *Bulletin de l'Institut Français d'Archéologie Orientale* 95, p. 60.
[7] J. H. Breasted, Ancient Records of Egypt, Vol. I - § 317.

The 6th Dynasty lasted for about 220 years — the time separating the Mercury shifts of 2,400 BCE and 2,180 BCE. Pharaoh Pepy II is known to have ruled over Egypt for as long as 94 years — although, more recently, historians have generally agreed on a estimation of about 57 years.[8] While an exact figure for the length of his reign can't be established with certainty, what is undisputable is that he had a very long reign. Queen Nictoris, the last ruler of the 6th Dynasty according to the Manethonian texts, was the wife of King Merenre II — the son of King Pepy II. The Turin Canon vindicates the Manethonian editors by listing her as 'King of Upper and Lower Egypt' immediately after her husband Merenre II, who himself reigned for only a year.

The Old Akkadian Empire
Contemporaneously with the 6th Dynasty in *c*.2,400 BCE, the competing amalgamation of independent Mesopotamian city-states characterizing the Early Dynastic era underwent significant changes with the accession of a new ruler: King Sargon. Considered by most ancient world scholars to have been a usurper of the line of succession at Kish,[9] King Sargon consolidated the first completely unified Mesopotamian state. The "Sargonic period" is synonymous with the term "Old Akkadian period" since King Sargon had established his capital at Akkad (also spelled Agade). Akkadian became the official language — displacing Sumerian which had been the predominant language during the Early Dynastic era. Sumerian culture would however continue to exist for centuries to come. The new centralized administration at Akkad continued to use Sumerian principally as a scholarly and liturgical language and royal inscriptions were now bilingual. Like the 6th Dynasty in Egypt, the five-ruler dynasty of Akkad came to a catastrophic end with the Mercury shift of 2,180 BCE which inaugurates Typhon Season #3.

The beginning of the Sargonic empire, again as was the case with Egypt's 6th Dynasty, was presaged by the earlier Mercury shift of 2,400 BCE. Sargon, finding the resulting chaos which had visited southern Anatolia, felt confident to undertake a massive northern campaign to suppress any potential opposition to his vast Mesopotamian empire. In the wide sweep of his conquests, one of the major city-states vanquished by the Akkadian king Sargon was Susa. The city of Susa, located in the modern region of Khuzestan, was the capital of Elam. From *c*.3,000 BCE to

---

[8] Nicholas Grimal (1992) *A History of Ancient Egypt*. Trans. by Ian Shaw. Blackwell: Oxford, U.K., p. 89.
[9] Norman Yoffee 'The Collapse of Ancient Mesopotamian States and Civilization.' In Cowgill, George L. & Yoffee, Norman (editors) (1988) *The Collapse of Ancient States and Civilizations*, p. 46.

about the time of the Babylonian king Hammurabi (early seventeenth century BCE[10]), the script then known to the Elamites was proto-Elamite. Following the conquest of ancient Susa by Sargon, important contacts were maintained between Elam and Mesopotamia throughout the Semitic Akkadian period. The circumstances under which King Sargon consolidated his prodigious empire, covered in much mystery in the minds of contemporary historians, are therefore seen to have been triggered by the civil chaos which accompanied the Mercury shift of 2,400 BCE. In a study on the collapse of the ancient Mesopotamian states, historian Norman Yoffee writes:

> The *Curse of Agade* (Cooper 1983) tells how Sargon rose to power with the help of the goddess Inanna and the god Enlil. The capital of Agade flourished with this divine favour until such time as Naram-Sin was reluctant to accept the prescribed ordinances and plundered Enlil's holy city of Nippur (whose scribes probably wrote this account). In revenge, Enlil called forth the host of Gutium people "with human instincts, but [of] canine intelligence and monkey's features" (Cooper 1983:57), from their Zargos Mountains home to devastate Agade."[11]

From the above reference to the effect that King Sargon rose to power with the aid of the notoriously tempestuous Sumerian gods Inanna and Enlil, one may indeed plausibly deduce that King Sargon's assent took place amid promethean cosmic tremors. Similarly, once the gods withdrew their favour from the Old Akkadian kingdom, they sent, through the agency of Typhon Season #3, multitudes of foreign invaders to utterly decimate Akkad. We again find the familiar theme of divine anger and retribution in response to the earthling leaders' transgressions.

The Sentence of the Heavens

> " At the conclusion of the Sixth Dynasty
> ... Egypt is suddenly blotted out from
> our sight as if some great catas-
> trophy had overwhelmed it."
>
> - G. A. Wainwright
> Egyptologist, 1930

The Old Kingdom in Egypt, analogously to the Old Akkadian period in Mesopotamia, came to an end in a ruinous social, cultural, natural and environmental

---

[10] According to the novel chronology.
[11] Norman Yoffee (1988) p. 62; Jerrold Cooper (1983) *The Curse of Agade*, Johns Hopkins University Press: Baltimore, MD.

CHAP. V: COPING WITH THE ASIATIC THREAT | 203

disaster. To cite American Egyptologist William A. Ward:

> Toward the close of the Sixth Dynasty (early 22nd century B.C.), a violent wave of destruction virtually wiped out Early Bronze culture in Palestine.[12]

As W. A. Ward delineates, this conflagration was far from being a mere local phenomenon. The outright collapse of Egypt's Old Kingdom must be seen within the context of a much larger wave of destructions. The real cause for the fall of the Old Kingdom far transcends mere internal political and/or class divisions. From the Nile Valley to Anatolia, overwhelming evidence for the two-pronged planetary cataclysm (Mercury shift of $c.2,180$ BCE and Venus shift of $c.2,130$ BCE) which terminated the early Bronze Age is there to be examined. As part of her analysis of the destruction of Byblos at the end of the Egyptian 6th Dynasty, the late British archaeologist Dame Kathleen Kenyon writes:

> ... evidence suggests that this break is associated with a great destruction by fire. ... A major event recorded by the stratification is a destruction by fire which left a deposit of ash up to 0.50 metre thick ... Beneath this were the objects that can be dated on epigraphic or other grounds to the time of the Old Kingdom of Egypt; objects with the name of Phiops II [Pepi II] were also included in the current material. ... Byblos therefore suffered a destruction at about the same period as that in which the incursions of Asiatics into Egypt broke up settlement government ...[13]

Those destructions at the end of the Old Kingdom occurred at the same time as other similar violent conflagrations at the close of Hissarlik's Troy II stratum, of Alisar, of Alaca Huyuk, of Tarsus, and other sites throughout Asia Minor.[14] What could have wrought such widespread havoc, from Troy to the Nile Valley, other than a universal cataclysm? During his 1930s excavations in Syria-Palestine and Anatolia, French archaeologist Claude F. Schaeffer found evidence of such ubiquitous destruction, over a great distance, that he simply could not accept the notion that this devastation could have been caused by invading armies, as conventional wisdom preached. As Kenyon maintained, Schaeffer's excavations had tho-

---

[12] W. A. Ward (1971) *Egypt and the East Mediterranean World: 2200-1900 B.C. (Studies in Egyptian Relations During the First Intermediate Period)*, American University of Beirut: Beirut, Lebanon, p. 11.
[13] Kathleen Kenyon (1966) *Amorites and Canaanites*, Oxford University Press: London, pp. 46-47.
[14] See Claude F. A. Schaeffer (1948) *Stratigraphie comparée et chronologie de l'Asie Occidentale (IIIe et IIe millénaires)*, Oxford University Press: London, p. 225.

roughly convinced him that the fiery destruction of Byblos was contemporary with the end of the 6th Dynasty in Egypt. He additionally correlates this destruction with the collapse of the second level-city of ancient Troy (Hissarlik):

> Indeed, there is not for us the slightest doubt that the conflagration of Troy II corresponds to the catastrophe that made an end to the habitations of the Old Bronze Age of Alaca Huyuk (level III), of Alisar (level IA), of Tarsus (level III, 12 to 13 metres below surface), and - [some 2,300 km east of Troy] - of Tepe Hissar (level IIB). In Syria this catastrophe incinerated Ancient Ugarit 2, the city of Byblos of Palestine.[15]

As the following table illustrates, Troy II indeed ends contemporaneously with the close of the 6th Dynasty.

Chronology of ancient Troy during the Early Bronze Age and nascent Middle Bronze Age

Troy I	3,000-2,500 BCE
	3,114 - 2,500 BCE (New Chronology)
Troy II	2,500 - 2,200 BCE
	2,200 - 2,180 BCE (New Chronology)
Troy III	2,200 - 2,050 BCE
	2,180 - 2,050 BCE (New Chronology)
Troy IV	2,050 - 1,900 BCE
	2,050 - 1,953 BCE (New Chronology)

Table 5-2

The cosmic disaster of 2,180 BCE caused seasonal rains to become very scarce — leading to heavy droughts which in turn contributed to the forced movement of vast numbers of city-dwellers and pastoral nomads — who deserted their towns and villages to seek refuge near rivers and streams.[16] Only decades after the Akkadians occupied the town of Tell Leilan and erected massive walls, renovated its religious quarters, and entirely overhauled its grain production system, the town was, quite inexplicably, suddenly abandoned.[17] Between 2,200 BCE and 2,100 BCE, according to archaeologist Rafique Mughal of the Pakistan Department of Archae-

---

[15] Claude F. Schaeffer (1948) *Stratigraphie comparée et chronologie de l'Asie Occidentale (IIIe et IIe millénaires)*, Oxford University Press: London, p. 225 (Trans. by G. Heinsohn).
[16] H. Weis, *The Sciences*, May/June 1996. Cited in Timo Niroma, http://www.personal.eunet.fi/pp/tilmari/tilmari2.htm
[17] Ibid.

CHAP. V: COPING WITH THE ASIATIC THREAT | 205

ology, the great cities of Mohenjodaro and Harappa in the Indus Valley unremittingly collapsed. Evidently, this catastrophe was truly global in nature. The hypothesis that enemy action could have been responsible for the downfall of all these ancient great centres of civilization is simply untenable.

Granted, evidence of foreign invasions do in fact accompany the archaeological and textual remains relating to the general conflagration of 2,180 BCE. But these were the *effect*, not the primary *cause* of the massive destructions of the Early Bronze IV cities and states. During the frenetic period immediately following the Mercury shift, the Asiatics, taking once more full advantage of the sociopolitical instability, invaded and occupied the Egyptian Delta. Egypt suddenly finding itself overrun, the pharaonic succession went into disarray. The Abydos king-list records 18 ephemeral kings after the reign of Pepy II. According to Egyptologists, the total sum of their reigns amounts to about twenty years. Those short-reigning pharaohs constitute the much-aggrieved 7th and 8th Dynasties. While Egyptologists generally ascribe a length of around twenty years to these dynasties, I would argue for a total length of about thirty years (from 2,180 to 2,150 BCE). The 8th Dynasty eventually lost control of most of the Two Lands — leaving an opening for various Nomes, especially to the south, to start gaining more and more independence. Consequently, Middle Egypt ultimately fell under the control of Herakleopolitan princes. Being relatively distant from the principal centre of the Asiatic dominion further to the north, the first Herakleopolitan king, Meryibre Khety I, was able to extend his influence as far south as Aswan, near the First Cataract. Egypt was more divided than ever. With no centralized power to contend with, the Asiatic invaders in the Delta remained virtually unchallenged for decades.

The Gutian Invasion of Akkad

Dynastic Egypt was not alone in dealing with foreign invaders at the heels of the ruinous Mercury shift of 2,180 BCE. The ancient Mesopotamian records indeed reveal that from the time of the Akkadian king Naram-Sin's reign, the grand-son of Sargon, a northern mountain people known as the Gutians (Guti or Quti) were attempting to belligerently penetrate Akkad's territory. The semi-nomadic Gutians, hailing from the mountains of modern Iran, finally succeeded in overwhelming the Akkadians, principally as a result of the Mercury shift, at the end of King Naram-Sin's reign. Much like King Khnum-Khufu in Egypt, Sumerian tradition maintains that King Naram-Sin's presumed iniquitous behaviour raised the indignation of the gods, the Sumerian chief deity Enlil in particular, and brought doom to the kingdom.

In a popular Old Akkadian text entitled "The Curse of Akkad," actually written down centuries after the calamity, the Sumerian scribes transmit that Akkad was completely razed by the barbarian invasion. To quote historian Walter R. Bodine:

> The devastation of the Gutians effected is portrayed in the "Curse of Akkad." In order to calm Enlil, eight of the leading deities pronounced a curse on Akkad, which was immediately carried out. In the world-view of the ancient Mesopotamian, the events of history were understood to be a playing out on the human level of the decisions made on the divine plane. Noteworthy in this composition is the attribution of the fall of Akkad to the act of Naram-Sin.[18]

As the following excerpt from "The Curse of Akkad" illuminates, Enlil caused the Gutians to descend *en masse* from the northern mountains to assail Akkad. Though the Gutians were certainly long predisposed to carry out that raid, it was the explicit will of Enlil which ultimately handed them the opportunity and the victory. Again, this and other barbarian assaults were the result, ignited by the planetary gods' wrath, and not the cause of the conflagrations.

> The roaring storm that subjugates the entire land,
> The rising deluge that cannot be confronted,
> Enlil, because his beloved Ekur (Enlil's temple at Nippur) was destroyed, what should he destroy (in revenge) for it?
> He looked towards the Gutian mountain ranges –
> Not classed among people, not reckoned as part of the land,
> Gutium, a people who know no inhibitions,
> With human instincts, but canine intelligence, and monkeys' features –
> Enlil brought them out of the mountains.
> Like herds of locust they lie over the land,
> Their arms are stretched over the plains for him (Enlil) like a snare for animals,
> Nothing leaves their arms,
> No one escapes their arms.
> Messengers no longer travel the highways,
> The courtier's boat no longer takes to the rivers.[19]

---

[18] Walter R. Bodine 'Sumerians.' In Alfred J. Hoerth, Gerald L. Mattingly & Edwin M. Yamauchi (editors) (1994) *Peoples of the Old Testament World*, p. 34.
[19] J. S. Cooper (1983) *The Curse of Agade*, Baltimore, pp. 142-63.

6

And the Waters of Heaven Came Down
(2,150 BCE to 1,953 BCE)

In the midst of civil disorder which followed the Mercury shift of 2,180 BCE, power in Egypt became highly decentralized. The monarchs of the 7th and 8th Dynasties where pharaohs only by title. It was only a matter of time before a more forceful dynastic line took over the reigns of power. But even that eventual consolidation of power, under the 9th and 10th Dynasty pharaohs of Herakleopolis, would not remained unchallenged. The historical period covered in this chapter, from 2,150 BCE to 1,953 BCE, was a period in which both the resolve and authority of the now mature dynastic Egyptian monarchy would be severely tested. These trying tests came from both the natural world and their foreign shores thronging with potential Asiatic enemies. This lethal combination of natural catastrophes and foreign intrusion, as seen earlier with the Gutian invasion, shaped every major aspect of pharaonic policy between the end of the Old Kingdom and the beginning of the Middle Kingdom. This period (from 2,180-1,953 BCE), traditional known as the First Intermediate Period, is, in the present reconstruction, called the Diluvian Period. The reason why I refer to this period as such is because it was during this era that the historical Great Flood, also recorded by various ancient sources, other than the Old Testament, took place. While the literal drowning of all humanity, as described in the Book of Genesis, never took place, the Great Flood nonetheless brought yet another end to one of the Jewish Aggada's Seven Creations — with the cataclysmic culmination of Typhon Season #3. For some reason, the ancients unanimously looked to the Venus shift of 2,130 BCE as having been responsible for a universal Great Flood. From Egypt to China, this Venus-induced axis shift enacted an era of momentous religious, astronomical and political changes. I believe that a vivid account of this Great Flood has survived in ancient Egyptian literature. It is by dating that long-neglected ancient Egyptian Flood story that I shall attempt to demonstrate its contemporaneity with the six hundredth year of the biblical Noah's life — the year in which the Book of Genesis' Great Flood took place. I will thereby argue that it isn't necessary for Bible students to search for the historical roots of Noah's Great Flood in shadowy neolithic times, but rather, as the Bible in its literal chronological sense communicates, during the twenty-second century BCE.

The Kings of Herakleopolis

Sometime after c.2,150 BCE, new pharaohs began ruling Egypt from the Delta town of Herakleopolis. There's no evidence that these Herakleopolitan kings ever directly ruled southern Egypt.[1] Essentially, their inability to maintain a grip over Upper Egypt was due to the seditious activities of rebellious Theban princes. While the 9th and 10th Dynasty Herakleopolitan kings do not mention these Theban dissidents by name, it is generally accepted that they were the forebears of the Theban monarchs of the 11th Dynasty (who would gain power after the Venus shift of 2,130 BCE).[2] Although the traditional territorial conflict between the competing followers of Horus and Seth, so typical of Typhon Seasons, is missing during Typhon Season #3, we nevertheless find that Egypt is, once more, divided between north and south. In essence, the rebellious elements were positioned in Upper Egypt. Equally typical of these periods of befuddlement, the deciding agent in settling the dispute between the feuding districts was the planet Venus.

The Great Flood

According to the Bible (Gen. 7:11), the Great Flood came upon the earth during the six hundredth year of Noah's life. Having established that the character of Noah is none other than a biblical metaphor for the Upper Egyptian sacred city of Thebes ("No" of the Book of Genesis), it should logically follow that the Great Flood manifested itself on the six hundredth year of the foundation of the Theban Nome. While the Khemetic district of Thebes itself is very ancient, as it was founded by the Anu, the actual establishment of the Nome of Thebes with Amun as its chief deity dates to the beginning of the Old Kingdom. Since King Sneferu inaugurated the twelve Nomes in 2,730 BCE, it would signify that the Great Flood came in 2,130 BCE — the year of the Venus shift which heralded the end of Typhon Season #3 (or to the Second Creation or the Sixth Adamah). Having placed the Great Flood of the biblical narratives at the end of the Early Bronze Age, it should then become relatively easy to also date when the sons of Noah (i.e. Ham, Shem and Japheth) lived. Like the vast majority of the major biblical characters from the Book of Genesis, the names attributed to the sons of Noah represent important territories or entire peoples — not individuals. Therefore, it is my belief that the biblical redactors purposely wrote the Scriptures so as to ensure

---

[1] W. A. Ward (1971) *Egypt and the East Mediterranean World: 2200-1900 B.C. (Studies in Egyptian Relations During the First Intermediate Period)*, American University of Beirut: Beirut, Lebanon, p. 7.

[2] See J. H. Breasted, *Ancient Records of Egypt*, Vol. I - § 391.

that the earliest narratives would be more metaphorical, figurative or symbolic representations within the confines of a much broader hidden historical context. As I've argued in the previous chapters, such was the case for the story of Cain and Abel — whose tribulations mask a proto-historical confrontation between the followers of Horus and Seth in Egypt. Following the Genesis narratives, the biblical protagonists begin to take on more realistic attributes identifiable with proper individuals. In fact, far less frequently, if ever again, do we find extravagant references to characters whose total life-time spans reach into the hundreds of years. Many historians argue that one of the principal reasons why the Bible cannot be taken seriously as an historical document is because of the highly unrealistic length of certain pivotal biblical patriarchs' lives. For instance, how could anyone take seriously the biblical claim that Noah lived 950 years?! Theologians and historians would indeed waste their time trying to rationalize this conundrum if they choose to hold on to the traditional view that Noah was a genuine individual.

When can we begin to speak about "historical" characters in the Old Testament narratives? At what point do the scriptural narratives become genuinely "Jewish" — and no longer biblical metaphors of Khemeto-Egyptian and Babylonian sagas? I believe that ancient Jewish history, as it relates to their identity as a distinct people among other Canaanites, really begins with the Great Flood of 2,130 BCE. It is only from that time forward, in my own view, that we can speak of historical biblical individuals, beginning with Abraham (whom I shall later argue was a contemporary of the metaphorical Noah). The three sons of Noah (Ham, Shem and Japheth), although not themselves genuine individuals, symbolise the various ethnic groups which interacted with Egypt (Noah-Thebes) around the time of the Great Flood. Therefore, the Old Testament's genealogy of Noah (see Table 6-1) should be interpreted as a "table of nations" which individually either had a relevant part to play in the formation of the early Hebrew state or were significant cultural entities or states at the time of the Great Flood. With regards to the roots of the ancient Hebrews, Shem is by far the most important of Noah's three sons. Shem was born during the five hundredth year of Noah's life (Gen. 5:32). Furthermore, Shem was not married and had no children when he entered the Ark. His first offspring, born soon after the Flood, was Elam — whom scholars identify with Persia. The other sons of Shem were Ashur (Assyria), Arphaxad (Chaldea), Lud (Lydia), and finally Aram (Syria). Therefore, Shem was the ancestor of the Near Eastern peoples in general, and of the Hebrews specifically. Archaeologically speaking, it is particularly telling that, during the time of Typhon Season #3, a considerable number of Semites lived in the land of Elam.[3] It is indeed quite striking that at this particular time of history, in the closing Early Bronze Age, all these nations or city-states of the ancient Near East were beginning their emergence into prosperous centres of civilization. The genealogy of Noah therefore could not have had any kind of historical basis prior to the Early Bronze IV period — simply because hardly any of these nations which the three sons of Noah engendered after the Flood even existed as organized states before then.

The era of wickedness in which the Scriptures tell us that Noah lived shortly before the Great Flood corresponds to the chaotic times characterizing Typhon Season #3. Observing that the world was filled with violence, corruption and rebellion, the Book of Genesis (6:5-7) relates that God planned to destroy his entire creation. We are again reminded of the sun-god Re who, seeing how the earth-dwellers had rebelled during Typhon Season #1, at once decreed the Destruction of Mankind (the primeval Flood of Gilgamesh's Epic). In both cases, God's fury manifested itself in the form of cosmic catastrophe involving the flood-carrying planet Venus. In Egypt, an important eye witness and contemporary to this Great Flood of 2,130 BCE is Pharaoh Akhtoy (Khety) III. In a document know as the "Instruction for Merikare," Akhtoy imparts to his son and immediate successor, Merikare, some valuable advice on the importance of being a righteous ruler. In what may be considered a lament, King Akhtoy III recounts how the inequity of Egypt during his rule warranted the wrath of God but that, in his mercy, god had "subdued the water monster"[4]:

> Provide for people, the cattle of God, for he made heaven and earth for their liking. He repelled the greed of the waters; he made the winds in order that their nostrils might breath; [for] they are likenesses of him that came forth from his flesh. He shines in the sky for their liking; he has made vegetation, small cattle, and fish for them to nourish them. He has killed his enemies and destroyed his own children, because they planned to make rebellion.[5]

As was the case at the end of six of the seven Creations, or World Ages, the ancients believed that God destroyed the world through the agency of the planet Venus, the Archangel of the Semites or goddess Hathor of the Nile Valley, in order to quell the

---

[3] See Edwin M. Yamauchi (1996) *Persia and the Bible*, Baker Books: Grand Rapids, Mich., p. 281.
[4] Donald B. Redford (1992) *Egypt, Canaan, and Israel in Ancient Times*, Princeton University Press: Princeton, NJ, p. 46.
[5] Leonard H. Lesko 'Ancient Egyptian Cosmogonies and Cosmology.' In Byron E. Shafer (editor) (1991) *Religion in Ancient Egypt (Gods, Myths, and Personal Practice)*, Cornell University Press: Ithaca & London, p. 103.

The Genealogy of Noah:

NOAH

SHEM

1. Elam (**Persia**)
2. Ashur (**Assyria**)
3. Arphaxad (**Chaldea**)
4. Lud (**Lydia**)
5. Aram (**Syria**)

5) <u>ARAM</u>
   begot: - Uz
          - Hul
          - Gether
          - Mash

HAM

1. Cush (**Euph./Africa**)
2. Mizraim (**Egypt**)
3. Put (**Libya**)
4. Canaan (**Phoenicia & Palestine**)

1) <u>CUSH</u>
   begot: - Seba
          - Havilah
          - Sabath
          - Raamah
            begot: - Sheba
                    - Dedan
          - Sabtechah
          - Nimrod
            begot from
            <u>Shinar</u>: - Babel
                    - Erech
                    - Accad
                    - Calneh
            from
            <u>Assyria</u>: - Nineveh
                    - Rehoboth
                    - Calah

4) <u>CANAAN</u>
   begot: - Sidon, - Heth, - the Jesubites,
          - the Amorites

JAPHETH

1. Gomer   5. Tubal
2. Magog   6. Meshech
3. Madai   7. Tiras
4. Javan

1) <u>GOMER</u>
   begot: - Ashkenaz
          - Riphatah
          - Togarmah

4) <u>JAVAN</u>
   begot: - Elishah
          - Tarshish
          - Kittim
          - Dodanim

Table 6-1

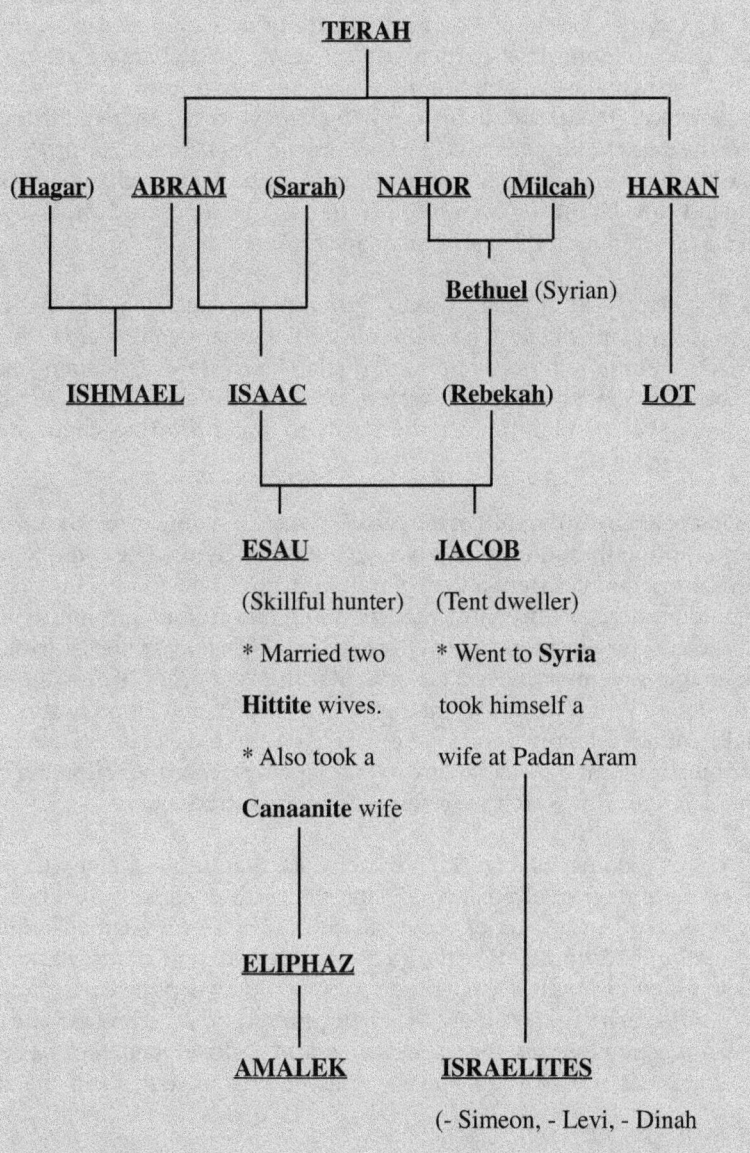

Table 6-2

CHAP. VI: AND THE WATERS OF HEAVEN CAME DOWN | 213

earthly rebellion of those (during a given Typhon Season) who had succumbed to Satan or Seth. In the above excerpt from the Instructions of Merikare, the familiar context of a Divine Creation followed by the deity's disappointment with his own creation is self-evident. In a particularly interesting side bar, we see above that Pharaoh Akhtoy makes an abundantly clear reference to torrents of water (*"the greed of the waters"*) that God, in his forgiving benevolence, removed from the face of the earth so as to allow his multifarious progeny to survive. Akhtoy's efforts to correlate the ruinous events of his own times to the watery chaos of primordial Creation indicates the sheer magnitude of the cataclysmic episode he is describing. As a series of prominent Bible scholars have claimed:

> The Flood was not simply a downpour of ordinary rain. The text indicates a cosmic upheaval. "The fountains of the great deep" were broken (Gen. 7:11). Perhaps there were earthquakes and the ocean floors may have been raised up until the waters covered the earth. By a supernatural upheaval, God returned the earth to the primitive chaos described in Genesis 1:2.[6]

Only a violent and sudden shift of the earth's polar axis could cause the ocean floors to rise, prompting the water to overwhelm inhabited lands. The consistent ancient traditions, from many distant and disparate cultures, concerning a universal Great Flood could hardly have been invented. Some common conflagration, experienced around the ancient world, must have served as a basis for all these stories. In the present chapter, we may indeed observe that the year 2,130 BCE is the common denominator, or reference point, linking the universal Great Flood traditions of the ancient Egyptians, Hebrews and Chinese. What could have happened in that year? At this point, it might be worthwhile to once again refer to the following quote by Immanuel Velikovsky, which we referred to in the Introduction:

> Let us assume, as a working hypothesis, that under the impact of a force or the influence of an agent — and the earth does not travel in an empty universe — the axis of the earth shifted or tilted. At that moment and earthquake would make the globe shudder. Air and water would continue to move through inertia; hurricanes would sweep the earth and the seas would rush over continents, carrying gravel and sand and marine animals, and casting them on the land. Heat would be developed, rocks would melt, volcanoes would erupt, lava would flow from fissures in the ruptured

---

[6] Lockyer, Herbert (editor) (1986) *Nelson's Illustrated Bible Dictionary*, Thomas Nelson: Nashville, p. 387.

ground and cover vast areas. Mountains would spring up from the plains and would travel and climb on the shoulders of other mountains, causing faults and rifts. Lakes would be tilted and emptied, rivers would change their beds; large land areas with their inhabitants would slip under the sea.[7]

Obviously, mere rainfall, no matter how unabated or prolonged, couldn't have produced the kind of devastation described in these ancient texts from Egypt to China. The watery paroxysm had been global in scope — causing the waters of the deep to rise to the surface and flooding many continents. As Immanuel Velikovsky imparts above, the Great Flood was provoked by a hurtling planetary body which passed dangerously close to the planet Earth. This agent was the planet Venus. As during the conclusion of every Typhonian fifty-two-year cycle, it violently veered from its prescribed orbital path and induced an axis shift which, in 2,130 BCE, produced a global fiery and watery conflagration.

The Hermopolitan Cosmogony: An Egyptian

Account of the Flood

The cataclysmic termination of this latest Typhon Season – in 2,130 BCE – heralded, once again, the reunification of the Two Lands under a novel dynasty. This time around, the rebellious forces were the victorious ones. The leaders of the Theban Nome, who had violently quarrelled with the Herakleopolitan kings through most of Typhon Season #3, abruptly put an end to Pharaoh Merikare's relatively short reign. The rise of the Theban rulers effectively brought to a close the Khemetic Renaissance begun under the 5th Dynasty. While the 11th Dynasty hailed from Upper Egypt, they actively sought to distance themselves from the cult of the sun-god Re. Theirs was a new era — a clean break from their processors' theological constructs. No more would the name of "Re" be found in the prenomens or throne names of the Theban pharaohs.

The unification of Egypt under the 11th Dynasty, following the Great Flood, occurred under some very unique circumstances. The preceding period of rebellion did not involve seditious Sethian disciples. The quarrel had been between the followers of Horus themselves. Yet, the divisions had been deep. Faced with an entirely new historical context, the Theban priests of the 11th Dynasty needed to devise a brand new cosmological construct to fit with the new reality. In addition to the purely political mutations, fundamental sociological changes affecting Egyptian domestic institutions had taken place. The end of the Old Kingdom had brought a rapid erosion of the authority of the Pharaoh as the predominant divine manifestation on earth. The increased power and influence of

---

[7] Immanuel Velikovsky (1955) *Earth in Upheaval*, Doubleday: Garden City, NY, p. 136.

the priesthood, who notoriously vied for their respective orders' and personal interests — to the ultimate expense of the Pharaoh, insured that the reigning king and his royal entourage or nobility would no longer have exclusive access to a prosperous afterlife. There is very little doubt that this "democratization" of the afterlife had greatly benefited the priesthood, as they could and probably did use it as a tool to undermine public support for the monarchy.

It was under this sociopolitical climate that the Theban 11th Dynasty came to power in Egypt. Quite understandably, the Theban priesthood of Amun freely capitalize on this general sentiment. Although, this time, the monarchy itself participated in the propaganda — quickly recognizing the political benefits they might gain from it. The new Theban pharaoh, Inyotef I, promised the populace that, unlike the preceding Herakleopolitan kings, the new Theban dynasty would rule as righteous servants of the people. As during the end of the First and Second Creations, the deposed monarchs had been accused of igniting the wrath of the heavens through their despotic and arrogant behaviour. Inyotef could therefore claim that he had been chosen by Heaven to exact the revenge of the gods upon the Herakleopolitan kings. Moreover, the Venus shift of 2,130 BCE had been particularly deadly — a situation which appears to have further emphasised, in the minds of the populace, the magnitude of Gods' anger. For while the planet Venus was known as an unpitying flood-carrier, the fact that ancient civilizations the world over chose to commemorate this particular Venus conflagration as the time of a universal "Great Flood," indicates that the axis shift had lifted an unusually large amount of water out of the ocean floors and into the inhabited lands. The resulting tumult disrupted the established social order — causing commoner to rise up against noble.

Our latest archaeotheological analysis of ancient Egyptian cosmogonies picks up here, immediately following the ruinous sociopolitical events engendered by the Great Flood. Neither the Heliopolitan or the Memphis Theologies were at that particular time appropriate cosmological constructs for the prevailing social order as the new Theban monarchs took over the reigns of the Two Lands from the Herakleopolitan pharaohs. A new cosmogony necessarily had to be formulated. That novel theology was developed around the Middle Egyptian town of Hermopolis, the city of Thoth. Unlike the more ancient Heliopolitan Ennead (which was composed of nine gods), the Hermopolitan cosmogony comprises of an "ogdoad" (a group of eight gods). These eight deities, the ogdoad, were divided into the following four couples: Nun and Naunet (were the watery abyss), Amun and Amaunet (represented hiddenness), Huh and Hauhet (were formlessness), and Kuk and Kauket (were darkness). Out of these eight gods came an egg bearing the creator-god responsible for all other deities, humans, and other living creatures. The Hermopolitan Theology has been interpreted by scholars as just another creation myth. In the eyes of most contemporary Western scholars, the ancient

Egyptians were merely adding more gods into their already crowded pantheon for the mere purpose of pleasing an ambitious priesthood, exponentially growing in power, and its legions of superstitious followers. Virtually no effort is made to try to find an historical foundation, or chronological sequence, for any of these theologies. To quote the American Egyptologist Leonard H. Lesko:

> Because it is impossible to know when each of the cosmogonical myths and cosmological concepts originated and how long each of them was prevalent, there is a definite tendency to ignore the problem and to present the phenomena as if all were applicable during the entire span of Egyptian history.[8]

However, I would challenge this dangerously defeatist belief among Egyptologists that it is "impossible" to date the creation and time-span of these ancient pharaonic cosmogonies. Our thorough archaeotheological analysis of the evolution of state theologies in ancient Khemeto-Egyptian society heretofore has, without a doubt, demonstrated that cosmogonical constructs followed very tangible historical patterns. In essence, the Hermopolitan cosmogony was a form of "Liberation Theology" which preached that the Great Flood had come along to democratize both the earthly society and the after world for the benefit of the commoner. This democratizing notion was most exhaustively articulated in a corpus of texts known collectively as the Book of the Two Ways. A guide-book to the beyond, excerpts from the Book of the Two Ways were inscribed inside the wooden coffins of all Egyptians — be they commoners or nobles. The "Coffin Texts," as they became more commonly known, promised that anyone could attain the same benefits of the afterlife as the Pharaoh, provided they could recite the spells.

Two versions of the Book of the Two Ways were apparently composed in the middle Egyptian town of Hermopolis. Coffin Text spell 130 recounts:

> **I made the great flood, that the poor man might have power like the great.**
> This is a deed thereof.
> I made every man like his fellow.
> **I did not command that they do evil.**
> **It is their hearts that disobey what I have said.**
> This is a deed thereof.
> I made their hearts to cease forgetting the West,
> in order to make divine offerings to the god
> of the nomes.
> This is a deed thereof. ...

---

[8] Leonard H. Lesko (1991) p. 122.

CHAP. VI: AND THE WATERS OF HEAVEN CAME DOWN | 217

As in the Bible, which quite significantly dates the Flood of Noah at the time when the Coffin Texts were composed, spell 130 communicates that the "Great Flood" came about as a direct result of humankind's inequity. By mercilessly destroying the evildoers, both in the Egyptian Book of the Two Ways and the Hebrew Book of Genesis, the Almighty manifests his preference for the meek of the earth. In the Coffin Texts, the weak are promised to go into the afterlife as "stars in the sky, alongside the moon god Thoth."[9] The eschatological destruction of the erring all-powerful rulers, once more, comes at the culmination of a Typhon Season. This Great Flood which democratized Egyptian society, by ousting the Herakleopolitan pharaohs, was evidently central to the emerging Hermopolitan Theology — as Coffin Text spell 76 illuminates:

> O you eight Heh (chaos) gods, keepers of the chambers of the sky, whom Shu made from the efflux of his limbs, who bound together the ladder of Atum, come in front of your father with me, give me your arms. Bind together the ladder for me; I am one who created you and made you, as I was created by your father, Atum.
>
> I am weary of the support of Shu since I raised up my daughter, Nut, from upon me, so that I might give her to my father Atum in his precinct. I have placed Geb under my feet. This god binds together the two lands for my father; he assembles for himself the Great Flood (heavenly cow). I have placed myself between them, so the Ennead cannot see me. I am Shu, whom Atum created, from whom Re came to be.
>
> I was not fashioned in the womb, I was not bound together in the egg, I was not conceived, but my father, Atum, spat me out in the spittle of his mouth, together with my sister, Tefnut. She went forth after me. I was covered with the breath of the throat.[10]

Although the 11th Dynasty pharaohs displaced the sun-god Re as the predominant state deity, in favour of the Theban god Amun, the above Coffin Text spell illustrates that the Heliopolitan Theology was skillfully remodelled in order to ensure a smooth transition between the Heliopolitan and Hermopolitan cosmogonies. The ennead (nine deities) are replaced by the ogdoad (eight deities) — among which we find Amun. In keeping with its archaeotheological context, the Hermopolitan Theology places the Great Flood at the genesis of the cosmogony.

---

[9] L. H. Lesko (1991) p. 102.
[10] R. O. Faulkner (1973-1978) *Ancient Egyptian Coffin Texts*. Vols. I-III. Aris & Phillips: Warminster, U.K., Vol. I: p. 77-80. Cited in Lesko (1991) pp. 94-95.

Other Flood Narratives from around the World

> " A god, Ifa, tired of living on earth and went to dwell in the firmament. Without his assistance, mankind couldn't interpret the desires of the gods, and one god, in a fit of rage, destroyed nearly everybody in a great flood."
>
> - Yoruba myth (southwest Nigeria)[11]

A vast number of ancient traditions relate that, in the antediluvian world (i.e. before the Great Flood), a race of giants peopled the earth. The precise meaning behind those ancient myths is difficult to ascertain. Nonetheless, for the purposes of dating the Great Flood, these myths are important bench markers. In ancient Mesoamerica, legend has it that these antediluvian giants instantly perished when the sky fell upon the earth at the end of the Second Sun (or Second Creation).[12] Moreover, as the Book of Genesis (6:4) makes clear, an enigmatic race of giants, presumably the same as the ancient Mesoamerican mythical giants, inhabited the earth before the Great Flood. Hence, we may safely deduce, from this tradition on antediluvian giants, that the Great Flood occurred in the year 2,130 BCE — at the close of the Second Creation. Also, in the Great Book of Barruch, it is narrated that the Great Flood destroyed four hundred thousand of the race of giants.

The memory of a great destruction of humankind by a universal Flood can be found in many ancient myths, the world over. We are, of course, familiar with the Gilgamesh Epic, recounting the fiery paroxysm of the planet Venus-Ishtar — which bears the blame for the primeval Flood:

> Ishtar, Goddess of Love and War, shrieked, cried out like a woman in labor: "How could I kill my own people, conspire with the gods against those to whom I gave birth?
> Their bodies float on the sea, swell like schools of dead fish."

The identification of the planet Venus as the primary agent of destruction sent by the gods to punish humankind is, judging from the above quotation, unequivocal. There were, in actual fact, three principal Venus-induced Floods during Antiquity: (1) the primordial Flood from the Epic of Gilgamesh dated to 3,114 BCE, (2) the Flood of Deucalion (in Greek mythology) or Great Flood of Noah in 2,130 BCE, and

---

[11] Hans Kelsen (1943) 'The principle of Retribution in the Flood and Catastrophe Myth.' In Alan Dundes (editor) (1988) *The Flood Myth*, University of California Press: Berkeley and London, p. 135.

[12] F. L. Gomara (1943) *Historia de la conquista de Mexico*, Mexico City, Vol. II: p. 261.

CHAP. VI: AND THE WATERS OF HEAVEN CAME DOWN | 219

(3) the Flood of Ogyges in 1,135 BCE. All of these manifested at the end of a Typhon Season — on the occasion of the Destruction of Mankind. The eighteenth century German scholar C.G.A. Oldendorp, reporting on an ancient flood legend carried into the West Indies by enslaved African, writes:

> About the history of creation I have found no trace among them; but I have here and there noted a vague and distorted knowledge about the destruction of the human race as the result of the great flood. Several Watje told me that at home they had heard about a general flood across the earth in which all human beings would have perished had they not immediately sought rescue on the highest mountain. Among the Kasenti is a tradition that God shall once again afflict humanity with such a flood as punishment. ... The Kanga and Loango [linguistically belonging to the Congo group] also have a tradition about a general extermination of the human race, which however was not caused by water, but by the collapse of the sky, and after all human beings had been crushed beneath its rubble, God produced a new human race.[13]

The catastrophist tradition is indeed very well embedded in the myths of the African continent. According to Emmi Kähler-Meyer: *"legends concerning the destruction of the human race and the formation of a new world are much more widespread even in Africa than was assumed in the old sources."*[14]

An ancient Far East Asian myth from Batak, Sumatra, narrates that Debata, the Creator, decided to send a great flood upon the earth when it had grown old and dirty. The last two survivors at once took refuge atop a mountain. When the flood waters had reached to their knees, Debata repented from his decision to destroy humankind. Lowering a clod of earth towards them, the last couple jumped onto it and were saved. As the couple and their offsprings multiplied, the clod of earth grew in size, becoming the earthly realm of today.[15] Another flood myth from Chingpaw, Upper Burma, relates that when the great deluge came, Pawpaw Nanchaung and his sister Chang-hko managed to save themselves by embarking on a large boat. Taking with them nine cocks and nine needles, they waited for the storm and rain to pass. When the tempest ended, they each day threw out one cock and one needle in order to assess the level of the waters. Finally, on the ninth day, they heard the sound of the cock crowing and the needle striking the ground.[16] Also, an ancient legend from Samoa recounts that, Fire and Water (offspring of the primeval octopus) confronted each other in a fierce battle. Faced with a globe

---

13 Quoted in Emmi Kähler-Meyer 'Myth Motifs in Flood Stories from the Grassland of Cameroon.' In Alan Dundes (editor) (1988) *The Flood Myth*, p. 251.
14 Ibid.
15 Theodore H. Gaster (1969) *Myth, Legend, and Custom in the Old Testament*, Harper & Row: New York, p. 100.
16 Ibid, pp. 97-98.

overrun by "boundless sea," the god Tan-galoa undertook to re-create the world.[17]

Turning to the Early Bronze Age Aegean. The end of Early Minoan II Crete, in 2,130 BCE, brought along with it, in the words of University of Sheffield archaeologist Keith Branigan, "social disruption and dislocation" as well as "the total destruction by fire of the hill-top houses at both Vasilike and Fournou Korifi (Myrtos)."[18] The exact cause of this conflagration is unknown. It was also during that time that many small towns of mainland Greece such as Agios Kosmas (Attica), Zygouries and Lerna (both in the Argolid) were likewise destroyed by fire.[19] Scholars often assume that these destructions are the work of foreign invaders — although they are unable to establish whence they came or even who they were. In Egypt and Syria-Palestine, the culmination of the Early Bronze IV period was, equally, characterized by "social disruption and dislocation." As we know, this was, in Egypt, the very turbulent period of the Herakleopolitan rulers' final demise. In Syria-Palestine, famine precipitantly set in; and massive nomadic movements of Asiatic peoples, in search of fertile lands, ensued.

Abraham Descends Into the Land of Pharaoh

I believe that it was during this very period of turmoil, consistently with the biblical narrative, that the Hebrew Patriarch Abraham and his family arrived in Egypt, for a short time, from Canaan (Gen. 12:10-20). Placing Abraham at this particular point in history naturally means that he was a contemporary of the symbolic biblical character Noah. The contemporaneity of Noah and Abraham is indeed illustrated in a pivotal, but little commented, passage in the Dead Sea Scrolls, which mentions that Noah *"gave the land to Abram, his beloved."*[20] Noah was, thus, obviously alive when Abraham, under the instructions of the Hebrew god, left Ur of the Chaldeans in southern Babylonia (Gen. 11:31) toward the land of Canaan. Therefore, the famine from which the Hebrews suffered in Abraham's time was actually caused by the conflagration attributed in the Bible to Noah's Flood.

Ancient Hebrew sources claim that the Great Flood was immediately preceded by an important cataclysmic event. In the Tractate Sanhedrin of the Talmud, it is revealed that: "Seven days before the deluge, the Holy One changed the primeval

---

[17] For this and other references to ancient Flood myth from around the globe, see http://pibweb.it.nwu.edu/~pib/flood.htm
[18] Keith Branigan 'Some Observations on State Formation in Crete.' In E. B. French & K. A. Wardle (1988) *Problems in Greek Prehistory (Papers Presented at the Centenary Conference of the British School of Archaeology at Athens, Manchester – April 1986)*, p. 67.
[19] J. Caskey (1960) 'The Early Helladic Period in the Argolid', *Hesperia* 29.
[20] *Dead Sea Scrolls*, 4Q252, fr. II.

CHAP. VI: AND THE WATERS OF HEAVEN CAME DOWN | 221

order and the sun rose in the west and set in the east."[21] In Egypt, this cataclysm induced the plague which visits Pharaoh's land at the time of Abraham's sojourn in the Nile Delta. This signifies that the pharaoh who initially welcomed Abraham and his family into Egypt was Akhtoy III. The biblical text imparts that the plagues which befell Pharaoh Akhtoy's land were caused by his, albeit unintentional, adulterous transgression with Abraham's wife, Sarah. Whether or not that particular illicit liaison ever took place, the fact remains that Pharaoh Akhtoy was aware that the pestilence visiting his country was an act of retribution by the Heavens.

> 17 And the Lord plagued Pharaoh and his house with great plagues because of Sarai Abram's wife.
> (Genesis 12:9-17)

The woes of Pharaoh were expressed, by his own hand, in the "Instructions for Merikare" — in which Akhtoy imparts to his son, Merikare, some advice for being a virtuous ruler. We detect in the tone of Pharaoh's speech a certain sentiment of guilt. As if he felt personally responsible for the numerous calamities which had fallen upon his country. He clearly hoped to encourage his son and successor to become a better king than he himself had been. Like the Khemetic king Khnum-Khufu, Pharaoh Akhtoy had "departed from the path of order" and, as a consequence, "the deity punishes this violation in accordance with almost [in this case quite literally] Biblical theodicy."[22]

Behold the Vile Asiatic!: The C-Group Nubians to the South and their Threat to Egyptian Hegemony

While Pharaoh Akhtoy was busy contending with the peaceful infiltration of Asiatics within his northern border, the C-Group Asiatics of Nubia, below the southern border, became more belligerent than ever. In his instructions to his son and heir, Merikare, King Akhtoy III warns him to be extremely wary of them. The Austrian excavator Prof. Manfred Bietak has subdivided the time-frame currently dealt with (2,200 to 1,950 BCE), in C-Group Nubia, into periods called Ia and Ib. With the new chronology, we can narrow down those parameters to 2,180–1,953 BCE. Likewise, the periods defined by Bietak as IIa and IIb (1,950–1,600 BCE) can be narrowed down to 1,953-1,628. Lastly, period III, which lasts through to the begin-

---

[21] Tractate Sanhedrin 108b.
[22] Siegfried Morenz (1973) *Egyptian Religion*. Trans. by Ann E. Keep. Cornell University Press: Ithaca, NY, p. 11. — Theodicy = A justification of God by attributing evil to man, who brought it about by his sinful conduct.

ning of Pharaoh Ahmose I's reign (Final Kerma), can be securely dated between 1,628 and 1,559 BCE. In his speech to his son, Pharaoh Akhtoy says: *"... look! the land which they destroyed is now made into townships and very many townspeople are there."* Where is this town which they destroyed? Where are the fortified cities they built on this land which they seemingly usurped? This land obviously could not be located in Canaan; because the Bible makes no mention of Canaanite enemies who posed a serious military threat to Abraham and his family during his journey out of Egypt — as we subsequently find in the Exodus story. What is more, the EB IV and MB I periods in Syria-Palestine were supposed to have been peopled by nomadic tribes. All the major cities in Syria-Palestine had been destroyed and abandoned at the end of the EB III period. Quoting W. F. Albright, Donald B. Redford describes it as *"a period of complete nomadic culture to the exclusion of city living."*[23] It does indeed seem odd that Pharaoh Akhtoy would, on the one hand, boast about his firm grip on his north-eastern frontier, and on the other hand seem apprehensive about the threat of an Asiatic incursion into Egypt. Since the Asiatics delineated in the "Instructions for Merikare" could not have "usurped" their own homeland farther East, the only plausible location left for these fortified towns would be below Egypt's southern border — the Kushite kingdom of Kerma. In fact, archaeologists agree that Lower Nubia represented a vibrant urban centre during the early part of the Middle Bronze Age.[24] According to Nubiologist P. L. Shinnie: *"Certainly, by about 2200 BC the area (Lower Nubia) was once more occupied and there was an increase in population."*[25] Pharaoh Akhtoy also says:

> But this further should be said because of the Bowman. Lo, the wretched Asiatic — it goes ill with the place where he is, afflicted with water, difficult from many trees, the ways thereof painful because of the mountains. He does not dwell in a single place, (but) his legs are made to go astray. He has been fighting (ever) since the time of Horus, (but) he does not conquer, nor yet can he be conquered. He does not announce a day in fighting, like a thief who ... for a gang.
> But as I live! (95) I am while I am! The bowmen, however, are a locked wall, opened ... I made the Northland smite them, I captured their inhabitants, and I took their cattle, to the disgust of the Asiatics in Egypt. Do not trouble thyself about him: he is (only) an Asiatic, one despised on his (own) coast. He may rob a single person, (but) he does not lead against a town of many citizens.[26]

---

[23] Donald B. Redford (1992) p. 65.
[24] Aminata Sackho-Autissier (1997) 'Soudan: Royaumes du Nil', *Archéologia* 331, p. 41.
[25] P. L. Shinnie (1996) *Ancient Nubia*, Kegan Paul International: London and New York, p. 55.
[26] James B. Pritchard (editor) (1955) *ANET*, pp. 414-418.

Again, we observe that King Akhtoy stressed the unpredictability of the Asiatic warriors — who have been fighting since the days of Horus (New Horus Period). Especially in times of universal chaos, they indiscriminately transgress all borders and settle where they do not belong. As Akhtoy increasingly became suspicious of the Asiatic immigrants and would-be invaders in the north as well, as is illustrated by his expulsion of Abraham, he guarded his northern frontier with great vigour. In some late Pyramid Texts dating to around the time of the Herakleopolitan kings, mention is made of "the Ram gate" which keeps Asiatic enemies at bay.[27] King Akhtoy makes reference to this very gate in his "Instructions for Merikare": *"But as I live! As long as I was around those bowmen were walled off, and the fortress that lay open I closed up on them."*

The picture which emerges of Pharaoh Akhtoy from his "Instructions," with regards, particularly, to his attitude towards the Asiatics from Canaan, concords remarkably well with the book of Genesis' portrayal of the pharaoh who expelled Abraham from Egypt. Moreover, the extant archeological record from that time has clearly revealed that the EB IV to MB I horizon on Syria-Palestine was largely one of nomadic peoples. According to ancient historian John Van Seters:

> One can only conclude from all these innovations that MB I represents the settling in Palestine of a new people.[28]

These new settlers who entered Palestine in early MBI were the proto-Hebrews of Abraham's time. Coming out of Egypt's eastern Delta following the chaotic aftermath of the Venus shift, they entered their Promised Land.

Birth of the Zodiacal Seasons

" Since all the practices of the Egyptians in their worship of animals are astonishing and beyond belief, they occasion much difficulty for those who would seek out their origins and causes. Now their priests have on this subject a teaching which may not be divulged ..."

- Diodorus of Sicily (Book I, 86)

The arrival of the Middle Bronze Age represented a vital turning point for the ancients in many ways. Not only did it establish the divide between the ante-diluvian and post-diluvian eras, but many ancient traditions maintain that the "Seasons," which began being religiously observed in the Middle Bronze Age,

---

[27] Donald B. Redford (1992) p. 63.
[28] Van Seters, John (1966) *The Hyksos (A New Investigation)*, Yale University Press: New Haven and London, p. 11.

had not existed in the antediluvian world. These "Seasons" were synonymous to the concept of World Ages. Each season was characterized by a particular zodiacal constellation of the vernal equinox's lengthy precessional cycle. But, as I've posited in the Introduction, the precessional cycle was violently periodically disturbed in Antiquity at the termination of Typhon Seasons. The ancients only began taking account of this change in the precessional cycle after the Great Flood of 2,130 BCE. According to the Aggadic cosmogony:

> To put a stop to the flood, God had to transfer two stars from the constellation of the Bear to the constellation of the Pleiades. That is why the Bear runs after the Pleiades. She wants her two children back, but they will be restored to her only in the future world.[29]

The astronomer-priests of Antiquity, from Egypt to China, remarked that the order of the firmament had changed after the Great Flood. Believing that the Flood was sent by Heaven as a punishment for the misconduct of humanity and as a harbinger of a new divine covenant, the swift alteration in the prescribed order of the precessional cycle thence came to be interpreted as a sign of God's renewed covenant. This novel archaeoastronomical concept was, in particular, vigorously solemnised in ancient China.

Between May 1996 and early 1999, a vast chronological project was undertaken, by a world-wide contingent of historians and archaeologists of Chinese descent, to scientifically date the Xia, Shang and Zhou Dynasties of ancient China.[30] The aim of this scholarly endeavour, to quote Chinese reporter Cui Lili, is "to finalize current findings that the earliest chronological record of Chinese history should start from 2241 BC instead of 841 BC."[31] An important reason why Chinese scholars feel such a pressing need to scientifically establish these dates is because contemporary Western scholarship has generally tended to mythologize early Chinese history.

The first step toward the demythologization of the early Chinese dynasties is to divine the esoteric meaning of one of their principal philosophical tenets: the *Tian-ming* or Mandate of Heaven. There were, in actual fact, three fundamental cornerstones, which have dominated China's conception of history for thousands of years. They are: *tian* (heaven), *Tianzi* (the son of Heaven or emperor) and *Tian-ming* (the Mandate of Heaven).[32] According to this notion, the ruler (i.e. the "son of

---

[29] Aggada.
[30] Cui Lili (1997) 'Project to Date China's Remote Ages', *Beijing Review* Vol. 40 - Num. 16, pp. 20-23.
[31] Ibid, p. 20.
[32] Martin Bernal (1991) *Black Athena (The Afroasiatic Roots of Classical Civilization) — Volume II: The Archaeological and Documentary Evidence*, Rutgers University Press: New Brunswick, NJ, p. 313.

Heaven") was granted divine right to govern, or rule over, China; but that any serious erring on his part would, at once, result in his mandate to rule being revoked. Explaining the immediate consequences of the emperor's transgression of the divine Mandate of Heaven, Professor Martin Bernal of Cornell University writes:

> ... The Mandate of Heaven is not constant. It was believed that misrule by an emperor could so upset the course of nature that *tian* - as high god or agent, or merely as an inert reaction - could manifest the disruption by prodigies: floods, droughts, earthquakes, the birth of freaks, etc.[33]

These are all calamities which befell the earth at the consummation of a Typhon Season. Like in Egypt, the ruling Chinese monarch often bore the responsibility for such grievous degenerations in the order of nature. Orthodox historians generally contend that this concept of the Mandate of Heaven was not devised in China until the time of the Zhou Dynasty, in the twelfth century BCE. But I purport that, in reality, the idea of the emperor being answerable to Heaven and, through the Mandate of Heaven, in charge of the well-being of the state, dates to the twenty-second century BCE. The earliest Chinese dynasties were founded on this important principle.

As we've seen, the notion of divine mandates, expiring in fiery catastrophes upon humanity's disobedience of divine laws, literally permeate both religious and secular texts of Antiquity. For instance in Plato's dialogues, we read:

> During a certain period God himself goes with the universe as guide in its revolving course, but at another epoch, when the cycles have at length reached the measure of his allotted time, he lets it go, and of its own accord it turns backward in the opposite direction ... the universe is guided at one time by an extrinsic divine cause, acquiring the power of living again and receiving renewed immortality from the Creator, and at another time it is left to itself and then moves by its own motion, being left to itself at such a moment that it moves backwards through countless ages, because it is immensely large and most evenly balanced, and turns upon the smallest pivot. ...
> And as the universe was turned back and there came the shock of collision, as the beginning and the end rushed in opposite directions, it produced a great earthquake within itself and caused a new destruction of all sorts of living creatures.
> (Plato, *Politicus*, 269-270;273)

---

[33] Ibid, p. 314.

Plato's catastrophic world-view, which he inherited from the actual experiences, shaped over several millennia, of African and Asiatic peoples, delineates the cataclysmic events which inevitably accompanied the swift deviations in the zodiacal precessional process. Once again, this unpredictable polar mechanism was the quintessence of the ancient Chinese notion of the Mandate of Heaven. Supporting this thesis, Dr. J. Needham of Cambridge University says:

> I think one could really say that the celestial pole was the fundamental basis of Chinese astronomy. It was connected also with the microscopic-macroscopic type of thinking, because the pole corresponded to the emperor on earth, around whom the vast system of the bureaucratic agrarian state revolved naturally and spontaneously. ... Moreover, just as the influence of the Son of Heaven on earth radiated in all directions, so the hour-circles radiated from the pole.[34]

The late French Sinologist Marcel Granet — formerly Director of Studies at L'École des Hautes Études, Professor at l'École des Langues Orientales, and Administrator of l'Institut des Haute Études de Paris, gives the following two models which have been advanced for the chronology of ancient China:

	I	II
Yao	2,357 - 2,256	2,145 - 2,043 BCE
Regency of Shun	2,285 - 2,256	
Shun	2,255 - 2,206	2,042 - 1,990
Regency of Yü	2,223 - 2,206	
Hsia (Xia) Dyn.	2,205 - 1,767	1,989 - 1,558
	17 kings = 439 years	17 kings = 432 years
		[or (*Annals*), 471 years.]
Shang Dynasty	1,766 - 1,123	1,557 - 1,050 BCE
	28 kings = 644 years	30 kings = 500 years
		[or (*Annals*), 471 years.]
Zhou Dynasty	1,122 BCE	1,049 BCE
King Wu	1,122 - 1,116	1,049 - 1,045
King Ch àng	1,115 - 1,079	1,044 - 1,008
.....		

Table 6-3

---

[34] J. Needham 'Astronomy in Ancient and Medieval China.' In The British Academy (1974) *The Place of Astronomy in the Ancient World (A Joint Symposium of the Royal Society and the British Academy)*, p. 68.

CHAP. VI: AND THE WATERS OF HEAVEN CAME DOWN | 227

These two chronological models have divided the favour of historians for generations. I chose to adopt the second model, devised by Pan Ku — the historian of the first Han — up until the end of the Shang Dynasty. From then on, I will rely on the first model. From my research, I have concluded that the Xia Dynasty ended exactly on the year 1,559 BCE. That date also marked the termination of the archaeological period known as the Middle Bronze Age. My theory is that the Xia Dynasty was a Middle Bronze Age empire, under the Mandate of Heaven characterized by the precessional sign of Aries. This dynasty was brought down by the arrival of the new precessional Mandate of Heaven of Leo, which in turn ushered in the Late Bronze Age. This means that the succeeding dynasty of Shang was itself a Late Bronze Age empire under the Mandate of Heaven of Leo. All this is in accord with the second model. However, I place the end of Shang to the year 1,135 BCE — which is more in twine with the first model. Again, this junction point establishes a change from the Mandate of Leo to the Mandate of Taurus — which belongs in the Iron Age. It follows, as well, that the dynasty which replaced Shang, the Zhou Dynasty, was an Iron Age empire ruling under the precessional Mandate of the Taurus.

The antiquity of this concept of Mandates of Heaven is, moreover, supported by the historical memoirs of *Se-Ma Ts'ien*. These records reveal that Emperor Yao "sent astronomers to the Valley of Obscurity and the Sombre Residence to observe the new movements of the sun and the moon and the Sygzygies or the orbital points of the conjunctions, also to investigate and inform the people of the order of the season."[35] The New Chronology Table indeed shows that Yao reigned over China at the time of the cycle-ending Venus shift of 2,130 BCE. It therefore comes as no surprise that he would make such observations. The first Chinese astronomers, the brothers Hsi and Hso, were commissioned by Emperor Yao to devise a calendar and observe the heavens. With these appointments, astronomical observation became tightly linked with the entire state apparatus.

> Thereupon Yaou [Yao] commanded He and Ho [Hsi and Hso], in reverent accordance with the wide heavens, to calculate and delineate the movements and appearances of the sun, the moon, the stars, and the zodiacal spaces; and to deliver respectfully the seasons to the people.[36]

The "zodiacal spaces" referred to above in the ancient Chinese sacred Book of *Shoo-king*, evidently represent the twelve different zodiacal constellations of the precessional cycle. Emperor Yao gave the astronomers the important task to figure out the length of these "Seasons" in order for the Chinese populace to be prepared for subsequent violent pole shifts.

---

[35] Immanuel Velikovsky (1950) *Worlds in Collision*, Doubleday & Co.: Garden City, N.Y.
[36] *The Shoo-king*.

Evidence of the observance of the swiftly shifting zodiacal constellations in the Nile Valley can, I believe, actually be found in the sacred rituals of the C-Group Nubians at Kerma. It is of interest to note that the Nubians at Kerma began practising ritual sacrifices of rams at the start of the second millennium BCE.[37] Numerous theories have been advanced by a variety of scholars to explain the Kerma Nubians' specific choice of the ram as a prime sacrificial animal. Since the sacrificed rams were all male, it has for instance been suggested that the Kerma people sought to curb population increase.[38] This hypothesis, however, is ruled out since it is now understood that the ritualistic practice was directly inspired by the ancients' newly-established observance of the revolving zodiacal seasons of the volatile precessional cycle. The zodiacal sign which ruled the vernal equinox at the time of these ram-burials at Kerma, of course, was the constellation of Aries.

The End of the Theban Supremacy

The suzerainty of the Theban rulers, which they acquired by defeating the Herakleopolitan dynasty at the heels of the Venus shift of 2,130 BCE, was relatively short-lived. Less than a hundred and fifty years after they seized the pharaonic throne, the new Theban dynasty would, in turn, find itself ousted by competing powers. Once again, the determining agent of the pharaonic dynasty's demise was the planet Venus. One hundred and seventy-seven years after the end of Typhon Season #3, in 1,953 BCE, the planet Venus once again veered from its orbital path and menaced the earth. Albeit less devastating than the previous Venus shift, in the sense that it did not provoke a major flood or radically shifted the course of the precessional cycle, this latest cataclysm had profound political effects for the reigning empires of the time.

The relative calm which reigned between the Venusian storms was, however, somewhat illusionary. The founder of the 11th Dynasty, Pharaoh Inyotef I, much disturbed by the presence of a large number of Asiatics in Egypt's north-eastern Delta, failed to secure the complete allegiance of Lower Egypt. In addition to the Asiatics, the Theban pharaohs had to contend with ferociously competing nomarchs in the district of Asyut. At the time of King Inyotef III's reign, also known as King Mentuhotep-S'ankhibtawy, the Thebans' direct influence extended merely from the First Cataract to the tenth Nome of Upper Egypt. The whole of Lower Egypt was controlled by the princes of Asyut.[39]

---

[37] Lucien Jourdan 'Sacrifices de moutons dans des tombes de Kerma de l'ile de Sai (Vallée du Nil, début du deuxième millénaire avant J.C. et leur signification rituelle).' In C.N.R.S. (1980) *Mémoires archéologiques* 1, pp. 6-82.
[38] Ibid, p. 82.
[39] Nicholas Grimal (1992) *A History of Ancient Egypt*. Trans. by Ian Shaw. Blackwell: Oxford, U.K., p. 155.

CHAP. VI: AND THE WATERS OF HEAVEN CAME DOWN | 229

The conventionally accepted version of how the stalemate was broken is that, following an uprising in the Thinite Nome, which served to destabilized, the northerners, King Mentuhotep-S'ankhibtawy seized the opportunity to move northwards and ultimately defeat the princes of Asyut. Once he reunified the Two Lands, it is then thought that Pharaoh Mentuhotep-S'ankhibtawy changed his name to Mentuhotep-Nebhepetre — Son of Re. The preeminent objective of the ensuing chapter will, however, be to demonstrate that Egyptologists have gone severely astray by making this assumption. I am entirely convinced that King Mentuhotep-S'ankhibtawy and King Mentuhotep-Nebhepetre were *not* one and the same person. These two different pharaohs were, in fact, separated in time by as much as 180 years! Therefore, as a direct result of the prevailing confusion, a period of almost two centuries in ancient Egyptian history has been literally skipped by historians.

The Third Dynasty of Ur

" *When the earth quakes through the whole day,*
there will be a destruction of the land. When it quakes
continually, there will be an invasion of the enemy."

- Ancient Babylonian belief.[40]

The Third Dynasty of Ur (Ur III) began in 2,113 BCE[41] — soon after the Great Flood — heralding what has been acclaimed by some scholars as a "Sumerian Renaissance."[42] The Third Dynasty of Ur reinstated Sumerian as the administrative language of Mesopotamia — replacing Akkadian as the lingua franca. The collapse of the Old Akkadian empire, occasioned by the Gutian invasion, ushered in a period of decentralization. In southern Mesopotamia, many city-states became increasingly autonomous, while others fell under the suzerainty of the Gutian invaders. The Gutians were finally repelled by Utu-hegal of Uruk, who instantaneously became a folk hero. Then, Ur-Nammu, the governor of Ur and brother of Utu-hegal, moved to seize control of the diverse neighbouring city-states.[43] Upon having successfully asserted his authority over the region, the deified King Ur-Nammu centralized Mesopotamian power around the city of Ur.

---

[40] R. C. Thompson (editor) (1900) *The Reports of the Magicians and Astrologers of Nineveh and Babylon in the British Museum*, Vol. II - Nums. 263, 265.
[41] Amélie Kuhrt (1997[1995]) *The Ancient Near East — c.3000– 330 BC* (Vol. I), Routledge: London and New York, p. 45.
[42] Ibid, p. 59.
[43] Norman Yoffee 'The Collapse of Ancient Mesopotamian States and Civilization.' In Cowgill, George L. & Yoffee, Norman (editors) (1988) *The Collapse of Ancient States and Civilizations*, p. 49.

King Ur-Nammu was succeeded by his son Shulgi, who maintained his father's centralization efforts. King Shulgi was then succeeded by two other heirs who reigned nine years each. Finally, the last ruler of Ur III, Ibbi-Sin reigned for twenty-four years. The last decades of the Third Dynasty of Ur were characterized by the Ur III rulers' heightened concern with potential foreign invasions and protecting their peripheral provinces as well their sphere of influence abroad.[44] Aside from possible external threats, Ur III rulers were doubtlessly likewise concerned about foreigners dwelling within their own borders. An important, and potentially explosive, distinction of Ur III society was the presence of a large contingent of "nomadic Amorites" from the Syrian desert. While the Ur III administration had attempted to build fortification walls to prevent the north-western nomadic intruders from settling *en masse* in the cities, their efforts appear to have been in vain. We can't speak of an Amorite invasion, but more of a gradual assimilation into Ur III society.[45] Under King Ibbi-Sin, the dynasty's hegemony began to crumble.[46] Various local city-state rulers, as in Mari on the Euphrates, started to challenge Ur's authority. Like in contemporary Egypt, the outcome of this tug of war would be ultimately decided by the latest Venus shift.

The collapse of Ur III in 1,953 BCE was the single event which, in my estimation, gave birth to the famous biblical story of the Tower of Babel (Gen. 11:1-19). In fact, the word "Babel" is actually Hebrew for Babylon.[47] The biblical motif of the tower was taken from the Babylonian stepped temple towers built during this time, known as "ziggurats." Interestingly enough, modern excavations, as well as ancient documents themselves, reveal that the first ziggurats had been erected soon after the Great Flood, as German Velikovskian scholar Gunnar Heinsohn explains:

> The smashed ziggurat is intriguing for being built upon the last and most voluminous flood stratum of Kish. Does it go far to be reminded of the Kabbalist tract *Jalkut Rubeni* (32b) which dates the building of the Tower of Babel right after the flood?[48]

According to the Jews held captive in Babylon, "the ziggurats were symbols of the

---

[44] Piotre Michalowsky (1976) *The Royal Correspondence of Ur*. Ph.D. dissertation. Yale University. Cited in Yoffee (1988).
[45] See G. G. Buccellati (1966) *The Amorites of the Ur III Period*, Naples.
[46] Thorkild Jacobsen (1953) 'The Reign of Ibbi-Sin', *Journal of Cuneiform Studies* 7, pp. 36-47.
[47] Richard Elliott Friedman (1997) *The Hidden Face of God*, Harper: San Fransisco, p. 8.
[48] Gunnar Heinsohn 'Destruction Layers in Archaeological Sites: The Stratigraphy of Armageddon.' In Zysman, Milton & Whelton, Clark (editors) (1990) *Catastrophism 2000 (A Sourcebook for the Conference: Reconsidering Velikovsky)*, pp. 238-239.

CHAP. VI: AND THE WATERS OF HEAVEN CAME DOWN | 231

arrogance and ambition of the heathen."[49] The ziggurat, "whose top may reach unto heaven,"[50] became the basis for the story of the Tower of Babel. It was in fact during the Third Dynasty of Ur that the first ziggurat was built.[51] Since stone was not available in Mesopotamia, the ziggurat was constructed of fired bricks and bituminous mortar[52] — just as the Bible (Gen. 11:3) describes. Another striking similarity to the biblical story is that, during Ur III, Akkadian, the ancient language of Mesopotamia, split into two other languages — raising the number of principal dialects to three: Akkadian, Babylonian and Assyrian. In all, no less than five languages were in common use; namely: Akkadian, Sumerian, Amorite, Elamite and Gutian. It is very probable then that the element of the confusion of languages found in the biblical story stems from this reality. Also chronologically significant is the fact that, in the Book of Genesis (10:8-10) it is said that after the Flood, the grandson of Noah and son of Cush, Nimrod, headed the kingdom of Babel. As the new chronology postulates, the constructions of the very first ziggurats, in Ur III Babylonia (Babel), began soon after the Great Flood of 2,130 BCE.

The collapse of the Third Dynasty of Ur elicited among the ancients, particularly among the enemies of the Babylonians (e.g. the ancient Israelites), very much the same comments which accompanied the collapse of Pharaoh Khnum-Khufu's, Pharaoh Akhtoy's, or the Chinese Dynasties' empires. They had all been punished by Heaven, it was believed, for their inequities. Once more, the planet Venus carried out the divine sentence. This Venusian shift of 1,953 BCE terminated the Middle Bronze I period. While the precessional order was not seriously affected, the ancients nonetheless were the spectators of yet another great heavenly battle. Chinese-American scholar (meteorologist) Kevin Pang reported that in the year 1,953 BCE, during the reign of Emperor Yü of China, the ancient Chinese recorded a conjunction of the five planets.[53] Such astronomical observations, whether they were actually accurate in every detail or not, usually meant that the peaceful order of the solar system had been disturbed.

Decimated by the Venus-induced disaster, the much-weakened dynasts of Ur III, became instantly vulnerable to foreign invasions. And surely, one invading group did come: the Elamites. Renowned ancient historian Edwin M. Yamauchi of Miami University, in line with orthodox scholarship, has dated the Elamite sack of Ur to c.1950 BCE.[54] This is a very credible date, since it synchronises perfectly with the Venus shift of 1,953 BCE.

---

[49] Evan Hadingham (1984) *Early Man and the Cosmos*, Walker & Co.: New York, pp. 3-4.
[50] Ibid, p. 4.
[51] Walter R. Bodine 'Sumerians.' In Alfred J. Hoerth, Gerald L. Mattingly & Edwin M. Yamauchi (editors) (1994) *Peoples of the Old Testament World*, p. 37.
[52] Lockyer (1986) p. 124.
[53] Martin Bernal (1991) *Black Athena II*, p. 282.
[54] Edwin M. Yamauchi (1996) *Persia and the Bible*, Baker: Grand Rapids, Michigan, p. 22.

The Elamite invasion is generally perceived as having been the primary cause for the downfall of the Third Dynasty of Ur. But this is inaccurate. The Elamites "took advantage" of the utter mayhem created by the cosmic catastrophe to invade Ur — which they probably could not have defeated otherwise. In a Babylonian document known as the 'Lamentations' over the destruction of Ur III, we can read:

> Hunger filled the city like water, it would not cease, ...
> They (the people) struck their necks with their hands and cried.
> They sought council with each other, they searched for clarification:
> '... How long until we are finished off by this calamity?
> Ur — inside it there is death, outside it there is death,
> Inside it we are being finished off by famine,
> **Outside it we are being finished off by Elamite weapons,**
> In Ur, the enemy has oppressed us, oh, we are finished!'[55]

The text is very explicit. The Elamites were *"finishing off"* the dynasts of Ur III. Therefore, it would be extremely misleading to assume, as most historians do, that the Elamites are to be blamed for *initiating* this state of chaos. The sheer expanse of the Venus-induced destruction of 1,953 BCE is evident, as outlined below by John Van Seters, from contemporary Syro-Palestinian devastations:

> The decline of MB I in Transjordan and the Negev is catastrophic. Very few settlements survived into the succeeding MB II period. In fact there is a general absence of sedentary life for several hundred years. Likewise in Palestine, MB I was very likely followed by a gap in settlement, but for a much shorter duration.[56]

In brief, by once again confirming the date, Van Seters goes on to say:

> The resulting chronology for MB I, based on ceramic evidence alone, would suggest the EB IV-MB I began in Transjordan by about 2300 B.C. and in Palestine and the Negev by 2200. Allowing a reasonable length of time for the period, **the final terminus would be about 1950 B.C.**[57]

---

[55] James B. Pritchard (editor) (1955) *ANET*, p. 611f; See also S. N. Kramer (1940) *Lamentation over the Destruction of Ur*, Chicago.
[56] John Van Seters (1966) *The Hyksos (A New Investigation)*, Yale University Press: New Haven and London, p. 13.
[57] Ibid, p. 17.

Pharaoh Mentuhotep-Nebhepetre, by author

Part III

Kingless Period
1,953 BCE to 1,820 BCE

Middle Kingdom
1,820 BCE to 1,559 BCE

Theban Renaissance
1,559 BCE to 1,330 BCE

7

A King-Less Egypt Under Foreign Occupation (1,953 BCE to 1,780 BCE)

My revised historical framework's proposition that the 11th Dynasty, in the midst of its reign, was suddenly overpowered and defeated by outside forces is, needless to say, in sharp contradiction with orthodox views about ancient Egyptian history. Moreover, it is quite universally agreed in scholarly circles that dynastic Egypt remained free of foreign invasions, until the advent of the Hyksos invaders during the so-called Second Intermediate Period, at the end of the Middle Bronze Age. Be that as it may, I shall suggest, however, that Asiatic forces initially took over the reigns of power in Egypt as early as the Middle Bronze IIa period. Following the Venus catastrophe of 1,953 BCE, I believe that an already quarrelling and divided Egypt (between the Thebans and the princes of Asyut) was, unexpectedly overrun by multitudes of Asiatic foes, taking advantage of the devastation caused by the cosmic upheaval — much like the Gutians and Elamites had done in Mesopotamia. Thus, faced with certain annihilation, the Thebans fled immediately to Ethiopia — where they, and their descendants, stayed for over a hundred and thirty years in forced exile. At the end of that lengthy period, they returned in strength, drove the Asiatics away, and at long last reunified the Two Lands.

Taking Advantage of Egypt's Nakedness
The first objection which most observers would likely level against such a revolutionary hypothesis is: where is the written evidence for this Asiatic invasion? One source where I believe this evidence exists is in the Hebrew Old Testament's Book of Genesis. According to the Bible, Mizraim, the son of Ham and brother of Cush, came to settle along the Nile from Mesopotamia with his children. Ham – the father of Cush, Mizraim, Put and Canaan – had seen the nakedness of his father Noah. The word "nakedness" is used repeatedly in the Bible to denote desolation. In Genesis 42:9, it is related that Joseph dreamt about spies transgressing the borders of an Egypt engulfed in famine and desolation to witness its "nakedness." An archaeotheological analysis of Gen. 9:21-27, the passage dealing with Ham's sin

against Noah, interestingly reveals, in my estimation, that No Amun (Noah) was attacked, sometime after the Great Flood, by Asiatics of Hamitic descent. Thus, Genesis 9:21-27 ought not be interpreted literally, in the sense that it involved particular individuals; namely Noah and Ham. As we already know, Noah represented the ancient Egyptian capital of Thebes (the biblical No Amun). Relatively shortly after the Great Flood, in 1,953 BCE, Egypt was overcome by another devastating Venus shift and, using the biblical terminology, found itself naked — or ravaged. As always, the state of chaos precipitated bellicose incursions into Egypt by Asiatic marauders eager to take full advantage of the resulting weakened condition of the Egyptian administration. Those who in fact raided Egypt on the heels of the Venus shift of 1,953 BCE, in biblical geographical terms, were Canaan, Put (Libyans), Cush (Kushites and Mesopotamians) and Mizraim (a band of native Egyptians of Asiatic descent). All of these nations represented Ham. The fact that, in the Book of Genesis, Shem and Japheth, turned away and did not see Noah's nakedness signifies that these peoples did not attack Egypt during its time of weakness. Thus, on the heels of the devastating Venus shift of 1,953 BCE, the population of Egypt was altered dramatically as waves of Asiatics such as Canaanites, Cushites and Libyans settled massively in the Nile Valley — altogether toppling the existing Egyptian monarchy.

Seeking Refuge in Ethiopia: The Egyptian Exodus

" *When Asia overwhelmed Egypt,*
Egypt sought refuge in Ethiopia [Nubia]
as a child returns to its mother ..."

- W.E.B. Du Bois
The World and Africa

Faced with this sudden invading influx of Asiatic foreigners, the native Egyptian monarchs, along with hosts of courtiers and loyal citizens, fled southward to Ethiopia. Moving along the route taken by the ancient Anu, on the opposite direction, the pharaohs of the 11th Dynasty returned to the ancestral homeland of pharaonic culture. As a result, the Thebans introduced the cult of the Theban god Amun further inland into the African continent. Whilst, during the third millennium BCE, Amun was exclusively a local dynastic Egyptian deity, it became widely accepted by the Khemites, or Ethiopians, living below the Fourth Cataract — once the Thebans introduced its cult there. Later on, in the Late Bronze Age, the popularity of the cult of Amun among the Ethiopians would flourish into a sophisticated cosmogony wholly independent of, though clearly related to, the older Egyptian Theban cult. The Theban exiles of the 11th Dynasty did not, however, only institute the dynastic cult of Amun into the more inland regions of Africa. They also imported into far-off, non-pharaonic, corners of Africa their ancient knowledge of astronomy. One of their destinations was West Africa. Discussing the obvious similarities between sacred cosmology of Dogon of Mali and that of the Egyptians, King's College, London professor of comparative religion, Julian Baldick writes:

> ... both the Egyptians and the Dogon see the universe as being formed by eight original gods; the Egyptian ram-god Amun, crowned with a solar disc, is like the African celestial ram, crowned with a gourd; Osiris is like the Dogon spirit called the Lebe, whose imminent resurrection is proclaimed by the emerging millet; and in both the Egyptian and African belief the individual has both a soul and a vital force or essence.[1]

The combination of the African "celestial ram" and the "cult of the ram-god Amun" freezes the time-frame for the original diffusion into West Africa from Egypt to the Middle Bronze Age — during the zodiacal Age of Aries. What is more, the particular focus placed by the Dogon on "eight" primeval gods is exceptionally reminiscent of the eight post-diluvian deities of the Hermopolitan ogdoad — prevalent in the Nile Valley during the era when the Thebans departed from Egypt and diffused their knowledge into West Africa. These two vital details, once reconciled with the archaeotheological framework of the new chronology, establishes both the time-frame and direction of the diffusion in question. The origins of the Dogon of Mali's ancient knowledge of astronomy, and their early cosmogony, must therefore be Egyptian — more specifically Theban. The Dogon of Mali are also known to have possessed for at least seven hundred years a very advanced knowledge and understanding with respect to the Sirius star system.[2] They also probably came to this knowledge during the Middle Bronze Age — at the time of the pharaonic return to the African interior during the 11th Dynasty. The research of French anthropologists Marcel Griaule and Germaine Dieterlen[3] has confirmed that the Dogon practice a world renovation ceremony in which the star Sirius, called sigui (sigutolo, "star of Sigui"), was honoured every sixty years. We know that the ancient Egyptians attached great importance to the cyclical motion of the star Sirius.

---

[1] Julian Baldick (1998) *Black God (The Afroasiatic Roots of the Jewish, Christian, and Muslim Religions)*, Syracuse University Press: Syracuse, NY, p. 50. See also Nicolas Grimal (1992) p. 45.
[2] See Ivan Van Sertima 'The Lost Sciences of Africa: An Overview.' In Ivan Van Sertima (editor) (1983) *Blacks in Science: Ancient and Modern*, Journal of African Civilizations / Transaction Books: New Brunswick, NJ, pp. 7-26.
[3] Marcel Griaule & Germaine Dieterlen (1950) 'Un système soudanais de Sirius', *Journal de la Société des Africanistes* 20, pp. 273-294.

Reunifying the Two Lands

The exile of the Thebans lasted for over one hundred and thirty years. Finally, in 1,820 BCE, an offensive to reclaim the Egyptian throne, by the descendants of the 11th Dynasty rulers, was carried out under the leadership of Pharaoh Mentuhotep-Nebhepetre. Conventionally dated to the middle of the 21st century BCE, King Mentuhotep-Nebhepetre's accession now moves downwards by over two centuries, at the other end of the 133-year-long Theban exile, and is now dated to c.1,820 BCE. Evidence for this conquering campaign is found on an inscribed block, now kept in Cairo, from a temple of Mentuhotep-Nebhepetre at Gebelen — which was rebuilt into a Ptolemaic temple wall during the Late Period. The story related on this block, which according to James Henry Breasted received remarkably scant attention from Egyptologists given its importance, clearly delineates a war of conquest against hosts of Asiatic usurpers of the Egyptian throne. Citing Breasted:

> The second block represents the king again smiting the enemy, four in number. The king bears the inscription: *"Son of Hathor, Mistress of Dendera, Mentuhotep."* The first enemy is without inscription, but represents an Egyptian! ... The king makes no distinction between his victories over foreign foes and his conquest of Egypt itself, and actually places the figure of the conquered Egyptian among those of the barbarians on the temple wall. Mentuhotep I [Nebhepetre] therefore acquired the land of Egypt by conquest ... [4]

The reason why Mentuhotep-Nebhepetre makes no apparent distinction between his victory over foreign foes and his actual conquest of Egypt is because those foreigners are the ones who were actually in power in Egypt at the time of his invasion. Thus, his victory was a liberation campaign against foreign occupation. Mentuhotep-Nebhepetre, like his ancestors of the first part of the 11th Dynasty, bore allegiance to the Theban war god Montu. He also carried the Horus name of Sematawy ("Uniter of the Two Lands"). Like his Theban predecessors, Mentuhotep-Nebhepetre instituted his funerary estate at Deir el-Bahari, in western Thebes. Indeed, inside that mortuary temple is prominently featured a pictorial account of an "Asiatic war" carried out victoriously by Mentuhotep-Nebhepetre. Describing this scene, Egyptologist William A. Ward writes:

> Foreigners are shown being slain or in obeisance before the king and "Asiatics" ... are mentioned twice. The location of these hostilities is unknown ...[5]

---

[4] J. H. Breasted, *Ancient Records of Egypt*, Vol. I - § 423H.
[5] W. A. Ward (1971) *Egypt and the East Mediterranean World: 2200-1900 B.C. (Studies in Egyptian Foreign Relations During the First Intermediate Period)*, American University of Beirut: Beirut, Lebanon, pp. 59-60.

Fig. 7a: Regiment of Nubian soldiers (Cush).

Fig. 7b: Regiment of Medjay soldiers (Mizraim).

Fig. 7c: King Mentuhotep-Nebhepetre (Cairo Museum).

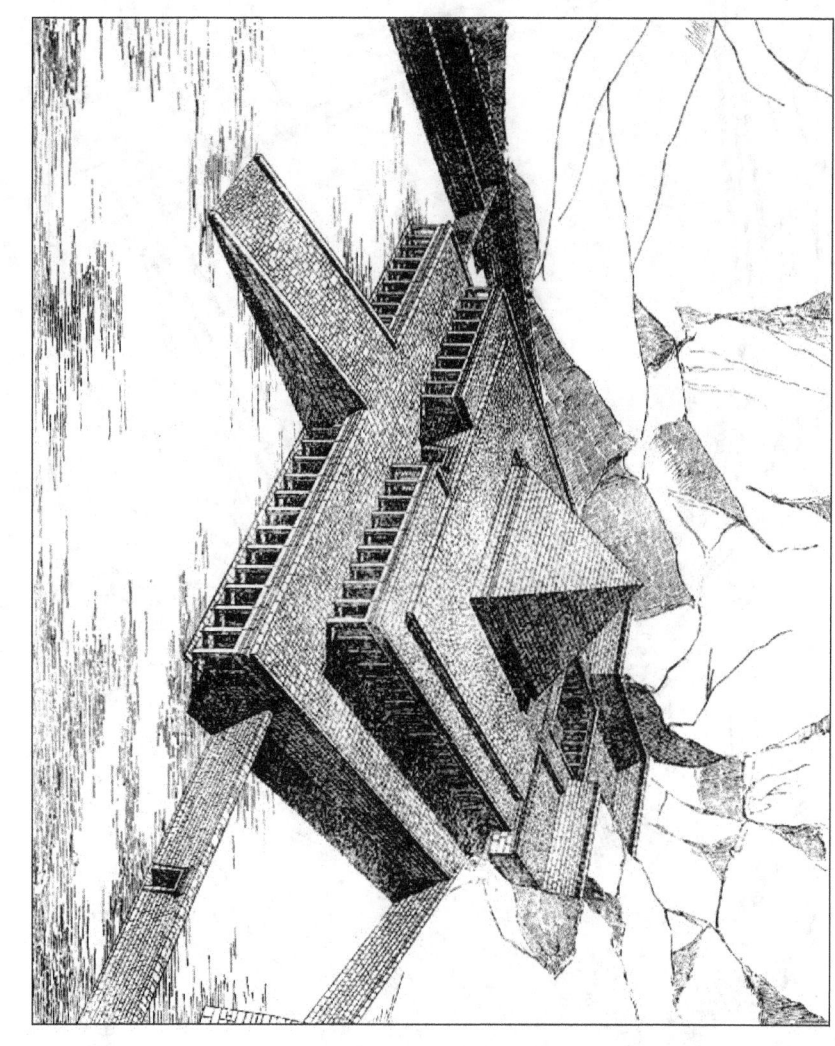

Fig. 7d: The 11th Dynasty temple at Deir el-Bahari [restored] (*from* Édouard Naville, 1910).

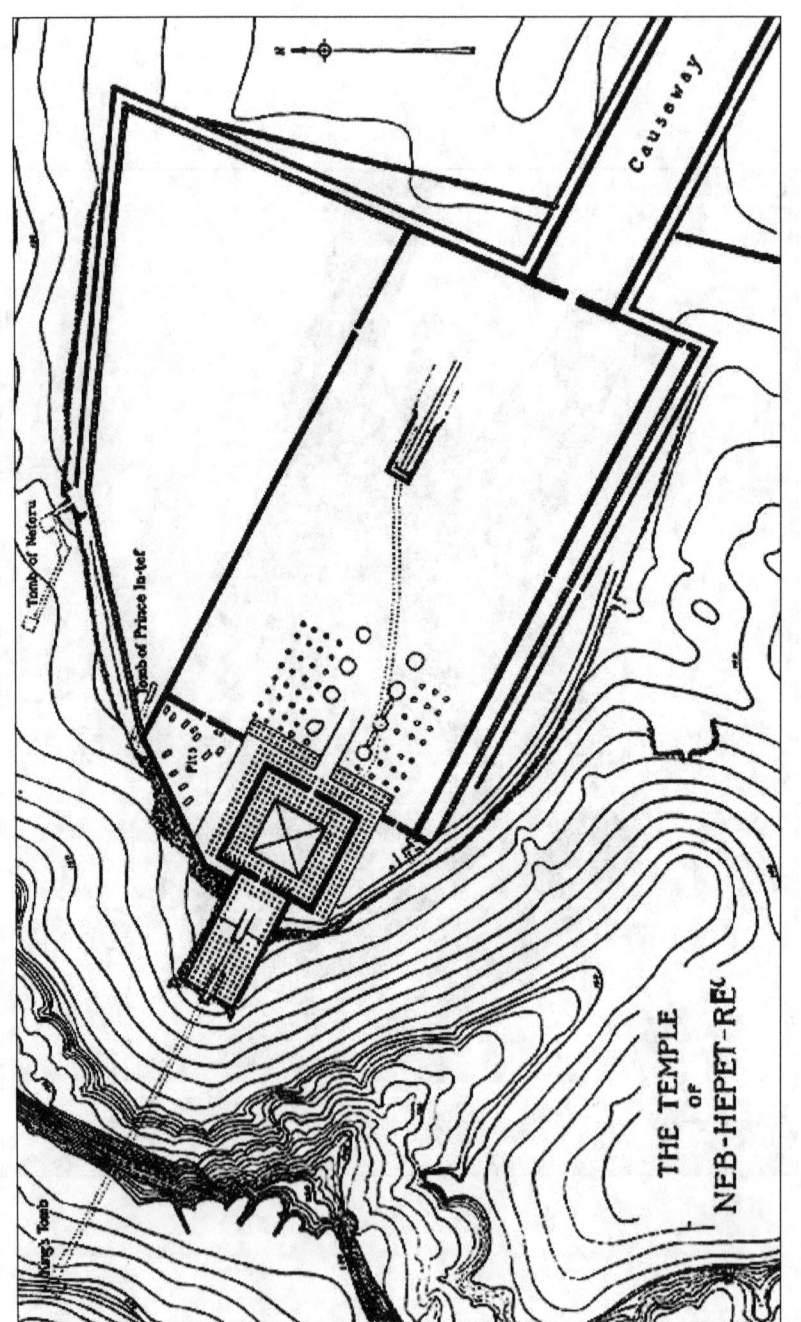

Fig. 7e: Overhead view of Pharaoh Mentuhotep-Nebhepetre's temple at Deir el-Bahari.

CHAP. VII: A KING-LESS EGYPT | 243

Ward conjectures that the Asiatic war might have taken place somewhere on the road to Sinai *"or even an Asiatic outpost in the eastern Delta itself ..."*[6] Evidently, since the battle fragments depict a walled fortress, Ward confirms that southern Palestine has to be ruled out because excavations have shown that such fortified towns did not yet exist there at the time. Another account pertaining to the Asiatic War under Mentuhotep-Nebhepetre is found in one of a number of stone blocks from a temple at Gebelin. There, the iconography is highly reminiscent of the traditional reunification palettes or stelae of Narmer and Sneferu. There, the king is shown smiting a row of Asiatics with his mace. A clear reference to the reunification of Egypt is made by Mentuhotep-Nebhepetre:

> Subduing the Chiefs of the Two Lands,
> establishing Upper and Lower Egypt,
> the highlands, the Two Banks and the Nine Bows.[7]

Why are the pharaoh's Asiatics enemies specifically referred to as "the Chiefs of the Two Lands [Egypt]?" Those Chiefs of the Two Lands are incidentally described as: "Nubians, Asiatics and Libyans." What kind of power could these traditional enemies of Egypt have possessed to earn the right to have been called, by Pharaoh Mentuhotep-Nebhepetre, "Chiefs of Upper and Lower Egypt?" Mentuhotep-Nebhepetre was expelling the sons of Ham, Cush, Mizraim, Put and Canaan, from the ancient Theban capital which they had defrauded at the time of its drunkenness, or weakness. Moreover, like his illustrious dynastic predecessor, Pharaohs Narmer and Sneferu, Mentuhotep-Nebhepetre united the Two Lands at the expense of the Sethian disciples. Thus, the obvious similarity in iconography between Mentuhotep-Nebhepetre's Asiatic wars and his subsequent unification accounts, as well as the earlier palette of Narmer and Sneferu's unification account are far from being coincidental. Pharaoh Mentuhotep-Nebhepetre, in an effort to forever eradicate the memory of the "Great Humiliation," picked up where the earlier kings of the 11th Dynasty had left off. Furthermore, like the editors of the Abydos King-lists would do many centuries later, the 11th Dynasty records remained completely silent about the Asiatic occupation. Hence, to this day, this pivotal episode has remained in the realm of the unknown.

---

[6] Ibid, p. 60ff.
[7] Ibid, p. 61.

Between the reign of King Mentuhotep-S'ankhibatwy over Thebes and Mentuhotep-Nebhepetre's reign over the whole of Egypt, lay a period of 133 years when Egypt was ruled by foreign kings. During that time of exile in the Black Land, the 11th Dynasty monarchs fused their traditional Theban religious concepts with the more ancient Khemetic traditions. The result, which translated itself during the Middle Kingdom's cosmogonical renaissance, was a dual allegiance to both their Theban deity Amun and the Heliopolitan sun-god Re. It is, moreover, important to note that *none* of the Theban kings of the 11th Dynasty who ruled before Mentuhotep-Nebhepetre *ever* wore the double crown.[8] The latter had evidently been much influenced by the Khemetic traditions during his dynasty's exile below the Fifth Cataract. A significant new artistic canon which Mentuhotep-Nebhepetre introduced into Egypt upon his dynasty's return from the Black Land was the "Osirid" statue. Such Osirid statues are attested in his mortuary temple at Deir el-Bahari. Those statues represent the king in the traditional guise of Osiris. This is also a clear return to Khemetic theology. Finally, a specific reference to Re, amalgamated with the traditional 11th Dynasty deity Montu, as in Mentuhotep, is evident from a offering table of Mentuhotep-Nebhepetre:

> Long live Horus he who reunited the Two Lands [...] king of Upper and Lower Egypt [Mentuhotep II] beloved of Hathor [...] son of Re Mentuhotep, given life forever! First *sed*-festival ...[9]

Once again, the latter makes a reference to the fact that he "reunited" the Two Lands. In an inscription on a chapel at Denderah, he specifies who his Asiatic enemies were:

> ... clubbing the eastern lands, striking down the hill countries, trampling the deserts, enslaving the Nubians, ... the Medjay and Wawat, the Libyans and the [Asiatics].

Mentuhotep-Nebhepetre describes the political situation in Egypt during the time immediately preceding his own reunification of the Two Lands as a period of disintegration. Egypt was said to have been divided into several autonomous chiefdoms with no central authority. As in the olden days, Upper and Lower Egypt were disunited. Mentuhotep-Nebhepetre established his seat of government, naturally, in Thebes. He also gave the princes of the "Oryx" Nome limited autonomy with the right to rule their own province. In all, Mentuhotep-Nebhepetre ruled

---

[8] William C. Hayes (1990 [1959]) *The Scepter of Egypt*, Vol. I: p. 148.
[9] Cauville & Gasse (1988) 'Fouilles de Dendera: Premiers résultats', *Bulletin de l'Institut Français d'Archéologie Orientale* 88, p. 27 (my translation).

CHAP. VII: A KING-LESS EGYPT | 245

for 51 years and was succeeded by his son and heir, King Mentuhotep III. Pharaoh Mentuhotep III is especially know for having carried on with the practice begun by Pharaoh Khety III of building fortification walls in the Egypt's eastern Delta to guard against potential bellicose Asiatic incursions.[10] Since Egyptian artifacts are very rare, and even absent, at many important MBIIa Syro-Palestinian sites,[11] it is evident that the 11th Dynasty pharaohs adopted an isolationist position with regards to the Asiatic lands. The official policy was one of containment. The expansionist age had not yet arrived. From as early as Mentuhotep-Nebhepetre's reign, we find references to a garrison of 3,000 soldiers stationed in "the Nomes of the northland." The policing of the eastern Delta was a major concern of the 11th Dynasty, and the Egyptian administration spared no expense to ensure its protection.[12]

Mesopotamia After the Elamites

After the Elamites displaced the Third Dynasty of Ur in 1,953 BCE, no single power held sway for nearly 250 years in Mesopotamia (from Ur to Carchemish). Various city-states enjoying varying degrees of power managed to form more or less successful alliances.[13] Around the start of the nineteenth century BCE, one of these Semitic groups, the Amorites managed to gain control of most of the Mesopotamian region. As a result, the onset of the Middle Bronze Age brought increased trade between the kingdoms of Anatolia, Mesopotamia and Syria-Palestine.[14] The Amorites established a centralized government in the city of Babylon. For this reason, the Amorites are commonly referred to as the "Old Babylonians" — and the period of their rule (c.1,890 BCE to 1,628 BCE) is commonly know as the Old Babylonian period. The Old Babylonians are famous for their set of laws. For example, criminals who committed crimes against the state were severely punished; and "bad behaviour in a bar" could result in the death penalty. The acknowledgement of the contemporary constellation of the vernal equinox (the Aries), may be traced in the development of new defence tactics such as the "battering ram" which developed in Mesopotamia.[15]

---

[10] Nicholas Grimal (1992) *A History of Ancient Egypt*. Trans. by Ian Shaw. Blackwell: Oxford, U.K., p. 157.
[11] James M. Weinstein (1975) 'Egyptian Relations with Palestine in the Middle Kingdom', *Bulletin of the American Schools of Oriental Research* 217, p. 2.
[12] Alessandra Nibbi (1975) *The Sea Peoples and Egypt*, Noyes Press: Park Ridge, N.J., p. 13.
[13] Kenneth A. Kitchen (1995) 'The Patriarchal Age: Myth or History', *Biblical Archaeology Review* Vol. 21 - Num. 2, p. 56.
[14] Gösta W. Ahlström (1993) *The History of Ancient Palestine From the Palaeolithic Period to Alexander's Conquest*, JSOT (Supplement Series 146): Sheffield, U.K., p. 174.
[15] Donald B. Redford (1992) *Egypt, Canaan, and Israel in Ancient Times*, Princeton University Press: Princeton, NJ, p. 96.

Joseph the Patriarch

The MBIIa and MBIIb periods in Palestine brought about a sharp increase in population, urban development and military fortification — particularly at the end of MBIIa. The nomadic age had definitely come to an end. Thus, the Egyptian concerns pertaining to security were much justified. The movement of Asiatics in the eastern Delta was constantly being watched. After the death of Mentuhotep III, his son Mentuhotep IV assumed the governance of Egypt. Things did not go as smoothly for him as they had for his deceased father. The Turin Canon makes mention of "seven empty years"[16] during Mentuhotep IV's reign. This, of course, reminds us of the biblical story of the vizier Joseph and the Egyptian famine. Could the patriarch Joseph have occupied his post in the court of Egypt during the reign of Pharaoh Mentuhotep IV? This is in fact precisely what I propose — since the historical context in Egypt described in the Hebrew Old Testament during Joseph's life-time is perfectly aligned with the sociopolitical realities of King Mentuhotep IV's reign. As the extant evidence from Egypt adduces, the Bible depicts an Egypt extremely weary of Canaanite incursions. Consequently, permission has to be granted by Pharaoh for the entry of any Asiatic individuals into Egypt.

According to the Book of Genesis, Joseph, who had been sold into slavery in Egypt by his jealous brothers (Gen. 37:22-36), rose to prominence in Pharaoh's court by interpreting the latter's dreams. Is it then possible to find a particular individual in Pharaoh Mentuhotep IV's court who might fit the profile of Joseph? If the Bible's account is to be relied upon, then it should not be too difficult to uncover evidence of this exalted royal official in his court from extant records. I believe that this evidence can be gleaned from a document commonly referred to as the Inscriptions of Mentuhotep. These were copied onto the mortuary stela of one Sehetepibre — a nobleman from the reigns of Pharaohs Sesostris III and Amenemhat II of the 12th Dynasty. The story of Mentuhotep, the royal official, apparently remained very popular in later times. As well, another nobleman, living during the 17th Dynasty, refers to such an illustrious Middle Kingdom official by the name of Mentuhotep. Since this last account of Mentuhotep's exploits begin with the name of Pharaoh Sesostris I, we may safely conjecture that Mentuhotep rose to prominence at the time of the former's predecessor, Pharaoh Mentuhotep IV. Interestingly, Mentuhotep, speaking in the first person, describes his actions and functions as follows:

> ... **sending forth two brothers** satisfied with the utterances of his mouth, upon whose tongue is the writing of Thoth, more accurate than the weight, likeness of balances, **fellow of the king in counselling** ... giving attention

---
[16] Nicholas Grimal (1992) p. 158.

to hear words, like a god in his hour, excellent in heart, skilled in his fingers, exercising an office like him who holds it, **favorite of the king before the Two Lands,** his beloved among the companions, powerful among the officials, **having an advanced seat to approach the throne of the king, a man of confidence to whom the heart opens.** [17]

Later in that very same text, this privileged official is described as a *"pilot of the people and giver of food,"* as an *"overseer of the double granary"*, and finally as *"chief treasurer."* Now turning to the Bible's description of Joseph's role in Pharaoh's court, we read:

> 39 And Pharaoh said unto Joseph, Forasmuch as God hath shewed thee all this, there is none so discreet and wise as thou art:
> 40 Thou shalt be over my house, and according unto thy word shall all my people be ruled: only in the throne will I be greater than thou.
> 41 And Pharaoh said unto Joseph, See, I have set thee over all the land of Egypt.
> (Genesis 41:39-41)

Need we look any further? What is more, the Egyptian text says that Mentuhotep "sent forth two brothers" after having given them some satisfying news! These brothers were none other than "Judah and his brethren" (Genesis 44: 14) — whom Joseph has sent back to Canaan to bring the good news to their father Jacob that his long-lost cherished son was still alive and now a governor in the land of Egypt. Although we know that Joseph had more than two brothers, it might be possible to explain the discrepancy in numbers between the Egyptian and Hebrew accounts by the simple fact that, from the Egyptian perspective, they would be more likely to remember the two brothers, Simeon and Benjamin, whom Joseph had held back as ransom.

The Venus Shift of 1,787 BCE and the Years of Want

"Ye are spies; to see the nakedness of the land yea are come."

- Genesis 42:9

In the above passage from the Book of Genesis, Pharaoh accuses the Israelites of being spies, much as in the earlier narrative of Noah and Ham, who transgressed the borders of Egypt to witness its nakedness. The allegorical meaning of Egypt's

---

[17] J. H. Breasted, *Ancient Records of Egypt*, Vol. I - § 531-533.

nakedness is, I believe, exactly similar to the meaning applied to it with respect to Noah-Thebes' nakedness after the Great Flood of 2,130 BCE. The chaotic agent which brought about the drunkenness and nakedness of Noah was exactly the same one that caused the nakedness, or seven years of famine, during the reign of Mentuhotep IV — which is the planet Venus. In 1,787 BCE, seven years before the advent of the 12th Dynasty, the planet Venus caused yet another natural disturbance on earth. In ancient Mesopotamia, the seven years of famine were intimately related to Ishtar, the planet Venus — as Cyrus Gordon delineates below:

> Anu reminds Ishtar that the slaying of the hero will bring on a seven-year famine, whereupon Ishtar assures Anu that she has laid up a seven-year supply of food. The notion that prolonged drought or famine will follow the death of a hero appears ... in both Ugaritic and biblical literature.[18]

It is likewise very significant that, during the course of the primeval Typhon Season, the vizier Imhotep warns Pharaoh Djoser-Netjerykhet, shortly prior to the Venus shift of 3,114 BCE that there would be seven years of famine — just as Anu cautions and as Joseph (who was perhaps consciously modelled after Imhotep) warns King Mentuhotep IV. The biblical symbolism of the seven cows also, incidentally, has a strong Typhonian theme underlying it. Indeed, the goddess Hathor was also widely worshipped in her multiple form of the "Seven Cows" or "Seven Hathors": Hathor of Thebes, Heliopolis, Aphroditopolis, Sinai, Momemphis, Herakleopolis, and Keset. These seven cows are seen by some scholars as "a sevenfold form of the goddess, analogous to her seven human form."[19] Like the Sumerian Ishtar, Hathor, in her Venusian aspect, was responsible for the Destruction of Mankind at the divinely appointed time. Again, the name "Hathor" is the Greek corruption of Het-Her (The Horus Above) and Het-Heru (The House of Horus). These appellations identify her as a sky goddess. For the priests of Heliopolis, Hathor was the consort of Re and the mother of Shu and Tefnut. In that capacity of a "Great Mother" and as the personification of the primeval waters of Nun, she was responsible, ultimately, for the general cosmic order. Therefore the seven leanfleshed cows which Pharaoh saw in his dream (Gen. 41:19) were interpreted by Joseph as seven years in which the cosmic order (Ma'at) would be disturbed (Gen. 41:27, 30-31). This Venus-induced universal conflagration took place in 1,787 BCE — which is seven years before the start of the 12th Dynasty.

---

[18] Cyrus Gordon (1962) *Before the Bible (The Common Background of Greek and Hebrew Civilizations)*, Collins: London, p. 69.
[19] See Geraldine Pinch (1993) *Votive Offerings to Hathor*, Griffith Institute/Ashmolean Museum: Oxford, U.K., p. 174.

CHAP. VII: A KING-LESS EGYPT | 249

Suddenly, the Egyptian administrators of the eastern desert found themselves confronted with a potentially dangerous political situation. But thanks to the comprehensive preparations undertaken throughout the 11th Dynasty, the situation did not degenerate into an uncontrolled influx of Asiatics into Egypt. At this time, the Egyptians began portraying Asiatics entering Egypt's eastern Delta, on the tomb walls at Beni Hassan.

> Their presence suggests that marauders or itinerants could have been infiltrating this region of the desert, crossing from the coast to the Nile Valley. ... The well-known representation of Abesha and a group of Asiatics in Tomb 3 (Khnumhotep) at Beni Hassan may depict this very activity. It is noteworthy that Gebel el-Zeit, near the Strait of Gubal and Wadi Abu Had, lies nearly opposite Minya (Menat Khufu), the seat of the nomarchs of the sixteenth Upper Egyptian nome.[20]

The Egypt-bound Midianite merchants to whom Jacob's other sons sold Joseph (Gen. 37:36) could have feasibly belonged to one of these Asiatic clans who entered Egypt at that time. Indeed, from ancient Near Eastern sources, modern scholars can evaluate the prices paid for slaves very accurately for the period ranging from 2,400 BCE to 400 BCE. It so happens that, at the time where I have placed Joseph in the new chronology (the eighteenth century BCE), we find a striking concordance. Indeed, as eminent Egyptologist Kenneth Kitchen writes: *"Joseph is sold to some passing Ishmaelites for 20 shekels (Genesis 37:28), the price of a slave in the Near East in about the 18th century B.C."*[21] Documents from the early Babylonian period, like the Laws of Hammurabi and the Mari archives, show that in this, and in no other period, were slaves worth twenty shekels. The Bible also says that "the Midianites sold him into Egypt unto Potiphar, an officer of Pharaoh's, and a captain of the guard." This reference to an "Egyptian guard" dealing with Asiatic merchants is, evidently, consistent with the historical picture which emerges at that time in Egypt. From the above quote, we can surmise that Joseph was sold to priests of the sixteenth Nome who bore special allegiance to the cult of the First Cataract deity Khnum. This may bear some additional significance since, during Typhon Season #1, Imhotep – who, like Joseph, spoke of seven years of famine in Egypt – resorts to the Khemetic god Khnum to appease the Typhonian deities.

---

[20] Ann Bomann & Robert Young (1994) 'Preliminary Survey in the Wadi Abu Had, Eastern Desert, 1992', *Journal of Egyptian Archaeology* 80, p. 30.
[21] Kenneth A. Kitchen (1995) 'The Patriarchal Age: Myth or History', p. 52.

8

The Pharaohs Who Knew Not Joseph (1,780 BCE to 1,628 BCE)

It is at the close of the "seven years of want" that King Amenemhat I, founder of the 12th Dynasty, takes over the throne of Egypt and establishes a new political order in Egypt. Most significantly, the capital is moved from Thebes in the south to Memphis to the north. The 12th Dynasty also displaced the cult of Montu, which had risen to prominence during the 11th Dynasty, and assimilated Montu's attributes into the new cult of Amun-Re. Despite having chosen to move Egypt's capital away from Thebes, the 12th Dynasty was Theban in origin — as is made evident by their choice of Amun, the Theban deity, as a chief god. The 12th Dynasty theologians made a concerted effort to consolidate both the Memphite (ithyphallic fertility god of Coptos, Min) and Heliopolitan (Khemetic primordial sun-god, Re) theologies with the Theban worship of Amun whilst nonetheless attempting to preserve the supremacy of the Theban theology of Amun. Amun-Re "King of the Gods" now reigned supreme. The new dynasty had not altogether abandoned Thebes however. In fact, it can be noticed that, much as in during Typhon Season #2, the 12th Dynasty symbolically divided Egypt's northern and southern parts between Horus and Seth. Upper Egypt, the realm of Seth, was ruled by the Sesostris line, while Lower Egypt, the domain of Horus, was ruled by the Amenemhat line. The Sethian root is obvious in the name "Sesostris." With the case of "Amenemhat," we can denote the name of the Theban god Amun. As the Thebans conceived of Amun as their chief deity, the pharaoh bearing the name of Amun was nothing less than a divine ruler on earth; the "first born" of God. Since Horus is the "first born" of Osiris, the former's association with Pharaoh Amenemhat was a natural one. The well-acknowledged fact among historians that the Amenemhat and Sesostris rulers of the 12th Dynasty ruled contemporaneously (i.e. as co-regents), is easily explained by this theological arrangement. The father, Amenemhat (the first born) administered the capital at Memphis in Lower Egypt, while the son, Sesostris, oversaw Upper Egypt. The 12th Dynasty pharaohs had been responsible for restoring order in Egypt after the seven years of famine which engulfed the Two Lands during Joseph's tenure as chief vizier. When the Bible speaks of that new king of Egypt "which knew not Joseph" (Exo. 1:8), we are most likely reading about Pharaoh Amenemhat I. I strongly doubt, however, the biblical redactor's contention that Amenemhat I had actively set out to oppress the Hebrews. Much to the contrary, under the benevolent reign of the 12th Dynasty, Joseph's brethren became princely rulers of the Delta city of Avaris (Pi-Ramses) in the land of Goshen.

Recovering from Civil Strife

In a document known as the Tod Inscription of Sesostris I, the 12th Dynasty king recounts the details of a "civil war" which engulfed Egypt immediately preceding his accession to the throne. Describing the savage vandalizing of an 11th Dynasty temple, Sesostris writes:

> It was a disaster that lay before me: all the walls were engulfed with fire, the temple priests were ignorant of the cults, vandals took to looting everywhere; the prisoners, who now meandered throughout the country, rejoiced about the civil war; ... each and every one was a pillager, and arsonists had overcome the temple. But those who had devastated this domain I have captured like fish without releasing neither man or woman ...[1]

The exact nature of this civil war has been the subject of much intrigue and debate among scholars. German Egyptologist Wolfgang Helck suggested linking those events to a palace intrigue which resulted in the murder of Amenemhat I.[2] I am however convinced that Sesostris I describes the chaotic events immediately preceding the accession of the 12th Dynasty — during the seven years of famine predicted by the Patriarch Joseph. The fact that the temple walls had been "engulfed with fire" and that the priests had grown "ignorant of the cults" must lead one to conclude that Pharaoh Sesostris I depicts a scene of immense chaos — a disturbance considerably more severe than a mere palace intrigue. The real culprit, once again, was the planet Venus — which violently shifted from it's set orbital path and disturbed earth's own polar stability in the year 1,787 BCE, causing a fiery cataclysm. The socioeconomic devastation was so complete that the 12th Dynasty saw it fit to inaugurate it's rule as a Renaissance Era. In column 35 of the Tod Inscription, King Sesostris I makes allusion to the "Repetition of Births."

---

[1] My own translation of French rendition quoted in Chr. Barbotin & J.-J. Clère (1991) *L'inscription de Sésostris Ier à Tôd'*, Bulletin de l'Institut Français d'Archéologie Orientale 91, p. 9.
[2] W. Helck 'Politische Spannungen zu Beginn des Mittleren Reiches.' In (1985) *Ägypten, Dauer und Wandel*, DAIAK Sonderschrift 18, p. 52.

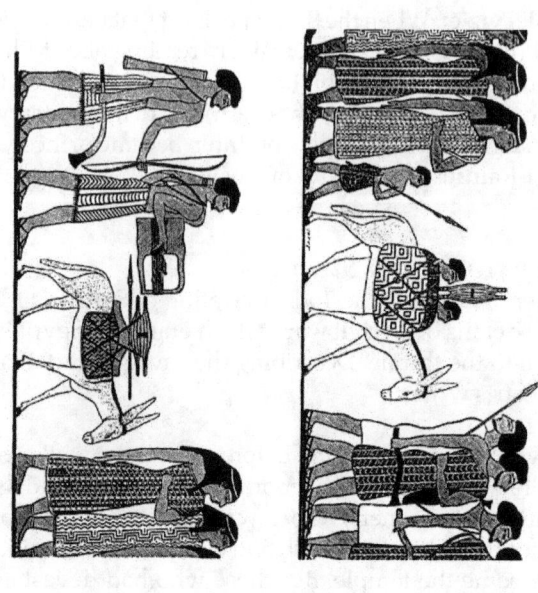

Fig. 8a: Scene from Beni Hassan tomb of the nomarch Khnumhotep depicting foreigners from Canaan arriving in Egypt.

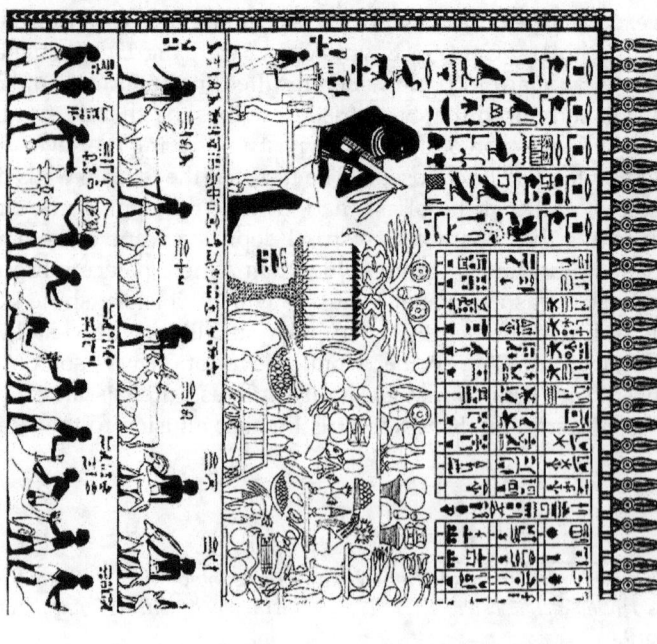

Fig. 8b: Scene of daily life at Beni Hassan.

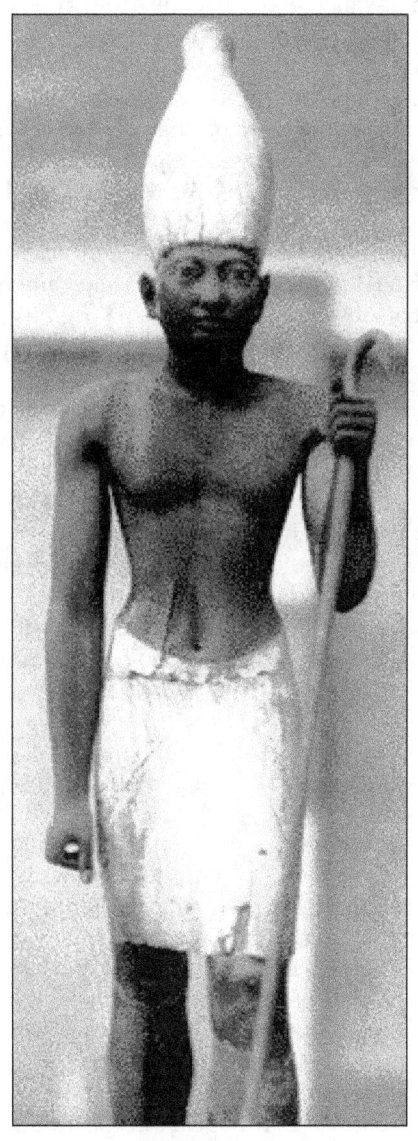

Fig. 8c: King Sesostris I (Cairo Museum).

CHAP. VIII: THE PHARAOHS WHO KNEW NOT JOSEPH

Throughout Egyptian history, Repetition of Birth eras signalled important transition periods (renaissance eras), usually from times of instability to more prosperous ones. The Horus name of Pharaoh Amenemhat I, *Wehem-meswt*, in fact means "He who repeats births."

It is under these conditions of renewed hope and newfound stability that the Hebrews, who had settled in the Land of Pharaoh under Joseph's administration, suddenly found themselves elevated to the status of royal nomarchs (i.e. Nome rulers). As the new chronology purports, the Middle Kingdom Pharaohs Wegaf to Neferhotep, conventionally dated to the 13th Dynasty, were really the contemporaries of Pharaohs Amenemhat I-IV. The former had in fact been highly Egyptianized Semites, like their brethren Joseph had been, who had gained the favour of Pharaoh Amenemhat I. The first of these Hebrew pharaohs, King Wegaf, belonged to the class of Hebrew nobles to whom King Mentuhotep IV had given the land of Goshen:

> 6 The land of Egypt is before thee; in the best of the land make thy father and brethren to dwell; in the land of Goshen let them dwell: and if thou knowest any men of activity among them, then make them rulers over my cattle. ...
> 11 And Joseph placed his father and his brethren, and gave them a possession in the land of Egypt, in the best of the land, in the land of Rameses, as Pharaoh had commended.
> 27 And Israel dwelt in the land of Egypt, in the country of Goshen; and they had possessions therein, and grew, and multiplied exceedingly.
> (Genesis 47:6, 11, 27)

The Hebrew Old Testament makes it clear that Pharaoh had given a portion of Egypt, the land of Goshen (Avaris or the Land of Ramses), to Joseph's Hebrew brethren. The Bible later goes on to say that these Hebrews, who "multiplied exceedingly" in the land of Goshen, subsequently were oppressed under a harsh pharaoh who knew not Joseph. Since Amenemhat I founded a new dynasty and inaugurated a Renaissance Era immediately after the end of Mentuhotep IV's reign, it's more than likely that Amenemhat I was the elusive new pharaoh of Egypt "which knew not Joseph" (Exo. 1:8). When the latter ascended Egypt's throne, he found Joseph's brethren dwelling in the land of Goshen. Contrary to what the Bible says, Pharaoh did not move to oppress the Hebrews of Goshen. In fact, he gave their ruler, Wegaf, full pharaonic titles. The reason why the biblical redactors sought to portray Joseph's brethren as downtrodden peasants is because they needed to justify the version of the Exodus story as it appears in the Torah. The oppression of the Israelites in the Land of Ramses, as I will be arguing later, occurred much later in history. Seeing that the biblical Exodus story is a composite of a series of historical events in ancient Israelite history, not all of these different components necessarily need to adhere to the oppression model.

The Move of the State Capital from Thebes to Lisht-Memphis: The Death of Noah

Before ascending the throne of Egypt, Pharaoh Amenemhat I had earlier been known as vizier Ammenemes under King Mentuhotep IV. Amenemhat's name meaning "Amun is the foremost," the latter's allegiance to the cult of Amun is well established. Despite that, King Amenemhat I abruptly decided to move Egypt's capital from Thebes, the domain of Amun, to Itjawy (modern Lisht) in Middle Egypt. This abandonment of Thebes (the biblical "No") as the capital of Egypt is reflected, in my opinion, within the Old Testament in the death of Noah. Seeing that the dynastic Theban Nome, established under Pharaoh Sneferu, was founded in 2,730 BCE, the year of Noah-Thebes' birth, the death of Noah 950 years later, in 1,780 BCE, must likewise reflect a pivotal event concerning Thebes.

> 28 And Noah lived after the flood **three hundred and fifty years.**
> 29 And all the days of Noah were **nine hundred and fifty years: and he died.**
> (Genesis 9:28-29)

Three hundred and fifty years after the Great Flood of 2,130 BCE comes down to the year 1,780 BCE — which is nine hundred and fifty years after 2,730 BCE. Hence, once Noah is recognized as a biblical metaphor for the ancient Egyptian capital of Thebes (No), Noah-Thebes thence becomes a crucial pillar unifying ancient Egyptian and Israelite history. Early Hebrew history owes a lot more to Egypt than the biblical redactors have been willing to openly concede. These historical links have instead been dissimulated under various allegorical characters and story lines. Many more of such metaphors will be uncovered in the chapters to come.

With the new capital now established at Lisht, the bulk of dynastic Egypt's economic and administrative activities now centred around Memphis, in Lower Egypt. The move also accompanied somewhat of a revival of the pyramid age. Though not coming anywhere near to achieving the splendours of the original pyramidal age, the 12th Dynasty kings attempted to revive the practice of pyramid building. The advent of the 12th Dynasty hence indeed lived up to its name as a true Renaissance Era. That renewal would however manifest itself in a lot more profound ways than in a mere architectural revival. The move of the centre of activity

CHAP. VIII: THE PHARAOHS WHO KNEW NOT JOSEPH | 257

to Lower Egypt, in itself, had infinitely greater meaning. As during the initial pyramid age, in Typhon Season #1, an attempt was made to symbolically divide Egypt between two separate kingships adhering to either Seth or Horus. For this Renaissance Era, the 12th Dynasty pharaohs and priests sought to recreate the predynastic era following the murder of Osiris. Reflecting the time of Djoser-Nejerykhet's reign, the administrative capital was again located in Memphis. A steadfast theological impulse had hence motivated the 12th Dynasty to move the capital out of Upper Egypt. Despite this not being a Typhonian era, no effort was spared to make it at least appear as such. Describing a throne dating to the 12th Dynasty found in their new capital of Lisht, Egyptologist Barry J. Kemp writes:

> On the Lisht thrones Horus and Seth are representatives of Upper and Lower Egypt of equal status. On the Shabaka Stone Seth's place is diminished: from an initial equality with Horus he is subsequently disinherited, though acquiescing in his new role. This text, and a mass of further ancient allusions on the same theme spread over a good part of Pharaonic history, poses a fundamental question. Does the myth mask a formative phase in the history of the Egyptian state?[3]

I believe that the answer to Barry J. Kemp's question is a resounding "yes." The Lisht throne, while not having been carved during a Typhon Season, commemorates those genuine historical eras when Upper and Lower Egypt were indeed bitterly divided between the followers of Horus and Seth. This dual allegiance of the 12th Dynasty kingship is reflected in the chosen throne names of pharaohs of that epoch: Amenemhat and Sesostris. The root of the name Amenemhat is obviously from the Theban god Amun, patron-deity of the Horus kingship from the preceding dynasty. The continuity of the traditional Horus supremacy was hence assured. The name Sesostris, on the other hand, has a distinctly Sethian origin. In the absence of a genuine Sethian rebellion, the 12th Dynasty was organized in such a way that a series of coregencies between the Horus elder, i.e. Amenemhat, and his eldest son, a Sethian figure named Sesostris, symbolically reenacted the primordial territorial division between Horus and Seth. It is therefore entirely probable that the administration of Upper Egypt and Nubia was more specifically relegated to the Sesostrises, as evidenced by the Nubian forts erected by King Sesostris III, while the Amenemhats oversaw the Delta region and Syria-Palestine. For about the next three hundred and sixty years, Egypt's Two Lands would be divided between two, and even a third (i.e. the Hebrew nobles and later the Hyksos), sets of rulers. Quoting Egyptologist Williams C. Hayes:

---

[3] Barry J. Kemp (1989) *Ancient Egypt: Anatomy of a Civilization*, Routledge: London and New York, p. 31.

The practice – an extremely sound one – was followed by most of Amunemhet's successors, and throughout the dynasty we find the succession assured by a series of coregencies between fathers and sons of the royal line.[4]

True to the conventional chronology, Hayes did not recognize the existence of a third line of legitimate rulers in the Delta. The biblical Joseph's brethren, Pharaohs Wegaf to Neferhotep, are traditionally believed to have been native Egyptian monarchs of the subsequent 13th Dynasty. How this confusion came about will be explored shortly. Also to be subsequently discussed is how, at the chaotic termination of the 12th Dynasty, the Hebrew pharaohs of Pi-Ramses (Avaris) were driven out by an invading horde of Hyksos rulers.

The fundamentally African origins of the 12th Dynasty pharaohs is evidenced by the fact that they were the direct descendants of the Theban pharaohs who, under Mentuhotep-Nebhepetre, came out of Ethiopia to reunify Egypt in 1,820 BCE. Surviving portrays of the 12th Dynasty kings likewise abundantly attest to their African origins (see Fig. 8d). As the dynastic Egyptian cult of the Theban god Amun journeyed in the Black Land, below the Fourth Cataract, during the time of the Asiatic occupation of Egypt, it soon began to acquire specifically Khemetic characteristics. So by the time Pharaoh Amenemhat I acceded to the throne of a unified Egypt, a historic fusion between the primordial Khemetic sun-god Re and the dynastic Egyptian god Amun of Thebes had materialized. King Amenemhat I, hailing from Elephantine near First Cataract, actively sought to once again give prominence to ancient Khemetic traditions by, amongst other things, resurrecting Heliopolitan theology. Revolutionizing ancient Egyptian religion, he elevated Amun-Re, the composite deity uniting the Khemetic sun-god Re and the Theban god Amun, to the status of state god. It is also very probable that the temple of Amun-Re at Karnak was first inaugurated under this king as a testament to this new theological fusion. Other building activities included, in the third year of Amenemhat I's reign, the restoration of the temple of Re-Atum at Heliopolis. All the ingredients are therefore in place to corroborate a vibrant return to Heliopolitan theology. Not since the days of King Khnum-Khufu had dynastic Egypt been so immersed in Khemetic traditions. The level of independence enjoyed by the dynastic Egyptian society of Asiatic origins between the 4th and 11th Dynasties would never again return during the Bronze Age. Following the return of the 11th Dynasty kings from the Ethiopian regions below the Fourth Cataract, the pharaohs of dynastic Egypt can for the first time be positively characterized, racially speaking, as Black. Indeed, from Pharaoh Mentuhotep-Nebhepetre up to the beginning of the new chronology's 18th Dynasty (with the exception of the 16th and 17th Dynasty), the Diopan model of a pre-eminently African pharaonic civilization is maintained by the present author.

---

[4] William C. Hayes (1990 [1959]) *The Scepter of Egypt*, Vol. I: p. 172.

The Influence of 12th Dynasty Kings in

Palestine and the Aegean

> "To abandon 1786 B.C. as the year when Dyn. XII
> ended would be to cast adrift from our only firm anchor,
> a course that would have serious consequences
> for the history, not of Egypt alone, but
> of the entire Middle East."
>
> - Sir Alan H. Gardiner
> *Egypt of the Pharaohs*

The extent of Egyptian influence in the Aegean during the Middle Kingdom has been, and definitely continues to be, the subject of much controversy within ancient world scholarship. In the midsts of the debate, African-centered scholars in particular have been vocally advocating the model of an Egyptian "colonization" of the Aegean and Palestine during the 12th Dynasty. However, both professional Aegean scholars and Egyptologists have generally been extremely reluctant to even admit to a substantial relationship between the two areas during the Middle Bronze Age — much less to the idea of an Egyptian colonization of the eastern Mediterranean. In modern scholarship's view, no such Egyptian empire existed at the time.[5] The principal argument used by archaeologists to refute the Afrocentrists' claim is that archaeological remains in Syria-Palestine and the Aegean do not support the thesis of a massive Egyptian presence in those regions. I now intend to cogently demonstrate that this ideological edifice of Eurocentric anti-diffusionism is built upon the quicksand of a faulty Egyptian chronology.

My own thesis is that the 12th Dynasty pharaohs sought to institute a kind of "Commonwealth" under Egyptian sovereignty throughout Syria-Palestine and the Aegean. While the various city-states of the Aegean and Syria-Palestine maintained their individual sovereignty, they were nonetheless under the military and economic tutelage of Egypt. It is evident that some hostile military expeditions had been dispatched by the 12th Dynasty kings into certain parts of Syria-Palestine to subdue occasional rebellions but, on the whole, the hereby proposed Commonwealth Model argues for a relatively uncontested, if not universally welcomed, Egyptian dominion over the eastern Mediterranean. Artisans and craftsmen from the Mediterranean world freely lived and worked

---

[5] See James M. Weinstein (1975) 'Egyptian Relations with Palestine in the Middle Kingdom', *Bulletin of the American Schools of Oriental Research* 217, pp. 1-16.

in Egypt, and certain aspects of Egyptian culture appear to have been adapted to the local culture in the foreign lands under pharaonic tutelage.

Incidentally, while this view of the relations between Egypt and the Syro-Palestinian & Mediterranean worlds during the Middle Kingdom has not traditionally held sway, more recent research and new evidence has been rapidly changing the view of some scholars, as Johns Hopkins University Egyptologist Prof. Hans Goedicke relates:

> A tenet of Egyptological historical research is the notion that the rulers of the Middle Kingdom concentrated their political efforts in the Nile Valley and were unconcerned with the Levant. ... For a decennium this idyllic picture has no longer been tenable due to new evidence.[6]

Among the available evidence, Dr. Goedicke names the Mit Rahineh inscription, which mentions at least three "bellicose actions" carried out by the Egyptian army in Asia. While it is important not to lose sight of the fact that many, if not most, of the relationships between 12th Dynasty Egypt and its contemporary Syro-Palestinian city-sates were commercial in nature, the Mit Rahineh inscription clearly speaks of the *"dispatch of soldiers together with the 'overseer of troops' and [the 'overseer of] soldiers' in order to hack up Asia."*[7] This belligerent action seems, according to Goedicke, to have taken place during the reign of Amenemhat II. Disagreeing with scholars like Goedicke who contend that Egypt exerted strong economic, political and military influence in Syria-Palestine during the Middle Kingdom, ancient historian James M. Weinstein has, for several years, been one of the most outspoken proponents of the orthodox viewpoint claiming that no such relationship ever existed. In Weinstein's view:

> The MBIIA Period in Palestine was basically a traditional phase from the semi-nomadic culture of MBI to the highly urbanized, economically prosperous, and militarily strong society of MBIIB-C. ... Through much of antiquity, Palestine was an economic, political, and military backwater ... The great expansion in relations between Palestine and Egypt occurred toward the end of the MBIIA Period and the beginning of MBIIB, i.e., in the late 12th—early 13th Dynasty, when Egypt was beginning to go into military and political decline, while the city-states of Palestine were gaining in power and wealth. It may seem strange that when Egypt was strong and Palestine weak (the conditions existing in MBIIA), trade was at a minimum, but that when Egypt's political and military fortunes declined and

---

[6] Hans Goedicke (1991) 'Egyptian Military Actions in "Asia" in the Middle Kingdom', *Revue d'Égyptologie* 42, p. 89.
[7] Ibid, p. 93.

CHAP. VIII: THE PHARAOHS WHO KNEW NOT JOSEPH | 261

Palestine's increased (the situation in late MBIIA and early MBIIB), trade rapidly expanded.[8]

I have absolutely no quarrel with James M. Weinstein as far as the socioeconomic situation of Syria-Palestine during MBIIa is concerned. Moreover, if one correlates this evidence with the traditional chronology of Egypt, Weinstein is absolutely right. Indeed, Egypt's 12th Dynasty definitely *could not* have wielded much influence in Palestine. But I maintain that the standard chronology of ancient Egypt is wrong. In the new chronology, we find the 12th Dynasty entering the scene at the end of MBIIa — at the exact time when, according to J. M. Weinstein, Syria-Palestine was also gaining in strength. Within the Commonwealth Model, one does not need to look very far for the cause of this sudden expansion in Syria-Palestine. In reality, both cultures, Egypt and Syria-Palestine, were peaking at the very same time! We can therefore naturally conclude, within the context of the new chronology, that Middle Kingdom Egypt served as the principal catalyst for Syria-Palestine's dazzlingly expeditious development during the MBIIb period. Describing this swift urban renewal at Shechem and Gezer, Joe D. Seger observes:

> In both sites [Shechem and Gezer], the earliest MB IIA city levels appear without any fortification walls, and the settlements are of rather modest size. However, in the succeeding MB IIB period, substantial city development and growth is witnessed.[9]

With their sudden wealth gained from their expansive trade relations with 12th Dynasty Egypt, coupled with the relative peace engendered by their new Commonwealth status under a major power, the Canaanites were able to begin building massive edifices and significantly improve their urban centres. The fortified cities of Hazor, Gezer and Schechem, which the Book of Joshua mentions during the Conquest accounts were all built during this period.

Having lowered the dates for the 12th Dynasty, we should hence expect that various material remains from the reigns of the Amenemhats and Sesostrises could be found among the Syro-Palestinian strata from the MBIIb period. This is indeed what we find. But archaeologists are, quite understandably, not too comfortable with these finds. Naturally, that's because Egyptological dogma dictates that the 12th Dynasty ended as the MBIIb period arose in the Levant. So finding artifacts belonging to 12th Dynasty pharaohs within MBIIb contexts presents serious problems for conventional scholarship. Outlining this apparent problem, Egyptologist William A. Ward wrote:

---

[8] James M. Weinstein (1975) 'Egyptian Relations with Palestine in the Middle Kingdom', *Bulletin of the American Schools of Oriental Research* 217, pp. 13-14.
[9] Joe D. Seger (1975) 'The MB II Fortifications at Schechem and Gezer: A Hyksos Retrospective', *Eretz-Israel* 12, p. 42.

> The numerous scarabs attributed to Sesostris I discovered at many Syro-Palestinian sites present special problems ... The strange circumstance pertaining to the scarabs is that wherever the archaeological context can be dated they appear in deposits no earlier than the MB IIA period (Albright), hence long after the reign of Sesostris himself. This obviously means that these objects are valueless as proofs of foreign relations during the lifetime of this king in spite of continuing attempts to use them so.[10]

The extent to which many ancient world scholars will go to defend the indefensible is glaringly displayed here. Once more, we have ample proof that the accepted dates for the 12th Dynasty are much too high, but the evidence is willfully ignored because it does not fit with preconceived notions. If the scarabs of Sesostris turn up in sites dating to long after the pharaoh's death, why should it be so illogical to reconsider the dates of his reign? One of the most important defining characteristics of the MBIIb-c era is the widespread, and supposedly unexplained, presence of Egyptian royal scarabs dating to the 12th Dynasty in Palestine.[11] Interestingly enough, similar 12th Dynasty scarabs were also found in Crete. The following table establishes the relationship between the different MBII strata in Syria-Palestine and the contemporary Middle Minoan Age in Crete:

Chronology of Protopalatial (or Old Palace) Crete:

MMI - MMIII	2,000 - 1,550 BCE
	1,953 - 1,559 BCE (New Chronology)
	MMI : 1,953 - 1,780 BCE — MB IIa
	MMII : 1,780 - 1,628 BCE — MB IIb
	MMIII : 1,628 - 1,559 BCE — MB IIc

Table 8-1

During the 1950's, archaeologist R. Weill[12] was ridiculed for suggesting that the pharaonic names inscribed on the scarabs uncovered in the Syro-Palestinian MBIIb-c strata were in fact carved during the reigns of these respective kings.

---

[10] W. A. Ward (1971) *Egypt and the East Mediterranean World: 2200-1900 B.C. (Studies in Egyptian Foreign Relations During the First Intermediate Period)*, American University of Beirut: Beirut, Lebanon, pp. 68-69.

[11] John Van Seters (1966) *The Hyksos (A New Investigation)*, Yale University Press: New Haven and London, p. 61.

[12] See R. Weill (1953) *XIIe Dynastie, royauté de Haute-Egypte et domination Hyksos dans le nord*, IFAOC Bibliotheque d'Etude, 26: Cairo.

CHAP. VIII: THE PHARAOHS WHO KNEW NOT JOSEPH | 263

Most scholars thought that such a proposition would require too much chronological gymnastics. Accepting Weill's theory would mean moving the twelfth dynasty down to the standard Second Intermediate Period (1,674 - 1,559 BCE) — long after the time when the 12th Dynasty is believed to have come to a close (in c.1780 BCE). On the other hand, in the novel chronology, the 12th Dynasty *does* fall within the period traditionally allotted to the so-called Second Intermediate Period. There is again absolutely no reason why the scarabs could not have been carved at the time when the 12th Dynasty rulers, whose names adorn them, reigned in Egypt. Weill having been unjustly discredited, the official interpretation still remains that the scarabs were manufactured *after* the end of the 12th Dynasty for purely amuletic purposes.[13] Proving once again that common sense is not always common, a fallacious interpretation of the evidence has been passed on as the evidence itself.

Besides, it is also evident, from examining the artistic style of several other MBIIb-c scarabs, that their design was significantly influenced by Minoan motifs.[14] Similar motifs were likewise widely in use both in Old Babylonian temples and in the Palace of King Zimri-Lim of Mari.[15] Not only is this irrefutable proof of intimate contact between 12th Dynasty Egypt and Middle Minoan Crete, but it also gives an inkling into the sheer expanse of Egyptian influence during the Middle Kingdom. As the following quote from the eminent classicist Sir Arthur Evans makes clear, the Cretan remains associated with the Egyptian 12th Dynasty belong to the archaeological period known as Middle Minoan II — which (as Table 8-1 delineates) incidentally corresponds with the Middle Bronze IIa period. Are those 12th Dynasty objects discovered in MBIIb context, in a distant island in the Aegean, again merely later replicas? How many "coincidences" must there be before the obvious may be acknowledged?

> ... Finally, this extensive Cretan influence on Middle Kingdom Egypt, to which the 'Great South Road' and its maritime outlet at Komò must have done so much to foment, has left its record ... in the remains of imported vessels of the **M.M. II** polychrome fabric on more than one Egyptian site. Of these the 'hole-mouthed' bridge-spouted pot from the Abydos cemetery ... is specially important form the chronological data as it supplies in connexion with a characteristic example of the **M.M. IIb** ceramic style. **It was found together with Twelfth Dynasty objects, including two glazed steatite cylinders of Sesostris (Sesostris II) and Amenemhat III ...**[16]

---

[13] John Van Seters (1966) p. 62.
[14] Ibid, pp. 62-63.
[15] A. Parrot (1958-59) *MAM*, 2, *Le Palais* – 3 parts. Geuthner: Paris. pp. I ff.
[16] Sir Arthur Evans (1921-1928) *The Palace of Minos at Knossos (A Comparative account of the Successive Stages of the Early Cretan Civilization as Illustrated by the Discoveries)* — Vol. II/Part I: Fresh lights on origins and External Relations – The Restoration in Town and Palace after Seismic Catastrophe Towards Close of M.M. III, and the Beginnings of the New Era. Macmillan: London, p. 209.

In addition to the MMIIb Cretan ceramic found at the Abydos cemetery, similar sherds of Cretan style were discovered near the pyramid of Pharaoh Sesostris II. Sir Evans concluded that the pottery came from a nearby settlement of Cretan workmen and skilled artisans hired to construct Sesostris II's pyramid. Naturally, as Evans himself theorized,[17] the members of the Cretan colony in Egypt certainly brought back to their homeland some of the various kinds of knowledge and customs they acquired in Egypt. A particular example of this influence can be attested through the proliferation in Crete, around the time of Sesostris II, of a new type of libation vases known as "ostrich-egg flasks." Similar ostrich-egg containers — which first came into use in Africa long before the beginning of dynastic Egypt — can still be found in modern Sudan. Since such vessels make their first appearance in the 11th Dynasty, it is more than likely that the Thebans adopted them during their exile in the Sudan, and brought them along to Egypt once they reunited the Two Lands under King Mentuhotep-Nebhepetre. The ostrich-egg containers continued to be used during the subsequent 12th Dynasty — where the Cretan workmen became familiar with them. Referring to those very same vessels found in Crete during the MMIIb-c period, Sir Arthur Evans says the following:

> It is indeed astonishing to find that a purely African form of vessel, at home in the Soudan and the Libyan Desert, should have been adapted to form what seems to have been a principal sacred utensil of Minoan cult, further implanted by Minoan expansion throughout Mainland Greece. That this 'rhyton' type should have been taken from such a quarter is a striking proof of the intensive personal contact of the Minoans with Nilotic regions far above the Delta.[18]

The Black kings of the 12th Dynasty, as is made amply evident in the above citation, exported African culture into the Middle Minoan Age Aegean. As mentioned earlier, it is also during that time, in MMII, that sphinx figures make their first appearance in Crete. The MMII Mediterranean lay in the midst of a an expansive pharaonic sphere of influence. From Memphis, to Crete, through Canaan and on to Mari, the 12th Dynasty kings made their presence felt. Such a vast international

---

[17] Ibid, p. 221.
[18] Ibid, p. 227.

Fig. 8d: Amenemhat III (Cairo Museum).

Fig. 8e: Amenemhat III as sphinx (Cairo Museum).

Fig. 8f: The fortress of Semneh (restored). *After* Chipiez (1882).

trading network naturally necessitated the maintenance of peace, stability and prosperity at home. Internal or neighbouring threats needed to be dealt with swiftly. The most pervasive menace came from the Asiatic C-Group Nubians dwelling below the southern border between the First and Fourth Cataracts.

The Nubian Policy

From very early on in the 12th Dynasty, the Khemeto-Egyptian rulers made it a top priority to overwhelm Nubia. In two military campaigns, Amenemhat I at once seized Gerf Hussain and the diorite quarries west of Toshka. Advancing further south, he occupied Korosko and, as many scholars believe, founded the fortress at Semneh (see Fig. 8c). King Sesostris I followed the same trail — both by military conquests and consolidation of Egyptian economic and administrative activities between the First and Second Cataracts. Infantry troops were strategically stationed in fortresses throughout the land of Wawat. On Year 5 of his reign, Sesostris I completed a fort at Buhen, in Lower Egypt. It is actually on his Buhen stela that we note the very first occurrence of the name "Kush" — which from then on became known as the Nubian territory between the Second and the Fourth Cataract. On the economic front, Nubia became an important source of gold, copper, amethyst, diorite and granite for Egypt — supplying much needed resources for Egypt's vast trading network. By the time Pharaohs Amenemhat II and Sesostris II became coregents, Egyptian domination of Nubia became so complete, that they no longer even faced any opposition from belligerent Nubian locals. Under King Sesostris III, the resulting scaling down of Egyptian military coercion encouraged some intrepid Nubian troops to start advancing north of the Second Cataract. Such an affront to Egyptian authority would not go unanswered. Sesostris III mounted at least four campaigns to push them back into Upper Nubia. Sesostris III is notorious for his particular hatred for his C-Group Asiatic foes to the south. His aversion was expressed, without reservation, in a Year 16 stela erected at Semneh. Calling the Asiatic Nubians "cowards" and "poltrons," Sesostris III wanted to make sure that his eventual successors would never relinquish Egypt's hold over Nubia. In Year 8, he formally established an Egyptian border at Semneh — forcefully forbidding any Nubian from crossing into Egyptian territory.

Having firmly established his administrative frontier at Semneh, Sesostris III had lived up to his theological duty as patron of Upper Egypt. The Nubian god Dedun, mentioned in the Pyramid Texts as 'Lord of Ta-Seti,' was worshipped along with the deified Sesostris III at Semneh.[19] Both being Sethian figures, the pairing was

---

[19] A. J. Arkell (1974 [1961]) *A History of the Sudan (From the Earliest Times to 1821)*, Greenwood Press: Westport, Conn., pp. 104-105.

well suited. By so naming the Kushite god Dedun "Lord of Ta-Seti," the dynastic Egyptians were obviously quick to correlate the ancient A-Group African Nubians with the later C-Group Asiatic Nubians who immigrated into the region during the EBIV period. While the A-Group and C-Group Nubians were not racially related, the latter Asiatic group, having immigrated into the same region, had come to adopt a similar culture as their A-Group predecessors. Again, the Asiatic origins of the C-Group Nubians are evidenced by, as John Van Seters remarks, in the Middle Kingdom Egyptian texts linking the Asiatics with the Nubians: *"[the] remarks against the Asiatics are bound up with those against the Nubia ..."*[20] Both groups of Asiatics, whether they dwelt below the southern border or in their homeland of Syria-Palestine, lived outside the regulated borders of the divinely ordered world (Ma'at) and, hence, had to be contained. In the eyes of the dynastic Egyptians, the new C-Group Nubians potentially posed the same threat to their internal stability as the ancient A-Group did. Yet, no matter what Sesostris III did, he could not have prevented the wrath of yet another fast-approaching cosmic catastrophe.

Year 7 of Sesostris III and the Threat of Doomsday

From an ancient Middle Kingdom document known as the El-Lahun papyrus, we learn that on the 120th year of the 12th Dynasty, the heliacal rising of Sirius was recorded on the 225th day of the year. Given the fact that I have earlier placed the beginning of the 12th Dynasty at 1,780 BCE, the 120th year of this dynasty would fall on the year 1,660 BCE. To understand what this all means, it might be useful to remind ourselves that the star of Sirius rises with the sun on the same day for four years. At the termination of this four-year cycle, its rise with the sun shifts one day later in the year — carrying on in the same fashion throughout the calendar. It takes a period of 1,460 years (a full sothic year) before Sirius' consecutive risings with the sun move through the entire cycle and returns to its point of departure. Since the rise of Sirius shifts one day later every four years, we can determine the date in which the last heliacal rising of Sirius occurred by multiplying 225 by 4 (which comes to 900 years) and then add that figure to the time when the subsequent observation was recorded — that is in 1,660 BCE (1,780 - 120 = 1,660). Amazingly, this ends up amounting to the year 2,560 BCE (1,660 + 900 = 2,560). This is the exact date when, according to William C. Hayes, the 5th Dynasty began — when the star shaft from the queen's chamber in the Pyramid of Khufu pointed directly to the star of Sirius. We've already seen that this event was greeted with immense importance during the Old Kingdom. Not only was this occasion recorded as a genuine heliacal rising of Sirius, but it also heralded a renaissance in the Osirian cult — which for the

---

[20] John Van Seters (1966) p. 80.

CHAP. VIII: THE PHARAOHS WHO KNEW NOT JOSEPH | 269

first time became officially recognized within dynastic Egypt. The role of the Great Pyramid's star shafts during the Early to Middle Bronze Ages has never been properly recognized by establishment scholars. But thanks to the work of Alexandre Badawy, Robert Bauval and Adrian Gilbert in recent years, these ancient "channels to the stars" have finally begun to be recognized as much more than mere ventilation shafts. The heliacal rising of Sirius recorded on the seventh year of King Sesostris III, in 1,660 BCE, obviously did not come at the end of the 1,460-year-long Sothic cycle begun in 2,953 BCE. The next heliacal rising was not due until the year 1,493 BCE. The presumed heliacal rising of Sirius recorded during the Middle Kingdom's 12th Dynasty was based on the Great Pyramid star shaft's periodic alignment with the star Sirius. The last time this had occurred was in 2,560 BCE — 900 years earlier.

Since the El-Lahun papyrus informs us that the so-called heliacal rising of Sirius recorded during the 12th Dynasty occurred on the 7th year of Sesostris III, which falls in 1,660 BCE, it becomes easy to determine the dates of his reign — given that we know how long he ruled. The reign of King Sesostris III is known to have lasted 39 years.[21] This ultimately means that the end of his reign came in the year 1,628 BCE (1,667 - 39 = 1,628). Incidentally, this date of 1,628 BCE is likewise famous because scientists have recently confirmed, based on frost-ring evidence,[22] that it was on this year that the volcanic eruption which destroyed the ancient Aegean island of Thera occurred. Given the widespread effects of this gargantuan eruption, there is very little doubt that its deleterious repercussions had affected Egypt. I will even go so far as asserting that the natural upheaval of 1,628 BCE was solely responsible for bringing down the 12th Dynasty in Egypt. Hence, the fact that the end of Pharaoh Sesostris III's reign happens to fall on the same year as the Thera eruption is no mere coincidence.

The volcanic island of Thera did not however just erupt by itself. I am indeed convinced that an outside destructive agent had precipitated the volcanic eruption. This time, not the planet Venus or Mercury, but the moon. Shortly before the time of the Thera eruption, the ancients astronomer-priests appear to have yet again feared that the world would be consumed by fire on account of the iniquitous behaviour of their rulers. For example, an Akkadian document from the reign of King Zimri-Lim in Mari, purported to be a divine revelation, foretells:

---

[21] Josef W. Wegner (1996) 'The Nature and Chronology of the Senwosret III - Amenemhat III Regnal Succession: Some Considerations Based on New Evidence from the Mortuary Temple of Senwosret III at Abydos', *Journal of Near Eastern Studies* Vol. 55 - Num. 4, p. 251.
[22] Valmore C. LaMarche, Jr. & Katherine K. Hirschboeck (1984) 'Frost Rings in Trees as Records of Major Volcanic Eruptions', *Nature* 307, pp. 121-126.

This eclipse, which (the moon) brought about in (the month of) Tebet, concerned the land of Amurru. **The king of the land of Amurru will die, his land will diminish, (or) in another interpretation, will disappear.** Surely the scholars can tell the king my lord something about the land of Amurru: the land of Amurru means the land of the Hittites and the land of the Sutaeans, (or) in another interpretation, the land of Chaldea. Someone or other of the kings of the land of the Hittites, or of the land of Chaldea, (reverse) or of the land of the Arabs, **must bear (the consequences of) this sign.** ... Either the king of Cush, or the king of [Tyre], or Mugallu must meet the appointed death ... [23]

The familiar theme of heavenly retribution here appears to be directly related to the erratic behaviour of the moon. A sign was read that the fires of heaven were at hand. It may therefore be no coincidence that many 12th Dynasty papyri "refer to lunar months in connection with regnal years"[24] in the days of Sesostris III and Amenemhat III. The moon was preeminent in the minds of the astronomer-priests because it was known that a cataclysmic lunar shift was on the verge of making the iniquitous rulers bear the consequences of their sin. It's hard to imagine how a simple eclipse could have been interpreted by the ancients as an ominous sign of the "appointed death" of powerful rulers. The ancient skies were messengers of dreadful omens to which the astronomer-priests paid great attention.

The Thera Eruption and the Papyrus Ipuwer

The end of Pharaohs Sesostris III and Amenemhat III's reigns simultaneously came under a violent cloud of ashes and volcanic smoke. As the Akkadian letter had accurately predicted, great rulers' lands had diminished, engulfed in death and foreign conquests. I believe that a vivid account of this calamitous event, as it manifested itself in the Nile Valley, has survived in an ancient Egyptian document known as the Papyrus Ipuwer, now kept in the Leiden Museum in the Netherlands. Scholars generally assume that the Papyrus Ipuwer is a surviving narrative of the dire state of Egypt's internal affairs during the so-called First Intermediate Period (2,180-2,040 BCE).[25] I however argue that the Papyrus Ipuwer was composed during the second half of the Middle Kingdom. In his

---

[23] James B. Pritchard (editor) (1955) *ANET*, p. 626.
[24] William. F. Edgerton (1942) 'Chronology of the Twelfth Dynasty', *Journal of Near Eastern Studies* 1, p. 310; Richard A. Parker (1980) 'The Sothic Dating of the Twelfth and Eighteenth Dynasties', *Kronos* Vol. 6 - Num. 1, p. 57.
[25] See I. V. Vinogradov 'The Middle Kingdom of Egypt and the Hyksos Invasion.' In I. M. Diakonoff (editor) (1991) *Early Antiquity,* pp.158-161.

CHAP. VIII: THE PHARAOHS WHO KNEW NOT JOSEPH | 271

1950 book *Worlds in Collision,* Dr Immanuel Velikovsky was the first historian to suggest that the Papyrus was an ancient Egyptian account of the disastrous effects of the Theran eruption in the Lower Nile Valley. Although, based on the now outdated estimation of the timing of the Thera eruption, Velikovsky had erroneously assumed that the cataclysm had occurred sometime around 1,500 BCE — at the close of the Middle Bronze Age. Now with the new scientifically approved date for the timing of the Thera eruption, in 1,628 BCE, it is necessary, should one still accept Velikovsky's theory, to redate the composition of the Papyrus Ipuwer as well. In the new chronology, we find that the chaotic events depicted in the Middle Kingdom scribe named Ipuwer's account fall at the end of the MBIIb period. As Velikovsky believed, a complete social breakdown in Egypt was prompted by this natural cataclysm. The monarchy in Egypt was instantaneously toppled, and the balance of power, from Upper Nubia to Syria-Palestine, would be entirely reshuffled.

Although the Thera eruption unleashed the full force of its furor in Crete and the other Aegean islands, it is logical to assume that other parts of the Mediterranean world were also severely affected. The Egyptian Delta, located approximately five hundred miles away from Santorini (i.e. Thera), would have certainly been "blacked out for a time by the ash cloud accompanying the major paroxysms."[26] As Prof. Hans Goedicke explains:

> There is no question that an eruption on Thera could be heard at Avaris, which is fairly close to the coastline. The precipitation in this case would not have been rain, but tephra falling out from the eruption. The general wind pattern would bring such ash to the northeastern Delta, as seabed core drilling in the Mediterranean has established.[27]

Undoubtedly, the volcanic eruption had been caused by a sudden lunar orbital shift, which resulted in a catastrophe of global proportion. The earth's crust quacked, huge winds and devastating tornadoes spread black volcanic dust everywhere. Day suddenly turned into night in many areas of the world. Seasons were altered, the pattern of the stars revolutionized. Accordingly, the Papyrus Ipuwer relates:

> 2:8 Forsooth, the land turns round as a potter's wheel.
> 2:10 Forsooth, gates, columns and walls are consumed by fire.
> 2:11 The towns are destroyed. Upper Egypt has become dry.
> 3:13 All is ruin!
> 4:2 ... Years of noise. There is no end to the noise.

---

[26] Dorothy B. Vitaliano (1973) *Legends of the Earth: Their Geologic Origins,* Indiana University Press: Bloomington and London, p. 252.
[27] Hans Goedicke 'The End of the Hyksos in Egypt.' In Leonard H. Lesko (editor) (1986) *Egyptological Studies in Honor of Richard A. Parker,* p. 41.

> 6:1 Oh, that the earth would cease from noise, and tumult (uproar) be no more.
> 7:14 The residence is overturned in a minute.
> 9:11 The land is not light [without light or dark]. ...

The Papyrus Ipuwer is not the only document describing the calamities caused by the lunar shift of 1,628 BCE. Velikovsky also turned to a premonition written by a scribe, Neferty, of the Old Kingdom. The prophecy of Neferty, as reported in the Hermitage Papyrus, is customarily thought to have been spoken during the reign of King Sneferu of the 4th Dynasty, and later committed to writing during the reign of King Amenemhat I of the 12th Dynasty.[28] Unlike the Papyrus Ipuwer, which describes events unfolding in the present tense or recent past, the Hermitage Papyrus is a prophecy written centuries before the actual events. Neferty's report commences with the description of a major upheaval in which the land of Egypt would, in the future, fall pray to Asiatic invaders infiltrating the eastern Delta. It ends with a prophecy concerning a king by the name of Ameny who would ultimately come as a saviour, and rid Egypt of the wicked occupants. Egyptologists believe that Amenemhat I used the prophecy of Neferty as a propaganda tool to legitimize his own claim to Egypt's throne. Chronologically speaking, as with the case of the Papyrus Ipuwer (or Leiden document), conventional scholarship assumes that the events prophetised in the Hermitage Papyrus mirror the tense relations between the Herakleopolitan kings and the marauding Asiatics of the standard First Intermediate Period (our Diluvian Period).

Scholars contend that Pharaoh Amenemhat I meant to convey to his people that "he" was the saviour named "Ameny" who saved his people from universal instability. This interpretation is, in my own view, quite wrong. If in fact this prophecy had been spoken during the reign of Pharaoh Sneferu, it may then have been written down and spread about during the dual reign of Amenemhat III and Sesostris III, in an effort to warn the inhabitants of Egypt of the impending catastrophe. That is, of course, assuming that the astronomer-priests had indeed been forewarned of the coming paroxysm by the erratic movements of the moon. They would have looked to this sign of the times as an expected fulfilment of the Prophecy of Neferty. Another possibility would be that the entire Neferty account was written *after* the Theran eruption by, as Egyptologists believe, a saviour-king who identified himself as the Ameny of the prophecy. But again, the reason why Egyptologists require the events described in the Leiden and Hermitage documents to have occurred *before* the reign of Amenemhat I (whom they've erroneously identified with the prophetised Ameny), is to find credible justification for a chaotic First

---

[28] James K. Hoffmeier 'Egyptians.' In Alfred J. Hoerth, Gerald L. Mattingly & Edwin M. Yamauchi (editors) (1994) Peoples of the Old Testament World, p. 267.

CHAP. VIII: THE PHARAOHS WHO KNEW NOT JOSEPH | 273

Intermediate Period. In the eyes of mainstream archaeological scholarship, the transition between the 12th and 13th Dynasties was a relatively smooth one.

In strongly disputing this traditional view, I maintain that the transition between the 12th and 13th Dynasties gave rise to the very tumultuous social and natural disorder predicted in the Prophecy of Neferty. The prosperous coregency of Pharaohs Sesostris III and Amenemhat III suddenly gave way to a murderous civil strife in which foreign invaders, entering from the eastern Delta, found Egypt defenceless and ravaged by heavenly fire. According to the Prophecy of Neferty:

> This land is (so) damaged (that) there is no one who is concerned with it, not one who speaks, no eye that weeps. How is this land? **The sun disc is covered over. It will not shine (so that) people may see.** No one can live when the clouds cover over (the sun). Then everybody is deaf for lack of it. ...
> **The rivers of Egypt are empty, (so that) the water is crossed on foot.** Men seek water for the ships to sail on it. Its course is [become] a sand-bank. ...
> The south wind will oppose the north wind; the skies are no (longer) in a single wind. **A foreign bird will be born in the marshes of the North-land.** ... Everything good is disappeared, and the land is prostrate because of woes from that flood, **the Asiatics who are throughout the land.**
> **Foes have arisen in the east, and Asiatics have come down into Egypt** ... No protector will listen.... Men will enter into the *fortresses*. ... If a statement is answered, an arm goes out with a stick, and men speak with: Kill him! ... **The land is diminished**, (but) its administrators are many; bare (but) its taxes are great; little in grain, (but) the measure is large ...
> (Then) it is that a king will come, belonging to the south, Ameni, the triumphant, his name. He is the son of a woman of the land of Nubia [Ta-Seti]; he is one born in Upper Egypt. He will take the [White] Crown; he will wear the Red Crown; he will unite the Two Mighty Ones; ... The Asiatics will fall to his sword, and the Libyans will fall to his flame. ... There will be built the Wall of the Ruler life, prosperity, health! and the Asiatics will not be permitted to come down into Egypt ... And justice will come into place, while wrong-doing is *driven* out.[29]

Exactly as the Akkadian divine revelation, dated to the reign of King Zimri-Lim in Mari, had predicted when it announced that the king of Amurru's *"land will dimi-*

---

[29] James B. Pritchard (editor) (1958) ANET, pp. 254-257.

nish," we again read above in the Prophecy of Neferty, concerning Egypt, that *"the land is diminished."* In both cases, this may have been a metaphor to explain the fact that prized land had been taken over by foreign invaders. In Egypt, these Asiatic foreigners had usurped the northern marshes of the Delta. As the waters from the sea swept from the ocean deep onto inhabited lands, torrential floods destroyed crops and disrupted the social order. The theory that Pharaoh's court, towards the end of the 12th Dynasty, fully expected this natural disaster to take place may be confirmed by the known fact that the rising levels of the Nile was anxiously monitored during the latter part of the 12th Dynasty. Observing extant evidence from Semneh, nineteenth century German Egyptologist Karl Richard Lepsius wrote:

> Semneh. The Nile is here compressed within a breadth of only about 1150 feet between high rocky shores. ... We found a considerable number of inscriptions from the Twelfth and Thirteenth Manethonic Dynasties. ... Many of them were intended to indicate the highest rising of the Nile during a series of years, especially in the reigns of Kings Amenemhet III and Sebekhotep I ...[30]

It is precisely between the reigns of Pharaohs Amenemhat III and Sobekhotep I that the devastating lunar upheaval took place. These exceptionally high Nile levels recorded at the end of Amenemhat III's reign, which certain scholars like Prof. Barbara Bell of Harvard University believe may have resulted in widespread famine, were likely caused by the lunar shift from 1,628 BCE. The flooding had been so widespread and debilitating that Sobek, the pharaonic divinity of floods, immediately became a central deity — both feared and revered for these demonstrated destructive powers. Thus, all of the pharaohs based in Lower Egypt, for the next two centuries, incorporated the name of Sobekhotep into their throne names. The first of these monarchs, who witnessed first-hand the ravages of the floods, was Queen Sobeknefru — the immediate successor to Pharaoh Amenemhat III. This sudden, and largely unexplained, appearance of a female pharaoh, the first since Queen Nictoris, has long intrigued historians.

At any rate, the end, and most probably the death, of Amenemhat III had come rather abruptly. Thus, Queen Sobeknefru ascended the throne at a time of great confusion and instability. Foreign multitudes were freely looting temples, nobles were being robbed of their possessions, and laws were no longer being respected. The utter pandemonium befell principally Lower Egypt, due to its relative proximity to Thera, and unfortunate status as the prime entry point for Asiatic invaders. If the Egyptians had any chance at all of restoring order, they would have to attack

---

[30] Karl R. Lepsius, *Letters from Egypt, Ethiopia and the Peninsula of Sinai*, pp. 19-20.

CHAP. VIII: THE PHARAOHS WHO KNEW NOT JOSEPH | 275

from Upper Egypt. Fulfilling the Prophecy of Neferty, Pharaoh Amenemhat IV, the real Ameny and brother of Queen Sobeknefru, managed to prevent the foreign invaders from altogether overrunning the Two Lands. Though he would not succeed in driving them out of the eastern Delta, King Amenemhat IV ensured that Egypt, with the 13th Dynasty, would continue to be ruled by native Egyptian pharaohs. He restored the priesthood, reopened the temples, and enforced the laws. Although he only briefly ruled from Lower Egypt, Ameny saved Egypt from another Kingless Period. But trouble, specifically within the eastern Delta town of Avaris, still threatened to disturb an already very fragile peace.

Death Upon the Firstborn of Egypt:
Of Exodus and Conquest

For millennia, those who have been raised within the Judeo-Christian tradition, have been made to believe that Joseph's brethren, the children of Israel, fled from Egypt's land of Goshen, or Pi-Ramses, under the enlightened leadership of Moses because they had suffered under Pharaoh Ramses II's merciless lash (the so-called Pharaoh of the Oppression). That picture couldn't in fact be further from the truth. The Hebrews who established themselves in the Delta town of Tell el-Dab'a (Avaris) during the reign of King Mentuhotep IV lived many centuries before Ramses II was ever even born. As I will fully demonstrate in Chapter 11, King Ramses II *did*, in fact, persecute the Israelites, and forced them to build his royal edifices in Pi-Ramses (the land of Ramses). However, this only happened during the Late Bronze III period. What the biblical redactors have tried to do in the Books of Genesis and Exodus is to merge, or condense, the Middle Bronze Age IIb Israelite experience in the land of Goshen with the subsequent Late Bronze Age III ordeal — when, in reality, nearly five hundred years separated the two Israelite settlements. The initial Hebrew sojourn in the land of Egypt was not only a peaceful one, but a prosperous one as well. Because of his love for Joseph, King Mentuhotep IV appointed the Hebrews as royal administrators of the land of Goshen. When King Amenemhat I of the 12th Dynasty ascended the Egyptian throne, the Hebrew leaders became fully fledged pharaohs with legitimate kingly titles. They ruled, alongside the 12th Dynasty pharaohs, over the Delta town of Avaris throughout the MBIIb period.

Precisely how I came to the conclusion that the first half of the standard 13th Dynasty ruled contemporaneously with the 12th Dynasty will be explained at length in the following chapter. Suffice it to say for now that I believe that Kings Wegaf to Neferhotep were actually Hebrew nobility who had been appointed as rulers of Avaris. Within the immediate vicinity of MBIIb Avaris, a large number of scarabs have been unearthed depicting Asiatic figures wearing kilts and elaborate robes which leave only one arm and shoulder free. Such garments are foreign to Egypt. It is therefore safe to assume that these people are foreigners. John Van Seters made the ingenious observation that this style of dress strongly resembles the kind of attire worn by the Asiatic immigrants depicted on the Beni Hassan tomb walls.[31] Agreeing with Van Seters' theory, this leaves little doubt, in my estimation, that these foreigners pictured on the scarabs were Israelites. Because, as Van Seters points out, the Asiatic figures delineated on the seals were most likely from the ruling class, the myth that Joseph's brethren had been slaves in Pharaoh's land is indubitably refuted.

With no tangible evidence of oppression, what could have possibly induced the Hebrews to hastily leave the land of Goshen and subsequently conquer Canaan — their new homeland? Two things: (1) the calamitous moon-induced Theran eruption in the Aegean and (2) the war-like Amalekite infiltration into Avaris. The Hebrew Exodus *out* of the Egyptian Delta therefore coincided with the invasion of the Asiatic Hyksos *into* Egypt's eastern Delta.[32] And like, Immanuel Velikovsky, I contend that the Hyksos were the Amalekites of the Bible.

Overwhelmed by the violent incursion of the Hyksos-Amalekites into their city of Avaris, and threatened by the civil uprisings in Egypt, the Hebrews finally decided, of their own volition, to depart from their adopted land and return to their ancestral home in Canaan. Two momentous obstacles however lay in their path. First, of course, they would necessarily have to get through the incoming Hyksos hordes — which would certainly be no easy task. Second, the Canaanites, with their imposing MBIIb fortresses, would definitely not be willing to bequeath their territory to Joseph's returning brethren. If the Israelites wanted the land back, they would have to acquire it by means of conquest. And this is exactly where the biblical Conquest narratives come into play. Archaeologically speaking, I firmly believe that the close of the MBIIb period is the only time in which Joshua's conquest could have taken place. Conventionally, Joshua's conquest is dated to the transition period between the end of the Late Bronze Age and the beginning of the Iron Age, in the twelfth century BCE. Needless to say, my own dating of Joshua's conquest to as much as five centuries prior to the traditional date, brings a lot into question. But Syro-Palestinian archaeologists have for some time now been seriously questioning the feasibility of the "Conquest Model" at the end of the Late Bronze Age. To quote Israeli archaeologist Israel Finkelstein:

---

31 John Van Seters (1966) p. 62.
32 Immanuel Velikovsky (1952) *Ages in Chaos,* Doubleday: Garden City, NY, p. 53. It must be borne in mind however that Velikovsky did believe that the Hebrews had been oppressed in Egypt during the Middle Kingdom and that, as in the biblical account, Pharaoh had gone after the fleeing Israelites in the desert.

CHAP. VIII: THE PHARAOHS WHO KNEW NOT JOSEPH | 277

No evidence of the Late Bronze Age period was ever unearthed at a number of sites central to the biblical account of the conquest of Canaan. For certain sites, this embarrassing state of affairs has been known for decades — and with the expansion of archaeological investigation, the phenomenon has turned out to be even more widespread than anyone imagined.[33]

Indeed, British archaeologist Dame Kathleen Kenyon's famous excavations at Jericho (Tell es-Sultan) in the 1950s led her to conclude that: *"When the material is analysed in light of our present knowledge, it becomes clear that there is a complete gap both on the tell and in the tombs between c.1580 B.C. and c. 1400 B.C."*[34] So, if there were no Late Bronze Age, or Early Iron Age, fortification walls indicating any sort of major settlement in sites like Jericho and Hazor (to corroborate the story of the tumbling walls and widespread conquests), then it could only mean that the traditional story of Joshua's conquest is nothing more than a myth. But is it really? What if the Conquest actually took place earlier – when there is evidence for major cities at Jericho and Hazor – like in the Middle Bronze Age?[35]

To begin with, the Bible estimates that the Hebrew Exodus took place 130 years after the death of Joseph. In the new chronology, assuming that the original Exodus occurred in 1,628 BCE, this figure would make a lot of sense. Since Joseph lived at the time of Pharaoh Mentuhotep IV and Amenemhat I's reigns, the Exodus and Conquest of Joseph's brethren find a comfortable place, chronologically speaking, at the termination of the MBIIb period. As I have already outlined in the Introduction, I believe that the traditional biblical account of the Hebrew Exodus is really a skilled amalgamation of no less than "four" historical Exoduses during the course of Israelite history. The Exodus which occurred during the Middle Bronze Age was the first of these four Exoduses. I believe that the Conquest Model is only applicable to the First Exodus. Moreover, as the familiar theme of oppression is entirely absent within the context of the First Exodus, the central figure of Moses, the liberator, is likewise necessarily absent during the Middle Bronze Age Exodus setting. The *only* pivotal character is that of Joshua. In actuality, the

---

[33] Israel Finkelstein (1988a) *The Archaeology of the Israelite Settlement*, Israel Exploration Society: Jerusalem, p. 296.
[34] Kathleen Kenyon (1970) *Archaeology in the Holy Land*. Third edition. Ernest Benn: London, p. 98.
[35] See David M. Rohl (1995) *A Test of Time — Vol. I: The Bible - From Myth to History*, Century: London, p. 302. Obviously, my own chronological reconstruction is incompatible with Rohl's view that the walls of Jericho came tumbling down at the end of the MB II period. Clearly, the walls of Jericho did fall down at the end of the Middle Bronze Age, but I doubt that this conflagration was caused by Joshua's conquest. As we shall see in Chapter 10, this and other destructions throughout Syria-Palestine at the end of the Middle Bronze Age were caused by the Venus shift of 1,559 BCE.

tradition of Moses would come later in Jewish historiography. When the Five Books of Moses were written, the biblical redactors artificially made Joshua and Moses contemporaries as they attempted to condense all of the Exodus traditions into a single coherent narrative. But in reality Joshua had never known Moses. He, Joshua, alone led the Hebrews through a victorious war of conquest against the powerful Canaanite city-states. Consequently, there had been no resistance from Pharaoh, no forty years of wandering in the desert, and no Ten Commandments. The conquest of Canaan had been swift and direct.

In the midst of thick volcanic smoke and raging heavens, Joshua led the Hebrews out of Avaris on the year of the Thera eruption. The biblical text makes it clear that the natural conflagration, which accompanied the Conquest, had stormed in under the influence of the sun and the moon's erratic motions:

> 12 Then spake Joshua to the Lord in the day when the Lord delivered up the Amorites before the children of Israel, and he said in the sight of Israel, Sun, stand thou still upon Gibeon; and thou, Moon, in the valley of Ajalon.
> 13 **And the sun stood still, and the moon stayed,** until the people had avenged themselves upon their enemies. Is not this written in the book of Jasher? So the sun stood still in the midst of heaven, and hasted not to go down about a whole day.
> 14 And there was no day like that before it or after it, that the Lord hearkened unto the voice of a man: for the Lord fought for Israel.
> (Joshua 10:12-14)

Like the people of Mari and Egypt, ancient Jewish tradition attests to the notably unusual behaviour of the moon in ancient times. The length of the day had been disrupted as the sun and the moon stood still on the Day of the Lord. The fact that the Bible states that the Lord fought on behalf of the Hebrews indicates that Joshua's forces' relatively easy defeat of the Canaanite rulers was mostly due to external factors. Without the destructive wrath of the cosmic upheaval, which utterly decimated many of the fortified towns of MBIIb Syria-Palestine, the Conquest certainly would not have been as successful, or even at all possible.

One of Joshua's most successful campaigns was against the king of Hazor, out of all the cities conquered by Joshua, Hazor alone was mercilessly burnt to the ground (Joshua 11:13). The king of Hazor who reigned at the time of the Conquest was named Yabin or Jabin. A crucial test for the new chronology would be to find solid proof that a ruler of Hazor named Jabin reigned during this pivotal MBIIb period. An important document from Mari indeed confirms the existence during MBIIb of a king of Hazor who bore the name of "Ibni-Hada" or "Yabin-Hadad." The Mari

CHAP. VIII: THE PHARAOHS WHO KNEW NOT JOSEPH | 279

archives further confirm that the latter was a contemporary of King Hammurabi in Babylon. We read in the text:

> 30 minas tin, for Ibni-Adad king of Hazor
> ...
> 20 minas tin for Ibni-Adad
> for the second time ...
> 20 minas tin for Ibni-Adad for the third time.

The Anglicized form of that name being "Yabin,"[36] we can establish that the powerful king of Hazor whom Joshua defeated during his conquest of Canaan was none other than King Ibni-Adad of the Mari archives. The extant archaeological evidence indeed confirms that Hazor was a very powerful capital during MBIIb. Hence, the biblical claim that "Hazor beforetime was the head of all those kingdoms" (Josh. 11:10) accurately reflects the prominent position of the kingdom of Hazor during the Middle Bronze II period. For the Israelites to have secured any effective control of Syria-Palestine, they inevitably had to confront the powerhouse which Middle Bronze Age Hazor represented. No such powerful fortresses existed in Late Bronze Age Hazor — at the time when most biblical scholars have traditionally dated Joshua's conquest. Quoting the late Israeli archaeologist Yigael Yadin:

> ... most of the archives are related to the last king of Mari, one Zimri-Lim, a contemporary of the great Hammurabi of Babylon. The documents, not all of which have been published, mention Hazor several times and in contexts that indicate **it was one of the most important cities in the entire Fertile Crescent.**[37]

Therefore, within the new chronology's Middle Bronze Age II context, not only do we have the architectural evidence for the mighty Hazor depicted in the Bible, but we also have proof of the existence of a king of Hazor named Jabin reigning at that time.

But arguably the most famous of the Conquest battles was the capture of Jericho, where Joshua struck first. Like ancient Hazor, Jericho, in central Canaan, was a heavily fortified city during the MBIIb period. The famous biblical tale about how these walls at Jericho came tumbling down have, over the centuries, inspired countless theological interpretations and scholarly debates. Between 1907 and 1911, Ger-

---

[36] Yigael Yadin (1975) *Hazor (The Rediscovery of a Great Citadel of the Bible)*, Random House: New York, pp. 14-16.
[37] Ibid.

man scholars Ernst Sellin and Carl Watzinger pioneered excavation efforts at the site. But much more thorough archaeological campaigns between 1930 and 1936 by British excavator John Garstang yielded infinitely more information. Garstang had been convinced that he had found ample evidence for Joshua's destruction of Jericho during the Late Bronze Age. But subsequently, another British archaeologist, Dame Kathleen Kenyon who excavated at Jericho in 1952, overturned his findings. She concluded that at the time when Bible scholars assume that the Conquest took place, Jericho had been an abandoned city. So once again, the traditional date for the conquest of Joshua does not hold up when confronted with the extant archaeological evidence.

Despite upholding, on the surface, a Late Bronze Age historical environment for the Conquest, I believe that the Scriptures nonetheless mask the true Middle Bronze Age context of Joshua's conquest of Jericho. The revelation is purposely vague and deliberately intended to be understood by an elite group of initiates only. Again, quoting the Maimonide rabbis concerning the seven World Ages:

> Whosoever should divine its true meaning, ought to take great care in not divulging it. This is a maxim, repeated to us by all our sages, principally concerning the understanding of the work of the six days.[38]

This ancient understanding of the work of the six days is skillfully dissimulated within the Book of Joshua in the following passage:

> 3 And ye shall compass the city, all ye men of war, and go round about it once. Thus shall thou do six days.
> 4 And seven priests shall bear before the ark seven trumpets of rams' horns: and the seventh day ye shall compass the city seven times, and the priests shall blow with the trumpets.
> 5 And it shall come to pass, that when they make a long blast with the ram's horn, and when ye hear the sound of the trumpet, all the people shall shout with a great shout; and the wall of the city shall fall down flat ...
> 6 And Joshua the son of Nun called the priests, and said unto them, Take up the ark of the covenant, and let seven priests bear seven trumpets of rams' horns ...
> (Joshua 6:3-6)

The six-day-long rotations around the city of Jericho by the men of war is meant to represent the six great cycle-ending Venusian destructions of the world prior to the

---

[38] In Charles François Dupuis (1984 [1872]) *The Origin of All Religious Worship*, Garland: New York and London, pp. 226-227.

CHAP. VIII: THE PHARAOHS WHO KNEW NOT JOSEPH | 281

Seventh Age, when the Book of Joshua was actually composed — centuries after the death of Joshua. The seven trumpets are metaphors for the Seven World Ages or Seven Creations. Finally, the ram's horns symbolize the actual age in which the walls tumbled at Jericho — the Aries Mandate, or the Third Creation. The vernal equinox was pointing to the constellation of Aries, during the Middle Bronze Age, when the ancient Israelites conquered the Canaanites under the leadership of Joshua. As already discussed in the previous chapter, the ram or the lamb motif is frequently utilized in numerous ancient traditions dating to the Middle Bronze Age. In the Hebrew tradition, the memory of the Aries Mandate remained inextricably tied to the lunar catastrophe which accompanied the First Exodus. In the words of Charles François Dupuis:

> ... This picture makes us remember the equinoctial feast of spring, celebrated in Egypt under Aries or under the Lamb, commemorative of the fire of Heaven, typifying the conflagration of the World. In that feast everything was marked red or of the color of fire, as in the Passover of the Jews or in their feast of the Lamb.[39]

Indeed, as both the Bible and the Papyrus Ipuwer relate, the Theran volcanic eruption had caused the rivers and streams in the Egyptian Delta to be filled with the reddish residue from the eruption. In the Papyrus Ipuwer, we read:

> 2:5-6 Plague is throughout the land. Blood is everywhere.
> 2:10 The river is blood. ... Men shrink from tasting [...] human beings, and thirst after water.

Analogously, the biblical Exodus narratives state:

> 21 And the fish that was in the river died; and the river stank, and the Egyptians could not drink of the water of the river; and there was blood throughout all the land of Egypt.
> (Exodus 7:21)

The similarities could not be more striking. It's more than obvious that these two texts refer to one and the same ruinous calamity which befell Egypt's Delta in ancient times. Also alike are the respective documents' details about the unfortunate fate of the children of the nobility and monarchy from Lower Egypt. The Papyrus Ipuwer says:

---

[39] Ibid, p. 254.

> 4:3, also 5:6 Forsooth, the children of princes are dashed against the wall.
> 6:12 Forsooth, the children of princes are cast out in the streets.
> 10:36 Lower Egypt weeps. ... The entire palace is without its revenues. To it belong (by right) wheat and barley, geese and fish.

Meanwhile, in the Bible, the princes and firstborns of Egypt, specifically Pharaoh's firstborn, are likewise threatened with persecution and death.

> 12 For I will pass through the land of Egypt this night, and will smite all the firstborn in the land of Egypt, both man and beast; and against all the gods of Egypt I will execute judgment: I am the Lord.
> (Exodus 12:12)

Evidently, the above must refer to the civil strife which engulfed the land of Egypt following the lunar shift — when commoner rose against noble and foreign invaders took pleasure in humiliating the nobles and monarchs of Egypt. But the Bible's eerie reference to the supernatural selection of the "firstborn" of Egypt for death on the appointed Day of the Lord is somewhat problematic. How could a global natural conflagration pick and choose, as could a thinking entity, among the earthlings, who would suffer from its ravages? Obviously, there is a hidden metaphor that needs to be elucidated. As the Hebrew Bible often, in a veiled manner, resorts to Egyptian theology, it would not be surprising to find that an explanation to the "firstborn" enigma can be found in Egyptian mythology.

I would propose that the elusive biblical reference to the firstborn of Egypt is in reality a cleaver allusion to the symbolic 12th Dynasty Horus kingship (the Amenemhats) which governed Lower Egypt at the time of the First Exodus. We must likewise recall that, speaking of Horus, the guardian of Lower Egypt in the Memphite Theology, Geb announces to the gathered Ennead: 'I have appointed Horus, the firstborn.' Therefore, since both the direct and derivative effects of the natural cataclysm of 1,628 BCE were most strongly felt in Lower Egypt, the domain of the firstborn of Geb, and that any Sethian attacks would naturally have more of a debilitating effect on the Horus kingship, then the biblical allegory is very appropriate. Moreover, it is clear that the Sethian kingship of Upper Egypt essentially takes over the place of the Horus kingship in Lower Egypt — with the pharaohs' obvious preference for the name "Sobekhotep."

9

The Hyksos Invasion (1,628 BCE to 1,559 BCE)

The Egyptian Middle Kingdom represents the watershed period in which the new chronology first deviates from the accepted ordering of the Egyptian dynasties. The first half of the 13th Dynasty is presented as having been contemporary with the 12th Dynasty and, from then on, the new chronology continues to differ sharply from the orthodox framework. The fascinating repercussions and underlying causes for this momentous incongruity will be the central focus of this chapter. The discrepancy in the official Egyptian king-lists has very similar sources as the chronological anomalies found in the biblical narratives. In both cases, the main motivations of the ancient scribes or redactors to alter the course their country's history had much to do with overriding nationalistic interests. The readers are therefore now asked to sail along the uncharted waters of an historical inquiry defined independently of the received official king-lists from dynastic Egypt and traditional biblical timetable. Such a bold endeavour asks of one to focus preeminently on the archaeological and historical evidence — totally free of preconceived notions. It is through this ground breaking trek that we shall uncover the hidden legacies of forgotten empires, exploits of unsung heroes, and the ghosts of silenced battles and defeats.

Where we last left off, the Hebrews were fleeing from the devastated town of Avaris. It had been argued that the Hebrews were not slaves in Egypt, but legitimate rulers of the Egyptian eastern Delta. The Hebrew pharaohs ruled alongside the 12th Dynasty monarchs in harmony. When the cataclysmic lunar shift, which terminated the 12th Dynasty, came along in 1,628 BCE, the Egyptianized Hebrews had no other choice but to depart from Egypt. Not only were the most dispossessed among the Egyptian populace rising up in droves against the nobility, but a horde of foreign invaders, in their destructive path, where heading straight towards Avaris. Those invading forces belonged to an Arabic ethnic group known as the Amalekites, also more popularly referred to as the Hyksos or shepherd-kings. In a matter of days, the Hyksos-Amalekites, taking advantage of Egypt's weakness, succeeded in taking over control of the Two Lands, until the Upper Egyptian saviour Ameny (Amenemhat IV) managed to restore native Egyptian rule and confine the Hyksos to Avaris. Though the native Egyptians had won the battle, the war was unquestionably far from over. Now sole masters of Avaris, the Hyksos wasted no time in taking full advantage of their strategic position to persecute the native Egyptian pharaohs to the south. Unlike what Egyptologists like to believe, the Hyksos invaders of the Middle Bronze Age had never been Egyptianized to the point of establishing a formal pharaonic dynasty and observing the cults of the local deities. They had thoroughly maintained their own cultural attributes. During the MBIIc period, Egypt was divided between three main centres of power. In keeping with Middle Kingdom tradition, the administration of Upper and Lower Egypt was divided between two pharaonic lines of the same dynasty. The Hyksos for their part altered the balance of power with their hold on Avaris.

Dismantling the Manethonian Framework

Having drastically lowered the dates for the 12th Dynasty, it becomes evident that not much room is left to include all of the late Middle Kingdom pharaohs enumerated in the Turin Canon into the revised chronology before the advent of King Ahmose in 1,559 BCE. A mere 69 years is left between the termination of the 12th Dynasty and the end of the Middle Kingdom. Yet, we're supposed to be able to fit the 13th, 14th, 15th, 16th and 17th Dynasties into that minuscule time period. Any reasonable observer could see, and logically deduce, that this is an impossible task. And if such is the case, is the new chronology thus irremediably flawed? Is there a viable way to manoeuvre past this seemingly insurmountable impasse? At any rate, we will forge ahead and resolve these and other questions pertinent to our study.

The Barbarus version of Manetho gives a figure of 153 years for the duration of the 13th Dynasty. This approximate view has also been adopted by modern Egyptologists like Kenneth A. Kitchen.[1] Ironically, if this period of 153 years is accounted for from the time of King Wegaf's reign in the New Chronology Table, we arrive at the year 1,627 BCE (1,780-153=1,627) — one year after the Thera eruption. Thus, the new chronology would suggest that Pharaoh Neferhotep's reign in Avaris was just coming to an end, following the Hyksos invasion. Hence, we find that in my revised framework, the traditionally allotted time period for the entire 13th Dynasty merely covers the reigns of Wegaf through Neferhotep. But even that is yet another illusion. I believe that the ancient authors of the Turin Canon knowingly falsified the genuine regnal order of the 13th Dynasty Kings. As Table 9-1 illustrates, for the 153-year-long period covering the reigns of Wegaf to Neferhotep, the Turing Canon plays a "left and right" game. As if placing two decks of playing cards upright side by side and then flipping them simultaneously, one card at a time, so as to ensure that the sets would be evenly mixed into a solitary deck,

---

[1] Kenneth A. Kitchen 'The Basics of Egyptian Chronology in Relation to the Bronze Age.' In Paul Åström (editor) (1987) *High, Middle or Low? (Acts of an International Colloquium on Absolute Chronology Held at the University of Gothenburg 20th - 22nd August 1987)*, Paul Åström Förlag: Gothenburg. Vol. I, pp. 37-55.

Reordering of the Conventional 13th Dynasty

Conventional 13th Dynasty		New (Delta) 12th Dynasty		New (MBIIC) 13th Dynasty
Wegaf	Wegaf	Wegaf		
Sobekhotep I	▲	Auyibre (Hor)		
Auyibre (Hor)	▼	Khendjer		
Sobekhotep II	Sobekhotep I	Neferhotep I		▲
Khendjer	Khendjer	▲		Sobekhotep I
Sobekhotep III	Neferhotep			Sobekhotep II
Neferhotep	Sobekhotep III			Sobekhotep III
Sobekhotep IV	Sobekhotep IV			Sobekhotep IV

Table 9-1

New Chronology's 12th and 13th Dynasties

Standard 13th Dyn.			Delta	12th Dynasty	
Wegaf	Wegaf		Wegaf	Senusret I	Amenemhat I
Sobekhotep I	Sobekhotep I		Auyibre (Hor)	Senusret II	Amenemhat II
Auyibre (Hor)	Auyibre (Hor)		Khendjer	Senusret III	Amenemhat III
Sobekhotep II	Sobekhotep II		Neferhotep	Sobeknefru	Amenemhat IV
Khendjer	Khendjer				(1,628 BCE)
Sobekhotep III	Sobekhotep III		**Thebes**	**13th Dynasty**	
Neferhotep	Neferhotep		Dudimose I	Sobekhotep I	
Sobekhotep IV	Sobekhotep IV		Men.-Emsaf	Sobekhotep II	
			Dudimose II	Sobekhotep III	
Sobekhotep V			Nehesy	Sobekhotep IV	
Sobekhotep VI				Sobekhotep V	(1,559 BCE)
Sobekhotep VII					
Sobekhotep VIII				Sobekhotep VI	
Dudimose I				Sobekhotep VII	
Menthu-Emsaf				Sobekhotep VIII	(1,418 BCE)
Dudimose II					
Nehesy					

Table 9-2

(1,780 BCE)

CHAPTER IX: THE HYKSOS INVASION | 287

the scribes managed to concoct an entirely fictitious dynasty! After King Neferhotep's reign, this "left and right" game ends; and, as Table 9-2 delineates, a new method is utilized by the scribes to further add to the fabricated 13th Dynasty of the Turin Canon. Hence, we see that Barbarus' figure of 153 years does after all have some meaning, but it is also a smoking gun at the chronological crime scene. It denotes a major demarcation point in the Turin Canon editors' misleading endeavour. Once we finally manage to disentangle the dynastic line up to Neferhotep (see Table 9-1), we find that the severed portion on the right (i.e. Wegaf to Neferhotep) represents the Egyptianized Hebrew kings who ruled Avaris during the 12th Dynasty. The second group of kings on the left (Sobekhotep I-IV) are the pharaohs of Lower Egypt who ruled during the MBIIc period. After Sobekhotep IV, the editors of the Turin Canon abruptly change tactics and then simply add on the names of Pharaohs Sobekhotep V, VI, VII and VIII. The remaining part of the chronology, following Sobekhotep VIII, is occupied by Kings Dudimose to Nehesy. But, in the New Chronology Table, we notice that these pharaohs in actual fact reigned contemporaneously with the 13th Dynasty Lower Egyptian rulers of the MBIIc period (Pharaohs Sobekhotep I-V). Since the Nile Valley flooding which accompanied the lunar shift of 1,628 BCE in the Delta, all the remaining Lower Egyptian rulers of the 13th Dynasty named themselves after Sobekhotep, the deity associated with floods.

The accumulated length of the pharaohs' reigns who make up the traditional 13th Dynasty far exceeds the 153-year period conventionally allotted. The new chronology allows for a total time span of 362 years between the beginning of Wegaf's reign and the end of Sobekhotep VIII's reign. Why would the ancients have attempted to condense this period into a mere 153 years? The chronology was drastically shortened because the 13th Dynasty had to fit into an already much amputated overall chronology of ancient Egyptian civilization contrived by the ancient Egyptians themselves. The Turin Canon, the Abydos king-lists and the Manethonian chronology all represent a gravely incomplete picture of ancient Egyptian history. The widespread misconception that all of these accounts were objective and disinterested records of pharaonic history has unfortunately blinded modern scholars. The simple basic truth, as I have firmly come to believe, is that the extant archaeological evidence, observed wholly independently, does not warrant the accuracy of any of those lists.

While it is still too early at this point to fully explain why the official king-lists are rigged, the Hyksos occupation of Egypt was a major motivation for the ancient Egyptian chroniclers' compression of the 13th Dynasty. The Hyksos occupation lasted for considerably longer than the *c.*110 years conventionally attributed to their rule. I would in fact argue that the Hyksos threat loomed over Egypt for over 500 years! It is this five hundred-year period which separated the initial Hyksos-Amalekite invasion and the advent of King Ahmose's 18th Dynasty which the redactors or editors of the various Egyptian king-lists felt compelled to reduce at all cost. The Manethonian chroniclers vigorously sought to portray the 18th Dynasty's final war of liberation from the Hyksos yoke as having taken place during the nascent Late Bronze Age. Since modern Egyptology depends heavily upon the Manethonian history of Egypt, this misleading view has been uncritically accepted. The reality is that the Hyksos invaders were only finally completely driven out of Avaris during the Iron Age, not in the early Late Bronze Age. There had been actually "two" periods when the Hyksos occupied the Delta town of Avaris (Tell el-Dab'a): during MBIIc-LBI and again during the close of LBIII. The 18th Dynasty, headed by Pharaoh Ahmose came along at the conclusion of the second, and last, period of Hyksos occupation. In the present chapter, however, we are uniquely concerned with the initial occupation.

A Change in the Balance of Power: The Hyksos in Avaris

The ethnic origin of the Hyksos invaders has long been a hotly debated subject among ancient historians. The current scholarly consensus rests upon their presumed Semitized Indo-Aryan roots. Diverse ancient traditions however vouch that the Hyksos were Arabians from the east. In the first century of the common era, the Jewish chronicler Flavius Josephus related:

> "Tutimaeus. In his reign, I know not why a **blast of God's displeasure** broke upon us. A people of ignoble origin from the east, whose coming was unforeseen, had the audacity to invade the country, which they mastered by main force without difficulty or even a battle. Having overpowered the chiefs, they then savagely burnt the cities, razed the temples of the gods to the ground, and treated the whole native population with the utmost cruelty, massacring some, and carrying off the wives and children of others into slavery. Finally they made one of their number, named Salatis, king. He resided at Memphis, exacted tribute from Upper and Lower Egypt, and left garrisons in the places most suited for defence. In particular he secured his eastern flank, as he foresaw that the Assyrians, as their power increased in the future, would covet and attack his realm. Having discovered in the Sethroite nome a city very favourably situated on the east of the Bubastis arm of the river, called after some ancient theological tradition Auaris, he rebuilt and strongly fortified it with walls, and established a garrison there numbering as many as two hundred and forty thousand armed men to protect his frontier. ... Their race bore the generic name of Hycsos, which means 'king-shepherds.'

For HYC in the sacred language denotes 'king,' and SOS in the common dialect means 'shepherd' or 'shepherds'; the combined words form Hycsos. **Some say they were Arabians."**
(Josephus, *Against Apion*, I, [14])

Several important bits of information, apart from the Hyksos' identification as Arabians, transpire from Josephus' account cited above. Firstly, the Hyksos invasion is dated to the reign of a pharaoh named "Tutimaeus" — whom ancient historians identify with King Dudimose I of the 13th Dynasty. Secondly, the invasion is said to have been unexpectedly prompted by "a blast of God's displeasure." Thirdly, Josephus' description of the chaotic events in Egypt resulting from the Hyksos incursion perfectly mirrors what is reported in both the Prophecy of Neferty and the Papyrus Ipuwer. In accordance with Josephus' report, we find that the New Chronology Table places Pharaoh Dudimose as a ruler of Upper Egypt on the year of the Thera eruption. The coregency of Queen Sobeknefru and Pharaoh Amenemhat IV appears to have indeed been exceedingly short, as in less than a year. Their immediate and respective successors, Pharaohs Dudimose I and Sobekhotep I, inherited a liberated Egypt, but were nonetheless confronted with a powerful and hostile Hyksos garrison in the eastern Delta. So while the blast of god, i.e. the lunar shift of 1,628 BCE, did not occur during the reign of Dudimose I as Josephus contends, it is true that the former, along with Sobekhotep I in Lower Egypt, were the ones who were left to deal with the Hyksos ruler Salatis (Sheshi I) once the dust had quite literally settled. Josephus further relates that, from his fortified northern capital, Salatis exacted tribute from *both* Upper and Lower Egypt. This represents a vitally important detail. It tells us that, in all probability, he did not directly rule the territory below Avaris. Native Egyptian pharaohs continued to rule on Upper and Lower Egypt separately — hence Flavius Josephus' specification that both territories paid tribute to Salatis.

The ancient belief that the Hyksos had been Arabians was resurrected in the 1950s by Immanuel Velikovsky. Identifying the Hyksos shepherd-kings with the biblical Amalekites, Velikovsky theorized, as we've seen in the previous chapter, that the Hyksos were the biblical Amalekites who obstructed the Hebrew's way out of Egypt's Delta and into Canaan during the Exodus. In his 1952 book *Ages in Chaos*, Immanuel Velikovsky proposed that the Hyksos-Amalekites had ruled over a vast Arabian empire from their principal seat of power in Mecca.[2] Immediately following a stupendous cosmic catastrophe, which befell Mecca, the Amalekites fled from their devastated homeland and proceeded to head toward Syria-Palestine and

---
[2] Immanuel Velikovsky (1952) *Ages in Chaos*, Doubleday: Garden City, N.Y., pp. 61, 91-92.

Egypt. Very long-standing traditions among Arab scholars indeed support Immanuel Velikovsky's bold historical reconstruction. For instance, in his book *Personal Narrative of a Pilgrimage to Al-Madinah and Meccah*, the famed nineteenth century British explorer Richard Francis Burton wrote:

> A tribe called Aulad Sam bin Nuh (the children of Shem), or Amalikah and Amalik, from their ancestor Amlak bin Arfakhshad bin Sam bin Nuh, was inspired with a knowledge of the Arabic tongue: it settled at Al-Madinah [Medina], and was the first to cultivate the ground and to plant palm-trees. In course of time these people extended over the whole tract between the seas of Al-Hijaz (the Gulf of Aqabah) and Al-Oman, (North-Western part of the Indian ocean), and they became the progenitors of the Jababirah (tyrants or "giants") of Syria, as well as the Farainah (Pharaohs) of Egypt ... [3]

As Amalek is a direct descendant of Esau (see Table 6-2), it leaves absolutely no doubt that the Amalekites descended from Shem — just like the ancient Arabic tribe of Amalikah. Evidently, they were one and the same. Moreover, it's remarkably telling that the Arabic legends reveal that the tribe of Amalik engendered a dynasty of Egyptian pharaohs. The Egyptians referred to the Amalekites as "the Amu" — denoting Asiatic bowmen. In the Instructions for Merikare, it is said of these Amu that: *"Although he possesses chattels and cattle, he is always on the move and perpetually in want."*[4] Their name of "shepherd-kings" hence must have something to do with the Amu's status as chattel and cattle herders. The biblical texts make similar observations about the Amalekites:

> 3 And so it was, when Israel had sown, that the Midianites came up, and the Amalekites, and the children of the east, even they came up against them.
> 4 And they encamped against them, and destroyed the increase of the earth, till thou come unto Gaza, and left no sustenance for Israel, neither sheep, nor ox, nor ass.
> 5 **For they came up with their cattle and their tents,** and they came as grasshoppers for multitude; for both they and their camels were without number: and they entered into the land to destroy it.
> (Judges 6:1-6)

---

[3] Sir Richard Francis Burton, *Personal Narrative of a Pilgrimage to Al-Madinah and Meccah*, Vol. I, p. 343.
[4] Donald B. Redford (1992) *Egypt, Canaan, and Israel in Ancient Times*, Princeton University Press: Princeton, NJ, p. 68.

It's difficult not to detect a pattern here. In Arabic, ancient Egyptian, and Hebrew texts, the Hyksos-Amalekites are described in virtually the exact same manner. They came from "the east" in a bloody path of destruction. They travelled with cattle, lived in tents and moved around in large groups. Finally, Flavius Josephus implicitly confirms the timing of their invasion: at the end of MBIIb.

Tell el-Dab'a After Pharaoh Neferhotep

The last of the Hebraic pharaohs to rule over MBIIb Avaris was King Neferhotep. Extant archaeological evidence shows that Pharaoh Neferhotep was a contemporary of King Yantin in Byblos — who was himself a contemporary of King Hammurabi in Babylonia. It thereby follows that Neferhotep was likewise a contemporary of King Zimri-Lim in Mari.[5] The Theran eruption having manifested itself precisely during the reign of Zimri-Lim, we should expect to find Pharaoh Neferhotep reigning at Avaris at the time of the Hyksos-Amalekite invasion of Egypt's Delta. Indeed, early in the last century, renowned British Egyptologist Arthur Weigall said the following about the invasion in question:

> ... it would seem that Lower Egypt was entirely lost some time during the reign of Neferhotpe. But it does not seem to have been conquered by the Pharaohs of the Fourteenth Dynasty ... I think that the loss of those regions of the Delta which were not already in the hands of the Fourteenth Dynasty was due to an Asiatic invasion ... A great horde of Semitic tribesmen seems to have poured into the eastern Delta along the Wadi Tumilat, and to have established its headquarters at Tell el-Yehudiyeh, on the edge of the eastern desert, some 30 miles north of Memphis, where Petrie found a great fortified camp of this period.[6]

This Asiatic invasion during the reign of Pharaoh Neferhotep which Weigall talks about was actually the Hyksos-Amalekite invasion of 1,628 BCE. As Josephus had earlier mentioned, the Hyksos built a number of heavily fortified camps north of Memphis. Tell el-Yehudiyeh was undoubtedly one of the towns where a major garrison was set up.

Recent excavations at Tell el-Dab'a (Avaris) undertaken by the Austrian archaeologist and Egyptologist Manfred Bietak have uncovered a wealth of information which go much further towards confirming that Pharaoh Neferhotep in-

---

[5] See David M. Rohl (1995) *A Test of Time — Vol. I*, Century: London, pp. 247-248.
[6] Arthur Weigall (1927) *A History of the Pharaohs — Vol. II: From the Accession of Amenemhat I of the Twelfth Dynasty to the Death of Thutmose III of the Eighteenth Dynasty, 2111 to 1441 B.C.*, Thornton Butterworth: London, pp. 159-160.

deed reigned during the MBIIb period. In fact, the Tell el-Dab'a finds represent a virtual gold-mine of evidence to support the new chronology. Bietak divided the different strata at Tell el-Dab'a in the following manner:

Bietak's Stratigraphy of Tell el-Dab'a		Bietak's Chronology	New Chronology
MBI	H = d/2	1,800 BCE	1,780 BCE MBIIb
	G/4 = d/1		
	G/1-3 = c		
MBIIa	F = b/3	1,700 BCE	
	E/3 = b/2		1, 628 BCE MBIIc
MBIIb	E/2-1 = b/1		
	E/1 = a/2	1,600 BCE	
MBIIc	D/3 = a/2		
	D/2	1,530 BCE	1,559 BCE

Table 9-3

(1) **Stratum G/4 = d/1**: It is to this period that Bietak ascribes Khendjer's rise to high position and eventually to kingship.
(2) **Stratum F = b/3**: The main temple (Temple III) was erected during this period according to Bietak.
(3) **Stratum E/3**: A corrupt form of the name Sobekhotep was found inscribed on a scarab.
(4) **Stratum E/2 = b/1**: First occurrence of a new style of scarab typical of the Hyksos period.
(5) **Stratum D/3 = a/2**: Discovery of the scarab belonging to a major Hyksos ruler by the name of Z-R Snsk whm 'nh. Bietak believes that this name is a long form of the popular name Ssy. Also in the same stratum were two bronze plates of King Neferhotep, which Bietak believes had been intentionally smashed with a hammer.

As shown above, my own chronological scheme for the stratification levels at Tell el-Dab'a does not differ much from Professor Bietak's own framework[7] — as far as absolute dates are concerned. Where I disagree with Bietak however is in his exce-

---

[7] See also Manfred Bietak (1984) 'Problems of Middle Bronze Age Chronology: New Evidence from Egypt', *American Journal of Archaeology* Vol. 88 - Num. 4, p. 471-485.

edingly low dating scheme for the beginning of the Middle Bronze Age. For instance, while I personally opt to endorse a date of 1,953 BCE for the beginning of MBIIa, Dr Bietak proposes dates ranging from as low as between 1710-1680 BCE for the transition period between MBI and MBIIa. Two scholars who have likewise, often vociferously, argued for a higher chronology at Tell el-Dab'a are University of Arizona excavator William G. Dever and the late Brown University Egyptologist William A. Ward.[8] One major difference between W. G. Dever and Bietak is that Dever pushes the beginning of the earliest phase at Avaris (Stratum H=d/2) all the way back to the mid-twentieth century BCE.[9] In Dever's own words:

> It has been clear almost from the beginning that the material culture of the lower levels Strata H, G and F is Canaanite (in my opinion specifically Palestinian) in character and represents an early Asiatic settlement in the Delta that is fascinating because it is "pre-Hyksos." ... he [Bietak] has drastically lowered the absolute dates of Dab'a Stratum E3 and on that basis has sought to adjust the entire Syro-Palestinian archaeological-chronological framework downward by as much as 125 years (especially for MBIIA).[10]

Unlike Professor Dever,[11] however, I refrain from, by placing the beginning of MBIIa back to 1,953 BCE, automatically moving Strata H to F up along with it. The Palestinian "pre-Hyksos" culture which W. G. Dever speaks of (the Hebrews) only settled and prospered in Tell el-Dab'a around 1,780 BCE. Moreover, I am of the opinion that Ward and Dever's high chronology (or "middle chronology" as they have more recently preferred to call it)[12] is not high enough. So where Dever and Ward would place the beginning of MBI (in $c.1,950$ BCE), I would instead place the beginning of MBIIa; and hence propose a date of $c.2,130$ BCE for the start of MBI. Since I also more or less adhere to Bietak's absolute dates for the stratified remains

---

[8] William A. Ward & William G. Dever (1994) *Scarab Typology and Archaeological Context: An Essay on Middle Bronze Age Chronology*, Van Siclen Books: San Antonio, TX.
[9] Ward goes as far back as 2,000 BCE.
[10] William G. Dever (1991) 'Tell el-Dab'a and Levantine Middle Bronze Age Chronology: A Rejoiner to Manfred Bietak', *Bulletin of the American Schools of Oriental Research* 281, p. 73.
[11] It must be noted that W. G. Dever, unlike the majority of Israeli archaeologists, prefers to equate the MBIIa period of the present scheme with MBI. The reason being that he does not consider the transitory stage of the late third millennium BCE to have been part of the Middle Bronze Age. See Dever (1987) p. 149.
[12] See James Weinstein (1996) 'A Wolf in Sheep's Clothing: How the High Chronology Became the Middle Chronology', *Bulletin of the American Schools of Oriental Research* 304, p. 56.

at Tell el-Dab'a, we now find Strata H, G, and F falling into the MBIIb period. That position is incidentally at odds with both Bietak and Dever whom, despite fundamental disagreements with regards to matters of absolute chronology, agree, for instance, to date Stratum G/4 = d/1 to the middle of the MBI period. But again, if, as I contend, the remains at Tell el-Dab'a are attributable to the Hebrews who arrived in Egypt in the days of Joseph, an MBI date for any stratified remains at Tell el-Dab'a would be much too early. What must be borne in mind is, in the words of James M. Weinstein, that: *"Palestine in MBI is almost completely dependent on Egyptian chronology."*[13] The Egyptian dynasty which is customarily linked with the MBI Syria-Palestine is the 12th Dynasty. So if 12th Dynasty artifacts are the main sources for dating Syro-Palestinian remains from the early strata at Tell el-Dab'a, then a lowered date for that dynasty automatically lowers the dates at Avaris.

Before starting to analyse the archaeological remains from each stratum, we shall add the following sixth set of evidence from Tell el-Dab'a as described by William G. Dever:

(6) **Stratum F:** A "duck-bill" axe of Syro-Palestinian type portrayed on a cylinder seal found in this stratum, is reminiscent of a similar object found in pre-Hammurabi destruction levels at Mari. Other such "duck-bill" axes have been unearthed in Ebla from the "Tomb of the Lord of Goats" dated by Dever to the MBIIb period.

This last piece of evidence is of crucial importance because it proves, at least in my opinion, that the Ebla site of MBIIb was indeed under the Age of Aries — as it is indicated by the official's title of "Lord of Goats." Moreover, seeing that the duck-bill axes unearthed attribute Stratum F at Tell el-Dab'a to the pre-Hammurabi period of the Mari empire, we therefore know that Stratum F preceded the Theran eruption. It then automatically follows that the great temple of Stratum F (Temple III), was built by W. G. Dever's "pre-Hyksos" Palestinians who resided in Avaris prior to the 1,628 BCE lunar catastrophe. Since Bietak reported that King Khendjer ruled during Stratum G, we can now deduce with near certainty that Khendjer was one of those Asiatic rulers from MBIIb Tell el-Dab'a. The termination of the pre-Hyksos Israelite settlement at Avaris is further confirmed by the discovery of two bronze plates belonging to King Neferhotep which, according to Bietak, had been intentionally smashed. This would further indicate that Tell el-Dab'a came under fierce Hyksos attack during the reign of Neferhotep. If these bronze plates had been purposely pulverised, the most plausible cause would have been attributed to enemy action.

---

[13] James M. Weinstein (1996) p. 60.

CHAPTER IX: THE HYKSOS INVASION | 295

As all of the various accounts of the Hyksos invasion transmit, the Amalekites mercilessly and indiscriminately destroyed temples, statues and artifacts all over Egypt, particularly in the Delta. Under such circumstances, it is therefore not surprising that archaeologists have also found a broken statuette of Queen Sobeknefru (a contemporary of Pharaoh Neferhotep) which had been reused in a wall footing at Gezer. Several other late 12th /early 13th Dynasty artifacts were likewise unearthed at Gezer. It's clear, in the minds of archaeologists, that the statues had not been manufactured at Gezer, but were brought over from Egypt. Since many, including the statuette of Queen Sobeknefru, are funerary objects, we must deduce that they were probably not meant to ever leave Egypt — as no Egyptian officials or monarchs would likely wish to be buried in Syria-Palestine.[14] In the excavation reports of Sir Flinders Petrie from the town of Kahun, originally built for the workers of the pyramid complex of Pharaoh Sesostris II in El-Lahun (which surrounded the town of Kahun), we learn that:

> During the latter part of the 12th Dynasty and the beginning of the 13th Dynasty, the inhabitants of the town [of Kahun] ransacked the tombs for materials and brought away many slabs of offerings, some of them inscribed, also stelae, statuettes and parts of tombs.[15]

It is obvious that the Amalekites (or Hyksos) were responsible for those reckless destructions. Petrie is wrong to conclude that the inhabitants of the Egyptian Delta ransacked their own towns. There was an invasion from without. It is true however that the Hebrews of Avaris were the ones who carried off the pillaged Egyptian artifacts to Syria-Palestine. But is there any firm evidence in the Bible that the Hebrews transported Egyptian burial remains to the Promised Land? I believe there is. A most striking bit of detail from the Book of Exodus (13:9) indeed reveals that the bones of Joseph were carried away to the Promised Land during the Exodus. Did the Hebrews actually exhume the body of Joseph? The Book of Genesis (50:25-26) makes it clear that Joseph was buried according to Egyptian customs and that, before dying, he'd expressed his wishes to have his remains brought along to the Promised Land with his descendants. Should we automatically take the biblical redactors at their word? We must remember that the Bible was only actually written down hundreds of years after the said events. The biblical redactors could have easily revised the course of events to suit their own purposes.

---

[14] James M. Weinstein (1974) 'A Statuette of the Princess Sobeknefru at Tell Gezer', *Bulletin of the American Schools of Oriental Research* 213, pp. 49-57.
[15] W.F.M Petrie (1890) *Kahun, Gurob, and Hawara*, Kegan Paul, Trench, Trübner: London, p. 31.

As always, archaeological evidence should take precedence over textual evidence. In this particular analysis, the archaeological evidence tells us that the Hyksos most likely plundered the tomb of Joseph. It is very easy to understand why the biblical redactors might have attempted to gloss over this fact. Surely, the remains of Joseph were taken to Palestine by the Hebrews on their way out of Egypt. But they had only done so out of respect for their revered ancestor whose tomb had been ransacked by the invading Amalekites — not because it had been Joseph's explicit wish. In the first volume of *A Test of Time*, David Rohl tried to show that a savagely attacked cult statue of an Asiatic high official found in Stratum F at Tell el-Dab'a was really a statue of Joseph the Patriarch.[16] While this particular theory is incompatible with my own chronological reconstruction, the battered state of the cult statue nonetheless serves, once again, to illustrate the chaotic state of affairs in Egypt prior to the First Exodus. In particular, the Asiatic official in question was obviously a very close contemporary of both Pharaoh Neferhotep and Queen Sobeknefru. Monuments dedicated to all three personages were ruthlessly attacked — obviously during the course of the very same upheaval. Once again, the scenario which I propose is that the Hyksos attacked and occupied Avaris in 1,628 BCE — while the MBIIb Asiatic occupants of Avaris (the Hebrews), who had been allowed to settle in the Egyptian Delta during the time of Joseph, journeyed to Palestine (the Conquest).

MBIIc in Palestine: The Hebrews After the Conquest

A crucial test to assess the theory that the Israelites entered Palestine during the Middle Bronze IIc period would be to find out if there is any archaeological evidence to support the sudden entry of a new group of people in Palestine at that time. This evidence does exist. Early in the MBIIc era, Syro-Palestinian archaeologists have uncovered new tomb types which did not exist in the area during the preceding MBIIb period. Following the lead of Flinders Petrie, the majority of archaeologists still, wrongly in my view, attribute the new tomb types and urban fortifications which suddenly appear at the onset of MBIIc in southern Palestine to the Hyksos. A leading authority on the sharp break between MBIIb and MBIIc in Palestine, Joe D. Seger writes:

> At this time [beginning of MBIIC], a wave of new and substantial fortification building takes place, and a fairly tight pattern of development emerges. At both Shechem and Gezer, the period is initiated by the construction of massive cyclopean fortification walls, in each case considerably expanding the size of the city. This fits the pattern observed at numerous other sites, from Hazor and Megiddo in the north to Tell Beit Mirsim and Lachish in the south.[17]

---

[16] David M. Rohl (1995) pp. 365-366.
[17] Joe D. Seger (1975) 'The MB II Fortifications at Schechem and Gezer: A Hyksos Retrospective', *Eretz-Israel* 12, p. 44.

Seger convincingly argues that there is little evidence to support the view of some scholars (e.g. Mazar) that these new buildings were erected by invading Indo-Aryans or Hurrians who overpowered and assimilated the local Semitic population.[18] However, Seger's own proposed solution that the urban development of MBIIc Palestine was "a direct effect of their [the Hyksos] consolidation of power"[19] in Egypt's eastern Delta is, in my own estimation, no more reliable. The new fortified buildings at Hazor, Megiddo and other sites, reflects the emergence of the biblical period of the Judges.

If the swift proliferation of fortified buildings in MBIIc Syria-Palestine was indeed a direct effect of the consolidation of Hyksos-Amalekite power in the Egyptian eastern Delta, it was more so in *reaction* to it. The Book of Judges indeed relates that the Amalekites, who supported the local Canaanites, hostile to the Israelites, often carried out raids against Israel.

> 3 And so it was, when Israel had sown, that the Midianites came up, and the Amalekites, and the children of the east, even they came up against them;
> 4 And the encamped against them, and destroyed the increase of the earth, till thou come unto Gaza, and left no sustenance for Israel, neither sheep, nor ox, nor ass.
> 5 **For they came up with their cattle and their tents, and they came as grasshoppers for multitude;** for both they and their camels entered the land and destroyed it.
> (Judges 6:3-5)

Incidentally, the above biblical description of the Hyksos-Amalekites, as one of the "children of the east," matches perfectly with the raid techniques used by the Amu who attacked Egypt![20] The Papyrus Hermitage 116b, recto, says:

> ... the Asiatics [Amu] approach in their might and their hearts rage against those who are gathering in the harvest, and they take away [their] kine from the ploughing. ... The land is utterly perished, and naught remains.[21]

---

[18] Ibid.
[19] Ibid.
[20] Immanuel Velikovsky (1952) *Ages in Chaos*, p. 74.
[21] Sir Alan H. Gardiner (1914) 'New Literary Works from Ancient Egypt', *Journal of Egyptian Archaeology* 1, p. 103.

Evidently, both the Israelites and the Egyptians are referring to the Hyksos-Amalekites, or king-shepherds. Faced with a hostile coalition of Hyksos and Canaanites, the Israelites' experience during the period of the Judges (i.e. the MBIIc period) was one of "national solidarity against foreign oppression."[22] In this climate, a succession of charismatic leaders came to rule the new nation of Israel — the Judges. The succession was not hereditary, as would be the case later during the United Monarchy, but one that was entirely based on the personal valour, courage, and moral fibre of the chosen leader. Hence, social class, status, or even gender, were not at all the criteria for leadership.[23] As sociologist Max Weber had argued, charismatic rule thrives during times of crisis for a nation. These Hebrew charismatic leaders, who governed during the MBIIc era, were, according to the Bible, Othniel, Ehud, Gideon, Deborah (and Barak), Jephthah and Samson. Other minor judges were Shamgar, Tola, Jair, Ibzan, Elon, and Abdon.

Conventional scholars place the period of the Judges between c.1,380-1,050 BCE. Not only is this much later than the period I propose in the new chronology for the period of the Judges, but it is also much longer. Both of these misconceptions have, quite naturally, been inherited from the Bible. However, I maintain that not only does the period of the Judges really belong in the closing Middle Bronze Age, but that it merely lasted less than a century. Evidence for both of these assertions can be gleaned from what scholars consider to be a serious chronological problem — but which, in the new chronology, makes perfect sense. This illusory conundrum has to do with the battle of Deborah and Barak against the Canaanites, headquartered at Hazor, and its eerie similarities with Joshua's earlier confrontation against the Canaanites at Hazor. In both instances, Hazor is portrayed as being at the centre of a vast and powerful Canaanite coalition. Modern archaeology has revealed that, at the time in which the Bible claims that Deborah led Israel, the Canaanite city of Hazor was a weak and unfortified town. How could it possibly have been at the head of an expansive Canaanite coalition? Furthermore, it is rather strange that, if the period of Judges really lasted over three hundred years, Joshua and Deborah could have fought against, possibly, the same Canaanite king of Hazor — Yabin (or Jabin). We recall that in the previous chapter, we've seen that Yabin, who was identified as King Ibni-Adad of the Mari archives, reigned over Hazor at a time when it was the head of many Canaanite kingdoms (Josh. 11: 10). Gravely misled by the over-extended biblical chronology of the period of Judges, historians have always assumed that the King Yabin whom Joshua defeated at the Waters of Merom (Josh. 11:1-4) and the King Yabin whom Deborah and

---

[22] H. H. Ben-Sasson (editor) (1976) *A History of the Jewish People*, Harvard University Press: Cambridge, Mass., p. 71.
[23] Ibid, p. 67.

Barak confronted at the River of Kishon (Judg. 4:2), were really two different Canaanite kings of Hazor. However, my belief is that they were in fact one and the same. The archaeological evidence says, incontrovertibly, that Yabin reigned over this powerful kingdom of Hazor during the Middle Bronze Age — not later.

The Hyksos Colonization of Crete and Greece

In his *Palace of Minos*, the famed excavator Sir Arthur Evans claimed that the Middle Minoan II period in the Aegean came to an abrupt end with a tremendous natural catastrophe.[24] This catastrophe marked the end of the Palatial Period. All three major palaces in Crete (Knossos, Mallia and Phaistos) were utterly destroyed. These heavy destructions of the Cretan palaces were, I believe, caused by the Thera eruption of 1,628 BCE which likewise wrought significant havoc upon the lands of Egypt and Syria-Palestine. In Crete, the upheaval heralded the new archaeological period of Middle Minoan III. During this period, we notice the first appearance of the "composite bow."[25] We recall that the Hyksos were known to the Egyptians as the "Bowmen" — an unambiguous reference to their weapon of choice: the bow. Prof. Martin Bernal of Cornell University made the ingenious proposition that this evidence could bear silent witness to a Hyksos invasion.[26] The million-dollar question is: did this invasion also spread to Crete — in addition to Egypt and Syria? This is in fact not at all impossible since, as Austrian excavator Prof. Manfred Bietak's research confirms, the Hyksos undertook maritime expeditions to Cyprus and Crete.[27] Therefore, it is indeed quite likely that the Hyksos-Amalekites, from their position of strength in Lower Egypt, exerted much influence over the Mediterranean region during the MBIIC era. Supporting this hypothesis, in 1973, excavator J.G.P. Best expressed his belief that between 2,100 and 1,600 BCE, the land of Greece was populated by Thracians of Indo-European stock — but that there appeared to have been some form of cultural shift at the onset of MM III.[28] There is no doubt that the population of Crete during the Middle Minoan III period was, at its base, Indo-European. Nevertheless, as Martin Bernal delineates below, there is strong evidence that a major Near Eastern cultural influx came into the Aegean at this time:

---

[24] Sir Arthur J. Evans (1921-35) *The Palace of Minos — Vol. III*, London, p. 14.
[25] H.L. Lorimer (1950) *Homer and the Monuments*, Macmillan: London, pp. 276-280.
[26] Martin Bernal (1991) *Black Athena (The Afroasiatic Roots of Classical Civilization) — Volume II: The Archaeological and Documentary Evidence*, Rutgers University Press: New Brunswick, NJ, p. 373.
[27] Manfred Bietak (1983) 'Some News about Trade and Trade Warfare in the Ancient Near East', *Marhaba* 3.83, pp. 41-43.
[28] J. G. P. Best & Y. Yadin (1973) *The Arrival of the Greeks*. Henri Frankfort Foundation, Hakkert: Amsterdam.

Nevertheless, there is little doubt that there was an intensification of Near Eastern and especially Egyptian influence on Cretan painting at the beginning of MM III. ... There are also reeds, which are painted precisely according to Egyptian convention, and papyrus, which if it was grown in the Aegean was not common there, as it was along the Nile; here too was close conformity to their representation in Egyptian paintings. The 'Nile scene' with a cat stalking or catching birds is attested in Egypt only from the New Kingdom. In the Aegean, however, it appears even earlier, in MM II/LM I in Crete and ... in 17th-century contexts from Thera and Mycenae.[29]

Moreover, the same types of daggers found in the Tell el-Ajjul (Sharuhen) levels associated with the Hyksos (City II — contemporary with MBIIc) are found in MM III Crete. Additionally, in the opinion of archaeologist Keith Branigan, during MM III and LM I, the Cretan style of weapon making shows unmistakable signs of Levantine influence.[30] Like Bernal,[31] I am convinced that the style of weaponry found in MM III Crete was derived from the powerful Hyksos culture to the south. Quite understandably, the artistic style of the Hyksos — which they imported into the Aegean — had, itself, been inevitably fashioned by the Egyptian artistic canons. Indeed, another important contribution of the Hyksos to the Aegean was their importation into Crete of their modified version of the traditional Egyptian sphinx: the griffin. The griffin, like the standard Egyptian sphinx, was a composite of lion and man — with the only difference being that the Hyksos, or Asiatic, variation had wings. The winged sphinx (griffin) was a distinctively Asiatic artistic innovation; and was often portrayed on Hyksos scarabs.[32] It is also worthy to point out that, given the fact that the Hyksos-Amalekites occupied the Egyptian Delta during Typhon Season #4 (1,579-1,559 BCE), their characteristic use of the griffin iconography was an early indication of their predilection for the god Seth. Indeed, the griffin was closely related to with the Khemeto-Egyptian Seth-animal.[33] The important fact, also, that the Cretan griffin does not appear on the island before MM III is a good indication of when this Sethian worship was being practiced.[34]

---

[29] Martin Bernal (1991) *Black Athena II*, p. 365.
[30] Keith Branigan (1968) 'A Transitional Phase in Minoan Metallurgy', *Bulletin of the British School in Athens* 63, p. 201.
[31] Martin Bernal (1991) *Black Athena II*, p. 369.
[32] See André Dessenne (1957) *Le Sphinx: Études iconographiques*, Bibliothèque des Écoles françaises d'Athènes et de Rome, 186: Paris.
[33] H. Te Velde (1967) *Seth, God of Confusion (A Study of His Role in Egyptian Mythology and Religion)*, E. J. Brill: London, p. 5.
[34] A. M. Bisi (1965) *Il Grifone: Storia di unn motivo iconographico nell'antico oriente mediterraneo*. Centro di studi semitici, Istituto di studi del vicino oriente-Università: Rome, p. 167.

Fig. 9a: Scene from the palace of King Zimri-Lim.

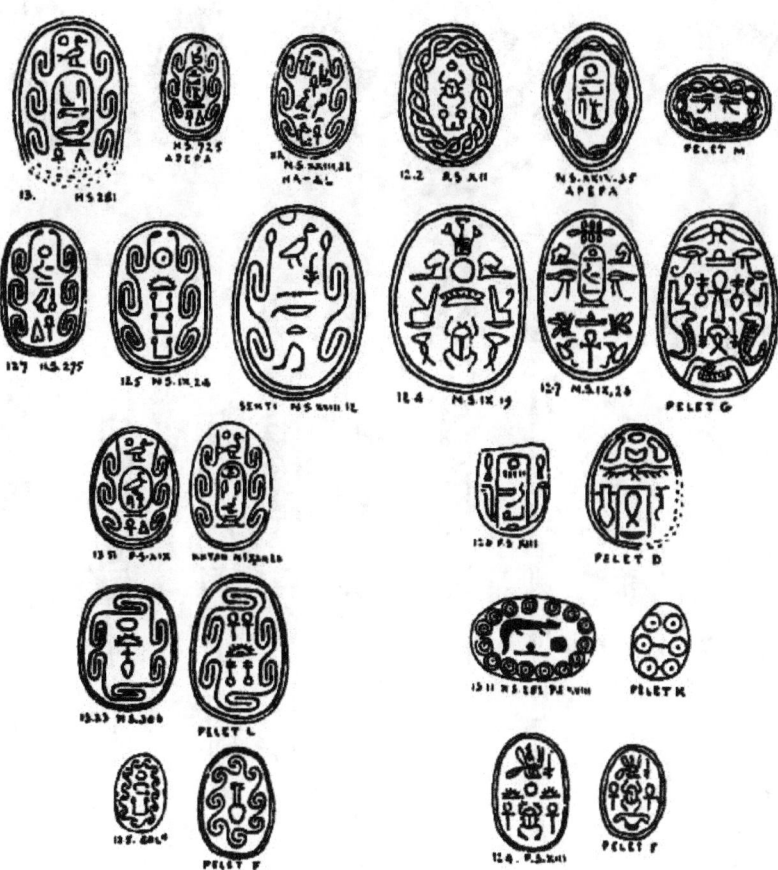

Fig. 9b: Hyksos scarabs. *From* Petrie (1939).

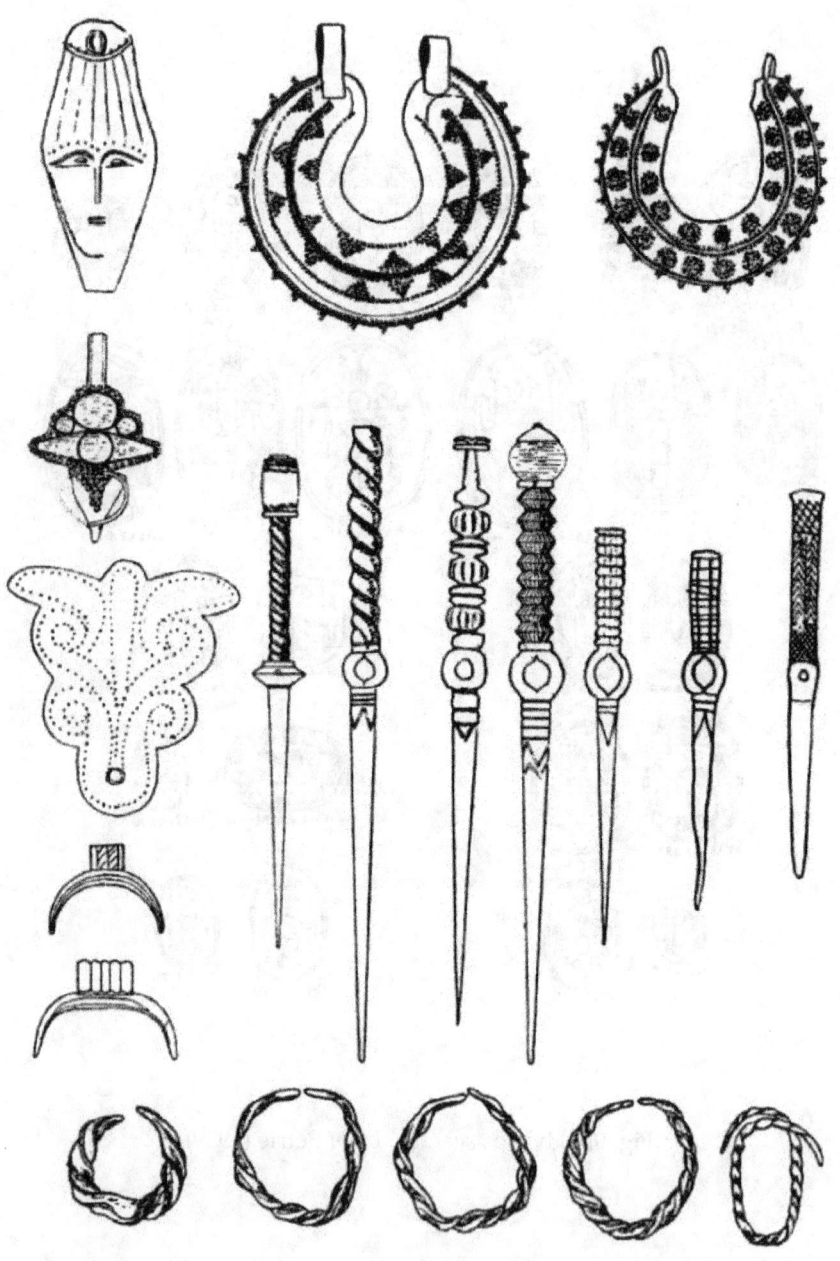

Fig. 9c: Hyksos jewellery and weaponry. *From* Petrie (1939).

Fig. 9d: Middle Minoan II palace (restored).

The MBIIc Indo-Aryan Invasions:

Why a Hurrian is Not a Hyksos

At the onset of MBIIc, Indo-European peoples, most prominently the Kassites, Hurrians, and the Hittites, began a vast and chaotic migration out of Europe toward India, Persia, and the ancient Near East. With them, they introduced a powerful new technology: the horse-drawn chariot. The advent of the Hyksos in the ancient Near East has adequately been chronologically connected by scholars with the massive migration of the Kassites into Babylon and that of the Hurrians into northern Mesopotamia at the end of MBIIb.[35] It would be a mistake, however, to assume, as a number scholars unfortunately still do, that the Hyksos and the Indo-Aryans were of the same racial stock. Indeed, to quote the renowned Swedish Egyptologist Torgny Säve-Söderbergh:

> The hypothesis that the Hyksos contained Hurrian elements seems also not to be supported by linguistic evidence. Most of the Hyksos names are pure Semitic, and those which cannot be thus explained are in any case hardly Hurrian.[36]

Scholars who still cling to a whole or partial Hurrian identity for the Hyksos are currently in the minority. Nevertheless, many scholars have been unable to resist justifying at least some link between the invading Hurrians of MBIIc and the Hyksos. Prof. Bernal, for instance, has argued for a "Hurrian and possibly even an Indo-Iranian element among the Hyksos," whilst, confronted with the linguistic evidence cited above, maintaining that they were "overwhelmingly Semitic-speaking."[37] Though it is, in fact, chronologically tempting to equate the incursion of the Hurrians with that of the Hyksos, given the clear contemporaneity of the two invasions, the two incoming streams must be kept separate. However, for scholars to acquiesce that both groups were of different racial origin and culture, would mean finding some unknown external cause that might have induced these disparate groups to "simultaneously" invade established powerhouses

---

[35] See William H. Stiebing, Jr. (1971) 'Hyksos Burials in Palestine: A Review of the Evidence', *Journal of Near Eastern Studies* Vol. 30 - Num. 2, p. 110.
[36] Torgny Säve-Söderbergh (1951) 'The Hyksos Rule in Egypt', *Journal of Egyptian Archaeology* 37, p. 58.
[37] Martin Bernal (1991) pp. 40-41.

of the Near East such as Egypt and Babylonia. The external factor was the moon-induced Thera eruption of 1,628 BCE. Certainly, one of the most damaging effects of this erroneous equation of the Hyksos with Indo-Aryan tribes, has been the belief that the Hyksos were responsible for introducing the horse and the horse-drawn chariot into Egypt. As a matter of fact, recent research has demonstrated that what were once thought to have been Hyksos horse burials, were in reality donkey burials. Referring to the work of Prof. Othmar Keel's study of MB II Canaan,[38] Prof. Aren M. Maeir of the Hebrew University's Institute of Archaeology writes:

> On the basis of previous publications, Keel demonstrated that the various equid burials found in MB II contexts in Egypt and Canaan, are of donkeys, not of horses as often suggested. Thus the centrality of the horse in "Hyksos culture" as often assumed in the past, is superfluous.[39]

While it is definitely true that the Hyksos of the Middle Bronze Age did not have horses, the "centrality of the horse in Hyksos culture," as we shall see in Chapter 12, is not at all "superfluous." In the new chronology, we shall attribute a length of over half a millennium to the Hyksos occupation of Lower Egypt and Canaan (although they were periodically driven back and then reinstated). It is really towards the end of their dominion over the ancient Near East, that is in the twelfth century BCE, that the horse (in the form of Poseidon: god of horses and chariots) finally became heavily associated with the Hyksos.

Typhon Season #4: Mercury and Venus Embark on Yet Another Collision Course with Earth

>   "... the earth trembled, and the heavens
>   dropped, the clouds also dropped water. The
>   mountains melted from before the Lord..."
>
>   - Judges 5:4-5

Less than half a century after the devastating moon-induced Thera eruption of 1,628 BCE, the ancient world was once again suddenly engulfed in a universal fiery cataclysm. This time, in 1,579 BCE, the culprit was the planet Mercury — which inaugurated Typhon Season #4. This particular Typhon Season seems to have

---

[38] See Othmar Keel (1993) 'Hyksos Horses or Hippopotamus Deities?', *Levant* 25, pp. 208-212.
[39] Aren M. Maeir (1994) 'Hyksos, Horses and Hippopotami: A Note', *Levant* 26, p. 231; (1989) 'Hyksos Miscellanea', *Discussions in Egyptology* 14, pp. 61-68.

been of exceptionally short duration — merely twenty years. From ancient Chinese records, it would appear that it lasted between 1,579 BCE and 1,559 BCE. This is as far cry from the traditional fifty-two years separating the Mercury and Venus catastrophes. A possible explanation might be that the relatively recent lunar shift delayed Mercury's orbital shift — which was due to occur in 1,611 BCE (just 17 years after the lunar shift). In any event, ancient Chinese chronicles reveal that the last ruler of the Xia Dynasty, Emperor Kwei, came to the throne in 1,589 BCE.[40] This date is of crucial importance to us because the annals of the *Bamboo Books* state that in the tenth year of Emperor Kwei, the eighteenth monarch since Yao, *"the five planets went out of their courses. In the night, stars fell like rain. The earth shook."*[41] This means that exactly on the year 1,579 BCE, an important cosmic disturbance occurred in the ancient skies. This event, the shift of the planet Mercury from its orbital path, inaugurated Typhon Season #4.

With the Mercury cataclysm and ensuing Typhon Season, three deities: Sobek, Neith and Nephthys became very popular towards the end of the 13th Dynasty. Sobek, the son of Neith, is the god of floods and riverbanks. His cult is the oldest one of the 13th Dynasty. Neith was identified as a controller of water. Her main role was that of a bovine deity associated with the Great Flood (Mht Wrt). We may recall that the previous Mercury catastrophe of 2,180 BCE caused the waters to raise significantly in Egypt. Just as Sobek was a god of the Fayum marshes, Neith, Sobek's mother, was a goddess affiliated with the Sais marshes in the Western Delta. Earlier Egyptian texts define Neith as a deity whose role it is to clear the land from the waters of the Great Flood (Mht Wrt) or primal water. In this capacity, Neith became known as a builder of canals and supervisor of irrigation projects.[42] The third deity of importance, Nephthys, was the sister of Isis and wife of Seth (Typhon). In Plutarch's *De Iside et Osiride*, he states:

> The outmost parts of the land beside the mountains and bordering on the sea the Egyptians call Nephthys. This is why they give to Nephthys the name of Finality [*teleut*] and say that she is the wife of Typhon. Whenever, then, the Nile overflows and with abounding waters spreads far away to those who dwell in the outermost regions, they call this the union of Osiris and Isis, which is proved by the uprising of plants.[43]

---

[40] Léon S. J. Wieger (1924) *La Chine à travers les ages*. Deuxième édition. Imprimerie de Hien-Hien: Hien-Hien, p. 16.

[41] James Legge (editor) *The Chinese Classics*, III, Pt. 1, 125. Cited in Immanuel Velikovsky (1950) *Worlds in Collision*, p. 254.

[42] *Pyramid Texts*, 508-509.

[43] Plutarch, *De Iside et Osiride*. In (1934-5) *Plutarch's Moralia*. Vols. I-XVI. Trans. by F.C. Babbit. Harvard University Press: Cambridge, Mass., Vol. V: p. 93.

Meanwhile, in MMIII Crete, vessels with loops in the shape of snakes were common place in newly-built "household shrines." These shrines were associated with the cult of the Snake Goddess.[44] The fact that these household shrines only appear during the MMIII period, replacing the peak sanctuaries, is an indication of the times in which they were manufactured.

To Divide and Conquer

Throughout Typhon Season #4, the Hyksos-Amalekites, stationed at Avaris in the eastern Delta, allowed the Egyptian monarchs of Upper and Lower Egypt to continue ruling as their vassals. Forging a strategic alliance with the Kushite from the Kingdom of Kerma, while encouraging divisions between Upper and Lower Egypt, the Hyksos-Amalekites managed to secure a strong foothold in the Nile Valley — while maintaining a relative distance in the northern lands. As Egyptologist Peter A. Piccione of the Oriental Institute of the University of Chicago relates:

> In the Thirteenth Dynasty, sometime between the reigns of **Neferhotep I** and **Sebekhotep IV** (ca. 1751-1730) [conventional chronology], commercial **contact between Kerma and Lower Egypt came to an end,** while contact with Upper Egypt remained constant. Similarly, archaeology reveals that Lower Egyptian pottery was abundant at *Buhen* early in the Thirteenth Dynasty, whereas later, only Upper Egyptian pottery existed there.[45]

What is known for sure is that Kerma's kingdom became even more powerful by allying itself with the invading Hyksos.[46] Indeed, a large number of Hyksos artifacts have been found in the cemeteries of Kerma. Ruling from Avaris, the Hyksos' strategy was obviously to "sandwich" the Lower Egyptians by establishing a strong presence in Upper Egypt, and forging an alliance with the Nubians. Isolated between a rock and a hard place, it is obvious, as P. Piccione points out, that the Lower Egyptians of the post-Thera eruption 13th Dynasty could not have had any relations with the Kerma people — since they were, now more than ever, sworn enemies. The Kushite were, in contrast, apparently quite free to enter and work in

---

[44] Keith Branigan (1988) *Pre-Palatial (The Foundations of Palatial Crete: A Survey of Crete in the Early Bronze Age).* Second updated edition. Adolf M. Hakkert: Amsterdam, p. 108.
[45] Peter A. Piccione 'Nubia: The Land Upriver —VII. Nubia in the Middle Kingdom', Internet resource: http://www.library.nwu.edu/class/history/B94/middle.html
[46] Peter Lacovara 'An Outline of Nubian History.' In Theodore Celenko (editor) (1996) *Egypt in Africa,* p. 93.

Upper Egypt. The throne name of one of the Upper Egyptian monarch of the 13th Dynasty, Pharaoh Nehesy (which literally means the Nubian), gives an inkling as to the power and influence of the Nubians in Upper Egypt at that time. The C-Group Kushites' increased prominence in Upper Egypt had, ironically, been triggered by the policies of the Egyptian kings themselves. When the 12th Dynasty pharaohs began holding garrisons in Nubia, soldiers were at the border forts in rotating service. After the Theran eruption, the Egyptian soldiers were no longer stationed in a rotational basis but were by then living in Nubia permanently. According to Nubiologist David O'Connor, there is a strong possibility that, as Egyptian control over Nubia waned, so did dynastic Egypt's hold over their own soldiers posted at the Second Cataract forts. He writes:

> As Egyptian control over the peripheral areas of its empire declined in the Late Middle Kingdom, the families and individuals who lived on at the forts appear to have switched their allegiance from Egypt to local Nubian rulers.[47]

Those defections were to play a determining role in how the MBIIc political and military climate would unfold between Egypt and Nubia. Much strengthened by the more experienced, highly trained, and not to mention strategically knowledgeable, Egyptian influx into their army, the Nubians could now pose a bigger threat to Egypt than ever before.

Egypto-Nubian Relations Under Sobekhotep IV and the Conquests of Moses

We observe the direct effects of the increased Nubian military prowess in the MB IIc period particularly during the reign of Sobekhotep IV. As David Rohl has suggested in *A Test of Time*, I believe that this pharaoh, also known as Khaneferre, was the father of the biblical Moses. The Egyptian name of Moses was Ahmose — the pharaoh who came to rule in Thebes at the beginning of the Late Bronze Age. Attempts to identify the biblical Moses with one or another ancient Egyptian pharaoh are nothing new.[48] Many such attempts have been inspired by Sigmund Freud's acclaimed book *Moses and Monotheism*. The Hebrew name of "Moses," as Freud

---

[47] David O'Connor 'The Hyksos Period in Egypt.' In Eliezer D. Oren (editor) (1997) *The Hyksos: New Historical and Archaeological Perspectives*, p. 72; H. S. Smith (1976) *The Fortress of Buhen: The Inscriptions*, Egypt Exploration Society: London.
[48] See Der Spiegel 'Was Moses Really Pharaoh?' In *World Press Review* (1997) Vol. 44 - Num. 12, p. 35.

remarked, is "an abridgement of a fuller" Egyptian name.[49] Again, I believe that this "fuller name" is that of Ahmose. Indeed, Freud expressed his surprise that James H. Breasted had not thought of Ahmose as a possible origin for the Hebrew name Moses among the list of Egyptian kings.[50]

In his archaeological search for the biblical Moses, David Rohl[51] turns to the early Christian historian Eusebius' work *Evangelicae Preparationis* (or Preparations for the Gospel). In that work, Eusebius refers to the writings of a Jewish historian by the name of Artapanus. Eusebius is only one of two sources[52] available for the analysis of Artapanus' scholarship since the latter's works haven't survived into our own times. During the late third century BCE, Artapanus compiled a history of the Israelite nation, presumably using authentic Egyptian records, which he entitled *Peri Ioudaion* (Concerning the Jews). Although rather convoluted, his detailed account on the origins of Moses reveals that Moses, as a Hebrew child, was adopted by the Egyptian princess Merris — who later married Pharaoh Khaneferre (Sobekhotep IV) of the 13th Dynasty. Having been educated as a royal prince of Egypt, Moses, as a grown man, helped his father Pharaoh Khaneferre to administer the land of Egypt. He showed great skill as an administrator, and became very well-liked and respected by the people of Egypt. Artapanus also tells us that "Prince Mousos" led a successful military campaign against the Nubians from the south — who had transgressed the borders of Egypt. In light of the body of evidence assessed thus far, it is evident that the Nubians would not have faced any serious opposition in Upper Egypt. Thus, Prince Mousos must have resided in Lower Egypt — where animosity towards the Nubians would have been at its highest. Interestingly enough, for the purposes of the new chronology, Artapanus recounts that during the time of Prince Mousos, "there were many kings of Egypt" and that Pharaoh Khaneferre (Sobekhotep IV) only ruled "over the regions beyond Memphis. Amazingly, this is *exactly* the political situation that the land of Egypt finds itself engulfed in during MBIIc! Hyksos kings attempted to rule Egypt from Tell el-Dab'a (Avaris) through a strategic coalition with the Nubians of the Kingdom of Kerma. All the while, the native Egyptian kings, as was the fashion during the Middle Kingdom, continued to administer Egypt under two contemporaneously ruling dynasties — one in Upper Egypt, the other in Lower Egypt. As Artapanus asserts, Pharaoh Khaneferre was a king of Lower Egypt (i.e. ruling over the regions beyond Memphis).

My identification of Artapanus' "Prince Mousos" (or the original Moses of the biblical narratives) with the Late Bronze Age Egyptian king Ahmose is a most vi-

---

[49] Sigmund Freud (1939) *Moses and Monotheism*. Trans. from the German by Katherine Jones. Hogarth Press/Institute of Psycho-Analysis: London, p. 13.
[50] Ibid, pp. 13-14.
[51] See David M. Rohl (1995) pp. 252-263.
[52] The other source being Clement's *Stromata*.

tal link for understanding the new chronology's transition from the Middle Kingdom to what I call the "Theban Renaissance" of the Late Bronze Age. The events in the life of Moses after his successful military campaign in Nubia are of main concern to us at present. The *Evangelicae Preparationis* transmits that Pharaoh Khaneferre was very jealous of his son Moses-Ahmose's triumph and attempted to have him killed. According to Artapanus, Moses-Ahmose was thus forced to flee to Arabia where he "lived with Raguel, the ruler of the region, whose daughter he married." Raguel, the King of Arabia, is then supposed to have ordered his Arab troops to plunder Egypt, but Moses is said to have been much concerned about the safety of his Hebrew brethren still in Egypt. Because of Moses' concerns, Raguel called off the retaliatory campaign. These particular details of Artapanus' story, claiming that Mousos journeyed to Arabia, and that Prince Mousos was racially related to them, are rather suspect since it is clear that the Hebrews were no longer dwelling in Egypt at that time. Prince Mousos, the son of Pharaoh Khaneferre, was definitely Egyptian. Whether he was Khaneferre's biological son, or a an adopted heir, as the Bible relates, is in itself a debatable issue — given the hostile relationships between them.

In any event, Prince Mousos eventually found it impossible to remain in Egypt — as he feared the wrath of Khaneferre. Confirming these events in Moses' life, which Artapanus relates, the Qur'an records:

> 19 A man from the farthest part of the city came running; said he: "O Moses, the nobles are taking counsel against thee, to kill thee; so go forth, verily I am one of those who give thee good advice."
> 20 So he went forth from it afraid and watchful; said he: "O my Lord, deliver me from the wrong-doing people."
> (Sura XXVIII: 19-20)

One important source however that contradicts Artapanus' theory as to where Moses-Ahmose fled to is the Jewish Talmud. According to the Talmud, Moses did not make his way to Arabia, but to Ethiopia. It is precisely through the Talmud that Egyptian-born historian Ahmed Osman, in his 1990 book *Moses: Pharaoh of Egypt (The Mystery of Akhenaten Resolved)*, theorizes that Moses found refuge in the court of the king of Ethiopia. While Osman and I disagree as to the general historical background of the Moses tradition, we do nonetheless agree on that particular point. Moses fled to Ethiopia — not Arabia. Jewish legend postulates that Moses became a favourite of King Kikanos and was appointed general of the Ethiopian army.[53] Upon the king's death, Moses succeeded King Kikanos, married his widow Adoniah, and ruled Ethiopia for forty years. Rabbinical texts hold that Moses refused to consummate the marriage with Queen Adoniah. At the end of the forty years, Adoniah, unable to bear the situation any longer, finally revealed to her people that Moses had never had sexual relations with her and had refused to honour the Ethiopian gods. Angered, Queen Adoniah told her people: "Why should this stranger continue to rule over you?" In the wake of these revelations and faced with the unhappiness of their queen, the Ethiopian populace grew very much perplexed — for they loved Moses but yet were uneasy with the situation. Ultimately, Moses-Ahmose chose to abdicate the Ethiopian throne and return to Egypt. Fearful of Pharaoh's reaction to his return to his estranged homeland, Moses decided to go live among the Medianites. According to Jewish legend, he met there his future wife Zipporah, at the same water well where Jacob had met Rachel. The ancient rabbis identified Zipporah, the daughter of the prophet Jethro, with the "Ethiopian woman" whom the Book of Numbers says Moses married. Ahmose-Moses did not have to wait too long before getting a chance to return to Egypt and actually ascend the throne meant for him. His long-awaited opportunity came with the sudden collapse of Egypt's Middle Kingdom — caused by the cycle-ending Venus catastrophe of 1,559 BCE at the end of Typhon Season #4.

The End of an Era: Venus, Ammisaduga and the Demise of the Xia Dynasty in China

> *" The people heard a great commotion in the heavens, and saw as if nine hundred of celestial mourners in the sky were deploring the end of the age."*
>
> - Jewish Aggada

The end of a World Age was, indeed, often perceived by the ancients as a time when a ruling dynasty or empire lost divine sanctioning to rule the regulated universe. Their failure to maintain the universal cosmic order resulted in their immediate overthrow, by a new ruler or dynasty, who allegedly represented a new and reinvigorated cycle. Given the extreme importance attached to these celestial signs, ancients astronomer-priests from around the globe, associated with both the existing powers and the potential usurpers, watched for any erratic movements of the planet Venus, in particular, during Typhon Seasons. At the time of Typhon Season #4, a very well-known case of such observations of the potentially erratic movement of the planet Venus was in ancient Sumeria. As Dr A. Sachs of Brown University observes:

---

[53] Louis Rapoport (1980) *The Lost Jews (Last of the Ethiopian Falashas)*, Stein and Day: New York, pp. 70-71.

CHAPTER IX: THE HYKSOS INVASION | 313

It is astonishing to find that somebody or other, for the whole of King Ammisaduqa's 21-year reign at so early a period, observed and recorded the Venus dates. Who was this observer? Did he have some reason to observe only Venus, or is it by chance that we do not have preserved his record of the dates of the other planets visible to the naked eye? Why just the reign of King Ammisaduqa? We have, alas, no answers to any of these questions either.[54]

The solution is, however, not far to be found — if it is recognized that Ammisaduga, as the New Chronology Table shows, reigned during the closing years of Typhon Season #4. His apparently eerie preoccupation with the planet Venus in particular comes from his people's vast experience with the devastating orbital errings of Venus at the conclusion of any given Typhon Season. Ishtar, the mythological incarnation of fiery Venus, came and destroyed everything in her wake. Velikovskian scholar Ev Cochrane, in his essay entitled 'Notes on Changes in the Cycle Times of Venus within Recorded History,'[55] citing several ancient sources, notes:

> As the various omens attached to the Venus-intervals confirm, the ancient Babylonians believed that Venus was capable of having an adverse influence on the affairs of men. The much older [than Ammisaduga's Venus observations] Sumerian hymns surrounding the planet-goddess Inanna presents a similar picture. There the planet-goddess was invoked as follows:

> "You make the heavens tremble and the earth quake. ... You flash like lightning over the highlands; you throw your fire-bands across the earth."[56]

Yet another hymn describes the planet-goddess as follows:

> Like a dragon you have deposited venom on the land. ... Oh foremost one, you are Inanna of heaven and earth! Raining the fanned fire down upon the nation ... Devastatrix of the lands ... At the sound of you the lands bow down.[57]

---

[54] A. Sachs 'Babylonian Observational Astronomy.' In The British Academy (1974) *The Place of Astronomy in the Ancient World (A Joint Symposium of the Royal Society and the British Academy)*, p. 44.
[55] See http://www.access.digex.net/~medev/vcycle
[56] D. Wolkstein & S. Kramer (1983) *Inanna*, p. 95.
[57] W. Hallo & J. Van Dijk (1968) *The Exaltation of Inanna*, pp. 15-17.

314 | PLANET OF THE GREEKS

In China, likewise, a changing of the Mandate of Heaven or World Age coincided with the cycle-ending Venus conflagration of 1,559 BCE. The termination of the Middle Bronze Age (of Syria-Palestine) witnesses the swift and bloody transition, in China, between the Xia and Shang Dynasties.

> Tradition relates that the last emperor of the first Dynasty *Kwei*, who had acceded to the throne in 1589, was corrupted by a woman; the infamous *Mei-hi*. The emperor succumbed to debauchery, and ordered the death of many innocent citizens. Warned that his actions jeopardized his throne, he replied: "I am to the Empire as the Sun is to the Heavens. When the Sun shall die, then shall I also be worried." In 1559, heading a coalition of peasants, T'ang, Lord of Shang, raised a rebellion and marched against the emperor. His army was comprised of many aborigines. It is especially to them that he addressed the following words before the battle of *Ming-t'iao*:
>
>> Gather around, multitude, and listen well as I speak. I, weak child, am not a rebel. The emperor, having committed many crimes, has caused the Heavens to call for his overthrow. You, multitudes, say that without pity for you, your prince forces you to neglect tending to your crops, for the simple pleasure of dethroning the emperor. This is not so. The emperor is guilty, and I must face him in battle lest I be myself punished by the Almighty up above. You shall help me, I your prince, to execute the sentencing of the Heavens. If you do it, I shall reward you largely, have no doubt. If you refuse to perform your duty, I shall exterminate you, as well as your families.
>
> *T'ang* was victorious. *Kwei* fled and died in exile. In 1558, *T'ang* assumed the throne, and founded the second Dynasty, which he called Shang; after the name of his principality.[58]

The culmination of the World Age, the Mandate of Aries was, therefore, interpreted by the ancient Chinese as a clear sign that a change of government was at hand. An old Chinese belief, carried through the ages, stated that "comets do foretell the death of princes."[59] In other words, some astronomical event always heralded the end of an empire. Elaborating on this concept, Needham writes:

---

[58] Père Léon S. J. Wieger (1924) *La Chine à travers les ages*, p. 16 (my translation).
[59] J. Needham 'Astronomy in Ancient and Medieval China.' In The British Academy (1974) *The Place of Astronomy in the Ancient World (A Joint Symposium of the Royal Society and the British Academy)*, p. 78.

CHAPTER IX: THE HYKSOS INVASION | 315

> It is interesting that inauspicious happenings were generally regarded as *chhien kao* or reprimands from heaven, and the emperor or some high official, very often the emperor himself, took the guilt upon him, prayed, fasted and promised to amend. Omens were regarded really as signs of bad government, and there would be trouble if things were not put in order ...[60]

Need we here be reminded of the similar woes which befell Pharaohs Akhtoy and Khnum-Khufu? As in the case of the last emperor of the great Xia Dynasty, Kwei, these earlier instances when a Pharaoh of Egypt endorsed personal blame for the collapse of the peaceful natural order. In all of the three cases, the cataclysm was caused by the drastic erring of the planet Venus from its set orbit, at the close of a Typhon Season. Ancient Chinese records postulate that during Emperor Kwei's reign, two bright stars battled in the firmament.

> At this time the two suns were seen to battle in the sky.
> The five planets were agitated by unusual movements.
> A part of Mount T'ai Chan fell down.[61]

Meanwhile, half-way across the globe in the ancient Near East and Africa, exactly similar destructions were taking place at Tell el-Dab'a (Avaris), at the close of the MBBIIc period, and further south in Nubia. According to Egyptologist Walter B. Emery, the Kerma forts of Nubia were *"overthrown"* and *" destroyed by fire"* at the end of the Middle Kingdom.[62]

---

[60] Ibid.
[61] L. Wieger (1922-23) *Textes historiques*, I, 50.
[62] See W. Y. Adams (1977) *Nubia: Corridor to Africa,* Princeton University Press: Princeton, NJ, pp. 189-190.

10

The Missing Link
(1,559 BCE to 1,330 BCE)

As the title of this chapter presages, the middle of the sixteenth century BCE marks an important turning point in the present historical reconstruction. Once radically reinterpreted, the pivotal historical developments from this unfortunately much-misunderstood period will, I believe, unlock several mysteries surrounding long lost chronicles of Antiquity. Obscure and discarded passages from the Manethonian texts, often summarily dismissed by ancient historians for their seeming incongruence, will suddenly be thrust back into the light of history. What's more, the legendary biblical kings, Saul, David and Solomon, will find a new place in the Late Bronze Age. The real identity of the Queen of Sheba, the magisterial Queen of the South who came to visit Solomon's court to test his wisdom, will likewise be investigated. Needless to say, such momentous shifts in the orthodox biblical time-line (which dates the United Monarchy to the Iron Age), are bound to have important repercussion for the overall chronology of the ancient world. Several questions naturally immediately arise: (1) How could a Solomonic empire, as described in the Bible, exist at a time when Egypt was supposedly a great power — wholly dominating Syria-Palestine? (2) Who was the pharaoh of Egypt during Solomon's reign? (3) Why doesn't the Bible mention him by name? Perhaps even more tantalising will be the quest, undertaken in the course of this and following chapters, to ascertain how and why the history of the vibrant Late Bronze Age has come down to us in such a confused state. For instance, why do so many of the Manethonian accounts, dealing with this particular period, find themselves in such conspicuous contradiction with the accepted chronology and of history Egypt? Evidently, Egyptologists have chosen to accept some accounts and altogether reject others. What was the criteria used to make these consequential choices? I will maintain that these decisions were based both on modern misconceptions and actual misleading reports from a number of ancient sources. The seeds of the powerful motivations which led later scribes or chroniclers, from ancient Egypt, Syria-Palestine and Greece, to intentionally misrepresent pivotal events from their respective histories, much to the detriment of modern scholarship, were largely sown during this very period of Antiquity. That is why the early Late Bronze Age is such a crucial period in the new chronology.

Was Ahmose Responsible for the Destruction of the Middle Bronze Age Canaanite Cities?

This missing link, heralded by the cycle-ending Venus shift of 1,559 BCE, began, as many other pivotal eras began and ended, in a great conflagration. The transition period from the Middle Bronze Age to the Late Bronze Age in Syria-Palestine has been the subject of incessant debate among historians and archaeologists. What has baffled these experts for years, is the widespread destruction of many important sites throughout the ancient Near East around the transition period between MBIIc and LBI, dated to around 1,550 BCE. Many of these towns were quickly rebuilt, while others laid utterly desolate for centuries. The most widely accepted version of events offered to explain such a disaster in the Syro-Palestinian horizon has been its attribution to an Egyptian military campaign.[1] In recent years, this assumption has come under attack by such scholars as Donald B. Redford and James K. Hoffmeier. Basing their arguments mainly on philological grounds (the interpretation of ancient texts), D. B. Redford and J. K. Hoffmeier claim that there's absolutely no evidence, from the extant pharaonic textual corpus, to justify an Egyptian military campaign responsible for such a fierce destruction of Syria-Palestine at the beginning of the Late Bronze Age. They instead believe in the concept of a long process (or *longue durée*) characterized by such factors as internal strife and socioeconomic problems.[2] Among those who favour the swift military raid model is William G. Dever, who claims that, regardless of what the Egyptian texts may say, the archaeological evidence proves, beyond the shadow of a doubt, that the destructions were severe and sudden. In response to his critics, Dever fires back: *"philology is not history."* With no conclusive answer in sight, the debate rages on.

The massive destruction of the Middle Bronze age Syro-Palestinian horizon is undeniable. Impressive fortified towns swiftly burned down and tumbled as if simultaneously hit by a massive plague of fiery devastation. Prof. William G. Dever describes the archaeological remains at the end of MBIIc as follows:

> My 1984 chart alone lists more than 20 Palestinian sites that attest destruction levels on the MBIIC/LBI horizon, and today there is considerable additional corroborative evidence. Taken together, these data demonstrate

---
[1] W. F. Albright (1949) *The Archaeology of Palestine,* p. 96; K. M. Kenyon (1973) 'Palestine in the Time of the Eighteenth Dynasty', *CAH* 2:1, pp. 555-556.
[2] Piotr Bienkowsky (1986) *Jericho in the Late Bronze Age,* Warminster, pp. 127-128.

CHAP. X: THE MISSING LINK | 319

data demonstrate beyond doubt that in the century between c.1550 and 1450 B.C. nearly every site of any importance was devastated by one and more destructions (Schechem has three). ... much of Palestine never recovered throughout the remainder of the Late Bronze Age.[3]

Similarly, James M. Weinstein[4] lists the following Palestinian sites which underwent heavy destruction in the mid-16th century BCE:

1. Tell el-Ajjûl (City III and Palace I)
2. Tell el-Far'ah (South)
3. Tell el-Hesi
4. Lachish
5. Tell Beit Mirsim
6. Jericho
7. Bethel
8. Schechem (Two closely-spaced ruins)
9. Tell el-Far'ah (North)
10. Beth-Shan (?)
11. Hazor
12. Dan
13. Tell en-Nagila
14. Malhata
15. Ashkelon
16. Beth-Zur
17. Beth-Shemesh
18. Gibeon (?)
19. Shiloh
20. Ta'anach

Another site that was severely destroyed at the end of the Middle Bronze Age is the town of Alalakh near Aleppo. Once again, this upheaval, dated between 1,560 and 1,550 BCE,[5] was attributed to enemy action. In this case, one candidate who has been suggested as a possible aggressor is the Hittite king Hattusilis I. However, scholars accept that King Hattusilis I ruled near the 1620s BCE.[6] Therefore, the military campaigns of Hattusilis I and the destruction of Alalakh in 1,559 BCE cannot be reconciled. It would instead seem that the city of Alalakh was destroyed during the time when, according to ancient historian Amélie Kuhrt, Zidanta I (1,560-1,550 BCE) ruled over the Hittite kingdom.[7] No such exploits have however been attributed to that king. Among the cities listed above, City IV at Jericho which, according to Kathleen Kenyon,[8] was destroyed around 1,550 BCE, is also believed by the latter to have been the target of both the fleeing Hyksos and their Egyptian pursuers — the army of Ahmose. Kenyon of course makes the assumption that the Hyksos were expelled from Avaris by Ahmose at the end of the Mid-

---

[3] William G. Dever (1990b) '"Hyksos", Egyptian Destructions, and the End of the Palestinian Middle Bronze Age', *Levant* 22, p. 76.
[4] James M. Weinstein (1981) 'The Egyptian Empire in Palestine: A Reassessment', *Bulletin of the American Schools of Oriental Research* 241, p. 2.
[5] Gates, Alalakh, 11, n.51; 27 – See Redford (1992) p.136.
[6] McMahon, Gregory (1989) 'The History of the Hittites', *Biblical Archaeologist* Vol. 52 - Nums. 2-3, p. 64. See also Amélie Kuhrt (1997 [1995]) *The Ancient Near East*, p. 230.
[7] A. Kuhrt (1997 [1995]) p. 230.
[8] Kathleen Kenyon (1957) *Digging Up Jericho*, Ernest Benn: London, p. 262.

dle Bronze Age. By associating the conflagration of City IV with the expulsion of the Hyksos from Egypt, she supposes that other Middle Bronze Age cities of Palestine, which met with the same fate as City IV, were destroyed by the alleged punitive expeditions of Ahmose. In his critique of Kenyon's conclusions however, archaeologist Bryant G. Wood remarks that Jericho's City IV was filled with food supplies at the time of its destruction — leading one to believe that its end came rather suddenly.[9] The reason why this information is meaningful is because the Egyptians always captured strongly fortified cities by means of a siege. To illustrate this argument, Wood points to the siege of Sahuren, which lasted for three years,[10] and the siege of Megiddo — which itself lasted for seven months.[11] Clearly, if the population of Jericho had been involved in such a confrontation with Ahmose, food supplies would not have been found in such abundance. It is also true, as Wood further comments, that the Egyptians customarily attacked their enemies just before harvest time — when food supplies would be at their lowest. Moreover, Redford and Hoffmeier question the ability of the Egyptian army of that time to capture and destroy major fortifications of Middle Bronze Age Palestine.[12] Hence, if we lack both means and motive, why do so many scholars[13] still continue to hold on to the Egyptian military raid model?

The reason is that some explanation has to be offered to account for such calamitous and widespread destruction all over Syria-Palestine. Professional archaeologists are accustomed to arbitrarily attribute massive conflagrations at the end of a given settlement strata to enemy action — even when they are unable to positively identify the ethnic origins or identity of these invading armies. In the case of the conflagrations which befell Syria-Palestine at the close of the Middle Bronze Age, real evidence for such a widespread Egyptian military campaign is particularly difficult to establish. The scholarly wars between philology and archaeology have engendered this present stalemate because

---

[9] Bryant G. Wood (1990a) 'Did the Israelites Conquer Jericho? (A New Look at the Archaeological Evidence', *Biblical Archaeology Review* Vol. 16 - Num. 5, p. 51.
[10] James B. Pritchard (editor) (1955) *ANET*, p. 233.
[11] Ibid, p. 238.
[12] James K. Hoffmeier (1989) 'Reconsidering Egypt's Part in the Termination of the Middle Bronze Age in Palestine', *Levant* 21, pp. 181-93.
[13] See James Weinstein (1991) 'Egypt and the Middle Bronze IIC/Late Bronze IA Transition in Palestine', *Levant* 23, pp. 105-115.

the lack of proof for an Egyptian invasion at the onset of LBI[14] is accompanied by overwhelming evidence of devastation at the close of MBIIc Syria-Palestine.

My own take on this rather pointless debate is that both camps are essentially correct. Much ink is currently being wasted on attempting to discredit perfectly viable sets of evidence. The solution that will unravel the jigsaw puzzle is to be found in a third heretofore unknown element: the planet Venus. As Redford and Hoffmeier rightly contend, Pharaoh Ahmose did not undertake a hugely scaled punitive military expedition into Canaan at the beginning of the Late Bronze Age. In fact, I would even go so far as saying that Ahmose did not even drive out the Hyksos out of the Egyptian Delta at the beginning of LBI. On the other hand, the excavation reports of Dever and Weinstein leave very little room to doubt the obvious fact that all the major fortified towns in Canaan underwent cataclysmic obliteration from *some* common cause from without at the close MBIIc. Again, this external element of destruction was the planet Venus — which, in the year 1,559 BCE, closed Typhon Season #4 with a devastating scorching of the earth's surface. The shifting in the earth's polar axis resulted in the destruction on the many fortified Middle Bronze Age Syro-Palestinian sites. These conflagration were not caused by an invading Egyptian army. So if the ancient Egyptians were *not* responsible for the demise of the MBIIc sites, and the Hyksos were *not* driven out of Avaris during the nascent Late Bronze Age, then the history of the ancient world has to be radically altered.

The Road Towards Peaceful Co-existence

While having attempted to demonstrate, in the New Chronology Table, that the 14th and 15th Dynasties were contemporaneous with the latter portion of the 13th Dynasty, one important point that attentive readers have surely observed is that I've, quite inexplicably, leapfrogged from the end of the 13th Dynasty, right to the reign of Ahmose — whom Egyptologists place in the 18th Dynasty. What happened to the two remaining dynasties which make up the traditional Second Intermediate Period? That is the 16th and 17th Dynasties? These last two dynasties are traditionally known to have marked the end of Hyksos rule in Egypt. As we have just seen, Pharaoh Ahmose is widely believed to have launched military raids

---

[14] See John J. Bimson & David Livingston (1987) 'Redating the Exodus', *Biblical Archaeology Review* Vol. 13 - Num. 5, p. 51. Bimson and Livingston believe that MBII did not end in the middle of the sixteenth century BCE, but in *c*.1,420 BCE. With this new lowered date in hand, they attempt to link the demise of Jericho with the biblical account of its destruction in the hands of Joshua. Serious problems are encountered, however, with such a late date for the end of the Middle Bronze Age — see Baruch Halpern (1987) 'Radical Exodus Redating Fatally Flawed', *Biblical Archaeology Review* Vol. 13 - Num. 6, pp. 56-61.

against the Hyksos rulers in Avaris at the end of the 17th Dynasty — thereby ushering in the New Kingdom. Where is that all-important 17th Dynasty in my revised model? How is one to account for the war of liberation undertaken by the Egyptians to free themselves form the oppressive yoke of the Hyksos?

Breaking with traditional scholarship, I hereby put forth the rabid thesis that the termination of the Middle Bronze Age did not mark the end of Hyksos rule in Egypt. Far from it actually. While losing much of their control over most of Middle Egypt, the Amalekite (or Hyksos) shepherd-kings in the land of Goshen retained their hold over Avaris throughout the LBI period and beyond! Egypt would not be totally free of the Hyksos spectre until well into the LBII period (in *c.*1,380 BCE). And still, the Egyptians would not have seen the end of them yet; even after a relatively short respite during the latter part of LB II and most of LBIII. As modern historians contend, the definite end of the Hyksos dominion over the Two Lands would indeed come at the end of the 17th Dynasty. But, according to the new chronology, the 17th Dynasty did not actually come along until well into LBIII — not the end of the Middle Bronze Age as commonly supposed. Indeed, what I will be intending to prove is that both the 16th and 17th Dynasties belong to the LBIII period, and that the final end of Hyksos influence over Egypt came in, or around, the year 1,117 BCE. Almost 450 years after Pharaoh Ahmose came to power in Egypt at the beginning of the Late Bronze Age.

Having abdicated the Ethiopian throne, Pharaoh Ahmose (son of Sobekhotep IV), returned to Egypt. Once there, most probably taking advantage of the state of utter chaos which had befallen his homeland as a result of the Venus-induced pole shift of 1,559 BCE, he founded the new 14th Dynasty. Much as was the case in China, Ahmose's new regime saw itself as a righteous administration coming along to replace an outdated Middle Kingdom which had lost its mandate to regulate the order of nature (Ma'at). King Ahmose does not appear to have held any particularly strong rancour against his father's dynasty since he allowed the 13th Dynasty to continue ruling Lower Egypt while his own dynasty retained suzerainty over Upper Egypt. In actuality, Ahmose was continuing the well-established practice of the Middle Kingdom to have different lines of rulers governing Upper and Lower Egypt. With regard to the king-shepherds ruling in Avaris, Pharaoh Ahmose actually adopted a policy of "Peaceful Coexistence" with the Hyksos-Amalekites. He never attempted to chase them out of the Egyptian Delta. In effect, the start of the Late Bronze Age never witnessed the kind of nationalistic warfare in Egypt that most historians proclaim.

The Hyksos-Amalekite royal line did not come to an abrupt end at the close of MBIIc; it was only getting started. Having lost their MBIIc sphere of influence south of Avaris with the accession of King Ahmose in Thebes, the Hyksos turned their attention to the Aegean. With their stepped-up colonizing drive in the Aegean,

CHAP. X: THE MISSING LINK | 323

Avaris continued to prosper and boasted many Minoan artisans. Commenting on his excavation campaigns at MBIIc-LBI Avaris, Prof. Manfred Bietak wrote:

> Dating from two hundred years after the palace of the early 13th Dynasty, there is evidence of further intensive contact between Egypt and the Minoan world, from the time of the late Hyksos period and the early 18th Dynasty. Within the western edge of the settlement of Tell el-Dab'a, which is now identified with the capital of the Hyksos, Avaris, and Piramesse, excavations at 'Ezbet Helmi have revealed an enormous compound, which should be identified as the citadel of Avaris during the late Hyksos period.[15]

Bietak also presumes that there "is no proof for any [Egypto-Minoan] contact in between"[16] the 13th and 18th Dynasties. In the traditional chronology, that hiatus would fall within the Second Intermediate Period. The second period of intense Egypto-Minoan contact, according to Bietak, would then come at the close of the SIP (from the late-17th to early-18th Dynasties). The new palace from Area H/I exhibits an impressive array of Minoan frescoes clearly analogous to the earlier Minoan material-remains uncovered in the 13th Dynasty settlement. What could have been the cause for the 200-year-long break in relations? History has no answer. Or is that historians have no answer? The new "palatial installations, forming a new royal citadel"[17] at Tell el-Dab'a (Area H/I-IV) has been dated to the 18th Dynasty because of extant contemporary sherds dating from the reigns of Kings Ahmose to Amenhotep II. Indeed, in a more recent paper, Bietak has revised his earlier theory, as quoted above, that the H/1 stratum dates to the so-called "Late Hyksos" period. In his words:

> Although originally we had thought that the platform in Area H/1 was Late Hyksos in date, since scarabs bearing the names of kings from Ahmose to Amenhotep II were deposited within the debris of the Eighteenth Dynasty settlement that succeeded it, the date of the platform now appears to be in the early Eighteenth Dynasty.[18]

---

[15] Manfred Bietak 'Connections Between Egypt and the Minoan World: New Results from Tell el-Dab'a/Avaris.' In W. Vivian Davies (editor) (1995) *Egypt, the Aegean and the Levant (Interconnections in the Second Millennium BC)*, p. 20.
[16] Ibid, p. 19.
[17] Manfred Bietak (1996) *Avaris: The Capital of the Hyksos (Recent Excavations at Tell el-Dab'a)'*, British Museum Press: London, p. 67.
[18] Manfred Bietak 'The Center of Hyksos Rule: Avaris (Tell el-Dab'a).' In Eliezer D. Oren (editor) (1997) *The Hyksos: New Historical and Archaeological Perspectives*, p. 117.

Within the context of the new chronology, we find that the kings of the early 18th Dynasty, whose sherds have been unearthed at Tell el-Dab'a's platform H/I, actually belong to the new 14th Dynasty of the Theban Renaissance. Under these new circumstances, the unexplained hiatus disappears! The Theban Renaissance *immediately* followed the end of the 13th Dynasty. The 18th Dynasty Egyptian King Ahmose, whom Prof. Bietak speaks of, did not come along until over 420 years after the beginning the *earlier* 14th Dynasty Pharaoh Ahmose's reign — whose scarabs have been unearthed at Avaris' Area H/1. Hence, Dr Bietak is the unwitting victim of a case of mistaken identity.[19] The continued, and seemingly even intensifying, prominence of the Amalekite-Hyksos town of Avaris during LBI further proves that Pharaoh Ahmose did not expel the Hyksos at the end of the Middle Bronze Age.

My use of the term "Theban Renaissance" as opposed to the traditionally utilized term "New Kingdom" to designate the period heralding the Late Bronze Age in Egypt, is precipitated by the fact that King Ahmose (1) did not institute a unified Egyptian kingdom at the onset of LBI, and (2) because ancient Thebes once again became the official capital of the Two Lands. The division of Egypt between the Theban new 14th Dynasty and the Sobek-named Lower Egyptian rulers would last throughout the LBI period. For instance, while King Amenhotep I, Ahmose's successor, undertook numerous building activities in Upper Egypt — namely in Elephantine, Kom Ombo and Abydos, there is little or no evidence to suggest that he, or his father Ahmose for that matter, ever built anything in Lower Egypt.[20]

A contemporary of both Ahmose and Amenhotep I was the Amalekite-Hyksos king Apophis. The latter did not wield nearly as much power over the dynastic Egyptians as his MBIIc Hyksos predecessors had. The nature of the relationship between the Egyptians and the Amalekites in the Northernlands had considerably changed with Ahmose's accession to the throne. The Nubian kingdom of Kerma had been utterly decimated. The Hyksos-Amalekite rulers no longer had them as key allies on Egypt's southern border. Having lost the control of Upper Egypt, the Hyksos refrained from extending their influence to the south of Tell el-Dab'a. So the Hyksos king under whom Amalekite military strategy shifted to compose with the new political realities of the early Late Bronze Age was King Apophis. While the strain of his city-state's dealings with the dynastic Egyptians were easing at the onset of LBI, King Apophis' foreign relations with the new kingdom of Israel was only

---

[19] This "double identity" will be further explored in Chapter 12 when we shall discover that the Pharaoh Ahmose, who founded the 18th Dynasty, came to rule over 400 years after the King Ahmose who reigned at the beginning of the Late Bronze Age. The traditional history of Egypt is therefore out of step by over four hundred years.

[20] Nicholas Grimal (1992) *A History of Ancient Egypt*. Trans. by Ian Shaw. Blackwell: Oxford, U.K., p. 206.

going from bad to worse. The nature of this tense relationship is reflected in the biblical texts through the narratives involving the Amalekite king Agag (or Agog) — who is here identified with King Apophis. This equation had been earlier made by Immanuel Velikovsky, who observed:

> The early Hebrew written signs as they are preserved on the stele of Mesha show a striking resemblance between the letters g (*gimel*) and p (*pei*). No other two letters are so much alike in shape as these: each is an oblique line connected to a shorter, more oblique line, and is similar to the written number 7; the size of the angle between the two oblique lines constitutes the only difference. Nevertheless, it seems that not the Hebrew reading rather the Egyptian must be corrected...[21]

Therefore, it will be assumed throughout the next few chapters that Apophis, Apap, Agag and Agog can all be used interchangeably. They're all variations of the same name. This Hyksos ruler's choice of that particular Egyptian god's name as the root of his throne name was not without meaning. Unlike Seth, the serpent Apophis wasn't a full-fledged god; but was nonetheless likened to Seth in the sense that he was an ever-present threat to the cosmic order (Ma'at). He relentlessly pursued the sun-god Re during his daily circuit through the sky. As the enemy of the sun-god, Apophis was seen as representing both darkness and chaos. Perhaps ironically, Seth was an enemy of Apophis — as the former periodically came to the defence of Re, as Apophis attacked. Since the pharaoh of Egypt is the incarnation of Re on earth, the enemies of Re, and hence of Pharaoh, were identified with Apophis. As intruders in the land of Egypt, the Hyksos, despite their more peaceful relations with the native Egyptians, remained an enemy of the sun-god Re. For as Queen Hatchepsut would later famously quip, "they ruled without Re, and he acted not by divine command." The new Hyksos king, Apophis, also saw in the cycle-ending Venusian catastrophe of 1,559 BCE a manifestation of Apophis' power.

Before going on to explore the details of the hostile relationship between the Hyksos and the Israelites during LBI, we will first look for evidence supporting my Peaceful Coexistence theory between the dynastic Egyptians and the Hyksos at that same time. As an initial piece of evidence, the New York Metropolitan Museum holds a scarab inscribed with the name of the Hyksos king Apap (Apophis) which was found in the tomb of Amenhotep I.[22] The scarab in question was part of an inscribed alabaster vase, which also bore the name of King Apophi's daughter, "Herit." Based on the fact that Herit was seemingly married to a contemporary Theban ruler, American Egyptologist W. C. Hayes rightly conjectured

---

[21] Immanuel Velikovsky (1952) *Ages in Chaos*, Doubleday: Garden City, NY, p. 72.
[22] William C. Hayes (1990 [1959]) *The Scepter of Egypt*, Vol. II: pp. 6-7.

that the two peoples must have been in good terms at this time. Similarly, Egyptologist Torgny Säve-Söderbergh relates that:

> ... the fact that an object inscribed with the name of a Hyksos, whom the Egyptians are supposed always to have hated bitterly, was found in the tomb of an Egyptian king may indicate that the earlier kings of the Eighteenth Dynasty had a more unbiased opinion of the Hyksos than that which reflected in the later sources.[23]

So if Ahmose maintained such close relations with King Agag, how could that be reconciled with the traditional view that Pharaoh Ahmose had eradicated all memory of the Hyksos occupation? The truth is that, as ancient historians relate, the native Egyptian war of liberation was waged by the kings of the early 18th Dynasty. The harshest episode of Hyksos rule took place during the time of the 17th Dynasty. After such atrocities, it would have been highly unlikely that any pharaoh of the 18th Dynasty could have married the daughter of a Hyksos ruler. Pharaoh Ahmose's assaults against the Hyksos capital of Avaris belong to the early Iron Age. At this point in the revised chronology, we find that the Late Bronze Age opens with the 14th Dynasty — not the 18th Dynasty. The confusing thing is that both dynasties were founded by a Theban king named Ahmose. The King Ahmose of the early Late Bronze Age had been the son of Pharaoh Sobekhotep IV of the 13th Dynasty. When he inherited the Egyptian crown, he established himself in Upper Egypt while allowing his deceased father's dynasty to continue ruling in Lower Egypt. There was probably no question however that the main seat of power was in Thebes. With the demise of the Kerma kingdom in Nubia, Ahmose no longer needed to fear the Hyksos as much. Though the native Egyptians could easily crush any potential Hyksos-Amalekite invasion from Avaris given their strong position in Upper Egypt, they still were not nearly strong enough to drive the Hyksos-Amalekites out of Tell el-Dab'a. The result was a stalemate which culminated into a necessary alliance, or principle of non-aggression. Pharaoh Ahmose married Herit, the daughter of the Hyksos king Apophis, in order to seal this amiable arrangement. Egypt was divided, but in peace.

The Osirid Statues of Late Bronze Age Egypt and the

Cult of Nebhepetre-Mentuhotep as Divine Ancestor

The Theban kings of new 14th Dynasty went out of their way to portray themselves as direct descendants of the illustrious Theban rulers of the 11th Dynasty —

---

[23] Torgny Säve-Söderbergh (1951) 'The Hyksos Rule in Egypt', *Journal of Egyptian Archaeology* 37, p. 69.

CHAP. X: THE MISSING LINK | 327

particularly Mentuhotep-Nebhepetre. This celebrated ancestor who reunified the Two Lands after over a century of foreign occupation, was, throughout the new 14th Dynasty, elevated to divine status. Indeed, during the Theban Renaissance, King Mentuhotep-Nebhepetre was deified in the form of "Osirid" cult statues. The Osirid statue (see Fig. 15-A) was actually first introduced by Mentuhotep-Nebhepetre himself during the 11th Dynasty. One such statue erected during the latter's own time was discovered by the French excavator Georges Legrain (1865-1917) at Karnak in 1905. We may be certain of its antiquity because of restoration cartouches found on it belonging to Sesostris II, Sesostris III, and Sobekhotep III. The actual "cult" of Mentuhotep-Nebhepetre would not however take form until the Late Bronze Age with the advent of the new 14th Dynasty. This new state of affairs is clearly and forcefully exhibited in numerous LBI-II documents from Egypt, as well as in religious practices of the time. In a stela from the British Museum (347/690), for instance, both Kings Amenhotep I and Mentuhotep-Nebhepetre are deified in the form of Osiris. The fact that Amenhotep I did not include his father Ahmose in the stela has led some scholars to speculate that Pharaoh Mentuhotep-Nebhepetre received the honour because the latter was perceived as a model ancestor.[24] A similar Late Bronze Age representation of Tuthmosis I and Mentuhotep-Nebhepetre also exists.[25] Egyptologist Édouard Naville's excavations at Deir el-Bahari have, quite interestingly, demonstrated that King Amenhotep I was the first pharaoh to build an edifice there since the reign of Mentuhotep-Nebhepetre.[26] It is in fact from the reign of Pharaoh Amenhotep I that the colossal Osirid statues depicted on the British Museum stela first began to appear. Furthermore, statues of Pharaoh Amenhotep I found by Naville at Deir el-Bahari (Cairo Museum no. 42.099 and Köfler-Truniger inv. a 105) are clearly African in appearance, and show marked resemblance to those of Mentuhotep-Nebhepetre. The attempt at reproduction in style is obvious. There appears to be no doubt that the new 14th Dynasty rulers were consciously attempting to revive the artistic canons of the latter part of the 11th Dynasty.

This revival in 11th Dynasty art and religious practices at the beginning of the Theban Renaissance was enacted in honour of King Ahmose's heroic retaking of the Theban capital from foreign tutelage. His exploits were likened to the reunification of the Two Lands by the Theban king Mentuhotep-Nebhepetre. Also, the Theban Renaissance reaffirmed the African attributes of pharaonic culture after a long period of Asiatic near-domination. Despite the Hyksos invasion of the Delta

---

[24] Christian Leblanc (1982) 'Le culte rendu aux colosses «Osiriaques» durant le Nouvel Empire', *Bulletin de l'Institut Français d'Archéologie Orientale* 82, p. 299.
[25] G. Davies, *Two Ramesside Tombs*, Pl. 13; C. Leblanc (1982) p. 311.
[26] Roland Tefnin (1968-1972) 'Contribution à l'iconographie d'Aménophis I: La statuette 42.099 du Musée du Caire', *Annuaire de l'Institut de Philologie et d'Histoire Orientales et Slaves* 20, pp. 433-434.

region, and their tutelage over Upper Egypt, the fundamental African roots of pharaonic culture continued to thrive throughout the Middle Kingdom. The Osirid statues introduced by Pharaoh Mentuhotep-Nebhepetre during the 11th Dynasty continued to be employed during the Hyksos occupation. But ancient historians have, once again, inserted a fictitious Dark Age in ancient Egyptian artistic styles. Egyptologists contend that Osirid statues were in use throughout the Middle Kingdom but were altogether abandoned during the so-called Second Intermediate Period — when the Hyksos-Amalekites invaded the eastern Delta. The Osirid colossi were then supposed to have suddenly reappeared with the New Kingdom's 18th Dynasty. Finally, Egyptologists believe that they abruptly went completely out of use at the end of the standard 20th Dynasty (late new 15th Dynasty).[27] In the new chronology, such a strange hiatus in artistic style is eliminated because we can trace a continuous tradition from the beginning of the Middle Kingdom, through the Theban Renaissance, and up until the end of the new 15th Dynasty. The New Chronology Table demonstrates that the 16th and 17th Dynasties which traditionally make up much of the Second Intermediate Period were ruled by Asiatic kings. Likewise, the Hyksos rulers listed in the conventional 15th Dynasty, under whom no Osirid statues were erected, reigned contemporaneously with the 16th and 17th Dynasties during the LBIII period. The Osirid statues were, for the last time, being used in Upper Egypt during that time. Since the Asiatic pharaohs further north were not erecting such statues, it can be conjectured that Osirid statues were indicative of the fundamentally African origins of the pharaohs who did portray themselves in that manner. Indeed, it is evident that the pharaohs of the 11th, 12th, 13th, new 14th and 15th Dynasties were all African rulers whose traditions had been shaped by Pharaoh Mentuhotep-Nebhepetre' reunification of Egypt out of Ethiopia during the MBIIa period.

It was particularly during the Theban Renaissance that the memory of Mentuhotep-Nebhepetre was most revered — with the exaltation of the Theban god Amun as Egypt's chief deity. During the LBII period, Queen Hatchepsut of the new 14th Dynasty built her own temple on the same site where Kings Mentuhotep-Nebhepetre and Amenhotep I had erected their buildings, at Deir el-Bahari. Once again, Pharaoh Mentuhotep-Nebhepetre's central position as a much-venerated deity, alongside the Theban god Amun, is made amply evident. Quoting Egyptologist Aidan Dodson:

> The reign of Hatshepsut has long been recognized as a period of particularly rich and varied foundation deposits, most notably those from the Great Temple at Deir el-Bahari. Amongst their contents were a few large calcite 'clamshells', inscribed with dedications to Amun ...

---

[27] Christian Leblanc (1982) p. 299.

Fig. 10a: Osirid statues from the Ramesseum.
After Perrot & Chipiez (1882).

Fig. 10b: The archangel Michael fighting the dragon
(from the Apocalypse by Dürer).

Superficially similar to the latter is a piece in Liverpool Museum [M 11929]... [The piece comprises of] a dedication whose formula essentially follows that found on the aforementioned pieces from Deir el-Bahari, but instead of Amun, the beneficiary of the queen's generosity is the Eleventh Dynasty king, Mentuhotpe II, owner of the adjacent temple.[28]

Dodson then goes on to comment that the *"piece is intriguing in that it is the first hint that Hatshepsut's relationship with her venerable predecessor was any more than that of neighbour and deriver of architectural inspiration."*[29] Egyptologists still debate over what that elusive relationship between Pharaoh Mentuhotep-Nebhepetre and Queen Hatchepsut actually was. The puzzling thing is that, in the Liverpool document, Queen Hatchepsut refers to the 11th Dynasty king as "her father." We know for sure that Mentuhotep-Nebhepetre couldn't possibly have been Hatchepsut's biological father. Therefore an alternative explanation has to be found. Moreover, several Osirid representations of Queen Hatchepsut can be found in her "temple of millions of years" at Deir el-Bahari. Additionally, a giant Osirid colossi found near the temple of Luxor, usurped by Ramses II, is believed to have originally belonged to Queen Hatchepsut.[30] It is obvious that the female pharaoh, like her LBI predecessors, actively sought to revive the legacy of the great 11th Dynasty Theban liberator. Like the latter's glorious dynasty, the new 14th Dynasty had emerged from Ethiopia to reclaim the Two Lands from Asiatic control. Thanks to these periodic "reinvigorations" of pharaonic culture from its native African sources, Khemetic tradition would continue to thrive in Egypt.

The Kingdom of Meroë: The Lion-God Apedemak and the Mandate of Leo

According to the Talmud, the walls of the Ethiopian kingdom which Ahmose-Moses came to rule over, had been heavily strengthened by a certain Bi'lam — one of Pharaoh's advisors (presumably Sobekhotep IV) who had been appointed by the king of Ethiopia as his interim representative during an internal rebellion in Nubia. After having successfully quelled the rebellion against the Ethiopian king, Bi'lam erected huge fortresses and proceeded to dig ditches and pits around the city — which I theorize was the Ethiopian town of Meroë. A very consequential bit of detail in the

---

[28] Aidan Dodson (1989) 'BRIEF COMMUNICATIONS: Hatshepsut and "her father" Mentuhotpe II', *Journal of Egyptian Archaeology* 75, pp. 224-225.
[29] Ibid, p. 226.
[30] Christian Leblanc (1982) pp. 301-302.

Talmudic account of Bi'lam's exploits is that the latter is said to have "deserted" the court of Pharaoh in Egypt in order to come to the aid of the king of Ethiopia — whom he later betrayed to usurp his throne. The reason why this information is so significant is because it mirrors the political situation between Egypt and Nubia during the Late Middle Kingdom in the New Chronology. We indeed recall that Nubiologist David O'Connor, in the previous chapter, spoke of such rampant defections of Egyptian soldiers and officials to the Nubian side during MBIIc. Clearly, those events must have taken place during the reign of Sobekhotep IV. Upon usurping the Ethiopian throne, Bi'lam immediately became engaged in a war, of 9 years in duration, against the embittered deposed king of Ethiopia — who had by then enlisted the services of Ahmose-Moses to his side against Bi'lam.

This kingdom of Ethiopia which Ahmose-Moses ruled over at the end of the MBIIc period was, in my opinion, the early kingdom of Meroë. Separated from the Nubians dwelling between the First and the Third Cataracts, these Ethiopians whom King Ahmose-Moses lived amongst after fleeing his father's court in Egypt had been the direct descendants of the classic Ptolemaic rulers whom Pharaoh Khnum-Khufu had expelled from Egypt at the onset of Typhon Season #2. The deposed Khemetic monarchy, and its priesthood, fled into forced exile south of the Fourth Cataract. There, what would later be known as the Meroitic kingdom evolved. It was at the beginning of the Late Bronze Age that the Meroitic kingdom, with a stable line of royal successors, emerged. Perhaps not coincidentally, Meroë's rise corresponded with the advent of the Theban Renaissance in Egypt. After having abdicated the Ethiopian throne, Ahmose returned to Egypt to inaugurate the Theban Renaissance. Much rejuvenated by Ahmose's brief reign, his Ethiopian successors instituted the Meroitic kingdom under the leonine deity Apedemak. The Meroitic script came into usage and an entire civilization blossomed.

To the vast majority of Nubiologists, my theory would be considered plain heresy. Indeed, the Meroitic kingdom, according to received wisdom, is not supposed to have flourished until the third century BCE! Yet, I hereby maintain that the first Meroitic king, Amanitekha, whose reign is conventionally believed to have fallen between 250 BCE and 235 BCE, was a contemporary of Pharaoh Ahmose, founder of the Theban Renaissance. But how, if I am correct, could the standard Nubian chronology be off by over a thousand years? Furthermore, how could generations of scholars have been so misled? One of the principal arguments Nubiologists would use to dismiss my theory is that the Meroitic culture exhibits very conspicuous Ptolemaic influences. Therefore, ancient historians, using the Greek Ptolemaic dynasty of Hellenistic times as a reference point, conclude that the Meroitic kingdom must necessarily postdate Alexander the Great. But in the new chronology, we know that a considerably more ancient Ptolemaic dynasty existed in Khemet during the Early Bronze II period. Again, I contend that the Meroitic

Fig. 10c: The lion-god Apademak of Meroë.

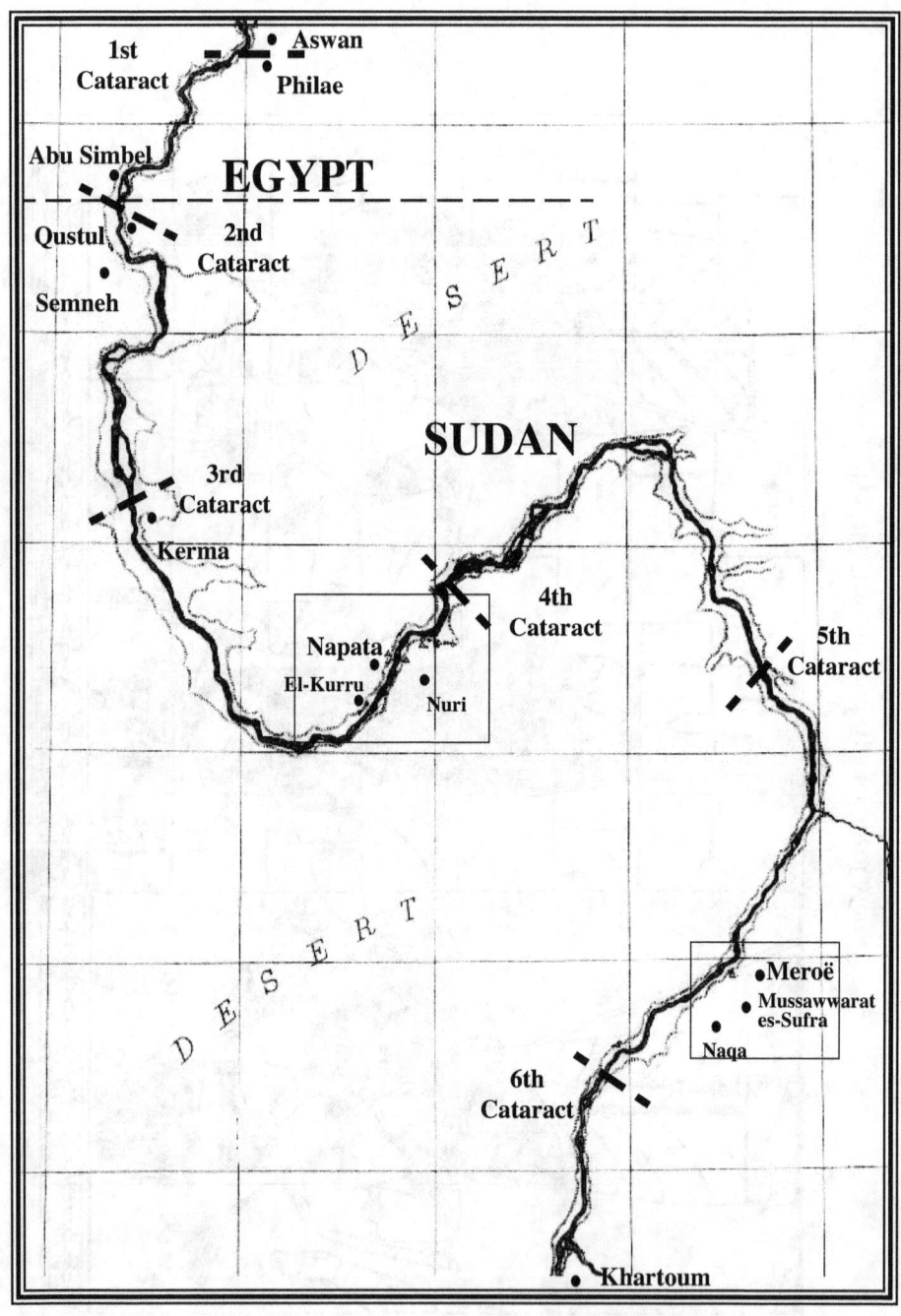

Fig. 10d: Map of Upper Egypt and Nubia (from Aswan to Khartoum).

kingdom which emerged during LBI was a remnant of the New Horus Period's Ptolemaic age. Quite literally turning the traditional Ethiopian chronology upside down, I will endeavour to demonstrate that the Meroitic culture actually *preceded* both the Napatan culture and the Ethiopian conventional 25th Dynasty in Egypt. But according to the accepted history of the ancient world, pharaonic culture in Ethiopia came about as a result of Egyptian colonization during the New Kingdom. Pharaoh Ahmose set up a viceregal administration (viceroys) in the land of Kush early on in the Late Bronze Age; and by the close of the so-called Third Intermediate Period, the colonized Nubians had become thoroughly Egyptianized — to the point of actually ruling Egypt itself, as the conventional 25th Dynasty, from Napata in the eighth century BCE. After the Napatans were defeated by the Macedonian standard 26th Dynasty, the Ethiopians, it is thought, moved their burial ground from El Kurru to Nuri (see Fig. 10d). Then, in c.295 BCE, the capital was permanently moved from Napata to Meroë — where it is believed that Meroitic culture, under Graeco-Roman influence, evolved until the fourth century of the common era. In this scenario, pharaonic Ethiopia is an offshoot or derivative of dynastic Egypt.

That accepted interpretation of ancient African history is however seriously flawed. In the new history I propose, the Egyptian viceregal administration was not set up in Nubia until the nascent Iron Age. As I have already outlined, Pharaoh Ahmose of the New Kingdom ascended the Egyptian throne in the second half of the twelfth century BCE. That is when the viceregal administration was set up in the land of Kush. Even then, there is no convincing evidence that dynastic Egypt's imperial influence spread below the Fourth Cataract — i.e. further than Napata. The punitive raids of the New Kingdom pharaohs were geared toward subduing the C-Group Asiatic Nubians dwelling between the First and the Fourth Cataracts. These rebellious Kushites had *never* been Egyptianized to the point of becoming pharaohs of Egypt. The C-Group Asiatic Nubians remained, throughout their history, a peripheral threat to the stability of the dynastic Egyptian state. It is very difficult to imagine how the native Egyptians could have welcomed Kushite pharaohs to Thebes in the eighth century BCE. In the new chronology, the Kushites were still being harshly colonized by the dynastic Egyptians at the time when the Ethiopian king Kashta acceded to the Egyptian throne in the middle of the eighth century BCE. This could only mean that Pharaoh Kashta's dynasty *did not* descend from the C-Group Nubian chieftains from the lands of Wawat and Kush. As the kings of Napata had themselves claimed, they were the descendants of ancient kings. Indeed, the Ethiopian pharaohs of the conventional 25th Dynasty were the last among a long line of independent Napatan and Meroitic rulers. The Nubians of Wawat and Kush (Lower and Upper Nubia), having immigrated into Nubia in the EBIV period from Syria-Palestine, were neither ethnically or culturally related to either the Napatans or the rulers of Meroë. The Napatans, as we'll see in the next chapter, descended from the A-Group Nubians of Ta-Seti. The first Napatan ruler, King Atlanarsa (whose reign is traditionally dated to between 653 BCE and 643 BCE), emerged, according to the new chronology, in the Late Bronze III period (in 1,187 BCE). So Atlanarsa preceded King Kashta at Napata by some 440 years — instead of succeeding the latter by about 90 years as conventional scholars would have it. For their part, I argue that the rulers of Meroë descended from the classic Ptolemaic monarchs of Khemet from the New Horus Period. They emerged as a fully-formed pharaonic state at the beginning of the Late Bronze Age. All this means that, from the Iron I to Iron IIb periods, the pharaohs of Napata and Meroë reigned contemporaneously in relative harmony. Hence, when the Ethiopian standard 25th Dynasty, headed by Pharaoh Kashta, emerged to rule Egypt at the end of Iron IIb, the royal line of Meroitic rulers buried at Meroë's North Cemetery had come to an end. Pharaoh Kashta's dynasty (which lasted from 747 BCE to 664 BCE) represented the very last set of Napatan monarchs to be buried at the royal cemeteries of El Kurru and Nuri.

By removing the influence of the dynastic Egyptian viceregal administration in Nubia as the fundamental force behind the ascension of the Napatan and Meroitic kingdoms, the entire structure of modern Nubiology falls apart. Once again, the accepted chronology of ancient Egypt is largely to blame. The great imperial age of the New Kingdom never greeted the end of the Middle Bronze Age as ancient historians believe. Not only were no belligerent military expeditions sent against the Hyksos stronghold in Avaris, but no viceregal administration was set up in Nubia during the Theban Renaissance. The expeditious demise of the Kerma kingdom at the end of MBIIc guaranteed that the lands of Wawat and Kush would no longer pose the immediate threat they once did for the time being. Additionally, having himself come forth from Ethiopia, King Ahmose had a stable ally in the new Meroitic kingdom. The sociopolitical situation during LBI-II did not lend itself to massive expansionist war efforts. In Egypt itself, the land was divided between three powers during LBI. Pharaoh Ahmose's main priority was to maintain these potentially fragile alliances.

Another important implication of this chronological revolution involves the development of the Meroitic alphabet. While the Meroitic alphabet was deciphered in 1910 by F. L. Griffith, scholars are still unable to actually read the Meroitic text — which has "not yet known its Champollion."[31] A major source of Meroitic texts is the temple of Musawwarat Es-Sufra in Meroë. Because of the presence of many graffiti in Egyptian demotic and Greek on the walls of this temple, scholars assume

---

[31] Marianne Cournevin (1998) *Secrets du continent Noir révélés par l'archéologie*, Maisonneuve et Larose: Paris, p. 183.

CHAP. X: THE MISSING LINK | 337

that the structure must have been erected around the first century CE. Archaeologists however generally push the genesis of the building activity at Meroë back to as early as the sixth century BCE.[32] But as Théophile Obenga rightly observes, the hieratic script (a cursive form of hieroglyphics) is attested from as early as the reign of King Djoser-Netjerykhet.[33] The demotic script is itself a derivative of the older hieratic script.[34] In opposition to the accepted view that demotic was first introduced by the standard 25th Dynasty pharaohs, in the eighth century BCE, I shall propose that its use originated in classic Ptolemaic times, and carried on again during the sixteenth century BCE with the Meroitic kings at Musawwarat Es-Sufra. The Ptolemaic rulers of the New Horus Period devised the demotic script as a derivative of the hieratic script introduced during the immediately preceding Memphite period. As the Meroitic monarchy descended from the classic Ptolemaic rulers, they naturally revived the use of demotic in Egypt during LBI. As we will see later, the Greek inscriptions were much later "added" onto the Meroitic temple at Musawwarat Es-Sufra. Indeed, it is evident that after the ancient capitals of Napata and Meroë ceased to be ruled by the pharaohs buried in their corresponding royal cemeteries, shortly after 664 BCE, the sites in question continued to be visited and inhabited by both Ethiopians and Mediterranean peoples throughout the time of the Roman empire and beyond.

It is also possible, in my view, to approximate the date of the building of the Meroitic temple at Musawwarat Es-Sufra by observing the religious iconography associated with the temple. The chief deity of the Meroitic Kingdom was the lion-god Apedemak (see Fig. 10c). Carved ram-headed leonine figures are likewise noticeable on the walls of the Lion-temple of Musawwarat Es-Sufra. Furthermore, in the north wall, the god Amun is depicted in the form of a ram. This dual emphasis on the ram and lion in Meroitic theology indicates that the religious traditions as Musawwarat Es-Sufra took shape during the transition period between the Aries and the Leo Mandates. The Venus shift of 1,559 BCE, which terminated the Middle Bronze Age, had occasioned, once more, a radical deviation of the earth's precessional cycle. In the year 1,559 BCE, the vernal sun moved from the constellation of Pisces, leapfrogging several constellations in the precessional order, to ultimately settle on the constellation of Leo. The sudden and disorderly move in the equinoctial points finally dictated the choice of the lion as the chief deity of the Meroitic kingdom. Since the immediately preceding constellation which ruled the

---

[32] P. L. Shinnie (1996) *Ancient Nubia*, Kegan Paul International: London and New York, p. 111.
[33] Théopile Obenga (1975) 'Contribution de l'Égyptologie au dévelopment de l'histoire africaine', *Présence Africaine* 94, p. 123; Jean Vercoutter (1992) *L'Égypte et la vallée du Nil — Tome I: Des Origines à la fin de l'Ancien Empire)*, Presses Universitaires de France: Paris, p. 71.
[34] Ibid.

vernal equinox was that of the Aries, it is easily understood why the deified ram likewise played an important role in Meroitic iconography at the start of the Late Bronze Age. The lion-god Apedemak symbolized the new Mandate of Leo which initiates the Late Bronze Age. We may furthermore establish a continuity in equinoctial worship with the ongoing devotion to the Theban god Amun in the form of a ram. Moreover, the contemporaneity of the nascent Meroitic kingdom with the Egyptian pharaohs of the Theban Renaissance is pertinently supported by both cultures' adherence to the Theban cult of Amun.

The Day of the Lord

> " Woe unto you that desire the day of the Lord!
> To what end is it for you? The day of the Lord is
> darkness, and no light. ... Shall not the day of the
> Lord be darkness, and no light? Even very
> dark, and no brightness in it? "
>
> - Amos 5:18, 20

So it was that the transition from the MBIIc to LBI eras took place amid massive destructions of fortified city-states and the resulting rise and fall of powerful kingdoms. One great era, or World Age, was annihilated to make way for another. Like the ancient Chinese doctrine of the changing Mandates of Heaven postulated, all major ancient Near Eastern cultures upheld the traditional belief that a cycle-ending cosmic catastrophe was a direct manifestation of divine will. God interfered in the historical process by destroying unrighteous kingdoms and appointing anointed rulers in their place. As we've seen with Joshua's conquest of Canaan, the cataclysmic movements of the heavenly bodies, affecting the outcome of great battles, were interpreted by the victors as a divine sanctioning of their power. In ancient Israelite tradition, those eschatological events were referred to as the Day of the Lord. In a 1976 article entitled 'The Sovereign's Day of Conquest,' Douglas Stuart of the Gordon-Conwell Theological Seminary observes:

> It seems to us equally possible that the prophetic concept of the Day of Yahweh may be influenced by a tradition not uniquely Israelite, but represented in a number of disparate Sumerian, Hittite, Egyptian, and Semitic texts from a variety of places and times. According to this apparently widespread ancient Near Eastern tradition, a truly great king or sovereign possessed such universal power and authority that he could complete a military campaign, or even an entire war of conquest against his enemy in a single day.[35]

---

[35] Douglas Stuart (1976) 'The Sovereign's Day of Conquest', *Bulletin of the American Schools of Oriental Research* 221, p. 159.

CHAP. X: THE MISSING LINK | 339

Other compelling evidence pointing to an ancient tradition about the "Day of the Lord" can be gleaned through extant sacred texts from Hazor, inscribed on a clay model of a cow's liver, uncovered by the late Israeli archaeologist Yigael Yadin (1917-1984) within a pile of discarded rubble. Yadin could deduce that the sacred omens inscribed in cuneiform on this object had been written down by temple diviners.[36] The interesting thing is that no other similar document had ever been found in Israel. This practice of liver divination was actually more common in Babylonia. Yadin believed that the ancient priests of Hazor must have acquired that tradition from them. While Yadin dated this document to the fifteenth century BCE, I believe that the omens were composed shortly before the Venus shift of the mid-sixteenth century BCE. The following excerpts from those sacred texts seem to give credence to my theory:

> **One king will bend down another**
> **An enemy will attack my country**
> [...]
> Forgiveness [will be granted] by the god of the men.
> A servant will rebel against his lord.

The other fragment reads:

> **Ishtar [?] will eat the land**
> Nergal will ...
> The gods of the city will back.[37]

The astronomer-priests of late MBIIc Hazor obviously were aware of the fact that the planet Venus (i.e. Ishtar) was travelling in a very erratic orbit and would inevitably provoke a cycle-ending conflagration of global scale (Ishtar will eat the land). As Yadin informs us that the above document was inspired by the Babylonians, we can deduce that the fragment is somewhat of an Israelite version of the Babylonian Ammisaduga Venus tablets. These indubitably contemporaneous sets of documents both lamented the imminent culmination of the prevailing World Age. The Hazor fragment predicts that the new world order would bring about a

---

[36] Yigael Yadin (1975) *Hazor (The Rediscovery of a Great Citadel of the Bible)*, Random House: New York, pp. 114-115.
[37] As translated by professors B. Landsberger and Haim Tadmor. Cited in Yadin (1975) p. 115.

confrontation between opposing rulers from different city-states. Effectively, two great Near Eastern kings met on the battlefield at the beginning of the Late Bronze Age: the Hyksos-Amalekite king Apophis (Agag) and the new Israelite king Saul. The cataclysmic close of the MBIIc period engendered the end of the biblical period of the Judges and the rise of the original kingdom of Israel. With the fast-changing political landscape which accompanied this critical transition period, several major ancient kingdoms rose and fell. The Hyksos-Amalekites, having suddenly lost their grip over southern Egypt, immediately turned their attention north toward Syria-Palestine and the Mediterranean. With the Canaanite cities finding themselves in a vulnerable position, it is entirely conceivable that King Agag attempted to overrun the weakened city of Hazor, as the above document postulates. Naturally, the Israelites would not leave such a threat unanswered and swiftly, emboldened by the spirit of the Day of the Lord, moved to curtail the Hyksos-Amalekites' advance into their territory. Such invasions from without were common-place at the end of great World Ages, and the ancients interpreted the commotion in the heavens as a manifestation of their god's power. Quoting Bible scholar James M. Connolly:

> The Day of the Lord as a final term of the historical process would be that day on which God's meaning would be evident. The eschaton, the last day, the Day of the Lord, is thus envisioned in Jewish Tradition as both historical (the end term of the historical process) and supra-historical (the explication of divine purpose). The eschaton expresses the real internal meaning for history, and it inaugurates a new age, the "age to come", and realizes God's eternal purpose.[38]

This coincides exactly with the events surrounding the end of a Typhon Season or World Age. The end of a Mandate of Heaven, or divine Covenant, marks the close of a particular historical process and the birth of a new one. The catastrophic shifting of the earth's polar axis, indicative of the Day of the Lord, indeed is intensely articulated in the Book of Amos:

> 8 Seek him that maketh the seven stars and Orion, and turneth the shadow of death into the morning, and maketh the day dark with night: that calleth for the waters of the sea, and poureth them upon the surface if the earth: The Lord is his name.
> (Amos 5:8)

---

[38] James M. Connolly (1965) *Human History and the Word of God (The Christian Meaning of History in Contemporary Thought)*, Macmillan: New York; Collier-Macmillan: London, p. 85.

CHAP. X: THE MISSING LINK | 341

The realization of God's purpose at the end of the period of the Judges was manifested by the founding of the United Monarchy under King Saul. Like a new Joshua, the Hebrew Scriptures represent King Saul as a great anointed leader of a war of conquest in which God's will for his people would be realized. By establishing the Israelite United Monarchy, King Saul acknowledged the new Covenant or Mandate of Heaven brought about by the new Age of Leo. Just as the Ethiopians had founded the Meroitic kingdom and the dynastic Egyptians inaugurated the Theban Renaissance, the Late Bronze Age introduced a new kingdom in Israel. The principal enemy of this new Israelite kingdom was the Hyksos-Amalekite king Agag (Apophis). In the book of Samuel, there is a vivid description of the confrontation between King Agag and King Saul. The Amalekites' destruction is called upon by God mainly for their iniquitous deeds against the children of Israel. The first Book of Samuel recounts:

> 2 Thus saith the Lord of hosts, I remember that which Amalek did to Israel, how he laid wait for him in the way, when he came up from Egypt.
> 3 Now go and smite Amalek, and utterly destroy all that they have, and spare them not; but slay both man and woman, infant and suckling, ox and sheep, camel and ass.
> (1 Samuel 15:2-3)

So King Saul drove the Hyksos-Amalekites out of Canaan but he did not totally exterminate King Agag's army. Saul only sought to contain the Amalekite threat within his own borders. Hence, he ceased pursuing the Hyksos-Amalekites at Egypt's northern border (1 Sam. 15:7). So, when the Bible recounts that Saul spared the best of Agag's possessions (1 Sam. 15:9) it means that Saul did not destroy the seat of Hyksos-Amalekite power at Tell el-Dab'a. In Chapter 13 we will better understand why the biblical text views King Saul's failure, or unwillingness, to fully carry out Agag's destruction in such a negative light. But I believe that in the early LBI phase, the Israelites did not have the military wherewithal to exterminate the Hyksos stronghold at Tell el-Dab'a. As the dynastic Egyptians were doing in the Nile Valley, the new Israelite kingdom could merely manage to stall the Hyksos expansion beyond their own borders.

Like the Meroitic temple at Musawwarat Es-Sufra, the iconography of the LBI city of Hazor can be used to date its remains to the Mandate of Leo. Indeed, Yigael Yadin reported that crouching stone lions guarded the entrance to the Late Bronze Age temple at Hazor.[39] The crouching lions symbolized the constellation of

---

[39] Yigael Yadin (1975) Hazor, pp. 104-109.

the vernal equinox at the time — which was that of Leo. I believe that this particular phase of the temple (stratum IB) had been built by King Solomon himself after Canaanite Hazor (stratum 2) suffered a massive destruction at the end of the Middle Bronze Age as predicted by the MBIIc diviner-priests of Hazor. Solomon, the builder king, thereafter rebuilt the city as part his reconstruction activities during the early Late Bronze Age. Yigael Yadin's excavations demonstrated conclusively that Hazor's stratum 2 (where the clay cow's liver was found), came to an abrupt end and was immediately thereafter abandoned by the people.[40] Like most scholars, Yadin attributed this massive conflagration at the end of the MBIIc period to some unidentified enemy attack — possibly the Egyptians. But, as I have sought to demonstrate, this is an unrealistic theory. The Venus-induced global cataclysm, or Day of the Lord, which terminated the Middle Bronze Age was the one and only culprit.

The Late Bronze Age Aegean: The Lost Pre-Homeric Civilization

> *" Thus, in many ways, what is known today as 'Mycenaean' material culture could usefully be seen as 'Hyksos' or at least the 'Hyksos of the non-Cretan Aegean.'"*
>
> - Martin Bernal
> *Black Athena II*

Having lost their hold over the Upper Nile Valley and Canaan at the start of the Late Bronze Age, the Hyksos immediately turned to the Aegean to quench their imperial thirst. King Apophis' preeminent claim to fame in ancient Hyksos history was his colonization drive of mainland Greece. He would be greatly revered by his Hyksos descendants, much as King Mentuhotep-Nebhepetre had been by his Egyptian descendants, for the great empire he established in the Aegean. The Minoans in Crete, whose kings maintained peaceful relations with King Apophis and his LBI successors, had however remained fully independent from the Hyksos. As evidenced by the Minoan frescoes discovered on the walls of the Hyksos palace at Tell el-Dab'a's platform H/I, the Minoans and the Hyksos had maintained strong trading links, as Minoan artisans continued to be employed at Avaris.

Clearly, my idea of a Hyksos Mycenaean empire during the LBI period is far from conventional. Classicists view the nascent Late Bronze Age Mediterranean as the

---

[40] Ibid, p. 115.

CHAP. X: THE MISSING LINK | 343

birthplace of Western culture. The great Homeric civilizations of Crete and Mycenae are allegedly not supposed to have been influenced, in any way whatsoever, by an Asiatic people like the Hyksos. Not only would this be impossible, in a strict chronological sense, in the view of mainstream scholarship but, also, the very idea that any Near Eastern people may have had such a direct hand in shaping early Western culture has traditionally been met with great resistance. One of a number of ancient historians who have challenged this widespread Eurocentric view of the Late Bronze Age Mediterranean is the Semitist Cyrus H. Gordon. Prof. Gordon's vision of the Late Bronze Age East Mediterranean amounts to an axis comprising of Syria-Palestine, the delta of Egypt, and Minoan Crete.[41] This is very much the perspective adopted in this volume. The Mediterranean world did not flourish in a vacuum — isolated from its Near Eastern neighbours. In fact, Crete very much owed its greatness to its intimate contacts with the Afroasiatic world. Referring once again to Cyrus H. Gordon, it has been argued that the still undeciphered Minoan Linear A script was actually a Phoenician language.[42] C. H. Gordon initially made this claim in April of 1962 but his proposal was never taken seriously — as Linear A still remains undeciphered. Nonetheless, Gordon was convinced that he had uncovered sufficient evidence to prove that the pre-Greek language of Late Bronze Age Crete was indeed fundamentally Phoenician.[43] But in his own words, "the Semitic decipherment of Linear A has been simply swept under the rug."[44] He then ponders: "How long will the comedy of denial go on I will not venture to predict."[45] Now while the Indo-European roots of Minoan civilization cannot be denied, it is evident that, from the Middle Bronze Age onwards, the island of Crete had been part of a vast network of trade and cultural exchange linking it to a number of major Near Eastern centres and the Nile Valley. Naturally, the Minoan script, Linear A, reflected this reality.

To recap, Minoan culture dates back to around 2,600 BCE. The island was settled by people from Asia Minor of Indo-European racial stock. As mentioned, it remains unknown what language they spoke, but scholars believe that it belonged to a separate category of the Mediterranean languages. At the turn of the last century, the celebrated British excavator Sir Arthur Evans divided the history of Crete into

---

[41] Howard Marblestone (1996) 'A "Mediterranean Synthesis": Professor Cyrus H. Gordon's Contribution to the Classics', *Biblical Archaeologist* Vol. 59 - Num. 1, p. 24.
[42] See Cyrus Gordon (1962) *Before the Bible (The Common Background of Greek and Hebrew Civilizations)*, Collins: London, pp. 215-217.
[43] Cyrus Gordon (1972) *Before Columbus (Links Between the Old World and Ancient America)*, Turnstone: London, p. 43.
[44] Cyrus Gordon (1993) 'BOOK REVIEW: 'Black Athena: The Afroasiatic Roots of Classical Civilization. Vol. I: The Fabrication of Ancient Greece, 1785-1985. M. Bernal. 1987', *Journal of Interdisciplinary History* Vol. 113 - Num. 3, p. 489.
[45] Ibid, p. 490.

three major sections: Early Minoan (2,600-2,130 BCE), Middle Minoan (2,130-1,559 BCE) and Late Minoan (1,559-1,135 BCE). Alternatively, classical archaeologists commonly use the following categorization: Prepalatial period (2,600-1,953 BCE), Protopalatial (i.e. Old Palace) period (1,953-1,628 BCE), New Palace period (1,628-1,380 BCE) and finally Postpalatial period (1,380-1,135 BCE). Scholars believe that after *c.*1,450 BCE, during the New Palace period, when Achaean rulers had supposedly established themselves in Crete, an archaic form of Greek gained widespread usage as the official language on Minoan civilization. Up until the 1950s however, classicists upheld the view that Greek had not been spoken in Crete during the Late Bronze Age. Indeed, to Arthur Evans, the Cretans had been the masters of the Late Bronze Age Aegean. He felt that known scripts used during the New Palace period (i.e. Linear A and Linear B) could not possibly be derived from the Greek. But in 1952, the British architect Michael Ventris at last successfully deciphered the Linear B tablets and proved that they were written in an archaic form of Greek. The earlier Minoan language spoken by Eteocretans (the native Cretans) is believed to have continued being used alongside Greek. The picture which classicists have devised of Late Bronze Age Crete therefore fits quite well with Homer's description of the Heroic Age. Homer contended that the inhabitants of Crete were divided into five distinct tribes: the Pelasgians, the Eteocretans, the Kydonians, the Achaeans and the Dorians — each speaking their own language. Again, this multicultural society is conventionally believed to have come about after the mainland Greeks, in about 1,450 BCE, took over the administration of the Cretan palaces, employing Minoan bureaucrats and scribes to carry on business, but using Greek (Linear B) as the *lingua franca*. The Mycenaeans are thought to have initially peacefully integrated the Minoans into their empire but that, in *c.*1,380 BCE, another wave of warlike Mycenaeans utterly decimated the palatial civilization of Crete.

In the revised history I propose, however, the Homeric Achaeans have no role to play in the Late Bronze Age Mediterranean. I believe that Palatial Minoan civilization had always maintained its linguistic and cultural individuality and independence. Homeric multicultural Crete, traditionally dated to the Late Bronze Age, as I shall argue in the following chapters, really belongs to the Iron Age period. The foundation of my thesis rests upon the assumption that the Linear A and Greek-based Linear B scripts had not, after all, been utilised contemporaneously in Late Bronze Age Crete. I contend that the Linear B script was devised by the Greeks from its Linear A base during the latter part of the twelfth century BCE — during the so-called Dark Age of Greece. Therefore, it means that Linear B was used in the Aegean alongside the Geometric script introduced by the Dorians in the early Iron Age. Hence, if Michael Ventris' discovery that the Linear B tablets found at Knossos in Crete were written in an archaic form of Greek compelled scholars to

CHAP. X: THE MISSING LINK | 345

conclude that Greeks had become the masters of Minoan civilization in the Late Bronze Age, wouldn't proving that the Linear B tablets really belonged to the Iron Age, the Dark Age period, significantly alter this picture? Indeed, I am thoroughly convinced that the Mycenaean Greeks never took over the Minoan trading empire during the Late Bronze Age. Minoan civilization remained, until its final demise in 1,380 BCE, a homogeneous culture composed of native Eteocretans. No Pelasgians, Kydonians, Achaeans or Dorians dwelt alongside the Eteocretan population during the Late Bronze Age. Returning to the old notion that the Palatial Minoan culture *did not* speak Greek, I maintain that only the Linear A script, attested from as early as around 1,750 BCE, derived from the undeciphered Middle Minoan hieroglyphic script (*c.*2,000-1,559 BCE), was employed during the Late Bronze Age. The Eteocretans, the direct descendants of the Palatial Minoans, persisted as an independent group until around 1,400 BCE. Eteocretan being a non-Hellenic language, the Greeks considered it a barbaric language — from the word "barbar" meaning "speaking nonsense." It does indeed seem quite odd that the Eteocretans, the supposed initiators of Greek civilization themselves, could have been viewed as barbarians by the Mycenaean Greeks. This ought to indicate some significant cultural detachment between the two peoples. Again, what I hypothesise is that not only culture and language but also chronology separated the Palatial Minoans and the Greeks. In Chapter 12, I will be arguing that the Greeks of Homer's heroic age were part of a horde of northern invaders who settled mainland Greece after the final collapse of the major Late Bronze Age civilizations. From there, meeting no resistance at all, they colonized an already destroyed Crete. The Greeks who ruled Homeric Crete, during the so-called Dark Age, rebuilt the great palace of Knossos upon the ruins of the previous Minoan civilization. This means that the Greek Linear B tablets found at Knossos, alongside the Linear A tablets, were carved between 1,135-750 BCE. So if the warlike Achaeans were not the masters of mainland Greece during the Late Bronze Age then who were? The answer is the Hyksos.

Chronology of Mycenaean-A Greece:

I. Late Helladic-A I (Mycenaean-A I)	1,550 - 1,450 BCE **1,559 - 1,418 BCE (New Chronology)**
II. Late Helladic-A II (Mycenaean-A II)	1,450 - 1,400 BCE **1,418 - 1,380 BCE (New Chronology)**
III. Late Helladic-A IIIa - c (Mycenaean-A IIIa-c)	1,400 - 1,050 BCE **1,380 - 1,135 BCE (New Chronology)** IIIa: 1,380 - 1,330 BCE IIIb: 1,330 - 1,187 BCE IIIc: 1,187 - 1,135 BCE

Table 10-1

The above chart outlines the archaeological classifications used by scholars to date Late Bronze Age Greece. The term of "Late Helladic period" is employed interchangeably with the term "Mycenaean period" because archaeologists believe that the Late Bronze Age ushered in Homer's Heroic Age of mainland Greece. But in the new chronology, I make a distinction between Mycenaean-A culture and the Mycenaean-B settlement. Since I believe that the Heroic Age belongs in the Iron Age – beginning at the end of the traditional Late Helladic period – the genuine Mycenaean Age starts over four hundred years later than customarily assumed. Nevertheless, Late Bronze Age Mycenae, following the Middle Helladic Period, must logically likewise be classified as a Late Helladic, or Mycenaean, settlement. Hence, I will designate the Hyksos-dominated Late Bronze Age mainland Greece as a Late Helladic-A, or Mycenaean-A, settlement while ascribing the later Greek Mycenaean culture of the Iron Age (1,135-747 BCE) to a Late Helladic-B, or Mycenaean-B, settlement. A similar distinction can be made between the conventional Late Minoan-A Crete inhabited by the native Eteocretans and the subsequent pseudo-Minoan culture that the Greeks introduced in the Iron Age, Late Minoan-B.

Arguably the most extraordinary discovery made in mainland Greece by the brilliant German amateur archaeologist Heinrich Schliemann (1822-1890) was the unearthing of the Shaft Graves of Mycenae. What classicist today refer to as "Mycenaean civilization" essentially represents this Late Bronze Age culture. The artifacts found buried with these early Mycenaean rulers show this culture to have been warlike. Chronologically speaking, the Shaft Graves definitely date to the early Late Bronze Age, since pottery dating to the Middle Helladic period abound among the artifacts. Moreover, African ostrich eggs, like the ones used in Middle Kingdom Egypt and MMIIb Crete (see p. 264) were found inside the graves. Additional evidence of the cosmopolitan nature of the Shaft Grave culture indicates that these rulers were new to Greece.[46] Again, I am wholly convinced that the monarchs buried in the Mycenaean Shaft Graves were Hyksos-Amalekite princes from Egypt's Delta.

King David and the Continuing Hyksos-Amalekite

Challenge

Completing Cyrus H. Gordon's Late Bronze Age axis of Crete and the Egyptian Delta was Syria-Palestine. As in the cases of the Egyptian Delta and Minoan civilization, my revised model unveils a dramatically different picture of Syria-Palestine during the Late Bronze Age than the one customarily portrayed by ancient

---

[46] Martin Bernal (1991) *Black Athena (The Afroasiatic Roots of Classical Civilization) — Volume II: The Archaeological and Documentary Evidence*, Rutgers University Press: New Brunswick, NJ, p. 44.

historians. In the new chronology, the Late Bronze I era corresponds with the biblical United Monarchy period. The troubles which King Saul, the first king of Israel, encountered with the Hyksos rulers in the Egyptian Delta, continued under his successor, King David. Originally an unlikely candidate to succeed Saul, David had, in his youth, been a harpist for King Saul. As a result of his bravery in battle, David became a hero in the eyes of the Israelite people — fuelling Saul's hostility towards him. On two occasion, Saul attempted to kill David with a spear. Realizing that his life was genuinely in danger, David fled King Saul's palace, where he had been staying, with Saul in pursuit. On a number of occasions, the Bible says that David had the chance to kill Saul, and claim the Hebrew throne, but refused to do so. But when Saul was defeated and killed in battle at Gilboa (2 Samuel 1), the tribe of Judah, to whom David belonged, elected him as their king at Gilboa. Meanwhile, the other remaining eleven tribes of Israel stayed steadfastly loyal to King Saul's family and elevated Ishbosheth, Saul's son, as their king in Mahanaim, east of the Jordan River. For the next two years, the two camps waged war against one another. The conflict finally ended with the assassination of Ishbosheth; and David was shortly thereafter anointed king of a unified Israel.

The biblical account of David's life and accession to power as king of Israel is undoubtedly at least partly fictitious. For instance, David's famous confrontation with Goliath, described as a Philistine, certainly could not have occurred during the Late Bronze Age; since the Philistines only entered Syria-Palestine during the early Iron Age. The possible reasons why the Philistines were woven into the history of the United Monarchy by the biblical redactors will be explored in Part IV. Nonetheless, other details of the story of David's life incontrovertibly point to a Late Bronze Age context. This evidence centres around the presence of threatening Hyksos-Amalekite forces to the south of Israel. In the Book of Samuel, the biblical redactors relate:

> 30 And it came to pass, when David and his men were come to Ziklag on the third day, that the Amalekites had invaded the south, and Ziklag, and smitten Ziklag, and burned it with fire ...
> 3 So David and his men came to the city, and behold, it was burned with fire; and their wives, and their sons, and their daughters were taken captives.
> (1 Samuel 30:1;3)

Evidently, the Hyksos-Amalekites, whom King Saul had waged war against, still had a strong foothold in Egypt's Delta. From this location, they were in a favourable position to invade the south of King David's kingdom. The presence of the Amalekites in Egypt during King David's reign is apparently further confirmed in the following except from the Book of Samuel:

13 And David said unto him, to whom belongest thou? and whence art thou? And he said, I am a young man of Egypt, servant of to an Amalekite; and my master left me, because three days agone I fell sick.
(1 Samuel 30:13)

In this passage, King David interrogates a meandering Egyptian in the field of his campaign against the Amalekites. The Egyptian reveals that he is the servant of the Amalekites. Knowing that the Amalekites were, in reality, one and the same as Hyksos hordes who overpowered the Egyptians, the fact that the Egyptian fugitive claims to be a servant of the Amalekites makes perfect sense. The Hyksos-Amalekites, as masters of Avaris during the reign of King David in Israel, naturally would make use of Egyptian servants and mercenaries.

Solomon the Builder King

Upon his death, King David was immediately succeeded on the throne of Israel's United Monarchy by his son Solomon. The Bible relates that King Solomon was a powerful king ruling, over a materially and spiritually prosperous Israel. His dominion covered about 50,000 square miles — stretching from the northern border of Egypt to Syria to the borders of Mesopotamia in the east.[47] Solomon completely revamped the administration of the Hebrew state by enlarging its government bureaucracy and commissioning ambitious building projects. To protect his kingdom, Solomon erected imposing double-wall fortresses and massive gateways at Gezer, Megiddo and Hazor. Basking in wealth and power, King Solomon established solid trading and diplomatic relations with numerous kings of neighbouring city-states. Through favourable treaties, Solomon was able to maintain peaceful relations with other Near Eastern nations.

Despite the numerous biblical claims of the magnificence of King Solomon's era, little, if any, archaeological evidence have been found by archaeologists to substantiate the Bible's assertions. The perplexing problem is that, at the time when the Bible contends that King Solomon ruled (during the tenth century BCE), the archaeological remains from Syria-Palestine far from reflects the wealth and cultural sophistication depicted in the Bible.[48] Finding absolutely no evidence for the massive fortresses and gateways at Gezer, Megiddo and Hazor during the Iron Age, many scholars have concluded that Solomon's kingdom never existed. In fact, the last time that such imposing structures were attested in Megiddo, and other large Syro-Palestinian city-centres, was during the Late Bronze Age. Stratum

---

[47] Herbert Lockyer (editor) *Nelson's Illustrated Bible Dictionary*, Thomas Nelson: Nashville, p. 1000.
[48] See James B. Pritchard (editor) (1974) *Solomon and Sheba*, Phaidon: London, p. 35; D. M. Rohl (1995) *A Test of Time — Vol. I, Century*: London, pp. 173-175.

VIIb (see Table 10-2) at Megiddo was the last period of effervescence comparable to Solomonic Israel as described in the biblical text.

Chronology of Megiddo from LBI to end of Iron IIb

LBI	Megiddo IX (Solomonic)	1,559 BCE - 1,380 BCE
LBII	Megiddo VIII	1,380 BCE - 1,330 BCE
LBIII	Megiddo VIIb	1,330 BCE - 1,135 BCE
Iron I	Megiddo VIIa	1,135 BCE - 945 BCE
Iron IIa	Megiddo VI-Vb	945 BCE - 828 BCE
Iron IIb	Megiddo Va-IVb	828 BCE - 747 BCE

Table 10-2

(1) Stratum VIII was contemporaneous with the reign of Amenhotep III and the time of the Amarna correspondences.
(2) Stratum VIIb marks the last great period of the city and was contemporaneous with Ramses II and Merneptah.

This signifies that the biblical King Solomon could only have ruled *before* or during the reigns of Ramses II and Amenhotep III of Egypt. In the new chronology, Solomon is, indeed, actually dated contemporaneously with the reigns of King Tuthmosis II and Queen Hatchepsut. His reign falls during Megiddo IX — in LBI period. Like the Megiddo VIII and VIIb strata, Megiddo IX exhibits a rich culture comparable to the Solomonic Megiddo described in the Bible. The richly stocked tombs of LBI Megiddo have, erroneously in my view, been attributed by some scholars to northern Indo-Aryan nobility.[49] But I believe that Megiddo Stratum IX must instead be seen as the burgeoning of ancient Megiddo, under the leadership of King Solomon.

At the culmination of King Solomon's reign however, the "LBI city at Megiddo ended in total devastation."[50] Again, that conflagration is, to quote Bible scholar Baruch Halpern, "universally attributed to Pharaoh Thutmosis III, who in a contemporary record recounts his campaign into Canaan and his destruction of Megiddo."[51] In disagreement with this theory, I instead maintain that the destruction

---

[49] Nadav Na'aman (1994) 'The Hurrians and the End of the Middle Bronze Age in Palestine, *Levant* 26, p. 179.
[50] Baruch Halpern (1987) 'Radical Exodus Redating Fatally Flawed', *Biblical Archaeology Review* Vol. 13 - Num. 6, p. 57.
[51] Ibid.

of Megiddo IX was precipitated by the combination of a cosmic upheaval and the victorious infiltration of the Hyksos-Amalekites into Syria-Palestine, from Avaris, in 1,380 BCE. King Solomon's empire was utterly defeated and a great hiatus in the history of the Hebrew people settled in.

A Peace Coming Undone: The Second Hyksos Invasion and Tuthmosis II's Reunification of the Two Lands

The close of the Late Bronze I era also brought significant changes in the political balance of power in the Nile Valley. The somewhat fragile peace which had been held together between the country's three principal centres of power (Upper Egypt, Lower Egypt and Avaris) since the termination of the Middle Bronze Age suddenly fell apart. Once again, Egypt was thrown into a state of chaos. This instability seems to have been caused by the accumulated effects of a series of unusually high Nile levels — much as had been experienced before the lunar shift of 1,628 BCE — during the reigns of Pharaohs Tuthmosis I and Sobekhotep VIII. The Egyptian state being much weakened, and already fragmented, by this latest challenge of nature, the Hyksos seized upon this opportunity to attempt to once more invade Egypt. An extant document dated to Year 4 of Pharaoh Sobekhotep VIII, known as the Inundation Stela, found in 1956 in the fill of the Third Pylon of the temple of Karnak, recounts the ravages of the annual inundation of the Nile.

> Living: The Son of Re, Sobekhotep, beloved of the great Hapy, given life forever.
> Year 4, 4th month of Shemu, the five days upon the year: before the said god who lives forever. The king's procession to the columned hall of this temple so that the great inundation could be witnessed. He came just as the columned hall of this temple was inundated with water. Then he waded in it together with the court.

On the basis of historical evidence which will be imparted shortly, the Egyptian state rapidly disintegrated in the latter years of King Sobekhotep VIII's reign. I would hypothesise that a primary cause for this decline of the Egyptian monarchy was the continually rising levels of the Nile over several years — leading to poor crops and economic dire straits. The reason why Sobekhotep VIII when through the exercise of describing in detail this "great inundation" may be because the rising levels of the Nile had indeed been uncharacteristically high. We are of course reminded of the very similar practices of Pharaoh Sesostris III before the planetary

CHAP. X: THE MISSING LINK | 351

cataclysm of 1,628 BCE. Only this time around, the resulting civil strife came about at the culmination of a much more gradual disintegration process. Closely mirroring the pattern of events following the Thera eruption, Egypt's monarchy, finding itself in a state of weakness, faced both external and internal challenges to its authority. The fabric of ordered society expeditiously collapsing, tomb robbers and vandals ran rampant all over Egypt. The similarity of these historical circumstances to the events surrounding the Thera eruption was not lost to the Hyksos rulers in Avaris. It is precisely at that time, I believe, that a new conquering Hyksos ruler took over the reigns of power in Avaris and set out to duplicate the exploit of his predecessor, Sheshi. Naturally, this new king decided to adopt the same name in honour of his revered ancestor. Knowing that Sheshi I invaded Egypt on the same year as the Thera eruption, in 1,628 BCE, we can work out when this new Sheshi came to power by referring to the length of the Hyksos rulers' reigns provided by the extant Manethonian texts.

Hyksos Kings	**Length of Reigns**	**Important Events**
Sheshi I (Salatis)	19 years 1,628 - 1,609 BCE	1st invasion of Egypt
Bnon	44 years 1,609 - 1,565 BCE	
Apachnas	36 years 1,565 - 1,529 BCE	
Apophis	61 years 1,529 - 1,468 BCE	
Jannas	50 years 1,468 - 1,418 BCE	
Sheshi II (Ashishi)	49 years 1,418 - 1,369 BCE	2nd invasion of Egypt

Table 10-3

The above chart indicates that Sheshi II became ruler of Avaris, as Sobekhotep VIII's reign came to an inevitable close, in 1,418 BCE. The Hyksos attempt to overthrow the existing Lower Egyptian government initially succeeded as, possibly overpowered by a combination of internal and external challenges, Sobekhotep VIII's reign came to an end — to be replaced by the equally ephemeral and mainly symbolic reign of Pharaoh Sobek-Emsaf I. Essentially, Lower Egypt had, for the second time, fallen into the hands of the Hyksos. In Upper Egypt, tensions ran high as memories of the harsh Hyksos occupation of the MBIIc period resurfaced. Unequivocally, the Hyksos could not be trusted in the Thebans' mind's eye. Unless they were driven out of Lower Egypt, it would not be very long before Thebes itself fell under Hyksos rule. So a great war of liberation broke out, headed by a new Theban pharaoh, to repel the Hyksos threat. Quoting Flavius Josephus:

> Then the kings of the Thebaid and of the rest of Egypt rose in revolt against the shepherds, and a great war broke out, which was of long du-

> ration. Under a king named Misphragmouthosis, the shepherds, he says, were defeated, driven out of all the rest of Egypt, and confined in a place called Auaris ...
> (Josephus, *Against Apion*, I [14])

This passage presents a number of problems for the accepted chronology of ancient Egypt. First of all, Josephus' "King Misphragmouthosis" is obviously a Tuthmoside pharaoh. If Ahmose had really driven the Hyksos out of Egypt at the beginning of the Late Bronze Age, why would a Tuthmoside pharaoh still be grappling with a clear and present Hyksos threat? Secondly, why would King Misphragmouthosis consider merely confining his Hyksos foes to Avaris a victory? Could it be that Tell el-Dab'a was considered, during the days of this Tuthmoside king, the home of the Hyksos? In the new chronology however, Josephus' statement makes perfect sense. We indeed find that the Hyksos incursion which he refers to was in fact their *second* invasion of Egypt. Originating from their domain in Avaris, that latest Hyksos foray came at the end of the LBI period, when a Tuthmoside pharaoh, Tuthmosis I, ruled in Thebes.

The next step now is to identify which of the Tuthmoside kings of the new 14th Dynasty was Josephus' King Misphragmouthosis. In my estimation, it was Pharaoh Tuthmosis II. There is a very intriguing passage in a Late Bronze Age document known as Biography of Ineni which reads:

> The Hawk in the nest [appeared as] the King of Upper and Lower Egypt, Okhepernere (... Thutmose II), he became king of the Black Land and Ruler of the Red Land, having taken possession of the Two Regions in triumph.[52]

Egyptologists know nothing of a unification campaign under King Tuthmosis II which could compare to the glorious unifications bouts of Narmer or Mentuhotep-Nebhepetre. Pharaoh Ahmose is supposed to have instituted a strong and unified Egyptian kingdom at the onset of the Late Bronze Age. Therefore why would any Tuthmoside king need to once again unify Upper and Lower Egypt? Yet, this is exactly what the Biography of Ineni postulates. Tuthmosis II became King of Upper and Lower Egypt by means of conquest because he successfully repelled the Hyksos invaders from Lower Egypt. Hence, for the first time in over three hundred and sixty years, the Two Lands were unified under the rule of a single pharaoh. But as Josephus posits, the Hyksos were not completely driven out of Egypt. King Tuthmosis II confined them to their fortress-city at Tell el-Dab'a. He had taken over the reigns of the Two Lands from Tuthmosis I and Sobek-Emsaf I — whom the Hyksos had overwhelmed.

---

[52] J. H. Breasted, *Ancient Records of Egypt*, Vol. II - § 116.

CHAP. X: THE MISSING LINK | 353

An interesting parallel can be found between these events in Tuthmosis II's reign and the annals of a pharaoh known to Egyptologists as Sobek-Emsaf III. Arthur Weigall argued that this king lived around the time of the Hyksos king Ashishi [our Sheshi II].[53] My argument however is that this king was in reality Pharaoh Sobek-Emsaf I himself, and that Sobek-Emsaf III never actually existed. The latter is merely an alter-ego of Pharaoh Sobek-Emsaf I. In the New Chronology Table, the first Sobek-Emsaf is shown to have been a contemporary of Sheshi II. Since it will be proven in the next chapter that Sobek-Emsaf II ruled in the first half of the fourteenth century BCE, this Sobek-Emsaf cannot therefore be the third in line. The relationship between Sobek-Emsaf I and Tuthmosis II's campaign annals is first noticeable by the fact that King Sobek-Emsaf I was also known by the name of Sekhemseshedetitouire; which translates as: "The Power Reclaiming the Two Lands of the Sun-god." The word *Shedeti* actually means "reclaiming."[54] Since, in the new chronology, Sobek-Emsaf I and Tuthmosis II were both contemporaries of Sheshi II, it may be deduced that both Egyptian pharaohs had as a main objective early in their reigns to recover the Two Lands from the clutches of the Hyksos invaders. Certainly, both references to the "reclaiming of the Two Lands" unambiguously describe the same historical event at the end of the LBI period. Ultimately, Pharaoh Tuthmosis II succeeded in containing the Hyksos' expansionary drive and confine them to Tell el-Dab'a.

Solomon and the Queen of Sheba
A great beneficiary of Pharaoh Tuthmosis II's northward punitive expedition was undoubtedly King Solomon in Canaan. Although it is difficult to estimate how the Hyksos' defeat in Lower Egypt might have curtailed their ability to threaten Solomon's kingdom, the diplomatic relations between King Solomon and Pharaoh Tuthmosis II were certainly reinforced by their common interest in keeping Sheshi II at Avaris in check. When Tuthmosis II died and was succeeded by his wife and half-sister Hatchepsut and his son Tuthmosis III, who both reigned as coregents, King Solomon still reigned in Syria-Palestine, and the courteous relationship between the two neighbours continued.

In his 1952 book Ages in Chaos, Immanuel Velikovsky had proposed the theory that Solomon's fame and reputation as a wise ruler had spread to the court of Queen Hatchepsut — whom he likewise believed was a contemporary of King Solomon. Velikovsky affirmed that Queen Hatchepsut was the biblical Queen of Sheba who had ventured to Solomon's court to witness for herself the extent of his wisdom.

---

[53] Arthur Weigall (1927) *A History of the Pharaohs — Vol. II: From the Accession of Amenemhat I of the Twelfth Dynasty to the Death of Thutmose III of the Eighteenth Dynasty, 2111 to 1441 B.C.*, Thornton Butterworth: London, p. 195.
[54] Ibid.

354 | PLANET OF THE GREEKS

Velikovsky looked to the famous reliefs of Queen Hatchepsut's great expedition to the Land of Punt from her temple at Deir el-Bahari as an authentic Egyptian version of the biblical narrative concerning the voyage of the Queen of Sheba to Israel. The very same hypothesis is here put forward but with the only exception that I place this event in the Late Bronze Age. Once again, we are confronted with the controversy surrounding the real location of the Land of Punt. Since scholars generally assume that the Land of Punt was located along the Red Sea coast of Somalia, Hatchepsut's expedition is believe to have been headed south toward Ethiopia. But as Velikovsky observes:

> The people of Pun [Punt], so admirably sculptured on the temple of Hatshepsut, are very closely like the high Egyptians. Further, the Egyptians called Pun "the land of the gods"; and they do not appear to have made war on the Punite race, but only to have had a peaceful intercourse of embassies and commerce. ... The name [Punt] is connected with Pœni, or Phœnicians, who appear to be a branch of that race.[55]

As I have already outlined in Chapter 2, I indeed believe that the true location of the Land of Punt, God's Land, was in Syria-Palestine. Queen Hatchepsut's final destination was not Ethiopia, but Solomonic Israel. Further making a case for this theory, Velikovsky writes:

> An official of the Sixth Dynasty left a laconic record stating that he visited Byblos and Punt eleven times.[56] Byblos was the old capital of Phoenicia; its ruins are eighteen miles north of Beirut. Having been visited eleven times by the officer coming from Egypt, and being mentioned together with Byblos, Punt must have been associated with Byblos.[57]

The text of the 6th Dynasty official might better be interpreted as referring to Byblos and Punt as synonyms. Or, accepting the view that the land of Punt or "God's Land" was a general reference to "the Orient,"[58] we may likewise assume that the official took it for granted that Byblos was part of the wider "Land of Punt." As Velikovsky remarked, it would seem quite odd that the official would consider visiting both

---

[55] Flinders Petrie (1894) *A History of Egypt* — Vol. I: *From the Earliest Times to the XVIth Dynasty*, Methuen: London, pp. 12-13.
[56] J. H. Breasted, *Ancient Records of Egypt*, Vol. II - § 892.
[57] Immanuel Velikovsky (1952) *Ages in Chaos*, pp. 109-110.
[58] Abdel-Aziz Saleh (1981) 'Notes on the Ancient Egyptian *t-ntr* "God's-Land"', *Bulletin de l'Institut Français d'Archéologie Orientale* 81, p. 107.

Fig. 10e: Queen Hatchepsut's temple at Deir el-Bahari (restored).
After Perrot & Chipiez (1882).

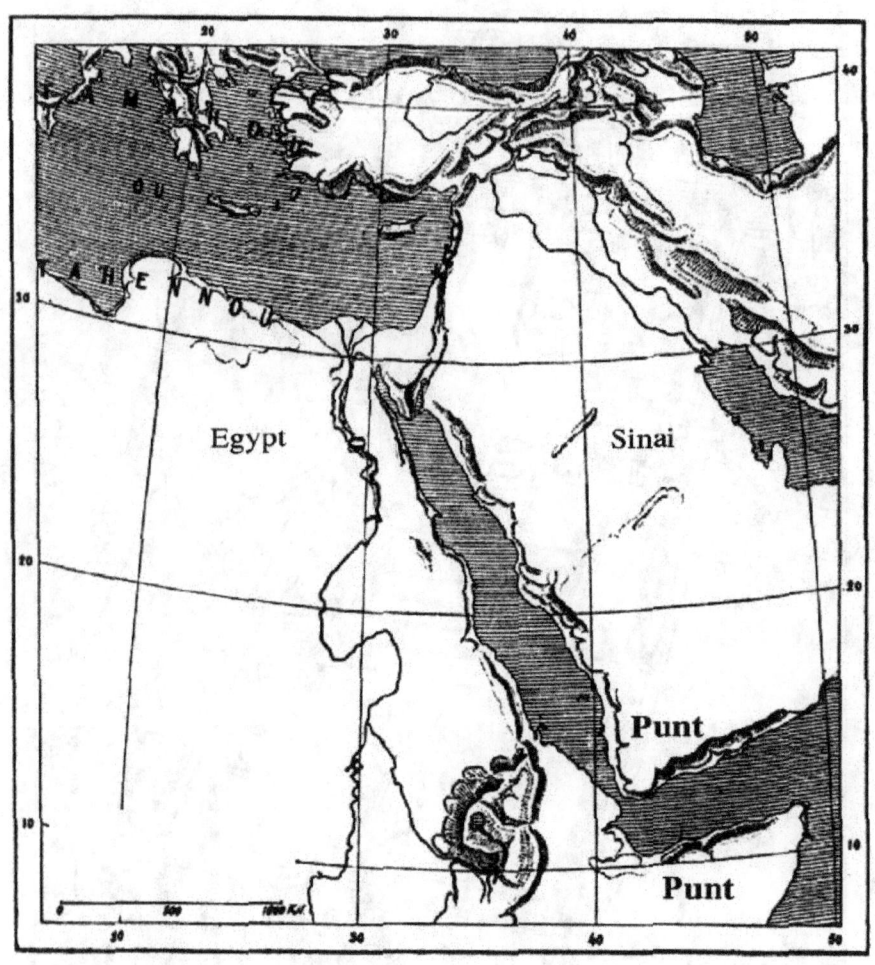

Fig. 10f: Conventionally accepted location of the Land of Punt.

CHAP. X: THE MISSING LINK | 357

Syria-Palestine and Ethiopia on each of his eleven trips. Clearly, in this particular case the Land of Punt was used by the official as a reference to Phoenicia.

Many critics of the theory that Queen Hatchepsut's Punt expedition reliefs at Deir el-Bahari depict scenes from Syria-Palestine have justifiably pointed out that the fauna displayed on the reliefs are definitely more African that Asiatic. Certain animals and dwelling units pictured could only have been found in Ethiopia — the generally accepted location of the Land of Punt. Admittedly, this represents a potentially fatal red herring for Dr Immanuel Velikovsky's theory. There is no doubt that, if Queen Hatchepsut indeed journeyed to Israel, she inevitably would have had to have stopped by the Red Sea's Somali cost first. But why? The texts from the Deir el-Bahari temple of Queen Hatchepsut intriguingly alludes to the fact that the land which she visited was located "on the two sides." This single most important description have led many scholars to conclude that the Land of Punt was located "on both coastal regions of the southernmost part of the Red Sea, where Africa and Arabia almost come together."[59] (see Fig. 10f) The picturing of both African and Asiatic types on the expedition reliefs was explained by this theory. But, as it was earlier argued in Chapter 5, Egyptians also occasionally referred to Kush as the Land of Punt because, during the Old Kingdom, a large number of Asiatics (C-Group settlers) came from God's Land (i.e. Syria-Palestine) to establish themselves below Egypt's southern border. So in it's broader meaning, God's Land also included the land of Kush since its population was predominantly of Asiatic racial stock. Hence, it may be argued that the reference to the "two sides" was meant to symbolize the entire Land of Punt on both sides of Egypt's major borders — the north-eastern and southern ones. But, as the following excerpt from an inscription of the New Kingdom pharaoh Seti I indicates, the primary location of the Land of Punt, or God's Land, was in Syria-Palestine — in the north-east:

> I turn my face to the east, I work a wonder for thee, I bind them all for thee, gathered in my grasp. I gather all the countries of Punt, all their tribute, of gum of myrrh, cinnamon, and all the pleasant sweet woods of God's-Land ... [60]

In the popular Middle Kingdom story of the Shipwrecked Sailor, we are privy to a discussion between Sinuhe and a giant talking serpent whose home is said to be in the Land of Punt. When Sinuhe imparts to the mythical serpent that, upon his return to Egypt, he would inform Pharaoh of the serpent's greatness, and see to it that

---

[59] See David M. Rohl (1998) *A Test of Time — Vol. II: Legend (The Genesis of Civilization)*, Century: London, p. 298.
[60] J. H. Breasted, *Ancient Records of Egypt*, Vol. III - § 116.

many luxury goods, such as incense, would be sent to him. The serpent immediately replies that he would have no need for such gifts because, in his own domain of Punt, those commodities were already widely produced and exported. Due to this clear reference to the land of Punt in the story, scholars have concluded that the magical island which Sinuhe visited lay somewhere in the Red Sea. But Sinuhe, throughout his lengthy travel account, mentions mainly sites in Syria and Lebanon. So how could he have ended up on the Sudanese coast off the Red Sea? If, as the story narrates, Sinuhe was running away from possible reprimand in Egypt, why take the completely unnecessary risk, once he was safely in Syria-Palestine, to cross the border back into Egypt and head on south towards Nubia? There is no doubt in my mind that the story of the Shipwrecked Sailor is set in Syria-Palestine and that the Land of Punt in the account refers to nowhere other than the ancient city of Byblos in Phoenicia. Indeed, as early as the 5th Dynasty, the term *fnhw* was employed by the Egyptians to designate a people from the Syrian region. Sinuhe uses that word to describe the lands he visited. Referring to the research of Claude Vandersleyen, Michael Green writes:

> Vandersleyen ... appears to regard *fnhw* as an Egyptian form of a Semitic word designating, amongst other ethnic groups, the inhabitants of the coastal plain of Canaan and serving as the etymological ancestor of the typonym "Phoenicia." ... According to Vandersleyen, "Phoenicia" is a Greek version of a local ethnic designation which was rendered *fnhw* in Egyptian.[61]

What is more, the Egyptian *f3w fnhw* "the land of the wood cutter" fits very well with Phoenicia's well-earned reputation as pharaonic Egypt's main provider of cedar wood and other resinous trees.

All this indicates that Queen Hatchepsut's expedition can be seen as a "grand tour" of God's Land — encompassing all the lands of the Asiatics, from Nubia to their homeland in Syria-Palestine. This actually explains why both African and Asiatic types are depicted in the Deir el-Bahari temple reliefs. The scenes were not meant to be chronologically or geographically accurate; as the many different types of peoples the queen encountered on her way were indiscriminately lumped together — representing the totality of Punt's population. But we must still answer why she chose this very long route to get to King Solomon's court. Couldn't she have just taken a caravan northwards from Thebes? Why head south along the Nile, cross over to the Arabian peninsula, and only then take a caravan route north to

---

[61] Michael Green (1983) 'The Syrian and Lebanese Topographical Data in the Story of Sinuhe', *Chronique d'Égypte* 58, p. 41.

CHAP. X: THE MISSING LINK | 359

Israel? Well for some reason, the God Amun, who had commissioned this expedition, was concerned for the safety of Queen Hatchepsut and specifically ordered that she undertake the trip on both land and sea. Quoting Egyptologist Abdel-Aziz Saleh:

> Amun, who is represented as very keen on the safety of the expedition, is said, in the texts, to have decided to conduct the voyage both on water and overland, in order to bring marvels from God's Land.
>
> Hatchepsut definitely stated that the object of her expedition was 'a sacred region of God's Land.'[62]

The fact that Queen Hatchepsut arrived in Israel from the Arabian peninsula is made evident from her name in biblical tradition as the: "Queen of Sheba" or "Queen of the South." She had to come in from Arabia, as opposed to the Egyptian Delta because of the hostile Hyksos rulers who still dwelt in Avaris at the time of the Punt expedition. Since Sheshi II's accession, the Hyksos were extremely aggressive and indubitably would not have hesitated one minute to attack Hatchepsut's convoy, loot all of the precious goods, and finally murder the Egyptian monarch. Even many hundreds of years after they had been expelled from the Egyptian Delta, the Hyksos, or king-shepherds, remained legendary for their ruthless piracy against passing caravans. In his writings, the Greek chronographer Strabo (58 BCE - 25 CE) related that:

> ... the harbour which Aegypt did have, the one at Pharos, gave no access, but was guarded by shepherds who were pirates and who attacked those who tried to bring ships to anchor there ...
> (Strabo, *Geography* Book XVII: 1, 19)

The name of "shepherds" used by Strabo to describe the pirates lurking at the Alexandrian harbor of Pharos appears to have been a throwback to the days when the Hyksos shepherd-kings were terrorizing passing ships and caravans journeying within Egypt's Delta. As completely nonsensical as it may seem to conventional historians and Egyptologists that Queen Hatchepsut could have had to worry about a Hyksos threat this late in the Late Bronze Age, that is exactly the situation she found herself in. For over two hundred years now, the Hyksos-Amalekites had been the sole masters of Avaris. A famous inscription of Queen Hatchepsut carved high upon the facade of her temple at Speos Artemidos comes to confirm, in my view, my hypothesis that the Hyksos had occupied Avaris in Hatchepsut's life time. In it, the queen writes:

---

[62] Abdel-Aziz Saleh (1972) 'Some Problems Relating to the Pwenet Reliefs at Deie el-Bahari', *Journal of Egyptian Archaeology* 58, p. 142.

> I have raised up what was dismembered, (even) from the first time when the Asiatics were in Avaris of the North Land (with) roving hordes in the midst of them overthrowing what had been made; they ruled without Re, and he acted not by divine command ...[63]

Egyptologists and ancient historians have long puzzled over the reasons why, seemingly out of the blue, Queen Hatchepsut would have, so passionately, resented the memory of the Hyksos occupation of Avaris whilst her Late Bronze I predecessors had refrained from displaying nearly as much animosity. Why this sudden outburst of anger? In the accepted framework, the Hyksos had been expelled by Ahmose for nearly a hundred years now. What took the Thebans so long to finally demolish the Hyksos buildings and start rebuilding Avaris? Well, the answer of course is that the Hyksos were only finally expelled from Avaris during the reign of Hatchepsut. And she saw it as her duty to rebuild the town in honour of the gods whom had been neglected by the Hyksos invaders. We know that the Speos Artemidos inscription can't be dated to any later than Hatchepsut's Year 9 since, in it, she refers to the Punt expedition. So the liberation of Avaris occurred during the latter years of Hatchepsut's reign — when her coregent Tuthmosis III was a grown man capable of governing on his own. It is under the leadership of Tuthmosis III, as we shall now see, that the Hyksos were banished from Avaris.

Tuthmosis III Drives the Hyksos out of Avaris

Probably while Hatchepsut was still in Syria-Palestine, tensions were building up to great heights between the Hyksos-Amalekites and the Thebans. The Egyptians, although they had driven the hated king-shepherds out of most of the Red Land, felt unbearably uneasy about their lingering presence in Avaris. Unlike what historians believe, the Tuthmoside kings of the Late Bronze Age had never acquired a great Asiatic empire. In fact, Egypt during much of the Theban Renaissance had remained quite an isolationistic power. Considering that the Hyksos-Amalekites still controlled the vital outpost of Avaris, their isolationism may have had more to do with circumstances than choice. Hence, there conceivably might have developed a strong nationalistic feeling of resentment against the Hyksos for continuing to isolate Egypt. The military success of Tuthmosis II had very much invigorated the Egyptians and they waited for the time when they could go all out and finally completely expel the Hyksos from their borders for good. That much-anticipated ideal time came during the reign of King Tuthmosis III, the son of the deliverer-king Tuthmosis II and coregent of Queen Hatchepsut. He resolved to

---

[63] Cited in Alan H. Gardiner (1946) 'Davis's Copy of the Great Speos Artemidos Inscription', *Journal of Egyptian Archaeology* 32, pp. 47-48.

CHAP. X: THE MISSING LINK | 361

erect a blockade around the fortress of Avaris and force the Hyksos out of Egypt. Describing these momentous events, Flavius Josephus writes:

> According to Manetho, the Shepherds enclosed this whole area [Avaris] with a high, strong wall, in order to safeguard all their possessions and spoils. Thummôsis, the son of Misphragmuthôsis (he continues), attempted by siege to force them to surrender, blockading the fortress with an army of 480,000 men. Finally, giving up the siege in despair, he concluded a treaty by which they should all depart from Egypt and go unmolested where they pleased. On these terms, the Shepherds, with their possessions and households complete, no fewer than 240,000 persons, left Egypt and journeyed over the desert to Syria. There, dreading the power of the Assyrians who were at that time masters of Asia, they built in the land now called Judaea a city large enough to hold all those thousands of people, and gave it the name of Jerusalem.
> (Manetho, *Aegyptiaca*, FR. 42)

Despite the presence of this passage in the Manethonian literature, Egyptologists have given very little, if any, credence to this version of how the Hyksos were driven out of Egypt. Quite simply, it doesn't fit with preconceived notions about the history of the Late Bronze Age. Some Bible historians in the past, on the other hand, have been slightly more interested in this passage because of its seeming allusions to the biblical Exodus. To more than a few biblically-inclined observers, this Manethonian reference proved that the Israelite Exodus had taken place during the reign of a Tuthmoside Egyptian pharaoh. As early as the second century CE, Theophilus, Bishop of Antioch, wrote: *"Moses was the leader of the Jews, as I have already said, when they had been expelled from Egypt by King Pharaoh whose name was Tethmôsis."*[64] Hence, on account of the Manethonian history of Egypt, it had become very customary to identify the ancient Israelites with the king-shepherds. Although this identification was indeed an erroneous one, I believe that the idea had been circulated in Antiquity long before the Manethonian history of Egypt was ever written — by the ancient Israelites themselves of all people. The reasons why the Israelites would have wanted to confound their own history with that of their sworn enemies, the Amalekites, are manifold. First of all, the biblical redactors who composed Israel's history during the Babylonian exile actively sought to *"blot out the remembrance of Amalek"* forever (Deut. 25:19).

One way in which they accomplished that was to take pivotal events from the history of the Amalekites and portray them in the Scriptures, with the necessary

---
[64] Manetho, Aegyptiaca, FR. 51.

modifications, as having been part of Israelite history. A prime example of that was the usurping of this particular story, as later related by Josephus, about the Hyksos' expulsion from Egypt and their subsequent founding of Jerusalem. As the biblical Exodus narratives are, in reality, an amalgamation of four different historical events separated in time by centuries, we find that the Hyksos expulsion out of Egypt in the LBII period during the reign of King Tuthmosis III (Thummosis, the son of Misphragmuthosis) symbolises the "Second Exodus." Furthermore, as the central biblical character of Moses in the Old Testament represents an equally complex intermingling of six different historical Moses figures, we additionally detect that this Second Exodus, which I date to 1,380 BCE, was led by the "Second Moses." What is particularly significant is that this was the first time that a Moses character headed and Exodus out of Egypt. We of course recall that during the First Exodus, in 1,628 BCE, there was no Moses. It is only with the advent of Ahmose, the apparently adopted son of King Sobekhotep IV, that the Mosaic tradition emerges with the "First Moses." It is indeed intriguing that the first two Moses figures were not Israelites themselves. Why the sixth century BCE biblical redactors chose to partially model the Hebrew Moses after these two individuals is obviously a mystery. Was there after all a specially meaningful relationship between the primordial Egyptian Moses and the subsequent Amalekite Moses? Maybe the Amalekite Moses, poised to undertake a war of conquest against Solomonic Judea, saw himself as a liberator of his people, much as Pharaoh Ahmose had been. Hence, he might have consciously chosen the name of Moses (a variation of Ahmose) to reflect that. The 240,000 people (probably an exaggerated number) whom Josephus says were forced to evacuate Avaris as a result of Tuthmosis III's siege no doubt had to have been led to Judea by a charismatic leader — whom I conjecture was the Second Moses. Without a doubt, that Second Moses could have been none other that King Sheshi II. He is the one who was ruler of Avaris at the time of King Tuthmosis III's blockade. His reign as king of the Amalekites seems to have lasted for over a decade after their expulsion from Avaris (i.e. until 1,369 BCE). Therefore, it was King Sheshi II who had led the Exodus to Jerusalem.

Another crucial bookend can be established between the First and Second Exoduses. I believe that in both instances, the flight from Egypt was accompanied by a massive natural cataclysm. Only this time around, the cause does not appear to have been the orbital shift of a planetary body but a meteorite shower. Probably, while the Amalekites were on their way toward exile in Syria-Palestine, the following events took place in the ancient skies according to the annals of Pharaoh Tuthmosis III:

> In the year 22, of the 3rd month of winter, sixth hour of the day. ... the scribes of the House of Life found it was a circle of fire that was coming in the sky ... it had no head, the breath of its mouth had a foul odor. Its body one rod long and one rod wide. It had no voice. Their hearts became confused through it: then they laid themselves on their bellies. ... They went to the Pharaoh ... to report it. His Majesty ordered... has been examined... as to all which is written in the papyrus rolls in the House of Life. His Majesty was meditating upon what happened. Now after some days had passed, these things became more numerous in the skies than ever. They shone more in the sky than the brightness of the sun, and extended to the limits of the four supports of the heavens ... Powerful was the position of the fire circles. The army of the Pharaoh looked on with him in their midst. It was after supper. Thereupon, these fire circles ascended higher in the sky towards the south. **Fishes and volatiles fell down from the sky. A marvel never before known since the foundation of their land.** And the Pharaoh caused incense to be brought to make peace on the earth .... And what happened was ordered by the Pharaoh to be written in the annals of the House of Life ... so that is be remembered forever.[65]

This very enigmatic text interestingly mirrors the biblical account of the Exodus in the sense that the "fishes and volatiles" which fell down from the sky could find their echo in the manna which fell from the sky (Ex. 16:15, 35) during the Hebrews' wanderings in the desert. Interestingly enough, as similarly described in the above account of Pharaoh Tuthmosis III, whatever that substance was which fell from the sky, the Bible conveys that it quickly began to stink if left uncollected on the ground (Ex. 16:20). Obviously, the notion that eatable stuff fell from the sky (i.e. fish and volatiles or manna) must communicate some sort of elusive metaphor. What the ancient Egyptians and Israelites really meant by that will most likely never be known. But what remains fascinating is how, just as we place the Second Exodus in the reign of Pharaoh Tuthmosis III, such a striking correlation can be found.

These "fire circles" which "shone more in the sky than the brightness of the sun" described by Tuthmosis III and which startled Pharaoh's army were probably in actual fact meteorites. While the destructive effects of these meteorites is not particularly made evident in Tuthmosis III's annals, the widespread destruction of many major cities of the Ancient Near east at the time in which I place the Second Exodus, in *c.*1,380 BCE, indicates that the meteor shower had indeed caused sig-

---

[65] Annals of Thutmose III — translated by Prince Boris de Rachewiltz.

nificant havoc — similar to a cataclysmic planetary orbital shift. At the Hittite capital of Hattusa (Boghazköy) in Anatolia, a tremendous destruction level has been recorder by archaeologist during the reign of King Tudhaliya III, in c.1,380 BCE. Given the sheer intensity of the devastation, scholars suppose that Boghazköy was invaded by enemies from all sides and burnt to the ground.[66] The evidence for the severe cataclysm is overwhelming but evidence for a foreign invasion is very slim. In fact, Suppiluliumas I, a close successor of Tudhaliya III, renovated the dilapidated buildings without ever putting the blame for their destruction upon foreign hordes. Not a single reference in Hittite records is made regarding civil strife or a break in the dynastic line between Tudhaliya III and Suppiluliumas I. The cause for the conflagration at Hattusa during LBII must be found somewhere else.

In his 1948 groundbreaking book *Stratigraphie Comparée et chronologie de l'Asie Occidentale*, the influential French archaeologist Claude F. Schaeffer (1898-1982) alleged to have uncovered massive evidence for a widespread catastrophic destruction of major Late Bronze Age Syro-Palestinian settlements in c.1,365 BCE.[67] This is the very same conflagration which I personally chose to date fifteen years earlier — to c.1,380 BCE. The astounding thing is that C. Schaeffer, two years before Immanuel Velikovsky's *Worlds in Collision* was published, was already entertaining the idea that those massive destructions were possibly the result of natural catastrophes in antiquity.[68] Actually, even as early as the 1930s, while excavating at Ugarit, Schaeffer came across destruction levels that were so widespread in sheer scope and intensity, that he began questioning the accepted view among archaeologists that the cities had been destroyed by invading armies.[69] In one of his correspondences with Immanuel Velikovsky on April 4th

---

[66] David Hawkins 'The Hittites and their Empire.' In Joan G. Westenholz (editor) (1996) *Royal Cities of the Biblical World*, p. 75.

[67] Claude F. A. Schaeffer (1948) *Stratigraphie comparée et chronologie de l'Asie Occidentale (IIIe et IIe millénaires)*, Oxford University Press: London, pp. 2, 5. Schaeffer's lower date [than my own date of 1,380 BCE] partly stems from his belief that the conflagration dated to the reign of Amenhotep IV. He has come to this conclusion on the sole account of a particular Amarna correspondence (EA 151) in which Abimilki, King of Tyre, writes to Pharaoh to tell him that a fiery catastrophe had decimated the palaces at Ugarit. Given that Ugarit was destroyed during LBII, Schaeffer believed that he had found archaeological confirmation for the event described in EA 151. I believe however that Abimilki lived during the Iron Age (see Chap. 15). As a result, the two events cannot be correlated. The need to have the LBII catastrophe at Ugarit happen during Pharaoh Amenhotep IV's reign is then nullified.

[68] Although Schaeffer did not make any such claims implicitly in *Stratigraphie Comparée*, he did ask: "... what is the nature of these events which destroyed the major cities from Anatolian Troy ... to the lands of Caucasus?" (1948, p. 535). While he did not venture to explain the actual nature of the conflagrations, he did realize he had to rule out human action.

[69] See Gunnar Heinsohn 'Destruction Layers in Archaeological Sites: The Stratigraphy of Armageddon.' In Milton Zysman & Clark Whelton (editors) (1990) *Catastrophism 2000 (A Sourcebook for the Conference: Reconsidering Velikovsky)*, p. 219.

1974, Schaeffer wrote: *"I am in full agreement with your theories of catastrophes caused by extraterrestrial agents in pre-historic and early historical times."*[70] Although, according to sources close to him, Schaeffer did not agree with Immanuel Velikovsky's chronological reconstructions, he nonetheless clearly believed in Velikovsky's scenario of global natural catastrophes in historical times. He reiterated his commitment to those revolutionary ideas ten years later when, on April 12th 1974, Schaeffer again wrote to Velikovsky saying: *"... how right you have been to date some of the great natural catastrophes in the early historical periods."*[71] There is therefore no doubt that Schaeffer would have been open to the suggestion that the destruction levels attested to in Syria-Palestine/Western-Asia during the early fourteenth century BCE could have been the result of a major cosmic catastrophe. To quote him directly:

> Our inquiry has shown that these successive crises which opened and closed the principal periods of the 3rd and 2nd millennia were not caused by the action of man. On the contrary, compared with the magnitude of these general crises and their profound effects, the exploits of conquerors and the schemes of political leaders seem very insignificant.[72]

The massive destructions caused by the meteorite shower of 1,380 BCE all over the ancient Near East and the Mediterranean were indeed responsible for the great movements of populations and political upheavals of the time. Like the Hebrews of the Middle Bronze Age had benefited from the lunar shift of 1,628 BCE as they entered the Promised Land, finding the Canaanite fortified towns ravaged by fire, so were the Hyksos-Amalekites' burden lightened by the sudden upheavals experienced by the great Solomonic cities now lying desolate in 1,380 BCE.

A Hyksos Palace in Jerusalem

> *" The function of war-god is*
> *for Seth a specialisation of his rule*
> *over foreign territories. A foreign country*
> *is a border region. That less orderly part*
> *of the world where he belongs."*
>
> - H. Te Velde
> *Seth, God of Confusion*

---

[70] *Biblical Archaeology Review* (1985) 'BARlines: Schaeffer's View of Velikovsky', Vol. 11 - Num. 1, p. 8.
[71] Ibid.
[72] C. F. Schaeffer (1948) p. 565. Cited in G. Heinsohn (1990) p. 221.

The claim made by Flavius Josephus that the Hyksos founded the city of Jerusalem following their expulsion from Avaris by King Tuthmosis III, if accurate, raises a number of interesting questions. The first major question of course has to be: how did the Hyksos-Amalekites, the traditional enemies of the Israelites, manage to enter into King Solomon's territory? Did they have to conquer Jerusalem? Secondly, is there any evidence of a Hyksos presence in Jerusalem during the Late Bronze II period? It is my contention that the answer to the first question is that the cosmic catastrophe of 1,380 BCE, coupled with the invasion of Syria-Palestine by horse-drawn chariot-riding Indo-Europeans such as Hurrians, Hittites and Amorites, completely decimated the United Monarchy of Israel. It is even very likely that King Solomon was killed by these invading hordes who sought to take over his territory. Needless to say, my hypothesis is very different from the traditional biblical account of how Israel's United Monarchy came to an end. But I believe that this humiliating episode was deliberately left out of the Hebrews' history by the biblical redactors during the Babylonian Exile for obvious reasons. Much more will later be said about the motives, means and repercussions of this clearly ideologically motivated omission. For the time being, we shall concentrate on the second question. Can we really prove that the Hyksos settled in Jerusalem during the LBII period? Again, I answer this question in the affirmative.

In recent years, Professor Gabriel Barkay of Tel Aviv University has brought the attention of the world's scholarly community to the presence in Jerusalem of Egyptian-style artifacts in a Late Bronze Age context. Piecing together evidence from a series of partially published archaeological surveys dating from the late nineteenth century, Prof. G. Barkay has successfully demonstrated that, north of Damascus Gate, outside the walled city of Herod's Jerusalem, laid an impressive array of pharaonic small artifacts that are for sure not local. Also found at the site were the remains of an Egyptian-style building. This area is now the site of both the École Biblique et Archéologique Française, and of the Dominican monastery of St-Étienne. The Dominican fathers began conducting archaeological excavations there from 1882.[73] Thirteen years later, a report was published by Père M. J. Lagrange entitled: 'Saint Étienne et son sanctuaire à Jerusalem.'[74] Over a century later, it was discovered that many of the finds documented in that report, had been dated incorrectly. In 1973, it became clear that the remains actually spread through a much earlier period than French Egyptologist Georges Legrain had originally surmised. While Legrain assumed that all the sites and objects unearthed were associated with the fifth century CE church built by the Byzantine Empress

---

[73] See Gabriel Barkay (1996) 'A Late Bronze Age Egyptian Temple in Jerusalem?', *Israel Exploration Journal* Vol. 46 - Num. 1, p. 23.

[74] M. J. Lagrange (1894) *Saint Étienne et son sanctuaire à Jerusalem*, Paris.

CHAP. X: THE MISSING LINK | 367

Eudocia, it was found that two caves were in fact from the period of the biblical Judean Monarchy (i.e. eighth to seventh centuries BCE conventionally).[75] Evidence of even earlier settlement and building activity is also evident. Indeed, Barkay directs us to an Egyptian stele fragment, and offering table, and an Egyptian-style capital, which have all been dated to the Late Bronze II period.

The small Egyptian stela, referred to as (SE17), was excavated by Père L. H. Vincent in the area of the Byzantine church, but was ironically given virtually no importance. The Egyptian stela in question was made of white stone and measures 13.5 cm in height, is *c*.12 cm wide, and 5 cm thick.[76] The inscriptions found on the stela fragment were published by Père V. Scheil in 1892.[77] Professor Barkay sums up its content as follows:

> The fragmentary inscription on the obverse contains 13 clear signs. It includes the title 'the foremost of Westerners,' which is the title of Osiris, the god of the dead who were buried on the western side of the Nile. Scheil suggested reading the inscription: **'[a stele to the god Seth who gave] strength** and long life of [Osiris the] foremost of westerners ... to the deceased ...' The name of Osiris also appears on an inscribed stele of Nubian sandstone discovered at Hazor and on stelae of local *kurkar* stone found at Deir el-Balah. Scheil claimed that part of the rectangular ear of the Egyptian god Seth is visible underneath the middle column of hieroglyphs ...[78]

What I should wish to bring particular attention to is the stela's author's obvious devotion to Seth, the Egyptian deity of chaos. Seth is a god who dwells at the periphery of Egypt — that is outside of Ma'at's divinely ordered world. Hence, Seth was widely identified with invading foreigners and chaos.[79] As the Hyksos-Amalekites had been exiled to the Asiatic lands by Tuthmosis III, beyond the divinely ordered land of Egypt, it is only natural that they would have identified themselves with Seth. Moreover, being the enemies of the dynastic Egyptians, the choice of Seth as their patron-deity was self-evident.

What is interesting about the second object: the offering table, is that Barkay identified it as being of the *htp* type — known in ancient Egypt from the Old King-

---

[75] G. Barkay and A. Kloner (1986) 'Jerusalem Tombs from the Days of the First Temple', *Biblical Archaeology Review* Vol. 12 - Num. 2, pp. 22-39; G. Barkay, A. Kroner & A. Mazar 'The Northern Necropolis of Jerusalem during the First Temple Period.' In H. Geva (editor) (1994) *Ancient Jerusalem Revealed, Jerusalem*, pp. 119-123.
[76] Gabriel Barkay (1996) 'A Late Bronze Age Egyptian Temple in Jerusalem?', p. 27.
[77] V. Scheil (1892): Varia, II, *RB* 1, pp. 116-117.
[78] Gabriel Barkay (1996) p. 28-29.
[79] See David Frankfurter (1993) *Elijah in Upper Egypt (The Apocalypse of Elijah and Early Egyptian Christianity)*, Fortress Press: Minneapolis, p. 164.

dom until the Late Period. He also remarks that similar objects were found in Late Bronze Age Canaanite temples.[80] Finally, the third artifact which is of significance to us, the Egyptian-style capital, was found near the entrance of a Garden Tomb. Upon observation of the capital's shape, Prof. Barkay concludes that it definitely does not belong to the Hellenistic or Byzantine Periods. He is convinced that it belongs to the time of the Egyptian New Kingdom. Describing the object in question, he writes:

> The capital's height is 54 cm.; the diameter of its base is 53 cm. (one royal Egyptian cubit?) and that of the top is about 80 cm. (1 1/2 cubits?). It is made of local limestone ... The type of stone appears to be similar to that used for the stele fragment with the hieroglyphic inscription. ... Eight leaves are modelled in low relief around the capital. The maximal width of each leaf is 22 cm. ... The shape of the capital resembles palm capitals of ancient Egyptian architecture. Many are known in Egypt from the New Kingdom period ... [81]

Of course, the New Kingdom period which Professor Gabriel Barkay speaks of also incorporates the Theban Renaissance in the new chronology. After having spent over two hundred years in Egypt's Delta, the Hyksos had naturally become partially Egyptianized. At the time of their Exodus from Egypt, their iconography would have certainly been analogous to Theban Renaissance art. All circumstances hence point to the obvious fact that the LBII Egyptian-style remains unearthed in Jerusalem must be classified as Hyksos artifacts.

The Men with Horses: The Hurrian Invasion of Canaan

and the Transmission of Horse-drawn Chariots in Egypt

Returning to the salient question of who held the political balance of power in Syria-Palestine following the cosmic cataclysm of 1,380 BCE and the resulting massive population movements, it is necessary to determine where exactly the new Hyksos capital in Jerusalem stood among the ancient Near Eastern powers of the time. With the demise of Solomonic Israel, did the Amalekites simply fill in the power vacuum? The truth is, the Hyksos-Amalekites were a minor power in LBII Syria-Palestine. The real power wielders were the Indo-Europeans who flooded the ancient Near East at the time of the meteor shower of 1,380 BCE. They were the ones who immediately took advantage of the chaos which accompanied the cosmic catastrophe to defeat King Solomon and establish a clear hegemony in the region. In

---

[80] Gabriel Barkay (1996) p. 31.
[81] Ibid, pp. 38-39.

CHAP. X: THE MISSING LINK | 369

a Late Bronze II document, dated to the reign of the Egyptian king Amenhotep II, known as the Elephantine Stela the latter records:

> Amenhotep (II), beloved of Harakhte and Amon, Lord of Thebes, Good God, creation of Re ... there is none fighting before him; an archer mighty in smiting; a wall protecting Egypt; firm of heart, [...] in the hour of [conflict]; trampling down those who rebel against him; [instantly] prevailing against all the barbarians with people and horses, when they came with myriads of men, while they knew not of Amon-Re ... [82]

In this text, King Amenhotep II refers clearly to the Indo-European invasion of Syria-Palestine which coincided with the Amalekite Exodus. These barbarian newcomers, evidently of Aryan origins, travelled with horses. While these Indo-European raiders did not conquer Egypt, their influence over Late Bronze Age Egypt would nonetheless be monumental. It was these Aryan tribes, not the Hyksos, who introduced the Egyptians to the horse and horse-drawn chariot. As historian Rivka Gonen remarks:

> The origin of the horse-drawn chariot has yet to be elucidated. The Egyptian word for chariot clearly indicates that it was brought to Egypt from Canaan, though Canaan was merely a way station on the route of its diffusion from the original source.[83]

As a result, I am thoroughly convinced that this crucial dissemination of the horse-drawn chariot from the homeland of the Indo-Europeans, through Canaan, and finally to Egypt, took place during the Late Bronze II era. Since the most prominent new Indo-Aryan ethnic group to enter Canaan during LBII were the Hurrians, the credit for introducing the horse to Egypt ought to be attributed to them.

> It is hardly accidental that from the time of Thutmose III onwards the Egyptians applied the term *H3rw* (i.e. Hurru) to the inhabitants of Syria-Palestine and that *H3rw* as a geographical name is known since the time of Thutmose IV. The penetration of large numbers of Hurrians into Canaan was dominant enough to justify the designation "Hurru" for the land and its inhabitants.[84]

---

[82] J. H. Breasted, *Ancient Records of Egypt*, Vol. II - § 792.
[83] Amnon Ben-Tor (editor) (1992) *The Archaeology of Ancient Israel*. Trans. by R. Greenberg. Yale University Press: New Haven and London; The Open University: Israel , p. 245.
[84] Nadav Na'aman (1994) 'The Hurrians and the End of the Middle Bronze Age in Palestine, *Levant* 26, p. 177.

The aforementioned observation by the eminent Levantine archaeologist Nadav Na'aman confirms that the ethnic identity of these Indo-Aryan newcomers to Canaan, contemporaries of the LBII pharaohs of Egypt, was Hurrian. Na'aman furthermore mentions that Pharaoh Tuthmosis IV cited Hurru-people who settled in Egypt after their capture from Gezer. Soon afterwards, King Amenhotep II recorded in his booty list thousands of Hurru-people, whom he captured in Canaan. In the presence of such overwhelming evidence, scholars virtually unanimously recognize that the LBII Egyptians regarded the people of Canaan as "Hurrians."

I further maintain that the Hyksos-Amalekites (or Amu) forged an alliance with these Hurrians — which allowed them to ensure not only a certain level of security in the region, but also gave them the clout to flex some political muscles of their own. With this newly-found alliance, the Hyksos eventually became the driving force behind the Late Bronze II kingdom of Amurru in northern Syria. Certain scholars believe that the state of Amurru might not have even existed until sometime after the reign of Egypt's King Amenhotep II.[85] While many scholars equate the "land of Amurru" which begins appearing in Levantine texts during the LBII period with the kingdom of the Amorites, I believe that the former was a distinct, and new, political entity. The fact that *"the land of Amurru"* seems to first appear in ancient texts precisely during the LB II period is very significant. Most historians contend that the term land of Amurru means "the West" or "the Western Land."[86] It is my own belief however that the population of Amurru must have consisted of a mixture of Amalekites, the "Amu", and of Hurrians, the "Hurru." This new kingdom emerged as a direct result of the arrival into Canaan of the Amalekites from the south and the Hurrians from the north, following the cosmic catastrophe of 1,380 BCE.

But the greatest power of the time in Western Asia were the Anatolian Hittites. Having successfully displaced the Mitannian hegemony in Syria, Hatti (the Hittite kingdom) penetrated as far as Damascus and the Lebanon Valley. Most Syro-Palestinian city-states came under the vassalage of the Hittite king — including Amurru. In a treaty between the Hittite king Suppiluliumas and Aziras, King of Amurru, the former wrote:

> I, the Sun, [made you my vassal.] And if you, [Aziras, 'protect' the king of the Hatti land, your master,] the king of the Hatti land, your master, will 'protect' you in the same way. ...

---

[85] Donald B. Redford (1992) *Egypt, Canaan, and Israel in Ancient Times*, Princeton University Press: Princeton, New Jersey, p. 170.
[86] Robert R. Stieglitz (1991) 'The City of Amurru', *Journal of Near Eastern Studies* Vol. 50 - Num. 1, p. 45.

CHAP. X: THE MISSING LINK | 371

> But Aziras, the king of [Amurru] land, parted from the gate of Egypt and became subservient to the Sun, the k[ing of H]atti land. And the Sun, the great king, was ve[ry happy] about .... that Aziras fell down at the feet of the Sun. Aziras parted from the gate of Egypt and fell d[own at the feet of the Sun.] I, the Sun, the great king, [accepted] Aziras [in vassalage] and added him to his brethren.[87]

When Suppiluliumas says that the king of Amurru "parted from the gate of Egypt," he may well have been referring to the exodus of the Amalekites from the land of Egypt during the reign of Tuthmosis III. As Egypt's rival, the Hittites gladly embraced the incoming Amalekites (now the Amu of Amurru) into their rapidly growing sphere of influence. In any event, the Hittites, now the dominant power in Syria, and Egypt promptly found themselves involved in a long-standing tug of war for control over Syria-Palestine.

The Tell el-Amarna and Boghazköy Records

Having finally removed the yoke of the Hyksos occupation in Avaris, the dynastic Egyptians, under the leadership of King Tuthmosis III, finally began, for the first time since the days of the illustrious 12th Dynasty, to look toward Western Asia with a conqueror's coveting eye. During the reigns of Pharaohs Tuthmosis III, Tuthmosis IV and Amenhotep II, military campaigns of varying scales began being launched from Egypt into Syria-Palestine. The numerous city-states which Egypt sought to subdue fought to maintain their independence. In a concerted effort to do just that, they frequently banded together in broad alliances headed by the Kingdom of Kadesh on the Orontes River in central Syria. They looked to the Kingdom of Mitanni for military backup — a major rival of Egypt in Syria.

The reign of Pharaoh Amenhotep III, however, signalled the end of the regular Egyptian military incursions into Syria-Palestine. Amenhotep III, and his successor Amenhotep IV, preferred to rule Egypt's hard-won Asiatic dominions from afar. Amenhotep III and Amenhotep IV also seem to have directed their attention toward establishing cordial diplomatic relations with the Ethiopians of Meroë. As will be made clear later in this chapter, these amiable relations with the kings of Ethiopia ultimately proved very beneficial for Amenhotep IV in particular. Nubiologists have long been intrigued by the presence of a temple-wall carving, from Meroë, of a the figure of a Pharaoh who bore exactly the same prenomen as King Amenhotep III (see Fig. 10g). The problem is that, according to the conventional Nubian chronology, this temple drawing was executed over a millennia after the reign of Amenhotep III. Scholars believe that the Ethiopians were merely attempting to

---

[87] James B. Pritchard (editor) (1955) *ANET*, pp. 529-530.

revive, or ensure the continuity, of pharaonic culture long after it had declined in Egypt. According to the new chronology, however, the Kingdom of Meroë was thriving at the time of Pharaoh Amenhotep III's reign in the Late Bronze Age. Therefore, there is no reason whatsoever that this figure of Amenhotep III from the Meroë temple-wall cannot be a genuine representation of the Late Bronze Age Egyptian pharaoh — carved during his lifetime.

The interest of Amenhotep III and Amenhotep IV in international relations was reflected in the establishment, in the latter years of Amenhotep III's reign, of a diplomatic correspondence centre at the capital-town of Tell el-Amarna in Upper Egypt (midway between Memphis and Thebes) — where the various Canaanite chieftains under Egypt's vassalage would regularly write to Pharaoh. An exhaustive archive of these correspondences were by chance found, in 1887, by an Egyptian peasant woman while sifting through the rubble of the ancient capital of Tell el-Amarna. The discovery of these tablets opened up a floodgate of information about Egypt's diplomatic relations with its Near Eastern neighbours. Between 1891 and 1892, eminent British Egyptologist Sir Flinders Petrie took over the task of excavating at Tell el-Amarna.

Another vital piece of the jigsaw puzzle was uncovered in 1906 when Hugo Winckler found an invaluable body of cuneiform texts at the ancient Hittite capital of Boghazköy (Hattusa). This archive (over ten thousand letters) was even more extensive than the one found at Tell el-Amarna nineteen years earlier. The Boghazköy records provided important missing detail, not already found in the Amarna letters, about the Egypto-Hittite relations during the Late Bronze Age. Among the important documents found at Boghazköy, is a copy of the peace treaty ratified by Hattusilis III and Ramses II following the Battle of Kadesh in the thirteenth century BCE. For the purposes of this chapter, we will concentrate on another Boghazköy document: *KUB*XIX 9. This text, dating also to the reign of Hattusilis III, narrates the important events in the reign of the latter's grandfather, Suppiluliumas I. The Anatolian archives come to an end not long after that with events dated to Suppiluliumas II's reign. With the collapse of the Hittite empire in the twelfth century BCE, Boghazköy was abandoned — as proven by an abrupt break in cuneiform correspondences.

The Amarna correspondences, as useful as they may be, must be assessed with extreme caution. I base this warning on my hypothesis that not all of the documents from Tell el-Amarna in fact date to the Late Bronze II period. As astonishing as this may seem, I contend that a vast number of these tablets actually date to the Iron Age. The scenario which I shall propose in Chapter 15 is that the well-known "Amarna revolution" headed by the heretic-king Akhenaten (customarily equated with the Late Bronze Age Egyptian king Amenhotep IV), really happened during the ninth

Fig. 10g: Pharaoh Tuthmosis III
(*by* Saint-Elme Gautier).

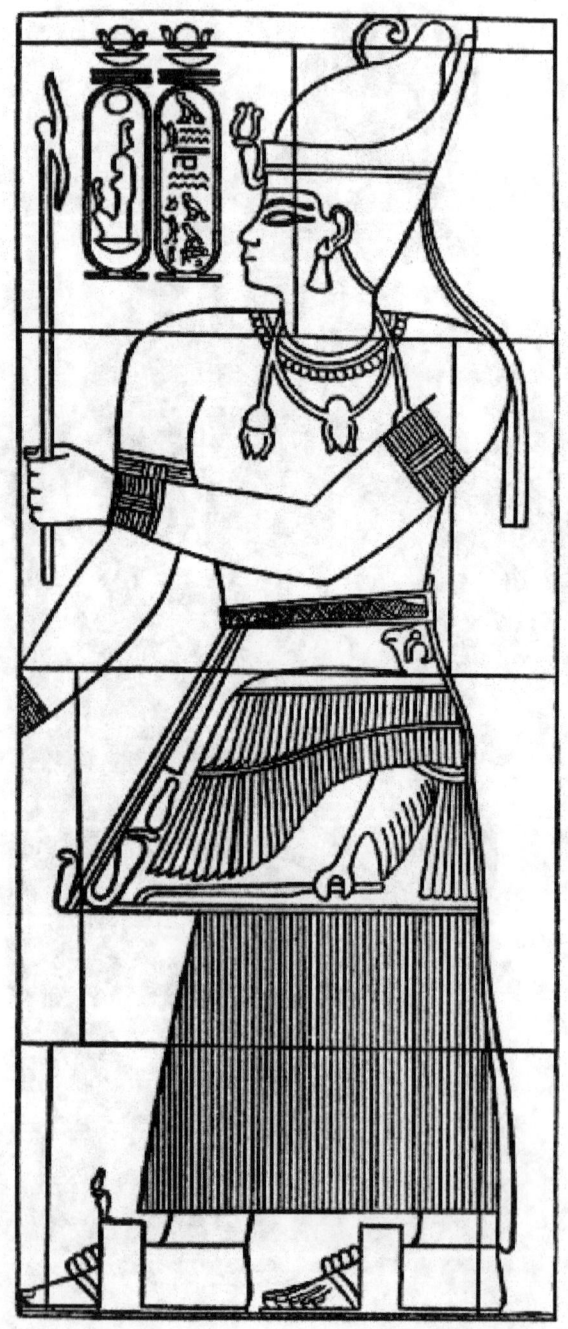

Fig. 10h: Pharaoh Amenhotep III in Meroë.

century BCE. As a result, the new chronology dissociates Pharaoh Akhenaten and Pharaoh Amenhotep IV. Moreover, it will be demonstrated later on that Akhenaten was not an alter-ego of Amenhotep IV, but in fact reigned some five centuries following the death of the latter. Although I maintain that the capital-city at Tell el-Amarna was indeed initially established during the Late Bronze Age II era, it can subsequently be argued that it once again became a vibrant correspondence centre during the Iron Age.

If I am indeed correct to assume that we must differentiate between two different sets of Amarna tablets – separated in time by half a millennium – then how ought one to go about differentiating between the two eras? For that purpose, the yardstick has to be the Boghazköy records. Since I am convinced of the accuracy of the orthodox dating for the Hittite tablets, the story lines from the Amarna tablets which unequivocally concur with the names, places and events from the Boghazköy records can therefore safely be dated to the LBII period.

Amenhotep IV and the Turbulent End
of the Theban Renaissance

If Amenhotep IV was not Akhenaten, then who was he? To answer that question, we must turn to Flavius Josephus:

> This king (Amenophis), he (Manetho) states, wishing to be granted, like Or, one of his predecessors on the throne, a vision of the gods, communicated his desire to his namesake, Amenophis, son of Paapis, whose wisdom and knowledge of the future were regarded as marks of divinity. This namesake replied that he would be able to see the gods if he purged the entire country of lepers and other polluted persons. Delighted at hearing this, the king collected all the maimed people in Egypt, numbering 80,000 and sent them to work, in the stone-quarries on the east of the Nile, segregated from the rest of the Egyptians. They included, he adds, some of the learned priests, who were afflicted with leprosy.
> (Josephus, *Against Apion*, I [26])

It is my contention that this King Amenophis was none other than the new 14th Dynasty's King Amenhotep IV. Eager to realize his strange ambition, Amenhotep IV was willing to go through great lengths. It's very unclear who "Or," his predecessor, was or what was meant by this "vision of the gods." Whatever the case may be, however, Pharaoh Amenhotep IV's decision to follow through with the advice of this diviner, Amenophis, son of Paapis, would have lasting effects on the course of Egyptian history. Thus, Pharaoh Amenhotep IV at once gathered all of those thousands of lepers and other handicapped people from all over Egypt and segregated them in the stone-quarry. But Amenophis, son of Paapis, had failed to forewarn Pharaoh Amenophis that he had also foreseen that these banished people would ultimately find a powerful ally and would eventually come to rule Egypt for 13 years. He instead left a written account of this to the king, and committed suicide. Josephus goes on:

> When the men in the stone-quarries had continued long in misery, the king acceded to their request to assign them for habitation and protection the abandoned city of the shepherds, called Auaris, and according to an ancient theological tradition dedicated to Typhon. Thither they went, and having now a place to serve as a base for revolt, they appointed as their leader one of the priests of Heliopolis called Osarsiph, and swore to obey all his orders.
> (Josephus, *Against Apion*, I [26])

Here we have an unambiguous reference to the old Hyksos capital in Avaris. It is described as the "abandoned" city of the king-shepherds. Evidently, the city had only recently been evacuated — as its history as a district where Seth was worshipped was fresh in the minds of the lepers and they felt quite comfortable with the prospect of going to dwell there. This could be an indication that most of the Hyksos buildings were still relatively intact, another indication of its recent occupation. Seemingly inspired by the legendary Hyksos resistance against Tuthmosis III, the lepers, who had themselves been relegated to the periphery of Egyptians society, found a powerful kindred spirit in the bygone Hyksos saga. Hence, they resolved to duplicate the feat accomplished by their newfound heroes.

Therefore, the choice of Avaris had, probably unbeknownst to King Amenhotep IV, been carefully calculated. The priest of Heliopolis, Osarsiph, who became the leader of the leapers at Avaris, fashioned himself as a new Sheshi-Moses. For this reason, I shall designate this Osarsiph as the Third Moses. Like the First and Second Moses before him, the biblical redactors have taken the events of his life to fashion the biblical Moses we are all familiar with. He gave the new hosts of Avaris laws and forbid them from associating with anyone outside their confederacy. He also ordered the citizens to repair the ancient city of Avaris and prepare for war against Pharaoh Amenhotep IV. As Amenophis, son of Paapis, had predicted, Osarsiph sent messengers to the Amalekites in their new homeland in Salem (ancient name of Jerusalem), and asked them to join him in an effort to overthrow Amenhotep IV. As Josephus relates:

> ... he (Osarsiph) sent an embassy to the shepherds who had been expelled by Tethmôsis (Tuthmosis III), in the city called Jerusalem; ... he begged them to unite wholeheartedly in an attack upon Egypt. He offered to conduct them first to their ancestral home at Auaris, to provide their hosts with lavish supplies, to fight on their behalf whenever need arose, and to bring Egypt without difficulty under their sway. Overjoyed by the proposal, all the Shepherds, to the number of 200, 000, eagerly set out, and before long arrived at Avaris.
> (Josephus, *Against Apion*, I [26])

Josephus describes the reaction of the pharaoh of Egypt as follows:

> The news of their invasion sorely perturbed Amenophis, king of Egypt, who recalled the prediction of Amenophis, son of Paapis. He began by assembling the Egyptians, and, after deliberation with their chiefs, sent for the sacred animals which were held in most reverence in his temples, and instructed the priests in each district to conceal the images of the gods as securely as possible. His five-year-old son Sethos, also called Ramesses after his grandfather Ra(m)pses, he entrusted to the care of a friend (the king of Ethiopia).
> (Josephus, *Against Apion*, I [26])

This passage is of extreme importance for validating the new chronology because, if the Amenophis of Manetho was indeed Amenhotep IV, we have the proof that he had a young son and future heir by the name of Ramses. I believe that this Crown Prince later became known as Pharaoh Ramses I — the first ruler of the new 15th Dynasty and, I believe, founder of the New Kingdom. The Manethonian accounts inform us that Amenophis (Amenhotep IV) crossed the Nile with 300,000 of his finest soldiers and marched towards his northern enemies.

Ironically, instead of confronting them, he abruptly retreats to Memphis — believing somehow that he would be fighting against the gods if he engaged in battle against the lepers and the shepherds. Once in Memphis, he picked up the Apis and other sacred animals he had previously ordered to be hidden there, and with all his army and populace, headed to Ethiopia for refuge. The Ethiopian king, who had been taking care of the young prince Ramses in the meantime, then welcomed Pharaoh Amenophis IV and his people into his country. He provided them with cities to dwell in for the predicted 13 year duration of Egypt's occupation. Meanwhile, in Egypt, the lepers and their allies *"treated the inhabitants in so sacrilegious a manner that the regime of the shepherds seemed like a golden age to those who now beheld the impieties of their present enemies."*[88] As a result, Amenophis' dire prediction had come true.

In the seventh tablet of a Hittite document known as "the Deeds of Suppiluliumas,"[89] we learn that the allegedly widowed queen of Egypt wrote to the Hittite king. In the correspondence, she pleads with Suppiluliumas to send her one of his sons in marriage to act as Pharaoh of Egypt — as her own husband, named Nibhururiya in the document, had died and left no heir to succeed him. Simply called "Dahamunzu" in the Hittite text, the widowed queen is generally identified as Akhesenamun — the wife of Tutankhamun. This is because scholarly opinion as to the identity of the deceased pharaoh, Nibhururiya, is divided between Pharaohs Akhenaten and Tutankhamun — with the latter gaining general consensus.[90] I argue, however, that King Nibhururiya was in fact neither. Kings Akhenaten and Tutankhamun, as I will attempt to further demonstrate in Chapter 15, were rulers of the ninth century BCE. The well-established theory that King Akhenaten was King Amenhotep IV of the fourteenth century BCE is, as I have claimed earlier, actually false. In the new history and revised chronology which I propose, Nibhururiya is to be identified with King Amenhotep IV but *not* with Akhenaten, and certainly not either with King Tutankhamun as conventionally believed. Quite evidently, as he fled to Ethiopia, King Amenhotep IV, perhaps because he had felt humiliated, had left his wife behind in Egypt. Believing that Pharaoh had perished in battle, Queen Dahamunzu looked for the assistance of the Hittite king. Alternatively, had Queen Dahamunzu actually been aware of her husband's self-imposed exile to Ethiopia, we may suppose that spreading the news of his death could have helped save Pharaoh's honour, and more importantly that of the Egyptian monarchy itself, among both Egypt's population and foreign lands.

Upon receiving Queen Dahamunzu' letter, Suppiluliumas was initially very reluctant to send his son, Zannanza, to Egypt. In order to ease his mind, he first dispatched an envoy from his court, Hattusaziti, to investigate matters. Why was the Hittite king so suspicious? Had he heard from certain sources that the king of Egypt wasn't really dead? Surely, he must have known that the king-sheperds and the lepers were threatening to, and in fact did ultimately, overrun Egypt! Was he concerned that the supposed widow of King Nibhururiya could have been a willing or unwilling agent of the invading shepherd-kings? I indeed believe that King Suppiluliumas interpreted the situation as a potential trap. In any event, here is how

---

[88] Josephus, *Against Apion*, I [26].

[89] This document, composed by Mursilis II, complements the *KUB* XIX 9 document dating to the reign of Hattusilis III.

[90] Trevor R. Bryce (1990) 'The Death of Niphururiya and its Aftermath', *Journal of Egyptian Archaeology* 76, p. 97.

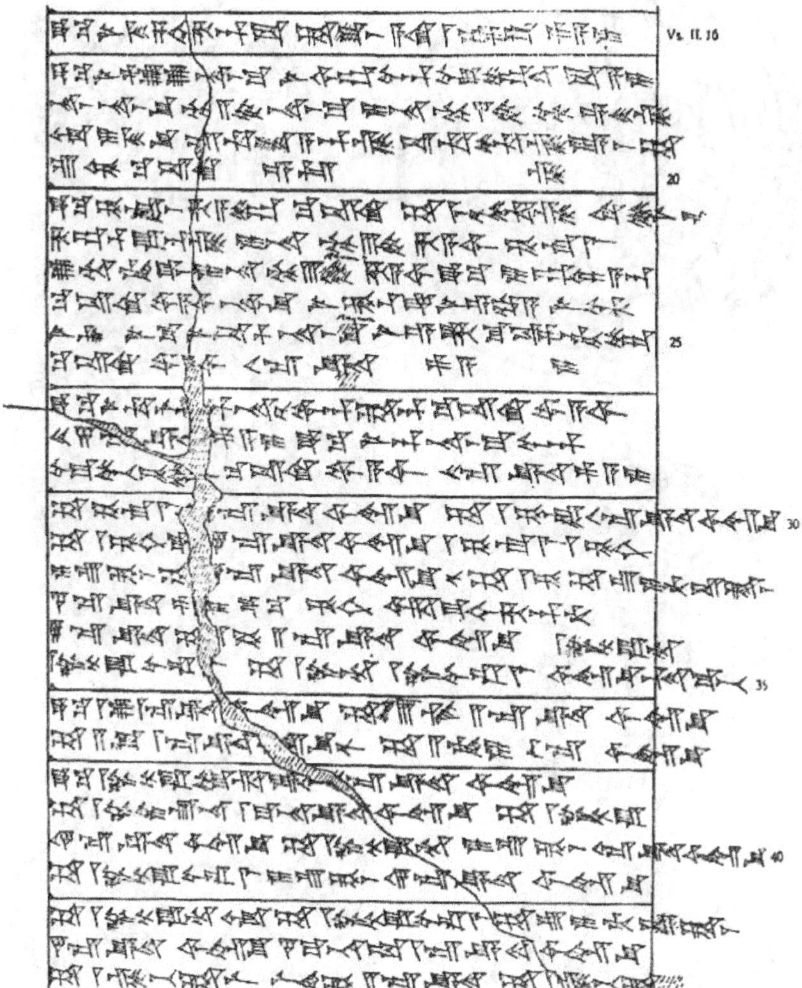

Fig. 10i: Boghazkhöy archive tablet.

Fig. 10j: Various Hittite royal sceals.

CHAP. X: THE MISSING LINK | 381

the events then unfolded, as explained by Trevor R. Bryce:

> (a) The Hittite envoy returns to Hattusa the following spring, accompanied by the Egyptian envoy Hani. Persuaded by the information he receives from them, Suppiluliuma sends his son Zannanza to Egypt for the intended marriage with the Egyptian queen.
> (b) Zannanza dies on the journey.
> (c) Suppiluliuma holds the Egyptians responsible for his son's death, and eventually launches a retaliatory attack on Egyptian territory (sc. in Syria).
> (d) Egyptian prisoners brought to Hatti **spread a plague throughout the Hittite population.**[91]

Who exactly were those plagued Egyptians being referred to? Moreover, doesn't that description sound eerily familiar? Obviously, these Egyptian prisoners who had plagued the Hittite population were none other than Josephus' "polluted" inhabitants of Egypt who had allied themselves with the Amalekites. Thus, the Hittite records and the Manethonian report of Josephus find an interesting parallel in the new chronology.

Finally, the Manethonian accounts relate that Amenophis (King Amenhotep IV) and his son Ramses (the future King Ramses I), probably after the prophesied 13 year-period had eventually elapsed, advanced from Ethiopia, each leading a large army, and *"defeated the shepherds and their polluted allies, killing many of them and pursuing the remainder to the frontiers of Syria."*[92] Knowing that the exile to Ethiopia lasted thirteen years, we can therefore establish when this latest Egyptian war of liberation took place — by approximating when Amenhotep IV retreated. For instance, on the year of Amenhotep IV (Nibhururiya)'s supposed death, began the Hittites' second Syrian war — which lasted six years. Suppiluliumas is known to have died at the end of this war. As a result, a firm chronological sequence can be gleaned from the following report, concerning the military accomplishments of Suppiluliumas, drafted by his grandson King Muwatalis II:

> These, (i.e. all the lost Anatolian territories) my grandfather Suppiluliuma brought back until he had reduced them to order. And he took 20 years until he had reconquered them. But when my grandfather Suppiluliuma entered the Hurri-land, then he vanquished all the Hurri-lands, and he fixed the boundary on yon side, (at) the land of Qadesh (and) the

---

[91] Trevor R. Bryce (1990) p. 99.
[92] Josephus, *Against Apion*, I [27].

land of Amurru, and vanquished the king of Egypt. But on this side, he destroyed the land of Irrite (and) the land of Suta and made the Mala river (=Euphrates) his boundary. And these (lands) he thus took into vassalage on the spot. And what was beside the Mala river, he vanquished by force. And his sons he made kings: — "in the land of Aleppo he made Telipinus king, in the land of Carchemish" he made Piyassilis king. My grandfather Suppiluliuma tarried the land of Amurru because the lands were strong, and he took 6 years before he had reduced them to order.[93]

Seeing that it has already been estimated that the last year of Suppiluliumas' reign fell in the year 1,340 BCE,[94] we must conclude, from the length of the war, that Amenhotep IV (Nibhururiya) was falsely reported dead in the year 1,346 BCE. On that year, the latter retreated to the Kingdom of Ethiopia for a thirteen-year period. This means Amenophis and Ramses reclaimed the Two Lands sometime around 1,333 BCE. Since that number represents a mere estimate, we can safely round it off to 1,330 BCE.

---

[93] Kenneth A. Kitchen (1962) *Suppiluliuma and the Amarna Pharaohs (A Study in Relative Chronology)*, Liverpool University Press, p. 3.
[94] Gregory McMahon (1989) 'The History of the Hittites', *Biblical Archaeologist* Vol. 52 - Nums. 2-3, p. 64.

Innermost coffin of Tutankhamun, by author

Part IV

New Kingdom

1,330 BCE to 747 BCE

11

The New Kingdom Begins (1,330 BCE to 1,187 BCE)

A truly gargantuan pillar of modern Egyptology comes crashing down with the new chronology's proposition that Pharaoh Ramses I, now founder of the New Kingdom, was indeed of royal blood and heir of a well-established pharaonic dynasty. The long-held view among several generations of scholars has so-far been that Ramses I's parental lineage hailed from the Egyptian army. It's always been thought that King Horemheb, who supposedly reigned in the fourteenth century BCE, having failed to produce a biological successor, appointed Ramses I as king to ensure the pharaonic succession. However, according to the new chronology, Horemheb really lived during the eighth century BCE — six hundred years after the accession of Pharaoh Ramses I. As we've seen in the last chapter, Ramses I was, in reality, the son of Pharaoh Amenhotep IV. Reclaiming the pharaonic throne, which his father had lost to a hostile coalition of Egyptian outcasts and Amalekites, Pharaoh Ramses I, in c.1,330 BCE, inaugurated the new 15th Dynasty. As his coronation name indicates, Menpehtyre (meaning "Stable is the power of Re"), Ramses I had gone to great lengths to reconsecrate Egypt to the sun-god Re-Atum and to enact a new era once again stressing the primacy of the Heliopolitan theology. Careful, however, not to alienate the Theban priesthood and its Amun theology, the new 15th Dynasty pharaohs skillfully combined the Theban cult of the preceding Theban Renaissance and the exceedingly more ancient Heliopolitan cult. The result was a return to the Middle Kingdom composite deity Amun-Re. The return to the Khemetic Heliopolitan Theology was, of course, the outcome of the new pharaohs' extended sojourn in the Black Land. Pharaoh Ramses I's successor, his son Seti I, continued in the same theological direction. Upon the death of Seti I, his own son and heir Ramses II travelled from the Delta down to Elephantine for his enthronement ceremony.[1] King Ramses II's selection of this city was not made at random. It was the home district of the Khemetic god Khnum, patron of the primordial Nome. King Ramses II erected a massive rock-cut temple at Abu-Simbel (see Fig. 11a). Acknowledging the primacy

---

[1] Donald B. Redford (1971) 'The Earliest Years of Ramses II, and the Building of the Ramesside Court at Luxor', *Journal of Egyptian Archaeology* 57, p. 111.

of both the Theban and Heliopolitan cults, Pharaoh Ramses II, in a dedicatory text from the Luxor Temple, portrays himself as a dedicated scholar who seeks to understand and appreciate the deep theological significance of the supremacy of Amun at Thebes.[2] What is more, the hieroglyphic text from Luxor positions the right eye of the sun-god in Thebes, and his left eye in Heliopolis.

Seti I's Victorious Campaigns in Asia

The New Kingdom pharaohs, motivated by the desire never again to experience the kind of humiliating defeat suffered at the hands of the Asiatics, embarked upon an ambitious empire-building project. Successful military expeditions of Seti into Canaan are recorded in several stelae (at Beth-Shan, Phoenicia and Tell esh-Shihab in northern Gilead). From the very first year of his reign, Seti I embarked on a military campaign in Syria-Palestine. Departing from the border fortress of Tjel (el-Qantara), he headed for Raphia. On his way to Raphia, he encountered a group of belligerent Shasu Bedouins. It appears that Seti I had been worried about the activities of the Shasu before undertaking his campaign, as he mentions on a Karnak relief dated to Year 1 of the Renaissance:

> One came to say to his majesty: "The vanquished Shasu, they plan a [rebellion]. Their tribal chiefs are gathered together, rising against the Asiatics of Kharu (Palestine). They have taken to cursing, and quarrelling, each of them slaying his neighbor, and they disregard the laws of the palace."[3]

Seti I ultimately vanquished and captured both Raphia and Gaza in Canaan. The obvious goal of the pharaoh was to establish an Egyptian empire in Asia. Taking advantage of obvious political instability in the ancient Near East at the time, he went on to annex several other city-states and turning them into vassals of the Egyptian crown. Other scenes from Karnak show Seti I attacking "the land of Amurru" and the Hittite forces at "the town of Kadesh" during the second leg of his Asiatic campaign in the following year. After having secured the allegiance of the Amurru, he then proceeded to attack the Libyans in a third campaign. After his fourth campaign, Egypt's military domination of Asia was unquestioned.

The fourth campaign, believed to have been against the Hittites, is immensely significant in the sense that it would arguably set the stage for the power struggle over the Asiatic lands between the two super-powers of the LBIII period: Egypt

---

[2] Mahmud Abd El-Razik (1975) 'The Dedicatory and Building Texts of Ramesses II in Luxor Temple — II: Interpretation', *Journal of Egyptian Archaeology* 61, p. 127.
[3] J. H. Breasted, *Ancient Records of Egypt*, Vol. III - § 101.

and the Anatolian Hittite empire. At the end of that fourth campaign, which set the boundary of Egypt's direct influence just south of the town of Kadesh, Seti I and the Hittite king Muwatalis II worked out a truce; but it was a peace in appearance only since, to quote French Egyptologist Nicholas Grimal, "the treaty simply gave both sides time to regain their strength."[4]

The Battle of Kadesh

Within the vast sweep of his foreign campaigns, Seti I had acquired the town of Kadesh, in northern Syria, as an Egyptian vassal. Understandably, this acquisition came as a threat to the Hittite Kingdom in Anatolia. From then on, it became a major priority for the Hittites to curb the expansion of the Egyptians into Syrian territory. The accession of a new king, Ramses II, in Egypt was seen by the Hittites as a golden opportunity to topple the balance of power. Taking advantage of this transition period, the Hittites immediately began courting the various Near Eastern rulers. In a letter written by the Hittite king Hattusilis III to the Babylonian ruler Kadashman-Enlil II much later in Ramses' reign, we read:

> Let me tell my brother the following, with respect to the messenger of the king of Egypt to whom my brother referred in his letter: Ever since your father and myself established diplomatic relations, and became like brothers, we agreed to the following: We are brothers, meaning that we are to be in hostile relations with each other's enemies and in friendly relations with each other's friends. When it happened that the King of Egypt (Ramses II) and I got angry with each other, I informed your father, Kadashman-Turgu, saying: "The King of Egypt has become my enemy," and your father answered as follows: "Should my brother march against Egypt, I will march with you; indeed, I will march personally with my infantry and my chariotry, as many as are available to go out with me." Ask your officials now, my dear brother; let them tell you how much infantry and chariotry your father actually promised to march out with me.

Such direct pressures applied by the Hittites were probably applied upon the various city-state rulers under the direct vassalage or influence of King Ramses II. Thus, the vassal-king of Kadesh's decision not to restore his allegiance to the Egyptian crown was based upon the political expediency, and apparent benefit, of not recognizing Seti I's heir, Ramses II, as his sovereign. Assuming that the king of

---

[4] Nicholas Grimal (1992) *A History of Ancient Egypt.* Trans. by Ian Shaw. Blackwell: Oxford, U.K., p. 247.

Kadesh took this bold step under the assurance of support from Muwatalis II, we may safely surmise that this single event could have triggered the entire conflict between Ramses II and the Hittites known as the Battle of Kadesh.[5]

Ramses II had secured the vassalage of the territory of Amurru in the fourth year of his reign. Setting out of Syria, he easily moved through Canaan until he reached the coast land of southern Phoenicia. After having subdued most of Phoenicia, he then moved inland through the eastern mountains towards the land of Amurru. Within two months, Amurru was his and, most importantly, Kadesh was now within reach.[6] Well aware of the danger Ramses' rapid advance posed to his empire's interests in the region, King Muwatalis II was determined not to allow Kadesh to fall, but he was even more intent on regaining the allegiance of the king of Amurru. All indications show that both parties expected to engage in a fierce duel of Titans. The Hittites had managed to secure in their camp northern Syrian as well as western and northern Anatolian troops. For his part, Pharaoh Ramses II divided his troops into four divisions: Amun, Re, Ptah and Seth. The Egyptians could likewise count on a multitude of conscripted foreign soldiers from the various city-states under their vassalage.

On Year 5, second month of the third season, of Pharaoh Usermare-Setepnere Ramses II's reign, his majesty boldly proceeded northward toward the highland of Kadesh. As King Ramses, with the Division of Amun marching behind him, crossed the channel of Orontes, they met with lurking Bedouins who, unbeknownst to Ramses, had been spies planted there by the Hittite king to misinform the Egyptian army. The Bedouins deliberately delivered a false report that the Hittite army was far away in the north Syrian town of Aleppo, some 120 miles away. Trusting this information, the Egyptians expected Muwatalis' forces to attack from the north or west. So Ramses and his division set up camp in the north-west of Kadesh. This apparently ideal location would later prove to be a trap as long as the other three divisions remained miles away. Indeed, soon after Ramses had pitched camp, two Bedouin counter-spies, rounded up by Egyptian reconnaissance forces, were brought over to Pharaoh Ramses and forced to confess that their brethren had earlier given him a false report. In reality, the Hittite army lay just behind Kadesh, less than two miles away. King Ramses II was wild with anger. Lying in ambush behind Kadesh, the Hittite army allowed Ramses II's first division of Amun to pass by, and then attacked the unprepared and stunned second division of Re while the third division of Ptah was still crossing the ford of Shabtuna. When Pharaoh heard

---

[5] Hans Goedicke (1966) 'Considerations on the Battle of Kadesh', *Journal of Egyptian Archaeology* 52, p. 71.
[6] Kenneth A. Kitchen (1982a) *Pharaoh Triumphant (The Life and Times of Ramses II, King of Egypt)*, Aris & Phillips: Warminster, U.K., p. 51.

the news, he raged "like his father Monthu" and, at once, charged toward the Hittite army alone — as his own troops had deserted him. In a heroic effort, Pharaoh Ramses narrowly prevailed against his immediate opposition and managed to save himself from certain death. Ramses had managed to draw out the fighting until the Na'arn (Seth) division came to save the Egyptian army from annihilation. The last remaining Ptah division subsequently arrived as Ramses' forces were struggling against the Hittite charioteers.

On the whole, the Battle of Kadesh was far from a victory for Ramses II. Having narrowly saved his own life and barely managed to rescue the remnant of his army whom he later severely and mercilessly punished, Ramses II finally agreed to sign a peace treaty with the Hittite king. Ramses had actually lost more than he had gained from the conflict since the Hittites had effectively regained control of the land of Amurru. Given such dismal results, modern historians are puzzled at the peculiar fact that Ramses overtly boasted about his "victory" at Kadesh. Following fifteen years of haggling between the Egyptians and the Hittites over dominance of the various Levantine city-sates, the two superpowers came to a virtual stalemate. So in Year 21 of Ramses II' reign, Egypt and Hatti signed a Peace Treaty, the first of its kind in history, which was later sealed by a marriage, in Year 34, between Ramses II and the daughter of King Hattusilis III.

Pharaoh Ramses II's "Hyksos" Division
The hypothesis that the land of Amurru's population was overwhelmingly of Hyksos extraction engenders the revolutionary notion that Pharaoh Ramses II reigned at a time when the Hyksos still represented a potential threat to the Egyptian state. After all, the grandfather of King Ramses II, Pharaoh Ramses I, had only recently undertaken a major liberation campaign against the Hyksos-Amalekites who had, once again, successfully invaded Egypt. Thenceforth, having learnt from Amenhotep IV's blunder, it became imperative for the new 15th Dynasty pharaohs to keep a stranglehold on the various Syro-Palestinian city-states — preventing them from forming any hostile alliances against the king of Egypt. All means were considered to ensure this objective's success. From Egyptianizing the Asiatics by allowing them to enrol in Pharaoh's army as well as permitting them to reside in Egypt as upwardly mobile citizens, to instituting vassal states all over western Asia. These were shrewd tactics which Pharaoh Ramses II employed with great success. At the very top of the latter's agenda was, of course, to prevent these vassal states from switching allegiance to the Hittite King.

Having firmly secured the allegiance of the land of Amurru prior to the outbreak of the war of Kadesh, King Ramses II could have thankfully counted on the services of the conscripts from Amurru — who came just at the right time to save him from certain death. The division of Seth was made-up of Canaanite soldiers called "Na'arn." These Na'arn hailed from the vassal sate of Amurru, in the region north of Byblos. As Hans Goedicke puts it: *"While the main body advanced from the south through the Bega', the division of Seth made its way through Amurru, the region north of Byblos."*[7] The reader's appreciation of the importance of this association of "Seth" with the land of Amurru is absolutely vital. We may recall from the Boghazköy annals that this is precisely where the Hyksos-Amalekites had settled *en masse* after their expulsion from Egypt under Pharaoh Tuthmosis III's reign. Moreover, the Hyksos' predilection for the storm-god Seth has already been amply demonstrated. Hence, I maintain that the name "Division of Seth" can be used interchange-ably with the term "Hyksos Division." The division of Seth was so named because it was made up mainly of Asiatic soldiers from foreign lands. Citing Prof. Julian Baldick:

> In Egypt itself Seth is worshipped in frontier regions, as the god of frontiers and other lands. When foreigners become influential in Egypt Seth is naturally given great veneration at pharaoh's court.[8]

Without a doubt, foreigners had indeed become very influential in Ramesside Egypt. The Hyksos immigrants in Egypt during the LBIII period were often referred to by the native Egyptians as "resident aliens."[9] A slightly more common appellation was that of "Foreign Chieftains." Modern scholars have also tended to refer to them as "Rulers of Foreign Lands." It is my contention that it is precisely because of the shepherd-kings' situation as resident aliens within Egypt's borders and as foreign chieftains in the Egyptian army during Ramses II's reign that they acquired the name of "Hyksos." Indeed, King Ramses II had gone to unusual lengths to accommodate the presence of two specific Asiatic groups in Egypt during the course of his reign: the Hyksos-Amalekites and the Phoenicians.

After Year 8: Foreigners in Pharaoh's Land

Why had there been so many foreigners in the land of Egypt during Ramses II's reign? The principal cause of the substantial influx of Asiatic blood into Egypt

---

[7] Hans Goedicke (1966) p. 79.
[8] Julian Baldick (1998) *Black God (The Afroasiatic Roots of the Jewish, Christian, and Muslim Religions)*, Syracuse University Press: Syracuse, NY, pp. 47-48.
[9] Hans Goedicke 'The End of the Hyksos in Egypt.' In Leonard H. Lesko (editor) (1986) *Egyptological Studies in Honor of Richard A. Parker*, Brown University Press: Hanover and London, p. 38.

CHAP. XI: THE NEW KINGDOM BEGINS | 391

during the second half of the fourteenth century BCE had, of course, been the invasion of Egypt by the lepers and shepherd-kings at the end of the Theban Renaissance. So when the pharaohs of the New Kingdom regained control of the country, after thirteen years of Asiatic occupation, they returned to a very different Egypt, ethnographically speaking. The challenge for the rulers of the new 15th Dynasty, for their very survival, was to promote the rapid Egyptianization of these foreigners. In the years immediately following the Battle of Kadesh, Pharaoh Ramses II, having lost the vassalage of the land of Amurru in Year 8 and coming to terms with the new political realities of the time, allowed the by then thoroughly Egyptianized Hyksos and Phoenicians dwelling in Egypt to constitute semi-independent dynasties of their own. These new dynasties, the 16th (Amalekite) and 17th (Phoenician) Dynasties, remained under the tutelage of King Ramses II in Thebes as vassal princes bearing full pharaonic titles. Politically, this arrangement benefited Ramses II since these northern foreign dynasties covered a strategic buffer zone in the remote eventuality of a Hittite invasion. The Hyksos and Phoenician origins of the 16th and 17th Dynasties are indeed confirmed in the Manethonian tradition by Eusebius:

> The Seventeenth Dynasty were Shepherds and brothers: **they were foreign kings from Phoenicia** who seized Memphis.
> (Manetho, *Aegyptiaca*, FR.48 [a])

Similarly, Sextus Julius Africanus wrote:

> The Seventeenth Dynasty were Shepherds and brothers: they were foreign kings from Phoenicia.
> (Manetho, *Aegyptiaca*, FR.47)

Both Eusebius and Africanus seem to have confused these 17th Dynasty Phoenician kings with the Hyksos invaders from the Middle Bronze Age. In the new chronology however, we find that these two dynasties, 16th and 17th, really belong in the closing Late Bronze Age. Furthermore, upon closer analysis, we may find that the source of this ancient erroneous equation between the Phoenicians and the shepherd-kings in fact point to a pivotal clue concerning a long-lost etymology. To be sure, should we accept the hypothesis earlier stipulated that the ancient Egyptian word "Hyksos," $Hk^3 H^3st$, meaning "Foreign Chieftains," was used to denote foreign rulers who dwelt in Egypt during King Ramses II's reign, then the name of Hyksos could equally be applied to the 17th Dynasty Phoenician kings. This is probably why Eusebius and Africanus refer to the Phoenicians as shepherd-kings. Far from being an indicator of any specific ethnicity or culture, the name of

"Hyksos," as renowned Egyptologist Donald B. Redford of the University of Pennsylvania states below, referred to an "alien authority."

> The use of the term $hk^3\ h^3s\ (w)t$ to designate power holders, but not those formally recognized by Pharaoh, presents a slight anomaly. As used in the Old and Middle Kingdom the term had come to mean an "alien authority."[10]

As alien authorities within LBIII Egypt, the Hyksos-Amalekite 16th Dynasty, as well as the Phoenician 17th Dynasty, reigned under the benevolent authority of King Ramses II. The Phoenicians were located in Thebes while the Amalekites governed their traditional territory of Avaris in Egypt's Delta. In order to safeguard his jurisdiction over his foreign-ruled principalities, Ramses II spent time in both his palaces in Thebes and Avaris. Recent archaeological excavations in Egypt's Delta have confirmed the presence, of the fabled Ramesside northern capital of Pi-Ramses (Estate of Ramses), the biblical Land of Ramses, in the region of Khatana/Kantir, just across the Nile's Pelusiac branch immediately to the north Avaris.

The first major question that immediately comes to mind for the biblically-inclined is of course: was this the site which the Hebrews were forced to build under the lash of the Pharaoh of the Oppression? For as the Book of Exodus relates:

> 11 Therefore they did set over them taskmasters to afflict them with their burdens. And they built for Pharaoh treasure cities, Pithom and Raamses.
> (Exodus 1:11)

Was Ramses II the biblical Pharaoh of the Oppression, as it is still generally accepted? I answer "yes" to these last two questions. Does this represent a contradiction given everything that I have said so far? Had not, according to my new chronology, Joshua's Conquest, the period of the Judges and that of the Israelite United Monarchy all come and gone by the time Pharaoh Ramses II acceded to Egypt's throne? How then could we now go back to the period of Hebrew bondage this late in the revised history? Well, the fact is that we still *have not* dealt with the critical period of Hebrew bondage. As we recall from Chapter 8, the king who knew not Joseph (Exodus 1:8) was Pharaoh Amenemhat III. I had besides argued that, contrary to the biblical version, this new king who reigned shortly after Joseph's death, had not oppressed the Hebrews, but actually elevated them to princely status. Thus, why would the biblical

---

[10] Donald B. Redford 'Textual Sources for the Hyksos Period.' In Eliezer D. Oren (editor) (1997) *The Hyksos: New Historical and Archaeological Perspectives*, p. 25.

CHAP. XI: THE NEW KINGDOM BEGINS | 393

redactors of the sixth century BCE completely concoct the story of the Hebrew bondage in Egypt? The truth is that they did not invent the story. What the biblical redactors skillfully did is to, once again, take two different series of events in Israelite history and artificially merge them into one. The result is a fictitious account based on fragments of genuine history. The first chapter of Exodus, albeit presented as a single short historical period, in itself covers a period of five hundred years. Exodus 1:8 which speaks of the king who knew not Joseph recounts an event from around 1,780 BCE, while Exodus 1:11, describing the Hebrews' ordeals in the Land of Ramses, retells happenings from the thirteenth century BCE.

So who exactly were these Israelites taken captive by King Ramses II to construct his palatial northern domain at Kantir? What had actually happened to the Israelite nation after it was quite literally swallowed up by the Indo-European invasion of Canaan in the Late Bronze II period? Having abruptly lost their long-held authority over their Promised Land, and suddenly finding themselves kingless, I propose that the once mighty nation of Israel instantly degenerated into a belligerent tribe of nomads known as the Shasu. The Shasu, first attested in ancient Egyptian literature during the reign of King Amenhotep III in the LBII period, dwelt principally in southern Canaan. The geographical lists of Pharaoh Ramses II specifically refer to their homeland as the 'land of Shasu Y-H-W (A).'[11] Many biblical scholars have enthusiastically pointed to this name, Y-H-W-(A), to argue that Yahwism, the religion of the ancient Hebrews based on the monotheistic worship of the god Yahweh, originated with the Shasu nomadic tribe. I believe that these Shasu were the carriers of the Israelite tradition and that, through them, the religion of Yahwism would reemerge, advocating a great renaissance of the Hebrew past, during the early Iron Age. Therefore, the Late Bronze III period can be interpreted as having been the "Dark Age of Israel."

I believe that Israelites arrived in Egypt's Delta during LBIII, unlike their ancestors, as prisoners of war at the time of King Ramses II. The latter had undertaken a major military campaign through Syria-Palestine — as part of the cold war waged between Egypt and the Hittites during the fifteen years following the Battle of Kadesh. Upon a block located atop the northern pylon of the Ramesseum (Ramses II's mortuary temple) in Thebes, is inscribed the following text: *"The town which the king (Ramses II) plundered in Year 8 — Shalem."* Shalem is the ancient name of the city of Jerusalem — which itself literally means the "City (or foundation) of Shalem."[12] King Ramses II's army, in the Year 8 campaign,

---

[11] H. H. Ben-Sasson (editor) (1976) *A History of the Jewish People*, Harvard University Press: Cambridge, Mass., pp. 17, 45.
[12] A. Jones (1990 [1856]) *Jones' Dictionary of Old Testament Proper Names*, Grand Rapids, p. 196. Cited in David M. Rohl (1995) *A Test of Time — Vol. I*, p. 149.

swept through Gaza, East Palestine, the Negev hills, the rift valley south of the Dead Sea, Edom-Seir, the land of Moab, as he *"swept round in a clockwise arc ... across the hilly central ridge of Canaan past Jerusalem, over the Jordan, past Jericho ..."*[13] The reliefs from Ramses' mortuary temple show Pharaoh bringing back lengthy rows of Syro-Palestinian captives back into Egypt from his Year 8 campaign. Among these multitudes of Asiatic captives, were the descendants of the kingdom of Israel. King Ramses II, as the Bible relates, coerced them into building his fortress-town of Pi-Ramses at Kantir.

Ramses II, after, in his own words, "plundering the chiefs of the Asiatics in their land," and turning those conquered lands into vassal sates, offered to his Syro-Palestinian subjects protection against outside conquering forces in return for their loyalty. In his Aswan Stela, Ramses wrote: "They sit in the shadow of his sword, and they fear not any country." For the dispossessed and landless Shasu-Israelites however, their status in Pharaoh Ramses' Egypt was that of slaves. Ramses II had apparently succeeded in governing a stable multicultural state. Hyksos-Amalekites, Phoenicians, other Asiatic peoples, Ethiopians and native Egyptians, all accepted the legitimacy of Pharaoh Ramses II's reign (1,290 - 1,224 BCE) which lasted for over sixty prosperous years. It was truly one of Egypt's golden eras. Over the few decades following King Ramses' reign however, a series of formidable ordeals would come along to test Egypt's authority, both on the domestic and international scenes.

The Rage of Typhon-Poseidon Strikes Again

One of the most severe of such ordeals was the renewed instability of the solar system which, in 1,187 BCE, occasioned yet another cycle-ending Typhon Season with a catastrophic orbital shift of the planet Mercury. Again, the results were large destructions of cities and swift invasions by foreign hordes. The ancient city of Emar in Syria, bordering the Euphrates Valley, which came under Hittite rule during the reign of King Mursilis II, suffered a massive destruction dated by scholars to the year 1,187 BCE.[14] According to Jean-Claude Margueron, this *"great cataclysm"* which visited Emar, is the very same agent responsible for the devastation of the Hittite empire at the end of the Late Bronze Age.[15] Once more, scholars claim that this violent conflagration was caused by a military raid carried out by a still undefined group of foreign invaders. But of late, certain scholars, like Nubiologist William Y. Adams, have been waking up to the fact that more complex

---

[13] Kenneth A. Kitchen (1982a) *Pharaoh Triumphant (The Life and Times of Ramses II, King of Egypt)*, Aris & Phillips: Warminster, U.K., p. 67. Cited in D. M. Rohl (1995) p.150.
[14] Jean-Claude Margueron (1995) 'Emar, Capital of Astata in the Fourteenth Century BCE', *Biblical Archaeologist* Vol. 58 - Num. 3, pp. 127-128.
[15] Ibid, p. 127.

explanations for the widespread destructions of major centres of civilizations of Antiquity must be found.[16] Once more, the cities were abandoned, never to be again inhabited during the entire first millennium BCE. In the case of Emar, the city lay in ruins until the Roman Era — at which time it was slowly reoccupied. But the great city was never rebuilt.[17] Elsewhere, in the mountain ranges of Asia, scientists have found that between c.1,200-1,150 BCE, glaciers in the Himalayan and Karakorum mountain ranges had severely retreated and that, in the Indus Valley, monsoon rains had drastically dipped to below normal levels.[18] Describing similar climatic deterioration spells during the same time in the eastern Mediterranean, William H. Stiebing, Jr. writes:

> The most persuasive data comes from the eastern Mediterranean itself. A log unearthed at Gordon in Asia Minor had series of very narrow tree-rings from around 1200 B.C.E., indicating a period of extremely dry years at that time.[19]

In China, ancient inscriptions from "oracle bones," datable to the twelfth century BCE, speak of "a year without harvest and with stunted seedlings."[20] As part of her studies on the Dark Age which engulfed the ancient Near East at the end of the Late Bronze Age, Professor Barbara Bell of Harvard University observed that such ubiquitous and intense conflagrations affecting the natural order were undoubtedly responsible for the unexplained collapse of the powerful Late Bronze Age cultural centres. Dr Bell writes:

> But even where it is clear that barbarian invasions did occur, we are left with the question of whether they are a sufficient cause or explanation for the destruction of a number of apparently powerful and prosperous states, and why so many different barbarian tribes were stirred to attack centers of civilization at the same time. Any one or two of the above disasters, standing alone, might be sufficiently explained by political factors. But the concentration of so many disasters and the universal absence of prosperity throughout the area strongly suggests a common underlying cause.[21]

---

[16] William Y. Adams (1968) 'Invasion, Diffusion, Evolution?', *Antiquity* 42, pp. 194-215.
[17] See also Daniel E. Fleming (1995) 'More Help from Syria: Introducing Emar to Biblical Study', *Biblical Archaeologist* Vol. 58 - Num. 3, pp. 139-147.
[18] Neumann and Parpola, Climatic Change, p. 167; Bryson and Murray, *Climates of Hunger: Mankind and the World's Changing Weather*, pp. 107-111.
[19] William H. Stiebing, Jr. (1994) 'Climate & Collapse (Did the Weather Make Israel's Emergence Possible?', *Bible Review* Vol. 10 - Num. 4, p. 25.
[20] K. D. Pang & H. H. Chou (1984) 'A Correlation between Greenland ice core climatic Horizons and Ancient Oriental Meteriological Records', *EOS* 65, p. 846.
[21] Barbara Bell (1971) 'The Dark Ages in Ancient History', *American Journal of Archaeology* 75, p. 2.

Indeed, the traditionally accepted theory that invading armies, whose ethnic origins historians are unable to securely determine, could have, in such unison, managed to simultaneously decimate powerful Late Bronze Age civilizations simply does not stand up to close scrutiny. This "common underlying cause" which Prof. Bell talks about was, in my own view, a very sudden and calamitous paroxysm of nature. The barbarian invasions were the "result" and not the cause of this planetary cataclysm. Without the common underlying cause, how could these northern invaders have garnered the sheer power, to so thoroughly pulverise such towering centres of civilization? Certainly, northern coalitions had indeed actively plotted to overrun the superpowers of the time in Egypt and Anatolia during the closing years of the Late Bronze Age. But the Mercury shift was the longed-for opportunity to achieve their ambition.

An Invasion from the North: The Sea Peoples

Storm Through Egypt and Libya

Even before the collapse of the major Late Bronze Age city-states accompanying the Mercury shift of 1,187 BCE, the stage was being set for the major population movements and foreign invasions which characterized the chaotic close of the Late Bronze Age in the ancient Near East. In a document dated to Year 5 Pharaoh Merneptah (1,220 BCE), not the Israel Stela, Ramses II's son and heir conveys the details of a massive offensive originating from the Libyan western desert. The Libyan king with his domestic and Meshwesh army, Meryry, were accompanied by a broad coalition of northern allies: the Sherden or Shardana (Sardinians), Lukka (Lycians), Teresh (Etruscans) and Shekelesh (Silicians), Ekwesh.[22] Merneptah's inscription concerning the Libyan campaign, found at Heliopolis, reads:

> Year 5, second month of summer, one came to say to His majesty: "The vile of the Libyans ... and every foreign land which is with him are penetrating to transgress the boundaries of Egypt." Then his majesty ordered [his] army to rise up against them.

Their objective was nothing less than the overthrow of the Egyptian government. The raid failed. Merneptah's army, in a fierce six-hour-long battle repelled the Libyans and their allies. Who were these various northern peoples who allied

---

[22] N. K. Sandars (1978) *The Sea Peoples (Warriors of the Ancient Mediterranean 1250-1150 BC)*, Thames and Hudson: London, pp. 105-106.

CHAP. XI: THE NEW KINGDOM BEGINS | 397

themselves with the Libyans? For one thing, it is certain that they were not indigenous to Africa but had arrived in Libya from the Mediterranean during the thirteenth century BCE. When, in 1860, the inscriptions of Merneptah were deciphered, it came as quite a shock to ancient historians and classicists to realize that north Mediterranean peoples had taken part in those ancient armed conflicts between Libya and Egypt.[23] Evidently, there had been a strong influx of European ethnic types into Libya early in the reign of Pharaoh Merneptah. Adhering to a very controversial theory by the late Harvard epigraphist Barry Fell (1917-1994), I contend that these Europeans who migrated to Libya had not hailed originally from the Mediterranean region, but had in fact come from northern Europe's Baltic region. Quoting Barry Fell:

> I must now express the view that the inscriptions have forced upon me: that I think it very probable that the Sea Peoples included substantial naval detachments from the Baltic region, that their language was a Nordic dialect of the Indo-European family, that the so-called "Libyan" alphabet is in fact of Nordic or at least northern European origin, and that it was taken to Libya by the defeated Sea Peoples who survived the Battle of the Nile. For some reason the alphabet they introduced has continued in use throughout subsequent Libyan history, whereas in its northern homeland it died out, to be replaced by runes. I would also hazard the guess that the blond Tuaregs who clung most tenaciously to the "Libyan" alphabet are probably descended from Nordic immigrants around the time of the Sea Peoples' invasion.[24]

Fell's argument, based on solid epigraphical grounds, that the Libyan alphabet stems from a Nordic dialect of the Indo-European family, has very interesting implications for the history of the ancient world. It would mean that, at some time during the closing Late Bronze Age, a horde of northern European immigrants descended upon the Aegean and, from there, subsequently settled in Libya. The prospect of a new Indo-European racial group suddenly entering the ancient Near East at the dawn of Merneptah's reign has also been explored by Immanuel Velikovsky:

> The Egyptians called the population of neighboring Libya Tehenu. The Tehenu were pictured with dark complexion and curly hair. Since the

---

[23] Immanuel Velikovsky (1978) *Ramses II and His Time*, Doubleday: Garden City, NY, pp. 196-197.
[24] Barry Fell (1982) *Bronze Age America*, Little, Brown & Co.: Boston and Toronto, p. 281.

First Dynasty of Egypt they had been known to the Egyptians by this name. But for some time another tribe, or race, named Temeh, was described and pictured as inhabiting Libya or its eastern part, Cyrenaica. "The Temehu were quite a different race whose skin was fair and who had blond hair and blue eyes. The home of those people cannot be Africa..."[25] They were clearly not of Semitic or Hamitic but of Aryan origin. Then who were they?[26]

It is my contention that these Nordic newcomers were the forebears of Homer's Mycenaean Greeks—the Achaeans or Danaans. As the ancient Greek legends relate, the Mycenaeans of Homer's Heroic Age had hailed from Libya. Of course, this idea runs smack against the prevailing model of autochthonous origins among Hellenic studies. In a paper presented at the centenary conference of the British School of Archaeology at Athens in 1986, classicist Steven Diamant boldly wrote:

> Some years ago, I began teaching in my classes, strictly as a devil's advocate position, the hypothesis of Mycenaeans as blond-[haired], blue-[eyed] invaders from the north, not only because it contradicted all the literature that I could give students to read, but also because it violated my own prejudices, which very much favour local evolution and not invasion/diffusionist explanations. The problem is that I slowly began to convince myself that I was right, and now I have to defend this somewhat risky proposition.[27]

A risky proposition it is indeed, but an accurate one in my estimation. Further adding to the controversy, I maintain that this Achaean/Danaan migration out of Libya and into mainland Greece occurred during the closing years of the Late Bronze Age. There is no doubt in my mind that the Achaean-Danaans belonged to one of the various invading northern European tribes collectively referred to by the ancient Egyptians as the Peoples of the Sea. Already counting among their ranks the Philistines, and associating themselves with the powerful Aegean-based Hyksos-Amalekites, and the Libyans, the Peoples of the Sea posed a substantial lingering threat to Egypt's security.

---

[25] Ahmed Fakhri (1944) *Siwa Oasis*, Cairo, p. 23.
[26] Immanuel Velikovsky (1977) *Peoples of the Sea*, Doubleday: Garden City, NY, p. 85.
[27] Steven Diamant 'Mycenaean Origins: Infiltration from the North?' In E. B. French & K. A. Wardle (1988) *Problems in Greek Prehistory (Papers Presented at the Centenary Conference of the British School of Archaeology at Athens, Manchester – April 1986)*, p. 153.

A Philistine Soldier in Meroë: A Look at an Inconceivable Idea

As the Philistines and the rest of the Peoples of the Sea were beginning to perturb the Egyptians, the Meroitic rulers in Ethiopia were likewise facing occasional raids by those same northern foes. According to the new chronology, the Meroitic king who reigned contemporaneously with King Merneptah in Egypt was King Natakamani. As a salient piece of pictorial evidence from the walls of the Meroitic temple of Naqa shows, which we shall examine momentarily, the Meroites had rendered the Sea Peoples tributary to them. This is unequivocal proof that the temple of Naqa must indeed date to the Late Bronze Age. Moreover, like the lion-temple of Musawwarat Es-Sufra, the new lion-temple at Naqa featured numerous representations of the leonine deity Apedemak — attesting to the continuity between the two temple complexes.[28] The temple of Naqa was constructed by King Natakamani and his wife, Queen Amanitere. Scholars believe that the temple's construction dates to the very beginning of the first century of the common era (2 to 23 CE). Again, I would argue that conventional wisdom is off-target by over a millennium. Just as the lion-temple of Musawwarat Es-Sufra was built immediately after the Venus catastrophe of 1,418 BCE, this lion-temple at Naqa was erected around the time of the Mercury shift of 1,187 BCE. What this means is that compelling theological and artistic similarities can be expected to be found between New Kingdom Egypt and Meroë at this time.

To begin with, we can observe a meaningful development in Meroitic theology which strikingly mirrors the theological reforms attested in early New Kingdom Egypt. As was the case during the Egyptian new 15th Dynasty, there was in Meroë a marked new adherence to the primordial Khemetic sun-god Re. The Heliopolitan divine triad, depicted piously on the temple walls at Naqa, was remarkably absent on the walls of the earlier (Theban Renaissance) temple of Musawwarat Es-Sufra. Nevertheless, the divine scenes illustrated on the temple-walls of Naqa are an obvious continuation of the earlier Theban religious themes found at Musawwarat Es-Sufra. According to noted Egyptologist and Nubiologist L. V. Zabkar:

> The divine triad composed of Apedemak, Isis and Horus is arranged on these reliefs [from temple at Naqa] in the same manner as the deities of the Theban triad of Amun, Mut and Khonsu, in that the father and son, Apedemak and Horus and Amon and Khonsu, are seen on the south wall in the procession of gods, and the divine mothers, Isis and Mut, on the north wall in the procession of goddesses.[29]

---

[28] F. Ll. Griffith (1911) *Meroitic Inscriptions I*, p. 65 – Pl.XXIII.
[29] L. V. Zabkar (1975) *Apedemak: Lion God of Meroe (A Study in Egyptian-Meroitic Syncretism)*, Aris & Phillips: Warminster, U.K., p. 9.

Indeed, the Meroitic divine triad of Apedemak, Isis and Horus at Naqa is represented in exactly the same fashion as the Theban divine triad of Amun, Mut and Khonsu in New Kingdom Egypt. As Griffith observed, the deities are classified by sex[30] — with the south wall representing Apedemak and Horus (Egyptian Amun and Khonsu) as father and son, and the north wall portraying the feminine figures: Isis and Mut as the divine mothers. The constant difference between Egypt and Meroë naturally remains with respect to the supremacy of Apedemak in Meroë – somewhat substituting the Theban god Amun – and the specifically Meroitic preference for the Hemhem crown. So the characteristic importance of Amun during LB I and LB II eras had not disappeared in Meroë during the LB III period. The historical relevance of Amun in Meroitic theology was preserved with the building of the temple of Amun at Naqa — erected during the reign of King Natakamani. The names of the king, the queen and their prince are all inscribed, in Meroitic script, on vertical columns separating the temple reliefs.[31] Even still, during the LB III period, Apedemak was elevated to the status of "sun-god" — making him, in many ways, the equal of the sun-god Osiris. Seeing that Osiris was also occasionally identified with the sun-god Re in Khemetic theology,[32] the influence of the new 15th Dynasty in Egypt is again made clear.

In addition to the above-mentioned similarities in theological observances, the contemporaneity of the Meroitic civilization and New Kingdom Egypt can be gleaned from equally analogous artistic styles and iconography. A quick examination of Figs. 11f-h reveals that there is a much more than passing similarity between the prisoner clubbing scenes from the temple-walls of Naqa and those from New Kingdom Egypt. Since the new 15th Dynasty Pharaohs such as Seti I and Ramses II emerged from Ethiopia during the LBIII period, it would be entirely logical to see the artistic style of this dynasty mirror that of the Meroë — as the prisoner scenes reflect. We indeed see, for instance, that the prisoners being smitten by Kings Seti I and Ramses II (see Fig. 11h), as well as by a number of other Ethiopian pharaohs of the time (see Figs. 11f-g), are illustrated, with remarkable affinity, in multiple super-imposed rows. Showing only one full figure of an Asiatic prisoner, the smiting reliefs all depict the remaining rows of captives with just their protruding limbs and head profiles. Again, I believe this to be a Meroitic artistic influence.

---

[30] F. Ll. Griffith (1911) *Meroitic Inscriptions I*, London, p. 57.
[31] Ibid, p. 63.
[32] L. V. Žabkar (1975) p. 18.

Fig. 11a: Entrance to Pharaoh Ramses II's temple at Abu-Simbel.

Fig. 11b: Sepulchral stela of a prince of Meroë paying homage to the god Osiris who wears the *atef*-crown. The throne of Osiris delineates the union of Black Land and the Red Land. Superseding the relief is a winged solar disk with a pair of cobras representing Horus the Behdetite (all of which indicate a classic Ptolemaic legacy).

Fig. 11c: Queen Amanishakete.

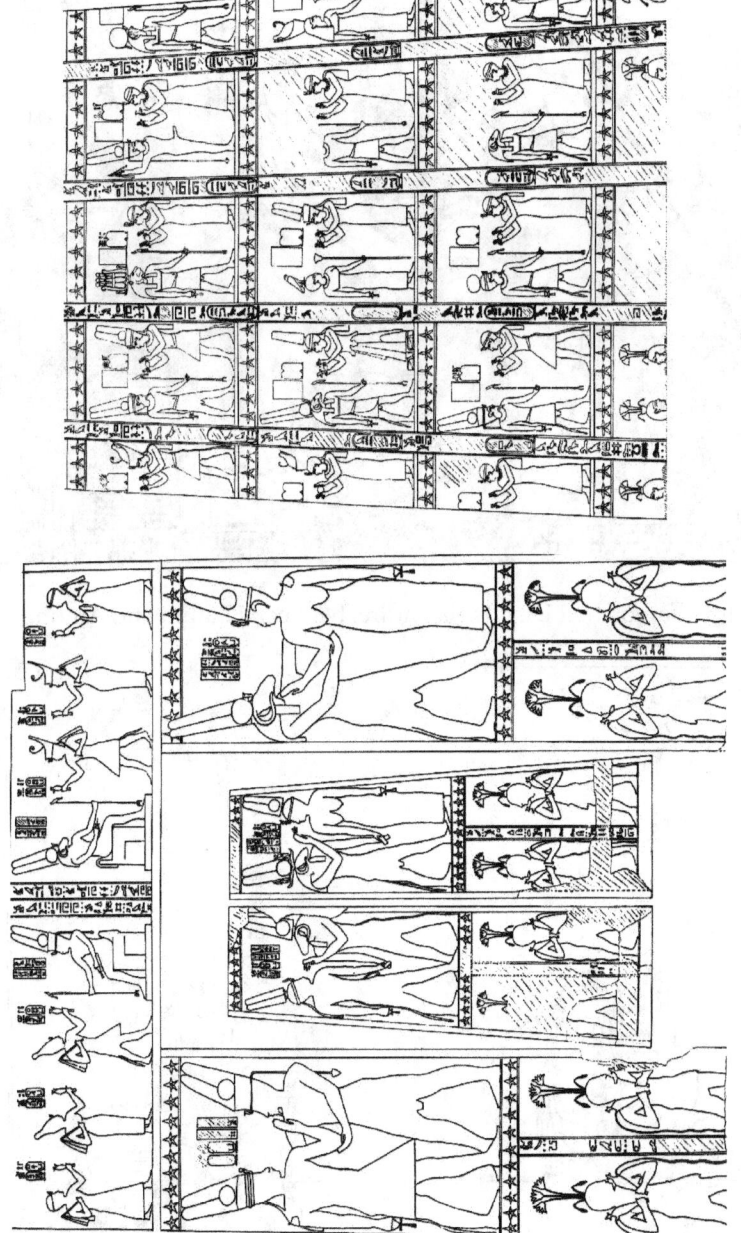

Fig. 11d: Scenes from Amun Temple of Naqa.

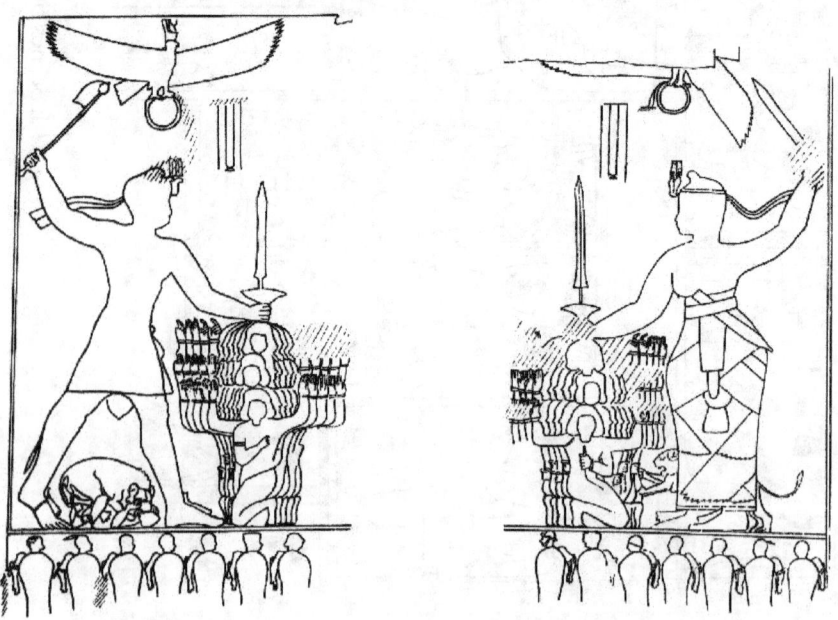

Fig. 11e: Pharaoh Seti I, in Osirian attire, between Khnum and Amun.

Fig. 11f: Smiting scenes from the temple of Naqa.

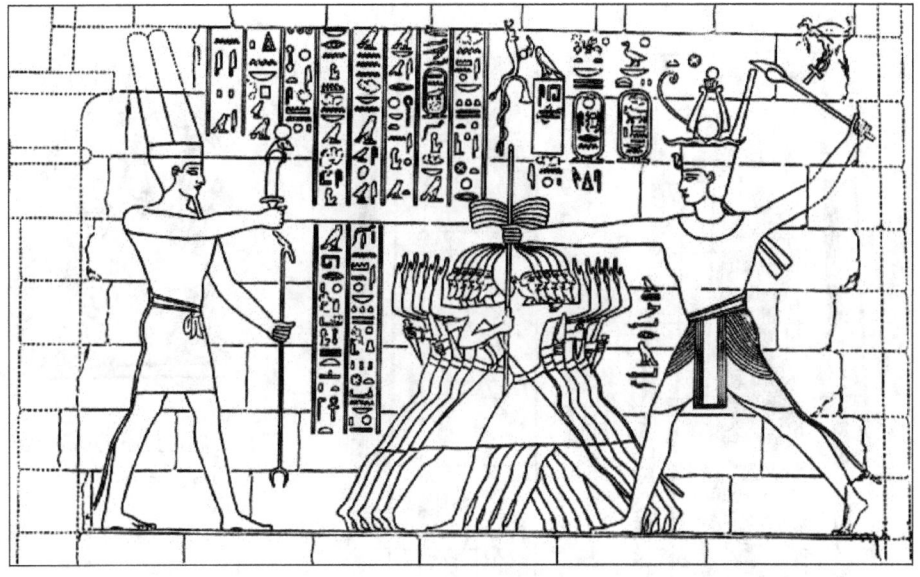

Fig. 11g: The Napatan king Senkamanisken smiting enemies in the presence of Amun-Re.

Fig. 11h: Pharaohs Ramses II and Seti I smiting enemies.

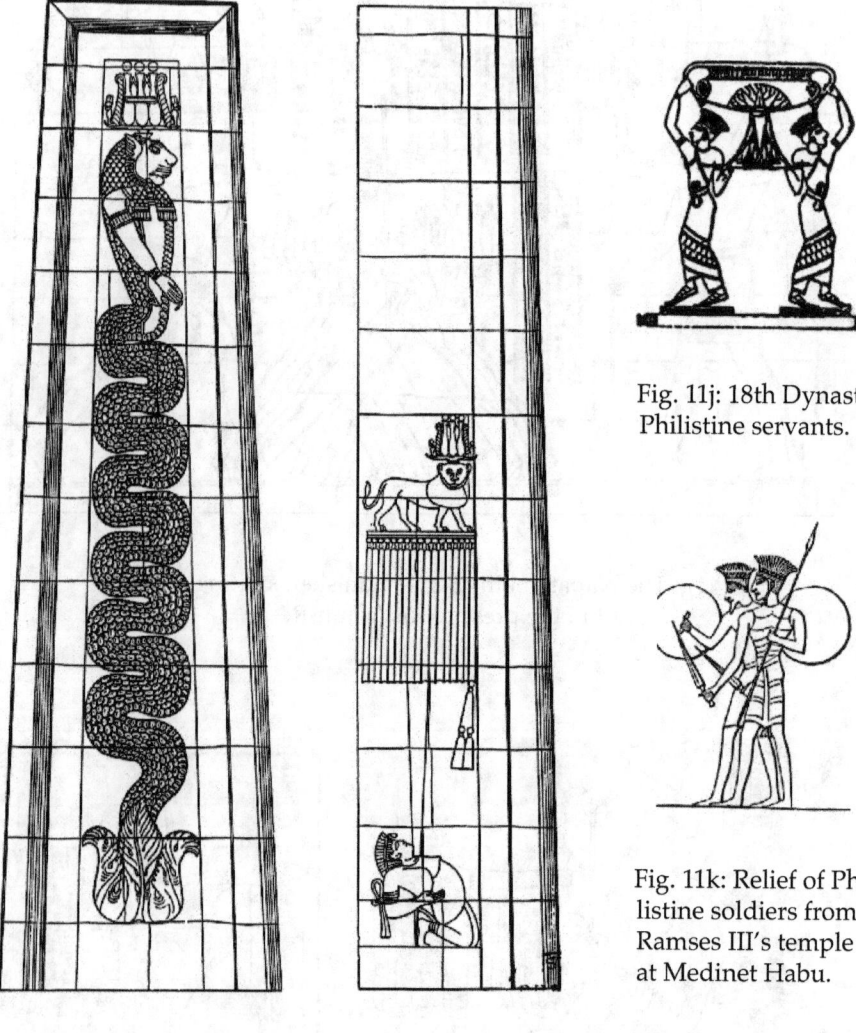

Fig. 11j: 18th Dynasty Philistine servants.

Fig. 11k: Relief of Philistine soldiers from Ramses III's temple at Medinet Habu.

Fig. 11i: Philistine captive represented on the temple of Naqa.

Chronology of the LB Age Ramesside Dynasty:

Kings	Dates of Reigns	Events of Significance
Ramses I	c.1,330 - 1,308 BCE	- Ousting of shepherds
Seti I	1,309 - 1,291 BCE	
Ramses II	1,290 - 1,224 BCE	- Battle of Kadesh-Orontes
Merneptah	1,224 - 1,214 BCE	- Infiltration of Libyans
Seti II	1,214 - 1,208 BCE	
Amenmesse	____-____	
Siptah	1,208 - 1,202 BCE	
Queen Twosre	1,202 - 1,194 BCE	
(Period of strife)	1,194 - 1,184 BCE	- Mercury Shift (1,187 BCE)
		- Invasion of the Atlanteans
		- Expulsion of Atlan[arsa]
Setnakhte	1,184 - 1,182 BCE	
Ramses III	1,182 - 1,151 BCE	- War against Sea Peoples
Ramses IV	1,151 - 1,145 BCE	
Ramses V	1,145 - 1,141 BCE	
Ramses VI	1,141 - 1,135 BCE	- Invasion of Agag II

Table 11-1

Fig 11l: Ramses II (Cairo Museum)

CHAP. XI: THE NEW KINGDOM BEGINS | 409

On the whole, the temple art from Naqa reveals one last momentous clue which, in my opinion, irrefutably proves that the temple of Naqa was built between the late thirteenth to early twelfth centuries BCE — at the time of the Peoples of the Sea infiltration. That pivotal indicator is the Ethiopians' depiction of a Philistine soldier (see Fig. 11i) on the wall of the temple of Queen Amanitere. There is indeed absolutely no question that the shackled captive portrayed on the temple of Naqa is indeed a Philistine. Comparing Fig. 11i with known representations of Philistine in Figs. 11j-k, it would be very difficult to conclude otherwise. But what would a Philistine soldier possibly be doing in Meroë in the first century BCE, during the reign of Queen Amanitere? Amazingly, scholars have been very quiet about this glaring anomaly. Not a single Nubiologist has ever raised the possibility that, based on the depiction of this Philistine soldier at Naqa, a fundamental reevaluation of the accepted chronology and history of Meroitic civilization ought to be considered. But as part of the new chronology, this is exactly the position which I endorse. The temple of Naqa was built during or around the time of King Merneptah in Egypt.

Arsa the Atlan and the Invasion of the Atlanteo-Napatans

> " *Howbeit Poseidon had gone among the far-off Ethiopians — the Ethiopians who dwell sundered in twain ...*"
>
> - Homer
> Odyssey, Book I: 22-23

The two to three decades following the death of Pharaoh Merneptah in Egypt were very turbulent ones. In 1,187 BCE, the calamitous start of Typhon Season #5 unleashed a veritable flood of invasions, rebellions, movements of population, and other sociopolitical upheavals. I contend that among these invasions was one which emanated from Ethiopia. This Ethiopian invasion would not only affect Egypt, but would likewise extend to Syria-Palestine. Conventional historians recall no such Ethiopian campaign in Antiquity. But a careful reexamination of the ancient literature from Ethiopia, Egypt and classical Greece can bring to light crucial pages which are currently missing from the history of ancient Africa and the world. We start with one of Greek Philosopher Plato's famous passage in the *Timaeus*:

> ... it related in our records how once upon a time your state stayed the course of a mighty host, which, starting from a distant point in the Atlantic Ocean, was insolently advancing to attack the whole of Europe and Asia to boot.

> For the ocean there was at one time navigable; for in front of the mouth which you Greeks call ... the pillars of Heracles there lay an island which was larger than Libya and Asia together; and it was possible for the travellers of that time to cross it to the other islands, and from the islands to the whole of the continent over against them which encompass that veritable ocean. For all that we have here, lying within the mouth of which we speak, is evidently a haven having a narrow entrance; but that yonder is a real ocean, and the land surrounding it may most rightly be called and in the fullest and truest sense, a continent. Now in this island of Atlantis there existed a confederation of kings, of great and marvellous power, which held sway over the island, and over many other islands also and parts of the continent; and moreover, of the lands here within the Straights they ruled over Libya as far as Egypt, and over Europe as far as Tuscany. So this host, being all gathered together, made an attempt one time to enslave by one single onslaught both your country and ours and the whole of the Straits. And then it was the manhood of your State showed itself conspicuous for valour in the sight of the world ... whereby it saved from slavery such as were not yet enslaved, and all the rest of us who dwell within the bounds of Heracles it ungrudgingly set free. But at a later time there occurred portentous earthquakes and floods, and one grievous night befell them, when the whole body of your warriors were swallowed up by the earth, and the island of Atlantis in like manner was swallowed up by the sea and vanished.
> (Plato, *Timaeus*, 24-5)

Who were these Atlantean invaders who, according to Plato, ruled over Libya and into Egypt? Where did they come from? In the Platonic dialogues, Hermocrates asks Critias to inform Socrates of an "ancient tradition" about the lost continent that once dwelled in the middle of the Atlantic ocean. In the discussion, Critias reveals that the inhabitants of Atlantis were descendants of Poseidon — the Egyptian Seth:

> I have before remarked in speaking of the allotments of the gods, that they distributed the whole earth into portions differing in extent, and made for themselves temples and instituted sacrifices. **And Poseidon, receiving for his lot the island of Atlantis,** begat children by a mortal woman, and settled them in part of the island ...

Hence, whoever these so-called Atlanteans were, they were indubitably followers of Seth — the notorious Egyptian deity of chaos. As Critias mentions that these Sethian disciples became masters of Atlantis at the time of Creation, we must return to the far-off days of the foundation of the First Creation, or the rabbinical Seventh

CHAP. XI: THE NEW KINGDOM BEGINS | 411

Erez, in the dawning third millennium BCE, to look for their origins. The very first step is to look for evidence of the existence of a Sethian clan. We have that evidence in the Nubian A-Group culture from the Qustul cemetery who, along with the Libyans, had been the valiant disciples of Seth. We recall that the Sethian A-Group Nubians of Qustul, to quote Nubiologist P. L. Shinnie, *"disappeared from archaeological view soon after 3000 BC."*[33] The telling question which must immediately follow is: where could they have gone? The answer is that they headed toward Atlantis.

But where was Atlantis? Clearly, there could not have been a huge land mass the size of Libya (Africa) and Asia combined lying in the middle of the Atlantic ocean at any time in Antiquity. Therefore, it would be entirely fatuous to take Plato's word at face value in looking for the location of Atlantis. In fact, I doubt that Atlantis was ever even an island, or that it existed in such remote times as Plato contends. I propose searching for the real location of Atlantis in West Africa. Indeed, the book by German ethnologist Leo Frobenius[34] (1873-1938) entitled *Mythology of Atlantis. The "Poseidon" of Black Africa. His Cult in Benin's Yoruba Culture*, published in 1949, induces us to consider a possible relationship between Plato's Atlantean Poseidon and the West African Poseidon. The "Black Atlantis"[35] of Frobenius is the real location of Atlantis — not a neo-Atlantean culture derived from the Aegean as Frobenius himself postulated. The worship of Seth was introduced into West Africa by the fleeing A-Group Nubians following their expulsion from Egypt by the proto-dynastic pharaoh Aha-Menes. The Yoruba sacred city of Ifé, within the kingdom of Benin, has a long tradition for being the home of Olokoun, god of the sea, and the equivalent of the Greek Poseidon.[36] Those later traditions stem from this very early diffusion from the Nile Valley.

As Seth or Poseidon had been responsible for the primeval breach in the cosmic order, it ought to be expected to find the West African Seth-Poseidon likewise asso-

---

[33] P. L. Shinnie (1996) *Ancient Nubia*, Kegan Paul International: New York and London, p. 52.
[34] Leo Frobenius (1949) *Mythologie de l'Atlantide. Le «Poseidon» de l'Afrique Noire. Son culte chez les Yoruba du Bénin,* Payot: Paris. Frobenius believed that Atlantis was located somewhere in the Mediterranean. Many African scholars, chief among them Cheikh Anta Diop, rejected Frobenius' theory because it implied that West African art originated in the West (i.e. Europe). Nonetheless, Diop had many praises for Frobenius.
[35] Suzanne Marchand (1997) 'Leo Frobenius and the Revolt Against the West', *Journal of Contemporary History* Vol. 32 - Num. 2, pp. 153-170.
[36] Leo Frobenius (1993) *L'Atlantide (Mythologies et cultes)*, Éditions du Rocher: Monaco, pp. 21-23.

ciated in some form with major planetary cataclysms — particularly involving the planet Mercury. While the Platonic dialogues assert that Atlantis went asunder some nine thousand years before the days of Solon (c.640-560 BCE), meaning in around 10,000 BCE, it's evident that the figure is overinflated. As with several other aspects of the story, the details have been much sensationalized. Nonetheless, I still believe that a genuine historical context can be gleaned from the tale. First and foremost, the association of a Sethian Atlantean culture with a great natural cataclysm, reflects Seth's infamous predilection for cosmic chaos. Significantly, the ancient Greeks designated Poseidon (Seth) as the father of Atlas. Hence, the destruction of Atlantis must have taken place at the start of a Typhon Season — a metaphor for Seth-Typhon's cyclical destruction of the world.

> After his fight with Heaven, Typhon descends to the Earth and destroys its products; he also assails the Mountains, the Seas, and the Rivers; he tears off whole islands, and flings the fragments violently against Heaven.[37]

I propose that the Typhonian conflagration which put an end to the historical Atlantis was the Mercury shift of 1,187 BCE. In his *Antiquities of the Jews*, Josephus[38] relates that because Adam had warned his descendants that sinful humanity would be destroyed in a deluge, the children of Seth raised two pillars, in anticipation of the flood, in order to preserve their science and philosophy. We recall from Chapter 2 that Adam had forewarned of two catastrophe: one by fire (Mercury shift) and the other by water (Venus shift). Since the children of Seth, Plato's Atlanteans in this case, built the Pillars of Herakles in anticipation of a devastating Venus-induced flood, they must have erected the pillars shortly after the Mercury shift of 1,187 BCE. The Pillars of Herakles were obviously located in the Atlanteans' homeland. According to Homer:

> ... Atlas of baneful mind, who knows the depths of every sea, and himself holds the tall pillars which keep earth and heaven apart.
> (Homer, *Odyssey*, Book I: 52-53)

In this capacity as one who ensures that earth and heaven are kept apart, we find that Atlas plays an analogous role in relation to Poseidon as does Ptah in relation to Seth in Egyptian mythology. Atlas' work became most vital during the perilous fifty-two-year periods when earth dwellers feared the eventual Venus catastrophe—

---

[37] Charles François Dupuis (1984 [1872]) *The Origin of All Religious Worship*, Garland: New York and London, p. 122.
[38] Flavius Josephus, *Antiquities of the Jews*, Book I: 2, 3.

CHAP. XI: THE NEW KINGDOM BEGINS | 413

having already been made to suffer the fiery rage of Poseidon-Mercury. By erecting the Pillars of Herakles, the deity responsible for the continuation of the precessional cycle, the Atlanteans were clearly aware that a World Age was coming to an end and being replaced by a new one.

Having identified West Africa as the location of Atlantis, the next step is to determine whether or not there is sufficient evidence for the presence of these Pillars of Herakles in West Africa. Turning to Prof. Martin Bernal:

> The first reference to Atlas as a toponym comes in Herodotos who refers to it not as a mountain range but as a single mountain with a slender cone, whose peaks are always covered in cloud. According to Herodotos **the local inhabitants were names Atlantes** after the mountain which they called 'the Pillar of the Sky'. Thus the original meaning seems to have been 'edge of the world' or Pillar of Herakles.[39]

So it was the West African Mount Atlas, whose peaks were always covered in clouds, which represented the genuine Pillars of Herakles. The Roman chronicler Pliny the Elder (c.23-79 CE) spoke of Mount Atlas as having been "the subject of much the most marvellous stories of all the mountains in Africa."[40] He also says that it is to this West African mountain that the Atlantic ocean owes its name.[41] Might this be a clue to the origin of Plato's story about a mythical island in the middle of the Atlantic? It seems indeed very probable that Plato, most likely aware of the ancient association between Mount Atlas and the adjacent Atlantic ocean, contrived his story around this correlation. In Chapter 14, we shall explore in further detail the possible origins of Plato's tale about this lost continent in the middle of the Atlantic. Suffice it to say for now that it is highly unlikely that such a land mass ever existed and that the real location of Atlantis was in West Africa's legendary Mount Atlas. The inhabitants of Mount Atlas were descended from the A-Group Nubians from Qustul who, in c.2,950 BCE, left Lower Nubia and diffused elements of pharaonic culture into West Africa.

The cultural continuity between West Africa, Nubia and Egypt had ardently been defended by Dr. Cheikh Anta Diop during his life time. According to Cheikh Anta Diop, traces of pharaonic culture could be found in the various customs, religions and languages of modern Africa. An important pillar of Diop's continuity theory was expressed in his linguistic correlations between ancient Egyptian language and

---

[39] Martin Bernal (1991) *Black Athena (The Afroasiatic Roots of Classical Civilization) — Volume II: The Archaeological and Documentary Evidence*, Rutgers University Press: New Brunswick, NJ, p. 299.
[40] Pliny, *Natural History*, Book V: 1, 6.
[41] Ibid.

the native West African language of Wolof.⁴² He found, among others, the following word-correlations to support his thesis on the probable Egyptian origins of several Wolof words:

Egyptian:	Wolof:
Tefnut = the divinity that Ra created by spitting her out.	*Tef-nit* = to spit out a human being; to have a human being come out of one's spittle, by spitting him out, hence *Teflit* = saliva.
Nen or *nwn* = the inert primordial water.	*Nen* = nothingness, non being.
	Nenn = inert.
noh	*noh* = the one who inflicts defeat.
nwn	*ñul* = black.
Tem = to stop doing something.	*Tem* = to stop doing something.
Seh, sih = noble.	*Seh* = dignitary.
Dtti = the desert, the savage country.	*Datti* = the savage brush, the uninhabited open country.
tak = to light up.	*tãl* = light up.
	tak = light up.
per = house.	*per* = the fence that surrounds the house.
p(a)mer = pyramid.	*ba-meel* = tomb, tomb stone.
gen = phallus.	*geño* = patrilinear line, stock, or clan.

The primordial home of pharaonic culture is to be found in Ethiopia — beyond the Fifth Cataract. Once it was brought into Khemet by the Anu, the local inhabitants of Lower Nubia, the African A-Group culture, adopted pharaonic religion and became disciples of the storm-god Seth. After having been routed out of Lower Nubia by Aha-Menes, the rudiments of pharaonic culture were then implanted into West Africa — where remains of this early influence can still be discerned today. Finally, in the twelfth century BCE, the Sethian disciples who had made their home in West Africa's Atlas mountains during the Early Bronze I period returned to their ancestral home in the southern Nile Valley. They settled in two places principally: the Ethiopian town of Napata, near the Fourth Cataract, and the Libyan oases.

Martin Bernal remarks that among the most famous tribes of Libya were the Nigretai or Nigretes —" *whose beautiful blackness was the source for the Latin word niger, from which the Portuguese, Spanish and English negro developed.*"⁴³ He also points out

---

⁴² Cheikh Anta Diop (1991) *Civilization or Barbarism (An Authentic Anthropology).* Trans. by Yaa-Lengi Meema Ngemi. Lawrence Hill Books: Brooklyn, NY, pp. 358-362, 379.
⁴³ Martin Bernal (1991) *Black Athena* II, p. 96.

CHAP. XI: THE NEW KINGDOM BEGINS | 415

that their name stems from the Semitic root (n)gr, meaning "water to flow into sand."⁴⁴ This particular etymology is also shared by the toponyms Gar, Ger, Nagar, Niger, and ultimately, the River Niger.⁴⁵ The reason why we should pay particularly attention to the River Niger is because "it flowed east away from the Atlantic, apparently into the desert." After the Mercury shift of 1,187 BCE, it was not only the water of the ancient Niger which flowed eastward — but its people. Those of them who established themselves in Nubia became known as the "Napatans." I am convinced that the name of this ancient Ethiopian town of Napata, Nbt or Nbyt is at the root of the Semitic nbt, which means "gush fort of water."⁴⁶ Hence, the link between the River Niger and the settlers of Napata is established by this common reference to flowing or gushing water. We already know why the River Niger was so categorized, but why were the Atlanteans of ancient Napata associated with "gushing water?" To find the answer we must once again resort to the writings of Pliny. The Roman chronicler mentions that the legendary Mount Atlas was renowned for its "gushing springs" which supplied its inhabitants with their water supply.⁴⁷ Pliny also provides a very specific definition of who the Nigretai were:

> In the interior circuit of Africa towards the south and beyond the Gaetulians, after an intermediate strip of desert, the first inhabitants of all are the Egyptian Libyans, and then the people called in Greek the White Ethiopians. **Beyond these are the Ethiopian clans of the Nigritae ...**
> (Pliny, Natural History, Book V: 8, 43.

Supporting the thesis which I have maintained all along, Pliny confirms that the Ethiopians dwelling below the Fourth Cataract were racially distinct from the Nubians of Upper and Lower Nubia residing between the First and Fourth Cataracts. The Greeks commonly referred to the latter as "White Ethiopians" because they, the Kushites, were the descendants of Asiatic immigrants. Black Ethiopians, the Meroites and Napatans (Nigretai), on the other hand were of purely African heritage. The Meroites, the direct descendants of the EBII classic Ptolemaic rulers of Khemet, had never left the Nile Valley and ensured the continuity of Khemetic tradition below the Fifth Cataract. For their part, the Napatans (Nabatu, Nabati or Nabateans), hailing from West Africa's Atlas mountains, emerged as an organize pharaonic state at the time of the Mercury shift of 1,187 BCE — faithful to their

---

44 Ibid.
45 Ibid.
46 Ibid.
47 Pliny, *Natural History*, Book V: 1, 6.

Sethian heritage. They immediately established peaceful relations with their Meroitic kin and, apparently renouncing their long-held allegiance to Seth, the Napatans began worshipping the Theban god Amun. Not all Napatans renounced their traditional Sethian heritage however. Those among them who found refuge in the Libyan oases piously held on to the worship of Seth. It should therefore come as no surprise that the Greek philosopher Maximus of Tyre (c.125-185 CE) related that "western Libyans" worshipped "Mount Atlas" jointly as a temple and a god.[48] There is no question that this is proof-positive that the Libyans had come under the influence of the Atlanteans of West Africa.

In the new chronology of the Sudan which I propose, the Napatan monarchy is instituted by Pharaoh Atlanarsa — the leader on the Nigretai immigrants in Napata. Since Pliny declares that the Napatans (or Nigretai) were once known as the "Atlantia,"[49] it is easy to find in Atlanarsa's name a reference to his Atlantean homeland. I maintain that this Napatan king's throne name of Atlanarsa was short for "Arsa the Atlan" or "Arsa of Atlantis." What makes me think that this king's name was "Arsa?" To understand how I have come to this conclusion, we need to turn to the Egyptian records from the turbulent years following the end of Pharaoh Merneptah's reign. In particular, we refer to the Great Papyrus Harris — a document dated to the reign of King Ramses III, now in the British Museum. Believed to have been composed by one of King Ramses III's sons, the papyrus describes the tumultuous state in which Egypt found itself before King Setnakhte, Ramses III's father, ascended the throne and "was victorious over his enemies." Astonishingly, the Great Papyrus Harris says that *"the land of Egypt was overthrown from without and every man was thrown out of his right."* Ancient historians know nothing of an "invasion from without" between the end of Merneptah's reign and the accession of Setnakhte. So this passage has been treated with much skepticism and caution. Yet, the Papyrus Harris is adamant that a foreign power, headed by a certain Arsa, succeeded in subduing Egypt for several years. The document relates that Egypt's central government had already collapsed for some time, with power falling into the hands of bickering town chiefs and rulers, before the foreign ruler Arsa ultimately enforced his will and made the whole country pay tribute to himself and his hosts. Although the Papyrus Harris identifies Arsa as a Syrian, there is no evidence that an LBIII Syro-Palestinian ruler could have been in a position to threatened Egypt in such manner. So Egyptologists have written off this account as no more than myth. However, I argue that Arsa was not a Syrian but an Ethiopian. More precisely, I identify him with the Napatan pharaoh Atlanarsa — "Arsa the Atlan."

---

[48] *Maximus Tyrius, Philosophumena – Dialexeis.* Edited by George L. Koniaris (1995) Walter de Gruyter, p. 25.
[49] Pliny, *Natural History*, Book VI: 35, 187.

By identifying this Arsa of the Great Papyrus Harris with the Napatan ruler Atlanarsa, we find that the story suddenly finds an interesting echo in Plato's Timaeus. Citing Plato again:

> Now in this island of Atlantis there existed a confederation of kings, of great and marvellous power, which held sway over the island, and over many other islands also and parts of the continent; and moreover, of the lands here within the Straights they ruled over Libya as far as Egypt, and over Europe as far as Tuscany. So this host, being all gathered together, made an attempt one time to enslave by one single onslaught both your country and ours and the whole of the Straits.

The widespread civil disorder into which Egypt was plunged had been caused by two main events: (1) the rapid and uncontrolled infiltration into the Egyptian Delta of the Libyans and their coalition of maritime peoples of the Mediterranean (from Sardina on the west to Asia Minor on the east) during the reign of Pharaoh Merneptah, and (2) the disastrous Mercury shift of 1,187 BCE. As was the case during most ruinous cosmic cataclysms, central governments came under overwhelming strain as both domestic and foreign rivals, taking full advantage of the widespread mayhem, belligerently sought to assert their own authority. After the death of Merneptah and the reign of Seti II, the Egyptian monarchy soon began falling into complete disarray as foreign hordes became increasingly powerful. Among these foreigners who hurriedly jostled for position, starting in 1,187 BCE, were the newly arrived Nigretai dwelling in Napata and the Libyan oases. As Plato's account reflects, these Atlanteans, after having settled heavily in Libya, also gained suzerainty over a fragile Egyptian state much weakened by the cosmic catastrophe of 1,187 BCE and long-standing domestic strife. The efforts, which Plato speaks of, by the Atlans to overrun the Aegean and vast parts of Europe will be dealt with in the following chapter. What is most important to comprehend for the time being is that the Nigretai or Napatans, under Pharaoh Atlanarsa, became the masters of Libya and Egypt between the year 1,187 BCE and the accession of the new 15th Dynasty Theban pharaoh Setnakhte — whose reign begins in c.1,184 BCE.

Dating the Napatan pharaoh Atlanarsa to the twelfth century BCE naturally runs against all logic as far as conventional historians are concerned. In the standard chronology, his reign falls between c.653-643 BCE — no less than half a millennium later. With very little evidence, or at least with very erroneous facts, to support his thesis, George Reisner had established that the Napatan king Atlanarsa was the son of Taharka of the standard 25th Dynasty (new 20th Dynasty).[50] No archaeolo-

---

[50] See George A. Reisner (1923) 'The Meroitic Kingdom of Ethiopia: A Chronological Outline', *Journal of Egyptian Archaeology* 9, pp. 34-77.

gists or ancient historians since then has come along to contradict him. Reisner' dating of the Meroitic/Napatan dynastic sequence has become a matter of faith. As will be further examined in chapters to come, George A. Reisner and other Nubiologists have been misled by the fallacious theory devised by Egyptologists that pharaonic Nubia was "civilized" by the New Kingdom's viceregal administration. That basic assumption had made it, and continues to make it, unthinkable in current learned circles that there could have been any kind of sophisticated royal dynasty in Napata or Meroë prior to the Ethiopian conventional 25th Dynasty in Egypt. Excavators have discovered two main burial places used by the Ethiopian kings of Napata, namely: El Kurru and Napata. The kings buried at El Kurru have always been thought to predate the Napatan kings buried at Nuri. This is because most of the kings buried at El Kurru belong to the standard 25th Dynasty. In the new chronology however, the order of burials are reversed. The burial complex at Nuri, which had for its first royal occupant Pharaoh Atlanarsa, was used from the twelfth century BCE to the mid-eighth century BCE. It was thereafter abandoned once the Napatan kings became the masters of dynastic Egypt in the second half of the eighth century BCE — albeit the illustrious standard 25th Dynasty pharaoh Taharka was buried at Nuri.

As the founder of the Napatan kingdom, Pharaoh Atlanarsa necessarily had to adhere to a specific theological construct or religious identity. Having been immensely influenced by Meroitic culture, King Atlanarsa abandoned his people's ancestral worship of Seth and instead paid tribute to both the Khemetic sun-god Re and "Amun of Napata." Again, this mixture of the Heliopolitan and Theban theologies fits perfectly well with the prevailing norm during the Late Bronze III period. Paying homage to Amun-Re, Atlanarsa writes:

> ... son of Re — Atlanersa, beloved of Amun of Napata; he made (it) as his monument for his father Amon-Re, lord of the thrones of the two lands; dwelling in the pure mountain, making for him a stand. ...
> A speech by Amun of Napata [to] the son of Re Atlanersa. "My heart is greatly content with what you do for me" ... "I give you upper and lower Egypt/the two lands in exchange for this monument.[51]

Among the body of evidence confirming the cultural near-continuity between Meroitic and Napatan civilizations is their common use of what Nubiologists call "thumb rings."[52] The lion-god Apedemak is shown wearing such rings on the south

---

[51] In John Baines (1985) *Fecundity Figures (Egyptian Personification and Iconology of a Genre)*, Bolchazy-Carducci: Chicago; Aris & Phillips: Warminster, U.K., p. 257.
[52] P. Shinnie (1967) *Meroe, a Civilization of the Sudan*, New York, p. 110f.

CHAP. XI: THE NEW KINGDOM BEGINS | 419

wall of the Musawwarat Temple.[53] Those same "thumb rings" continued being used by the Napatans, as is attested in a stone fragment from the tomb of the wife of King Aspelta[54] (a contemporary of the 17th Dynasty king Sekenenre in the new chronology). Historians however believe that the order of influence is reversed. Since it is commonly thought that Aspelta reigned between 593-568 BCE – supposedly about three centuries before the time Apedemak's temple is believed to have been built – the accepted view is that Aspelta was probably the earliest Ethiopian king to have worn this thumb ring. In the new chronology however, it is clear that Aspelta actually carried on the practice of the earlier Meroitic kings. The Ethiopian kings buried at Napata (Nuri) and Meroë (North Cemetery) ruled contemporaneously in harmony until the middle of the eighth century BCE — when the El Kurru pharaohs took over control of Ethiopia and Egypt.

In short, in the years immediately preceding the accession of Pharaoh Setnakhte, the Khemetic empire which Pharaohs Seti I and Ramses II had so valiantly laboured to establish was coming apart at the seam as the Libyans and Napatans threatened not only Egypt itself, but also its Syro-Palestinian vassals. From Egypt, King Atlanarsa devised to launch conquering campaigns to subdue as many lands or city-states of the Mediterranean and Syria-Palestine as he could. The big question was: who would stop him?

---

[53] L. V. Zabkar (1975) p. 14.
[54] D. Dunham (1955) *Nuri*, Boston, pp. 119-120.

12

Learning the Art of Chariot Warfare (1,187 BCE to 1,117 BCE)

> " *The Late Bronze Age did not die a slow, lingering death. It came to a swift end in the 12th century B.C.E., marked by sudden cultural collapse and widespread population shifts. Out of the ashes of the Bronze Age destructions emerged classical Greek culture and biblical Israel.*"
>
> - William H. Stiebing, Jr.
> 'Climate & Collapse'

The nascent twelfth century BCE, in the ancient Near East and Mediterranean world, was characterized by an unforeseen destabilizing power vacuum which derived from the sudden collapse of the great Hittite empire in Anatolia and from Egypt falling prey to foreign usurpers. In 1,187 BCE, Libya and the Nile Valley were ruled by the Napatan pharaoh Atlanarsa. Having consolidated his power over those regions, Atlanarsa next sought to lay claim to the Aegean and western Asia. Again, this episode is, I believe, documented in Critias' account in Plato's *Timaeus*:

> So this host, being all gathered together, made an attempt one time to enslave by one single onslaught both your country and ours and the whole of the Straits. And then it was the manhood of your State showed itself conspicuous for valour in the sight of the world ... whereby it saved from slavery such as were not yet enslaved, and all the rest of us who dwell within the bounds of Heracles it ungrudgingly set free.
> (Plato, *Timaeus*, 24-5)

Who were these warriors from the Greek mainland who successfully repelled the military advances of Atlanarsa? These Mycenaeans were the Hyksos who were still the masters of mainland Greece at the close of the Late Bronze Age. While the Hyksos rulers in Egypt's eastern Delta and Syria-Palestine had ultimately been subdued by the LBII-III Egyptian pharaohs, those of them who controlled Late Helladic-A mainland Greece had retained virtually complete independence. The

Mycenaean-A Hyksos were undoubtedly the ones who ultimately benefited the most from the power vacuum left by the demise of Hatti and the weakening of Egypt. As the uncontested rulers of the Aegean, they naturally came into close contact with the invading Sea Peoples from the Baltic region. They immediately integrated these northern Indo-European mercenaries into a warlike coalition headed by them and, as a result, greatly increased their military capabilities. But, as the Egyptian battle reliefs from the reign of Ramses III indicate, the Peoples of the Sea offered their services to diverse powers — often depending on where particular detachments found refuge. The first major battle which this new Aegean coalition, headed by the Mycenaean-A Hyksos, waged was against the Nigretai army of Atlanarsa and his Libyan allies. In fact, as the *Timaeus* postulates, it was precisely to meet the Napatan menace head on that this new Aegean Hyksos dynasty was inaugurated. Finding inspiration in their illustrious ancestor King Agag, the Hyksos rulers of the closing LBIII period chose to name themselves Agag as well. So in order to differentiate these Hyksos kings from their LBI predecessor, the former shall be designated as the "Agagite Dynasty" — since there had been three Agag kings in the Mycenaean-A Aegean between 1,187 BCE and 1,117 BCE.

Agag I finally prevailed against Atlanarsa and became a hero both amongst his own people and abroad. With Arsa of Atlantis gone, Pharaoh Setnakhte in Egypt managed to restore the monarchy and ensure the continuation of the new 15th Dynasty. But as the Papyrus Harris demonstrates, the Mycenaean-A Hyksos were not given proper credit by the Egyptians for successfully containing the Napatan threat. Instead, a hostile relationship developed between the new superpowers of the ancient Near East. The two sides did not immediately come to blows, however, as the Mycenaean-A Hyksos King Agag I, a contemporary of Pharaohs Setnakhte and Ramses III, concentrated his conquering efforts on the north of Asia Minor and Europe. Nonetheless, the meteoric rise of this Hyksos power within the Mediterranean basin was of very grave concern to the Theban pharaohs — since the vassal princes of 16th Dynasty at Avaris were likewise of Hyksos heritage. These fears soon proved to be justified as the vassal 16th Dynasty princes became the Egyptian emissaries and allies of their bellicose Aegean confreres. Faced once again with this unfortunately self-imposed Hyksos threat in the north, the Thebans were thoroughly poised for yet another, and this time final, war of liberation against their traditional enemies.

The Hyksos Once Again

The timing for the inauguration of this new Agagite dynasty very much dictated its religious allegiances. The Agagite rulers dedicated their crown to Apophis, the serpent who constantly pursued the sun-god Re. Given the central importance accorded to Apophis by the priests of Ptah, and hence Apophis' close affiliation with the Typhonian Apis bull, it's definitely no small coincidence that the Agagite line would appear precisely during Typhon Season #5. Apophis was always considered as an equal, in strength, to Seth. The two were the only ones who could withstand each other.[1] Therefore, the gargantuan battle waged between the Nigretai, the children of Seth, and the Agagite dynasty, the fervent followers of Apophis, carrier a very profound symbolism which the two opponents were undoubtedly aware of. The Mycenaean-A Hyksos' choice to adopt Apophis as their patron deity was very likely motivated by the knowledge that they would confront a Sethian enemy in the midst of a Typhon Season. As Egyptologist J. F. Borghouts relates:

> ... it may be clear that one of the terrible weapons to be feared from the demon of chaos [Apophis] is his malevolent eye. When the sun-boat would be caught by its glance, **a cosmic calamity might be the result.** The danger is countered by averting the glance in some magical way — or by defying it; but the latter can only be done by someone equal to Apopis, like Seth, or the sun-god's eye itself.[2]

The sacred Apis bull is, of course, an indispensable emblem of any Typhon Season. The name Epaphus, the Greek equivalent of the Egyptian Apis, frequently appears in Aischylos' *The Suppliants*. Indeed, in Aischylos' writings, the identification of the Hyksos dynasty in Egypt with Apophis and Apis is very strong. I would argue that the "Aegyptos" of Aischylos is really a synonym for the Hyksos rulers (foreign chiefs) of the 16th and 17th Dynasties.

By historically setting the narratives from Aischylos' *The Suppliant* during Typhon Season #5, I consequently pose the radical hypothesis that the proto-Hellenic (or proto-Homeric) Danaans, Danaos of the Greek epics, arrived in mainland Greece during Typhon Season #5, and were culturally nurtured by the Mycenaean-A Hyksos. In the Greek legends, Aegyptus (the Hyksos) and Danaos (the Danaans/Greeks) are said to have been brothers. Their portrayal as brothers in Greek mythology would not necessarily mean that they were genetically related, but that their alliance was a strong and mutually beneficial one. Quoting from Martin Bernal's *Black Athena* (Vol. I):

> There is also *epinoia,* which means both the gentle breathing of Zeus that impregnates Io and later the storm that threatens the Danaids. Even beyond these and Apia(n), another connection to the name Epaphos has been sug-

---

[1] J. F. Borghouts (1973) 'The Evil Eye of Apopis', *The Journal of Egyptian Archaeology* 59, p. 114.
[2] Ibid, p. 120.

gested by Jean Bérard: the name ›Ip.py was that of two or three Hyksos pharaohs and was conventionally rendered in Greek as Ap(h)ophis.[3]

In the new chronology, these three Hyksos pharaohs named Apophis (Agag) reigned between 1,187 BCE and 1,117 BCE. As will be argued shortly, it is precisely during this time period that the legend of Io, the Greek goddess of Argos, and Aischylos' colonization narratives must be placed. Under the tutelage of these three Hyksos rulers, and of their contemporaries in Egypt (the 16th and 17th Dynasties), Homeric Greece was shaped. The Typhonian themes common to all of these aforementioned peoples and dynasties' literature, personal names, theology, art and aesthetics incontrovertible point to the fact that they lived and evolved during a Typhon Season.

The Horse-drawn Chariot: An African War Apparatus

Changes the Course of Egyptian History

My hypothesis arguing for the presence of a Hyksos empire in the Aegean, the Egyptian Delta and Syria-Palestine decades after the death Pharaoh Ramses II is definitely the epitome of heresies as far as traditional ancient historians are concerned. After all, weren't the Hyksos, during the closing Middle Bronze Age, supposed to have been responsible for introducing the horse-drawn chariots into Egypt — which permitted the Tuthmoside and Ramesside kings to establish their vast Late Bronze Age Asiatic empires? As we've seen in Chapter 9, the entire basis of this fallacious argument rests on the assumption that the Hyksos were Indo-Europeans. The Indo-Aryan tribes who invaded the ancient Near East during the Middle Bronze Age were evidently responsible for bringing in the horse-drawn chariots — a war instrument which drastically influenced power relations between the various city-states and empires of the Late Bronze Age. The Hittites of Anatolia, for example, owed much of their privileged political and military position to the horse-drawn chariot. But having already concluded that the Hyksos were not Indo-Europeans, I cannot therefore concur with the accepted theory that the Hyksos invaders were the ones who introduced the horse-drawn chariots into Egypt. The Hyksos-Amalekites who established themselves in MBIIc Syria-Palestine and Tell el-Dab'a in Lower Egypt had not domesticated, or even known, the horse but instead made extensive use of the donkey. In order to simply keep up with the Hittite army, the Egyptians unquestionably had, out

---

[3] Martin Bernal (1987a) *Black Athena (The Afroasiatic Roots of Classical Civilization) — Volume I: The Fabrication of Ancient Greece 1785-1985*, Vintage: London, p. 92; A. F. Garvie (1969) *Aeschylus' Supplices: Play and Trilogy*, Cambridge University Press: London, p. 72; J. Bérard (1952) 'Les Hyksos et la légende d'Io: Recherches sur la période pré-mycenienne', *Syria* 29, p. 35.

CHAP. XII: LEARNING THE ART OF CHARIOT WARFARE | 425

of necessity, to master the art of chariot warfare from at least as early as the LBII era. With the breakneck influx into Canaan of the charioteer-warriors of Hurrian and Indo-Aryan descent in the fourteenth century BCE, horses and horse-drawn chariots, had eventually become common currency in Egypt.

Notwithstanding, the swift, light-weight, manoeuvrable vehicles which modern Egyptologists customarily associate with New Kingdom empire building did not, in actuality, come to exist until the time of Typhon Season #5. The Egyptians' expert mastery of the horse-drawn chariot was not acquired from the Hyksos, or the Indo-Europeans, but from the Ethiopians of Napata. Like has been discussed earlier, once the Atlans, the sons of Poseidon, came to establish themselves in the Libyans oases from their home in the Atlas mountains (Atlantis) in West Africa, they soon became know for their use of horses. In her 1997 article entitled "The Horses of Kush,"[4] Egyptologist Lisa Heidorn, from the University of Helsinki, has convincingly demonstrated that the ancients indeed looked upon the Ethiopians from Napata as preeminent horse breeders and standard-pioneering makers of horse-drawn chariots. Moreover, as the late nineteenth century U.S. congressman and historian Ignatius Donnelly related:

> Poseidon was a sea-god because he ruled over a great land in the sea, and was the national god of a maritime people; he is associated with horses, because in Atlantis the horse was first domesticated; and, as Plato shows, the Atlanteans had great race-courses for the development of speed in horses; and Poseidon is represented as standing in a war-chariot, because doubtless wheeled vehicles were first invented by the same people who tamed the horses; and they transmitted these war-chariots to their descendants from Egypt and Britain. We know that horses were the favorite objects chosen for sacrifice to Poseidon by the nations of antiquity within the Historical Period; they were killed, and cast into the sea from high precipices.[5]

Accepting that the Napatans came from the Atlas mountains in West Africa, and were the direct descendants of the A-Group Seth-worshipping Nubians, we can safely deduce that Plato's story is based on solid historical evidence. Now whether the Napatans had in fact invented their own form of war-chariot in their homeland in the Atlas mountains of West Africa, or had only began domesticating horses and training them for war whilst in the Libyan oases, is a question open to de-

---

[4] Lisa A. Heidorn (1997) 'The Horses of Kush', *Journal of Near Eastern Studies* Vol. 56 - Num. 2, pp. 105-114.
[5] Ignatius Donnelly (1882) *Atlantis: The Antediluvian World*, Harper & Brothers: New York, p. 25.

bate. But most scholars believe that the ancient presence of horses in the Libyan oases had been the result of Indo-European invasions into Libya.[6] A much more compelling case could be made for the theory that the Atlanteans, the sons of Poseidon, had mastered the horse only whilst in Libya since unequivocally proving the presence of horse-drawn chariots in such remote times in West Africa would be very difficult. What seems quite evident however is that King Arsa of Atlantis and his Napatan forces had spread the cult of the Typhonic horse through much of the ancient world. For instance, there is extensive evidence of similar chariot-horse sacrifices, as described above by Plato, during the corresponding latter part of the Shang Dynasty in China (during Typhon Season #5). Both the horses and drivers were "slaughtered and buried with the chariots in specially prepared pits around tombs used in the after-life."[7] The practice was carried on through the Zhou Dynasty, and down to the Qin-Han period (221 BCE - 220 AD). No doubt, the Greek tale of the wooden horse of Troy and the Hellenic association of the earth-shaker Poseidon with a horse as well the latter's esteemed status as the "patron of chariots," likewise must stem directly from the Napatan influence during Typhon Season #5.

In an unpublished essay by Martin Bernal, commissioned for *The Encyclopedia of African American Culture and History*, but which was incidentally rejected for its "controversial" nature, Bernal writes:

> Classical writings refer to a people called Nigretai, Nigretes or Negritai, who were Western Ethiopians or live to the west of the Ethiopians. Together with their neighbours the Pharusai they were described as having ridden across the desert on horses and chariots to raid and destroy 300 Phoenician cities on the coast. The Roman writer Pliny (23-79 C.E.) believed they came from the Niger but it would seem more plausible to suggest that they came from the Saharan oases (v.43). There is no doubt that they appeared as "black" to the people of the coast.

Again, confirming Plato's accounts, it is evident that the Ethiopian army of Arsa the Atlan had made significant conquests over a vast portion of the Aegean and Syria-Palestine before being ultimately repelled by Agag I, the Hyksos king of the new Agagite line. The history books have not retained any traces of this short but ever so consequential Ethiopian foray into ancient military history. As seen above, however, certain ancient traditions *have* carried along the memory of those Ethio-

---

[6] See Martin Bernal (1991) *Black Athena (The Afroasiatic Roots of Classical Civilization) — Volume II: The Archaeological and Documentary Evidence*, Rutgers University Press: New Brunswick, NJ, p. 95.

[7] Lu Liancheng (1993) 'Chariot and Horse Burials in Ancient China', *Antiquity* Vol. 67 - Num. 257, p. 824.

pian conquerors. The Napatans' truly momentous contribution to ancient warfare – through perfecting the art of horse-drawn chariot warfare – would have an immeasurable impact of the shaping of both the military and political maps of the ancient Near East during the Iron Age.

Where the impact of the new horse-drawn chariot technology would most immediately be felt was during the great battle waged between Pharaoh Ramses III and the Peoples of the Sea coalition. In his war annals, Ramses III recounted the capture of nearly one hundred chariots from the Libyans.[8] The Libyan forces had evidently acquired the necessary skill to build and use these war chariots from the Napatans — their allies.

King Ramses III, the Great Papyrus Harris, and

the Battle of the Peoples of the Sea

The Great Papyrus Harris, dating to the reign of Ramses III, now in the British Museum, which speaks of Arsa and of the troubled times immediately preceding Ramses III's accession, also imparts the details of a great battle waged during Year 8 of the latter's reign. This war was carried out against a military coalition of various petty northern powers collectively known as the Peoples of the Sea. The inscriptions from Ramses III's temple at Medinet Habu describe the events as follows:

> ... as for the foreign countries, they made a conspiracy in their islands. All at once the lands [i.e. the people] were on the move, scattered in war. No country could stand before their arms. Hatti, Kode [Kizzuwatna], Carchemish, Arzawa and Alashiya. They were cut off. ... They were advancing on Egypt while the flame [perhaps the Egyptian navy or a reference to scorched earth tactics] was prepared before them. Their league was Peleset, Tjeker, Shelkelesh, Denyen and Weshesh, united lands [i.e. people]. They laid their hands upon the lands to the very circuit of the earth, their hearts confident and trusting: 'Our plans will succeed'.[9]

Pharaoh Ramses III prepared for the impending Sea Peoples' invasion by setting up a garrison in Djahi, somewhere between the Nile Delta and Palestine. He set up a "wall of warships" at Egypt's northern frontier. The Egyptian navy and army

---

[8] J. H. Breasted, *Ancient Records of Egypt*, Vol. IV - § 111.
[9] In N. K. Sandars (1978) *The Sea Peoples (Warriors of the Ancient Mediterranean 1250-1150 BC)*, Thames and Hudson: London, p. 119.

were made up of brave Egyptian conscripts called upon to defend their native land. During the land battle, Egypt's enemies, the Peleset (with feathered crowns) and the Shardana (adorned with horned helmets) advance with the aid of ox-carts often loaded with their wives and children — showing that they were, to quote N. K. Sandars "a people on the move in search of a new home."[10] The sea battle (see Fig. 12a) was waged within the Nile's Delta. The Egyptian navy utterly annihilated the invaders, who massively drowned as theirs boats capsized.

The Sea Peoples depicted in Fig. 12a fighting against Ramses III's Egyptian navy, shown wearing the Viking-like horned helmets, were, I argue, the same invaders from the Baltic region who, according to Barry Fell, spoke a "Nordic dialect of the Indo-European family." These people, I identify as the Danaans of Homer's narratives who settled in Libya prior to Danaos and Aegyptus' legendary colonization of mainland Greece. As Prof. Cyrus Gordon explains, they were they were the ancestors of the classical Greeks:

> Early in the twelfth century B.C., the Danites were allies of their fellow Sea Peoples the Philistines in assaulting Egypt during the reign of Ramses III ... The Danites were widespread. Cyprus was called Ia-Dnan "The island of Da(an)." The same people were called Danuna, and under this name they appear as rulers of the Plain of Adana in Cilicia. Greek tradition has their eponymous ancestor, Danaos, migrating from the Nile Delta to Greece where he became king of Argos. So important was this movement that the Greeks afterward called themselves Danaoi for centuries. Vergil also designated the Greeks as "Danai."[11]

Some may object to this identification by saying that this particular detachment of Sea Peoples could hardly have been Homer's Danaans, since the name which the Egyptians gave them, the "Shardana," sounds somewhat different from the name of "Danaan" (although the "dana" at the end bears a close resemblance to Danaan). But while the Shardana are listed in the Papyrus Harris, they are not mentioned in the Year 8 sea battle reliefs from Medinet Habu. Hence, the invading sailors with the horned helmets, to again quote ancient historian N. K. Sandars, are "not necessarily Shardana."[12] In actual fact, the great Papyrus Harris mentions "the fallen ones of Denyen" who accompany the "fallen ones of Peleset." Thus, the names Shardana and Denyen (Danaan) can be used alternately.

---

[10] Ibid, pp. 120-121.
[11] Cyrus H. Gordon (1972) *Before Columbus (Links Between the Old World and Ancient America)*, Turnstone: London, pp. 110-111.
[12] N. K. Sandars (1978) p. 127.

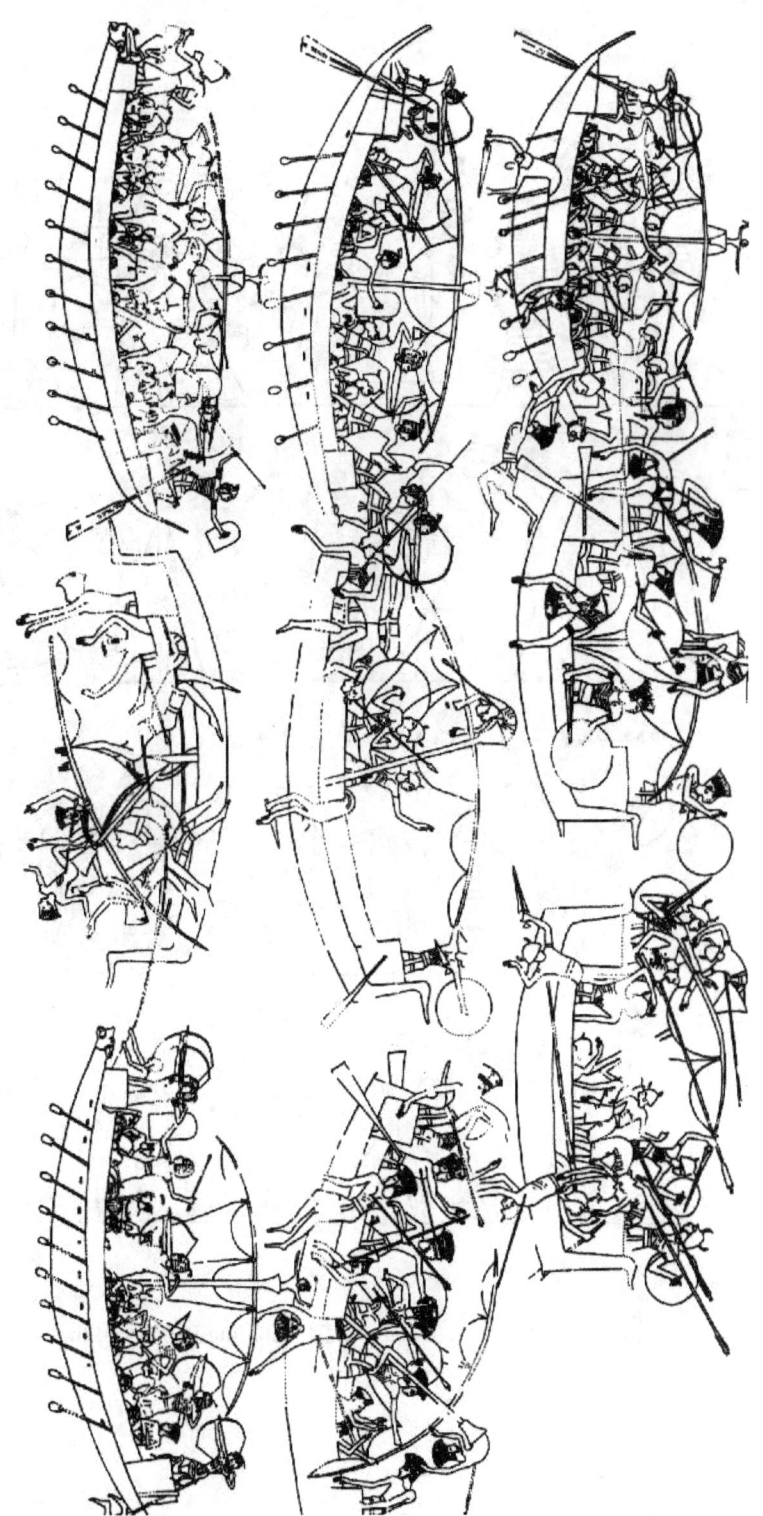

Fig. 12a: Naval battle between Egyptian forces and the Peoples of the Sea.

Fig. 12b: Prisoners of Ramses III including Peoples of the Sea.

CHAP. XII: LEARNING THE ART OF CHARIOT WARFARE | 431

The Danaans, or proto-Hellenic Greeks, were eventually altogether expelled from Egypt and settled *en masse* in mainland Greece — from whence they had journeyed to Libya and Egypt's Delta after arriving in Argos from their aboriginal Nordic homeland early in King Merneptah's reign. As Diodorus of Sicily relates:

> They say also that those who set forth with Danaus, likewise from Egypt, settled what is practically the oldest city of Greece, Argos, and that the nation of the Colchi in Pontus and that of the Jews, which lies in between Arabia and Syria, were founded as colonies by certain emigrants from their country; and this is the reason why it is a long-established institution among these two peoples to circumcise their male children, the custom having been brought over from Egypt.
> (Diodorus of Sicily, Book I, 27. 6-28. 4)

This statement from Diodorus of Sicily has, over recent years, been eagerly retaken by several Afrocentric scholars as evidence of the African roots of Greek civilization. Cheikh Anta Diop, a leading proponent of this theory, deduced that Danaos had been an Egyptian. But, as classicist Mary R. Lefkowitz postulates, it must be borne in mind that Danaos' family, although he had lived in Egypt, had arrived there from Argos. Nevertheless, this reality does not take away from the fact that the Danaans, as Danaos' bond with Aegyptus demonstrates, acquired in Egypt the very building blocks of Greek civilizations — which they later exported to the mainland along with Aegyptus.

> Diop's suggestion that Danaus was Egyptian is slightly less farfetched. He was Egyptian, in the sense that he was born in Egypt. But according to the myth, his family was Greek in origin. His great-grandfather, Epaphus, was born in Egypt, after his mother, Io, the daughter of the river Inachus in Argos, had come to the Nile Delta. Io (Danaus' greatgrandmother) had been compelled to leave Greece because the Greek god Zeus had fallen in love with her, and in jealousy his wife, Hera, turned her into a cow.[13]

Known as "the maiden with cow-horns"[14] Io, the Argive Isis, had been the object of Zeus' love and desire whom Hera had changed into a cow. Smitten by his love for Io, Zeus had rendered her pregnant simply by touching her with his hand. Io bore

---

[13] Mary R. Lefkowitz (1997) *Not Out of Africa (How Afrocentrism Became an Excuse to Teach Myth as History)*. Second revised edition. BasicBooks: New York, p. 18.
[14] *Prometheus Bound*, 585.

a son named Epaphos (the Apis Bull) who was born in Libya. Therefore, as a cow-figure, Io was closely identified with the Egyptian bovine deity Apis.[15] Again, the archaeotheological timing of this myth, in the new chronology, to the disorderly days of Typhon Season #5 provides an important anchor point. Through the distinguished progeny engendered by the union of Zeus and Io came two brothers, Danaos and Aegyptus (the Danaans and the Hyksos vassal princes in Egypt). Danaos had fathered fifty girls while Aegyptus had fathered fifty sons. A conflict arose when the sons of Aegyptus expressed their desire to marry their cousins, the fifty Danaans. The Danaans refused the proposed union and, rather than being forced to submit to the sons of Aegyptus, decided to flee the land of Egypt and return to their adopted homeland in Argos. Much of the rest of this chapter will be focused on proving the veiled historicity of this ancient Greek legend.

The Trojan War and Stonehenge Revisited

In the eighth year of his reign, Pharaoh Ramses III recorded that the Peoples of the Sea attacked *both* Egypt and the Asiatic mainland. Among the Asiatic towns destroyed by the multicultural northern invaders were Cyprus, Carchemish, Arzawa and Hatti. Many scholars recognize that Ramses III's description of the events "must reflect some reality."[16] If the proto-Hellenic Greeks, or Danaans, who made up an important part the Sea People armada, managed to advance all the way through to Boghazköy, would it then be so far fetched to assume that they could have also conquered the ancient city of Troy? The traditional Greek date for the Homeric Trojan War, as given by Eratosthenes, is 1,184 BCE.[17] Although certain classicists and ancient historians dismiss this date as being around half a century too late, that date fits perfectly with the new chronology. The Greek attack against Troy therefore took place soon after the devastating Mercury shift of 1,187 BCE.

In addition, Hesiod wrote that the heroes of the Trojan War lived during the "Fourth Age of men." After the Fourth Age was destroyed by the wrath of the planetary gods, Hesiod says that a Fifth Age of iron emerged.[18] Could we possibly get any clearer indications than that?! Typhon Season #5 brought the collapse of Hesiod's Fourth Age. The ensuing Fifth Age, starting in 1,135 BCE ushered in none other than the Iron Age — Hesiod's "Fifth Age of iron!" Or the Jewish Aggada's Fifth Creation and, as we will see in Chapter 14, the ancient Mesoamericans' Fifth Sun.

---

[15] Martin Bernal (1987a) *Black Athena* I, p. 92.
[16] Oscar White Muscarella (1995) 'The Iron Age Background to the Formation of the Phrygian State', *Bulletin of the American Schools of Oriental Research* 299-300, pp. 91-92.
[17] Lord William Taylour (1990) *The Mycenaeans*. Revised edition. Thames and Hudson: London, p. 159.
[18] Hesiod, *Works and Days*, l. 169.

CHAP. XII: LEARNING THE ART OF CHARIOT WARFARE | 433

In 1,184 BCE, the master of Asia was the Hyksos king Agag I (Apap I or Apophis I). No campaign of such massive scale by the Peoples of the Sea could've been undertaken without Hyksos approval and assistance. In actuality, it is virtually certain, under the circumstances, that the Hyksos held a leadership role in not only the Peoples of the Sea's vast sweeping offensive north of Syria, but the Hyksos must have also orchestrated their war effort against the Theban forces. King Agag I, as the head of this large coalition, wielded immense power. He is the one who led the proto-Hellenic Danaans in their belligerent offensive against the Indo-European Trojans. All those cities which Ramses III mentions, where the Danaans and the Philistines ravaged in their path, had already been severely weakened by the devastating Mercury-induced destruction of just three years earlier — in 1,187 BCE. The name of the leader of the Homeric expedition against Troy, Agamemnon, is based on the name of the Hyksos king Agag — who is the real hero of the Trojan War. The origin of the additional name of "Memnon" in Agamemnon's name (Agag + Memnon) will be explained in Chapter 16.

Amid the rubble of the collapsed walls of Troy VIIb1, Agag I and the proto-Hellenic Danaans decimated the last remaining survivors of the Late Bronze Age Indo-European settlement in the plains of Hissarlik. The Danaan's ambitions would not stop at Troy however. Already very familiar with the lands of northern Europe, given their Nordic origins, the Danaans further went on to colonize ancient England and Ireland. While etymologists in England and Ireland have traditionally opposed the theory of a Mediterranean origin for the early settlers of their respective homelands, a considerable number of British archaeologists and anthropologists have been surprisingly open to such speculations. A popular theory among the latter is that the early settlers who cultivated barley on the southern plains of England, some two thousand years before the birth of Christ, and who built Stonehenge, were "related culturally and ethnically to the Homeric civilization of Mycenae and Crete."[19] Author John Philip Cohane, in his 1969 book *The Key*, has traced important similarities between the building techniques at Stonehenge, the Salisbury Plain in Wiltshire, Avebury, and those of the Postern Gate at Mycenae.[20] Armed with this evidence, Cohane searched for supplementary proof of an ancient link between Homeric Greece and the builders of Stonehenge in Irish mythology:

> The die-hard attitude of the Dublin traditionalists toward a Mediterranean ancestry is especially difficult to understand in view of material contained in early Irish mythology. Various legends, in particular the ninth-century

---

[19] John Philip Cohane (1969) *The Key*, Crown: New York, pp. 28-29.
[20] See Ibid, Plate 5.

> *Lebor Gabala Erenn*, trace in minute detail the voyages of at least one group of early Irish from Egypt and Libya to Crete and Sicily, then Spain and on to Ireland.[21]

Later on, Cohane writes:

> One finds two other parts of parallel names, one in Ireland, the other in the Mediterranean. In Irish mythology, Oc and Ogma reign over the Tuatha De *Dan*aan, the "Children of the goddess *Dan*aan." Throughout the *Iliad* and the *Odyssey* Homer uses interchangeably the two terms *Ach*aean and *Dan*aean as names for the early Greeks. Only once throughout both epics does he refer to them as Hellenes. In each case the name Oc/Og and Dan/Don are closely identified with one another."[22]

The reason why Homer designated the early Greeks as Achaeans and Danaans interchangeably, is because the Danaans were the proto-Hellenic Greeks. Because the Danaans learned the art of warfare from the Agagite Amalekites, the Hyksos king Agag I, or Ogyges I, was honoured as a god in the mythology of the Danaans who had followed him to Troy. Hence, the Gaelic deity Og or Ogam is none other than a divine incarnation of the Hyksos king Ogyges I (or Agag I). In author Anne Ross' book entitled *The Folklore of the Scottish Highlands*, for which she extensively researched ancient Gaelic tales, legends and songs passed on over countless generations, she speaks of an ancient Celtic god named "Ogmios" (Ogma) — the god of knowledge.[23] In fact, according to British author James Bailey: *"It is Og who gives the Irish the only prehistoric script the British Isles have used, Ogham ..."*[24] This ancient script which the Danaans introduced into the British Isles, bearing the imprint of the great Hyksos king Agag I, was Phoenician in origin. The proto-Hellenic Greeks indeed owed their alphabet to the Phoenicians. The American epigraphist Barry Fell, for instance, had for many years argued that the ancient Celtic script of Ogam "is not an ancient Gaelic alphabet as it has always been thought" but, in reality, was a form of Phoenician.[25] This relationship between the Phoenicians and the Danaans was forged during their stay in Egypt — when Thebes was ruled by a dynasty of Phoenician kings (the 17th Dynasty).

---

[21] John Philip Cohane (1969) p. 34.
[22] Ibid, p. 104.
[23] Ann Ross (1976) *The Folklore of the Scottish Highlands*, B. T. Batsford: London, p. 12; Barry Fell (1982) *Bronze Age America*, Little, Brown & Co.: Boston and Toronto, p. 156.
[24] James Bailey (1973) *The God-Kings & the Titans (The New World Ascendancy in Ancient Times)*, St. Martin's Press: New York, p. 181.
[25] Barry Fell (1976) *America B.C. (Ancient Settlers in the New World)*, Wildwood House: London, p. 64.

A Fight for Avaris

*" No man rests, being wasted through servitude
of the Asiatics. I will grapple with him and rip open his
belly, for my desire is to deliver Egypt and
to smite the Asiatics."*

- King Kamose

*" And when he looked on Amalek, he took
up his parable, and said, Amalek was the first of the
nations; but his latter end shall be that
he perish for ever."*

- Numbers 24:20

Since King Agag I had been, without a doubt, the most illustrious of the Hyksos rulers, those who followed him had a very tough act to follow indeed. King Agag I's son and successor Agag (Apap) II was left with a grand empire and, as a direct consequence, likewise found himself with a great deal more to lose. Under King Apap II's rule, the Thebans monarchs in the south, the native Khemeto-Egyptian 15th Dynasty and the Phoenician 17th Dynasty, became increasingly defiant and began preparing themselves for a fierce war of independence to once and for all rid themselves of the Hyksos yoke. Pharaoh Ramses III had dealt with the then much more pressing threat from the Peoples of the Sea — leaving the increasingly nationalist Hyksos in the north much room to manoeuvre and grow in strength. After the death of Ramses III, Hyksos power and influence had spread to such a monumental extent that they were by then the undisputed masters of Egypt and Syria-Palestine. Historians generally ascribe the clear loss of Egyptian imperial trappings over Canaan, as well as the declining authority of the Pharaoh over his own people and priesthood, following the death of Ramses III, to internal strife between the king's legitimate heirs and widespread tomb robbing in the Theban necropolis. However, I would instead argue that the real reason for this decline in Theban power at the end of LBIII was the renewed Hyksos supremacy in Avaris. Power had shifted to the north.

Those who will be found at the vanguard of this emancipating quest are the Theban pharaohs of the 17th Dynasty. The hostilities appear to have begun under Pharaoh Sekenenre (Tao II). The New Chronology Table offers us a very interesting parallel which helps to clarify the nature of the animosities between Sekenenre in Thebes and Apap II in Avaris. As we can observe in the chronological table, there is a more than striking resemblance between the names of two contemporaneous rulers of the 16th and 17th Dynasties. Alongside Pharaoh Sekenenre of the 17th

Dynasty, we find a certain Sekhenre of the 16th Dynasty ruling in Avaris. I am absolutely convinced that these two rulers were one and the same person. King Tao II–"the Brave" (Sekenenre), undoubtedly conquered the Hyksos city of Avaris, and was incidentally recorded as a ruler of the 16th Dynasty as well! This belligerent attack is what sparked the tense relationship between him and Apap II. What most likely occurred is that Apap II retaliated by attacking Avaris and then declaring himself, once again, "Lord of Avaris." As the reconsecrated ruler of Avaris, he made Sekenenre his subject. The fact that King Apap II appears to have left Avaris vulnerable to Theban attack could indicate that, as a ruler of large coalition of powers, Apap II may have taken residence elsewhere — perhaps in the Aegean of Syria-Palestine. The established practice of the Agagite rulers appears to have been to acquiesce the day-to-day governorship of Avaris in the hands of their Hyksos brethren of the 16th dynasty, while they themselves attended to the broader affairs of the Hyksos empire. The unsuspected Theban raid seems to have finally compelled the Hyksos king to adopt Avaris as his permanent residence in order to more effectively contend with the Theban nationalistic threat. Evidently concerned that the rebellious spirit might spread further, King Apap II also carried on his punitive expedition further south. He expeditiously put an end to the Khemeto-Egyptian 15th Dynasty by defeating King Ramses VI and appointing his son Khyan as overseer of his new southern frontier. It is indeed well-known from extant evidence that from the very first year of Ramses VI's reign, foreign enemy hordes were terrorising the Egyptian population.[26] Egyptians stopped working because of their "fear of the enemy" who "destroyed everything" and "burned men alive."[27] Egyptologist Amin A.M.A. Amer, following eminent Egyptologist Jaroslav Cerny, assumed that the presence of "the enemy" within the land of Egypt might point to evidence of a civil war. He writes:

> This enemy was rumoured to have threatened Per-Nebyt (north of Thebes?), destroying everything and burning its people. This would show some serious trouble which had broken out early in the reign.[28]

These "enemies" were none other than the Hyksos. The chaotic political situation is very well described in a papyrus from the British Museum — in which the Hyksos king "Apophis" is mentioned. Dr E. L. Lushington, in his *Transactions of the Society of Biblical Archaeology*, translate the papyrus in question as follows:

---

[26] Andrzej Niwinsky (1995) 'Le Passage de la XXe à la XXIIe dynastie: Chronologie et histoire politique', *Bulletin de l'Institut Français d'Archéologie Orientale* 95, p. 330.
[27] J. Cerny 'Egypt: from the Death of Ramses III to the End of the Twenty-First Dynasty.' In *Cambridge Ancient History* (1975) Third edition, Vol. II/2, p. 613, K. A. Kitchen (1983) *Ramesside Inscriptions, Historical and Biographical* (Vol. IV), Oxford, p. 342.
[28] Amin A.M.A. Amer (1985) 'Reflections on the Reign of Ramesses VI', *Journal of Egyptian Archaeology* 71, p. 67.

CHAP. XII: LEARNING THE ART OF CHARIOT WARFARE | 437

> It came to pass that the land of Kemi [Khemet] belonged to the enemies. And nobody was lord in the day when that happened. At that time there was in deed a king Ra-Sekenen [Sekhenre], but he was only a Hak of the city of the South, but the enemies sat in the town of the Amu, and Apopi was king in the city of Avaris. And the whole world brought him its productions, also the North country did likewise with all the good things of Tameri. And the king Apopi chose the god Set for his divine lord, and he did not serve any of the gods which he worshipped in the whole land. He built him a temple of glorious work, the last for ages [...And the king] Apopi [appointed] feasts [and] days to offer [the sacrifices] at every season to the god Sutekh.[29]

The British Museum papyrus outlines, in truly amazing detail, the prevailing political situation at the time, according to my revised scheme, when the Hyksos king Apap II raided the south of Egypt following Sekenenre's bold foray into Avaris. It is clear, from Lushington's translation, that Sekenenre had been a ruler of the south. The enemies of Sekenenre — called the Amu (Amalekites) — occupied the northern part of Egypt, specifically the Hyksos city of Avaris dedicated to the storm-god Seth. When King Apap II drove King Sekenenre's Theban forces out of the Delta, he did not have the rebellious Theban monarch immediately killed. Other extant sources reveal to us that Sekenenre was first forcibly subjected to various humiliations by Apap II. Pharaoh Sekenenre was afterwards executed by a violent blow to the head — as revealed by the king's mummy. The British Museum papyrus' statement to the effect that the land of Kemi (Khemet) belonged to the enemies, is proof that the Black Land (Upper Egypt) was now under Hyksos control. Another document bearing the name of Apap (Agag II) reveals that "his father Seth, lord of Auaris [Avaris], had set all foreign countries under his feet."[30] As Lushington's translation further illuminates, the Amu king Apap who reigned in the north while King Sekenenre ruled in the south, consecrated himself to Seth and had a temple built in honour of this god in Avaris.

The suggestion that the Hyksos could have invaded Thebes as late as during the reign of Ramses VI is, of course, a completely ridiculous idea as far as conventional Egyptologists and ancient historians are concerned. Those events recounted in the British Museum papyrus are supposed to have been separated in time from the reign

---

[29] Dr E. L. Lushington, *Transactions of the Society of Biblical Archaeology*, Vol. IV: p. 263.
[30] Immanuel Velikovsky (1952) *Age in Chaos*, Doubleday: Garden City, NY, p. 68.

of Ramses VI by over four hundred years! The much hated Hyksos were supposed to have been long gone — a distant memory Ramses VI and his subjects had much preferred to forget. This could not be further from the truth. Ramses VI, Sekenenre, and Apap II were all contemporaries. The audacious attack of Sekenenre had so incensed Apap II, that he would have Pharaoh Ramses VI pay for the affront as well. The New Kingdom Ramesside dynasty did not survive the wrath of the Hyksos king. Indeed, I believe that the very last Ramesside pharaoh to rule Late Bronze Age Egypt was Ramses VI. The later Ramesside rulers known as Ramses VII through XII of the standard 20th Dynasty, as will be explained in Chapter 18, actually reigned during the last two centuries before the common era. Indeed, the last significant remains of any Ramesside king from the standard 20th Dynasty (latter part of the new 15th Dynasty) found in Late Bronze Age/Early Iron Age Syria-Palestine belong to Ramses VI.[31] In the words of archaeologist Israel Finkelstein:

> In fact, there is good reason to suggest that the Egyptian domination in southern Canaan lasted until the days of Ramses VI, that is, up to c.1135 BCE.[32]

While we can hardly talk of Ramesside domination of Canaan following the death of Ramses III, there is no question that the abrupt break in archaeological remains belonging to Ramesside kings in Canaan in c.1,135 BCE means that the New Kingdom Ramesside line ended with Ramses VI. Remains of further Ramesside kings have not been found because those kings never followed King Ramses VI of the Late Bronze Age. After the Hyksos King Agag II banished Ramses VI, he replaced him with his own son Khyan. Although a lid belonging to Khyan found in the Aegean has been dated to the Middle Minoan III period, or MBIIIc, it is quite probable that this archaeological verdict was rendered with the accepted chronology in mind. Indeed, following the renowned classicist L. R. Palmer's lead, several modern scholars, including Sturt Manning, believe that *"the Khyan lid should no longer be used to date the MM III period."*[33] With the Hyksos gaining partial control of Upper Egypt, the Theban 17th Dynasty under King Kamose, Sekenenre's successor, became increasingly isolated. The political situation does not seem to have differed much from the time of the late Middle Bronze Age

---

[31] Peter James *et al* (1991a) *Centuries of Darkness (A Challenge to the Conventional Chronology of Old World Archaeology)*, Jonathan Cape: London, p. 247.

[32] Israel Finkelstein (1996) 'The Archaeology of the United Monarchy: An Alternative View', *Levant* 28, p. 180.

[33] Sturt Manning (1988) 'The Bronze Age Eruption of Thera: Absolute Dating, Aegean Chronology and Mediterranean Cultural Interrelations', *Journal of Mediterranean Archaeology* Vol. 1 - Num. 1, p. 31.

CHAP. XII: LEARNING THE ART OF CHARIOT WARFARE | 439

when the Hyksos had likewise isolated the Egyptian 13th Dynasty. Again, the Hyksos kings, having learned from their MBIIc ancestors, made a strategic alliance with the Kushites of the land of Wawat. This is confirmed by the following message sent by Agag II to his son in the land of Kush — which King Kamose had inadvertently intercepted:

> Aa-user-Re, the Son of Re: Apophis, sending greetings to my son, the ruler of Cush. Why do you arise as a ruler without letting me know? Do you see what Egypt has done to me: the ruler who is in it, Kamose the Strong, given life, attacking me on my own soil, (although) I had not assailed him – just like everything that he has done to you? He picks out these two lands to persecute them, my land and yours. He has destroyed them. Come north. *Do not falter.* See, he is here in my land, and there is no one who is waiting for you in this (part of) Egypt. ... Then we shall divide the towns of this Egypt, and our *[two lands]* will be happy in joy.[34]

It is unclear whether Agag II (Apophis) is writing to his real son Khyan (who may have unexpectedly been crowned king of the Kushites), or if he refers to the Kushite king as his son as a sign of his acknowledgement of their vigorous bond. Either way, it's clearly evident that the Cushites had joined into an alliance with the Hyksos and were menacing Egypt. According to the New Chronology Table, the Napatan ruler who reigned at the time of this Kushite-Hyksos alliance was Aspelta. In the latter's official annals it was in fact duly recorded on the "Accession Stela of Aspelta" that *"the army of Cush was at the Pure Mountain, threatening Egypt."*[35] Mount Barkal, or Gebel Barkal, was known in ancient Egyptian inscriptions as "Ta-ab" — meaning "Pure, or Holy Mountain."[36] Although Aspelta described those events, it was not the Napatan forces who had entered into the Hyksos alliance against the Thebans, but the Kushites who dwelt principally between the First and the Third Cataracts — the descendants of the C-Group Asiatic immigrants. This is an important distinction to be made. Once again, the revised Napatan chronology has found an important pillar. King Aspelta plainly recounts the same dire situation the Thebans in Egypt found themselves in — opposed to belligerent Kushite forces — as transpires from the message intercepted by King Kamose. Nubiologists, who conventionally date the reign of King Aspelta to

---

[34] James B. Pritchard (editor) (1955) *ANET*, pp. 554-555.
[35] A. J. Arkell (1974 [1961]) *A History of the Sudan (From the Earliest Times to 1821)*, Greenwood Press: Westport, Conn., p. 145.
[36] W. A. Wallis Budge (1976 [1907]) *The Egyptian Sudan (Its History and Monuments)*, AMS Press: New York, Vol. I: p. 130.

593-568 BCE, have much to explain since no such event could possibly have taken place during that time. Actually, historian are faced with a glaring contradiction since King Psamtik II of the standard 26th Dynasty, who is erroneously believed to have been a contemporary of Aspelta, is supposed to have utterly annihilated the Nubians — who were at that time in no position to threaten Egypt.

Meanwhile, Pharaoh Kamose in Thebes was fiercely determined to meet the Hyksos challenge head on. Not only would he not yield to Agag II's threats, but he would even be so bold as to attack the Hyksos realm itself — much like his predecessor, Sekenenre, had done to his imminent peril. As University of Chicago Egyptologist Frank J. Yurco relates:

> Kamose's second stela mentions some Hyksos ships that he captured in the waters near Avaris. They were filled with weaponry and other goods, including much wood from Syria and perhaps elsewhere.[37]

King Kamose would not be able to defeat the Hyksos alone however. Both his southern and northern fronts were teeming with hostile enemy soldiers. Nothing could be done until Upper Egypt was delivered first. If not Kamose himself, then a new Theban conqueror had to come along to fully deliver Thebes. This saviour did come. It was Ahmose, the brother of Kamose.

Ahmose the Saviour

> *" Events are often duplicates;*
> *many battles are shadows; many speeches*
> *are echoes; many treaties are copies;*
> *even some empires are phantoms."*
>
> *- Immanuel Velikovsky*
> *Ages in Chaos*

The political and social climate at the closing stages of Typhon Season #5 was eerily similar to the conditions we found in Egypt at the end of Typhon Season #4. In both eras, the Hyksos had managed to isolate the native Egyptian kings by establishing a presence in Upper Egypt and forging a strategic military alliance with the Kushites. In both cases, the Egyptian dynasts urgently needed to reclaim Upper Egypt. One could easily understand how the two periods, albeit separated in time by over four hundred years, may have been compared — even to the extent of fusing them into one. I believe that this is indeed exactly what the ancients did. As author Richard E. Friedman observes, the ancients' perception

---

[37] Frank J. Yurco 'Black Athena: An Egyptological Review.' In Mary R. Lefkowitz & Guy M. Rogers (editors) (1996) *Black Athena Revisited*, p. 63.

CHAP. XII: LEARNING THE ART OF CHARIOT WARFARE | 441

of the universe was shaped by their vision of a *"cyclical time of nature rather than one of a linear time of history."*[38] This made it a lot easier for them to justify the creation of a "Great Time Warp of History." Amply aware of those similarities, the younger brother of Kamose, who fancied himself as the deliverer of the Hyksos-beleaguered Theban capital, chose to name himself Ahmose — like the great Theban ancestor who had reclaimed Thebes from the hands of those very same foreign usurpers and their Nubian collaborators. We now pick up where Egyptologists believe we should have proceeded all the way back at the end of the Middle Bronze Age! Much of the nearly four hundred and twenty-five years of history which we have been studying since the end of the Middle Bronze Age up to this point "never" happened according to modern scholars. The trouble is, what we shall now describe as early Iron Age events, are interpreted as early Late Bronze Age events by Egyptologists and ancient historians.

Like his Theban ancestor and namesake, the Iron Age Pharaoh Ahmose would refrain from altogether expelling the Hyksos from the Egyptian Delta town of Avaris. All indications however show that the Theban relationship with the Hyksos in the north was certainly not as courteous as they were at the beginning of the Late Bronze Age. The extant Egyptian records relating Ahmose's raids against Avaris are understandably much more likely to belong to this period, given the similar Theban campaigns during Typhon Season #5. Ahmose's attacks would however be no more successful than they had been under his immediate predecessors Sekenenre and Kamose. Indubitably, the Theban forays against Avaris must have somewhat destabilized the Hyksos garrisons, but they had not succeed in permanently removing the Hyksos from the region. In essence, the new King Ahmose's chief achievement was to regain Egyptian control of Thebes and the rest of Upper Egypt from the crippling influence of the Hyksos and the Kushites. In order to prevent further Nubian threats against Thebes, Ahmose at once appointed his own son Ahmose Si-Ta-yit as King's Son and Overseer of the Southern Country. The latter's successor, Thuwre, was however a non-royal. Ahmose thereby established a permanent Egyptian administration in the land of Kush that would be known as the "viceregal administration" headed by an appointed viceroy. As the Kushites became increasingly Egyptianized, it was rationalized, they would be much less likely to pose further threats to Egyptian interests. Coercive measures were nonetheless frequently and forcefully applied to curb any Kushite resistance or drive for independence.

An inscribed alabaster vase identifies Ahmose's wife as Ahmose Nefretiry. From other evidence, Egyptologists also know that this queen was the daughter of Pharaoh Sekenenre and the mother of Amenhotep I — Ahmose's successor. The royal continuity was hence legitimately established. The thorny issue of the ethnicity of the ancient Egyptian monarchs ought to, at this pivotal junction, be tho-

---

[38] Richard Elliott Friedman (1997) *The Hidden Face of God*, Harper: San Fransisco, p. 88.

roughly addressed. As we know by now, the 16th Dynasty was made up of rulers of Phoenician descent. Consequently, it would be quite inappropriate to classify them as having been "Black" in the strict Diopan sense. The same ambivalence in not found in the Theban Renaissance whose pharaohs were incontrovertibly African. The nascent Iron Age Egyptian kings of Phoenician descent whom we later find occupying the pharaonic throne are essentially usurpers of the earlier Black pharaohs' titles. The latter part of the twelfth century BCE introduces a form of "re-Levantization" of dynastic Egypt's monarchy after the dynastic throne of the Two Lands had been occupied by Black pharaohs since the time of King Mentuhotep-Nebhepetre. The Asiatic vassal-kings who settled in Egypt during the reign of the African pharaoh Ramses II were now the sole masters of Egypt. What's more, they would not hesitate to use the entire Late Bronze Age Khemeto-Egyptian king-list as a model for their own "alter ego" dynastic line. When modern Western European scholars attempt to ascertain the racial makeup of the dynastic Egyptians, it is to these phantom rulers that they base their research on; since many of the extant mummies dated to the New Kingdom belong to these pharaohs of Levantine descent. As the more recent of the two identical dynastic lines, it is only natural that their artifacts and various self-portraits would have eclipsed much of the earlier African relics.

Drastically lowering the date for the beginning of the 18th Dynasty by over four hundred years – to 1,135 BCE – unquestionably precipitates fundamental changes affecting far more than mere chronology. For instance, Ahmose, founder of the 18th Dynasty, is no longer considered as the founder of the New Kingdom. Also, like the original Ahmose of the new 14th Dynasty, he is no longer credited with driving the Hyksos out of Avaris. Both Ahmoses became illustrious figures by freeing Thebes and the rest of Upper Egypt from Hyksos tyranny. Perhaps the most significant revolutionary by-product of this much lowered date is its ultimate effect on Hyksos history. According to Josephus, the Hittite empire lasted for over five hundred years.[39] Historians have never taken this figure seriously because the accepted chronology and history of ancient Egypt allows for a maximum of about one hundred and fifteen years, the total length of the so-called Second Intermediate Period, for any Hyksos influence over Egypt. But in the new chronology, we see that this so-called Second Intermediate Period has quite literally swallowed up the entire four hundred-year period that has vanished from history. Rulers from the MBIIc period have been dated contemporaneously with kings from the 16th and 17th Dynasties. My drastic leap from the 13th Dynasty to what Egyptologists consider to have been the 18th Dynasty was no phantasmagoric leap after all. The new 14th Dynasty takes the place of its later Levantine alter ego, the 18th Dynasty.

---

[39] Josephus, *Against Apion*, Book I: 84.

CHAP. XII: LEARNING THE ART OF CHARIOT WARFARE | 443

Flavius Josephus is therefore vindicated. There is indeed no question that the Hyksos continued to pose a lingering threat to the dynastic Egyptian state well beyond the close of the Middle Bronze Age.

With the end tail of Hyksos power crossing the threshold of the Iron Age, we face myriads of heretofore unforeseen possibilities. Historical evidence which didn't appear to make sense at the end of the Middle Bronze Age now fit right into the mould of a closing Late Bronze Age environment. It is imperative to differentiate between the 18th Dynasty Pharaoh Ahmose and his new 14th Dynasty alter-ego and predecessor. Indeed, the traditional picture of a bellicose transition from Hyksos rule in Egypt to Theban liberation with the advent of the Late Bronze Age, stems primarily from the annals of the 18th Dynasty Ahmose. It is he who carries out hostile raids into the Hyksos northern realm. The records of the later King Ahmose indicate that the Egyptians army had access to swift two-wheeled horse-drawn chariots in their assault against the Hyksos. Ancient historians generally assume that the ancient Egyptians had acquired the horse-drawn chariot from the Hyksos invaders. Professor Amélie Kuhrt of University College, London describes the position of most ancient world scholars:

> ... it is possible that one of the tangible legacies of Hyksos rule was the introduction of the **fast, two-wheeled, horse-drawn chariot** into Egypt, which now became [at the time of King Ahmose's 18th Dynasty] the most important weapon of the Egyptian army. The new militaristic emphasis, it has been argued, is reflected be a new item of royal head-gear. **This is the blue crown** ... [40]

That "new militaristic emphasis" is a product of political developments during Typhon Season #5 — not the reality of the transition phase between MBIIc and LBI. Furthermore, the Hyksos were not the ones who introduced the swift two-wheeled horse-drawn chariot into Egypt — it was the Napatans. Consequently, the militaristic "blue crown" (or khepresh) which was first worn by the pharaohs of the 18th Dynasty, is inevitably to be seen as a distinguishing feature of Iron Age pharaohs. The crucial importance of this distinction could not be stressed enough. Since we now have to contend with two virtually identical dynastic lines of succession, we need something tangible to help us differentiate between the Late Bronze Age pharaohs and their Iron Age alter egos. That salient feature is the blue crown. None of the pharaohs who ruled before the 18th Dynasty wore that particular crown. It was an innovation of the Theban monarchs who,

---

[40] Amélie Kuhrt (1997 [1995]) *The Ancient Near East (c.3000 – 330 BC)*, Routledge: London and New York, Vol. I: p. 190.

under the oppressive regime of the Hyksos at the close of the Late Bronze Age, adopted the khepresh headgear as a war-like symbol of their hard won independence. Since the blue crown's war-like characteristics was intimately linked with horse-drawn chariot, its inception must inevitably post-date Arsa the Atlan's pugnacious expedition from the Libyan oases.

It is thoroughly inconceivable that Pharaoh Ahmose of the new 14th Dynasty could have had access to such horse-drawn chariots. The simple and unavoidable fact is that horses didn't even yet exist in Egypt at the end of the Middle Bronze Age. Burial evidence that some scholars have pointed to in a vain attempt to authenticate the presence of horses in MBIIc Egypt have turned out to be burials of donkeys — not of horses. As University of Uppsala Egyptologist Torgny Säve-Söderbergh remarked:

> At Tell el-'Ajjul in southern Palestine Petrie found rich tombs where horses and asses had been buried with the dead, an he regarded this as a definite proof on the one hand that the Hyksos used the horse, and on the other hand that the tombs in question belonged to the Hyksos. But these tombs date from the very end of the Hyksos period, possibly even only from the Eighteenth Dynasty. Not a single buried horse nor even a bone of a horse has been found in any of the numerous tombs from the Hyksos period in Egypt, and there is not a single picture of a horse, despite the fact that all sorts of different animals are depicted on the scarabs of this time.[41]

Undoubtedly, the Hyksos *did* use horses to terrorize the Thebans during Typhon Season #5; but the MBIIc burial grounds excavated by Petrie have erroneously been interpreted as "late Hyksos" — when in reality, they were "early Hyksos" burials. Therefore, it is not necessary to artificially turn donkeys into horses in order simply to make sense of the 18th Dynasty evidence. Once again, this is a needless conflict between archaeology and philology. Both the Hyksos and the Egyptians would have plenty of time to get themselves acquainted with the horse. But as things stood at the end of the Middle Bronze Age, neither of them had been at all familiar with horses — much less with horse-drawn chariots. The earliest references to chariotry troops in the Egyptian records, according to the conventional chronology, date to the reign of Kamose.[42] If we accept the new chronology, we know that horse-drawn chariots had only begun to make their way into Egypt during the LBII period.

---

[41] Torgny Säve-Söderbergh (1951) 'The Hyksos Rule in Egypt', *Journal of Egyptian Archaeology* 37, pp. 59-60.
[42] Jaromir Malek (1989) 'An Early Eighteenth Dynasty Monument of Sipar from Saqqâra', *Journal of Egyptian Archaeology* 75, pp. 71-72; L. Habachi (1972) *The Second Stela of Kamose*, Glückstadt, p. 36.

Pharaoh Ahmose had yet another compelling reason to find inspiration in his Theban ancestor and namesake Ahmose. Not only were the sociopolitical conditions in their respective times immensely analogous, but they also both acceded to the Egyptian throne on the year in which a Typhon Season came to a thunderous end with a Venus-induced global cataclysm. I may even go so far as saying that the coming Venus shift was more than likely interpreted by Pharaoh Ahmose as an omen portending the imminent demise of the Hyksos occupation in his homeland. Consequently, he envisioned himself as the new Ahmose — who had been called upon by the great god to inflict upon the woeful Hyksos his divine punishment. The violent termination of the World Age, or Mandate of Heaven, was an urgent call, in the minds of the ancients, to repentance in the face of God's eschatological manifestation. The full significance of this Venusian paroxysm of 1,135 BCE is conveyed in Pharaoh Ahmose's Tempest Stela:

> (8) ... The gods [caused] the sky to come in a tempest of r[ain], with darkness in the western region and the sky being
> (9) unleashed without [cessation, louder than] the cries of the masses, more powerful than [...], [while the rain raged (?)] on the mountains louder than the noise of the cataract which is Elephantine. Every house, every quarter that they reached ...
> (12) while a torch could not be lit in the Two Lands. Then His majesty said: "How much greater this than the wrath of the great god, than the plans of the gods!" Then His Majesty descended
> (13) to his boat, with his council following him, while the crowds on the East and West had hidden faces, having no clothing on them
> (14) after the manifestation of God's wrath. ...
> (15) Then His Majesty began to reestablish the Two Lands ...[43]

Attempts have been made by some scholars to correlate the ruinous events described in Ahmose's Tempest Stela with the Theran eruption.[44] Such an interpretation would however necessitate maintaining the now discarded date of c.1,500 BCE for the Theran eruption. In any event, this would not change anything since Pharaoh Ahmose wrote his Tempest Stela in 1,135 BCE — the year of the Venus Shift which terminated the Age of Leo and immediately heralded the Mandate of Taurus.

---

[43] Karen P. Foster & Robert K. Ritner (1996) 'Texts, Storms, and the Thera Eruption', *Journal of Near Eastern Studies* Vol. 55 - Num. 1, p. 11.

[44] The main proponents of this theory are C. Vandersleyen, H. Goedicke, E. N. Davis, K. P. Foster and R. K. Ritner (1996, p. 10). For a critique of their position see Malcolm H. Wiener & James P. Allen (1998) 'Separate Lives: The Ahmose Tempest Stela and the Theran Eruption', *Journal of Near Eastern Studies* Vol. 57 - Num. 1, pp. 1-28.

The advent of the new divine covenant consuming the Fourth Creation is acknowledged by Pharaoh Ahmose when he says that the populace had "hidden faces, having no clothing on them after the manifestation of God's wrath." We are of course reminded of the well-known Genesis account of the primordial Creation in which Adam and Eve, who had heretofore dwelt freely naked in the Garden of Eden quite suddenly, in their shame, "hid themselves from the presence of God ..." (Gen. 3:8) — having abruptly been made aware of their nakedness. The theme of nakedness, as already analysed in the case of Noah-Thebes after the Venus-induced Great Flood, denotes a Venusian eschatological destruction of civilization which causes the chastised sufferers to atone to their angered deity — in humble repentance for their human inequity. The consummation of the age was a periodic reminder to ruler and commoner alike that the day of judgment, the Day of the Lord, is never far away and that one must continuously live in righteousness in respect of the divine order (Ma'at).

The Great Exodus

Pharaoh Ahmose's resolve to, in his own words, "reestablish the Two Lands" by restoring political and religious order was soon put to the test by the people of Egypt. No sooner had Ahmose ascended the Egyptian throne that the populace began to complain to their newly crowned pharaoh that the cosmic tumult which befell Egypt was due to the excessive numbers of foreigners who dwelt within their borders. They wondered how they could possibly be expected to please the Creator if so many different people who did not share the same religious beliefs were freely allowed to live in their midst — completely oblivious to the collective duty to live according to the divine precepts of Ma'at. The devastating wrath of the planet Venus upon Egypt was certainly, in their own mind's eye, to be blamed upon the iniquitous foreigners such as the Phoenicians, Hebrews, and Amalekites whose ancestors had been permitted to settle massively in Egypt, during the reign of Ramses II. According to Diodorus of Sicily:

> When in ancient times a pestilence arose in Egypt, the common people ascribed their troubles to the workings of a divine agency; for indeed with many strangers of all sorts dwelling in their midst and practising different rites of religion and sacrifice, their own traditional observances in honour of the gods had fallen into disuse. Hence the natives of the land surmised that unless they removed the foreigners, their troubles would never be resolved. At once, therefore, the aliens were driven from the country, and the most outstanding and active among them banded together and, as some say, were cast ashore in Greece and certain other regions; their lead-

ers were notable men, chief among them being Danaus and Kadmos. But the greater number were driven into what is now Judaea, which is not far distant from Egypt and was at that time utterly uninhabited. The colony was headed by a man called Moses, outstanding both for his wisdom and for his courage.
(Diodorus of Sicily, Book XL: 3, 2)

However, post-Ramsesside Egypt had become so multicultural that one must assume that the litmus test for "native Egyptianess" was to what extent these foreigners had become "Egyptianized." Most of those who bitterly complained to Pharaoh about the iniquitous foreigners in Egypt had probably been descendants of immigrants themselves, but resented those who had resisted becoming Egyptianized. They were blamed for arousing the gods of Egypt's indignation. An interesting parallel could be logically made with the modern nation of the United-States. America is a nation of immigrants and, despite being a relatively young nation, waves of anti-immigrant feelings, especially in times of economic distress and war, have been well documented by historians and sociologists. Pharaoh Ahmose himself was of Phoenician extraction as a matter of fact. The pestilence which arose in Egypt at this time according to Diodorus of Sicily was of course caused by the immense upheaval of nature described in Pharaoh Ahmose's Tempest Stela. Once again, we are referred to the biblical Moses tradition. As was the case during the two previous Exoduses, this latest episode takes place amidst a tremendous natural catastrophe. This Third Exodus, involving the Fourth Moses, coincided with a similar massive departure from Egypt of the proto-Hellenic Greeks (i.e. Danaos) and the Egypto-Phoenicians (i.e. Kadmos). According to some Egyptian priests who lived in the first century BCE, their ancestors had "sent forth numerous colonies to many parts of the inhabited world, by reason of the preeminence of their former kings and their excessive population."[45] Again, Diodorus of Sicily writes:

> Now the Egyptians say that also after these events a great number of colonies were spread from Egypt over all the inhabited world. To Babylon, for instance, colonists were led by Belus, who was held to be the son of Poseidon and Libya; and after establishing himself on the Euphrates river he appointed priests, called Chaldaeans by the Babylonians ... They say also that those who set forth with Danaus, likewise from Egypt, settled what is practically the oldest city of Greece, Argos, and that the nation of the Colchis in Pontus and that the nation of the Jews, which lies between Arabia and Syria, were founded as colonies by certain emigrants from their country; and this is the reason why it is a long-established institution among

---

[45] Diodorus of Sicily, Book I: 29.

> these two peoples to circumcise their male children, the custom having been brought from Egypt. Even the Athenians, they say, are colonists from Sais in Egypt ...
> (Diodorus of Sicily, Book I: 28)

This "nation of the Jews" which was founded by the Fourth Moses and his followers following their expulsion from Egypt's Delta under Pharaoh Ahmose at the dawn of the Iron Age was a rejuvenation of the old nation of Israel which crumbled during the Late Bronze II period. Confirming the existence of the new chronology's Fourth Moses during the reign of Pharaoh Ahmose, Julius Africanus writes:

> The Eighteenth Dynasty consisted of 16 kings of Diospolis. The first of these was Amôs, in whose reign Moses went forth from Egypt, as I here declare ...
> (Manetho, *Aegyptiaca*, FR. 52)

The group of Jews which the Fourth Moses led out of bondage in Egypt were the descendants of the southern Canaanite slaves whom King Ramses II had captured from the land of Shasu Y-H-W (A) as part of his Year 8 campaign. Held prisoners in the Land of Ramses to build the fortress at Kantir in Egypt's eastern Delta, under the shadow of their archenemies the Hyksos, the Yahwists welcomed the opportunity to depart from this land of bondage completely unmolested. As it unequivocally was Pharaoh's, as well as his people's, desire to see all foreigners leave Egypt at once, no efforts were made to hinder the Israelites' exodus toward their ancestral Promised Land.

The Egypto-Phoenician Colonization of the Aegean at the End of the Late Bronze Age

Diodorus of Sicily's statement to the effect that even the Athenians had been colonists from Egypt has been greeted with much skepticism by classicists and ancient historians. Yet, evidence for the Egypto-Phoenician roots of the Greek alphabet is overwhelming. Mainland Greece at the end of the Late Bronze Age was left devastated by the Venus shift of 1,135 BCE. The Mycenaean-A Hyksos empire having been considerably weakened by their rapidly loosening grip over the Egyptian Delta and complete loss of Upper Egypt, though Avaris and much of Canaan still firmly remained in Hyksos hands, a kind of power shift was taking place in the Aegean. The 17th Dynasty Phoenician vassal pharaohs, along with their Egypto-Phoenician officials and subjects, who were being driven out of Egypt,

CHAP. XII: LEARNING THE ART OF CHARIOT WARFARE | 449

massively ventured to colonize mainland Greece. Led by this dynasty's last ruler, King Kamose, the Egypto-Phoenicians probably elected to settle in Greece because any potential challenge posed by the Hyksos would have been conceivably harsher in Canaan. What's more, Syria-Palestine had by that time been literally overrun by the Philistines — who no doubt would have waged war against the former Thebans. In the Mediterranean, the territories were more scattered. Pharaoh Kamose, whom I identify with the Greek hero Kadmos who founded the fabled "seven-gated" Thebes in Greece — in remembrance of the Egyptian Thebes, civilized an emerging proto-Hellenic population ravaged by the recent Venus shift of 1,135 BCE.

> The land of Greece, on the contrary, has experienced countless catastrophes, which have obliterated the memory of the past; and as one civilization succeeded another the men of each epoch believed that the world began with them. They were late in learning the alphabet and found the lesson difficult; for those who would assign the earliest date to its use pride themselves on having learnt it from the Phoenicians and Kadmos.
> (Josephus, *Against Apion*, I: 10)

As Josephus relates above, the latest catastrophe had been especially harsh on Greece. The land which Kadmos and his Phoenician hordes found was wholly ravaged. The local inhabitants, composed largely of newcomers from the north who settled mainland Greece during LBIII, were illiterate and in search of a new sense of cultural identity. The arrival of the Egypto-Phoenicians provided the proto-Hellenic Greeks with the model and inspiration to institute the fundamental pillars of Homer's Heroic Age. The most pivotal of these building tools was of course the alphabet. Josephus is not alone in claiming that the Phoenicians introduced the alphabet in Greece. Herodotus reported the same fact:

> These Phoenicians who came with Kadmos at their settlement in this country, among many other kinds of learning, brought into Hellas the alphabet, which had hitherto been unknown, as I think, to the Greeks; ... At this time the Greeks that dwelt round them for the most part were Ionians; who, having been taught the letters by the Phoenicians, used them with some few changes of form ...
> (Herodotus, Book V: 58)

Indeed, the Greeks of antiquity never referred to their own script as the "Greek alphabet," but always as the "Phoenician letters" or the "Kadmean letters" —

after the Phoenician king, Kadmos, who gave Greece its alphabet.[46] Roger D. Woodward offers the following arguments to support, in his words, "the case that the Greeks acquired their alphabet from some Semitic-speaking peoples (i.e. the Phoenicians)":

> (1) the characters of the most archaic Greek scripts closely match those of the Phoenician script;
> (2) the sequence of characters is almost the same in the Greek and Phoenician scripts; and
> (3) the characters of the two scripts have very similar Semitic (and not Greek) names.[47]

Although conventional wisdom would have it that the introduction into Greece of the Phoenician alphabet occurred in the eighth century BCE, an increasingly large number of classicists are now open to the idea of a twelfth century BCE borrowing.[48] The repercussions of this admission become infinitely multiplied if one accepts the novel chronology's proposition that the Greek alphabet was first devised in the twelfth century BCE as a result of Egypto-Phoenician colonization. Some critics of Prof. Martin Bernal have chided him for failing to make any clear distinction between "Egyptian" and "Phoenician" colonization of the Aegean. Prof. Patricia Maynor Bikai of UCLA's Department of Classics, on that very point, writes:

> ... nowhere is any real distinction drawn between the two peoples. He [Martin Bernal] speaks of 'Egyptian-Phoenician invasions' (*BA* I, p. 81) 'Egypto-Phoenician invaders of Boiotia', 'Egypto-Phoenician colonizations' (p. 110), etc. This creates the paradox that while *Black Athena* appears to revive the Phoenicians, it does so just long enough to drown them in the Nile. The 'hyphenization' of the Phoenicians is an old and revered custom ...[49]

The reason why this "hyphenization" which "drowns the Phoenicians into the Nile" has survived throughout the centuries is because it is based on fact. The hyphena-

---

[46] Cyrus Gordon (1993) 'BOOK REVIEW: 'Black Athena: The Afroasiatic Roots of Classical Civilization. Vol. I: The Fabrication of Ancient Greece, 1785-1985. M. Bernal. 1987', Journal of *Interdisciplinary History* Vol. 113 - Num. 3, p. 489.

[47] Roger D. Woodward (1997) *Greek Writing from Knossos to Homer (A Linguistic Interpretation of the Origin of the Greek Alphabet and the Continuity of Ancient Literacy)*, Oxford University Press: London and New York, pp. 133-134.

[48] Louis H. Feldman (1996) 'Homer and the Near East: The Rise of the Greek Genius', *Biblical Archaeologist* Vol. 59 - Num. 1, pp. 13-21.

[49] Patricia Maynor Bikai (1990) 'Black Athena and the Phoenicians', *Journal of Mediterranean Archaeology* Vol. 3 - Num. 1, p. 69.

tion is justified because the Phoenicians who colonized Greece in the 12th century BCE had been part of a pharaonic Phoenician dynasty from Thebes in Egypt. In his famous *Mémoire*, read at the Académie des Inscriptions et Belles-Lettres in 1859, French Egyptologist Emmanuel de Rougé (1811-1872), a former pupil of Jean-François Champollion and chair of the department of Egyptian archaeology at the Collège de France (from 1860), proclaimed that the Phoenician alphabet was derived from Egypt's hieroglyphics.[50] Professor de Rougé's find vindicates that the Phoenicians had indeed maintained intimate contacts with the Egyptians at the time of their script's formulation. As a last piece of evidence, in Euripides' *The Phoenician Women*, we are told that Kadmos "came from Tyre to see the downfall of his dynasty."[51] This statement is breathtakingly consistent with the new chronology since we know that King Kamose (Kadmos) was the last ruler of the 17th Dynasty.

Elsewhere, Professor Martin Bernal shows remarkable insight by correlating the events described in Aischylos' *The Suppliants* with a historical settlement of Greece by Aigyptos (the Hyksos) and Danaos (the Danaans/Greeks).[52] In the new chronology, however, the time-frame of these formative events is drastically lowered to the latter part of the twelfth century BCE.[53] Referring to *The Suppliants*, Bernal brings particular attention to the name "Hikesios" — the central byname of Zeus:

> It is also interesting to note that the two plays called *Hiketides* both refer to Argos, the city later especially associated with the Hyksos colonization. Hikesios strikingly resembles the Egyptian *Hk3 h3st*, which in the 3rd century BC was rendered into Greek as Hyksos.[54]

---

[50] Emmanuel de Rougé (1874) *Mémoire sur l'origine égyptienne de l'alphabet phénicien*, Imprimerie Nationale: Paris.
[51] Euripides, *The Phoenician Women*, 202-249.
[52] See Martin Bernal (1987a) *Black Athena* I, pp. 88-98.
[53] In Cadmean Letters, M. Bernal proposes a high date (before 1,400 BCE) for the Greeks' borrowing of the Phoenician alphabet. Bernal's argument rests mainly on his proposed raising of the dates of the famous inscriptions of King Ahiram of Phoenicia (conventionally dated to *c*.1,000 BCE — Bernal argues for a thirteenth century BCE date). Hence, raising the date for Ahiram, in whose time a fully developed Phoenician script existed, would automatically justify raising the dates of Phoenician diffusion. Agreeing with Edward M. Cook [(1994) 'On the Linguistic Dating of the Phoenician Ahiram Inscription (KAI 1), *Journal of Near Eastern Studies* Vol. 53 - Num. 1, pp. 33-36] however, I doubt that King Ahiram could have reigned in the thirteenth century BCE. My own revised chronology requires him (Ahiram) to remain in the accepted time-line in order to make him a contemporary of the Iron Age Egyptian king Tuthmosis III (the second biblical Solomon). The Bible clearly states that Solomon was a contemporary of Ahiram in the Iron Age. Since the Greeks could not have borrowed the Phoenician alphabet before the twelfth century BCE, the King Ahiram of 2 Chronicles 2:3 could only have been a contemporary of the second Solomon.
[54] Martin Bernal (1987a) *Black Athena* I, p. 97.

Since both the 16th Amalekite Dynasty and the 17th Phoenician Dynasty were equally considered as "Hyksos" in Ramesside times, Aischylos' identification of Argos with the name "Hikesios" is not coincidental. To quote Prof. Martin Bernal: "... *the pun was an old one, and it is very unlikely that it originated with Aischylos.*"[55]

The Egypto-Phoenician colonization of mainland Greece having taken place during a Typhon Season, one should likewise expect the Greek legends to take account of this factor. Indeed, Diodorus of Sicily relates (Book V: 58) that, at the time of the Aegean's colonization by Danaos and Kadmos, a temple to Typhon (Seth), was erected on the island of Rhodes. Once again, the new chronology is vindicated. The Hyksos king Agag II, as we have seen, erected a temple to Seth shortly before the foreigners were driven out of Egypt. The context is therefore ideal for the building of a similar temple in the Aegean by Kadmos and Danaos. Martin Bernal has also suggested that the "Apia" of Aischylos, which refers to the Argolid, may in effect be etymologically linked with the "Apis" of the Egyptians.[56] As Seth and Apophis are inextricably linked with cyclical Typhon Seasons, the extensive references to Epaphos and Apis (both variants of Apophis)[57] in *The Suppliants*, and the choice of Typhon (Seth) by Danaos and Kadmos as their deity, make perfect sense. More archaeotheological evidence which could help us to date the foundation of the Athenian state can be gleaned from the Greek tale about the epic battle between Athena and Poseidon. Bernal has cleverly demonstrated that Neit's city of Sais, *Ht Nt* — "House of Neit," could well be the equivalent of the Greek "Athens."[58] If this identification is correct, which I believe it indeed is, then, archaeotheologically speaking, one must assume that the Greek city of Athens was established during one of the Typhon Seasons. Is it at all a coincidence that the goddess Athena battled against Poseidon — the Sethian arch-demon of chaos? As all cosmic battles were reproduced on earth in the form of wars between the supporters of each deity involved, it is possible to identify, as L. R. Farnell has done, the actors who took part in this cultic struggle:

> ... the Attic legend of the rivalry of Poseidon and Athena and many other similar theomachies, probably all contain a kernel of historical fact, an actual conflict of worships – an earlier cherished by the aboriginal men of the locality, and a later introduced by the new settlers. Athena was the goddess

---

[55] Ibid.
[56] Ibid, pp. 92-93.
[57] See Jean Bérard (1952) 'Les Hyksos et la légende d'Io. Recherches sur la période prémycenièune', *Syria* 29, p. 35.
[58] Martin Bernal (1991) *Black Athena* II, p. 87.

of Attica, Poseidon the great god of the Ionians; the strife and the friendship between the two deities on the Acropolis may have been the religious counterpart of the conflict and union of the old Attic and Ionic elements of the population.[59]

The battle between Poseidon and Athena in Athens was the Greek version of the conflict between Neit and Seth (Typhon) at Ht Nt/Sais.[60] As a righteous leader, Kamose' mission was to reconcile, or appease, these forces of chaos and restore order. Some inhabitants of ancient Greek Thebes in fact believed themselves to be descendants of the "sow men" who emanated from the teeth of the dragon slain by the founder of their city, Kadmos.[61]

The Birth of Mycenaean-B Culture:

Homers' Heroic Age Begins

Classical scholars divide the history of Greece into three main periods: Helladic, Hellenic, and Hellenistic. The Helladic period, which includes Mycenaean civilization, conventionally comes to a close in *c.*1,200 BCE — after the fall of Troy. Then, a Dark Age of about 500 years is believed to have stood between the end of the Helladic period and the beginning of the Hellenic period — which falls in *c.*700 BCE. Finally, the Hellenistic period was ushered in by the advent of Alexander in *c.*330 BCE, and lasted until the Roman Conquest of Egypt in 31 BCE. I am however of the opinion that the five centuries of darkness which engulf the Aegean at the end of the Helladic period, are in reality nothing more than a pure fabrication of modern scholars. Like Velikovskian scholar Clark Whelton said it so well: *"... the lights did not go out on the Dark Age until the switch was flipped by modern archaeology."*[62] As an example of evidence pointing to the nonexistence of a Dark Age of illiteracy in Greece is, firstly, the rather serendipitous fact that at the very time when it is known that Greeks lived in Phoenicia, in the ninth century BCE, Phoenician inscriptions dating from the ninth century BCE were found in Cyprus and Sardina. This proves that the Greeks and Phoenicians had close relations during the so-called Dark Age.[63] We must assume that the Greeks had already borrowed the

---

[59] L. R. Farnell (1895-1909) *The Cults of the Greek States.* Vols. I-V. Clarendon Press: Oxford, pp. 270-271.
[60] Martin Bernal (1991) *Black Athena* II, p. 90.
[61] Mary R. Lefkowitz 'Ancient History, Modern Myths.' In Mary R. Lefkowitz & Guy MacLean Rogers (editors) (1996) *Black Athena Revisited*, p.10.
[62] Clark Whelton 'Velikovsky's "Dark Age of Greece".' In Milton Zysman & Clark Whelton (editors) (1990) *Catastrophism 2000 (A Sourcebook for the Conference: Reconsidering Velikovsky)*, p. 255.
[63] Louis H. Feldman (1996) p. 16.

Phoenician alphabet by then. Secondly, archaeologists working in Crete near Knossos unearthed a bowl with an inscription on it dating to the late eleventh century BCE.[64] Evidently, the ancient Greeks knew how to write at that time — in the middle of a supposed Dark Age. A lot more will be said about the so-called Dark Age of Greece in Chapter 15.

Nonetheless, the period in Aegean history which we are currently dealing with, the Late Helladic period, is conventionally believed to have hosted the epic Homeric civilizations of Crete and Mycenae. Classicists date the Late Helladic period from *c.*1,550 BCE to *c.*1,100 BCE. In the new chronology, this period corresponds to Late Helladic-A or Mycenaean-A (1,159-1,135 BCE). This period in the history of the Aegean, I have determined, was dominated by the Hyksos-Amalekites and the Cretans. Therefore, Homer's conquering Achaeans have essentially no place in the new chronology's Helladic period. It's only from the conventional Late Helladic IIIc period that the Greeks (meaning the Danaans or Achaeans) make their initial appearance. These I have labelled the "proto-Hellenic Greeks" because they are the precursors of the Greeks of the classical age. They grew in power and influence in the middle of the supposed Dark Age of Greece. Also joining them at the end of the standard LHIIIc period were the Dorians. The Dorian invasion, referred to as "the return of the Heraklids" in the Greek legends, characterised, in my view, the return to Hellas of some of the Danaans who had accompanied King Agag I (Agamemnon) in his northern conquests following the Mercury shift of 1,187 BCE — when Herakles held the fate of the earth in a precarious balance. Since they had not been present at the time of the Egypto-Phoenician colonization, the Dorians brought in a different script — known as "Geometric." This Dorian Geometric script continued being used alongside Greek until the close of the Late Helladic-B or Mycenaean-B period. Analysing the finds of archaeologists dating to this period is very enlightening for the purposes of the new chronology.

> The chronology of the Aegean/Greek world in the period between c.1200 BC and 700 BC has long been accepted as problematic: Late Helladic (LH) IIIC pottery, and the related 'Philistine pottery', occurs in contexts in the Levant and Palestine from around the time of Ramesses III to Ramesses VI, and then nothing is known until the 8th-7th centuries BC ...[65]

Again, it is consequential to retain from the above statement that any reliable Late Bronze Age archaeological sequence ends with Ramses VI. The fact that the historical evidence gets blurred after the reign of King Ramses VI goes a long way in

---

[64] F. M. Cross (1980) 'Newly Found Inscriptions in Old Canaanite and Early Phoenician Script', *Bulletin of the American Schools of Oriental Research* 238, p. 15-17.
[65] Sturt W. Manning & Bernhard Weninger (1992) 'A Light in the Dark: Archaeological Wiggle Matching and the Absolute Chronology of the Close of the Aegean Late Bronze Age', *Antiquity* 66, p. 636.

CHAP. XII: LEARNING THE ART OF CHARIOT WARFARE | 455

confirming my contention that the Late Bronze Age Ramesside line ended with this king. The Late Helladic IIIc pottery found between the reigns of Ramses III and Ramses VI definitely belong to the Mycenean-A IIIc era. But it is a grave mistake to assume that the Aegean was plunged into a mysterious Dark Age after this. The numerous 18th Dynasty objects found alongside Mediterranean artifacts inscribed with Greek letters must indeed belong to the new chronology's 18th-19th Dynasties — dating from 1,135 BCE to 747 BCE. This entire era covers the Mycenaean-B period outlined below:

Chronology of Mycenaean-B Greece:

I. Late Helladic I	1,550 - 1,450 BCE
(Mycenaean-B I)	**1,135 - 1,117 BCE (New Chronology)**
II. Late Helladic II	1,450 - 1,400 BCE
(Mycenaean-B II)	**1,117 - 945 BCE (New Chronology)**
III. Late Helladic IIIa - c	1,400 - 1,050 BCE
(Mycenaean-B IIIa-c)	**945 - 747 BCE (New Chronology)**
	IIIa: 945 - 828 BCE
	IIIb: 828 - 776 BCE
	IIIc: 776 - 747 BCE

Table 12-2

It is genuinely necessary to differentiate between the Mycenaean-A and Mycenaean-B cultures because they are not only separated by chronology but also by culture. The Mycenaean-A Hyksos-Amalekites responsible for the Late Bronze era Shaft Grave culture had never known the Greek alphabet. The Mediterranean script they were familiar with was the Minoan script of Linear-A. When the proto-Hellenic (Mycenaean-B) Greeks gained control of the Aegean at the end of the Late Bronze Age with the massive immigration of the Danaans, the latter adapted the earlier Minoan Linear-A script with their newly-acquired alphabet to ultimately devise the Linear-B script. The Mycenaean-B inhabitants soon controlled the entire Aegean.

A Change of Seasons in China

Halfway around the globe meanwhile, in the last years of the Shang Dynasty, the ancient Chinese recorded the appearance of "tow suns" in the sky.[66] We're immediately reminded of the similar cosmic disturbances which accompanied the

---

[66] Martin Bernal (1991) p. 283; see also Pang. K. D. & Chou, H. H. (1985) 'Three Very Large Volcanic Eruptions in Antiquity and their Effects on the Climate of the Ancient World', paper abstracts, *Eos* 66, p. 816.

end of the preceding Xia Dynasty. The outcome had been a devastating Venus catastrophe which terminated the Middle Bronze Age. This time around, the cosmic disturbances witnessed in the final days of the Shang Dynasty portended the fiery destruction of the Late Bronze Age. What is more, we can now observe a striking parallel between the events occurring in ancient China during the reign of the Pharaoh Ahmose in the mid-sixteenth century BCE, and those relating to the Chinese king Wen Wang during the reign of the King Ahmose in the twelfth century BCE. Just like T'ang, Lord of Shang, Wen Wang, Lord of Zhou, was preparing to overthrow the Chinese emperor of his time. The reasons given for his actions are exactly similar to those of T'ang. A new age or "Mandate of Heaven" had dawned, so it was time for the sitting Dynasty to be replaced. The conventionally accepted date for the attack of Wen Wang on the last dynast of Shang is 1,122 BCE.[67] The timing of this attack therefore comes relatively shortly after the Venus shift which terminated Typhon Season #5. Again, we find ourselves at another crossroads between the World Ages. This time, the transition marked the move from the Mandate of Leo to Taurus. Describing this major event in China, Père Léon S. J. Wieger writes:

> ... *Fa* (Wen Wang) of Zhou, defeated and killed Sinn, the last sovereign of the second Dynasty. According to tradition, his army was made up of four thousand chariots of war; which then suggest a total number of three hundred thousand warriors, not including the jockeys. The emperor had, for his part, seven hundred men at his disposal to face Wen Wang. Before the battle of Mu-ye, *Fa* (Wen Wang) addressed his troops:

> ... You have come this far, men of the West. My friends princes, ministers, officers, chiefs of thousands, chiefs of hundreds, and your warriors of different races bring your bows to your feet, rest your armours on the ground, for I shall speak. The Ancients say that the house in which the hen crows (instead of the rooster), shall be ruined. The current emperor of Shang only listens to his wife *(Tan-ki)*. Fooled by debauchery, he has forsaken his ancestors and his parents. He has delegated his powers to evil-doers who have gained his trust. The empire of Shang has degenerated into tyranny. I Fa (Wen Wang), will administer to those criminals the sentencing of the Heavens. We shall attack. Each time you advance six or seven paces, stop yourselves and tighten the ranks. Charge like tigers, like panthers, like bears; but let the enemies who flee go unmolested, for they shall be of use to us later. Courage warriors! All cowards will be punished with death.

---

[67] Kwang-chih Chang 'Sandai Archaeology and the Formation of States in Ancient China: Processual Aspects of the Origins of Chinese Civilization.' In David N. Keightley (editor) (1983) *The Origins of Chinese Civilization*, p. 497.

CHAP. XII: LEARNING THE ART OF CHARIOT WARFARE | 457

Fa (Wen Wang) of Zhou was victorious. The emperor committed suicide or was killed. *Fa* (Wen Wang) assumed the throne and founded the third Dynasty, which he called Zhou, after the name of his principality.[68]

Preserved in the Chinese *Book of History*, are a series of proclamations which are said to have been delivered to the defeated people of Shang by the Zhou conquerors. The Zhou rulers placed much emphasis on the fact that Heaven had decreed a new *t'ien-ming* (Mandate of Heaven). They reminded their defeated foes that Heaven traditionally chose certain men to exercise the Heaven-sanctioned power over the people of China; so long as the elected kings ruled with wisdom and justice. In the eyes of the new rulers, the Shang Dynasty kings had turned away from the righteous path and had, in direct consequence, incurred the wrath of Heaven. The new Zhou Dynasty had been chosen by Heaven to replace the cruel and degenerate Shang Dynasty.

> Thus the Chou [Zhou] rulers explained the change of dynasties not as a purely human action by which a strong state overthrew a weak one, but as a divinely directed process in which a new group of wise and virtuous leaders was substituted for an old group whose members, by their evil actions, had disqualified themselves from the right to rule. To reinforce this view, the Chou leaders advised the people of Shang to look back to their own history, in which this same process had taken place when King T'ang, the virtuous founder of the Shang dynasty, had been directed by Heaven to overthrow the degenerate ruler of the old Hsia [Xia] dynasty and institute a new rule. ... from Chou times down to the present day, this description of the dynastic cycle and the concept of the heavenly mandate has been accepted by nearly all Chinese as the correct interpretation of history.[69]

This cyclical vision of history was a fundamental philosophy of the ancients the world over. It was perfectly understood that civilisations or regimes rose and fell abruptly depending on the movement of the planetary bodies.

---

[68] Père Léon S. J. Wieger (1924) *La Chine à travers les ages*. Deuxième édition. Imprimerie de Hien-Hien: Hien-Hien, p. 19 (my translation).
[69] Wm. Theodore de Bary (editor) (1966) *Sources of Chinese Tradition*, Columbia University Press: New York and London, pp. 8-9.

Moses the Lawgiver and the Hyksos Giants

For the ancient Israelites, periodic cosmic conflagrations were all part of Yahweh's grand design. The Day of the Lord. Yahweh is portrayed in the Bible as a deity who turns the waters into blood (Psalm 105:29) and who commands the stormy winds (Psalm 107:25). Citing Martin Bernal: *"Yahweh is chiefly to be seen, with Seth, Yam and Poseidon, as a divinity of unpredictable disruption and especially of volcanic disturbance."*[70] It's therefore not surprising that the Manethonian texts identify Moses, Yahweh's servant, with the storm-god Typhon. According to rabbinical sources, the course of the planets became confounded in the time of Moses.[71] This age-old association of Moses with Poseidon and the various Typhon Seasons stems from the fact that the Third Exodus came at the end of the Fourth Creation. The image of Yahweh, as it transpires in the Old Testament, takes roots principally at the time of the Third Exodus because it is precisely then that Yahwism is resurrected along with the liberation of the people of Israel from bondage in Egypt. In the Jewish Fourth Book of Ezra, it is written:

> I sent him [Moses] and led my people out of Egypt, and brought them to Mount Sinai, and held him by me for many days. I told him many wondrous things, shown him the secrets of the times, declared to him the end of the seasons.[72]

What the ancient rabbis dissimulated in this metaphorical portrayal of Yahweh teaching Moses the secrets of "the end of the seasons" is, yet again, a hint that Moses led the Israelites out of captivity at the end of a World Age or Typhon Season. The Fourth Moses understood, as the ancient Chinese of the Zhou Dynasty did, that the termination of the Leo Mandate inaugurated a new divine covenant. As part of this new Mandate of Heaven, the evil doers from the previous World Age faced severe punishment for their inequities. An anointed leader, such as Moses or Wen Wang, was then to arise in order to carry out the righteous will of Heaven.

The manner in which the Fourth Creation, or Mandate of Leo, came to a close was through a Venus-induced flood. This major flood, which was of lesser but similar magnitude to the Great Flood at the end of Typhon Season #3, ravaged mainly the Aegean. It was called the Flood of Ogyges — after the ruler of the Mediterranean region at the time, the Mycenaean-A Hyksos king, Apophis II (or Agag/Ogyges). According to Julius Africanus:

---

[70] Martin Bernal (1991) *Black Athena* II, p. 292.
[71] Pirkei Rabbi Elieser.
[72] IV Ezra 14:4.

CHAP. XII: LEARNING THE ART OF CHARIOT WARFARE | 459

> We affirm that Ogygus [Ogyges] from whom the first flood [in Attica] derived its name, and who was saved when many perished, lived at the time of the Exodus of the people from Egypt along with Moses.
> (*The Ante-Nicene Fathers*)

Moreover, according to rabbinical tradition, Og was the sole survivor of a major flood. In the Book of Deuteronomy (3:11) Og had a bed of iron and was the last survivor of a race of giants. He was a contemporary of Moses. These two clues from the Book of Deuteronomy: (1) the bed of iron is to be seen as a reference to the time in which King Og lived — the dawning Iron Age; and (2) that he was the last of a race of giants indicates that he was the last ruler of a great empire. After King Agag II's reign, the Hyksos lost control of much of the Aegean and were on the verge of altogether losing their status as a major power. In Greek legend, Ogyges or Ogygus, the Aegean monarch who ruled during the Flood of Ogyges (Agag II), reigned over Greek Boeotia — which was believed in ancient times to have been the oldest city in Greece. Thus, Greek history begins after the Flood of Ogyges. Indeed, the colonizing Egypto-Phoenician kings who arrived in Boeotia and founded Greek Thebes settled immediately after the Flood of Ogyges had subsided. The correlation between Ogyges, the Flood of Attica and the Venus shift is brilliantly illustrated here by John Philip Cohane:

> In view of what follows, the most significant aspect of the legends concerning Ogygios is that he is closely identified with a great flood or series of floods in Boeotia and elsewhere. In one legend he is said to have perished in a flood. Later Ogygios and Noah were often confused in people's minds. Varro states that in the time of Ogygios the planet Venus went through a marked change in color and shape, a phenomenon related to the floods.[73]

For starters, it is extremely consequential, as Cohane illuminates, that Varro (116-27 BCE), well renowned as "the greatest scholar among the Romans of his time,"[74] would say that the properties of the planet Venus radically changed at the time of the Ogyges flood. Varro's characterization of the planet Venus as a carrier of floods has extensively been corroborated throughout this book. Those major floods often came at the close of Typhon Seasons. The most severe ones having occurred at the end of Typhon Season #1 (the primeval flood of the Gilgamesh Epic), Typhon Season #3 (the universal "Great Flood" or the classical deluge of Deucalion), and

---

[73] John Philip Cohane (1969) *The Key*, p. 110.
[74] N.G.L. Hammond & H. H. Scullard (editors) (1970) *The Oxford Classical Dictionary*, Clarendon Press: Oxford, U.K.

Typhon Season #5 (the Flood of Ogyges). King Og is said to have been the only survivor of that last flood. But since the tradition of the Flood of Ogyges had, over-time, been confused with the story of Noah, it was also believed that Og saved himself by climbing onto the roof of Noah's ark. Hence, he and Noah's people would have been the only survivors. The two tales must have been combined for a reason — through some important common denominator. That common denominator was the planet Venus — the ferocious carrier of floods. Since Africanus tells us that Ogyges reigned at the time of the Hebrew Exodus from Egypt, we must conclude that the latter lived during Typhon Season #5. That goes without saying since, not only having already identified him as King Agag II, the disturbance of the planet Venus described by Varro accompanying the Exodus could only have occurred during the Third Exodus of 1,135 BCE. This means that the Flood of Ogyges, contrary to what Graeco-Roman tradition itself postulates, took place *after* the Flood of Deucalion. It's highly probable that the ancient Graeco-Roman historians made the Flood of Ogyges precede the Flood of Deucalion in their folk myths in an effort to give Greek culture older roots. The nationalistic ends must have been thought to justify the means. For instance, Varro says that the Flood of Ogyges occurred twenty-one hundred years before the time when he was writing.[75] Since he wrote in around 30 BCE, it's obvious that he is in fact referring to the Great Flood of 2,130 BCE. Finally, my contention that the Flood of Deucalion is the same as that of Noah is furthermore supported by the fact that Apollodorus describes Deucalion and his wife Pyrrha as journeying inside a "floating chest."[76] As we know, that floating chest, which Apollodorus speaks of, is the equivalent of Noah's ark.

Since the Third Exodus, led by Moses-Typhon (the Fourth Moses), took place concurrently with the Flood of Ogyges, it is evident that Typhonian themes in the Exodus story abound. Fleeing from bondage in Egypt, the Israelites found themselves confronted with a prodigious Sethian enemy, the Hyksos-Amalekites, blocking their way into their ancestral Promised Land. In the Old Testament, the Hyksos and their allies are referred to as a race of giants. The Book of Numbers (13:33) relates that Moses had sent out twelve spies to the land of Canaan who returned with the frightening report that they saw "giants" who made them feel like "grasshoppers" in comparison. The Hyksos-Amalekite giants, a reference to their sheer strength and number in Canaan at the time of Typhon Season #5, headed a coalition of Rephraim (Valley of Giants) composed of Canaanites, Edomites, Moabites, and Ammonites. As Martin Bernal observes, these "giants" were all associated with the Typhonian snake:

---

[75] Sir James George Frazer (1923) *Folk-Lore in the Old Testament (Studies in Comparative Religion Legend and Law)*, Tudor: New York, p. 71.
[76] See David M. Rohl (1998) *A Test of Time — Vol. II: Legend (The Genesis of Civilization)*, Century: London, p. 145.

Ôg was strikingly similar to Ogygos. He was seen in the Bible as the last of the Rephaim, a race of aboriginal giants associated with the watery slush of the underworld. In opposition to these characteristics the Rephaim were also associated with healing and the snakes connected in both Greece and the Levant with medicine. They were also linked to life, rebirth and fertility.[77]

As disciples of Seth, the Hyksos-Amalekites, headed by their king Apophis II (Ogygos), naturally identified with the serpentine aspects of this deity of chaos. As was outlined in Chapter 2, Typhon Seasons largely came to be associated with serpents because reptiles were commonly known to surface in large numbers as a consequence of the earth's torments. To retake the quote from the Greek dramatist Aischylos' *The Suppliant Maidens* already cited:

> For Apis, seer and leech, the son of Apollo, came from Naupaktos on the farther shore and purged well this land of monsters deadly to man, which Earth, defiled by the bloody deeds of yore, caused to spring up — plagues charged with wrath, a baleful colony of swarming serpents. Of these plagues Apis worked a cure by surgery and spells ...
> (Aischylos, *The Suppliant Maidens*, 260-265)

As the repeller of Typhonian chaos, Apis rescued the earth dwellers from the ravages of the Sethian snakes. In the Book of Numbers, an unambiguous reference is made to these Typhonian snakes:

> 6 And the Lord sent fiery serpents among the people, and they bit the people; and much people of Israel died.
> (Numbers 21:6)

The theme of the snake in the Exodus account is furthermore illustrated in the Book of Numbers (21:7-9) when Moses is instructed by Yahweh to make a fiery serpent of his own, the bronze serpent, upon a pole. Thenceforth, whenever Israelites fell victim to the serpents' bite, they beheld Moses' brass serpent and were cured. Moses' brass serpent was the equivalent of the Khemetic Neheb-kau serpent who, in Heliopolitan theology, represented the vertebra of Atum.

> Thus one passage makes passing reference to "the adze of Atum which is in the vertebra of the Neheb-kau serpent which brings an end to the strife in

---
[77] Martin Bernal (1991) *Black Athena* II, p. 84.

Heliopolis"; another qualifies Atum as "he who quelled the raging in heaven, the strife in Heliopolis (at) the great battle." The latter is further described as when Re had transformed himself into an ichneumon of 46 cubits (long) to fell Apophis in his rage."[78]

As eminent Egyptologist Donald B. Redford describes above, Atum, as the Neheb-kau serpent, endeavoured to quell the rebellion of Apophis as the heavens raged. Apophis and his disciples were therefore agents of chaos. It was of course with that in mind that the Egyptians expelled the Sethian tribes from Egypt. These "giants" whom the Israelites encountered during the course of the Third Exodus were inevitably those very same castaways from Egypt; namely: the Canaanites, Edomites, Ammonites, and Moabites — whom the Bible (Nums. 24: 17) identifies as "the children of Seth." Citing Herodotus:

> ... the Ammonians, who are colonists from Egypt and Ethiopia and speak a language compounded of the tongues of both countries. It was from this, I think, that the Ammonians got their name too; for Amun is the Egyptian name for Zeus.
> (Herodotus, Book II: 42)

In the same vein, it is perfectly evident that the Ammonites of the Bible, who played an important role in the Exodus story had hailed from Egypt. The Bible tells us that the Ammonites were allies of both the Hyksos and the Philistines.[79] That might also help explain why they were expelled from Egypt. It likewise certainly confirms the historical context at the height of the Ammonites' power. They (i.e. the Edomites, Ammonites, and Moabites) could only have been present during the Third Exodus — not before or after. The earliest extra-biblical reference to the Edomites for instance dates to the reign of Merneptah.[80] Moreover, according to biblical archaeologist Baruch Halpern:

> There is simply no evidence of Moabite, Ammonite or Edomite Kingdoms in MB II or LB I or LB IIA. This is admittedly an argument from silence. But it is a silence of about 300 years duration.[81]

Faced with these hostile giants occupying several key sectors of the Promised Land, the Fourth Moses had no other choice but to retreat to the Sinai desert. This

---

[78] Donald B. Redford (1992) *Egypt, Canaan, and Israel in Ancient Times*, Princeton University Press: Princeton, New Jersey, pp. 44-47.

[79] Judges 3:13, 10:7-8.

[80] Itzhaq Beit-Arieh (1996) 'Edomite Advance into Judah', *Biblical Archaeology Review* Vol. 22 - Num. 6, p. 31.

[81] Baruch Halpern (1987) 'Radical Exodus Redating Fatally Flawed', *Biblical Archaeology Review* Vol. 13 - Num. 6, p. 59.

CHAP. XII: LEARNING THE ART OF CHARIOT WARFARE | 463

is where the tradition of the forty-year-long wanderings of the Hebrew people in the Sinai comes from. The ancient Israelites of the Third Exodus did not possess the military wherewithal to undertake a massive conquest of Canaan as their Middle Bronze Age ancestors did. Several clues confirm beyond the shadow of a doubt that, if the ancient Israelites really had wandered in the Sinai Peninsula for forty years, it could only have happened during the Third Exodus. For instance, the Old Testament (Ex. 13:17) reveals that the Israelites initially lost their way in the Egyptian Delta soon after having left Kantir because Yahweh had not wished them to encounter the Philistines lest they "repent when they see war, and they return to Egypt." It was the Peoples of the Sea invasion after the reign of Ramses II which brought the Philistines into this region. Hence, this part of the Exodus story cannot be attributed to the period preceding Joshua's Conquest in the Middle Bronze Age. The traditional date for the Exodus, as given by modern scholars, of between 1,314-1,194 BCE, likewise stands on very shaky ground since, as ancient historian William H. Stiebing, Jr. observes below:

> ... there appears to have been no human occupation in Sinai in the 13th century B.C., the G.A.D. [Generally Accepted Date] for the Exodus. Indeed, there was no human occupation in the Sinai, as demonstrated by the archaeological evidence, during the entire Late Bronze Age (1550-1200 B.C.).
>
> In contrast, archaeologists have found abundant evidence of human occupation in the Sinai during almost every archaeological period both before and after the G.A.D. for the Exodus, that is before and after the Late Bronze Age.[82]

Hence, the Second Exodus is also an improbable candidate for the Sinai wanderings. The early Iron Age provides the proper archaeological context for the Israelites' forty-year-long ordeal. But as it's been extensively argued in Part III, the critical transition period between the Late Bronze and Iron Ages, upon which the traditional Exodus date rests, provides no archaeological evidence for the Book of Joshua's Conquest Model. This tale, as the new chronology postulates, belongs in the Middle Bronze Age. How then did the wandering Israelites enter Canaan? This is a necessary question to be answered.

---

82 William H. Stiebing, Jr. (1985) 'Should the Exodus and the Israelite Settlement be Redated?', *Biblical Archaeology Review* Vol. 11 - Num. 4, p. 58; see also Itzhaq Beith-Arieh (1984) 'Fifteen Years in the Sinai (Israeli Archaeologists Discover a New World', *Biblical Archaeology Review* Vol. 10 - Num. 4, pp. 26-39, 46-54.

13

The Imperialistic Age: In Search of the Glory of Saul, David and Solomon (1,117 BCE to 945 BCE)

> *"The hardest mysteries to solve are frequently those that have multiple causes."*
>
> - Richard E. Friedman
> *The Hidden Face of God*

The eleventh to tenth centuries BCE in Egypt, the early part of the so-called Third Intermediate Period in the standard chronology, is generally believed to have been an epoch of rapidly stagnating domestic and international power for Egypt's monarchy. According to ancient historians, the erosion of pharaonic authority after the reign of Pharaoh Ramses III was so severe, that genuine power fell into the hands of high priests of Thebes and Tanis. Under such dire circumstances, it is evident that professional Egyptologists completely rule out the existence of an Egyptian Asiatic empire, like was known in the Late Bronze Age, during this period. But we must now remember that, in the novel chronology, the conventional Late Bronze Age in Egypt, characterized by the meteoric ascent of the 18th Dynasty, actually ventures forth with the advent of the Iron Age. Contrary to the orthodox view, I contend that the fall of the Late Bronze Age in no way marked the end of the imperialistic age in Egypt. In fact, it was reaching it's apogee during the Iron I period. In Syria-Palestine, the new Tuthmoside line of the 18th Dynasty consolidated a vast sphere of influence reaching all the way to Mesopotamia. The illustrious 18th Dynasty pharaoh Tuthmosis III received tribute from Aegean chieftains as well as from the Kushites to the south. The Anatolian Hittites decimated by the cataclysmic end of the Late Bronze Age, Egypt suddenly found itself being the sole super-power in the ancient Near East. It was truly a golden era. Only the neo-Hittites, a remnant of the befallen Anatolian Hittite empire, based in Carchemish, still proved a potential danger.

In Israel, the close of the Late Bronze Age brought significant changes. Controlled by the Hyksos Agagite dynasty for decades, Palestine finally fell under Egyptian tutelage when King Tuthmosis I of the 18th Dynasty successfully drove the Hyksos-Amalekites out, for good, from Avaris and southern Canaan. The removal of the Hyksos garrisons from southern Canaan left the door open for the wandering Israelites in the Sinai desert to reenter Palestine soon after 1,117 BCE. The biblical redactors, writing in the sixth century BCE, made the extremely consequential choice of using this particular historical setting to relate the Conquest story of Joshua, which, as we know, in fact took place in the Middle Bronze Age. Similarly, the period of the Judges and the United Monarchy were lowered chronologically by several centuries. Thus, pivotal events from the seventeenth century became artificially contemporary with an eleventh century BCE background. The ancient city of Jericho, which was an abandoned ruin when the Israelites returned from their sojourn in the Sinai, suddenly returned to its Middle Bronze Age magnificence in the immortal pages of the Bible. Archaeologically, this makes little sense; but for the nationalistic purposes of the biblical redactors, it was a necessary thing to do.

In their efforts to turn the chronicles of Judges into an Iron Age narrative, the biblical redactors used central stories such as Samson's conflicts against the Philistines (Judges 15:15). Samson the Nazarite, a man reportedly of truly imposing physical strength and a member of the tribe of Dan, was, in reality, a metaphor for the Greek deity Herakles — a character of analogous strength and overseer of the rotating World Ages of the precessional cycle. As the twelve labours of Herakles denote the "orb of heaven that turns around like a millstone and ever does something bad,"[1] the Bible's imagery of Samson "eyeless in Gaza at the mill with slaves,"[2] symbolises the tight and volatile balance in the cosmic order. Like the Pillars of Herakles which held up the universe in times of Typhonian chaos, the two temple pillars which Samson toppled inside the Philistine temple, killing everyone including himself (Judges 16:29-31), illustrated the cycle-ending Venusian conflagration which befell the ancient Near East in 1,135 BCE. To be sure, it is quite unlikely that Samson, as portrayed in the Bible, was an actual historical figure. The Book of Judges' explicit declaration that Samson lived at a time when the Philistines ruled over the Israelites (15:11) incontrovertibly disassociates him from the genuine period of the Judges — which belongs in the closing Middle Bronze Age. The Philistines only came onto the scene in Syria-Palestine during Typhon Season #5. Therefore, it would be imperative to find a link between Samson and the period at hand. The primary clue can be found in the name of the tribe to which Samson belonged: the tribe of Dan. I believe that the tribe of Dan represents the Danaans who still dwelt in Canaan or returned from the Agagite conquests (as in the return

---

[1] Trimalcho in Petronisu. Cited in Giorgio de Santillana & Hertha von Dechend (1969) *Hamlet's Mill*, p. 137.
[2] John Milton, Samson Agonistes, I:41. Cited in Graham Hancock (1996) *Fingerprints of the Gods*, p. 267.

of the Heraklids) at the close of Typhon Season #5. Probably, these bands of Heraklids formed the basis of the story of Samson the Danite — the biblical counterpart of Herakles, patron of the Danaans.

Can the Real Israels Please Stand in Line?

Over the last generation, three main models or theories have been offered by Bible scholars to explain the rise of biblical Israel as a state in Palestine. The three approaches are: (1) the maximalist theory which holds that the Hebrew army under Joshua conquered Canaan; (2) the theory postulating that the various Israelite tribes settled peacefully into Canaan; and (3) the notion that the early Israelites were indigenous to Canaan and that they became a nation through a "social revolution" or "internal revolt." The Conquest Model, widely associated with the renowned late American biblical archaeologist William F. Albright (1891-1971), based on the narratives from the Book of Joshua, enjoyed widespread support among biblical scholars and archaeologists alike for many years — specifically from the 1940s through to the 1970s. However, the apparent lack of archaeological evidence to support the idea of a conquest of Israel from without, at the close of the Bronze Age, has led most scholars, over more recent years, to altogether abandon the Albrightian model. In the wake of the shattering demise of the Conquest Model, two novel paradigms have emerged: the "Peaceful Infiltration" and the "Peasant Revolt" models. These two models now dominate the field.[3]

The Peaceful Infiltration Model is also known by the names of its two principal founding proponents, namely: Albrecht Alt (1883-1956) and Martin Noth (1902-1968). The Alt-Noth Model contends that there never was a single short-term thrust of Hebrew tribes into Palestine as the Conquest Model postulates, but that there were, in actual fact, "a series of movement by single tribes and bands which may well have lasted for several centuries."[4] According to Alt and Noth, these Hebrew tribes did not encounter serious resistance from the Canaanites already established there. The different Hebrew tribes, it is alleged, migrated and settled separately and were isolated from one another "by chains of non-Israelite townships."[5] The reason why there were no large Canaanite armies against which the Israelites could have faced opposition is because, to quote Prof. Martin Noth, "the tribes of Israel entered those parts of the country that had only been

---

[3] William G. Dever 'The Late Bronze-Early Iron I Horizon in Syria-Palestine: Egyptians, Canaanites, "Sea Peoples," and Proto-Israelites.' In William A. Ward & Martha S. Joukowsky (editors) (1992b) *The Crisis Years: The 12th century B.C. (From Beyond the Danube to the Tigris)*, p. 103.
[4] Albrecht Alt (1968) *Essays on Old Testament History and Religion*. Trans. by R. A. Wilson. Anchor Books/Doubleday: Garden City, NY, p. 228.
[5] Ibid.

inhabited sparsely or not at all in the Bronze Age."[6] The archaeological evidence indeed confirms that the new Iron I settlements in the Canaanite highlands grew on territories which remained largely unoccupied throughout the Late Bronze Age.

In an even more radical departure from the traditional Conquest Model from the biblical texts, the Peasant Revolt model, attributed to George E. Mendenhall and Norman K. Gottwald, denies the very notion of any sizable incursion of ancient Israelites into Canaan from the outside. Norman K. Gottwald sees no great difference, as far as underlying assumptions go, between the Conquest model adherents and those who would argue for gradual, peaceful infiltration. In his mind, these two schools of thought hold one common fallacious assumption: that the "Israelites came as pastoral nomads from the desert steppes."[7] Instead, Gottwald and Mendenhall categorize these new Iron I settlers as refugees hailing from Late Bronze Age Canaan's exploited lower classes — not as incoming pastoral nomads. Gottwald and Mendenhall did not agree on all specific points however; since Mendenhall deplored the "Marxist bend" which Gottwald later applied to his social revolution theory.[8] In a nutshell, the Mendenhall-Gottwald social revolution theory maintains that the nation of Israel crystallized, as a socio-religious entity, from the withdrawal of exploited low-land peasants from the degenerate urban Canaanite society. Soon after the collapse of the Late Bronze Age, the low-land dwellers moved into the Canaanite Highlands and constituted a novel cultural entity. Again, this development, according to the Mendenhall-Gottwald Model, is evidence of a social revolution. But I would instead venture to propose that this relocation of the low-land peoples coincided, and was part of, the much wider displacement of populations, throughout the ancient Near East and Mediterranean region, at the heels of the devastating Venus shift of 1,135 BCE. The Canaanite low-land dwellers could have, in actual fact, sought refuge in higher altitudes (Canaanite Highlands) in order to escape from the flooded low-land territories. As Prof. William G. Dever of the University of Arizona delineates below, the two centuries which followed the collapse of the Late Bronze Age were characterized by the simultaneous emergence of several city-states. Evidently, a common cause must have been at the root of such social transformations.

> The nascent tenth-century Iron Age cultures in Israel would then correspond to the rise of the Neo-Hittite and Aramaean city-states in Syria, as well as contemporary early state formation processes in Ammon, Moab, and

---

[6] Martin Noth (1958) *The History of Israel,* Adams & Charles Black: London, p. 68.
[7] Norman K. Gottwald (1978) 'Were the Early Israelites Pastoral Nomads?', *Biblical Archaeology Review* Vol. 4 - Num. 2, p. 2.
[8] See James K. Hoffmeier (1997) *Israel in Egypt (The Evidence for the Authenticity of the Exodus Tradition),* Oxford University Press: Oxford and New York, p. 6.

Edom in Transjordan. Thus within the course of some two centuries, new "petty states" — and, of course, new ethnic groups — have replaced the typical socioeconomic structures and political configurations of Middle-Late Bronze Age Canaan. Anyone who thinks that such a major upheaval ending the 2,000 year old Bronze Age in the southern Levant — took place without sweeping movements of peoples, as well as far-reaching changes in ethnic consciousness, will have a lot of explaining to do, not to mention explaining away a mass of archaeological evidence.[9]

Such "sweeping movements" had indeed been plentiful. The Iron I settlements in Palestine, which Dever refers to as "proto-Israelite," may in my opinion be largely identified with the biblical Israelite.[10] However, given the fact that, according to my historical reconstruction, we are now dealing with the Third Exodus and that the age of Solomon had already passed, Dever's designation of the Iron I Canaanite populace as "proto"-Israelite is not very appropriate. Instead, I would here label them as "proto-Yahwists" — as I propose that the religious identification of the Jewish people's ancestors with the god Yahweh cemented itself during the Great Exodus of Asiatic foreigners from Egypt during Typhon Season #5.

The sudden increase in population, as well as the marked shift in settlement style (from large urban centres to small villages), leads Dever to conclude that we are dealing with "*an increase that cannot be due to natural growth rates alone but must have resulted from immigration.*"[11] Broadly adhering to the Mendenhall-Gottwald social revolution theory, William G. Dever and Baruch Halpern however believe that these new immigrants came from somewhere in Canaan. Dever nonetheless considers the "peasant revolt" model to be *passé* in the sense that he would instead propose a model of "indigenous origins" or a Symbiosis Model.[12] They (Dever and Halpern) both dismiss the Bible's account of a mass exodus from Egypt, followed

---

[9] William G. Dever (1995a) 'Ceramics, Ethnicity, and the Question of Israel's Origins', *Biblical Archaeologist* Vol. 58 - Num. 4, p. .206.
[10] W. G. Dever believes that the "proto-Israelites" could well be identified as the biblical Israelites, but is more tentative in making the equation because he believes that biblical Israel was still in formation at the time. He nonetheless maintains that the continuity of material culture between Iron I and Iron II Canaan proves that proto-Israelite culture is the "precursor of the full-fledged later Israel."
[11] William G. Dever (1995a) 'Ceramics, Ethnicity, and the Question of Israel's Origins', *Biblical Archaeologist* Vol. 58 - Num. 4, p. 208.
[12] W. G. Dever 'Israelite Origins and the "Nomadic Ideal": Can Archaeology Separate Fact from Fiction?' In S. Gitin *et al.* (editors) (1998) *Mediterranean Peoples in Transition*, p. 220. According to Dever, the entire notion that the proto-Israelites had been pastoral nomads who *immigrated* into Canaan is better left in the past. He prefers viewing them as indigenous to Canaan.

by a war of conquest, because Merneptah's so-called "Israel Stela" records the existence, in Year 5, of Israelite people in Palestine. If one were to accept the traditional view that Ramses II was the Pharaoh of the Oppression, how could the Israelites have already been established in Canaan after just four years — when the Bible says that they wandered in the desert for forty years?

They therefore argue that accepting the common belief that Merneptah was the Pharaoh of the Exodus and that Ramses II, the father of Merneptah, was the Pharaoh of the Oppression, poses a serious contradiction. Many Bible scholars are of the same opinion, and chose to either ignore the story that the Israelites built the store-cities of Ramses and Pithom (preferring to assume that they built the site of Tell el-Dab'a in the mid-eighteenth century BCE) or instead to "disassociate the Exodus from the Conquest." The latter option, preferred by Baruch Halpern[13] and William Dever,[14] proposes a "Homesteading Model" — where the Israelites would have been part of a much larger Iron I mixed population of displaced urban Canaanite colonists. They argue that the so-called proto-Israelites used Yahwism as a unifying religion in an effort to differentiate themselves from their Transjordanian counterparts in Ammon, Moab and Edom. Indeed, for a large number of archaeologists, the Israelites may never have even dwelt in Egypt! While some accept the idea that at least a certain number of Israelites could have lived and worked in Egypt as artisans or indentured servants from as early as the eighteenth century BCE, the "Exodus-Conquest" model has been largely discounted.

As I have already demonstrated however, discarding the Albrightian interpretation of an historical Exodus based on the biblical framework (Conquest Model) would be a mistake. First of all, the most important piece of evidence which the above scholars rely on to question the Exodus scenario, the Israel Stela (an Egyptian document which refers to "Israelites living in Canaan), is actually irrelevant for our current purposes. As heretical as this may seem, the Merneptah Stela was not carved until the seventh century BCE — well after the time when the nation of Israel had been firmly established![15] Secondly, there is no need to look for any evidence of the Conquest at this particular time since it really occurred all the way back in the seventeenth century BCE. Hence, divorcing the Exodus from the Conquest does not necessitate the repudiation of either tradition. It is only necessary to acknowledge that the biblical Exodus account is a composite record of events in the Israelites' history which spans many centuries.

---

[13] Baruch Halpern 'The Exodus from Egypt: Myth or Reality?' In Hershel Shanks *et al* (1992) *The Rise of Ancient Israel*. Symposium at the Smithsonian Institution – October 26, 1991. Biblical Archaeology Society: Washington, DC, pp. 86-117.
[14] W. G. Dever (1995a) p. 211.
[15] This topic will be further explored in Chapter 17.

CHAP. XIII: THE IMPERIALISTIC AGE | 471

In any case, the Third Exodus, of 1,135 BCE, shaped much of what would be known as the "Nation of Israel" in the Iron Age. The Hebrews who returned from the Sinai wanderings were the ones who resuscitated the old notion of the Israelite nation, epitomized in Solomonic times, which had prevailed during the latter Middle and early Late Bronze Ages. Thirteenth century BCE Canaanite society had been completely alien to the tenets of Yahwism — as a result of the invasions of the Hurrians, Hittites and other foreign powers after the fall of the United Monarchy. So the thirteenth century BCE represents a Dark Age in biblical Israel. Consequently, I would agree with archaeologist Israel Finkelstein's belief that William Dever contradicts himself when, on the one hand, he claims that the new Iron I settlements in the Canaanite highlands show no significant break from the previous Late Bronze Age material culture until around 1,100 BCE,[16] while still maintaining that the new ethnic group established itself in the thirteenth century BCE.[17] However, I would not go so far as Finkelstein does — who points to this apparent contradiction as evidence that no significant break in culture occurred. Actually, the reason why no significant cultural departure is observed until around 1,100 BCE is because it is only during that time that the massive population movements took place (in *c.*1,135 BCE). Moreover, accepting the date of 1,135 BCE as the terminal point of the Late Bronze Age eliminates the strain of accounting for Dever's gap between the late-thirteenth century and late-twelfth to eleventh centuries BCE. Dever's late thirteenth century date for the beginning of the new Iron I Canaanite culture seems to rest entirely on the dates of King Merneptah's reign in Egypt. Summarizing this point, Finkelstein writes:

> Based on the testimony of the Merneptah Stele, Dever dates the foundation of the Iron I highlands sites to the late-thirteenth century BCE. But from a pure archaeological point of view, it is extremely difficult to provide a precise date for the beginning of the Iron I wave of settlement in the highlands. Moreover, most of the sites were probably established in the late-twelfth, if not in the eleventh century BCE.[18]

But since I argue that there is no extant evidence to prove that the Late Bronze Age Merneptah ever spoke of Israelites living in Canaan, we can move the mass migrations of the proto-Yahwists to *c.*1,135 BCE — as Finkelstein argues. The Israelites who returned from their forty-year-long wanderings in the Sinai desert probably found a highly sympathetic audience open to nationalistic propaganda

---

[16] W. G. Dever (1995a) p. 206.
[17] Israel Finkelstein (1996) 'Ethnicity and Origin of the Iron I Settlers in the Highlands of Canaan: Can the Real Israel Stand Up?', *Biblical Archaeologist* Vol. 59 - Num. 4, p. 198.
[18] Ibid, Notes: (1).

among the Iron I Canaanite settlers who lived "precisely in those areas that were not heavily occupied in the fourteenth-thirteenth century BCE or dominated by Late Bronze Age Canaanite city-states."[19] All the ingredients were there to build a new nation on the pattern of the old nation of Israel which was swallowed up amid foreign occupation. Yahwism gained widespread following among the Iron I settlers who were *already* living in the Canaanite highlands when the wandering Yahwists from the Sinai desert arrived. The new "ethnic consciousness," expressed through the unifying agent of Yahwism, brought to the Iron I Canaanite peasant classes by the Israelites (or Shasu), who had departed from Egypt at the end of the Late Bronze Age, salvaged Hebrew historiography from certain demise.

Out of the four Exoduses which have been identified in this book, the Third Exodus was most likely the one in which the Israelite Ten Commandments (or at the very least the basic notion of a series of divinely ordained Commandments) could have been devised, and Yahwism solidified. I say this because the Third Exodus, as one of two Exoduses to have occurred at the end of a Typhon Season, would be a likely candidate to have inspired the Yahwists with the need to devise a new covenant (a new Mandate of Heaven) to appease an angered deity. Moreover, as the one Exodus in which a long journey in the Sinai desert is most likely, the Third Exodus is surely to be seen as the event which gave birth to Yahwism. What is more, the memory of the Third Moses, who decreed a series of laws in Avaris was still fresh in the minds of the Israelites of the time. With regards to the observance of the new Mandate of Heaven, it is also interesting to note that the new era of the Taurus had brought to prominence the cult of El — as evidenced by the "Bull Site" in the Samarian highlands.[20] Despite the primacy of Yahwism, there is in fact little to prove that the ancient Israelites were entirely monotheists in those remote times. Later in this section, it will be suggested that the strict monotheism that we find in the later books of the Prophets, emerged chiefly during the Divided Monarchy period during the eighth century BCE. The nation of Israel which emerged early in the Iron Age was the result of the amalgamation of a vast array of Canaanite peoples from diverse religious and ethnic backgrounds. A highly revealing passage from the Book of Ezekiel indeed remarks:

> 3 And say, Thus saith the Lord God unto Jerusalem; Thy birth and thy nativity is of the land of Canaan; thy father was an Amorite, and thy mother an Hittite.
> (Ezekiel 16:3)

---

[19] W. G. Dever (1992b) p. 103.
[20] See A. Mazar (1982) 'The Bull Site" — An Iron I Open Cult Place', *Bulletin of the American Schools of Oriental Research* 273, pp. 37-55.

The fact that the prophet Ezekiel says that the Israelites' ancestors were the Amorites and the Hittites clearly demonstrates that he is referring to the Iron Age Yahwists. Among the peoples who overran the original United Monarchy in the Late Bronze II period were indeed the Amorites and the Hittites. The swift demise of the Solomonic empire propelled the Hebrews into the direct tutelage of these peoples.

Hail the King: Tuthmosis I as the Founder of the New United Monarchy

Having established both the provenance and ethnic identity of the Iron I Canaanite settlers who formed the nation of Israel under the banner of Yahwism, the question posed at the end of chapter 12 still has to be answered. How did the Yahwists from the Sinai desert enter Canaan? Since the enslaved Hebrews left Egypt in 1,135 BCE, and their wanderings lasted for forty years according to the Bible, it would mean that the Yahwists entered the Canaanite highlands in *c.*1,095 BCE. What happened between 1,135 BCE and 1,095 BCE to suddenly permit the Israelites to enter Canaan? We've seen in the previous chapter that the principal reason why the Israelites could not enter Canaan in 1,135 BCE was because hostile Hyksos garrisons were still occupying southern Canaan at the end of Typhon Season #5. Did the Israelites defeat those same Hyksos in battle in 1,095 — analogously to the Conquest Model? I do not believe so. Instead, I would suggest that the Hyksos forces at Avaris and Southern Canaan were finally defeated by the dynastic Egyptians in 1,117 BCE. Having gotten wind of the Hyksos' overthrow whilst in the Sinai, the Yahwists returned to their ancestral homeland in safety.

My date of 1,117 BCE for the final expulsion of the Hyksos from Avaris and southern Canaan comes from the writings of Flavius Josephus — who postulates that the period of Hyksos domination lasted a grand total of five hundred and eleven years.[21] Accepting that the initial Hyksos-Amalekite penetration into Egypt's eastern Delta took place in 1,628 BCE, means concluding that Hyksos influence in Egypt and the Near East came to a definite close in 1,117 BCE (1,628 - 511 = 1,117). As a result, the Iron Age dynastic Egyptian pharaoh whom I argue was responsible for this victorious campaign was Tuthmosis I. The Tuthmoside line of the Iron Age, even more than their Late Bronze Age alter-egos, were a dynasty of great conquerors. Between *c.*1,117 BCE and *c.*945 BCE, it could be argued that Egypt went through its most prosperous and powerful period ever — as far as exercising its suzerainty over foreign territories. The great power of

---

[21] Josephus, *Against Apion*, Book I: 84.

the Anatolian Hittites gone, Egypt now found itself the sole superpower of the ancient Near East. The 18th Dynasty, therefore, really came into its own with the ascent of Tuthmosis I. The latter, by at very long last ridding Egypt of the Hyksos menace, for good this time, accomplished what Ahmose I, the founder of the 18th Dynasty, could not do. A record of Tuthmosis I's victorious campaign against the Hyksos is kept in the annals of Ahmose, son of Ebana — an army officer who served under Pharaohs Ahmose, Amenhotep I, and Tuthmosis I (of the Iron Age). Ahmose of Ebana describes, on the walls of his tomb, the numerous campaigns against the Hyksos in which he took part. As my historical reconstruction delineates, Ahmose of Ebana lived in a time of continual struggle against the Hyksos enemy in the north. In his inscriptions, Ahmose of Ebana writes:

> I followed the king on foot when he rode abroad in his chariot. One besieged the city of Avaris; I showed valor on foot before his majesty ... One fought on the water in the canal [riverbed] of Avaris ... then there was again fighting at this place; I again fought. ... One fought in this Egypt, south of this city; then I brought away a living captive. ... One captured Avaris ... One besieged Sharuhen [s'-r'-h'-n] for six years [and] his majesty took it ... [22]

Biographies of high officials assisting their Pharaoh while the latter annihilated his enemies are a very common feature of early 18th Dynasty times.[23] The majesty whom Ahmose of Ebana speaks of above was none other than King Tuthmosis I — the last pharaoh under whom he served. The town of Avaris was taken, not under Ahmose, but under Tuthmosis I. Once the Hyksos-Amalekites were defeated, they fled to Sharuhen, in southern Palestine, but Tuthmosis I followed them and besieged them there as well.[24] In his book *Ages in Chaos*, Dr Immanuel Velikovsky made a very interesting parallel between the annals of Ahmose of Ebana and the Book of Samuel. Like in the Ahmose inscription, Samuel describes the feat of a monarch, King Saul, who undertakes to annihilate the Amalekites in their city in northern Egypt. The hero-monarch in the Ahmose inscription is Pharaoh Tuthmosis I. Like King Saul, Tuthmosis I leads a decisive final battle against the Amalekite-Hyksos in Avaris. In the Book of Samuel, King Saul's exploits are described as follows:

> 5 And Saul came to the city of Amalek, and laid wait in the valley.
> 7 And Saul smote the Amalekites from Havilah until thou comest to Shur, that is over against Egypt.

---

[22] J. H. Breasted, *Ancient Records of Egypt*, Vol. II - § 7-8.
[23] See John Baines (1986) 'The Stela of Emhab: Innovation, Tradition, Hierarchy', *Journal of Egyptian Archaeology* 72, pp. 41-53.
[24] Josephus, *Against Apion*, Book I: 76.

CHAP. XIII: THE IMPERIALISTIC AGE | 475

> 8 And he took Agag the king of the Amalekites alive, and utterly destroyed the people with the edge of the sword.
> (1 Samuel 15:5, 7-8)

The Amalekite territories which King Saul overruns are exactly the areas under the control of the Hyksos at the beginning of the 18th Dynasty — according to this historical reconstruction. The Amalekite king whom Saul slaughtered was none other than King Agag III, ruler of Avaris. Unlike the original King Saul, of Chapter 10, who could not overwhelm the Hyksos-Amalekite garrisons at Avaris, the King Saul of the Iron Age was successful in doing so. Whoever the later King Saul was, he was certainly a very powerful king.

Since we know that a King Saul already existed during the Late Bronze Age, must we assume that there was another Hebrew king, named Saul, who inaugurated a new United Monarchy era in Israel in the Iron Age — much as in the case of the two Pharaoh Ahmoses in Egypt? This is unnecessary. I actually believe that the biblical redactors of the sixth century BCE remodelled the exploits of Saul after the military campaign of the Iron Age Egyptian pharaoh Tuthmosis I. Their objective was to move the beginning of the Iron age, chronologically speaking, all the way up to the end of the Middle Bronze IIc era. Equating the 18th Dynasty pharaoh Tuthmosis I with King Saul did just that. Where the latter had failed, militarily, the former had been immensely successful.

Tuthmosis I gained the admiration of the Israelites because he had defeated and driven out their archenemies — the Hyksos-Amalekites. Hence, the Tuthmoside pharaohs of the 18th Dynasty became the new Israelite kings of the proto-Yahwists of the Iron Age. As a matter of fact, it was precisely because Tuthmosis I had withdrawn the threat of the Hyksos-Amalekites in southern Palestine that the wanderings Yahwists in the Sinai desert were finally able to reenter Canaan. Having, in this manner, solidified his credibility among the Asiatics of Syria-Palestine, Pharaoh Tuthmosis I, and his immediate successors, reigned largely unopposed over Egypt's Syro-Palestinian vassals. Pharaoh Tuthmosis I's Iron Age empire was truly gargantuan — stretching from the Euphrates to Nubia. In his analysis of an inscription dated to the second year of Tuthmosis I near the island of Tomâs, Prof. Hans Goedicke of Johns Hopkins university writes:

> ... the extent of Tuthmosis I's authority, with the southern border at the Fifth Cataract and the northern border at the river "which flows down in flowing south," the latter considered a poetical description of the Euphrates. This rendering involves major chronological problems, in that it suggests that Tuthmosis I had been recognized as sovereign in the Levant at the same time as he became king in Egypt.[25]

---

[25] Hans Goedicke (1996) 'The Thutmosis I Inscription Near Tomâs', *Journal of Near Eastern Studies* Vol. 55 - Num. 3, p. 172.

He goes on to say that:

> The initial success of Tuthmosis I in exercising authority over the Levant was not based on military force but appears to have been a voluntary move on the part of the Levantine city-states. ... Iconographically, it is unquestionably not an indication of military achievement but of political consolidation.[26]

This scenario could not have taken place in the Late Bronze I era — when the initial Tuthmosis I, of the new 14th Dynasty reigned. The chief reason for that is that, at this earlier time, the Hyksos still controlled the Delta — blocking Egypt's expansion into the Levant. If we move down, in the new chronology, to the 18th Dynasty, we find that such a great empire could have indeed been established by King Tuthmosis I — now head of the only super-power left in the ancient Near East after the swift collapse of the Late Bronze Age. According again to Prof. Goedicke, *"foreigners from the South and others from the North travel to Egypt as soon as the news of Tuthmosis I's ascent to the throne becomes known."*[27] This is of course entirely consistent with my hypothesis that the proto-Yahwists of the Canaanite highlands elected Pharaoh Tuthmosis I as their legitimate ruler — the new King Saul. Therefore, throughout the neo-Tuthmoside era, the pharaohs of Egypt were considered the legitimate rulers of the newly reinvigorated nation of Israel. Pharaoh Tuthmosis I incarnated King Saul, Tuthmosis II was the new King David and finally Tuthmosis III was the later embodiment of King Solomon. There was, of course, no period of the Judges in the Iron Age. So the new Egyptian-based United Monarchy period was the only link between the Third Exodus and the era of the Divided Monarchy. As we shall discover in Chapter 15, the biblical pharaoh Shishak (Shoshenk I) — who is supposed to have attacked Israel shortly after the death of King Solomon, was in fact the immediate successor of Pharaoh Tuthmosis III, of the 18th Dynasty, on the Egyptian throne.

The Mycenaean-B Domination of Crete

In addition to its suzerainty of the Levant, the neo-Tuthmoside line also exercised considerable influence over the Aegean. Newly colonized by Phoenician and Egyptian learned migrants from the Nile Valley, the Mediterranean region quite naturally became an integral part of the 18th Dynasty's sphere of influence. Iron Age Crete, during the reign of Tuthmosis III experienced very important changes.

---

[26] Ibid, p. 176.
[27] Ibid, p. 165.

Since the establishment of the Danaans and Egypto-Phoenicians in mainland Greece during Typhon Season #5, Crete was for the first time overrun *en masse* by the new Mycenaeans. Between the sudden collapse of Palatial Crete during the Late Bronze II era and the advent of King Tuthmosis III, (the Postpalatial period) Crete had essentially remained in a decadent transitional phase. The architectural and cultural glory of the Eteocretans of the New Palace period, the founders of the Linear A script, following this long period of stagnation, was resurrected by the Mycenaean Greeks during the reign of Tuthmosis III. While it is widely believed that the Greeks conquered Crete at the beginning of the LMII period, sometime around 1,450 BCE, I maintain that the importation of the Greek alphabet into Crete, which served as a basis for the Minoan Linear B script, took place in the Iron Age. Therefore, Minoan palaces in which Linear B tablets were found, conventionally dated to the Late Minoan II period, must be redated to the nascent Iron Age.

The Linear B script can't possibly date to the Late Bronze Age since Greek itself, upon which Linear B is based, did come actually come into being until Typhon Season #5 — with the pivotal Egypto-Phoenician colonization of mainland Greece. The Mycenaean Greeks who colonized Greece were not the Hyksos of the Late Bronze Age (Mycenaean-A culture) but the proto-Hellenic Danaans, influenced by the Egypto-Phoenicians, of the ending Late Bronze Age and early Iron Age. This later Greek culture, I have labelled as Mycenaean-B. Similarly, a distinction is made between the native Eteocretans of the Middle and Late Bronze Age (Minoan-A culture) and the subsequent Iron Age, neo-Minoan, Cretan palatial era inaugurated by the proto-Hellenic Greeks (Minoan-B culture).

In short, it seems evident that the Mycenaean-B Greeks constituted the Iron Age Palatial era in Crete during the reign of Pharaoh Tuthmosis III of the 18th Dynasty. This crucial transition in the political and cultural landscape of Iron Age Crete is attested in the tomb of the vizier Rekhmire. Rekhmire was the son of a priest of Amun, Nefer Weben, and became the most powerful commoner under the reign of Tuthmosis III during the 18th Dynasty. His tomb, located in the Theban necropolis, depicts him as having been, among other things, responsible for the overseeing of foreign embassies and tributes. The elaborate tribute scenes from his tomb-walls show that there was an important transition of Cretan kilt styles from a purely Minoan to mainland Greek genre during his times as vizier of Egypt. As Ian Wilson elaborates below, it has long been recognized that the sudden change indicates an evolution in the cultural history of Crete.

> Close examination has revealed that the Mycenaean Greek-style kilts worn by these men have been painted over what were formerly Minoan-style cod-pieces. Egyptologists suggest that this denotes a change of regime on Crete while Rekhmire was vizier.[28]

Some scholars conjecture that this sudden change of costumes indicates *"a shift from Minoan to Mycenaean rule in the palace of Knossos."*[29] Speaking of these paintings from Rekhmire's tomb, Prof. J. V. Luce of Trinity College says: *"He [Rekhmire] could be regarded as Egypt's foreign minister. The change in his tomb decoration can hardly be discounted as a mere artistic whim. It must surely have had political significance. By ordering kilts to be painted over, Rekhmire was giving diplomatic recognition to a change of regime at Knossos."* In fact, the last prosperous phase of the palace of Knossos, containing Linear B tablets, which classical archaeologists date to the Late Bronze Age, begins in the eleventh century BCE. A particularly interesting bit of detail in the vizier Rekhmire's tribute indicate, in my estimation, the time in which these scenes were depicted — shortly following the transition from the Mandate of Leo to the Mandate Taurus. As Dr. Cheikh Anta Diop observes:

> In the tomb of Rekhmira, vizier of Thutmose III, precisely, the Cretans, called Keftiu ..., are represented, ... paying their annual tribute, consisting of vases in the form of the heads of bulls and lions, goblets, daggers, needles, all of these in gold and silver.[30]

The bulls and lions may well have been symbols of the changing precessional seasons.

The Neo-Hittites: An Intermediary Iron Age Power

The only significant opponents to the powerful Tuthmoside pharaohs of the 18th Dynasty were the neo-Hittites. The neo-Hittite culture, as its name implies, was an Iron Age remnant of Hittite civilization. They were a mixture of Hittites, Hurrians, Hattians and others who occupied a series of city-states in the northern regions of modern-day Syria and southern Turkey. Their capital was established a the city of

---

[28] Ian Wilson (1986) *Exodus: The True Story Behind the Biblical Account*, Harper Collins: New York, p. 140.
[29] Harmut Matthäus (1995) 'Representations of Keftiu in Egyptian Tombs and the Absolute Chronology of the Aegean Late Bronze Age', *Bulletin of the Institute of Classical Studies* 40, p. 183.
[30] Cheikh A. Diop (1991) *Civilization or Barbarism (An Authentic Anthropology)*. Trans. by Yaa-Lengi Meema Ngemi. Lawrence Hill Books: Brooklyn, NY, p. 91.

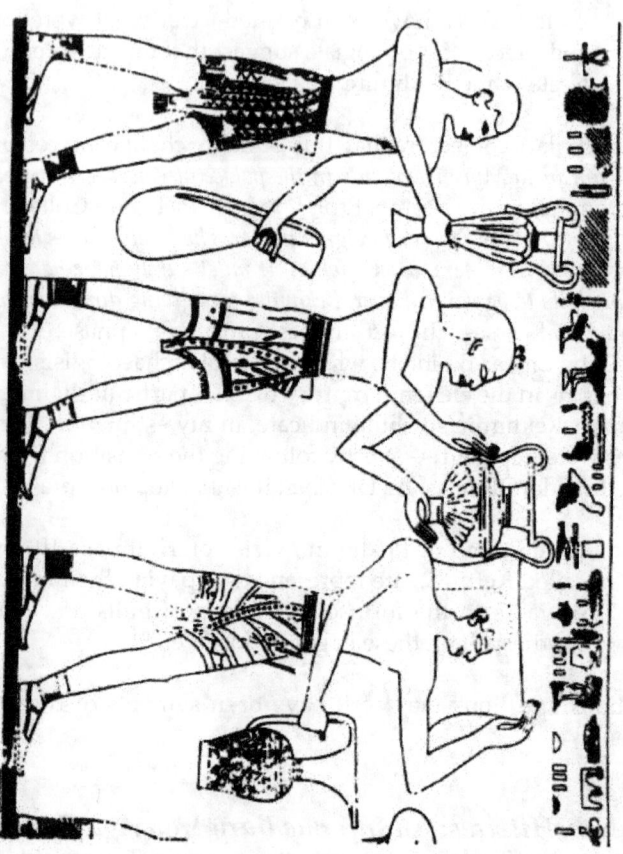

Fig. 13a: Greek tribute bearers from tomb of Rekhmire.

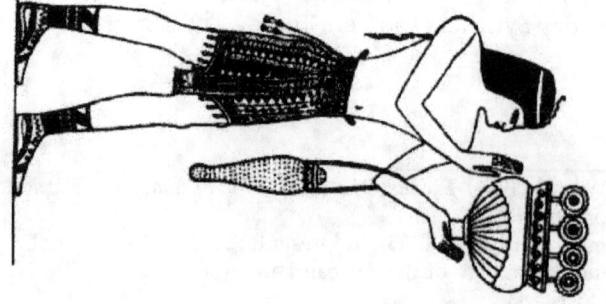

Fig. 13b: Representation of Phoenician from Medinet Habu temple of Ramses III.

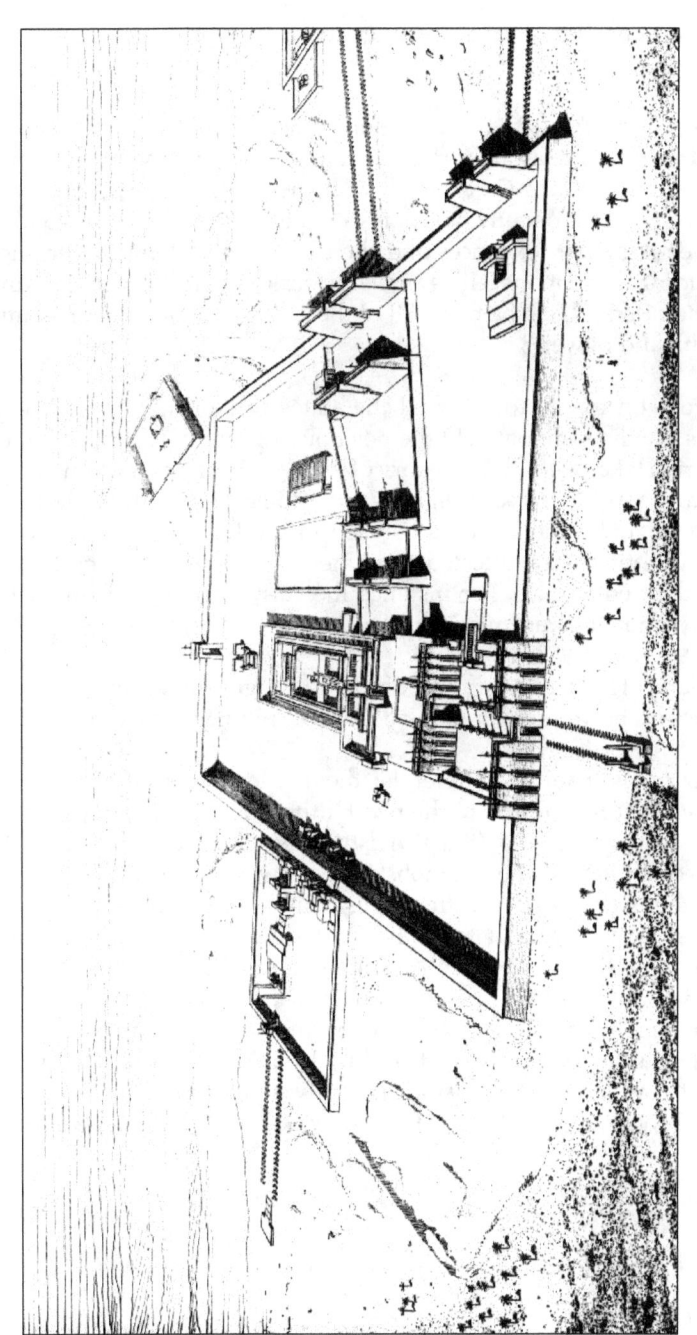

Fig. 13c: Overhead view of Karnak (restored). *After* Chipiez (1882).

Carchemish in northern Syria. Writing about ancient Carchemish, scholar Irene J. Winter relates:

> Perhaps no other site in the region of northern Syria and south-eastern Anatolia played as important a role in the history of the early first millennium B.C. as Carchemish, "on the banks of the Euphrates." It is one of the best-documented sites of the period, due to a combination of Neo-Assyrian references and the excavated material of the site itself, including inscriptions reliefs and large-scale architectural projects initiated by the rulers of Carchemish. All of these documents attest to its immense wealth and power.[31]

Dr Winter goes on to say that "of all the states of North Syria and Southeast Anatolia, it is Carchemish that held the position of primary economic importance prior to Assyrian take-over."[32] The history of the neo-Hittites runs from the collapse of the Late Bronze Age to the early eighth century BCE. During this time, numerous references to "Hatti" – the same name used in the Late Bronze Age to refer to the Anatolian Hittites – are attested in numerous sources from the Iron Age in reference to the neo-Hittites. For instance the Assyrian king Shalmaneser III, a contemporary Ahab in Israel, records:

> The land of Hatti to its farthest border I brought under my sway. From the source of the Tigris to the source of the Euphrates my hands conquered.[33]

No special effort is made to differential them from the earlier Hittites. It was simply a given that he referred to the neo-Hittites. Similarly, I believe that when the Tuthmoside rulers of the 18th Dynasty referred to the land of Hatti, they meant the neo-Hittites. In the pharaohs' case, however, the equation of the two Hattis, from the Late Bronze and Iron Ages, may have served a special purpose. It allowed them to better emulate, in the recounting of their exploits to the gods at Karnak, their earlier Late Bronze Age alter-egos. In fact, I believe that most of the Tuthmoside battle scenes depicted on the wall of Karnak, especially those where Pharaoh is shown wearing the blue crown, were in reality Iron Age scenes. The elaborate Karnak battle scenes from the Iron Age often represented a delicate balance between Iron Age historical reality and a grandiose fictional retelling of a Late Bronze Age past. A perfect example of that, as will be examined in

---

[31] Irene J. Winter (1983) 'Carchemish Sa Kisad Puratti', *Anatolian Studies* 33, p. 177.
[32] Ibid, p. 195.
[33] Daniel D. Luckenbill (1968 [1928]) *Ancient Records of Assyria and Babylonia*, Vol. I - Sec. 641.

Chapter 17, is the retelling of the epic Battle of Kadesh. I, indeed, very much doubt that the Egyptian account that contemporary scholars have of this battle between the Egyptians and the Hittites really dates to the Late Bronze Age. As I will argue later, I maintain that the only document relating the outcome of the Battle of Kadesh, which was actually contemporary with the war in question, was the Hittite account found at Boghazköy. This is not to say that the Egyptian version of the events was entirely fictitious, but that it was written in an Iron Age context. Hence, the details of this account inevitably betray it's Iron Age context in numerous details. Moreover, the overall story was written in a manner which suited the revered memory of the ancestral Pharaoh — in that case, Ramses II. More often, however, it was the posterity of the reigning Iron Age pharaoh, whose own legacy depended on how his ancient alter-ego was seen, which was at stake since the objective was to render the two reigns undistinguishable.

The Many Layers of the Temple of Karnak:

A series of strange archaeological anomalies may set us on the path to proving that we are in fact dealing with two Tuthmoside lines separated by as much as five hundred years. The first of these anomalies is, as J. H. Breasted observed, the: *"systematic insertion of the names of Thutmose I and Thutmose II together, over the name of Hatshepsut on buildings erected by her together with Thutmose III ..."*[34] How could that be? Egyptologists believe that the inscriptions prove that Tuthmosis I & II reigned a short time after the co-regency of Hatchepsut and Tuthmosis III had begun. But Tuthmosis I & II were Tuthmosis III's grandfather and father respectively, and the latter would logically have still been alive during the desecration of his building. Why would Tuthmosis I & II show such blatant disrespect to their progeny? Moreover, what would be the political justification for seeing two previous kings suddenly retaking power several years after their reign ended? Where is the evidence for such a strange turn of events in the records of any of the kings concerned? The answer, of course, is that the Tuthmoside pharaohs who usurped the buildings of Queen Hatchepsut, of the Late Bronze Age's new 14th Dynasty, were the Iron Age rulers of the 18th Dynasty.

Secondly, in the temple of Amun-Re at Karnak, it is known that Tuthmosis I built two great pylons (pylons IV and V), as well as a hypostyle room in between them. But what baffles archaeologists is the fact that Queen Hatchepsut, his daughter, later erected two obelisks at the door of the Vth pylon —within the edifice. The problem is that, in light of the fact that Queen Hatchepsut "succeeded" Tuthmosis I, there's absolutely no way she could have managed to fit the obelisks within the

---

[34] J. H. Breasted, *Ancient Records of Egypt*, Vol. II - § 128.

CHAP. XIII: THE IMPERIALISTIC AGE | 483

structure without altogether dismantling the pylon and then rebuilding it again around the obelisks she had inserted! While the obelisks stand to about 30 metres, the actual room, although quite large at 70 metres in length, has a depth of only 10 metres. This architectural feat defies all logic.[35] Why go through all this trouble? French Egyptologist Christiane Wallet-Lebrun has suggested that Hatchepsut must have been motivated by some "serious religious reasons" to even attempt to undertake such a dumb founding exploit.[36] But no extant ancient texts give out any hints whatsoever about what those enigmatic reasons might have been. No Egyptologist,[37] as of yet, has offered a convincing explanation for this conundrum. As the following evidence will hopefully prove, I contend that the two obelisks had been erected by Hatchepsut in the Late Bronze Age long before Pylons IV and V were built by King Tuthmosis I in the Iron Age.

At the base of another monument (her Northern obelisk), Hatchepsut decided to record, for posterity, her building achievements — particularly the history of her obelisks. There, she expressed her wish to erect two obelisks between the great pylons of her father Tuthmosis I, in honour of the god Amun-Re.[38] Do we then have proof that she actually did erect these strangely placed obelisks? I am not so convinced. The texts from the Karnak obelisks themselves tell us that Queen Hatchepsut inaugurated the monuments for *"her father Amun, Lord of the thrones of the Two Lands."*[39] But on the Northern obelisk inscription, she does not refer to the god Amun as her divine father, but rather to Amun-Re.[40] This detail automatically rules out the Late Bronze Age Hatchepsut as a candidate for the authorship of the Northern obelisk inscription — since the god Amun-Re was not the state god during the LB I-II period.

The proposition that there was a second Queen Hatchepsut who reigned during the Iron Age automatically begs the question of what was the relationship with the Tuthmoside pharaohs. An exactly analogous familial relationship as during the new 14th Dynasty would naturally be very unlikely. In the 18th Dynasty, it appears that Hatchepsut and Tuthmosis III were sister and brother — i.e. both children of Pharaoh Tuthmosis II. A statue of a certain nobleman named Enebini, now in the British Museum, dated to the 18th Dynasty, indeed postulates that Hatchepsut and Tuthmosis III were sister and brother:

---

[35] Christiane Wallet-Lebrun (1982) 'Notes sur le temple d'Amon-Rê à Karnak (I)', *Bulletin de l'Institut Français d'Archéologie Orientale* 82, pp. 355.
[36] Ibid, p. 356.
[37] Although, faced with multiple anomalies, Christiane Wallet-Lebrun (1984, p. 331) supposes that Pylon IV was really constructed by Tuthmosis III and not Tuthmosis I as traditionally believed. But that theory is not without its flaws.
[38] K. Sethe & W. Helck, *Urk. IV*, 365, 1. 1
[39] Ibid, 357, 1. 4-5.
[40] Christiane Wallet-Lebrun (1982) p. 357.

> Made as favor of the Good Goddess, Mistress of the Two Lands, Maka-re (Hatchepsut), living and abiding like Re, and her brother the Good God, Lord of Offering, Menkheperre (Thutmose III), who is given life like Re, forever.[41]

The central importance given to the sun-god Re, in the above inscription, is yet another indication that this Queen Hatchepsut did not rule during the Theban Renaissance. It's more likely that the Iron Age Queen Hatchepsut was a mere figurehead and co-regent of her brother Tuthmosis III. Her principal role was most probably to ensure the exact reproduction of the Iron Age alter-ego dynasty. The peculiar omission of Hatchepsut's name from later official king-lists, like the Abydos king-list, is likely an indication of her minor role in the 18th Dynasty.

---

[41] J. H. Breasted, *Ancient Records of Egypt*, Vol. II - § 213.

14

The Western Hemisphere

The issue of Transatlantic pre-Columbian travels from Africa and the ancient Near East, particularly during the early Iron Age, has sparked many heated debates in scholarly circles. To most scholars of ancient Mesoamerica, the very notion that sea-bound Iron Age peoples from Africa and the ancient Near East could have travelled to America is preposterous. Nevertheless, certain venturesome scholars, like Barry Fell, Ivan Van Sertima and Cyrus H. Gordon to name a few, have, for many years, contended that such ancient contacts in fact did take place. Generally speaking, those who espouse this belief, argue that the magnificent Classical period of ancient Mexico represented a flowering of the influence of these much earlier contacts. The Classic period in Mesoamerican history, which spanned from 150 CE to 900 CE was, to quote Americanist Michael D. Coe, the "Golden Age of Mesoamerica, when the seeds that were planted during the Preclassical [period] reached fruition."[1] The great civilizations of the Aztecs and Maya blossomed during those prosperous times of the Classical period. Did those seed from the Preclassical period, upon which the Aztec and Maya cultures (among others) grew out of, indigenous to the Americas or had they been imported from somewhere else? This is the main question which will be explored in this chapter.

The reason why this topic is relevant to our study of the new chronology in the Old World is because it ties in directly with some of the material covered in Chapters 11 and 12 — specifically with respect to the Atlanteans and Danaans. For the purposes of this chapter, we take ourselves back to the beginning of Typhon Season #5 — in 1,187 BCE. This is the time when I believe that the civilizing seeds, attributable to the Preclassical period in Mesoamerica, were planted. My basic hypothesis is that the Atlans of West Africa, whom I contend were ancestors of the Olmecs in Mesoamerica, came to the new world, following the Mercury shift of 1,187 BCE, with their knowledge of the calendar, astronomy, art and religion. The mixture of this scientific influx from abroad and the already existing knowledge-base of the local inhabitants, ultimately led to the creation of Olmec culture — which went on to serve as a vital underpinning for later Mesoamerican civilizations. In his seminal book *They Came Before Columbus*, originally published in 1976, Rutgers University anthropol-

---

[1] Michael D. Coe (1994 [1962]) *Mexico: From the Olmecs to the Aztecs*, Thames and Hudson: London, p. 89.

ogist Ivan Van Sertima had likewise advanced the theory that the Olmecs were of African ancestry. Professor Van Sertima pointed, for instance, to the obvious African characteristics of the seventeen colossal stone heads, each weighting around 20 tons and ranging from 5 to 11 feet in height, carved by the Olmecs between the twelfth and tenth centuries BCE. Also utilizing evidence from burial remains found there, he writes:

> ... these skulls in Olmec strata are of continental African type, such as we find in West Africa today, and not those of Pacific negritos, who could have come in much earlier.[2]

The time frame for the initial carving of the colossal Olmec heads perfectly coincides with the period in which I believe these African migrants arrived in ancient Mexico from the Atlas mountains. Scholars indeed agree that the Olmecs first arrived in South America during the twelfth century BCE.[3] According to renowned Americanist, Michael D. Coe: *"... we can only guess from where they came."*[4] But despite this uncertainty about the origins of Olmec culture, Coe, an ardent isolationist, still discounts the possibility of outside influence from across the Atlantic ocean. It is interesting, however, to point out that, quoting Ignatius Donnelly, that the "Toltecs traced their migration back to a starting-point called 'Atlan.' This could be no other than Atlantis."[5]

The Fifth Sun at the End of the Second World

The Fifth Sun or the Fifth Age of Man, the equivalent of Hesiod's Fifth Age of iron, again, marks the era when I propose that Old World culture was exported to the New World. This was at the close of precessional mandate of Leo — when a new Sun, or World Age, was expected to soon appear after a tumultuous period of cosmic disorder. The tail-end of the Mandate of Leo in Mesoamerica, the ancient Near East and China exhibit, for instance, noticeable artistic similarities. Those are manifested in the resemblance between antrhropomorphic seated statues of feline deities found in both Olmec South-America (Puebla, Mexico, c.1,150 BCE) and late Shang Dynasty sacred art in China.[6] Equally uncanny is the resemblance between

---

[2] Ivan Van Sertima (1987) 'Egypto-Nubian Presence in Ancient Mexico.' In *African Presence in Early America*, p. 40.
[3] Michael D. Coe 'San Loranzo and the Olmec Civilization.' In E. Benson (editor) (1968) *Dumbarton Oaks Conference on the Olmec*, p. 61.
[4] Ibid.
[5] Ignatius Donnelly (1882) *Atlantis: The Antediluvian World*, Harper & Brothers: New York, p. 105.
[6] For photographs see Wayne B. Chandler 'Trait-Influences in Meso-America: The African-Asian Connection.' In Ivan Van Sertima (editor) (1987) *African Presence in Early America*, pp. 302-303.

Olmec and Shang Dynasty figures of a jaguar figure protecting a child.[7] All of these leonine symbols obviously relate to the Sun Age which was coming to an end at the onset of Typhon Season #5. According to the African-centered scholar Wayne B. Chandler:

> Ennobled as a symbol of power and strength, the great cats — *Tiger* in China, *Jaguar* in Mexico, and *Lion* in Africa are also classified as earth gods in all religions. Motif imagery and time sequence are also in order for this category.[8]

The Sun Age which came about at the end of Typhon Season #5 was, of course, the Fifth Sun. The succession of the World Ages was absolutely central to Mesoamerican culture — as Burr Cartwright Brundage outlines below:

> The Aztec myth of the five ages of the world describes four abortive attempts to create a viable world order. each of the four early suns finally weakened and fell from its station in the heavens, the disaster in each case being accompanied by a cosmic holocaust.[9]

The Hopi, for their part, referred to the zodiacal "Seasons" which began after the Great Flood to mark their World Ages — as opposed to the Typhon Season system used by the Olmecs and the Maya. Since we know that the Great Flood triggered the observance of the precessional movement of the vernal constellations, the Hopi's World Ages corresponded to the astrological ages of Aries, Leo, Taurus and Pisces. As a result, the end of the Hopi's Second World would correspond with the end of the Mayan Fourth Sun. Describing the end of the Second World, Hopi tradition relates:

> (So again) as on the First World, Sotuknang called on the Ant people to open up their underground world for the chosen people. When they were safely underground, Sotuknang commanded the twins, Palonga-whoya and Poganghoya, to leave their posts at the north and south ends of the world's axis where they were stationed to keep the earth properly rotating. The twins had hardly abandoned their stations when the world with no one to control it, teetered off balance, spun around crazily, then rolled over

---

[7] Ibid, pp. 316-317.
[8] Wayne B. Chandler 'Trait-Influences in Meso-America: The African-Asian Connection.' In Ivan Van Sertima (editor) (1987) *African Presence in Early America*, p. 290.
[9] Burr Cartwright Brundage (1979) *The Fifth Sun (Aztec Gods, Aztec World)*, University of Texas Press: Austin and London, p. 164.

twice. Mountains plunged into seas with a great splash, seas and lakes splashed over the land; and as the world spun through cold and fireless space, it froze into solid ice.[10]

So as the Second World, or Second Mandate (of Leo) abruptly came to an end, the Third World, or Third Sun, would appear. The following is a description of the exact same catastrophe as described by the Hopi people — only this time viewed from the perspective of the ensuing Third world, as enunciated by Ignatius Donnelly:

> The "Codex Chimalpoca"—a Nahua, Central American record— tells us that the third era of the world, or "third sun," is called *Quia Tonatiuh*, or sun of rain, "because in this age there fell a rain of fire, all which existed burned, and there fell a rain of gravel;" the rocks "boiled with tumult, and there also arose the rocks of vermilion color." In other words, the traditions of these people go back to a great cataclysm of fire, when the earth possibly encountered, as in the Egyptian story, one of "the bodies moving round the earth and in the heavens;" they had also memories of "the Drift Period," and of the outburst of Plutonic rocks.[11]

Again, the end of the Hopi's Second World (the end of the Leo Mandate) can be correlated with the end of the Mayan Fourth Sun and the arrival of their Fifth Sun (as heralded by Typhon Season #5). Gómar, a Spaniard who visited the Western Hemisphere during the middle of the sixteenth century CE, and who paid particular interest to the ancient texts of the New World, wrote:

> After the destruction of the fourth sun, the world plunged in darkness during the space of twenty-five years. Amid this profound obscurity, ten years before the appearance of the fifth sun, mankind was regenerated.[12]

It was during this period of obscurity that the Qiché tribe migrated to Mexico. Meanwhile, in the ancient Near East, a Great Exodus out of Egypt was taking place. In both hemispheres, the birth of the Fifth Sun was characterized by vast migratory movements of peoples in search of a better land. The dawning new World Age brought hopes of a better life in a Promised Land.

---

[10] Patrick Doran 'The Social Impact of Velikovsky on Our Generation.' In Nahum Ravel (editor) (1975) *From Past to Prophecy: Velikovsky's Challenge to Conventional Beliefs* (Proceedings of the Symposium held at the Saidye Bronfman Centre, Montreal, Quebec – January 10th-12th, 1975), p. 72.

[11] Ignatius Donnelly (1882) *Atlantis: The Antediluvian World*, Harper & Brothers: New York, p. 145.

[12] Gómara, *Conquista de Mexico*, II, 261.

CHAP. XIV: THE WESTERN HEMISPHERE | 489

Quite clearly the basis of the Hopi Cosmology is a catastrophic view of existence. They, like the Israelites, began this age amidst a violent upheaval which initiated their migrations in search of their chosen land. Their goal, on the bleak mesas of the American southwest.[13]

The planet Venus naturally occupied a preeminent position in the formation of these ancient theological constructs. It was the common denominator, incarnated in diverse deities all around the world, which cements archaeotheological links between Old and New World cosmogonies. In his 1974 essay entitled 'Maya Astronomy,' J. E. S. Thompson of the National University of Mexico's Centre of Maya Studies wrote:

> From Mexican sources it is known that Venus was much feared at heliacal rising after inferior conjunction; its rays then slew various categories of persons or personified manifestations of nature. Illustrations (from Maya Venus table) ... show Venus gods hurling spears earthward, and, below the slain victims. The accompanying glyphs, with very few exceptions are direful: 'Woe to the maize, woe to the corn fields, drought, misery, affliction of war' and so on. By predicting the day of the heliacal rising, the priests were able to warn the threatened group, so that it could take protective measures. For instance, we know from Mexican sources that 'when it [Venus] emerged much fear came over them; all were frightened. Everywhere the outlets and openings [of houses] were closed up. It was said that perchance [the light] might bring a cause of sickness, something evil when it came to emerge.' The spear represents the 'death ray.'... the Maya were certainly more interested in Venus than in any other planet ... We know neither names nor glyphs of any planet other than Venus.[14]

With regards to the 52-year cycle, Thomson later says:

> The Aztec are said to have held their great ceremony of rekindling fire at the end of the 52-year cycle when the Pleiades reached the zenith at midnight ...[15]

---

[13] Patrick Doran 'Living with Velikovsky: Catastrophism as World View.' In E.R. Milton (editor) (1978) *Recollections of a Fallen Sky: Velikovsky and Cultural Amnesia (Papers presented at the University of Lethbridge — May 9 and 10 1974)*, Unileth Press: Lethbridge, Alberta, p. 145.

[14] J. E. S. Thompson 'Maya Astronomy.' In The British Academy (1974) *The Place of Astronomy in the Ancient World (A Joint Symposium of the Royal Society and the British Academy)*, pp. 87-88.

[15] Ibid, p. 92.

Also, Burr Cartwright Brundage writes:

> To the Aztecs the planet Venus was a warrior, a valiant champion whose challenges to the sun were dire and constant. The malevolence of Venus was well known ...[16]

The Venus calendar found in the Dresden Codex is believed to have been compiled shortly after 1,000 CE in the northern Yucatán, but evidence suggests that it was based on earlier texts.[17] No doubt, the native Mesoamericans were already aware of the recurring Venusian catastrophes long before they came into contact with the Atlans during Typhon Season #5, but the idea, and composition, of the Venus calendar, at least in the form it has survived in the Classical period, may well have had its origins in the Old World. As we'll explore shortly, the similarity of the Mesoamerican Venus calendar to its much earlier Egyptian equivalent are astounding.

Olmec Civilization

Although Olmec civlization only flourished in the twelfth century BCE[18] — on the coast of Veracruz and Tabasco, Mexico — Americanists contend that the Olmecs' ancestors were Native Americans whose "Ice Age ancestors entered the New World from northern Asia via the Bering Strait land bridge."[19] My question is: what caused the native inhabitants of La Venta, Mexico to all of a sudden, in the twelfth century BCE, pretty much abandon their traditional beliefs in an egalitarian society? Why, without apparent explanation, abruptly move from a culture devoid of social status or wealth accumulation, to one of complex hierarchical rule and sophisticated religious and ceremonial observances? The "flood of new features in iconography, rituals, ceramics and tools"[20] which suddenly appears

---

[16] Burr Cartwright Brundage (1979) *The Fifth Sun*, pp. 7-8.
[17] Evan Hadingham (1984) *Early Man and the Cosmos*, Walker: New York, p. 219.
[18] Michael D. Coe, Richard A. Diehl & Minze Stuiver (1967) 'Olmec Civilization, Vera Cruz, Mexico: Dating the San Lorenzo Phaze', *Science* 155, p. 1400; Micheal D, Coe & Richard A. Diehl (1980) *In the Land of the Olmecs: Archaeology of San Lorenzo Tenochtitlan.* Vols. I-II. University of Texas Press: Austin, TX.
[19] Michael D. Coe and Richard A. Diel (1980), p. 11. Many Native-American scholars have however been very critical of the Eurocentric Bering Strait theory. Since that controversial topic is beyond the scope of this book, the reader is referred to the works of Vine Deloria, Jr.
[20] Muriel Porter Weaver (1993) *The Aztecs, Maya, and their Predecessors (Archaeology of Mesoamerica).* Third edition. Academic Press: San Diego, Cal., p. 31.

in the Basin of Mexico between c.1,200 BCE to c.1,100 BCE can hardly, in my view, be attributed to some mysterious local impulse as academics contend. Describing this leap between Olmec I (c.1,500-c.1,200 BCE) and Olmec II (c.1,200-c.600 BCE) as *"an extraordinary elaboration of the earlier village type,"*[21] eminent Mesoamerican scholar Ignacio Bernal prefers to classify the Olmec I phase as an advanced culture rather than as a classical "civilization" in terms of urban planning or monumental sculptures. But again, Ignacio Bernal prefers to *"reject the idea that Olmec culture was created in another region."* Opting instead to hold on to the view that *"Its roots are in its own territory."*[22] Ivan Van Sertima has come under fierce attack by Americanists for allegedly denigrating the value of Mesoamerican culture by claiming that Olmec civilization flourished under African influences.[23] But I do not believe that this is what Professor Van Sertima's hypothesis entails at all. There is indeed no question that much of Olmec civilization was, at its base, Native American. However, during the twelfth century BCE, there undeniably was an important cultural revival, or influx, that changed La Venta for ever.

I strongly believe that this cultural impulse came from the east — from West Africa. Those Bronze Age West Africans, the Atlanteans (descendants of the A-Group disciples of Seth from Nubia), introduced the fruits of pharaonic culture to the New World. The most obvious sign of this diffusion is the presence of step-pyramids in ancient Mexico. While one of the arguments used to dispel this hypothesis has been that the ancient Egyptians had long abandoned step-pyramid technology by the time such Transatlantic voyages could have taken place, we must recall that at the time of the A-Group's cultural height in the Nile Valley, the only pyramid structure which they were familiar with was that of Djoser-Netjerykhet — a step-pyramid.

Professor Ivan Van Sertima has moreover presented an excellent case for the identification of parallel ritual traits and techniques between the pharaonic (or Egypto-Nubian world) and the Olmec civilization. Among such similarities are the use of the royal flail, the artificial beard, and the practice of the "Opening of the Mouth Ceremony."[24] Referring specifically to what he perceives as being a clear

---

[21] Ignacio Bernal (1969) *The Olmec World*. Trans. by Doris Heyden and Fernando Horcasitas. University of California Press: Berkeley and Los Angeles, p. 110.
[22] Ibid.
[23] See Martin Bernal (1998) 'On "Robbing Native American Cultures"', *Current Anthropology* Vol. 39 - Num. 4, pp. 512-514.
[24] See Ivan Van Sertima (1987) 'Egypto-Nubian Presence in Ancient Mexico.' In *African Presence in Early America*, pp. 29-55.

relationship between the eighth century BCE Ethiopian pharaohs and the Olmec world, Van Sertima says the following:

> The Nubian pharaohs donned the double crown of the two lands in the 8th century B.C. when they regained their power over the north. The double crown appears on an Olmec dignitary at Cerro de la Piedra. He is seen offering a glyph (symbolic object) with the Egyptian cross motif to a seated figure that has African features and African-type hair.[25]

I, however, part company with Prof. Van Sertima in my belief that the above mentioned pharaonic characteristics found in Olmec art were in fact part of an *early* case of Old World diffusion into the New World; specifically through the Atlanteo-Napatan culture in the twelfth century BCE. Further corroborating the theory of an African influx into the New World in Antiquity, Cyrus H. Gordon, speaking about a Mixtec Negro head from Oaxaca, Mexico, writes:

> The black color and the features, such as thick lips, leave no doubt in anyone's mind that the artist has portrayed a Negro. No artist can "invent" authentic races of mankind, such as the types we are examining. The implication is simply that early America was the meeting ground of various races of men from the Old World who were eventually absorbed into modern Indian populations.[26]

The Feathered Serpent from the East: The Hyksos, the Danaans and Phoenicians Beyond the Pillars of Herakles

Studies on the possible historicity of pre-Columbian transoceanic travels have been dismissed by many established specialists as: *"romantic ruminations of arm-chair historians."*[27] Indeed, recent proponents of this "hyperdiffusionist" approach, like Ivan Van Sertima and Cyrus H. Gordon, have been strongly attacked by mainstream scholars.[28] But the physiological, linguistic, and cultural evidence for the multi-ethnic composition of ancient Mesoamerican civilization, incorporating cul-

---

[25] Ibid, p. 46.
[26] Cyrus H. Gordon (1972) *Before Columbus (Links Between the Old World and Ancient America)*, Turnstone: London, p. 22.
[27] Philip J. Arnold III (1995) Ethnicity, Pottery, and the Gulf Olmec of Ancient Veracruz, Mexico', *Biblical Archaeologist* Vol. 58 - Num. 4, p. 191.
[28] See Bernard Ortiz de Montellano, Gabriel Haslip-Viera & Warren Barbour (1997) 'They were Not Here Before Columbus: Afrocentric Hyperdiffusionism in the 1990s', *Ethnohistory* Vol. 44 - Num. 2, pp. 199-234.

CHAP. XIV: THE WESTERN HEMISPHERE | 493

tures from the Old World, is more than circumstantial. These foreign elements were not only Afroasiatic, but also even European. Indeed, in the ancient Mexican city of La Venta, an Olmec legend related that a "Man in Snake," depicted as a light-skinned and bearded figure, had come to La Venta from the east.[29] Prof. Cyrus H. Gordon had, incidentally, brought attention to "bearded human head feathered serpents" from an archaic Greek temple on the Athenian necropolis.[30] Could that "Man in Snake" have come from the Mediterranean region? According to ancient Mesoamerican legend, citing Fray Bernandino Sahgún, those light-skinned gods from the east *"could do practically anything, nothing seemed too difficult for them; they cut the greenstone, they melted gold, and all this came from Quetzalcoatl — arts and knowledge."* Quetzalcoatl's "mission was with humanity of the Fifth Age."[31] Quetzalcoatl literally means "plumed serpent."

The timing of Quetzalcoatl's arrival in ancient Mexico is hence securely situated during Typhon Season #5 — analogously to the arrival of the Atlans. But does that mean that Quetzalcoatl represented these West African migrants? That would be very unlikely, since Quetzalcoatl had white skin. So who were these light-skinned people from the east who arrived in Mesoamerica during Typhon Season #5. I believe that they were made up of a diverse coalition of Hyksos from the Mediterranean Agagite dynasty, Danaans and Phoenicians. Their seaward travels to the New World were part of the grand migration of the Heraklids, headed by the Agagite Hyksos, following the Trojan War. Not only had the Danaans and Hyksos reached ancient British Isles, but other detachments had gone off as far as ancient Mexico. Their knowledge of the arts and sciences which they brought to the New World, given the timing of their transmission, was considered "Sethian knowledge." Much as in the Old Testament's Book of Creation, the carrier of this cycle-ending knowledge was identified with a Typhonian serpent. We know that the ancient Egyptians equated this serpent of knowledge with Apophis, and that Apophis (Agag), albeit occasionally presented as a rival of Seth, was himself, in its function as a Typhonian deity, closely linked with the latter.

To the ancient Greeks, Ogyges was a form of Okeanos[32] — a probable root of the modern word "ocean." Moreover, fairly close links can be established in Greek mythology between Atlas and Okeanos. According to the poet Homer, Atlas was:

---

[29] Graham Hancock (1996 [1995]) *Fingerprints of the Gods (A Quest for the Beginning and the End)*, Seal Books: Toronto, p. 165.
[30] See Cyrus H. Gordon (1972) *Before Columbus*, p. 52.
[31] Graham Hancock (1996 [1995]) *Fingerprints of the Gods*, p. 177.
[32] Joseph Fontrose (1959) *Python (A Study of Delphic Myth and its Origins)*, University of California Press: Berkeley, Cal., p. 311; Martin Bernal (1991) *Black Athena II*, p. 301.

> ... a baneful mind, who knows the depths of every sea, and himself holds the tall pillars which keep heaven and earth apart.
> (Homer, *Odyssey*, Book I: 52)

The reputation earned by both Atlas and Ogyges for their profound knowledge of the high seas stems directly from their fabled explorations of the Atlantic Ocean and the lands laying beyond its horizon. Plato might have known that the Atlanteans of Mount Atlas had discovered America and incorporated it in his story concerning Atlantis. For centuries, readers of Plato's text have wondered if the latter was referring to America when he spoke of a mysterious island larger than Libya laying in the middle of the Atlantic ocean. As I have outlined in Chapter 11, however, I maintain that Plato's Atlantis was located in West Africa. However, his attempt to make Atlantis into a large island in the middle of the Atlantic ocean can be understood, as mentioned above, within the context of these West Africans' travels to America. Plato was not the only one to hint at an ancient knowledge of the Americas. Diodorus of Sicily makes an equally intriguing statement:

> For there lies out in the deep off Libya an island of considerable size, and situated as it is in the ocean it is distant from Libya a voyage of a number of days to the west. Its land is fruitful, much of it being mountainous and a little being a level plain of surpassing beauty. ...
>
> In ancient times this island remained undiscovered because of its distance from the inhabited world ...
> (Diodorus of Sicily, Book V: 19, 1-2 and 20, 1)

This large landmass, situated to the west of Libya (Africa), sounds surprisingly like the Americas. For his part, Strabo speaks of Phoenician travels during Typhon Season #5 (after the Trojan War) which extended "beyond the Pillars of Hercules."

> [far-famed] are the voyages of the, Phoenicians, who, a short time after the Trojan War, explored the regions beyond the Pillars of Hercules and founded cities both there and in the central parts of the Libyan sea-board.
> (Strabo, Book I: 3, 2)

Since, as Diodorus claims, the Phoenicians "planted many colonies throughout Libya" (V: 20,1), it may be safe to conjecture that the Phoenicians must have heard about the existence of the Americas through their contacts with the West African Atlantes who had settled heavily into Libya in the twelfth century BCE. The know-

CHAP. XIV: THE WESTERN HEMISPHERE | 495

ledge of the Americas' existence could have then been passed on, perhaps through the Phoenicians (who likewise had a strong presence in the Aegean), to the Agagite Hyksos-Amalekite dynasty in the Mediterranean. In the early 1960s, author Pierre Honoré in his book *In Quest of the White God*, made the following comparative analysis of certain letters of the Greek, Phoenician, and Mayan alphabet, in that order[33] :

    Alpha, alep, ahau   Iota, iud, ik
    Beta, bejt, baaz   Kappa, koph, queh
    Gamma, gimel, ghanan   Lambda, lamed, lamat
    Epsilon, eh, eb   Tau, tav, tihax

I am indeed thoroughly convinced that a link existed, during the twelfth century BCE, between the ancient Near East, the Aegean, and Preclassical Mesoamerica which contributed to this striking similarity between these alphabets. The hieroglyphic nature of the Mayan script must, for its part, stem from Olmec influence. Hence, the basis of Classical Mayan culture is the result of the primeval mixture of all of these Old World influences during the early days of the Fifth Sun and the then existing Preclassical Mesoamerican local culture. Not only was the basis of the Maya alphabet fomented during Typhon Season #5, but also the major scientific advances like the Mayan Venus calendar.

The Venus Calendar

The Mayan Venus calendar comprised of 2,920 days (twice the 1,460 day period in Egypt's Venus calendar; hence why the Mayan period of 8 years of 365 days [8 x 365 = 2,920] is double that of Egypt's 4 years of 365 days [4 x 365 = 1,460]). As will be demonstrated in the next chapter, these periods of four and eight years played an important cultic role in the sacred festivals of both the Eastern and Western Hemispheres. The relationship between the ancient Mayan and Egyptian sacred calendars have long been underestimated, and most often altogether ignored, by scholars. The reason, of course, is that the idea of contact between the Old World and the New World in such remote times has traditionally been met with much resistance. However, the similarity between the two systems is, in my view, much too striking to ignore. Venus was the centre piece of Mayan cosmology and mythology. Like in the Old World, its was feared as an agent of destruction and cycle-ending doom. In the *Dresden Codex*, one of the few surviving Mayan books, the "1 Ahau" was the traditional Sacred Day of Venus. Linguistically, the word Ahau

---

[33] Pierre Honoré (1963) *In Quest of the White God (The Mysterious Heritage of South American Civilization)*. Trans. from the German by Olivier Corburn and Ursula Lehrburger. Hutchinson: London, p. 37.

stands for either "Lord" or "Sun." The Maya, like the Babylonians many centuries before them, carefully tracked the movements of the planet Venus. Two distinct cycles were involved in the calendric system: (1) the 365-day cycle — the *Haab*, and (2) the sacred cycle of 260 days — the *Tzolkin*. These two cycles periodically came in synch with each other every 52 years, in a period called the Calendar Round. Needless to say, this period of 52 years symbolized the Typhon Seasons which stood between the succeeding World Ages of Suns. Since Venus was the primary agent in ending and heralding these great Suns, the 52-year period was skillfully incorporated into the Venus calendar. The fact that the double calendric system was used during the Ptolemaic period[34] (which would mean, from the perspective of the new chronology, that it originated in the fourth millennium BCE) suggests that the Atlanteans must have learned it from the Khemites and later transported it to the new world. Equally similar to Khemeto-Egyptian tradition, the Maya 365-day calendar was made up of 18 months of 20 days each — with five days added on at the end.[35] Again, the similarities are very striking.

According to the Maya of the Classic period, the universe's cyclical pattern of destruction and rebirth, as described in the *Popol Vuh* creation myth, and the *Dresden Codex*, could be appeased, or at the very least regularized, through the ritualistic practice of human sacrifice. As in most of the Old World traditions, the cataclysmic culmination of a World Age signalled a major rupture in the stable relationship between the gods and humanity. In the Mayan creation myth, the Hero Twins, Hunapu (associated with the firmament, the sun, and life) and Xbalanque (associated with the underworld, the jaguar, Venus, and death), tricked the gods of death by transforming themselves into the sun and Venus. Therefore, finding inspiration in the myth of the Hero Twins, the Maya believed that human beings, in imitation of the Hero Twins, could serve as channels of cosmic rebirth, and outwit the gods of death, through blood sacrifice. This Mesoamerican practice of blood sacrifice somewhat resembles the practice of Typhonian bull and Asiatic prisoner sacrifices in Egypt during Typhon Seasons — as described in Chapter 2. Naturally, at the time when these human sacrifices were taking place in Mesoamerica of the Classic period (250-900 CE), the last Typhon Season had long passed and the once turbulent solar system had long been permanently stabilized. Nevertheless, the Maya were, apparently expecting the solar system to eventually once again fall into chaos, reenacting rituals performed by their distant Preclassical ancestors of the nascent Fifth Sun. Evidently, the planet Venus was preeminent in these cosmic rebirth rituals. In an-

---

[34] Immanuel Velikovsky (1977) *Peoples of the Sea*, p. 240.
[35] J. E. S. Thompson (1974), p. 84. Thompson discounts any Old World/New World connections.

tiquity, the Venus cycle of 8 years, during which Venus runs its synodic course five times, was pivotal to Babylonian, Chinese and Mayan astronomy.[36] As translated in the various Old World myths cited below, the movement of the planet Venus was ritually associated with human sacrifice in the ancient Aegean as well.

> Theseus killed the Minotaur who demanded human sacrifice every eight years;
> Cadmus struck dead the Theban serpent which swallowed human beings. As a punishment he had to serve Ares for eight years;
> Apollo killed Python and had to serve Admetos for eight years;
> Heracles killed the Hydra and King Faunus who sacrificed human beings. He had to serve Eurysteus foe eight years;
> Oedipus killed the Sphinx which had sacrificed human beings.[37]

This eight year period relates, again, to the Venus cycle of 8 years. The association of the planet Venus with decapitation rituals was likewise accepted, even before the Maya, by the Teotihuacan — who were contemporaries of the Maya. Like many other Mesoamerican cultures, the people of ancient Teotihuacan, in the Andes, also believed that the end of the Fourth Age came in devastating blaze of fire and destruction. The flooded land, as we are told, was engulfed in total darkness. The sun would not shine for many days. For the inhabitants of Teotihuacan, the only way that the sun would ever shine again was if someone offered himself in sacrifice. In the words of David Carrasco of the University of Colorado:

> For 52 years following the end of the four ages, the world was in darkness. "When no sun had shown and no dawn had broken," the gods gathered at Teotihuacán so they could create a new age. They asked: "Who will carry the burden? Who will take it upon himself to be the sun, to bring the dawn?"[38]

---

[36] A. Aaboe 'Scientific Astronomy in Antiquity.' In The British Academy (1974) *The Place of Astronomy in the Ancient World (A Joint Symposium of the Royal Society and the British Academy)*, p. 22. Aaboe considers "absurd" the idea that Babylonian, Chinese and Mayan astronomy could be connected in any way.

[37] Benny Peiser 'Post-Mycenaean Greek History Begins in the 6th Century BC: The Controversy about the Olympic Victor List and its Implications for Early Greek Chronology.' In Milton Zysman & Clark Whelton (editors) (1990) *Catastrophism 2000 (A Sourcebook for the Conference: Reconsidering Velikovsky)*, p. 271.

[38] David Carrasco (1982) *Quetzalcoatl and the Irony of Empire (Myths and Prophecies in the Aztec Tradition)*, University of Chicago Press: Chicago and London, p. 96.

The Aztecs: Carriers of a Lost Knowledge

> *" And in all the [Aztec] temples there was the singing of fitting chants; there was an uproar; there were war cries. It was thus said ' If the eclipse of the sun is complete, it will be dark forever! The demons of darkness will come down; they will eat men!'"*
>
> - Sahagún, Spanish chronicler (16th century CE)

The Aztecs very much looked to the past for inspiration.[39] The great majority of their religious practices were patterned after considerably older Mesoamerican traditions. Indeed, the Aztecs inherited most of their traditions from the ancient Teotihuacan — through the Toltecs as well as other peoples of ancient Mexico.[40] Again, the time of the Fifth Sun was seen as the genesis of all knowledge. It was said by the Aztec priests that Teotihuacan was the sacred place where the Fifth Sun was created through the god's self-sacrifice. In Aztec culture, two men were considered the equals of Quetzalcoatl: King Nazahualpilli of Tezcuco and King Montezuma. Both living Aztec rulers had the reputation of being great astrologers. They prided themselves on their knowledge of the motions of the celestial bodies. Sometime after the accession of Montezuma, it was his fellow king Nazahualpilli who warned the former, on account of his stargazing, of an imminent cosmic catastrophe. Nazahualpilli prophetised that the time allotted by Heaven for the Aztec empire was coming to a close. The end would inevitably come with the slaughter of the Aztec people, and the utter destruction of the civilization. Something had to be done. A severe famine which occurred in the year 1505 of the Julian calendar, followed by an eclipse two years later, were seen by the Aztec astrologers as omens of the impending cataclysm. When, in 1508 CE, King Montezuma was handed an ashen-faced crane-like bird whilst meditating in his study at his celestial school at Tlillancalmocatl, he was more than ever convinced that the end of his empire was near. Gazing inside the crest attached to the bird's head, the Aztec king saw a reflection of the heavens and planets being struck by flame-generating fire sticks. Then, as reported, the picture changed — to be replaced with a vision of invading bearded conquerors from the east. In what probably was one of the most

---

[39] Burr Cartwright Brundage (1979) *The Fifth Sun*, p. 30.
[40] Esther Pasztory (1997) *Teotihuacan (An Experiment in Living)*, University of Oklahoma Press: Norman and London, pp. 15-29.

consequential coincidences in history, during the predicted period, white-skinned and bearded men in ships, the Spaniards, sailed into the New World from the east. Naturally, the Aztecs "immediately accepted the Spaniards as the White Gods who had returned."[41] Moreover, the Spanish ships arrived, by sheer coincidence, just at the beginning of a new 52-year sacred cycle. In the Aztecs' mind, to once again quote Carrasco: *"Like famine and military defeat, they were viewed partly as cosmological communications reflecting the destiny of the fifth sun."*[42] The demise of their civilization had been ordained by "the pattern of Heaven."[43] So the Spaniards' arrival, combined with the natural upheavals, thoroughly convinced Montezuma that the Fifth Sun was due to perish, along with own his reign. Turning to John Philip Cohane:

> It is an accepted historical fact that one of the reasons, if not the chief reason, for the downfall of Montezuma's well-organized Aztec Empire was the belief held by the natives, rulers and ruled alike, from time immemorial that the founders of their ancient civilization had been "bearded white gods" who had first appeared in sailing ships "from the east." The tradition had been handed down from generation to generation that these strangers, having passed on their wisdom and scientific knowledge to the Mexicans, had departed with the promise that they would someday return.[44]

While the Aztecs were, in reality, living in the current Seventh Sun, their belief that they lived in the Fifth Creation, comes from the fact that they had, much later, come to adopt religious traditions of their Iron I ancestors — who had themselves come into contact with Quetzalcoatl. Hence, it was believed that the Fifth Sun could not come to an end until Quetzalcoatl, who brought the knowledge of the arts and sciences, along with cosmic disturbances, at the beginning of the Fifth Sun, returned from the east. The principal reason why the Aztecs believed that the return of Quetzalcoatl should be accompanied with irregularities in the order of nature is because the original Quetzalcoatl came during a Typhon Season. Specifically at the end of Typhon Season #5 — hence Quetzalcoatl's intimate association with the cycle-ending planet Venus. The bearded white-skinned invaders with 'caskets upon their heads,' whose imminent return was expected had originally, in the Fifth Creation, been diverse bands of Sea Peoples, Phoenicians and Hyksos. Millennia later, these white-skinned invaders were the Spaniards.

---

[41] Pierre Honoré (1963) *In Quest of the White God (The Mysterious Heritage of South American Civilization)*, p. 17.
[42] David Carrasco (1982) *Quetzalcoatl and the Irony of Empire (Myths and Prophecies in the Aztec Tradition)*, p. 187.
[43] Ibid, p. 191.
[44] John Philip Cohane (1969) *The Key*, Crown: New York, p. 24.

The Legacy of the Catastrophic World View

in Native American Traditions

The memory of world-wide cosmic conflagrations in Antiquity is not only limited to the civilizations of Mesoamerica in the New World. Native nations of North America also transmit many accounts of such universal planetary cataclysms. These oral traditions are amazingly similar to the catastrophist traditions of the Old World and Mesoamerica. Confirming this, prolific Native-American scholar, Vine Deloria, Jr., of the University of Colorado's Center for Native American Studies writes:

> The idea of world ages, held by some tribes, is comparable in many ways to the world age concepts held in India. The flood stories, even the most remote, gave rise to the belief that the world is periodically destroyed by flood, fire, or other natural catastrophes, and this idea was held by a number of tribes with stories of some antiquity. Some substance was given to the belief in periodic destruction by particular stories, and in this sense the people could be said to have had a conception of history. For example, the Sioux explanation was framed in familiar terminology. They held that the world was protected by a huge buffalo that stood at the western gate of the universe and held back the waters that periodically flooded the world. Every year the buffalo lost a hair on one of its legs. Every age it lost a leg. When the buffalo had lost all its legs and was no longer able to hold back the waters, the world was flooded and renewed.[45]

Moreover, in his extensive study of the age-old oral traditions of the Native-American nations of California at the turn of the century, the natural scientist C. Hart Merriam observes:

> Some explain the origin of thunder, lightning, the rainbow, and other natural phenomena; some tell of a flood, when only the tops of the highest mountains broke the waves; others of a cheerless period of cold and darkness before the acquisition of the coveted heat and light-giving substance, which finally was stolen and brought home to the people. ... the Tu'-le-yo'me say that when *Sah'-te'* set the world on fire, Coyote-man made the flood and put out the fire. Other local myths are ... that *Cha'-ke* the Tule-wren, a poor despised orphan boy, shot out the sun, leaving the world in total darkness ...[46]

---

[45] Vine Deloria, Jr. (1994 [1972]) *God is Red (A Native View of Religion)*. Updated edition. Fulcrum: Golden, Colorado, p. 102.

[46] C. Hart Merriam (1993 [1910]) *The Dawn of the World (Myths and Tales of the Miwok Indians of California)*, University of Nebraska Press: Lincoln and London, pp. 17;20.

CHAP. XIV: THE WESTERN HEMISPHERE | 501

In his book The Sun Came Down, Blackfeet Native-American scholar Percy Bullchild also spoke of ancient Native American and Canadian legends describing similar natural conflagrations in the form of cosmic justice carried out by the "Creator Sun."[47] Additionally, in their 1995 book entitled *When the Sky Fell*, authors Rand and Rose Flem-Ath relate the following tale of the Utes nation (after whom the State of Utah was named) of the American West's myth of the taming of the sun-god — taken from a nineteenth century article by J. W. Powell entitled 'Mythologic Philosophy':

> Once upon a time Ta-wats, the hare-god, was sitting with his family by the camp-fire in the solemn woods, anxiously waiting for the return of Ta-vi, the wayward sun-god. Wearied with long watching, the hare-god fell asleep, and the sun-god came so near that he scorched the naked shoulder of Ta-wats. Foreseeing the vengeance which would be thus provoked, he fled to his cave beneath the earth.
>
> Ta-wats awoke in great anger, and speedily determined to go and fight the sun-god. After a long journey of many adventures the hare-god came to the brink of the earth, and there watched long and patiently, till at last the sun-god coming out he shot an arrow at his face, but the fierce heat consumed the arrow ere it had finished its intended course; then another was sped, but that also was consumed; and another, and still another, till only one remained in his quiver, but this was the magical arrow that had never failed its mark.
>
> Ta-wats, holding it in his hand, lifted the barb to his eye and baptized it in a divine tear; then the arrow was sped and struck the sun-god full in the face, and the sun was shivered into a thousand fragments which fell to the earth, causing a general conflagration.
>
> Then Ta-wats, the hare-god, fled before the destruction he had wrought, and as he fled the burning earth consumed his feet, consumed his legs, consumed his body, consumed his hands and his arms — all were consumed but the head alone, which bowled across valleys and over mountains, fleeing the destruction from the burning earth, until at last, swollen with heat, the eyes of the god burst and the tears gushed forth in a flood which spread over the earth and extinguished the fire.
>
> The sun-god was now conquered, and he appeared before a council of the gods to await sentence. In that long council were established the days and the nights, the seasons and the years, with the length thereof, and the sun was condemned to travel across the firmament by the same trail day after day till the end of time.[48]

---

[47] Percy Bullchild (1985) *The Sun Came Down*, Harper & Row: San Fransisco.
[48] Major J. W. Powell (1880) 'Mythologic Philosophy', *Popular Science Monthly* 15, pp. 795-808.

Similarly, the Kutenai nation of the Canadian province of British-Columbia, to whom the Utes are ethnically related, speak of their fear of the world coming to a catastrophic end should the sky become unstable.[49] All this further proves that the cosmic conflagrations had really been global in nature and that the memory of these planetary upheavals have survived for many millennia after the solar system had finally stabilized itself.

The Seventh Sun

The aboriginals of Sarawak and Sabah recall that "six Suns perished" and that "at present the world is illuminated by the seventh Sun."[50] Indeed, the end of the last Typhon Season (#7), in 612 BCE, brought along the demise of the Sixth Sun, and ushered in the present Seventh Age or Sun. The current age is characterized by the zodiacal sign of Pisces. Buddhist tradition holds that "the universe is conceived as having seven stages with the summit located in the cosmic North, or the Pole Star."[51] Hindus believe that the establishment of a New World "procured from the depths of the celestial ocean," must be dedicated by the "Seven Sages."[52] Evidently, the oft-recurring number seven is a direct reference to the seven Creations or Suns of the world's catastrophic Antiquity. But as Immanuel Velikovsky outlines below, this notion of the Seven World Ages has filtered into much more subtle symbols and conventions which we have adopted from Antiquity:

> The naming of the seven days of the week in honor of the seven planets is not only an act of reverence apportioned to these gods, but also a memorial to the seven ages that were governed by each of the seven planets in succession. This idea can be traced in the establishment of the Jewish week with its Sabbath. ... The meaning of this passage [Gen. 2:2] is that in six world ages the heavens and earth were finally established, and that now, in the seventh age, no further changes in the cosmic order should be expected.[53]

---

[49] Harry Robert Turney-High (1974) *Ethnology of the Kutenai*, Draus: Mildwood, NY, p. 96.
[50] Dixon, *Oceanic Mythology*, p. 178.
[51] Christopher Lamb 'Buddhism.' In Jean Holm (editor) (1994) *Myth and History*, p. 29.
[52] Giorgio de Santillana & Hertha von Dechend (1969) *Hamlet's Mill (An Essay on Myth and the Frame of Time)*, Gambit: Boston, p. 3.
[53] Immanuel Velikovsky 'In the Beginning': unpublished material.

CHAP. XIV: THE WESTERN HEMISPHERE | 503

The very important concept that the Seventh Creation, the present one, is the last World Age, and that no further disturbances in the solar system ought be feared will be dealt with at length in later chapters. Suffice it to say for now, however, that the ancient astronomer-priests virtually universally appear to have agreed that Typhon Season #7 marked the very last time when a drastic shift in the precessional cycle would take place. Secure in that knowledge, the number seven became the preeminent esoteric numeral — employed in countless mythological and theological constructs. As Velikovsky argues above, another noticeable usage of the potent symbolism of the seven World Ages is in the formulation of the modern seven-day calendar week. Each of the week's seven days was, additionally, given a name based on one of the seven visible planets of the solar system.

Roman	English	German	French
dies Solis (Sun)	Sunday	Sonntang	
dies Lunae (Moon)	Monday	Montag	lundi
dies Mars (Mars)	Italian	Spanish	mardi
dies Jovis (Jupiter)	Giovedi	jueves	Jeudi
dies Veneris (Venus)	English	viernes	vendredi
dies Saturinis (Saturn)	Saturday	sabado	samedi

Table 14-1

According to the fourth century BCE Roman author Dio Cassius, the practice of dividing the week into seven days, in honour of the seven planets, was initiated by the Egyptians, and was later diffused to other places.[54] The French and Spanish words for Sunday, dimanche and domingo, from their Latin root signify "Day of the Lord." And sabado, Saturday, is from "Sabbath." The esoteric order of the seven days, differing slightly from the modern sequence, had Sunday, the Day of the Lord in the Judeao-Christian tradition, as the last of the seven days. Therefore, the sixth day, symbolising the Sixth Creation, was the Sabbath. As the end and beginning of the Sun Ages manifested themselves in a series of planetary cataclysms, "the ancients ... maintained that the successive ages were initiated

---

[54] Dio Cassius, 37: 186.

by planets: Moon, Saturn, Mercury, Jupiter, Venus, Mars. Therefore the sun-ages could also have been called planet ages."[55] These symbolic affiliations between the various celestial bodies and the world ages do not necessarily entail, as Velikovsky has alluded to in the previous quote, that each planet age's length was determined by a given period when a specific planet was more conspicuous than the others in the ancient skies. In most cases, the seven ages were each attributed an arbitrary length of one thousand years. The Syrian devil-worshipping sect of the Yezidis for example believed that the planetary gods would descend in turns upon the earth every thousand years to establish a new world order. In much the same vein, Julius Africanus wrote of historical ages governed under planets taking turns as celestial rulers.[56] Also, in their Sidra Rabba, the Mandaeans, while not subscribing to the length of a thousand years per age, professed that the seven world ages ending in catastrophe were each ruled by one of these seven planets. Although the World Ages were, in actual fact, really separated by the periodic tandem cataclysmic actions of the planets Mercury and Venus, it became a matter of convention to ascribe each of the World Ages to one of the seven visible planets of the solar system. The ancients' conviction that each one of the six World Ages which preceded the Seventh Creation were terminated in catastrophes, lends considerable credence to the catastrophist position that the planetary bodies, or "wanderers" of the solar system were not seen in ancient times as having always kept a stable orbital path.

---

[55] Immanuel Velikovsky 'Planet Ages': unpublished material.
[56] Cited in ibid.

15

The Libyans and Ethiopians Take Control of the Two Lands (945 BCE to 747 BCE)

The middle of the tenth century BCE, when the reign of the 18th Dynasty pharaoh Tuthmosis III came to an end, introduced an important new era in Egypt's history. This period saw the emergence of the Libyans to unprecedented power in the Nile Valley. Taking advantage of the power vacuum created by the death of King Tuthmosis III, the Libyans seized power in Egypt and established a new capital at Tanis, in Lower Egypt. The ascent of the Libyans in pharaonic Egypt during the middle of the tenth century BCE is not at all a novel concept. It is, in fact, the orthodox view among Egyptologists. Where the new chronology breaks with tradition is in my belief that the pharaoh whom Shoshenk I, the first king of the new Libyan dynasty, followed upon Egypt's throne was Tuthmosis III. The conventional framework, of course, places the reign of King Tuthmosis III in the Late Bronze Age. Completely unaware of the Great Time Warp of History, ancient historians believe that King Shoshenk I succeeded the standard 21st Dynasty — at a time when Egypt had fallen into the hands of powerful Theban priests. Conventionally known as the Third Intermediate Period, the era covered in this chapter will be shown to have really represented the remaining portion of the prosperous New Kingdom.

The Libyans were not, however, the only foreign power to dominate the late New Kingdom in Egypt. Soon after the Libyans gained supremacy in Tanis, the Ethiopians from the Kingdom of Napata, during the reign of the Judean king Asa, became the masters of Thebes — setting the stage for their eventual take over of the whole of Egypt in the middle of the eighth century BCE. This cohabitation of the Libyans and Ethiopians, in turn, coincided with the Homeric Heroic Age of the Greek King Minos — master of the Aegean. Again, this is a radical departure from orthodox scholarship. On the basis of Egyptian archaeological remains found in the Aegean, scholars have dated the legendary King Minos to the Late Bronze Age. But, as it's been abundantly made clear by now, the Egyptian relics unearthed together with the Linear-B tablets, in reality, belong to the Iron Age. It is the remains of the new chronology's late New Kingdom Libyan and Ethiopian pharaohs which, I believe, were discovered in the Aegean. This realization is the key behind the unravelling of the mystery of the Dark Age of Greece.

The Libyan Renaissance Era

The new chronology's contention that the Libyan Dynasty immediately followed the end of the Late Bronze Age, and Tuthmoside line of the 18th Dynasty, brings up an important question. What became of the rest of the 18th Dynasty — as it is conventionally known? Supporting the idea that this Iron Age 18th Dynasty's succession line is relatively faithful to the conventionally accepted framework, then where are Pharaohs Amenhotep II, Akhenaten, Horemheb and the others in the new chronology? To be sure, those pertinent questions had not escaped the new Libyan dynasts of the tenth century BCE either. They were indeed well-aware of the fact that the New Kingdom's 18th Dynasty had been in the process of attempting to imitate the dynastic succession of the Theban Renaissance's 14th Dynasty. The new Libyan pharaohs' ultimate decision to carry on with this entire ploy would have devastatingly confounding effects on modern scholarship. Indeed, it is my belief that, as it can be observed in the New Chronology Table, Pharaoh Shoshenk I, as well as several of the remaining Libyan pharaohs of the Iron IIa-b period, deliberately chose to take on a second royal name from the 18th Dynasty. Thus, they would ultimately be known by the gods, when in Lower Egypt, in their original Libyan throne name, and when they went to Thebes, in Upper Egypt, they would be referred to in their phantom 18th Dynasty names. My contention is therefore that Shoshenk I's alter ego was the 18th Dynasty's Pharaoh Amenhotep II, and that King Osorkon I is to be identified with Tuthmosis IV — while Shoshenk III chose to identify himself with Amenhotep III.

In Amenhotep II's Great Karnak Stela, we can find striking similarities with Shishak's campaigns in the Levant. The following excerpt from Stela in question records a battle in and around the vicinity of the Orontes on Year 2:

> First month of the third season (ninth month), day 26; his majesty crossed over the ford of the Orontes on this day, caused to cross [...] like the might of Montu of Thebes. His majesty raised his arm, in order to see the end of the earth; his majesty described a few Asiatics (*Sttyw*) coming on horses [...] coming at a [gallop] (*rkrk*). Behold, his majesty was equipped with his weapons of battle, his majesty conquered with the might [of Set] in his hour. They retreated when his majesty looked at one of them. Then his majesty himself overthrew their [...], with his spear [...]. Behold, he carried away this Asiatic [...], his horses, his chariots, and all his weapons of battle. His majesty returned with joy of heart [to] his father, Amon; he (his majesty) gave to him a feast [...].[1]

---

[1] J. H. Breasted, *Ancient Records of Egypt*, Vol. II - § 784.

CHAP. XV: THE LIBYANS AND ETHIOPIANS TAKE CONTROL | 507

The Great Karnak stela also informs us that Amenhotep II had a son who later became king Tuthmosis IV. In the Theban Renaissance, we know that Tuthmosis IV was the son of *Tuthmosis III* — not of Amenhotep II. Like Shishak, Amenhotep II is said to have conquered Asiatics and taken possession of their belongings. The reference to a highly organized chariotry force among the Asiatics further, in light of my revised historical scheme, serves to confirm the fact that Amenhotep II's campaign must have taken place during, and only in, the Iron Age. The description of Amenhotep II having "carried away" the spoils of the Asiatics to Egypt is highly reminiscent of the biblical account of Pharaoh Shishak who "took away the treasures of the king's house... took all ... [and] carried away also the shields of gold" belonging to the Israelites (2 Chr. 12:9). It is impossible, granted, to say with absolute certainty whether the two texts are in fact attempting to describe one and the same event but, at the very least, the context is very much similar.

The Theban succession sequence adopted by the Libyans did not exactly mirror that of the earlier Theban Renaissance's 14th Dynasty. As specified above, the Iron Age Amenhotep II (or Shishak I) had a son and heir named Tuthmosis IV — while during the Late Bronze Age, Amenhotep II and Tuthmosis IV (who himself ruled *earlier*) were most likely brothers. The revised framework also dictates that the Iron Age Amenhotep II would ascend the throne relatively abruptly — having not been raised as an heir to the Egyptian crown. As a matter of fact, a large stela, uncovered during the 1920s near the Great Sphinx at Gizah, bearing the name of Amenhotep II alludes precisely to such an unusual situation. On this particular document, Amenhotep II claims that he was chosen by the oracle of the Great Sphinx to be king. In gratitude, he built a chapel in honour of the oracle. If Amenhotep II was born as an heir to his divine father, Pharaoh of Egypt, why should he have been elated to, might I add *unexpectedly*, hear the news, relatively late in his young life, that he would one day be king?

It is interesting to note in addition that the Libyans, as evidenced by historical accounts from the time of Alexander the Great, were famous for their oracles. Evidently, the King Amenhotep II who received this revelation was not expecting to ever become Pharaoh of Egypt. An unexpected turn of events only could have caused him to accede to the throne. That watershed event was the Libyan invasion of Egypt at the end of the New Kingdom's Tuthmoside line of in Egypt. The reference to the oracle is a hint pointing to the Libyan origins of Amenhotep II/Shoshenk I. It is likewise of interest to note that a particular stela (see Fig. 15d) shows Tuthmosis IV (Osorkon I) — wearing the blue crown (a clear indication of its Iron Age status) — honouring a sphinx figure. Since King Tuthmosis IV/Osorkon I was the son of King Amenhotep II/Shoshenk I, it may quite safely be surmised that King Tuthmosis IV/Osorkon I continued being grateful to the Great Sphinx for the favour the latter had bequeathed upon his family.

Another indication of the newness of Shoshenk I/Amenhotep II's rule is the latter's inauguration of a "Renaissance Era." As Pharaoh Seti I had done as he turned a new militaristic page in Egypt's history early in the New Kingdom, Pharaoh Shoshenk I/Amenhotep II marked the new Libyan rule of Egypt by inaugurating the Renaissance Era. An inscription on the Festival Hall of Amenhotep II at Karnak mentions the Year 7 of the Renaissance Era.[2] No Pharaoh would have ever decreed a Renaissance Era unless a pivotal historical development was at hand.

The Biblical Shishak

Ever since Jean-François Champollion's identification of Pharaoh Shoshenk I as the biblical Shishak, one of only a very few firm archaeological links became, at long last, established between the biblical narratives and archaeology. While some scholars (e.g. Velikovsky and Rohl) have come along since then to challenge this basic link, it is still widely accepted as an accurate anchor point among scholarly circles. From that basic contention, I do not intend to waver. In fact, a stela of Shoshenk I (Shishak) was found in Megiddo during a 1925 excavation at the site by the University of Chicago's Oriental Institute. Scholars have long debated over which Strata at Megiddo relates to Shishak's campaign. My own view is that it occurred during Megiddo VI. The following table outlines the stratified levels at Megiddo during the Iron Age:

Chronology of Iron Age Megiddo:

Iron I	Megiddo VIIa	1,135 BCE - 945 BCE
Iron IIa	Megiddo VI-Vb	945 BCE - 828 BCE
- Invasion of Shoshenk I (Shishak) during Stratum VI.		
Iron IIb	Megiddo Va-IVb	828 BCE - 747 BCE
- Destruction of Va-IVa phase by Mars shift in 747 BCE.		

Table 15-1

---

[2] Charles F. Nims (1948) 'An Oracle Dated in "The Repeating of Births"', *Journal of Near Eastern Studies* Vol. 7 - Num. 3, pp. 157-162.

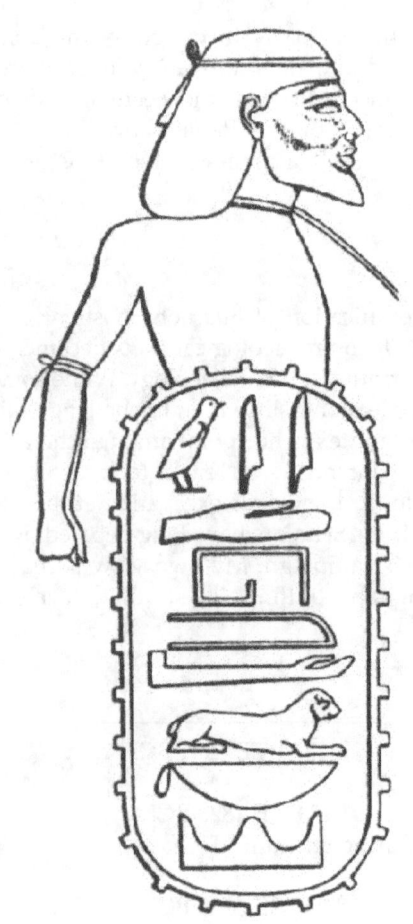

Fig. 15a: Captive from King Shoshenk's campaign believed to represent Israel.

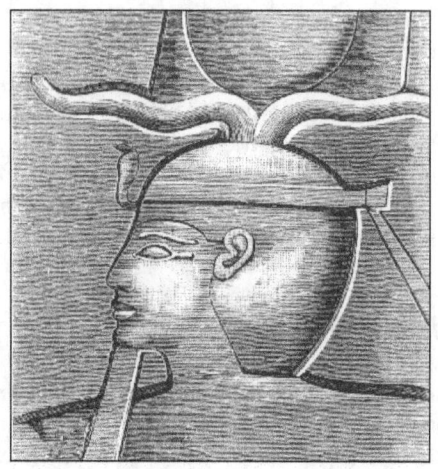

Fig. 15b: King Shoshenk I (Shishak).

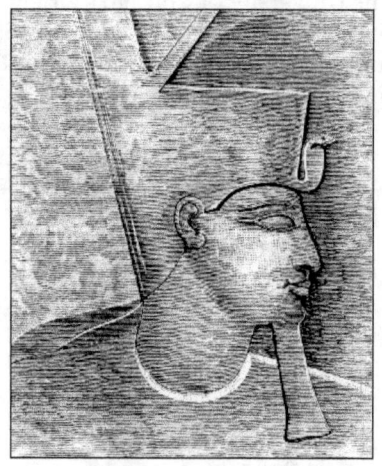

Fig. 15c: King Osorkon II.

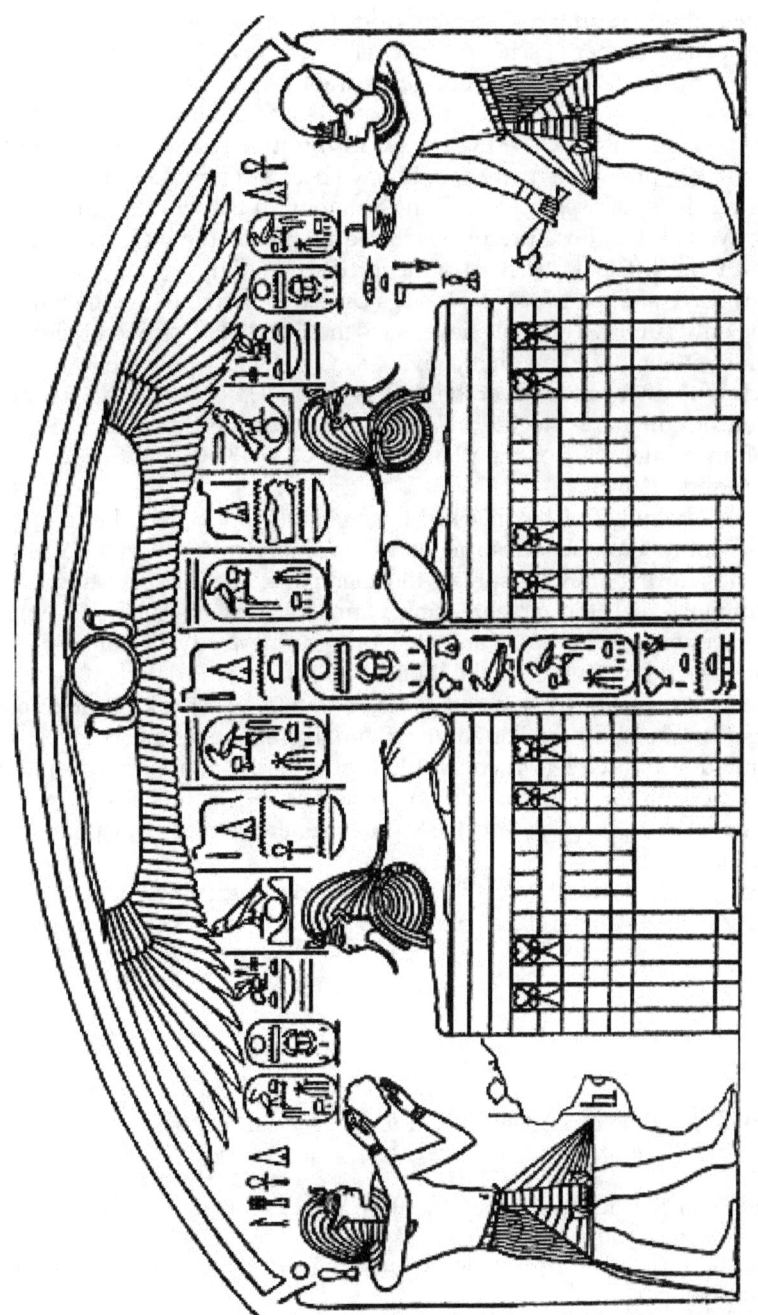

Fig. 15d: Tuthmosis IV (Osorkon I) making offerings to the Great Sphinx.

CHAP. XV: THE LIBYANS AND ETHIOPIANS TAKE CONTROL | 511

It is well known that Stratum Va-IVb were destroyed by a huge fire.[3] Based on that evidence, a vast number of scholars have felt it safe to deduce that this phase was annihilated by the attacking troops of Pharaoh Shishak.[4] This is how the end of Stratum Va-IVb at Megiddo came to be dated to *c.*925 BCE. Those dates are however much too high.[5] The high dates for Stratum Va-IVb result mainly from scholars' assumption that there should have been strongly fortified walls at Megiddo during the supposed reign of King Solomon in the tenth century BCE. Since Stratum Va-IVb fits those preconceived requirements, the high chronology became the orthodoxy. The destruction of the fortified buildings could only, in the minds of many, have marked the end of Israel's United Monarchy — with Pharaoh Shishak as the only culprit. The Bible never says that Shishak destroyed Megiddo however. In fact, it is more likely that activity, as G. I. Davies points out,[6] could have only picked up after he took over the city. As we shall later see, the destruction of the fortified buildings of Megiddo Va-IVb and other area sites, came about as a result of an orbital shift of the planet Mars in 747 BCE — not as a result of Shishak's raid in 925 BCE.

Therefore, the advent of Shishak marked the *beginning* of a new building phase at Megiddo — not its imminent destruction as a primary cultural centre. Similar building activity during Iron IIa spread to other parts of Syria-Palestine. Like Solomon (Tuthmosis III), the Israelite king Omri solicited the help of foreign architects from Phoenicia to build and decorate the new city of Samaria. He associated himself with King Ethbaal (Elibaal's son) — who later offered his daughter in marriage to Omri's son and successor Ahab. Shoshenk I's victorious campaign against the southern kingdom of Judah, following the split of the so-called United Monarchy (which would perhaps be more appropriately referred to as the "Tuthmoside Era") in the wake of King Tuthmosis-Solomon's death (1 Kings 14:25), served as a catalyst for a renewed period of pharaonic tutelage over the Israelites.

As Prof. Donald B. Redford of Pennsylvania State University noted, the accounts of Shoshenk I's military campaigns displayed at Karnak, bear striking resemblance

---

[3] David Ussishkin (1990) 'Notes on Megiddo, Gezer, Ashdod, and Tel Batash in the Tenth to Ninth Centuries B.C.', *Bulletin of the American Research Center in Egypt* 277-278, p. 74.
[4] See ibid, p. 73.
[5] Contra Yigael Yadin 'Solomon's City Wall and the Gate at Gezer.' In Harry M. Orlinsky (editor) (1981) *Israel Exploration Journal Reader*. Vols. I-II. KTVA: New York, pp. 132-138. Yadin saw the fortified walls of Megiddo Stratum IVB as evidence "of the historical authenticity of 1 Kings 9:15."
[6] G. I. Davies (1986) *Megiddo*, Lutterworth: Cambridge, p. 96.

to Pharaoh Tuthmosis III's military reliefs from the same temple complex.[7] Both Breasted and Velikovsky[8] had likewise made mention of that fact. This, in my opinion, is no accident. Unlike what Egyptologists may wish to think, and have us all believe, no period of five hundred years separated the two campaign reliefs. I would, instead suggest that Shoshenk I immediately succeeded Tuthmosis III, and used the latter's records as a source of inspiration for his own reliefs. The various Karnak battle scenes of the Late Bronze Age and early Iron Age pharaohs (Ramses II and Tuthmosis III in particular), would in fact serve as models for several of the new Libyan rulers. However, Shoshenk I would not merely be content with emulating Tuthmosis. The entire original dynastic line of the Late Bronze Age's Theban Renaissance would, for lack of a better word, be wholly "recycled" throughout the Iron Age. So here we are faced with the first example of two Dynasties being melted into one. Not only are we dealing with a literally "cloned" Dynastic line, but also with pharaohs adopting a "double identity." In the final analysis, we can see, as Donald B. Redford put it, that a lot of "role play"[9] was going on during the early 19th Dynasty of the revised chronology.

The war inscriptions from the Karnak temple's influence on the new 19th Dynasty of Libyan kings is not the only evidence putting them in a New Kingdom context. In the Berlin Staatliche Museum, there is a canopic chest[10] belonging to King Shoshenk I which bears unmistakably New Kingdom features. What makes this particular artifact an unusual object, artistically speaking, is that canopic chests — according to most Egyptologists — stopped being used at the end of the New Kingdom.[11] Therefore, in the standard chronology, the sudden re-emergence of its use following a presumed hiatus of over a century, is understandably rather puzzling. The conundrum is even more perplexing when one considers the fact that no such artifacts have been attributed to the standard 21st Dynasty kings — the dynasty which is thought to have immediately preceded Shoshenk I's line and followed the last conventional New Kingdom dynasty. If the standard 21st Dynasty, as received wisdom would have it, came immediately after the end of the New Kingdom, why is the change in artistic style so drastic? The truth is, the gap of over a century which separates the last Late Bronze Age Ramesside kings from

---

[7] Donald B. Redford (1992) *Egypt, Canaan, and Israel in Ancient Times*, Princeton University Press: Princeton, NJ, p. 314.
[8] Immanuel Velikovsky (1952) *Ages in Chaos*, Doubleday: Garden City, NY, p. 174. Velikovsky believed that Shishak and Tuthmosis III were one and the same person.
[9] Donald B. Redford (1973b) 'Studies in Relations Between Palestine and Egypt During the First Millennium B.C.', *Journal of the American Oriental Society* Vol. 93 - Num. 1, p. 13.
[10] Canopic jar/chest: A container in which the ancient Egyptians preserved the viscera of a deceased person usually for burial with the mummy.
[11] David M. Rohl (1995) *A Test of Time — Vol. I: The Bible (From Myth to History)*, Century: London, p. 378.

CHAP. XV: THE LIBYANS AND ETHIOPIANS TAKE CONTROL | 513

Shoshenk I, was not filled by the so-called 21st Dynasty, but by the new "alter ego" line begun under Ahmose in 1,135 BCE. This so-called 21st Dynasty will become, in the modified chronology, the very last Dynasty of pharaonic Egypt — the 31st Dynasty.

Evidently, a strong case can be presented to support my theory that Shoshenk I and Osorkon I closely followed Tuthmosis III (the biblical King Solomon) by examining some carved inscriptions found on two statues of the Libyan kings in question. First, the upper part of a statue of Osorkon I, found in Byblos in the 1890's, bears the following inscription:

> Statue which Elibaal, king of Byblos, son of Yehimilk, [king of Byblos], made [for] Baalat-Gebel, his lady. May Baalat-[Gebel] prolong [the days of] Elibaal and his years over [Byblos].

Several scholars, including Albright, have rightly concluded that this statement carved on Osorkon I's statue proves that this Libyan pharaoh and King Elibaal of Phoenicia were contemporaries. Second, the Shoshenk I statue, found in 1894, bears an inscription which clearly states that the statue was a gift from Egypt to the Phoenician king Abibaal — the immediate predecessor of Yehimilk, and a successor of King Ahiram. Now knowing, from the biblical texts, that Ahiram was a contemporary of King Solomon (2 Sam. 5:11; 1 Kings 10:11, 22; 2 Chr. 8:2), it would automatically follow that Shoshenk I and Osorkon I ruled in Egypt shortly after Solomon's reign. Since, in the new chronology, Kings Solomon and Tuthmosis III are shown to have been one and the same person, it follows that Shoshenk I acceded to Egypt's throne towards the end of Pharaoh Tuthmosis III's reign. As we've already seen, the evidence from Karnak seems to back up this theory. Using the stratigraphy of Megiddo as a reference guide for dating Shishak's campaign in Israel, we find that his punitive expedition occurred at the end of Stratum VIa.[12] Accepting archaeologist Israel Finkelstein's model, I would therefore suggest lowering Stratum Va-IVb at Megiddo (commonly believed to be the Solomonic city) to the ninth through eighth centuries BCE.[13]

The Ethiopian Invasion

The Libyans' claim over the Egyptian kingdom left behind by the New Kingdom Tuthmoside pharaohs wouldn't go unchallenged for very long. That challenge came from the south — Ethiopia. The Napatans, since King Atlanarsa's bold military foray into the Near Eastern world, had not lost their imperialistic *elan vital*. Some

---

[12] Israel Finkelstein (1996) 'The Archaeology of the United Monarchy: an Alternative View', *Levant* 28, p. 183.
[13] Ibid.

two hundred and ninety years later, they were now at it again. This time, the Napatan pharaoh responsible for the latest Ethiopian invasion was King Harsiotef. This theory is undoubtedly about to raise an awful lot of scholarly eyebrows. To begin with, the Napatan pharaoh Harsiotef is not supposed to have acceded to the Napatan throne until the year 404 BCE — according to historians. But in the new chronology which I propose, the Napatan kingly line buried at Nuri is aligned with King Atlanarsa (Arsa the Atlan) in the year 1,187 BCE. So there's about a five hundred-year gap between the conventional and revised schemes. In the revised chronology, the Ethiopian monarch who occupied the Napatan throne at the end of Osorkon I's reign in Egypt was King Harsiotef.

Evidence for an Ethiopian imperialistic push during the time of the Divided Monarchy in Israel can be found in the Second Book of Chronicles. In the reign of King Asa of Judah (913-873 BCE), a mighty Ethiopian army is said to have invaded Canaan from Egypt.

> 9 And there came out against them Zerah the Ethiopian with an host of a thousand, and three hundred chariots; and came unto Mareshah.
> 10 Then Asa went out against him, and they set the battle in array in the valley of Zephathah at Mareshah.
> (2 Chronicles 14:9-10)

Who was that Zerah who came out of Ethiopia to conquer Palestine? Why did he set out on this quest? And, perhaps most importantly, "how" did he reach Syria-Palestine? These are all very important questions which beg to be answered since, as Immanuel Velikovsky sagaciously observes:

> The way from Ethiopia to Palestine is along the valley of the Nile, and an Ethiopian army, in order to reach Palestine, would have had to conquer Egypt first.[14]

Had Egypt been conquered by the Ethiopians prior to Zerah's raid into Palestine? My theory is that Zerah was a general of the Napatan ruler Harsiotef who had, prior to Zerah's campaign, taken over Upper Egypt and had begun to rule from Thebes.

For a long time, many conventional historians have and still identify the biblical Zerah as the Libyan king Osorkon I.[15] But the Bible makes it clear that Zerah was an Ethiopian. There could not have been any confusion, in the mind of the Israelites, as far as distinguishing between Ethiopians and Libyans. In the Book of Chronicles,

---

[14] Immanuel Velikovsky (1952) *Ages in Chaos*, p. 209.
[15] See Edward H. Sugden (1928) *Israel's Debt to Egypt,* Epworth Press: London, p. 41.

CHAP. XV: THE LIBYANS AND ETHIOPIANS TAKE CONTROL | 515

Zerah the Ethiopian is said to have had a large contingent of Libyan soldiers among his troops (2 Chronicles 16:8). Hence if Zerah was a Libyan, he would have clearly been identified as such. He is said to have been Ethiopian because he *was* Ethiopian. To get around that hurdle, others have tried to suggest that Zerah was in fact a general of Osorkon I.[16] The rationale being that, since he commanded Libyan troops, Zerah must have been hired for his services by a Libyan pharaoh. Again, I emphatically disagree. General Zerah commanded Libyan troops because his Ethiopian pharaoh, Harsiotef, had seized the Upper Egyptian throne in Thebes and had subdued, apparently without much resistance, the Libyans monarchs in Tanis. Actually, a sort of alliance seems to have been struck between the Ethiopians and the Libyans at that time. The Ethiopians seem to have been contented to govern Upper Egypt, while the Libyans carried on ruling from their administrative centre at Tanis. The standard 22nd Dynasty (new 19th Dynasty) rulers are indeed recognized as having been Tanite kings. Thus, it would logically follow suit that King Harsiotef ought to have been a Theban monarch. Although this is evident in the new chronology, Egyptologists have not recognized him as such. Besides, at the same time when I place the Napatan king Harsiotef's arrival in Thebes, conventional historians record the existence of a Libyan pharaoh of Thebes by the name of "Harsiese." This Theban king's reign represents somewhat of a puzzle for Egyptologists because, despite being traditionally relegated to the conventional 22nd Dynasty (a Tanite dynasty), he clearly is a Theban ruler. Perplexed by this anomaly, Egyptologist D. A. Aston argues that Harsiese should be eliminated from the list of Tanite kings of the standard 22nd Dynasty (new 19th Dynasty). He explains:

> The Twenty-second Dynasty was definitely Tanite, whereas Harsiese, known only from Theban monuments, was clearly a Theban king ...[17]

The similarity between the two names, Harsiotef and Harsiese, is by no means a mere coincidence. King Harsiotef and Pharaoh Harsiese were one and the same person. Harsiese, as Aston postulates, does not belong in the new 19th Dynasty because he simply has no place there. He was not a Libyan Tanite dynast but was, in reality, an Ethiopian king — Harsiotef. Harsiese, his Egyptian name, has been included, in the Manethonian framework, as part of the Libyan standard 22nd Dynasty because of Harsiotef's contemporaneity with that dynasty.

On a stela found at Gebel Barkal in the Sudan, dated to the 35th year of King Harsiotef, the latter recounts how he learned in a dream that Amun had chosen

---

[16] See J. Daniel Hays (1998) 'From the Land of the Bow: Black Soldiers in the Ancient Near East', *Bible Review* Vol. 14 - Num. 4, p. 32.
[17] D. A. Aston (1989) 'Takelot II — A King of the "Theban Twenty-Third Dynasty"?', *Journal of Egyptian Archaeology* 75, pp. 139-140.

him to occupy the Egyptian throne.[18] Déjà vu? Didn't the Libyan pharaoh Shoshenk I have a dramatically similar dream (only with the Great Sphinx as bearer of the message instead of Amun)? Mere coincidence? Or indisputable proof of contemporaneity? After having been called upon by Amun, Harsiotef journeyed to Napata for his coronation. It's obvious that Harsiotef/Harsiese had been inspired by the tale of Shoshenk I/Amenhotep II. Both of them came to power in Egypt, not as legitimate heirs, but after having "acquired" legitimacy through a successful conquest from without.

If my new chronology is accurate, it would mean that the Napatan kings conventionally dated to the fourth century BCE were, in reality, ruling contemporarily with the eighth century BCE Libyan rulers of the standard 22nd Dynasty (new 19th Dynasty). This finding is further confirmed by the work of ancient historians and new chronologists Peter James, and his several associates, who, referring to the following two fourth century BCE Ethiopian kings: Menmaetre-setepen-Amun and Ary-mery-Amun, observe:

> Both of these Nubian kings have been dated to the 4th century BC, but a number of factors suggest that they were contemporary with the Libyan rules of Egypt in the post-Ramesside period.[19]

Among these factors is the fact that King Ary-mery-Amun (again conventionally dated to the fourth century BCE), "adopted the same throne-names as Shoshenk III of the 22nd Dynasty."[20] James *et al.* also remark that, in the case of King Menmaetre-setepen-Amun, whose supposed fourth century BCE cartouches were found at Kawa and Gebel Barkal, there is strong evidence of a late New Kingdom influence in his chosen throne name. Therefore, if we accept that King Harsiotef (who is also presumed to have been a fourth century BCE Napatan ruler) was none other than King Harsiese of the standard 22nd Dynasty, we may hope to find similar traces of New Kingdom influence associated with the latter. Such confirming evidence is indeed available.

A fragment from the Pennsylvania University Museum (E.16186), may help us to prove both of the new chronology's propositions that King Harsiese ruled during the New Kingdom *and* during the ninth century BCE. The object in question is a wooden fragment from Abydos, inscribed with the name of the daughter of King Harsiese. The fragment apparently comes from a coffin. Egyptologist John H. Taylor believes that the name should be read: *T-di-t-nbt-hn*. He paid particular attention to the last part of the name: *hn*.

---

[18] A. J. Arkell (1974 [1961]) *A History of the Sudan (From the Earliest Times to 1821)*, Greenwood Press: Westport, Conn., p. 155.
[19] Peter James *et al.* (1991a) *Centuries of Darkness (A Challenge to the Conventional Chronology of Old World Archaeology)*, Jonathan Cape: London, p. 217.
[20] Ibid.

> At the top of the fragment are the legs and feet of a bird, followed by the *nb* hieroglyph and a sign which is a form of the box *hn*. This last is a very rare element in personal names. ... the phrase may refer to Nut's well-known symbolic association with the coffin, since *hn* **sometimes occurs as a word for 'coffin' in the New Kingdom.**[21]

Later, Taylor states:

> ... Thus all the available evidence indicates that the name *T-di-t-nb(t)-hn* was typical of the period between *c.*900 and *c.*700 BC, in the first half of which Harsiese's rule falls.[22]

The fragment originally belonged to a coffin; and we know that the rare element of her name: *hn*, was used in the New Kingdom to refer to a "coffin." Finally, Taylor confirms that the fragment fits within the new chronology dates for Harsiese of the ninth century BCE. Given this scenario, it is not surprising that the daughter of Harsiotef would identify herself with Nut, and hence to the coffin. As in the case of Pharaoh Shoshenk I's canopic chest, we again find ourselves confronted with a New Kingdom practice in a tenth to ninth century BCE context.

Akhenaten: The Heretic King

Pharaoh Harsiotef would be followed on the Theban and Napatan thrones by his son and heir Akhraten. The latter did not have the expansionistic ambitions which his father had. In fact, King Akhraten was very much of a pacifist and, to boot, the father of our commonly familiar form of monotheism. The readers may have already understood that my intention is to equate the Napatan king Akhraten with the dynastic Egyptian king Akhenaten of the conventional 18th Dynasty. To begin with, the names are strikingly similar. What is more, it would appear that Akhraten likewise distanced himself from the traditional cult of Amun. The Napatan cult of Amun was at Pnubs, situated in the region north of Kawa between Dongola and Tumbos at the southern limit of the Third Cataract.

> A temple of importance dedicated to Amun existed at Pnubs during the time of the early Kushite kings since it figures among the four great centres of Amun-worship to which King Anlamani dedicated his four sisters as

---
[21] John H. Taylor (1988) 'BRIEF COMMUNICATIONS: A daughter of King Harsiese', *Journal of Egyptian Archaeology* 74, p. 230.
[22] John H. Taylor (1988) p. 231.

sistrum players, and it was visited by Anam-nete-yerike, Harsiotef, and Nastasen during the coronation voyages. The three other centres of Amun-worship, Gebel Barkal, Sanam, and Kawa, boasted temples built by the Twenty-fifth Dynasty kings, at the first by Piankhy and the last by Taharqa.[23]

It is interesting to note that King Akhraten, who reigned between Harsiotef and Nastasen (who were both crowned at the temple of Amun), is not listed as a contributor to the cult of Amun at Pnubs. Why the conspicuous sudden break with tradition on the part of Akhraten? The apparent discontinuity in the Napatan Amun worship during the reign of Pharaoh Akhraten can be explained by the fact that he had renounced the Theban god Amun, in favour of the solar worship of Aten. Overlooking his father's Egyptian capital at Thebes, Akhenaten (or Akhraten) decided to establish his own Egyptian capital at the ancient Upper Egyptian town of Tell el-Amarna. Akhenaten's traditional association with the Late Bronze Age pharaoh Amenhotep IV stems from the former's consequential choice of Tell el-Amarna as his Egyptian capital. Akhenaten himself evidently laid the foundations for this modern misconception by, in the same fashion as the Libyan Lower Egyptian pharaohs of his day were doing, consciously identifying himself with the long-deceased pharaoh.

Led astray by the Great Time Warp of History, Egyptologists have erroneously deduced that Akhenaten was the son of the Late Bronze Age pharaoh Amenhotep III. But Akhenaten never claimed to have been the son of Amenhotep III. The one and only piece of evidence which scholars cling to, in terms of identifying Akhenaten as King Amenhotep III's son, is the identification in the Amarna and Boghazköy records which mention Nibhururiya (Amenhotep IV) as the son of Naphuria (Amenhotep III). But, in the new chronology, we find that Pharaoh Akhenaten in fact ruled numerous centuries after the Boghazköy records were written. Moreover, these Hurrian-sounding names undoubtedly belong in a historical context where the Hurrians were in a position of influence. As we know, when Pharaoh Amenhotep IV reigned at Tell el-Amarna, the Hurrians were the preeminent ethnic group in Canaan. Therefore, it is entirely conceivable that Amenhotep III and Amenhotep IV adopted Hurrian names in order, perhaps, to further legitimize their suzerainty over the Hurrians of Canaan. However, on the other hand, Akhenaten could not possibly have had any dealings whatsoever with the Hurrians since their empire had completely disappeared by the end of the Late Bronze Age.

On the basis of this supposed link between Hurrians and Akhenaten, ancient historians have tended to look for an Indo-Aryan origin for his revolutionary brand of monotheism. Delineating this tendency, Martin Bernal writes:

---

[23] Helen Jacquet-Gordon, Charles Bonnet & Jean Jacquet (1969) 'Pnubs and the Temple of Tabo on Argo Island', *Journal of Egyptian Archaeology* 55, p. 110.

Egyptologists paid particular attention to giving him and his new religion Aryan, or at least northern, credentials. Petrie claimed that the religion had originated in the Hurrian-speaking northern kingdom of Mitanni, from where, he alleged, Akhenaton's grandfather, mother and wife had all come.[24]

Obviously, Pharaoh Akhenaten's family, or his religious movement, could not have hailed from an Indo-Aryan kingdom. By this time, the Late Bronze Age empire of Mitanni had already disappeared over half a millennium ago; and the once mighty Anatolian Hittite empire was nothing but a distant memory. The origins of Akhenaten's Amarnian revolution stem from the Black Land. It was an adaptation of the primordial Heliopolitan solar cult, as D. W. Thomas outlines below:

> ... There is, however, a continually increasing body of evidence which points to the fact that the cult of Ten had developed before the time of Amenhotep IV [Akhenaten], indeed probably as early as the reign of Thutmose IV (c.1411-1397 B.C.). It is likely that the worship of Ten developed from the ancient cult of the Heliopolitan sun-god Re. In the course of time the syncretistic character of Egyptian religious thinking had led to the fusion of the god Re with many other deities such as Atum, Horus, and Amun, with the consequent assimilation of their characteristics and functions. The new cult paid homage to the physical orb of the sun (for which the Egyptian word was Ten) ... Central to the new faith was the idea of "living on ma'at." This important term ma'at, variously translated "righteousness, justice," or "truth," meant basically the divinely ordained cosmic order. By the Middle Kingdom it had acquired the overtones of social justice.[25]

Ten or Tum was actually a form of "Atum" in Heliopolitan theology. Indeed, basing his argument on Donald B. Redford's book Akhenaton, Egyptologist Ian Shaw explains that *"the Heliopolitan cult of the sun is widely considered to have exerted a considerable influence on the roots of Atenism."*[26] Shaw also notices that Akhenaten seemed to have acknowledged this debt by erecting a temple called "Which-lifts-Re-in-Heliopolis-of-Re."[27]

---

[24] Martin G. Bernal (1987a) *Black Athena (The Afroasiatic Roots of Classical Civilization) — Volume I: The Fabrication of Ancient Greece 1785-1985*, Vintage: London, p. 383.
[25] D. Winton Thomas (editor) (1958) *Documents from Old Testament Times*, Thomas Nelson: London.
[26] Ian Shaw (1994) 'Balustrades, Stairs and Altars in the Cult of the Aten at El-Amarna', *Journal of Egyptian Archaeology* 80, pp. 119-121.
[27] Ian Shaw (1994) pp. 119-121.

In addition, the Khemetic roots of Akhenaten are further confirmed by his particular predilection for the classic Ptolemaic *hemhem*-crown. Surveying the long history of the usage of this specific crown, Nubiologist L. V. Zabkar observes:

> Now, the hemhem-crown certainly originated in Egypt, probably during the Eighteenth Dynasty. Its oldest occurrences seem to be in the representation of Akhenaton in the tomb of Panehesi at Amarna, and on the back of Tutankhamun's gold-plated throne. From Egypt, probably during the Nineteenth Dynasty, this crown passed into the Egyptian temples of Nubia then further into Napata... and finally into Meroe. In Egypt it was widely used by Ptolemaic kings... From then on it is represented so frequently in the reliefs of the temples of Philae, Edfu, Kom Ombo, Dendera, and elsewhere, that is seems unnecessary to refer to its occurrence in a more detailed manner.[28]

Within the context of the new chronology, this order is completely reversed. In reality, the usage of the *hemhem*-crown originated, as we've seen in Chapter 2, with the Khemetic Horus-the-Elder pharaohs of the New Horus Period. Subsequently, it was transported into Ethiopia, as the Horus-the-Child pharaohs of dynastic Egypt never adopted it. It thereafter resurfaced in Egypt during the New Kingdom. The founding pharaohs of the standard 19th Dynasty (new 15th Dynasty), after having sojourned at length in the Kingdom of Meroë (where the *hemhem*-crown was naturally much revered), were the very first dynastic pharaohs to wear this distinctly Khemetic crown. While the Napatan and Meroitic pharaohs continued to wear it, the native Egyptian kings of the 18th Dynasty again abandoned it. Finally, it was Akhraten, the Napatan monarch, along with his father's conquering Napatan dynasty, who once again made the *hemhem*-crown a much-esteemed kingly symbol. A very similar history can be traced for the Khemetic double-plume crown — which Akhenaten also characteristically wore.[29]

The Amarna Letters: A Continuing Story

At any rate, Pharaoh Akhraten did significantly more than merely symbolically adopt Amenhotep IV's ancient capital. He also reinstituted Tell el-Amarna as a centre of correspondences with the various chiefdoms and city-states of Syria-Palestine. Like I have postulated earlier in Chapter 10, a second corpus of texts began circulating at the site in the ninth century BCE. These were stored on top of the much older correspondences. The new archives were also apparently modelled

---

[28] L. V. Zabkar (1975) *Apedemak: Lion God of Meroe (A Study in Egyptian-Meroitic Syncretism)*, Aris & Phillips: Warminster, U.K., pp. 102-103.
[29] See Julia Samson (1977) 'Nefertiti's Regality', *Journal of Egyptian Archaeology* 63, p. 93.

CHAP. XV: THE LIBYANS AND ETHIOPIANS TAKE CONTROL | 521

after the Late Bronze Age II cuneiform letters. I am not the first author to suggest such a drastic shift in the accepted dates for the Amarna correspondences. In the 1950s, Immanuel Velikovsky wrote:

> According to my chronological scheme, the letters of el-Amarna, sent and received by Amenhotep III and Akhenaton, were written, not in −1410 to −1370 as is generally accepted, but in −870 to −840, at the time of King Jehosaphat in Jerusalem.[30]

Although Immanuel Velikovsky and I have arrived at this conclusion by using different methods, unlike his chronological scheme, I maintain that an original Late Bronze Age archive existed before the ninth century letters. Moreover, dating the reign of King Akhenaten to c.860-828 BCE, I concur with Immanuel Velikovsky's hypothesis that the former was a contemporary of the Judean king Jehosaphat. While most Egyptologists believe that Akhenaten ruled for only 17 years, evidence does exist to support the view that he may have indeed reigned longer. For example, extant documents mention "Year 18"[31] and "Year 21"[32] of his reign. Despite this clear evidence, as Egyptologist Keith Seele illuminates, *"these were discarded by the members of the expedition [of the Egypt Exploration Society at Amarna] owing to their preconceived notions of the chronology of Akhenaton's reign."*[33] Modern scholars' preconceived notions have, in fact, led to very grave misinterpretations about Akhenaten and his reign. Chief among these misconceptions is ancient historian's erroneous belief that Akhenaten ruled in the Late Bronze Age. In fact, several Amarna correspondences indicate that letters were sent to Akhenaten from Syria-Palestine during the Divided Monarchy period of Israel.

About sixty letters found at the site of Tell el-Amarna were written by the king of "Sumur." The latter wrote so much that Akhenaten replied: "Thou writest to me more than all the regents." This land of Sumur (also Sumura) must actually be recognized as the biblical Samaria (Semer or Somron in Hebrew).[34] Samaria was only built during the reign of Omri, father of Ahab (1 Kings 16:24). Therefore, the Amarna letters, which mention the town of Sumura (Samaria) over one hundred times, could not possibly predate the reign of King Omri (880-873 BCE). In addition, the city of "Urusalim" mentioned in the Amarna letters can be none other than Jerusalem. We may recall that during the reign of the original Amenhotep IV, in

---

[30] Immanuel Velikovsky (1952) *Ages in Chaos*, p. 229.
[31] Fairman in *City of Akhenaten*, Part II, 104, n. 1.
[32] Gunn in *City of Akhenaten*, Part I, 165, n. 1.
[33] Keith C. Seele (1955) 'King Ay and the Close of the Amarna Age', *Journal of Near Eastern Studies* Vol. 14 - Num. 3, p. 175.
[34] Immanuel Velikovsky (1952) *Ages in Chaos*, pp. 229-330.

the LBII period, the city of Jerusalem did not yet bare that name, but was known simply as "Salem." Also, Professor Nadav Na'aman from Tel Aviv University conveys that *"Urusalim* is undoubtedly identical with Jerusalem ..."[35] Since the name of Jerusalem did not actually come into use until the Iron Age, we must therefore conclude that the Amarna letters, referring to the city of Urusalem (Jerusalem), should likewise be dated to the Iron Age.

Another city frequently mentioned in the Amarna archives is that of "Gubla" — believed by some to be the city of Byblos (Gwal of the Phoenicians). Disputing this hypothesis, Dr Velikovsky argues instead that Gubla was really Jezreel — the other capital in Israel during the Divided Monarchy period.[36] Indeed, the king of Gubla repeatedly makes clear of his intentions to supplant Sumur (Samaria) as capital of Israel from the hands of the Syrians — which he eventually succeeds in doing. Since Samaria was built by Omri, and Jezreel by his son Ahab, we may suppose that the "King of Gubla" mentioned in the Amarna letters was none other than King Ahab himself. In the New Chronology Table, we see that Ahab would indeed have been a contemporary of Akhenaten. Incidentally, Velikovsky also believed that the Stela of King Mesha of Moab, as well as the inscriptions of the Assyrian king Shalmanaser III, must all be contemporaneous with the el-Amarna letters of Pharaoh Akhenaten's time.[37] Again, the New Chronology Table confirms this inference. In the final analysis, between *c.*860 BCE and 828 BCE, we find Pharaoh Akhenaten ruling in Egypt, Jehosaphat in Jerusalem, Ahab in Samaria, Ben-Hadad in Damascus, and Shalmanaser III in Assyria. In Phoenicia, King Abimilku was the ruler. In one of the Amarna letters (EA 89), we learn that, following the murder of the king of Phoenicia, Pharaoh at once intervened and personally appointed a certain "Abimilku" as king of Tyre.

In line 52 of a particular Amarna correspondence (EA 151) addressed to King Akhenaten, from the vassal king Abimilku of Tyre, is mentioned "the country of Danuna." Several scholars were initially of the view that Abimilku spoke of the Greek Danaans — proving that there were contacts between Greece and Phoenicia at the time of the Amarna correspondences. That idea makes perfect sense; but a serious problem arises if we hold on to the traditional date for Akhenaten's reign. Conventional historians maintain that EA 151 was written sometime around 1,365 BCE. But since we know, according to the present revised history, that the Nordic Danaans did not arrive in Egypt, or the Near East, prior to the time of Pharaoh Merneptah, then Abimilku could not have written about "the country of Danuna"

---

[35] Nadav Na'aman (1996) 'The Contribution of the Amarna Letters to the Debate on Jerusalem's Political Position in the Tenth Century B.C.E.', *Bulletin of the American Schools of Oriental Research* 304, p. 19; H. J. Franken & M. L. Steiner (1992) 'Urusalim and Jebus', *Zeitschrift für die alttestamentliche Wissenschaft* 104, pp. 110-111.
[36] Immanuel Velikovsky (1952) *Ages in Chaos*, p. 232.
[37] Ibid, p. 229.

prior to the reign of Merneptah! Few scholars have seriously considered the relationship between the Danaans of the Amarna archives and those of Merneptah's reign and of the Peoples of the Sea war. William F. Albright, obviously speaking of the Danaans that King Abimilku described in the ninth century BCE, writes:

> ... But there can be no reasonable doubt in the first centuries of the Iron Age *Danana* or *Danona* did refer to the tribes of Greek Affiliation, since it appears in Phoenician inscriptions of the 9th and 8th centuries as the name of the peoples of Cilicia ...[38]

Thus, there is strong corroborating evidence for dating EA 151 to the ninth century BCE. Moreover, from solid surviving epigraphic evidence, we *know* that the Phoenicians had contacts with Greek "Danaans" in the ninth century BCE — since they *tell* us so. Incidentally, proving such contacts in the fourteenth century BCE is a bit more problematic. Critiquing Albright's above statement, Michael C. Astour writes:

> But both Albright and Hanfmann did not take into consideration, or have deliberately by-passed a difficulty which cannot be harmonized with their construction; the presence in this very same spot, two centuries before the migration of the Peoples of the Sea, of a country with the very same name of Danuna, clearly attested in the Amarna letter of Abimilki.[39]

Michael C. Astour gets around this problem by differentiating between the Iron Age inhabitants of Cilicia — whom he personally prefers to call the "Danunians," and the Homeric "Danaans." His theory is that the Cilician Danunians were the direct descendants of the Homeric Danaans.[40] Consequently, I believe that such a distinction is baseless and illusionary. No Danaans roamed around anywhere near Phoenicia two centuries before the Peoples of the Sea invasion. Since Homer's Heroic Age is now found in the Iron Age, no elaborate theory needs to be devised to account for a problem that does not exist. The Cilician Danaans (Astour's Danunians) were one and the same as the Homeric Danaans. They became major players in the Mediterranean world in, and only in, the Iron Age.

Another important group of people mentioned in the Tell el-Amarna archives are the "Habiru." From the correspondences sent to Akhenaten, we learn that the

---

[38] William F. Albright (1950) 'Some Oriental Glosses on the Homeric Problem', *American Journal of Archaeology* 54, p. 172.
[39] Michael C. Astour (1967) *Hellenosemitica (An Ethnic and Cultural Study in West Semitic Impact on Mycenaean Greece)*, E. J. Brill: Leiden, p. 15.
[40] Ibid, p. 15.

king of Jerusalem implored Pharaoh to send troops to defend his city-state from the sustained attacks of foreign invaders. Among these foreign hordes were the infamous Habiru — invading from the east; and the army of the King of Hatti (neo-Hittites) menacing from the north. At this juncture, is there any evidence of heavy fortifications in Canaan during this time, which might corroborate the inhabitants' fear of a foreign invasion? In fact, there is. Having lowered the chronology of the Iron Age fortifications in Syria-Palestine, we now find that the monumental buildings of Megiddo, and other major biblical sites, first began appearing in the ninth century BCE — not during the accepted time-frame for the United Monarchy.[41] These are now placed in the historical context of the Omrid dynasty. However, many biblical scholars, accepting the "Myth of Solomon," still contend that the fortified towns of Iron Age Palestine belong to the tenth century BCE.[42] But that argument has been refuted by Kathleen Kenyon, who wrote:

> In spite of the attraction of the theory that the buildings represent one of Solomon's chariot cities, planning, building style and pottery evidence all point to the approximate contemporaneity of this stratum [Megiddo IV] with the first layout of Samaria.[43]

According to Kenyon, Omri had founded Samaria "on virgin soil"[44] six years after his accession in 880 BCE. Moreover, by lowering Megiddo's Stratum Va-IVb slightly further than Dame Kenyon has, I should instead propose that Stratum Va-IVb immediately *succeeded* the Omrid dynasty. Nonetheless, it is wholly evident that King Omri provided the initial impulse for the imposing Israelite building styles contemporary with King Akhenaten's Amarnian period and the latter's successor, Amenhotep III. It is quite probable that such strong fortifications had become necessary to withstand the repeated attacks of the bellicose Habiru — whom I identify as the Aramaeans.[45]

The Aramaeans, hailing from the land of Aram, occupied a region extending from the Lebanon Mountains on the west, eastward to the Euphrates river, and on the north from the Taurus Mountains and southward to Damascus.[46] An ancient people which traces is roots back to the Early Bronze IV era, they finally became an organized kingdom after the collapse of the Hittite empire at the culmination of the

---

[41] See G. J. Wightman (1990) 'The Myth of Solomon', *Bulletin of the American Schools of Oriental Research* 277-278, pp. 5-20.
[42] That position was adopted by, among others, W. F. Albright and Y. Yadin.
[43] Kathleen Kenyon (1970) *Archaeology in the Holy Land*. Third edition. Ernest Benn: London, p. 271.
[44] Ibid, p. 33.
[45] Israel Finkelstein (1996) p. 185.
[46] Herbert Lockyer (editor) *Nelson's Illustrated Bible Dictionary*, Thomas Nelson: Nashville, p. 83.

CHAP. XV: THE LIBYANS AND ETHIOPIANS TAKE CONTROL | 525

Late Bronze Age. Describing how these Aramaeans rose to power in the Iron Age, Professor Hélène Sader of the American University of Beirut writes:

> ... The breakdown of Hittite power also freed the North Syrian vassal city-states from foreign hegemony, leaving them at the same time without military support. In the absence of written documentation from North Syria dating to that period, we can make only one observation: the Late Bronze Age North Syrian kingdoms ceased to exist: Tunip, Nila, Qatna, Amurru, Nukhashe, disappear from the texts and from the map. They were replaced in the 10th century by new geopolitical entities: the Aramaean kingdoms.[47]

In brief, the Aramaean confederation of the Iron Age came to existence as a result of the collapse of the Anatolian Hittite empire. The LBII kingdom of Amurru disintegrated into an impoverished clan-based community of peasants by the time Akhenaten and Ahab came to power in their respective states. As the Amurru were known as the Habiru at the time of Suppiluliumas, it was only logical for the Aramaeans, as the direct descendants of the Amurru, to be referred to as Habirus as well. Like the Habirus of the Amarna letters, Dr Sader, quoting from the Assyrian texts, describes the Iron Age Aramaeans as *"extremely mobile ... without king or chief, kingdom or fortified cities."*[48] Therefore, the Habiru were a stateless people living in the hill-country, selling their services as mercenaries to different rulers.

The Dark Age of Greece

Evidence for placing Akhenaten's reign in the ninth century BCE does not only exist in Syria-Palestine, but also in the Aegean. The problem is that I believe archaeologists have mistakenly dated these ancient relics to the Late Bronze Age — having been lead astray by the conventional chronology of ancient Egypt. As discussed before, this is the primary cause behind the creation of the fallacious concept of the Dark Age of Greece. In fact, before 1870, the very notion of a Dark Age of Greece did not even exist in ancient world scholarship. Prior to that time, the Heroic Age described by Homer was thought of as a legend — probably based on ninth to eighth centuries BCE Greece.[49] After 1870 however, the following two

---

[47] Hélène Sader 'The 12th Century B.C. in Syria; The Problem of the Rise of the Aramaeans.' In William A. Ward & Martha Sharp Joukowsky (editors) (1992) *The Crisis Years: The 12th Century B.C. (From Beyond the Danube to the Tigris)*, p. 159.
[48] Ibid.
[49] See Ian Morris 'Periodization and the Heroes: Inventing a Dark Age.' In Mark Golden & Peter Toohey (editors) (1997) *Inventing Ancient Culture (Historicism, Periodization, and the Ancient World)*, pp. 96-131.

landmark events would come along to radically alter this accepted image: (1) German merchant Heinrich Schliemann's (1822-1890) acclaimed discovery of the Greek Bronze Age and (2) Egyptologist Sir Flinders Petrie's (1853-1942) synchronism of Mycenaean Greece with Egypt's conventional 18th Dynasty. A pre-twelfth century BCE Heroic Age was then immediately catapulted out of the realms of legend and into historical reality — separated by no less than five centuries from the age of the lyric poets.

Schliemann set out to ancient Troy, Hissarlik, with the intention of taking Homer seriously. His ambition was, from the onset, to discover the ruins of the legendary ancient Troy. As an amateur archaeologist, his unrefined excavation techniques destroyed much of the evidence; but what he found at Hissarlik and the Aegean revolutionized ancient world scholarship. In Mycenae, Heinrich Schliemann unearthed several Egyptian artifacts bearing the royal cartouches of Pharaohs Amenhotep II, Amenhotep III, Akhenaten, and Queen Tiy. In his mind, this was undeniable proof that the Greek Mycenaean Age of the classical epics, along with Homer's Troy, belonged in the Late Bronze Age. Subsequently, the noted British Egyptologist Sir Flinders Petrie, gave Egyptology's seal of approval to the theory based on the correlation between Mycenaean Greece and Late Bronze Age Egypt. Another British excavator, Sir Arthur Evans (1851-1941), finally analogized Schliemann's Mycenaean Greece with the Late Minoan period in Crete — which he called Minoan civilization. In Crete, was found a circular seal belonging to Queen Tiy, the wife of King Amenhotep III — apparently further vindicating Arthur Evans' hypothesis. With these sacred pillars, the foundations of modern classical archaeology were erected.

In the spring of 1880, Heinrich Schliemann met a young architect by the name of Wilhelm Dörpfeld, who would later become his assistant during his last campaign at Troy. Arthur Evans later described Dörpfeld as "Schliemann's greatest find." Wilhelm Dörpfeld was one of the very first archaeologists to notice that all was not well with the idyllic picture drawn up of the Late Bronze Age Aegean since Schliemann's excavations. Dörpfeld remained entirely convinced, until the time of his death, that the Greek geometric ware and Dorian pottery discovered in the Aegean – which are dated to the first millennium BCE – were in fact contemporaneous with, or even preceded, Mycenaean Greece (of the second millennium BCE). According to Dörpfeld, geometric and Mycenaean ware were found together in Olympia, Troy and Tiryns.[50] In Dörpfeld's words: *"This geometric style is very old; it existed before and next to the Mycenaean art, nor was it replaced by it."*[51]

The dilemma was clear but unsolvable. How could Iron Age artifacts be found in a clearly Late Bronze Age context, and vice-versa? Many scholars, chief among

---

[50] Clark Whelton 'Velikovsky's "Dark Age of Greece".' In Milton Zysman & Clark Whelton (editors) (1990) *Catastrophism 2000 (A Sourcebook for the Conference: Reconsidering Velikovsky)*, p. 258.
[51] Wilhelm Dörpfeld (1935) *Alt-Olympia*, Berlin, Vol. I: p. 12.

Fig. 15e: King Akhenaten, Queen Nefertiti and children worshipping the Aten sun-disc.

Fig. 15f: King Shoshenk-Amenhotep III and Queen Tiy (Cairo Museum).

CHAP. XV: THE LIBYANS AND ETHIOPIANS TAKE CONTROL | 529

whom Adolf Furtwangler, dismissed Dörpfeld as an "ignoramus" — pointing out that Greek geometric ware could not possibly belong to the Late Bronze Age. The tide in the academic world swept in the favour of Dörpelfd's detractors. In the end, Dörpfeld's own students distanced themselves from him. In his review of Dörpfeld's work, Immanuel Velikovsky writes:

> The archaeological work that brought him to his theories was impeccable. His theories were wild mainly because he did not make the final step and free Greek archaeology from the erroneous Egyptian time-table. The contemporaneity of Mycenaean and early geometric ware, if true, contains the clue to the removal of the last argument for the preservation of the Dark Age between the Mycenaean and Greek periods of history.[52]

The solution is not, as Dörpfeld had argued, that the geometric ware dated to the Late Bronze Age, but that Mycenaean Greece and Minoan Crete, with the palaces of Knossos and Tyrins containing Linear-B tablets, belong to the ninth century BCE.

Early Geometric	900 BCE to 850 BCE
	900 BCE to 828 BCE (New Chronology)
Middle Geometric	850 BCE to 750 BCE
	828 BCE to 747 BCE (New Chronology)
Late Geometric	750 BCE to 700 BCE
	747 BCE to 687 BCE (New Chronology)

Table 15-2

As the above table illustrates, the Dorians introduced the geometric ware into the Aegean during the early ninth century BCE — when Akhenaten, Amenhotep III and Queen Tiy ruled in Egypt. The stratigraphical evidence from numerous Mycenaean sites, in fact, is littered with geometric ware. Describing the stratigraphical remains from a burnt stratum at Mycenae, Lord William Taylour says:

> ... the palace of Nestor, according to Blegen, was completely destroyed by a devastating fire at the end of LH IIIB or c.1200 BC. This is a period that saw the destruction and desolation of many sites. The great citadels on the mainland: Mycenae, Tiryns, Midea as well as Pylos suffered disastrous fires. Others such as Gla, Korakou, Zygouries, Prosymna, Berbati were either abandoned or destroyed about this time.[53]

---

[52] Quoted in C. Whelton (1990) p. 258.
[53] William Taylour (1990) *The Mycenaeans*. Revised edition. Thames and Hudson: London, p. 161.

Within the rubble of the palace of Pylos' final destruction, Carl Blegen reported having found, in the upper black layer, "along with the usual Mycenaean pottery, a few glazed sherds of Late Geometric style."[54] The question that now begs to be answered is *when* did the final destruction of the palace at Pylos occur? If Late Geometric sherds are present among the destruction debris, how is one to defend the theory that the palace was destroyed in *c.*1,200 BCE? Should not an eighth to seventh century BCE date be more appropriate? Blegen tried to get around the problem by suggesting that there might have been "fairly widespread activity on the site in Late Geometric times."[55] But, as Jan Sammer, a former research assistant of Immanuel Velikovsky, astutely observed, since Carl Blegen also earlier claimed that the destruction of Nestor's palace marked *"the end of human occupation on the site,"*[56] how is one then to reconcile with Blegen's seemingly contradictory statement that the presence of Late Geometric ware is the product of a later occupation? Similar contradictions plague the dating of the archaeological remains from other areas in the Aegean.

In his review of an article written by Immanuel Velikovsky — about an 1896 dig at Enkomi, Cyprus conducted under A. S. Murray of the British Museum — published in *Pensée*, Velikovskian scholar Clark Whelton says the following about the excavation in question:

> The tombs all belonged to the Mycenaean Age, and Egyptian artifacts were found from the time of Amenhotep III and Akhnaton, supposedly of the 14th century BCE. But other objects in the sepulchral chambers closely resembled ware dated to the seventh century. Ivories and bronzes were found similar to one discovered at Nimrud, capital of Assyria. A box of Assyrian design was also unearthed. Silver vases were "obviously Mycenaean in shape" but they shared distinctive features with silver rings with engravings very much like those "seen on Assyrian sculpture from Nimrud of **Assurnazirpal (884-860)**..." A porcelain head of a woman "seems to [be] Greek, not only in her features but also in the way in which her hair is gathered up at the back in a net, just as on the sixth century vases of this shape." Phoenician glass was found next to an amulet with the cartouche of Tutankhamen. Murray was baffled. He dared not challenge the Egyptologists ...[57]

---

[54] Carl Blegen, *Palace of Nestor*, p. 300.
[55] Ibid, p. 294.
[56] Ibid, p. 42.
[57] Clark Whelton (1990) pp. 258-259.

CHAP. XV: THE LIBYANS AND ETHIOPIANS TAKE CONTROL | 531

In the words of A. S. Murray himself: *"... there was not apparent in the tombs we opened any wide differences of epoch. For all we could say, the whole burying-ground may have been the work of a century."*[58] Within a stratified surface of merely "one century" in duration, Egyptian objects supposedly datable to the fifteenth to fourteenth centuries BCE were found intermingled with Assyrian artifacts themselves dating to the ninth century BCE. The first solution that came to Murray was to drastically reduce the accepted dates for the Mycenaean age; but that proposal was rejected by the scholarly world. Murray never dared to even suggest that the Egyptian chronology could have been off-track. Aware of the possibly devastating implications of A. S. Murray and his team's speculations upon the orthodox chronology, Arthur J. Evans lashed out at the Enkomi excavators. Foreseeing the controversial conclusions which might be drawn from all of this, Evans feared that A. S. Murray's findings pointed to "a chronology which brings the pure Mycenaean style down to the Age of the Tyrants" of the eighth century BCE — making it "the immediate predecessor of the Ionian Greek art of the seventh century B.C."[59]

The conclusions which Evans feared Murray could reach are exactly the ones which he *should* have reached. Most scholars can detect a continuity between Mycenaean tradition and seventh century BCE Ionian art; but the unnecessary gap of several centuries between the Mycenaeans and the Ionians stems entirely from Mycenaean connections with the reigns of Amenhotep III, Akhenaten and Tutankhamun. To quote the renowned ancient historian H. R. Hall earlier in this century: *"The chronological scheme depends ultimately upon Egyptian datings of Aegean pottery."*[60] Yet, from the archaeological findings enumerated above unearthed at Enkomi, it ought to be clear to any impartial observer, untainted by the conventional chronology of ancient Egypt, that Kings Amenhotep III, Akhenaten, and Tutankhamun all reigned during the ninth to eighth centuries BCE. Again pondering on the fictitious Dark Age of Greece, Velikovsky observes:

> The removal of the Dark Age from the historical sequence unshackles what was for centuries shackled, and releases the scholarly endeavour from

---

[58] A. S. Murray 'Excavations at Enkomi.' In Murray *et al.* (1900) *Excavations in Cyprus*, British Museum: London.
[59] Sir Arthur Evans (1900) 'Mycenaean Cyprus as Illustrated in the British Museum Excavations', *Journal of the Royal Anthropological Institute* 30, p. 199ff.
[60] H. R. Hall (1915) *Aegean Archaeology*, London, p. 2.

travelling on the same circular paths with no exit, the modern version of the Cretan Labyrinth. Moreover, it rehabilitates scholars accused of ignorance and negligence, their having been guilty only of not perceiving that the problems they dealt with were not problems at all, as soon as unreal centuries are stricken out.[61]

The End of the Amarnian Heresy

In Chapter 10, we discovered that Pharaoh Amenhotep IV's reign ended in a very different manner than traditionally believed. It was demonstrated that, based on the Manethonian texts, Amenhotep and his young son Ramses fled to Ethiopia in c.1,346 BCE after being overwhelmed by a hostile coalition comprising of impaired native Egyptians and Hyksos-Amalekites from the land of Amurru. Egyptologists have rejected unanimously this version of the events because, in their view, it does not fit with the extant archaeological evidence. Should one accept that King Amenhotep IV was indeed King Akhenaten, then it is entirely illogical to accept the Manethonian tradition's contention that the latter had a son and heir named Ramses and that he hastily departed from Egypt — leaving the throne vacant. Extant documents from Egypt clearly state that, soon after King Akhenaten's reign, which ends somewhat in mystery, the priests of Amun, whom the former had suppressed during his reign, backed as his successor Pharaoh Tutankhamun. The link between Tutankhamun, the son of Akhenaten, and the Amarnian era is undeniable. We know that King Tutankhamun, when he ascended the throne, changed his name from Tutankhaten to Tutankhamun, in order to reassure the now powerful priests of Amun of his allegiance to the Theban cult. But having dissociated, in the novel chronology, the LBII Amenhotep II from Akhenaten (who now belongs in the ninth century BCE), it is evident that Pharaoh Tutankhamun belongs in the Iron Age. Orthodox scholarship, by mistakenly considering Amenhotep IV and Akhenaten as one and the same individual, has thrown off the entire history of the ancient world in a whirlwind of confusion.

All the while, we must remember that, in the new chronology, Egypt was divided between the Ethiopians in the south and the Libyans in the north. During Akhenaten's reign, the Libyan pharaoh Takelot I was ruling Lower Egypt. But in 828 BCE, both Akhenaten and Takelot I were replaced by a new Libyan pharaoh named Shoshenk III. In keeping with his dynasty's tradition, Shoshenk III adopted a second Theban throne name: Amenhotep III. Shoshenk III was the first new 19th Dynasty Libyan monarch since King Osorkon I to adopt a Theban name modelled after the new 14th Dynasty of the Theban Renaissance. That's, of course,

---

[61] Quoted in C. Whelton (1990) p. 262.

CHAP. XV: THE LIBYANS AND ETHIOPIANS TAKE CONTROL | 533

because when the Napatans suddenly took control of Thebes under the leadership of King Harsiotef, the Libyans could no longer claim suzerainty over Upper Egypt. Thus, the Libyan kings Shoshenk II and Takelot I remained at Tanis and were forced to discontinue the alter-ego line. But a dramatic turn of events at the end of Pharaoh Akhenaten's reign once again thrust Thebes into the hands of the Libyans. This defining factor was Typhon Season #6. In 828 BCE, the erring planet Mercury once again wrought ravages upon the earth's surface. The prophecy of a potter from the court of Shoshenk-Amenhotep III has come down in which a turbulent period called "Typhon time" is said to have been at hand. The extant document, written in Greek, is understandably not believed to date from the New Kingdom (at the time when Egyptologists believe Amenhotep reigned). Evidently, that's because scholars could not justify the fact that it was written in Greek. In the new chronology, however, Pharaoh Amenhotep III (Shoshenk III's alter-ego) *does* reign in a time when the text could have indeed been written in Greek. The potter's report reveals that:

> The waterless Nile will be filled, the displaced winter will come in its own season. The sun will resume its course and the winds be restrained. For in the Typhon time the sun is veiled.[62]

All these are very clear indications of the effects of a Typhon Season. What's more the term "Typhon time" is even utilised. I believe that Typhon Season #6 (828-776 BCE) began on the year of Shoshenk-Amenhotep III's accession to the throne. His reigned, spanning 52 years,[63] lasted exactly as long as the Typhon Season. Ironically, the same chaotic circumstances which brought Shoshenk-Amenhotep III to the Theban throne in 828 BCE would, in turn, cause his own ousting in 776 BCE — when the planet Venus put a cataclysmic end to Typhon Season #6. This time, it would be the Theban monarch Horemheb who would take advantage of the cosmic tumult to lay claim to Upper Egypt. This massive flooding of the Nile's waters onto the banks of Egypt, which accompanied the introduction of Typhon Season #6, is described by Strabo below:

> They say that Typhon (who, they add, was a dragon), when struck by the bolts of lightning, fled in search of a descent underground; that he not only cut the earth with furrows and formed the bed of the river, but also descended underground and caused the fountain to break forth to the surface ...
> (Strabo, *Geography*, 16. 2. 6-7)

---

[62] Immanuel Velikovsky (1952) *Ages in Chaos*, p. 47.
[63] Kenneth A. Kitchen (1973) *The Third Intermediate Period in Egypt (1100 - 650 B.C.)*, Aris & Phillips: Warminster, U.K., p. 103.

The devastating climatic effects of the Typhon Season were also recorded by the Libyan king, and contemporary of Shoshenk-Amenhotep III, Osorkon II — as Immanuel Velikovsky, quoting from James H. Breasted's Ancient Records, relates:

> In the reign of Osorkon II of the Libyan Dynasty in Egypt, in the third year, the first month of the second season, on the twelfth day, according to a damaged inscription, "the flood came on, in this whole land ... this land was in its power like the sea; there was no dyke of the people to withstand its fury. All the people were like birds upon it ... the tempest ... suspended ... like the heavens. All the temples of Thebes were like marshes."[64]

Like the Libyan king Shoshenk-Amenhotep III, the Tanite pharaoh Osorkon II's reign coincided with the advent of Typhon Season #6. Although, as will be explained shortly, Osorkon II was crowned in Lower Egypt eight years after Shoshenk-Amenhotep III was crowned in Thebes. In the mean time, it is probable that Takelot I continued reigning from Tanis until Osorkon II's eventual accession. So, in 828 BCE, two different Libyan pharaohs were masters of the Two Lands — one in Upper Egypt and the other in Lower Egypt.

According to my chronological reconstruction, there were no familial links whatsoever between the Iron Age Amenhotep III and Akhenaten. Since the former succeeded the latter, it is completely understandable that Akhenaten would have made no mention at all of Amenhotep III. Believing that Amenhotep III was the father of Akhenaten, conventional scholars are baffled by this apparent omission. Many theories have been offered to explain this non-existent problem. The majority opinion is that because Akhenaten had been neglected as a child by his father, Amenhotep III, once he became pharaoh, Akhenaten, in turn, made no effort to honour his legacy. This is, unfortunately, another mere scholarly hypothesis which passes on as fact. Akhenaten did not mention Amenhotep III simply because the latter was his successor. Moreover, Akhenaten's father was not Amenhotep III, but Harsiotef.

French Egyptologists Luc Gabolde and Vincent Rondot, in the course of their study of the Amenhotep III's temple of Montu at North Karnak, came across a perplexing anomaly which they reported in a 1993 article in the *Bulletin de l'Institut Français d'Archaeologie Orientale*. To their amazement, they discovered a section of Pharaoh Amenhotep III's temple which had been founded upon blocks belonging to Amenhotep III, but which had themselves been usurped by Akhenaten! What is

---

[64] Immanuel Velikovsky (1950) *Worlds in Collision*, Doubleday: Garden City, NY, p. 209; J. H. Breasted, *Ancient Records of Egypt*, Vol. IV - § 743.

more, Amenhotep III's blocks which had been usurped by Akhenaten had somehow been actually later "restored" by Amenhotep III.

> Would it not be appropriate to reconsider the accepted dates for the temple's construction and attempt to explain the anomaly observed by the improbable posthumous decoration under the name of Amenhotep III?[65]

The Amarnian revolution initiated by Akhenaten preceded King Amenhotep III's reign. Evidence of this can be, for instance, gleaned from an androgynous-looking statue of a headless Amenhotep III at the Metropolitan Museum of Art in New York — showing unmistakably clear signs of Amarnian artistic influences. What's more, in the great religious centre in Heliopolis, Amenhotep III acknowledges Aton's solar cult — although he does not give it supremacy.[66]

Bubastis, Soleb and the Heb-Sed Festival

The Libyan pharaohs Shoshenk-Amenhotep III and Osorkon II both chose a religious capital, in the Black Land and Red Land respectively, in order to perform rituals to appease Ptah, the Typhonian deity responsible for maintaining universal order during Typhon Seasons. In Lower Egypt, King Osorkon II chose the city of Bubastis. We may in fact recall that, in Chapter 2, Bubastis served the very same function during Typhon Season #2. For his part, Pharaoh Shoshenk-Amenhotep III chose the town of Soleb in Nubia.

> In Nubia ... at Soleb, between Wady Halfa and Dongola, Amenophis III ... built a temple ... In this temple, which he dedicated to "his living image on earth," to himself, represented as a man with the horns of Amon, Amenophis III is seen celebrating a festival which is in an abridged form exactly the same as at Bubastis ... Amenophis is seen carried on his litter, holding the same emblems as Osorkon [II]. The inscription is much weathered, but what remains of it is identical with that of Bubastis... The two pavilions of Soleb and Bubastis are very much alike; at Soleb, in front of it, are the remains of an inscription nearly destroyed: "The access (?) to the Sed-festival." This proves that the ceremony at Bubastis was also a *Sed*-festival. ... A mention of the *Sed*-festival is found in the

---

[65] Luc Gabolde & Vincent Rondot (1993) 'Une catastrophe antique dans le temple de Montou à Karnak-Nord', *Bulletin de l'Institut Français d'Archéologie Orientale* 93, p. 250 (my translation).
[66] Jean Leclant 'Aménophis III : Un Pharaon et l'Afrique.' In Charles-André Julien (editor) (1977) *Les Africains* - Tome I, Editions J. A.: Paris, pp. 91-92.

great Harris papyrus of the British Museum. There Ramses III, speaking of what he has done at Memphis says: "I made thee the first *Sed*-festival of Tonen. ..." This sounds very like a description of what is represented at Bubastis. There are some remarkable coincidences. ... Ramses III, informs us that the first *Sed*-festival of his reign was to coincide with *the great festivals of Tonen*. This god being a form of Ptah, the god of Memphis ... at Bubastis the same thing occurs.[67]

In actuality, the two scenes, from Soleb and Bubastis, are so similar that Prof. Charles Cornell Van Siclen III of the University of Chicago's Oriental Institute came to the amazing conclusion that: *"While the Bubastis version is not an exact copy of the Soleb text, it is so close as to presuppose a common source from which both texts were taken."*[68] The amazing similarities incontrovertibly come from the fact that both temples were built contemporaneously by two pharaoh who ruled at the same time, but from different capitals. The *Heb*-Sed festival, celebrated in honour of the Memphite deity Ptah, in the form of the Apis bull, in both locations during Typhon Season #6. In Soleb, it was celebrated on the thirtieth year of Amenhotep III's reign — in keeping with tradition.

On the thirtieth regnal year of a pharaoh, especially if he ruled during a Typhon Season, a *Heb-Sed* festival was held to celebrate Pharaoh's vitality and regenerate his strength. Egyptologists are, however, much-confounded by the fact that Pharaoh Osorkon II celebrated his *Heb-Sed* festival eight years prematurely, on Year 22 of his reign. As the Swiss Egyptologist Édouard Naville (1844-1926) observed: "how can Osorkon II celebrate it in the twenty-second year of his reign?"[69] The answer to that question is that Year 30 of Pharaoh Shoshenk-Amenhotep III in Thebes corresponded with Year 22 of Pharaoh Osorkon II at Bubastis. Since King Shoshenk-Amenhotep celebrated his festival on the thirtieth year of the Typhon Season, his contemporary, Osorkon II, saw it fit, perhaps for the sake of unity or plain convenience, to celebrate his own *Heb-Sed* festival in Bubastis at the same time.

The Temple of Osiris-Apis

As part of the *Heb-Sed* festival, it was customary for Pharaoh to wear a bull's tail as he ceremoniously ran between the territorial cairns. According to Barbara Adams, the act represented "a connection with the symbolism of the king as the bull god Apis

---

[67] Édouard Naville (1892) *The Festival-Hall of Osorkon II in the Great Temple of Bubastis (1887-1889)*, Egypt Exploration Fund: London, pp. 4-5.
[68] Charles Cornell Van Siclen III (1973) 'The Accession Date of Amenhotep III and the Jubilee', *Journal of Near Eastern Studies* Vol. 32 - Num. 3, p. 296.
[69] Édouard Naville (1892) p. 6.

CHAP. XV: THE LIBYANS AND ETHIOPIANS TAKE CONTROL | 537

when he takes his run of renewal."[70] As the god of inundation, Apis, in his incarnation of Hapy, naturally became a prominent deity at this particular time. So preeminent was the cult of the Apis bull during Typhon Season #6, that a mortuary temple for the cult of the dead Apis bull was instituted. Although the name "Serapeum" is commonly used to designate this mortuary temple, this name is actually a misnomer. The proper term is "Temple of Osiris-Apis." We owe the commonly applied term of "Serapeum" to the French excavator Auguste Mariette (1821-1881) who, upon discovering the ancient bull burial site, was immediately reminded of the famous passage in Strabo's *Geography* in which the latter describes a temple of "Serapis" that was located near ancient Memphis. But what Strabo described as the temple of Serapis at Saqqara was, in actual fact, the temple of Osiris-Apis (reflecting the belief that when the Apis, the physical embodiment of Ptah, died he became Osiris just like the king). The Osiris-Apis temple at Saqqara was built centuries before the institution of the worship of Serapis — a Hellenistic god. The cult of Serapis, inspired by the more ancient cult of Osiris-Apis, had been quite literally invented by the Ptolemaic Greek rulers of Alexandria in an attempt to build a rapport with the native Egyptians and, thus, confer greater legitimacy to their reign.

Mariette reported that, depicted on decorated walls of an Apis burial chamber known as Chapel 1, one could clearly see the figure of Pharaoh Amenhotep III, accompanied by his son Djhutmose, offering incense to the Apis bull. The name of the royal prince (Djhutmose B) was also inscribed on several calcite and pottery vases.[71] Other artifacts have identified the numerous titles of the prince-priest Djhutmose as that of "Crown Prince," "Overseer of the Priests of Upper and Lower Egypt," "High Priest of Ptah in Memphis" and finally "*sem*-priest of Ptah."[72] On the basis of evidence unearthed, Egyptologists have concluded that Djhutmose was the eldest son of King Amenhotep III. Pharaoh Shoshenk-Amenhotep III bestowed the title of HPP (High Priest of Ptah) to his eldest son. As early as the classic Ptolemaic age, the *sem*-priest title was held by the chief clergyman at Memphis. In those ancient Typhonian days, the Sethian animals (as the red bull) were killed in sacrificial rituals held at Sokaris.[73] The importance of the HPP at the time of Shoshenk-Amenhotep III's reign was obviously compounded by the fact that Egypt was at that time engulfed in a Typhon Season. The HPP would ensure, by ceremo-

---

[70] Barbara Adams (1990) 'An Enigmatic Sealing from Abydos', *Eretz-Israel* 21, p. 4.
[71] Aidan Dodson (1990) 'Crown Prince Djhutmose and the Royal Sons of the Eighteenth Dynasty', *Journal of Egyptian Archaeology* 76, p. 88.
[72] Ibid, p. 88.
[73] Sylvie Cauville (1988) 'Les mystères d'Osiris à Dendera (Interprétation des chapelles osiriennes)', *Bulletin de la Société Française d'Égyptologie* 112, p. 32.

niously appeasing Ptah—the Demiurge, that Egypt would be spared from the customary plagues of Typhon Season. In addition, it is clear that Amenhotep-Shoshenk III gave much importance to the worship of Sekhmet — the ferocious lion-goddess closely assimilated to Bastet, mistress of Bubastis. Her role was, as in early and proto-dynastic times, to repel the archdemon Apophis, destroy the enemies of the Egyptian state, punish wrong-doers and maintain the cosmic order.[74] All those were very important concerns during a Typhon Season. Similar importance was given to a rejuvenated cult of the Memphite Hathor (as a human goddess with a bovine head) who, as a female counterpart of Ptah—the Demiurge, joined forces with Sekhmet to maintain the universal order.[75] Pharaoh Shoshenk-Amenhotep III saw Ptah and his female counterparts Sekhmet and the Memphite Hathor as forming a powerful "Typhonic divine triad."[76] Finally, the close proximity of the Osiris-Apis Temple from the northern section of the pyramid complex of Pharaoh Djoser-Netjerykhet, who performed a *Heb-Sed* festival during Typhon Season #1, is not accidental. As in previous Typhon Seasons, the Memphite Theology once again took centre stage.

What is extremely consequential to point out at this stage is that prior to the advent of Typhon Season #6, the temple of Osiris-Apis, where the sacred Apis bulls were buried, did not exist. In opposition to current Egyptological scholarship, I maintain that not even a single Apis burial was performed in Egypt during the Bronze Age. The foundation chapel at the temple of Osiris-Apis was erected under King Shoshenk-Amenhotep III. The early date of the chapel is confirmed by the fact that it was constructed *before* the establishment of the well-known Lesser Vaults. Indeed, before the larger Apis bull burial chambers of the Lesser Vault began being built under the Iron Age king Ramses II (whom I will argue in Chapter 17 was an alter-ego of Pharaoh Nekau II of the seventh century BCE), the Apis bull tombs comprised of a free-standing chapel.[77]

King Moeris & the Labyrinth

Pharaoh Shoshenk-Amenhotep III, in addition to inaugurating the temple of Osiris-Apis, embarked on grandiose building projects in Egypt. Not since Pharaoh Ramses II's reign had a pharaoh of Egypt enjoyed such a lengthy reign and was so well-known around the ancient Near East and the Mediterranean. In spite of his impos-

---

[74] Jean Yoyotte (1980) 'Une monumentale litanie de granit (Les Sekhmet d'Aménophis III et la conjuration permanente de la déesse dangereuse', *Bulletin de la Société Française d'Égyptologie* 87-88, p. 56.

[75] See Jocelyne Berlandini (1983) 'La déesse bucéphale: Une iconographie particulière de l'Hathor Memphite', *Bulletin de l'Institut Français d'Archéologie Orientale* 83, pp. 33-52.

[76] This Typhonic divine triad also seems to have been of importance during the reign of Ramses III in Typhon Season #5 — see Berlandini (1983, pp. 45-46).

[77] Aidan Dodson (1990) p. 88.

CHAP. XV: THE LIBYANS AND ETHIOPIANS TAKE CONTROL | 539

ing stature, Pharaoh Shoshenk-Amenhotep III conducted no military expeditions into Syria-Palestine or the Aegean. Perhaps somewhat inspired by his Theban predecessor Akhraten, his was a benevolent and prosperous reign. One of his greatest architectural achievements was the construction of a magnificent labyrinth. I believe that this monument was one and the same as the famous Labyrinth of King Moeris. That hypothesis, of course, entails that the legendary King Moeris was actually none other than Shoshenk-Amenhotep III.

Because the Labyrinth was built adjacently to Pharaoh Amenemhat III's pyramid at Hawara, in the Fayum, it has, for time immemorial been assumed that the Labyrinth was constructed by King Amenemhat III as well. But I am convinced that the Labyrinth was constructed many centuries after the death of Amenemhat III. There is in fact no conclusive evidence that the two structures, the Labyrinth and the adjacent Hawara pyramid, had been constructed at the same time. Actually, it would appear that the two edifices served independent functions.[78] What's more, Egyptologist Alan B. Lloyd has interestingly pointed out that:

> Mortuary temples at this period [Middle Kingdom] are always built adjacent to the tomb which they are intended to serve. The only unusual feature is that the building lies to the south of the Pyramid, whereas mortuary temples normally lie to the east facing in the direction of the valley.[79]

The explanation which I propose for the proximity of the Labyrinth of King Moeris (Shoshenk-Amenhotep III) to the pyramid of King Amenemhat III at Hawara is that the former had a keen interest in the Middle Kingdom, particularly the 13th Dynasty, along with its religious practices and art. Diodorus of Sicily described King Moeris as follows:

> ... they (the Egyptians) appointed a native king Mendes, whom some call Marrus. Though he was responsible for no military achievements whatsoever, he did build himself what is called the Labyrinth as a tomb, an edifice which is wonderful not so much for its size as for the inimitable skill with which it was built; for, once in, it is impossible to find one's way out again without difficulty, unless one lights upon a guide who is perfectly acquainted with it.
> (Diodorus of Sicily, Book I: 61)

---
[78] See David M. Rohl (1995) *A Test of Time — Vol. I*, p. 345.
[79] Alan B. Lloyd (1970) 'The Egyptian Labyrinth', *Journal of Egyptian Archaeology* 56, p. 95.

The Greek historian Herodotus (II: 148) reports having seen for himself the Labyrinth of King Moeris. He also says (II: 13) that King Moeris *"was not yet nine hundred years dead"* when he journeyed to Egypt. Therefore, according to Herodotus, King Moeris could not have reigned during the Middle Bronze Age — when modern historians place King Moeris.

Complementing the above quote by Diodorus of Sicily, the earlier chronicles of Herodotus further comment that Moeris built his Labyrinth "in the vicinity of the city called the City of Crocodiles." He claims that the buildings of the Greeks paled in comparison to this enormous structure, worthy of ten pyramids, which consisted "of twelve courts which have their gates opposite one another, six facing northwards and six facing south." (II: 148) Describing the Labyrinth's chambers, Herodotus says:

> The chambers above ground I myself saw as I passed through them and I speak of them on the basis of my own observation, but the subterranean group I heard of only by oral report. For the Egyptians in charge refused flatly to show them, saying that there lay the tombs not only of the kings who had caused the Labyrinth to be built in the beginning but also those of the sacred crocodiles. So my statements on the lower chambers are based on hearsay, though I speak of the upper chambers from my own observation.
> (Herodotus, Book II: 148)

It is interesting to note that in his excavation of the 13th Dynasty stratum at Tell el-Dab'a, Professor Manfred Bietak of the Austrian Archaeological Institute in Cairo, states the following in his description of the Stratum $d/1 = G/4$ palace built there (contemporaneously with the 12th Dynasty):

> Some of the older tombs got new superstructures, aligned to the orientation of the new palace. In a later phase of this stratum, rows of new tombs were sunk into the gardens. Each had subterranean chambers and was covered by a vault consisting of two layers of brick.[80]

It is important to note that the ancient Egyptians identified the crocodile, a sacred denizen of the Nile, with the god Sobek.[81] Herodotus' statement leads us to believe that the underground crocodile tomb-chambers were older than the Labyrinth built atop of it. Since the Egyptians of Herodotus' time obviously still held those ancient crocodile burials as sacred, it would be logical to assume that King Shoshenk-Amenhotep III built the Labyrinth on top of these Middle Kingdom croco-

---

[80] Manfred Bietak (1991) 'Egypt and Canaan During the Middle Bronze Age', *Bulletin of the American Schools of Oriental Research* 281, p. 34.
[81] William C. Hayes (1990 [1959]) *The Scepter of Egypt*, Vol. I: p. 45.

CHAP. XV: THE LIBYANS AND ETHIOPIANS TAKE CONTROL | 541

dile burials for very specific reasons. One plausible explanation is that, as a Typhonian deity, Sobek – god of crocodiles – could protect Egypt against the ravages of Typhon Season #6.

Herodotus is not the only ancient chronicler who indicates that King Moeris lived in much later times than contemporary Egyptologists believe. In his own accounts, citing Herodotus, the Roman historian Pliny writes:

> We must mention also the labyrinths, quite the most abnormal achievement on which man has spent his resources, but by no means a fictitious one, as might well be supposed. One still exists in Egypt, in the nome of Heracleopolis. This, the first ever to be constructed, was built, according to tradition, 3600 years ago by King Petesuchis or King Tithoes, although Herodotus attributes the whole work to the 'twelve kings,' the last of whom was Psammetichus. Various reasons are suggested for its construction. Demoteles supposes it to have been the palace of Moeris, and Lyceas the tomb of Moeris ... Whatever the truth may be, there is no doubt that Daedalus adopted it as the model for the labyrinth built by him in Crete ...
> (Pliny, *Natural History*, Book XXXVI: 19, 84-85)

If the Labyrinth represented the work of "twelve kings, the last of whom was Psammetichus (Psamtik)," then it must follow that King Moeris was the first of these twelve pharaohs. As Table 15-3 illustrates below, listing down the Theban pharaohs who ruled after King Shoshenk-Amenhotep III, according to the New Chronology Table, we amazingly discover that the twelfth ruler in line is none other than Psamtik I — just as Pliny postulates!

12th:	Psamtik I	6th:	Piye
11th:	Nekau I	5th:	Kashta
10th:	Tanutamun	4th:	Horemheb
9th:	Taharka	3rd:	Ay
8th:	Shebitku	2nd:	Tutankhamun
7th:	Shabaka	1st:	Amenhotep III (Shoshenk III)

Table 15-3

Having, thus, attributed the reign of King Moeris to the Iron Age, Pliny's final statement, to the effect that the fabled Cretan architect Daedalus had modelled the Labyrinth of King Minos after the Labyrinth of King Moeris, takes on vital consequences.

King Minos, Ruler of the Iron IIb Aegean, and the Sethian Minotaur

It had long been thought by a great number of classicists that English archaeologist Sir Arthur Evans' discovery of what he called "Minoan Crete" had irrevocably overturned Schliemann's idea of a truly Homeric Aegean. Furthermore, at the turn of the 20th century, the consensus hovered around the theory that it was really the Cretans, not the Mycenaeans, who were the true masters of the Late Bronze Age Aegean. In the final analysis, the Minoans, according to Sir Evans, had colonized Mycenaean Greece — not the other way around. Since Evans had dated the end of imperial Minoan Crete to around 1,400 BCE, after which time Mycenae supposedly lay decadent, Homer's Trojan War could only have been nothing more than a myth.

However, many questions remained unanswered. Chief among them: the Linear B texts. Sir Arthur Evans was convinced that Linear B could not possibly be Greek. Many voices were raised to question Evans' views. An important dissenting voice was that of Carl Blegen — an American archaeologist who was convinced Evans' so-called "decadent" fourteenth to thirteenth centuries BCE Mycenae was in fact none other than the heroic Greece of Homer's *Iliad*. Guided by the Trojan Epic, Blegen excavated at Pylos, on the Greek mainland's western Peloponnese, where he found evidence of a magnificent palace. The culture uncovered there was clearly related to that of Sir Arthur Evans' Cretan palace. Numerous clay tablets written in the still elusive Linear B script were also uncovered at Pylos. Blegen was well on his way to proving that Mycenae had indeed been independent of Crete. But until the Linear B tablets could be at last deciphered, the case could not be proven. Believing that he had uncovered the evidence for the existence of a strong Mycenaean empire during the thirteenth century BCE, Blegen went on to conclude that the destruction level at the end of Troy VIIa (in *c.*1,260 BCE) was the smoking gun for Homer's Trojan War.

When Michael Ventris' tremendous breakthrough came in 1952, proving that the Linear B script was indeed an archaic form of Greek, Homer had at last been vindicated. King Minos, who ruled the Aegean from Crete, had indeed been a Greek king. The over 3,000 clays tablets, thought to date to between around 1,400 BCE to 1,240 BCE, are believed to chronicle the time of the Greek Heroic Age through the end of the Trojan War. Since the ancient tablets were written in Greek, this was proof the it was the *Greeks* who held suzerainty over the Late Bronze Age Aegean, not the Cretans. Thus, Carl Blegen's vision of a vibrant Mycenaean empire during the fourteenth through thirteenth centuries BCE, from which an expedition towards Troy could have indeed set off, suddenly

CHAP. XV: THE LIBYANS AND ETHIOPIANS TAKE CONTROL | 543

became a reality for ancient historians. But, as I have abundantly argued thus far, the Trojan War was in reality the *beginning* of the Greek Heroic Age. The Greek language, which served as a base for the Linear B script, was not devised until the very end of the Late Bronze Age.

As Evans had maintained, I believe that Late Bronze Age Crete had always remained independent of Hyksos-dominated Greece. Again as Arthur Evans postulated, Late Minoan-A Crete was devastated early in the fourteenth century BCE and the Aegean remained relatively desolate until the rise of the Hyksos Agagite dynasty in the twelfth century BCE. After the demise of the Agagite dynasty, mainland Greece came under the domination of the Mycenaean-B culture — representing mainly Danaans from the north (People of the Sea) whose newly-emerging civilization had been much influenced by the large colonizing influx of Phoenicians from Egypt. These were the Greeks of Homer's Heroic Age who, after a long period of decadence, resettled the island of Crete and resurrected the vanished Palatial Minoan culture from the LB I-II period. From the older Linear A script devised by the Eteocretans (whom they incidentally considered as barbarians), they developed a modernized script, Linear B, using their own newly-constituted language, Greek.

The Linear B tablets deciphered by Michael Ventris in 1952, with the help of classicist John Chadwick, must, therefore, necessarily date to the Iron Age. From the Egyptian artifacts found alongside the Linear B tablets in Crete, it would appear as though the famed place of Knossos, or at least its latest incarnation, was erected during Typhon Season #6 — shortly after the Mercury catastrophe of 828 BCE. The Egyptian royal cartouches from Knossos indeed begin with the reigns of Pharaohs Akhenaten, followed by Amenhotep III (with Queen Tiy) and Tutankhamun. This signifies that the legendary King Minos, who ruled over the entire Aegean from Knossos, was a contemporary of these Egyptian pharaohs of the 18th Dynasty. Interestingly, it is recounted in Greek mythology that King Minos obtained the Cretan throne at Knossos through the aid of Poseidon. To prove his gratitude, King Minos promised Poseidon to offer him back in sacrifice anything that the latter sent to Crete. The details of the story strongly indicate that King Minos ruled Knossos during a Typhon Season — specifically Typhon Season #6. Like his Egyptian contemporary, King Shoshenk-Amenhotep III, King Minos acceded to the Cretan throne on the year of the Seth/Poseidon/Mercury-induced global cataclysm of 828 BCE. Hence, it is entirely understandable that the Greek legend would claim that the sea and storm-god Poseidon permitted King Minos to rule Crete — because this is exactly what happened. Equally logical, given the Typhonian context, is that the motif of the bull became very prominent in Crete during King Minos' rule. For example, bull sacrifices and bull leaping ceremonies were performed — while in Egypt, the cult of the Apis bull was diligently observed. Evidently, the Cretan Minotaur, a ferocious monster which was half man and half bull, provides an interesting counterpart to the Egyptian Apis or Typhonian bull. Poseidon had sent a bull to Crete — fully expecting King Minos to offer the bovine in sacrifice, as he had promised. But Minos felt that the bull was much too beautiful to offer back to Poseidon in sacrifice, so he killed another bull. Angered at Minos for breaking his word, Poseidon made the bull rampage all over Crete — spreading terror in his wake. Poseidon also made Minos' wife, Pasiphae, fall deeply in love with the animal. As a result, Pasiphae gave birth to the Minotaur — the half man, half bull monstrous creature. King Minos confined the Minotaur inside a huge labyrinth which Daedalus, the illustrious Athenian craftsman, had designed. As in ancient Mesoamerica, there is evidence that the Cretans performed human sacrifices to the Minotaur.[82] Most often, those sacrificed were Athenian prisoners. It was believed that such rites would appease the terrible bull responsible for "all the destructive forces of nature, the terrible earthquakes and the might of the stormy sea."[83] In the midst of a ruinous Typhon Season, the Cretans – as did the Egyptians and Mesoamericans – looked to appease the god of chaos in the hopes of ensuring a rejuvenating transition to the ensuing World Age.

Since King Minos was a contemporary of Pharaoh Shoshenk-Amenhotep III, the Cretan Labyrinth, as we've seen earlier form the works of Pliny, was definitely constructed in the same era of King Moeris' Labyrinth. Diodorus of Sicily, in fact, claims the same thing:

> And some say that Daedalus, visiting Egypt and admiring the skill shown in the building (the Egyptian Labyrinth), also constructed for Minos, the king of Crete, a labyrinth like the one in Egypt, in which was kept, as the myth relates, the beast called Minotaur.
> (Diodorus of Sicily, Book I: 60)

Other ancient chroniclers' descriptions of the Cretan Labyrinth and the events surrounding King Minos' reign, as well as Thucydides' account, also help to locate its construction during the Iron Age, as I postulate in the new chronology.

> Minos is the earliest of all those known to us by tradition who acquired a navy. He made himself master of a very great part of what is now called the Hellenic Sea, and became lord of the Cyclades islands and first colonizer of most of them, driving out the Carians and establishing his own sons in them as governors.
> (Thucydides, Book I: 4)

---

[82] Yu. V. Andreyev 'The World of Crete and Mycenae.' In I. M. Diakonoff (editor) *Early Antiquity*, p. 312.
[83] Ibid.

Fig. 15g: Ram of Amun made by Shoshenk-Amenhotep III found at the temple of Soleb.

Fig. 15h: Crouching lion attributed to Amenhotep III.

Fig. 15i: The bull of Minos.

Fig. 15j: The golden mask of Tutankhamun.

Fig. 15k: Canopic chest of King Tutankhamun.

CHAP. XV: THE LIBYANS AND ETHIOPIANS TAKE CONTROL | 549

Based on the observation from the accounts of Thucydides, we can surmise that Minos' reign coincided with the presence of the Carians in the Mediterranean nation. Analogously, Herodotus (I: 171) says that the Carians paid tribute to King Minos. Where this is strange, if one is to rely on the orthodox chronology and history of the Aegean, is that the Carians are an Iron Age people. They only become visible in the historical records from the eighth century BCE onwards, at the earliest. Evidently, if the Carians are to be contemporaries of King Minos, then King Moeris and his Egyptian Labyrinth must likewise be moved down into the Iron Age.

Chariots of Fire: Venus and the Olympiads

The inauguration, in 776 BCE, of the Olympic games in Greece was one of the landmark events which took place during the time-span of Typhon Season #6. The importance of the symbolism for the timing of this particular event cannot be stressed enough. Like Immanuel Velikovsky, it is my assertion that the Olympic games in Greece began on the year of a cosmic catastrophe involving the planet Venus. Furthermore, it would be a mistake to assume that the year of the inauguration, 776 BCE, and the interval period of four years for the scheduling of the next Olympiad were decided upon haphazardly. As we've seen in the previous chapter, a much deeper cultic design was at work in the minds of the ancients. Dr Immanuel Velikovsky was the first modern historian to critically put forth the theory that the Greeks' festival of the Olympic Games was established on the basis of an ancient Egyptian Venus calendar. In this way, he followed the lead of the fifth century BCE Greek poet Pindar (Ol. Od. III, 35) who claimed that the Olympian months Parthenios and Appolonios were identical with the months of Thoth and Mesori of the Egyptian calendar.

We may recall that the Sothic "great year" of 1,460 years begins with the year when the heliacal rising of the dog star Sirius is on the first of the month of Thoth. After four years, it would then rise on the second of Thoth. During the 1930s, astronomer M. Knapp brought attention to what he perceived as being a very close relationship between the Sothic cycle and the planet Venus.[84] This theory slides at the heart of my own assertion that the cultic meaning of the Olympiads in Greece stems out of a mixture of Egypt's Sothic cycle, of elements from the Venus calendar and finally of the usual planetary catastrophes accompanying the Typhon Seasons (particularly with regards to the planet Venus). Horapollo[85] spoke of the fact that the Egyptian year was made up of four years. The ancient Greeks knew that the Egyptians' year consisted of four years — which is the same length as the Olympic

---

[84] M. Knapp (1934) *Pentagramma Veneris*, Basel, p. 22.
[85] "A year among the Egyptians consists of four years." *Horapollo*, II, lxxxix. See J. G. Wilkinson in G. Rawlinson (1858-60) *The History of Herodotus*, London, Vol. II: p. 285.

550 | PLANET OF THE GREEKS

cycle. Turning to Immanuel Velikovsky for an explanation of this Venus calendar hypothesis, we learn that:

> The Venus calendar shows a close coincidence with the year of 365 days at intervals of eight years. The eight-year period could easily be divided in half, each half composed of two and a half synodic periods of Venus, with the inferior conjunction and the middle of the superior being the dividing points. Accordingly, the Venus year in Egypt was equal to four years of 365 days.[86]

Adding to the above statement by Velikovsky, catastrophist historian Benny Peiser writes:

> ...it is perfectly clear that the early octaeteris and pentaeteris festival periods of Greece were religious and cultic at their very beginning, calculated only by observing the synodical revolutions of (the goddess) Venus.[87]

The focus on the planet Venus, on that pivotal year, commemorated the cataclysmic end of Typhon Season #6. In Greek mythology, it's stated that Herakles, in one of his labours, drove the Minotaur out of Crete. On that very same year halfway around the world, in ancient China, "the text of the ancient Chinese book of Shiking refers to some celestial phenomenon in the days of the king Yen-Yang, in 776 BC: the sun was obscured."[88] Like the dynasty of Xia at the end of Typhon Season #4 and the dynasty of Shang at the end of Typhon Season #5, the Dynasty of Western Zhou came to an abrupt end at the end of Typhon Season #6. Chinese scholars agree that, somewhere around 770 BCE, under the pressure of western nomads from Shenshi, the "Chou [Zhou] people abandoned their former capital."[89] T. V. Stepugina describes the situation as follows:

> After the transfer of the Chou capital to Luoyi, internecine wars and dissension within the ruling house of the *wang* weakened Chou to such an extent that other, stronger states of the Huang Ho basin placed it, as the cultic center of the Celestial Empire, under their own protection. The military

---

[86] Immanuel Velikovsky (1977) *Peoples of the Sea*, Doubleday: Garden City, NY, p. 240.
[87] Benny Peiser 'Post-Mycenaean Greek History Begins in the 6th Century BC: The Controversy about the Olympic Victor List and its Implications for early Greek Chronology.' In Zysman, Milton & Whelton, Clark (editors) (1990) *Catastrophism 2000 (A Sourcebook for the Conference: Reconsidering Velikovsky)*, p. 278.
[88] Immanuel Velikovsky (1950) *Worlds in Collision*, p. 211.
[89] T. V. Stepugina 'China in the First Half of the First Millennium B.C.' In I. M. Diakonoff (editor) (1991) *Early Antiquity*, p. 420.

CHAP. XV: THE LIBYANS AND ETHIOPIANS TAKE CONTROL | 551

> and priestly powers, which had earlier seemed inseparable, came to be regarded as independent from one another, and the militarily stronger ruler now acquired a new and important function: the military protection of the *wang* of Chou, the supreme religious leader of the Celestial Empire, the Son of Heaven. The concept of the "universal" character of the royal state power of the wangs of Chou developed precisely during this period. ... The idea of the divine origin of the Chou dynasty was supposed to lay the foundation for a stable cultic leadership of the *wangs* of Chou. A story was circulated about the Hsiah [Xia] and Yin [Shang] dynasties, which preceded the Chou dynasty, as "rejected by heaven."[90]

This indubitably confirms that 776 BCE was a year, like in 1,559 BCE and 1,135 BCE beforehand, when a World Age came to its sudden culmination, accompanied by a violent Venusian cataclysm.

The Freudian Moses, the Fourth Exodus,

and the Pharaoh of the Exodus

> *" The universal experience of Canaanites ... was that in times of famine, Canaanites were sent down to Egypt."*
>
> - Baruch Halpern
> Pennsylvania State University

The fall of state governments and empires which had suddenly been "rejected by heaven," and the sweeping movements of dispossessed peoples, which accompanied the latest Venusian cataclysm of 776 BCE were, naturally, not only restricted to China. The entire ancient Near East, and the Mediterranean region, was thrown into upheaval. In Egypt, the reign of King Shoshenk-Amenhotep III came to an abrupt end. His immediate successor, Pharaoh Horemheb, soon inherited the responsibility to restore order and divine balance in a land ravaged by chaos. In an intriguing account known as the Cairo Fragments, Horemheb describes the state of Egypt, on the year of the Venus shift of 776 BCE. On the document's principal relief, superseded with eight vertical descriptive lines, is portrayed Horemheb, giving advice to a group of royal officials about the handling of a group of Asiatic refugees, who had recently settled in Egypt. According to the American Egyptologist James Henry Breasted,

---

[90] Ibid, p. 421-422.

this scene depicts events which occurred during, or shortly after the reign of Akhenaten. But Breasted is working within the framework of the conventional chronology. In the new chronology, Horemheb is the immediate successor of Shoshenk-Amenhotep III. The lines above the relief scene go as follows:

> ... Asiatics; others have been placed in their abodes [...] they have been destroyed, and their town laid waste, and fire had been thrown [...]; [they have come to entreat] the Great in Strength to send his mighty sword before [...]. Their countries are starving, they live like goats of the mountain, [their] children [...] saying: "A few of the Asiatics, who knew not how they should live, **have come [beggling [a home in the domain] of Pharaoh, ... after the manner of your fathers' fathers since the beginning,** under [...]. Now, the Pharaoh, ... gives them into your hand, to protect their borders."[91]

From the above-cited text, we can surmise that the cycle-ending Venus shift of 776 BCE had wrought such havoc in Palestine that many Asiatics, among them certainly Israelites, sought refuge in Egypt. Pharaoh Horemheb mentions that these distressed Asiatics came beseeching the Egyptians to grant them hospitality, in their time of misfortune, in the manner of their ancestors. The Israelites' ancestors, such as Abraham and Jacob, had indeed sought refuge and assistance in the land of Pharaoh in dire times. While the Bible makes no mention of a massive settling of Egypt by Israelites in the land of Egypt during the period of the Divided Monarchy, I believe that several members of a particular Hebrew tribe, that of Manasseh, descended into Egypt contemporaneously with the accession of Pharaoh Horemheb. Restless and directionless in a foreign land, they chose as a charismatic leader, issued from the Egyptian ruling class, who showed compassion for their cause. That charismatic leader, who eventually led them out of Egypt in Horemheb's reign, was the Fifth Moses. In fact, it is even possible that the biblical redactors of the sixth century BCE gave that tribe this particular name because of its association with a prominent Mosaic figure. Incidentally, according to theologian Lester L. Grabbe:

> The name "Moses"(*msh*) has been altered in the text by the addition of an -n- to make it Manasseh (*mnsh*), but the additional letter is written partly above the line. It is generally accepted that the original is Moses. However, not only is the "pagan" priest a descendant of Moses, his ancestor Gershom is said to be a son of Moses, whereas he is normally said to be a son of Araon (e.g. 1 Chron 6:1). This is clearly a different tradition and an embarrassing one. It seems to be the remnant of a Mosaic priesthood otherwise unrecorded in the OT tradition. No wonder a scribe attempted to change the name Moses to Manasseh![92]

---

[91] J. H. Breasted, *Ancient Records of Egypt*, Vol. III - § 11.
[92] Lester L. Grabbe (1995) *Priests, Prophets, Diviners, Sages (A Socio-Historical Study of Religious Specialists in Ancient Israel)*, Trinity Press International: Valley Forge, Penn., p. 43.

CHAP. XV: THE LIBYANS AND ETHIOPIANS TAKE CONTROL | 553

This "remnant of a Mosaic priesthood," which Lester L. Grabbe alludes to, has its origins in this breakaway group of Israelites who left Syria-Palestine to go to Egypt and, as we'll see shortly, ultimately to Ethiopia. Traditions identifying the tribe of Manasseh as a "lost tribe" indeed abound. On the border between Burma and the Indian provinces of Manipur and Mizoram, in Asia, for instance, a people identifying themselves as the "Children of Menmasseh" believe themselves to be descendants of the ancient Israelites. The Bnai Menashe believe that they had once been enslaved in a hostile foreign country and departed from their bondage amid pillars of cloud and fire. Based on evidence of a Jewish community in China dating to the time of the First Temple, some historians have hypothesized that the Bnai Menashe may have reached the province of Manipur via the silk route towards China.[93] In any event, it is evident that the tribe of Manasseh has long been linked with far-off wanderings from the bulk of the Israelite tribes. These traditions have a strong historical basis — as I hope to be able to demonstrate. Moreover, as Lester L. Grabbe outlines above, there are likewise indications of a lost Mosaic priesthood which the Old Testament redactors have kept quite about — at least overtly.

This fifth Moses figure, whose name has been lent to the tribe of Manasseh, appears to have had been deeply influenced by Pharaoh Akhenaten's Amarnian revolutionary and monotheist philosophy. For these reasons, I shall dub him the "Freudian Moses." The Fifth Moses seems to fit remarkably well with the description given of the biblical Moses by Sigmund Freud:

> Let us assume that Moses was a noble and distinguished man: perhaps indeed a member of the royal house, as the myth has it. He must have been conscious of his great abilities, ambitious and energetic; perhaps he saw himself in a dim future as the leader of his people, the governor of the Empire. In close contact with Pharaoh he was a convinced adherent of the new religion, whose basic principles he fully understood and had made his own. With the king's death and the subsequent reaction he saw all his hopes and prospects destroyed. If he was not to recant the convictions so dear to him then Egypt had no more to give him; he had lost his native country. In this hour of need he found an unusual solution. The dreamer Ikhnaton had estranged himself from his people, had let his world empire crumble. Moses' active nature conceived the plan of founding a new empire, of

---

[93] Internet resource: http://www.bnaimenashe.com/pages/history.html

> finding a new people, to whom he could give the religion that Egypt disdained. It was, as we perceive, an heroic attempt to struggle against his fate, to find compensation in two directions for the losses he had suffered through Ikhnaton's catastrophe. ... He established relations with them [the Jews], placed himself at their head and directed the Exodus "by strength of hand."[94]

Unlike Freud however, I do not believe that this Exodus "passed off peacefully and without pursuit." Like the tradition of the Bnai Menashe recounts, the departure of the Tribe of Manasseh from Egypt, with the Fifth Moses at their head, I believe, was accompanied by clouds of smoke and pillars of fire. These extensive upheavals of nature had been caused by the cycle-ending fury of the planet Venus in 776 BCE. As Freud postulates, the Fifth Moses was not himself a Hebrew, but an aristocratic Egyptian. Longing to reinvigorate the banned religion of Pharaoh Akhenaten, under whose reign the Fifth Moses probably lived, he saw in these Asiatics who entered Egypt in a time a of chaos an opportunity to pass on the ideals of monotheism, developed by Akhenaten, after the Amarnian philosophy had been forcefully suppressed during the lengthy reign of Pharaoh Shoshenk-Amenhotep III. Actually, long before Freud came along with the hypothesis that Moses was an Egyptian educated aristocrat and contemporary of King Akhenaten, the editors of Manetho's *History of Egypt*, had written:

> Moses, a son of the tribe of Levi, educated in Egypt and initiated at Heliopolis, became a High Priest of the Brotherhood under the reign of Pharaoh Amenhotep. He was elected by the Hebrews as their chief and he adapted to the ideas of his people the science and philosophy which he had obtained in the Egyptian mysteries, proofs of this are to be found in the symbols in the Initiations, and in the precepts and commandments. ... the dogma of an "only god" which he taught was the Egyptian Brotherhood interpretation and teaching of the Pharaoh who established the first monotheistic religion known to man.

The above passage provides many vital clues which incontrovertibly indicate that we are indeed dealing with the Fifth Moses, who lived during and after the time of the Amarnian revolution. I would as well contend that the Fifth Moses was still a very young man at the close of Pharaoh Akhenaten's Amarnian era. Given the

---

[94] Sigmund Freud (1939) *Moses and Monotheism*. Trans. from the German by Katherine Jones. Hogarth Press/Institute of Psycho-Analysis: London, pp. 46-47.

CHAP. XV: THE LIBYANS AND ETHIOPIANS TAKE CONTROL | 555

rather lengthy reign of Pharaoh Shoshenk-Amenhotep III, it is evident that, if the Fifth Moses assumed a leadership role early in the reign of Horemheb, he must have been appointed to high office in the court of Shoshenk-Amenhotep III (Pharaoh Amenhotep of the Manethonian text — not Pharaoh Akhenaten as scholars have suggested). The traditional biblical assumption, from the Book of Genesis, which maintains that the composite Moses was a Jewish child who grew up as an Egyptian "learned in all the wisdom of the Egyptians" (Acts 7:22) comes from the life of the Fifth Moses. Although it would have been very unlikely that he was the son of Hebrew slaves. That particular element was probably introduced by the biblical redactors in an attempt to harmonize all of the historical Moses into the composite Moses whose "factional" life (a mixture of fact and fiction) is described in the Bible. A much more credible scenario, given the historical circumstances of the eighth century BCE, would be that the Freudian Moses was born into a very Egyptianized aristocratic Israelite family who had probably been in Egypt for several generations. Witnessing the massive influx and subsequent encampment of the Israelites from the tribe of Manasseh, under the orders of the new Pharaoh Horemheb, the Fifth Moses was stirred to act on behalf of his brethren. Perhaps in opposition to the ruling Egyptian court, the Fifth Moses rallied the Israelites under his leadership on the basis of the forbidden Amarnian teachings of monotheism. As a priest of Heliopolis, he was very much acquainted, and evidently much in agreement with the religion of the Aten sun-disk — which had incidentally sprung from the Heliopolitan Theology. Understandably, the new pharaoh, Horemheb, immediately went out of his way to severely crush any potential rekindling of the Amarnian revolution. From his perspective, this was a clear an present threat to his power in Egypt. Thus, the only option left for the Freudian Moses and his Asiatic followers was to flee Egypt. As in the previous Exoduses, their journey took place at a time of great cosmic tremors. It was the culmination of Typhon Season #6.

It was in 1890 that the inscriptions from a shrine of black granite from el-Arish were published by F. Ll. Griffith.[95] The monument in question, first discovered in the 1860's, had for several generations been used by local Arab villagers as a cattle through. The inscribed stone was finally brought to the Museum of Ismailia sometime during the first decades of the last century. The monolith dates from the Hellenistic ages but actually refers to events from a much earlier period. Upon the Stone Shrine at el-Arish is inscribed:

> Trouble has beset the eyes. ... For nine days nobody has left the palace. There have been nine days of violence and tempest. Nobody, neither God

---

[95] F. Ll. Griffith (1890) *The Antiquities of Tell el Yahûdiyeh*, The Egypt Exploration Fund: London.

or man, is able to see his neighbor's face. We do not know what has happened throughout the Earth ... It is a confusion that you brought upon the entire Earth with the sound of an uproar. ... Oh, let the Earth stop rumbling. ... Towns are destroyed ... Upper Egypt is devastated ... Blood is everywhere ... Pestilence, looting are everywhere on Earth.

Likewise, in Asia, Buddhist tradition postulates that at the beginning of the Sixth Sun (end of Typhon Season #6), *"the whole world becomes filled with smoke and saturated with greasiness of that smoke."* There was *"no distinction of day and night."* The conflagration was created by a *"cycle-destroying great cloud"* of cosmic nature.[96] The el-Arish document is indeed very reminiscent of the climatic conditions during the composite Exodus.

In all of the three previous Exoduses which we've examined so far, no where has mention yet been made of the Pharaoh of the Exodus — who, despite his promise to free his Hebrew slaves, pursued the fleeing Israelites as they prepared to cross the Red Sea. In all previous occasions, Pharaoh had not objected to, and even actually encouraged, the Hebrews' flight from Egypt. Was this central detail of the composite Exodus entirely fabricated by the biblical redactors? This, in my estimation, is highly unlikely. It is indeed quite difficult to imagine how such a vital element of the Exodus story could not bear at least some element of truth in it. I believe that solid evidence for the historicity of this event, which I argue took place during the Fourth Exodus, can be gleaned from the following fascinating passage from the el-Arish Stone:

> His Majesty [...] finds on this place called Pi-Kharoti.
> Now when the majesty of Ra-Harmachis [Harakhte] fought with the evil-doers in this pool, the Place of the Whirlpool, the evil-doers prevailed not over his majesty leapt over the so-called Place of the Whirlpool.
> (Stone Shrine at el-Arish)

Analogously to the Bible, the document clearly alludes to a very large watery whirlwind which the elusive Egyptian pharaoh – Harakhte – had to contend with. Unlike in the biblical text, however, the Hebrews (the evil-doers) do not prevail. The passage from the Stone Shrine at el-Arish, may in fact be an account of the Pharaoh of the Exodus' famed pursuit of the Israelites — told from the perspective of the Egyptians. Pharaoh Horemheb, a contemporary of both Kings Tutankhamun and Ay, wrote in his hymn to Re-Harakhte: *"Harakhte, only god, king of the gods; he rises in the west, he sendeth his beauty ..."*[97] Therefore, it is entirely likely that either Horemheb,

---

[96] H. C. Warren (1896) *Buddhism in Translations*, pp. 322-327.
[97] J. H. Breasted, *Ancient Records of Egypt*, Vol. III - § 18.

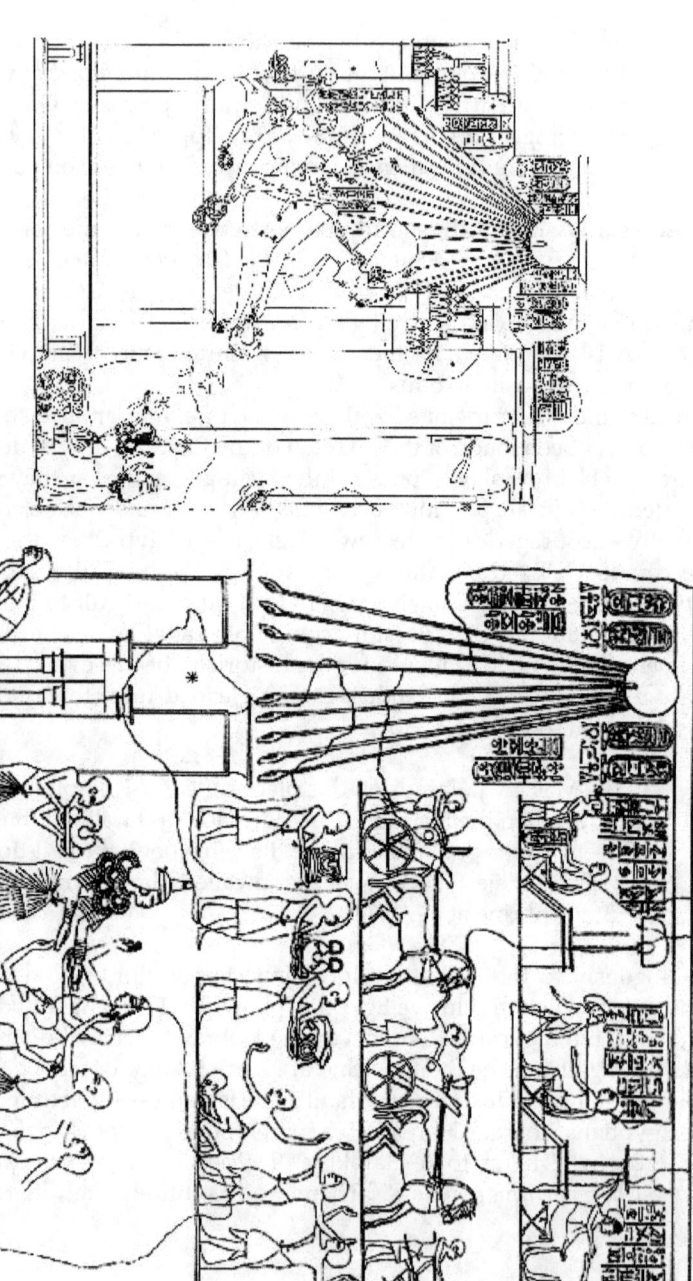

Fig. 151: Relief from the Amarnian tomb of King Ay, 'Master of the Horse.'

New Chronology of the Late New Kingdom Through to the End of Napatan Rule:

	Tanis		
	Shoshenk I		945 BCE
Thebes	Osorkon I		
Harsiese	Shoshenk II		
Akhenaten	Takelot I		
Shoshenk III	Osorkon II (820 - 791 BCE)		- Mercury shift (-828)
(828-776 BCE)	Takelot II (807- 781 BCE)		
Tutankhamun/Ay	Osorkon III (781- 747 BCE) /		
Horemheb (776-47)	Takelot III (757 - 747)		- Venus shift (-776)
Napata	**Thebes**	**Tanis**	
Kashta	Rudamon	Pedubast	- Mars shift (-747)
Pi-Ankhy	Iuput, Pimay	Nimlot	
Shabaka	Osorkon IV	Tefnakht	
Shebitku	Shoshenk IV	Bocchoris	
Taharka	Osorkon V	Shoshenk V	
Tanutamon			664 BCE

Table 15-4

Fig. 15m: Pharaoh Ay in his Chariot.

Fig. 15n: Objects from the tomb of Tutankhamun.

CHAP. XV: THE LIBYANS AND ETHIOPIANS TAKE CONTROL | 559

Tutankhamun or Ay could have gone by the name of: His Majesty of Re-Harmachis (Harakhte). Amazingly, in addition, the place-name Pi-Kharoti on the el-Arish Stone (where Pharaoh Harakhte meets with the "evil-doers"), appears in the Book of Exodus in reference to the place where Pharaoh and his horsemen met with the Israelites:

> But the Egyptians pursued after them, all the horses and chariots of Pharaoh, and his horsemen, and his army, and overtook them encamping by the sea, beside Pi-Kharoti [Khiroth].
> For the horse of the Pharaoh went in with his chariots and with his horsemen into the sea, and the Lord brought again the waters of the sea upon them.
> (Exodus 14:9, 15:19)

There is no doubt that "Pi-Kharoti" of the el-Arish document and "Pi-Khiroth" of the Bible refer to one and the same place.[98] With regards to the identity of King Harakhte (Pharaoh of the Exodus), I propose that he was Pharaoh Ay, the successor of Tutankhamun at Thebes and a contemporary of King Shoshenk-Amenhotep III, and briefly of Horemheb. Thus, Pharaoh Ay is now identified as the Pharaoh of the Exodus who actually pursued the Israelites as they fled Egypt, while Horemheb was the pharaoh who had initially allowed these Israelites from the tribe of Manasseh to settle in Egypt. The year of the Venusian turbulence, 776 BCE, covered the Asiatics' entrance into Egypt, their choice of the Freudian Moses as their leader, and the pursuit of Pharaoh Ay-Harakhte. An important clue that Ay could have indeed been the Pharaoh of the Exodus comes from the latter's former army title of "Commander of the Horses" — as Keith Seele remarks below.

> He [Ay] was "Commander of all the Horses of his Majesty." This title clearly indicates Ay to have been a military officer of high rank, and I believe that it would be proper to interpret it as something like "General of the Royal Chariotry" ...[99]

If we rely on the biblical accounts, the Pharaoh of the Exodus perished in the Red Sea — as god caused the walls of waters, miraculously erected to allow the Israelites to cross the waters on foot, to suddenly collapse on top of the Egyptian chariotry (Exodus 14:27-29). Evidently, the splitting of the Red Sea in two is a symbolic des-

---

[98] Immanuel Velikovsky (1952) *Ages in Chaos*, p. 44.
[99] Keith C. Seele (1955) 'King Ay and the Close of the Amarna Age', *Journal of Near Eastern Studies* Vol. 14 - Num. 3, p. 168.

cription of the planetary tug of war which resulted in the upturning of the earth's watery masses at the close of every Typhon Season. The Jewish Midrash[100] incidentally narrates that, during the Exodus, the Archangel Michael transformed himself into "a wall of fire" between the fleeing Hebrews and the pursuing Egyptian army.

> The celestial struggle at the Sea of Passage is depicted in the familiar image of the Archangel Michael slaying the dragon. Michael produces fire by touching the earth, and it was the emanation of this arch-angel that was seen in the burning bush. He has his abode in heaven and is the forerunner of Shehina or God's presence, but as Lucifer, Michael falls from heaven and his hands are bound by God. All these attributes and acts of the Archangel Michael lead us to recognize which planet he represents: it is Venus.[101]

It is, incidentally, very interesting to note that King Akhenaten had ordered a tomb to be made for King Ay at Tell el-Amarna, but the tomb was, mysteriously, never finished and never occupied.[102] Did Ay perish in the watery whirlwind? While this probably may never be known for sure, the circumstances certainly seem to point to this conclusion.

The Ethiopia-Bound Israelites and the Ark of the Covenant

Placing another Israelite Exodus out of Egypt this late in the history of Syria-Palestine naturally excludes the notion that the destination of these wanderers would be Canaan. At the close of Typhon Season #6, biblical Israel was already well established. Moreover, the Bible would certainly never have been so completely silent about the divinely-assisted return of the children of Manasseh from the land of Egypt. I am, thus, convinced that expatriate members of the lost tribe of Manasseh, after their very short sojourn in Egypt, headed south toward Ethiopia. With them, they brought the newly-formulated monotheistic belief system, taught by the Fifth Moses, along with the long and rich traditions of their Hebrew culture. It is evident that the Israelites had already developed a brand of monotheism long before the Amarnian revolution, but there is in fact very little, if anything, to prove that the Syro-Palestinians of the burgeoning Iron Age were steadfast monotheists. After all, we must bear in mind that the Israelites remained under the direct suzerainty of the Tuthmoside kings during the entire

---

[100] Pirkei Rabbi Elieser 42.
[101] Immanuel Velikovsky (1950) *Worlds in Collision*, p. 293.
[102] Percy E. Newberry (1932) 'King Ay, the Successor of Tut'ankhamun', *Journal of Egyptian Archaeology* 18, p. 50.

CHAP. XV: THE LIBYANS AND ETHIOPIANS TAKE CONTROL | 561

Iron I period. What the Freudian Moses preached was a mixture of the traditional Hebrew Yahwism and the main monotheistic tenets of the Amarnian philosophy. Inspired by the tradition of the previous Moses, the Fifth Moses established laws and religious standards for the community's relationship with God. Among the material symbols of the Freudian Moses', and his Canaanite followers', sacred union with the divine world was the legendary Ark of the Covenant.

According to the biblical texts, the Ark of the Covenant was a sacred portable chest. In the Book of Exodus, it's made evident that the Ark was the most important sacred object of the Hebrews during the wilderness wanderings — when it was carried by the sons of Levi (Deut. 31:9). At the time of the Conquest, recounted in the Book of Joshua, the Ark was carried at the fall of Jericho (Josh. 6:4-11). Subsequently, the Israelites took it along into their battle against the Philistines, but were comprehensively defeated (1 Sam. 4:1-11). The Philistines captured the Ark but later returned it after their camp was struck by a sudden disaster (1 Sam. 5-6). The Ark was at last welcomed back into Jerusalem by King David; and Solomon later established it in the Holy of Holies of the Temple which he erected. The sacred Ark, containing the two tablets of the Law of Moses, is last mentioned in the Bible in the First Book of Kings. The Ark of the Covenant then disappeared altogether from history when the Babylonian king Nebuchadnezzar and his army destroyed Jerusalem in 586 BCE. After the Israelites' return from captivity in Babylon, the Bible, mysteriously, no longer says anything at all about the Ark of the Covenant. Therefore, the Holy of Holies within what is called the Second Temple in Jerusalem, erected in the time of Ezra and Zechariah, did not contain the sacred Ark of the Covenant. After his conquest of Jerusalem, in 63 BCE, the Roman general Pompey demanded the privilege to enter the Holy of Holies. But when he discovered that it was an empty room, he wondered why the sanctuary was the object of such reverence by the Jews.

The basic reason why I believe that the history of the Ark of the Covenant is so sketchy is because it was never really part of the history of Israel. To begin with, it is impossible, according to my revised history of biblical Israel that Joshua could have had access to any documents passed on by Moses — since the First Moses only came around decades after the Conquest. Thus, from the outset, it is evident that the symbol of the Ark was a later addition to the narrative of Joshua's Conquest. As a matter of fact, the Ark of the Covenant was not even part of the First Temple of Solomon in the Late Bronze Age. Nor was it existent in the Iron I era when the Bible, misleadingly, dates the United Monarchy of Israel. The genuine history of the Ark of the Covenant begins on the year 776 BCE. It was built by the lost tribe of Manasseh in Egypt under the directions of the Fifth Moses. It's design was very much influenced, quite naturally, by the Egyptian artistic canons of the post-Amarnian era.

Recalling one of his visits to the Cairo Egyptian Museum's permanent exhibition of objects from the tomb of Tutankhamun, author Graham Hancock describes "dozens of Ark-like chests ... conceptually similar to the Ark of the Covenant."[103] He also points to the presence of deities with wings spread upwards "just like the cherubim referred to in the biblical description of the Ark"[104] on the doors and rear walls of the shrines. Ingeniously linking those Ark-like chests of King Tutankhamun's reign to his Ethiopian voyages, Hancock demonstrates, in his international best-seller *The Sign and the Seal (The Quest for the Lost Ark of the Covenant)*, the truly astounding resemblance between a given chest from King Tutankhamun's tomb and a carved relief of a very similar artifact from a fallen stela in Axum.[105] Where Hancock believes that he has found extant pictorial replicas of the long-lost Ark of the Covenant is in Ethiopia. This evidence can be gleaned from the ancient traditions of the Felasha — the Ethiopian Jewry whose priests maintain that they (the Beta Israel) had settled in Abyssinia (i.e. Ethiopia) in ancient times from pharaonic Egypt. According to Ethiopian national legend, the community of Ethiopian Jews currently dwelling in Abyssinia was originally founded by one Menelik — whom the legend holds was the son of the Queen of Sheba and King Solomon. The last monarch of this royal dynasty is purported to have been Negus (Emperor) Haile Selassie. The Ethiopian Jews themselves do not however generally accept this legend. Most of them consider themselves to be the remnants of lost tribe of Dan. Known as the Beta Israel (House of Israel), the Abyssinian Jews live in accordance with the Law of Moses. As the University of Alabama's Durrenda Ojanuga outlines:

> No one is really sure of their [the Jews of Ethiopia] origin; however, they lived in the mountains of Ethiopia, isolated from the Jewish community at large, for over 2,000 years, practising a traditional form of Judaism. When Ethiopian Jews had their first encounter with Europeans, they were surprised to find that there were White Jews, as they believed themselves to be the only Jewish people in the world.[106]

These Ethiopian Jews, who have been living in accordance to the Law of Moses for millennia, are the descendants of the members of the lost tribe of Manasseh who fled from Egypt, under the leadership of the Fifth Moses, during the rule of King

---

[103] Graham Hancock (1992) *The Sign and the Seal (The Quest for the Lost Ark of the Covenant)*, Doubleday Canada: Toronto, p. 288.
[104] Ibid.
[105] See ibid, Figs 56 and 57.
[106] Durrenda Ojanuga (1993) 'The Ethiopian Jewish Experience as Blacks in Israel', *Journal of Black Studies* Vol. 24 - Num. 2, p. 147; D. Kessler (1985) *The Falashas: The Forgotten Jews of Ethiopia*, Schocker: New York.

CHAP. XV: THE LIBYANS AND ETHIOPIANS TAKE CONTROL | 563

Horemheb. In fact, there is a very telling passage in the Dead Sea Scrolls which bears witness to the Fourth Exodus:

> Do you act better than Am[mon, seated between] the Niles? ... Its interpretation: **Amon is Manasseh and the Niles are the important people of Manasseh,** the nobles of the [people who surround Ma[nasseh] [...] **Water surrounds the one whose rampart was the sea, and the water her walls.** [...] Its interpretation: they are men at arms, her mighty warriors. **Ethiopia was her strength [and Egypt, without end.]** ... Put and Libya [were her guards]
> (Dead Sea Scrolls: 4QNahum Pesher [4Q169 4 – *Frags*. 3-4 / *Column* III])

In the above citation, Manasseh is clearly equated with Amon — the Egyptian deity or Theban cult. The fact that the Manasseh are said to have been a people of the Nile Valley, arguably, indicates that members of the Tribe of Manasseh must have indeed sojourned in Egypt in massive numbers. Moreover, the reference to waters of the sea who served as a rampart for the tribe of Manasseh, a wall of water, must certainly be a reference to the metaphorical account of the parting of the Red Sea found in the Bible. The episode of the composite Exodus story where a pharaoh of Egypt, and his chariotry forces, chased the Israelites up to Pi-Kharoti, in fact, takes place during the Fourth Exodus. The Pharaoh of the Exodus was actually none other than King Ay, who lived during Typhon Season #6. Finally, the Dead Sea Scrolls make abundantly clear that at the time when this particular episode took place, the Ethiopians and the Libyans were very powerful in Egypt. Indeed, we find in the novel chronology that, precisely during the Iron II period, the Ethiopians and Libyans were the uncontested masters of the Nile Valley. Further confirming this fact, the Second Book of Chronicles, covering that very period when the Tribe of Manasseh, is emphatic about the dominance of the Ethiopians and Libyans:

> 8 Were not the Ethiopians and the Lubims [Libyans] a huge host, with very many chariots and horsemen?
> (2 Chronicles 16: 8)

Evidently, the Dead Sea Scrolls describe the historical situation of the time very accurately. The assertion that the Manasseh of the Nile were supported by the strength of the Ethiopians and guarded by the Libyans, reflects the hospitality which they, at least initially, granted the newly-arrived Asiatics at the heels of the Venus shift. The Fifth Moses who, given his ties to the cult of Aten and of Re at Heliopolis, likely hailed from an Ethiopian family. He provided the Manasseh with guidance in times of great distress. Out of Egypt, he led them towards Ethiopia — their new home. This is precisely why, as I believe the Book of Amos alludes to below, the fleeing Manasseh of the Nile became known as "the children of the Ethiopians."

> 7 **Are ye not as children of the Ethiopians unto me,** O children of Israel? saith the Lord. Have I not brought up Israel out of the land of Egypt? ...
> (Amos 9:7)

Why does Amos specifically states the "children of the Ethiopians" as reference used by God to explain his power of deliverance from lands of affliction to the Israelites? The assumption is, evidently, that the Israelites would understand this reference to the Ethiopians' experience perfectly well. But nowhere in the Bible is a proper context given to evaluate this assertion. The interesting thing is that Amos, a contemporary of the Israelite king Jeroboam II, lived at the time of the Fourth Exodus towards Ethiopia!

A Changing of the Guard

Despite the demise of King Akhraten's Amarnian era, the power and influence of the Ethiopians in the Nile Valley had not diminished in the Nile Valley. Though they no longer, for the time being (the Iron IIb period), exercised direct suzerainty of dynastic Egypt, the Ethiopians' temples and administrative centres continued to be look up to reverently by the Libyans — who had, in the interim, reclaimed direct control of Thebes. Pharaoh Shoshenk-Amenhotep III erected temples at Soleb and Sedeinga, below the Fourth Cataract — dedicated, respectively, to a cult of himself, and the second temple for the worship of his Chief Queen Tiy, who was an Ethiopian herself. An avenue of granite ram-sphinxes was also constructed by King Shoshenk-Amenhotep III at the temple of Soleb in Nubia. We know that the temple at Soleb must be dated to the ninth century BCE Amenhotep III because, along with the rams, were found two lions which, incidentally, bear the inscription of King Tutankhamun. This means that Tutankhamun, a contemporary of Shoshenk-Amenhotep III, completed work on the unfinished crouching lions (see Fig. 11h, now in the British Museum). Moreover, one of the granite rams was taken from Soleb to Barkal by the Ethiopian kings of the standard 25th Dynasty (new 20th Dynasty). In the new chronology, this sequence of events makes perfect sense, since the new 20th Dynasty immediately follows Shoshenk III's 19th Dynasty. The standard chronology places a hiatus of about 650 years between the time when the ram figure was erected in its original emplacement at Soleb, and the time when the Ethiopians carried it away to Gebel Barkal.

CHAP. XV: THE LIBYANS AND ETHIOPIANS TAKE CONTROL | 565

Therefore, the transition between the reasserted Libyan rule during the Iron IIb era and the return of Napatan dominance, in 747 BCE, went through quite smoothly — as the two peoples had remained in good terms. The successor of the Libyan king Shoshenk-Amenhotep III, Horemheb, ensured the seamless continuity. The latter was likely neither a Libyan or an Ethiopian, but a native Egyptian. It would appear that he was appointed to the Theban throne by the outgoing pharaoh Shoshenk-Amenhotep III — who perhaps felt that he no longer had the mandate to rule following the disastrous upheaval of nature which befell Egypt at the close of the Fifth Sun. Thus, the *Cairo fragments* relate that:

> Chosen of the king, presider over the Two Lands, in order to carry on the administration of the Two Lands, general of generals of the Lord of the Two Lands; for the ka of the real king's-scribe, his beloved, Harmhab (Horemheb).[107]

The name of the king who favoured him is not mentioned, but it couldn't have been anyone else than Pharaoh Amenhotep-Shoshenk III. Given the apparent haste with which Horemheb was appointed, one may assume that his rule was but a temporary arrangement.

In 1942, the Memphite tomb of a certain Prince Shoshenk, Son of Osorkon II, and of his wife Karoma was discovered. The clearing out and publication tasks were carried out by Egyptologist Ahmad Badawi.[108] Prince Shoshenk, Osorkon II's heir apparent and high priest of Ptah, had died relatively young during his fathers' reign and, thus, never ascended the pharaonic throne. When the archaeological campaign got underway, a perplexing puzzle awaited the archaeologists at the entrance of this tomb. On the tomb's lintel doorway, Badawi was amazed to discover that an incised relief showing a kneeling figure representing Pharaoh Horemheb himself making funerary offerings. Immediately behind Horemheb, was none other than the deceased Prince Shoshenk, also in a kneeling position! The big question is: what could a portrait of King Horemheb possibly be doing in the tomb of Prince Shoshenk? If the former had died, according to the accepted chronology, some six hundred years before the birth of Prince Shoshenk? Although the cartouche of Pharaoh Horemheb had been somewhat damaged, as a result of an obviously deliberate attempt to erase it, there was no doubt in Badawi's mind that here was a figure of Pharaoh Horemheb. Given Horemheb's ephemeral and largely uneventful reign, what could have induced the Libyan dynasts to go out of their way to include such a conspicuous portrait, along with the cartouche, of a pharaoh

---

[107] J. H. Breasted, *Ancient Records of Egypt*, Vol. III - § 20.
[108] Ahmad Badawi (1956) 'Das Grab des Kronenprinzen Scheschonk, Sohnes Osorkon's II. und Hohenpriesters von Memphis', *Annales du Service des Antiquités* 54, p. 159, Pl. IV.

who had died some six hundred years earlier?[109] Customarily, had a revered royal ancestor been deified long after his death, he would have been portrayed as a deceased deity; but King Horemheb is obviously alive in the relief. In fact, all indications show that he had actually survived Prince Osorkon since he is shown paying tribute to him in his tomb. It is obvious that it was in fact Pharaoh Horemheb who had this scene painted in Prince Shoshenk's tomb just a few decades after the latter's death.

Setting the Record Straight

In any case, it is possible to get a better idea about the transition period between the Libyan and Ethiopian pharaohs by turning our attention to the temple of Osiris — Ruler of Eternity in Karnak. The two rooms at the rear of the temple are considered by archaeologists as being the earliest structure of the building. It is believed that the rooms were erected by Osorkon III and Takelot III of the standard 23rd Dynasty.[110] It is also clear that the temple underwent modification under the Ethiopian king Shabaka. Of great importance for our analysis, is a decorative scene from the inner sanctum of the temple in which are depicted the family members of Osorkon III. The cartouches of Osorkon III, his co-regent Takelot III, his son Rudamon and of the God's Wife Shepenwepet all appear. The God's Wife Shepenwepet is also accompanied by an adopted God's Wife by the name of Amenirdis.[111] An important detail to note is that this Amenirdis was the daughter of the Ethiopian king Kashta. This last detail chronologically freezes the entire sequence of events, relating to this temple, to a time span covering the new chronology's 19th Dynasty up to the end of Kashta's reign (around 747 BCE). In the new chronology, I have taken the last two pharaohs of the standard 23rd Dynasty, Rudamon and Iuput, and combined them with the kings of the conventional 24th Dynasty to form part of the new 21st Dynasty. Likewise, all the kings who usually follow Shoshenk III of the standard 22nd Dynasty (Pimay, Shoshenk IV-V and Osorkon IV-V), end up following Rudamon and Iuput of the new 21st Dynasty. Similarly, King Pedubast, traditionally placed *before* Osorkon III, now also moves to the new 21st Dynasty. Therefore, Rudamon, the son of Osorkon III portrayed in the temple of Osiris, went on to form a new dynasty towards the end of Pharaoh Kashta's reign. Since Rudamon's predecessors, Takelot III and Osorkon III of the standard 23rd Dynasty are now incorporated within the standard 22nd Dynasty at Tanis (new 19th Dynasty), the phantom standard 23rd Dynasty proves to serve no purpose at all.

---

[109] Immanuel Velikovsky 'The Assyrian Conquest': unpublished material.
[110] Donald Redford (1973a) 'An Interim Report on the Second Season of Work at the Temple of Osiris, Ruler of Eternity, Karnak', *Journal of Egyptian Archaeology* 59, p. 16.
[111] David M. Rohl (1995) *A Test of Time* I, p. 372.

CHAP. XV: THE LIBYANS AND ETHIOPIANS TAKE CONTROL | 567

In the final analysis, we find Osorkon III ascending to the throne at Tanis immediately after Takelot II — while Amenhotep-Shoshenk III, the predecessor of King Horemheb, reigned in Thebes. As a result, the questions to be now asked are: who were Osorkon III and Takelot III, and when did their co-regency take place? To partly answer those questions, I must first voice my own opinion that Osorkon III was actually Prince Osorkon of the standard 22nd Dynasty (new 19th Dynasty). I am also of the view that Prince Osorkon did not wait several decades before becoming king, but actually took over during the turbulent period following the 26th year of his father's reign —Takelot II. The co-regency between Osorkon III and Takelot III began on Year 24 of the former — in 757 BCE. From Prince Osorkon's Chronicle, we learn that he was attested as high priest of Karnak in Year 11 of his father Takelot II. The violent civil war which broke out in Year 15 of Takelot II went on until Year 24 of his reign. On Year 26, King Takelot II dies and the hostilities resume. Since the evidence tells us that the co-regency between Osorkon III and Takelot III began in 757 BCE, the temple of Osiris — Ruler of Eternity must have been erected between 757 and 747 BCE — when King Kashta's reign comes to an end. Hence, Osorkon III's co-regency with Takelot III must have lasted exactly ten years — while Horemheb reigned in Thebes. There is also another document from the West Quay at Karnak which mentions a high priest by the name of Osorkon in the 39th year of Shoshenk III — in 789 BCE. Prince Osorkon served as high priest of his father Takelot II's court from 796 BCE until he became king in his own right in 781 BCE. Obviously, as most scholars would attest to, the high priest Osorkon of Shoshenk III's reign was one and the same as Prince Osorkon of Takelot II's court — hence allowing for a co-regency between Amenhotep-Shoshenk III and Takelot II.

Mars: The Velikovskian Scenario

> *" And it shall come to pass in that day,*
> *saith the Lord God, that I will cause the sun*
> *to go down at noon, and I will darken*
> *the earth in the clear day ..."*
>
> - Amos 8:9

Horemheb reigned as pharaoh for 28 years.[112] This means that he ceased ruling Egypt in 747 BCE (776 - 28 = 747). Could his own reign have ended, as in the case

---

[112] See Peter A. Clayton (1994) *Chronicle of the Pharaohs (The Reign-by-Reign Record of the Rulers and Dynasties of Ancient Egypt)*, Thames and Hudson: London.

of his predecessor, King Moeris, in the shadow of a cosmic catastrophe? Is there any evidence of yet another planetary cataclysm at that time? According to Immanuel Velikovsky, such a disaster occurred exactly on the last year of King Horemheb's reign, in 747 BCE. This time, the cosmic disturbance involved the planet Mars. In Babylonia and Assyria, the planet Mars was given the name of "Nergal." The planet Mars was known in both cultures, from the eighth century BCE on, as "the lord of destruction."[113] Why had Nergal, the planet Mars, become so feared? Why was Mars-Nergal described as a warrior-deity who "causes the earth to shudder"?[114] What could the ancients have possibly meant when they said of Mars-Nergal: "The heaven he makes dark, he moves the Earth off its hinges"?[115] To Immanuel Velikovsky, the answer was clear. He pointed to the introduction of new calendars appearing on that year — ushered in by some event of great significance.[116] As at the end of Shoshenk-Amenhotep III's reign, Pharaoh Horemheb was hastily succeeded at the heels of yet another planetary cataclysm.

Meanwhile in the Aegean, the devastating effects of this latest orbital shift led to vast movements of population across the ancient Mediterranean islands and cities. The Mars catastrophe of 747 BCE was, in fact, one of the preeminent catalysts for the emergence of classical Greece. The settling of new territories, which serve as a historical background and inspiration for Homer's Odyssey, are to be set in this time. The Mars shift of 747 BCE comes along to round off a series of cosmic catastrophes, during the early history of the Mycenaean-B culture, which provided the founding structure for the mythology and poetry of the Hellenic age. For instance, the tale of Odysseus appears to have been based on the symbolism of the Typhon Seasons.

> And now the sun, leaving the beauteous mere, sprang up into the brazen heaven to give light to the immortals and to mortal men on the earth, the giver of grain; and they came to Pylos, the well-built citadel of Neleus. Here the townsfolk on the shore of the sea were offering sacrifice of black bulls to the dark-haired Earth-shaker.
> (Homer, *Odyssey*, Book III: 1-6)

Here, Homer makes an undeniably clear reference to the Apis bull cult practised by the Egyptians during the Typhon Seasons. As we know, Poseidon-Seth was indeed known to the ancient Greeks as the "Earth-shaker"[117] or "Earth-enfolder."[118]

---

[113] Langdon (1909) *Sumerian and Babylonian Psalms*, p. 85.
[114] Ibid, p. 79.
[115] Böllenrücher, *Gebete und Hymnen an Nergal*, p. 9.
[116] Immanuel Velikovsky (1950) *Worlds in Collision*, p. 210.
[117] Homer, *Odyssey*, Book VII: 273 and Hesiod, *Theogony*, 15.
[118] *Odyssey*, Book III: 55.

CHAP. XV: THE LIBYANS AND ETHIOPIANS TAKE CONTROL | 569

Like their Greek contemporaries in Crete within Minos's court at Knossos, the Mycenaean-B townsfolk from Pylos sought to appease the wrath of Typhon — the earth-shaker who mercilessly pours the turbulent waters of the sea upon inhabited lands.

Since this scene takes place at Pylos, the Iron Age citadel built by Neleus, we know that the Greeks must have been performing the bovine rituals during Typhon Season #6. This was only the second Typhon Seasons in the history of the Mycenaean-B Greeks. Unlike their much more ancient Afroasiatic neighbours, the Greeks did not remember the previous cataclysms. A brand new cosmogony, evidently partially borrowed from the Afroasiatic myths, emerged early during the time of the Fifth Creation.

> From that time forth Poseidon the earth-shaker, does not indeed slay Odysseus, but makes him a wanderer from his native land.
> (Homer, *Odyssey*, Book I: 74-75)

Those wanderings of Odysseus are dated by Homer to shortly after the sack of Troy.[119] They record the earliest memories of the Greeks of a universal catastrophe followed by broad displacements of peoples. Homer's *Odyssey* draws from the experiences of Odysseus and the returning Danaans to describe the similar migrations which immediately followed the Mars shift of 747. Incidentally, this cataclysm coincides with the catastrophic collapse of Knossos and the end of King Minos' Mediterranean empire. On the likely Iron Age context of an historical *Odyssey*, classicist Ian Morris writes:

> A few archaeologists in the 1890s also argued that even if Homer's Heroic Age did largely reproduce the Mycenaean world, since he had probably lived in the eighth century, the ship scenes on the Late Geometric pottery could illuminate the *Odyssey* ...[120]

In fact, many classical scholars contend that there was a "population explosion" in eighth century Greece — urging the Greeks to send out colonies.[121] The eminent classicist A. M. Snodgrass estimates that "in the space of two thirty-year generation, between 780 and 720 B.C., the population [of Attica] may have multiplied itself by a factor of approximately seven."[122] Like Odysseus, who was forced to

---

[119] *Odyssey*, Book I: 1-2.
[120] Ian Morris (1997) p. 112.
[121] G. L. Cawkwell (1992) 'Early Colonization', *Classical Quarterly* Vol. 42 - Num. 2, p. 289.
[122] A. M. Snodgrass (1980) *Archaic Greece (The Age of Experiment)*, J. M. Dent & Sons: London, p. 18.

wander through foreign lands on account of Poseidon's persecution, the Mycenaean-B inhabitants of the Greek mainland and Crete, sent out numerous colonies abroad as Poseidon's wrath raged during Typhon Season #6. Since the Late Geometric phase, the time in which the Odyssey is set, lasted between c.750-700 BCE, it in fact falls immediately after the Mars shift of 747 BCE.

The vizier Nespekashuti, by author

Part V

Napatan Period
747 BCE to 664 BCE

Macedonian Period
664 BCE to 561 BCE

Ethiopian and Persian Conquests
561 BCE to 404 BCE

16

Descendants of Ancient Kings (747 BCE to 664 BCE)

> " Now the Ethiopians, as historians
> relate, were the first of all men and the proofs
> of this statement, they say, are manifest."
>
> - Diodorus of Sicily
> (Book III: 2)

One of the most consequential effects of lowering the date for the beginning of the 18th Dynasty in Egypt, by over four centuries, is the complete shattering of the orthodox history of the C-Group Kushites. Conventional wisdom contends that the Ethiopian kings of the standard 25th Dynasty (new 20th Dynasty) had been Egyptianized Kushites who'd been exposed to pharaonic culture through the viceregal administration set up in Nubia by the pharaohs of the 18th Dynasty. Theban priests of Amun, sent to Gebel Barkal during the New kingdom, are believed to have introduced the Ethiopians to the worship of Amun. Later on, those same Ethiopians allegedly managed to conquer their Egyptian tutors' homeland and, somehow, were received in Thebes as genuine pharaohs in the mid-eighth century BCE. Thus, in the standard framework, the Kushites' rise from subordinate pupil to sudden master of the Nile Valley spanned over eight hundred years. Reducing that period in half, by lowering the dates of the 18th Dynasty, can understandably be met with much resistance by modern Nubiologists. Since, according to the orthodox history and chronology of the Nile Valley, the late twelfth century BCE was a period of imperial decline in dynastic Egypt, the presence of an effective Egyptian viceregal administration in Nubia, vigorously dominating Nubia, would be seen as rather fanciful.

It is in fact entirely true that the earlier pharaohs of the 18th Dynasty were notoriously eager to maintain an authoritative Egyptian presence in the land of Kush. For example, King Amenhotep I had set up Egypt's southern frontier at Semneh on the Third Cataract. Subsequently, Pharaoh Tuthmosis I successfully broke through the Third Cataract point and, through intemperate military conquest, pushed the Egyptian border further south. After a series of punitive expedition, Tuthmosis I stopped at the door of Meroë and went no further.[1] Historians have difficulty explaining why Tuthmosis I's army would stop

---

[1] Hans Goedicke (1996) p. 175.

short of conquering Meroë — seeing that his Egyptian forces had made it that far without facing any opposition from the helpless Nubian garrisons. Napata was the limit of Egypt's southern empire during the New Kingdom. This is confirmed by the fact that no *in situ* New Kingdom archaeological remains have been found at or below Napata.[2] The Egyptian southern frontier at the Fourth Cataract was not established until the forty-seventh regnal year of Pharaoh Tuthmosis III. But, I'm proposing that this pharaoh, of the New Kingdom's 18th Dynasty, lived in the Iron Age I era — where I believe that dynastic Egypt was at the height of its imperial power. The 18th Dynasty's Tuthmosis III was the first Egyptian king to reach Gebel Barkal.[3] No other Egyptian monarch before him had ever done so. Thus, the Ethiopian region below the Fourth Cataract had, throughout the Late Bronze Age, remained free of Egyptian imperial intervention. And even when the powerful Tuthmoside pharaohs of the 18th Dynasty came along, they refrained from pushing too far below the Fourth Cataract — toward the kingdom of Meroë. The reason for that is that the Khemetic kingdoms of Napata and Meroë had always remained fully independent of the Dynastic Egyptians. The dynastic Egyptian punitive raids had consistently been targeted against the non-pharaonic C-Group Nubians dwelling between the Second and Fourth Cataracts.

The accepted notion that the Ethiopian pharaohs who came to rule Egypt in the middle of the eighth century BCE came from among the C-Group Kushites is one of the greatest, and most damaging, myths of ancient world scholarship. As I have outlined in previous chapters, the C-Group Asiatic Nubians from the lands of Kush and Wawat never, in reality, developed a sophisticated pharaonic-style monarchy. Nor would the Egyptians ever have welcome them as legitimate rulers of the Two Lands. As late as the reign of Tutankhamun, the latter was conducting fierce punitive military expeditions below the Second Cataract. If, as I have demonstrated King Tutankhamun reigned just a few decades before the advent of Napatan rule in Thebes, how is one to justify their sudden acceptance as legitimate pharaohs in Egypt? The truth is, King Tutankhamun was of Napatan heritage himself, through his father King Akhraten. The Kushites whom he attacked were viewed, both by the Ethiopians and the Egyptians, as belligerent peoples of Asiatic descent — agents and disciples of the storm-god Seth. Their very presence was seen as threat to the divinely ordained natural order (Ma'at). As classicists Frank Snowden observes:

> A few pieces from Egyptian workshops dating to the reign of Tutankhamun illustrate the pharaonic practice of symbolizing Egypt's power and might by portraying both Asians [Asiatics] and Kushites as

---

[2] Charles-André Julien (editor) (1977) *Les Africains*, Éditions J. A.: Paris, Tome I: pp. 87-88.
[3] Robert G. Morkot 'Nubia in the New Kingdom: The Limits of Egyptian Control.' In W. Vivian Davies (editor) (1991) *Egypt and Africa (Nubia from Prehistory to Islam)*, p. 294.

CHAP. XVI: DESCENDANTS OF ANCIENT KINGS | 575

humiliated foes: a wooden chest depicting the pharaoh slaughtering Syrians on one side and Kushites on the other; a foot-stool decorated with alternating Kushites and Asiatic captives dressed in their native garb; and a ceremonial throwing stick combining a black African in ebony and a bearded Asiatic in ivory.[4]

Again, the reason why the Kushites and the Asiatics are represented together is because the two sets of peoples are culturally linked. Neither of them belong to the realm of pharaonic culture. Even the ancient Greek chroniclers recognized this fact.

> ... but the parts on the left side of the course of the Nile, in Libya, are inhabited by the Nubae, a large tribe, who, beginning at Meroë, extend as far as the bends of the river, and are not subject to the Aethiopians but are divided into several separate kingdoms.
> (Strabo, *Geography* Vol. XVII: 1, 2)

By erroneously equating the Asiatic Nubians of the lands of Kush and Wawat, modern scholars have developed a completely warped purview of pharaonic history in Ethiopia. This confusion was further amplified by the misaligned orthodox chronology of Egypt.

A Dark Age in Nubia?

In fact, it is precisely the inaccurate chronology of dynastic Egypt which provides a basis for the confused history of Nubia. The viceregal administration instituted in Nubia by the 18th Dynasty pharaohs, allegedly during the Late Bronze Age, is supposed to have been the catalyst for the eventual "Egyptianizing" of the Kushites. Yet, this model is in itself rife with contradictions, as Peter James delineates below:

> Having created a Dark Age in Nubia, it is not surprising that historians have treated the appearance of the Egyptianized 'Kingdom of Kurru' in the mid-9th century BC as a new beginning, largely unrelated to the end of the Viceregal period. ... Indeed, few writers considering the end of the viceregal administration and the rise of the Kingdom of Kurru discuss the Dark Age itself; most restrict themselves to a passing comment on the lack of evidence from this period. Accordingly, the sudden expansion of Kurru power in the second half of the 8th century BC has baffled Nubian archaeologists.[5]

---

[4] Frank M. Snowden, Jr. (1993) 'Images and Attitudes: Ancient Views of Nubia and the Nubians', *Expedition* Vol. 35 - Num. 2, p. 43.
[5] Peter James *et al.* (1991) *Centuries of Darkness (A Challenge to the Conventional Chronology of Old World Archaeology)*, Jonathan Cape: London, p. 208.

How is it possible that, in the words of Nubiologist William Y. Adams, "Nubia vanished entirely from history," only to have its native rulers "emerge with a vengeance three centuries later"?[6] What happened in the meantime to the viceregal infrastructures so painstakingly enforced over a period of five hundred years? Can we really be expected to believe that Nubian society reverted to a "tribal level"[7] after the Egyptians' supposed withdrawal at the end of the New Kingdom? Adams and another prominent Nubiologist Bruce Trigger of McGill University have come under constant criticism from African-centered scholars for claiming that the C-Group Nubian culture had permanently been a colonial derivative of the Egyptian powerhouse in the north. Although I personally do not find anything improper with their interpretation of the Nubian archaeological evidence, were I *do* quarrel with Adams and Trigger, though, is with their assumption that it was those obsequious Kushites, dwelling between the Second and Fourth Cataracts, who later founded the conventional 25th Dynasty (new 20th Dynasty).

The so-called Dark Age of Nubia, as with the Dark Age of Greece, is simply an unnecessary by-product of the faulty accepted chronology of ancient Egyptian civilization. Though, in the new chronology, this problem simply disappears by lowering the dates of the Egyptian viceregal administration by several centuries, still another conundrum would present itself when considering that, from one day to the next, these C-Group Nubians would go from subservient lackeys to masters of the Nile Valley. Thus, in either case, linking the Egyptian viceregal administration in the lands of Kush and Wawat with the subsequent rise of the Napatan dynasty in Thebes, proves extremely problematic. The one, and only, solution is to recognize that there was a continuous pharaonic culture, south of the Fourth Cataract, which actually preceded the 18th Dynasty Egyptian viceregal administration by millennia. It was, in fact, as the cultural inheritors of the ancient Khemetic kingdoms of the Anu, Meroites, and Napatans of Nuri, that the Napatan kings of El Kurru, starting in the ninth century BCE, emerged as a force to be reckoned with in the Nile valley. They owed absolutely nothing and, as Strabo relates, were in no way connected with the Asiatic Nubians from the lands of Kush and Wawat. The entire era of the Egyptian viceregal administration during the 18th Dynasty did not concern them directly since the Tuthmoside Kings'

---

[6] William Y. Adams (1964) 'Post-Pharaonic Nubia in the Light of Archaeology, I', *Journal of Egyptian Archaeology* 50, pp. 114-115.
[7] Bruce Trigger (1976) *Nubia Under the Pharaohs*, Thames & Hudson: London, p. 140.

Standard Chronology of the Napatan and Meroitic Kings

Napata (El Kurru) (806-653 BCE)	Meroë (295 BCE to 320 CE)
Kashta	Arkakamani (South Cemetery)
Pi-Ankhy	Amanislo " "
Shabaka	Queen Bartare " "
Shebitku	Amanitekha (North Cemetery)
Taharka	Arnekhamani
Tanutamun	Arqamani
	Tabirqa (200-185 BCE)
Napata (Nuri) (653-295 BCE)	Queen Shanakdakhete
Atlanarsa	Tanyidamani
Senkamanisken	Amanirenas
Anlamani	Akinadad
Aspalta	Queen Amanishakhete
Amtalqa	Natakamani
Malenaqen	Amanitere
Analmaye	Sherkarer (12-17 CE)
Amani-nataki-lebte	Pisakar
Karkamani (519-510 BCE)	Amanitaraqide
Amaniastabarqa	Amanitenmemide
Siaspiqa	Queen Amanikhatashan
Nasakhmani	Tarekeniwal
Malewiebamani	Takideamani
Talakhamani	Aryesbekhe
Aman-nete-yerike	Teritnide
Baskakeren	Aretnide
Harsiotef	Teqerideamani
Akhraten	Yesbekheamani
Amanibakhi (310-295 BCE)	Maleqerabar (308-320 CE)
	(N.B.: 15 rulers have been omitted)

Table 16-1

Fig. 16a: Pharaoh Shabaka.

southern frontier ended just below the Fourth Cataract. There could, actually, have been some form of alliance between the Napatan pharaohs of Nuri and the Tuthmoside pharaohs to keep the Asiatic Nubians in check, as there is evidence that during the course of the Tuthmoside Nubian campaigns, Kushites were hanged on the walls of Napata in order to discourage further rebellion against the Egyptian crown.

To recapitulate, the revised chronology of Ethiopian pharaonic civilization literally reverses the order of the traditionally accepted succession (see Table 16-1) of the Napatan and Meroitic pharaohs. In the new chronology, the succession line starts with the Meroitic pharaohs buried in Meroë's North Cemetery, later followed with a series of contemporary Napatan kings from Nuri, and lastly come the Napatan rulers of El Kurru (of the standard 25th Dynasty). The kings buried at the South Cemetery of Meroë must have, for their part, ruled after the Amarnian era; since King Amanislo inscribed his name on both lions made for Pharaoh Shoshenk-Amenhotep III at his Soleb temple. It would seem that the Meroitic kings of the South Cemetery simply followed the line of kings buried in the North Cemetery. Hence, we should assume that King Maleqerabar was a close predecessor of Pharaoh Arkakamani — himself a likely contemporary of Amenhotep-Shoshenk III. Conventional historians, however, contend that after the South Cemetery at Meroë became full, it was abandoned by the Meroitic kings — who were consequently later buried in the North Cemetery. The extant archaeological evidence, on the basis of the novel chronology, however, demonstrates that the South Cemetery succeeded the North Cemetery. What we should instead conclude is that Queen Bartare was the last monarch to be buried in Meroë, in the South Cemetery. The Napatan pharaohs of El-Kurru then immediately took over the Meroitic sites and, during the eighth and seventh centuries BCE, had their own lesser royals and officials buried there.[8]

All of this signifies that, during the Tuthmoside imperialistic age in Egypt, the 18th Dynasty ruled contemporaneously with the Napatans of Nuri and the Meroites of the North Cemetery. In his 1975 book *Apedemak: Lion God of Meroë*, Nubiologist L. V. Zabkar outlines the obvious similarities between the artistic techniques used in Meroitic and Napatan Nubia and 18th Dynasty Egypt as follows:

> This technique of the Naqa designer could well be part of an Egyptian tradition which appeared in Nubia in the 18th Dynasty, and which was then adopted by the Napatan and Meroitic sculptors and applied in a variety of ways to statuary and reliefs. It will be remembered that the inscribed rams of Amenhotep III from Jebel Barkal have their fleece marked by large elon-

---

[8] See Mark Lehner (1997) *The Complete Pyramids*, Thames and Hudson: London, p. 198.

gated tufts, and the same sculptor's device can also be seen on the rams of Amun protecting King Taharqa on the statues from Gebel Barkal, as well as those at Kawa, in which the fleece of the rams is indicated by the same large tufts probably modelled on those of Amenhotep's rams. The granite rams at Naqa and the rams flanking the approach of the temple of Amun at Meroe, have their fleece indicated on their bodies by spiral-like circular marks, and a similar device was also used in miniature sculpture.[9]

Unlike Zabkar, I do not believe that the artists who built the temple at Naqa were influenced by the artisans of Amenhotep III. My own historical reconstruction postulates instead that it was Shoshenk-Amenhotep III himself who looked to the Ethiopians for inspiration. Once again, we find undeniably contemporary artistic styles and practices between the Napatans and New Kingdom Egyptians — all in a time when they were supposed, according to conventional wisdom, to have been separated in time by several centuries. Additionally, pointing to linguistic evidence, eminent French Egyptologist Jean Yoyotte remarks:

> Two words belonging to the Meroitic vocabulary, qêré, "king" and atê, "water," appear in Egyptian texts from the New Kingdom; the first one before the year 1,000 [BCE], the second around 1,300 [BCE]. At this date, consequently, people who spoke the Meroitic language were feasibly already established in the Sudan.[10]

A Chronological Enigma at Gebel Barkal

The truth about the anteriority of the Meroitic and Napatan cultures has thus been a prisoner, condemned in perpetuity, of the orthodox chronology of ancient Egypt. Blindly accepting the Egyptological establishment's framework, Nubiologists continually fail to understand the nature and time line of pharaonic culture in Ethiopia. Even excavations which yield potentially valuable clues toward the proper reconstruction of Nubian chronology, are summarily made to fit into the standard Egyptological mould. One such case, I believe, was a series of excavations conducted at the sacred mountain of Gebel Barkal in this century. During three seasons in 1970, 1986, and 1987, the Boston Museum of Fine Arts undertook the project of further supplementing the archaeological data

---

[9] L. V. Zabkar (1975) *Apedemak: Lion God of Meroe (A Study in Egyptian-Meroitic Syncretism)*, Aris & Phillips: Warminster, U.K., p. 39.
[10] Jean Yoyotte (1954-57) 'Le toponyme «Napata» comme témoin linguistique', *GLECS* 8, p. 108 (my translation).

CHAP. XVI: DESCENDANTS OF ANCIENT KINGS | 581

compiled by George Reisner at Napata between 1916 and 1920. Indeed, Reisner's findings had taken a long time to be published (in 1950, 1955 and even as late as 1970) and needed to be updated. The director of the campaign was Timothy Kendall, then keeper of the Egypt and Near East Department at the museum. The stated objective of the American mission was to excavate the Napatan temples situated at the bottom of the sacred mountain of Gebel Barkal. In between the time when Reisner had completed his initial excavation and the beginning of the Boston Museum campaign, many tourists who visited the ancient Napatan site were intrigued with what appeared to have been an unfinished colossal statue of a Napatan king protruding from the mountain side. In 1941, two such tourists, while examining the mysterious pinnacle with the aid of binoculars, discovered what appeared to have been traces of an inscription near the peak of the structure, at some 75 metres from the ground. In 1953, Nubiologist A. J. Arkell again observed these inscriptions, armed with a surveyor's telescope; and identified two royal cartouches near the top of the pinnacle. The finds of Dr Arkell established the following:

> It will be seen that there are four cartouches visible, together with top of a fifth near the upper horizontal line. The two complete names are, presumably, Nastasen, and clearly Taharqa. ... First, since the signs read from left to right (presumably in vertical columns) Nastasen appears to be named well before Taharqa, who, in fact, lived nearly four hundred years earlier.[11]

The subsequent work of Kendall at Gebel Barkal in the late 1980s would come along to confirm Arkell's reading of the two best preserved cartouches. Initially, Kendall tried to observe the cartouches with the aid of a telescope, but he did not get far. Undaunted by this, Kendall decided to go see the inscription for himself on top of the mountain. He enlisted the help of Paul Duval, an expert alpinist, to help him climb the mountain. So on February 22nd 1987, the pair set out for the adventure. Unbeknownst to them, they were about to discover something of important significance. Upon close inspection, Kendall was able to decipher two cartouches: one bearing the name of Taharka, the other inscribed with the name of Nastasen. The accompanying text seemed to refer to some victorious campaigns these two pharaohs had waged against the "Bedouins of Asia" and the "Libyan nomads."[12] The inscriptions were carved above where an enshrined statue of King Taharka once stood. No one then or since have been able to explain what could have motivated these kings to inscribe their names in such

---

[11] H. N. Chittick (1957) 'An Inscription on Gebel Barkal', *Journal of Egyptian Archaeology* 43, p. 43.
[12] Marianne Cournevin (1998) p. 178.

an inaccessible location. It is ironically assumed by Nubiologists that Nastasen's and Taharka's reigns were separated by nearly four hundred years. But it is clear from the American mission's excavation reports that a large series of grooves, meant to uphold wooden beams, carved in between the main mountain rock and the protruding rock containing the shrine with the inscriptions, had been utilized by the Ethiopian masons to access the shrine. Can one seriously assume that, four hundred years after this delicate system was constructed, Nastasen would risk sending his men upon such a perilous quest simply to carve his name next to his ancestor? How could the wooden beams have remained solid and safe after nearly four centuries? The new chronology solves this mystery. Being the immediate successor of Akhenaten in Nubia, Nastasen was most likely a contemporary of Kashta — the founder of Taharka's Dynasty. Therefore, it is entirely probable that the construction project, meant to connect the Gebel Barkal sacred mountain's main body and its semi-detached pinnacle, went on interrupted, albeit slowly, from the reigns of Nastasen to Taharka. The actual time-gap between the two Ethiopian rulers probably did not exceed a century — if that much.

Governing Petty Kings

Like Pharaoh Shoshenk-Amenhotep III passed on the reigns of power to King Horemheb after the Venus cataclysm of 776 BCE, so the latter relinquished his throne to the Ethiopian king Taharka on the year of the Mars shift of 747 BCE. The transition occurred relatively smoothly, as the Ethiopians and the Libyan pharaohs of the new 19th Dynasty had maintained good relations. Pharaoh Osorkon II had even insisted that Ethiopians should be present at his *Heb-Sed* festival at Bubastis.[13] Puzzled by this fact Egyptologist Édouard Naville was forced to ask himself the question: "Why did Osorkon [II] wish that Ethiopians should be present at his festival in the Delta? Had he any special connection with Ethiopia, by birth or by conquest?—These are questions to which we can give no answer..."[14] The answer, however, only remains a mystery within the fallacious context of the accepted histories and chronologies of Egypt and Nubia. The dynastic Egyptians had always held the Ethiopians in very high regard for their ancient knowledge base and overall antiquity. As a matter of fact, when Napatans of Kurru took over the reigns of power in the Theban capital, they legitimized their rule to the native Egyptian populace by claiming that they were descendants of ancient kings. This assertion has traditionally been met with much skepticism among modern Egyptologists and Nubiologists — given the incompatibility of this statement with the orthodox interpretation of Ethiopia's histo-

---

[13] Édouard Naville (1892) *The Festival-Hall of Osorkon II in the Great Temple of Bubastis (1887-1889)*, Egypt Exploration Fund: London, p. 25.
[14] Ibid.

CHAP. XVI: DESCENDANTS OF ANCIENT KINGS | 583

ry. The evidence presented in this book, however, very much vindicates the claim of the El Kurru pharaohs. As Napatan rulers, their most ancient pharaonic ancestors were the A-Group Ta-Seti Nubians — who precede the advent of the first dynastic Egyptian king. Being extremely proud of their Khemetic origins, the Ethiopian pharaohs of the new 20th Dynasty *never* wore the "khepresh" or blue crown of the later dynastic Egyptian pharaohs.[15] They also did not wish to associate themselves with the alter ego line which begun with King Ahmose of the 18th Dynasty. Affirming their anteriority, they wore two urae on their crown — as a sign that they ruled both the Black Land and the Red Land.[16]

Pharaoh Piye (formerly read Pi-Ankhy), Taharka's successor, held his coronation ceremony at Heliopolis. As in the Khemetic tradition, Piye paid homage to Re and Atum in the presence of the sacred *ben-ben* stone:

> Mounting the stairs to the great window to view Re in the Pyramidion House. The king stood by himself alone. Breaking the seals of the bolts, opening the doors; viewing his father Re in the holy Pyramidion House; adorning the Morning Bark of Re and the Evening Bark of Atum.

A devout disciple of the Theban deity Amun as well, Piye adopted the same Horus name as Mentuhotep-Nebhepetre, Sematawy, which means "Unifier of the Two Lands." Piye was not interested in residing in the Egyptian capital, or in Egypt itself for that matter. So he allowed the local Egyptian dynasts to continue ruling as vassals from Thebes and Tanis (new 21st Dynasty). The Piye Stela offers us ample proof that the local dynasts were ruling in Egypt at the same time as the Ethiopians. Piye, for example, describes King Tefnakht as the "Great Chief of the Libu [Libyans]" ruling in Sais. Other "pharaohs" mentioned are Osorkon IV, Iuput, and Nimlot. The dynasty of local petty kings reigning under the tutelage of the Napatans at El Kurru represents the 21st Dynasty in the new chronology which I propose. This new 21st Dynasty is a rearranged amalgamation of some of the pharaohs listed in the conventional 22nd through 24th Dynasties. Inconsistencies within the succession of reigns in the so-called Third Intermediate Period have indeed been observed for some time by Egyptologists — as D. A. Aston remarks below:

> Osorkon IV, although of the Tanite line, probably does not belong to the Twenty-second Dynasty either. Priese was the first to suggest that he be-

---

[15] Bruce Trigger *et al.* (1983) *Ancient Egypt: A Social History*, Cambridge University Press: Cambridge, U.K., p. 289.
[16] Marianne Cournevin (1998) *Secrets du continent Noir révélés par l'archéologie*, Maisonneuve et Larose: Paris, p. 179.

longed with Manetho's Twenty-third Dynasty, and this idea has recently been strengthened by Lehy who demonstrated that the Pedubast and Osorkon with whom Manetho's Twenty-third Dynasty begins are probably Pedubast II and Osorkon IV.[17]

Once we remove Osorkon III and Takelot III from the so-called 23rd Dynasty, and place them in the new 19th Dynasty, we can automatically equate the standard 23rd Dynasty with the new 21st Dynasty. The reason why Egyptologists have been misled in placing Osorkon III after Pedubast is because Manetho's 23rd Dynasty has an Osorkon following Pedubast. Like Priese and Lehy however, I believe that the Osorkon of Manetho was actually Osorkon IV. Since there would then no longer be any evidence for the existence of a Pedubast before Osorkon III, I would further suggest that there was only ever *one* Pedubast. We now understand why historians artificially introduced Osorkon III and Takelot III within the standard 23rd Dynasty. They wrongly assumed that the Osorkon of Manetho's 23rd Dynasty (new 21st Dynasty) was Osorkon III, when he was really Osorkon IV — a contemporary of Piye and Shabaka. Confusion about the genuine order of succession of these petty monarchs, and about their contemporaneity with the Napatan pharaohs of the El Kurru, has even led to the unnecessary creation of duplicate pharaohs. This fact can be gleaned from the following quote by eminent Egyptologist Kenneth A. Kitchen:

> That there were *two* kings Iuput emerges from the chronology of the Libyan period, whereby the king Iuput of the time of the Nubian Pi-ankhy can hardly be the same as the Iuput who was co-regent of Pedubast, the traditional founder of the 23rd Dynasty! To crush that entire dynasty into the modest interval between the invasions of Egypt by Piankhy and his successor Shabako is just not feasible.[18]

From the New Chronology Table, however, we immediately discern that all of these kings, Piye (Pi-Ankhy), Iuput, and Pedubast, were in fact contemporaries. Another interesting implication of the reordering of the successions, is the possibility of finally identifying who precisely was the Ethiopian "King So" from the Bible's Book of Kings (2 Kings 17:4). The subject of his exact identity has been the cause of intense debate among ancient historians.[19] The Israelite king Hoshea, who was caught in between a tremendous tug of war between the Ethiopians in Egypt and the Assy-

---

[17] D. A. Aston (1989) 'Takelot II — A King of the "Theban Twenty-Third Dynasty"?', *Journal of Egyptian Archaeology* 75, p. 140.
[18] Kenneth A. Kitchen (1973) *The Third Intermediate Period in Egypt*, § 79 – p. 97.
[19] See Alberto R. W. Green (1993) 'The Identity of King So of Egypt — An Alternative Interpretation', *Journal of Near Eastern Studies* Vol. 52 - Num. 2, pp. 99-108.

Fig. 16b: King Sargon II of Assyria (*by* Saint-Elme Gautier).

Fig. 16c: Assyrian palace [restored] (*from* Chipiez, 1884).

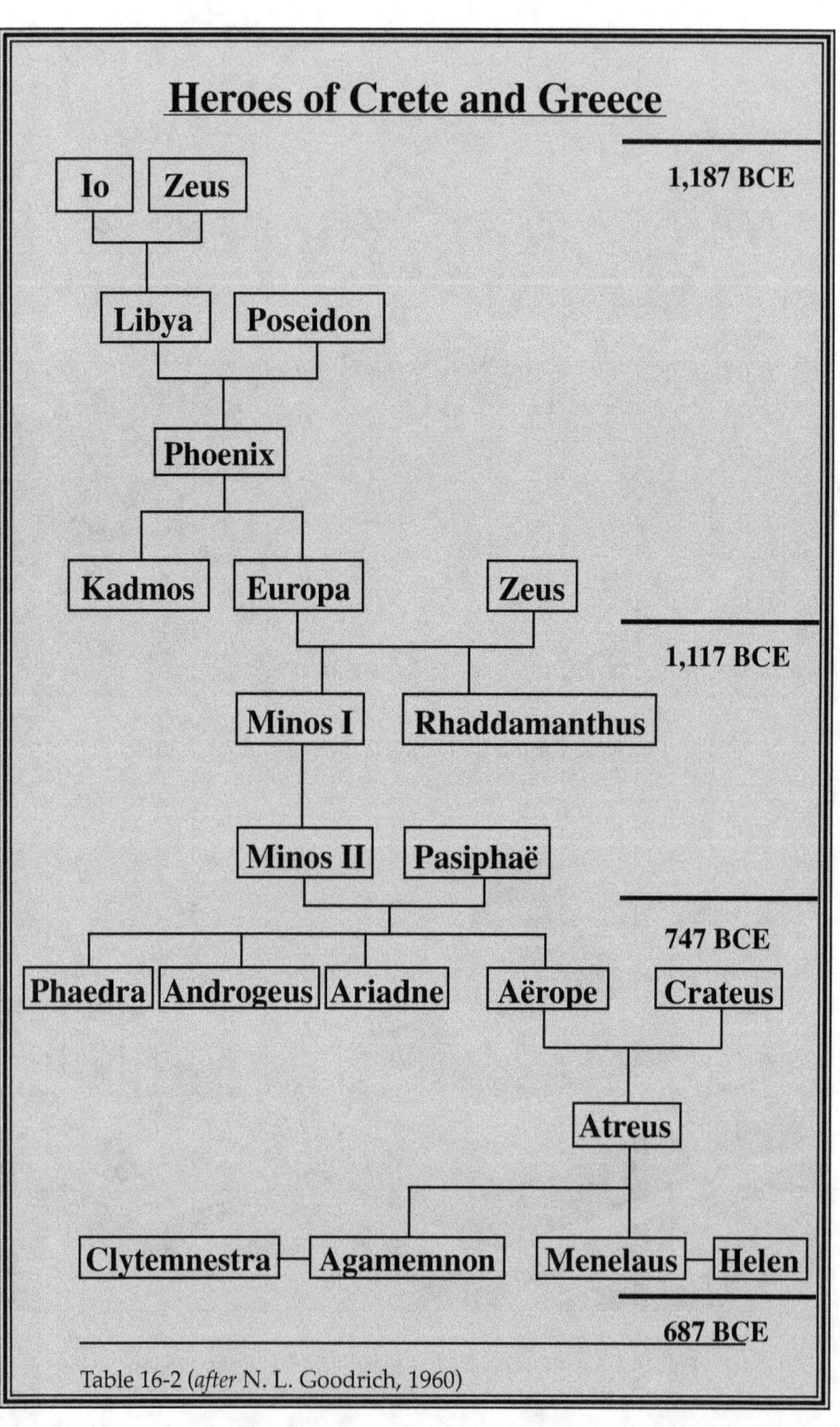

Table 16-2 (*after* N. L. Goodrich, 1960)

rians over power and influence in the ancient Near East, was a contemporary of the Assyrian King Shalmanaser V and the Ethiopian pharaoh So. Looking at the New Chronology Table, I believe that we must conclude that "So" was none other than King Shoshenk V, the Theban petty ruler of the new 21st Dynasty. According to Albert R. W. Green of Rutgers University:

> In translating 2 Kings 17:4, the Lucianic Version of the Septuagint adds "Adrammelech the Ethiopian, living in Egypt" for "So King of Egypt." What we clearly have is an interpretation, not just a translation. ... According to the translator, it was a Nubian or Ethiopian king who was residing in Egypt at the time that was the object of this request for help.[20]

Prof. Green goes on to conclude that this Ethiopian king was Piye. For his part, Donald B. Redford of the University of Toronto — assuming that "So" is really a transcription of "Sais" — feels that "there can be no doubt" that the Egyptian king whom Hoshea contacted was Tefnakht — not an Ethiopian.[21] Yet earlier in the last century, Sir Flinders Petrie[22] had assumed that King So was really Shabaka, while C. F. Lehnmann-Haupt[23] opted for Shebitku. Though I would agree with Lehnmann-Haupt that the Ethiopian king who ruled Egypt at the time of Hoshea was Shebitku, I would not however identify him as the King So of 2 Kings 17:4. The fact is, both Shebitku and king So (Shoshenk V), in addition to Bocchoris in Tanis, reigned contemporaneously with Hoshea in Israel.

Mars, Venus, and the Trojan War
The period immediately following the close of King Hoshea's reign in Israel brought yet another era of cosmic upheaval in the ancient world. As Immanuel Velikovsky argued in *Worlds in Collision*, less than a century after it wrought significant havoc

---

[20] A. R. W. Green (1993) p. 101.
[21] Donald B. Redford (1985) 'Sais and the Kushite Invasions of the Eighth Century B.C.', *Journal of the American Research Center in Egypt* 22, p. 15. The exact same position was adopted earlier by Hans Goedicke in 1963. Assuming that So was really Sais would however necessitates modifying the biblical text to make it read: "to Sais, to the king of Egypt" (A. Green [1993], p. 102). In that fashion, the pharaoh in question is no longer identified by name. Hencewhy Redford and Goedicke are able to assume that Egyptian king of 2 Kings 17:4 was the Saite pharaoh Tefnakht. I find this theory rather unconvincing because, as K. Kitchen points out, the "place name" theory requires an emendation of the original biblical text.
[21] Sir Flinders Petrie (1912) *Egypt and Israel*, London, pp. 75-77.
[22] C. F. Lehmann-Haupt (1911) *Israel: Seine Entwicklung im Rahmen der Weltgeschichte*, Tübinge, pp. 100-104.

upon the earth, the planet Mars, in 687 BCE, once again left its stable orbital course. Defending his hypothesis, Velikovsky writes:

> The Talmudic and Midrashic sources, which relate that the army of Sennacherib was destroyed by a blast and scourge accompanied by a terrible din on the night following the day when the shadow of the sun returned ten degrees, are more specific: the scourge was inflicted by the Archangel Gabriel "in the guise of a column of fire." In the present research it has been established that it was the work of Mars.[24]

The memory of that catastrophic event lived on in the mythologies of many ancient peoples. That is why, in the eighth century BCE, the Babylonian king Shamash-shum-ukin wrote: "Nergal (the Assyrian and Babylonian Mars), the most violent among the gods." Likewise, in Assyria, King Esarhaddon uttered: "Nergal, the almighty among the gods, fear, terror, awe-inspiring splendor."[25] King Ashurbanipal of the seventh century BCE spoke of Nergal (Mars) as the god who brought defeat: "Nergal, the perfect warrior, the most powerful one among the gods, the preeminent hero, the mighty lord, king of battle, lord of power and might, lord of the storm, who brings defeat."[26] Even up until the time of the Roman Empire, we find the chronicler Pliny describing Mars as a feared warrior: "We also see at Rome goblets of iron dedicated in the temple of Mars the Avenger."[27]

The reader is certainly versed enough in ancient mythology by now to know that the same hero-god in one culture, can often be portrayed as an evil force, or arch-demon, in another culture. In many instances, the followers of one particular god waged war on the people who bore allegiance to the enemy-god of their own deity. One mythic arena in which I believe the belligerent planet Mars is made a central character is Homer's tale of Troy. Homer is believed to have lived during the Iron IIc-IIIa period. Though I believe his account of the Trojan War is based on genuine historical events dating to the end of the Late Bronze Age, it is evident that Homer incorporated many elements to the story from his own day. Classicists indeed often point out that Homeric poetry is an intricate mixture of references from pre-Dark Age and Hellenic Greece. Therefore, what Homer came up with in the *Iliad* &*Odyssey* can be seen as a jigsaw puzzle — begging to be unravelled to discern which components are really from the Late Bronze Age and which

---

24 Immanuel Velikovsky (1950) *Worlds in Collision*, p. 291; Babylonian Talmud, Tractate Sanhedrin 95b; Tosefta Targum Isaiah 10:32; Aggadat Shir 5, 39 and 8, 45; Jerome on Isaiah 30:2.
25 Daniel D. Luckenbill (1968 [1928]) *Ancient Records of Assyria and Babylonia*, Vol. II - Sec. 508.
26 Ibid, Sec. 922.
27 Pliny, *Natural History*, Book XXXIV: 40, 141.

ones date to his own day. In this very same investigative quest, Dr Immanuel Velikovsky pays particulat attention to Homer's repeated references to the planet Mars as a war-like deity. Velikovsky cleverly observed that if Homer speaks of Ares, the Mars of the Greeks, in his epic story then one must assume that the Trojan War was fought *after* 747 BCE — when Ares/Nergal became a popular god.[28]

The reason why Ares became a major deity in the Greek pantheon is because the planet Mars had caused, in recent memory in the Aegean, a major natural conflagration. The migrations which characterized the Late Geometric phase had resulted from the Mars-induced cosmic upheaval. Incidentally, I personally disagree with Immanuel Velikovsky's hypothesis that the Trojan War was actually "fought" in the eighth or seventh century BCE. What I believe that Homer attempted to accomplish, however, is to retell the epic of Troy, a Late Bronze Age story, by using his own time as a setting. Indeed, Homer mentions the Phrygians among the allies of the Trojans. But like the Carians, Phrygian conquerors leave no sign of their occupation of Asia minor until *c.*750 BCE. The first evidence of armed conflict between the Phrygians and other ancient Near Eastern powers occurs during the reign of the Assyrian king Sargon II — who expeditiously moved to halt their expansion into Assyrian territory.

In his unpublished works, Immanuel Velikovsky puts forth the theory that Phrygian culture was destroyed by the same natural catastrophe which decimated Sennacherib's army in 687 BCE — to then be replaced by the short-lived Cimmerian empire. Evidence does exists however to support the view that a Phrygian kingdom survived the Cimmerian attack, albeit much weakened and of considerably smaller scale. For instance, Phrygian sites were rebuilt in purely Phrygian style. Herodotus (Book I: 35) also points to the existence of a Phrygian royal household in the sixth century BCE. Since the Phrygians, according to Homer's *Iliad*, took part in the Trojan War, and that Mars, in his capacity as a war-hero appears repeatedly in the text, it is beyond doubt that the composition of Homer's *Iliad* dates to the turbulent era between the two Mars catastrophes of 747 and 687 BCE — which is actually consistent with the actual time of Homer's life. Interestingly, in his posthumous work entitled *The Chronology of Ancient Kingdoms Amended*, published in 1728, Sir Isaac Newton had proposed, like Immanuel Velikovsky, an eighth century BCE date for the Trojan War.

Several neo-Velikovskian scholars have likewise attempted to establish an eighth to seventh century BCE date for a historical Trojan war. One of them is Clark Whelton, who writes:

> As a final piece of literary-historical evidence for dating the Trojan War, Velikovsky cites a passage from Book XI of the "Iliad." Nestor, the aged king

---

[28] Immanuel Velikovsky (1950) *Worlds in Collision*, p. 247.

> of Pylos, while convincing Patroclus to take the field in Achilles' place, mentions a four-horse chariot team which his father Neleus sent to the land of Elis to "run in the games and compete for the tripod." An important event in the ancient Olympic games was a race between chariots drawn by four-horse teams. It is firmly established that the first Olympiad was held in the eighth century BCE, most likely in -776. Olympia was located in the land of Elis, in the western Peloponnese. Neither Neleus nor Nestor could have known of the Olympic games if they lived in the 12th century ...[29]

Hence, as we know from the previous chapter, Nestor, the king of Pylos, must have lived during the time of the first Olympiad. Furthermore, Neleus and Nestor could not have lived at the time of the original Trojan War, conducted under the leadership of Agag since the four-hourse chariot did not make its way into Greece until the time of the Libyan (i.e. Danaan) and Egypto-Phoenician and colonisation of mainland Greece — which immediately *post-dates* the Agagite Trojan War.

> According to Herodotus [Book IV, 189], quadrigas, or four-horse chariots, were introduced to Greece from Libya. As Homer mentions their use, this must have been before 800 BC and may well have been even earlier, **the most likely period being the 12th century when Libyans and Greeks were allied as Peoples of the Sea.**[30]

Homer's own Trojan War epic, albeit based on the much earlier Agagite Trojan saga, is, at its very core, an Iron Age story shaped by Iron Age events. Following the Peoples of the Sea war, the now "Hellenic" Greeks came of age. Before Homer's Trojan War could take place, the nascent Hellenic culture had to first and foremost evolve. The following timetable shows it would have been impossible, on the basis of my historical reconstruction, for Homer's Trojan War, as described in the *Iliad*, to have taken place before the eighth century BCE:

(1) Mycenaeans sack Troy in 1,184 BCE.
(2) Greek Thebes was founded by Kadmos in 1,135 BCE.
(3) Oedipus was a descendant of Kadmos.
(4) Sons of Oedipus die in war of the Seven against Greek Thebes.
(5) Greek Thebes, a generation after the war of Seven, is finally
    defeated by the Epigonoi — around which time, Homer says,
    that the Trojan War took place.

---

[29] Clark Whelton 'Velikovsky's "Dark Age of Greece".' In Milton Zysman & Clark Whelton (editors) (1990) *Catastrophism 2000 (A Sourcebook for the Conference: Reconsidering Velikovsky)*, p.257.
[30] Martin Bernal (1991) *Black Athena* II, p. 96.

CHAP. XVI: DESCENDANTS OF ANCIENT KINGS | 591

According to Homer himself, Kadmos predates the Trojan War by several centuries. If my identification of Kadmos as Pharaoh Kamose of the new chronology's 18th Dynasty is accurate, this automatically means that Homer's Trojan War took place long after 1,135 BCE. With the war of Seven and Oedipus belonging to the Iron IIb period,[31] it becomes easy to date the events narrated in the *Iliad* to the Iron IIIa period — a generation after the war of Seven.

Another valuable point to be raised is that if Homer's version of the Trojan War had really taken place during the twelfth century BCE, without as I argue setting it in his own time, the people of Troy should have been portrayed in the *Iliad* as Indo-European people who spoke a language related to Hittite. The intriguing fact that Homer describes the Trojans as being very similar to the Greeks themselves, in terms of cultural and linguistic attributes,[32] ought to be an indication to us as to "when" exactly Homer's version of the events occurred. If traces of the Hittites are nowhere to be found, we must look to the Iron Age for an "Iliadesque" Anatolia.

On the whole, there is no doubt in my mind that the actual siege of Troy in fact belongs in the end of the Late Bronze Age. There indeed appears to be very little evidence to support a foreign invasion of Troy during Iron IIIa. How then is Homer's Iron Age saga to be rationalized? Well, quite simply that Homer's epic is an intricate and masterful amalgamation of two very different historical periods brought together to form a semi-fictitious tale. These two historical periods are namely (1) the Agagite imperial age of Typhon Season #5 and (2) the Napatan era of supremacy over Egypt during the Iron IIc and Iron IIIa periods. Attributes from both of these periods, as well as from the intervening 18th Dynasty rule (as evidenced by the reference to Nestor, king of Pylos), form the backbone of the *Iliad*.

A perfect example of this is Homer's creation of the character of Agamemnon — who was really a composite hero comprising of an Ethiopian hero "Memnon" from his *Iliad* — certainly inspired by the powerful Napatan rulers of his own day, and the long gone Amalekite hero "Agag." The latter was a hero to the Greeks because he led the Achaeans into a successful battle against the Trojans at the conclusion of the Late Bronze Age. The Ethiopian pharaohs of the new 20th Dynasty's reputation, to quote D. B. Redford, as "redoutable warriors, endowed with an élan vital and a swiftness in battle"[33] again inspired Homer to associate the character of Memnon

---

31 See Immanuel Velikovsky (1960) *Oedipus and Akhnaton*, Doubleday: Garden City, NY.
32 Mary R. Lefkowitz (1996) 'Ancient History, Modern Myths.' In Mary R. Lefkowitz & Guy MacLean Rogers (editors) (1996) *Black Athena Revisited*, p. 11.
33 Donald B. Redford (1993) 'Taharqa in Western Asia', *Eretz-Israel* 24, p. 190.

The Typhonian Cycle and the End
of Napatan Dominance

with Ethiopia. It is also probably unlikely that the El Kurru pharaohs ever conducted any sort of military campaign in Greece. Homer, who must have certainly been aware of the Ethiopians' great reputation as warriors, introduced this element from his day in the *Iliad*.

The status of the Ethiopians of El Kurru as the most powerful rulers of the ancient world came to a sudden end in 664 BCE. This was the year when the Assyrians, the Napatans' principal rivals, sacked the Egyptian southern capital of Thebes. This attack, I believe, coincided with a Mercury shift which inaugurated Typhon Season #7. There is evidence that this cataclysm was expected by the astronomer-priests of Antiquity. For instance, in a foreboding letter addressed to the Assyrian King Ashurbanipal (668-627 BCE), evidently written shortly before the Mercury attack, from a servant named Adad-sumi-usur, we may read:

> Good health to Your Majesty! May the gods Ashur, Sin, Samas, Bel, Nabû, and Nergal bless Your Majesty many times.
> The sun did not have an eclipse, it let (the computed event) pass by.
> The planet Venus will reach the constellation of Virgo; the heliacal rising of the planet Mercury is near; there will be a hard rain and the storm god Adad will thunder. Your majesty should know [all this].[34]

The fact that the astronomer-priests had specifically identified the planets Mercury and Venus in association with the storm-god Adad was not at all coincidental. Of course, these are the two planets which periodically shift from their regular orbital path and cause great destructions during Typhon Seasons. Evidently, this message addressed to Ashurbanipal was meant to warn him of the impending fiery consummation of the prevailing World Age. The observation of eclipses and other unusual movements of the planets, particularly Mercury and Venus, were carefully recorded and analysed for indications of possible cosmic danger. In his *Naturales quaestiones*, Seneca retakes the catastrophic concepts of Berosus in the following manner:

> Berosus, the translator of Bel, attributed to the planets the cause of these perturbations. ... His certainty in this matter was so great as to fix the dates of the universal conflagration and deluge. Everything terrestrial, he says,

---

[34] R. F. Harper, *Assyrian and Babylonian Letters*, 657.

will be burned, when the stars which now follow different orbits will reunite in the sign of Cancer, and will place themselves in one line, so that a straight line would pass through the centers of all these globes. The deluge will come when the same planets will have conjunction in Capricorn.

It was probably Ashurbanipal's advance knowledge of the coming Mercurian cataclysm which allowed him to prepare and take advantage of the period of chaos which befell the entire ancient Near East on that year.

17

Changing the Course of History: The Tale of the Victor (664 BCE to 404 BCE)

During the course of the historical period examined in this chapter, two bodies of texts, which came to shape human history from the time of their composition to the present, were produced by ancient scribes of Egypt and Israel. These documents were: the "Abydos King-lists" and the "Five Books of Moses" — or the Torah. What these two ancient records have in common is that, in my estimation, they were politically and ideologically motivated. Traditionally, ancient historians have tended to be considerably more skeptical of the Five Books of Moses than they have been of the Abydos King-lists — believed to have been devise by the Egyptians during the LBIII period. Reflecting this common skepticism about the Old Testament, Syro-Palestinian archaeologist William G. Dever observes: *"The biblical writers are not telling it the way it was, but the way it would have been had they been in charge."*[1]

However, I would also contend that the same could be said about the dynastic Egyptians. Why assume that the Egyptian records would be any more, or any less for that matter, reliable than the ancient biblical records? As I shall endeavour to demonstrate shortly, Pharaoh Seti I's famed Abydos King-list, which serves as an important backbone for modern Egyptian chronology, was such an attempt to present the history of Egypt as it would have been had King Seti I been in charge. Where the plot thickens further still, is with my revolutionary assertion that this Pharaoh Seti who had the Abydos King-list carved was not the Seti I of the Late Bronze Age, but an Iron Age Seti I who reigned in the seventh century BCE.

In putting forth this hypothesis, I tread on a path already set by Dr Immanuel Velikovsky over two decades ago in his book *Ramses II and his Time*. In this work, Velikovsky attempted to equate the standard 19th Dynasty, which modern Egyptologists date to the Late Bronze Age, with the conventional Macedonian 26th Dynasty of the seventh century BCE. To justify his position, Velikovsky argued:

---
[1] William G. Dever 'How to Tell a Canaanite from an Israelite.' In Hershel Shanks *et al.* (1992) *The Rise of Ancient Israel*, p. 28.

Suffice it to say here that the Eighteenth and Nineteenth Dynasties are notable for the *dissimilarity* of their style of art, language, and religion, while many features of Libyan and Ethiopian style mimic closely the uses of the Eighteenth and Nineteenth Dynasties respectively, reviving them, supposedly but inexplicably, after a hiatus of many hundreds of years.[2]

Those similarities which Velikovsky points to, between the 18th and 19th Dynasties and the linguistics and artistic canons of the Ethiopian and Libyan dynasties from the tenth to seventh centuries BCE, are indeed entirely consistent within the context of the novel chronology. We know that the 18th Dynasty (or new 19th Dynasty) was, in fact, contemporary with and even synonymous with, the Libyans and Ethiopian dynastic lines. Hence, there never was a hiatus of many hundred years in which the artistic styles of the New Kingdom disappeared — only to suddenly resurface during the time of Libyan and Ethiopian dynasties. Ethiopian and Libyan monarchs had *themselves* been New Kingdom pharaohs. After the end Pharaoh Horemheb's reign in 747 BCE, the Ethiopians established a new dynasty in Thebes. The immediate successors of that Napatan dynasty were the Macedonians of the standard 26th Dynasty. The latter are the pharaohs whom Immanuel Velikovsky as well as this author equates with the conventional 19th Dynasty. Any of the artistic styles analogous to the Ethiopian and Libyan dynasties, attributable to the orthodox 19th Dynasty, necessarily belong to this alter-ego dynasty from the seventh century BCE.

The Abydos King-Lists and the Dark Age

of Egyptian History

For generations, a source of incessant intrigue and debate among Egyptologists has been the uncanny omission by ancient Egyptian scribes of a period of about five hundred years of Egyptian history from the official Egyptian records. For some elusive reason, the Egyptian king-lists at Abydos, in Upper Egypt, jump from Amenemhat IV to Ahmose I, and completely ignore all the pharaohs who ruled in between. Why this glaring omission? Basing their observations on the standard history of ancient Egypt, scholars generally assume that the ancient Egyptians simply refused the record the names of the hated Hyksos invaders who ruled Egypt with an iron fist during that intervening period. While this might have indeed been an important part of their motivation, an even more central reason was that it proved to be a necessary thing to do in order to carry on the alter-ego line of pharaohs.

---

[2] Immanuel Velikovsky (1978) *Ramses II and His Time*, Doubleday: Garden City, NY, p. 207.

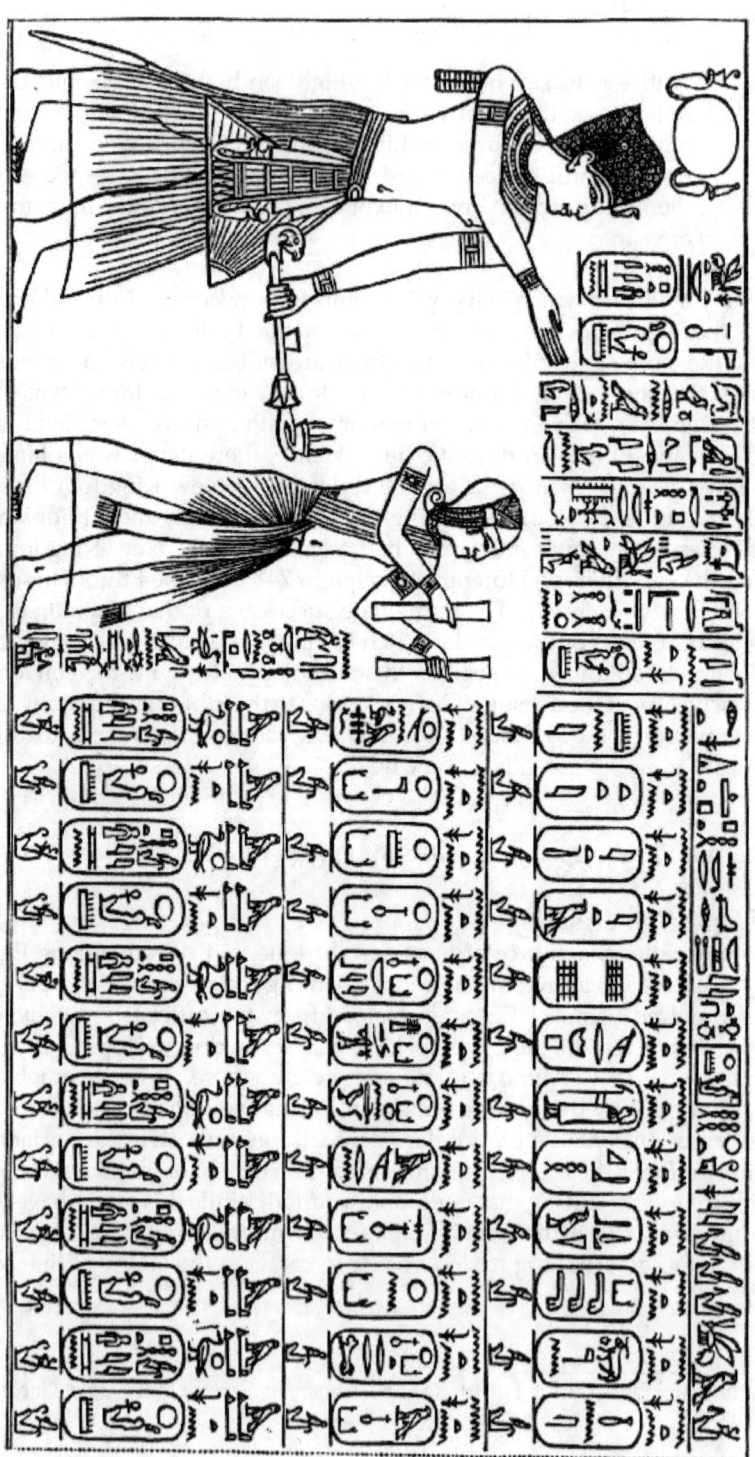

Fig. 17a: The Abydos King-list. After Lenormant (1882).

Fig. 17b: King Nekau-Ramses II (*by* Saint-Elme Gautier).

CHAP. XVII: CHANGING THE COURSE OF HISTORY | 599

As part of this process, not only did the displeasing memory of the Hyksos need to be erased, but also all mention of the Napatan era which stood between the end of Horemheb's reign and the accession of the new Ramses I (Nekau I) in 664 BCE. The objective was to move upwards by several centuries the advent of the 18th Dynasty — thus eliminated what I have identified as the new 14th and 15th Dynasties, as well as the 16th and 17th Dynasties. Also, the period of the 13th Dynasty which was contemporary with the Hyksos occupation of the eastern Delta had to be disposed of. The result was that, in the Abydos King-lists, Pharaoh Ahmose I (the successor of the 17th Dynasty) became the immediate successor of Amenemhat IV. The Ahmose I which follows Amenemhat IV in the Abydos King-lists is, evidently, not the Ahmose of the sixteenth century BCE, but rather, the Levantine ruler of the twelfth century BCE.

As a result, four hundred years were, quite literally, made to disappear in thin air. To be sure, the list starts with the proto-dynastic king Menes, then carries on relatively correctly through to the end of the 12th dynasty, then ends as follows: Ahmose, Amenhotep I, Tuthmosis I, Tuthmosis II, Tuthmosis III, Amenhotep II, Tuthmosis IV, Amenhotep III, Horemheb, Ramses I, Seti I. Egyptologists were surprised to notice that the names of Pharaohs Akhenaten and Tutankhamun are missing from the list. Again, it is believed that the reason for these omissions is pre-eminently political in nature. All traces of the Amarnian heresy had to be eradicated. Evidently, however, the Ethiopian origins of Pharaohs Akhenaten and Tutankhamun, just like the Libyan identity of the Iron IIa-b alter-ego pharaohs, were perilous red herrings for the sustainability of the revised history of Egypt which they wished to pass on to posterity. The Abydos King-lists were essentially very Egypto-centric (as in "dynastic" Egypt). Any rulers who came before the proto-dynastic king Menes, or who were not dynastic rulers, were not included in these lists. Thus, the Abydos King-lists, or their contemporary royal list known as the Turin Canon, never were complete records of the Nile Valley's pharaonic history.

We now enter another major episode of the "Great Time Warp of History." After the Assyrians invaded Egypt in 664 BCE, they placed a dynasty of Macedonian rulers to govern Egypt on their behalf as a self-contained vassal state. This dynasty of Macedonian kings is the one commonly known to Egyptologists as the 26th Dynasty. The first of those Macedonian rulers, King Nekau I, came to the throne after the Ethiopian line of the traditional 25th Dynasty had been defeated by the Assyrian king Esarhaddon. Turning again to Dr Immanuel Velikovsky, who outlines the alter-ego line of succession below, I maintain that a second, and most importantly "distinct," Ramses I, Seti I and Ramses II ruled in Egypt during the seventh century BCE.

> My effort at reconstructing the history of the Nineteenth Dynasty has led me to identify the father of Necho II, Psammetichus, with Seti the Great

(Ptah Maat), and the grandfather of Necho II, Necho I, with Ramses I. I show that Ramses I was appointed to rule Egypt by Assurbanipal after the sack of Thebes in – 663.[3]

Where I believe that Immanuel Velikovsky erred, however, is in not recognizing that there indeed had been an earlier Ramesside dynasty during the Late Bronze Age — as conventional ancient historians believe. Moreover, having established, through the novel chronology, that most dynastic Egyptian pharaohs of the Late Bronze Age had subsequent Iron Age alter-egos, one should expect to find at least some evidence for the existence of these later kings in extant archaeological records. For instance, French Egyptologists Luc Gabolde and Vincent Rondot found inscriptions by Seti I on the Temple of Montu, built under Amenhotep III. Since this temple could have been built by the first Amenhotep III of the fourteenth century BCE, there is no paradox there with regards to the conventional chronology. But Gabolde and Rondot reported that Pharaoh Seti I's inscription *followed* those of Tutankhamun and Horemheb.[4] Having hypothesized that Pharaohs Tutankhamun and Horemheb ruled in the *eighth* century BCE, we must then concede, that this King Seti I *necessarily* had to have ruled after that time — i.e. after the mid eighth century BCE. Therefore, the latter can't possibly be the original Seti I of the fourteenth century BCE.

Another uncanny archaeological conundrum, relating to Ramses II, involves, as Velikovsky pointed out,[5] the presence of a commemorative document carved by the former on a rock at Nahr el-Kelb (Dog River). It stands immediately next to a similar tablet erected by the Assyrian king Esarhaddon. The obvious question is: why would either ruler choose to carve a record of his own exploits next to the victory tablet of an enemy king? Given what we know of the importance of military propaganda in the mind of the ancients, why weren't the enemy's tablets destroyed at once? Conventional wisdom has it that the tablet of Ramses II stood there for some six hundred years before King Esarhaddon, in an act of irony,[6] carved his own tablet next to it. Like Velikovsky, however, I believe that Esarhaddon's document was inscribed shortly *before* that of Ramses II, and that "there was no irony on the part of either the Assyrian king or the pharaoh."[7] The Assyrians had actually made it possible for Nekau II's (Ramses II) dynasty to rule over Egypt.

---

[3] Immanuel Velikovsky (1978) *Ramses II and His Time*, pp. 4-5.
[4] Luc Gabolde & Vincent Rondot (1993) 'Une catastrophe antique dans le temple de Montou à Karnak-Nord', *Bulletin de l'Institut Français d'Archéologie Orientale* 93, p. 246.
[5] Immanuel Velikovsky (1978) p. 9.
[6] Daniel D. Luckenbill (1968 [1928]) *Ancient Records of Assyria and Babylonia*, Vol. II - Sect. 479.
[7] Immanuel Velikovsky (1978) p. 9.

The Move to Tanis and the Four-Hundred-Year Stela

When was the ancient city of Tanis built? While it is known that 12th Dynasty kings first made use of it, archaeologically speaking, excavators can record datable structures attributable to a centre of power and authority only from the so-called Third Intermediate Period. With the sole exception of the 12th Dynasty, no evidence has transpired which would link any previous dynasties to this site. Therefore, that automatically eliminates any Late Bronze Age activity. Moreover, Tanis was, without a doubt, a city built *after* the New Kingdom of the standard chronology.[8] But once again, there is an anomaly. Several building blocks inscribed with the cartouche of Ramses II have been uncovered at Tanis by excavators. The official explanation is that those blocks had been transported, in antiquity, from Pi-Ramses (or Kantir near Avaris) to Tanis — long after Ramses II had died. By who, why or how? No one knows exactly. What would have motivated Ramses II to suddenly dismantle and displace parts of his buildings, which he had so painstakingly built at Pi-Ramses, to a new location? I am convinced that most of the Ramesside blocks were in fact indigenous to Tanis. It was Nekau II, the Iron Age Ramses II, who was responsible for inscribing these blocks.

The town of Tanis, properly speaking, was founded by Shoshenk I. The idea upheld by modern historians that the city's origins date to the so-called 21st Dynasty is, as I shall outline in Chapter 18, wrong since that particular dynasty did not come into being until the second century BCE. Starting in 1860, Auguste Mariette, who three years earlier had been appointed director of the Antiquities Service of Egypt — which he set up under the viceroy of Egypt, began extensive excavations at ancient Tanis (or Tell San el-Hagar). Concentrating his efforts on the temple of Amun, Mariette found King Ramses II's name inscribed on an exceptionally large amount of objects and monuments. Confronted with such overwhelming evidence, Mariette's team coined an equation which came to be adhered to for nearly a century: "Tanis = Pi-Ramses = Avaris."[9] Indeed, scholars were convinced that they had at last found the biblical "Land of Ramses" where the Israelites had slaved under the lash of Pharaoh. Thus, it is evident that the Book of Exodus was not very far in the back of the heads of those who excavated at Tanis at the turn of the last century. As we know by now, more recent research had come along to dispel this notion.

An important Tanite document used by scholars to date the beginning of Hyksos rule in Egypt is the so-called Four-Hundred-Year Stela. The stela, found inside the Temple of Amun in Tanis, is said to have been erected during the reign of Pharaoh

---

[8] Philippe Brissaud 'Tanis (Tell San el-Hagar).' In Joan Goodnick Westenholz (editor) (1996) *Royal Cities of the Biblical World*, p. 130.
[9] See Raymond Weill (1935) 'The Problem of the Site of Avaris', *Journal of Egyptian Archaeology* 21, pp. 10-25.

Ramses II. Since Ramses II is depicted with the blue crown on top of the stela, we know that it does not date to the Late Bronze Age, but rather to the time of Nekau-Ramses II. What is more, the simple fact that the document in question was found "inside" the Amun Temple at Tanis indicates that it *could not possibly* date to anytime before the reign of Pharaoh Shoshenk I. The Four-Hundred-Year Stela recounts the celebration, by the future pharaohs Ramses I and Seti I, of a jubilee of 400 years of the cult of Seth in Tanis. Clearly, the commemoration is implied to have taken place during the reign of Horemheb — as it is claimed that Ramses and Seti both served as officers in the army of Pharaohs Horemheb at the time. But for the reasons outlined earlier, this line of succession was wholly fictional. It was a blatant fabrication by the rulers of the new 22nd Dynasty to revise the history of Egypt. Obviously, their plan worked. But, as James H. Breasted plainly acknowledged: *"It is impossible to discover any certain connection between him [Horemheb] and Ramses I, who now succeeded him."*[10] Not everything on the Four-Hundred-Year Stela is fictional however. The four hundredth year anniversary of the founding of the temple of Seth, incidentally, came around during the reign of Pharaoh Horemheb. Taking the arbitrary reference point of Year 17 of Horemheb's reign, in 760 BCE, we come to the year 1,160 BCE (760 + 400 = 1160). Interestingly, this date happens to fall *exactly* during the time when Agag (Apophis) II ruled in Avaris and built a temple to Seth!

> King Apophis chose for his lord the god Seth.
> He did not worship any other deity in the whole land except Seth.[11]

Once the Napatan new 20th Dynasty was erased from history, it became possible for Pharaoh Nekau-Ramses I to claim that he immediately succeeded Horemheb. Having erroneously accepted that Pharaoh Horemheb reigned during the Late Bronze Age, ancient historians began looking for the beginning of an official cult of Seth in the Egyptian Delta during the Middle kingdom. The trend was, and to some extent still is, to automatically date the entry of the Hyksos into Egypt to four hundred years before the time of Pharaoh Horemheb. Ironically, this dating scheme is consistent with both the traditional date for the rule of King Horemheb and the new chronology dates. If the conventionally accepted late fourteenth to early thirteenth century BCE dates are adhered to, then the four hundred year

---

[10] James H. Breasted 'Chapt. 7: The Age of Ramses II.' In J. B. Bury *et al.* (editors) (1924) *Cambridge Ancient History — Vol. II: (The Egyptian and Hittite Empires to 1000 B.C.)*, Cambridge University Press: Cambridge, U.K., p. 135.
[11] Papyrus Sallier I, 1.2-3. In Sir Alan H. Gardiner (1932) *Late-Egyptian Stories*, Bibliotheca Aegyptiaca 1, Éditions de la Fondation Égyptologique Reine Elizabeth: Brussels, p. 85.

CHAP. XVII: CHANGING THE COURSE OF HISTORY | 603

period starts around the time of the initial Hyksos entry into the Egyptian Delta in the seventeenth century BCE. On the other hand, as we've just seen, the new chronology scheme instead takes us to the middle of Typhon Season #5 — during the "second," and final, period of Hyksos domination. The temple of Seth was not built during the Middle Bronze Age but in the closing Late Bronze Age. To the biblically inclined scholars who attempted to equate the Hyksos with the Israelites, or at the very least placing the time of the Hebrew sojourn in Egypt in Hyksos times, the Four-Hundred-Year Stela was of particular significance. Hence, I would definitely agree with Baruch Halpern when he theorizes that:

> ... the image of Ramses II determined the reconstruction of the Exodus story. ... Historically, one might conclude that Semites, subjected to forced labor in the Delta, expressed their natural desire to turn the tables in the form of identification with the Hyksos.[12]

Indeed, as we read in the Book of Acts:

> And God spake on this wise, that his seed should sojourn in a strange land; and that they should treat them evil four hundred years.
> (Acts 7:6)

So the Four-Hundred-Year Stela appears to have served as an important document for the Jewish biblical redactors. As Halpern contends, it probably "inspired the tradition of a four-hundred-year sojourn in Egypt."[13] Needless to say, however, Jewish chronology was radically thrown off by the fact that the biblical Pharaoh of the Oppression was not the man behind the Four-Hundred-Year Stela (who himself really lived during the new 22nd Dynasty), but rather the Ramses II who ruled in the Late Bronze Age. If Nekau-Ramses II's deception worked in the sixth century BCE, one can only imagine what kind devastating effect it's had on modern historiography. Accepting the idea that the Hyksos ruled four hundred years before Ramses II, many modern historians came to believe that Joseph rose to prominence during the Hyksos occupation of Egypt. Hence, it became widely accepted that "the new king" (or dynasty) "which knew not Joseph" (Exodus 1:8) was naturally to be equated with the 18th Dynasty rulers of the New Kingdom under whom the Hyksos were expelled.[14]
Other obvious references to Egyptian royal documents by the Jewish biblical re-

---

12 Baruch Halpern (1993) 'The Exodus and the Israelite Historians', *Eretz-Israel* 24, p. 92.
13 Ibid.
14 Edward H. Sugden (1928) *Israel's Debt to Egypt*, Epworth Press: London, pp. 22-23.

dactors of the sixth century BCE — which served as a basis for well-known scriptural accounts are, for example, Tuthmosis III's highly enigmatic House of Life memoirs, written concurrently with the time of the Second Exodus, in which he made reference to fishes that fell from the sky (presumably the "manna" of the Scriptures). Or again, Ahmose's Tempest Stela — itself referring to the violent cycle-ending cataclysm of 1,135 BCE in which the world's men and women had *"hidden faces, having no clothing on them after the manifestation of God's wrath."* That clearly having been a backdrop for the story of Adam and Eve in the garden of Eden after having eaten of the forbidden fruit — thereby incurring "the wrath of God."

The Community of Workmen at Deir el-Medina:

A Post-Napatan Ramesside Town

A well-known workmen's village at Deir el-Medina was significantly settled and urbanized during the reign of Horemheb. Soon after, Taharka built a chapel to Osiris there. Egyptologists include the standard 19th Dynasty as a heyday period for the Deir el-Medina workmen's village.[15] I would instead propose that, in reality, the 19th Dynasty occupation was really a Saite (new 22nd Dynasty) occupation level.

It's difficult to deny the fact that the pyramids built at Deir el-Medina and Abydos during the Saite Dynasty bear more than striking resemblance with the Napatan pyramids constructed at El-Kurru by such kings as Kashta and Shabaka. University of Chicago Egyptologist Mark Lehner also brought attention to the equally strong similarity between the El-Kurru pyramids and the 18th Dynasty private pyramids built for high officials.[16] Describing these workmen's tombs, Brown University Egyptologists Leonard H. Lesko and Barbara Lesko write:

> Just outside the walls of their village, the wealthiest workers at Deir el-Medina built their own tombs ... The worker's tombs were typically marked by small, steep brick pyramids topped by a stone pyramidion, or miniature pyramid ... These pyramids contained tiny aboveground chapels in which were recorded the images and names of the persons buried in the crypt below.[17]

---

[15] Nicholas Grimal (1992) *A History of Ancient Egypt*. Trans. by Ian Shaw. Blackwell: Oxford, U.K., p. 278.
[16] See Mark Lehner (1997) *The Complete Pyramids*, Thames and Hudson: London, pp. 192-199.
[17] Leonard H. Lesko & Barbara Lesko (1999) 'Pharaoh's Workers (How the Israelite Lived in Egypt)', *Biblical Archaeology Review* Vol. 25 - Num. 1, p. 42.

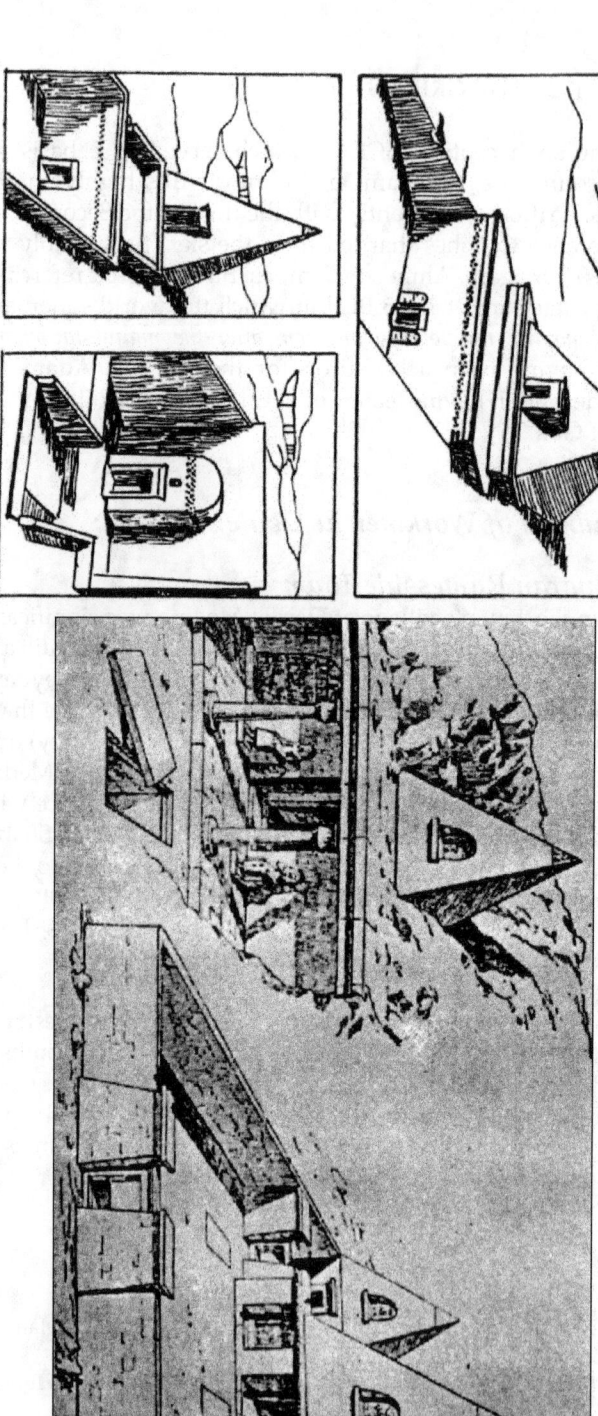

Fig. 17c: Theban rock-cut tombs of the conventional New Kingdom.

Fig. 17d: Tombs of workmen's community at Deir el-Medina.

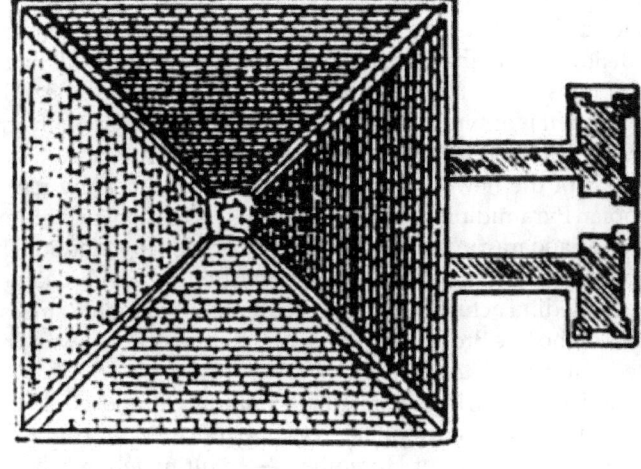
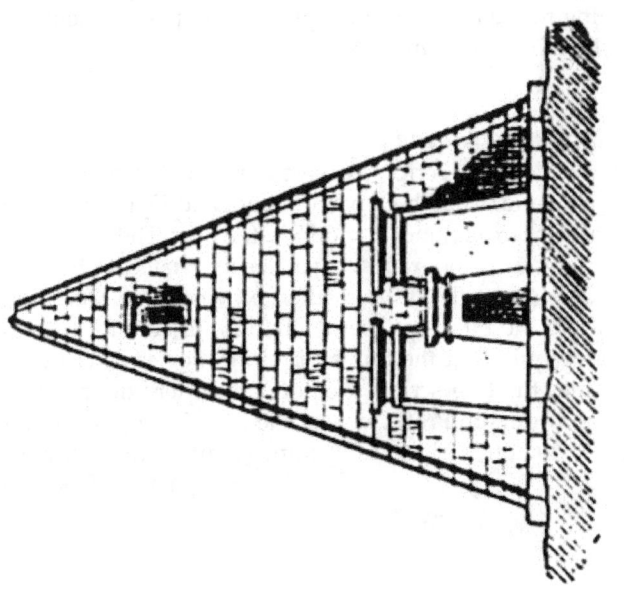

Fig. 17e: Pyramid of Meroë.

CHAP. XVII: CHANGING THE COURSE OF HISTORY | 607

As the Leskos outline in the above reference, the tomb monuments in question, called 'Pyramidion House' by the Ethiopians, were comprised of a small mastaba within a sandstone pyramid. Again, scholars would have us all believe that the Ethiopian pyramids at El-Kurru were later replicas of the New Kingdom structures (see Figs. 17c-e). Believing that the Ethiopian pyramids were first built by the kings of El-Kurru, Egyptologists assert that Kashta was the first king in some 800 years to be buried in a pyramid. It is assumed that the kings of Nuri carried on the tradition, and were themselves followed in this practice by the Meroitic kings.

Within the context of the new chronology however, the uncanny resemblance between the Ethiopian Pyramidion Houses and the New Kingdom private pyramids at Deir el-Medina and Saqqara can more logically be attributed to a Meroitic/Napatan influence in Egypt from as early as the Late Bronze Age. The earliest settlement of workmen at Deir el-Medina actually dates to the reign of Pharaoh Ramses III. Following the collapse of the late Bronze Age, the number of workmen was drastically reduced and faded into complete oblivion.

After a likely resettlement during the reign of Pharaoh Tuthmosis III, in the Iron Age, the Deir el-Medina workmen's village was only once again truly resurrected to its past status during the reign of Horemheb — to ultimately reach its apogee during the Saite Dynasty. Hence, the seemingly unexplained hiatus of 800 years in pyramid building is then automatically eliminated. The fact that, as Grimal remarks, no Deir el-Medina workmen were "implicated in the pillaging of the necropolis that took place in the reign of Ramses IX"[18] is easily explained by the simple fact that Ramses IX, according to the novel chronology, lived in the first century BCE — long after the demise of the Saite Dynasty.

The Myth of the Transfer to Meroë

Scholars believe that the demotic script (cursive form of hieroglyphics) first came into use during the standard 26th Dynasty (new 22nd Dynasty). Based on a comparative analysis of Meroitic and demotic letters, Dr Theophile Obenga has demonstrated that demotic orthography is so closely related to the Meroitic script, that a reader of demotic could easily read a text written in Meroitic without prior knowledge of the Meroitic alphabet.[19] Taking into account the lengthy and strenuous processes required of the human brain to devise a script, Professor Obenga concludes that the two scripts, demotic and Meroitic, must have a common origin. Since, according to Prof. Obenga, the Meroitic alphabet does not appear to derive from the demotic script, the Meroitic language must have served

---

[18] Nicholas Grimal (1992) p. 280.
[19] Théophile Obenga (1973) *L'Afrique dans l'Antiquité (Egypte pharaonique — Afrique noire)*. Présence Africaine: Paris, pp. 110-115.

as a basis for demotic scribes of the new 22nd Dynasty. If the order of script development needs to be reversed, should not the same be true of the cultural entities themselves?

To modern historians, such a speculation is pure heresy. It is pretty much the Gospel in ancient world scholarship that after the standard 25th Dynasty (new 20th Dynasty) was defeated and ousted from Egypt by the Macedonian Saite Dynasty, the Napatan rulers relocated their burial ground to Nuri, and later went on to establish themselves in Meroë — further south. The old capital at Napata was abandoned and a whole new dynastic line was begun in Meroë. From two inscriptions of Psamtik II and other Carian records scribbled on the walls of the temple of Abu Simbel, it is indeed well-known that Psamtik II carried out a devastating attack on Napata in 591 BCE. According to Nubiologist A. J. Arkell:

> This sack of Napata explains the broken statues of Taharka, Tan-wetamani, Senkamanisken, Anlamani and Aspelta found at Barkal, and the erasure of royal names on stelae, and it must have caused the transfer of the capital to Meroë. That Aspelta made Meroë his capital is supported by objects and those of two successors from the palace near the great temple, also by pieces of a stela from the Sun Temple. Indeed, on the Tanis stela of Psammetik II, the residence of the ruler of Cush may already be given as Meroë.[20]

This entire idea that Aspelta (whose reign is conventionally dated to 593-568 BCE) and his immediate predecessors were *themselves* responsible for instituting the Ethiopian capital at Meroë is, as I have been endeavouring to demonstrate, a mere fanciful speculation of modern scholarship. In reality, Pharaoh Psammetik II's punitive expedition, finishing off what the Assyrians began in 664 BCE, altogether put an end to the Meroitic-Napatan dynastic line whose remains have been found at El Kurru, Nuri and Meroë. No longer were Ethiopian kings buried in those pyramidion-cemeteries after the sixth century BCE. As we'll subsequently see, there would indeed be further settlements on those Sudanese sites, all the way up to the end of the Roman empire, but no more would a complex pharaonic culture thrive in those centres.

The Battle of Kadesh: An Iron Age Poetic Account

The Abydos King-lists and the Turin Canon are not the only two Iron Age dynastic Egyptian bodies of texts which modern Egyptologists have mistakenly dated to the Late Bronze Age. Another such pivotal sets of documents are the accounts of the

---

[20] A. J. Arkell (1974 [1961]) *A History of the Sudan (From the Earliest Times to 1821)*, Greenwood Press: Westport, Conn., pp. 145-146.

Fig. 17f: King Ashurbanipal of Assyria.

Fig. 17g: Pharaoh Ramses II attacking enemies in his chariot.

Fig. 17h: Hittite enemies from the Battle of Kadesh reliefs.

CHAP. XVII: CHANGING THE COURSE OF HISTORY | 611

Battle of Kadesh which were allegedly composed during the reign of Ramses II. As I have briefly touched on in Chapter 11, historians have long been puzzled by the stark discrepancy between the accounts of the same battle which the Hittites and Egyptians recorded. As we've seen in Part IV, the duel was very much of a draw, and much closer to a humiliating defeat than a glorious victory for Ramses II. The Anatolian Hittite records from Boghazköy indeed reflect this reality. On the other hand, the Egyptian account, both from a document known as the "Poem of Pentaur" and the battle reliefs from the Temple of Karnak, boast of a decisive victory for the undaunted Pharaoh Ramses II. Faced with this obvious contradiction, Egyptologists generally agree that Ramses II's version of the conflict against his Hittite archenemies is a grotesquely embellished account meant to please the gods of Karnak. But, once more, I strongly disagree with the orthodox view. I am thoroughly convinced that King Ramses II of the new chronology's 15th Dynasty, from the Late Bronze Age, never in fact composed the extant Egyptian accounts of this battle. The famous Poem of Pentaur was, in a figurative manner of speaking, dynastic Egypt's equivalent of the *Iliad*. In this analogy, Homer would be Pharaoh Nekau-Ramses II of the new 20th Dynasty.

Like the *Iliad*, an Iron Age tale, which describes a battle waged in the closing Late Bronze Age, but using a Hellenic historical context, so does the extant Egyptian accounts of the Battle of Kadesh delineates a Late Bronze Age conflict obviously set in an Iron Age setting. Wishing to appropriate for himself the legacy of Ramses the Great, the Macedonian king Nekau II rewrote history in the most flagrant way. The Poem of Pentaur, like the Turin Canon, was written during the reign of King Nekau-Ramses II. The poem in question, describing Pharaoh Ramses II as a great warrior and leader, betrays its Iron Age origins. For instance, by referring to such Iron Age peoples as the Carians and Lydians, serving as mercenaries, in Pharaoh's army. Acknowledging this perplexing problem, Professor Ekrem Akurgal of the University of Ankara writes:

> Today (1961), despite all industrious archaeological exploration of the last decades, the period from 1200 to 750 for most parts of the Anatolian region lies still in complete darkness. The old nations of Asia Minor, like the Lycians and the Carians, the names of which are mentioned in the documents of the second half of the second millennium, are archaeologically first noticeable about 700 or later ... Hence the cultural remains of the time between 1200 and 750 in central Anatolia, especially on the plateau, seem to be quite irretrievably lost for us.[21]

---

[21] See Clark Whelton 'Velikovsky's "Dark Age of Greece".' In Milton Zysman & Clark Whelton (editors) (1990) *Catastrophism 2000 (A Sourcebook for the Conference: Reconsidering Velikovsky)*, p. 255.

Scholars are aware of the fact that King Gyges (680-652 BCE) of Lydia supplied Greek and Carian soldiers to Psamtik I (Seti I),[22] the father of Nekau II (Ramses II), as a token of alliance. Herodotus (Book II: 152) refers to those Ionian Greek and Carian mercenaries sent to Psamtik I as "men of bronze" from the sea. On that very topic, Cambridge Egyptologist John D. Ray writes:

> ... Psammetichus handed an independent and essentially prosperous country to his son Necho, and all seemed well. But this was the sort of independence and prosperity which came with a price tag, in that success had been gained by the widespread use of foreign mercenaries. Most of these were Greeks, more specifically Ionians from the eastern coast of the Aegean, and others were Carians ...[23]

The army of Nekau-Ramses II was, thus, full of these Iron Age peoples. Unlike the original King Ramses II though, Nekau II never faced the Anatolian Hittites. By the time the latter came around, the principle enemy of the dynastic Egyptians was the Neo-Babylonian empire headed by King Nebuchadnezzar. In his book *Ramses II and His Time*, Dr Immanuel Velikovsky had awkwardly attempted to equate this Neo-Babylonian dynasty with the Hittite empire of Hattusilis III. Not recognizing that the seventh-century BCE King Ramses II was not only an alter-ego of Nekau II, but also a duplicate of an earlier Pharaoh Ramses II, who indeed battled against the Late Bronze Age Hittites, Velikovsky's framework was significantly discredited. Nevertheless, as I have just argued, I do believe that historical elements from the extant Egyptian accounts of the Battle of Kadesh may be found in the Iron Age duel between Nekau II and Nebuchadnezzar.

The Two Chief Queens of Ramses II: Myth or Reality?

A confounding issue which has intrigued many Egyptologists for a long time, is the relationship between the supposed two chief queens of Pharaoh Ramses II. It is still not clear to scholars why Ramses II would have chosen to elect two chief queens. They are even more mystified by the apparent lack of palace intrigues — which should have naturally resulted from such an awkward arrangement. The two chief queens in question are Nofretari and Isis-Nofret. Though Ramses II had many wives, these two are the only ones who bore the title of Chief Queen. Of the two queens, Nofretari enjoyed the highest public profile. Ramses II had a small temple

---

[22] Amélie Kuhrt (1997 [1995]) *The Ancient Near East (c.3000 – 330 BC)*, Routledge: London and New York, Vol. II: p. 569.
[23] John D. Ray (1996) 'Amasis: The Pharaoh with no Illusions', *History Today* Vol. 46 - Num. 3, p. 27.

erected in her honour at Abu Simbel, as well as having an ominous house of eternity built for her in the Valley of the Queens. Isis-Nofret, on the other hand, despite having been the mother of Merneptah (the heir to Ramses' throne), benefited from much less pomp and circumstance. If Queen Isis-Nofret was the mother of the next king, why didn't she receive the highest honours? In spite of some scholars claims[24] that jealousy and rivalry existed between them, no clear evidence gives credence to this theory; and no correspondence literature between the two queens has transpired. Furthermore, I am convinced that the reason why scholars have been unable to satisfactorily explain their complex relationship is because they *didn't* have any such relationship. These two chief queens were, in reality, the wives of two different pharaohs known as Ramses II — separated in time by over six hundred years! I would propose that Queen Nofretari was the original King Ramses II' chief queen in the LB III period, while Queen Isis-Nofret bore the same title under Nekau-Ramses II's reign.

Being aware by now of the very different political situations characterizing these two pharaohs' reigns, it becomes possible to analyse the extant archaeological evidence relating to the two chief queens, to positively establish their proper place in history. Here, I have found it necessary to only look at Isis-Nofret's case — as I believe that it alone settles the issue convincingly. The most important distinguishing piece of evidence is a small monument of Queen Isis-Nofret sold to the Louvre Museum in Paris in 1842 by Nestor L'Hôte.[25] The monument is undoubtedly of Memphite origin. From it, we learn that Isis-Nofret, in addition to being the royal wife of King Ramses II, was also the mother of both the *sem*-priest Khamweset and the royal scribe and generalissimo Ramessou. This alone leaves no doubt that Isis-Nofret was indeed the wife of Nekau II. The *sem*-priest Khamweset (also known as King Psamtik II) was an official of the temple of Osiris-Apis (Serapeum) — which did not exist during the time of the Late Bronze Age Ramses II. Moreover, strong evidence has already been presented for the seventh century BCE dating for the generalissimo Ramessou. What is more, we find a common pattern for the use of Isis-Nofret as a name for royal women of that time (during Typhon Season #7). Other extant evidence identifies a Queen Isis-Nofret as the royal wife of King Merneptah (Apries), the daughter of Ramses II (Nekau II), as well as the daughter of the *sem*-priest Khamweset.[26] Moreover, the fact that the Louvre Museum monument was found in Memphis is also of some importance — given the Typhonian times in which I believe it was composed. Furthermore, the

---

[24] See K. A. Kitchen's *Ramses II, Pharaoh Triumphant*.
[25] Christian Leblanc (1993) 'Isis-Nofret, Grande Épouse royale de Ramsès II (la reine, sa famille et Nofretari)', *Bulletin de l'Institut Français d'Archéologie Orientale* 93, p. 314-315.
[26] Ibid, p. 313.

department of archaeology of the University of Cairo has recently discovered in the Ramesside necropolis of Saqqara at Memphis, two limestone blocs identifying Isis-Nofret as the royal wife of Ramses II.[27] Other finds in Saqqara include another similar bloc discovered near the temple of Osiris-Apis (Serapeum) in 1986 by Prof. Mohammed Ibrahim Ali, again inscribed with the name of the chief queen Isis-Nofret.[28] And finally, to put the last nail in the coffin, we turn our attention to the discovery in Gibel El-Silsila of alterations which were made by Ramses II, or possibly by the *sm*-priest Khamweset, to a temple built by Horemheb. On the renovated structure, is carved a great stela representing Isis-Nofret accompanied by Ramses II himself and her son Khamweset. The inscription under the relief also mentions the generalissimo Ramessou, as well as the crown prince Merneptah.[29] Since this relief was carved on top of a building erected by Horemheb, of the eighth century BCE, it logically follows that Isis-Nofret, Ramses II, Khamweset, Ramessou, and Merneptah, all must be dated to a later date (i.e. the seventh century BCE). If we are to also look for evidence to authenticate Nofretari as the Late Bronze Age chief queen, we can find this confirmation in the fact that she is the one whom Pudukhepa, the wife of the Hittite king Hattusilis III, refers to in her letters as the royal wife of Ramses II.[30] This evidence was interpreted by some scholars as a possible indication of Nofretari's role as the diplomatic or stately wife; hence justifying her higher profile.

The obvious importance of the Memphite necropolis during the new 22nd Dynasty naturally reflects the fact that these monarchs lived during a Typhon Season. The *sem*-priest title, which Khamweset bore, was held by the chief clergyman at Memphis since the very first Typhon Season. Egyptologists believe that while the site of the temple of Osiris-Apis at Saqqara, where the deceased Apis bull was worshipped, was used as a cemetery for bulls from as early as *c.*1,400 BCE, it was Pharaoh Ramses II who first designed a main gallery and subsidiary catacomb chambers to house the massive coffins of the deceased Apis bulls — who in death became Osiris. It is maintained that later pharaohs came along and enlarged the original catacomb — burying more Apis bulls. Since we've established that the *sem*-priest Khamweset, the son of Isis-Nofret, was also the son of King Nekau-Ramses II, it becomes evident that the Ramesside Apis bulls buried at Saqqara date from the seventh century BCE at the earliest.

As I have argued in Chapter 15, Pharaoh Shoshenk-Amenhotep III was in fact the "first" one to bury an Apis bull in the temple. Since he is the alter-ego of Pharaoh Amenhotep III, in whose time Egyptologists assume the Apis cemetery was initial-

---

[27] Ibid, p. 316.
[28] Ibid.
[29] Ibid, p. 317.
[30] Ibid, p. 320.

ly begun on the site of the eventual Apis catacomb, it fits remarkably well with the fact that King Amenhotep III of the 18th Dynasty and Shoshenk III, who is believed to have buried an Apis bull centuries after Pharaoh Ramses II, were one and the same individual. Thus, it was King Shoshenk-Amenhotep III who was the very first monarch to both inaugurate the Apis cemetery and design a complex gallery for the ceremonial burial of the deceased Apis bull on the site the Osiris-Apis temple at Saqqara.

The Ashkelon Wall and the Ramesside Succession Line

Since a second King Ramses II ruled Egypt, posing as the original Ramses the Great, during the seventh century BCE, it can well be understood how the records of this later impostor may be easily misconstrued by modern historians as original Late bronze Age accounts of the original Pharaoh Ramses II. As long as the subterfuge continues to go wholly unnoticed, or be denied, the entire history of the ancient world will hang in the balance. Like we have seen earlier, one of these misdated documents which have mislead generations of Egyptologists is the Poem of Pentaur. But other equally vital accounts which I believe were composed by Pharaoh Nekau-Ramses II continue to falsely pass for genuine Late Bronze Age records. These are, among others, the so-called "Gezer" reliefs from Karnak — which are part of the grand "Ashkelon Wall" describing the various military campaigns of Ramses II. Establishing the Iron Age context of the Ashkelon Wall reliefs will likewise go a long way towards proving that the composition date of the Poem of Pentaur must likewise be moved down into the Iron Age.

For the following analysis, I will stick to David Rohl's view, as expressed in *A Test of Time*, that Pharaoh Ramses II originally carved the campaign scene of the "Gezer" register found on the Ashkelon Wall. Though this position was originally accepted before the late 1970s, it has since been generally accepted that it was instead carved by Merneptah. This latter opinion was originally advanced in 1977 by American Egyptologist Frank Yurco who, believing that the Ashkelon Wall recorded the same events described in Merneptah's famous Victory Stela, claimed to have found evidence linking the Gezer scene to the latter's reign.[31] He based his argument on his observation of a damaged cartouche from the Gezer scene which he believes originally read "Merneptah." That cartouche belonging to King Merneptah had clearly been overwritten or usurped by both Amenmesse and Seti II.[32] On account of this fact, Yurco argued that Ramses II could not possibly have built the Ashkelon Wall since the material used to built it obviously post-dated his reign.

---

[31] See Frank J. Yurco (1990) '3,200-Year-Old Picture of Israelites Found in Egypt', *Biblical Archaeology Review* Vol. 16 - Num. 5, pp. 20-38; David Rohl (1995) pp. 164-165.
[32] Frank J. Yurco (1990) p. 25.

Based on the new chronology however, we know that Amenmesse and Seti II belong in the thirteenth century BCE. So logically, the Merneptah whose name they effaced, must necessarily have been the "Late Bronze Age" King Merneptah. Following Yurco's logic, it goes without saying that the Khemeto-Egyptian Pharaoh Ramses II of the LBIII period could not have logically constructed the Gezer scene, or the Ashkelon Wall for that matter. My theory is that Ramses II (Nekau II) of the seventh century BCE, *reused* that block, which was by then centuries old, to record his own campaign in Gezer. To further confirm the attribution of the Ashkelon Wall to King Ramses II, Rohl points to the Hattian Treaty on Year 21 of Ramses II, which *follows* the Gezer register. If the Ashkelon Wall was really to be credited to Merneptah, we would face a serious chronological anomaly — as the Gezer scene is sandwiched between the "Kharru" campaign record and the Hattian Treaty. Both records being unmistakably Ramesside. Moreover, we can clearly see, depicted on the Gezer scene, a well-defined figure of the *sem*-priest Prince Khamweset — the son of King Ramses II. The only way to explain Frank Yurco's scenario would be, as Rohl puts it, that the Late Bronze Age Ramses II could have actually left a blank wall for his eventual successors to fill in.[33] Such a thing would be highly unlikely. The above body of evidence incontrovertibly points to the fact that King Nekau-Ramses II was the author of the Ashkelon Wall battle scenes.

As a final piece of chronological detective work, it is of interest to note that Pharaoh Shoshenk I's campaign relief actually immediately precedes Ramses II's Kharru campaign scene. Based on the new chronology, it would seem to me that all those reliefs were carved in chronological order. The string of reliefs actually start on the eastern extremity of the temple of Karnak Great Court's Second Pylon — just beside Ramses III's temple; and carry on in sequence until they hit a corner. From that point on, it is immediately followed to the right by the Yenoam and Gezer scenes, and carries on with the Hattian Treaty until we reach the last triumphal scenes. It seems strange that Pharaoh Ramses II would not have started carving his reliefs at the base of the Second Pylon; as he obviously had to overcome the temple wall's abrupt corner to carry on depicting his battle scenes. Wouldn't it have been a lot more convenient for him to just record the whole set of scenes on one wall had it been possible? Why leave the beginning of the wall blank so that Shoshenk I could fill it in centuries later? Obviously, according to the new chronology, Shoshenk I's battle relief was "already" there when Nekau-Ramses II began depicting his own battle scenes. He simply carried on where Shoshenk I had left off some three hundred years earlier.

---

[33] David Rohl (1995) p. 167.

Venus, the Solar Eclipse and the Northern Coalition

The end of the Saite new 22nd Dynasty was far from peaceful. The much troubled times began during the reign of King Psamtik II. The source of these chaotic times came from both natural and political disorder. Firstly, with the consummation of Typhon Season #7, in 612 BCE, the earth once again — and for the very last time — came under the fiery wrath of the planet Venus. As was usually the case, the Venusian paroxysm engendered political chaos — as empires crumbled and rose. Two years later, in 610 BCE, a solar eclipse would induce a coalition of northern vandals to invade Palestine and Egypt.

Those events are not, however, supposed to have happened during the reign of Psamtik II if we were to rely on the accepted chronology of ancient Egypt. Historians date the reign of Psamtik II to 595-589 BCE.[34] Yet, in my revised scheme, Psamtik II's reign ends in 610 BCE. To understand where, in my opinion, Egyptologists have gone wrong, we must take a look at a pivotal piece of evidence. A demotic papyrus from Egypt has transpired in which we learn that, shortly following the death of Psammetichus, a solar eclipse occurred on 30 September 610 BCE.[35] Modern Egyptologists have used this evidence to date the reign of the "first" Psammetichus (Psamtik I) from 664 BCE to around 610 BCE. I believe instead that this Psammetichus from the demotic papyrus whose death occurred near September 610 BCE was not Psamtik I, but actually Psamtik II.

That single mistake has thrown off the real dating for the Saite Dynasty by several years. According to the new chronology, we in fact find King Nekau I coming to power as a vassal ruler of the Assyrians in 664 BCE; to then be followed by Psamtik-Sethos I, his son Nekau-Ramses II, and finally by Psamtik II. But unlike how traditional scholarship would have it, the total time-span of these reigns lasted from 664 BCE to 610 BCE, not from 664 BCE to 589 BCE. The difference of about two decades, as we shall shortly see, will make a significant difference in how the transition period from the seventh to sixth centuries BCE unfolds.

I believe that we find a Greek corroborating record of the same solar eclipse, as described in the demotic papyrus, in the following account of Herodotus:

> ... there was war between the **Lydians and the Medes** for five years, each won many victories over the other, and once they fought a battle by night. They were still warring with equal success, when it chanced, at an encounter which happened in the sixth year, that during the battle **the day was suddenly turned to night.** Thales of Miletus had foretold this loss of

---

[34] After Gardiner (1961) *Egypt of the Pharaohs*.
[35] Kenneth Kitchen (1991) 'The Chronology of Ancient Egypt', *World Archaeology* Vol. 23 - Num. 2, p. 204.

> daylight to the Ionians, fixing it within the year in which the change did indeed happen. So when the Lydians and Medes saw the day turned to night they ceased from fighting, and both were the more zealous to make peace. Those who reconciled them were Syennesis the Cilician and Labynetus the Babylonian; ... These nations make sworn compacts as do the Greeks; moreover, they cut the skin of their arms and lick each other's blood.
> (Herodotus, Book I: 74)

Historians date the above events, as described by Herodotus, to May 585 BCE — at which time it is widely believed that a solar eclipse occurred in the ancient skies. But in the presently revised history, that battle between the Lydians and the Medes when "the day was suddenly turned to night," is instead dated to the 30th of September 610 BCE. On that day, they cemented a deadly alliance that would soon wreck havoc upon their southernly neighbours. This passage from the writings of Herodotus is also of crucial importance for our attempts at confirming the accuracy of certain of the biblical accounts from the books of the prophets. With amazing accuracy we indeed find the very same historical event described in the Book of Jeremiah:

> 9 For, lo, I will raise and cause to come up against Babylon **an assembly of great nations from the north country**: and they shall set themselves in array against her; from thence she shall be taken: their arrows shall be as of a mighty expert man; none shall return in vain. ...
> 41 Behold, a people shall come from the north, and a great nation, and many kings shall be raised up from the coasts of the earth.
> 51:11 Make bright the arrows; gather the shields: the Lord hath raised up the spirit of the **kings of the Medes**: for his device is against Babylon ...
> 28 **Prepare against her the nations with the kings of the Medes, the captains thereof, and all the rulers thereof, and all the land of his dominion.**
> (Jeremiah 50:9, 41 and 51:11, 28)

All this means that a war broke out between the Lydians and the Medes in 615 BCE (five years before the solar eclipse), in which both side suffered many casualties as well as gaining ground. In the middle of a fierce battle on September 30th 610 BCE, the day of the solar eclipse, day turned into night. This event caused the rulers and captains of the Lydian and Medes nations to put their differences aside and form a coalition. This coalition, which Jeremiah refers to (51:28) as an assembly of great nations from the north, would ultimately be responsible for the downfall of the

CHAP. XVII: CHANGING THE COURSE OF HISTORY | 619

Chaldean empire. Could the striking resemblance between the demotic papyrus, the accounts of Herodotus and the prophecy of Jeremiah be attributed to mere coincidence? All the dates fit perfectly with the sequence of events described in the new chronology.

Two years before the momentous events of 610 BCE, a natural disturbance of much greater impact shook the ancient world. The fifty-two-year cycle which had heralded Typhon Season #7 in 664 BCE, now came to an end with the usual cataclysmic Venusian orbital shift in 612 BCE. Incidentally, this bookend year of 612 BCE also witnessed, as was the case with the Assyrian sack of Thebes in 664 BCE, the invasion of yet another vital centre of Near Eastern civilization — Nineveh, in Assyria itself this time. Prophetising Nineveh's imminent destruction in 612 BCE the prophet Nahum writes of the Lord's coming wrath as follows:

> 5 The mountains quake at him, and the hills melt, and the earth is burned at his presence, yea, the world and all that dwell therein.
> 6 ... his fury is poured out like fire, and the rocks are thrown down by him.
> (Nahum 1:5-6)

The devastation of Nineveh, as described by Nahum, is equated to a "Day of the Lord." We know that the Day of the Lord is an occasion of cosmic retribution against earth dwellers who have gone astray at the end of a World Age or Mandate of Heaven. According to Nahum, the Lord warns the Assyrians of Nineveh that: "I will discover thy skirts upon thys face, and I will shew the nations thy nakedness ..." (3:5). With the Venus shift of 612 BCE bringing to a close the Sixth Creation, the earthlings are once again found naked and aware of their iniquity in the face of God. The Bible does not acknowledge the fact that the Israelites themselves were certainly likewise overcome by the conflagration, but it is obvious that the catastrophe was universal. Where Nineveh had been singled out however is when, probably shortly after the Venus shift, it suddenly came under a forceful raid carried out by the Chaldeans and the Medes. Nineveh was left desolate, as the prophet Zephaniah recounts:

> 13 And he will stretch out his hand, and destroy Assyria; and will make Nineveh a desolation, and dry like the wilderness.
> (Zephaniah 2:13)

Nineveh was not the only city which lay in "desolation" after the Venus shift of 612 BCE. Jerusalem itself was another one. In Pharaoh Merneptah's famous Israel Stela, several Syro-Palestinian cities, including Jerusalem, are said to have lain desolate. But historians suppose that Merneptah is describing Jerusalem sometime during the latter quarter of the thirteenth century BCE. With virtually no opposition, that hypothesis has served as a benchmark for scores of biblical archaeologists. Entire scholarly careers are currently based on this single inference. How secure is it though? I am thoroughly convinced that, once again, historians have been gravely misled by the Egyptological evidence. As Immanuel Velikovsky hereby describes, the Pharaoh Merneptah who carved the Israel Stela lived in the seventh to sixth centuries BCE.

> The pharaoh, whose name is read Binere'-meramun Merenptah-hotphi(r)ma'e and who followed Ramses II, is the pharaoh Hophra of Jeremiah. The reading hotphi(r)ma'e should be repaired to hophrama'e. The letter *t* in *hotep* ("beloved") was apparently not sounded (Amenhotep, likewise, is Amenophis in Greek) and thus Hotphir was transliterated Hophra in Hebrew and Apries in Greek. ... According to both Jeremiah and Herodotus, Hophra-Apries followed Necho-Nekos closely. ... But how wide of a mark! Merneptah was not the Pharaoh of Joseph, or of the Exodus, but the Pharaoh of the Exile.[36]

The top relief of the Israel Stela depicts Pharaoh Merneptah wearing a "blue crown" (see Fig. 17j). The Late Bronze Age King Merneptah couldn't have possibly worn the blue crown because it simply hadn't yet come into use, as part of official pharaonic regalia, during his time. Therefore, the events which this pharaoh describes in this great stela cannot date to the Late Bronze Age either. The document reads:

> The kings are overthrown saying: Mercy!
> Not one holds up his head among the Nine Bows.
> Wasted is Tehenu,
> Kheta [Hatti] is pacified,
> Plundered is Pekanaan (The Canaan),
> With every evil,
> Carried off is Ashkelon,
> Seized upon is Gaza,
> Yenoam is made a thing not existing.
> Israel is laid waste, his seed is no more;
> Palestine has become a widow for Egypt.
> All lands are united, they are pacified;
> Every one that is turbulent is bound by king
> Merneptah, given life like Re, everyday.

---

[36] Immanuel Velikovsky (1978) pp. 190-191.

Fig. 17i: Queen Nefertari (13th century BCE).

Fig. 17j: Top relief of Israel Stela showing Arpies-Merneptah wearing the blue crown (digitally restored).

Fig. 17k: King Merneptah of the Late Bronze Age wearing the double crown.

King Apries-Merneptah, here, is describing the political situation around him near the time of his accession in 610 BCE, in the wake of the Venusian shift of 612 BCE. Contented with their successful plunder of the Assyrian city of Nineveh, the Chaldeans (Kheta) were now at peace. Nebuchadnezzar had also mercilessly ransacked Canaan and expelled the Israelites from their land — leaving Jerusalem in shambles, as the prophet Jeremiah relates:

> 2 Thus saith the Lord of hosts, the God of Israel; Ye have seen all the evil that I have brought upon Jerusalem, and upon all the cities of Judah; and, behold, this day they are a desolation, and no man dwelleth therein. ...
> 6 Wherefore my fury and mine anger was poured forth, and was kindled in the cities of Judah and in the streets of Jerusalem; and they are wasted and desolate, as at this day.
> (Jeremiah 44:2, 6)

The prophet Jeremiah offers exactly the same description of the state of the land of Israel as does Apries-Merneptah — his contemporary. Jeremiah says that Jerusalem is "wasted and desolate" — as Apries-Merneptah relates that "Israel is laid waste, his seed is no more." Moreover, Velikovsky[37] quotes a passage from the Lamentations of Jeremiah in which the latter proclaims: "How doth the city sit solitary, that was full of people! How is she become as a widow!" We recall that Pharaoh Apries-Merneptah likewise recounts that "Palestine has become a widow for Egypt." Further echoing Apries-Merneptah's line: "Carried off is Ashkalon, Seized upon is Gaza," Jeremiah (47:5) writes: "Baldness has come upon Gaza; Ashkelon is cut off with the remnant of their valley..." Virtually word for word are, within the Book of Jeremiah, the exact contents of Merneptah's Israel Stela! Once again, is this yet another case of sheer coincidence? I certainly would argue against that. The prophet Jeremiah and the author of Merneptah's Israel Stela, King Apries-Merneptah himself, were evidently contemporaries describing one and the same series of dramatic events. As a final observation, Apries-Merneptah's commentary that Israel's "seed is no more" very probably refers to the fact that, subsequently to Jerusalem's destruction by natural and military forces, the people (his seed) of Israel were sent into forced exile by the Neo-Babylonians.

---

[37] Immanuel Velikovsky (1978) *Ramses II and His Time*, p. 194.

The End of the Sixth Sun

As was unfailingly the case at the conclusion of all World Ages, a great Venusian conflagration spread confusion, war, exile and precipitous urban decline. The chaotic situation described in Apries-Merneptah's so-called Israel Stela was but one of the extant ancient accounts of this tumultuous period. Others, in Israel and Greece, for instance, were acknowledging the power of the Heavens to exact its revenge upon an iniquitous population. In Israel, the prophet Jeremiah, whom as we know was a contemporary of Pharaoh Apries-Merneptah, spoke of the wrath of the elusive "Queen of Heaven."

> 18 But since we stopped burning incense to the queen of heaven and pouring out drink offerings to her, we have lacked everything and have been consumed by the sword and famine. ...
> 20 Then Jeremiah spoke to all the people – the men, the women, and all the people who had given him that answer – saying:
> 21 The incense that you burned in the cities of Judah and in the streets of Jerusalem, you and your fathers, your kings and your princes, and the people of the land, did not the Lord remember them, and did it not come into His mind?
> 22 So the Lord could no longer bear it, because of the evil of your doings and because of the abominations which you committed. Therefore your land is a desolation, an astonishment, a curse, and without an inhabitant, as it is this day.
> (Jeremiah 44:18, 20-22)

Who was this elusive Queen of Heaven? How odd for such a staunchly monotheistic people such as the ancient Israelites to have made burnt incense offerings to a celestial deity other than Yahweh. As Velikovsky hypothesise below, I propose that the Queen of Heaven was the planets Venus. Knowing that they lived in the middle of a Typhon Season, experience had though the ancients, including the Israelites, that the ferocious planet Venus, i.e. the Queen of Heaven, would sooner or later depart from its increasingly troubled orbit and cause a tremendous natural upheaval. Jeremiah 44:22 clearly refers to the concept of the waning Mandate of Heaven — when the chief deity becomes disillusioned with his Creation and plots to destroy it.

> It is apparent from this passage (Jeremiah 44:17-18) that the population of Jerusalem that sought refuge in Egypt thought the national catastrophe fell upon their people, not because they had left the Lord God, but because in

the days of Josiah and his sons they had ceased to worship the planetary gods of Manasseh and especially the Queen of Heaven, the planet Venus.[38]

The prophet Isaiah holds up a similar discourse when describing the calamity which had abruptly befell the Israelites, and the rest of the ancient world, at the termination of the Sixth Creation, in 612 BCE.

> 5 The earth also is defiled under the inhabitants thereof; because they have transgressed the laws, changed the ordinance, broken the everlasting covenant.
> 6 Therefore hath the curse devoured the earth, and they that dwell therein are desolate: therefore the inhabitants of the earth are burned, and few men left. ...
> 12 In the city is left desolation, and the gate is smitten with destruction. ...
> 18 And it shall come to pass, that he who fleeth from the noise of the fear shall fall into the pit; and he that cometh up out of the midst of the pit shall be taken in the snare: for the windows from on high are open, and the foundations of the earth do shake.
> 19 The earth is utterly broken down, the earth is clean dissolved, the earth is moved exceedingly.
> 20 The earth shall reel to and fro like a drunkard ...
> (Isaiah 24: 5-6, 12, 18-20)

Again the ever-recurring notion that the earth dwellers had somehow "transgressed the laws" and "broken the everlasting covenant," altogether typical of the ancients' discourse following a cycle-ending Venus conflagration, resurfaces in the Book of Isaiah. The unbearable noise emanating from the firmament, the perilous cracking and shifting of the earth's crust, and the bobbing motion of the earth's equatorial bulge which the prophet Isaiah describes, in amazing detail, could not have been a mere figment of his imagination. Other peoples were likewise describing the same events. For instance, Isaiah's assertion that "few men [were] left" (24:6) following the Venusian conflagration, again reappears in Plato's *Critias*—in reference to the account of Solon (incidentally a contemporary of Isaiah). After Pharaoh Amasis forcefully obtained power in Egypt by leading a mutinous band of Egyptians against Apries, Plato recounts that Solon travelled to Egypt to gather various forms of knowledge from the priests of Egypt. These Saite priests addressed Solon as follows:

---

[38] Immanuel Velikovsky (1950) *Worlds in Collision*, p. 296.

> O Solon, Solon, you Hellenes are never anything but children, and there is not an old man among you. Solon in return asked him what he meant. I mean to say, he replied, that in mind you are all young; there is no old opinion handed down among you by ancient tradition, nor any science which is hoary with age. And I will tell you why. There have been, and will be again, many destructions of mankind arising out of many causes; the greatest have been brought about by the agencies of fire and water, and other lesser ones by innumerable other causes. There is a story, which even you have preserved that once upon a time Phaëthon, the son of Helios, having yoked the steeds in his father's chariot, because he was not able to drive them in the path of his father, burnt up all that was upon the earth, and was himself destroyed by a thunderbolt. Now this has the form of a myth, but really signifies a declination of the bodies moving in the heavens around the earth, and a great conflagration of things upon the earth, which recurs after long intervals; at such times those who live upon the mountains and in dry and lofty places are more liable to destruction than those who dwell by rivers or on the sea-shore. And from this calamity we are preserved by the liberation of the Nile, who is our never-failing saviour. When, on the other hand, the gods purge the earth with a deluge of water, the survivors in you country are herdsmen and shepherds who dwell on the mountains, but those who, like you, live in the cities are carried by the rivers into the sea. Whereas in this land, neither then nor at any other time, does the water come down from above on the fields, having always a tendency to come up from below; for which reason the traditions preserved here are the most ancient.

The pivotal notion, explored throughout this volume, that many ancient myths are in fact allegorized memoirs of great natural cataclysms, is clearly evoked above by Plato. Due to its favoured geographical position and antiquity, Egypt was always in a position to perpetuate the memory of these cosmic upheaval, described as Sethian degenerations into chaos, and guide and offer assistance to less fortunate victims of such periodic universal chaos. Given the circumstances, the ancient Egyptians were the carriers of an array of esoteric knowledge which the Greeks were eager to learn. From the writings of Censorinus, among others, it is evident that the ancient Greeks and Romans took great interest in such topics:

> There is a period called "the supreme year" by Aristotle, at the end of which the sun, moon, and all the planets return to their original position. This "su-

preme year" has a great winter, called by the Greeks *kataklysmos*, which means deluge, and a great summer, called by the Greeks *ekpyrosis*, or combustion of the world. The world, actually, seems to be inundated and burned alternately in each of these epochs.[39]

A Funny Thing Happened on the Way to Ethiopia

In the conventional chronology of ancient Egypt, the Saite dynasty was immediately followed by the first era of Persian rule. The Persian king Cambyses II is believed to have been a ruthless conqueror who committed many sacrileges in his quest to dominate Egypt. This picture of Cambyses II comes mainly from the accounts of Herodotus, who recounts:

> On the tenth day after the surrender of the walled city of Memphis, Cambyses took Psammenitus [Psamtik III] king of Egypt, who had reigned for six months, and set him down in the outer part of the city with other Egyptians, to do him despite; having so done he made trial of Psammenitus' spirit ...
> (Herodotus, Book III: 14)

The evidence and various accounts concerning Cambyses II's behaviour in Egypt often contradict each other, however, and have led to some disagreement between ancient historians. Some scholars have come to believe that Herodotus' version of the conquest of Cambyses does not reflect reality at all because it is known that Cambyses II assumed the full titulary of an Egyptian Pharaoh and paid tribute to the Delta goddesses Neith and Sais. Thus, they argue that his bad reputation was due to later propaganda against the Persians, since Cambyses II had obviously honoured the traditional Egyptian deities and not defiled them as Herodotus claims. My personal belief, however, is that Herodotus was not referring to the pious Persian king Cambyses II, but to his forefather Cambyses I. The latter is really the one who terminated the Saite dynasty in Egypt. Between the ephemeral rule of Cambyses I and the more stable rule of Cambyses II, there is a long-lost vital period of transition which I believe is described accurately below by Diodorus of Sicily:

> Now four Ethiopians held the throne, not consecutively but with intervals between, for a little less than thirty-six years in all; and the Persians, after their king Cambyses had subdued the nation by arms, ruled for one hun-

---
[39] Censorinus, *Liber de die natali*, xviii.

dred and thirty-five years, including the periods of revolt on the part of the Egyptians which they raised because they were unable to endure the harshness of their dominion and their lack of respect for their native gods. Last of all the Macedonians and their dynasty held rule for two hundred and seventy-six years.
(Diodorus of Sicily, Book I: 44)

Who were these four Ethiopians who ruled Egypt before Cambyses II? Historians assume that Diodorus of Sicily is referring to the Ethiopian kings of the standard 25th Dynasty (new 20th Dynasty). The problem that poses itself however is that this Ethiopian dynasty lasted for much longer than 36 years — two and a half times longer to be exact. I am actually convinced that another Ethiopian dynasty ruled Egypt *just prior* to Cambyses II's conquest of the Two Lands. Diodorus of Sicily, in the above passage, indeed, seems to imply that the Persian king immediately succeeded the Ethiopian rulers. The latter clearly outlines a *continuous* sequence of events in Egyptian history up to his own time. First there are the Ethiopians, then the Persians, including the periods of native Egyptian rule, and lastly, the Macedonian and Ptolemaic kingship. If Diodorus of Sicily meant to refer to the dynasty of King Taharka, which did not last 36 years, he would have mentioned, in his sequence of events, the Macedonian dynasty that, in the conventional chronology, immediately precedes the Persian conquest. He does not. Clearly, a previously unknown line of Ethiopian kings ruled Egypt between the end of Psamtik III's reign and the conquest of Cambyses II.

But exactly thirty-six years prior to the conquest of King Cambyses II, immediately before the Ethiopians seized power in Egypt for the last time, an earlier Persian monarch, King Cambyses I succeeded in ousting Psamtik III of the Saite Dynasty. King Cambyses I's dominion over Egypt did not last even a few months — for he soon involved himself in a perilous conflict with the Ethiopians. Soon after having conquered Egypt, King Cambyses I sent out Persian spies to Ethiopia for the purpose of gathering information on their way of life. Perceiving that his unexpected visitors were malicious spies, the Ethiopian king spoke thus of Cambyses: "It is not because he sets great store by my friendship that the Persian King sends you with gifts, nor do you speak the truth (for you have come to spy out my dominion), nor is your king a righteous man..." The king of Ethiopia then sent the spies away with the following message for their Persian king :

... when the Persians can draw a bow of this greatness as easily as I do, then to bring overwhelming odds to attack the long-lived Ethiopians; but till then, to thank the gods who put it not in the minds of the sons of the Ethiopians to win more territory than they have.
(Herodotus, Book III: 21)

CHAP. XVII: CHANGING THE COURSE OF HISTORY | 629

Meanwhile, back in Egypt, Cambyses continued to show growing disrespect for Egyptian customs, as Herodotus further recounts:

> When the priests led Apis in, Cambyses—for he was well-nigh mad—drew his dagger and made to stab the calf in the belly, but smote the thigh; then laughing he said to the priests: "Wretched wights, are these your gods, creatures of flesh and blood that can feel weapons of Iron? That is a god worthy of the Egyptians.
> (Herodotus, Book III: 29)

Immediately afterwards, Cambyses proclaimed that he would at once put to death any priest he saw performing rites in honour of the Apis. Meanwhile, the Apis bull finally succumbed to its wound, died, and was buried "without Cambyses' knowledge." Egyptologists are however very quick to question that classical perception of Cambyses. Indeed, modern archaeological research has proven, beyond the shadow of a doubt, that Cambyses II was actually very respectful of Egyptian religious cults. Auguste Mariette's 1850 excavations at the Memphite temple of Osiris-Apis uncovered evidence that two Apis bulls had lived during the reign of Cambyses II (Apis XLII and Apis XLIV).[40] Apis XLIV was born in Year 5 of Cambyses II[41] and went on to live for over seven years. If, as Herodotus claims, the invading Persian king so forcibly forbad the worship of the Apis as soon as he ascended the Egyptian throne, why was the Apis bull still being worshipped so long after Year 5 of Cambyses II? Not to mention the obvious point that since Apis XLII died in Year 5 of Cambyses II, the year of Apis XLIV's birth, it should then logically be safe to assume that religious rituals at the temple of Osiris-Apis went on uninterrupted despite Cambyses II's accession. In fact, we know that the sarcophagus of Apis XLII *"was even a personal gift of Cambyses as its inscription indicates."*[42] Why would Cambyses go through the trouble of "donating" that sarcophagus if he hated the Apis so much? In any event, according to Herodotus, the very fact that the Apis bull was even buried at all was kept secret from King Cambyses — so as not to offend him. The priests knew that they would automatically be killed if Cambyses knew anything about it. And finally, how can one possibly explain the surviving iconography showing Cambyses II, himself, paying tribute to the living Apis bull!? Again, we are evidently faced with a case of mistaken identity. The Cambyses of Herodotus simply cannot be the Cambyses of the modern historians.

---

[40] Leo Depuydt (1995) 'Murder in Memphis: The Story of Cambyses's Mortal Wounding of the Apis Bull (ca. 523 B.C.E.)', *Journal of Near Eastern Studies* Vol. 54 - Num. 2, p. 120.
[41] According to stela now in Paris, France's Louvre Museum (Louvre IM.4187).
[42] L. Depuydt (1995) p. 121.

Once Cambyses's emissaries returned from Ethiopia, Herodotus describes the reaction of Cambyses as follows:

> Having viewed all, the spies departed back again. When they reported all this, Cambyses was angry, and marched forthwith against the Ethiopians, neither giving command for any provision of food nor considering that he was about to lead his army to the ends of the earth; and being not in his right mind but mad, he marched at once ...
> (Herodotus, Book III: 25)

Strangely enough, Herodotus then says that, due to lack of provisions, Cambyses abruptly changed his mind and returned, at once, to Thebes—not having completed a fifth of his journey! But, oddly enough, Strabo completely contradicts this when he says that Cambyses actually reached Meroë:

> ... when Cambyses took possession of Aegypt, he advanced with the Aegyptians as far as Meroë; and indeed this name was given by him to both the island and the city, it is said, because his sister Meroë—some say his wife—died there.
> (Strabo, *Geography* Vol. XVII: 1, 5)

While Strabo makes no allusion to a bloody conflict between Cambyses and the king of the Ethiopians, the obvious discrepancy in the ancient accounts raises a red flag. Moreover, Herodotus never said that Cambyses ever returned to Ethiopia after his failed attempt. So *did* Cambyses ever make it to Ethiopia? It's in fact probable that he did. As a matter of fact, I believe that Cambyses I was defeated, whether in actual battle or in a duel of will, by the Ethiopians and was forced to relinquish the entire Nile Valley to the king of the Ethiopians. Confirming that King Cambyses I indeed lost control of Egypt as a result of his poor showing in the battle against the king of Ethiopia, Diodorus of Sicily says:

> And they say that, by reason of their [the Ethiopians] piety towards the deity, they manifestly enjoy the favour of the gods, inasmuch as they have never experienced the rule of an invader from abroad; for from all time they have enjoyed a state of freedom and peace one with another, and although many and powerful rulers have made war upon them, not one of these has succeeded in his undertaking.
> Cambyses, for instance, they say, who made war upon them with a great force, both lost all his army and was himself exposed to the greatest peril ...
> (Diodorus of Sicily, Book III: 2,3)

CHAP. XVII: CHANGING THE COURSE OF HISTORY | 631

Herodotus wrote his *History* in *c*.450 BCE — after the Persian conquest of Egypt in 525 BCE. Over a century had passed since Cambyses I's defeat at the hands of the Ethiopians. Since Herodotus was a host of the Persians, could he have been intentionally misled by the latter about the history of the Persian conquest of Egypt? Knowing what we now about the unscrupulous editing tactics of the ancients with respect to their own history, this hypothesis cannot be ignored. There is actually very little doubt in my mind that what was related to Herodotus by the Persian was a composite account of both Cambyses' forays into the Two Lands.

The ruthlessness of the original King Cambyses was maintained, but the defeat strategically concealed — hence the improbable scenario of a hurried pull-back. The truth is, Cambyses I's offensive against the Ethiopians failed — which resulted in the Persians' loss of Egypt. Probably having learnt from the errors of his forefather, King Cambyses II, in his own conquest of Egypt thirty-six years later, in 525 BCE, was much better organized and definitely more considering and respectful of local customs and religious beliefs. This attitude, in contrast to the image of the composite Cambyses of Herodotus' account, is confirmed in an extant text from a statue of Udjahorresnet, a native Egyptian official, erected within the temple of Neith at Sais during the reign of Darius I. Commenting on the document in question, Egyptologist Alan B. Lloyd writes:

> It will be observed that Udjahorresnet dwells with particular insistence on the way in which Cambyses had accepted the traditional model of Egyptian kingship, and regulated his behaviour by it. Sais was a royal city, and Cambyses is represented as showing that city and its cults particular respect.[43]

This is certainly not the kind of behaviour we find in Herodotus' description of Cambyses' actions. Llyod continues:

> The more circumspect reader might be inclined to question the historicity of all this in view of the tradition of Cambyses' gross impiety towards Egyptian cults which is preserved in Classical sources. Such doubts are, however, unjustified. Not only do contemporary Egyptian texts confirm the stance described in our inscription, but there are excellent reasons for rejecting the historicity of the Classical tradition itself.[44]

---

[43] Alan B. Lloyd (1982) 'The Inscription of Udjahorresnet: A Collaborator's Testament', *Journal of Egyptian Archaeology* 68, p. 170.
[44] Ibid, p. 173.

Wholly dismissing Herodotus' accounts, however, simply because they are "inconvenient," is not good enough, and much too easy. To quote M. Miller: "... *the Apis story in Herodotus seems to be a pure fiction, yet it is the hinge of a whole narrative, and it is most difficult to believe that there was not some remote foundation for it.*"[45] The new chronology gives the answer. Herodotus' account describes the impieties of Cambyses I, not the actions of the later Persian king Cambyses II.

The utter mayhem and senseless desecration of monuments throughout Egypt caused by Cambyses I's wild rampage, followed by the return to peace and order under the new Ethiopian kings who drove out the invading Persians is, in my view, recounted in a biography of Petrosiris at Tûna el-Gebel.[46] Thought by most scholars to have carved this story sometime after the reign of Saite dynasty, Petrosiris relates that Egypt had come under the chaotic rule of a certain *hk3 h3swt* (Ruler of foreigners). That elusive foreign ruler caused great "displacements" and "fighting" throughout Egypt. The religious cults in the sacred temples, apparently under his direct orders, were abruptly suspended. No one was safe. Then Petrosiris contends that the end of chaos came with the sudden arrival of a *hk3 Kmt* (Ruler of Khemet). Under the new Khemetic ruler, he says, "everything became splendid which was found collapsed." Petrosiris was soon returned to his old post as a high official of Egypt and he at once set about putting everything into place.

This apparently crucial set of events in Egypt's history has received remarkably little attention. The reason for that is obvious. Historians just don't know what to make of it. To this day, no definite explanation has been offered to account for the actual events themselves, or to positively establish the real identity of either the "Ruler of foreigners" or the "Ruler of Khemet." It is entirely evident to the author however that these were, respectively, Cambyses I and the Ethiopian king who defeated the latter.

The Identity of the "Ruler of Khemet"

The first two of the four Ethiopian rulers who came to rule dynastic Egypt between the reigns of Cambyses I and Cambyses II were King Actisanes, who took on the name of Amenemhat and his son who adopted the name of Sesostris — evidently in an effort to mirror the Middle Bronze Age 12th Dynasty royal succession. These two were followed by two other Ethiopian rulers whose short-lived reigns preceded the conquest of Cambyses II in 525 BCE. In the new chronology, this long-lost ephemeral Ethiopian occupation of Egypt represents the 23rd Dynasty. I believe that these kings were the remnant of the great Napatan civilization which came to

---

[45] M. Miller (1959) 'The Early Persian Dates in Herodotus', *Klio: Beiträge zur alten Geschichte* 37, p. 35.
[46] Text in G. Lefebvre (1923) *Le tombeau de Petosiris*, II, Cairo, 53ff.

an end at the onset of Typhon Season #7. These Ethiopians, who came to power in Egypt in 561 BCE, launched extensive military conquests in Syria-Palestine and southern Europe. I am confident that the military exploits of Kings Actisanes-Amenemhat and Sesostris have formed the backbone of the classical Greek legends of the mighty Ethiopian-Egyptian rulers Memnon and Sesostris. Herodotus (II: 103-105) claims that an Egyptian pharaoh by the name of Sesostris conquered Colchis — located along the eastern coast of the Black Sea south of the Caucasus. Therefore, Herodotus asserts that the dark-skinned inhabitants of Colchis descended from the Ethiopian king of Egypt's army who settled there. Although dark-skinned people are known to have resided there, scholars do not believe that an Egyptian pharaoh ever reached such far corners of Europe. Egyptologists are particularly skeptical because, by erroneously identifying Herodotus' King Sesostris with a composite figure of the Sesostris pharaohs of the Middle Bronze Age, they doubt that an Egyptian king could have launched such an ambitious series of campaigns into Europe during the Middle Kingdom. But I contend that Herodotus is not talking about a Middle Bronze Age king, but of one who actually lived in his own era — in the Iron Age. Crucial details from the Herodotus' narration indeed unequivocally prove Sesostris could only have conducted his campaigns during the Iron Age.

> The pillars which Sesostris erected in the conquered countries have for the most part disappeared; but in the part of Syria called Palestine, I myself saw them standing, with the writing above-mentioned, and the emblem distinctly visible. In Ionia also, there are two representations of this prince engraved upon rocks, one on the road from Ephesus to Phocaea, the other between Sardis and Smyrna.
> (Herodotus, Book II: 106)

How could any Sesostride pharaohs from the Middle Kingdom have possibly invaded these specific Ionian cities when these were only instituted during the second half of the eighth century BCE? Moreover, the itinerary which Sesostris followed evidently shows that he had targeted cities which only existed during the Iron Age. Additionally, having established that King Moeris of the Greek texts lived in the ninth century BCE, it is useful to point out that, according to Diodorus of Sicily, King Sesostris ruled "seven generations" after King Moeris.

> ... Now this is the account which the Egyptians give of Moeris. Sesoösis (Sesostris), they say, who became king seven generations later, performed more renowned and greater deeds than did any of his predecessors.
> (Diodorus of Sicily, Book I: 52-53)

Sesostris, whom Herodotus (II: 110) says "was king not only of Egypt, but also of Ethiopia," exceeded the deeds of his Napatan and Egyptian predecessors in the sense that he, and his father and immediate predecessor King Actisanes-Amenemhat (Memnon), were the first to successfully invade such distant parts of Europe. Like his predecessors, King Sesostris of the new 23rd Dynasty very much revered the memory of another great conquering ruler of Egypt: Pharaoh Mentuhotep-Nebhepetre. Dedicatory objects, made in the honour of Mentuhotep-Nebhepetre, and attributed to Pharaoh Sesostris were found in Thebes, as Egyptologist William C. Hays delineates below.

> An exceptionally interesting small object ... from Thebes, is a ceremonial instrument called a *posesh-kef*, made of hornblende granite and dedicated by one of the Se'n-Wosrets (I or III) [Sesostris] to his revered "ancestor" Montuhotpe II of the Eleventh Dynasty.[47]

Pharaoh Sesostris, however, refers to a much more distant ancestor, in this particular object, than Egyptologists believe. The following citation by William C. Hays comes along to confirm my hypothesis that the King Sesostris who composed this dedicatory *posesh-kef*, and other objects traditionally believed to date to the 12th Dynasty, was the ruler of an Ethiopian dynasty which immediately followed the Macedonian Saite Dynasty of Egypt's Late Period.

> Fragments of relief from a limestone gateway found at Memphis in the ruins of the palace of King Ha'a'-yeb-Re' (Apries) of the Twenty-Sixth Dynasty have been dated by Petrie to the reign of Se'n-Wosret I [Sesostris]. **The work, however, appears to be more consistent with the archaizing style of the Twenty Sixth Dynasty and it is probable that the reliefs are contemporary with the building in which they were found.**[48]

Petrie only dated the fragments of Sesostris to the Middle Kingdom because he was completely unaware that an Iron Age pharaoh also named Sesostris ruled Egypt shortly after the reign of Apries. There should, in actual fact, be nothing unusual with the discovery of artifacts belonging to a Sesostride king exhibiting clear Saitic

---

[47] William C. Hayes (1990 [1959]) *The Scepter of Egypt*, Vol. II: p. 181.
[48] Ibid, p. 182.

manufacturing style. And, to boot, located "inside" a temple of Pharaoh Apries! Regardless of certain inconsistencies, the Greek historians of the classical era also give a distinct picture that Pharaoh Memnon and Sesostris of the new 23rd Dynasty ruled immediately after the Macedonian Saite dynasty. Diodorus of Sicily, for instance, claims that a certain Ethiopian king by the name of Actisanes (commonly believed to be the alter ego of Shabaka) "lead an army against Amasis" and "Egypt fell under the rule of the Ethiopians" (Book I: 60). Ironically, Diodorus of Sicily goes on to say that Pharaoh Moeris came to rule immediately after King Actisanes! This obviously does not make any sense since it stands in stark contradiction to his earlier statements saying that King Moeris ruled "seven generations" (Book I: 53) before Sesostris — who himself reigned "many generations" (Book I: 60) before Amasis.[49] So how could the Ethiopian king Actisanes have followed Amasis — only to then himself be followed by Moeris — a supposed ancestor of Amasis?! Diodorus of Sicily was evidently struggling to piece together a genuine historical account while being confronted with a contradictory chronology of Egypt set down by the pharaohs of Egypt themselves.

The account of an Ethiopian ruler following the Saite Dynasty of Amasis[50] is, therefore, probably an echo of the lost Ethiopian dynasty which ruled Egypt between the era following the end of Psamtik III's reign and Cambyses II's conquest of Egypt. King Actisanes may be seen as the Ethiopian ruler who defeated Cambyses I in battle. Like Herodotus who was given contradictory information by the Persians about the composite Cambyses, it is likewise highly possible that Diodorus of Sicily may have been the unwitting victim of this same ideological and political revision of history which denied that these Ethiopian rulers ever existed. We already know that historians, ancient and modern, have identified King Actisanes with the Napatan pharaoh Shabaka of the standard 25th Dynasty.[51] Thus, it may not be entirely a coincidence that early Egyptologists, following classical tradition, believed that Shabaka, and not Pi-Ankhy (or Piye), had invaded Egypt. The Manethonian texts, indeed, altogether ignore Pi-Ankhy, as Sir Alan H. Gardiner observes:

> It is strange ... that Manetho makes no mention of the great Sudanese or Cushite warrior Pi'ankhy who about 730 B.C. suddenly altered the entire complexion of Egyptian affairs.[52]

---

[49] Based on the observations of James Henry Breasted (*A History of Egypt*, p. 189), who theorized that the Greeks might have attributed to Sesostris the triumphs of several prominent kings, it has been suggested by some scholars that the earlier Sesostris might have been none other than Pharaoh Ramses II of the Late Bronze Age.
[50] Herodotus, Book II: 137.
[51] Indeed, Herodotus seems to have equated the Actisanes of Diodorus of Sicily with Shabaka. Both Ethiopian rulers are said to have conquered Egypt during the reign of King Amasis. We can only conclude that they were alter egos.
[52] Sir Alan H. Gardiner (1961) *Egypt of the Pharaohs*, Oxford University Press: Oxford, p. 335.

For that reason, I believe that later Graeco-Roman editors of the Manethonian texts had actually confused the two episodes of Ethiopian dominance. Pharaoh Piankhy was ignored because it was believed that King Shabaka, erroneously equated with Actisanes, was really the one who conquered Egypt. King Actisanes-Amenemhat, the father and predecessor of King Sesostris, thus, founded the new 23rd Dynasty. He did not become Pharaoh of Egypt by invading the Saite Dynasty, but rather by prevailing over the Persian invader Cambyses I who had issued him a challenge. The close relationship between Memnon and Sesostris seems to be confirmed by Herodotus' statement (II: 106) to the effect that the statues of the Ethiopian conqueror Sesostris, erected in Ionia, were often mistakenly attributed to King Memnon. It is evident that King Memnon, in order to have been so compared to his son Sesostris, must have likewise engaged in far-off conquering expeditions. Indeed, Herodotus describes the town of Susa, in Elam, as the "city of Memnon."[53] As in the case of Sesostris, modern historians believe that this legendary "Memnon" of the Greeks was a Middle Kingdom pharaoh — in this case, King Amenhotep III. This attribution comes from the fact that the ancient Greeks themselves had decided that two colossal seventy-foot-tall seated statues of Pharaoh Amenhotep III, still standing in Thebes, represented their Ethiopian hero Memnon — who fought bravely at Troy and was slain by Achilles. But as Prof. Martin Bernal outlines below, linguistically speaking, the Greek name Memnon correlates much better with the pharaonic name "Amenemhat."

> Thus, while some Egyptians appear to have objected to the name Memnon being applied to a statue of Amenophis, others identified it with Ammenemes. imn m ht/Amenemhe/Ammenemes is a more plausible origin for Memnon than imn htp/Amenhotep/Amenophis.[54]

The reason why the Greeks specifically chose to refer to the Ethiopian pharaoh Actisane-Amenemhat by the legendary name of Memnon is because he reminded them of the Homeric hero Memnon from the *Iliad*. As soon as Actisanes arrived in southern Europe with his conquering army, the association was the echo of Homer's epic sprung into the minds of the Greek populace. Many ancient accounts retell the conquests of this great Ethiopian pharaoh, as in Pausanias' chronicles:

---

[53] Herodotus Book V: 54; Book VII: 151.
[54] Martin Bernal (1991) *Black Athena (The Afroasiatic Roots of Classical Civilization) — Volume II: The Archaeological and Documentary Evidence*, Rutgers University Press: New Brunswick, NJ, p. 268.

CHAP. XVII: CHANGING THE COURSE OF HISTORY | 637

> In Egyptian Thebes where you cross the Nile to the Reeds, as they call it, I saw a sounding statue of a seated figure. Most people call him Memnon who marched into Egypt and as far as Susa out of Aithiopia; on the other hand the Thebans say that this is not Memnon, but a statue of Phamenoph who lived in their region.[55]

As with the case of Kings Apries-Merneptah and Sesostris, archaeological evidence which is customarily dated to the Late Bronze Age by Egyptologists can, I believe, be shown to support my hypothesis of the existence of an Iron Age pharaoh by the name of Amenemhat. This same evidence can be gleaned from Tanite statues attributed to King Amenemhat III's reign (see Figs. 17m-n). Quite inexplicably, they drastically break with the established artistic canons of Middle Kingdom Egypt. One of them, a bust of Pharaoh Amenemhat III (Fig. 17m), portrays him with uncharacteristic hair-locks — of a particular sort nowhere else seen in ancient Egyptian art. Similar hair-locks are attested on two standing statues of the deities Hapy and Iakes — together presenting "fish offerings" in the Temple of Amun. These were discovered by Auguste Mariette during his Tanis excavations in 1862. Commenting on this so-called "artistic heresy" or "strange style,"[56] H. R. Hall writes:

> Why the king bade himself and his gods to be represented thus strangely we do not know. It was an aberration from the conventional canons only once paralleled in later days, and that by a king who was half mad and wholly a heretic, in religion as well as art, Akhenaten. We cannot assume any religious heresy in Lamaris, but [that] he was a monarch of original and powerful mind is obvious.[57]

The statues of Hapy and Iakes, dated to the reign of Amenemhat III, bear a later inscription added by Psusennes I — who's reign falls in the standard 21st Dynasty (new 31st Dynasty). They are shown presenting fish-offerings to the gods. The accepted interpretation is that the statues were carved during the Middle Kingdom's 12th Dynasty under Amenemhat III, and were later usurped by Psusennes I of the standard 21st Dynasty sometime in the mid-eleventh century BCE. I would however suggest a much different scenario. In the new chronology, we find *another* king by the name of Amenemhat ruling in the 6th century BCE — under the Age of Pisces. I believe that it was *this* Amenemhat who was actually

---

[55] Pausanias, I: 42, 1.
[56] Philippe Brissaud (1996) 'Tanis (Tell San el-Hagar)', p. 119.
[57] H. R. Hall (1916) *The Ancient History of the Near East (From the Earliest Times to the Battle of Salamis)*, Methuen: London, p. 164.

responsible for the carving of those statues. Since that king ruled under the Age of Pisces, it would have made perfect sense for Amenemhat to picture Hapy and Iakes as presenting fish-offerings to Amun. The fact that the statues were *later* inscribed by Pharaoh Psusennes I poses no problem for my revised history since, in the novel chronology, Psusennes I reigns during the first century BCE — almost an entire millennium later than in the orthodox chronology. Finally, the unusual hair styles attested in both monuments are indicative of their late artistic traditions. After having abandoned Napata, the Ethiopians became less and less attached to the rigorous traditional tenets of pharaonic religion, art and culture. A somewhat similar phenomenon, albeit at a much less hurried pace, was taking place in Egypt. As we'll see in the following chapter, however, a tremendous cultural renewal would eventually take place in Egypt — partly in response to the centuries of foreign occupation. But in Ethiopia, ironically, the sack of Napata by the Assyrians signalled the beginning of a permanent downfall of pharaonic culture. Increasingly, the Ethiopian rulers were moving toward a new cultural identity. I believe that the highly unorthodox style of the new 23rd Dynasty Amenemhat was a clear indication of that.

The reigns of Kings Actisanes-Amenemhat and Sesostris were the only active reigns, with respect to military forays abroad, of the new 23rd Dynasty. Herodotus says that the son of Sesostris was a peaceful ruler.

> When Sesostris died, he was succeeded in the kingship (so said the priests) by his son Pheros. This king made no wars; and it happened that he became blind, for the following reason: the Nile came down in a flood such as never before, rising to a height of eight cubits, and the water which overflowed was roughened by a strong wind ...
> (Herodotus, Book II: 111)

Since we know that there were four Ethiopian kings in the new 23rd Dynasty, another ruler, perhaps a brother of King Pheros, must have ruled briefly after the latter became incapacitated. The Persians soon realized how vulnerable their Ethiopian enemies in Egypt were; and headed by their King Cambyses II, they successfully invaded Egypt and, at once, turned the country into a Persian satrapy.

The Second Persian Invasion and the Completion of the Red Sea Canal

Once Cambyses II took control of Egypt in 525 BCE, he appointed administrators from Persia in all major cities of Egypt. Perhaps to ensure that the Ethiopians would not attempt to overrun the Persian army again, he also penetrated Nubia and es-

Fig. 171: Statues of Amenhotep III traditionally referred to as the Colossi of Memnon.

Fig. 17m: Bust of Pharaoh Actisanes-Amenemhat.

Fig. 17n: Hapy and Iakes making fish offerings (*by* Bourgoin).

tablished garrison at Egypt's southern border. Cambyses II's reign was very short however and, in 522 BCE, he was succeeded by Darius I. Darius I, the Great, was a highly efficient king. He spent three years putting down rebellions at the farthest outskirts of his empire. Once he secured the full consolidation of his power, he divided the Persian Empire into twenty-nine satrapies, or provinces, each governed by an appointed Persian or Median official of the noble class. Darius chose Susa as his new capital and enacted a series of laws governing the empire which were very similar to the ancient Code of Hammurabi. He was also very mindful of ensuring the proper administration of trading networks, the up keeping of roads and many other such civic necessities. During his reign, classical sources tell us, King Darius the Great completed work on the construction of a Red Sea canal. Herodotus relates that the canal's construction was begun under Pharaoh Nekau II of the Saite Dynasty.

> Psammetichus had a son Necos, who became king of Egypt. It was he who began the making of the canal into the Red Sea, which was finished by Darius the Persian.
> (Herodotus, Book II: 158)

Herodotus records that Nekau II abandoned the project after 120,000 workmen died in its construction and because an oracle informed him that his labour would ultimately benefit foreigners. The Late Period seems to have been a period consumed with irrigation and the watering of the Nile's banks — as the accident suffered by King Pheros, son and heir of Sesostris, seems to further indicate. In fact, Sesostris himself, according to Aristotle (*Meteorology* I: 15) initiated the construction of a canal crossing the Ithmus to the Erythraean Sea. But Aristotle relates that Sesostris, like his successor Darius, had been forced to completely abandon the project when it was realized that the level of the land was lower than that of the sea. This is confirmed by Diodorus of Sicily — who visited Egypt in 59 BCE:

> From the Pelusiac mouth there is an artificial canal to the Arabian Gulf and the Red Sea. The first to undertake the construction of this was Necho the son of Psammetichus, and after him Darius the Persian made progress with the work for a time but finally left it unfinished; for he was informed by certain persons that if he dug through the neck of land he would be responsible for the submergence of Egypt, for they pointed out to him that the Red Sea was higher than Egypt.
> (Diodorus of Sicily, Book I: 33)

We see that Aristotle is at odds with Herodotus and Diodorus of Sicily as to the identity of the pharaoh who first began construction on the canal. Was it Necho II or Sesostris? Pliny comes along to somewhat even the score by claiming that the idea for the construction of the canal was initially conceived by Sesostris and later again contemplated by Darius, but that it was really Ptolemy II who finally began work on it. In the final analysis, the weight of the evidence points to Nekau-Ramses II as the real initiator of the project.[58] This means that the bulk of the work on the Red Sea canal could only have been produced between the reigns of Kings Nekau-Ramses II and Darius I. Where does this leave Pharaoh Sesostris?

Certainly, the considerable amount of tradition claiming that Sesostris worked on, or even initiated, the Red Sea canal project must be based on *some* factual memory. Various theories have been offered by scholars to explain why the classical Greek narratives identify Sesostris in particular as a conqueror and builder of the Red Sea Canal. Some excavators have pointed to evidence from monuments on the Red Sea shore bearing the name "Sesostris" as evidence of the historicity, albeit much embellished, of the Sesostris legends — which they place in the Middle Kingdom[59] According to Strabo, however, work on the canal was begun under Sesostris and then *later* continued under Nekau II. That could well indicate that these two pharaohs must have lived around the same time. Thus, how could a project started under a Middle Kingdom pharaoh be left unfinished, only to be picked up again over a thousand years later by a Saite ruler? Furthermore, how could they have faced the exact same engineering obstacles? Wouldn't those engineering lessons have been learnt over the centuries? I believe that Strabo had most likely been misled by the flawed chronology of Herodotus by placing Sesostris before Nekau II. Strabo's own version of events, compounded with the accounts of other ancient chroniclers, who believed that Sesostris pioneered the construction of the Red Sea canal, make it clear that the latter ruled during the same era as Nekau and Darius. According to the new chronology, construction on the canal was initially undertaken by Nekau-Ramses II, to be later carried on under Sesostris, and finally completed by Darius I. Therefore, Darius actually erected four stelae in commemoration of the canal's excavation.[60]

---

[58] Carol A. Redmount (1995) 'The Wadi Tumilat and the "Canal of the Pharaohs"', *Journal of Near Eastern Studies* Vol. 54 - Num. 2, p. 135.
[59] See Abdel Monem A. H. Sayed (1983) 'New Light on the Recently Discovered Port on the Red Sea Shore', *Chronique d'Égypte* 58, p. 33.
[60] Carol A. Redmount (1995) p. 127.

Child of Jacob, Where's Thy Brother?

> " Was not Esau Jacob's brother? saith the Lord:
> yet I loved Jacob. And I hated Esau, and laid his
> mountains and his heritage waste for the
> dragons of the wilderness."
>
> - Malachi 1:2-3

> " ... thou shalt blot out the remembrance
> of Amalek from under heaven ..."
>
> - Deuteronomy 25:19

> " Ezra exalted the role of Moses ... and lifted
> him above all other authority and above what Moses'
> authority had been during the existence of the
> First Commonwealth. ... In the rabbinical
> tradition Ezra is second only to Moses."
>
> - Immanuel Velikovsky
> *Peoples of the Sea*

In Syria-Palestine, Darius the Great continued the policy adopted by his predeces-sor Cyrus II to restore the state of Israel by encouraging and assisting in the return of the Jewish exiles from Babylon. In the second year of Darius I's reign, work on the Temple of Jerusalem was resumed. The Persian king provided generously for the building efforts (Ezra 6: 1-12). By the sixth year of his reign, in 515 BCE, the Temple was completed. The return from the Babylonian Exile was a vital turning point in the history of the Israelites. As some theologians like to say, they left Judeans and returned Jews. What this essentially means is that the very foundation of Judaism was fomented in Babylon during the exile. This was the era when the religious elite of the Israelite people converged to look back at the entire history of their people and attempted to formulate a concise, coherent, and uniform record — from the primeval Creation to the Babylonian Exile. Out of these concerted efforts was born the Torah (Pentateuch) or the Five Books of Moses — i.e. Genesis, Exodus, Leviticus, Numbers and Deuteronomy. All of these Books were, I believe, written, from start to finish, during the Babylonian Exile. Also composed during the exile in Babylon by the religious elite were the Books of Joshua, Judges, Ruth, Samuel, Kings, and Chronicles. Actually, the only Books of the Bible which I believe existed prior to the Babylonian Exile are the Books of the prophets — from Isaiah to Malachi.

Like the Egyptians of the new 22nd Dynasty, the Jews during the Babylonian Exile composed a nationalistic history, or an idealized version of their ancient past. The chief editor, I contend, was Ezra — who I incidentally identify as the Sixth, and final, Moses. Thus, the ancient Jewish tradition which holds that the Torah was written down by Moses himself, is really a hidden reference to the Sixth Moses — Ezra. The Jewish priests who searched for ancient records of humanity, under the leadership of Ezra, while in Babylon, had evidently had access to very detailed historical and religious records from diverse great cultures of the ancient Near East. The composite account of the Exodus and the life of Moses were clearly based on a very detailed understanding of the complex history of their own people and likewise of the peoples whom they fought against. One of those enemies whom they were particular aware of, and also whose place in the overall scheme of things they were particular eager to minimize in their national history, were the Hyksos-Amalekites. The memory of their great empire was virtually annihilated from the pages of the Bible. It is also, in passing, quite consequential that the dynastic Egyptians attempted to do the very same thing just a few centuries earlier. The combined effect of these nationalistic historical revisions, specifically meant to deny the Hyksos-Amalekites of their rightful place in history, still powerfully reverberate, to this day, through modern scholars' virtually complete ignorance of the sheer extent of the Hyksos' real power in the Late Bronze Age.

Like the Egyptians, the Jews had suffered much under the yoke of the Hyksos-Amalekites. From the time of the First Exodus, the ancient Hebrews and the Amalekites entered into a tumultuous relationship which lasted for centuries. To illustrate the utter hatred which the Israelites held for the Amalekites, Velikovsky referred to a Jewish legend in which it is claimed that:

> So long as the seed of Amalek exists, the face of God is, as it were, covered, and will only then come to view when the seed of Amalek shall have been exterminated.[61]

Another tradition said that "God bade Moses impress upon the Jews to repulse no heathen should desire conversion, but never accept an Amalekite as a proselyte." It was furthermore taught that Amalek would be "the first to descend to hell." And that "God himself took up war against Amalek."[62] Why did God forsake his eldest son?

> Timnah was the concubine of Eliphaz, Esau's son, and she bore him Amaleq. (Dead Sea Scrolls: 4QGenesis Peshera [4Q252 – *column* 4])

---

[61] Ginzberg, *Legends*, III, p. 62.
[62] Immanuel Velikovsky (1952) *Ages in Chaos*, Doubleday & Co.: Garden City, NY, p. 95.

CHAP. XVII: CHANGING THE COURSE OF HISTORY | 645

The Old Testament was written by the sons of Jacob: the Israelites. From the time of the First Exodus, the Israelites had been perpetually at odds with the sons of Esau: the Amalekites. Thus, the biblical antagonism between Jacob and Esau is a metaphor for the historical rivalry between the Israelites (the descendants of Jacob) and the Amalekites (the descendants of Esau). As we know, any attempt to form an understanding of Israelite origins solely on the basis of the biblical narratives is a very dangerous endeavour indeed — as most texts were specifically written to justify their political and ideological interpretation of history.[63] Divine sanction for the obliteration of the Amalekites, who incidentally once mastered the land of Israel and helped shape the Mosaic tradition, was sought to secure Ezra's vision of an ethnically unified Israel. To quote Roger Syrén: *"After his departure from Jacob, Esau vanished into the unknown."*[64] All the Bible tells us is that Esau went into Ishmael (Exodus 28:9) and became the ancestor of the modern Arabs.

Debates have raged among biblical scholars concerning the date of the biblical texts' composition. Also in contention are, naturally, the level of reliability of these texts as historical records. The two antagonistic camps are basically divided between the so-called maximalists (those who believe the biblical texts to be relatively accurate and actually written in or around the time the authors claim they were) and the minimalists (who, on the contrary, believe that the Old Testament narratives are a complete invention of post-Exilic Jews who likely committed these tales to writing many centuries after the said events). Leaning more toward the maximalist view, though probably not a staunch maximalist himself, Swiss Egyptologist Édouard Naville wrote:

> I believe therefore that it is to Ezra that must be attributed the turning of the old Mosaic cuneiform writings into Aramaic, which was the script and idiom of that time; besides, there was no other ... How did Ezra come to have these writings of Moses 'in his hand'?[65]

Naville's hypothesis is that the cuneiform tablets of the law of Moses, which were supposedly kept in the temple of Jerusalem at the time of Nebuchadnezzar II's conquest, were carried away to Babylon — where Ezra later had access to them. Naville goes on to say:

---

[63] See Michael Prior (1997) *The Bible and Colonialism: A Moral Critique*, Sheffield Academic Press: Sheffield, U.K., p. 250.
[64] Roger Syrén (1993) *The Forsaken First-Born (A Study of a Recurrent Motif in the Patriarchal Narratives)*, JSOT (Supplement Series 133): Sheffield, U.K., p. 66.
[65] Édouard Naville (1915) *The Text of the Old Testament*, The British Academy: London, pp. 67-68.

> It seems probable that when Ezra turned the law of Moses into Aramaic, he divided them into five books. ... Ezra may also have arranged these tablets in order, putting each of them in its proper place, so as to make a running and continuous text, which, having been turned into Aramaic, was on a roll of skin.[66]

Thus, Naville accepts that the main outlines of the story of Moses in the Torah must have been based on a genuine Mosaic tradition. Naville, rightfully in my view, doubts that Ezra could have garnered the necessary authority to impose a completely fabricated tradition to his people. Expressing his disagreement with those who held that view, Naville adds:

> If, according to Eduard Meyer, Ezra had brought them [the Israelites] a law of his own invention, which he had concocted with the well-to-do Jews of Babylon, would the Jews of Jerusalem have submitted at once, would they so easily have dismissed their wives? For where would Ezra have found the authority to enforce the law upon them?[67]

As Naville supposes, there certainly was a previous Mosaic tradition to act as a basis for his laws. But German historian Eduard Meyer still isn't too far from the mark when he claims that Ezra literally "invented" both Jewish Mosaic tradition and the Five Books of Moses. Indeed, as many modern Bible scholars contend (e.g. Wagner, Winnett, Rendtorff, Schmid & Mayes), I believe that there was no Torah (Law of Moses) or Pentateuch in existence until the time of the Babylonian exile.[68] However, Ezra *was* able, by claiming to be the latest Mosaic figure, to rely on the genuine historical records of the periodic advent of a Messianic leader — specially anointed to deliver his people on the Day of the Lord. Evidently, different generations of people or tribes within the overall Jewish population may have cherished the memory of a particular Moses over the others. But Ezra was able to unite all of these people by presenting them a composite Moses who represented all of their hopes and aspirations for the Jewish people.

Édouard Naville also makes the interesting observation that, as is the case with the biblical Moses, Ezra was born in a foreign land — in the latter's case Mesopotamia — and instructed in the wisdom of his people's captors. Ezra's own life experiences, which somewhat mirrored the circumstances of the preceding Moses archetypes, made him a suitable candidate for assuming the responsibilities of a new Mosaic figure for the Jewish people.

---

[66] Ibid, p. 69.
[67] Édouard Naville (1915) *The Text of the Old Testament*, The British Academy: London, p. 70.
[68] See R. N. Whybray (1987) *The Making of the Pentateuch: A Methodological Study*, JSOT (Supplement Series 53): Sheffield, U.K., p. 221.

CHAP. XVII: CHANGING THE COURSE OF HISTORY | 647

Ezra, however, apparently did not wish for it to be know to posterity that he had fomented a composite Moses. Though the fact that the Torah is still being called the Five Books of Moses, it is clear that following generations had lost the knowledge of the identity of the Moses who composed the Pentateuch. It simply became taken for granted that the composite Moses had been then author. Even the very notion that the biblical Moses was an amalgamation of several ancient Jewish Messianic figures became the sole knowledge of the initiated.

King Psusennes I, by author

Part VI

Independent Dynasties & Second Persian Period

404 BCE to 333 BCE

Late Period

333 BCE to 31 BCE

18

The Last Centuries (404 BCE to 31 BCE)

The Persian occupation of Egypt under King Darius I (522-486 BCE) of the new 24th Dynasty (standard 27th Dynasty) had been relatively beneficial for Egyptians of the learned classes and the priesthood. King Darius the Great's policies of instituting a strict code of law in Egypt, restoring temples and financing irrigation projects and business ventures, had been used as a tactic to maintain Egypt within the Persian Empire. However, following the Persians' defeat at the hands of the Athenians at Marathon in 490 BCE, things began to go from bad to worse. The death of Darius the Great in 486 BCE unleashed growing resentment in Egypt against the Persian occupants and a revolt erupted in the Delta under the leadership of Libyans from the West Delta. In response to the uprising, the reigning Persian monarch, King Xerxes, immediately reduced the status of Egypt within the Persian Empire to a mere conquered province. A much disliked king in Egypt, Xerxes never even visited Egypt and even apparently barred Egyptians from occupying high positions within his administration. In 465 BCE, King Xerxes was murdered and, once again, the Libyans in the Delta used this opportunity to rise up against the Persians. This time around, the rebels, headed by one Inaros, were supported by Athenian forces hostile to the Persians as well. But Inaros was crucified by the Persians in 454 BCE after the Delta region was retaken by the new Persian king, Artaxerxes I. Despite this latest show of force by the Persians, the reigns of Artaxerxes I (465-424 BCE) and Darius II (424-404 BCE) were characterized by great instability in Egypt, with numerous rebellions, of varying scales and success, succeeding each other. Finally, the death of Darius II, in 404 BCE, unleashed a final rebellion which succeeded in removing the Persians' stranglehold over Egypt. A new dynasty made up of a single individual, King Amyrtaeus (404-399 BCE), at last restored native Egyptian control of the Nile Valley.

Pharaoh Amyrtaeus established his dynasty at Sais, but growing domestic power struggles led to the advent of a new dynasty, based in Mendes, the new 26th Dynasty (standard 29th Dynasty) which ruled from 399 BCE to 380 BCE. The new 26th Dynasty restored a certain level of normalcy in Egypt's domestic and international affairs. The building of monuments resumed and trade and military alliances were now being forged with Persia's enemies. Following the ephemeral rule of the new 26th Dynasty's last ruler, King Nepherites II (who reigned a mere four months), Nectanebo I of Sebennytos, a general, usurped the throne and established the new 27th Dynasty (standard 30th Dynasty). Narrowly averting a decisive Persian invasion in 373 BCE, the new 27th Dynasty enjoyed very prosperous times. In my revised history of Egypt, this period is of critical importance because it is precisely at this time that a great religious renaissance took place — which I believe forever altered the history of the ancient world. This Renaissance Period marked a forceful return to the artistic canons, religious cosmogonies, and even cultural attributes of the classic Ptolemaic line of the Early Bronze I-II period. Perhaps this sudden return to the primeval origins of pharaonic culture, after centuries of foreign occupation, was meant to reaffirm dynastic Egypt's heritage in times of obvious cultural instability. This cultural return to the New Horus Period of long-ago, evidently, led to the rise in prominence of the traditional myth of Isis and Osiris. Also, the Memphite cosmogony became increasingly popular as the inspiration behind the designs of official tombs, cult centres and artistic styles in general.

The Great Religious Renewal

It was in North Saqqara, near the temple of Osiris-Apis, that Prof. Walter B. Emery discovered, in 1964, a sacred animal necropolis containing millions of mummified remains of three main sacred animals: the ibis, the baboon (both symbols for the god Ptah) and the Hawk (representing Horus). Inside the various terraces, temples and galleries could be found the mummified carcasses of no less than four million ibis, five hundred baboons and five hundred thousand hawks.[1] In addition to the three catacombs containing the mummies of these three animals: (1) the Hawk Catacomb, (2) the South Ibis Catacomb and (3) the Baboon Catacomb, could also be found (4) the South Ibis Catacomb — containing cow remains — dedicated to Isis, the mother of the Apis bull. Emery carried on excavating the site until the time of his death in 1971. He was then succeeded by Geoffrey T. Martin and Harry S. Smith who went on excavating until 1976.[2] More recently, between November 25th and December 20th of 1992, a mission at the Sacred Animal Necropolis was undertaken by the Egyptian Exploration Society. The aim of the dig was to supplement Egyptologists' knowledge of the ceramics and animal bone remains previously recorded in this area during the 1960s and 1970s. In a summary report of the 1992 excavation, Paul T. Nicholson outlines that each catacomb is composed of several galleries, all

---

[1] Edwin M. Yamauchi (1996) *Persia and the Bible*, Baker Books: Grand Rapids, Mich., p. 119.
[2] See W. B. Emery (1971) 'Preliminary Report on the Excavations at North Saqqara, 1969-70', *Journal of Egyptian Archaeology* 57, pp. 3-13; H. S. Smith (1972) 'Dates of the Obsequies of the Mothers of Apis', *Revue d'Egyptologie* 24, pp. 176-87.

CHAP. XVIII: THE LAST CENTURIES | 653

numbered by excavators. Within several of the galleries, various vessels and remains of mummified birds were discovered. Not all of the Hawk mummies found contained actual deceased hawks, or even birds. Some of them contained only parts of a genuine hawk, mixed in with various other elements. It is worthy to note, incidentally, that the mummies have only one modelled eye, with the other left as an empty socket.[3] Nicholson suggests that this was an obvious reference to the struggle between Horus and Seth — when Horus lost an eye during his conflict with his uncle. A relevant clue, which helps us to identify the period in which these animal catacombs were originally built, is the discovery, in the South Ibis Catacomb, of a blocking shaft dated to the Old Kingdom.[4] This, therefore, indicates that the catacombs were originally built during, or before, the Old Kingdom.

In the case of the South Ibis Catacomb, animal bone analyst Dr Barbara Ghaleb concluded that most of the mummies from that catacomb, were indeed those of genuine ibis.[5] The reason for the disparity between the Hawk and South Ibis catacomb mummies was attributed to the fact that hawks were a much more difficult species to breed in captivity than the ibis. At any rate, it is evident that these ancient catacombs were reused during Egypt's Late Period (fourth century BCE) since, to quote Paul T. Nicholson:

> The non-mummy pottery from around the South Ibis Catacomb includes some sherds of the Ptolemaic and Roman periods. Janine Bourriau [ceramicist] has not so far had time to examine this area in detail, but it is possible that use of this Catacomb extended beyond the main period of use for the Hawk Catacomb.[6]

The late date of the sacred animal burial is also confirmed by the presence of demotic, Greek and Carian documents associated with the "Iseum" which housed cow remains meant to represent the goddess Isis, the mother of the Apis bull.[7] Also uncovered were numerous statues of Isis and Osiris, as well as a statuette of Imhotep, from the North Saqqara deposits of Pharaoh Nectanebo II's time.[8] Like the rulers of the classic Ptolemaic dynasty, the rulers of the new 27th Dynasty, keeping pace with the New Horus Period religious renaissance theme,

---

[3] Paul T. Nicholson (1994) 'Preliminary Report on Work at the Sacred Animal Necropolis, North Saqqara, 1992', *Journal of Egyptian Archaeology* 80, p. 6.
[4] Ibid.
[5] Ibid, p. 9.
[6] Ibid.
[7] Geoffrey T. Martin *et al.* (1971) 'The Excavations at North Saqqara, 1969-70', *Journal of Egyptian Archaeology* 57, pp. 11-12.
[8] See Walter B. Emery (1970) 'Preliminary Report on the Excavations at North Saqqara, 1968-9', *Journal of Egyptian Archaeology* 56, p. 6.

were particularly fond of the exceedingly ancient cult of the deified vizier Imhotep. What is more, we know that the ibis was a sacred bird to both Thoth and Imhotep. In fact, not only were the kings of the new 27th Dynasty attempting to emulate the Khemetic rulers of the New Horus Period, but of very close concern to them was also the Typhonian era (TS#1) in which the vizier Imhotep actually lived — during the reign of Pharaoh Djoser-Netjerykhet. This, of course, is only logical since the promethean conflict between Horus and Seth, evidently symbolized in the Sacred Animal Necropolis, played itself out during the primeval Typhon Season. Incidentally, excavator Walter B. Emery found evidence that the galleries were connected to a 3rd Dynasty burial chamber.[9] This burial chamber, I would instead date to the predynastic days of Imhotep since Emery found numerous limestone false-door stela, inscribed with Carian texts, which are extremely reminiscent of well-known mastabas of Djoser-Netjerykhet's time.[10]

Nectanebo II extensively renovated the Osiris-Apis temple at Memphis and gave renewed importance to the cult of Ptah.[11] Likewise, a relief of Nectanebo II being embraced by Isis at the temple of Osiris-Apis at Saqqara[12] exhibits clear Ptolemaic influences. In it, Isis is portrayed exactly as on the classic Ptolemaic temple reliefs. In fact, one of the leading authorities on the Ptolemaic temples, French Egyptologist Sylvie Cauville, has remarked that: "... *It is of interest to note that the artistic style of the Late Period Ptolemaic temples is very much reminiscent of the Nectanebo kings' buildings.*"[13] These obvious similarities are in fact there because it is my belief that King Nectanebo II, probably completing work already done by his two predecessors of the new 27th Dynasty, endeavoured to extensively restore, and even entirely rebuild, the over two and a half millennia-old classical Ptolemaic temples of the First Cataract. Essentially, what survives now of the Ptolemaic temples represents the work of the new 27th Dynasty pharaohs. It is actually a long-standing gigantic myth that the Ptolemaic temples near the First Cataract in Upper Egypt were constructed during the post-Alexandrian Greek occupation of Egypt. Years before Alexander the Great ever even entered Egypt, Pharaoh Nectanebo II had already finished putting the finishing touches to the reconstructed edifices of the great classic Ptolemaic era. It is clear, however, that the Greek Ptolemaic kings also inherited the same fascination with the First Cataract temples, as will now be seen.

---

[9] Walter B. Emery (1970) p. 7.
[10] See Walter B. Emery (1970) Plate XV.
[11] See Michael Jones (1990) 'The Temple of Apis in Memphis', *Journal of Egyptian Archaeology* 76, pp. 141, 145-147.
[12] See Cyril Aldred (1980) *Egyptian Art (in the days of the Pharaohs — 3100-320 BC)*, Thames and Hudson: London, p. 234, Pl. 194.
[13] Sylvie Cauville (1989) 'La chapelle de Thot-Ibis à Dendera', *Bulletin de l'Institut Français d'Archéologie Orientale* 89, p. 45. (My translation)

CHAP. XVIII: THE LAST CENTURIES | 655

The Second Persian Occupation, Alexander the Great and the Advent of the Greek Ptolemaic Dynasty

To begin with, in 343 BCE, the Persians, under King Artaxerxes III (Ochus) regained control of Egypt. Artaxerxes ruled Egypt with an iron fist. He showed very little respect for the local temples and the native populace in general. He stormed city walls, freely pillaged the local resources — all in an attempt to thwart any potential Egyptian revolts. Artaxerxes had been king of Persia for twenty years before the Persians defeated the Egyptians. He ruled over Egypt for six years and was murdered in 338 BCE by his own commander Bagoas. Afterwards, there was a period of chaos, between 338-335 BCE where it appears that a Nubian prince by the name of Khabbash gained control of Egypt. But the Persians reasserted themselves in 335 BCE under Darius III. There is however evidence that a certain Arses, the youngest son of Ochus, ruled during that same period of confusion. Perhaps that period was one in which Kabbash and Arses competed for power. At any rate, order was restored in 335 BCE, when the last Persian king to rule Egypt, Darius III, ascended the throne. He ruled for three years until, in 332 BCE, Alexander the Great, commanding a mixed army of Macedonians and Greeks, put an end to Persian domination in Egypt.

Eager to rid themselves of the oppressive Persian yoke, the Egyptians welcomed Alexander and hailed him as a liberator. Conquering Egypt without a battle, Alexander journeyed to the Siwa Oasis in the Western Delta to visit the Oracle of Amun, and was declared son of Amun. His coronation subsequently took place in Memphis. As a result, romantic myths attributed to him parental lineage to the last native pharaoh, and religious innovator, Nectanebo II. This connection with the new 27th Dynasty (standard 30th Dynasty) which enacted the great Khemetic Renaissance is of pivotal interest because it lays the background for the revival of the Memphite cult in Alexandria during the Hellenistic period. I believe that the cult of Serapis, which developed in Alexandria at this time was intimately related to, and was a conscious continuation, of the religious renaissance of the new 27th Dynasty. Alexander initiated the building of Alexandria, giving prominence to a Hellenized version of the ancient Memphite cult, but he never lived to see the completed city. He left Egypt in 331 BCE and delegated authority to Cleomenes and Naukratis. When Alexander died, in 323 BCE, a Macedonian general who called himself Ptolemy I Soter, became ruler of Egypt. He assumed the official title of satrap of Egypt but his powers definitely transcended those of a mere viceroy. He styled himself as a legitimate Horus king. Greek Ptolemaic rulers went on ruling in Alexandria until the death of Cleopatra VII on August 12th, 30 BCE.

The Alexandrian rulers established the Serapeum, their centre of worship of the Hellenistic version of the Egyptian Memphite deity Apis, called Serapis, modelled after the temple of Osiris-Apis located next to the temple of the deceased pharaoh Nectanebo II in Memphis — who was himself the object of a local cult as a falcon-god.[14] According to the Rosetta stone, the Greek Ptolemaic kings were crowned in Memphis. These are extremely important clues for my our historical reconstruction. I believe that the Serapeum built in Alexandria was meant as a northern replica, or counterpart, of the temple of Osiris-Apis in Memphis. Evidently, the cult of Serapis was closely related to the previous Memphis renaissance of the new 27th Dynasty. In effect, I will contend that the Macedonians would have never instituted the worship of this Hellenized version of the Egyptian Apis had it not been for the previous religious renaissance of the new 27th Dynasty. Hence, Alexander the Great, by linking himself, through his mother Olympias, to the deceased Egyptian pharaoh Nectanebo II, was making a conscious effort to link himself and his dynasty to the Ptolemaic cultural renaissance.

By building a replica of the Serapeum next to the temple of Nectanebo II, the Ptolemaic rulers were fulfilling Alexander's vision. Evidently, the choice of the name of "Ptolemy" by Alexander's general as his throne name as satrap of Egypt was an acknowledgement of this crucial link between the two dynasties. Thus, my hypothesis is that Ptolemy was not Soter I's real name, but rather a name that he adopted from the New Horus Period and which was revived during the new religious renaissance. The Macedonian-Greek Ptolemaic dynasty was, in reality, an alter-ego or reincarnation of the classic Ptolemaic dynasty of the New Horus Period from the Early Bronze I-II era. As a result, I doubt that the Ptolemaic temples north of the First Cataract, which incidentally were erected during the new 27th Dynasty on top of the earlier New Horus Period buildings, were constructed by the native Egyptians in honour of their Greek overlords. Since these temples were already standing at Edfu and Dendera at the time of Alexander the Great's arrival, they had obviously served as a model for the Macedonians of Alexandria — who attempted to reproduce these artistic canons further north.

There is indeed a clear difference in quality and style between the Ptolemaic relics, such as statues, stelae and temple reliefs, in Edfu and Alexandria. The common explanation is that the art produced in the south was the work of native Egyptian artisans, working for the benefit of their Greek occupiers, and that the much lesser quality busts and other reproductions in the north, were made by the Macedonians themselves. But why had such an obvious discrepancy in styles been maintained for so long? Couldn't the native Egyptian masons travel to Alexandria? Similarly, why hadn't the Alexandrian Hellenistic statues made their way in Upper Egypt? Other related anomalies present themselves. For

---

[14] Dorothy J. Thompson (1988) *Memphis Under the Ptolemies*, Princeton University Press: Princeton, N.J., p. 212.

instance, while the pharaohs of the new 27th Dynasty, reflecting the royal regalia of their own time, had depicted the classic Ptolemaic monarch wearing the dynastic blue crown, the later Alexandrian Ptolemies never portrayed themselves wearing this symbol of dynastic Egypt. As American Egyptologist Robert S. Bianchi astutely observed, there are "no unequivocally identified examples in sculpture in the round" of any Greek Ptolemaic kings wearing the blue crown.[15] I, however, find Professor Bianchi's explanation that the Greek pharaohs were denied this "symbol of legitimacy" by the Egyptian priesthood because of their foreign origin, rather unconvincing. Why would the Greek Ptolemaic kings be repeatedly depicted wearing a blue crown on the temples walls of Upper Egypt, and never on their three dimensional representations from Alexandria? If the Egyptian priesthood really did wish to deny them this privilege, wouldn't that situation have been reversed? To quote Egyptologist Anthony Leahy: " ... *it is hard to see why it should be allowed in one medium and not in another when the physical context of the two — a native temple — was essentially the same.*"[16] Moreover, the basic physical appearance of the Ptolemies depicted in Edfu and Alexandria are completely at odds. The extant pictorial evidence delineating the physical appearance of the Ptolemies and Cleopatras, as Classicists Mary Lefkowitz explains below, has very little to do with how they are portrayed in the Ptolemaic temples in Upper Egypt.

> She [Cleopatra] chose to portray herself as an Egyptian not because she was Egyptian, but because she was ambitious to stay in power. In her surviving portraits on coins and in sculpture she appears to be impressive rather than beautiful, Mediterranean in appearance, with straight hair and a hooked nose.[17]

While the Romans, for reasons which will be made clear in the next chapter, tried to depict Cleopatra VII as an Egyptian, the fact is she was not. Though she wore pharaonic dress, as all other Greek Ptolemaic rulers, their culture was, evidently, Hellenic. The rigid pharaonic regalia seen on the classic Ptolemaic rulers' depictions at Edfu was not so strictly adhered to in Alexandria.

The other Ptolemaic pharaoh who followed Soter I in Alexandria, Ptolemy II Philadelphus, continued to recognize the interest of the Greeks and Macedonians to dominate the Nile Valley. Their objective was to integrate its people and resources firmly toward the Hellenic culture and interests of the Mediterranean world. Pto-

---

[15] Robert S. Bianchi, *Cleopatra's Egypt*, p. 143 (no. 48).
[16] See Anthony Leahy (1992) 'Royal Iconography and Dynastic Change, 750-525 BC: The Blue and Cap Crowns', *Journal of Egyptian Archaeology* 78, p. 226.
[17] Mary R. Lefkowitz (1997 [1996])*Not Out of Africa (How Afrocentrism Became an Excuse to teach Myth as History)*. Second revised edition. BasicBooks: New York, p. 35.

lemy II Philadelphus also carried this objective south of Egypt's First Cataract border into Ethiopia. It was indeed during the reign of King Philadelphus that the Greeks first invaded Ethiopia. Timosthenes, the admiral of Ptolemy II, went as far as Meroë itself. At this particular junction point, we get another chance to test my revised chronology of Meroitic civilization. Diodorus of Sicily (Book III: 6) speaks of a certain "Ergamenes," whom he describes as a king of Ethiopia who had received a Greek education in philosophy during the reign of Ptolemy II Philadelphus. This king was apparently the first Ethiopian king to openly defy the powerful priesthood of his court. He had all the temple priests slain and, thereafter, ran matters according to his own will. Nubiologists have attempted to identify this Ergamenes with one of the Meroitic rulers who, according to the conventional chronology of the Kingdom of Meroë, reigned contemporaneously with Ptolemy II Philadelphus. But the Meroitic king-list does not include this name. Consequently, varying close substitutes have been suggested.

The one most commonly retained is King Arqamani from Meroë's North Cemetery — who is conventionally believed to have reigned between 218-200 BCE. Based on the new chronology, however, we know that Arqamani ruled about twelve hundred years before the advent of Ptolemy II Philadelphus. According to my revised historical framework, the complex Meroitic civilization which produced the Lion-temples of Musawwarat Es-Sufra and Naqa, had ceased to exist, as a fundamentally pharaonic entity, in the middle of the eighth century BCE. The little that remained of that pharaonic civilization came undone during the reign of King Ergamenes — with the murder of the priests and the irreversible Hellenization, and later Christianization, of Nubia. Outlining the major anomalies associated with identifying Ergamenes with Arqamani, or other Meroitic pharaohs, Prof. Edwyn Bevan of Oxford University, in the 1920s, wrote:

> Yet, if Ergamenes himself took to Greek philosophy, the court and kingdom, to judge by the monumental remains, continued in externals to be Pharaonic. **There is no trace, so far as I know, of Hellenistic influence in the temples and pyramids of Meroe or the remains of its art.** The temple built by Ergamenes at Dakkeh is on purely Egyptian lines. And when he died, his mummy was laid to rest in a pyramid near Meroe, decorated with copies of scenes from the Book of the Dead according to the correct Egyptian tradition. It has even been observed that the hieroglyphics inscribed for Ergamenes are of such a good Pharaonic type as to make it likely that he procured priestly craftsmen from Egypt. This would not invalidate the story of his having had personally Greek ideas, since we can see, in the case of the Ptolemies, that no inference can be made from the style of the Egyptian temples built at the king's command to the king's own culture.[18]

---

[18] Edwyn Bevan (1927) *A History of Egypt Under the Ptolemaic Dynasty*, Methuen: London, p. 245.

Professor Bevan avoids dealing with the blatant contradiction by resorting to the equally flawed example of the Ptolemaic temples who were allegedly built by native Egyptians for the benefit of the Greek occupants. In both cases, the logic presented is seriously flawed. The pyramids and various funerary objects from Meroë show no sign of a Hellenistic influence simply because these artifacts "predate" the Hellenistic era.

The Cult of the Fish

The religious renewals which symbolized the Independent Dynasties and Late Period in Egypt, again, show an impressive continuity. For instance, a scribe of Amun-Re by the name of Hor constructed, under the reign of Ptolemy I Soter, a chapel dedicated to Thoth-Ibis at Dendera.[19] Therefore, it is evident that the Ptolemies promoted the worship of sacred animals in Egypt. Further confirming this continuity hypothesis, it appears that Hor renovated several buildings erected under the Nectanebos.[20] Additionally, the construction of underground animal catacombs was pursued by King Ptolemy I Soter at Touna el-Gebel. The scribe Hor is known to have restored earlier cult sites dedicated to the sacred ibis and falcon bird-gods. In addition to Touna el-Gebel, the divine association of the ibis and falcon is attested in Kom Ombo, Diospolis, Abydos and Saqqara. Besides, as it was during the Second Persian Period, the baboon, in the form of Thoth, was also of central importance.

Another sacred animal which was preeminently revered during these periods of religious renewal was the fish. In the temple of Pharaoh Nectanebo I is illustrated, to quote Egyptologist Robert K. Ritner, "a problematic scene."[21] There, Anubis, the god of mummification, bends over a large smooth disk — presiding over the divine birth of the pharaoh. This scene is exactly similar to an earlier relief depicting Queen Hatchepsut's divine birth. It later became a standard iconography in the Graeco-Roman birth houses, and is found at Edfu, Philae and Dendera. Where this role of Anubis, as the presider over divine rebirth, is linked with animal worship can be gleaned from as early as, and even long before, the time of Typhon Season #7. In the Theban tomb of one official Khabekhnet, Anubis presides over the divine birth of a giant fish.

---

[19] See Sylvie Cauville (1989) pp. 44-66.
[20] Ibid, pp. 48-49.
[21] Robert K. Ritner (1985) 'Anubis and the Lunar Disc', *Journal of Egyptian Archaeology* 71, p. 149.

> The substitution of a symbol for the body of Osiris is well known in Egyptian representations. ... A specific example of a substitution for the body of Osiris in a mummification scene is found in the tomb of Khabekhnet (Theban tomb 2) in which a mammoth *bdw*-fish occupies the bier over which Anubis bends.[22]

This official, Khabekhnet (son of Senedjem), lived during the reign of Pharaoh Nekau-Ramses II. Egyptologist date this wall painting to Ramses II's reign in the Late Bronze Age,[23] but again, given the context, I am persuaded that he lived during the reign of the *"Iron Age"* Ramses II. The Egyptian priests who lived during Typhon Season #7 were undoubtedly aware that the next constellation due to appear on the vernal equinox would be that of Pisces. Anubis, in his traditional role as a guarantor of rebirth, was meant to be portrayed, in the mural, as ensuring a smooth transition to the Age of Pisces. The Pisces Mandate introduced an era where Osiris adopted a new form: that of a fish. Other artifacts, dated to the Pisces Mandate, come to reinforce this theory. Indeed, during the 1970s, American Egyptologist Bob Brier obtained, in Egypt, a series of mummified fish dating to the Greek Ptolemaic period.[24] In fact, all of the mummified sacred fishes discovered are dated to the Late Period.[25] The conventional Late Period starts with the Saite Dynasty of Nekau-Ramses II. If the wall painting in Khabekhnet's tomb really dated to the Late Bronze Age, as Egyptologists contend, how then could one explain the absence of any such mummified fish (either pictured of actual) between the end of Ramses II's LBIII rule and the Late Period?[26]

The archaeotheological link between Osiris and the changing constellations of the precessional cycle was an old one. It is, for instance, very revealing that Osiris was represented at Heliopolis, *for the very first time* in dynastic Egyptian history, in the form of a bull during the time of the Ethiopian novel 20th Dynasty (conventional 25th dynasty).[27] Likewise, during the immediately succeeding Saite dynasty, Osiris is referred to as "the bull in Heliopolis." These references to Osiris in the form of a bull evidently symbolize the Age of Taurus, during which the Egyptians lived when these iconographies were devised.

---

[22] Robert K. Ritner (1985) p. 152.
[23] See C. F. Nims & W. Swaan (1965) *Thebes of the Pharaohs*, London, p. 195, Pl. 97.
[24] Bob Brier & M. V. L. Bennet (1979) 'Autopsies on Fish Mummies (Possible Identification of the Classical Phagrus)', *Journal of Egyptian Archaeology* 65, pp. 128-133. See also F. Filce Leek (1976) 'An Ancient Egyptian Mummified Fish', *Journal of Egyptian Archaeology* 62, pp. 131-133.
[25] Bob Brier & M. V. L. Bennet (1979) p. 132.
[26] As is supposed by F. Filce Leek (1976) p. 131.
[27] Essam El-Banna (1989) 'À propos des aspects héliopolitains d'Osiris', *Bulletin de l'Institut Français d'Archéologie Orientale* 89, p. 124.

CHAP. XVIII: THE LAST CENTURIES | 661

In the Middle Kingdom, King Neferhotep visited "the house of writings" in order to "discover the correct form of a new statue of Osiris, laid down by the gods themselves at the beginning of time."[28] Why did Neferhotep feel that it was time to change the form of Osiris? Could it be that he presumed that the lunar shift of 1,628 BCE would herald the advent a new constellation at the vernal equinox? That is a strong possibility. Indeed, the ancient Egyptians also looked upon Osiris as a fearful god in his hour of anger.

> L. Kákosy, in his recent article on Osiris as a bellicose god, quoted two pertinent texts from the shrines of Tut'ankhamun, in which Osiris is referred to as one whose heart 'inflicts all carnage ...' on his enemies 'who cannot be saved from his arm'; when Osiris come forth against them, 'they are fallen, for ever and ever ...' Already in the hymns of the Middle Kingdom Osiris is called 'Lord of fear ...', and 'great of terror ...'[29]

As the god Osiris transformed himself through his various zodiacal incarnations at the close of a given World Age or Mandate of Heaven, he spread terror across the earth. At the culmination of Typhon Season #7, Osiris metamorphosed himself from a bull into a fish. Thus, throughout Egypt's Late Period, the fish had become regarded as a sacred animal. Emory University's Michael C. Carlos Museum holds in its permanent collection a bronze, lapis lazuli and red glass statuette of a large fish receiving tribute by an Egyptian. This piece, named "Oxyrhynchus Fish with Donor," is dated to the Late Period. Oxyrhynchus was a Late Period Hellenized Egyptian town located in the 19th Upper Egyptian Nome of the western edge of the Nile Valley, just south of the Fayum oasis, or about 160 km southwest of Memphis. In that Middle Egyptian city, the fish was deified "as a sort of *genius loci*."[30] Plutarch related a very interesting story that when, at a particular time, the Oxyrhynchites' nearby neighbours, the Kynopolites, sought to provoke the latter by eating fish in front of them, the Oxyrhynchites were so outraged that they at once invaded Kynopolites.

---

[28] Barry J. Kemp (1989) *Ancient Egypt: Anatomy of a Civilization*, Routledge: London and New York, p. 26.

[29] L. V. Zabkar (1983) 'Six Hymns to Isis in the Sanctuary of Her Temple at Philae and their Theological Significance — Part I', *Journal of Egyptian Archaeology* 69, p. 125; L. Kákosy 'Ein literarisch-mythologisches Motiv: Osiris als Gott des Kampfes und der Rache.' In J. Assman et al. (editors) (1977) *Fragen an die altägyptische Literatur*, Wiesbaden, pp. 285-288; A. Piankoff (1952) *Les chapelles de Tout-ankh-Amon*, Cairo, p. 75 - Il. 34-35.

[30] Hugh MacLennan (1968) *Oxyrhynchus: An Economic and Social Study*, Adolf M. Hakkert: Amsterdam, p. 11.

The Revolt in the South

During the reign of Ptolemy V Epiphanes, the native Egyptian and Ethiopian revolts, which had begun under Philopator, began intensifying. Two of the rebel leaders went under the names of Anmachis and Hermachis. They were either nationalistic Egyptians who sought to cleanse the throne of Egypt from Greek rule, or possibly Ethiopians who had raided Upper Egypt. In any event, a fragment dated to Ptolemy V Epiphanes' reign reads: "Ptolemy formed a corps of 500 horsemen from Greece for his war against the Ethiopians."[31] As the political situation worsened, the Macedonians' hold on Upper Egypt inevitably began to wane as famine and revolts became common place in Nubia.[32]

> When we inquire into the factors which brought about the spirit of nationalist revolt under the later Ptolemies, especially in Upper Egypt, an important one was probably the continued maintenance of the Pharaonic tradition in the Nile country to the south of Egypt. The Greek conquerors had subjugated Egypt, but they had not subjugated the whole realm of the ancient Pharaohs, the whole area of Egyptian culture; and so long as the Egyptian nationalists saw their old tradition still ruling, there just beyond the southern frontier, they might well refuse to believe that it had been crushed for good.[33]

As Edwyn Bevan outlined above, the Greek Ptolemaic rulers had to continually contend with a threat of rebellion in Upper Egypt and the land of Wawat. In fact, it would not be long before a successful rebellion, inspired by the Upper Egyptians and Nubians, ended the Alexandrian dynasty's (new 29th Dynasty) dominion over much of Egypt outside of their own territory in the north. This, naturally, is a very radical hypothesis. Ancient historians have always maintained that the Greek Ptolemaic rulers retained control of the entire territory of Egypt until the defeat of Cleopatra VII in 31 BCE.

This orthodox interpretation is, in my view, inaccurate. During reigns of Ptolemy V Epiphanes and Ptolemy VI Philometor, the Alexandrians' power in Egypt began to erode significantly. The circumstances accompanying the accession of the very youthful Epiphanes are mired by royal court intrigue. Within the few short years which followed, massive native revolts were beginning to seriously undermine Macedonian authority in Egypt. Undoubtedly, claimants to the throne manifested themselves at an increasingly frequent rate. As the Ptolemies' overseas campaign defeats became more and more commonplace, leading by 196 BCE to a substantial

---

[31] *Geog. Græc. Min.* i. p. 119.
[32] Nicholas Grimal (1992) *A History of Ancient Egypt*. Trans. by Ian Shaw. Blackwell: Oxford, U.K., p. 65.
[33] Edwyn Bevan (1927) *A History of Egypt Under the Ptolemaic Dynasty*, pp. 260-261.

shrinking of the Ptolemaic overseas empire, their credibility in Egypt suffered immensely. As a result, more and more of the native Egyptians were joining forces with the rebels. To make matters worse, the Syrian king Antiochus IV, in 170 BCE, invaded Egypt and established a protectorate. In 168 BCE, he returned to be crowned in Memphis and installed a Seleucid governor. That renewed conflict with the Seleucids in the reign of Ptolemy VI Philometor signalled the beginning of the end for the Greek Ptolemies outside of Alexandria. Despite the Romans' intervention in the summer of 168 BCE which forced the Seleucids out of Egypt, it was already too late for the much-beleaguered Alexandrians. By the middle of the second century BCE, two contemporaneous native Egyptian dynasty were established in Thebes and Tanis.

Ramses III: Ruler of the Greek Ptolemaic Age

The new native Egyptian dynasty which arose in Thebes sometime around 145 BCE did not attempt to drive out the Macedonians from Alexandria. Until the arrival of the Romans in 31 BCE, the native monarchs, representing the new 30th and 31st Dynasties, and the Greek Ptolemaic rulers, the new 29th Dynasty, reigned in Egypt peacefully and independent of each other. The Alexandrians understood well that there was nothing much they could do to reclaim Egypt, and the native Egyptians were happy to have finally regained control of the main city-centres of their country. I believe that the charismatic native Egyptian leader who reconquered Thebes adopted the name of Pharaoh Ramses III and established a royal capital at Medinet Habu in Upper Egypt — a very conscious decision obviously, as he sought to emulate his illustrious distant ancestor from the Late Bronze Age. The reason why this ruler chose the name of Ramses III is because this is where the alter-ego line, interrupted at the end of the Saite Dynasty (new 22nd Dynasty), actually left off.

The coming to power of the new Ramses III during the Late Period was the catalyst for the inauguration of a Renaissance Era known as that of: *"The Repetition of Births."* We may recall that the ancient Pharaohs Amenemhat I, Seti I, an Amenhotep II (Shoshenk I) had all likewise proclaimed this same "new era" at the beginning of their respective reigns. The beginning of all of these kings' reigns indeed signalled the beginning of a new period — radically altering the political landscape in Egypt. In the new Ramses III's case, this renaissance era signalled the return of Egypt under native rule after years of foreign occupation. An oracle of the high priest Pi-Ankhy, who would later be crowned king of Thebes after Ramses III's reign, found at Karnak, makes mention of the Year 7 of the "Renaissance era."[34]

---

[34] Kenneth A. Kitchen (1973) *The Third Intermediate Period in Egypt (1100 - 650 B.C.)*, Aris & Phillips: Warminster, U.K., p. 17.

I believe that Egyptologists are mistaken by equating this Year 7 of the Renaissance Era with the Year 1 of the Renaissance Era on the 19th year of Pharaoh Ramses XI's reign. These two observations were actually separated in time by almost a century. While Pi-Ankhy's Renaissance Era denoted the new political developments (as heralded by the new King Ramses III's reign), the Renaissance Era recorded during Pharaoh Ramses XI's reign was initiated by a change in the administration style in the Two Lands. In Part IV, I arrived at the conclusion that the Late Bronze Age Ramesside line of the new 15th Dynasty ended with Ramses VI. Therefore, it becomes evident that, according to the new chronology, Ramses XI belongs to the last Ramesside dynasty of the Hellenistic age.

In all of his correspondences, Pi-Ankhy constantly referred to himself as "the general of the Pharaoh." Who was this pharaoh? Egyptologists believe that this pharaoh whom he spoke of was Ramses XI. This is mainly because, in the standard chronology, Pi-Ankhy, who was one of the founding kings of the conventional 21st Dynasty (new 31st Dynasty), is widely thought to have immediately followed the late Ramesside kings of the orthodox 20th Dynasty. The new chronology, however, asserts that Pi-Ankhy was in fact a contemporary of the new Ramses III of the Late Period. Differentiating the Renaissance eras from Pi-Ankhy's and Ramses XI's lifetimes, therefore, automatically renders the new 30th Dynasty and the new 31st Dynasty contemporaneous. Moreover, immediately after the death of Ramses III, or perhaps in the latter years of his short reign, a dynasty of priestly rulers, based in Thebes and Tanis, was inaugurated. With time, they became increasingly independent of the Ramesside rulers in Thebes — whose power became essentially symbolic.

But what evidence really exists to demonstrate that a pharaoh by the name of Ramses III ruled during the Late Period in Egypt? Like Immanuel Velikovsky, I believe that this evidence can be found in the remains of a palace attributed to Ramses III at Tell el-Yahudiya — in Egypt's Delta. This site was excavated, during the late nineteenth century, by Egyptologist Édouard Naville — who reported several glaring anomalies among the relics uncovered there:

> There is a curious fact about the disks which have been found in such large numbers; some of them are inscribed on the back with Greek letters A, E, ..., X, while others bear Egyptian signs. The Greek letters show that strangers were at some time employed in the work. The greatest part of the building was however thoroughly Egyptian in style, as may be judged from the remains of columns still *in situ*. The enamel ornaments, though unusual, cannot be considered as a foreign import, as something similar has already been found in one of the pyramids of Sakkarah. It is not likely that later kings, such as the Saites or the Ptolemies,

CHAP. XVIII: THE LAST CENTURIES | 665

should have taken the trouble to build for their predecessor, Ramses III, such a beautiful chamber ... I believe, therefore, that the chamber of Ramses III was built under his order ... One of the subsequent kings, probably Ptolemy, may have had it repaired in the same style by the hands of Greek workmen.[35]

The palace of King Ramses III had never been renovated by the Ptolemies. The reason why Greek letters have been found on the palace tiles at Tell el-Yahudiya is because there was a new Pharaoh Ramses III who reigned in Egypt at the time when the Greek Ptolemaic kings ruled in Alexandria. To highlight the unlikelihood of Naville's explanation, that Ramses III's palace had been much later renovated by the Ptolemies, Velikovsky quotes orientalist and art expert T. H. Lewis who judged that:

The most noticeable feature is that several of the rosettes have Greek letters at the back, evidently stamped during the process of making.[36]

This could indicate that the tiles, and thus the palace, had been specifically made for this pharaoh from their very inception. Judging from the presence of the letter *alpha* on the tiles, an element characteristic of the classical age of Plato, Lewis came to the conclusion that the tiles from Ramses III's palace at Tell el-Yahudiya must be dated to the last few centuries before the common era.[37] Following Lewis' lead, other scholars, like Emil Brugsch, actually dated the tiles to the time of the Greek Ptolemaic kings of Egypt:

The Greek letters, and especially *alpha*, found on the fragments and disks leave no room for doubt that the work was executed during the last centuries of the Egyptian Empire and probably in the time of the Ptolemies; but the matter becomes more difficult if we ask who the author of this work was.[38]

In the final analysis, one thing is for sure: the palace chamber for which the tiles were used was especially built for King Ramses III. The pharaoh's name is clearly inscribed on the front of tiles containing the classical Greek letters on their backs.

---

[35] Édouard Naville (1890) *The Mound of the Jew and the City of Onias*, Egypt Exploration Fund: London, pp. 6-7.
[36] T. H. Lewis (1881-82) 'Tel-el-Yahoudeh', *Transactions of the Society of Biblical Archaeology* 7, p. 182.
[37] Ibid, p. 189.
[38] Emil Brugsch (1886) 'On et Onion', *Receuil de travaux relatifs à la philologie et à l'archéologie égyptiennes et assyriennes* 8, p. 5.

Velikovsky also brought attention to some perplexing evidence uncovered in an ancient cemetery just about a mile away from Tell el-Yahudiya.

While excavating that site in the early 1900s, Édouard Naville and F. Ll. Griffith concluded, from the burial remains, that the necropolis could be dated no earlier than to the time of the early Ptolemies.[39] What complicates matters, for conventional historians, is the embarrassing presence of a scarab belonging to King Ramses III among the artifacts found within the funerary complex. What's more, Naville observed that the decorative paintings on the coffins belonging to the cemetery exhibited unmistakable Greek and Roman influences. How could that be? Once again, late Greek letters (M and C) were inscribed on vases discovered inside various tombs from the necropolis! Since the vases would then logically have to be dated to the time of Pharaoh Ramses III, scholars had initially concluded that the vases were manufactured during the twelfth century BCE. The inescapable dilemma however soon became apparent. The Cypriot pottery in question was, stylistically, of a late date. Other similar artifacts had been unearthed by Flinders Petrie in Greek military settlements in Egypt — thereby fixing the earliest possible date for their manufacturing to around the seventh century BCE.[40]

It is certainly of great significance that around the same time when Ramses III had his temple built at Tell el-Yahudiya — over the closing years of the reign of Ptolemy VI (Philometor) — that the Greek Ptolemaic king allowed Onias, a Jewish priest, to build a temple at Tell el-Yahudiya. What now has to be determined is: which temple came first? My own theory is that, upon the untimely death of Philometor in Palestine, in 145 BCE, the native Egyptians took advantage of the Greek king's sudden death in battle against Alexander Balas to overthrow his Jewish protegé, Onias, and at long last reestablish a native Egyptian dynasty.

It would nevertheless seem that Ramses III allowed the Jews to continue worshipping in their temple. The Greek Ptolemaic dynasty's power and ability to rule beyond Alexandria was greatly reduced after Philometor's defeat in Syria. The Seleucid boy-king Demetrius II seized upon this opportunity to obliterate Ptolemaic hegemony in the Near East. Philometor's soldiers were either forced to join the Seleucid army, or retreat, with their tails between their legs, to Egypt. Alexandria was now divided between the supporters of the new queen, Cleopatra II and her son, and those who wished for Philometor's younger sibling, Ptolemy "the Brother" (Euergetes II), to ascend the throne. Under such circumstances, it would be easy to understand how the Egyptian nationalists could have achieved independence in Upper Egypt.

---

[39] Immanuel Velikovsky (1977) *Peoples of the Sea*, Doubleday: Garden City, NY, pp. 13-14.
40 Ibid, p. 15.

Fig. 18a: Alexander III (the Great).

Fig. 18b: Temple of Medinet Habu at Thebes (restored). *After* Chipiez (1882).

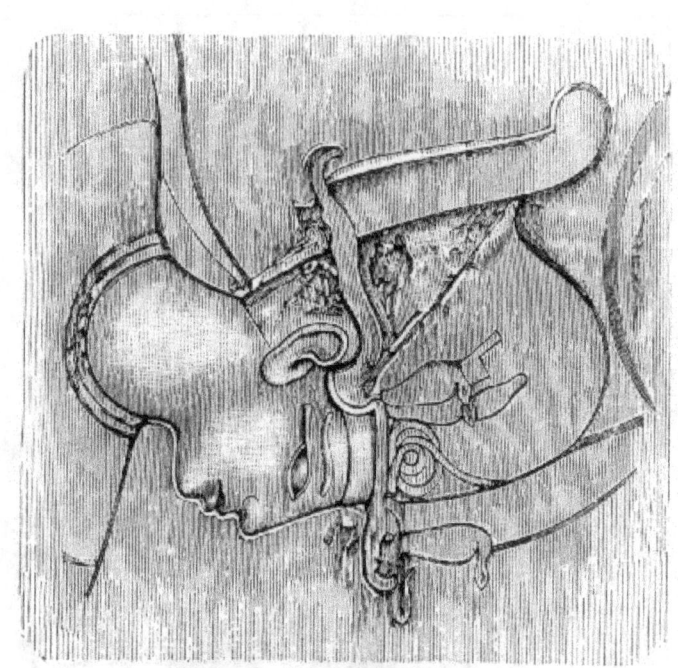

Fig. 18c: King Ramses III (2nd century BCE).

Fig. 18d: King Ramses IV (2nd cent. BCE).

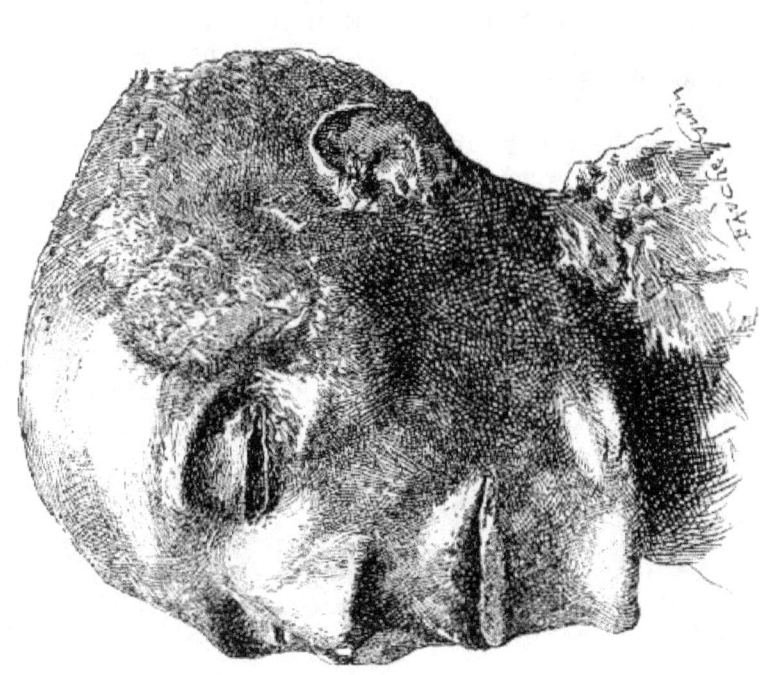

Fig. 18e: Mummy of Psamtik-Seti I.

Fig. 18f: Mummy of Nekau-Ramses II.

CHAP. XVIII: THE LAST CENTURIES | 671

In addition to building a new palace at Tell el-Yahudiya, King Ramses III of the new 30th Dynasty also renovated the Late Bronze Age temple at Medinet Habu of his new 15th Dynasty name-sake. Since not a single figure depicted on facade of the temple at Medinet Habu is shown wearing the blue crown of the alter-ego dynasties, we may surmise that this part of the temple remained relatively intact, and is identical to how it looked during the close of the Late Bronze Age. Where the new 30th Dynasty Ramses III of the Late Period made changes is in the battle scenes depicted on the temple-walls. Just as the extant Karnak battle reliefs of Ramses II were largely Iron Age carvings of Nekau-Ramses II illustrating the Late Bronze Age exploits of the latter's predecessor, I propose that much of the pictorial records of the Peoples of the Sea Battle at Medinet Habu were likewise carved, or re-executed, during the Late Period. Similarly, Immanuel Velikovsky argued for a late stylistic date for the various Medinet Habu hunting scenes. He directs our attention to the obvious similarity between them and the well know style of similar Assyrians reliefs of the ninth to seventh centuries BCE. This similarity has indeed been observed, long before Velikovsky, by conventional scholars. It has widely been argued that Ramses III's scenes were used as models, by the Assyrians, for their own reliefs.

In the new chronology, however, the order of influence is reversed. The Assyrian reliefs must definitely have been the original ones. In the 1920's, Louis Speleers made a thorough comparative study of those Egyptian and Assyrian scenes.[41] After careful examination, he reported that the Assyrian reliefs had been much more carefully, and skillfully, carved. The Assyrian scenes were clearly the originals. In the words of Speleers:

> Far from claiming that the Assyrians have copied from the Egyptians, it ought to be asked whether the latter have not borrowed the motifs from the Asians because it is undeniable that the Assyrian motifs that seemed to have pointed to an Egyptian origin actually came from Asia.[42]

Of course, this caused a significant problem: the Assyrian reliefs were not supposed to have been carved until several centuries after the reign of Ramses III. So how could Ramses III, of the twelfth century BCE, have borrowed the artistic style of Ashurbanipal's seventh century BCE artisans? This Persian influence is, moreover, evident in the other temple of the new Ramses III at Tell el-Yahudiya. Quoting Édouard Naville's *The Mound of the Jew*, Dr Velikovsky writes:

---

[41] Louis Speleers (1923) 'Les scènes de chasse assyriennes et égyptiennes', *Recueil de travaux relatifs à la philologie et l'archaéologie égyptiennes et assyriennes* 40, pp. 158-176.
[42] Ibid, p. 173.

Naville says, "This work strikingly reminds us of Persian art, both modern and antique. In Persia it seems to have been made on a larger scale than in Egypt." This observation adds a "Persian problem" to the "Greek problem" if the tiles were manufactured more than six hundred years before Cambyses subjugated Egypt.[43]

Indeed, more evidence will be presented later in this chapter to show the extent of Persian influence on the new 30th and 31st Dynasties of the Late Period. These are, of course, indications of the fact that these late Ramessides pharaohs reigned, not during the Late Bronze Age and early Iron Age, but after the Persians had occupied Egypt.

The Rise of the Priest-Kings

As we have seen earlier, historians have wrongly equated the "Year 7" of the Renaissance Era recorded during Pi-Ankhy's pontificate with "Year 1" of the Renaissance dated to the 19th year of Ramses XI's reign. Needless to say, this error has devastating consequences on our view of the past. Thus, in the standard chronology of ancient Egypt, Pi-Ankhy follows Ramses XI — partially on account of this faulty dating of the Renaissance Era. Furthermore, because other records make mention of "Year 5" and "Year 6" of the Renaissance Era during the pontificate of the high priest Herihor – a contemporary of Pi-Ankhy – Egyptologists place Herihor between Ramses XI and Pi-Ankhy. Moreover, since it is known that the high priest Smendes was a contemporary of Herihor, Smendes is likewise thought to have preceded Pi-Ankhy. Since there is apparently evidence for the existence of yet another Herihor, as well as a second Smendes, several generations *after* the reign of Pi-Ankhy, Egyptologists tell us there really were *two* Herihors as well as *two* Smendeses. Once again, this is false. There, in fact, never was a second Herihor or Smendes. Both sets of priest-kings were in reality one and the same! Both belong to the *later* Renaissance Era — that which was inaugurated by Ramses XI around the mid-first century BCE. All this means is that the standard 21st Dynasty (new 31st Dynasty) began with Pi-Ankhy ruling in Thebes, and Amenemnisu reigning in Tanis. Herihor never preceded Pi-Ankhy in Thebes, nor did Smendes come before Amenemnisu in Tanis.

The most likely scenario is that Pi-Ankhy had been a high priest at Karnak during the reign of Ramses III, and subsequently became priest-king at Tanis during the reign of Ramses IV. Therefore, Pi-Ankhy could not have been king yet when he recorded the 7th year of the new Era since the accompanying relief refers to him as:

---

[43] Immanuel Velikovsky (1977) *Peoples of the Sea*, Doubleday: Garden City, NY, pp. 11-12.

CHAP. XVIII: THE LAST CENTURIES | 673

"Fanbearer, Viceroy of Nubia, high priest of Amun, General and Army-leader".[44] We now for sure that the Late Period Ramses III ruled for at least seven years (from the "Year 7" inscription of Pi-Ankhy at Karnak). What is less certain, however, is how long he went on to rule after that seventh year. But it would appear that his reign did not last for very long after Year 7. Records from the latter Ramessides' reigns reveal that Ramses III was assassinated in a palace intrigue. The hostile jostling for position and palace tumult which followed his murder was probably the catalyst which led to the establishment of an independent priestly dynasty, with seats in Thebes and Tanis, while Ramses III's sons were bickering in Thebes over the succession of their father. But despite having formed a separate dynasty, the priests-kings were not totally free of the tutelage of the Ramesside kings. The Ramessides, as will be demonstrated shortly, still had the power to appoint and dismiss the priest-kings in Thebes and Tanis.

The priestly dynasty's administrative and religious centres in Thebes and Tanis were respectively inaugurated by Pi-Ankhy and Amenemnisu. Each centre was devoted to a specific deity. In Thebes, it was Khonsu who was paid tribute to in the temple of Khons-in-Thebes. Whereas in Tanis, the main focus was place upon "Horus-of-the-Camp." This latest Tanite incarnation of Horus had not existed prior to the rise of the priestly dynasty. This particular Horus cult was, thus, an innovation of the new 31st Dynasty. As Egyptologist Kim Ryholt explains below, the cult of Horus-of-the Camp is completely unknown in the dynasties which precede and follow the conventional 21st Dynasty (new 31st Dynasty).

> To say that Horus-of-the-Camp is obscure is to put it mildly. No temple or other monument that can be directly related to this god has so far been published [1993], although a temple of his once stood in his residence of el-Hiba. Part of an archive of two scribes belonging to this temple has come to light. The archive is dated to the Twenty-first Dynasty by the mention of the high priests Masaharta and Menkheperre. As Cerny observed, el-Hiba apparently served as the residence of the high priest of Amun.[45]

The dearth of evidence relating to the cult of Horus-of-the-Camp before or after the new 31st Dynasty indicates: (1) that this particular cult did not exist prior to the advent of that dynasty and (2) that the 31st Dynasty was likely the last pharaonic dynasty in Egypt. The late formulation of the cult of Horus-of-the-Camp is proven

---

[44] Kenneth A. Kitchen (1973) *The Third Intermediate Period in Egypt*, pp. 17-18.
[45] Kim Ryholt (1993) 'A Pair of Oracle Petitions Addressed to Horus-of-the-Camp', *Journal of Egyptian Archaeology* 79, pp. 195-196.

by the fact that the context through which it evolved was characterized by the legacy of the Persian occupation of Egypt. Turning to Immanuel Velikovsky:

> Taking care of the **military outposts entrusted to the command of priests who had the status of princes,** Darius obviously was concerned with the protection of the western frontier of Egypt against the incursion of Libyan bands; or it is entirely possible that he was mindful of the growing might of Carthage, farther west. ... **It (the priestly outposts) became famous because of its oracle,** and Ammon of the Oracle (the Greeks wrote the name with a double *m*) was highly regarded among the Libyans and the Egyptians and its fame spread abroad. ... Egypt, which had lost its independence under the Persians and been made into a satrapy, had, nevertheless, a measure of self-rule as a theocratic state. **Priests were made into military commanders, the temples enjoyed certain protection, and the land, without an autonomous civil government of its own, fell into a fief-like dependence on the temples and their priesthood.** ... Amon priests of the oases were also in charge of the sacred center in Karnak (Thebes). ... the authority of the Amon priests, entrusted also with the command of the garrison troops, was very pronounced.[46]

Therefore, the ascent of these new 31st Dynasty powerful priests, in Tanis and Thebes, during the Late Period was not at all a sudden occurrence. The priests of Amun, since the early days of the Persian occupation, has been accustomed to wield important military, political, and economic power over the Egyptian populace. The choice of "Horus-of-the-Camp" as the deity honoured in Tanis reflects these priests' role, under the Persians, as commanders and administrators of soldiers' camps in the Delta. These camps had in fact existed before the Persian occupation — as they were first established during the Saite Period.

> After Psammetichus (I) had established his authority over the entire kingdom he built for the god in Memphis the east propylon and the enclosure about the temple, supporting it with colossi twelve cubits high in the place of pillars; and among **the mercenaries** he distributed notable gifts over and above their promised pay, **gave them the region called The Camps to dwell in** ...
> (Diodorus of Sicily, Book I: 67)

Complementing Diodorus of Sicily's above statement, Herodotus writes:

---
[46] Immanuel Velikovsky (1977) *Peoples of the Sea*, pp. 119-120, 124.

CHAP. XVIII: THE LAST CENTURIES | 675

> The Ionians and Carians who had helped him to conquer were given by Psammetichus places to dwell in called The Camps ...
> (Herodotus, Book II: 154)

Also, it is of particular significance that special emphasis was put on Pi-Ankhy's function as a military general in the reliefs at Karnak.[47] All extant evidence seem to confirm that Pi-Ankhy was indeed regarded *primarily* as the "Pharaohs' General" or "Generalissimo." So the latter was quite evidently a priestly official in charge of soldiers and mercenaries. Equally noteworthy is the fact that, not only was Pi-Ankhy a priest of Amun (Ammon), but that the Karnak inscriptions describing Pi-Ankhy are considered by Egyptologists to be "oracle texts." Again, this is consistent with the famous tradition of the Oracle of Ammon (Amun) aligned with the priestly generals of the Egyptian Delta. Moreover, Herodotus' contention that these "Camps" comprised largely of Ionina and Carian mercenaries situates the inauguration of these camps after the middle of the eighth century BCE.

> The Ionians and the Carians who had helped him to conquer were given by Psammetichus places to dwell in called "The Camps," opposite to each other on either side of the Nile; and besides this he paid them all that he had promised. Moreover he put Egyptian boys in their hands to be taught the Greek tongue ... The Ionians and Carians dwelt a long time in these places, which are near the sea, on the arm of the Nile called the Pelusian, a little way below the town of Bubastis.
> (Herodotus, Book II: 154)

Thus, the new 31st Dynasty (standard 21st Dynasty) Tanite cult of Horus-of-the-Camp could not possibly have existed during the eleventh to tenth centuries BCE, as orthodox scholarship maintains, because it stemmed from political realities dating to the time of the Saite Dynasty and the Persian occupation of Egypt. The Camps which were administered by the native Egyptian priest-generals, which inspired the cult of Horus-of-the Camp, had originally been instituted by Psamtik I — long after the time when Egyptologists erroneously believe that the Tanite priestly dynasty had ended.

Since I argue that this priestly dynasty was an echo of the same powerful native Egyptian priesthood that the Persians appointed, at the site of the Saite military camps, to regulate the daily affairs of Egypt in the absence of an autonomous native monarchy, it means that the accepted dates for the standard 21st Dynasty have to be lowered drastically by several centuries. In the novel chronology, it becomes

---

[47] Kenneth A. Kitchen (1973) *The Third Intermediate Period in Egypt*, §15 – p. 18.

the Late Period's 31st Dynasty — which begins after the middle of the second century BCE. The Tanite priest-kings shared their limited power with other priest-king located Thebes. But overseeing, with varying degrees of authority, the priest-kings of Thebes and Tanis, were Ramesside pharaohs also based in Thebes (Pharaohs Ramses IV-XII). Evidence of the priestly dynasty's Ramesside allegiance can be gleaned from the throne names of the priest-kings — as Egyptologist Kenneth A. Kitchen describes:

> These compound names, Ramses-Psusennes and Ramses-Ankhefenmut, are wholly in the style of those of the sons and successors of Ramses III in the 20th Dynasty, and suggest that Psusennes I and his son claimed a link with the Ramessides... [48]

Later on, Prof. Kitchen refers to the presence of this Ramesside element in both full names of Psusennes I and his son as *"an unresolved enigma."* Consequently, we can clearly understand why Egyptologists, misled by the orthodox chronology, would find it difficult to explain why the later priest-kings of the standard 21st Dynasty would still allude to some link with the preceding Ramesside dynasty. In the new chronology, however, the contemporaneity of the late Ramesside dynasty and the priestly dynasty offers an appropriate circumstance for the Ramesside elements within Psusennes I and his son's names.

The Khonsu Cosmogony

The Khonsu cosmogony, a Theban creation story, was inscribed onto the temple walls of the Khonsu (or Khons) Temple at Karnak. Egyptologists assume it to be a Ptolemaic text, but I propose instead that it was composed by the priest-class from Thebes during the Late Period. The Khonsu cosmogony is an interesting mixture of the Heliopolitan, Hermopolitan and Memphite theologies. Since the Hermopolitan cosmogony (which originally dates to c.2,130 BCE) is an integral part of the Khonsu theology, we must conclude that this cosmogonical construct was surely not devised during the classical Ptolemaic age. Given its Ptolemaic influence, it must therefore have been composed *after* the religious renaissance enacted by the Nectanebos. It is difficult to say if the Khonsu cosmogony did not exist in some form prior to the new 27th Dynasty, but it's at least clear that the version of it which has survived on the walls of the Khonsu Temple at Karnak dates to the time of the new 31st Dynasty. Indeed, under the suzerainty of the later Ramessides and priest-kings of the new 31st Dynasty, the moon god Khonsu along with Amun and Mut, his parents, appeared as the dominant Theban divine triad at Karnak. The cult of Khons-in-Thebes became the principal theological construct in Thebes.

---

[48] Kenneth A. Kitchen (1973) *The Third Intermediate Period in Egypt*, §41 – p. 48.

The Anomalies from Tanis

> *"The end of the Twenty-first Dynasty and its transition into the Twenty-second is one of the more obscure parts of the notoriously opaque Third Intermediate Period."*
>
> - Aidan Dodson[49]

The new chronology's contention that the conventional 21st Dynasty followed, by several centuries, and not preceded the standard 22nd Dynasty, plainly calls for a radical reinterpretation of the archaeological evidence. I shall now advance a series of arguments, based on the archaeological evidence from Tanis, to demonstrate that these two dynasties were indeed separated in time by around six hundred years. The three major anomalies which we will now examine, shed some serious doubts on the accepted interpretation of the evidence from Tanis. Firstly, according to Egyptologist Philippe Brissaud of the Mission Française des Fouilles de Tanis (French team excavating at Tanis): *"... no remains pre-dating the Twenty-Second Dynasty have been recovered except for some primitive graves."*[50] At the Temple of Amun in Tanis. Brisson believes that the Tanite temple's first pylon already stood during the time of Pharaoh Shoshenk III of the ninth century BCE. The gate erected by this latter king was built without any substructure, and no such gate datable to Psusennes I of the 21st Dynasty (our 31st Dynasty) has ever been discovered. This makes sense since while Shoshenk III ruled in the ninth century BCE, Psusennes I did not reign until the second century BCE. Thus, he definitely could not have built a gate before Shoshenk III did. Moreover, it is an undisputed fact that Shoshenk III carried out major building projects and reorganizations in Tanis. But the south-western corner of Psusennes I's temenos, showing obvious architectural defects, was left untouched by Shoshenk III.[51] Scholars have suggested that the ill-conceived structure, built on a sandy spur, was deliberately bypassed by Shoshenk. I believe that Shoshenk III did not fail to renovate it because he chose to omit it, but because Psusennes I's temenos didn't yet exist during his time.

Secondly, in 1951, Montet discovered in the debris of the Temple of Khonsu in Tanis, a series of granite statues of baboons. The statues were associated with the

---

[49] Aidan Dodson (1993) 'BRIEF COMMUNICATIONS: Psusennes II and Shoshenq I', *Journal of Egyptian Archaeology* 79, p. 267.
[50] Philippe Brissaud 'Tanis (Tell San El-Hagar).' In Joan G. Westenholz (editor) (1996) *Royal Cities of the Biblical World*, p. 136.
[51] Ibid, pp. 137-138.

temple as decorative ornaments. This temple, dedicated to the moon-god Khonsu, is dated to the standard 30th Dynasty (new 27th Dynasty). It is believed to have been built by King Nectanebo I.[52] But again, there is a problem. Montet's team discovered, on one of the baboons, an inscription of Psusennes I who supposedly reigned centuries earlier.[53] How could Psusennes I have inscribed his name on the temple's baboon if the structure was not even built until long after his death? Scholars get around this anomaly by saying that the temple was originally built under Psusennes I, but was later rebuilt or renovated under the 30th Dynasty. This signifies that Egyptologists assume that this temple of Khonsu in Tanis held a long history. The consensus is that it was built between 1,040 and 992 BCE, in the reign of Psusennes I, and went on being in use until the conventional 30th Dynasty some 650 years later and beyond. Ironically, historians still insist on classifying it as a 30th Dynasty temple. What we can however, surmise from the new chronology, is that the temple was indeed erected during the new 27th Dynasty under King Nectanebo I and went on being used until at least the time of the new 31st Dynasty up to three centuries later. As a result, the finding of a granite baboon inscribed with the name of Psusennes I in a fourth century BCE temple, is no longer a glaring anomaly. But again, orthodox ancient world scholarship had found yet another explanation to justify the impossible.

The third and final anomaly is already familiar to those who've hitherto read the works of Velikovsky and David Rohl. This is the well-know case of the misdated tombs at Tanis. Rohl[54] remarked that the tomb of Psusennes I of the 21st Dynasty (new 31st Dynasty) cuts into the tomb of Osorkon II of the 22nd Dynasty (new 19th Dynasty). This means that the tomb of Psusennes I was built after the tomb of Osorkon II which in turn signifies that Psusennes I died after Osorkon II. If Psusennes I's dynasty came before Osorkon II's dynasty, how can one explain this perplexing abnormality? We shall leave this headache to conventional scholars because, in the novel chronology, this makes perfect sense. No less than seven centuries actually separated the two rulers. When the Tanite priest-kings assumed rulership over the ancient city of Tanis during the second century BCE, they saw fit to carry on the previous burial traditions of their tenth to eighth centuries BCE ancestors. So, in addition to building new tombs on top of the old Tanite tombs, they usurped and re-used the earlier pharaohs' sarcophagi and funerary objects for their own burials.

When Montet's team excavated the tombs at Tanis, it was clearly observed that the tomb of Osorkon II had been robbed in antiquity. The ancient thieves had left vir-

---

[52] Pierre Montet (1952) 'Sur une statue de babouin et quelques blocs récemment trouvés à Tanis', *Bulletin Trimestriel de la Société Française d'Égyptologie* 10, p. 45.
[53] Philippe Brissaud (1996) p. 127.
[54] See David Rohl (1995) *A Test of Time — Vol. I: The Bible (From Myth to History)*, Century: London, pp. 91-107.

CHAP. XVIII: THE LAST CENTURIES | 679

tually nothing behind — the tomb was, for all intents and purpose, devoid of any artifacts of value. Much to Montet's surprise however, the tomb of Psusennes I, which stands immediately next to that of Osorkon II, had not been emptied of its treasures. Could the ancient robbers have actually missed Psusennes' tomb? As Montet observed:

> The thieves who pillaged the tomb of Osorkon II, adjacent to that of Psusennes, having made numerous trial diggings all around and having found nothing, abandoned their search.[55]

Why would the ancient tomb robbers have put themselves through the trouble of digging trenches all around Osorkon II's tombs to make sure their hadn't missed any treasures, and simply ignore the richly stocked tomb of Psusennes I's tomb right next to it?[56] Evidently, it's because King Psusennes I's tomb was not there at the time. The tomb of Psusennes I was first opened in 1939. Present for the event were King Farouk of Egypt and Etienne Drioton, director of the Antiquities Services of Egypt. Below, Montet describes how he, along with Drioton, took on the task of opening the coffin of the ancient pharaoh:

> I helped him to place the [silver] lid alongside the coffin that contained the mummy and its jewels in a gilded cartonnage. At this moment it was observed that the coffin was of an unknown king, Heqa-kheper-ê Chéchanq [Sheshonk], who could not have reigned less than a century after Psusennes.[57]

Furthermore, on one of the many bracelets found in Psusennes I's tomb, scholars were faced with a strange set of circumstances. For instance, the inscription from the bracelet in question spells the word "king" (n-s-w) in a manner only known to Greek Ptolemaic times. Montet also paid particular attention to an inscription from a wall in Psusennes I's tomb in which the king pays tribute to the goddess Mut — who is referred to as: "the heavenly lady, suzerin of the Two Lands, mistress of the Hellenic coast. ..."[58] Commenting on this puzzling fact, Dr Immanuel Velikovsky writes:

> The "Hellenic coast" referred to in the tomb of Psusennes had its beginning in the days of Amasis ... With Psusennes, together with the entire so-called Twenty-first Dynasty, removed to the time preceding Amasis by five hun-

---

[55] Montet (1951) *Psousennènes*, Paris, p. 8.
[56] Immanuel Velikovsky (1977) *Peoples of the Sea*, pp. 155.
[57] Montet (1951) p. 20.
[58] See Velikovsky (1977) p. 158.

dred years, the anachronism of the reference to the Hellenic coast in Egypt is an unsolvable problem. ... His writing the title "king" in a manner in use in the Ptolemaic period and his referring to the coast west of Damietta as Hellenic point in the same direction as his use of a Persian title in his cartouche.[59]

For his part, Pierre Montet comments:

> The sea of the Hellenes (*Helou-nebout*) was for the Egyptians the Mediterranean from Alexandria to Rosetta. The seaboard of the Hellenes was the portion of the Egyptian west of Damietta.[60]

The new 31st Dynasty pharaoh's tomb remains clearly confirm his chronological place in the history of Egypt. King Psusennes I's reference to the Hellenic coast demonstrates that he was indeed a contemporary of the Greek Ptolemies in Alexandria. Moreover, his use of a Persian title in his royal cartouche clearly shows that he reigned *after* the Persian occupation of Egypt.

There is yet another compelling set of evidence which seems to confirm the course of events outlined in the new chronology. In an article published in 1988 by Egyptologist Aly Abdalla entitled 'A Group of Osiris-Cloths of the Twenty-First Dynasty in the Cairo Museum,' Abdalla discusses the finds of archaeologists Daressy and Grebaut's excavation of a cache full of standard 21st Dynasty (new 31st Dynasty) mummies at Deir El-Bahari in 1891. These mummies were of lower rank priests and priestesses connected with the cult of Amun in Thebes. The main focus of the article centres on the thick linen cloths which were used to wrap the mummies, and the iconographical characteristics of the representations of the god Osiris painted on them. Daressy reported that the coffins were found in great disorder — which could suggest that the catacomb may have been robbed in Antiquity. The funerary garments, known as Osiris-cloths, had stopped being used after the 17th Dynasty, and had only been used again for burials during the Persian and Graeco-Roman eras. Therefore, during the time when the priestly dynasty is supposed to have ruled Egypt, according to the orthodox chronology, the use of Osiris-cloths for funerary purposes had long been abandoned. Elaboration of this, Aly Abdalla writes:

> This practice of providing sheets or shrouds of this nature seems to have fallen away, but, **towards the end of the Twentieth Dynasty, individual bandages were inscribed with spells from the Book of the Dead.** ... The

---

[59] Ibid, pp. 158-159.
[60] Montet (1951) p. 92.

practice of providing cloth inscribed with spells and vignettes from the Book of the Dead was briefly revived in the Persian to Ptolemaic Period. In the Graeco-Roman period the decoration of the outer shroud reached its greatest development ... [61]

This Dark Age in the use of the Osiris-cloths is wholly unnecessary since, based on the new chronology, we know that the late Ramesside pharaohs of the conventional 20th Dynasty, and those of the standard 21st Dynasty, reigned during the Hellenistic age. The funerary trend had been revived by the Persians and later followed during the Greek Ptolemaic age and was then, quite naturally, adopted by the later Ramessides and priest-kings from Thebes and Tanis. The dilapidated state of the sepulchres containing the shrouded mummies uncovered by Daressy left no doubt that the 21st Dynasty tombs had been plundered in Antiquity. The cause and effects of these robberies also have important consequences for the chronology of Egypt.

The Tomb Robberies and the Renaissance Era

Immediately following Psusennes I in Tanis, came Osorkon The Elder (the Manethonic Osochor). In all likeliness, he mounted the throne at a relatively old age. His throne name, Osorkon, the same as some of the earlier Tanite pharaohs of the new 19th Dynasty, may indicate that some of the new 31st Dynasty priest-kings were of Libyan origin. This may explain the close connections between the burials of these two dynasties' pharaohs. Out of his six-year reign, it's believed by some historians that he spent three years as a co-regent of his successor, Amenenope. While this has been, for many years, ground for debate among scholars, I believe that the truth is with those who support a long reign for Amenenope. The controversy stems form diverging interpretations of two particular pieces of evidence. On the one hand, is the mummy-bandage found at Deir el-Bahari which mentions "Year 49" of Amenenope. On the other hand, is the claim by the Manethonian texts that Amenenope ruled for 9 years. The Manethonian tradition also claims that Psusennes I, Amenenope's immediate predecessor, reigned for 46 or 41 years. Obviously, both priest-kings could not have ruled for that long. The long reign must necessarily be attributed to either one or the other. The reason why I believe that the longer reign ought to be granted to Amenenope is because the Theban kings Menkheperre, Smendes and Pinedjem II were all contemporaries of this pharaoh.[62] Evidence will be given later in this, and the next, chapter

---

[61] Aly Abdalla (1988) 'A Group of Osiris-Cloths of the Twenty-First Dynasty in the Cairo Museum', *Journal of Egyptian Archaeology* 74, pp. 158, 163-64.
[62] See Kitchen's *Third Intermediate Period in Egypt*, §22 – pp. 24-25.

to support the unreliability of the Manethonian accounts with respect to this dynasty in particular. These ancient priest-kings reigned during a very turbulent era of the Late Period — when tomb robberies and trials had been conducted. An ancient Egyptian document known as the Mayer A papyrus, reports that in the lifetime of the high priest Amenhotep:

> He said, "The Barbarians came and seized the Temple while I was in charge of some asses belonging to my father. Peheti, a barbarian, seized hold of me and took me to I-pip, it being for as long as six months (already) since Amenhotep, who used to be High Priest of Amon, had been suppressed." The witness testified that he was permitted to return to his domicile after "nine whole months of the suppression of Amenhotep who used to be High Priest of Amon."[63]

We know that Amenhotep was high priest of Amun during the reign of Ramses IX, since a bas-relief shows Amenhotep paying tribute to the latter. It is thus safe to assumed that the high priest Amenhotep could have been suppressed by the barbarian invaders sometime during the reign of Pharaoh Ramses IX. During this period of chaos, many tombs of the ancient pharaohs were desecrated and these barbarians seem to have briefly taken control of the Delta. Soon after this "war against Amenhotep" had been quelled, efforts were undertaken to ensure the proper reburial of the looted sepulchres.

A Theban viceroy by the name of Pinehas, under the orders of Ramses IX, undertook to rid Egypt of the barbarians and punish all wrong-doers. The process of re-burying the looted sarcophagi took many years. The majority of the reburials were completed during the reigns of Pharaohs Ramses X and Ramses XI. This can be ascertained from the fact that inside the *undisturbed* burial of King Psusennes I, Montet found bracelets on which are recorded the name of the high priest Smendes son of Menkheperre — a contemporary of Ramses X. Thus, my hypothesis is that the barbarians had desecrated the original tomb of Psusennes during the reign of Ramses IX, and that the high priest Smendes helped his father, King Menkheperre (a contemporary of Ramses IX), in the handling of the remaining mummies. Psusennes was properly *re-entombed* immediately next to the tomb of Osorkon II. The indications of a hasty burial in the tomb of Pharaoh Psusennes I are obvious. Some scholars have pointed to the reference to Smendes on those bracelets as evidence for a supposed long reign of Psusennes I — to the expense of Amenenope.[64] In my historical reconstruction, the problem no longer poses itself. A short reign for Psusennes I remains entirely probable.

---

[63] T. E. Peet (1920) *The Mayer Papyri A and B*, London; T. E. Peet (1930) *The Great Tomb Robberies of the Twentieth Egyptian Dynasty* Vol. 2, p.xxiv; E. F. Wente (1966) 'The Suppression of the high priest Amenhotep', *Journal of Near Eastern Studies* 25, p. 2.
[64] See Kitchen's *Third Intermediate Period in Egypt*, §25 – pp. 28-29.

CHAP. XVIII: THE LAST CENTURIES | 683

At any rate, I believe that Menkheperre, the father of the high priest Smendes, was appointed king on Year 25 of Ramses IX's reign.[65] The former must have been appointed at Thebes shortly after the barbarian attack and the sending of Pinehas to restore order. The period of recovery from the barbarian invasion went on until Pharaoh Ramses XI declared a Renaissance Era to mark the return to political stability in Egypt. The official Pinehas (also spelled Panhesy) is known to have held the office of Viceroy of Kush up to the 17th year of Ramses XI's reign.[66] Pinehas certainly held a very high position in Ramses XI's court as evidenced by his other titles of: "Fan-bearer on the right of the king (the king's right-hand man), Royal Scribe, General, Overseer of the granaries of the Pharaoh, Officer of the southern lands, and Leader of the troops of Pharaoh.[67] He is first attested on Year 12 of Ramses XI.[68]

Therefore, it seems quite probable that Pinehas exercised his duties for a period of five years. On Year 17 of King Ramses XI, these functions were assumed by the high priest Herihor — after which time Pinehas disappears from the records. It seems that the latter had been expelled back to Nubia by Ramses IX. All this paints a very clear picture which develops as follows:

1) During the reign of Ramses IX, a group of barbarians (led by Peheti) stormed the city of Thebes — robbing the tombs of the ancient pharaohs and usurping power in Tanis for about nine months.
2) During those nine months, the Theban high priest Amenhotep is forcibly carried away from his post.
3) While Ramses IX still occupied the throne, Pinehas punishes the barbarians and reinstates the high priest Amenhotep to his post.[69]
4) On Year 12 of Ramses XI's reign, Pinehas becomes a high official in Pharaoh's court.
5) He serves in this capacity for five years, and then replaces Amenhotep as high priest of Amun with Herihor. After that time (Year 17), it is not clear what becomes of Pinehas.
(6) On Year 19 of Ramses XI (year of the Renaissance), a report recounting the suppression of the high priest Amenhotep surfaces during tomb-robbery trial.

---

[65] A document known as the Maunier stela says that the high priest Menkheperre was appointed king on Year 25 of some unnamed ruler. Kitchen identifies him as the fictitious Smendes I.
[66] K. A. Kitchen (1973) *The Third Intermediate Period in Egypt*, p. 16.
[67] Sir A. Gardiner (1948) *Ramesside Administrative Documents*, Oxford University Press: London, p. 36.
[68] Cyril Aldred 'More Light on the Ramesside Tomb Robberies.' In John Ruffle, G. A. Gaballa & Kenneth A. Kitchen (editors) (1979) *Glimpses of Ancient Egypt (Studies in Honour of H. W. Fairman)*, p. 94.
[69] Cerny believes that Amenhotep was high priest during Year 3 of Ramses X.

Before returning to Nubia, however, Pinehas had appointed a new high priest by the name of "Herihor" to replace Amenhotep. This Theban priest was subsequently crowned in Tanis as King Siamun — as I propose in my revised history. An inscription from the temple of Khonsu refers to *Siamun* as: *"Siamon-Herihor, beloved of Mut the great ..."*[70] Also, on the east wall of the same Khonsu Temple at Karnak, Amun-Re addresses *Herihor* as follows:

> Welcome! Welcome! My son, my beloved, **Siamun, Herihor.** My heart is pleased with thy offering. I accept what thou hast made. thou hast made bright Benben in newness.[71]

It is evident that both Siamun and Herihor bore the same name of "Siamun-Herihor." They could only have been, in reality, one and the same person! The king known to Egyptologists as Herihor — founder of the standard 21st Dynasty (new 31st Dynasty), never existed. The real Herihor was none other than King Siamun — a *late* ruler of the new 31st Dynasty. It is more likely that Herihor was Siamun's personal name, or possibly his religious name as high priest of Karnak. If Siamun only used his name of Herihor as high priest of Karnak, the following riddle raised by Prof. Kenneth Kitchen could be solved:

> There is so far no evidence at all that Herihor's 'kingship' was ever recognized in his lifetime anywhere beyond the cloistered courts of Karnak, nor did any successor ever boast of descent from 'king' Herihor. ... The reason for Herihor's adoption of kingly titles is unknown.[72]

Herihor was not to be recognized as pharaoh once outside of Karnak because he would then revert to his royal name of "Siamun." The reason why Egyptologists aren't willing to admit the undeniable fact that Siamun and Herihor were one and the same person is obvious. The equation of the two rulers clashes with the accepted view of Egyptian history.

As a result, in the standard chronology, the 20th Dynasty of the late Ramesside kings immediately precedes that of King Herihor's 21st Dynasty. Evidence for that is found in the fact that Herihor was appointed as high priest of Amun near the end of the conventional 20th Dynasty. It would therefore seem logical to assume that Herihor was the founder of the succeeding dynasty. On the other hand, if Herihor is identified with Siamun, as in the new chronology, then scholars would automatically be forced to concede that both dynasties ruled at the same time. All the pha-

---

[70] J. H. Breasted, *Ancient Records of Egypt*, Vol. IV - § 623.
[71] Khonsu, No. 146.
[72] Kenneth A. Kitchen (1973) *The Third Intermediate Period in Egypt*, §17 – p. 21.

Fig. 18g: Temple of Khons at Karnak (restored). *After* Perrot & Chipiez (1882).

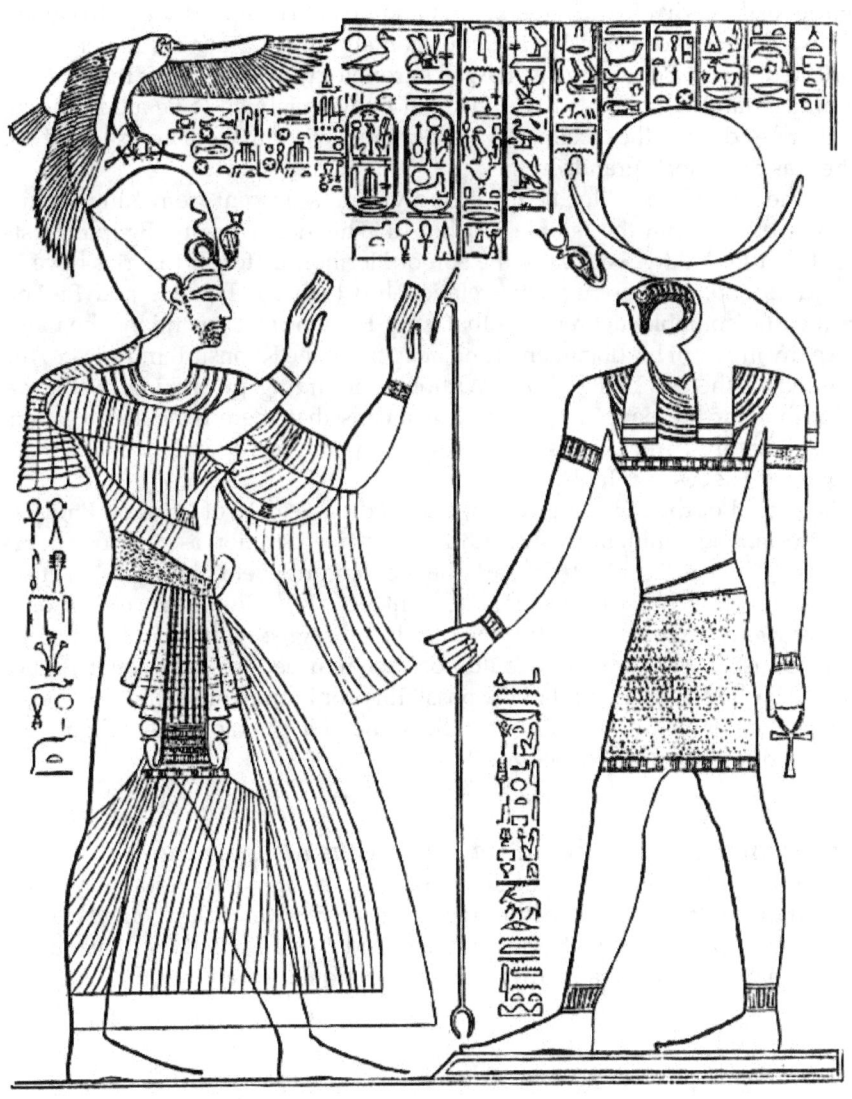

Fig. 18h: Pharaoh Ramses X worshipping Khonsu.
After Lenormant (1882).

raohs who preceded Siamun-Herihor then, necessarily, need to have been contemporaries of the earlier Ramessides of the standard 20th Dynasty (new 30th Dynasty). This is why Herihor I and his fictitious contemporary, Smendes I, were literally fabricated to suit Egyptologists' flawed chronology. In the light of these facts, we can understand why it was that Pinedjem I never claimed to be a descendent of Herihor[73] — despite the fact that, as conventional wisdom would erroneously have it, he was the latter's grandson.

On the other hand, Pinedjem I proudly claims descent from King Pi-Ankhy on inscriptions from the temple of Khonsu. This has led some Egyptologists to doubt that Pi-Ankhy was really the son of Herihor. Different theories have been offered to explain the enigmatic relationship between Herihor and Pi-Ankhy, but the undisputable fact remains that King Herihor *never* mentions the name of Pi-Ankhy in any of his documents; and *nowhere* in the Khonsu Temple is Pi-Ankhy recorded as the son of Herihor.[74] Without a founding priest-king by the name of Herihor for the new 31st Dynasty, it means that there is neither a Smendes I. Pi-Ankhy and Amenemnisu were, in reality, the real founders of the priestly dynasty at Thebes and Tanis.

The period of the Renaissance Era, declared on Year 19 of Pharaoh Ramses XI, was proclaimed simultaneously with Herihor's recognition as ruler of Thebes at Karnak's Khonsu Temple.[75] To mark the momentous event, there was an effort in Thebes to portray the recent past as a decadent period. The Renaissance Era promised a "happy end" to the instability.[76] Naturally, I disagree with the opinion of many Egyptologists[77] that Ramses XI could not have returned to Thebes after the accession of Herihor — on account of the possibility for imminent conflict. The political arrangement of the time ensured that the Ramesside pharaohs ruled Egypt jointly with the priest-kings of Thebes and Tanis.

The Mummies of the Royal Cache and the Missing Bulls

Since the era coinciding with the accession of Herihor was a period of renewal in which the tumultuous events of the preceding decades were at last being put behind, its entirely appropriate that Herihor was, indeed, the one to put the final touches to the reburial of the desecrated royal sarcophagi from the Valley of the Kings. Early

---

[73] See Edward F. Wente (1967) 'On the Chronology of the Twenty-first Dynasty', *Journal of Near Eastern Studies*; E. F. Wente (1967) *Late Ramesside Letters*— Letters in Ancient Oriental Civilizations - Num. 3, University of Chicago Press: Chicago.

[74] Beatrice L. Goff (1979) *Symbols of Ancient Egypt in the Late Period (The Twenty-first Dynasty)*, Mouton: The Hague, p. 53.

[75] Andrzej Niwinsky (1995) 'Le passage de la XXe à la XXIIe dynastie: Chronology et histoire politique', *Bulletin de l'Institut Français d'Archéologie Orientale* 95, p. 340.

[76] Ibid, p. 341.

[77] See Ibid.

in Pharaoh Ramses XI's Renaissance era, the bodies of the pharaohs were rewrapped for final burial, in a secluded and secret location atop a mountainous area in Deir el-Bahari, by Siamun-Herihor himself under Ramses XII's reign.[78] The timing of these tomb robberies and subsequent reburial appears to be confirmed by Diodorus of Sicily, reporting what Egyptian priests told him when he visited Egypt during the 180th Olympiad (60-56 BCE):

> Now the priests said that in their records they find forty-seven tombs of kings; but down to the time of Ptolemy son of Lagus, they say, only fifteen remained, most of which had been destroyed at the time we visited those regions, in the One Hundred and Eightieth Olympiad. Not only do the priests of Egypt give these facts from their records, but many also of the Greeks who visited Thebes in the time of Ptolemy son of Lagus and composed histories of Egypt, one of whom was Hecataeus, agree with what we have said.
> (Diodorus of Sicily, Book I: 46)

Diodorus of Sicily specifically says that the sepulchres had been intentionally "destroyed" — presumably by looters. These events, I contend, were analogous to the tomb robberies from the reign of Ramses IX; since, according to the new chronology, Ramses IX reigned during the time of the Grecian 180th Olympiad. Other helpful chronological bearings can be gleaned from the bandages wrapped around the bodies of the pharaohs. On both the sarcophagi of Psamtik-Seti I and Nekau-Ramses II is inscribed: "Year 6 of the Renaissance Era."[79] This confirms that Herihor was still high priest of Amun when he re-entombed the mummies of these pharaohs. That may have been a year before he became priest-king under the name of Siamun. We know that because Herihor ceases to be mentioned after Year 7 of Ramses XI.[80] As we will see, by the time he finally sealed the royal cache, he was already known as "King" Siamun-Herihor.

However, we seem to encounter a red herring in attempting to prove that the ancient tombs were desecrated during the reign of Ramses IX. On the actual bandages found on the mummies is, in seven occasions, apparent evidence that the re-burials were performed by Pinedjem I. On the mummies of Tuthmosis II and Amenhotep II is written Year 6 of Pinedjem I. The mummy of Ahmose bears an inscription dated to Year 8 of that same king. The same scenario is repeated in

---

[78] J. H. Breasted, *Ancient Records of Egypt*, Vol. II - § 592.
[79] H. Gauthier, *Le livre des rois d'Egypte* 3, 220, II, III.
[80] Beatrice L. Goff (1979) *Symbols of Ancient Egypt in the Late Period (The Twenty-first Dynasty)*, p. 51.

CHAP. XVIII: THE LAST CENTURIES | 689

the cases of Ramses III (Year 9), Seti I (Year 10), and finally Ramses II (Year 15). This causes an obvious problem for the new chronology. Pinedjem I is supposed to have been already dead by the time the tombs were robbed during the reign of King Ramses IX. Equally puzzling is the fact that an inscription mentioning Year 16 of Masaherta, the son of Pinedjem I, appears on the mummy of Amenhotep I. At first glance, it would seem logical to assume that Masaherta carried on the earlier work of his father. But as Beatrice L. Goff recounts:

> All the dates from year 6 to 15 of Pinedjem and 16 to 19 of Masaherta are assigned by most scholars to other rulers than Pinedjem I and Masaherta. There is no agreement as to who these rulers were.[81]

The reasons for this uncertainty are manifold. It is not clear whether the Pinedjem who presided over the reburial of the ancient kings resided in Tanis or in Thebes. Moreover, the inscriptions of Years 6, 9, 10, 13, and 15 refer to him solely as high priest — not as King.[82] Scholars have therefore concluded that King Pinedjem I had first been high priest before becoming Pharaoh. This interpretation is likewise problematic since, in some occasions, Pinedjem was recognized as high priest *after* the death of King Pinedjem I.[83] I would propose that the "high priest" Pinedjem was not the same person as "King" Pinedjem. There is no doubt that King Pinedjem I, son of Pi-Ankhy, existed as is evidenced by the following inscription on the forecourt of the temple of Khonsu: "Live the Horus, Strong Bull, Beloved of Amun, King of Upper and Lower Egypt, Who pleases the gods, Who does benefactions for their kas, the high priest of Amun-Re King of the Gods, Pinedjem, son of Piankh."[84]

However, while Pinedjem I bore both the titles of high priest and Pharaoh, the Pinedjem who reburied the desecrated mummies only bore the title of high priest. Besides, for the case of the Years 16 to 19 inscriptions of King Masaherta, we can see from the New Chronology Table that King Masaherta was a contemporary of Ramses IX. This means that King Masaherta was most probably the earliest priest-king to have re-embalmed the mummies of the ancient pharaohs. Confirmation of the fact that Masaherta ruled during the time of Ramses IX can be gleaned from the fact that King Menkheperre, the immediate successor of Masaherta, was name king on Year 25 of Ramses IX. It also follows that, as the inscription "Year 6 of Menkheper-

---

[81] Beatrice L. Goff (1979) *Symbols of Ancient Egypt in the Late Period (The Twenty-first Dynasty)*, p. 56.
[82] Ibid, p. 57.
[83] Ibid.
[84] R. Lepsius (1849-56) *Denkmäler aus Aegypten und Aethiopien*, Nicolai: Berlin, 3, pl. 249 c-e.

re" on the bandages from the desecrated mummy of Seti I[85] suggests, Menkheperre carried on the work of his predecessor, and was himself *later* followed by the high priest Pinedjem. E. F. Wente[86] has even gone as far as suggesting that the high priest Pinedjem who oversaw part of the reburials was in reality King Smendes. This hypothesis certainly would not be entirely inconsistent with the new chronology, but whether or not King Smendes was known as high priest Pinedjem before his coronation must, for now at least, remain in the realm of speculation.

Evidently, one of the first issues that comes to mind when analysing the funerary contents of the Deir el-Bahari royal cache is: were these pharaohs' mummies those of the original rulers of the Late Bronze Age, or are we in fact confronted with the remains of the alter-ego monarchs of the Iron Age. My assertion is that the latter is true. My principal argument to support this thesis is based on the order in which the royal sarcophagi were placed into the cache. According to Gaston Maspero, who cleared the royal cache in 1881, the coffin of a Tanite official of Libyan origin by the name of Djedptahefankh was deposited deep inside the tomb. The reason why this is so significant is because the official Djedptahefankh, Second Prophet of Amun during the new 19th Dynasty (standard 22nd Dynasty), was entombed in the cache *before* the priest-kings of the new 31st Dynasty placed the newly embalmed body of Pharaoh Seti I in the same royal cache's narrow passage way. In *A Test of Time,* David M. Rohl demonstrated that, based on the dimensions of both coffins and the size of the descending corridor of the royal cache, there was absolutely no way that the coffin of Djedptahefankh could have been manoeuvred past the sarcophagi of Seti I which blocked the entrance way. Logically, the coffin of Seti I must have been placed there last.[87] In fact, the coffin of Djedptahefankh was, in order of emplacement, the earliest sepulchre to be deposited in the Deir el-Bahari royal cache — making it the oldest mummy from the rock-cut mausoleum. Therefore, I contend that all of the royal mummies date from the Iron Age.

Djedptahefankh, as can be gleaned from his mummy's bandages, was buried on Year 10 of Pharaoh Shoshenk I. According to the orthodox chronology, King Shoshenk I founded the dynasty which succeeded that of the priest-kings from Thebes and Tanis — in the tenth century BCE. Egyptologists have worked out that Year 11 of Shoshenk I came thirty-four years after Year 10 of Herihor — when the Deir el-Bahari royal cache was sealed. This is why the presence of Djedptahefankh's coffin in the rock-cut mausoleum has been such a perplexing anomaly for conventional

---

[85] Gaston Maspero (1889) Les momies royales de Deir el Bahari. in *Memoires ... de la Mission Archéologique française au Caire* Tome I, p. 555.
[86] Edward F. Wente (1967) 'On the Chronology of the Twenty-first Dynasty', *Journal of Near Eastern Studies* Vol. 26 - Num. 3, pp. 155-176.
[87] *See* David M. Rohl (1995) p. 76.

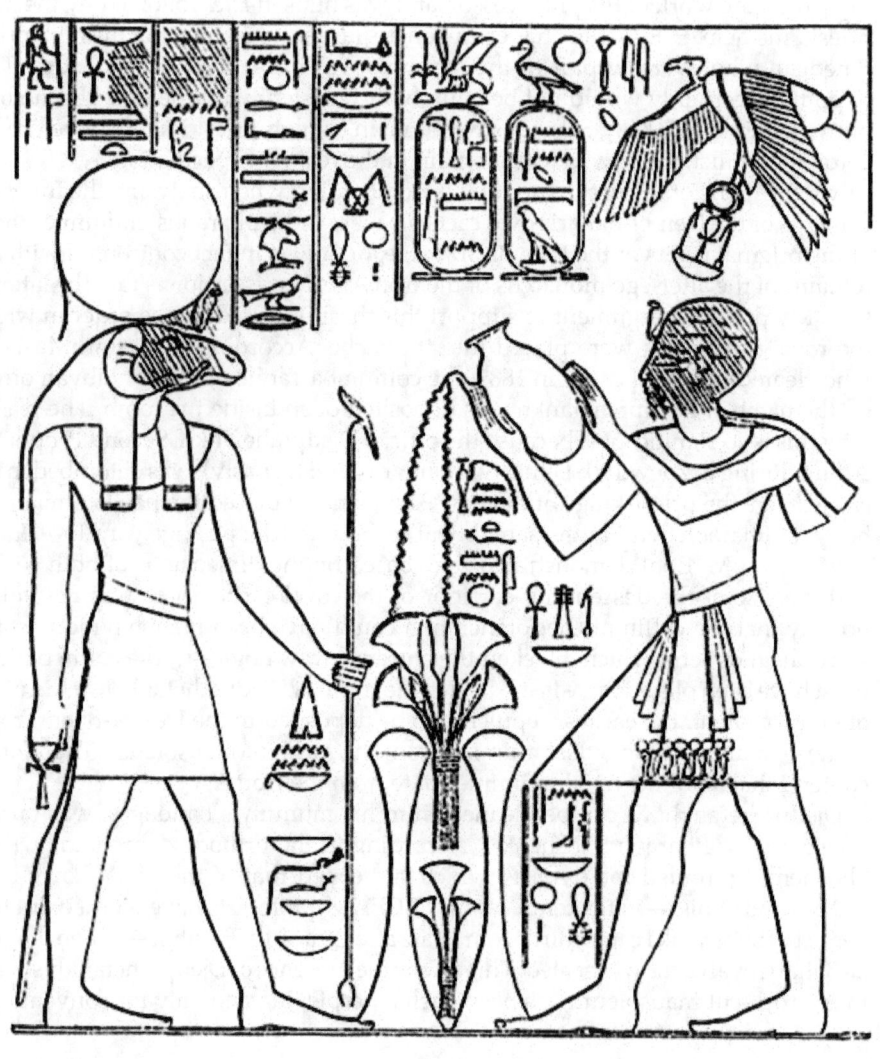

Fig. 18i: Herihor making offerings to Amun. *After* Lenormant (1882).

Record of Apis Bull Burials in Order of Reigns

Standard Chronology: (c.1,290 BCE to 643 BCE)	New Chronology: (828 BCE to c.50 BCE)
1. Ramses II (Year 30/ Stela 5)	1. Shoshenk-Amenhotep III
2. Ramses II (Year ??)	2. Takelot I
3. Ramses II (Year ??)	3. Osorkon II
4. Ramses II (Year 55?)	4. Pimay
5. Ramses II (Year??)	5. Bocchoris
6. Ramses-Siptah (Year ??)	6. Taharka
7. Ramses III (Year ??)	7. Shoshenk V
8. Ramses VI (Year ??)	8. Taharka
9. Ramses IX (Year ??)	9. Shoshenk V
10. Ramses XI (Year ??)	10. Taharka
11. Ramses XI (Year ??)	11. Psamtik- Seti I
12. Ramses XI (Year ??)	12. Ramses-Nekau II
13. Takelot I (Year ??/ Stela 19)	13. Ramses-Nekau II
14. Osorkon II (Year 23/ Stela 18)	14. Ramses-Nekau II
15. Shoshenk III (Year 28/ Stela 21)	15. Ramses-Nekau II
16. Pimay (Year 2/ Stela 22)	16. Ramses-Nekau II
17. Shoshenk V (Year 11/ Stela 27)	17. Ramses-Siptah
18. Shoshenk V (Year 37/ Stela 31)	18. Ramses III
19. Bocchoris (Year 6/ Stela 91)	19. Ramses VI
20. Taharka? (Year 4/ Stela 129)	20. Ramses IX
21. Taharka (Year 14)	21. Ramses XI
22. Taharka (Year 24/ Stela 125)	22. Ramses XI
23. Psamtik I (Year 21/ Stela 192)	23. Ramses XI

Table 18-1

CHAP. XVIII: THE LAST CENTURIES | 693

scholars. Many historians simply attempt to dismiss the entire problem by proposing the unlikely scenario that the sealed mausoleum was reopened, after Siamun's reign, to allow for the inclusion of Djedptahefankh's coffin. As we've seen, however, that would have been structurally unfeasible. Other unyielding historians have suggested that, in the hurried pace of the nineteenth century excavators, working with much less sophisticated methods than today, the sarcophagi were mislabelled and their real order confused. With little concrete evidence to back up these hypotheses, the mystery has remained unsolved.

The answer, I am convinced, lays in the new chronological framework hereby presented. Since King Shoshenk I really ruled many centuries before Siamun, the presence of Djedptahefankh's coffin in the Deir el-Bahari royal cache is no mystery at all. Evidently, Djedptahefankh's mummy was one of the very first ones to be installed there. Centuries later, analogously to the reappropriation of the Tanite tombs, the priest-kings of the new 31st Dynasty reused the hidden sepulchre to re-entomb the bodies of the Theban pharaohs. All of the kings whose original tombs had been ransacked (i.e. Ahmose, Amenhotep II, Tuthmosis III) during the turbulent new 31st Dynasty most likely belong to the Iron Age dynasties. This would make sense, as they were the latest Theban kings to be buried in Egypt who bore those names. Concurring with the idea of an Iron Age dating span for the mummies of the royal cache, Velikovsky writes:

> Soon you will be able to judge as right or wrong my unqualified statement that carbon analysis of the wooden sarcophagi of Seti, Ramses II, Merneptah, and Ramses III, or of the furniture and sacred boats of Tuthmose III or Tutankhamen, would yield dates five to seven hundred years younger than those assigned by adherents of the conventional chronology. Then you will know for certain whether the conventional or the revised history of the lands of the ancient East for twelve hundred years is authentic and true.[88]

For instance, the blond-haired mummy of Pharaoh Ramses II found in the royal cache was actually that of the Macedonian king Nekau II of the seventh century BCE. He was not the pharaoh known to all as "Ramses the Great" who fought against the Late Bronze Age Anatolian Hittites. That Ramses II was unquestionably of Ethiopic race. His mummy may still be buried somewhere in Egypt's soil.

The royal mummies from the Deir el-Bahari cache are not, however, the only extant pharaonic sepulchres to have been wrongly dated by modern Egyptologists to the

---

[88] Immanuel Velikovsky 'Worlds in Collision in the Light of Recent Finds in Archaeology, Geology, and Astronomy.' In (1955) *Earth in Upheaval*, p. 278.

Late Bronze Age. The accepted sequence of the Apis bull burials at Saqqara is likewise severely misaligned. When French Egyptologist Auguste Mariette discovered the so-called Serapeum (Greek *Sarapieion*) at Saqqara in 1851, the complex mausoleum was found to be comprised of a series of huge sepulchral chambers each containing the mummified remains of an Apis bull. The massive basalt sarcophagi housing the bovine mummies were each dated to the reign of a particular pharaoh. It is through the names of the pharaohs associated with the Apis bulls that scholars have reconstructed the history of the temple of Osiris-Apis. Thus, as Egyptologist Michael Jones puts it, orthodox scholars believe that "a continuous cult of Apis was maintained from the reign of Ramses II [of the Late Bronze Age] down to Darius I."[89] According to my revised chronology however (see Table 18-1), the pharaoh who inaugurated the temple of Osiris-Apis at Saqqara, and who buried the first bull, was in fact King Shoshenk-Amenhotep III. As we've seen in Chapter 15, it was under the latter's reign that the cult of the living Apis bull, prompted by Typhon Season #6, rose to unprecedented prominence. This signifies that the Apis bull dated to the reign of Ramses II really belongs to Pharaoh Nekau-Ramses II. A review of a strange anomaly from the Osiris-Apis Temple, indeed, appears to confirm this fact. This irregularity is the mysterious absence of any Apis bulls buried during the conventional 21st Dynasty and early 22nd Dynasty. Having accepted that the first Apis bull was buried during the reign of the standard 19th Dynasty, preceding further bull burials during the time of later Ramessides, Egyptologists have found it difficult to explain this hiatus in bull burials. Supposedly, the Apis burials carried on subsequently after the middle of the standard 22nd Dynasty — until the advent of the Persian king Darius.

Why would the pharaohs of the orthodox 21st and early 22nd Dynasty suddenly abandon the practice? This has long been an enigma. Many ancient historians believe that these ancient bovine sepulchres simply haven't been unearthed yet. Disputing this generally accepted hypothesis, I instead propose that these bulls never existed. Since, in the novel chronology, King Shoshenk-Amenhotep III ascends the throne in the middle of the conventional 22nd Dynasty (new 19th Dynasty), it becomes clear, given that the latter inaugurated the ritualistic burials of bull as Saqqara, why none of his Libyan predecessors recorded the burial of any Apis bulls. Moreover, since we have radically shifted downward the date of the orthodox 21st Dynasty (new 31st Dynasty), the absence of any Apis bull burials during this dynasty's time is easily explained by the fact that the priest-kings ruled centuries after Darius. Nonetheless, the later Ramessides of the new 30th Dynasty (Ramses III-XI) did resurrect the practice during their reigns. But the scale or importance of the event was obviously less ponderous than in previous times — as the priest-kings obviously neglected it.

---

[89] Michael Jones (1990) 'The Temple of Apis in Memphis', p. 143.

The Ourmai Papyrus: Record of the End of a Civilization

Despite the illusory peace which Egypt enjoyed after the affairs of the State had been at last reordered, Ramses XI's Renaissance era would come to a violent end. In 1891, Russian Egyptologist V. S. Golenishchev purchased from an antique dealer in Cairo a series of papyri which included a lament written by a certain Ourmai. This Ourmai, son of Khevi, lived during the standard 21st Dynasty (new 31st Dynasty). Along with Ourmai's letter of laments, the series of papyri purchased by Golenishchev also comprised of the record of Wenamon's errand abroad. In fact, it became immediately clear that both documents were written by the same hand. From the time that Ourmai's letter of laments was first published, in 1961, Egyptologists have pondered on the elusive meaning of the strange events described in it. Ourmai, a noble man of the temple of Heliopolis, writes to Re Nekht, a royal scribe in Herakleopolis, and wails about the desolation and terror of which the land of Egypt had apparently become host. Ourmai writes:

> I was carried away unjustly, I am bereft of all, I am speechless [to protest], I am robbed, though I did no wrong; I am thrown out of my city, the property is seized, nothing is left [to me]. I am [defenceless] before the mighty wrongdoers.
> ...
> They (Ourmai's colleagues) are torn away from me; their wives are killed [before them]; their children are dispersed, some thrown into prison, others seized as prey.
> I am thrown out of my yesterday's domicile, compelled to roam in harsh wanderings. **The land is engulfed by enemy's fire. South, north, west, and east belong to him.**
> ...
> Bodies [of the dead] and bones [are] thrown out upon the ground, and who will cover them? ...
> I suffer hunger ... my grain that was given to me by soldiers ... his taxes are heavy ...
> Thy power, O lord creator, should manifest itself. Come save me from them.

Who were these "mighty wrongdoers" who wrought so much havoc upon the people of Egypt? What foreign power seized control of the land's temples — to ultimately impose heavy taxes upon the people and leave Egypt's dispossessed aristocracy to beg their cruel assailants for food? Why is it that no royal house appears to exist in Egypt after the foreign hordes (representing "him" who invaded north, south, east and west) had ransacked the land? Historians have, unfortunately, yet to satisfactorily answer any of these questions. The accepted history of Egypt makes no mention of a foreign invasion during the standard 21st Dynasty. The transitions between the conventional 20th and 21st Dynasties, as well as between the standard 21st and 22nd Dynasties, are supposed to have been relatively smooth ones. As a result, the events described in Ourmai's letter of laments appear, to every historian, wholly enigmatic.

The scenario I put forward is that the Ourmai document recounts the Roman invasion of Egypt shortly after the Battle of Actium on September 2nd 31 BCE. After having conquered Alexandria, the Romans moved southward in order to establish their suzerainty over the Thebaid and Nubia. Octavian's triumph put an irreversible end to pharaonic Egypt's independence and even very existence.

The Roman Colosseum, by author

Part VII

Returning to Caesar what belongs to Ceasar

19

After Cleopatra: The Rise of Rome and the Uniformitarian World View

> *" I added Egypt to the Empire of the Roman people."*
>
> - Emperor Augustus

Once the Romans acquired control of Egypt, following the Battle of Actium, it became a Roman province governed by a viceroy directly responsible to the Emperor. The first viceroy, under Emperor Augustus, was the Roman poet and soldier Cornelius Gallus. Egypt was without a doubt the most wealthy of the Roman provinces. To protect Roman interest there, Augustus appointed three six thousand-men-strong legions. In this chapter, I shall refrain from delving into the royal succession details of the Roman emperors since they are already widely known and I do not hereby offer any new or revised schemes. What will be mainly of interest is the influence which ancient Rome continues to have on modern scholars' understanding of the history of the ancient world as a whole — particularly pharaonic Egypt. The Romans, indeed, had an immense interest in Egypt. But, given the history of the Romans' interactions with dynastic Egypt during the Hellenistic period, their understanding of Egyptian history and culture was chiefly centred on Ptolemaic Alexandria. Attaching much value to Hellenic culture during their occupation of Egypt, as evidenced by their characteristic classification and social control of the populace based on ethnic origins, my premise is that the Romans eagerly sought to hand over to posterity a vision of Egyptian history which favoured their Greek predecessors. As was the case in countless instances before the Romans, history was shaped by the cultural allegiances of those with the ultimate power to define historical reality. Alexandria became the cultural capital of Egypt during Roman times. In 12 BCE, the Romans transported two obelisks of Pharaoh Tuthmosis III from their original emplacement in Heliopolis and erected them at Alexandria in front of the Caesarion, a temple dedicated to August Caesar. Alexandria remained a prime centre of learning throughout the duration of the Roman Empire — remaining so until the Arab conquest in the seventh century CE. Therefore, much of what later became known about ancient Egyptian civilization in Europe before the Napoleonic expedition, came from what remained of the burnt library of Alexandria, founded under Ptolemy I and containing over 700,000 scrolls, after the Arabs conquered Alexandria in 642 A.D.

Manetho's History of Egypt

Without a doubt, the most influential document which was produced in Alexandria, during the Roman occupation, was Manetho's History of Egypt. Historians believe that, during the Greek Ptolemaic period, King Ptolemy II Philadelphus, wishing to acquaint his court's ruling class with the history of Egypt, commissioned a native Egyptian priest from Sebennytos by the name of Manetho to compile a history of Egypt in the Greek language. Egyptologists believe that Manetho, having access to many ancient annals, was able to devise a relatively accurate list of the Egyptians kings, from the proto-dynastic era to the epoch of the Greek Ptolemies, in an orderly succession of dynasties. Manetho's framework still serves as the cornerstone of the currently accepted chronology of ancient Egypt. Ironically though, the actual work of this Manetho has not survived to our day. What academics know of it are taken from the chronicles of later historians, such as Sextus Julius Africanus, Eusebius and George Syncellus, who wrote their own accounts centuries after Manetho of Sebennytos' presumed death. The discrepancies between these later scholars' transmission of Manetho's work have been ascribed by historians to careless copying and recopying of the original Alexandrian document. Challenging received wisdom, I instead propose that the fundamental reason why such discrepancies occur, and that the original Manethonian text is missing, is because Manetho of Sebennytos never existed. I believe that he was an complete invention of the Romans — who sought to establish some credibility for their own version of Egyptian history.

My main argument to support this thesis is that, according to the new chronology, it is impossible that Manetho could have written a complete list of the Egyptian dynasties during the reign of the Alexandrian Pharaoh Ptolemy II Philadelphus. Indeed, he could not have possibly known of the existence of the pharaohs of the new 31st Dynasty (standard 21st Dynasty), or of the later Ramesside pharaohs for that matter, if he indeed had lived during the early decades of the Greek Ptolemaic era. Moreover, how can one explain Diodorus of Sicily's total ignorance of the existence of Manetho's writings on the history and chronology of ancient Egypt? Despite having reportedly spoken to many authorities on dynastic Egypt and gathered a vast amount of recorded traditions and histories from the Land of the Pharaohs, not even once in his entire body of work does Diodorus of Sicily mention Manetho! How could this be?

Manetho's failure to acknowledge that the Greek Ptolemaic line was different from, and much later than, the Ptolemaic dynasty responsible for initially building the Ptolemaic temples at the First Cataract and establishing the cult of Horus of Behdet, is certainly no innocent oversight. It's obvious that the Romans, then the sole superpower of the ancient world, wanted to write a history which would continue to focus solely on dynastic Egypt and also misleadingly attribute all Ptolemaic innovations to the Greek Alexandrians from the Hellenistic period. Moreover, it is evident that the political role of the Greek Ptolemaic dynasty in Egypt during the century and a half preceding the Battle of Actium was grossly overblown by the blatant omission of the native new 30th and 31st Dynasties. The Manethonian history of Egypt, wholly fabricated during the Roman occupation, annexed the latter dynasties as a continuation of the early Abydos and Turin King-lists.

Like the seventh century BCE Macedonian scribes who concocted these king-lists, the Romans essentially faced no opposition in the accomplishment of their scheme. In the name of the Empire, nationalistic propaganda took precedence over historical accuracy. In light of all that we've seen so far, it's a highly debatable issue as to whether or not the ancients, regardless of their cultural heritage, ever really put historical accuracy ahead of political or ideological interest. Certainly, my undaunted contention that the Romans could actually have gone to such lengths to ensure the glorious legacy of Graeco-Roman culture may seem highly questionable to many. Certainly, Graeco-Roman culture having been, for so long, held upon a pedestal of dispassionate, rational, objective and democratic discourse, the very thought of abandoning this perspective as a reliable yardstick, without a doubt, opens up many new avenues for a radical reinterpretation of ancient world historiography.

At any rate, during the nineteenth century, Western scholarship has often, even unconsciously, tended to apply a debilitating kind of Eurocentric colonialist view upon it's understanding of the relations between the Graeco-Roman world and Egypt, both during and after the Hellenistic age. The Manethonian framework, with regards to Ptolemaic rule in particular, has fit that preconceived picture like a glove. It is no secret that scholars are much influenced by the times in which they live, as in cultural or temporal biases, when attempting to interpret historical evidence. Given Western Europe's relatively recent history of colonialism, it would not be wholly unreasonable to hypothesise that, despite their best intentions, modern Western scholars' historiography could have been tainted by this legacy. Just to outline what I believe to be one of many such glaring examples, is the following statement by author Beatrice L. Goff:

> Their [the Egyptians] unquestioned acceptance of inconsistency as basic to the world about them did not immediately change when they came under the influence of the disciples of Socrates, Plato, Aristotle, and the other philosophers; but gradually the Egyptians of the Ptolemaic and Roman Periods acquired new attitudes. ... The Ptolemies took pride in exhibiting

their ancestral traditions. Furthermore, when they found themselves competing with people who valued clarity of thinking, they superimposed upon their ancestral traditions a clarity of concept that cannot be substantiated by resort to texts of earlier periods. ... it was to the Egyptians' obvious advantage to present the religion of their ancestors in an intelligible form that would seem admirable in their own intellectually stimulating day.[1]

Hence, the Greek Ptolemies are supposed to have introduced "clarity of thinking" into an Egypt tormented by self-imposed "inconsistency." The architectural and cultural rejuvenation of pharaonic Egypt during the Hellenistic period was, according to this Eurocentric model, a natural result of the Egyptians' exposure to the superior post-Socratic logic of the Greeks. A proper historical-critical analysis of the ancient Egyptian textual and archaeological evidence should, however, reveal that the maximalist interpretation of the Manethonian tradition is, again, highly misleading. The Greek Ptolemaic rulers were actually the ones who had been inspired by Khemeto-Egyptian theological genius. Awed by the classical Ptolemaic temples which the Nectanebos had "renovated," the Macedonians under Alexander merely "imitated" without, I believed, any initial attempt to claim the building exploits for the First Cataract temples. Unfortunately, we owe the illusory association of the Upper Egyptian Ptolemaic temples with the Alexandrian Macedonians to the Romans.

Ethiopia During the Graeco-Roman Era
The imperialistic ambitions of Augustus during the first decades of the Roman occupation of Egypt led, among other destinations, to an expedition by the prefect Aelius Gallus, in *c*.25 BCE, to Arabia. But, given the fierce resistance from the Nabataeans, the Romans encountered much difficulties in annexing this region — which retained its independence until 106 CE. It was because of the Romans' major preoccupation with Arabia under Gallus that the Ethiopians of Meroë, wielding influence over Nubia up to the First Cataract, mounted a surprise attack against Thebes. This led the next prefect of Rome, Petronius, to retaliate by launching two military campaigns against Meroë, between 24-22 BCE — razing several towns and forcing the submission of the legendary one-eyed Meroitic queen Candace. This Queen Candace was, I believe, one of a series of monarchs so-named. These illustrious Candace queens, as the consecutive Caesar dynastic line in Egypt, were part of a hereditary succession line. Only they, having come along centuries after the

---
[1] Beatrice L. Goff (1979) *Symbols of Ancient Egypt in the Late Period (The Twenty-first Dynasty)*, Mouton Publishers: The Hague, p. 37.

Fig. 19a: Roman kiosk adjacent to the ancient temple of Naqa.

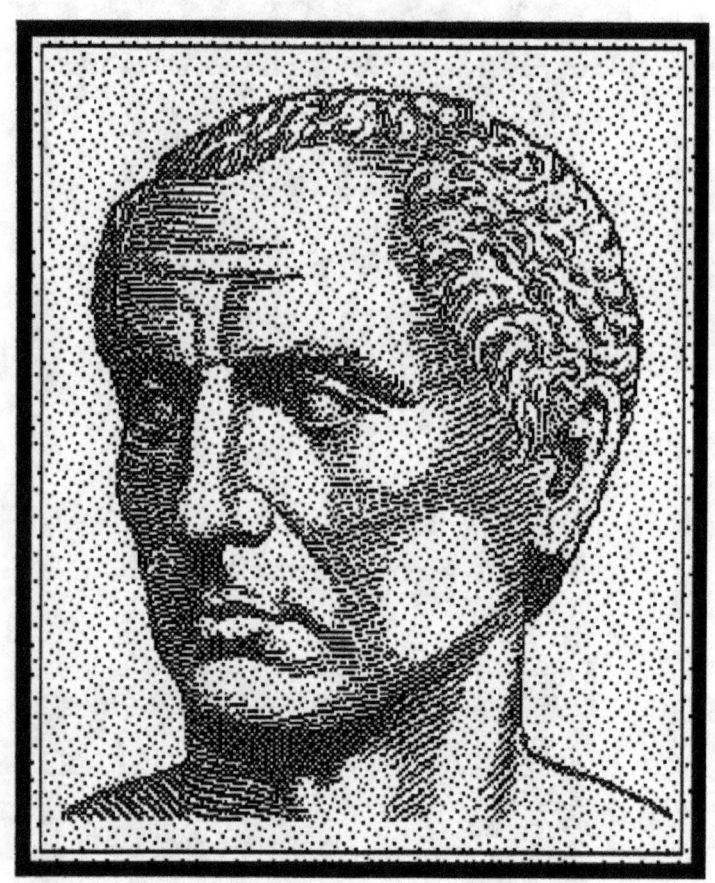

Fig. 19b: The Emperor Ceasar.

CHAP. XIX: AFTER CLEOPATRA: THE RISE OF ROME | 705

final ousting of the Napatans from Egypt, did not rule over a classically speaking pharaonic civilization by that time. Meroë, as the following statement by Pliny indicates, was evidently the capital of the Ethiopian monarchy during the reign of the Roman emperor Augustus, but all of the Meroitic pharaohs' pyramidal tombs had already been erected by the time of the first Candace's advent. From there, the famous one-eyed Candace ruled Ethiopian up to the First Cataract.

> The actual town of Meroë ... They say that it is ruled by a woman, Candace, **a name that has passed on through a succession of queens for many years ...**
> (Pliny, *Natural History*, Book VI: 35, 186-187)

The matriarchal nature of Ethiopia's monarchy at the turn of the first millennium CE is, additionally, made evident by Eusebius:

> ... from the land of the Ethiopians an officer of the queen of that land, for the nation, following ancestral customs, is still ruled by a woman.
> (Eusebius, *Ecclesiastical History*, Book II: 1)

The New Testament's Book of Acts (8:27) likewise acknowledges the existence of a Queen Candace — whose eunuch was converted to Christianity and baptized by St. Philip. Queen Candace, according to the Bible, came to Jerusalem to worship — which would certainly seem like an odd journey for the head of a pharaonic state. This instead indicates, in my view, the growing influence of Christianity in Nubia during that time. In fact, many modern Sudanese Christians believe that Christianity arrived in the Sudan with the conversion of Queen Candace recounted in the Book of Acts. Scholars have actually suggested that the earliest Axiumite Christian churches, founded by African pilgrims returning from the Holy Land, were built during the early Roman era. Moreover, during the third century, many Egyptian Christians fled to Ethiopia to escape persecution from the Roman emperors Decius and Diocletian. While the Christian religion only became the official religion of the Kingdom of Nubia during the late sixth century CE, it is evident that, from the middle of the first century CE, Christianity had a strong presence in Ethiopia. It is thus quite difficult to reconcile this fact with the traditionally held belief that Ethiopia was still a strongly pharaonic culture up until the middle of the fourth century CE.

My hypothesis that, contrary to the belief of modern Nubiologists, pharaonic culture was essentially dead in Ethiopia by the end of Egypt's Late Period is, apparently, supported by the following citation from the works of Pliny:

> These are the places that were reported as far as Meroë, though at the present day hardly any of them still exist on either side of the river; at all events an exploring party of praetorian troops under the command of a tribune lately sent by the emperor Nero, when among the rest of his wars he was actually contemplating an attack on Ethiopia reported that there was nothing but desert. ... but nevertheless it was not the arms of Rome that made the country a desert: Ethiopia was worn out by alternate periods of dominance and subjugation in a series of wars with Egypt, having been a famous and powerful country even down to the Trojan wars, when Memnon was king ...
> (Pliny, *Natural History*, Book VI: 35, 181-182)

Pliny portrays Ethiopia's great pharaonic period as belonging to the past. Like several earlier classical Greek chroniclers, he does indeed acknowledge that Ethiopia had once been a mighty kingdom among nations. That, was obviously no longer the case during the days of Emperor Nero (54-68 CE). Ethiopia no longer wielded any actual or potential power over Egypt and the ancient Near East. Despite their isolation during the Roman era, historians are dumbfounded by the sheer boldness expressed in scenes and inscriptions from the Meroitic temples which boast of their continuing power in Egypt. Until the middle of the fourth century BCE, according to Nubiologists, the Ethiopian kings at Meroë carried on this so-called pretence of familiarity with the arts and religion of Egypt even though pharaonic culture in Egypt itself, decimated by the advent of the Christians, had long ceased to thrive. But as I have been arguing, the truth is pharaonic culture declined in ancient Nubia long before it had in Egypt. These Meroitic temples, describing intimate relations with Egypt, belong to a much earlier period than conventionally believed.

During the matriarchal rule of the Candaces, the Kingdom of Ethiopia was ruled from both the ancient capitals of Napata and Meroë but, from at least as early as the days of Alexander the Great, Graeco-Roman culture had much altered the face of ancient Nubia. According to Strabo:

> Among these fugitives (fleeing from Petronius) were the generals of Queen Candace, who was ruler of the Aethiopians in my time —a masculine sort of woman, and blind in one eye. ... After this he (Petronius) set out for Napata. This was the royal residence of Candace; ... Petronius attacked and captured Napata too, from which her son had fled, and rased it to the ground; and having enslaved its inhabitants, he turned back again with the booty ... Meantime Candace marched against the garrison with many thousands of men ...
> (Strabo, *Geography*, Book XVII: 1, 54)

CHAP. XIX: AFTER CLEOPATRA: THE RISE OF ROME | 707

Therefore, it is entirely evident that, during the early decades of the Roman occupation of Egypt, Roman culture became a mainstay of the Kingdom of Nubia. A kiosk built in Roman style stands in front of the Lion-temple at Naqa. Other evidence of a late occupation of these ancient Nubian sites can be attested by the remains of a Roman bath near the palaces at Meroë.[2] In addition to that, an inscription in Latin was carved by a visitor on the wall of a building at Musawwarat.[3] According to L. V. Zabkar: " *It is as yet impossible to determine who built the 'Kiosk' at Naqa.*"[4] For his part, F. Ll. Griffith was rightly convinced that the Kiosk at Naqa was built in Roman times.[5] But to then go on and assume, as most scholars do, that the Lion-temple of Naqa was contemporary with the Roman kiosk is inaccurate. The Romans erected these facilities many centuries after the last Meroitic pharaoh built a pyramid there.

Although Nubiologists maintain that the X-Group Nubians – attested from the fourth century CE – whose tombs have been excavated at Qustul and Ballâna in Lower Nubia, are the immediate inheritors of the Meroitic pharaohs, there is no evidence whatsoever that X-Group Nubians ever used the Meroitic script![6] Could these Nubians have, all of a sudden, forgotten how to read and write? Adding to this mystery, pyramid-building appears to have come to a sudden end with the fall of the Meroitic kingdom — only to be replaced by mere earth mounds in Lower Nubia. Puzzled by these inconsistencies, Bruce Trigger of McGill University writes:

> The disappearance of the Meroitic script is well attested throughout the region (Lower Nubia), but nowhere is the negative evidence more striking tha[n] at Qustul and Ballâna, where it might have been expected to survive as a script at the royal court.[7]

With regards to the pyramids, he says:

> If pyramids were built in Lower Nubia during the Meroitic period, the abandonment of this shape in Ballâna (X-Group) times remains to be explained. Even if they were not, we must query why the rulers buried at Qustul and Ballâna, when they adopted the other attributes of the Meroitic royal funerary ritual, did not adopt this symbol as well.[8]

---

[2] A. J. Arkell (1974) p. 168.
[3] Lepsius (1849-59) VI, 101, 56.
[4] L. V. Zabkar (1975) *Apedemak: Lion God of Meroe (A Study in Egyptian-Meroitic Syncretism)*, Aris & Phillips: Warminster, England, p. 40.
[5] F. Ll. Griffith, *Meroitic Inscriptions* (Part I), p. 61.
[6] Bruce Trigger (1969) 'The Royal Tombs at Qustul and Ballâna and their Meroitic Antecedents', *Journal of Egyptian Archaeology* 55, p. 124.
[7] Ibid.
[8] Ibid, p. 120.

As a result, it is conventionally believed that the kings of Meroë held sway over Lower Nubia until the supposed end of the Meroitic kingdom in the fourth century CE. That argument is used to explain the continuity in culture exhibited by Meroitic influences in X-Group Lower Nubia. No satisfactory explanation has however been offered to account for the sharp discontinuity in script and funerary practices. The only answer to this riddle is, in my opinion, to admit that many centuries lay between the end of the Meroitic kingdom and the subsequent X-Group culture of Lower Nubia.

Mankind in Amnesia? (Stolen Legacies, Fallen Skies and the Triumph of the Axial Age)

The lasting influence of Graeco-Roman culture on the modern interpretation of the ancient world in the West, and the rest of the world, in fact spreads far beyond the realm of historiography. The way in which the universe, and humanity's interaction with it, was perceived also changed dramatically. The proliferation of archaeotheological cosmogonies, dissimulating symbolic historical records, became less and less frequent and even understood. The general trend, throughout much of the ancient world, after the culmination of Typhon Season #7, was to move away from the traditional catastrophic world view to a more uniformitarian view of the solar system. Somehow, the ancients had come to the accurate conclusion that they no longer needed to fear the destruction of the Seventh Sun. Two peoples who spearheaded the implementation of this paradigm shift: were the Jews and the Greeks. The prophet Ezra, the Sixth Moses, was convinced that the Almighty, through His fiery destruction of the Sixth Creation, had completed his divine ordering of the Heavens. No more would the Creator be required to directly intervene, as a severe arbiter, in the matters of humankind. In essence, the Heavens had suddenly grown silent and humanity was left with the responsibility to live their lives, as mature individuals, in accordance to divine law.

Meanwhile, in ancient Greece, Socrates and Plato were developing concepts of human nature and the universe which signalled a major departure from the hitherto dominant paradigms of a chaotic universe dominated by warring planetary gods. Thus, history would no longer be viewed as being part of a cyclical process of rising and falling civilizations, but rather as part of a linear process. But despite this precipitous paradigmatic shift, certain notions or concepts of the catastrophic world view were incorporated, in a symbolic manner, into newly emerging sacred texts and philosophical tenets of the Seventh Creation. For instance, the number seven,

CHAP. XIX: AFTER CLEOPATRA: THE RISE OF ROME | 709

representing the seven World Ages separated by planetary catastrophes, became a sacred number in the Jewish Torah — representing the divine itself. The six heavens preceding the seventh realm, which represented the completion of God's Creation (as in the seven days of Creation) symbolized the material world. Thus, the knowledge of the revolving World Ages of the past became incorporated in a kind of mystery system. Furthermore, as the pioneering creators of these complex cosmogonies, the Egyptians naturally were pivotal transmitters of these mysteries. Like certain classical authors postulated, I believe that not only the Bible was influenced greatly by these Egyptian mysteries, but also some of the works of the early Greek philosophers. In his chronicle *Geography*, Strabo goes as far as claiming that Plato and Eudoxus studied philosophy and astronomy in Egypt for thirteen years.

> ... for since the priests excelled in their knowledge of the heavenly bodies, albeit secretive and slow to impart it, Plato and Eudoxus prevailed upon them in time and by courting their favour to let them learn some of the principles and doctrines; but the barbarians concealed most things. However, these men did teach them the fractions of the day and the night which, running over and above the three hundred and sixty-five days, fill out the time of the true year.
> (Strabo, *Geography* XVII: 1, 29)

Plato's description of the shifting of the heavenly bodies at the end of the ages, which appears to contradict the Socratic school, certainly seems to hint at his possible exposure to the ancient catastrophic world view. Moreover, it is interesting to note that Herodotus heard from the priests of Egypt that there had been four reversals of the world's cosmic order. Herodotus visited Egypt during the Age of Pisces — the fourth zodiacal age of antiquity. The four reversals which the Egyptian priests spoke of occurred in 1559, 1135, 776 and 612 BCE. Is it possible that Plato could have been in contact with this very same Egyptian priesthood? I believe that Plato, though dedicated to the Socratic vision of a stable universe, was nonetheless aware of, and accepted, the fact that, prior to the advent of the Seventh Age, planetary catastrophes had occurred periodically. In this belief, he had a counterpart in his Judean contemporary Ezra (the Sixth Moses). Incidentally, in the minds of the post-Exilic Jewish priesthood which rallied around Ezra, the end of the Sixth Age signalled the end of any further cosmic changes. According to Immanuel Velikovsky:

> The sabbath, the seventh day, is a symbol and assurance that no other metagenetic catastrophe will come. In keeping with this solemn day of rest, the creator is implored to refrain from reshaping the earth ...[9]

---

[9] Immanuel Velikovsky 'A Hebrew Cosmogony': unpublished material.

The legacy of the catastrophic world view is indeed wholly evident throughout the pages of the Bible. Like Plato, Ezra understood the reality of past cosmic conflagrations. In his drama *Sisyphus*, Critias, the cousin of Plato's mother, demonstrated that the cult of planetary gods was linked to a terrifying beliefs in world conflagrations. Plato, himself, spoke of periodic floods which were accompanied by massive cataclysms resulting from the moving away of the planets from their set course. On this matter, Friedrich Solmsen observes:

> Already in Plato emphasis is put in the regularity with which the catastrophes occur. There is some indication that this element of order and regularity is related to the heavenly movements. However, Plato refrains from developing this idea; all he actually says is that these catastrophes reflect a displacement or "derangement of the bodies in heaven which circle around the earth." The notion that heavenly movements could affect things on earth would strike the men of the Academy as not nearly so absurd as the reverse doctrine which Aristotle scornfully rejects (to wit, that changes between land and sea should have a bearing on the history of the entire Cosmos). ...
>
> In its original form, however, the Academic doctrine knew more than one kind of catastrophe. Not only floods but great conflagrations too were held to occur at regular intervals.[10]

Plato also speaks of these catastrophes as having caused "the periodic disappearance of human civilization after a time of hopeful progress."[11] Those similarities between Plato and Ezra may have been the inspiration behind Numenius' enigmatic statement that Plato was "Moses speaking in an Attic dialect."[12] Similarly, Aristobulus, an Alexandrian Jew who lived during the second half of the second century BCE, had claimed that Plato had been a student of Moses. There appears to be little doubt that the "Moses" that Numenius and Aristobulus are talking about was Ezra, the Sixth Moses. Evidently, we know that he was indeed a contemporary of Plato.

The highly elitist and secretive trait of Khemeto-Egyptian culture, which Cheikh Anta Diop described as its "major weakness," ensured that the masses of the peo-

---

[10] Friedrich Solmsen (1960) *Aristotle's System of the Physical World: A Comparison with His Predecessors*, Cornell University Press: Ithaca, NY, pp. 431-432; Plato, *Timaeus* 22d1, cf 23a7; Aristotle, *Meteorological* I, 14.352a26ff. (cf. a17ff.)

[11] Friedrich Solmsen (1960) p. 432.

[12] Quoted in Clement of Alexandria, *Stromata*, Vio. I: 153.4; Eusebius, *Praeparatio Evangelica*, IX.6.9.

CHAP. XIX: AFTER CLEOPATRA: THE RISE OF ROME | 711

ple in Egypt received only an exoteric education with respect to the Ages of Man and the cyclical movements of the heavenly bodies. Unlike the Greek philosophers who freely divulged their knowledge to the masses in an effort to make a name for themselves, Egyptian priests preferred to jealously keep their scientific knowledge among themselves.[13] Such secrecy has unfortunately served to confuse, not only modern observers, but perhaps more importantly the early Greek chroniclers — from whom contemporary scholars gain some of their understanding of ancient Egypt. To this day, Egyptologists have pretty much the same exoteric understanding of ancient Egyptian religion as did the ancient Egyptian laity or Greek visitors to the Land of the Pharaohs. That is to say a purely agrarian and solar interpretation of Khemetic mythology. Further hindering this understanding, professional Egyptologists have traditionally been very patronizing with respect to the ability of the ancient Egyptians to devise a system of restricted knowledge. But in the words of Oxford Egyptologist John Baines: *"These attitudes are limiting because they discourage the search for system and complexity."*[14] This attitude comes partly from the fact that pharaonic Egypt is seen by modern Western observers as a "pre-logical" civilization. Meaning that its essential cultural, philosophical and religious underpinnings were formed prior to the rise of the rational mode of thought — attributed preeminently to the Greeks.

During the course of the late nineteenth and emerging twentieth centuries, European scholars, among them German historian an philosopher Karl Jaspers, came with the concept known of the "Axial Age."[15] According to this model, the middle of the first millennium BCE quite inexplicably heralded, through much of the ancient world (e.g. Israel, Greece, China, Iran and India), a simultaneous religious, philosophical, and scientific break from past forms of esoteric speculations to a more "rational" of "modern" mode of thought. In Greece, that revolution first manifests itself with Socrates and Plato. This notion has come to dominate modern scientific thought; and, as Boston University geologist Robert M. Schoch elaborates below, has significantly shaped our modern understanding of the ancients:

> Looking back, we moderns may appreciate the literary quality of Gilgamesh or the Homeric epics, but we reject the accuracy of their content. The ancients were, we seem to believe, psychological primitives who lived in

---

[13] Cheikh Anta Diop (1962) 'Histoire primitive de l'Humanité: Évolution du monde noir', *Bulletin de l'IFAN* Vol. 24 (Série B) - Num. 3-4, p. pp. 526-528.
[14] John Baines (1990) 'Restricted Knowledge, Hierarchy and Decorum: Modern Perceptions and Ancient Institutions', *Journal of the American Research Center in Egypt* 27, p. 2.
[15] See Martin Bernal (1991) *Black Athena (The Afroasiatic Roots of Classical Civilization) — Volume II: The Archaeological and Documentary Evidence*, Rutgers University Press: New Brunswick, NJ, pp. 309-310.

quaking fear of the heavens. They were much like children who invent monsters under the bed and in the closet, and keep themselves awake at night, worrying about fangs and claws. Yet how can we be sure of our intellectual and psychological superiority? Could we, in so smug and easy a dismissal, be missing something critically important?[16]

The legacy of the Axial Age's main drawback is that we have lost the ability to understand the allegorical catastrophic meanings within the ancients' theological constructs. Aristotle, who "considered all non-Hellenes innately inferior,"[17] arrogantly assessed pre-Socratic philosophy "as no more than a stammering attempt to say what only he, at last, was able to articulate with fluency."[18] The Socratic and Aristotelian paradigms, which have come to dominate post-Axial Age science, essentially put and end to the catastrophic world view. In the words of Livo C. Stecchini:

> By rationalizing the beliefs in the heavenly bodies as gods and making them the expression of a higher realm (higher physically and morally) which is rational, regular, and unalterable, Aristotle set up the foundations of classical science.[19]

Indeed, following the Dark Ages in Europe (from the conquest of Rome by the Goths and Vandals in the fifth century to the beginning of the Renaissance and Reformation in the fifteenth century), Aristotelianism became the order of the day. In his highly influential *Traité de mécanique céleste,* Pierre Simon Laplace (1779-1825) later declared that the solar system was governed by gravitation and that the planets' orbital paths were eternally stable. However in Aristotle's own time, catastrophism was widely discussed. As a matter of fact, "Stoic philosophers taught the recurrent conflagrations of the world; the Pythagoreans were immersed in speculations of cosmic order and disorder ..."[20] Likewise, in the first century BCE, Lucretius in his *On the Nature of Things,* spoke of recurring cosmic catastrophes. In Rome, Pliny wrote: "*Heavenly fire is spit forth by the planets as crackling charcoal flies from a burning log.*"[21] If the catastrophic world view had indeed been such an integral part of

---

[16] Robert M. Schoch (1999) *Voices of the Rocks (A Scientist Looks at Catastrophes and Ancient Civilizations).* With Robert Aquinas McNally. Harmony Books: New York, p.15.
[17] Alan Davies (1988) p. 4.
[18] Peter Kingsley (1995) *Ancient Philosophy, Mystery, and Magic (Empedocles and Pythagorean Tradition),* Clarendon Press: Oxford, U.K., p. 3.
[19] Livio C. Stecchini (1963) 'The Inconsistant Heavens: Velikovsky in Relation to Some Past Cosmic Perplexities', *American Behavioral Scientist* Vol. 67 - Num. 1, p. 20.
[20] Immanuel Velikovsky (1982) *Mankind in Amnesia,* Doubleday: Garden City, NY, p. 48.
[21] Pliny, *Natural History,* Book II: 18.

the ancients' collective psyche, then why would it have, at this particular time, been abandoned and even denied? I believe that this has much to do with the political situation around the world during the time of the Axial Age — in addition to the realization that revolving cycle of the World Ages had come to an end. Longing to rid themselves of the uncertainty of constantly expecting a collapse of their civilization, and the accompanying political threat of rising charismatic leaders claiming to hold the Mandate of Heaven, the secular and religious leaders of most ancient societies actively discouraged the adherence to the catastrophic world view. Turning to Lynn E. Rose in conclusion:

> It can be argued that *all* of the leading and distinctive features of Aristotle's system served, in one way or another, to soothe Aristotle's deep-seated fear of planetary catastrophes. His denial of what had happened in the past went to such extremes that he created a system in which interplanetary near-collisions not only did not happen, but could not possibly happen. Aristotle and Aristotelianism came to be *the* principal theoretical obstacle to catastrophism. No one, in the entire history of recorded thought did more than Aristotle in an effort to de-legitimize catastrophism.[22]

---

[22] Cited in Velikovsky (1982) p. 53.

20

Catastrophist Christology and the New Testament

The highly charged political nature of the ancient catastrophic world view in the post Axial Age era manifested itself, I believe, most strongly in the rise of diverse Messianic movements — starting during the second half of the first century BCE. My theory is that the swift surge of the Messianic ideal at this particular time coincided with the expected heliacal rising of the star of Sirius. We recall that the last time this astronomical event had occurred before then was in 1,493 BCE — on Year 9 of Pharaoh Amenhotep I. In my new chronology of the ancient world, we find that King David in Israel was a contemporary of Pharaoh Amenhotep I. The heliacal rising of Sirius in 1,493 BCE, therefore, likewise took place during the lifetime of King David. This fact was certainly not lost by the biblical redactors. In the Book of Chronicles, the following reference was, I believe, a symbolic description of the constellation of Orion — the constellation accompanied by the star Sirius.

> 16 And David lifted up his eyes, and saw the angel of the Lord stand between the earth and the heaven, having drawn sword in his hand stretched out over Jerusalem.
> (1 Chronicles 21:16)

As we've discussed in Chapter 1, the constellation of Orion was perceived by the ancients as a standing man with a sword. The association between the reign of the mighty King David in Israel during the Late Bronze Age and the heliacal rising of Sirius in 1,493 BCE remained a preeminent esoteric feature of Jewish religion. But, given the allegorical nature of the biblical texts, and Ezra's concern with distancing himself from pagan religions, this fact remained hidden. The title of "Son of David" was not perceived as a political one by the New Testament writers.[1] The charismatic Jewish leader who was prophesied to be the "Son of David" was one who would be born around the time of the next heliacal rising of Sirius, in c.33 BCE. The elusive star which guided the Magi on the year of Christ's birth

---

[1] Stephen H. Smith (1996) 'The Function of the Son of David Tradition in Mark's Gospel', *New Testament Studies* Vol. 42 - Num. 4, pp. 523-539.

in the New Testament, the "Star of David," was really a reference to the heliacal rising of the star Sirius. Therefore, when the Magi and Pharisees informed the Roman governor, King Herod, of the birth of a Jewish king, heralded by a star in the east (Matt. 2:1-4), he resolved to annihilate him.

The New Moses: The Jesus Narratives and their Old Testament Sources

> " History has become our fate.
> We must, therefore, pass everything which we think, say and believe about Jesus through the sieve of strict methodological consideration, through the fire of historical criticism."
>
> - Heinz Zahrnt
> *The Historical Jesus*

According to the Gospel of Matthew, Jesus was born "in the days of Herod the king" (Mtt 2:1). Herod the Great, founder of the Herodian dynasty, ruled over Palestine from 37 BCE until March-April 4 BCE. It has long been customary to date the birth Christ towards the end of Herod's reign.[2] This is on account of the fact that Matthew (2:19) places the death of Herod the Great during the infant Jesus' flight to Egypt with Joseph and Mary. However, my thesis will argue that Jesus-Christ was born on the fifth year of Herod's reign, in 33 BCE. This is when, according to the Sothic sequence adopted here, based on the heliacal risings from protodynastic times and Year 9 of Amenhotep I, that the heliacal rising took place. Historians, on the other hand, generally accept a later date of 139 CE for this heliacal rising — based on the observations of Censorinus. But Censorinus' date fails to align with the Egyptian evidence. The Sothic period which began on Year 9 of Pharaoh Amenhotep I could not have happened so late. What's more, the majority of New Testament scholars conjecture that the Book of Matthew was written down in its present form sometime around 80 CE.[3] Thus, if a correlation can be established between King David and Jesus-Christ through the Sothic cycle, as I will argue, then Censorinus' date is certainly too late.

King Herod's decision to slay all the newborn male children in Bethlehem in an attempt (Matt. 2:16), to prevent the rise of this rival "King of the Jews", is certainly

---

[2] Gerard Mussies (1998) 'The Date of Jesus' Birth in Jewish and Samaritan Sources', *Journal for the Study of Judaism: in the Persian, Hellenistic and Roman Period* Vol. 29 - Num. 4, pp. 416-437.

[3] Raymond E. Brown (1993) *The Birth of the Messiah (A Commentary on the Infancy Narratives in the Gospels of Matthew and Luke)*, Doubleday: New York, p. 45.

very similar to the events in the life of the infant composite Moses in the Old Testament. Bible scholars have, for a long time, been particularly interested in the obvious similarities between the narratives of the life of Jesus-Christ and the Old Testament story of Moses. Incidentally, Moses is mentioned more than eighty times in the New Testament — more than any other Old Testament figure.[4] According to New Testament scholar Dale C. Allison, as he mentions in his 1993 book The New Moses, this belief among the early editors of the New Testament that Jesus-Christ was the new Moses shaped how the Jesus tradition was transmitted. Also, in a 1986 article entitled 'From Moses to Jesus: Parallel Themes', Bible scholar John Dominic Crossan makes a brilliant analysis of the striking similarities between the infancy narratives of Moses (both biblical and extra-biblical) and Jesus.[5] Paralleling Pharaoh and Herod, Crossan writes:

The Plot Against the Children:

by Pharaoh	by Herod
Scene I: A sign in the form of a predilection or dream. (As in Josephus' *Antiquities*)	A sign in the form of a star. (Matthew 2:1-2)
Scn. II: Pharaoh and his courtiers' fear.	Herod's fear. (Matthew 2:3)
Scn. III: Pharaoh consults with courtiers.	Herod consults with priests and scribes (Matthew 2:4)
Scn. IV: Pharaoh decides to massacre male Hebrew children. (Exodus 1:16, 22)	Herod decides to massacre all male children two years old and under. (Matthew 2:16)

Another old testament parallel found in Jesus' infancy narratives is in Luke's description of Mary and Joseph's presentation of Jesus in the temples. That scene is highly reminiscent of Samuel's presentation by his parents in the central shrine, where Eli received him (1 Samuel 1:24; 2:20).[6] These and other references to the Old Testament lead Bible scholars to conjecture that "much of the story of Jesus' infancy was not based on eyewitness memory but was shaped by OT models."[7] The infancy narratives in the New Testament are not the only passages which were obviously based on the life of Moses in the Old Testament. As biblical scholar Daniel

---

[4] Daniel Jeremy Silver (1982) *Images of Moses*, Basic Books: New York, p. 136.
[5] John Dominic Crossan (1986) 'From Moses to Jesus: Parallel Themes', *Bible Review* Vol. 11 - Num. 2, pp. 18-27.
[6] Raymond E. Brown *et al.* (editors) (1978) *Mary in the New Testament*, p. 14.
[7] Ibid.

Jeremy Silver observes, the New Testament accounts of Jesus' later years likewise mirror the life of the composite Moses:

> The Sermon on the Mount is a sermon on the mount so that Jesus may be seen in the same situation as Moses on Sinai. His speech concluded, Jesus performs ten miracles which clearly are intended to parallel the ten plagues – miracles – that Moses performed in Egypt. Matthew declares that Jesus, as a Second Moses, surpasses the first. Why else should God send another? Moses was the prophet of the first redemption, Jesus is the prophet of the second redemption.[8]

In the history of the Jewish nation, the Moses figures were essentially deliverers of their people during times of captivity. Often, the given Messianic figure emerged during the time of an impending cosmic catastrophe, or at the termination of a Typhon Season. The composite Moses, in the Jewish pseudographical literature, is said to have learned the mysteries of the season. This intrinsically means that he had become wise in the knowledge of the revolving World Ages and the divines forces and justifications accompanying these eschatological cataclysms. The Old Testament's composite Moses served as a vital link between God and His people, as a transmitter of the terms and conditions of the new covenant at the crossroads of ending and beginning World Ages or Divine Mandates/Covenants. Similarly, the New Testament writers wanted to portray Jesus-Christ as just such a divine redeeming link. The fundamental idea was that Jesus came to earth to herald a new era or Divine Covenant. The New Testament writers were, however, convinced that while the composite Moses had offered temporary salvation for humanity, Jesus-Christ, instead, came to offer eternal redemption.

Jesus-Christ as Catastrophist

The fact that Christ had come to earth after, according to the universal Axial Age belief, the time when heavens had gone silent and the planets had finally stabilized themselves meant for the initiated early Christians that Jesus had come along to ensure, or confirm, God's mercy for humanity. He was the saviour of the Ages of Pisces, which began in 612 BCE. By offering himself in sacrifice, Christ guaranteed the renewal of God's Covenant without the customary cataclysmic end of the zodiacal World Age. Despite this assurance, however, early Christians, as Christ preached himself, were convinced that a manifestation of God's power, or Day of the Lord, in the form of a cosmic disturbance was very close at hand. This cosmic disturbance would not involve a cycle-ending Venusian conflagration, but a less

---

[8] Daniel Jeremy Silver (1982) pp. 137-138.

CHAP. XX: CATASTROPHIST CHRISTOLOGY | 719

severe lunar upheaval. This resurgence of the catastrophic world view, during the second half of the first century BCE, was not only akin to the followers of Jesus, but common to most of the Messianic cults which emerged around that time.

Undoubtedly, there was a foreboding sense, among several of these Messianic sects and other religious orders, that the end of the World Age was near. This sense of imminent doom is evident, for example, in the Book of Enoch — considered to have been the most important pseudopigraph of the first two centuries BCE. The most common version of the Book of Enoch is the Ethiopic one — known as "1 Enoch" to Bible scholars. The original Aramaic version of this work was thought to have been lost until the Dead Sea scrolls were discovered. As 1 Enoch is preserved in full (108 chapters divided into five parts and one appended chapter), most commentaries on the Book of Enoch focus on the Ethiopic version. In it, we may read:

> 4. And the moon shall alter her order, and not appear at her time.
> 5. And in those days the sun shall be seen and he shall journey in the evening on the extremity of the great chariot in the west ...
> 6. And many chiefs of the stars shall transgress the order (prescribed). And these shall alter their orbits and tasks, and not appear at the seasons prescribed to them.
> 7. And the whole order of the stars shall be concealed from the sinners, and the thoughts of those on earth shall err concerning them, [and they shall be altered from their ways]. Yea they shall err and take them to be gods.
> (Book of Enoch 80:4-7)

This all seems very similar to the astronomical and eschatological cataclysmic conditions prevailing at the end of a World Age. Quite evidently, the Book of Enoch's authors were heavily relying upon the traditional esoteric knowledge of the revolving World Ages. As in earlier Antiquity, this premonitioned catastrophe was seen as an impending judgment of God. Jude, in the first century BCE, who considered the Book of Enoch as being "divinely inspired,"[9] wrote of this judgment:

> In the seventh (generation) from Adam, Enoch also prophesied these things, saying: 'Behold, the Lord came with his holy myriads, to execute judgment on all and to convict all the ungodly of all their ungodly deeds which they have committed in such an ungodly way, and of all the harsh things which ungodly sinners spoke against him.'
> (Jude 14-15)

---

[9] R. H. Charles (editor) (1979) *The Book of Enoch*, Makor: Jerusalem, pp. xii-xiv. See also Norman Golb (1995) *Who Wrote the Dead Sea Scrolls? (The Search for the Secret of Qumran)*, Scribner: New York, p. 366.

God's judgment was, thus, expected during the Seventh Creation — the Age of Pisces. Incidentally, Jesus had conceived his earthly mission as that of putting an end to Satan's reign over the earth (Luke 10:17-18).[10] As the new Moses, and the manifestation of God on earth, Jesus-Christ was portrayed as embodying both the roles of redeemer and executor of divine judgment. Whether or not this lunar disturbance occurred or not, the New Testament does make mention of a sudden darkness which engulfed the earth at the time of Christ's crucifixion.

> 44 And it was about the sixth hour, and there was darkness over all the earth until the ninth hours.
> 45 And the sun was darkened, and the veil of the temple was rent in the midst.
> (Luke 23:44-45)

I believe that the New Testament writers included this passage to underline the fact that the death of Christ heralded a new era or Divine Covenant. In this case, we also know that it "renewed" the zodiacal Age of Pisces and prevented it from coming to a cataclysmic end. Furthermore, I would tentatively place the year of Christ's death to the year zero. Since I believe that the heliacal rising of the star Sirius, which accompanied Christ's birth, took place during the second half of the first century BCE, I have simply equated the accepted date of Christ's birth with the year of his death. Since Jesus-Christ is known to have lived 33 years, I have concluded that the heliacal rising of Sirius occurred in c.33 BCE.

This link between Jesus-Christ's ministry and the vast esoteric knowledge of the pre-Axial Age era's so-called paganism can, I earnestly contend, be understood by the acknowled-gement of the much-debated theory that Christ had spent his formative years (the Lost Years) in Egypt. Most likely, given his followers' evident predilection for cultic fish imagery in the pages of the New Testament, Jesus must have spent some time at Oxyrhynchus while in Egypt. In fact, Christianity implanted itself in the Nome of Oxyrhynchus from as early as the second century CE.[11] That could underline the close relationship between Christianity and the fish cult. An important archive of papyri, among them early Christian apocryphal texts, dating from 250 BCE to 700 CE establish a continuity between the earlier pagan cults and Christianity.

Certainly, one of the most important links between Christianity and Egyptian religion is the esoteric symbolism of the heliacal rising of Sirius and the accompany-

---

[10] Gerald O'Collins (1995) *Christology (A Biblical, Historical, and Systematic Study of Jesus)*, Oxford University Press: Oxford and New York, p. 57.
[11] Cf. Lequien, *Oriens Christianus* 2,577.

CHAP. XX: CATASTROPHIST CHRISTOLOGY | 721

ing symbolism of the constellation of Orion. As Diodorus of Sicily corroborates below, the ancient land of Babylon, where the Magi who first noticed the "star in the east" came from, had themselves been highly influenced by Egyptian astronomy.

> ... the Chaldaeans of Babylon, being colonists from Egypt, enjoy the fame which they have for their astrology because they learned that science from the priests of Egypt.
> (Diodorus of Sicily, Book I: 81)

The traditional symbolic attributes of the star Sirius, the star which the Magi were referring to, or the Star of David, can actually be gleaned from a certain description of Christ in the New Testament as one who smites the nations with a sword (Rev. 19:15). In Antiquity, as evidenced by the following citation from Homer's *Odyssey*, the constellation of Orion did in fact symbolize a figure holding a weapon (like a sword, rod of club in his hand).

> ... I saw huge Orion in a meadow full of asphodel, driving the ghosts of the wild beasts that he had killed upon the mountains, and he had a great bronze club in his hand, unbreakable for ever and ever.
> (Homer, *Odyssey*, Book XI)

In the Book of Revelation, we read:

> 5 And she brought forth a man child, who was to rule all nations with a rod of iron: and her child was caught up unto God, and to his throne.
> (Revelation 12:5)

Early Christianity was, indeed, closely intertwined with surrounding religious cults and traditions which were considered pagan. Preeminent among those was the cult of Mithras. The cult of Mithras, an Aryan sun-god, was imported into the Roman empire during the first century CE from the east — specifically from Sanskrit and Persian literature which go back to around 1,400 BCE. There were many hundreds of Mithraic temples in the Roman empire. Mithras' most important function was sacrificing a bull — symbolizing evil in the world. Similar to ancient sacrificial bull cult devoted to Poseidon the Earth-shaker in Homer's *Odyssey*, the Mithraic cult incorporated other Typhonian elements such as evil snakes who would attack Mithras' testicles — who nonetheless prevailed. The mystery religions, of which the cult of Mithras was arguably the most significant one, were practised throughout the Roman empire during the time of the apostle Paul of Tarsus, and undoubtedly had a significant influence upon the latter. We indeed find numerous Mithraic influences in the New Testament. For instance, Mithras was: (1) Born of a virgin in a manger during the winter solstice on December 25th in the Julian calendar. This date was declared the official birth date of Mithras by emperor Aurelian in c.270 CE. Legend also relates that shepherds had brought gifts to the infant Mithras. (2) Mithras is said to have taken a last supper with his followers before returning to his heavenly father. (3) He was believed not to have died but to have ascended to the heavens, whence he would return at the end of time to exact judgment upon the world. The structure of the Mithraic cult was extremely hierarchical. Moreover, members of Mithraea, the Mithraic temples, were required to go through a series of seven grades, each of which had a special symbol and titular planet. There is absolutely no doubt in my mind that this was a ritualistic reenactment of the seven World Ages and their arbitrarily corresponding seven planets —as was outlined in Chapter 14.

Our attention will now be turned toward attempting to uncover similar allegorical references, inside the New Testament, to the seven World Ages and the seven intervening cataclysmic Typhon Seasons. To begin with, it would be useful to consider the following quotation from Professor William Mullen of Bard College:

> ... The difficulty of sustaining such tension also in due time produced an apocalyptic literature among the Jews, but the rabbinical tradition worked against it, and it remains peripheral to the Jewish religion. Nevertheless, when Jesus of Nazareth entered his public ministry the apocalyptic notions were at his disposal; and in some sense the gospels may be characterized as a teaching of the ethics of the last days. If this historical figure was convinced of an imminent end of the world, he must also have been passionately concerned to tell people how they should act in regard to it. There is a different aspect of Jesus, though, which may have been available to the minds of his contemporaries, and was in any case soon developed by Paul into an essential part of Christianity. That is Christ in the ancient pattern of a dying and reborn god whose death and resurrection promise salvation to mankind, whether salvation in the sense of life after the human death, or finally salvation as survival during the process by which heaven and earth are next remade.[12]

---

[12] William Mullen 'Structuring the Apocalypse (Old and New World Variations).' In E. R. Milton (editor) (1978) *Recollections of a Fallen Sky: Velikovsky and Cultural Amnesia (Papers presented at the University of Lethbridge — May 9 and 10 1974)*, Unileth Press: Lethbridge, Alberta, p. 73.

CHAP. XX: CATASTROPHIST CHRISTOLOGY | 723

Since Jesus-Christ's mission, according to the New Testament, was to be sacrificed in order to safe keep the Divine Covenant between God and humanity, it is evident that his primary goal was to prevent the cataclysmic cessation of the Age of Pisces. In order to do that, the decadent Seventh Creation had to be renewed through a new Covenant. The previous six Creations' endings, when humans suddenly found themselves naked and ashamed, newly aware of their transgressions against Heaven, through divine mercy, would no longer occur. The biblical theme of nakedness as symbolizing the eschatological destruction of a the World Ages has been reviewed thoroughly in previous chapters. Jesus-Christ stressed that, in order to prevent, or alleviate, the shame of nakedness, one needed to become as a child. In the early apocryphal documents known as the Papyrus Oxyrhynchus and the Nag Hammadi Codex, it is recounted about Jesus and his disciples:

> His disciples say to him, "When will you be revealed to us and when shall we see you?" He says, "When you take off your clothes and are not ashamed [...]"
> (Papyrus Oxyrhynchus, 655, 17-24)
>
> His disciples said, "When will you be revealed to us and when will we see you?" Jesus said, "When you take your clothing without being ashamed, and take your clothes and put them under your feet as the little children and tread on them, then [you shall behold] the Son of the Living (One) and you shall not fear.
> (Nag Hammadi Codex, 11, 39:27-40:2)

What Christ meant through this parable is that humanity will only be saved when they no longer fear God's judgment. This judgment is specifically one which relates to the end of the World Ages. Thus, the arrival of Jesus-Christ, as the divine saviour who sacrifices himself to safeguard and renew the decadent World Age, allows his disciples, once they recognize who he is and his role, to become children again. The theme of humanity returning to the mentality of children during the close of a World Age is also tackled in classical Greek literature. The Eleatic Stranger of the Platonic dialogues describes to Socrates, in the following manner, the state of the world when the Creator had decreed a new World Age by allowing the course of the heavenly bodies to be rearranged:

> First the age of animals, whatever it was at the moment, stood still, and every mortal creature stopped growing older in appearance and then re-

> versed its growth and became, as it were, younger and more tender; the hoary locks of the old men grew dark, and bearded cheeks grew smooth again as their possessors reverted to their earlier ages, and the bodies of young men grew smoother and smaller day by day and night by night, **until they became new-born babes,** to which they were likened in mind and body ...
> (Plato, *Politicus*, 270)

The Greeks believed, for their part, that when an overspent World Age came to an end and was replaced by a new vibrant one, the earth dwellers likewise became rejuvenated in every way. Those who survived the pole shift became like new-born babes. This, naturally reflects, Jesus-Christ's preoccupation with his followers to be "born again" into the new Divine Covenant. As the Stranger in the Platonic dialogues says: "*It is a natural consequence of the return of the old to childhood that those who are dead and lying in the earth take shape and come to life again, since the process of birth is reversed along with the reversal of the world's revolution."* Additionally, again strikingly echoing the New Testament, the Eleatic Stranger makes numerous references to the "golden lamb" and the "divine shepherd."

> 7 But the heavens and the earth, which are now, by the same word are kept in store, reserved unto fire against the day of judgment and perdition of ungodly men.
> 8 But, beloved, be not ignorant of this one thing, that one day is with the lord as a thousand years, and a thousand years as one day. ...
> 10 But the day of the lord will come as a thief in the night; in the which the heavens shall pass away with a great noise, and the elements shall melt with the fervent heat, the earth also and the works that are therein shall be burned up.
> (2 Peter 3:7-8, 10)

As the above quote from the New Testament further demonstrates, Messianism was intimately related to the catastrophic world view. Not only is this evident in the New Testament, but also in the numerous contemporary apocryphal texts, like the Apocalypse of Elijah.

The Apocalypse of Elijah is arguably the most important record for the study of the development of Christianity in Egypt during the Roman Era. Paleographically and historically, the text is dated to the latter half of the third century of the common era.[13] Much like the community at Qumran had been, the Apocalypse of Eli-

---

13 David Frankfurter (1993) *Elijah in Upper Egypt (The Apocalypse of Elijah and Early Egyptian Christianity)*, Fortress Press: Minneapolis, p. 2.

jah came out of a group that chose to exclude themselves from the main urban settings. The members of the community were "overwhelmingly concerned with the end of the world as they knew it."[14] Their's was not a political struggle, or a protest movement against an oppressive Roman regime, but rather a yearning to acquire eschatological salvation in the coming new World Age.

> 7. Then, in that time, the earth will tremble; the sun will grow dark. Peace will be removed from upon the earth and under heaven ... The trees will be uprooted and toppled over. Wild beasts and farm animals will die in a catastrophe.
> 8. Birds will fall on the ground dead,
> 9. [The earth will parch,] and the waters of the sea will dry up.[15]

On the Osirian Aspects of Christ

The authors of the Apocalypse of Elijah were deeply entrenched within the traditional pharaonic religious traditions of their homeland. More than any other pseudographal literature of its time, the Apocalypse of Elijah forcefully and skillfully positions the nascent Christian tradition within its Khemetic context. There is in fact much to warrant a strong relationship between the story of Jesus and the Virgin Mary in the New Testament and the Khemeto-Egyptian myth of Osiris, Horus and Isis. Like the Old Testament redactors, the New Testament writers, much learned in the ancient mysteries, drew on ancient pharaonic mythology to shape the Jesus narratives. For example, as Gerald Massey outlined, when the Egyptian texts speak of "Horus [who] came by water as Ichtus the fish who gave himself for food,"[16] we cannot help but see an antecedent to Christic theology. The Coffin Texts of Egypt's 5th Dynasty, in particular, appear to have served as an important source of inspiration to the New Testament writers. We begin our comparative analysis with Coffin Text Spell 148:

A. The Announcement of the Pregnancy of Isis
209d [After] the blast of a meteorite such that [even] the gods fear
210a Isis awoke pregnant by the seed of her brother Osiris!
210b Thus the woman raised herself abruptly,
210c her heart pleased with the seed of her brother Osiris, ...
212b-c I [Isis] have conceived the form of a god within the ovary as my

---

[14] Ibid.
[15] David Frankfurter (1993) p. 323.
[16] Gerald Massey (1970) *Ancient Egypt (The Light of the World)*, Samuel Weiser: New York, p. 291.

son,
212c-d the foremost of the Ennead, who will rule this land, who will be the heir to Geb,
213a-b who will argue on behalf of his father, [and] who will slay Seth the enemy of his father Osiris.[17]

Like Isis, the Virgin Mary is impregnated with the seed of the son of heaven suddenly. Like the infant Horus, Christ, according to the Book of Revelation, would grow up to slay Seth and his followers.

> 17 ... there shall come a Star out of Jacob, and a Sceptre shall rise out of Israel, and shall smite the corners of Moab, and destroy all the children of Seth.
> (Numbers 24:17)

Because of the potential threat that the divine infant poses, he is relentlessly hounded by his enemies. In the Pyramid Texts, Isis must hide the infant Horus from Seth and his hosts.

C. Atum-Re's Advice to Exercise Discretion
217c-e Then Atum-Re said, 'As you are pregnant, then that which you should conceal, O mistress, is that your pregnancy is [to result in] your giving birth to godhead which was [formerly] the seed of Osiris,
217e-f lest that [very] enemy come who slew his father
217g that he might break the seed within its infancy,
218a [the one] whom [even] The-Great-of-Magic fears.'[18]

Similarly, the Book of Revelation says:

> 3 And there appeared another wonder in heaven; and behold a great red dragon, having seven heads and ten horns, and seven crowns upon his heads.
> 4 And his tail drew the third part of the stars of heaven, and cast them to the earth: and the dragon stood before the woman which was ready to deliver, for to devour her child as soon as it was born.
> 5 And she brought forth a man child, who was to rule all nations with a rod of Iron: and her child was caught up unto God, and to his throne.
> 6 And the woman fled into the wilderness, where she hath a place pre-

---

[17] Robert H. O'Connell (1983) 'The Emergence of Horus (An Analysis of Coffin Text Spell 148)', *Journal of Egyptian Archaeology* 69, pp. 72-73.
[18] Robert H. O'Connell (1983) pp. 73-74.

CHAP. XX: CATASTROPHIST CHRISTOLOGY | 727

> pared of God, that they should feed her there a thousand two-hundred and threescore days.
> (Revelation 12:3-6)

That "dragon" is obviously Typhon. We recognize the role he, as the primeval serpent, has traditionally been assigned in countless myths of antiquity. In addition, we know that there had been exactly "seven" Typhon Seasons before the Book of Revelation was written. So the reference to the Typhonic dragon's "seven heads" & "seven crowns" is most likely a symbol of the number of Typhon Seasons which had occurred prior to the coming of Christ. As the saviour of the world, Jesus-Christ had for his sole mission to ensure the continuation of humanity and the maintaining of divine order by defeating the Typhonian devil, or cosmic serpent.

> 9 And the great dragon was cast out, that old serpent, called the Devil, and Satan, which deceiveth the whole world: he was cast out into the earth, and his angels were cast out with him.
> 10 And I heard a loud voice saying in heaven, Now is come salvation, and strength, and the kingdom of our God ...
> (Revelation 12:9-10)

So, the Kingdom of God is established when the forces of chaos, incarnated in Typhon, are tamed. The important message of the Book of Revelation however is that, although defeated and humiliated, the dragon is never totally eliminated. When he comes, "he hath but a short time" (Rev. 12:12) and he always seeks revenge. Could that "short time" be the infamous 52-year cycle? If we recall, at the end of every Typhon Seasons, when the primeval dragon is at last defeated, great floods cover the earth. Amazingly enough, the Book of Revelation says:

> 13 And when the dragon saw that he was cast unto the earth, he persecuted the woman which brought forth the man child. ...
> 15 And the serpent cast out of his mouth water as a flood after the woman, that he might cause he to be carried away of the flood.
> (Revelation 12:13,15)

The theme of the dragon chasing after the mother of the divine child-saviour — in whose hands he meets his end — is the striking common denominator between Coffin Text Spell 148 and Revelation 12. Mere coincidence? Not likely in my estimation.

Aaboe, A. 'Scientific Astronomy in Antiquity.' In The British Academy (1974) *The Place of Astronomy in the Ancient World (A Joint Symposium of the Royal Society and the British Academy)*, pp. 21-42.
Abdalla, Aly O. A. (1988) 'A Group of Osiris-Cloths of the Twenty-First Dynasty in the Cairo Museum', *Journal of Egyptian Archaeology* 74, pp. 157-164.
Adams, Barbara (1990) 'An Enigmatic Sealing from Abydos', *Eretz-Israel* 21, pp. 1-9.
Adams, William Y. (1968) 'Invasion, Diffusion, Evolution?', *Antiquity* 42, pp. 194-215.
────── (1977) *Nubia: Corridor to Africa*, Princeton University Press: Princeton, NJ.
────── (1985) 'Doubts about the Lost Pharaohs', *Journal of Near Eastern Studies* Vol. 44 - Num. 3, pp. 185-192.
Ahituv, Shmuel (1996) 'Sources for the Study of the Egyptian-Canaanite Border Administration', *Israel Exploration Journal* Vol. 46 - Num. 2, pp. 219-224.
Ahlström, Gösta W. (1990) 'The Bull Figurine from Dhahrat et-Tawileh', *Bulletin of the American Schools of Oriental Research* 280, pp. 77-82.
────── (1993) *The History of Ancient Palestine from the Palaeolithic Period to Alexander's Conquest* — Supplement Series 146, JSOT Press: Sheffield, U.K.
Ahmed, Salah El-Din M. 'Le royaume de Napata.' In *La Nubie (L'archéologie au Soudan)* (1994) Éditions Faton: Dijon, pp. 42-45.
Albright, William F. (1920) 'Menes and Narâm-Sin', *Journal of Egyptian Archaeology* 6, pp. 89-98.
────── (1942) 'A Teacher to a Man of Shechem about 1400 B.C.', *Bulletin of the American Schools of Oriental Research* 86, pp. 28-31.

———— 'Some Remarks on the Archaeological Chronology of Palestine before about 1500 B.C.', In Ehrich, Robert W. (editor) (1965) *Chronologies in Old World Archaeology*, pp. 47-60.
Alcina, José (1978) *L'art pré-colombien*, Éditions d'art Lucien Mazenod: Paris.
Aldred, Cyril 'More Light on the Ramesside Tomb Robberies.' In John Ruffle, G. A. Gaballa and Kenneth A. Kitchen (editors) (1979) *Glimpses of Ancient Egypt (Studies in Honour of H. W. Fairman)*, pp. 92-99.
———— (1980) *Egyptian Art (in the Days of the Pharaohs — 3100-320 BC)*, Thames and Hudson: London.
Alexander, Robert L. (1991) 'Sausga and the Hittite Ivory from Megiddo', *Journal of Near Eastern Studies* Vol. 50 - Num. 3, pp. 161-182.
Aling, Charles F. (1981) *Egypt and Bible History (From Earliest Times to 1000 B.C.)*, Baker House: Grand Rapids, Mich.
Allison, Dale C., Jr. (1993a) *The New Moses (A Matthean Typology)*, Fortress Press: Minneapolis.
———— (1993b) 'What Was the Star that Guided the Magi?', *Bible Review* Vol. 9 - Num. 6, pp. 21-24;63.
Alt, Albrecht (1968) *Essays on Old Testament History and Religion*. Trans. by R. A. Wilson. Anchor Books/Doubleday: Garden City, N.Y.
Altizer, Thomas J. J. (1990) *Genesis and Apocalypse (A Theological Voyage Toward Authentic Christianity)*, Westminster/John Knox Press: Louisville, Kentucky.
Amer, Amin A.M.A. (1985) 'Reflections on the Reign of Ramesses VI', *Journal of Egyptian Archaeology* 71, pp. 66-70.
Amiran, Ruth (1974) 'An Egyptian Jar Fragment with the Name of Narmer from Arad', *Israel Exploration Journal* Vol. 24 - Num. 1, pp. 4-12.
Anderson, Bernhard W. (editor) (1984) *Creation in the Old Testament*, Fortress Press: Philadelphia; SPCK: London.
Andjembe, Léonard (1989) 'Sur la rupture opérée par Cheikh Anta Diop dans l'historiographie négro-africaine', *Présence Africaine* 149-150, pp. 10-19.
Andreyev, Yu. V. 'The World of Crete and Mycenae.' In I. M. Diakonoff (editor) (1991) *Early Antiquity*, pp. 309-327.
Ani, Marimba (Dona Richards) (1979) 'The Ideology of European Dominance', *Présence Africaine* 111, pp. 3-18.
———— (1994)*Yurugu (An African-centered Critique of European Cultural Thought and Behavior)*, Africa World Press: Trenton, NJ.
Anthony, David W. (1995) 'Horses, Wagons & Chariots: Indo-European Languages and Archaeology', *Antiquity* Vol. 69 - Num. 264, pp. 554-564.
Anthony, David W. & Brown, Dorcas R. (1991) 'The Origins of Horseback Riding', *Antiquity* Vol. 65 - Num. 246, pp. 22-38.

Armayor, O. Kimball (1978) 'Did Herodotus Ever Go to Egypt?', *Journal of the American Research Center inEgypt* 15, pp. 59-73.
Arkell, A. J. (1974 [1961]) *A History of the Sudan (From the Earliest Times to 1821)*, Greenwood Press: Westport, Conn.
Armour, Robert A. (1986) *Gods and Myths of Ancient Egypt*, The American University in Cairo Press: Cairo.
Arnold, Philip J., III (1995) 'Ethnicity, Pottery and the Gulf Olmec of Ancient Veracruz, Mexico', *Biblical Archaeologist* Vol. 58 - Num. 4, pp. 191-198.
Artzy, Michal (1987) 'On Boats and Sea Peoples', *Bulletin of the American Schools of Oriental Research* 266, pp. 75-84.
Asante, Molefi Kete (1987) *The Afrocentric Idea*, Temple University Press: Philadelphia.
———— (1988) *Afrocentricity*, Africa World Press: Trenton, NJ.
———— (1990) *Kemet, Afrocentricity and Knowledge*, Africa World Press: Trenton, NJ.
———— (1991) 'Putting Africa at the Center', *Newsweek* 118 (September 23), p. 46.
———— (1992) 'Afrocentric Concepts in African Historiography: A Review Essay', *Research in African Literatures* Vol. 23 - Num. 1, pp. 191-195.
———— 'Early African Cultures: An Afrocentric Perspective.' In Celenko, Theodore (editor) (1996) *Egypt in Africa*, p. 33.
———— 'European Racism Regarding Ancient Egypt.' In ibid, pp. 116-117.
———— (1998) *The Afrocentric Idea*. Revised and expanded edition. Temple University Press: Philadelphia.
Asante, Molefi Kete & Abarry, Abu (editors) (1996) *African Intellectual Heritage: A Book of Sources*, Temple University Press: Philadelphia.
Asante, Molefi Kete & Ravitch, Diane (1991) 'Multiculturalism: An Exchange', *American Scholar* 60 (Spring), pp. 267-276.
Assmann, Jan (1997) *Moses the Egyptian (The Memory of Egypt in Western Monotheism)*, Harvard University Press: Cambridge, Mass.
Aston, D. A. (1989) 'Takeloth II -A king of the "Theban Twenty-Third Dynasty"?', *Journal of Egyptian Archaeology* 75, pp. 139-153.
Astour, Michael C. (1967) *Hellenosemitica (An Ethnic and Cultural Study in West Semitic Impact on Mycenean Greece)*, E. J. Brill: Leiden.
Auld, Graeme (1992) 'BOOK REVIEW: Centuries of Darkness: A Challenge to the Conventional Chronology of Old World Archaeology. P. James *et al.* 1991', *Journal of Theological Studies* Vol. 43 - Num. 1, pp. 141-142.
Aventi, Anthony F. (editor) (1975) *Archaeastronomy in Pre-Columbian America*, University of Texas Press: Austin and London.

Awadalla, Atef (1989) 'Une stèle d'Amenemhat Imy-st-n-imn', *Bulletin de l'Institut Français d'Archéologie Orientale* 89, pp. 25-40.

Baer, Klaus (1973) 'The Libyan and Nubian Kings of Egypt: Notes on the Chronology of Dynasties XII to XXVI', *Journal of Near Eastern Studies* Vol. 32 - Nums. 1-2, pp. 4-5.

Bailey, James R. (1973) *The God-Kings & the Titans (The New World Ascendancy in Ancient Times)*, St. Martin's Press: New York.

Baines, John (1982) 'Interpreting Sinuhe', *Journal of Egyptian Archaeology* 68, pp. 31-44.

———— (1985) *Fecundity Figures (Egyptian Personification and the Iconology of a Genre)*, Aris & Phillips: Warminster, U.K.; Bolchazy Carducci Publishers: Chicago, Ill.

———— (1986) 'The Stela of Emhab: Innovation, Tradition, Hierarchy', *Journal of Egyptian Archaeology* 72, pp. 41-53.

———— (1990a) 'Trône et Dieu: Aspects du symbolisme royal et divin des temps archaiques', *Bulletin de la Société Française d'Égyptologie* 118, pp. 5-32.

———— (1990b) 'Restricted Knowledge, Hierarchy, and Decorum: Modern Perceptions and Ancient Institutions', *Journal of the American Research Center in Egypt* 27, pp. 1-23.

———— (1991a) 'Was Civilization Made in Africa?', *New York Times Book Review* (August 11), pp. 12-13.

———— (1991b) 'Egyptian Myth and Discourse: Myth, Gods, and the Early Written and Iconographic Record', *Journal of Near Eastern Studies* Vol. 50 - Num. 2, pp. 81-105.

———— 'The Aims and Methods of Black Athena.' In Lefkowitz, Mary R. & Rogers, Guy M. (editors) (1996) *Black Athena Revisited*, pp. 27-48.

Baines, John and Malek, Jaromir (1980) *Atlas of Ancient Egypt*, Facts on File: New York.

John Baines Baines, T.G.H. James, Anthony Leahy & A. F. Shore (editors) (1988) *Pyramid Studies and other Essays — Presented to I.E.S. Edwards*, Egypt Exploration Society: London.

Baldick, Julian (1998) *Black God (The Afroasiatic Roots of the Jewish, Christian, and Muslim Religions)*, Syracuse University Press: Syracuse, NY.

Barbotin, Chr. & Clère, J.-J. (1991) ' L'inscription de Sésostris Ier à Tôd', *Bulletin de l'Institut Français d'Archéologie Orientale* 91, pp. 1-32.

Barkay, Gabriel (1996) 'A Late Bronze Age Egyptian Temple in Jerusalem?', *Israel Exploration Journal* Vol.46 - Num.1, pp. 23-43.

Barker, Margaret (1992) *The Great Angel (A Study of Israel's Second God)*, Westminster /John Knox Press: Louisville, Kentucky.

Barrett, C. K. (editor) (1989) *The New Testament Background (Writings from Ancient Greece and the Roman Empire that Illuminate Christian Origins)*. Revised edition. HarperCollins: New York.

Bartlett, John R. (1984) *Jews in the Hellenistic World (Josephus, Aristea, the Sibylline Oracles, Eupolrmus)*. Commentaries on Writings of the Jewish and Christian World 200 BC to AD 200 — Vol. II. Cambridge University Press: Cambridge, Mass.

Barton, John (1997) *Reading the Old Testament (Method in Biblical Study)*, Westminster John Knox Press: Louisville, Kentucky.

Barzun, Jacques 'History, Popular and Unpopular.' In Strayer, Joseph R. (editor) (1943) *The Interpretation of History*, pp. 27-57.

Bauckham, Richard (1993) *The Climax of Prophecy (Studies on the Book of Revelation)*, T&T Clark: Edinburgh, U.K.

——— (1993) *The Theology of the Book of Revelation*, Cambridge University Press: Cambridge, Mass.

Baud, Michel & Dobrev, Vassil (1995) 'De nouvelles annales de l'Ancien Empire égyptien (Une «Pierre de Palerme» pour la VIe dynastie)', *Bulletin de l'Institut Français d'Archéologie Orientale* 95, pp. 23-63.

Bauer, Henry H. (1984) *Beyond Velikovsky (The History of a Public Controversy)*, University of Illinois Press: Urbana and Chicago.

——— (1988) 'L'Affaire Velikovsky', *La Recherche* 205, pp. 1448-1455.

Baumgartel, Elise J. (1975) 'Some Remarks on the Origins of the Titles of the Archaic Egyptian Kings', *Journal of Egyptian Archaeology* 61, pp. 28-32.

Bauval, Robert & Gilbert, Adrian (1994) *The Orion Mystery (Unlocking the Secrets of the Pyramids)*, Doubleday Canada: Toronto.

Bawer, Bruce (1998) 'Public Intellectuals: an Endangered Species?' *Chronicle of Higher Education* (April 24), p. A72.

Beaux, Nathalie (1994) 'La douat dans les Textes des Pyramides (Espace et temps de gestation)', *Bulletin de l'Institut Français d'Archéologie Orientale* 94, pp. 1-6.

Begg, Ean (1985) *The Cult of the Black Virgin*, Arkana: London.

Beit-Arieh, Itzhaq (1996) 'Edomite Advances Into Judah', *Biblical Archaeology Review* Vol. 22 - Num. 6, pp. 28-36.

Bell, Barbara (1971) 'The Dark Ages in Ancient History', *American Journal of Archaeology* 75, pp. 1-26.

Bell, H. I. (1944) 'Evidences of Christianity in Egypt During the Roman Period', *Harvard Theological Review* Vol. 37 — Num. 2, pp. 185-208.

Ben-Jochannan, Yosef A. A. (1970) *African Origins of Major Western Religions*, Alkebu-lan Books: New York.

——— (1972) *Black Man of the Nile and his Family (African Foundations of Civilization and Thought)*, Alkebu-lan Books: New York.

——— (1988) *Africa: Mother of Western Civilization*, Black Classic Press: Baltimore, MD.

Ben-Sasson, H. H. (editor) (1976) *A History of the Jewish People*, Harvard University Press: Cambridge, Mass.

Ben-Tor, Amnon (1991) 'New Light on the Relations Between Egypt and Southern Palestine During the Early Bronze Age', *Bulletin of the American Schools of Oriental Research* 281, pp. 3-10.

——— (editor) (1992) *The Archaeology of Ancient Israel*. Trans. by R. Greenberg. Yale University Press: New Haven and London; The Open University: Israel.

Ben-Tor, Daphna (1994) 'The Historical Implications of Middle Kingdom Scarabs Found in Palestine Bearing Private Names and Titles of Officials', *Bulletin of the American Schools of Oriental Research* 294, pp. 7-22.

Benson, Elizabeth P. & de la Fuente, Beatriz (editors) (1996) *Olmec Art of Ancient Mexico*, National Gallery of Art: Washington.

Bérard, Jean (1952) 'Les derniers Hyksôs et la légende d'Io', *Bulletin de la Société Française d'Égyptologie* 10, pp. 41-43.

Bérard, Victor (1927) *Les phéniciens et l'Odyssée*. Vols. I-II. Armand Colin: Paris.

Berkeley, Heather (1976) *The Velikovsky Controversy (The Capering Comet and Minds in Collision)*. M.A. Thesis: University of Toronto.

Berlandini, Jocelyne (1983) 'La déesse bucéphale: une iconographie particulière de l'Hathor memphite', *Bulletin de l'Institut Français d'Archéologie Orientale* 83, pp. 33-49.

——— (1995) 'Ptah-demiurge et l'exaltation du Ciel', *Revue d'Égyptologie* 46, pp. 9-41.

Bernal, Ignacio (1969) *The Olmec World*. Trans. by Doris Heyden and Fernando Horcasitas. University of California Press: Berkeley and Los Angeles.

Bernal, Martin G. 'Black Athena: The African and Levantine Roots of Greece.' In Van Sertima, Ivan (editor) (1985) *African Presence in Early Europe*, pp. 66-82.

——— (1986) 'Black Athena Denied: The Tyranny of Germany over Greece and the Rejection of the Afroasiatic Roots of Europe 1780-1980', *Comparative Criticism* 8, pp. 3-69.

——— (1987a) *Black Athena (The Afroasiatic Roots of Classical Civilization) — Volume I: The Fabrication of Ancient Greece 1785-1985*, Vintage: London.

——— (1987b) 'On the Transmission of the Alphabet to the Aegean Before 1400 BC', *Bulletin of the American Schools of Oriental Research* 267, pp. 1-19.
——— 'First Land then Sea: Thoughts about the Social Formation of the Mediterranean and Greece.' In E. Genovese & L. Hochberg (editors) (1987c) *Geography in Historical Perspectives*, Blackwell: New York, pp. 50-55.
——— (1989a) 'Black Athena and the APA', *Arethusa* Special Fall Issue, pp. 17-38.
——— (1989b) 'Response to Professor Snowden', *Arethusa* Special Fall Issue, pp. 30-32.
——— 'Classics in Crisis: An Outsider's View In.' In Phyllis Culham, Lowell Edmunds & Alden Smith (editors) (1989) *Classics: A Discipline and Profession in Crisis*, pp. 67-74.
——— (1990a) *Cadmean Letters (The Transmission of the Alphabet to the Aegean and Further West before 1400 B.C.)*, Eisenbrauns: Winona Lake, Indiana.
——— (1990b) 'Response to Critical Reviews of Black Athena: The Afro-asiatic Roots of Classical Civilization. Volume I: The Fabrication of Ancient Greece 1785-1985', *Journal of Mediterranean Archaeology* Vol. 3 - Num. 1, pp. 111-137.
——— (1991) *Black Athena (The Afroasiatic Roots of Classical Civilization) — Volume II: The Archaeological and Documentary Evidence*, Rutgers University Press: New Brunswick, NJ.
——— (1992a) 'Response to Edith Hall', *Arethusa* 25, pp. 203-214.
——— (1992b) 'The Case for Massive Egyptian Influence in the Aegean', *Archaeology* Vol. 45 - Num. 5, pp. 53-55, 82-86.
——— (1992c) 'Animadversions on the Origins of Western Science', *Isis* Vol. 83 - Num. 4, pp. 596-607.
——— (1993a) 'Response to S. O. Y. Keita', *Arethusa* 26, pp. 315-319.
——— (1993b) 'Response', *Journal of Women's History* Vol. 4 - Num. 3, pp. 119-135.
——— (1995) 'Race, Class, and Gender in the Formation of the Aryan Model of Greek Origins', *South Atlantic Quarterly* Vol. 94 - Num. 4, pp. 987-1008.
——— (1998) 'On "Robbing Native American Cultures"', *Current Anthropology* Vol. 39 - Num. 4, pp. 512-514.
Bernal, Martin & Lefkowitz, Mary R. (1992) 'Correspondance: Martin Bernal Responds to Afrocentric "Myths": An Exchange', *New Republic* (March 9), pp. 4-5.
Bernand, André (1994) *Leçon de civilisation*, Fayard: Paris.

Best, J. G. P. & Yadin, Y. (1973) *The Arrival of the Greeks*. Henri Frankfort Foundation, Hakkert: Amsterdam.

Betancourt, Philip 'Relations Between the Aegean and the Hyksos at the End of the Middle Bronze Age.' In Oren, Eliezer (editor) (1997) *The Hyksos: New Historical and Archaeological Perspectives*, pp. 429-432.

Bevan, Edwyn (1927) *A History of Egypt Under the Ptolemaic Dynasty*, Methuen: London.

Biallas, Leonard J. (1986) *Myths (Gods, Heroes, and Saviors)*, Twenty-Third Publications: Mystic, Conn.

Bianchi, Robert Steven (editor) (1995) *Who's Who in Egyptian Mythology*. Second revised edition. The Scarecrow Press: Metuchen, NJ and London.

───────── Foreword to Rohl, David M. (1995) *A Test of Time — Vol. I: The Bible (From Myth to History)*, pp. i-iii.

Biblical Archaeology Review (1985) 'BARlines: Schaeffer's View of Velikovsky', Vol. 11 - Num. 1, p. 8.

Bienkowski, Piotr (1986) *Jericho in the Late Bronze Age*, Warminster, U.K.

───────── (1989) 'The Division of Middle Bronze IIB-C in Palestine', *Levant* 21, pp. 169-179.

───────── (1990) 'Jericho was Destroyed in the Middle Bronze Age, Not the Late Bronze Age', *Biblical Archaeology Review* Vol. 16 - Num. 5, pp. 45-46, 69.

Bierling, Neal (1992) *Giving Goliath His Due (New Archaeological Light on the Philistines)*, Baker Books: Grand Rapids, Mich.

Bietak, Manfred (1979a) 'The Present State of Egyptian Archaeology', *Journal of Egyptian Archaeology* 65, pp. 156-160.

───────── (1979b) 'Avaris and Piramesse: Archaeological Exploration in the Eastern Nile Delta', *Proceedings of the British Academy* 65, pp. 225-290.

───────── (1984) 'Problems of Middle Bronze Age Chronology: New Evidence from Egypt', *American Journal of Archaeology* Vol. 88 - Num. 4, pp. 471-485.

───────── (1988) 'Contra Bimson, Bietak Says Late Bronze Age Cannot Begin as Late as 1400 B.C.', *Biblical Archaeology Review* Vol. 14 - Num. 4, pp. 54-55.

───────── (1990) 'The Concept of Eternity in Ancient Egypt and the Bronze Age World: An Archaeological Approach', *Eretz-Israel* 21, pp. 10-17.

───────── (1991) 'Egypt and Canaan During the Middle Bronze Age', *Bulletin of the American Schools of Oriental Research* 281, pp. 27-72.

───────── (1992) 'Minoan Wall-Paintings Unearthed at Ancient Avaris.' *Egyptian Archaeology* 2, pp. 26-28.

――― 'The Sea Peoples and the End of the Egyptian Administration in Canaan.' In Biran, A. & Aviram, J. (editors) (1993) *Biblical Archaeology Today, 1990 (Proceedings of the Second International Congress on Biblical Archaeology — Jerusalem, June-July 1990)*, pp. 292-306.

――― 'Connections Between Egypt and the Minoan World: New Results from Tell el-Dab'a/Avaris.' In Davies, W. V. & Schofield, Louise (editors) (1995) *Egypt, the Aegean and the Levant (Interconnections in the Second Millennium BC)*, pp. 19-28.

――― (1996) *Avaris: The Capital of the Hyksos (Recent Excavations at Tell el-Dab'a)*, British Museum Press: London.

――― 'The Center of Hyksos Rule: Avaris (Tell el-Dab'a).' In Oren, Eliezer D. (editor) (1997) *The Hyksos: New Historical and Archaeological Perspectives*, pp. 87-139.

Bietak, Manfred & Marinatos, Nanno (1995) 'The Minoan Wall Paintings from Avaris', *Ägypten und Levante* 5, pp. 49-71.

Bikai, Patricia Maynor (1990) 'Black Athena and the Phoenicians', *Journal of Mediterranean Archaeology* Vol. 3 - Num. 1, pp. 67-75.

Bilger, Burkard (1997) 'The Last Black Classicist', *The Sciences* Vol. 37 - Num. 2, pp. 16-19.

Bimson, John J. (1978) *Redating the Exodus and Conquest*, JSOT: Sheffield, U.K.

――― (1988) 'A Reply to Baruch Halpern's "Radical Exodus Redating Fatally Flawed," in BAR, November/December 1987', *Biblical Archaeology Review* Vol. 14 - Num. 4, pp. 52-55.

Bimson, John J. & Livingston, David (1987) 'Redating the Exodus', *Biblical Archaeology Review* Vol. 13 - Num. 5, pp. 40-53, 66-68.

Bilolo, Mubabinge (1989) 'La civilisation pharaonique était-elle KAME/KMT/NÈGRE? (L'état de la question en égyptologie avant et après «Nations Nègres et Culture»', *Présence Africaine* 149-150, pp. 68-100.

Biran, A. & Aviram, J. (editors) (1993) *Biblical Archaeology Today, 1990 (Proceedings of the Second International Congress on Biblical Archaeology — Jerusalem, June-July 1990)*, Israel Exploration Society/Israel Academy of Science and Humanities: Jerusalem.

Blacker, Carmen & Loewe, Michael (editors) (1975) *Ancient Cosmologies*, George Allen & Unwin: London.

Blackman, Aylward Manley (1923) *Luxor & its Temples*, A&C Black : London.

Blakey, Michael L. 'Race, Nationalism, and the Afrocentric Past.' Schmidt, Peter R. & Patterson, Thomas C. (editors) (1995) *Making Alternative Histories (The Practice of Archaeology and History in Non-Western Settings)*, pp. 213-228.

Bledstein, Burton J. (1976) *The Culture of Professionalism (The Middle Class and the Development of Higher Education in America)*, W. W. Norton: New York.
Blegen, Carl W. (1963) *Troy and the Trojans*, Thames and Hudson: London.
Bodine, Walter R. 'Sumerians.' In Alfred J. Hoerth, Gerald L. Mattingly & Edwin M. Yamauchi (editors) (1994) *Peoples of the Old Testament World*, pp. 19-42.
Ann Bomann & Robert Young (1994) 'Preliminary Survey in the Wadi Abu Had, Eastern Desert, 1992', *Journal of Egyptian Archaeology* 80, pp. 23-44.
Bonnet, Charles (1992) 'Excavations at the Nubian Royal Town of Kerma: 1975-91', *Antiquity* Vol. 66 - Num. 252, pp. 611-625.
———— (1994) 'Palais et temples dans la topographie urbaine: Les exemples du bassin de Kerma', *Revue d'Égyptologie* 45, pp. 41-48.
Bonvin, Jacques (1988) *Vierges Noires (La réponse vient de la terre)*, Dervy-Livres: Paris.
Boone, Elizabeth Hill (1994) *The Aztec World*, St. Remy Press: Montréal; Smithsonian Books: Washington, DC.
Borg, Marcus J. (1994) *Jesus in Contemporary Scholarship*, Trinity Press International: Valley Forge, Penn.
Borgen, Peder (1996) *Early Christianity and Hellenistic Judaism*, T&T Clark: Edinburgh, U.K.
Borghouts, J. F. (1973) 'The Evil Eye of Apopis', *Journal of Egyptian Archaeology* 59, pp. 114-150.
Bork, Paul F. (1978) *The World of Moses*, Southern Pub. Association: Nashville, Tenn.
Bottéro, Jean (1994) *Babylone et la Bible* — Entretiens avec Hélène Monsacré, Les Belles Lettres: Paris.
Jean Bottéro, Clarisse Herrenschmidt, Jean-Pierre Vernant (1996) *L'Orient ancient et nous (L'Écriture, la raison, les dieux)*, Albin Michel: Paris.
Bovon, François (1993) *Révélations et écritures (Nouveau Testament et littérature apocryphe chrétienne)* — Recueil d'articles, Éditions Labor et Fidels: Genève.
Bowman, Alan K. (1986) *Egypt after the Pharaohs (332 BC - AD 642 from Alexander to the Arab Conquest)*, British Museum Publications: London.
Brandl, Baruch (1996a) 'A "Hyksos" Scarab from a Burial Cave on Mt. Canaan, Zefat (Wadi Hamra)', *'Atiqot 29*, pp. 1-5.
———— (1996b) 'A "Hyksos" Scarab and a Cylinder Seal from a Burial Cave at Moza 'Illit', *'Atiqot 29*, pp. 7-14.
Branigan, Keith (1988) *Pre-Palatial (The Fondations of Palatial Crete: A Survey of Crete in the Early Bronze Age)*. Second updated edition. Adolf M. Hakkert: Amsterdam.

---------- 'Some Observations on State Formation in Crete.' In French, E. B. & Wardle, K. A. (editors) (1988) *Problems in Greek Prehistory (Papers Presented at the Centenary Conference of the British School of Archaeology at Athens, Manchester – April 1986)*, pp. 63-68.

Breasted, James H. (1959 [1902]) *Development of Religion and Thought in Ancient Egypt*, Harper & Row: New York.

---------- (1962[1906])*Ancient Records of Egypt: Historical Documents from the Earliest Times*. Vols. I-V. Russell & Russell: New York.

Bremmer, Jan (editor) (1987) *Interpretation of Greek Mythology*, Barnes & Nobles Books: Totowa, NJ.

Bricault, Laurent & Pezin, Michel (1993) 'Une nouvelle «triade» pathyrite', *Bulletin de l'Institut Français d'Archéologie Orientale* 93, pp. 67-77.

Brier, B. & Bennett, M.V.L. (1979) 'Autopsies on Fish Mummies (Possible Identification of the Classical Phagrus)', *Journal of Egyptian Archaeology* 65, pp. 128-133.

Brissaud, Philippe 'Tanis (Tell San El-Hagar).' In Westenholz, Joan Goodnick (editor) (1996) *Royal Cities of the Biblical World*, pp. 113-149.

The British Academy (1974) *The Place of Astronomy in the Ancient World (A Joint Symposium of the Royal Society and the British Academy)*, Oxford University Press: London.

Brodie, Thomas L. (1993) *The Quest for the Origin of John's Gospel (A Source-Oriented Appoach)*, Oxford University Press: New York and Oxford.

Broodbank, Cyprian & Strasser, Thomas F. (1991) 'Migrant Farmers and the Neolithic Colonization of Crete', *Antiquity* Vol. 65 - Num. 247, pp. 233-245.

Browder, Anthony T. (1992) *Nile Valley Contributions to Civilization*, IKG: Washington, DC.

Brown, Donald E. (1988) *Hierarchy, History, and Human Nature (The Social Origins of Historical Consciousness)*, University of Arizona Press: Tucson.

Brown, Raymond E. (1993) *The Birth of the Messiah (A Commentary on the Infancy Narratives in the Gospels of Matthew and Luke)*, Doubleday: New York.

---------- (1994) *The Death of the Messiah (A Commentary on the Passion Narratives in the Four Gospels)*. Vols. I-II. Anchor Bible Reference Library. Doubleday: New York.

Raymond E. Brown, Karl P. Donfried, Joseph A. Fitzmyer & John Reumann (editors) (1978) *Mary in the New Testament (A Collaborative Assessment by Protestant and Roman Catholic Scholars)*, Paulist Press: New York and Mahwah.

Brug, John Frederick (1986) *A Literary and Archeological Study of the Philistines*. Vols. I-II. University Microfilms International: Ann Arbor, Mich.

Brundage, Burr Cartwright (1979) *The Fifth Sun (Aztec Gods, Aztec World)*, University of Texas Press: Austin and London.

Brunson, James 'The African Presence in the Ancient Mediterranean Isles and Mainland Greece.' In Van Sertima, Ivan (editor) (1985) *African Presence in Early Europe*, pp. 36-65.

Bruwier, Marie-Cécile (1989) 'Deux fragments d'une statue colossale de reine ptolemaiques à Mariemont', *Chronique d'Égypte* 64, pp. 25-43.

Bryce, Trevor R. (1989) 'Some Observations on the Chronology of Suppiluliuma's Reign', *Anatolian Studies* 39, pp. 19-30.

———— (1990) 'The Death of Niphururiya and its Aftermath', *Journal of Egyptian Archaeology* 76, pp. 97-106.

Budge, Wallis E. A. (1894) *Saint Michael the Archangel (Three Encomiums by Theodosius - Archbishop of Alexandria, Severus - Patriarch of Antioch, and Eustathius – Bishop of Trake)*, Kegan Paul, Trench, Trübner: London.

———— (1904) *The Gods of the Egyptians (or Studies in Egyptian Mythology)*. Vols. I-II. Methuen: London.

———— (1910)*The Nile (Notes for Travellers in Egypt and in the Egyptian Sudan)*. Eleventh edition. Thos. Cook & Son: London and Cairo.

———— (1911) *Osiris and the Egyptian Resurection*. Vols. I-II. The Medici Society: London.

———— (1928) *A History of Ethiopia: Nubia & Abyssinia (According to the Hieroglyphic Inscriptions of Egypt and Nubia, and the Ethiopian Chronicles)*. Vol. I. Methuen: London.

———— (1933) *Legends of Our Lady Mary the Perpetual Virgin and Her Mother Hannâ*. Trans. from the Ethiopic manuscripts collected by King Theodore at Makdalâ and now in the British Museum. Oxford University Press: London.

———— (1934) *From Fetish to God in Ancient Egypt*, Oxford University Press: London.

———— (1961) *Osiris (The Egyptian Religion of Resurrection)*, University Books: New Hyde Park, NY.

———— (1976 [1907]) *The Egyptian Sudan (Its History and Monuments)*. Vols. I-II, AMS Press: New York.

Bullchild, Percy (1985) *The Sun Came Down*, HarperCollins: New York.

Burkert, Walter (1992) *The Orientalizing Revolution (Near Eastern Influence on Greek Culture in the Early Archaic Age)*, Harvard University Press: Cambridge, Mass.

Burl, Aubrey (1981) *Rites of the Gods*, J. M. Dent & Sons: London.
Burland, C. A. (1972) *Montezuma (Lord of the Aztecs)*, Weidenfeld and Nicolson: London.
Burstein, Stanley M. (1981) 'Axum and the Fall of Meroe', *Journal of the American Research Center inEgypt* 15, pp. 47-49.
Burn, Jerome (1978) 'Velikovsky Spawns More Controversy', *New Scientist* Vol. 78 - Num. 1099, p. 134.
Buswell, James O., III (1964) *Slavery, Segregation and Scripture*, William B. Eerdmans: Grand Rapids, Mich.
Butterfield, Herbert (1958) *The Origins of Modern Science: 1300-1800*, G. Bell and Sons: London.
Calame, Claude (1996) *Thésée et l'imaginaire athénien (Légende et culte en Grèce antique)*. Deuxième édition revue et corrigée. Éditions Payot Lausanne: Paris.
Caldwell, Richard (1989) *The Origin of the Gods (A Psychoanalytic Study of Greek Theogonic Myth)*, Oxford University Press: New York and Oxford.
Campbell, John Kerr (1898) *Bible Hieroglyphics — or The Gospel in Similitudes*, S.W. Patridge: London.
Campbell, Joseph (1962) *The Masks of God: Oriental Mythology*, Viking Press: New York.
Carmichael, Joel (1995) *The Unriddling of Christian Origins (A Secular Account)*, Prometheus Books: Amherst, NY.
Carr, David M. (1996) *Reading the Fractures of Genesis (Historical and Literary Approaches)*, Westminster / John Knox Press: Louisville, Kentucky.
Carrasco, David (1982) *Quetzalcoatl and the Irony of Empire (Myths and Prophecies in the Aztec Tradition)*, University of Chicago Press: Chicago and London.
——— (editor) (1991) *To Change Place (Aztec Ceremonial Landscapes)*, University Press of Colorado: Niwot, Col.
Carruthers, Jacob H. (1986) see Karenga, Maulana.
——— (1992) 'OUTSIDE ACADEMIA: Bernal's Critique of Black Champions of Ancient Egypt', *Journal of Black Studies* Vol. 22 - Num. 4, pp. 459-476.
——— (1995) *MDW NTR—Divine Speech (A Historical Reflection of African Deep Thought from the Time of the Pharaohs to the Present)*, Karnak House: London; Red Sea Press: Lawrenceville, NJ.
Carson, D. A. & Woodbridge, John D. (editors) (1983) *Scripture and Truth*, Zondervan: Grand Rapids, Mich.

Case, Frederick Ivor & Case, Marcel Ivor (1989) 'L'héritage égyptien: Perspectives culturelles de l'œvre de Cheikh Anta Diop', *Présence Africaine* 149-150, pp. 101-109.
Cassagnes-Brouquet, Sophie (1990) *Vierges Noires (Regard et fascination)*, Éditions du Rouergue: Rodez, France.
Catchpole, David R. (1993) *The Quest for Q*, T&T Clark: Edinburgh, U.K.
Cauville, Sylvie (1983) *La théologie d'Osiris à Edfou*, Institut Français d'Archéologie Orientale: Caire.
——— (1987) *Essai sur la théologie du temple d'Horus à Edfou*, Institut Français d'Archéologie Orientale: Caire.
——— (1988) 'Les mystères d'Osiris à Dendera (Interprétation des chapelles osiriennes)', *Bulletin de la Société Française d'Égyptologie* 112, pp. 23-35.
——— (1989) 'La chapelle de Thot-Ibis à Dendera édifiée sous Ptolémée Ier par Hor, scribe d'Amon-Rê', *Bulletin de l'Institut Français d'Archéologie Orientale* 89, pp. 43-66.
——— (1990) 'Les inscriptions dédicatoires du temple d'Hathor à Dendera', *Bulletin de l'Institut Français d'Archéologie Orientale* 90, pp. 83-114.
——— (1992) 'Le temple d'Isis à Dendera', *Bulletin de la Société Française d'Égyptologie* 123, pp. 31-43.
——— (1993) 'La chapelle de la barque à Dendera', *Bulletin de l'Institut Français d'Archéologie Orientale* 93, pp. 79-172.
Cauville, Sylvie & Gasse, Annie (1988) 'Fouilles de Dendera: Premiers résultats', *Bulletin de l'Institut Français d'Archéologie Orientale* 88, pp. 25-32.
Cawkwell, G. L. (1992) 'Early Colonization', *Classical Quarterly* Vol. 42 - Num. 2, pp. 289-303.
Cazelles, Henri (1991) 'Historiographies bibliques et prébibliques', *Revue Biblique* T. 98 - 4, pp. 481-512.
Celenko, Theodore (editor) (1996) *Egypt in Africa*, Indianapolis Museum of Art: Indianapolis, Ind.
Centre Franco-Égyptien d'Études des Temples de Karnak (1970) *Karnak (1968-1969)*, Librairie Orientaliste Paul Geuthner: Paris.
——— (1975) *Karnak V (1970-1972)*, IFAO: Cairo.
——— (1980) *Karnak VI (1973-1977)*, IFAO : Cairo.
——— (1982) *Karnak VII (1978-1981)*, Éditions Recherche sur les Civilisations: Paris.
Cerny, Jaroslav (1946) 'Studies in the Chronology of the Twenty-First Dynasty', *Journal of Egyptian Archaeology* 32, pp. 24-30.

Chadwick, John (1976) *The Mycenaean World*, Cambridge University Press: Cambridge, Mass.
Chandler, Wayne B. 'Trait-Influences in Meso-America: The African-Asian Connection.' In Van Sertima, Ivan (editor) (1987) *African Presence in Early America*, pp. 274-334.
——— 'Of Gods and Men: Egypt's Old Kingdom.' In Van Sertima, Ivan (editor) (1989) *Egypt Revisited*, pp. 117-182.
Chang, Kwang-Chih 'Relative Chronologies of China to the End of Chou.' In Ehrich, Robert W. (editor) (1965) *Chronologies in Old World Archaeology*, pp. 503-526.
——— (1971) *The Archaeology of Ancient China*. Revised and enlarged edition. Yale University Press: New Haven and London.
——— (1980) *Shang Civilization*, Yale University Press: New Haven and London.
——— 'Sandai Archaeology and the Formation of States in Ancient China: Processual Aspects of the Origins of Chinese Civilization.' In Keightley, David N. (editor) (1983) *The Origins of Chinese Civilization*, pp. 495-521.
Charlesworth, James H. (editor) (1994) *The Dead Sea Scrolls (Hebrew, Aramaic, and Greek Texts with English Translations)* —Vol.1 (Rule of the Community and Related Documents). With F. M. Cross, J. Milgrom, E. Qimron, L. H. Schiffman, L. T. Stuckenbruck and R. E. Whitaker. J. C. B. Morh (Paul Siebeck): Tübinger; Westminster /John Knox Press: Louisville.
——— (editor) (1992) *Jesus and the Dead Sea Scrolls*, Doubleday: New York.
——— (editor) (1992) *The Messiah (Developments in Earliest Judaism and Christianity)*. The First Princeton Symposium on Judaism and Christian Origins. Fortress Press: Minneapolis.
Chavalas, Mark (1996) 'Terqa and the Kingdom of Khana', *Biblical Archaeologist* Vol. 59 - Num. 2, pp. 90-101.
Ching, Julia (1993) *Chinese Religion*, Orbis Books: Maryknoll, NY.
Clark, Daima M. 'Similarities Between Egyptian and Dogon Perceptions of Man, God and Nature.' In Karenga, Maulana & Carruthers, Jacob H. (editors) (1986) *Kemet and the African Worldview*, pp. 119-130.
Clarke, John Henrik (1971) 'The Impact of the African on the New World: A Reappraisal', *Présence Africaine* 79, pp. 3-16.

———— (1976) '"The Cultural Unity of Negro Africa": A Reappraisal (Cheikh Anta Diop Opens Another Door to African History)', *Présence Africaine* 97, pp. 148-164.

———— Introduction to Diop, Cheikh Anta (1978 [1959]) *The Cultural Unity of Black Africa (The Domains of Patriarchy and Matriarchy in Classical Antiquity)*, pp. i-xv.

———— (1979) 'African-American Historians and the Reclaiming of African History', *Présence Africaine* 110, pp. 29-48.

———— (1981) 'African Culture as the Basis of World Culture', *Présence Africaine* 117-118, pp. 123-129.

———— (1984) 'Ancient Civilizations of Africa: The Missing Pages in World History', *Présence Africaine* 130, pp. 148-158.

———— (1988) 'Pan-Africanism: A Brief History of An Idea in the African World', *Présence Africaine* 145, pp. 26-56.

———— (1989) 'The Historical Legacy of Cheikh Anta Diop: His Contributions to a New Concept of African History', *Présence Africaine* 149-150, pp. 110-120.

———— (1991) *Africans at the Crossroads (Notes for an African World Revolution)*, Africa World Press: Trenton, NJ.

———— Introduction to Ani, Marimba (1994) *Yurugu (An African-centered Critique of European Cultural Thought and Behavior)*, pp. xv-xvii.

Clayton, Peter A. (1993) 'Nubia: A Drowned Land and its Re-emerging Civilization', *Minerva* Vol. 4 - Num. 1, pp. 26-29.

———— (1994) *Chronicle of the Pharaohs (The Reign-by-Reign Record of the Rulers and Dynasties of Ancient Egypt)*, Thames and Hudson: London.

Clegg, Legrand H., II 'The First Americans.' In Van Sertima, Ivan (editor) (1987) *African Presence in Early America*, pp. 144-165.

———— 'Black Rulers of the Golden Age.' In Van Sertima, Ivan (editor) (1988) *Great Black Leaders: Ancient and Modern*, pp. 239-260 (or pp. 144-165).

Clendinnen, Inga (1991) *Aztecs (An Interpretation)*, Cambridge University Press: Cambridge, U.K.

Cline, Eric H. (1991) 'Hittite Objects in the Bronze Age Aegean', *Anatolian Studies* 41, pp. 133-143.

———— (1996) 'BOOK REVIEW: Black Athena Revisited. M. R. Lefkowitz & G. M. Rogers (editors) (1996)', *American Journal of Archaeology* Vol. 100 - Num. 4, pp. 781-782.

Coe, Michael D. (1994 [1962]) *Mexico: From the Olmecs to the Aztecs*, Thames and Hudson: London.

Michael D. Coe, Richard A. Diehl & Minze Stuiver (1967) 'Olmec Civilization, Vera Cruz, Mexico: Dating the San Lorenzo Phaze', *Science* 155, pp. 1399-1401.

Coe, Michael D. & Diehl, Richard A. (1980) *In the Land of the Olmecs: Archaeology of San Lorenzo Tenochtitlan*. Vols. I-II. University of Texas Press: Austin, TX.
Cohane, John Philip (1969) *The Key*, Crown: New York.
Cohen, Kenneth J. (1994) 'King Saul: A Bungler from the Beginning', *Bible Review* Vol. 10 - Num. 5, pp. 34-39; 56.
Coleman, John E. (1992) 'Did Egypt Shape the Glory that Was Greece? (The Case Against Bernal), *Archaeology* Vol. 45 - Num. 5, pp. 48-52; 77-81.
Collier, Sandra (1993) 'The Khepresh Crown of Pharaoh', *UFAHAMU* Vol. 21- Nums. 1& 2, pp. 137-151.
Collins, John J. (1993) 'A Pre-Christian Son of God Among the Dead Sea Scrolls', *Bible Review* Vol. 9 - Num. 3, pp. 34-38.
────── (1993) 'The suffering Servant at Qumran?', *Bible Review* Vol. 9 - Num. 6, pp. 25-27, 63.
Collins, John J. (1995) *The Scepter and the Star (The Messiah of the Dead Sea Scrolls and Other Ancient Literature)*, Doubleday: New York.
Comfort, Philip Wesley (1992) *The Quest for the Original Text of the New Testament*, Baker Books: Grand Rapids, Mich.
Coogan, Michael D. (1995) '10 Great Finds', *Biblical Archaeology Review* Vol. 21 - Num. 3, pp. 36-47.
Cook, Edward M. (1994) 'On the Linguistic Dating of the Phoenician Ahiram Inscription (KAI 1)', *Journal of Near Eastern Studies* Vol. 53 - Num.1, pp. 33-36.
Cook, Erwin F. (1995) *The Odyssey in Athens (Myths of Cultural Origins)*, Cornell University Press: Ithaca and London.
Cook, Stephen L. (1995) *Prophecy & Apocalypticism (The Postexilic Social Setting)*, Fortress Press: Minneapolis.
Cooper, Jerrold S. & Schwartz, Glenn M. (editors) (1996) *The Study of the Ancient Near East in the Twenty-First Century*, Eisenbrauns: Winona Lake, Ind.
Cornevin, Marianne (1993) *Archéologie africaine (À la lumière des découvertes récentes)*, Maisonneuve et Larose: Paris.
────── (1998) *Secrets du continent Noir révélés par l'archéologie*, Maisonneuve et Larose: Paris.
Corrasco, David (1982) *Quetzalcoatl and the Irony of Empire (Myths and Prophecies in the Aztec Tradition)*, University of Chicago Press: Chicago and London.
Cottrell, Leonard (1965) *The Land of Shinar*, Souvenir Press: London.
Couroyer, L. B. (1990) 'L'Exode et la bataille de Qadesh', *Revue Biblique* T. 97-3, pp. 321-358.

Cowgill, George L. & Yoffee, Norman (editors) (1988) *The Collapse of Ancient States and Civilizations*, University of Arizona Press: Tucson.
Coyle, Kathleen (1996) *Mary in the Christian Tradition: From a Contemporary Perspective*, Gracewing House: Leominster, Herefordshire; Twenty-Third Publications: Mystic, Conn.
Crawford, Harriet (1991) *Sumer and the Sumerians*, Cambridge University Press: Cambridge, U.K.
Crossan, John Dominic (1986) 'From Moses to Jesus: Parallel Themes', *Bible Review* Vol. 11 - Num. 2, pp. 18-27.
——— (1991) *The Historical Jesus (The Life of a Mediterranean Jewish Peasant)*, HarperCollins: New York.
——— (1998) *The Birth of Christianity (Discovering What Happened in the Years after the Execution of Jesus)*, HarperCollins: New York.
Crowfoot, J.W. (1911) *The Island of Meroë*, Egypt Exploration Fund: London.
Csorba, Mrea (1996) 'The Chinese Northern Frontier: Reassessment of the Bronze Age Burials from Baifu', *Antiquity* Vol. 70 - Num. 269, pp. 564-586.
Phyllis Culham, Lowell Edmunds & Alden Smith (editors) (1989) *Classics: A Discipline and Profession in Crisis*, University Press of America: Lanham and New York.
Cunneen, Sally (1996) *In Search of Mary (The Woman and the Symbol)*, Ballantine Books: New York.
Damrosch, David (1995) *We Scholars (Changing the Culture of the University)*, Harvard University Press: Cambridge, Mass.
Daniélou, Jean (1968) *The Infancy Narratives*. Trans. from the French by Rosemary Sheed. Burns & Oates: London.
Dathorne, O. R. (1989) 'Africa As Ancestor: Diop As Unifier', *Présence Africaine* 149-150, pp. 121-133.
David, Rosalie (1981) *A Guide to Religious Rituals at Abydos*, Aris & Phillips: Warminster, U.K.
——— (1996) *The Pyramid Builders of Ancient Egypt (A Modern Investigation of Pharaoh's Workforce)*, Routledge: London and New York.
Davidson, Basil (1974 [1968]) *Africa in History (Themes and Outlines)*, Collier: New York.
Davidson, Hilda Ellis (1993) *The Lost Beliefs of Northern Europe*, Routledge: London and New York.
Davies, Gordon F. (1992) *Israel in Egypt (Reading Exodus 1-2)*, JSOT (Supplement Series 135): Sheffield, U.K.
Davies, Nigel (1979) *Voyagers to the New World*, William Morrow: New York.
——— (1982) *The Ancient Kingdoms of Mexico*, Allen Lane: London.

Davies, Norman de Garis (1906) *The Rock Tombs of El Amarna — Part IV: Tombs of Penthu, Mahu, and Others,* The Egypt Exploration Fund: London.

——— (1908) *The Rock Tombs of El Amarna — Part VI: Tombs of Parennefer, Tutu, and Aÿ,* The Egypt Exploration Fund: London.

Davies, Philip R. (1998) *Scribes and Schools (The Canonization of the Hebrew Scriptures),* Westminster John Knox Press: Louisville, Kentucky.

Davies, W. Vivian (1982) 'The Origin of the Blue Crown', *Journal of Egyptian Archaeology* 68, pp. 69-76.

——— (editor) (1991) *Egypt and Africa (Nubia from Prehistory to Islam),* British Museum Press: London.

Davies, W. Vivian & Schofield, Louise (editors) (1995) *Egypt, the Aegean and the Levant (Interconnections in the Second Millennium BC),* British Museum Press: London.

Davis, Whitney M. (1979) 'Plato on Egyptian Art', *Journal of Egyptian Archaeology* 65, pp. 121-127.

Davila, James R. (1995) 'The Flood Hero as King and Priest', *Journal of Near Eastern Studies* Vol. 54 - Num. 3, pp. 199-214.

de Bary, Wm. Theodore (editor) (1966) *Sources of Chinese Tradition,* Columbia University Press: New York and London.

de Durand-Forest, Jacqueline & Baudot, Georges (directeurs) (1995) *Mille ans de civilisation mésoaméricaine (Des Mayas aux Aztèques).* Vols. I-II. L'Harmattan: Paris.

de Grazia, Alfred (1963) 'The Scientific Reception System and Dr. Velikovsky', *American Behavioral Scientist* Vol. 7 - Num. 1, pp. 45-68.

——— (editor) (1966) *The Velikovsky Affair (The Warfare of Science and Scientism),* University Books: New York.

——— 'The Coming Cosmic Debate in the Science and Humanities: Revolutionary VS. Evolutionary Primevology.' In Ravel, N. (editor) (1975) *From Past to Prophecy: Velikovsky's Challenge to Conventional Beliefs (Proceedings of the Symposium held at the Saidye Bronfman Centre, Montreal, Quebec – January 10th-12th, 1975),* pp. 21-40.

Bernard Ortiz de Montellano, Gabriel Haslip-Viera & Warren Barbour (1997) 'They were Not Here Before Columbus: Afrocentric Hyperdiffusionism in the 1990s', *Ethnohistory* Vol. 44 - Num. 2, pp. 199-234.

De Romilly, Jacqueline (1992) *Pourquoi la Grèce?,* Éditions de Fallois: Paris.

de Santillana, Giorgio & von Dechend, Hertha (1969) *Hamlet's Mill (An Essay on Myth and the Frame of Time),* Gambit: Boston, Mass.

Deiss, Lucien Rev. (1972) *Mary, Daughter of Sion.* Trans. by Barbara T. Blair. Liturgical Press: Collegeville, Minn.

Delebecque, Édouard (1992) *L'Apocalypse de Jean (Introduction, traduction, annotations),* Mame: Paris.

Deloria, Vine, Jr. (1994 [1972]) *God is Red (A Native View of Religion)*, Updated edition. Fulcrum: Golden, Col.

——— (1997) *Red Earth, White Lies (Native Americans and the Myth of Scientific Fact)*, Scribner: New York.

Deman, Albert (1985) 'Présence des Égyptiens dans la seconde guerre médique (480-479 av. J.-Chr.)', *Chronique d'Égypte* 60, pp. 56-74.

Desautels, Jacques (1988) *Dieux et mythes de l a Grèce ancienne (La mythologie gréco-romaine)*, Presses de l'Université Laval: Québec.

Dentan, Robert C. (editor) (1967) *The Idea of History in the Ancient Near East*, Yale University Press: New Haven and London.

Depuydt, Leo (1995) 'Murder in Memphis: the Story of Cambyses's Mortal Wounding of the Apis Bull (ca. 523 B.C.E.)', *Journal of Near Eastern Studies* Vol. 54 - Num. 2, pp. 119-126.

Derchain, Philippe (1978) '«En l'an 365 de Sa Majesté le Roi de Haute et Basse Égypte Râ-Harakhty vivant par-delà le Temps et l 'Espace»', *Chronique d'Égypte* 53, pp. 48-56.

——— (1985) see Verhoeven, Ursula.

——— (1987) 'Magie et politique (A propos de l'hymne à Sésostris III)', *Chronique d'Égypte* 62, pp. 21-29.

Derchain-Urtel, Marie-Theresia (1981) *Rites égyptiens III — Thot (à travers ses épithètes dans les scènes d'offrande des temples d'époque gréco-romaine)*, Fondation Égyptologique Reine Élisabeth: Bruxelles.

Derry, D. E. (1956) 'The Dynastic Race in Egypt', *Journal of Egyptian Archaeology* 42, pp. 80-85.

Desroches-Noblecourt, Ch. (1969) 'Le nouveau Site d'Abou-Simbel et son petit temple', *Bulletin de la Sociéte Française d'Égyptologie* 53-54, pp. 9-30.

Dever, William G. (1975) 'MB IIA Cemeteries at 'Ain es-Sâmiyeh and Sinjil', *Bulletin of the American Schools of Oriental Research* 217, pp. 23-36.

——— (1980) 'New Vistas on the EB IV ("MB I") Horizon in Syria-Palestine', *Bulletin of the American Schools of Oriental Research* 237, pp. 35-64.

——— (1981) 'The Impact of the New Archaeology on Syro-Palestinian Archaeology', *Bulletin of the American Schools of Oriental Research* 242, pp. 15-22.

——— (1987) 'The Middle Bronze Age: The Zenith of the Urban Canaanite Era', *Biblical Archaeologist* Vol. 50 - Num. 3, pp. 148-177.

——— (1990a) *Recent Archaeological Discoveries and Biblical Research*, University of Washington Press: Seattle and London.

——— (1990b) '"Hyksos", Egyptian Destructions, and the End of the Palestinian Middle Bronze Age', *Levant* 22, pp. 75-79.

———— (1991) 'Tell el-Dab'a and Levantine Middle Bronze Age Chronology: A Rejoiner to Manfred Bietak', *Bulletin of the American Schools of Oriental Research* 281, pp. 73-79.

———— (1992a) 'The Chronology of Syria-Palestine in the Second Millenium B.C.E.: A Review of Current Issues', *Bulletin of the American Schools of Oriental Research* 288, pp. 1-25.

———— 'The Late Bronze-Early Iron I Horizon in Syria-Palestine: Egyptians, Canaanites, "Sea Peoples," and Proto-Israelites.' In Ward, William A. & Joukowsky, Martha Sharp (editors) (1992b) *The Crisis Years: The 12th Century B.C. (From Beyond the Danube to the Tigris)*, pp. 99-110.

———— (1992c) see Shanks, Hershel.

———— 'Biblical Archaeology: Death and Rebirth.' In Biran, A. & Aviram, J. (editors) (1993a) *Biblical Archaeology Today, 1990 (Proceedings of the Second International Congress on Biblical Archaeology — Jerusalem, June-July 1990)*, pp. 706-722.

———— (1993b) 'Cultural Continuity, Ethnicity in the Archaeological Record and the Question of Israelite Origins', *Eretz-Israel* 24, pp. 22-33.

———— (1995a) 'Ceramics, Ethnicity, and the Question of Israel's Origins', *Biblical Archaeologist* Vol. 58 - Num. 4, pp. 200-211.

———— (1995b) '"Will the Real Israel Please Stand Up?" Archaeology and Israelite Historiography. (Part I)', *Bulletin of the American Schools of Oriental Research* 297, pp. 61-80.

———— (1995c) '"Will the Real Israel Please Stand Up?" Part II: Archaeology and the Religions of Ancient Israel', *Bulletin of the American Schools of Oriental Research* 298, pp. 37-58.

———— (1996a) 'Revisionist Israel Revisited: A Rejoinder to Niels Peter Lemche', *Currents in Research: Biblical Studies* 4, pp. 35-50.

———— (1996b) 'Archaeology and the Current Crisis in Israelite Historiography', *Eretz-Israel* 25, pp. 18-27.

———— 'Settlement Patterns and Chronology of Palestine in the Middle Bronze Age.' In Oren, Eliezer D. (editor) (1997) *The Hyksos: New Historical and Archaeological Perspectives*, pp. 285-301.

———— 'Israelite Origins and the "Nomadic Israel": Can Archaeology Separate Fact from Fiction?' In Gitin, S. et al. (editors) (1998) *Mediterranean Peoples in Transition*, pp. 220-237.

Diakonoff, Igor M. (editor) (1991) *Early Antiquity*, University of Chicago Press: Chicago and London.

Diansseny, Dorank Assifat (1989) 'Les fondements philosophiques de la problématique culturelle et politique de Cheikh Anta Diop', *Présence Africaine* 149-150, pp. 134-142.

Diop, Alioune (1947) 'Niam n'goura ou les raisons d'être de Présence Africaine', *Présence Africaine* 1, pp. 7-14.

────── (1973) 'Pour une politique de la civilisation noire', *Présence Africaine* 85, pp. 139-1

Diop, Cheikh Anta (1956) 'Apports et perspectives culturels de l'Afrique', *Présence Africaine* 8-10, pp. 339-346.

────── (1959a) *L'unité culturelle de l'Afrique Noire (Domaines du patriarcat et du matriarcat dans l'antiquité classique)*, Présence Africaine.

────── (1959b) 'L'unité culturelle africaine', *Présence Africaine* 24-25, pp. 60-65.

────── (1960a) 'Les intellectuels doivent étudier le passé non pour s'y complaire mais pour y puiser des leçons', *La Vie Africaine*, Paris, 6 (mars-avril), pp. 10-11.

────── (1960b) *L'Afrique Noire pre-coloniale (Étude comparée des systèmes politiques et sociaux de l'Europe et de l'Afrique Noire, de l'antiquité à la formation des états modernes)*, Présence Africaine: Paris.

────── (1962a) 'Histoire primitive de l'humanité: Évolution du monde noire', *Bulletin de l'IFAN* Vol. 24 (série B) - Num. 3-4, pp. 449-541.

────── (1962b) 'Réponse à quelques critiques', *Bulletin de l'IFAN* Vol. 24 (série B) - Num. 3-4, pp. 542-574.

────── (1967) *Antériorite des civilizations nègres: Mythe ou vérité historique?*, Présence Africaine: Paris.

────── (1973) 'Introduction à l'étude des migrations en Afrique centrale et occidentale. Identification du berceau nilotique du peuple sénégalais', *Bulletin de l'IFAN* Vol. 35 (série B) - Num. 4, pp. 769-792.

────── Preface to Obenga, Théophile (1973) *L'Afrique dans l'Antiquité (Egypte pharaonique — Afrique Noire)*, pp. ix-xii.

────── (1974) *The African Origin of Civilization: Myth or Reality?*, Lawrence Hill: Westport, Conn.

────── (1978 [1959]) *The Cultural Unity of Black Africa (The Domains of Patriarchy and Matriarchy in Classical Antiquity)*, Third World Press: Chicago, Ill.

────── (1979) *Parenté génétique de l'égyptien pharaonique et des langues négro-africaines*. IFAN-NEA: Dakar.

────── (1979 [1954]) *Nations nègres et culture (De l'antiquité Nègre égyptienne aux problèmes de l'Afrique Noire d'aujourd'hui)*. Troisième édition Tomes I-II. Présence Africaine: Paris.

────── 'Origine des anciens Egyptiens.' In Mokhtar, G. (editor) (1980) *Histoire Générale de l'Afrique — Volume II: Afrique ancienne*, UNESCO: Paris, pp. 39-72.

——— (1981) 'L'apport de l'Égypte à la civilisation grecque', *Afrique Histoire* 2, pp. 26-29.

——— (1981) *Civilisation ou barbarie (Anthropologie sans complaisance)*, Présence Africaine: Paris.

——— (1987) *Precolonial Black Africa*, Lawrence Hill: Westport, Conn.

——— (1991) *Civilization or Barbarism (An Authentic Anthropology)*. Trans. by Yaa-Lengi Meema Ngemi. Lawrence Hill Books: Brooklyn, NY.

Diouf, Mamadou & Mbodj, Mohamad 'The Shadow of Cheikh Anta Diop.' In V. Y. Mudimbe (editors) (1992) *The Surreptitious Speech: Présence Africaine and the Politics of Otherness 1947-1987*, pp. 118-135.

Dixon, D. M. (1964) 'The Origin of the Kingdom of Kush', *Journal of Egyptian Archaeology* 50, pp. 121-132.

Dobrev, Vassil (1993) 'Les titulatures des rois de la IVe Dynastie', *Bulletin de l'Institut Français d'Archéologie Orientale* 93, pp. 180-204.

Dodson, Aidan (1985) 'BRIEF COMMUNICATIONS: A fragment of canopic chests in Sir John Sloane's museum', *Journal of Egyptian Archaeology* 71, pp. 177-179.

——— (1988) 'Some Notes Concerning the Royal Tombs at Tanis', *Chronique d'Égypte* 63 - Num. 126, pp. 221-233.

——— (1989) 'BRIEF COMMUNICATIONS: Hatshepsut and "her father" Mentuhotpe II', *Journal of Egyptian Archaeology* 75, pp. 224-226.

——— (1990) 'Crown Prince Djhutmose and the Royal Sons of the Eighteenth Dynasty', *Journal of Egyptian Archaeology* 76, pp. 87-96.

——— (1993) 'BRIEF COMMUNICATIONS: Psusennes II and Shoshenq I', *Journal of Egyptian Archaeology* 79, pp. 267-268.

Dommergues, André (1980) 'Le culte du serpent en Afrique noire', *Présence Africaine* 114, pp. 132-143.

Donahue, V. A. (1992) 'The Goddess of the Theban Mountain', *Antiquity* Vol. 66 - Num. 253, pp. 871-885.

Donnelly, Ignatius (1882) *Atlantis: The Antediluvian World*, Harper & Brothers: New York.

——— (1883) *Ragnarok: The Age of Fire and Gravel*, D. Appleton & Co.: New York.

Doran, Patrick 'The Social Impact of Velikovsky on Our Generation.' In Ravel, N. (editor) (1975) *From Past to Prophecy: Velikovsky's Challenge to Conventional Beliefs* (Proceedings of the Symposium held at the Saidye Bronfman Centre, Montreal, Quebec – January 10th-12th, 1975), pp. 66-74.

———— 'Living with Velikovsky: Catastrophism as World View.' In Milton, E. R. (editor) (1978) *Recollections of a Fallen Sky: Velikovsky and Cultural Amnesia (Papers presented at the University of Lethbridge May 9 and 10, 1974)*, pp. 139-146.

Dothan, Trude & Dothan, Moshe (1992) *People of the Sea (The Search for the Philistines)*, Macmillan: New York and Toronto.

Doumas, Christos G. (1983) *Thera: Pompeii of the Ancient Aegean (Excavations at Akrotiri 1967-79)*, Thames and Hudson: London.

———— (1991) 'High Art from the Time of Abraham', *Biblical Archaeology Review* Vol.17 - Num.1, pp. 40-51.

Drake, St. Clair (1987-1990) *Black Folk Here and There (An Essay in History and Anthropology)*. Vols. I-II. Center for Afro-American Studies/University of California: Los Angeles.

Du Bois, W.E.B (1976) *The World and Africa*, Kraus-Thomson: Millwood, New York.

Dundes, Alan (editor) (1988) *The Flood Myth*, University of California Press: Berkeley and Los Angeles.

Dunham, Dows (1950) *The Royal Cemeteries of Kush (El Kurru)*, Harvard University Press: Cambridge, Mass.

Dupuis, Charles François (1984 [1872]) *The Origins of All Religious Worship*, Garland: New York and London.

Durán, Fray Diego (1971) *Book of the Gods and Rites and the Ancient Calendar*. Trans. and edited by Fernando Horcasitas and Doris Heyden. University of Oklahoma Press: Norman.

Duran, J.-M. (1985) 'La situation historique des Sakkanakku: Nouvelle approche', *Mari Annales Recherches Interdisciplinaires* 4:147-72.

Eaton-Krauss, Marianne (1990) 'The Coffins of Queen Ahhotep', Consort of Seqenien-Re and Mother of Ahmose', *Chronique d'Égypte* 65, pp. 195-205.

Edmons, I. G. (1977) *The Mysteries of Troy*, Thomas Nelson: Nashville and New York.

———— (1981) *The Mysteries of Homer's Greeks*, Elsevier/Nelson Books: New York.

Edmuns, Lowell (editor) (1990) *Approaches to Greek Myth*, Johns Hopkins University Press: Baltimore and London.

Edwards, David N. 'La forteresse de Qasr Ibrim.' In *La Nubie (L'archéologie au Soudan)* (1994) Éditions Faton: Dijon, pp. 64-69.

Ehret, Christopher (1995) 'The African Sources of Egyptian Culture and Language', *UFAHAMU* Vol. 23 - Num. 3, pp. 34-46.

Ehrich, Robert W. (editor) (1965) *Chronologies in Old World Archaeology*, University of Chicago Press: Chicago and London.

Eisenman, Robert H. & Wise, Michael (1993) *The Dead Sea Scrolls Uncovered (The First Complete Translation and Interpretation of 50 Key Documents Withheld for Over 35 Years)*, Element: Shaftesbury, Dorset; Rockport, Mass.; Brisbane, Queensland.
El-Banna, Essam (1989) 'À propos des aspects Héliopolitains d'Osiris', *Bulletin de l'Institut Français d'Archéologie Orientale* 89, pp. 101-126.
El-Kordy, Zeinab (1984) 'Établissement du pouvoir royal à Min, dieu parède à Edfou', *Bulletin de l'Institut Français d'Archéologie Orientale* 84, pp. 121-126.
El-Razik, Mahmud (1975) 'The Dedicatory and Building Texts of Ramses II in Luxor Temple — II: Interpretation', *Journal of Egyptian Archaeology* 61, pp. 125-136.
Ela, Jean-Marc (1989a) *Cheikh Anta Diop ou l'honneur de penser*, L'Harmattan: Paris.
———— (1989b) 'Conscience historique et révolution africaine chez Cheikh Anta Diop', *Présence Africaine* 149-150, pp. 161-192.
Elliot, J. K. (editor) (1996) *The Apocryphal Jesus (Legends of the Early Church)*, Oxford University Press: Oxford and New York.
Emery, Walter B. (1967) *Lost Land Emerging*, Charles Scribner's Sons: New York.
———— (1969) 'Preliminary Report on the Excavations at North Saqqâra, 1968', *Journal of Egyptian Archaeology* 55, pp. 31-35.
———— (1970) 'Preliminary Report on the Excavations at North Saqqâra, 1968-9', *Journal of Egyptian Archaeology* 56, pp. 5-11.
Erwin, Lorna & Maclennan, David (editors) (1994) *Sociology of Education in Canada (Critical Persective on Theory, Research & Practice)*, Copp Clark Longman: Toronto.
Es-Saghir, Mohamed & Valbelle, Dominique (1983) 'I: The Discovery of Komir Temple (Preliminary Report) / II: Deux hymnes aux divinités de Komir, Anoukis et Nephthys', *Bulletin de l'Institut Français d'Archéologie Orientale* 83, pp. 149-170.
Evans, Arthur (1921-1928) *The Palace of Minos at Knossos (A Comparative account of the Successive Stages of the Early Cretan Civilization as Illustrated by the Discoveries)* — Vol. II / Part I: Fresh lights on origins and External Relations – The Restoration in Town and Palace after Seismic Catastrophe Towards Close of M.M. III, and the Beginnings of the New Era. Macmillan: London.
Exum, J. Cheryl & Clines, David J. (editors) (1993) *The New Literary Criticism and the Hebrew Bible*, JSOT Press: Sheffield, U.K.

Christopher Eyre, Anthony Leahy & Lisa Montagano Leahy (editors) (1994) *The Unbroken Reed (Studies in the Culture and Heritage of Ancient Egypt — In Honour of A. F. Shore)*, Egypt Exploration Society: London.
Fagan, Brian M. (1984) *The Aztecs*, W. H. Freeman: New York.
Fairservis, W. A., Jr. (1962) *The Ancient Kingdoms of the Nile (And the Doomed Monuments of Nubia)*, Thomas Y. Cromwell: New York.
——— (1991) 'A Revised View of the Na'rmr Palette', *Journal of the American Research Center in Egypt* 28, pp. 1-20.
Farnell, L. R. (1895-1909) *The Cults of the Greek States*. Vols. I-V. Clarendon Press: Oxford.
Faulkner (1973) *The Ancient Egyptian Coffin Texts*. Vols. I-III. Aris & Phillips: Warminster, U.K.
Fauvelle, François-Xavier (1996) *L'Afrique de Cheikh Anta Diop (Histoire et idéologie)*, Karathala / Centre de recherches africaines: Paris.
——— (1997) 'Cheikh Anta Diop dix ans apres: L'historien et son double', *Afrique Contemporaine* 181, pp. 3-11.
Feder, Kenneth L. (1990) *Frauds, Myth, and Mysteries: Science and Pseudo-science in Archaeology*, Mayfield: Mountain View, Cal.
Felder, Cain Hope (1991) *Stony the Road We Trod (African American Biblical Interpretation)*, Fortress Press: Minneapolis.
——— (1992) 'Afrocentrism and Biblical Authority', *Theology Today* Vol. 49 - Num. 3, pp. 357-366.
——— (1993) 'Afrocentrism, the Bible, and the Politics of Difference', *The Journal of Religious Thought* Vol. 50 - Num. 1-2, pp. 45-46.
Feldman, Louis H. (1996) 'Homer and the Near East: The Rise of the Greek Genius', *Biblical Archaeologist* Vol. 59 - Num. 1, pp. 13-19.
Fell, Barry (1976) *America B.C. (Ancient Settlers in the New World)*, Wildwood House: London.
——— (1982) *Bronze Age America*, Little, Brown & Co.: Boston and Toronto.
Finch, Charles S. 'The Black Roots of Egypt's Glory.' In Van Sertima, Ivan (editor) (1988) *Great Black Leaders: Ancient and Modern*, pp.139-143.
——— 'Imhotep the Physician: Archetype of the Great Man.' In Van Sertima, Ivan (editor) (1989a) Egypt Revisited, pp. 213-231.
——— (1989b) 'Interview with Cheikh Anta Diop', *Présence Africaine* 149-150, pp. 361-373.
Finegan, Jack (1969) *Hidden Records of the Life of Jesus*, Pilgrim Press: Philadelphia and Boston.
——— (1992) *The Archeology of the New Testament (The Life of Jesus and the Beginning of the Early Church)*. Revised edition. Princeton University Press: Princeton, NJ.

Finkelstein, Israel (1988a) *The Archaeology of the Israelite Settlement*, Israel Exploration Society: Jerusalem.

──────── (1988b) 'Searching for Israelite Origins', *Biblical Archaeology Review* Vol. 14 - Num. 5, pp. 34-45, 58.

──────── (1990) 'On Archaeological Methods and Historical Considerations: Iron Age II Gezer and Samaria', *Bulletin of the American Schools of Oriental Research* 277-278, pp. 109-119.

──────── (1996) 'The Archaeology of the United Monarchy: an Alternative View', *Levant* 28, pp. 177-185.

Finkelstein, Israel & Na'aman, Nadav (editors) (1994) *From Nomadism to Monarchy (Archaeological and Historical Aspects of Early Israel)*, Yad Izhak Ben-Zvi & Israel Exploration Society: Jerusalem; Biblical Archaeology Society: Washington.

──────── (1996) 'Ethnicity and Origin of the Iron I Settlers in the Highlands of Canaan: Can the Real Israel Stand Up?', *Biblical Archaeologist* Vol. 59 - Num. 4, pp. 198-209.

Fitton, J. Lesley (1996) *The Discovery of the Greek Bronze Age*, Harvard University Press: Cambridge, Mass.

Flem-Ath, Rand & Flem-Ath, Rose (1995) *When the Sky Fell (In Search of Atlantis)*, Stoddart: Toronto.

Fleming, Daniel E. (1995) 'More Help from Syria: Introducing Emar to Biblical Study', *Biblical Archaeologist* Vol. 58 - Num. 3, pp. 139-147.

Fontenrose, Joseph (1959) *Python (A Study of Delphic Myth and its Origins)*, University of California Press: Berkeley, Cal.

──────── (1981) *Orion: The Myth of the Hunter and the Huntress*, University of California Press: Berkeley, Cal.

Fontinoy, Charles (1989) 'Les noms de l'Égypte en hébreu et leur étymologie', *Chronique d'Égypte* 64, pp. 90-97.

Forsyth, Phyllis Young (1980) *Atlantis (The Making of Myth)*, McGill-Queen's University Press: Montreal; Croom Helm: London.

Fortin, Michel (1984) 'Archaeological Notes: "The Enkomi Tower"', *Levant* 16, pp. 173-176.

Foster, Karen Polinger & Ritner, Robert K. (1996) 'Texts, Storms, and the Thera Eruption', *Journal of Near Eastern Studies* Vol. 55 - Num. 1, pp. 1-15.

France, Peter (1991) *The Rape of Egypt (How the Europeans Stripped Egypt of its Heritage)*, Barrie & Jenkins: London.

Franke, Detlef (1985) 'BRIEF COMMUNICATIONS: An important family from Abydos of the Seventeenth Dynasty', *Journal of Egyptian Archaeology* 71, pp. 175-176.

Frankfort, H. (1933) *The Cenotaph of Seti I at Abydos*, The Egypt Exploration Society: London.

Fankfurter, David (1993) *Elijah in Upper Egypt (The Apocalypse of Elijah and Early Egyptian Christianity)*, Fortress Press: Minneapolis.

Frazer, James George, Sir (1923) *Folk-Lore in the Old Testament (Studies in Comparative Religion Legend and Law)*, Tudor: New York.

French, E. B. & Wardle, K. A. (editors) (1988) *Problems in Greek Prehistory (Papers Presented at the Centenary Conference of the British School of Archaeology at Athens, Manchester – April 1986)*, Bristol Classic Press (General Editor: John H. Betts): Bristol, U.K.

Freud, Sigmund (1939) *Moses and Monotheism*. Trans. from the German by Katherine Jones. Hogarth Press/Institute of Psycho-Analysis: London.

Friedman, Richard Elliott (1987) *Who Wrote the Bible?*, Summit Books: New York.

——— (1997) *The Hidden Face of God*, HarperCollins: New York.

Frobenius, Leo (1949) *Mythologie de l'Atlantide: Le «Poseidon» de l'Afrique noire. Son culte chez les Yoruba du Bénin*, Payot: Paris.

——— (1993) *L'Atlantide (Mythologies et cultes)*. Trans. from the German by F. Gidon. Édition du Rocher: Monaco.

Froment, Alain (1991) 'Origine et évolution de l'homme dans la pensée de Cheikh Anta Diop: Une analyse critique', *Cahiers d'Études Africaines* 121-122 – XXX: 1-2, pp. 29-64.

Frykenberg, Robert Eric (1996) *History and Belief (The Foundations of Historical Understanding)*, William B. Eerdmans: Grand Rapids, Mich.

Gabolde, Luc & Rondot, Vincent (1993) 'Une catastrophe antique dans le temple de Montou à Karnak-Nord', *Bulletin de l'Institut Français d'Archéologie Orientale* 93, pp. 245-264.

Gabolde, Marc (1995) 'L'inondation sous les pieds d'Amon', *Bulletin de l'Institut Français d'Archéologie Orientale* 95, p. 235-258.

Galan, José M. (1992) 'EA 164 and the God Amun', *Journal of Near Eastern Studies* Vol. 51 - Num. 4, pp. 287-291.

Gardiner, Alan H. (1914) 'New Literary Works from Ancient Egypt', *Journal of Egyptian Archaeology* 1, pp. 100-106.

——— (1946) 'Davis's Copy of the Great Speos Artemidos Inscription', *Journal of Egyptian Archaeology* 32, pp. 43-56.

——— (1947) *Ancient Egyptian Onomastica*, I-III, Oxford.

——— (1961) *Egypt of the Pharaohs*, Oxford University Press: Oxford.

Gardiner, Juliet (editor) (1990) *The History Debate*, Collins & Brown: London.

Garstang, John (1931) *Joshua, Judges*, Constable: London.

——— (1934)*The Heritage of Solomon (An Historical Introduction to the Sociology of Ancient Palestine)*, Williams and Norgate: London.

Garstang, John & Garstang, J.B.E. (1948) *The Story of Jericho*, Marshall, Morgan & Scott: London and Edinburgh.

Garstang, John & Gurney, O. R. (1959) *The Geography of the Hittite Empire*, The British Institute of Archaeology at Ankara: London.

Gates, Henry Louis, Jr. (1991) 'Beware the New Pharaohs', *Newsweek* 118 (September 23), p. 47.

Gatore-Oswald (1977) 'Theophile Obenga et les paradoxes de l'ethnocentrisme', *Présence Africaine* 103, pp. 109-125.

Gersh, Stephen & Kannengiesser, Charles (editors) (1992) *Platonism in Late Antiquity*, University of Notre Dame Press: Notre Dame, Ind.

Gerson, L. P. (1990) *God and Greek Philosophy (Studies in the Early History of Natural Theology)*, Routledge: London and New York.

Ghali, Ibrahim Amin (1969) *L'Égypte et les Juifs dans l'antiquté*, Éditions Cujas: Paris.

Gibbs, Lee W. & Stevenson, W. Taylor (editors) (1975) *Myth and the Crisis of Historical Consciousness*, Scholars Press: Missoula, Montana.

Giles, Herbert A. (1969) *Religions of Ancient China*, Books for Libraries Press: Freeport, NY.

Gimbutas, Marija (1982) *The Goddesses and Gods of Old Europe (6500 – 3500 BC: Myths and Cult Images)*, University of California Press: Berkeley.

Ginenthal, Charles (editor) (1976) *Stephen Jay Gould and Immanuel Velikovsky (Essays in the Continuing Velikovsky Affair)*, IVY Press: Forest Hill, NY.

────── (1995) *Carl Sagan & Immanuel Velikovsky*, New Falcon: Tempe, AZ.

Gingerich, Owen (1996) 'Neptune, Velikovsky and the Name of the Game', *Scientific American* Vol. 275 - Num. 3, pp. 181-183.

Girardot, N. J. (1983) *Myth and Meaning in Early Taoism (The Theme of Chaos)*, University of California Press: Berkeley and Los Angeles.

Seymour Gitin, Amihai Mazar & Ephraim Stern (editors) (1998) *Mediterranean Peoples in Transition (Thirteenth to Early Tenth Centuries BCE)*, Israel Exploration Society: Jerusalem.

Glasson, T. F. (1980) *Jesus and the End of the World*, Saint Andrew Press: Edinburgh, U.K.

Goedicke, Hans (1963) 'The End of "So, King of Egypt"', *Bulletin of the American Schools of Oriental Research* 171, pp. 64-66.

────── (1966) 'Considerations on the Battle of Kadesh', *Journal of Egyptian Archaeology* 52, pp. 71-80.

────── (1974) 'Some Remarks Concerning the Inscription of Ahmose, Son of Ebana', *Journal of the American Research Center in Egypt* 11, pp. 31-41.

———— (1975) *The Report of Wenamun*, Johns Hopkins University Press: Baltimore and London.

———— (editor) (1985) *Perspectives on the Battle of Kadesh*, Halgo: Baltimore, MD.

———— 'The End of the Hyksos in Egypt.' In Lesko, Leonard H. (editor) (1986) *Egyptological Studies in Honor of Richard A. Parker*, pp. 37-47.

———— (1991) 'Egyptian Military Actions in "Asia" in the Middle Kingdom', *Revue d'Égyptologie* 42, pp. 89-94.

———— (1996) 'The Thutmosis I Inscription Near Tomâs', *Journal of Near Eastern Studies* Vol. 55 - Num. 3, pp. 161-176.

Goff, Beatrice L. (1979) *Symbols of Ancient Egypt in the Late Period (The Twenty-first Dynasty)*, Mouton Publishers: The Hague.

Golb, Norman (1995) *Who Wrote the Dead Sea Scrolls? (The Search for the Secret of Qumran)*, Scribner: New York.

Golden, Mark & Toohey, Peter (editors) (1997) *Inventing Ancient Culture (Historicism, Periodization, and the Ancient World)*, Routledge: London and New York.

Goldsmith, Donald (editor) (1977) *Scientists Confront Velikovsky*, Cornell University Press: Ithaca, NY.

Goodrich, Norma Lorre (1960) *Ancient Myths*, New American Library: New York.

Gordon, Cyrus H. (1962) *Before the Bible (The Common Background of Greek and Hebrew Civilisations)*, Collins: London.

———— Foreword to Astour, M. C. (1967) *Hellenosemitica (An Ethnic and Cultural Study in West Semitic Impact on Mycenean Greece)*, p. xi.

———— Preface to Cohane, John Philip (1969) *The Key*, pp. 13-16.

———— (1972) *Before Columbus (Links Between the Old World and Ancient America)*, Turnstone: London.

———— 'The Mediterranean Synthesis.' In Ward, William A. & Joukowsky, Martha Sharp (editors) (1992) *The Crisis Years: The 12th Century B.C. (From Beyond the Danube to the Tigris)*, pp. 188-196.

———— (1993) 'BOOK REVIEW: 'Black Athena: The Afroasiatic Roots of Classical Civilization. Vol. I: The Fabrication of Ancient Greece, 1785-1985. M. Bernal. 1987', *Journal of Interdisciplinary History* Vol. 113 - Num. 3, pp. 489-490.

Gordon, Gérard (1974) 'L'Éléphantine-du-Sud', *Chronique d'Égypte* 51, pp. 238-253.

Gorenstein, Shirley (1975) *Not Forever on Earth (Prehistory of Mexico)*, Charles Scribner's Sons: New York.

Gottwald, Norman K. (1978) 'Were the Early Israelites Pastoral Nomads?', *Biblical Archaeology Review* Vol. 4 - Num. 2, pp. 2-7.

——— (1979) *The Tribes of Yahweh (A Sociology of the Religion of Liberated Israel 1250-1050 B.C.E.)*, Orbis Books: Maryknoll, NY.
Gould, Stephen Jay (1996 [1981]) *The Mismeasure of Man.* Revised and expanded edition. W. W. Norton: New York and London.
Goyon, Jean-Claude (1978) 'Hededyt: Isis-Scorpion et Isis au Scorpion (en marge du papyrus de Brooklyn 47.218.50-III)', *Bulletin de l'Institut Français d'Archéologie Orientale* 78 (2), pp. 439-457.
——— (1985) *Les dieux-gardiens et la Genèse des temples (D'après les textes égyptiens de l'époque gréco-romaine).* Vols. I-II. Institut Français d'Archéologie Orientale du Caire: Caire.
Grabbe, Lester L. (1995) *Priests, Prophets, Diviners, Sages (A Socio-Historical Study of Religious Specialists in Ancient Israel)*, Trinity Press International: Valley Forge, Penn.
Graham. Lloyd (1997[1975]) *Deceptions and Myths of the Bible*, Carol: Secaucus, NJ.
Granet, Marcel (1948) *La civilisation chinoise (La vie publique et la vie privée)*, Éditions Albin Michel: Paris.
——— (1959) *Chinese Civilization.* Trans. by Kathleen E. Innes and Mabel R. Brailsford. Meridian Books: New York.
Grant, Michael (1982) *From Alexander to Cleopatra (The Hellenistic World)*, Weidenfeld & Nicholson: London.
——— (1995 [1970]) *The Ancient Historians*, Duckworth: London.
Gray, Chris (1989) *Concepts of History in the Works of Cheikh Anta Diop and Theophile Obenga*, Karnak House: London.
Green, Alberto R.W. (1993) 'The Identity of King So of Egypt - An Alternative Interpretation', *Journal of Near Eastern Studies* Vol. 52 - Num. 2, pp. 99-108.
Green, Joel B. & Turner, Max (editors) (1994) *Jesus of Nazareth: Lord and Christ (Essays on the Historical Jesus and New Testament Christology)*, William B. Eerdmans: Grand Rapids, Mich.; Paternoster Press: Carlisle, U.K.
Green, Michael (1983) 'The Syrian and Lebanese Topographical Data in the Story of Sinuhe', *Chronique d'Égypte* 58, pp. 38-59.
Green, Tamara M. (1989) 'Black Athena and Classical Historiography: Other Approaches, Other Views', *Arethusa* (Fall - Special Issue), pp. 55-65.
Greenberg, Lewis M. & Sizemore, Warner B. (1977) *Velikovsky and Establishment Science*, Kronos: Glassboro, NJ.
Griffith, F. Ll. (1890) *The Antiquities of Tell el Yahûdiyeh*, Egypt Exploration Fund: London.
Griffiths, John Gwyn (1960) *The Conflict of Horus and Seth (From Egyptian and Classical Sources)*, Liverpool University Press: Liverpool, U.K.

———— (1970a) *Plutarch's De Iside et Osiride*, University of Wales Press: Swansea, Wales.

———— (1970b) 'BRIEF COMMUNICATIONS: "The Pregnancy of Isis": a comment', *Journal of Egyptian Archaeology* 55, pp. 194-195.

———— (1976) 'BRIEF COMMUNICATIONS: A refrain in the texts of the Edfu Temple', *Journal of Egyptian Archaeology* 62, pp. 186-187.

———— (1980) *The Origins of Osiris and His Cult*, E. J. Brill: London.

Grimal, Nicolas (1992) *A History of Ancient Egypt*. Trans. by Ian Shaw. Blackwell: Oxford, U.K.

Grinnel, George 'The Intellectual Context of Velikovsky's Thought.' In Ravel, Nahum (editor) (1975) *From Past to Prophecy: Velikovsky's Challenge to Conventional Beliefs* (Proceedings of the Symposium held at the Saidye Bronfman Centre, Montreal, Quebec – January 10th-12th, 1975), pp. 52-65.

Paul R. Gross, Norman Levitt & Martin W. Lewis (editors) (1996) *The Flight from Science and Reason*. Annals of the New York Academy of Sciences. Vol. 775. New York Academy of Sciences: New York.

Gutbub, Adolphe (1973) *Textes fondamentaux de la theologie de Kom Ombo*. Thèse pour le Doctorat ès Lettres présentée à la faculté des lettres et sciences humaines de l'Université de Paris.

———— (1984) 'Kom Ombo et son relief culturel', *Bulletin de la Sociéte Française d'Égyptologie* 101, pp. 21-44.

Gyles, Anna Benson & Sayer, Chloë (1980) *Of God and Men (The Heritage of Ancient Mexico)*, HarperCollins: New York.

Hable-Sellassie, Sergew (1972) *Ancient and Medieval Ethiopian History to 1270*, [s.n.]: Addis Ababa.

Hadingham, Evan (1984) *Early Man and the Cosmos*, Walker & Co.: New York.

Haeny, Gerhard (1985) 'A Short Architectural History of Philae', *Bulletin de l'Institut Français d'Archéologie Orientale* 85, pp. 197-233.

Hall, H. R. (1913) see Naville, E.

———— (1916) *The Ancient History of the Near East (From the Earliest Times to the Battle of Salamis)*, Methuen: London.

Hall, Robert G. (1991) *Revealed Histories (Techniques for Ancient Jewish and Christian Historiography)*, JSOT Press: Sheffield, U.K.

Hallager, Erik (1977) *The Mycenean Palace at Knossos (Evidence for Final Destruction in the IIIB Period)*, Medelhavsmuseet: Stockholm.

Halpern, Baruch (1987) 'Radical Exodus Redating Fatally Flawed', *Biblical Archaeology Review* Vol. 13 - Num. 6, pp. 56-61.

———— (1988) *The First Historians (The Hebrew Bible and History)*, HarperCollins: New York.

———— (1992) see Shanks, Hershel.

———— (1993) 'The Exodus and the Israelite Historians', *Eretz-Israel* 24, pp. 89-96.
Hamington, Maurice (1995) *Hail Mary? (The Struggle for Ultimate Womanhood in Catholicism)*, Routledge: New York and London.
Hammond, N.G.L. & Scullard H. H. (editors) (1970) *The Oxford Classical Dictionary*, Clarendon Press: Oxford, U.K.
Hancock, Graham (1992) *The Sign and the Seal (The Quest for the Lost Arch of the Covenant)*, Doubleday Canada: Toronto.
———— (1996 [1995]) *Fingerprints of the Gods (A Quest for the Beginning and the End)*, Seal Books: Toronto.
Hankey, Vronwy (1989) see Warren, P.
———— (1990) 'Petrie, Mycenae & Egypt', *Minerva* Vol. 1 - Num. 3, pp. 12-15.
———— (1993) 'Egypt, the Aegean and the Levant', *Egyptian Archaeology* 3, pp. 27-29.
Haran, Menahem 'The Disappearance of the Ark.' In *Israel Exploration Journal Reader* (1981) with a prolegomenon by Harry M. Orlinsky. Vol. I. KTAV: New York, pp. 262-274.
———— (1995) 'Altar-ed States (Incense Theory Goes Up in Smoke)', *Bible Review* Vol. 11 - Num.1, pp. 31-37.
Hare, Douglas R. A. (1990) *The Son of Man Tradition*, Fortress Press: Minneapolis.
Hari, Robert (1976) 'La reine d'Horemheb était-elle la soeur de Neferetiti?', *Chronique d'Égypte* 51 - Num. 101, pp. 39-46.
———— (1976) 'Un nouvel élément de la Corégence Aménophis III — Akhenaton', *Chronique d'Égypte* 51, pp. 252-260.
Hasel, Michel G. (1994) 'Israel in the Merneptah Stela', *Bulletin of the American Schools of Oriental Research* 296, pp. 45-61.
Hawass, Zahi (1994) 'A fragmentary Monument of Djoser from Saqqara', *Journal of Egyptian Archaeology* 80, pp. 45-56.
Hawkins, David 'The Hittites and their Empire.' In Westenholz, Joan Goodnick (editor) (1996) *Royal Cities of the Biblical World*, pp. 69-79.
Hawks, Francis L. (1850) *The Monuments of Egypt; or, Egypt a Witness for the Bible*, Geo. P. Putnam: New York.
Haycock, B. G. (1972) 'Landmarks in Cushite History', *Journal of Egyptian Archaeology* 58, pp. 225-244.
Hayes, William C. (1990 [1959]) *The Scepter of Egypt (A Background for the Study of the Egyptian Antiquities in The Metropolitan Museum of Art) — Vol. I: From the Earliest Times to the end of the Middle Kingdom*, The Metropolitan Museum of Art: New York.

―――― (1990 [1959]) *The Scepter of Egypt (A Background for the Study of the Egyptian Antiquities in The Metropolitan Museum of Art) — Vol. II: The Hyksos Period and Kingdom (1675-1080 B.C.)*, Metropolitan Museum of Art: New York.

Hays, J. Daniel (1998) 'From the Land of the Bow: Black Soldiers in the Ancient Near East', *Bible Review* Vol. 14 - Num. 4, pp. 28-33, 50-51.

Heidorn, Lisa A. (1997) 'The Horses of Kush', *Journal of Near Eastern Studies* Vol. 56 - Num. 2, pp. 105-114.

Heinsohn, Gunnar 'Destruction Layers in Archaeological Sites: The Stratigraphy of Armageddon.' In Zysman, Milton & Whelton, Clark (editors) (1990) *Catastrophism 2000 (A Sourcebook for the Conference: Reconsidering Velikovsky)*, pp. 213 - 247.

Hengel, Martin (1995) *Studies in Early Christology*, T&T Clark: Edinburgh.

Herman, Edward S. & Chomsky, Noam (1988) *Manufacturing Consent (The Political Economy of the Mass Media)*, Pantheon Books: New York.

Herr, Larry G. (1993) 'What Ever Happened to the Ammonites?', *Biblical Archaeology Review* Vol. 19 - Num. 6, pp. 26-35, 68.

―――― (1997) 'The Iron II Period: Emerging Nations', *Biblical Archaeologist* Vol. 60 - Num. 3, pp. 114-183.

Hess, Richard S. (1997) 'Hurrians and Other Inhabitants of Late Bronze Age Palestine', *Levant* 29, pp. 153-155.

Hilliard, Asa G. 'Are Africans Africans? Scholarship and Propaganda, Valid Discourse on Kemetic Origins.' In Celenko, Theodore (editor) (1996) *Egypt in Africa*, pp. 112-115.

Hinkel, Friedrich W. 'Les pyramides de Méroé.' In *La Nubie (L'archéologie au Soudan)* (1994) Éditions Faton: Dijon, pp. 60-63.

Hodder, Ian et al. (editors) (1995) *Interpreting Archaeology (Finding Meaning in the Past)*, Routledge: London and New York.

Alfred J. Hoerth, Gerald L. Mattingly & Edwin M. Yamauchi (editors) (1994) *Peoples of the Old Testament World*, Baker Books: Grand Rapids, Michigan.

Hoffman, Michael A. (1979) *Egypt Before the Pharaohs (The Prehistoric Foundations of Egyptian Civilization)*, Alfred A. Knopf: New York.

Hoffmeier, James K. (1989) 'Reconsidering Egypt's Part in the Termination of the Middle Bronze Age', *Levant* 21, pp. 181-193.

―――― (1990) 'Some Thoughts on William G. Dever's "'Hyksos', Egyptian Destructions, and the End of the Palestinian Middle Bronze Age"', *Levant* 22, pp. 83-89.

―――― 'Egyptians.' In Alfred J. Hoerth, Gerald L. Mattingly & Edwin M. Yamauchi (editors) (1994a) *Peoples of the Old Testament World*, pp. 251-290.

——— (1994b) Millard, Alan R.
——— (1997) *Israel in Egypt (The Evidence for the Authenticity of the Exodus Tradition)*, Oxford University Press: Oxford and New York.
Hoffner, Harry A., Jr. 'Hittites.' In Alfred J. Hoerth, Gerald L. Mattingly & Edwin M. Yamauchi (editors) (1994) *Peoples of the Old Testament World*, pp. 127-155.
Hoffner, Harry A., Jr. & Beckman, Gary M. (1990) *Hittite Myths*. Scholars Press: Atlanta, Ga.
Holl, Augustin F. C. 'African History: Past, Present, and Future.' In Schmidt, Peter R. & Patterson, Thomas C. (editors) (1995) *Making Alternative Histories (The Practice of Archaeology and History in Non-Western Settings)*, pp. 183-211.
Holladay, A. J. (1989) 'The Hellenic Disaster in Egypt', *Journal of Hellenic Studies* 109, pp. 176-182.
Holm, Jean (editor) (1994) *Myth and History*, Pinter: London and New York.
Homet, Marcel F. (1965) *On the Trial of the Sun Gods*. Trans. from the French by Elizabeth Reynolds Hapgood. Neville Spearman: London.
Honoré, Pierre (1963) *In Quest of the White God (The Mysterious Heritage of South American Civilization)*. Trans. from the German by Olivier Corburn and Ursula Lehrburger. Hutchinson: London.
Hopfe, Lewis M. (editor) (1994) *Uncovering Ancient Stones (Essays in Memory of H. Neil Richardson)*, Eisenbrauns: Winona Lake, Ind.
Hornung, Erik (1982) *Conceptions of God in Ancient Egypt (The One and the Many)*. Trans. from the German by J. Baines. Cornell University Press: Ithaca, NY.
Houston, Drusilla Dunjee (1985[1926]) *Wonderful Ethiopians of the Ancient Kushite Empire*, Black Classic Press: Baltimore, MD.
Houston, Jean (1992) *The Hero and the Goddess (The Odyssey as Mystery and Initiation)*, Ballantine Books: New York.
Houston, Stephen & Stuart, David (1996) 'Of Gods, Glyphs and Kings: Divinity and Rulership Among the Classic Maya', *Antiquity* Vol. 70 - Num. 268, pp. 289-309.
Howe, Stephen (1998) *Afrocentrism: Mythical Pasts and Imagined Homes*, Verso: London and New York.
Huot, Jean-Louis (1994) *Les Premiers Villageois de Mésopotamie (Du village à la ville)*, Armand Colin: Paris.
Hurowitz, Victor (1994) 'Inside Solomon's Temple', *Bible Review* Vol. 10 - Num. 2, pp. 25-37;50.
——— (1994) 'Did King Solomon Violate the Second Commandment?', *Bible Review* Vol. 10 - Num. 5, pp. 26-33.

Hurry, Jamieson B. (1978 [1928]) *Imhotep: The Vizier and Physician of King Zoser and Afterwards the Egyptian God of Medicine*. Second revised edition. Oxford University Press/AMS Press: New York.

Hutchinson, R. W. (1948) 'Notes on Minoan Chronology', *Antiquity* Vol. 22 - Num. 85, pp. 61-74.

Huxley, G. L. (1965) *Achaeans and Hittites*, The Queen's University: Belfast.

Ingham, M. F. (1969) 'The Length of the Sothic Cycle', *Journal of Egyptian Archaeology* 55, pp. 36-40.

Ivimy, John (1975) *The Sphinx & the Megaliths*, HarperCollins: New York.

Jack, J. W. (1925) *The Date of the Exodus (In Light of External Evidence)*, T & T Clark: Edinburgh, U.K.

Jackson, Howard M. (1995) 'The Shadow of Pharaoh, Your Lord, Falls Upon You: Once Again Wenamun 2.46', *Journal of Near Eastern Studies* Vol. 54 - Num. 4, pp. 273-286.

Jackson, John G. (1974) *Introduction to African Civilizations*, Citadel Press: Secaucus, NJ.

———— (1993) *Man, God, and Civilization*, Carol: New York.

Jacobson, Thorkild (1976) *The Treasures of Darkness (A History of Mesopotamian Religion)*, Yale University Press: New Haven and London.

Jacot, Louis (1986) *A Heretical Cosmology (The Catastrophic Dislocations of Galaxies, Stars and Planets)*, Exposition-Banner: Pompano Beach, Fl.

Jacquet-Gordon, Helen (1981) 'Fragments of a Topographical List Dating to the Reign of Tuthmosis I', *Bulletin de l'Institut Français d'Archéologie Orientale* 81 (Supplément), pp. 41-46.

Helen Jacquet-Gordon, Charles Bonnet, & Jean Jacquet (1969) 'Pnubs and the Temple of Tabo on Argo Island', *Journal of Egyptian Archaeology* 55, pp. 103-111.

Jairazbhoy, R. A. (1974) *Ancient Egyptians and Chinese in America*, Rowman and Littlefield: Totowa, NJ.

———— 'The Egyptian Presence in South America.' In Van Sertima, Ivan (editor) (1987) *African Presence in Early America*, pp. 76-135.

James, George G. M. (1992 [1954]) *Stolen Legacy (Greek Philosophy is Stolen Egyptian Philosophy)*, AfricaWorld Press: Trenton, NJ.

James, Peter (in collaboration with I. J. Thorpe, Nikos Kokkinos, Robert Morkot and John Frankish) (1991a) *Centuries of Darkness (A Challenge to the Conventional Chronology of Old World Archaeology)*, Jonathan Cape: London.

———— (1991b) 'Centuries of Darkness: Context, Methodology and Implications', *Cambridge Archaeological Journal* 1, pp. 228-235.

———— (1992) 'Centuries of Darkness: A Reply to Critics', *Cambridge Archaeological Journal* 2, pp. 127-144.

Jaritz, Horst & Bickel, Susanne (1994) 'Une porte monumentale d'Amenhotep III. Second rapport préliminaire sur les blocs réemployés dans le temple de Merenptah à Gourna', *Bulletin de l'Institut Français d'Archéologie Orientale* 94, pp. 277-285.

Jones, M. E. Moncton (1924) *Ancient Egypt from the Records*, Methuen: London.

Jones, Major J. (1987) *The Color of God (The Concept of God in Afro-American Thought)*, Mercer: Macon, Ga.

Jones, Michael (1990) 'The Temple of Apis in Memphis', *Journal of Egyptian Archaeology* 76, pp. 141-147.

Jones, P.V. (1992) 'The Past in Homer's Odyssey', *Journal of Hellenic Studies* 112, pp. 74-90.

Jourdan, Lucien 'Sacrifices de moutons dans des tombes de Kerma de l'ile de Saisi (Vallée du Nil, début du deuxième millénaire avant J.C. et leur signification rituelle.' In C.N.R.S. (1980) *Mémoires archéologiques* — n° 1, pp. 6-82.

Juel, Donald (1988) *Messianic Exegegis (Christological Interpretation of the Old Testament in Early Christianity)*, Fortress Press: Philadelphia.

Juergens, Ralph E. (1963) 'Minds in Chaos: A Recital of the Velikovsky Story', *American Behavioral Scientist* Vol. 7 - Num. 1, pp. 4-17.

Kadry, Ahmed (1981) 'Some Comments on the Qadesh Battle', *Bulletin de l'Institut Français d'Archéologie Orientale* 81 (Supplément), pp. 47-55.

Kähler-Meyer, Emmi 'Myth Motifs in Flood Stories from the Grassland of Cameroon.' In Dundes, Alan (editor) (1988) *The Flood Myth*, pp. 249-259.

Kaiser, Water C., Jr. (1995) *The Messiah in the Old Testament*, Zondervan: Grand Rapids, Mich.

Kantor, Helene J. 'The Relative Chronology of Egypt and Its Foreign Correlations before the Late Bronze Age.' In Ehrich, Robert W. (editor) (1965) *Chronologies in Old World Archaeology*, pp. 1-46.

Karenga, Maulana (1988) 'Black Studies and the Problematic of Paradigm: The Philosophical Dimension', *Journal of Black Studies* Vol. 18 - Num. 4, pp. 395-414.

Karenga, Maulana & Carruthers, Jacob H. (editors) (1986) *Kemet and the African Worldview (Research, Rescue and Restoration)*, University of Sankore Press: Los Angeles.

Kee, Howard Clark (1984) *The New Testament in Context (Sources and Documents)*, Prentice-Hall: Englewood Cliffs, NJ.

Keel, Othmar (1993) 'Hyksos Horses or Hippopotamus Deities?', *Levant* 25, pp. 208-212.

Keightley, David N. (editor) (1983) *The Origins of Chinese Civilization*, University of California Press: Berkeley and Los Angeles.

Kelly, David H. (1991) 'Egyptians and Ethiopians: Color, Race, and Racism', *Classical Outlook* 68 (Spring), pp. 77-82.
Kemp, Barry J. (1983) see Trigger, Bruce.
────── (1989) *Ancient Egypt: Anatomy of a Civilization*, Routledge: London and New York.
Kemp, Barry J. et al. (1997) 'BOOK REVIEW: Askut in Nubia (The Economics and Ideology of Egyptian Imperialism in the Second Millennium B.C.). S. T. Smith. 1995', *Cambridge Archaeological Journal* Vol. 7 - Num. 1, pp. 123-137.
Kendall, Timothy 'Le Djebel Barkal: la Karnak de Koush.' In *La Nubie (L'archéologie au Soudan)* (1994) Éditions Faton: Dijon, pp. 46-53.
Kenyon, Kathleen M. (1957) *Digging Up Jericho*, Ernest Benn: London.
────── (1965) *Excavations at Jericho — Vol. II: The Tombs Excavated in 1955-8*, British School of Archaeology in Jerusalem: London.
────── (1966) *Amorites and Canaanites*, Oxford University Press: London.
────── (1970) *Archaeology in the Holy Land*. Third edition. Ernest Benn: London.
────── (1971) *Royal Cities of the Old Testament*, Barrie & Jenkins: London.
────── (1978) *The Bible and Recent Archaeology*, John Knox Press: Atlanta.
────── (1981) *Excavations at Jericho — Vol. III: The Architecture and Stratigraphy of the Tell*. Edited by Thomas A. Holland. British School of Archaeology in Jerusalem: London.
────── (1987) *The Bible and Recent Archaeology*. Revised edition by P.R.S. Moorey. John Knox Press: Atlanta, Ga.
Kerisel, J. (1993) 'Le conduit de la chambre de la reine dans la pyramide de Chéops.' *Bulletin de la Sociéte Française d'Égyptologie* 127, pp. 38-43.
Kesteloot, Lylian (1989) 'Du pouvoir à la métaphysique dans le mythe de Seth et Horus', *Présence Africaine* 149-150, pp. 193-202.
King, Katherine Callen (editor) (1994) *Homer*, Garland: New York.
King, Philip J. (1994) 'Jeremiah's Polemic Against Idols (What Archaeology Can Teach Us)', *Bible Review* Vol. 10 - Num. 6, pp. 23-29.
Kitchen, Kenneth Anderson (1962) *Suppiluliuma and the Amarna Pharaohs (A Study in Relative Chronology)*, Liverpool University Press.
────── (1966) *Ancient Orient and Old Testament*, Tyndale Press: London.
────── (1968) 'Further Notes on New Kingdom Chronology and History', *Chronique d'Égypte* 43, pp. 313-324.
────── (1972) 'Ramesses VII and the Twentieth Dynasty', *Journal of Egyptian Archaeology* 58, pp. 182-194.
────── (1973) *The Third Intermediate Period in Egypt (1100 - 650 B.C.)*, Aris & Phillips: Warminster, U.K.

——— (1977a) *The Bible in its World (Archaeology and the Bible Today)*, The Paternoster Press: Exeter, U.K.
——— (1977b) 'On the Princedoms of Late-Libyan Egypt', *Chronique d'Égypte* 52, pp. 40-48.
——— (1979) see Ruffle, John.
——— (1982a) *Pharaoh Triumphant (The Life and Times of Ramses II, King of Egypt)*, Aris & Phillips: Warminster, U.K.
——— (1982b) 'The Twentieth Dynasty Revisited', *Journal of Egyptian Archaeology* 68, pp. 116-125.
——— (1989a) 'Where Did Solomon's Gold Go?', *Biblical Archaeology Review* Vol. 15 - Num. 3, p. 31.
——— (1989b) 'Shishak's Military Campaign in Israel Confirmed', *Biblical Archaeology Review* Vol. 15 - Num. 3, p. 33.
——— 'The Arrival of the Libyans in Late New Kingdom Egypt.' In Leahy, Anthony (editor) (1990) *Libya and Egypt (c.1300-750 BC)*, pp. 15-27.
——— (1991a) 'The Chronology of Ancient Egypt', *World Archaeology* Vol. 23 - Num. 2, pp. 201-208.
——— (1991b) 'Egyptian Chronology: Problem or Solution?', *Cambridge Archaeological Journal* I, pp. 235-239.
——— (1993a) 'L'Égypte ancienne, et Ancient Testament: apperçus nouveaux', *Bulletin de la Société Française d'Égyptologie* 128, pp. 15-27.
——— 'New Directions in Biblical Archaeology: Historical and Biblical Aspects.' In Biran, A. & Aviram, J. (editors) (1993b) *Biblical Archaeology Today, 1990 (Proceedings of the Second International Congress on Biblical Archaeology — Jerusalem, June-July 1990)*, pp. 34-52.
——— (1995) 'The Patriarchal Age: Myth or History?', *Biblical Archaeology Review* Vol. 21 - Num. 2, pp. 48-55, 88.
Knapp, Bernard A. (1992a) 'Bronze Age Mediterranean Island Cultures and the Ancient Near East, Part 1', *Biblical Archaeologist* Vol. 55 - Num. 2, pp. 52-72.
——— (1992b) 'Bronze Age Mediterranean Island Cultures and the Ancient Near East, Part 2', *Biblical Archaeologist* Vol. 55 - Num. 3, pp. 112-128.
Kohl, Philip L. (1995) 'BOOK REVIEW: Centuries of Darkness: A Challenge to the Conventional Chronology of Old World Archaeology. P. James *et al.* 1995', *Journal of Interdisciplinary History* Vol. 26 - Num. 2, pp. 274-275.
Kruchten, Jean-Marie (1985) 'Un instrument politique original: La «belle fête de *pn-ntr*» des rois-prêtres de la XXI ^{ieme} dynastie', *Bulletin de la Société Française d'Égyptologie* 103, pp. 6-23.

——— (1989) *Les annales des pràtres de Karnak (XXI -XIII^(mes)Dynasties) et autres textes contemporains relatifs à l'initiation des prêtres d'Amon*, Département Oriëntalistiek: Leuven.
Krupp, E. C. (1983) *Echoes of the Ancient Skies (The Astronomy of Lost Civilizations)*, HarperCollins: New York.
Kugler, Robert A. (1996) *From Patriarch to Priest (The Levi-Priestly Tradition from Aramaic Levi to Testament of Levi)*, Scholars Press: Atlanta, Ga.
Kuhn, Thomas S. (1970) *The Structure of Scientific Revolutions*. Second edition. University of Chicago Press: Chicago, Ill.
Kuhrt, Amélie (1997 [1995]) *The Ancient Near East (c.3000 – 330 BC)*. Vols. I- II. Routledge: London and New York.
Labrousse, Audran 'Sedeinga, métrolope régionale au coeur de l'Empire méroitique.' In *La Nubie (L'archéologie au Soudan)* (1994) Éditions Faton: Dijon, pp. 34-39.
Lacovara, Peter 'An Outline of Nubian History.' In Celenko, Theodore (editor) (1996) *Egypt in Africa*, pp. 92-94.
Lam, Aboubacry Moussa (1989) 'Égypte ancienne et Afrique noire chez Cheikh Anta Diop', *Présence Africaine* 149-150, pp. 203-213.
LaMarche, Valmore C., Jr. & Hirschboeck, Katherine K. (1984) 'Frost Rings in Trees as Records of Major Volcanic Eruptions', *Nature* 307, pp. 121-126.
Lamberg-Karlovsky, C. C. & Sabloff, Jeremy A. (1979) *Ancient Civilizations (The Near East and Mesoamerica)*, Benjamin/Cummings: Menlo Park, Cal.
Lamberton, Robert & Keany, John J. (editors) (1992) *Homer's Ancient Readers (The Hermeneutics of Greek Epic's Earliest Exegetes)*, Princeton University Press: Princeton, NJ.
Lambropoulos, Vassilis (1993) *The Rise of Eurocentrism (Anatomy of Interpretation)*, Princeton University Press: Princeton, NJ.
Lanfranchi, Giovanni B. 'Assyrian Culture.' In Westenholz, Joan Goodnick (editor) (1996) *Royal Cities of the Biblical World*, pp. 171-193.
Lapis, I. A. 'The Culture of Ancient Egypt.' In Diakonoff, I. M. (editor) (1991) *Early Antiquity*, pp. 193-213.
Lapp, Paul W. (1969) 'The 1968 Excavations at Tell Ta'annek', *Bulletin of the American Schools of Oriental Research* 195, pp. 2-49.
Lauer, Jean-Philippe (1976) *Saqqara (The Royal Cemetery of Memphis: Excavations and Discoveries since 1850)*, Thames and Hudson: London.
Laurentin, René (1996) *Vie authentique de Jésus Christ*, Fayard: Paris.
Leahy, Anthony (1988a) 'The Earliest Dated Monuments of Amasis and the End of the Reign of Apries', *Journal of Egyptian Archaeology* 74, pp. 183-199.

────── (editor) (1988b) see Baines, John et al.
────── (editor) (1990) *Libya and Egypt (c.1300-750 BC)*, SOAS: London.
────── (1992) 'Royal Iconography and Dynastic Change, 750-525 BC: The Blue and Cap Crowns', *Journal of Egyptian Archaeology* 78, pp. 223-240.
────── (1994) see Eyre, Christopher
Leblanc, Christian (1982) 'Le culte rendu aux colosses «Osiriaques» durant le Nouvel Empire', *Bulletin de l'Institut Français d'Archéologie Orientale* 82, pp. 295-311.
────── (1993) 'Isis-Nofret, Grande Épouse royale de Ramsès II (la reine, sa famille et Nofretari)', *Bulletin de l'Institut Français d'Archéologie Orientale* 93, pp. 313-333.
Leek, F. Filce (1976) 'An Ancient Egyptian Mummified Fish', *Journal of Egyptian Archaeology* 62, pp. 131-133.
Leeming, David Adams (1990) *The World of Myth*, Oxford University Press: New York and Oxford.
Lefkowitz, Mary R. (1981) *The Lives of the Greek Poets*, Johns Hopkins University Press: Baltimore, MD.
────── (1992a) 'Not Out of Africa (The Origins of Greece and the Illusions of Afrocentrists)', *New Republic* (February 10), pp. 29-36.
────── (1992b) 'Reply to Martin Bernal', *New Republic* (March 9), p. 5.
────── (1992c) 'Afrocentrism Poses a Threat to the Rationalist Tradition', *Chronicle of Higher Education* (May 6), p. A52.
────── (1992d) see Bernal, Martin
────── (1993a) 'Afrocentrists Wage War on Ancient Greeks',*Wall Street Journal* (April 7), p. A14.
────── (1993b) 'Multiculturalism, Uniculturalism, or Anticulturalism?', *Partisan Review* Vol. 60 - Num. 4, pp. 590-596.
────── (1994a) 'Combating False Theories in the Classroom', *The Chronicle of Higher Education* (January 19), pp. B1-B3.
────── (1994b) 'The Myth of a "Stolen Legacy"', *Society* Vol. 31 - Num. 3, pp. 27-33.
────── (1997 [1996]) *Not Out of Africa (How Afrocentrism Became an Excuse to teach Myth as History)*. Second revised edition. BasicBooks: New York.
Lefkowitz, Mary R. & Rogers, G. M. (editors) (1996) *Black Athena Revisited*, University of North Carolina Press: Chapel Hill and London.
Lehner, Mark (1997) *The Complete Pyramids*, Thames and Hudson: London.
Lemche, Niels Peter (1990) *Ancient Israel (A New History of Israelite Society)*, JSOT Press: Sheffield, U.K.

——— (1996) 'Early Israel Revisited', *Currents in Research: Biblical Studies* 4, pp. 9-34.

Lemire, Laurent (1989) 'Jean Yoyotte ou l'Égypte san pharaon', *L'Histoire* 122, pp. 80-83.

Lenormant, François (1881) *Histoire ancienne de l'Orient jusqu'aux guerres médiques — Tome I: Les origines. – Les races et les langues*, A. Levy: Paris.

——— (1882) *Histoire ancienne de l'Orient jusqu'aux guerres médiques — Tome II: Les égyptiens*, A. Levy: Paris.

Leonard, Albert, Jr. (1981) 'Considerations of Morphological Variation in the Mycenaean Pottery from the Southeastern Mediterranean', *Bulletin of the American Schools of Oriental Research* 241, pp. 87-100.

Lepsius, Richard (1853) *Letters from Egypt, Ethiopia, and the Peninsula of Sinai*, Henry G. Bohn: London.

Lesko, Leonard H. (editor) (1986) *Egyptological Studies in Honor of Richard A. Parker*, Brown University Press: Hanover and London.

——— (1988) see Parker, R. A.

——— 'Ancient Egyptian Cosmogonies and Cosmology.' In Shafer, Byron E. (editor) (1991) *Religion in Ancient Egypt (Gods, Myths, and Personal Practice)*, pp. 88-122.

——— 'Egypt in the 12th Century B.C.' In Ward, William A. & Joukowsky, Martha Sharp (editors) (1992) *The Crisis Years: The 12th Century B.C. (From Beyond the Danube to the Tigris)*, pp. 151-156.

Lesko, Leonard H. & Lesko, Barbara (1999) 'Pharaoh's Workers (How the Israelites Lived in Egypt)', *Biblical Archaeology Review* Vol. 25 - Num. 1, pp. 36-45.

Levine, Molly Myerowitz (1989) 'The Challenge of Black Athena to Classics Today', *Arethusa* 22 (Fall - Special Issue), pp. 7-16.

——— (1990) 'Classical Scholarship: Anti-Black & Anti-Semitic? (Have Classical Historians Suppressed the Black and Semitic Roots of Greek Civilization?', *Bible Review* Vol.6 - Num. 3, pp. 32-36, 40.

——— (1992) 'The Use and Abuse of Black Athena', *American Historical Review* Vol. 97 - Num. 2, pp. 440-460.

Thomas E. Levy, Edwin C. M. van der Brink, Yuval Goren, & David Alon (1995) 'New Light on King Narmer and the Protodynastic Egyptian Presence in Canaan', *Biblical Archaeologist* Vol. 58 - Num. 1, pp. 26-34.

Lewis, Naphtali (1986) *Greeks in Ptolemaic Egypt (Case Studies in the Social History of the Hellenistic World)*, Clarendon Press: Oxford.

Liancheng, Lu (1993) 'Chariot and Horse Burials in Ancient China', *Antiquity* Vol. 67- Num. 257, pp. 824-837.

Lichtheim, Miriam (1973) *Ancient Egyptian Literature — A Book of Readings I: The Old and Middle Kingdom*, Berkeley, Ca.

Lili, Cui (1997) 'Project to Date China's Remote Ages', *Beijing Review* Vol. 40 - Num. 16, pp. 20-23.

Lilyquist, Christine (1993) 'Granulation and Glass: Chronological and Stylistic Investigations at Selected Sites, *ca.* 2500-1400 B.C.E.', *Bulletin of the American Schools of Oriental Research* 290-291, pp. 29-94.

Lipinski, E. (editor) (1991) *Phoenicia and the Bible (Proceedings of the Conference held at the University of Leuven on the 15th and 16th of March 1990)*, Departement Oriëntalistiek: Leuven and Uitgeverij Peeters: Leuven.

Liverani, Mario (editor) (1993) *Akkad: The First World Empire (Structure, Ideology, Traditions)*, Sargon: Padova.

Lloyd, Alan B. (1970) 'The Egyptian Labyrinth', *Journal of Egyptian Archaeology* 56, pp. 81-100.

——— (1972) 'Triremes and the Saite Navy', *Journal of Egyptian Archaeology* 58, pp. 268-279.

——— (1977) 'Necho and the Red Sea: Some Considerations', *Journal of Egyptian Archaeology* 63, pp. 142-155.

——— (1982) 'The Inscription of Udjahorresnet: A Collaborator's Testament', *Journal of Egyptian Archaeology* 68, pp. 166-180.

——— (1983) see Trigger, Bruce.

——— (editor) (1992) *Studies in Pharaonic Religion and Society (In Honour of J. Gwyn Griffiths)*, The Egypt Exploration Society: London.

——— 'Cambyses in Late Tradition.' In Eyre, Christopher et al. (editors) (1994) *The Unbroken Reed (Studies in the Culture and Heritage of Ancient Egypt — In Honour of A. F. Shore)*, pp. 195-204.

Logan, Alastair H. B. (1996) *Gnostic Truth and Christian Heresy (A Study in the History of Gnosticism)*, T&T Clark: Edinburgh, U.K.

Lucas, Jonathan Olumide (1970) *Religions in West Africa and Ancient Egypt*, Nigerian National Press: Apapa.

Luckenbill, Daniel D. (1968 [1928]) *Ancient Records of Assyria and Babylonia — Vol. I: Historical Records of Assyria from the Earliest Times to Sargon*, Greenwood Press: New York.

——— (1968 [1928]) *Ancient Records of Assyria and Babylonia — Vol. II: Historical Records of Assyria from Sargon to the End*, Greenwood Press: New York.

Luckert, Karl W. (1991) *Egyptian Light and Hebrew Fire (Theological and Philosophical Roots of Christendom in Evolutionary Perspective)*, State University of New York Press: Albany, NY.

Lüdemann, Gerd (1997) *The Unholy in Holy Scripture (The Dark Side of the Bible)*. Trans. from the German by John Bowden. Westminster John Knox Press: Louisville, Kentucky.

Machlin, Milt (1991) *Joshua's Altar (The Dig at Mount Ebal)*, William Morrow: New York.

Mack, Burton L. (1996) *Who Wrote the New Testament? (The Making of the Christian Myth)*, HarperCollins: New York.

Mackenzie, Donald Alexander (1917) *Myths of Crete & Pre-Hellenic Europe*, Gresham: London.

────── (1923) *Myths of Pre-Columbian America*, Gresham: London.

Maeir, Aren M. (1994) 'Hyksos, Horses and Hippopotami: A Note', *Levant* 26, pp. 231.

Malamud, Martha A. (1989) 'BOOK REVIEW: 'Black Athena: The Afroasiatic Roots of Classical Civilization. Vol. I: The Fabrication of Ancient Greece, 1785-1985. M. Bernal. 1987', *Criticism* Vol. 31 - Num. 3, pp. 317-322.

Malek, Jaromir (1982) 'The Original Version of the Royal Canon of Turin', *Journal of Egyptian Archaeology* 68, pp. 93-106.

────── (1986) 'The Monuments Recorded by Alice Lieder in the "Temple of Vulcan" at Memphis in May 1853', *Journal of Egyptian Archaeology* 72, pp. 101-112.

────── (1989) 'An Early Eighteenth Dynasty Monument of Sipair from Saqqâra', *Journal of Egyptian Archaeology* 75, pp. 61-76.

────── (1996) 'The Egyptian Text on the Seal Impression from Alalakh (Tell Atchana)', *Levant* 28, pp. 173-176.

Manning, Sturt W. (1988) 'The Bronze Age Eruption of Thera: Absolute Dating, Aegean Chronology and Mediterranean Cultural Interrelations', *Journal of Mediterranean Archaeology* Vol. 1 - Num. 1, pp. 17-82.

────── (1990) 'Frames of Reference for the Past: Some Thoughts on Bernal, Truth and Reality', *Journal of Mediterranean Archaeology* Vol. 3 - Num. 2, pp. 255-274.

Manning, Sturt W. & Weninger, Bernhard (1992) 'A Light in the Dark: Archaeological Wiggle Matching and the Absolute Chronology of the Close of the Aegean Late Bronze Age', *Antiquity* 66, pp. 636-663.

Marblestone, Howard (1996) 'A "Mediterranean Synthesis": Professor Cyrus H. Gordon's Contribution to the Classics', *Biblical Archaeologist* Vol. 59 - Num. 1, pp. 22-30.

Marchand, Suzanne (1997) 'Leo Frobenius and the Revolt Against the West', *Journal of Contemporary History* Vol. 32 - Num. 2, pp. 153-170.

Margueron, Jean-Claude (1995) 'Emar, Capital of Astata in the Fourteenth Century BCE', *Biblical Archaeologist* Vol. 58 - Num. 3, pp. 126-138.

Marinatos, Nanno (1993) *Minoan Religion (Ritual, Image, and Symbol)*, University of South Carolina Press: Colombia.
Marinatos, Spyridon (1973) 'The First Mycenaeans in Greece', in R. A. Crossland and A. Birchall (editors), *Bronze Age Migrations in the Agean*, pp. 107-113.
Markoe, Glenn E. (1990) 'The Emergence of Phoenician Art', *Bulletin of the American Schools of Oriental Research* 279, pp. 13-26.
Martin, Frank (1984) 'The Egyptian Ethnicity Controversy and the Sociology of Knowledge', *Journal of Black Studies* Vol. 14 - Num. 3, pp. 295-325.
Martin, Geoffrey T. (1976) 'Excavations at the Memphite Tomb of Horemheb, 1975: Preliminary Report', *Journal of Egyptian Archaeology* 62, pp. 5-13.
———— (1978) 'Excavations at the Memphite Tomb of Horemheb, 1977: Preliminary Report', *Journal of Egyptian Archaeology* 64, pp. 5-9.
———— (1979) 'Excavations at the Memphite Tomb of Horemheb, 1978: Preliminary Report', *Journal of Egyptian Archaeology* 65, pp. 13-16.
Martin, Luther H. (1987) *Hellenistic Religion (An Introduction)*, Oxford University Press: New York and Oxford.
Martin, James (1996) 'Dating Solomon's Wife', *America* Vol. 174 - Num. 1, p. 15.
Martin, Thomas R. (1996) *Ancient Greece (From Prehistoric to Hellenistic Times)*, Yale University Press: New Haven and London.
Marty, Martin E. (1994) 'Literalism & Everything Else: A Continuing Conflict', *Bible Review* Vol. 10 - Num. 2, pp. 39-43;50.
Marxsen, Willi (1990) *Jesus and Easter (Did God Raise the Historical Jesus from the Dead?)*. Trans. by Victor Paul Furnish. Abingdon Press: Nashville, Tenn.
Maspero, Gaston (1893) *Études de mythologie et d'archéologie égyptiennes*. Paris.
———— (1893) *Lectures historiques (histoire ancienne)*. Paris.
———— (1923) *Au temps de Ramsès et d'Assourbanipal (Égypte et Assyrie Anciennes)*. 7ième édition. Hachette: Paris.
———— (1926) *Manual of Egyptian Archaeology (and Guide to the Study of Antiquities in Egypt. For the Use of Students and Travellers)*. Trans. by Agnes S. Johns. Sixth English edition. G. P. Putnam's Sons: New York.
Massey, Gerald (1970) *Ancient Egypt (The Light of the World)*, Samuel Weiser: New York.
Mastorakis, Michel & von Effenterre, Micheline (1991) *Les minoens (L'âge d'or de la Crète)*, Éditions Errance: Paris.

Matthäus, Harmut (1995) 'Representations of Keftiu in Egyptian Tombs and the Absolute Chronology of the Aegean Late Bronze Age', *Bulletin of the Institute of Classical Studies* 40, pp. 177-194.

Matthews, Victor H. & Benjamin, Don C. (1991) *Old Testament Parallels (Laws and Stories from the Ancient Near East)*, Paulist Press: New York and Mahwah, NJ.

Mayerson, Philip (1978) 'Anti-Black Sentiment in the VITAE PATRUM', *Harvard Theological Review* Vol. 71 - Num. 3-4, pp. 304-311.

Mazar, Amihai (1990) *Archaeology of the Land of the Bible — 10,000 - 586 B.C.E.*, Doubleday: New York.

——— (1998) see Gitin, Seymour.

McAnany, Patricia A. (1995) *Living with the Ancestors (Kinship and Kingship in Ancient Maya Society)*, University of Texas Press: Austin, TX.

McCaffree, Joe E. (1982) *Bible and I Ching Relationships*, South Sky Book Co.: Hong Kong and Seattle.

McCurly, Foster R. (1983) *Ancient Myths and Biblical Faith (Scriptural Transformations)*, Fortress Press: Philadelphia.

McDonald, Lee M. (1995) *The Formation of the Christian Biblical Canon*. Revised and expanded edition. Hendrickson: Peabody, Mass.

McEvenue, Sean (1990) *Interpreting the Pentateuch*, Liturgical Press: Collegeville, Minn.

McGregor, Malcolm F. (1987) *The Athenians and their Empire*, University of British Columbia Press: Vancouver.

McHugh, John (1975) *The Mother of Jesus in the New Testament*, Darton, Longman & Todd: London.

McMahon, Gregory (1989) 'The History of the Hittites', *Biblical Archaeologist* Vol. 52 - Nums. 2-3, pp. 62-77.

Mead, George Robert Stow (1968 [1903]) *Did Jesus Live 100 B.C.? (An Enquiry into the Talmud Jesus Stories, the Toldoth Jeschu, and some Curious Statements of Epiphanus: Being a Contribution to the Study of Christian Origins)*, University Books: New York.

Mellaart, James (1978) *The Archaeology of Ancient Turkey*, Rowman and Littlefield: Totowa, NJ.

Meltzer, Edmund S. (1988) 'Ancient Egypt through Three Windows', *Journal of the American Oriental Society* Vol. 108 - Num. 2, pp. 285-290.

Memmi, Albert (1990) *The Colonizer and the Colonized*. Trans. by Howard Greenfeld. Earthscan: London.

Ménard, René (1878) *La mythologie dans l'art ancient et moderne*, Librairie Ch. Delagrave: Paris.

Mendenhall, George E. (1962) 'The Hebrew Conquest of Palestine', *Biblical Archaeologist* Vol. 25 - Num. 3, pp. 66-87.

——— (1973) *The Tenth Generation (The Origins of the Biblical Tradition)*, Johns Hopkins University Press: Baltimore and London.
Menu, Bernadette (1988) 'Les actes de vente en Egypte ancienne, particulièrement sous les rois Kouchites et Saites', *Journal of Egyptian Archaeology* 74, pp. 165-171.
Mercer, Samuel A. B. (1942) *Horus: Royal God of Egypt*, Society of Oriental Research: Grafton, Mass.
Merriam, C. Hart (editor) (1993 [1910]) *The Dawn of the World (Myths and Tales of the Miwok Indians of California)*, University of Nebraska Press: Lincoln and London.
Meyer, Marvin W. (editor) (1987) *The Ancient Mysteries — A Sourcebook (Sacred Texts of the Mystery Religions of the Ancient Mediterranean World)*, HarperCollins: New York.
Meyers, Eric M. (1994) 'Second Temple Studies in the Light of Recent Archaeology — Part I: The Persian and Hellenistic Periods', *Currents in Research: Biblical Studies* 2, pp. 147-179.
Millard, Alan R. (1989) 'Does the Bible Exaggerate King Solomon's Golden Wealth?', *Biblical Archaeology Review*, Vol. 15 - Num. 3, pp. 21-30.
——— (1990) 'King Og's Iron Bed: Fact or Fancy?', *Bible Review* Vol. 6 - Num. 2; pp. 16-21.
——— (1994) 'Recreating the Tablets of the Law', *Bible Review* Vol. 10 - Num. 1, pp. 49-53.
Alan R. Millard, James K. Hoffmeier & David W. Baker (editors) (1994) *Faith, Tradition, and History (Old Testament Historiography in Its Near Eastern Context)*, Eisenbrauns: Winona Lake, Ind.
Miller, Alicia (1977) *Index to the Works of Immanuel Velikovsky*, Glassboro State College: Glassboro.
Milton, E. R. (editor) (1978) *Recollections of a Fallen Sky: Velikovsky and Cultural Amnesia (Papers presented at the University of Lethbridge May 9 and 10, 1974)*, Unileth Press: Lethbridge, Alberta.
Minault-Gout, Anne (1996) 'Une tête de la reine Tiyi découverte dans l'ile de Sai, au Soudan', *Revue d'Égyptologie* 47, pp. 37-41.
Miscall, Peter D. (1993) *Isiah*, JSOT Press: Sheffield, U.K.
Mitchell, T. C. (1988) *The Bible in the British Museum (Interpreting the Evidence)*, British Museum Publications: London.
Modrzejewski, Joseph Mélèze (1997) *The Jews of Egypt (From Ramses II to the Emperor Hadrian)*. Trans. from the French by Robert Cornman. Princeton University Press: Princeton, NJ.
Monnet Saleh, Janine (1986) 'Interprétation globale des documents concernant l'unification de l'Égypte, *Bulletin de l'Institut Français d'Archéologie Orientale* 86, pp. 227-238.

───── (1990) 'Interprétation globale des documents concernant l'unification de l'Égypte (suite)', *Bulletin de l'Institut Français d'Archéologie Orientale* 90, pp. 261-279.

Montet, Pierre (1952) 'Sur une statue de babouin et quelques blocs récemment trouvés à Tanis', *Bulletin Société Française d'Égyptologie*10, pp. 45-48.

Carlos Moore, Tanya R. Saunders & Shawna Moore (editors) (1995) *African Presence in the Americas,* Africa World Press: Trenton, NJ.

Moorehead, Caroline (1996) *Lost and Found (the 9,000 Treasures of Troy),* Viking Penguin: New York.

Moorey, P.R.S. (1982) *Ur of the Chaldees. A revised and updated edition of Sir Leonard Wolley's Excavations at Ur,* Cornell University Press: Ithaca, NY.

Moran, William L. (editor) (1992) *The Amarna Letters,* Johns Hopkins University Press: Baltimore and London.

Morenz, Siegfried (1973) *Egyptian Religion.* Trans. by Ann E. Keep, Cornell University Press: Ithaca, NY.

Moreux, Théophile Abbé (1924) *L'Atlantide a-t-elle existé?,* Gaston Doin: Paris.

Morkot, Robert G. (1990) '*Nb-mt-r* - United-With-Ptah', *Journal of Near Eastern Studies* Vol. 49 - Num. 4, pp. 323-337.

───── 'Nubia in the New Kingdom: The Limits of Egyptian Control.' In Davies, W. Vivian (editor) (1991) *Egypt and Africa (Nubia from Prehistory to Islam),* pp. 294-301.

Morris, Ian 'Periodization and the Heroes: Inventing a Dark Age.' In Golden, Mark & Toohey, Peter (editors) (1997) *Inventing Ancient History (Historicism, Periodization, and the Ancient World),* pp. 96-131.

Morris, Sarah P. (1989) 'Daidalos and Kadmos: Classicism and 'Orientalism'', *Arethusa* (Fall - Special Issue), pp. 39-54.

───── (1990) 'Greece and the Levant', *Journal of Mediterranean Archaeology* Vol. 3 - Num. 1, pp. 57-66.

Morrison, M. A. & Owen, D. I. (editors) (1981) *Studies on the Civilization and Culture of Nuzi and the Hurrians,* Eisenbrauns: Winona Lake, Ind.

Moule, Charles Francis Digby (1977) *The Origins of Christology,* Cambridge University Press: Cambridge, U.K.

Mountjoy, P. A. (1997) 'The Destruction of the Palace at Pylos Reconsidered', *Annual of the British School at Athens* 92, pp. 109-137.

Mudimbe, V.Y. (editor) (1992) *The Surreptitious Speech (Présence Africaine and the Politics of Otherness 1947-1987),* University of Chicago Press: Chicago and London.

Muhly, James D. (1990) 'Black Athena versus Traditional Scholarship', *Journal of Mediterranean Archaeology* Vol. 3 - Num. 1, pp. 83-110.
Mulholland, J. Derral 'Movements of Celestial Bodies —Velikovsky's Fatal Flaw.' In Goldsmith, Donald (editor) (1977) *Scientists Confront Velikovsky*, pp. 105-115.
Mullen, William 'Structuring the Apocalypse (Old and New World Variations.' In Milton, E. R. (editor) (1978) *Recollections of a Fallen Sky: Velikovsky and Cultural Amnesia (Papers presented at the University of Lethbridge May 9 and 10, 1974)*, pp. 67-78.
Murphy, Frederick J. (1994) 'Apocalypse and Apocalypticsm: The State of the Question', *Currents in Research: Biblical Studies* 2, pp. 147-179.
——— (1994) 'The Book of Revelation', *Currents in Research: Biblical Studies* 2, pp. 181-225.
Murphy, Raymond 'A Weberian Approach to Credentials: Credentials as a Code of Exclusionary Closure.' In Lorna Erwin & David Maclennan (editors) (1994) *Sociology of Education in Canada (Critical Persective on Theory, Research & Practice)*, pp. 102-119.
Muscarella, Oscar White (1995) 'The Iron Age Background to the Formation of the Phrygian State', *Bulletin of the American Schools of Oriental Research* 299-300, pp. 91-101.
Mussies, Gerard (1998) 'The Date of Jesus' Birth in Jewish and Samaritan Sources', *Journal for the Study of Judaism: in the Persian, Hellenistic and Roman Period* Vol. 29 - Num. 4, pp. 416-437.
Mwadilifu, Mwalimu I. (editor) (1984) *Cheikh Anta Diop an African Scientist (An Axiomatic Overview of his Teachings and Thoughts)*, ECA Associates: Chesapeake, NY.
Na'aman, Nadav 'Pharaonic Lands in the Jezreel Valley in the Late Bronze Age.' In M. Heltzer & E. Lipinski (editors) (1988) *Society and Economy in the Eastern Mediterranean (c.1500-1000 B.C.)*, Leuven, pp.177-185.
——— (1994a) 'The Hurrians and the End of the Middle Bronze Age in Palestine', *Levant* 26, pp. 175-184.
——— (1994b) see Finkelstein, Israel.
——— (1996) 'The Contribution of the Amarna Letters to the Debate on Jerusalem's Political Position in the Tenth Century B.C.E.', *Bulletin of the American Schools of Oriental Research* 304, pp. 17-27.
Naddaf, Gerard (1998) 'Lefkowitz and the Afrocentric Question', *Philosophy of the Social Sciences* Vol. 28 - Num. 3, pp. 451-470.
Nagy, Gregory (1990) *Pindar's Homer (The Lyric Possession of an Epic Past)*, Johns Hopkins University Press: Baltimore and London.
Naville, Édouard (1888) *The Shrine of Saft el Hennett and the Land of Goshen (1885)*, Egypt Exploration Fund: London.

——— (1890) *The Mound of the Jew and the City of Onias*, Egypt Exploration Fund: London.

——— (1891) *Bubastis (1887-1889)*, Egypt Exploration Fund: London.

——— (1892) *The Festival-Hall of Osorkon II in the Great Temple of Bubastis (1887-1889)*, The Egypt Exploration Fund: London.

——— (1903) *The Store-City of Pithom and the Route of the Exodus*, The Egypt Exploration Fund: London.

——— (1905) *The Text of the Old Testament*, The British Academy: London.

——— (1910) *The XIth Dynasty Temple at Deir El-Bahari (Part II)*, The Egypt Exploration Fund: London.

——— (1914) *The Cemeteries of Abydos (Part I - 1909-1910) (The Mixed Cemetery and Umm Le-Ga'ab)*, Egypt Exploration Fund: London.

Naville, E. & Hall, H. R. (1913) *The XIth Dynasty Temple at Deir El-Bahari (Part III)*, Egypt Exploration Fund: London.

Needham, J. 'Astronomy in Ancient and Medieval China.' In The British Academy (1974) *The Place of Astronomy in the Ancient World (A Joint Symposium of the Royal Society and the British Academy)*, pp. 67-82.

Newberry, Percy E. (1893) *Beni Hasan (PartI)*, Kegan Paul, Trench, Trübner & Co.: London.

——— (1932) 'King Ay, the Successor of Tut'ankhamun', *Journal of Egyptian Archaeology* 18, pp. 50-52.

Ngom, Gilbert (1989) ' L'Égyptien et les langues bantu: Le cas du duala', *Présence Africaine 149-150*, pp. 203-213.

Nibbi, Alessandra (1975) *The Sea Peoples and Egypt*, Noyes Press: Park Ridge, NJ.

Nicholson, Paul T. (1994) 'Preliminary Report on Work at the Sacred Animal Necropolis, North Saqqara, 1992', *Journal of Egyptian Archaeology* 80, pp. 1-10.

——— (1994) 'Archaeology Beneath Saqqara', *Egyptian Archaeology* 4, pp. 7-8.

——— (1996) 'The North Ibis Catacomb at North Saqqara', *Egyptian Archaeology* 9, pp. 16-18.

Niehaus, Jeffrey J. (1995) *God at Sinai (Covenant & Theophany in the Bible and Ancient Near East)*, Zondervan: Grand Rapids, Mich.

Nilsson, Martin P. (1986) *Homer and Mycenae*, Cooper Square: New York.

Nims, Charles F. (1948) 'An Oracle Dated in "The Repeating of Births"', *Journal of Near Eastern Studies* Vol. 7 - Num. 3, pp. 157-162.

Niwinsky, Andrzej (1995) 'Le passage de la XXe à la XXIIe dynastie (Chronologie et histoire politique)', *Bulletin de l'Institut Français d'Archéologie Orientale* 95, pp. 329-360.

Nobles, Vera L. (1996) 'Nubia and Egypt: Is it Ella or a Copy?', *Journal of Black Studies* Vol. 26 - Num. 4, pp. 431-446.
Nodet, Étienne (1993) 'Flavius Josèphe: Création et histoire', *Revue Biblique* T. 100-1, pp. 5-40.
Noguera, Anthony (1976) *How African was Egygt? (A Comparative Study of Ancient Egyptian and Black African Cultures)*, Vantage: New York.
Nolan, Albert (1978) *Jesus Before Christianity*, Orbis Books: Maryknoll, NY.
Noth, Martin (1958) *The History of Israel*, Adam & Charles Black: London.
Obenga, Théophile (1969) 'L'Afrique dans l'Antiquité', *Présence Africaine* 72, pp. 73-84.

─────── (1970) 'Méthode et conception historique de Cheikh Anta Diop', *Présence Africaine* 74, pp. 3-28.

─────── (1973) *L'Afrique dans l'Antiquité (Egypte pharaonique — Afrique noire)*. Présence Africaine: Paris.

─────── (1974) 'Les 20 ans de Nations nègres et culture ', *Présence Africaine* 89, pp. 214-223.

─────── (1975) 'Contribution de l'Egyptologie au dévelopment de l'histoire africaine', *Présence Africaine* 94, pp. 119-139.

─────── (1978) 'Cheikh Anta Diop et les autres', *Présence Africaine* 105-106, pp. 29-44.

─────── (1978) 'Parenté linguistique génétique entre l'égyptien (ancient égyptien et copte) et les langues négro-africaines modernes', *Le peuplement de l'Egypte ancienne et le déchiffrement de l'écriture meroitique*. Actes du colloque tenu au Caire du 28 janvier au 3 février 1974. Collection: Histoire Générale de l'Afrique, Études et documents n° 1., pp. 65-71, UNESCO: Paris.

─────── (1980a) *Pour une Nouvelle Histoire*, Présence Africaine: Paris.

─────── (1980b) 'Formation du pluriel en Sémitique et en Egyptien', *Cahiers Congolais d'Anthropologie et d'Histoire* 5, pp. 31-38.

─────── (1983) 'Les origines des Pharaons sont africaines', *Afrique Histoire* 7, pp. 47-48.

─────── (1986a) 'Le message de Cheikh Anta Diop', *Revue Culturelle Malienne* 7, p. 16.

─────── (1986b) 'La philosophie pharaonique', *Présence Africaine* 137-138, pp. 3-24.

─────── (1987) 'L'univers puissant et multiple de Cheikh Anta Diop', *Ethiopiques, Revue trimestrielle de culture négro-africaines* IV, 1-2, 9-16.

─────── (1988) 'Esquisse d'une histoire culturelle de l'Afrique par la lexicologie', *Présence Africaine* 145, pp. 3-25.

─────── (1989a) 'L'économie de la nature ou le Grand Hymne à Aton', *Présence Africaine* 149-150, pp. 249-266.

———— 'African Philosophy of the Pharaonic Period.' In Van Sertima, Ivan (editor) (1989b) *Egypt Revisited*, pp. 286-324.

———— (1990) *La philosophie africaine de la période pharaonique 2780-330 avant notre ère*, L'Harmattan: Paris.

———— (1996) *Cheikh Anta Diop, Volney et le Sphinx (Contribution de Cheikh Anta Diop à l'historiographie mondiale)*, Présence Africaine: Paris; Khepera: Gif-sur-Yvette, France.

———— (1998) *African Philosophy in World History*, Sungai: Princeton, NJ.

O'Brien, Joan V. (1993) *The Transformation of Hera (A Study of Ritual, Hero, and the Goddess in Iliad)*, Rowman & Littlefield: Lanham, Maryland.

Ockinga, Boyo G. (1987) 'On the Interpretation of the Kadesh Record', *Chronique d'Égypte* 62, pp. 38-48.

O'Collins, Gerald (1995) *Christology (A Biblical, Historical, and Systematic Study of Jesus)*, Oxford University Press: Oxford and New York.

O'Connell, Robert H. (1983) 'The Emergence of Horus (An Analysis of Coffin Text Spell 148)', *Journal of Egyptian Archaeology* 69, pp. 66-87.

O'Connor, David (1983) see Trigger, Bruce.

———— (1987) 'The Location of Irem', *Journal of Egyptian Archaeology* 73, pp. 99-136.

———— 'The Nature of Tjemhu (Libyan) Society in the Later New Kingdom.' In Leahy, Anthony (editor) (1990) *Libya and Egypt (c.1300-750 BC)*, pp. 29-113.

———— 'Early States Along the Nubian Nile.' In Davies, W. Vivian (editor) (1991) *Egypt and Africa (Nubia from Prehistory to Islam)*, pp. 145-165.

———— (1993) *Ancient Nubia: Egypt's Rival in Africa*, University Museum of Archaeology – University of Pennsylvania: Philadelphia.

———— 'Egypt and Greece: The Bronze Age Evidence.' In Lefkowitz, Mary R. & Rogers, Guy M. (editors) (1996) *Black Athena Revisited*, pp. 49-61.

———— 'The Hyksos Period in Egypt.' In Oren, Eliezer D. (editor) (1997) *The Hyksos: New Historical and Archaeological Perspectives*, pp. 45-83.

Okpewho, Isidore (1981) 'Cheikh Anta Diop: The Search for a Philosophy of African Culture', *Cahiers d'Études Africaines* 84 – XXI: 4, pp. 587-602.

Oppenheim, A. Leo (1967) *Letters from Mesopotamia (Official, Business, and Private Letters on Clay Tablets from Two Millennia)*, University of Chicago Press: Chicago and London.

Oren, Eliezer D. (editor) (1997) *The Hyksos: New Historical and Archaeological Perspectives*, University Museum of the University of Pennsylvania: Philadelphia.

Osman, Ahmed (1991) *Moses: Pharaoh of Egypt (The Mystery of Akhenaten Resolved)*, Paladin: London.
Page, Sydney H. T. (1995) *Powers of Evil (A Biblical Study of Satan and Demons)*, Baker Books: Grand Rapids, Mich.; Apollos: Leicester, U.K.
Pagels, Elaine (1988) *Adam, Eve, and the Serpent*, Random House: New York.
─────── (1991) 'The Social History of Satan, the "Intimate Enemy": A Preliminary Sketch', *Harvard Theological Review* 84:2, pp. 105-128.
Palmer, Leonard R. (1965) *Mycenaeans and Minoans (Agean Prehistory in the Light of the Linear B Tablets)*. Second revised edition. Faber and Faber: London.
Parker, G. W. (1917) 'The Aryan Origin of Grecian Civilization', *Journal of Negro History* 2, pp. 334-344.
Parker, Richard A. 'Ancient Egyptian Astronomy.' In The British Academy (1974) *The Place of Astronomy in the Ancient World (A Joint Symposium of the Royal Society and the British Academy)*, pp. 51-65.
Parker, R. A. & Lesko, Leonard H. 'The Khonsu Cosmogony.' In Baines, John *et al.* (editors) (1988) *Pyramid Studies and other Essays*, pp. 168-174.
Parpola, Simo (1983) *Letters from Assyrian Scholars to the Kings Esarhaddon and Assurbanipal*. Vols. I-II. Butzon & Bercker: Kevelaer.
Pasztory, Esther (1997) *Teotihuacan (An Experiment in Living)*, University of Oklahoma Press: Norman and London.
Patterson, Orlando (1971) 'Rethinking Black History', *Harvard Educational Review* 41, pp. 297-315.
─────── (1977) *Ethnic Chauvanism (The Reactionary Impulse)*, Stein and Day: New York.
Pearce, Sarah (1995) 'Josephus as Interpreter of Biblical Law: The Representation of the High Court of Deut.17:8-12 according to Jewish Antiquities 4.218', *Journal of Jewish Studies* Vol. 46 - Nums.1-2, pp. 30-42.
Peet, Thomas Eric (1914) *The Cemeteries of Abydos (Part II. 1911-1912)*, Egypt Exploration Fund: London.
Peiser, Benny 'Post-Mycenaean Greek History Begins in the 6th Century BC: The Controversy about the Olympic Victor List and its Implications for early Greek Chronology.' In Zysman, Milton & Whelton, Clark (editors) (1990) *Catastrophism 2000 (A Sourcebook for the Conference: Reconsidering Velikovsky)*, pp. 265-288.
Pensée (editors) (1976) *Velikovsky Reconsidered*, Doubleday: Garden City, NY.
Leo G. Perdu, Lawrence E. Toombs & Gary L. Johnson (editors) (1987) *Archaeology and Biblical Interpretation (Essays in Memory of D. Glenn Rose)*, John Knox Press: Atlanta, Ga.

Perrot, G. & Chipiez, C. (1882) *Histoire de l'art dans l'antiquité (Égypte, Assyrie, Phénicie, Judée, Asie Mineure, Perse, Grèce, Étrurie, Rome)* — Tome I: *L'Égypte*, Hachette: Paris.

───── (1882) *Histoire de l'art dans l'antiquité (Égypte, Assyrie, Phénicie, Judée, Asie Mineure, Perse, Grèce, Étrurie, Rome)* — Tome II: *Chaldée et Assyrie*, Hachette: Paris.

───── (1885) *History of Art in Phoenicia and its Dependencies*. Vol. I. Trans. & edited by Walter Armstrong. Chapman and Hall: London.

───── (1887) *Histoire de l'art dans l'antiquité (Égypte, Assyrie, Phénicie, Judée, Asie Mineure, Perse, Grèce, Étrurie, Rome)* — Tome IV: *Judée (Sardaigne, Syrie, Cappadoce)*, Hachette: Paris.

───── (1890) *Histoire de l'art dans l'antiquité (Égypte, Assyrie, Phénicie, Judée, Asie Mineure, Perse, Grèce, Étrurie, Rome)* — TomeV: *Perse (Phrygie, Lydie et Carie, Lycie)*, Hachette: Paris.

Peters, Ted (editor) (1989) *Cosmos as Creation (Theology and Science in Consonance)*, Abingdon Press: Nashville, Tenn.

Petrie, William Matthew Flinders (1890) *Kahun, Gurob, and Hawara*, Kegan Paul, Trench, Trübner: London.

───── (1894 -1905) *A History of Egypt*. Vols. I-VI. Methuen: London.

───── (1900) *The Royal Tombs of the First Dynasty (1900 - Part I)*, Egypt Exploration Fund: London.

───── (1901) *The Royal Tombs of the Earliest Dynasties (1901- Part II)*, Egypt Exploration Fund: London.

───── (1902) *Abydos (Part I. 1902)*, Egypt Exploration Fund: London.

───── (1905) *Ehnasya (1904)*, Egypt Exploration Fund: London.

───── (1939) *The Making of Egypt*, Sheldon Press: London.

Pfouma, Oscar (1989) 'L'héritage pharaonique: Hommage à Cheikh Anta Diop', *Présence Africaine* 149-150, pp. 267-282.

───── (1993) *Histoire culturelle de l'Afrique noire*, Éditions Publisud: Paris.

Piérart, Marcel & Touchais, Gilles (1996) *Argos (Une ville grecque de 6000 ans)*, Editions Paris-Méditerranée / CNRS: Paris.

Pierron, Véronique (1996) 'L'histoire manipulée', *Sciences et Avenir* (March), pp. 90-92.

Pinch, Geraldine (1993) *Votive Offerings to Hathor*, Griffith Institute / Ashmolean Museum: Oxford, U.K.

Piñero, A. (1993) 'Angels and Demons in the Greek Life of Adam and Eve', *Journal for the Study of Judaism (in the Persian, Hellenistic and Roman Period)* Vol. 24 - Num. 2, pp. 191-214.

Pippin, Tina (1996) 'Ideology, Ideological Criticism, and the Bible', *Currents in Research:Biblical Studies* 4, pp. 51-78.

Plumley, Martin J. 'Gods and Pharaohs at Qasr Ibrim.' In John Ruffle, G. A. Gaballa and Kenneth A. Kitchen (editors) (1979) *Glimpses of Ancient Egypt (Studies in Honour of H. W. Fairman)*, pp. 127-131.
Pobi-Asamani, Kwadwo O. (1994) *W.E.B. Du Bois (His Contributions to Pan-Africanism)*, Borgo Press: San Bernardino, Cal.
Podany, A. (1988) *The Chronology and History of the Hana Period*. Ph.D. diss., UCLA.
Poe, Richard (1997) *Black Spark, White Fire (Did African Explorers Civilize Ancient Europe?)*, Prime: Rocklin, Cal.
Porada, Edith (1984) 'The Cylinder Seal from Tell el Dab'a', *American Journal of Archaeology* Vol. 88 - Num.4, pp. 485-488.
Porten, Bezalel (1968) *Archives from Elephantine (The Life of an Ancient Jewish Military Colony)*, University of California Press: Berkely and Los Angeles.
────── (1995) 'Did the Ark Stop at Elephantine?', *Biblical Archaeology Review* Vol. 21- Num. 3, pp. 54-67, 76-77.
Postgate, J. N. (1994) *Early Mesopotamia (Society and Economy at the Dawn of History)*, Routledge: London and New York.
Potter, Charles Francis (1964) *The Lost Years of Jesus*, University Books: New Hyde Park, NY.
Prag, Kay (1986) 'Byblos and Egypt in the Fourth Millenium B.C.', *Levant* 18, pp. 59-73.
Préaux, Claire (1992) *Le monde hellénistique (La Grèce et l'Orient de la mort d'Alexandre à la conquête de la Grèce 323-146 AVANT J.-C.)* Tome 2. Presses Universitaires de France: Paris.
Prior, Michael (1997) *The Bible and Colonialism: A Moral Critique*, Sheffield Academic Press: Sheffield, U.K.
Pritchard, James B. (editor) (1955) *Ancient Near Eastern Texts (Relating to the Old Testament)*. 2nd edition. Princeton University Press: Princeton, NJ.
────── (editor) (1958) *The Ancient Near East (An Anthology of Texts and Pictures)*, Oxford University Press: Oxford and New York.
────── (editor) (1974) *Solomon and Sheba*, Phaidon: London.
────── (editor) (1975) *The Ancient Near East — Volume II: A New Anthology of the Texts and Pictures*, Princeton University Press: Princeton, NJ.
Puhvel, Jaan (1987) *Comparative Mythology*, Johns Hopkins University Press: Baltimore and London.
Rainey, Anson F. (1978) *El Amarna Tablets 359-379*. Supplement to J. A. Knudtzon, Die El-Armana-Tafeln. 2nd edition, revised. Kevelaer, Butzon & Bercker /Neukirchen-Vluyn, Neukirchener Verlag.
Räisänen, Heikki (1990) *The Messianic Secret in Mark's Gospel*. Trans. by Christopher Tuckett. T&T Clark: Edinburgh, U.K.

Rambova, N. (1977) *The Shrine of Tut-Ankh-Amon*, Princeton University Press: Princeton, NJ.
Ransom, C. J. 'Science's Unscientific Reception of Velikovsky.' In Ravel, N. (editor) (1975) *From Past to Prophecy: Velikovsky's Challenge to Conventional Beliefs (Proceedings of the Symposium held at the Saidye Bronfman Centre, Montreal, Quebec – January 10th-12th, 1975)*, pp. 15-20.
——— (1976) *The Age of Velikovsky*, Delta: New York.
——— 'How Stable is the Solar System?' In Pensée (editors) (1976a) *Velikovsky Reconsidered*, Doubleday: Garden City, NY, pp. 95-100.
Ransom, C. J. & Hoffee, L. H. 'The Orbits of Venus.' In ibid (1976b), pp. 103-110.
Rapoport, Louis (1980) *The Lost Jews (Last of the Ethiopan Falashas)*, Stein and Day: New York.
Raschke, Wendy J. (editor) (1988) *The Archaeology of the Olympics (The Olympics and other Festivals in Antiquity)*, University of Wisconsin Press: Madison.
Rashidi, Runoko & Van Sertima, Ivan (editors) (1995) *African Presence in Early Asia*, Journal of African Civilization/Transaction: New Brunswick, NJ.
Ravel, Nahum (editor) (1975) *From Past to Prophecy: Velikovsky's Challenge to Conventional Beliefs (Proceedings of the Symposium held at the Saidye Bronfman Centre, Montreal, Quebec – January 10th-12th, 1975)*, YM / YWHA & NHS: Montreal, QC.
Ravitch, Diane (1990) 'Multiculturalism: E Pluribus Plure', *American Scholar* 59 (Summer), pp. 337-354.
——— (1991) see Asante, Molefi Kete.
Rawlinson, George (1882) *History of Ancient Egypt*. Vol. II. S. E. Cassino: Boston; Porter and Coates: Philadelphia.
——— (1897) *Ancient Egypt*, T. Fisher Unwin: London; G. P. Putnam's Sons: New York.
Rawson, Jessica (1993) 'Ancient Chinese Ritual Bronzes: The Evidence from Tombs and Hoards of the Shang (c.1500-1050 BC) and Western Zhou (c.1050-771 BC) Periods', *Antiquity* Vol. 67 - Num. 257, pp. 805-820.
Ray, John D. (1990) 'An Egyptian Perspective', *Journal of Mediterranean Archaeology* Vol. 3 - Num. 1, pp. 77-81.
——— (1996) 'Amasis: The Pharaoh with no Illusions', *History Today* Vol. 46 - Num. 3, pp. 27-31.
Redd, Danita 'Black Madonnas of Europe: Diffusion of the African Isis', In Van Sertima, Ivan (editor) (1985) *African Presence in Early Europe*, pp. 108-133.

Redford, Donald B. (1967) *History and Chronology of the Eighteeth Dynasty of Egypt: Seven Studies*, University of Toronto Press: Toronto.
——— (1971) 'The Earliest Years of Ramses II, and the Building of the Ramesside Court at Luxor', *Journal of Egyptian Archaeology* 57, pp. 110-119.
——— (1973a) 'An Interim Report on the Second Season of Work at the Temple of Osiris, Ruler of Eternity, Karnak', *Journal of Egyptian Archaeology* 59, pp. 16-30.
——— (1973b) 'Studies in Relations Between Palestine and Egypt During the First Millennium B.C.', *Journal of the American Oriental Society* Vol. 93 - Num. 1, pp. 3-17.
——— (1985) 'Sais and the Kushite Invasions of the Eighth Century B.C.', *Journal of the American Research Center in Egypt* 22, pp. 5-15.
——— 'The Name Manetho.' In Lesko, Leonard H. (editor) (1986) *Egyptological Studies in Honor of Richard A. Parker*, pp. 118-121.
——— (1986) *Pharaonic King-Lists, Annals and Day-Books (A Contribution to the Study of the Egyptian Sense of History)*, Benben Publications: Mississauga, Ont.
——— (1992) *Egypt, Canaan, and Israel in Ancient Times*, Princeton University Press: Princeton, NJ.
——— (1993) 'Taharqa in Western Asia and Libya', *Eretz-Israel* 24, pp. 188-191.
——— 'Textual Sources for the Hyksos Period.' In Oren, Eliezer D. (editor) (1997) *The Hyksos: New Historical and Archaeological Perspectives*, pp. 1-44.
Redmount, Carol A. (1995) 'The Wadi Tumilat and the "Canal of the Pharaohs"', *Journal of Near Eastern Studies* Vol. 54 - Num. 2, pp. 127-135.
Rehak, Paul & Younger, John G. (1998) 'Review of Aegean Prehistory VII: Neo-palatial, Final Palatial, and Postpalatial Crete, *American Journal of Archaeology* Vol. 102 - Num. 1, pp. 91-173.
Reichard, Gladys A. (1977 [1950]) *Navaho Religion (A Study of Symbolism)*, Princeton University Press: Princeton, NJ.
Reisner, George A. (1923) 'The Meroitic Kingdom of Ethiopia: A Chronological Outline', *Journal of Egyptian Archaeology* 9, pp. 34-77.
Renfrew, Colin (1972) *The Emergence of Civilisation (The Cyclades and the Aegean in the Third Millennium B.C.)*, Methuen: London.
——— (1990 [1987]) *Archaeology and Language (The Puzzle of Indo-European Origins)*, Cambridge University Press: Cambridge, U.K.
——— Foreword to James, Peter *et al.* (1991) *Centuries of Darkness (A Challenge to the Conventional Chronology of Old World Archaeology)*, pp. xiii-xv.

Rice, Michael (1991) *Egypt's Making (The Origins of Ancient Egypt 5000-2000 BC)*, Routledge: London and New York.
Richard, Earl (1988) *Jesus: One and Many (The Christological Concept of New Testament Authors)*, Michael Glazier: Wilmington, Del.
Richards, Dona (see Ani, Marimba)
Richardson, Alan (1954) *History Sacred and Profane*, Westminster Press: Philadelphia.
Ries, Julien (éditeur) (1982) *Gnosticisme et monde hellénistique (Actes du colloque de Louvain-la-Neuve ‹11-14 mars 1980›)*. Avec collaboration de Yvonne Janssens et de Jean-Marie Servin. Université catholique de Louvin, Institut Orientaliste: Louvin-la-Neuve.
Ritner, Robert K. (1985) 'Anubis and the Lunar Disc', *Journal of Egyptian Archaeology* 71, pp. 149-155.
Rochberg-Halton, F. (1991) 'Between Observation and Theory in Babylonian Astronomical Texts', *Journal of Near Eastern Studies* Vol. 50 - Num. 2, pp. 107-120.
Rohl, David M. (1992) 'Some Chronological Conundrums of the 21st Dynasty', *Ägypten und Levante* 3, pp. 137-139.
────── (1995) *A Test of Time — Vol. I: The Bible (From Myth to History)*, Century: London.
────── (1998) *A Test of Time — Vol. II: Legend (The Genesis of Civilisation)*, Century: London.
Rohr, Richard (1996) *Jesus' Plan for a New World (The Sermon on the Mount)*. In collaboration with J. B. Feister. St. Anthony Messanger Press: Cincinnati, Ohio.
Rollins, Wayne G. (1983) *Jung and the Bible*, John Knox Press: Atlanta, Ga.
Rose, Lynn E. 'The Censorship of Velikovsky's Interdisciplinary Synthesis.' In Pensée (editors) (1976) *Velikovsky Reconsidered*, Doubleday: Garden City, NY, pp. 13-20.
────── Preface to Velikovsky, Immanuel (1982) *Mankind in Amnesia*, Doubleday: Garden City, NY, pp. vii-ix.
────── (1994) 'The Astronomical Evidence for Dating the End of the Middle Kingdom of Ancient Egypt to the Early Second Millenium: A Reassessment', *Journal of Near Eastern Studies* Vol. 53 - Num. 4, pp. 237-261.
Ross, Anne (1976) *The Folklore of the Scottish Highlands*, B. T. Batsford: London.
Roth, Ann Macy (1988) 'The Organization of Royal Cemeteries at Saqqara in the Old Kingdom', *Journal of the American Research Center in Egypt* 25, pp. 201-214.

―――― 'Building Bridges to Afrocentrism: A Letter to My Egyptological Colleagues.' In Gross, Levitt, & Lewis (1996) *The Flight from Science and Reason*, pp. 313-326. Also available on the Internet at http://www.sas.upenn.edu/African_Studies/Articles_Gen/afrocent_roth.html

―――― (1997) 'BOOK REVIEW: Not Out of Africa: How Afrocentrism Became an Excuse to Teach Myth as History. M. R. Lefkowitz. 1996; Black Athena Revisited. M. R. Lefkowitz & G. M. Rogers. 1996', *American Historical Review* Vol. 102 - Num. 2, pp. 493-495.

John Ruffle, G. A. Gaballa and Kenneth A. Kitchen (editors) (1979) *Glimpses of Ancient Egypt (Studies in Honour of H. W. Fairman)*, Aris & Phillips: Warminster, U.K.

Robert John Russell, Nancey Murphy and C. J. Isham (editors) (1996) *Quantum Cosmology and the Laws of Nature (Scientific Perspectives on Divine Action)*. Second edition. Vatican Observatory Publications: Vatican City State; The Center for Theology and the Natural Sciences: Berkeley, Cal.

Russell, John Malcolm 'Nineveh.' In Westenholz, Joan G. (editor) (1996) *Royal Cities of the Biblical World*, pp. 153-170.

Ryhiner, Marie-Louise (1986) *Rites égyptiens VI — L'offrande du lotus (dans les temples égyptiens de l'époque tardive)*, Fondation Égyptologique Reine Élisabeth: Bruxelles.

Ryholt, Kim S. B. (1993) 'A Pair of Oracle Petitions Addressed to Horus-of-the-Camp', *Journal of Egyptian Archaeology* 79, pp. 189-198.

Sachs, A. 'Babylonian Observational Astronomy.' In The British Academy (1974) *The Place of Astronomy in the Ancient World (A Joint Symposium of the Royal Society and the British Academy)*, pp. 43-50.

Sackho-Autissier, Aminata (1997) 'Soudan: Royaumes du Nil', *Archéologia* 331, pp. 36-45.

Sader, Hélène 'The 12th Century B.C. in Syria; The Problem of the Rise of the Aramaeans.' In Ward, William A. & Joukowsky, Martha Sharp (editors) (1992) *The Crisis Years: The 12th Century B.C. (From Beyond the Danube to the Tigris)*, pp. 157-163.

Sagan, Carl 'An Analysis of Worlds in Collision.' In Goldsmith, Donald (editor) (1977) *Scientists Confront Velikovsky*, pp. 41-104.

―――― (1979) *Broca's Brain (Reflections on the Romance of Science)*, Random House: New York.

Saleh, Abdel-Aziz (1972) 'Some Problems Relating to the Pwenet Reliefs at Deir el-Bahari', *Journal of Egyptian Archaeology* 58, pp. 140-158.

―――― (1981) 'Notes on the Ancient Egyptian *t-ntr* "God's-Land"', *Bulletin de l'Institut Français d'Archéologie Orientale* 81 (Supplément), pp. 107-117.

Sales, Véronique (1996) 'Moise, les hébreux et Pharaon (Entretien avec Jean Yoyotte)', *l'Histoire* 205, pp. 76-83.
Sall, Babacar (1989) 'Histoire et conscience historique: De la philosophie de l'histoire dans l'œuvre de Cheikh Anta Diop', *Présence Africaine* 149-150, pp. 283-291.
Samartha, S. J. (1991) *One Christ — Many Religions (Toward a Revised Christology)*, Orbis Books: Maryknoll, NY.
Sambin, Chantal (1992) 'Les portes de Médamoud du musée de Lyon', *Bulletin de l'Institut Français d'Archéologie Orientale* 92, pp. 147-184.
Samson, Julia (1977) 'Nefertiti's Regality', *Journal of Egyptian Archaeology* 63, pp. 88-97.
Sandars, N. K. (1978) *The Sea Peoples (Warriors of the Ancient Mediterranean 1250-1150 BC)*, Thames and Hudson: London.
Sanders, Ed Parish (1992) *Judaism (Practice and Belief 63 BCE-66CE)*, SCM Press: London, Trinity Press International: Philadelphia.
Sanders, Prince E. (editor) (1969) *Haytian Papers*. Reprint. Negro Universities Press: Westport, Conn.
Sarna, Nahum M. (1986) *Exploring Exodus (The Heritage of Biblical Israel)*, Schocken Books: New York.
Satlow, Michael L. (1997) 'Jewish Constructions of Nakedness in Late Antiquity', *Journal of Biblical Literature* Vol. 116 - Num. 3, pp. 429-454.
Sauneron, Serge (1957) *The Priests of Ancient Egypt*. Trans. by Ann Morrissett. Grove Press: New York; Evergreen Books: London.
Säve-Söderberg, Torgny (1951) 'The Hyksos Rule in Egypt', *Journal of Egyptology Archaeology* 37, pp. 53-71.
Sayed, Abdel Monem A. H. (1983) 'New Light on the Recently Discovered Port on the Red Sea Shore', *Chronique d'Égypte* 58, pp. 23-37.
Scarborough, Vernon L. & Wilcox, David R. (editors) (1991) *The Mesoamerican Ball-game*, University of Arizona Press: Tucson.
Schaeffer, Claude Frédéric-Armand (1948) *Stratigraphie comparée et chronologie de l'Asie Occidentale (IIIe et IIe millénaires)*, Oxford University Press: London.
Schäfer, Heinrich (1974) *Principles of Egyptian Art*. Trans. and ed. by John Baines. Clarendon Press: Oxford, U.K.
Schele, Linda & Freidel, David (1990) *A Forest of Kings (The Untold Story of the Ancient Maya)*, William Morrow: New York.
Schele, Linda & Miller, Mary Ellen (1986) *The Blood of Kings (Dynasty Ritual in Maya Art)*, George Braziller: New York; Kimbell Art Museum: Fort Worth, TX.
Schilling, Harold K. (1973) *The New Consciousness in Science and Religion*, United Church Press: Philadelphia.

Schlagel, Richard H. (1995) *From Myth to Modern Mind (A Study of the Origins and Growth of Scientific Thought) — Vol. I: Theogony Through Ptolemy*, Peter Lang: New York.
Schliemann, Heinrich (1881) *Ilios (The City and Country of the Trojans)*, Harper & Brothers: New York.
Schmidt, Peter R. & Patterson, Thomas C. (editors) (1995) *Making Alternative Histories (The Practice of Archaeology and History in Non-Western Settings)*, School of American Research Press: Sante Fe, Mexico.
Schoch, Robert M. (1999) *Voices of the Rocks (A Scientist Looks at Catastrophes and Ancient Civilizations)*. With Robert Aquinas McNally. Harmony Books: New York.
Schreiter, Robert J. (editor) (1991) *Faces of Jesus in Africa*, Orbis Books: Maryknoll, NY.
Schwartz, Benjamin I. (1985) *The World of Thought in Ancient China*, Harvard University Press: Cambridge, Mass.
Schwartz, Regina W. (1997) *The Curse of Cain (The Violent Legacy of Monotheism)*, University of Chicago Press: Chicago and London.
Scully, Stephen (1990) *Homer and the Sacred City*, Cornell University Press: Ithaca and London.
Seele, Keith C. (1955) 'King Ay and the Close of the Amarna Age', *Journal of Near Eastern Studies* Vol. 14 - Num. 3, pp. 168-180.
——— (1957) see Steindorff, George.
Seger, Joe D. (1975) 'The MB II Fortifications at Shechem and Gezer: A Hyksos Retrospective', *Eretz-Israel* 12, pp. 34-45.
Sellers, Jane B. (1992) *The Death of Gods in Ancient Egypt (An Essay on Egyptian Religion and the Frame of Time)*, Penguin Books: New York.
Sexton, James D. (trans./ed.) (1992) *Mayan Folktales (Folklore from Lake Atitlán, Guatemala)*, Anchor Books/Doubleday: New York and London.
Shafer, Byron E. (editor) (1991) *Religion in Ancient Egypt (Gods, Myths, and Personal Practice)*, Cornell University Press: Ithaca, NY.
Hershel Shanks, William G. Dever, Baruch Halpern & P. Kyle McCarter, Jr. (1992) *The Rise of Ancient Israel*. Symposium at the Smithsonian Institution - October 26, 1991. Biblical Archaeology Society: Washington, D.C.
Shaw, Ian (1994) 'Balustrades, Stairs and Altars in the Cult of the Aten at El-Amarna', *Journal of Egyptian Archaeology* 80, pp. 109-127.
Shaw, Maria C. (1996) 'The Bull-Leaping Fresco from Below the Ramp House at Mycenae: A Study in Iconography and Artistic Transmission', *Annual of the British School at Athens* 91, pp. 167-191.
Sherratt, E. S. (1990) 'Reading the Texts: Archaeology and the Homeric Question', *Antiquity* Vol. 64 - Num. 245, pp. 807-824.

Shinnie, P. L. (1967) *Meroe (A Civilization of the Sudan)*, Frederick A. Praeger: New York and Washington.

——— 'Urbanism in the Ancient Sudan.' In John Ruffle, G. A. Gaballa and Kenneth A. Kitchen (editors) (1979) *Glimpses of Ancient Egypt (Studies in Honour of H. W. Fairman)*, pp. 123-126.

——— (1996) *Ancient Nubia*, Kegan Paul Intl.: London and New York.

Shires, Henry M. (1974) *Finding the Old Testament in the New*, Westminster Press: Philadelphia.

Silver, Daniel Jeremy (1982) *Images of Moses*, Basic Books: New York.

Silverman, Neil Asher (1982) *Digging for God and Country (Exploration, Archaeology, and the Secret Struggle for the Holy Land 1799-1917)*, Alfred A. Knopf: New York.

Simonnet, Dominique & Stavridès, Yves (1996) "Égyptologie: «Il ne suffit pas de lire les hiéroglyphes.» — Un entretien avec le Pr Jean Yoyotte', *L'Express* 2372, pp. 110-112.

Singer, Itamar (1983) 'Western Anatolia in the Thirteenth Century B.C. According to the Hittite Sources', *Anatolian Studies* 33, pp. 205-217.

——— (1995) 'A Hittite Seal from Megiddo', *Biblical Archaeologist* Vol. 58 - Num. 2, pp. 91- 92.

Sloyan, Gerard S. (1995) *The Crucifixion of Jesus (History, Myth, Faith)*, Fortress Press: Minneapolis.

Smart, Ninian & Hecht, Richard D. (editors) (1982) *Sacred Texts of the World (A Universal Anthology)*, Crossroad: New York.

Smelik, Klaas A. D. (1991) *Writings from Ancient Israel (A Handbook of Historical and Religious Documents)*. Trans. by G. I. Davies. Westminster / John Knox Press: Louisville, Kentucky.

Smith, H. S. (1976) 'Preliminary Report on Excavations in the Sacred Animal Necropolis (Season 1974-1975)', *Journal of Egyptian Archaeology* 62, pp. 14-17.

Smith, H. S. & Jeffreys, D. G. (1977) 'The Sacred Animal Necropolis, North Saqqâra: 1975/6', *Journal of Egyptian Archaeology* 63, pp. 20-28.

Smith, Mark S. (1996) 'The Literary Arrangement of the Priestly Redaction of Exodus: A Preliminary Investigation', *Catholic Biblical Quarterly* Vol. 58 - Num. 4, pp. 523-539.

Smith, Michael E. (1996) *The Aztecs*, Blackwell: Oxford, U.K.

Smith, Stephen H. (1996) 'The Function of the Son of David Tradition in Mark's Gospel', *New Testament Studies* Vol. 42 - Num. 4, pp. 523-539.

Smith, Stuart Tyson (1995) *Askut in Nubia (The Economics and Ideology of Egyptian Imperialism in the Second Millennium B.C.)*, Paul Kegan International: London and New York.

Smoller, Laura Ackerman (1994) *History, Prophecy, and the Stars (The Christian Astrology of Pierre D'Ailly, 1350 - 1420)*, Princeton University Press: Princeton, NJ.

Snodgrass, Anthony M. (1971) *The Dark Age of Greece (An Archaeological Survey of the Eleventh to Eighth Centuries BC)*, Edinburgh University Press: Edinburgh, U.K.

────── (1980) *Archaic Greece (The Age of Experiment)*, J M Dent & Sons: London.

Snowden, Frank (1948) 'The Negro in Ancient Greece', *American Anthropologist* 50, pp. 31-44.

────── (1970) *Blacks in Antiquity: Ethiopians in the Greco-Roman Experience*, Harvard University Press: Cambridge, Mass.

────── (1983) *Before Color Prejudice: The Ancient View of the Blacks*, Harvard University Press: Cambridge, Mass.

────── (1989) 'Bernal's "Blacks," Herodotus, and Other Classical Evidence', *Arethusa* (Fall - Special Issue), pp. 83-95.

────── (1990) 'Did Herodotus Say the Egyptians Were Black?', *Biblical Archaeology Review* Vol. 16 - Num. 2, pp. 72-74.

────── (1993) 'Images and Attitudes: Ancient Views of Nubia and the Nubians', *Expedition* Vol. 35 - Num. 2, pp. 40-50.

────── 'Bernal's "Blacks" and the Afrocentrists.' In Lefkowitz, Mary R. & Rogers, Guy M. (editors) (1996) *Black Athena Revisited*, pp. 112-128.

────── 'The Physical Characteristics of Egyptians and their Southern Neighbors: The Classical Evidence.' In Celenko, Theodore (editor) (1996) *Egypt in Africa*, pp. 106-108.

Solmsen, Friedrich (1960) *Aristotle's System of the Physical World: A Comparison with His Predecessors*, Cornell University Press: Ithaca, NY.

────── (1979) *Isis among the Greeks and Romans*, Harvard University Press: Cambridge, Mass.

Solomon, Robert C. & Higgins, Kathleen M. (editors) (1993) *From Africa to Zen (An Invitation to World Philosophy)*, Rowman & Littlefield: Lanham, MD.

Souffrant, Claude (1970) 'Catholicisme et négritude à l'heure du Black Power', *Présence Africaine* 75, pp. 131-140.

Sours, Michael (1991) *The Prophecies of Jesus*, Oneworld Publications: Oxford, U.K.

Soustelle, Jacques (1984) *The Olmecs (The Oldest Civilization in Mexico)*. Trans. from the French by Helen R. Lane. Doubleday: Garden City, NY.

Spady, James (1989) 'Dr. Cheikh Anta Diop and the Background of Scholarship on Black Interest in Egyptology and Nile Valley Civilizations', *Présence Africaine* 149-150, pp. 292-312.

Spalinger, Anthony J. (1980) 'Historical Observations on the Military Reliefs Reliefs of Abu Simbel and Other Ramesside Temples in Nubia', *Journal of Egyptian Archaeology* 66, pp. 83-99.

─────── (1995) 'Some Remarks on the Epagomenal Days in Ancient Egypt', *Journal of Near Eastern Studies* Vol. 54 - Num. 1, pp. 33-47.

Sproul, Barbara C. (1991) *Primal Myths (Creation Myths Around the World)*, HarperCollins: New York.

Stager, Lawrence E. (1985) 'Merneptah, Israel and Sea Peoples: New Light on an Old Relief', *Eretz-Israel* 18, pp. 56-64.

Stambaugh, John E. (1972) *Sarapis Under the Early Ptolemies*, E. J. Brill: Leiden, Netherlands.

Stanesby, Derek (1985) *Science, Reason & Religion*, Croom Helm: London.

Stecchini, Livio C. (1963) 'The Inconsistant Heavens: Velikovsky in Relation to some Past Cosmic Perplexities', *American Behavioral Scientist* Vol. 7 - Num. 1, pp. 19-44.

Steindorff, George & Seele, Keith C. (1957) *When Egypt Ruled the East*, University of Chicago Press: Chicago and London.

Stepugina, T. V. 'China in the First Half of the First Millenium B.C.' In Diakonoff, I. M. (editor) (1991) *Early Antiquity*, pp. 420-432.

Stevenson, W. Taylor (1969) *History as Myth (The Import for Contemporary Theology)*, Seabury Press: New York.

Stiebing, William H., Jr. (1971) 'Hyksos Burials in Palestine: A Review of the Evidence', *Journal of Near Eastern Studies* Vol. 30 - Num. 2, pp. 110-117.

─────── (1980) 'The End of the Mycenaean Age', *Biblical Archaeologist* Vol. 43 - Num. 1, pp. 7-21.

─────── (1985) 'Should the Exodus and the Israelite Settlement be Redated?', *Biblical Archaeology Review* Vol. 11 - Num. 4, pp. 58-67.

─────── (1989) *Out of the Desert? (Archaeology and the Exodus/Conquest Narratives)*, Prometheus Books: Buffalo, NY.

─────── (1994) 'Climate & Collapse (Did the Weather Make Israel's Emergence Possible?', *Bible Review* Vol. 10 - Num. 4, pp. 19-27, 54.

Stieglitz, Robert R. (1990) 'The Geopolitics of the Phoenician Littoral in the Early Iron Age', *Bulletin of the American Schools of Oriental Research* 279, pp. 9-12.

─────── (1991) 'The City of Amurru', *Journal of Near Eastern Studies* Vol. 50 - Num. 1, pp. 45-48.

Stone, Bryan Jack (1995) 'The Philistines and Acculturation: Culture Change and Ethnic Continuity in the Iron Age', *Bulletin of the American Schools of Oriental Research* 298, pp. 7-27.

Storer, Norman W. 'The Sociological Context of the Velikovsky Controversy.' In Goldsmith, Donald (editor) (1977) *Scientists Confront Velikovsky*, pp. 29-39.
Stove, David 'The Scientific Mafia.' In Pensée (editors) (1976) *Velikovsky Reconsidered*, Doubleday: Garden City, NY, pp. 5-13.
Strachan, Gordon (1985) *Christ and the Cosmos*, Labarum Publications: Dunbar, Scotland.
Strayer, Joseph R. (editor) (1943) *The Interpretation of History*, Princeton University Press: Princeton, NJ.
Stuart, Douglas (1976) 'The Sovereign's Day of Conquest', *Bulletin of the American Schools of Oriental Research* 221, pp. 159-164.
Sugden, Edward H. (1928) *Israel's Debt to Egypt*, Epworth Press: London.
Sweeney, Marvin A. (1993) 'The Book of Isaiah in Recent Research', *Currents in Research: Biblical Studies* 1, pp. 141-162.
Syrén, Roger (1993) *The Forsaken First-Born (A Study of a Recurrent Motif in the Patriarchal Narratives)* JSOT(Supplement Series 133): Sheffield, U.K.
Talbott, Stephen L. (1966-1976) *Velikovsky Reconsidered*, Warner: New York.
Taylor, John H. (1988) 'BRIEF COMMUNICATIONS: A daughter of King Harsiese', *Journal of Egyptian Archaeology* 74, pp. 230-231.
Taylour, William, Lord (1990) *The Mycenaeans*. Revised edition. Thames and Hudson: London.
Te Velde, H. (1967) *Seth, God of Confusion (A Study of His Role in Egyptian Mythology and Religion)*. Trans. by G. E. van Baaren-Pape. E. J. Brill: Leiden.
───── (1971) 'Some Remarks on the Structure of Egyptian Divine Triads', *Journal of Egyptian Archaeology* 57, pp. 80-86.
Tefnin, Roland (1968-1972) 'Contribution à l'iconographie d'Aménophis I: La statuette 42.099 du Musée du Caire', *Annuaire de l'Institut de Philologie et d'Histoire Orientales et Slaves* 20, pp. 433-437.
Templeton, John M. (1995) *The Humble Approach (Scientists Discover God)*. Revised edition. Continuum: New York.
Tessier, Beatrice (1990) 'The Seal Impression Alalakh 194: A New Aspect of Egypto-Levantine Relations in the Middle Kingdom', *Levant* 22, pp. 65-71.
Thompson, Dorothy J. (1988) *Memphis Under the Ptolemies*, Princeton University Press.
Thompson, J. Eric S. (1970) *The Rise and Fall of Maya Civilization*. Second enlarged edition. University of Oklahoma Press: Norman.

―――― 'Maya Astronomy.' In The British Academy (1974) *The Place of Astronomy in the Ancient World (A Joint Symposium of the Royal Society and the British Academy)*, pp. 83-98.

―――― (1990) *Maya History & Religion*, University of Oklahoma Press: Norman.

Thompson, Stephen E. (1990) 'The Origin of the Pyramid Texts Found on Middle Kingdom Saqqâra Coffins', *Journal of Egyptian Archaeology* 76, pp. 17-25.

Townsend, Richard F. (editor) (1992) *The Ancient Americas (Art from Sacred Landscapes)*, Art Institute of Chicago: Prestel Verlag, Munich.

Claude Traunecker, Françoise Le Saout & Olivier Masson (1981) *La chapelle d'Achôris à Karnak — II (Texte et documents)*. Centre franco-égyptien d'étude des temples de Karnak. Éditions ADPF: Paris.

Trigger, Bruce G. (1969) 'The Royal Tombs at Qustul and Ballâna and their Meroitic Antecedents', *Journal of Egyptian Archaeology* 55, pp. 117-128.

―――― (1976) *Nubia Under the Pharaohs*, Westview Press: Boulder, Col.

―――― (1980) *Gordon Childe (Revolutions in Archaeology)*, Columbia University Press: New York.

―――― (1987) 'Egypt: A Fledging Nation', *Journal of the Society for the Study of Egyptian Antiquities* Vol. 17 - Num. 1-2, pp. 58-65.

―――― (1989) *A History of Archaeological Thought*, Cambridge University Press: Cambridge, U.K.

―――― (1993) *Early Civilizations: Ancient Egypt in Context*, American University in Cairo Press: Cairo.

―――― (1992) 'Brown Athena: A Postprocessual Goddess?', *Current Anthropology* Vol. 33 - Num. 1, pp. 121-123.

―――― (1994) 'BOOK REVIEW: Centuries of Darkness: A Challenge to the Conventional Chronology of Old World Archaeology. P. James *et al.* 1991', *American Historical Review* Vol. 99 - Num. 3, pp. 872-873.

―――― (1997) see Kemp, Barry J. et al.

―――― (1998) 'Archaeology and Epistemology: Dialoguing across the Darwinian Chasm', *American Journal of Archaeology* Vol. 102 - Num. 1, pp. 1-34.

Bruce G. Trigger, Barry J. Kemp, David O'Connor & Alan B. Lloyd (1983) *Ancient Egypt: A Social History*, Cambridge University Press: Cambridge, U.K.

Trimier, Jacqueline 'The Myth of Authenticity: Personhood, Traditional Culture, and African Philosophy.' In Solomon, Robert C. & Higgins, Kathleen M. (editors) (1993) *From Africa to Zen (An Invitation to World Philosophy)*, pp. 187-219.

Triomphe, Robert (1989) *Le lion, la vierge et le miel,* Les Belles Lettres: Paris.
Trouillot, Michel-Rolph (1995) *Silencing the Past (Power and the Production of History),* Beacon Press: Boston, Mass.
Turner, Frank M. (1989) 'Martin Bernal's Black Athena: A Dissent', *Arethusa* (Fall - Special Issue), pp. 97-109.
Ulansey, David (1994) 'Solving the Mithraic Mysteries', *Biblical Archaeology Review* Vol. 20 - Num. 5, pp. 40-53, 79.
Uphill, E. P. (1984) *The Temple of Per Ramesses,* Aris & Phillips: Warminster, U.K.
Ussishkin, David (1980) 'Was the "Solomonic" City Gate at Megiddo Built by King Solomon?', *Bulletin of the American Schools of Oriental Research* 239, pp. 1-18.
——— 'King Solomon's Palace and Building 1723 in Megiddo.' In *Israel Exploration Journal Reader* (1981) with a prolegomenon by Harry M. Orlinsky. Vol. I. KTAV: New York, pp. 284-296.
——— (1990) 'Notes on Megiddo, Gezer, Ashdod, and Tel Batash in the Tenth to Ninth Centuries B.C.', *Bulletin of the American Schools of Oriental Research* 277-278, pp. 71-91.
van Der Woude, Adam s. (1995) 'Tracing the Evolution of the Hebrew Bible (What the Dead Sea Scrolls Teach Us)', *Bible Review* Vol. 11 - Num.1, pp. 42-45.
Van Groningen, Gerard (1990) *Messianic Revelation in the Old Testament,* Baker Books: Grand Rapids, Mich.
Van Sertima, Ivan (1976) *They Came Before Columbus,* Random House: New York.
——— (editor) (1985) *African Presence in Early Europe,* Journal of African Civilizations / Transaction Books: New Brunswick, NJ.
——— (editor) (1987) *African Presence in Early America,* Journal of African Civilizations / Transaction Books: New Brunswick, NJ.
——— (1988) *Great Black Leaders (ancient and Modern),* Journal of African Civilizations / Transaction Books: New Brunswick, NJ.
——— (editor) (1989a) *Egypty Revisited,* Journal of African Civilizations/ Transaction Books: New Brunswick, NJ.
——— (1989b) 'Death Shall Not Find Us Thinking That We Die', *Présence Africaine* 149-150, pp. 321-330.
——— (editor) (1992) *Great African Thinkers Cheikh Anta Diop,* Journal of African Civilizations / Transaction Books: New Brunswick, NJ.
——— (editor) (1994) *Egypt: Child of Africa,* Journal of African Civilizations / Transaction Books: New Brunswick, NJ.
——— (1995) see Rashidi, Runoko.

Van Seters, John (1966) *The Hyksos (A New Investigation)*, Yale University Press: New Haven and London.
——— (1983) *In Search of History (Historiography in the Ancient World and the Origins of Biblical History)*, Yale University Press: New Haven and London.
Van Siclen, Charles Cornell, III (1973) 'The Accession Date of Amenhotep III and the Jubilee', *Journal of Near Eastern Studies* Vol. 32 - Num. 3, pp. 290-300.
Vandenberg, Philipp (1979) *Ramses II*. Traduit de l'allemand par Jeanne-Marie Gaillard-Paquet. Pierre Belfond: Paris.
——— (1979) *The Mystery of the Oracles (World-Famous Archaeologists Reveal the Best-Kept Secrets of Antiquity)*, Macmillan: New York.
Vandersleyen, Claude (1977) 'Une stèle de l'an 18 d'Ahmosis à Hanovre', *Chronique d'Égypte* 52, pp. 223-244.
——— (1988) 'Les deux jeunesses d'Amenhotep III', *Bulletin de la Sociéte Françaíse d'Égyptologie* 111, pp. 9-27.
Vardaman, Jerry & Yamauchi, Edwin M. (editors) (1989) *Chronos, Kairos, Christos (Nativity and Chronological Studies)*. Presented to Jack Finegan. Eisenbrauns: Winona Lake, Ind.
Vaughn, Wally G. (1991) *From the Descent to the Exodus: Five Unresolved Issues*, Peter E. Randall: Portsmouth, NH.
Velikovsky, Immanuel (1950) *Worlds in Collision*, Doubleday: Garden City, NY.
——— (1952) *Ages In Chaos — Vol. I: From the Exodus to King Akhnaton*, Doubleday: Garden City, NY.
——— (1955) *Earth in Upheaval*, Doubleday: Garden City, NY.
——— (1960) *Oedipus and Akhnaton*, Doubleday: Garden City, NY.
——— (1963) 'Some Additional Examples of Correct Prognosis', *American Behavioral Scientist* Vol. 7 - Num. 1, pp. 50-54.
——— 'Additional Examples of Correct Prognosis.' In de Grazia, Alfred (editor) (1966) *The Velikovsky Affair (The Warfare of Science and Scientism)*, pp. 232-245.
——— (1977a) *Peoples of the Sea*, Doubleday: Garden City, NY.
——— 'My Challenge to Conventional Views in Science.' In Greenberg, Lewis M. & Sizemore, Warner B. (1977b) *Velikovsky and Establishment Science*, pp. 5-17.
——— 'The Ten Points of Sagan.' In ibid (1977c), pp. 32-48.
——— (1978) *Ramses II and His Time*, Doubleday: Garden City, NY.

────── 'Cultural Amnesia: The Submergence of Terrifying Events in the Racial Memory and their Later Emergence.' In Milton, E. R. (editor) (1978) *Recollections of a Fallen Sky: Velikovsky and Cultural Amnesia (Papers presented at the University of Lethbridge May 9 and 10, 1974)*, pp. 21-28.
────── Afterword to Milton, E. R. (editor) (1978) pp. 149-153.
────── (1982) *Mankind in Amnesia*, Doubleday: Garden City, NY.
────── (1983) *Stargazers and Gravediggers (Memoirs to Worlds in Collision)*, William Morrow: New York.
────── For extensive archive of Velikovsky's unpublished works on the Internet, see http://www.varchive.org/
Verbruggen, H. (1981) *Le Zeus crétois*, Les Belles Lettres: Paris.
Vercoutter, Jean (1956) *L'Égypte et le monde égéen préhellénique (Études critiques des sources égyptiennes: Du début de la XVIIe à la fin de la XIXe Dynastie)*, IFAO: Cairo.
────── (1992) *L'Égypte et la vallée du Nil — Tome I: Des origines à la fin de l'Ancien Empire*, Presses Universitaires de France: Paris.
Verhoeven, Ursula & Derchain, Philippe (1985) *Rites égyptiens V — Le voyage de la déesse libyque (Ein Text aus dem «Mutritual» des Pap. Berlin 3053)*, Fondation Égyptologique Reine Élisabeth: Bruxelles.
Vernienne, Marc (editor) (1996) *Studies in the Book of Exodus (Redaction, Reception, Interpretation)*, Leuven University Press: Leuven, Belgium.
Vernus, P. (1978) 'L'apport des sources égyptiennes au problème hourrite', *Revue Hittite et Asianique* 36, pp. 189-197.
Vinogradov, I. V. 'The Middle Kingdom of Egypt and the Hyksos Invasion.' In Diakonoff, I. M. (editor) (1991) *Early Antiquity*, pp. 158-171.
Vitaliano, Dorothy B. (1973) *Legends of the Earth: Their Geologic Origins*, Indiana University Press: Bloomington and London.
von Känel, Frédérique (1984) *Les prêtres-ouab de Sekhmet et les conjurateurs de Serket*, Presses Universitaires de France: Paris.
von Rad, Gerhard (1991) *Holy War in Ancient Israel*, Trans. & edited by Marva J. Dawn. William B. Eerdmans: Grand Rapids, Mich.
Wainwright, Arthur W. (1993) *Mysterious Apocalypse (Interpreting the Book of Revelations)*, Abingdon Press: Nashville, Tenn.
Wainwright, G. A. (1923) 'The Red Crown in Early Prehistoric Times', *Journal of Egyptian ARchaeology* 9, pp. 26-33.
────── (1936) 'Orion and the Great Star', *Journal of Egyptian Archaeology* 22, pp. 45-46.
────── (1946) 'Zeberged: The Shipwrecked Sailor's Island', *Journal of Egyptian Archaeology* 32, pp. 31-38.

―――― (1961) 'Some Sea-Peoples', *Journal of Egyptian Archaeology* 47, pp. 71-90.
―――― (1963) 'The Origin of Storm-Gods in Egypt', *Journal of Egyptian Archaeology* 63, pp. 13-20.
Walker, J. D. (1995) 'The Misrepresentation of Diop's Views', *Journal of Black Studies* Vol. 26 - Num. 1, pp. 77-85.
Wallet-Lebrun, Christiane (1982) 'Notes sur le temple d'Amon-Rà à Karnak (I)', *Bulletin de l'Institut Français d'Archéologie Orientale* 82, pp. 355-362.
―――― (1984) 'Notes sur le temple d'Amon-Rê à Karnak', *Bulletin de l'Institut Français d'Archéologie Orientale* 84, pp. 317-333.
Ward, William A. (1971) *Egypt and the East Mediterranean World: 2200-1900 B.C. (Studies in Egyptian Foreign Relations During the First Intermediate Period)*, American University of Beirut: Beirut, Lebanon.
―――― (1992) 'The Present Status of Egyptian Chronology', *Bulletin of the American Schools of Oriental Research* 288, pp. 53-66.
Ward, William A. & Joukowsky, Martha Sharp (editors) (1992) *The Crisis Years: The 12th Century B.C. (From Beyond the Danube to the Tigris)*, Kendall/Hunt: Dubuque, Iowa.
Warren, P. & Hankey, V. (1989) *Aegean Bronze Age Chronology*, Bristol Classic Press: Bristol, U.K.
Watterson, Barbara (1984) *The Gods of Ancient Egypt*, Facts on File Publications: New York and Bicester, U.K.
Weaver, Muriel Porter (1972) *The Aztecs, Maya, and their Predecessors (Archaeology of Mesoamerica)*, Seminar Press: New York and London.
Weeks, Kent R. (1998) *The Lost Tomb*, William Morris: New York.
Wegner, Josef W. (1996) 'The Nature and Chronology of the Senwosret III – Amenemhat III Regnal Succession: Some Considerations Based on New Evidence from the Mortuary Temple of Senwosret III at Abydos', *Journal of Near Eastern Studies* Vol. 55 - Num. 4, pp. 249-279.
―――― 'Interaction between the Nubian A-Group and Predynastic Egypt: The Significance of the Qustul Incense Burner.' In Theodore Celenko (editor) (1996) *Egypt in Africa*, pp. 98-100.
Weigall, Arthur (1925) *A History of the Pharaohs — Vol. I: The First Eleven Dynasties*, Thornton Butterworth: London.
―――― (1927) *A History of the Pharaohs — Vol. II: From the Accession of Amenemhat I of the Twelfth Dynasty to the Death of Thutmose III of the Eighteenth Dynasty, 2111 to 1441 B.C.*, Thornton Butterworth: London.
―――― (1934) *The Life and Times of Akhnaton — Pharaoh of Egypt*, Thornton Butterworth: London.

Weiger, Léon S. J. (1924) *La Chine à travers les ages.* Deuxième édition. Imprimerie Hien-Hien: Hien-Hien.

────── (1929) *Textes historiques — Histoire politique de la chine.* Tome I. Troisième édtion. Imprimerie Hien-Hien: Hien-Hien.

Weinstein, James M. (1974) 'A Statuette of the Princess Sobeknefru at Tell Gezer', *Bulletin of the American Schools of Oriental Research* 213, pp. 49-57.

────── (1975) 'Egyptian Relations with Palestine in the Middle Kingdom', *Bulletin of the American Schools of Oriental Research* 217, pp. 1-16.

────── (1981) 'The Egyptian Empire in Palestine: A Reassessment', *Bulletin of the American Schools of Oriental Research* 241, pp. 1-23.

────── (1991) 'Egypt and the Middle Bronze IIC - Late Bronze IA Transition in Palestine', *Levant* 23, pp.105-113.

────── (1992a) 'The Chronology of Palestine in the Early Second Millennium B.C.E.', *Bulletin of the American Schools of Oriental Research* 288, pp. 27-46.

────── (1992b) 'BOOK REVIEW: Black Athena: The Afroasiatic Roots of Classical Civilization. Vol. II: The Archaeological and Documentary Evidence. M. Bernal. 1987', *American Journal of Archaeology* 96, pp. 381-383.

────── 'The Collapse of the Egyptian Empire in the Southern Levant.' In Ward, William A. & Joukowsky, Martha Sharp (editors) (1992c) *The Crisis Years: The 12th Century B.C. (From Beyond the Danube to the Tigris),* pp. 142-150.

────── (1992d) 'The Chronology of Palestine in the Second Millenium B.C.E.', *Bulletin of the American Schools of Oriental Research* 288, pp. 27-38.

────── 'Reflections on the Chronology of Tell el-Dab'a.' In Davies, W. V. & Schofield, Louise (editors) (1995) *Egypt, the Aegean and the Levant (Interconnections in the Second Millennium BC),* pp. 84-90.

────── (1996) 'A Wolf in Sheep's Clothing: How the High Chronology Became the Middle Chronology', *Bulletin of the American Schools of Oriental Research* 304, pp. 55-63.

Weisberg, David 'The Neo-Babylonian Empire.' In Westenholz, Joan Goodnick (editor) (1996) *Royal Cities of the Biblical World,* pp. 221-233.

Wenham, David (1995) *Paul: Follower of Jesus or Founder of Christianity?,* William B. Eerdmans: Grand Rapids, Mich.

Wente, Edward F. (1967) 'On the Chronology of the Twenty-first Dynasty', *Journal of Near Eastern Studies* Vol. 26 - Num. 3, pp. 155-176.

West, John Anthony (1979) *Serpent in the Sky (The High Wisdom of Ancient Egypt),* Harper & Row: New York.

Westenholz, Joan Goodnick (editor) (1996) *Royal Cities of the Biblical World*, Bible Lands Museum Jerusalem: Jerusalem.

Whelton, Clark 'Velikovsky, Fundamentalism, and the Revised Chronology.' In Zysman, Milton & Whelton, Clark (editors) (1990) *Catastrophism 2000 (A Sourcebook for the Conference: Reconsidering Velikovsky)*, pp. 203-212.

——— 'Velikovsky's "Dark Age of Greece."' In ibid, pp. 251-263.

Whitelam, Keith W. (1996) *The Invention of Ancient Israel (The Silencing of Palestinian History)*, Routledge: London and New York.

Whitley, A.J.M. (1988) 'Early States and Hero Cults: A Re-appraisal', *The Journal of Hellenic Studies* 108, pp. 173-182.

Whybray, R. N. (1987) *The Making of the Pentateuch: A Methodological Study*, JSOT (Supplement Series 53): Sheffield, U.K.

Wieger, Léon S. J. (1924) *La Chine à travers les ages*. Deuxième édition. Imprimerie de Hien-Hien: Hien-Hien.

——— (1929) *Textes historiques: Histoire politique de la Chine*. Tome I. Troisième édition. Imprimerie Hien-Hien: Hien-Hien.

Wiener, Malcolm H. & Allen, James P. (1998) 'Separate Lives: The Ahmose Tempest Stela and the Theran Eruption', *Journal of Near Eastern Studies* Vol. 57 - Num. 1, pp. 1-28.

Wightman, G. J. (1990) 'The Myth of Solomon', *Bulletin of the American Schools of Oriental Research* 277-278, pp. 5-22.

Wilhelm, Worringer (1928) *Egyptian Art*. Trans. by Bernard Rackham. G. P. Putnam's Sons: London.

Wilkinson, J. G. (1854) *A Popular Account of the Ancient Egyptians*. Vol. I. John Murrey, Albemarle Street: London.

Wilkinson, Richard H. (1992) *Reading Egyptian Art (A Hieroglyphic Guide to Ancient Egyptian Painting and Sculpture)*, Thames and Hudson: London.

Willetts, R. F. (1980) *Cretan Cults and Festivals*, Greenwood Press: Westport, Conn.

Willhelm, Sidney M. 'The Velikovskian Upheaval: A Temporocentric Challenge.' In Greenberg, Lewis M. & Sizemore, Warner B. (1977) *Velikovsky and Establishment Science*, pp. 49-61.

Williams, Bruce (1980) 'The Lost Pharaohs of Nubia', *Archaeology* Vol. 33 - Num. 5, pp. 12-21.

——— (1985) 'A Chronology of Meroitic Occupation Below the Fourth Cataract', *Journal of the American Research Center in Egypt* 22, pp. 149-195.

——— (1986) *Excavations between Abu Simbel and the Sudan Frontier*, Chicago.

——— (1987) 'Forebears of Menes in Nubia: Myth or Reality?', *Journal of Near Eastern Studies* Vol. 46 - Num. 1, pp. 15-26.

——— (1988) 'Narmer and the Coptos Colossi', *Journal of the American Research Center in Egypt* 25, pp. 35-59.

——— 'A Prospectus for Exploring the Historical Essence of Ancient Nubia.' In Davies, W. Vivian (editor) (1991) *Egypt and Africa (Nubia from Prehistory to Islam)*, pp. 74-91.

——— 'The Qustul Incense Burner and the Case for a Nubian Origin of Ancient Egyptian Kingship.' In Celenko, Theodore (editor) (1996) *Egypt in Africa*, pp. 95-97.

Williams, Bruce & Logan, Thomas J. (1987) 'The Metropolitan Museum Knife Handle and Aspects of Pharaonic Imagery Before Narmer', *Journal of Near Eastern Studies* Vol. 46 - Num. 4, pp. 245-285.

Williams, Chancellor (1987) *The Destruction of Black Civilization (Great Issues of a Race from 4,500 B.C. to 2,000 A.D.)*, Third World Press: Chicago, Ill.

——— (1993 [1961]) *The Rebirth of African Civilization*, Third World Press: Chicago, Ill.

Williams, Norman Powell (1929) *The Ideas of the Fall and Original Sin (A Historical and Critical Study)*, Longmans, Green & Co.: London.

Wilson, Ian (1985) *The Exodus Enigma*, Weidenfeld and Nicolson: London.

——— (1986) *Exodus: The True Story Behind the Biblical Account*, Harper Collins: New York.

Wilson, John A. (1968) *The Culture of Ancient Egypt*, University of Chicago Press: Chicago and London.

Winter, Irene J. (1983) 'Carchemish Sa Kisad Puratti', *Anatolian Studies* 33, pp. 177-197.

Winters, Clyde Ahmad (1994) 'Afrocentrism: A Valid Frame of Reference', *Journal of Black Studies* Vol. 25 - Num. 2, pp. 170-190.

Wise, Michael Owen (1990) *A Critical Study of the Temple Scroll from Qumran Cave 11*, Oriental Institute of the University of Chicago: Chicago, Ill.

——— (1993) see Eisenman, Robert H.

Witherington, Ben III (1990) *The Christology of Jesus*, Fortress Press: Minneapolis.

Wolf, Irving 'Introduction to Velikovsky.' In Ravel, Nahum (editor) (1975) *From Past to Prophecy: Velikovsky's Challenge to Conventional beliefs (Proceedings of the Symposium held at the Saidye Bronfman Centre, Montreal, Quebec – January 10th-12th, 1975)*, pp. 2-14.

Wolff, Samuel R. (1996) 'Archaeology in Israel', *American Journal of Archaeology* Vol. 100 - Num. 4, pp. 725-768.

Wondji, Christophe (1989) 'Pour une histoire africaine engagée et responsable', *Présence Africaine* 149-150, pp. 331-346.

Wood, Bryant G. (1990a) 'Did the Israelites Conquer Jericho? (A New Look at the Archaeological Evidence', *Biblical Archaeology Review* Vol. 16 - Num. 5, pp. 44-58.

—— (1990b) 'Dating Jericho's Destruction: Bienkowsky is Wrong on All Counts', ibid, pp. 45-49, 68-69.

—— (1991) 'The Philistines Enter Canaan (Were they Egyptian Lackeys or Invading Conquerors?', *Biblical Archaeology Review* Vol. 17 - Num. 6, pp. 44-52, 89-92.

Woodward, Roger D. (1997) *Greek Writing from Knossos to Homer (A Linguistic Interpretation of the Origins of the Greek Alphabet and the Continuity of Ancient Literacy)*, Oxford University Press: London and New York.

Würthwein, Ernst (1995) *The Text of the Old Testament (An Introduction to the Biblia Hebraica)*. Second edition. Trans. by Erroll F. Rhodes. William B. Eerdmans: Grand Rapids, Mich.

Yadin, Yigael (1955) 'The Earliest Record of Egypt's Military Penetration into Asia? (Some Aspects of the Narmer Palette, the 'Desert Kites' and Mesopotamian Seal Cylinders)', *Israel Exploration Journal* Vol. 5 - Num. 1, pp. 1-16.

—— (1975) *Hazor (The Rediscovery of a Great Citadel of the Bible)*, Random House: New York.

—— 'Solomon's City Wall and Gate at Gezer.' In *Israel Exploration Journal Reader* (1981) with a prolegomenon by Harry M. Orlinsky. Vol. I. KTAV: New York, pp. 132-138.

Yakar, Jak 'Hattusa-Bogazkoy: Aspects of Hittite Architecture.' In Westenholz, Joan Goodnick (editor) (1996) *Royal Cities of the Biblical World*, pp. 53-68.

Yamauchi, Edwin M. (1967) *Greece and Babylon (Early Contacts Between the Aegean and the Near East)*, Baker Book House: Grand Rapids, Mich.

—— (1980) *The Archaeology of New Testament Cities in Western Asia Minor)*, Baker Books: Grand Rapids, Mich.

—— (1989) See Vardaman, Jerry

——— 'Persians.' In Alfred J. Hoerth, Gerald L. Mattingly & Edwin M. Yamauchi (editors) (1994a) *Peoples of the Old Testament World*, pp. 107-124.

——— 'The Current State of Old Testament Historiography.' In A. R. Millard, James K. Hoffmeier & David W. Baker (editors) (1994b) *Faith, Tradition, and History*, pp. 1-36.

——— (1996) *Persia and the Bible*, Baker Books: Grand Rapids, Mich.

Yoffee, Norman 'The Collapse of Ancient Mesopotamian States and Civilization.' In Cowgill, George L. & Yoffee, Norman (editors) (1988) *The Collapse of Ancient States and Civilizations*, pp. 44-68.

Yoshimura, Sakuji & Takamiya, Izumi (1994) 'A Monument of Khaemweset at Saqqara', *Egyptian Archaeology* 5, pp. 19-23.

Yoyotte, Jean (1976-77) '«Osorkon fils de Mehytouskhé» un pharaon oublié?', *Bulletin de la Sociéte Française d'Égyptologie* 77-78, pp. 39-51.

——— (1980) 'Une monumentale litanie de granit (Les Sekhmet d'Amenophis III et la conjuration permanente de la déesse dangereuse)', *Bulletin de la Sociéte Française d'Égyptologie* 87-88, pp. 47-71.

——— (1982) 'Champollion et le panthéon égyptien', *Bulletin de la Sociéte Française d'Égyptologie* 95, pp. 76-103.

——— (1989) 'Le roi Mer-djefa-Rà et le dieu Sopdou (Un monument de la XIVe dynastie)', *Bulletin de la Sociéte Française d'Égyptologie* 114, pp. 17-58.

Yurco, Frank J. (1989) 'Were the Ancient Egyptians Black or White?', *Biblical Archaeology Review* Vol. 15 - Num. 5, pp. 24-29, 58.

——— (1990) '3,200-Year-Old Picture of Israelites Found in Egypt', *Biblical Archaeology Review* Vol. 16 - Num. 5, pp. 20-38.

——— 'Black Athena: An Egyptological Review.' In Lefkowitz, Mary R. & Rogers, Guy M. (editors) (1996) *Black Athena Revisited*, pp. 62-100.

——— 'The Origins and Development of Ancient Nile Valley Writing.' In Celenko, Theodore (editor) (1996a) *Egypt in Africa*, p. 34-37.

——— 'Mother and Child Imagery in Egypt and Its Influence on Christianity.' In (1996b) ibid, p. 43-45.

Zabkar, Louis V. (1975) *Apedemak: Lion God of Meroe (A Study in Egyptian-Meroitic Syncretism)*, Aris & Phillips: Warminster, U.K.

——— (1983) 'Six Hymns to Isis in the Sanctuary of Her Temple at Philae and their Theological Significance — Part I', *Journal of Egyptian Archaeology* 69, pp. 115-137.

——— (1988) *Hymns to Isis in Her Temple at Philae*, Brandeis University Press/University Press of New England: Hanover and London.

Zahrnt, Heinz (1963) *The Historical Jesus*, Collins: London.

Zangger, Eberhard (1992) *The Flood from Heaven (Deciphering the Atlantis Legend)*, William Morrow: New York.

Ziony Zevit, Seymour Gitin & Michael S. Koloff (editors) (1995) *Solving Riddles and Untying Knots (Biblical Epigraphic, and Semitic Studies)*. In honor of Jonas C. Greenfield. Eisenbrauns: Winona Lake, Indiana.

Ziegler, Christiane (1981) 'Une découverte inédite de Mariette, les bronzes du Sérapéum', *Bulletin de la Sociéte Française d'Égyptologie* 90, pp. 29- 44.

Zysman, Milton & Whelton, Clark (editors) (1990) *Catastrophism 2000 (A Sourcebook for the Conference: Reconsidering Velikovsky). August 17-19, 1990 – University of Toronto*. Heretic Press: Toronto.

www.ingramcontent.com/pod-product-compliance
Lightning Source LLC
Chambersburg PA
CBHW050416240426
43661CB00055B/2170